SIPRI Yearbook 2007
Armaments, Disarmament and International Security

SIPRI Yearbook 2007

Armaments, Disarmament and International Security

Stockholm International Peace Research Institute

OXFORD UNIVERSITY PRESS
2007

OXFORD

UNIVERSITY PRESS

Great Clarendon Street, Oxford OX2 6DP

Oxford University Press is a department of the University of Oxford.
It furthers the University's objective of excellence in research, scholarship,
and education by publishing worldwide in

Oxford New York

Auckland Cape Town Dar es Salaam Hong Kong Karachi
Kuala Lumpur Madrid Melbourne Mexico City Nairobi
New Delhi Shanghai Taipei Toronto

With offices in

Argentina Austria Brazil Chile Czech Republic France Greece
Guatemala Hungary Italy Japan Poland Portugal Singapore
South Korea Switzerland Thailand Turkey Ukraine Vietnam

Oxford is a registered trade mark of Oxford University Press
in the UK and in certain other countries

Published in the United States
by Oxford University Press Inc., New York

© SIPRI 2007

*Yearbooks before 1987 were published under the title
'World Armaments and Disarmament:
SIPRI Yearbook [year of publication]'*

British Library Cataloguing in Publication Data
Data available

Library of Congress Cataloging in Publication Data
Data available

Typeset and originated by Stockholm International Peace Research Institute
Printed and bound in Great Britain
on acid-free paper by
Biddles Ltd, King's Lynn, Norfolk

ISSN 0953–0282
ISBN 978–0–19–923021–1

Contents

Part II. Military spending and armaments, 2006

Part III. Non-proliferation, arms control and disarmament, 2006

Appendix 12B. Nuclear explosions, 1945–2006 552
Vitaly Fedchenko and and Ragnhild Ferm Hellgren

Appendix 12C. Fissile materials: global stocks, production and elimination 558
Harold Feiveson, Alexander Glaser, Zia Mian and Frank von Hippel

13. Chemical and biological weapon developments and arms control 577
John Hart and Frida Kuhlau

Annexes

Preface

With the publication of *SIPRI Yearbook 2006*, SIPRI marked the 40th year since the institute's creation. The anniversary year of 2006 proved full of action and variety. SIPRI hosted a high-level commemorative seminar, linked with a lecture dedicated to the memories of Sweden's Olof Palme and Anna Lindh, at Stockholm in December. Several smaller seminars and conferences on historical or functional topics important for SIPRI's traditions were held in Sweden and other countries in cooperation with the institute's close partners. Four interns from backgrounds in remote or conflict-burdened regions were offered a free stay at SIPRI to help launch their careers in peace research or policymaking. A book of records and reminiscences from SIPRI's four decades was published by the institute and can be accessed, together with many other anniversary-related materials, at http://anniversary.sipri.org.

As the present edition of the Yearbook goes to press in spring 2007, the institute's attention is turning towards new beginnings. This autumn, Dr Bates Gill, a well-known US expert on East Asian affairs as well as security and arms control, will take over as the Director of SIPRI. This edition of the Yearbook is, therefore, the last as well as the fifth that I will have presided over personally during my tenure. Perhaps appropriately, many of its contents—apart from the traditional statistics and reportage functions—have a questioning and forward-looking tone. One theme that runs through many of them, and not for the first time, is the challenge of devising policies and, above all, restraints for a security environment that is now powerfully shaped by non-state actors and transnational forces as well as traditional state-based diplomacy. Another question asked by several contributors, including myself in the volume's Introduction, is how we should extend our concepts of risk to human life to cover all the various hazards affecting both richer and poorer populations (including the subset of dangers linked with armed violence)—and how to design, and prioritize, the right policies and resource uses to deal with them. Although not confronted directly in this volume, the huge emerging issue of the management of climate change is an example of a challenge that embodies and illustrates all these points. The 2007 edition of the Yearbook provides, at least, one of the necessary building blocks for approaching it with the chapter contributed by guest author Kamila Pronińska on energy and security.

At all times, SIPRI has faced the challenge of keeping its standards and values steady while adapting the focus and even the manner of its work to new security developments. During my years as Director, the adaptations made in institute methods and publications have included more focus on non-state partners (NGOs, scientists and the private sector), more use—though it still needs to go much further—of new electronic media, and more study of regional and well as global institutional dynamics. The theme of transparency has hardly been new since it was one of SIPRI's first core values, but it is now being pursued in new ways, including a more active media and event promotion policy, and—not least—experimentation with new ways of capitalizing on this Yearbook itself. The 2006 edition of the Yearbook was translated in full into Arabic, Chinese, Japanese, Russian and Ukrainian, an all-time record for such foreign-language versions. The range of the pocket-sized summary versions of the Yearbook, which can be found online at http://books.spri.org, has grown to include most recently Catalan and Dutch as well as English, Swedish, French, German and Spanish. All further offers of partnership in translating either or both versions into new languages will be warmly received.

The time of leaving an institute is also a time to look back and give thanks. First and foremost, these should go out to SIPRI's partners, supporters and readers and to the users of all our various services around the globe. SIPRI was conceived as a resource for the world, not as an end in itself. The demand that the institute experiences and the response it receives to its outputs and efforts are the surest measure of whether it is both fulfilling a needed function and staying on the proper track. The experience of the past five years suggests that a positive answer can be given to these questions, but also that there is less room than ever for any complacency. The road to peace, freedom and stability gets more entangled almost by the day and the traps and barriers more daunting. I wish my own successor, and the Governing Board and all staff at SIPRI, success and steadfastness in carrying the institute's work to new and higher levels as the 21st century unfolds.

For this yearbook in particular, I would like to thank all the authors and other contributors from both inside and outside SIPRI; and all the editing team, now consisting of David Cruickshank, Tom Gill, Jetta Gilligan Borg, Caspar Trimmer and Connie Wall. Special and indispensable roles are further played by SIPRI's Deputy Director Daniel Nord and Research Coordinator Ian Anthony; Nenne Bodell and the Library staff; Head of Administration and Finance Anna Helleday, who deals with the funding of translations; Gerd Hagemeyer-Gaverus and the IT department; Peter Rea, the indexer; and my own, infallibly steady and hard-working Assistant, Cynthia Loo. Even if the burden of work on the Yearbook itself is something that I lay down with a certain relief, the process of working on it with all these exceptional people is something that I will sorely miss.

Alyson J. K. Bailes
SIPRI Director
May 2007

Glossary

NENNE BODELL and CONNIE WALL

Abbreviations

ABM	Anti-ballistic missile	CEMAC	Communauté Economique et Monétaire d'Afrique Centrale (Economic Community of Central African States)
ACV	Armoured combat vehicle		
AG	Australia Group		
ALCM	Air-launched cruise missile		
APC	Armoured personnel carrier	CFE	Conventional Armed Forces in Europe (Treaty)
APEC	Asia–Pacific Economic Cooperation		
APM	Anti-personnel mine	CFSP	Common Foreign and Security Policy
APT	ASEAN Plus Three	CICA	Conference on Interaction and Confidence-building Measures in Asia
ARF	ASEAN Regional Forum		
ASEAN	Association of South East Asian Nations		
ATT	Arms trade treaty	CIS	Commonwealth of Independent States
ATTU	Atlantic-to-the Urals (zone)	CSBM	Confidence- and security-building measure
AU	African Union		
BMD	Ballistic missile defence	CSCAP	Council for Security Cooperation in the Asia Pacific
BSEC	Organization of the Black Sea Economic Cooperation		
BTWC	Biological and Toxin Weapons Convention	CSTO	Collective Security Treaty Organization
BW	Biological weapon/warfare	CTBT	Comprehensive Nuclear Test-Ban Treaty
CADSP	Common African Defence and Security Policy	CTBTO	Comprehensive Nuclear Test-Ban Treaty Organization
CAR	Central African Republic		
CBM	Confidence-building measure	CTR	Co-operative Threat Reduction
CBSS	Council of the Baltic Sea States	CW	Chemical weapon/warfare
		CWC	Chemical Weapons Convention
CBW	Chemical and biological weapon/warfare	D-8	Developing Eight (countries)
CCW	Certain Conventional Weapons (Convention)	DDR	Disarmament, demobilization and reintegration
CD	Conference on Disarmament		
CEI	Central European Initiative	DPKO	Department of Peacckeeping Operations

DRC	Democratic Republic of the Congo	ICC	International Criminal Court
EAEC	European Atomic Energy Community (*also* Euratom)	ICJ	International Court of Justice
EAPC	Euro-Atlantic Partnership Council	ICTY	International Criminal Tribunal for former Yugoslavia
ECOWAS	Economic Community of West African States	IGAD	Intergovernmental Authority on Development
EDA	European Defence Agency	IGC	Intergovernmental Conference
EMU	European Monetary Union		
ENP	European Neighbourhood Policy	IMF	International Monetary Fund
ERW	Explosive remnants of war	INDA	International non-proliferation and disarmament assistance
ESDP	European Security and Defence Policy		
EU	European Union	INF	Intermediate-range Nuclear Forces (Treaty)
FMCT	Fissile material cut-off treaty	IRBM	Intermediate-range ballistic missile
FSC	Forum for Security Co-operation	IST	Iraqi Special Tribunal
FY	Financial year	JCG	Joint Consultative Group
FYROM	Former Yugoslav Republic of Macedonia	JCIC	Joint Compliance and Inspection Commission
G8	Group of Eight (industrialized nations)	JHA	Justice and Home Affairs
		LEU	Low-enriched uranium
GAERC	General Affairs and External Relations Council	MANPADS	Man-portable air defence system
GCC	Gulf Cooperation Council	MDGs	Millennium Development Goals
GDP	Gross domestic product		
GLCM	Ground-launched cruise missile	MER	Market exchange rate
		MERCOSUR	Mercado Común del Sur (Southern Common Market)
GNEP	Global Nuclear Energy Partnership		
GNI	Gross national income	MIRV	Multiple, independently targetable re-entry vehicle
GNP	Gross national product		
GTRI	Global Threat Reduction Initiative	MOTAPM	Mines other than anti-personnel mines
GUAM	Georgia, Ukraine, Azerbaijan and Moldova	MTCR	Missile Technology Control Regime
HCOC	Hague Code of Conduct	NAM	Non-Aligned Movement
HEU	Highly enriched uranium	NATO	North Atlantic Treaty Organization
IAEA	International Atomic Energy Agency	NBC	Nuclear, biological and chemical (weapons)
ICBM	Intercontinental ballistic missile	NGO	Non-governmental organization

NNWS	Non-nuclear weapon state	SCO	Shanghai Cooperation Organization
NPT	Non-Proliferation Treaty	SECI	Southeast European Cooperative Initiative
NRF	NATO Response Force		
NSG	Nuclear Suppliers Group	SLBM	Submarine-launched ballistic missile
NSS	National Security Strategy		
NWS	Nuclear weapon state	SLCM	Sea-launched cruise missile
OAS	Organization of American States		
		SORT	Strategic Offensive Reductions Treaty
OCCAR	Organisation Conjointe de Coopération en matière d'Armement	SRBM	Short-range ballistic missile
ODA	Official development assistance	SRCC	Sub-Regional Consultative Commission
OECD	Organisation for Economic Co-operation and Development	SSM	Surface-to-surface missile
		SSR	Security sector reform
		START	Strategic Arms Reduction Treaty
OIC	Organization of the Islamic Conference		
OPANAL	Agency for the Prohibition of Nuclear Weapons in Latin America and the Caribbean	TLE	Treaty-limited equipment
		UAE	United Arab Emirates
		UAV	Unmanned aerial vehicle
		UCAV	Unmanned combat air vehicle
OPCW	Organisation for the Prohibition of Chemical Weapons		
		USAID	US Agency for International Development
OPEC	Organization of the Petroleum Exporting Countries	UN	United Nations
		UNDP	UN Development Programme
OSCC	Open Skies Consultative Commission	UNHCR	UN High Commissioner for Refugees
OSCE	Organization for Security and Co-operation in Europe	UNMOVIC	UN Monitoring, Verification and Inspection Commission
PFP	Partnership for Peace		
PPP	Purchasing power parity	UNROCA	UN Register of Conventional Arms
PSI	Proliferation Security Initiative	UNSCOM	UN Special Commission on Iraq
QDR	Quadrennial Defense Review	WA	Wassenaar Arrangement
		WEU	Western European Union
R&D	Research and development	WMD	Weapon(s) of mass destruction
SAARC	South Asian Association for Regional Co-operation		
SADC	Southern African Development Community		
SALW	Small arms and light weapons		
SAM	Surface-to-air missile		

Intergovernmental bodies and international organizations

The main organizations and export control regimes discussed in this edition of the Yearbook are described in the glossary. Members or participants are listed on pages xxix–xxxvi. On the arms control and disarmament agreements mentioned in the glossary, see annex A in this volume.

African Union (AU)	The Constitutive Act of the African Union entered into force in 2001, formally establishing the AU. Its headquarters are in Addis Ababa, Ethiopia, and membership is open to all African states. In 2002 it replaced the Organization for African Unity. The AU promotes unity, security and conflict resolution, democracy, human rights, and political, social and economic integration in Africa. *See* the list of members.
Agency for the Prohibition of Nuclear Weapons in Latin America and the Caribbean (OPANAL)	Established by the 1967 Treaty of Tlatelolco to resolve, together with the IAEA, questions of compliance with the treaty. Its seat is in Mexico City, Mexico.
Arab League	The League of Arab States, established in 1945, with Permanent Headquarters in Cairo, Egypt. Its principal objective is to form closer union among Arab states and foster political and economic cooperation. An agreement for collective defence and economic cooperation among the members was signed in 1950. *See* the list of members.
Asia–Pacific Economic Cooperation (APEC)	Established in 1989 to enhance economic growth and security in the Asia–Pacific region, with its seat in Singapore. Its member economies engage in dialogue and enter into non-binding commitments on e.g. combating terrorism, non-proliferation of weapons of mass destruction and effective export control systems. *See* the list of member economies.
Association of South East Asian Nations (ASEAN)	Established in 1967 to promote economic, social and cultural development as well as regional peace and security in South-East Asia. The seat of the Secretariat is in Jakarta, Indonesia. The ASEAN Regional Forum (ARF) was established in 1994 to address security issues. Cooperation on political and security issues in the ASEAN Plus Three forum started in 1997 and was institutionalized in 1999. *See* the lists of the members of ASEAN, ARF and ASEAN Plus Three.
Australia Group (AG)	Group of states, formed in 1985, which meets informally each year to monitor the proliferation of chemical and biological products and to discuss chemical and biological weapon-related items which should be subject to national regulatory measures. *See* the list of participants.
Black Sea Economic Cooperation (BSEC)	*See* Organization of the Black Sea Economic Cooperation.

Central European Initiative (CEI)

Established in 1989 to promote cooperation among members in the political and economic spheres. It provides support to its non-EU members in their process of accession to the EU. The seat of the Executive Secretariat is in Trieste, Italy. *See* the list of members.

Collective Security Treaty Organization (CSTO)

Formally established in 2002–2003 by six signatories of the 1992 Collective Security Treaty, the CSTO aims to promote cooperation among the members. An objective is to provide a more efficient response to strategic problems such as terrorism and narcotics trafficking. Its seat is in Moscow, Russia. *See* the list of members.

Commonwealth of Independent States (CIS)

Established in 1991 as a framework for multilateral cooperation among former Soviet republics, with headquarters in Minsk, Belarus. *See* the list of members.

Commonwealth of Nations

An organization, established in 1949, of developed and developing countries whose aim is to advance democracy, human rights, and sustainable economic and social development within its member states and beyond. Its Secretariat is in London, UK. *See* the list of members.

Comprehensive Nuclear-Test-Ban Treaty Organization (CTBTO)

Established by the 1996 CTBT to resolve questions of compliance with the treaty and as a forum for consultation and cooperation among the states parties. The CTBTO will become operational when the CTBT has entered into force. A Preparatory Commission was established to prepare for the work of the CTBTO, in particular by establishing the International Monitoring System, consisting of seismic, hydroacoustic, infra-sound and radionuclide stations from which data are transmitted to the CTBTO International Data Centre. Its seat is in Vienna, Austria.

Conference on Disarmament (CD)

A multilateral arms control negotiating body that has been enlarged and renamed several times since 1959 and has been called the Conference on Disarmament since 1984. It is not a UN body but reports to the UN General Assembly. The CD is based in Geneva, Switzerland. *See* the list of members under United Nations.

Conference on Interaction and Confidence-building Measures in Asia (CICA)

Initiated in 1992, and established by the 1999 Declaration on the Principles Guiding Relations among the CICA Member States, as a forum to enhance security cooperation and confidence-building measures among the member states. It also promotes economic, social and cultural cooperation. *See* the list of members.

Council for Security Cooperation in the Asia Pacific (CSCAP)

Established in 1993 as an informal, non-governmental process for regional confidence building and security cooperation through dialogue and consultation on security matters in the Asia–Pacific region. *See* the list of member committees.

Council of Europe	Established in 1949, with its seat in Strasbourg, France, the Council is open to membership of all the European states that accept the principle of the rule of law and guarantee their citizens' human rights and fundamental freedoms. Among its organs are the European Court of Human Rights and the Council of Europe Development Bank. *See* the list of members.
Council of the Baltic Sea States (CBSS)	Established in 1992 as a regional intergovernmental organization for cooperation among the states of the Baltic Sea region. Its secretariat is located in Stockholm, Sweden. *See* the list of members.
Developing Eight (D-8)	A group of states established in 1997 to improve the developing countries' positions in the world economy and enhance participation in decision making at the international level. It holds summit meetings every two years. The Council is composed of ministers of foreign affairs and is the political decision-making organ. The Commission is the executive organ. The Secretariat is in Istanbul, Turkey. *See* the list of members.
Economic Community of West African States (ECOWAS)	A regional organization established in 1975, with its Executive Secretariat in Lagos, Nigeria, to promote trade and cooperation and contribute to development in West Africa. In 1981 it adopted the Protocol on Mutual Assistance in Defence Matters. *See* the list of members.
European Atomic Energy Community (Euratom, or EAEC)	Created by the 1957 Treaty Establishing the European Atomic Energy Community (Euratom Treaty) to promote the development of nuclear energy for peaceful purposes and to administer the multinational regional safeguards system covering the EU member states. Euratom is located in Brussels, Belgium. The members of Euratom are the EU member states.
European Defence Agency (EDA)	An agency of the European Union (see below), under the direction of the Council, that was established in 2004 to help develop European defence capabilities, to promote European armaments cooperation and to work for a strong European defence technological and industrial base. The Steering Board, composed of the defence ministers of the EU member states (except Denmark) and the European Commission, is the decision-making body. It is located in Brussels. *See* the list of members.

European Union (EU)   Organization of European states, with its headquarters in Brussels, Belgium. The 2000 Treaty of Nice entered into force on 1 February 2003. The three EU 'pillars' are: the Community dimension, including the Single European Market, the Economic and Monetary Union (EMU) and the Euratom Treaty; the Common Foreign and Security Policy (CFSP); and cooperation in Justice and Home Affairs (JHA). The Treaty establishing a Constitution for Europe was signed by the EU heads of state or government in October 2004, but it will not enter into force until all the EU governments have ratified it, by a parliamentary vote or a referendum. *See* the list of members and *see also* European Atomic Energy Community.

Group of Eight (G8)   Group of eight (originally seven) leading industrialized nations which have met informally, at the level of heads of state or government, since the 1970s. *See* the list of members.

Gulf Cooperation Council (GCC)   The Cooperation Council for the Arab States of the Gulf, known as the GCC and with its headquarters in Riyadh, Saudi Arabia, was created in 1981 to promote regional integration in such areas as economy, finance, trade, administration and legislation and to foster scientific and technical progress. The members also cooperate in areas of foreign policy and military and security matters. The Supreme Council is the highest GCC authority. *See* the list of members.

Hague Code of Conduct against Ballistic Missile Proliferation (HCOC)   The 2002 HCOC is subscribed to by a group of states which recognize its principles, primarily the need to prevent and curb the proliferation of ballistic missile systems capable of delivering weapons of mass destruction and the importance of strengthening multilateral disarmament and non-proliferation mechanisms. The Austrian Ministry of Foreign Affairs, Vienna, Austria, acts as the HCOC Secretariat. *See* the list of subscribing states.

Intergovernmental Authority on Development (IGAD)   Initiated in 1986 as the Intergovernmental Authority on Drought and Development, IGAD was formally established in 1996 to promote peace and stability in the Horn of Africa and to create mechanisms for conflict prevention, management and resolution. Its Secretariat is in Djibouti. *See* the list of members.

International Atomic Energy Agency (IAEA)   An intergovernmental organization within the UN system, with headquarters in Vienna, Austria. The IAEA is endowed by its Statute, which entered into force in 1957, to promote the peaceful uses of atomic energy and ensure that nuclear activities are not used to further any military purpose. Under the Non-Proliferation Treaty and the nuclear weapon-free zone treaties, non-nuclear weapon states must accept IAEA nuclear safeguards to demonstrate the fulfilment of their obligation not to manufacture nuclear weapons. *See* the list of IAEA members under United Nations.

Joint Compliance and Inspection Commission (JCIC)	The forum established by the 1991 START I Treaty in which the two parties (Russia and the United States) exchange data, resolve questions of compliance, clarify ambiguities and discuss ways to improve implementation of the START treaties. It convenes at the request of at least one of the parties.
Joint Consultative Group (JCG)	Established by the 1990 CFE Treaty to promote the objectives and implementation of the treaty by reconciling ambiguities of interpretation and implementation. Its seat is in Vienna, Austria.
Mercado Común del Sur (MERCOSUR)	*See* Southern Common Market.
Missile Technology Control Regime (MTCR)	An informal military-related export control regime which in 1987 produced the Guidelines for Sensitive Missile-Relevant Transfers (subsequently revised). Its goal is to limit the spread of weapons of mass destruction by controlling ballistic missile delivery systems. *See* the list of participants.
NATO–Russia Council	Established in 2002 as a mechanism for consultation, consensus building, cooperation, and joint decisions and action on security issues, focusing on areas of mutual interest identified in the 1997 NATO–Russia Founding Act on Mutual Relations, Cooperation and Security and new areas, such as terrorism, crisis management and non-proliferation.
NATO–Ukraine Commission	Established in 1997 for consultations on political and security issues, conflict prevention and resolution, non-proliferation, arms exports and technology transfers, and other subjects of common concern.
Non-Aligned Movement (NAM)	Established in 1961 as a forum for consultations and coordination of positions in the United Nations on political, economic and arms control issues among non-aligned states. *See* the list of members.
North Atlantic Treaty Organization (NATO)	Established in 1949 by the North Atlantic Treaty (Washington Treaty) as a Western defence alliance. Article 5 of the treaty defines the members' commitment to respond to an armed attack against any party to the treaty. Its institutional headquarters are in Brussels, Belgium. The NATO Euro-Atlantic Partnership Council (EAPC), established in 1997, is the forum for cooperation between NATO and its Partnership for Peace partners. *See* the lists of NATO and EAPC members.
Nuclear Suppliers Group (NSG)	Established in 1975 and also known as the London Club, the NSG coordinates national export controls on nuclear materials according to its Guidelines for Nuclear Transfers (London Guidelines), which contain a 'trigger list' of materials that should trigger IAEA safeguards when they are to be exported for peaceful purposes to any non-nuclear weapon state, and the Guidelines for Transfers of Nuclear-Related Dual-Use Equipment, Materials, Software and Related Technology (Warsaw Guidelines). *See* the list of participants.

Open Skies Consultative Commission (OSCC)	Established by the 1992 Open Skies Treaty to resolve questions of compliance with the treaty.
Organisation Conjointe de Coopération en matière d'Armement (OCCAR)	Established in 1996, with legal status since 2001, by four European states. Its aim is to provide more effective and efficient arrangements for the management of specific collaborative armament programmes. Its headquarters are in Bonn, Germany. *See* the list of members.
Organisation for Economic Co-operation and Development (OECD)	Established in 1961, its objectives are to promote economic and social welfare by coordinating policies among the member states. Its headquarters are in Paris, France. *See* the list of members.
Organisation for the Prohibition of Chemical Weapons (OPCW)	Established by the 1993 Chemical Weapons Convention as a body for the parties to oversee implementation of the convention and resolve questions of compliance. Its seat is in The Hague, the Netherlands.
Organization for Democracy and Economic Development–GUAM	A group of four states whose history goes back to 1997, established to promote stability and strengthen security. The members cooperate to promote social and economic development and trade in seven working groups. Its Information Office, which functions as a secretariat, is in Kyiv, Ukraine. *See* the list of members.
Organization for Security and Co-operation in Europe (OSCE)	Initiated in 1973 as the Conference on Security and Co-operation in Europe (CSCE), in 1995 it was renamed the OSCE and transformed into an organization, with headquarters in Vienna, Austria, as a primary instrument for early warning, conflict prevention and crisis management. Its Forum for Security Co-operation (FSC), also in Vienna, deals with arms control and confidence- and security-building measures. The OSCE comprises several institutions, all located in Europe. *See* the list of members and *see also* Stability Pact for South Eastern Europe.
Organization of American States (OAS)	Group of states in the Americas which adopted its charter in 1948, with the objective of strengthening peace and security in the western hemisphere. The General Secretariat is in Washington, DC, USA. *See* the list of members.
Organization of the Black Sea Economic Cooperation (BSEC)	Established in 1992, with its Permanent Secretariat in Istanbul, Turkey. Its aims are to ensure peace, stability and prosperity in the Black Sea region and to promote and develop economic cooperation and progress. *See* the list of members.
Organization of the Islamic Conference (OIC)	Established in 1969 by Islamic states to promote cooperation among the members and to support peace, security and the struggle of the people of Palestine and all Muslim people. Its Secretariat is in Jeddah, Saudi Arabia. *See* the list of members.
Pacific Islands Forum	Founded in 1971, a group of South Pacific states that proposed the South Pacific Nuclear Free Zone, embodied in the 1985 Treaty of Rarotonga, and contribute to monitoring implementation of the treaty. The Secretariat is in Suva, Fiji. *See* the list of members.

Proliferation Security Initiative (PSI)	Based on a US initiative announced in 2003, the PSI is a multilateral activity focusing on law enforcement cooperation for the interdiction and seizure of illegal weapons of mass destruction, missile technologies and related materials when in transit on land, in the air or at sea. The PSI Statement of Interdiction Principles was issued in 2003. More than 70 states support and participate in the PSI, and other states participate in certain activities as observers.
Shanghai Cooperation Organization (SCO)	The predecessor group the Shanghai Five was founded in 1996; it was renamed the SCO in 2001 and opened for membership of all states that support its aims. The member states cooperate on confidence-building measures and regional security and in the economic sphere. The SCO Secretariat is in Beijing, China. *See* the list of members.
South Asian Association for Regional Co-operation (SAARC)	Created in 1985 as an association of states to promote political and economic regional cooperation, with its secretariat in Kathmandu, Nepal. *See* the list of members.
Southeast European Cooperative Initiative (SECI)	An initiative launched by the USA in 1996 to promote cooperation and stability among the countries of south-eastern Europe and facilitate their accession to the European Union. The SECI Secretariat is located in the OSCE offices in Vienna. *See* the list of members.
Southern African Development Community (SADC)	Established in 1992 to promote regional economic development and fundamental principles of sovereignty, peace and security, human rights and democracy. The Secretariat is in Gaborone, Botswana. *See* the list of members.
Southern Common Market (MERCOSUR)	Established in 1991 to achieve economic integration between the South American states. In 1996 it adopted a decision that only countries with democratic, accountable institutions in place would be allowed to participate. The Common Market Council is the highest decision-making body, and the Common Market Group is the permanent executive body. The Secretariat and Parliament are located in Montevideo, Uruguay. *See* the list of members.
Stability Pact for South Eastern Europe	Initiated by the EU at the 1999 Conference on South Eastern Europe and subsequently placed under OSCE auspices, the Pact is intended to provide the subregion with a comprehensive, long-term conflict prevention strategy by promoting political and economic reforms, development and enhanced security, and integration of South-East European countries into the Euro-Atlantic institutions. Its activities are coordinated by the South Eastern Europe Regional Table and chaired by the Special Co-ordinator of the Stability Pact. The seat of the Special Co-ordinator is in Brussels, Belgium. *See* the list of partners.
Sub-Regional Consultative Commission (SRCC)	Established by the 1996 Agreement on Sub-Regional Arms Control (Florence Agreement) as the forum in which the parties resolve questions of compliance with the agreement.

United Nations (UN)

The world intergovernmental organization with headquarters in New York, USA. It was founded in 1945 through the adoption of its Charter. The six principal UN organs are the General Assembly, the Security Council, the Economic and Social Council (ECOSOC), the Trusteeship Council (which suspended operation in 1994), the International Court of Justice (ICJ) and the Secretariat. The UN also has a large number of specialized agencies and other autonomous bodies. *See* the list of members.

Wassenaar Arrangement (WA)

The Wassenaar Arrangement on Export Controls for Conventional Arms and Dual-Use Goods and Technologies was formally established in 1996, with its secretariat in Vienna, Austria. It aims to prevent the acquisition of armaments and sensitive dual-use goods and technologies for military uses by states whose behaviour is cause for concern to the member states. *See* the list of participants.

Western European Union (WEU)

Established by the 1954 Modified Brussels Treaty. The seat of the WEU is in Brussels, Belgium. WEU operational activities (the Petersberg Tasks) were transferred to the EU in 2000. The Assembly of WEU, Interparliamentary European Security and Defence Assembly, seated in Paris, France, scrutinizes intergovernmental cooperation in armaments and arms research and development. *See* the list of members.

Zangger Committee

Established in 1971, the Nuclear Exporters Committee, called the Zangger Committee, is a group of nuclear supplier countries that meets informally twice a year to coordinate export controls on nuclear materials according to its regularly updated trigger list of items which, when exported, must be subject to IAEA safeguards. It complements the work of the NSG (*see* Nuclear Suppliers Group). *See* the list of participants.

Membership of intergovernmental bodies and international organizations as of 1 January 2007

The UN member states and organizations within the UN system are listed first, followed by all other organizations in alphabetical order. Note that not all members or participants of the organizations are UN member states. The address of an Internet site with information about each organization is provided where available.

United Nations members (192) and year of membership
<http://www.un.org>

Afghanistan, 1946
Albania, 1955
Algeria, 1962
Andorra, 1993
Angola, 1976
Antigua and Barbuda, 1981
Argentina, 1945
Armenia, 1992
Australia, 1945
Austria, 1955
Azerbaijan, 1992
Bahamas, 1973
Bahrain, 1971
Bangladesh, 1974
Barbados, 1966
Belarus, 1945
Belgium, 1945
Belize, 1981
Benin, 1960
Bhutan, 1971
Bolivia, 1945
Bosnia and Herzegovina, 1992
Botswana, 1966
Brazil, 1945
Brunei Darussalam, 1984
Bulgaria, 1955
Burkina Faso, 1960
Burundi, 1962
Cambodia, 1955
Cameroon, 1960
Canada, 1945
Cape Verde, 1975
Central African Republic, 1960
Chad, 1960
Chile, 1945
China, 1945
Colombia, 1945
Comoros, 1975
Congo, Democratic Republic of the, 1960
Congo, Republic of the, 1960
Costa Rica, 1945
Côte d'Ivoire, 1960
Croatia, 1992
Cuba, 1945
Cyprus, 1960

Czech Republic, 1993
Denmark, 1945
Djibouti, 1977
Dominica, 1978
Dominican Republic, 1945
Ecuador, 1945
Egypt, 1945
El Salvador, 1945
Equatorial Guinea, 1968
Eritrea, 1993
Estonia, 1991
Ethiopia, 1945
Fiji, 1970
Finland, 1955
France, 1945
Gabon, 1960
Gambia, 1965
Georgia, 1992
Germany, 1973
Ghana, 1957
Greece, 1945
Grenada, 1974
Guatemala, 1945
Guinea, 1958
Guinea-Bissau, 1974
Guyana, 1966
Haiti, 1945
Honduras, 1945
Hungary, 1955
Iceland, 1946
India, 1945
Indonesia, 1950
Iran, 1945
Iraq, 1945
Ireland, 1955
Israel, 1949
Italy, 1955
Jamaica, 1962
Japan, 1956
Jordan, 1955
Kazakhstan, 1992
Kenya, 1963
Kiribati, 1999
Korea, Democratic People's Republic of (North Korea), 1991

Korea, Republic of (South Korea), 1991
Kuwait, 1963
Kyrgyzstan, 1992
Laos, 1955
Latvia, 1991
Lebanon, 1945
Lesotho, 1966
Liberia, 1945
Libya, 1955
Liechtenstein, 1990
Lithuania, 1991
Luxembourg, 1945
Macedonia, Former Yugoslav Republic of, 1993
Madagascar, 1960
Malawi, 1964
Malaysia, 1957
Maldives, 1965
Mali, 1960
Malta, 1964
Marshall Islands, 1991
Mauritania, 1961
Mauritius, 1968
Mexico, 1945
Micronesia, 1991
Moldova, 1992
Monaco, 1993
Mongolia, 1961
Montenegro, 2006
Morocco, 1956
Mozambique, 1975
Myanmar, 1948
Namibia, 1990
Nauru, 1999
Nepal, 1955
Netherlands, 1945
New Zealand, 1945
Nicaragua, 1945
Niger, 1960
Nigeria, 1960
Norway, 1945
Oman, 1971
Pakistan, 1947
Palau, 1994
Panama, 1945

Papua New Guinea, 1975
Paraguay, 1945
Peru, 1945
Philippines, 1945
Poland, 1945
Portugal, 1955
Qatar, 1971
Romania, 1955
Russia, 1945
Rwanda, 1962
Saint Kitts and Nevis, 1983
Saint Lucia, 1979
Saint Vincent and the
  Grenadines, 1980
Samoa, 1976
San Marino, 1992
Sao Tome and Principe, 1975
Saudi Arabia, 1945
Senegal, 1960
Serbia, 2000

Seychelles, 1976
Sierra Leone, 1961
Singapore, 1965
Slovakia, 1993
Slovenia, 1992
Solomon Islands, 1978
Somalia, 1960
South Africa, 1945
Spain, 1955
Sri Lanka, 1955
Sudan, 1956
Suriname, 1975
Swaziland, 1968
Sweden, 1946
Switzerland, 2002
Syria, 1945
Tajikistan, 1992
Tanzania, 1961
Thailand, 1946
Timor-Leste, 2002

Togo, 1960
Tonga, 1999
Trinidad and Tobago, 1962
Tunisia, 1956
Turkey, 1945
Turkmenistan, 1992
Tuvalu, 2000
Uganda, 1962
UK, 1945
Ukraine, 1945
United Arab Emirates, 1971
Uruguay, 1945
USA, 1945
Uzbekistan, 1992
Vanuatu, 1981
Venezuela, 1945
Viet Nam, 1977
Yemen, 1947
Zambia, 1964
Zimbabwe, 1980

UN Security Council

<http://www.un.org/Docs/sc/>

Permanent members (the P5): China, France, Russia, UK, USA

Non-permanent members in 2007 (elected by the UN General Assembly for two-year terms; the year in brackets is the year at the end of which the term expires): Belgium (2008), Congo, Republic of the (2007), Ghana (2007), Indonesia (2008), Italy (2008), Panama (2008), Peru (2007), Qatar (2007), Slovakia (2007), South Africa (2008)

Conference on Disarmament (CD)

<http://disarmament2.un.org/cd>

Algeria, Argentina, Australia, Austria, Bangladesh, Belarus, Belgium, Brazil, Bulgaria, Cameroon, Canada, Chile, China, Colombia, Congo (Democratic Republic of the), Cuba, Ecuador, Egypt, Ethiopia, Finland, France, Germany, Hungary, India, Indonesia, Iran, Iraq, Ireland, Israel, Italy, Japan, Kazakhstan, Kenya, Korea (North), Korea (South), Malaysia, Mexico, Mongolia, Morocco, Myanmar, Netherlands, New Zealand, Nigeria, Norway, Pakistan, Peru, Poland, Romania, Russia, Senegal, Slovakia, South Africa, Spain, Sri Lanka, Sweden, Switzerland, Syria, Tunisia, Turkey, UK, Ukraine, USA, Venezuela, Viet Nam, Zimbabwe

International Atomic Energy Agency (IAEA)

<http://www.iaea.org>

Afghanistan, Albania, Algeria, Angola, Argentina, Armenia, Australia, Austria, Azerbaijan, Bangladesh, Belarus, Belgium, Belize, Benin, Bolivia, Bosnia and Herzegovina, Botswana, Brazil, Bulgaria, Burkina Faso, Cameroon, Canada, Central African Republic, Chad, Chile, China, Colombia, Congo (Democratic Republic of the), Costa Rica, Côte d'Ivoire, Croatia, Cuba, Cyprus, Czech Republic, Denmark, Dominican Republic, Ecuador, Egypt, El Salvador, Eritrea, Estonia, Ethiopia, Finland, France, Gabon, Georgia, Germany, Ghana, Greece, Guatemala, Haiti, Holy See, Honduras, Hungary, Iceland, India, Indonesia, Iran, Iraq, Ireland, Israel, Italy, Jamaica, Japan, Jordan, Kazakhstan, Kenya, Korea (South), Kuwait, Kyrgyzstan, Latvia, Lebanon, Liberia, Libya, Liechtenstein, Lithuania, Luxembourg, Macedonia (Former Yugoslav Republic of), Madagascar, Malawi, Malaysia, Mali, Malta, Marshall Islands, Mauritania, Mauritius, Mexico, Moldova, Monaco, Mongolia, Montenegro, Morocco, Myanmar, Namibia, Netherlands, New Zealand, Nicaragua, Niger, Nigeria, Norway, Pakistan, Panama, Paraguay, Peru, Philippines, Poland, Portugal, Qatar, Romania, Russia, Saudi Arabia, Senegal, Serbia, Seychelles, Sierra Leone, Singapore, Slovakia, Slovenia, South Africa, Spain, Sri Lanka, Sudan, Sweden, Switzerland, Syria, Tajikistan, Tanzania, Thailand, Tunisia, Turkey, Uganda, UK, Ukraine, United Arab Emirates, Uruguay, USA, Uzbekistan, Venezuela, Viet Nam, Yemen, Zambia, Zimbabwe

Note: North Korea was a member of the IAEA until June 1994. Cambodia withdrew its membership as of March 2003.

African Union (AU)
<http://www.africa-union.org>

Algeria, Angola, Benin, Botswana, Burkina Faso, Burundi, Cameroon, Cape Verde, Central African Republic, Chad, Comoros, Congo (Democratic Republic of the), Congo (Republic of the), Côte d'Ivoire, Djibouti, Egypt, Equatorial Guinea, Eritrea, Ethiopia, Gabon, Gambia, Ghana, Guinea, Guinea-Bissau, Kenya, Lesotho, Liberia, Libya, Madagascar, Malawi, Mali, Mauritania, Mauritius, Mozambique, Namibia, Niger, Nigeria, Rwanda, Western Sahara (Sahrawi Arab Democratic Republic, SADR), Sao Tome and Principe, Senegal, Seychelles, Sierra Leone, Somalia, South Africa, Sudan, Swaziland, Tanzania, Togo, Tunisia, Uganda, Zambia, Zimbabwe

Arab League
<http://www.arableagueonline.org/>

Algeria, Bahrain, Comoros, Djibouti, Egypt, Iraq, Jordan, Kuwait, Lebanon, Libya, Mauritania, Morocco, Oman, Palestine, Qatar, Saudi Arabia, Somalia, Sudan, Syria, Tunisia, United Arab Emirates, Yemen

Asia–Pacific Economic Cooperation (APEC)
<http://www.apec.org>

Australia, Brunei Darussalam, Canada, Chile, China, Hong Kong, Indonesia, Japan, Korea (South), Malaysia, Mexico, New Zealand, Papua New Guinea, Peru, Philippines, Russia, Singapore, Taiwan, Thailand, USA, Viet Nam

Association of South East Asian Nations (ASEAN)
<http://www.aseansec.org>

Brunei Darussalam, Cambodia, Indonesia, Laos, Malaysia, Myanmar, Philippines, Singapore, Thailand, Viet Nam

ASEAN Regional Forum (ARF)
<http://www.aseanregionalforum.org>

The ASEAN member states plus Australia, Bangladesh, Canada, China, European Union, India, Japan, Korea (North), Korea (South), Mongolia, New Zealand, Pakistan, Papua New Guinea, Russia, Timor-Leste, USA

ASEAN Plus Three
<http://www.aseansec.org/16580.htm>

The ASEAN member states plus China, Japan and Korea (South)

Australia Group (AG)
<http://www.australiagroup.net>

Argentina, Australia, Austria, Belgium, Bulgaria, Canada, Cyprus, Czech Republic, Denmark, Estonia, European Commission, Finland, France, Germany, Greece, Hungary, Iceland, Ireland, Italy, Japan, Korea (South), Latvia, Lithuania, Luxembourg, Malta, Netherlands, New Zealand, Norway, Poland, Portugal, Romania, Slovakia, Slovenia, Spain, Sweden, Switzerland, Turkey, UK, Ukraine, USA

Central European Initiative (CEI)
<http://www.ceinet.org>

Albania, Austria, Belarus, Bosnia and Herzegovina, Bulgaria, Croatia, Czech Republic, Hungary, Italy, Macedonia (Former Yugoslav Republic of), Moldova, Montenegro, Poland, Romania, Serbia, Slovakia, Slovenia, Ukraine

Collective Security Treaty Organization (CSTO)

Armenia, Belarus, Kazakhstan, Kyrgyzstan, Russia, Tajikistan, Uzbekistan

Commonwealth of Independent States (CIS)
<http://www.cis.minsk.by>

Armenia, Azerbaijan, Belarus, Georgia, Kazakhstan, Kyrgyzstan, Moldova, Russia, Tajikistan, Ukraine, Uzbekistan

Commonwealth of Nations
<http://www.thecommonwealth.org>

Antigua and Barbuda, Australia, Bahamas, Bangladesh, Barbados, Belize, Botswana, Brunei Darussalam, Cameroon, Canada, Cyprus, Dominica, Fiji, Gambia, Ghana, Grenada, Guyana, India, Jamaica, Kenya, Kiribati, Lesotho, Malawi, Malaysia, Maldives, Malta, Mauritius, Mozambique, Namibia, Nauru, New Zealand, Nigeria, Pakistan, Papua New Guinea, Saint Kitts and Nevis, Saint Lucia, Saint Vincent and the Grenadines, Samoa, Seychelles, Sierra Leone, Singapore, Solomon Islands, South Africa, Sri Lanka, Swaziland, Tanzania, Tonga, Trinidad and Tobago, Tuvalu, Uganda, UK, Vanuatu, Zambia

Conference on Interaction and Confidence-building Measures in Asia (CICA)
<http://www.kazakhstanembassy.org.uk/cgi-bin/index/128>

Afghanistan, Azerbaijan, China, Egypt, India, Iran, Israel, Kazakhstan, Kyrgyzstan, Mongolia, Pakistan, Palestine, Russia, Tajikistan, Thailand, Turkey, Uzbekistan

Council for Security Cooperation in the Asia Pacific (CSCAP)
<http://www.cscap.org>

Member committees: Australia, Brunei Darussalam, Cambodia, Canada, China, CSCAP Europe, India, Indonesia, Japan, Korea (North), Korea (South), Malaysia, Mongolia, New Zealand, Papua New Guinea, Philippines, Russia, Singapore, Thailand, USA, Viet Nam

Council of Europe
<http://www.coe.int>

Albania, Andorra, Armenia, Austria, Azerbaijan, Belgium, Bosnia and Herzegovina, Bulgaria, Croatia, Cyprus, Czech Republic, Denmark, Estonia, Finland, France, Georgia, Germany, Greece, Hungary, Iceland, Ireland, Italy, Latvia, Liechtenstein, Lithuania, Luxembourg, Macedonia (Former Yugoslav Republic of), Malta, Moldova, Monaco, Netherlands, Norway, Poland, Portugal, Romania, Russia, San Marino, Serbia, Slovakia, Slovenia, Spain, Sweden, Switzerland, Turkey, UK, Ukraine

Council of the Baltic Sea States (CBSS)
<http://www.cbss.st>

Denmark, Estonia, European Commission, Finland, Germany, Iceland, Latvia, Lithuania, Norway, Poland, Russia, Sweden

Developing Eight (D-8)
<http://www.developing8.org/index.php>

Bangladesh, Egypt, Indonesia, Iran, Malaysia, Nigeria, Pakistan, Turkey

Economic Community of West African States (ECOWAS)
<http://www.ecowas.int>

Benin, Burkina Faso, Cape Verde, Côte d'Ivoire, Gambia, Ghana, Guinea, Guinea-Bissau, Liberia, Mali, Niger, Nigeria, Senegal, Sierra Leone, Togo

European Defence Agency
<http://www.eda.europa.eu>

Austria, Belgium, Bulgaria, Cyprus, Czech Republic, Estonia, Finland, France, Germany, Greece, Hungary, Ireland, Italy, Latvia, Lithuania, Luxembourg, Malta, Netherlands, Poland, Portugal, Romania, Slovakia, Slovenia, Spain, Sweden, UK

European Union (EU)
<http://europa.eu.int>

Austria, Belgium, Bulgaria, Cyprus, Czech Republic, Denmark, Estonia, Finland, France, Germany, Greece, Hungary, Ireland, Italy, Latvia, Lithuania, Luxembourg, Malta, Netherlands, Poland, Portugal, Romania, Slovakia, Slovenia, Spain, Sweden, UK

Group of Eight (G8)
<http://www.g8.utoronto.ca>

Canada, France, Germany, Italy, Japan, Russia, UK, USA

Gulf Cooperation Council (GCC)
<http://www.gcc-sg.org>

Bahrain, Kuwait, Oman, Qatar, Saudi Arabia, United Arab Emirates

Hague Code of Conduct against Ballistic Missile Proliferation (HCOC)
<http://www.bmaa.gv.at/view.php3?f_id=54&LNG=en&version=>

Afghanistan, Albania, Andorra, Argentina, Armenia, Australia, Austria, Azerbaijan, Belarus, Belgium, Benin, Bosnia and Herzegovina, Bulgaria, Burkina Faso, Burundi, Cambodia, Cameroon, Canada, Cape Verde, Chad, Chile, Colombia, Comoros, Cook Islands, Costa Rica, Croatia, Cyprus, Czech Republic, Denmark, Ecuador, El Salvador, Eritrea, Estonia, Ethiopia, Fiji, Finland, France, Gabon, Gambia, Georgia, Germany, Ghana, Greece, Guatemala, Guinea, Guinea-Bissau, Guyana, Haiti, Holy See, Honduras, Hungary, Iceland, Ireland, Italy, Japan, Jordan, Kazakhstan, Kenya, Kiribati, Korea (South), Latvia, Liberia, Libya, Liechtenstein, Lithuania, Luxembourg, Macedonia (Former Yugoslav Republic of), Madagascar, Malawi, Mali, Malta, Marshall Islands, Mauritania, Micronesia, Moldova, Monaco, Mongolia, Montenegro, Morocco, Mozambique, Netherlands, New Zealand, Nicaragua, Niger, Nigeria, Norway, Palau, Panama, Papua New Guinea, Paraguay, Peru, Philippines, Poland, Portugal, Romania, Russia, Rwanda, Senegal, Serbia, Seychelles, Sierra Leone, Slovakia, Slovenia, South Africa, Spain, Sudan, Suriname, Sweden, Switzerland, Tajikistan, Tanzania, Timor-Leste, Tonga, Tunisia, Turkey, Turkmenistan, Tuvalu, Uganda, UK, Ukraine, Uruguay, USA, Uzbekistan, Vanuatu, Venezuela, Zambia

Intergovernmental Authority on Development (IGAD)
<http://www.igad.org>

Djibouti, Eritrea, Ethiopia, Kenya, Somalia, Sudan, Uganda

Missile Technology Control Regime (MTCR)
<http://www.mtcr.info>

Argentina, Australia, Austria, Belgium, Brazil, Bulgaria, Canada, Czech Republic, Denmark, Finland, France, Germany, Greece, Hungary, Iceland, Ireland, Italy, Japan, Korea (South), Luxembourg, Netherlands, New Zealand, Norway, Poland, Portugal, Russia, South Africa, Spain, Sweden, Switzerland, Turkey, UK, Ukraine, USA

Non-Aligned Movement (NAM)
<http://www.cubanoal.cu/ingles/index.html>

Afghanistan, Algeria, Angola, Antigua and Barbuda, Bahamas, Bahrain, Bangladesh, Barbados, Belarus, Belize, Benin, Bhutan, Bolivia, Botswana, Brunei Darussalam, Burkina Faso, Burundi, Cambodia, Cameroon, Cape Verde, Central African Republic, Chad, Chile, Colombia, Comoros, Congo (Democratic Republic of the), Congo (Republic of the), Côte d'Ivoire, Cuba, Djibouti, Dominica, Dominican Republic, Ecuador, Egypt, Equatorial Guinea, Eritrea, Ethiopia, Gabon, Gambia, Ghana, Grenada, Guatemala, Guinea, Guinea-Bissau, Guyana, Honduras, India, Indonesia, Iran, Iraq, Jamaica, Jordan, Kenya, Korea (North), Kuwait, Laos, Lebanon, Lesotho, Liberia, Libya, Madagascar, Malawi, Malaysia, Maldives, Mali, Mauritania, Mauritius, Mongolia, Morocco, Mozambique, Myanmar, Namibia, Nepal, Nicaragua, Niger, Nigeria, Oman, Pakistan, Palestine Liberation Organization, Panama, Papua New Guinea, Peru, Philippines, Qatar, Rwanda, Saint Lucia, Saint Vincent and the Grenadines, Sao Tome and Principe, Saudi Arabia, Senegal, Seychelles, Sierra Leone, Singapore, Somalia, South

Africa, Sri Lanka, Sudan, Suriname, Swaziland, Syria, Tanzania, Thailand, Timor-Leste, Togo, Trinidad and Tobago, Tunisia, Turkmenistan, Uganda, United Arab Emirates, Uzbekistan, Vanuatu, Venezuela, Viet Nam, Yemen, Zambia, Zimbabwe

North Atlantic Treaty Organization (NATO)
<http://www.nato.int>

Belgium, Bulgaria, Canada, Czech Republic, Denmark, Estonia, France*, Germany, Greece, Hungary, Iceland, Italy, Latvia, Lithuania, Luxembourg, Netherlands, Norway, Poland, Portugal, Romania, Slovakia, Slovenia, Spain, Turkey, UK, USA

* France is not in the integrated military structures of NATO.

Euro-Atlantic Partnership Council (EAPC)
<http://www.nato.int/issues/eapc>

The NATO member states plus Albania, Armenia, Austria, Azerbaijan, Belarus, Bosnia and Herzegovina, Croatia, Finland, Georgia, Ireland, Kazakhstan, Kyrgyzstan, Macedonia (Former Yugoslav Republic of), Moldova, Montenegro, Russia, Serbia, Sweden, Switzerland, Tajikistan, Turkmenistan, Ukraine, Uzbekistan

Nuclear Suppliers Group (NSG)
<http://www.nuclearsuppliersgroup.org>

Argentina, Australia, Austria, Belarus, Belgium, Brazil, Bulgaria, Canada, China, Croatia, Cyprus, Czech Republic, Denmark, Estonia, Finland, France, Germany, Greece, Hungary, Ireland, Italy, Japan, Kazakhstan, Korea (South), Latvia, Lithuania, Luxembourg, Malta, Netherlands, New Zealand, Norway, Poland, Portugal, Romania, Russia, Slovakia, Slovenia, South Africa, Spain, Sweden, Switzerland, Turkey, UK, Ukraine, USA

Organisation Conjointe de Coopération en matière d'Armement (OCCAR)
<http://www.occar-ea.org>

Belgium, France, Germany, Italy, Spain, UK

Organisation for Economic Co-operation and Development (OECD)
<http://www.oecd.org>

Australia, Austria, Belgium, Canada, Czech Republic, Denmark, Finland, France, Germany, Greece, Hungary, Iceland, Ireland, Italy, Japan, Korea (South), Luxembourg, Mexico, Netherlands, New Zealand, Norway, Poland, Portugal, Slovakia, Spain, Sweden, Switzerland, Turkey, UK, USA

Organization for Democracy and Economic Development–GUAM
<http://www.guam.org.ua/en.phtml>

Azerbaijan, Georgia, Moldova, Ukraine

Organization for Security and Co-operation in Europe (OSCE)
<http://www.osce.org>

Albania, Andorra, Armenia, Austria, Azerbaijan, Belarus, Belgium, Bosnia and Herzegovina, Bulgaria, Canada, Croatia, Cyprus, Czech Republic, Denmark, Estonia, Finland, France, Georgia, Germany, Greece, Holy See, Hungary, Iceland, Ireland, Italy, Kazakhstan, Kyrgyzstan, Latvia, Liechtenstein, Lithuania, Luxembourg, Macedonia (Former Yugoslav Republic of), Malta, Moldova, Monaco, Montenegro, Netherlands, Norway, Poland, Portugal, Romania, Russia, San Marino, Serbia, Slovakia, Slovenia, Spain, Sweden, Switzerland, Tajikistan, Turkey, Turkmenistan, UK, Ukraine, USA, Uzbekistan

Organization of American States (OAS)
<http://www.oas.org>

Antigua and Barbuda, Argentina, Bahamas, Barbados, Belize, Bolivia, Brazil, Canada, Chile, Colombia, Costa Rica, Cuba*, Dominica, Dominican Republic, Ecuador, El Salvador, Grenada, Guatemala, Guyana, Haiti, Honduras, Jamaica, Mexico, Nicaragua, Panama, Paraguay, Peru, Saint Kitts and Nevis, Saint Lucia, Saint Vincent and the Grenadines, Suriname, Trinidad and Tobago, Uruguay, USA, Venezuela

* Cuba has been excluded from participation in the OAS since 1962.

Organization of the Black Sea Economic Cooperation (BSEC)
<http://www.bsec-organization.org>

Albania, Armenia, Azerbaijan, Bulgaria, Georgia, Greece, Moldova, Romania, Russia, Serbia, Turkey, Ukraine

Organization of the Islamic Conference (OIC)
<http://www.oic-oci.org>

Afghanistan, Albania, Algeria, Azerbaijan, Bahrain, Bangladesh, Benin, Brunei Darussalam, Burkina Faso, Cameroon, Chad, Comoros, Côte d'Ivoire, Djibouti, Egypt, Gabon, Gambia, Guinea, Guinea-Bissau, Guyana, Indonesia, Iran, Iraq, Jordan, Kazakhstan, Kuwait, Kyrgyzstan, Lebanon, Libya, Malaysia, Maldives, Mali, Mauritania, Morocco, Mozambique, Niger, Nigeria, Oman, Pakistan, Palestine, Qatar, Saudi Arabia, Senegal, Sierra Leone, Somalia, Sudan, Suriname, Syria, Tajikistan, Togo, Tunisia, Turkey, Turkmenistan, Uganda, United Arab Emirates, Uzbekistan, Yemen

Pacific Islands Forum
<http://www.forumsec.org.fj>

Australia, Cook Islands, Fiji, Kiribati, Marshall Islands, Micronesia, Nauru, New Zealand, Niue, Palau, Papua New Guinea, Samoa, Solomon Islands, Tonga, Tuvalu, Vanuatu

Shanghai Cooperation Organization (SCO)
<http://www.sectsco.org>

China, Kazakhstan, Kyrgyzstan, Russia, Tajikistan, Uzbekistan

South Asian Association for Regional Co-operation (SAARC)
<http://www.saarc-sec.org>

Afghanistan, Bangladesh, Bhutan, India, Maldives, Nepal, Pakistan, Sri Lanka

Southeast European Cooperative Initiative (SECI)
<http://www.secicenter.org>

Albania, Bosnia and Herzegovina, Bulgaria, Croatia, Greece, Hungary, Macedonia (Former Yugoslav Republic of), Moldova, Romania, Serbia, Slovenia, Turkey

Southern African Development Community (SADC)
<http://www.sadc.int>

Angola, Botswana, Congo (Democratic Republic of the), Lesotho, Madagascar, Malawi, Mauritius, Mozambique, Namibia, South Africa, Swaziland, Tanzania, Zambia, Zimbabwe

Southern Common Market (Mercado Común del Sur, MERCOSUR)
<http://www.mercosur.org.uy>

Argentina, Brazil, Paraguay, Uruguay, Venezuela

Stability Pact for South Eastern Europe
<http://www.stabilitypact.org>

Country partners: Albania, Austria, Belgium, Bosnia and Herzegovina, Bulgaria, Canada, Croatia, Cyprus, Czech Republic, Denmark, Estonia, Finland, France, Germany, Greece, Hungary, Ireland, Italy,

Japan, Latvia, Lithuania, Luxembourg, Macedonia (Former Yugoslav Republic of), Malta, Moldova, Montenegro, Netherlands, Norway, Poland, Portugal, Romania, Russia, Serbia, Slovakia, Slovenia, Spain, Sweden, Switzerland, Turkey, UK, USA

Other partners: Central European Initiative, Council of Europe (Council of Europe Development Bank), European Bank for Reconstruction and Development, European Investment Bank, European Union (Council of the European Union, European Agency for Reconstruction, European Commission, European Parliament, Office for South Eastern Europe), International Finance Corporation, International Monetary Fund, International Organization for Migration, North Atlantic Treaty Organization, Office of the High Representative in Bosnia and Herzegovina, Organisation for Economic Co-operation and Development, Organization for Security and Co-operation in Europe, Organization of the Black Sea Economic Cooperation, Southeast European Cooperative Initiative, South-East European Cooperation Process, United Nations (UN Development Programme, UN High Commissioner for Refugees, UN Mission in Kosovo), World Bank

Wassenaar Arrangement (WA)
<http://www.wassenaar.org>

Argentina, Australia, Austria, Belgium, Bulgaria, Canada, Croatia, Czech Republic, Denmark, Estonia, Finland, France, Germany, Greece, Hungary, Ireland, Italy, Japan, Korea (South), Latvia, Lithuania, Luxembourg, Malta, Netherlands, New Zealand, Norway, Poland, Portugal, Romania, Russia, Slovakia, Slovenia, South Africa, Spain, Sweden, Switzerland, Turkey, UK, Ukraine, USA

Western European Union (WEU)
<http://www.weu.int>

Belgium, France, Germany, Greece, Italy, Luxembourg, Netherlands, Portugal, Spain, UK

Zangger Committee
<http://www.zanggercommittee.org/Zangger/default.htm>

Argentina, Australia, Austria, Belgium, Bulgaria, Canada, China, Croatia, Cyprus, Czech Republic, Denmark, Finland, France, Germany, Greece, Hungary, Ireland, Italy, Japan, Korea (South), Luxembourg, Netherlands, Norway, Poland, Portugal, Romania, Russia, Slovakia, Slovenia, South Africa, Spain, Sweden, Switzerland, Turkey, UK, Ukraine, USA

Conventions

. .	Data not available or not applicable
–	Nil or a negligible figure
( )	Uncertain data
b.	Billion (thousand million)
kg	Kilogram
km	Kilometre (1000 metres)
kt	Kiloton (1000 tons)
m.	Million
Mt	Megaton (1 million tons)
th.	Thousand
tr.	Trillion (million million)
$	US dollars, unless otherwise indicated
€	Euros

Introduction
A world of risk

ALYSON J. K. BAILES

I. Introduction

It seems to be a pattern in human existence that feelings of insecurity expand to fill the space left by the passing of earlier threats and fears. Although the shadow of nuclear extinction has been lifted from the world with the ending of the cold war and the phenomenon of major armed conflict has gradually been reduced to fewer than 20 cases (all of which are intra-state conflicts),[1] the security behaviour of the world's largest power—the United States—has been dominated in recent years by its often costly effort to block new perceived sources of vulnerability. More broadly, advances in world prosperity are giving those who benefit from them the sense of having more to lose, while those whose position has actually or relatively worsened have reason to resent their situation more. The boom in global travel, communications and economic interdependence of all kinds is exposing more and more people to unfamiliar environments and contacts, with all the attendant hazards.

Increasingly, analysts in the field of public security policy are trying to capture all these different dimensions of security challenge by using the word 'risk'—a term perhaps more familiar in the past from business analysis or from more specialized uses in individual and social psychology. Section II of this chapter discusses the reasons why this may be so. Section III addresses the difficulties of defining and assessing 'risk' in such a way that it can be a useful tool of defensive or constructive security policy. Section IV considers the range of different responses to risk, with their strengths and weaknesses, and concludes that active and forceful efforts to eliminate risks (especially those of human origin) sometimes do more damage than their necessarily imperfect results can justify. Section V draws together the results of the analysis and relates them to the critique of contemporary security policies offered under different headings in recent editions of the SIPRI Yearbook. It suggests that a risk-based analysis can give new force to the arguments for a global, cooperative framework for response based on shared human vulnerabilities and the consequent shared interests.

---

[1] This estimate uses the definition of a major armed conflict as one that has at some stage caused at least 1000 battle-related deaths in a year; on this and other definitions of armed conflict see appendices 2A–2C in this volume.

II. Risk as a new security paradigm

Since the early 1990s a school of security analysis has developed that focuses on the 'risk society' as a new framework for the making of security policy.[2] Simultaneously, the language of risk has become more widely used by security analysts, commentators and practitioners—including many of SIPRI's own authors—even without their being aware of its theoretical underpinnings. One reason for this is fairly obvious: the word can capture a much wider range of problematic security phenomena than the traditional term 'threat' or even the more general term 'challenge'. 'Threat' was reserved, and perhaps still should be, for problems that are consciously and actively created by one security actor—ranging from an individual person to a state, alliance or international movement—for another. Finding the right way to apply the traditional term is tricky in the case of modern transnational phenomena such as terrorism. Terrorist actions targeted against a particular nation or society can fairly be called a threat to that nation or society. However, since their most characteristic modus operandi is to kill at random, the likelihood that any individual— who may not even be part of the target community but, say, a tourist—will get caught up in a terrorist action may better be defined as a risk than a threat for that person. At the same time, those who are targeted may subjectively feel 'threatened' by terrorism in ways not very different from how they once worried about nuclear war. This helps to explain why, as discussed further below, governments are also tempted to respond to the new problem in ways that are analogous to the old problems.

Modern definitions of 'human' (or comprehensive, or multifunctional) security include many types of danger and damage that do not involve armed violence or where such violence takes forms purely internal to a society, such as gang warfare, gender-based violence or extreme physical oppresssion by the state.[3] To the extent that these represent intentional human behaviour, it is not illogical to say that populations and persons may be threatened or at least feel threatened by them. Yet the range of appropriate responses in this case clearly lies well outside the traditional, state-based security discourse. This is even more the case for dangers that arise from unintentional human behaviour, such as accidents and negligence—as occurred, for example, in Chernobyl in 1986—or those that have causes essentially beyond human control, even if

---

[2] 'Risk society' as a concept was coined by the sociologist Ulrich Beck. For an introduction see Beck, U., *Risk Society: Towards a New Modernity* (Sage Publications: London, 1992). For application of the concept in the realm of security studies see e.g. Coker, C., International Institute for Strategic Studies, *Globalisation and Insecurity in the Twenty-first Century: NATO and the Management of Risk*, Adelphi Paper no. 345 (Oxford University Press: Oxford, 2002); and Rasmussen, M. V., '"A parallel globalization of terror": 9-11, security and globalization', *Cooperation and Conflict*, vol. 37, no. 3 (Sep. 2002), pp. 323–49.

[3] On the concept of human security see Study Group on Europe's Security Capabilities, 'A human security doctrine for Europe', London School of Economics and Political Science, Centre for the Study of Global Governance, London, Sep. 2004, URL <http://www.lse.ac.uk/Depts/global/Publications/HumanSecurityDoctrine.pdf>; and University of British Columbia, Human Security Centre, *Human Security Report 2005: War and Peace in the 21st Century* (Oxford University Press: New York, N.Y., 2005), URL <http://www.humansecurityreport.info/>.

human actions can both aggravate and palliate them—for example, natural disasters, the effects of climate change, and epidemic diseases of people, animals and crops.

However inexact, the word 'risk' is likely to be readily understood when it is used to gather all these different kinds of problem into one security perspective. The argument in favour of trying to do so is not just a matter of theory. There has been a growing understanding in recent years that it is difficult to assure the security of a society, a state or an integrated region without taking into account the full range of challenges it faces and, in particular, understanding the ways in which they interrelate. The effort to plan corrective strategies that encompass many fields of security at the same time characterizes the latest thinking about crisis management and post-conflict peacebuilding, as well as many countries' homeland security policies.[4] Any attempt to deal with any type of security threat, challenge or risk will use resources—including intangible ones such as the support or acquiescence of the population—and the only fully rational resource strategy is one that identifies all the areas of related spending before setting priorities and, ideally, seeking synergies among them.[5] If the language and concept of risk can help decision makers and opinion formers to design more comprehensive frameworks of this kind and to avoid priority setting based purely on habit and prejudice, then this alone would demonstrate their practical usefulness.

The notion of risk also carries some baggage from its past applications and current usage in non-security realms, which may give new insights into modern security challenges. Risk is reflexive in that it is human beings' decisions to live in a certain way, to engage in certain activities and to go to certain places that expose them to the hazards concerned in the first place.[6] Just as the financial investments that bring the highest returns are normally also those with the greatest financial risk, the benefits of living in an open, globalized society have multiple risks as their obverse: exposure to terrorist infiltration and attack, aggravation of environmental pollution, exposure to disease, or the collapse of fragile and complicated material and social support systems.

A further level of reflexivity—or feedback—arises from the ways in which individuals and societies perceive and choose to respond to the risks that affect them. One person or group may see more clearly the necessary connections between their own choices and the risks attached and as a result be more ready to live with the latter; another may fail to see the connections and so be less

---

[4] See Dwan, R., and Wiharta, S., 'Multilateral peace missions: challenges of peace-building', *SIPRI Yearbook 2005: Armaments, Disarmament and International Security* (Oxford University Press: Oxford, 2005), pp. 139–66. See also chapter 3 in this volume; and Hansen, A. S. and Wiharta, S., *The Transition to a Just Order: Establishing Local Ownership after Conflict, A Policy Guide* (Folke Bernadotte Academy Publications: Stockholm, 2007).

[5] Hagelin, B. and Sköns, E., 'The military sector in a changing context', *SIPRI Yearbook 2003: Armaments, Disarmament and International Security* (Oxford University Press: Oxford, 2003), pp. 281–300.

[6] See e.g. Beck, U., Bonss, W. and Lau, C., 'The theory of reflexive modernization: problematic, hypotheses and research programme', *Theory, Culture and Society*, vol. 20, no. 2 (Apr. 2003), pp. 1–33; and Rasmussen, M. V., '"It sounds like a riddle": security studies, the war on terror and risk', *Millennium: Journal of International Studies*, vol. 33, no. 2 (Mar. 2004), pp. 381–95.

ready to accept the consequences of their own actions. One country may grasp that risk is endemic and conclude that even its extreme forms, such as terrorism or the use of weapons of mass destruction (WMD), can only ever be minimized and controlled, rather than tracked to their roots and eliminated. Like a business operating in a high-risk market, such a country will emphasize prevention, defensive measures, resilience and survival strategies in the event of a calamity, alongside whatever equivalent it can find to liability insurance. Another country may view the same risks as unacceptable—without necessarily being ready to give up the types of behaviour that have aggravated them—and will be drawn towards stronger measures including, in the extreme case, forceful pre-emption. The many-layered subjectivity of such judgements is explored further in the next section, and the choice of responses is discussed again in section IV.

III. Measuring the immeasurable

In common with the handling of earlier threats, creating policies to respond to risk calls for the clear identification and, ideally, quantification of the challenge that needs to be met. Even in the context of more traditional military confrontations, such assessments are not easy: data on the other side's military holdings may be hard to obtain or deliberately distorted; judgements need to be made on quality, intention and probability as well as quantitative potential, and so on.[7] When trying to bring the much larger range of risk factors relevant to security within the span of a single assessment, these difficulties are multiplied. This section addresses the complications that arise at the objective, the subjective and the methodological levels, in turn.

Objective definition and assessment

An obvious objective difficulty in assessing security risks is that there are so many that are relevant to the survival and welfare of a present-day population, state or multi-state organization. The chances of a direct military attack may have been greatly reduced for certain states, such as the members of the European Union (EU) and the North Atlantic Treaty Organization (NATO), but none can entirely ignore them. Calculating them is already hard enough for a state that has several obvious potential adversaries or several vulnerabilities. Then come the risks of, and risks created by, internal armed conflicts: both for the territories where they occur and for their neighbours, and often also for

---

[7] A common analytical (and political) mistake is to draw conclusions about a country's defence capability and perhaps even its strategic intentions directly from its level of military expenditure. In reality a country's capability consists of the cumulative resources acquired usually over a long period, including some elements that were purchased at market price and others that were not (e.g. gifts of equipment and the services of conscripts). The capability is further conditioned by factors of quality, appropriateness and will. On the difficulty of assessing and applying military expenditure data see Ward, M., 'International comparisons of military expenditure: issues and challenges of using purchasing power parities', *SIPRI Yearbook 2006: Armaments, Disarmament and International Security* (Oxford University Press: Oxford, 2006), pp. 369–86.

quite remote states that have ties with the scene of the conflict or stand to be affected by refugee flows. Local and transnational terrorist activity, although often linked with the issues of a specific conflict, is notoriously much harder to identify, analyse and anticipate.[8]

A range of other, intentional but less physically violent, human actions can pose substantial risks for both their perpetrators and others: the acquisition of or intent to acquire WMD; denial of or interference with vital energy supplies, other strategic commodities (including foodstuffs) and natural assets (e.g. water), international lines of transport and communication, or international financial systems and relationships; attacks on the Internet and other information technology assets; and deliberate damage to the environment. Internal abuses of human and civic rights have become a 'risk' that affects not only the local victims but, potentially, any responsible state since the international community feels an increasing pressure and duty to intervene in cases where a state maltreats or fatally neglects its own population.[9]

On top of all these risks of conscious human origin come those that have origins that could not be controllable by humans (even if human activities have contributed to them): accidents of all kinds and one-off natural disasters; disease epidemics affecting people, animals or crops; and more gradual or long-term changes in local habitats and the global environment, including the much-discussed (but negligible) risk of a large meteorite or asteroid strike.

Even when addressed from the perspective of a single state or society, these risks are so diverse in nature, origin and degree of 'knowability' that many different experts and disciplines would need to be called upon for a combined assessment. Hitherto, neither governments' security work nor independent security research has generally been organized in a way that brings these different sources of expertise together.[10] Even if all the experts could be gathered in one room, they would still have to face the many practical challenges of building a multi-risk analytical model. What to include and what to leave out can be a subject of almost endless debate, especially when it comes to social and economic factors such as the impact of ageing societies on the viability and external competitiveness of national economic and social welfare systems, or the putative connections between high immigration, multi-ethnic communities, internal disorder and the roots of terrorism. Aberrant internal forces such as terrorists and criminals clearly need to be counted as threat or risk factors. However, should the rest of society be seen as the target on which these and other dangers impact, as some might prefer, or as part of the problem? It cannot be denied that recognizing the intrinsic vulnerabilities of a given society is important for understanding the way in which the events more

---

[8] On transnational conflicts see chapter 2 in this volume.

[9] The outcome document of the Sep. 2005 UN World Summit contains important new agreed formulations on the duty of any government to ensure its people's welfare. UN General Assembly Resolution 60/1, 24 Oct. 2005, URL <http://www.un.org/Depts/dhl/resguide/r60.htm>.

[10] Before 11 Sep. 2001 it was unusual for governments of developed countries even to assess external and internal security threats through the same bureaucratic processes. Conflict-ridden developing countries did not have the luxury of distinguishing between them.

readily characterized as risks would impact on it. For example, one epidemic may strike harder against an ageing population, another where there are more children; a divided and unruly society makes it harder both to control crime and terrorism internally and to withstand an outside attack or natural disaster; a society with existing inter-ethnic tensions or high unemployment is likely to have more trouble with a flood of new refugees, and so on. Once more, the logic here seems to point to the desirability of making the work of risk definition, analysis and the study of interconnections as inclusive as possible.

Some traps of subjectivity

Once the scene is set for an overall risk assessment, it is important to be on guard against the many ways in which human perceptions and attitudes may distort the results. All humans face decisions involving the judgement of risk all the time—if only over what to eat and what means of transport to use—yet the human mind is notoriously ill-adapted for the task, at least at the conscious level. Non-experts persistently misunderstand the scientific rules of probability and misread quantified statements about odds and the incidence of various dangers.[11] Further distortions arise, however, from the specific situations of different human observers and the contexts in which opinions about risk are formed. Some of the most obvious examples follow.

1. Unfamiliarity and difference cause a risk to be subjectively rated higher, while familiarity leads to acceptance or even complacency. A US tourist or businessman will accept advice that it is too risky to go to country A at all, while women native to that country are still managing to bear and raise children there.[12] Tourists from country B may meanwhile think it too risky to go to some (or some parts) of the USA's own cities because of levels of street crime. People in country A itself might not want their women to face the sexual and cultural risks that they see as rampant in US society.

2. 'New' risks—especially if highly publicized—tend to drive 'old' ones out of people's minds, so much so that links between the older and newer manifestations and valuable lessons from past experience are commonly missed.

3. Risks on which information is readily available are addressed preferentially over those that are harder to define and quantify.

4. Short-term risks of relatively clear and compact origin are given priority as targets for active policy over longer-term, gradually evolving, more insidious ones.

5. Risk perceptions are skewed not only by the interests but also by the self-defined roles and responsibilities of those making the judgements. Different actors prefer to look for and address the risks that fall within their own per-

[11] Probably the best-known example is that if a tossed coin has come down heads 10 times running, most people will believe it more likely to come down tails the next time, whereas in fact the odds remain 50 : 50 on both results.

[12] The advice may of course be logically defended if US citizens, as such, are likely to be selectively targeted for attack.

ceived competences, duties and capabilities. Governments are entrusted with protecting their whole territory and population and possess special powers, ranging from making war to passing binding laws, to do so. Thus, they will naturally be drawn towards risks of definable human origin where there is a target to attack or to negotiate with. They may easily be tempted to use their strongest attribute—military power—for the purpose.[13] Companies that feel primarily responsible for their own operations, profits, suppliers and markets are most interested in risks arising in and directly impacting on the related economic fields, so that, for example, damage to their corporate image, punitive lawsuits or inadequate insurance may come higher on their list of risks than terrorist attack, even if they are constantly exposed to the latter.[14] Citizens, and the civil society groups that represent them, may meanwhile see wrong actions and misuse of power by both government and business—not least when carried out in the name of risk management—as risks they need to mobilize against.

Section IV returns to how these subjectively determined views of risk shape patterns of response. One last complication should be noted here, however: the different degrees to which different human risk perceptions may become combined or interact. Much of the dialogue between the developed states of the North and the less-developed states of the South is about the efforts of the states of the South to make the North recognize and help with their greater exposure to a range of more consistently destructive risk factors. A powerful state (or multi-state organization) can impose its subjectively generated perceptions of threat and priorities on many others who, perhaps, do not objectively share the given problem let alone the same inherent preferences for dealing with it. Similarly, within a country government is normally well placed to impose its own characteristic risk vision on business and society, but it also happens that a business lobby or citizen's movement can impel government to give a higher priority to some risks than it would otherwise have done (for better or worse). All that said, problems arise far more often from the failure of different states and groupings to share and compare their visions, or of governments to discuss these matters with their own business constituencies and with civil society representatives.[15]

---

[13] This attitude may be encouraged by the discourse recently prevailing in the field of conflict management that emphasizes the importance of restoring the central authority's 'monopoly of force'. This doctrine might be less prone to misunderstanding and abuse if it were always stressed that good governance is needed to legitimize the state monopoly, and that less use of force rather than more is usually one of the ways a 'good' government is identified.

[14] Ilmonen, U., 'Survival planning for business: a view from Nokia', eds A. J. K. Bailes and I. Frommelt, SIPRI, *Business and Security: Public–Private Sector Relationships in a New Security Environment* (Oxford University Press: Oxford, 2004), pp. 183–86.

[15] Governments addressing themselves to functional aspects of security, such as protecting critical infrastructure or stockpiling drugs, can hardly avoid working with the private sector. However, if such consultation is limited to only a few fields, it merely aggravates the problem of achieving consistency and optimal resource use across the whole field of risk assessment and response.

Methodological complications

Any attempt to assess and prioritize risks more objectively must return to the mundane questions of what is being measured, in what setting, from whose perspective and to what end. The very semantics of the word 'risk' associate it—more so than 'threat'—with notions of incidence and probability. A high risk of phenomenon X is most naturally understood as an increased likelihood that X will happen in a given environment or during a given period. For the purposes of security analysis, however, it is not just frequency or likelihood that is relevant. It may actually be easier for people to adjust to a harmful phenomenon (below the level of mass destruction) that recurs often in a given environment and for government to anticipate and handle that phenomenon in a resource-efficient way. If the aim of analysis is not just to catalogue risks but to improve the quality of policy response, it is equally important to be able to assess the relative gravity of the impact of different events—including their secondary effects—and to judge correctly how far a public policy response is feasible and efficient. When making such judgements, the kind of question to ask is whether human authorities can hope to anticipate, prevent or palliate the eventuation of the risk, or whether thay can only demonstrate their effectiveness in clearing up afterwards. Assessing the factor of connectivity is also very important for policy choices: a type of event that can be triggered by several different causes and that, in turn, can trigger multiple problems in other dimensions should prima facie attract more attention and resources than one that stands alone, however much damage it does at the time.[16]

Where or in what context the risk is being measured is a point that needs reflection. Commercial risk-assessment services, used notably by private business, have now become very sophisticated but still typically take a country-by-country approach that lends itself to portrayal in maps. The indicators measured can range from individual exposure to disease, street crime, kidnapping and so on, to systemic levels of political risk (including armed conflict but also the risk of sudden dispossession by the government) and economic risk (including such basic features of the economy as currency stability or security of supply but also human factors like the adequacy of regulation, policy stability and the degree of corruption). These are tools that are well matched to customers that have to choose between one country and another, be it a business deciding where to trade, a newspaper deciding where to send reporters or a tourist deciding where to travel. However, most such consumers are not the same as those who carry responsibility (in any sense) either for the creation of risks or for the response to them. The government of the country in question, its neighbours and other states or institutions that have an interest or duty to

---

[16] This reasoning led a major multifunctional study commissioned in 1991 by the Government of Switzerland to identify a widespread and sustained electricity blackout as the single greatest danger facing the country. Comprehensive Risk Analysis Switzerland, 'Comprehensive Risk Analysis Switzerland (1991–1999)', Swiss Federal Institute of Technology, Zurich, 1999, URL <http://www.crn.ethz.ch/projects/ComprehensiveRiskAnalysis1999.cfm>. See also Braun, H., 'The non-military threat spectrum', *SIPRI Yearbook 2003* (note 5), pp. 33–43.

influence conditions there need analysis that tells them much more about both the causation and the consequences of each major risk factor. Neither of these can easily be confined to the limits of a single state.

This is easy to see in the context of transnational threats and natural challenges, ranging from the operations of global terrorist networks to the spread of epidemics, but it is also true of many intra-state conflicts and even of single policy acts. To take a topical example, it may have seemed natural for a professional risk consultant drawing up a risk map of the world to inscribe the 'risk' of North Korea's testing a nuclear device on North Korea itself. However, the factors that determined the timing of the test doubtless included various features of North Korea's relations with outside players, while the constituencies affected by the test ranged from those in nearby Seoul, Tokyo and Beijing all the way to Canberra, Washington and New York. For people on the streets of Pyongyang, however, the test itself was not a 'risk' in any direct sense, although the consequences of international reactions to it might well be.[17] Again, a map that shows how likely conflict is to break out in country X in the near future cannot answer the other very important questions of which other countries (and non-state actors) may have an interest in starting or stopping the conflict and how likely it is to lead to some form of national, multinational or institutional intervention.

On this showing, country-by-country risk measurement needs to be supplemented by something else in order to capture many of the dynamics relevant for successful forecasting and anticipation, or for determining policy priorities and responses. Larger maps that demonstrate intra- and interregional flows and influences are already used to present single-dimension challenges like the spead of HIV/AIDS, the spread of avian influenza, the estimated impact of climate change, terrorist networks, drug-smuggling routes, and so on. Other security-related phenomena (such as linkages and overspills between different conflicts, flows of armaments and other conflict commodities), certain economic interactions (including energy and investment flows) and some human ones (like migration, outsourcing or the flow of remittances from migrant workers) could all be pictured in the same way. Whether separately or combined, the pattern they formed could inform risk estimates by drawing attention to critical nodes, cases of high dependency, rapid shifts in relationships and suchlike. To arrive at a regional or a global equivalent of national risk mapping, it would be desirable not only to integrate as many of these different factors as possible but to begin to sketch the interplay between them. For policymakers who seek (just as at the national level) some sense of the impact of risk, however, another dimension would still need to be added: the vulnerability of the global system and the international human community to a particular risk or set of risks. This, in turn, demands an assessment of international society's capacity to respond (actively or by absorbing the losses) and an opinion on whether such responses would in real life be rational or would tend to make things worse.

---

[17] See chapter 12 and appendix 12B in this volume.

If the terminology used here is a little reminiscent of discussions about the international monetary system, this is a useful reminder that economic analysts (both governmental and business-based) have to make similar judgements about a highly connective and interdependent global scene. It would be an interesting exercise to compare and, where possible, combine the techniques of risk assessment and management used in business and other economic contexts with those being developed by governments and multilateral organizations in the context of multifunctional security. The differences in goals and cultures of the two approaches are precisely what make the attempt worthwhile. The dispassionate qualities of a good private-sector assessment of security risk, which prosaically calculates probabilities and costs rather than labelling perpetrators as 'evil' or their acts as 'shocking', may sometimes be a good corrective to public judgements swayed by the subjectivity mentioned above. Private-sector leaders would no doubt also want to urge politicians to take more seriously the security implications of issues that hit business first and foremost, such as overstretched insurance capacity or cyber-sabotage. Government for its part could point out to private actors the many ways in which their own actions or oversights might aggravate risks and the need for them to cooperate positively with both official and social authorities to reduce the damage. Indeed, the more widely the definitions of a modern public security policy are drawn, the clearer it becomes that the private sector today is often the most exposed to functional and transnational risks and among the best placed to devise solutions. This in turn suggests the need for a blending of public and private risk analyses and response strategies, rather than one-sided imposition of a paradigm.[18]

IV. The risks of risk management

This section returns to the challenges that exclusively concern public policy-makers in the field of security, together with those who are consulted by such authorities or who seek to control them. It is argued, first, that a number of factors are combining to promote a more active or preventative approach to security risk by some of today's greatest powers and major institutions; but, second, that such behaviour can be counterproductive in at least three ways if pushed to extremes.

The temptation to act

Any security risk that has origins or causes that are susceptible to human influence has the potential to be eliminated, reduced or contained through policy. As noted above, such action will almost invariably have costs, in cash and

---

[18] On the issues discussed in this passage see eds Bailes and Frommelt (note 14); and Bailes, A. J. K., 'Private sector, public security', eds A. Bryden and M. Caparini, Geneva Centre for the Democratic Control of Armed Forces (DCAF), *Private Actors and Security Governance* (Lit: Zurich, 2006), URL <http://www.dcaf.ch/publications/kms/details.cfm?id=25736>, pp. 41–63.

other resources, including the cost of diverting resources from other potential uses. However, there are also risks involved in the very process of acting against risk. In the field of traditional, interstate security relations these 'process' risks can be categorized as: (*a*) retaliation by the object of the action, leading possibly to escalation; (*b*) retaliation by another party either supporting the attacked party or simply taking advantage of the occasion; (*c*) domestic risks such as popular objections leading to loss of political support and credibility or, in the extreme case, collapse of the responsible regime; and (*d*) what might be called the moral risk of breaking any relevant normative rules, which could also lead to a type of altruistic retaliation such as sanctions or even forceful intervention by the relevant international bodies.

These points apply *mutatis mutandis* not just to military actions but to other, for example economic, tools used with coercive intent. Although the picture they present is complex, state authorities have long experience of calculating process risks and are familiar with the most obvious secondary choices that may be made in order to minimize them. These include: (*a*) seeking first to overcome the problem cooperatively (e.g. with a non-aggression pact or arms control agreement); (*b*) solving it in a way that avoids or reduces the risk of direct confrontation (examples range from deterrent military postures, through negotiated confidence-building measures, to buying off the opponent or diverting its attention towards another target); (*c*) acquiring allies or creating mutual support groupings to share the liability; and (*d*) seeking prior approval from a higher authority such as the United Nations, or even getting that body to tackle the target itself. Last but not least, in cases where the risk concerned does not jeopardize either the community's or the government's own survival, the calculation of these process risks may produce a rational decision to do nothing or to engage only in preparations designed to cushion the eventual impact.

The challenge for today's policymakers could be defined as the need to extend and adapt this traditional wisdom to the altered, and generally much wider, range of risks that are within the scope of security policy today. New scope for miscalculation exists even in relation to threats of the more familiar interstate type. For a start, the motive to address residual risks actively, and to use more ambitious (pre-emptive) policies, has been strengthened by the removal of the very large risks of retaliation and escalation inherent in the East–West stand-off of cold war times. The means to act are available in abundance, most obviously to the USA as the only remaining military superpower, but also to all the other states that have chosen not to cut their defence effort in proportion to the drop in proximate military threats.[19]

As to the four types of process risks, the USA no longer has reason to fear retaliation by any power of its own size, nor to expect that any of the larger powers would intervene to protect its likely targets, nor that anyone would dream of exploiting the overseas deployment of US troops to venture a mili-

---

[19] World military expenditure in 2006 was $1.2 trillion, which is just below its real value at the height of the cold war. The USA accounted for 46% of this total spending. See chapter 8 in this volume.

tary attack on the homeland.[20] The kind of retaliation that might, nonetheless, be expected from different potential US military targets is harder to assess than it was in the case of the Soviet Union because intelligence on them is more scarce, cultural interpretation is harder and their own policies are sometimes inherently unpredictable. The circumstances of the early 21st century have kept the risk of domestic retaliation relatively low for both the US and the Russian administrations. Finally, the policy of the two US Administrations of President George W. Bush has been to downgrade, at both theoretical and practical levels, the importance—and even the legitimacy—of international rules and institutions that might attach moral risk to pre-emptive action.

All these factors could have been expected to generate a more adventurous anti-risk strategy both by the USA and by other powers making similar calculations (e.g. Israel), even in the absence of the terrorist attacks of 11 September 2001. They have, however, also opened the way for many developments that are more widely welcomed by world opinion, such as the proliferation of international peace missions of all kinds; the freedom for NATO to engage itself militarily in Afghanistan; the openings for the EU to develop itself as an intervening power, even in such sensitive locations as the Palestinian territories; and the decisions of the UN World Summit of September 2005 to adopt principles that underpin humanitarian intervention in cases such as genocide.[21] The relaxation of cold war disciplines has allowed former adversaries to accede to what used to be an enemy institution or to work together in ad hoc peace deployments, as in the Western Balkans.[22] The same picture is seen in the building of institutions and action networks to tackle new shared functional threats, sometimes through novel uses of military assets.[23] The fact that so many states have been able to face and overcome the risks involved in transition to a democratic mode of governance in the past 15 years can be traced back in large part to the same strategic shifts, and to their impact on both global diplomacy and global economics. If, therefore, blame needs to be attributed for recent cases of apparently excessive activism linked with false risk calculation, the answer may best be sought in the combination of major changes in realpolitik with new and urgent demands for response to other categories of human risk—including the 'new threats' of terrorism and WMD proliferation—for which recent history offers no single tried and tested model.

Notoriously, part of the USA's stated justification for its 'global war on terrorism' is the principle that one can neither negotiate with terrorists nor

---

[20] The same could be said of China or Russia, unless they were to attack the USA itself or one of its allies.

[21] See note 9.

[22] Examples of accession to formerly enemy institutions are the entries of Cambodia and Viet Nam to the Association of South East Asian Nations (ASEAN), 10 Central European countries to NATO in 1999–2004 and 8 Central European countries to the EU in 2004. For the current membership of these bodies see the glossary in this volume. Russian troops were deployed in conjunction with NATO forces in Bosnia and Herzegovina and Kosovo during the 1990s.

[23] E.g. the Proliferation Security Initiative was set up in 2003 to tackle the unlawful transfer of WMD-related consignments by sea. See e.g. Ahlström, C., 'The Proliferation Security Initiative: international law aspects of the Statement of Interdiction Principles', *SIPRI Yearbook 2005* (note 4), pp. 741–67.

deter them by the traditional interstate means. The current US Administration has also applied this principle to its dealings with states potentially engaged in nuclear proliferation. It maintains that negotiation with such states (at least, in bilateral form) is neither morally acceptable nor productive, while the methods of deterrence and containment are too slow and uncertain. The discarding of these familiar policy tools has left the USA with the main options of 'hardening' itself as a target (with missile defences, controls on immigrant and non-immigrant entry, and various counterterrorist measures at home) and of forcefully and actively intervening against the supposed sources of danger abroad. The actual costs and risks that are associated with the choices are addressed in the next subsection. At this point, it may be suggested that the USA's most fateful steps overall have been (*a*) to favour traditional military power in its policy against new threats and (*b*) to assume that the same risk calculus attaches to it as to the tackling of states and other geographically based adversaries in post-cold war conditions, as described above. Not only is military coercion an approach of limited value for eliminating terrorism as such, but when used against targets defined by an anti-terrorist or anti-proliferation logic it has turned out to be more prone to evoke retaliation and less likely to be rewarded or at least tolerated by the relevant domestic and international constituencies than could be expected in the case of other bilateral interventions and peace missions (whether legally mandated or not).[24]

A more open but intriguing question is how far the USA's and other powers' thinking about active and coercive approaches to risk has been influenced by the integration of other risks of non-intentional or non-human origin into the officially recognized security spectrum. Destructive forces such as epidemic disease or natural calamities cannot be negotiated with; unintentional human errors cannot be deterred; and even some types of intentional human behaviour that affect international security relations—such as mass migration—or internal social viability—such as having more or fewer children than the authorities recommend—can only be influenced with a rather narrow and uncertain range of means. Moreover, in none of these areas does strong corrective intervention carry much risk of retaliation as such; and if it misfires or rebounds in other ways, people are less likely to condemn the government for failure than in the case of miscalculations against 'manageable' human opponents. The chance that an active policy of risk elimination or reduction in these fields will run into international legal obstacles or moral prohibitions is relatively low, although it is perhaps highest in the fields of migration and population control. Overall, therefore, it may be posited that these new dimensions of security have helped to steer many governments' preferences towards a type of response that places relative emphasis on prevention or pre-emption—even if the means chosen for it are often 'peaceful' and internation-

---

[24] For this purpose, contrast the scale of repercussions created by the invasion of Iraq with those of US military actions since the end of the cold war in Panama (1989), the 1991 Gulf War, its handling of peace missions in Somalia, etc. The new ambition and scale of the US action in Afghanistan and Iraq also helps to explain why the international fallout has been greater than in earlier terrorist-related actions such as bombings carried out against targets in Libya in 1986, Sudan in 1998 and Yemen in 2002.

ally cooperative ones—and where the rest of the policy arsenal is reduced to measures for improved resistance and for damage limitation. It is tempting to speculate on how far this model may have influenced paradigms of anti-terrorist policy and, in particular, may have discouraged recourse to the tools of discussion and negotiation (with the basis of human understanding that they require), even among states that do not favour the use of military force for the purpose.

At any rate, consideration of current responses to human security risks serves to underline yet again the variety and subjectivity of national judgements both on the severity of risk and on the merits of specific responses. China has been criticized for setting the risks of loss of face and foreign intrusion above those of spread of infection in the early stages of its response to the SARS crisis of 2003 and possibly to the more recent avian influenza threat.[25] In Russia, concerns in certain quarters about military and scientific confidentiality have sometimes hampered acceptance of international help to reduce risks from leftover and unwanted nuclear, biological and chemical materials.[26] The USA's policy on the global risk of fast population growth is conditioned, in a way that few of its Western partners' policies are, by perceived risks to the sanctity of human life.[27] Conversely, European countries (and many others) have been prepared to accept significant new constraints and short-term sacrifices to help control global warming, while the US authorities both dispute the scale of this risk and reject the economic costs that they associate with the currently available countermeasures. Such examples underline that it is not so much the idea of preventing, pre-empting or eliminating risk as such that has divided the world so sharply in recent years, but rather the question of priorities and of suitable cases, rules and instruments for its application.

Counterproductive approaches

Another important question for analysis is 'what works?' This final subsection looks at a range of ways in which active approaches to countering risk may do more harm than good, for those who embark on them and for the global system at large.

---

[25] Njuguna, J. T., 'The SARS epidemic: the control of infectious diseases and biological weapon threats', *SIPRI Yearbook 2004: Armaments, Disarmament and International Security* (Oxford University Press: Oxford, 2004), pp. 697–712.

[26] See Anthony, I., *Reducing Threats at the Source: A European Perspective on Cooperative Threat Reduction*, SIPRI Research Report no. 19 (Oxford University Press: Oxford, 2003). Russia's persistent cover-up of its cold war biological weapon research and production programmes and of the scale of the leftover hazards is perhaps the single most glaring and dangerous example. See e.g. Hagelin, B. et al., 'Transparency in the arms life cycle', *SIPRI Yearbook 2006* (note 7), pp. 253–54.

[27] Population growth was identified as a risk to US national security in a 1974 National Security Council report. US National Security Council, 'Implications of worldwide population growth for U.S. security and overseas interests', National Security Study Memorandum no. 200, Washington, DC, 10 Dec. 1974. Since the 1980s US administrations have adapted the 1974 policy according to their different views on birth control and abortion.

First, what could be called the traditional varieties of backlash, familiar from earlier experience of interstate conflict, are still extant and often defy prediction, even when the power taking action is apparently much stronger than the target. Thus, President Saddam Hussein's forces collapsed surprisingly fast in Iraq in 2003 but the Taliban have proved to be much tougher than expected in Afghanistan, like the North Vietnamese in the past or the Chechens. Second, a risk that has apparently been eliminated can reappear in another place or in a different form. Iraq exhibits many varieties of this, from Baathists turning to terrorism after their military defeat, to other types of terrorist moving from their (possibly threatened) home territories to Iraq, and the insurgency resuming in new places after US troops believe they have gained control of some of its strongholds. Interveners are not immune from such problems even when acting altruistically, as shown by the number of cases of would-be conflict resolution where violence has broken out in new areas or contexts after a peace settlement was agreed and seemed to have been successful.[28] There are also examples in fields not involving armed violence, such as the ability of terrorists, criminals and smugglers to find new avenues for their financing, procurement and movement after others are blocked, or the opportunistic spread of new diseases in populations that have eliminated—but also lost their resistance to—older ones.

Retaliation by a protective power or other third party against the state or states taking the action remains rather rare but may be detected in new forms involving non-traditional actors: as when terrorists step up their violence in response to actions that they disapprove of against populations elsewhere or when Iran aggravates the West's problems by supporting Hezbollah and Hamas. It has been argued more broadly that the US-led coalition's action in Iraq, far from breaking up the so-called Axis of Evil, has actually encouraged previously unrelated terrorist groups to establish new links under the brand name of al-Qaeda.[29] In the diplomatic sphere, China has been observed systematically making new friends (principally through oil contracts) with countries that have fallen under US disfavour, such as Guatemala, Iran and Venezuela.[30]

Domestic backlash is still a real risk for most countries, as the former government of Spain found to its cost when it lost the 2004 elections as a result of its response to the Madrid bombings of 11 March 2004, coming on top of its high-risk decision to send troops to Iraq. Most other European governments which joined the US-led coalition have since paid some price, electorally or in opinion ratings, despite the fact that they were often acting on

---

[28] Sudan is a well-known case. For this and other examples see Dwan, R. and Holmqvist, C., 'Major armed conflicts', *SIPRI Yearbook 2005* (note 4), pp. 83–120.

[29] US Department of State, Office of the Coordinator for Counterterrorism, *Country Reports on Terrorism 2005* (US Department of State: Washington, DC, Apr. 2006), URL <http://www.state.gov/s/ct/rls/crt/c17689.htm>, pp. 11–15.

[30] See chapter 6 in this volume.

a quite sophisticated multiple risk analysis.[31] The US President himself managed to win re-election in 2004 but has seen his approval ratings wane in the second term and the opposition Democratic Party seize control of the Congress in the November 2006 mid-term elections. The USA has had to pay a higher than expected human and budgetary price for the Afghanistan and Iraq interventions and homeland security, in turn leading to various new exposures and uncertainties on the national and global economic front. Last but not least, the continued relevance of what is defined above as moral risk has been made abundantly clear in the Iraqi case. The US Administration's policies have reduced trust in and support of, and raised the level of antipathy towards, the USA in all world regions and have seriously strained—if not yet broken— communities like NATO that were designed precisely for shared risk management.[32] Some US policymakers, at their most extreme, have attempted to define this type of risk out of existence by categorizing alliances and international rules as handicaps. However, this approach has demonstrated its futility on every occasion since 11 September 2001 when the USA has needed the help of allies and international organizations or, indeed, has been driven to create new rule-based constructs in the service of its chosen policy towards 'new' threats.[33]

There are two further dimensions, however, that may be added to the risk calculus and that perhaps particularly deserve to be in present globalized conditions: one concerns the rationality of transferring or displacing risk and the other the failure to adapt analysis of the reflexive nature of risk to state policy.

In models of confrontation involving states, or the use of traditional force against new actors, successfully reducing the risks for one party almost invariably means creating more risks for others. The cold war strategies of deterrence (such as mutual assured destruction and flexible response) deliberately set out to create a sense of risk, fear and uncertainty on the other side in order to reduce the probability of an attack. US leaders since 2001 have also often used the language of 'making the world unsafe' for their opponents, of inducing 'shock and awe' among them and so on. This represents a kind of zero-sum approach to the distribution of risk, just as there is a traditional zero-sum philosophy of security.

This approach is not inherently wrong. Generally accepted policies for reducing everyday risk in societies also entail deliberately raising the level of

[31] Their analyses attempted to address not just the direct threat from Saddam Hussein, but also the risk that abstention represented for bilateral and Europe-wide relations with the USA and the risk of how the USA might behave if it intervened alone.

[32] On antipathy towards the USA see Pew Research Center, 'America's image slips, but allies share U.S. concerns over Iran, Hamas', Pew Global Attitudes Project Report, Washington, DC, Sep. 2006, URL <http://pewglobal.org/reports/display.php?ReportID=252>.

[33] Examples include the USA's attempts in 2004–2005 to obtain assistance from NATO as an institution in Iraq; the need for a new UN resolution to legalize the occupation of Iraq after Apr. 2003; the USA's reliance on the EU for cooperation in travel security and immigration control; the multilateral frameworks that the USA has participated in for the attempted solution of nuclear proliferation problems in Iran and North Korea; and the USA's initiatives in the International Maritime Organization for new maritime security rules and in the UN itself for Security Council Resolution 1373 on terrorist financing and Resolution 1540 on WMD. On Security Council Resolution 1540 see appendix 11A in this volume.

risk for thieves, murderers, drug pedlars, speeding drivers, environmental pol-
luters and others who contravene the laws of society. Finding a way to make
life more difficult and dangerous for terrorists, while if possible avoiding the
creation of martyrs, is a core challenge of anti-terrorist action. The new focus
on post-conflict justice is largely driven by the need to make war crimes peril-
ous for their perpetrators, not just for the victims.[34] Nevertheless, modern
security risks rarely have the simplicity of a 'High Noon' scenario where only
the bad guy has to pay the price for the good guy's survival. There are two
obvious ways in which the active combating of risks of human origin can end
by spreading risk more widely—over and above the indirect variants of
rebound, where all US citizens may, for example, face more hostility abroad
because of a few leaders' actions.

The first way is the equivalent of collateral damage, where conditions
become more risky for populations close to or associated with the target without themselves being to blame. This is the situation of Palestinians and Lebanese affected en masse by Israeli reprisals; of the constantly growing proportion of civilians who are consciously targeted, not just hit by side effects, in
intra-state conflicts; or of ordinary citizens in many parts of Afghanistan and
Iraq following the US-led interventions.[35] Even leaving aside purely moral
objections, anti-risk policies that create, as it were, such a large and non-
functional surplus of risk must be open to question.

The second way is the displacement of risk, when a risk reappears in a new
location after it has supposedly been eliminated. Cases are mentioned above
where this takes the form of a new challenge for the original actor, but there
are also many ways in which third parties can be affected by such displacement. If one country or province cracks down on illegal immigrants, they will
look for other more porous borders. Terrorist groups that are rooted out from
certain countries will settle in others that may be less vigilant and able to contain their activities. A ballistic missile shield that covers only certain European
countries would leave others more exposed. Poland and the Baltic states see an
oil pipeline that bypasses them in the interests of an assured supply from
Russia to Germany as making their own energy security (or even their general
security) more uncertain. Wastes that are not permitted to be buried in one
country's soil or emptied into its waters will be exported to another country,
possibly one that is less competent to store them safely. If countries that are
able to produce effective anti-epidemic vaccines choose to hoard them for
themselves, mortality in other countries will be higher.

As these last few cases should hint, displacing risk is not just morally
questionable. In conditions of growing global interdependence it is always
prone to rebound on the first actor sooner or later, even if in very indirect
ways. This is particularly the case with action in spheres that are inherently
transnational, such as terrorism, WMD proliferation, malfunctioning of the

---

[34] Wiharta, S., 'The International Criminal Court', *SIPRI Yearbook 2003* (note 5), pp. 153–66.

[35] On the Israeli action in Lebanon in the summer of 2006 see chapter 2 in this volume. On the targeting of civilians see Dwan and Holmqvist (note 28), pp. 96–102.

energy market, migration, environmental damage and disease. It is no accident that in these dimensions even unilateralist countries and countries with a risk philosophy that tends towards a zero-sum attitude regularly find themselves drawn back towards more cooperative responses that seek to reduce risk exposure and increase resilience for as many people as possible and for the global system as such. No country today is, metaphorically speaking, an island and none can succeed in becoming the equivalent of a gated community either. The countries and institutions with the most advanced and coherent security philosophies today are the ones that have projected this truth back into the handling of risk in more traditional dimensions of defence and security, and have adjusted their policies accordingly.

One final, and more general, way in which national or institutional approaches to risk may become counterproductive is by failing to adapt to state policy the latest analytical understanding (as explained in section III) of the reflexive nature of risk. Very often in the world of security, as in business and in people's daily lives, a given risk is the direct concomitant—the price or cost—of a self-chosen pattern of behaviour. The fact that the behaviour in question may not be wrong in itself—as Western populations may incur the wrath of certain terrorists by allowing free speech or giving women equal rights—does not invalidate the linkage, just as the supremely unselfish action of saving another person can often mean risking one's own life. In such cases, a policy that aims to eliminate the risk without changing the behaviour that caused it is very likely to fail or, even if it momentarily succeeds, to entail a major displacement of risk. If behaviour change is not an option—for example, because the behaviour is an expression of human rights or is required for a certain level of economic development—a policy that accepts the inevitability of some risk, and that aims rather to maximize prediction skills, minimize impact and optimize the population's resilience, may represent the most effective balancing of resources as well as being less likely to run into normative barriers. For countries acting on the international stage, the equivalent strategies for risk management are those that focus on containment, solidarity and mutual assistance in dealing with consequences, and (where possible) dialogue with and the gradual transformation of the problematic elements. Forming multi-state groupings for direct or indirect security purposes can bring the same benefits of risk suppression within the community, and of resistance and resilience across a wide spectrum of external threats, as good policy can within a single state—without compromising and while even enhancing the chosen values and way of life of the participants.[36] At global level, and as suggested in section II, universal human risks can be seen as the price of increasingly universal human interconnection and mobility and are demonstrably best met by universal cooperation.

Much the same policy prescriptions could be arrived at from an alternative starting point that sees risk as a necessary constraint on human or national

---

[36] Bailes, A. J. K. and Cottey, A., 'Regional security cooperation in the early 21st century', *SIPRI Yearbook 2006* (note 7), pp. 195–223.

self-assertion, and a deterrent to unbridled experimentation with the very powerful instruments that humankind possesses today. The human tendency to behave more recklessly in proportion to (or even faster than) the rate at which proximate risks are reduced is well documented in other contexts. When cars are given new safety features, the number of accidents may go down but the overall number of deaths (mainly of people outside the cars) can increase as people drive more boldly.[37] A similar correlation is mooted above between the USA's perception of new risks to its population (terrorism), the reduced proximate risk involved in the use of US military resources to tackle this challenge in post-cold war times, and the cost now accumulating from that action in terms of process risk, spillover affecting bystanders and displaced risk to third parties. From one point of view this would suggest that the mechanisms of risk, and especially its reflexive character, offer one of the few remaining constraints on a power that no longer faces a similarly strong state adversary—if the risk is correctly perceived and calculated in the first place. From another, it leads to the unpalatable conclusion that even if human policy could give certain parties the option of eliminating security risk altogether, it would not be good for humanity at large or even for themselves that they should do so.

V. Concluding remarks

Little is new in the above analysis; several of the points made were, indeed, mentioned in other recent editions of the SIPRI Yearbook. The idea that the leading powers' choice of methods in pursuit of security may have shifted too much towards action and away from restraint was presented in the Introduction to *SIPRI Yearbook 2003* and again, linked with an argument about the growth of armaments, in *SIPRI Yearbook 2006*.[38] Limitations on the successful use of military power, and the various kinds of process and moral risks it entails, were identified in the Introduction to *SIPRI Yearbook 2006* among others.[39] The argument for greater recognition of interdependence between different world constituencies, and hence the need for more sheltered societies to help in easing the risk burden of less fortunate ones, was made in the Introduction to *SIPRI Yearbook 2005* as part of a discussion of global governance.[40]

The conclusions emerging—in favour of policies based less on self-interest and short-term calculation, and more on cooperation and a comprehensive grasp of security interactions—may seem almost too banal to be worth repeating. They represent, however, a prescription that has repeatedly been found to

---

[37] The author is indebted to Michael Brzoska for this point in the argument.

[38] Bailes, A. J. K., 'Trends and challenges in international security', *SIPRI Yearbook 2003* (note 5), pp. 11–16; and Bailes, A. J. K., 'The world of security and peace research in a 40-year perspective', *SIPRI Yearbook 2006* (note 7), pp. 17–28.

[39] Bailes (note 38), pp. 10–17.

[40] Bailes, A. J. K., 'Global security governance: a world of change and challenge', *SIPRI Yearbook 2005* (note 4), pp. 13–21.

have evolutionary advantages at the individual human level, as well as in international politics. As noted elsewhere, there is a current trend towards the growth of regional and other (e.g. functional) multi-state groupings for security cooperation that are driven by similar reasoning, and which by their very existence subtly curtail their members' scope as well as need for risk taking.[41] It is commonly pointed out that such institutions find it hard to actively confront and check the more extreme kinds of external risk or threat, but it is less often noted that none has yet been destroyed as a result of any such threat being actualized.[42] Does this model, with its apparently risk-absorbing qualities, survive only because other powers, such as the USA, are ready to fill the gap by actively confronting the worst risks and being ready in their turn to absorb the costs involved? That is one tenable explanation of what is observed in the field of traditional and terrorist-related security action; but it needs to be offset by recognition of the USA's relative underperformance in combating other risks like climate change, population growth or the alienation of the Muslim world.

There has for at least a century been speculation about an alternative global solution that would pool states' strengths in a global security mechanism. Such a mechanism would be used to tackle the toughest threats of common concern to humanity, both of intentional human origin—where it would incidentally spread the process risks more efficiently—and of non-intentional origin. Whether or not the United Nations in its present form comes anywhere near to fulfilling this ideal function, the above analysis suggests that the prescription as such is more logical and realistic than many of today's self-proclaimed realists would admit.

---

[41] See e.g. Bailes and Cottey (note 36).

[42] NATO's vulnerability, should it fail in its self-assigned task in Afghanistan, might turn out to be an exception.

Part I. Security and conflicts, 2006

Chapter 1. Euro-Atlantic security and institutions

Chapter 2. Major armed conflicts

Chapter 3. Peacekeeping: keeping pace with changes in conflict

Chapter 4. Regional security cooperation in the former Soviet area

Chapter 5. Democratic accountability of intelligence services

Chapter 6. Energy and security: regional and global dimensions

1. Euro-Atlantic security and institutions

PÁL DUNAY and ZDZISLAW LACHOWSKI

I. Introduction

Factors of both continuity and change coexisted in Euro-Atlantic security in 2006. The United States and its coalition partners continued their operations in Iraq in spite of mounting domestic disillusion and protest, above all in the USA itself. At the same time, other areas of cooperation between the USA and European countries were pursued pragmatically, including the increasingly difficult North Atlantic Treaty Organization (NATO) operation in Afghanistan. Such shared liabilities, combined with gradual US policy shifts in some areas, had a steadying effect on European–US relations overall.

The impasse over the 2003 Constitutional Treaty and enlargement issues dominated the agenda of the European Union (EU) but did not prevent further incremental developments in EU external security roles (including crisis-management missions) that point in the direction of growing global ambitions. NATO member states debated further reforms and increased their involvement in Afghanistan as part of efforts to bolster the organization's own relevance. In the Western Balkans, the complexity of the Kosovo problem became more obvious the closer the international community came to addressing concrete proposals for the province's separate future.

The interruptions of energy supplies from Russia to its western neighbours at the end of 2005 and the beginning of 2006 made energy security a central topic. There were other signs, too, of Russia using its latest economic gains and growing confidence to assert its interests more forcefully in relation to both the West and its own near neighbours. Its disputes with Georgia were kept under control with some difficulty. Ukraine's politics, including its engagement with Western institutions, showed signs of having reached a stalemate.

Section II of this chapter addresses developments in US policies on Euro-Atlantic issues. Sections III and IV review developments in the EU and NATO, respectively. Section V examines events in Kosovo and section VI in the former Soviet area. Section VII presents the conclusions.

II. The United States

The principles of US external policy, a matter of the highest importance for the world, were developed with the publication in 2006 of two major documents: the National Security Strategy (NSS) and the Quadrennial Defense

Review (QDR).[1] At the same time, events abroad and in the USA called into question the longer-term continuance of the robust policies that these documents reflected. US strategy in Iraq was under particular fire by the end of the year—and new divisions were looming over the challenge of Iran[2]—against a background of increasing interplay with US domestic politics, including the outcome of mid-term elections to the US Congress.

The US Administration of President George W. Bush issued its second National Security Strategy in March 2006. Unlike the previous version of 2002,[3] the new NSS neither reflects any one clear shift in prevailing circumstances nor shows a convincing adaptation to existing and prospective changes. It starts from the same basic threat analysis and objectives as the 2002 NSS but claims that since then 'the world has seen extraordinary progress in the expansion of freedom, democracy, and human dignity'. For example, it states that the 'peoples of Afghanistan and Iraq have replaced tyrannies with democracies', but there is no reference to external forces that contributed to the change. Since 'tyranny'—apparently selected as a more flexible term than dictatorship—threatens 'the world's interest in freedom's expansion', the goal is to eliminate it. A list of examples of such dangerous regimes includes North Korea, Iran, Syria, Cuba, Belarus, Myanmar (Burma) and Zimbabwe—countries that the NSS also claims 'in their pursuit of [weapons of mass destruction] or sponsorship of terrorism, threaten our immediate security interests'. The report also identifies Iran as posing the single most urgent threat of this kind.[4]

The world view of the document is explicitly dualistic, comparing the post-September 2001 battle of ideas between democracy and tyranny with the ideological contest of the cold war between democracy and communism. Perpetuating the pre-emption notion that was so controversial in the 2002 NSS, the 2006 NSS states that the USA does 'not rule out the use of force before attacks occur, even if uncertainty remains as to the time and place of the enemy's attack'.[5]

The 2006 NSS gives some evidence of changed thinking by the US Government, however. Emphasis is put on multilateral cooperation, particularly with the oldest and closest allies of the USA, but not excluding a role for the United Nations or formal regional structures. The section on post-conflict stabilization and reconstruction, not present in the previous NSS, shows a softening of the negative US attitude to activities such as state building and calls for cooperation with others working in the field. Space is given to global and

---

[1] The White House, 'The National Security Strategy of the United States of America', Washington, DC, Mar. 2006, URL <http://www.whitehouse.gov/nsc/nss/2006/>; and US Department of Defense, 'Quadrennial Defense Review report', Washington, DC, 6 Feb. 2006, URL <http://www.defenselink.mil/qdr/>.

[2] On Iran's nuclear programme and related policy issues see chapter 12 in this volume.

[3] The White House, 'The National Security Strategy of the United States of America', Washington, DC, Sep. 2002, URL <http://www.whitehouse.gov/nsc/nss/2002/>.

[4] The White House (note 1), pp. 2, 3, 20.

[5] The White House (note 1), p. 23. See also 'President Bush's National Security Strategy unveiled', *Peace Watch*, vol. 12, no. 2 (Apr./May 2006), pp. 6–7.

transnational threats such as avian influenza, AIDS, environmental destruction and natural disasters.[6]

The report of the Quadrennial Defense Review was also published in early 2006. It is a reflection of the lessons learned by the US Administration and US military leadership in the first four years of the 'global war on terrorism'. As the war is expected to be of indefinite duration, the QDR makes clear that it is not designed as a 'new beginning'. It defines two fundamental imperatives for the US Department of Defense (DOD): continuing to reorient its capabilities and forces to give more flexibility in response to asymmetric challenges and to hedge against uncertainty over the next 20 years; and making comprehensive changes to ensure that organizational structures, processes and procedures effectively support its strategic direction.[7] The document shows that the USA intends to maintain its predominance in traditional warfare while improving its ability to address the non-traditional, asymmetric military challenges.

As noted by the chairman of the US Joint Chiefs of Staff, 'The 2006 QDR was the first contemporary defence review to coincide with an ongoing major conflict.'[8] It was published against the background of an increasing challenge to the 'transformationalist' policies associated with the Secretary of Defense, Donald Rumsfeld—which prescribe the use of smaller forces equipped with high technology[9]—from 'traditionalists' both inside and outside the US armed forces, who argued that only the presence of a mass ground force can hope to hold territory in the face of low-intensity insurgency. Supporters of this view have called for the US Army to grow by several thousand troops per year in the near future and have drawn attention to evidence of the forces already in the field being overstretched and under-equipped.[10]

The 2006 QDR calls for an increase in the USA's deployable (i.e. fully equipped and fully manned) forces and a rebalancing between active and reserve forces. Specifically, it prescribes more special operations forces and special forces battalions.[11] In a related development, in December 2006 the US military issued a new army and marine force manual on counter-insurgency operations (the first for 20 years), reflecting its concern about its limited ability to cope with insurgencies in the light of experiences in Afghanistan and Iraq.[12] The manual recognizes the complexity of the tasks facing troops who

[6] The White House (note 1), pp. 16, 38, 47.

[7] US Department of Defense (note 1), pp. v, 1.

[8] US Department of Defense (note 1), p. A-3.

[9] Hoffman, F., 'Warfare—past and present: what has changed and what remains constant?', *Armed Forces Journal*, Nov. 2006.

[10] Kagan, F. W., 'The U.S. military's manpower crisis', *Foreign Affairs*, vol. 85, no. 4 (July/Aug. 2006), pp. 97–110; and Scott Tyson, A., 'General says army will need to grow', *Washington Post*, 15 Dec. 2006, p. A01. President Bush has proposed that the size of the US Army and US Marine Corps grows by 92 000 over the next 5 years. The White House, 'President Bush delivers State of the Union address', Press release, Washington, DC, 23 Jan. 2007, URL <http://www.whitehouse.gov/stateofthe union/2007/>.

[11] US Department of Defense (note 1), pp. 42–45.

[12] US Department of the Army, Headquarters, *Counterinsurgency*, Field Manual no. 3-24 and Marine Corps Warfighting Publication no. 3-33.5 (Department of the Army: Washington, DC, Dec. 2006), URL <http://usacac.army.mil/CAC/Repository/Materials/COIN-FM3-24.pdf>.

have also to assist in the rebuilding of infrastructure and facilitate the establishment of local governance and the rule of law.

In the US domestic context, the QDR stresses the inter-agency approach to providing security, and its reference to 'better fusion of intelligence and operations' may or may not be made in this context.[13] Such references raise the question of there being a blurring of roles between the DOD and other government agencies, including those responsible for intelligence. It is known that the DOD has used the operations in Afghanistan and Iraq as an opportunity to expand its autonomous intelligence activity.[14] This has sometimes resulted in overlaps, duplication of effort and even major differences of assessment between various agencies. The 2006 QDR, while understandably stressing the intelligence needs of the armed forces, avoids commenting on the problem of reconciling the many institutions that are active in this area.[15] Although the establishment of the post of Director of National Intelligence in 2004 has reduced the problem, it apparently has not resolved it.

The QDR aims to accelerate military transformation by focusing on the needs of combatant commanders (who head unified combatant commands) and on developing joint capabilities.[16] Effective network-centric warfare continues to be an objective.[17] If such qualitative improvements and tactical lessons learned from recent combat experience take effect, this may widen the problematic technology gap between US and other coalition armed forces, unless experience is shared with and digested by at least the main partner countries.

The Iraq operation and the US domestic debate

The Iraq operation entered its fourth year in 2006 and increasingly affected US domestic politics. As so often with major military actions carried out far from home, support has declined for several reasons. There has been an erosion in the US public's trust in the ability of the president to lead generally and, more specifically, in the winnability of the Iraq conflict as the situation there has become hard to characterize as anything other than a civil war.[18] While it remains a delicate matter for the US Democratic Party to take any stand that could be criticized as failing to 'support the troops', partisan debate on the issue started to become more open and polarized even before the mid-term elections to the US Congress in November 2006, which gave the Democratic Party control of both houses. Overall, while US popular support for the

---

[13] US Department of Defense (note 1), p. vi.

[14] For more details see Dunay, P. and Lachowski, Z., 'Euro-Atlantic security and institutions', *SIPRI Yearbook 2006: Armaments, Disarmament and International Security* (Oxford University Press: Oxford, 2006), pp. 39–41.

[15] US Department of Defense (note 1), pp. 55–58.

[16] US Department of Defense (note 1), p. 4.

[17] On network-centric warfare and related policies see chapter 9 in this volume.

[18] See Fearon, J. D., 'Iraq's civil war', *Foreign Affairs*, vol. 86, no. 2 (Mar./Apr. 2007), pp. 2–15.

war in Iraq was more than 70 per cent in the spring of 2003, by 2006 the majority had concluded that the war was a mistake.[19]

Deaths of US military personnel reached 3000 by the end of 2006 and were particularly high in the last three months of the year.[20] However, the overall fatality rate in 2006 was not significantly different from previous years.[21] The casualty rate for Iraqi police and security forces is roughly twice the rate of that for all coalition forces, which is a serious problem not least in view of the plans to gradually hand over responsibility for the country's security to Iraqi units.[22] Perhaps even more significant as a motive for revision of the US strategy is the steadily increasing number of enemy-initiated attacks since May 2003, and the rise in the average number of attacks per day since the beginning of 2006.[23] Both trends indicate that the coalition is not controlling the situation and have fuelled the widespread concern that it may deteriorate further.

The views of the US Administration itself evolved during 2006. At the start of the year, President Bush reiterated that 'The road of victory is the road that will take our troops home.'[24] By the autumn most members of the administration were finding it necessary to nuance this view, although Vice-President Dick Cheney still emphasized that 'we are not looking for an exit strategy; we're looking for victory'.[25] The president in his turn said that the US goal in Iraq 'is clear and unchanging' and rightly pointed out the risks of a hasty withdrawal: 'A failed Iraq in the heart of the Middle East will provide safe haven for terrorists and extremists.'[26] By the end of the year, after much similar criticism at home as well as abroad and the elections to the Congress, the president was ready to recognize that 'We're not winning, we're not losing', a formula also employed by the chairman of the Joint Chiefs of Staff.[27]

---

[19] Gordon, P. H., 'The end of the Bush revolution', *Foreign Affairs*, vol. 85, no. 4 (July/Aug. 2006), p. 79.

[20] The precise figure is 3003 deaths. Fatality figures are taken from the Iraq Coalition Casualty Count website, URL <http://www.icasualties.org/>.

[21] The total number of coalition fatalities was 897 in 2005 and fell to 871 in 2006. Iraq Coalition Casualty Count (note 20).

[22] Fischer, H., *Iraqi Police and Security Forces Casualty Estimates*, US Library of Congress, Congressional Research Service (CRS) Report for Congress RS22532 (CRS: Washington, DC, 17 Nov. 2006), URL <http:// fpc.state.gov/fpc/c19485.htm>, p. 1.

[23] Woodward, B., *State of Denial: Bush at War, Part III* (Simon & Schuster: New York, N.Y., 2006), pp. 472–73.

[24] The White House, 'President Bush delivers State of the Union address', Press release, Washington, DC, 31 Jan. 2006, URL <http://www.whitehouse.gov/stateoftheunion/2006/>.

[25] The White House, 'Interview of the Vice President by Time magazine', Washington, DC, 18 Oct. 2006, URL <http://www.whitehouse.gov/vicepresident/news-speeches/>, p. 6.

[26] Scott Tyson, A. and Fletcher, M. A., 'Bush, Rumsfeld defend strategy', *Washington Post*, 21 Oct. 2006, p. A01; and The White House, 'Press conference by the President', Washington, DC, 21 Aug. 2006, URL <http://www.whitehouse.gov/news/releases/2006/08/>. The UN Secretary-General, Kofi Annan, acknowledged the same danger. United Nations, 'Annan speaks with US Iraq Study Group as sectarian violence soars', News item, New York, N.Y., 27 Nov. 2006, URL <http://www.un.org/apps/news/story.asp?NewsID=20741>.

[27] Baker, P., 'U.S. not winning war in Iraq, Bush says for 1st time', *Washington Post*, 20 Dec. 2006, p. A01.

The question was, of course, what alternative strategy might produce better results for the interveners or, indeed, for Iraq. During 2006 various bodies started to work on ideas for withdrawal from Iraq, and the US Administration launched its own bipartisan Iraq Study Group (ISG) in March, led by former Secretary of State James Baker and former congressman Lee Hamilton. The ISG's report, published in December 2006, starts from a grim picture of the situation in Iraq, which it argues could not improve without reconciliation among various population groups.[28] The report sets aside the much-discussed option of decentralizing Iraq into three regions, concluding that the ethnic and religious groups are too mixed to be neatly separated. Its two most important recommendations are to change the role and reduce the number of coalition troops in Iraq and to launch a major diplomatic offensive that would reconnect the process of Iraqi reconciliation with the peace process in the Middle East, including by opening a dialogue with Iran and Syria.[29] Within Iraq, the report calls for a revision of the current US approach, with more emphasis on the political process, including state building. Specifically, it recommends the withdrawal 'of all combat brigades not necessary for force protection' by the first quarter of 2008 on the condition that 'additional Iraqi brigades are being deployed'.

The questioning of US strategy also extended in 2006 to the link between Iraq and anti-terrorism policy. According to the reported results of a national intelligence estimate that addressed this topic for the first time since March 2003, the 'invasion and occupation of Iraq has helped spawn a new generation of Islamic radicalism' and 'New jihadist networks and cells, sometimes united by little more than their anti-Western agendas, are increasingly likely to emerge'.[30] This official US analysis, increasingly also supported by US and British public opinion, underlined that arresting the trend of violence in Iraq would be crucial for success in reducing terrorist activity globally.[31]

Within the US establishment, the military has opposed reductions in coalition troop numbers, but the military also objected to another widely canvassed idea—sending additional troops to stabilize some of the hot spots in Iraq, including Baghdad, as a step towards making large-scale withdrawals possible

---

[28] Baker, J. A. III and Hamilton, L. H. (co-chairs), *The Iraq Study Group Report: The Way Forward—A New Approach* (Vintage: New York, N.Y., Dec. 2006); the text is also available at URL <http://usip.org/isg/>.

[29] In this respect the ISG echoes the judgement of many observers that the Iraq invasion did not, as the US Administration hoped, bring closer a breakthrough in Israeli–Palestinian and Israeli–Arab relations. Instead, it complicated the prospects for such a breakthrough, while inadvertently giving greater leverage to radical Shia elements backed by Iran.

[30] Office of the Director of National Intelligence, 'Declassified key judgments of the national intelligence estimate "Trends in global terrorism: implications for the United States" dated April 2006', Press release, Washington, DC, 26 Sep. 2006, URL <http://www.dni.gov/press_releases/press_releases.htm>; and Mazzetti, M., 'Spy agencies say Iraq war worsens terrorism threat', *New York Times*, 24 Sep. 2006.

[31] Bowman, K., 'Public opinion on the war with Iraq', AEI Public Opinion Studies, American Enterprise Institute (AEI), Washington, DC, 5 Apr. 2007, URL <http://www.aei.org/publications/filter.all, pubID.22142/pub_detail.asp>; and Bowman, K., 'U.S. public opinion and the terrorist threat', *One Issue, Two Voices*, no. 4 (Oct. 2005), pp. 2–9.

thereafter.[32] According to one report, the 'Pentagon has warned that any short-term mission may only set up the United States for bigger problems when it ends'.[33]

President Bush announced his own new Iraq strategy in January 2007. Its most important element was the sending of more than 20 000 additional troops to Iraq in order to gain control over the insurgency, particularly in Baghdad and its vicinity, because 'Eighty percent of Iraq's sectarian violence occurs within 30 miles [50 kilometres] of the capital'.[34] The troops thus committed to Iraq would work alongside Iraqi units (one US battalion to each Iraqi brigade) and have some elements embedded in the latter.[35] The president made no mention of subsequent troop withdrawals, except to remark that the USA's commitment 'is not open-ended'. He did not signal any diplomatic opening towards Iran and Syria, but stressed that the USA would 'interrupt the flow of support from Iran and Syria' and that the USA would do more to make its friends in the Middle East understand their own interest in the stability of Iraq.

In the new stage of debate the Iraq operation is being increasingly compared with events during the Viet Nam War in the 1950s–70s in terms of the escalating demand for US forces, the failure of the latter to master the situation in spite of superior technology and the disappointment of hopes that local military forces could be sufficiently prepared to take their place. In one respect, the Iraqi conundrum appears more difficult because, while the US retreat left Viet Nam on the road towards unification, Iraq seems more likely to end up dismembered.

Whatever military measures may be taken in the short term, the Iraq conflict seems to have demonstrated that the 'Bush revolution' in foreign affairs based on the combination of 'hyper-realism and transformational zeal'[36] has been at least partially exhausted. Domestic criticism is continuing to mount over the president's use of his executive powers on matters concerning Iraq and security generally, while the growing boldness of the Democratic Party has been matched by loss of cohesion in the Republican Party.[37] If the documents published by the US Administration in 2006 show a limited readiness to rethink, influential groups of experts are already elaborating alternative strategies to help the USA lead the international system in a more cooperative and liberal direction in the future.[38] In the meantime the Iraq conflict has contributed to

---

[32] Baker, P., 'President confronts dissent on troop levels', *Washington Post*, 21 Dec. 2006, p. A01.

[33] Wright, R. and Baker, P., 'White House, Joint Chiefs at odds on adding troops', *Washington Post*, 19 Dec. 2006, p. A01.

[34] The White House, 'President's address to the nation', Press release, Washington, DC, 10 Jan. 2007, URL <http://www.whitehouse.gov/news/releases/2007/01/>.

[35] Pace, P. (Gen.), Chairman of the Joint Chiefs of Staff, Testimony before the US House of Representatives Armed Services Committee, 11 Jan. 2007. Transcript available at URL <http://www.washingtonpost.com/wp-dyn/content/article/2007/01/11/AR2007011101273.html>.

[36] These terms are used in Krepon, M., 'Negating American power', Henry L. Stimson Center, Washington, DC, 1 Nov. 2006, URL <http://www.stimson.org/pub.cfm?ID=345>.

[37] DeYoung, K., 'Skepticism over Iraq haunts U.S. Iran policy', *Washington Post*, 15 Feb. 2007, p. A01.

[38] Ikenberry, G. J. and Slaughter, A.-M. (co-directors), *Forging a World of Liberty under Law: U.S. National Security in the 21st Century*, Final report of the Princeton Project on National Security (Prince-

the growing prominence of security as an issue in US politics and has been a massive drain on US resources,[39] making the country more vulnerable to reversals in foreign trade and in the monetary sphere. Judgement should perhaps still be suspended, however, on how far the outcome reflects the shortcomings of the 'Bush doctrine', as such, and how far the problems have flowed from selecting some of the toughest available targets for action and from specific mistakes committed there.

The USA and Europe: concord and discord

The discord that prevailed in European–US relations in 2002–2003 has gradually given way to pragmatism, as the great majority of European governments have accepted the need to return to cooperation with the USA across a broad front. The underlying disagreements, however, are based on different perceptions of security. Public opinion polls show that every threat experienced by both sides—with the exception of global warming—is graded as more acute by US citizens than by Europeans. In consequence, the USA sees its international environment as more hostile, and security as a higher priority overall, than Europe does.[40] This gives the US leadership scope to spend more resources on security, and even to take steps in pursuit of it that may contradict the rule of law, with (at least) mainstream popular support.

Consistent with these findings, European public opinion has remained sceptical towards the USA even while official elites have become more accommodating. The proportion of favourable opinions on the USA have continued to fall practically everywhere in Europe and in many countries no longer represent the majority.[41] A recent poll found that US leadership in world affairs was regarded as desirable by only 37 per cent of European respondents, and only three countries—the Netherlands, Romania and the United Kingdom—viewed it more positively than negatively.[42] Even Tony Blair, the strongly pro-US British Prime Minister, called in 2006 for a revision of strategy on Afghanistan, Iraq and extremism more broadly. In a speech in August 2006 he suggested that the banner should not be 'regime change' but 'values change' and that popular support could only be maintained if policy 'is not just about interests but about values, not just about what is necessary but about what is right'. He stated that 'the stronger and more appealing our world-view is, the more it is seen as based not just on power but on justice, the easier it

---

ton University, Woodrow Wilson School of Public and International Affairs: Princeton, N.J., Sep. 2006), p. 6.

[39] See chapter 8 in this volume.

[40] Transatlantic Trends, *Transatlantic Trends: Key Findings 2006* (German Marshall Fund of the United States: Washington, DC, 2006), URL <http://www.transatlantictrends.org/>, p. 7.

[41] Pew Global Attitudes Project, 'America's image slips, but allies share U.S. concerns over Iran, Hamas', Survey report, Washington, DC, 13 June 2006, URL <http://www.pewglobal.org/reports/display.php?ReportID=252>, p. 1.

[42] Transatlantic Trends (note 40), p. 5.

will be for us to shape the future' and that 'whereas unilateral action can never be ruled out, it is not the preference'.[43]

A particularly acute difference between the current US and European leaderships concerns the relationship between the rule of law and security, particularly in the context of countering terrorism. It is also a divisive issue within the USA. There have been domestic as well as foreign protests over the US Administration's detention of foreigners on its territory without being convicted and without access to due process of law, and the US Supreme Court has challenged some of those practices.[44] During 2006, Republican and Democratic congressmen alike voiced their concerns over the torture of terrorism suspects and achieved a revision of a draft bill that sets clearer limits to interrogation techniques.[45] It is fair to add that there were similar internal divides in European states over some governmental counterterrorism proposals liable to affect personal freedoms.

During 2006 the Parliamentary Assembly of the Council of Europe carried out an investigation into the much-publicized reports of terrorist suspects being secretly detained and unlawfully transferred between countries ('rendition') by the USA with help or connivance from Council of Europe member states. The stories included alleged flights commanded by the US Central Intelligence Agency (CIA) through European bases, detention without rights at sites other than the Guantánamo Bay detention camp and rendition of some suspects to their home countries, where they were likely to be tortured. The Parliamentary Assembly condemned 'the systematic exclusion of all forms of judicial protection' and called on the USA 'to dismantle its system of secret detentions and unlawful inter-state transfers' and to 'prohibit the "extra-legal" transfer of persons suspected of involvement in terrorist organisations and all forcible transfers of persons from any country to countries that practise torture or that fail to guarantee the right to a fair trial'.[46] In a separate report, the Secretary General of the Council of Europe, Terry Davis, highlighted various weaknesses in the control mechanisms over intelligence services and the lack of adequate human rights safeguards for civil air traffic.[47] These conclusions,

---

[43] Blair, T., Speech to the Los Angeles World Affairs Council, 1 Aug. 2006, URL <http://www.number10.gov.uk/output/page9948.asp>.

[44] On 29 June 2006 the judgement given by the Supreme Court in the case *Hamdan v. Rumsfeld, Secretary of Defense et al.* (no. 05-184) indicated that the US President exceeded his authority when he ordered military tribunals for the Guantánamo Bay detainees. The opinion of the court is available at URL <http://www.supremecourtus.gov/opinions/05slipopinion.html>. For a summary see 'U.S.: military tribunal ruling second setback for Bush', Radio Free Europe/Radio Liberty, 30 June 2006, URL <http://www.rferl.org/specials/9112001/>.

[45] 'Letter: Powell says Bush plan to authorize torture "would put troops at risk"', Think Progress, Center for American Progress Action Fund, 14 Sep. 2006, URL <http//thinkprogress.org/2006/09/14/powell-letter/>; and Babington, C., 'House approves bill on detainees', *Washington Post*, 28 Sep. 2006, p. A01. The bill became the 2006 Military Commissions Act, US Public Law 109-366, which was signed into law on 17 Oct. 2006.

[46] Council of Europe Parliamentary Assembly, Resolution 1507(2006), 27 June 2006, URL <http://assembly.coe.int/Main.asp?link=/Documents/AdoptedText/ta06/Eres1507.htm>.

[47] Council of Europe, 'Supplementary report by the Secretary General on the use of his powers under Article 52 of the European Convention on Human Rights in the light of reports suggesting that individuals, notably persons suspected of involvement in acts of terrorism, may have been arrested and

even if not binding on European governments, may be expected to discourage them from considering or condoning similar practices in future.

European–US differences also crystallized around the balance to be struck between, on the one hand, the security interests of airlines and flight destination and departure countries and, on the other, the right of passengers to privacy. Following the terrorist attacks of 11 September 2001, the USA passed legislation requiring airlines operating flights to, from or across US territory to give US authorities electronic access to the data contained in their reservation and departure control systems, called passenger name records (PNR). Implementation in Europe was a matter for the European Union to rule on, given its competence in the area of aviation. In 2004 the European Commission had assessed that the US Customs and Border Protection agency could provide enough protection of passenger data to meet European privacy standards. In the same year the EU Council of Ministers had approved the conclusion of an agreement with the USA on the processing and transfer of PNR. The European Parliament, however, applied to the European Court of Justice for the annulment of these decisions on the grounds that there was no basis for such action in EU law, and in May 2006 the court duly annulled both the Commission and Council measures, thereby forcing the reopening of EU–US negotiations.[48] The EU now rejected the US demand for routine sharing of passenger data among US law enforcement agencies and barred the US Department of Homeland Security from extracting data automatically from European airlines' computer systems, safeguards that were enshrined in the new agreement that was reached in October 2006.[49]

With some delay on the European side, biometric passports were introduced at the end of August 2006 for visitors entitled to visa-free entry to the USA through a major airport or seaport.[50] The US Department of Homeland Security is now considering the extension of the Visa Waiver Programme in response to 'the increased interest among some international allies' of the USA.[51]

detained, or transported while deprived of their liberty, by or at the instigation of foreign agencies'. Information Document SG/Inf. (2006) 13, Council of Europe, Strasbourg, 14 June 2006, URL <https://wcd.coe.int/ViewDoc.jsp?id=1010167>. On the general problem of democratic accountability of intelligence services see chapter 5 in this volume.

[48] For details and the legal reasoning see European Court of Justice, 'The Court annuls the Council decision concerning the conclusion of an agreement between the European Community and the United States of America on the processing and transfer of personal data and the Commission decision on the adequate protection of those data', Press Release no. 46/2006, Luxembourg, 30 May 2006, URL <http://curia.europa.eu/en/actu/communiques/cp06/aff/>. For the text of the judgement see URL <http://curia.europa.eu/jurisp/cgi-bin/form.pl?lang=EN&Submit=rechercher&numaff=C-317/04>.

[49] The Agreement between the European Union and the United States of America on the Processing and Transfer of Passenger Name Record (PNR) Data by Air Carriers to the United States Department of Homeland Security was signed on 16 and 19 Oct. 2006. Its text is reproduced in *Official Journal of the European Union*, L298 (27 Oct. 2006), pp. 29–31.

[50] European Commission, 'New, secure biometric passport in the EU, strengthens security and data protection and facilitates travelling', Press release no. IP/06/872, Brussels, 29 June 2006, URL <http://europa.eu/rapid/pressReleasesAction.do?reference=IP06/872>.

[51] US Department of Homeland Security, 'Statement by Homeland Security Secretary Michael Chertoff on security improvements to the visa waiver program', Press release, Washington, DC, 28 Nov. 2006, URL <http://www.dhs.gov/xnews/releases/pr_1164753617598.shtm>.

III. The European Union

In 2006 the European Union remained in a state of transition. In the wake of the negative referendum results on the 2003 Constitutional Treaty in France and the Netherlands in 2005, EU leaders had announced an indefinite period of 'reflection'.[52] It was clear by 2006 that the constitution's failure had left Europe uncertain about fundamental questions regarding its future, purpose and course, including the best way to handle divisive debates both among governments and between governments and the people.[53] The idea of European solidarity is being challenged by several different 'patriotisms' arising in the political, ethnic, economic and even linguistic spheres. The current mood of pessimism and confusion has spread beyond traditionally Euro-sceptical countries to affect even the EU's new members, which have appeared increasingly inward-looking and hardly able to forge consensus regionally, let alone EU-wide.[54] The constitutional stalemate has also increasingly affected plans for the further enlargement of the EU, thus reviving the old widening-versus-deepening dilemma (whether new members can be absorbed in the absence of deeper institutional and financial reforms). It remains to be seen whether the departures and arrivals of leading politicians in the governments of the large EU members in 2006–2007 can open the way to a deeper transformation of the European political landscape.

The Constitutional Treaty deadlock

The prospects for an EU relaunch were brightened somewhat by the agreement of the outline of the EU budget for 2007–13 at the December 2005 European Council. However, over the next year the member governments remained deeply divided over whether, how and when the constitution should be resurrected. It was evident that the issue would not be tackled until mid-2007 at the earliest, and attention became focused on the plans of Germany, the EU Presidency holder in the first half of 2007. Given the presidential election in France and the planned change of prime minister in the UK about that

---

[52] The Treaty Establishing a Constitution for Europe was signed on 30 Sep. 2003 but has not been fully ratified. The text of the treaty is available at URL <http://europa.eu/constitution/>. To enter into force, the treaty must be ratified by all 27 EU member states. Belgium, Estonia and Finland ratified the treaty in 2006 to bring the total number of ratifications to 16. The 13 earlier ratifications were by Austria, Bulgaria, Cyprus, Greece, Hungary, Italy, Latvia, Lithuania, Luxembourg, Malta, Romania, Slovenia, Spain. In addition, the treaty has been approved by the German and Slovak parliaments, but ratification is delayed pending court cases. The treaty was rejected in referendums in France (in May 2005) and the Netherlands (in June 2005). 'EU constitution: where member states stand', BBC News, 28 Feb. 2007, URL <http://news.bbc.co.uk/2/3954327.stm>.

[53] For the causes of such malaise see Dunay and Lachowski (note 14), pp. 44–45.

[54] In contrast, the 2004 enlargement has produced tangible benefits for the EU in the world at large by increasing trade, investment and competitiveness. Blanke, J., *Lisbon Review 2006: Measuring Europe's Progress in Reform* (World Economic Forum: Geneva, 2006), URL <http://www.weforum.org/en/initiatives/gcp/Lisbon Review/>.

time, however, the room for early progress by Germany looked narrow.[55] In the meantime, the process of ratification of the Constitutional Treaty continued: altogether 16 member states had ratified it by the end of 2006, showing their determination to keep the matter on the agenda symbolically in the absence of any more practical way forward.[56]

Enlargement

Some effort was made in 2006 to confront the EU's increasingly evident enlargement fatigue. The planned admission of Bulgaria and Romania in 2007 became a test case: would it be seen as the completion of the May 2004 enlargement phase, followed by an indefinite pause, or as a prelude to further expansion? Should enlargement in general be considered a success story worth continuing, or had the EU's capacity to absorb new members been exhausted politically even if not in objective economic terms?[57]

The treaties of accession with Bulgaria and Romania had been signed on 25 April 2005, with the aim of full entry in January 2007. A monitoring report by the European Commission in May 2006 gave qualified approval for the accession of both states but deferred a final decision until early October 2006.[58] The report called on both countries to address a number of outstanding issues, including greater efforts to fight corruption and crime, and judicial reforms for greater transparency, efficiency and impartiality. Bulgaria was indirectly warned that, failing such improvements, the Commission could recommend deferring its accession. On 26 September a new monitoring report stated that the two countries were 'sufficiently prepared' to meet the political, economic and *acquis* criteria by 1 January 2007 but proposed the unprecedented step of creating a mechanism to promote and verify both states' progress after accession in certain areas.[59]

In the light of the experience with these two states and the talks with other current and potential candidates, the December 2006 European Council set a number of new criteria for future admissions. First, it was agreed that the enlargement strategy would henceforth be based on 'consolidation, conditionality and communication', combined with the EU's capacity to integrate new

---

[55] The German ambassador to the UK gave a signal by speaking of his country's commitment to the 'constitutional process' rather than the 'constitution'. Tempest, M., 'Q&A: Wolfgang Ischinger, German ambassador to the UK', *The Guardian*, 1 Dec. 2006.

[56] See note 52.

[57] In this context, *The Economist* rightly noted that the EU 'is not a club with a fixed lump of benefits that get used up when it adds new members. It is more like a network in which the benefits of membership increase as more members join.' 'The absorption puzzle', *The Economist*, 29 June 2006. For arguments on absorption capacity see also Bildt, C., 'Open wide Europe's door', *International Herald Tribune*, 7 Nov. 2006.

[58] European Commission, 'Bulgaria: May 2006 monitoring report', Brussels, 16 May 2006; and European Commission, 'Romania: May 2006 monitoring report', Brussels, 16 May 2006—both at URL <http://ec.europa.eu/enlargement/key_documents/reports_2006_en.htm>.

[59] European Commission, 'Monitoring report on the state of preparedness for EU membership of Bulgaria and Romania', Brussels, 26 Sep. 2006, URL <http://ec.europa.eu/enlargement/key_documents/reports_sept_2006_en.htm>, pp. 9–13.

members. Second, 'difficult issues', such as judicial reforms and fighting corruption, would be addressed early in accession talks. Finally, 'the pace of the accession process depends on the results of the reforms' in the applicant country and the EU would no longer set target dates for accession until and unless negotiations were close to completion.[60] These new criteria will apply first and foremost to Turkey and the Western Balkan applicants—the candidate countries Croatia and the Former Yugoslav Republic of Macedonia (FYROM) and the potential candidates Albania, Bosnia and Herzegovina, Kosovo, Montenegro and Serbia. Meanwhile, Croatia was commended for the progress it had made in the past year.

On the Western Balkans, generally, the December 2006 European Council reaffirmed that the future of the region 'lies in the European Union', but this did not stop local states worrying that the EU's new mood and new admission criteria might leave them outside the EU for the indefinite future.[61] No new commitments or hints of membership were offered to other interested countries, such as Georgia or Ukraine. Meanwhile, the Stabilization and Association Agreement negotiations with Serbia and Montenegro were called off on 3 May 2006 because its government failed to meet its commitments on cooperation with the International Criminal Tribunal for the former Yugoslavia (ICTY) to catch General Ratko Mladić, charged with war crimes.[62]

Turkey's EU membership negotiations ran into increasing difficulties in 2006. Formally, Turkey has to negotiate and conclude 35 'chapters' on issues including trade, economy, information, foreign, security and defence policy, the legal and judiciary system, religious and democratic freedoms, the rule of law, human rights and the protection of minorities.[63] Enthusiasm for the process declined during 2006 on both sides. Militant Islamic radicalism and the war in Iraq confirmed the scepticism of some in the EU and strengthened concerns about letting a large Muslim country into the Union.[64] In turn, Turkey slowed its political reforms and continued to refuse to recognize the Republic of Cyprus (now an EU member) without a comprehensive deal to end the long-standing division of the island.[65] Popular support for EU membership in

---

[60] Council of the European Union, 'Presidency conclusions', European Council, Brussels, 14–15 Dec. 2006, URL <http://europa.eu/european_council/conclusions/index_en.htm>, pp. 2–3.

[61] Council of the European Union (note 60), p. 3.

[62] European Commission, 'Serbia 2006 progress report', Brussels, 8 Nov. 2006, URL <http://ec.europa.eu/enlargement/key_documents/reports_nov_2006_en.htm>. Following Montenegro's declaration of independence on 3 June 2006, the EU established diplomatic relations with it on 12 June.

[63] In 2006 the EU agreed only one chapter, concerning science and research. European Commission, 'Turkey 2006 progress report', Brussels, 8 Nov. 2006, URL <http://ec.europa.eu/enlargement/key_documents/reports_nov_2006_en.htm>, p. 4.

[64] Islam was not the only issue for the anti-Turkish lobby: in Nov. 2006 the lower house of the French Parliament approved a law making it an offence to deny that there was a genocide of Armenians in Turkey in 1915–17. In response, Turkey suspended its military relations with France. Shihab, S., 'Génocide arménien : le Parlement turc dénonce l'attitude de la France' [Armenian genocide: the Turkish Parliament denounces the French standpoint], Le Monde, 19 Oct. 2006.

[65] Turkey has not fully implemented the additional protocol extending its customs union to the 10 new EU members admitted in 2004 and has denied access to its ports to vessels flying the Republic of Cyprus flag or whose last port of call was Cyprus.

Turkey has fallen to 35 per cent from almost 80 per cent in 2003.[66] This was mirrored by a similar average level of support (39%) from EU citizens for Turkish membership of the Union.[67] A November 2006 European Commission report bluntly warned Turkey over the Cyprus issue and criticized other short-comings ranging from minority rights to freedom of expression.[68] In the autumn, EU member states remained divided over the importance as well as the possibility of avoiding an impending collapse in the negotiations over Turkish membership. In face of continued Turkish intransigence regarding the Cyprus deadlock, in December the EU foreign ministers agreed to suspend negotiations on eight chapters that were directly relevant to Turkey's behaviour in this context but, in a compromise, did not set a deadline for compliance.[69]

The European Neighbourhood Policy

As the enlargement of the EU is increasingly showing signs of exhaustion, the European Neighbourhood Policy (ENP)—which at present covers only non-candidate countries—is attracting new attention as a possible long-term alternative.[70] Even if some thinkers still maintain that enlargement is 'not just the EU's best foreign policy; it's their only foreign policy',[71] neighbourhood policy is moving to the centre of debate. The present ENP proceeds by means of negotiations between the EU and individual 'neighbours', giving flexibility to adjust the rate of 'Europeanization' to the ambitions of the two sides. However, some eastern neighbours—such as Georgia, Moldova and Ukraine—would clearly like to move on to become candidates for accession. Ukraine has made some progress towards European standards, despite difficulties stemming from internal divisions in its political institutions, and Moldova is closely watching and trying to copy its example.[72] The ENP has different dynamics with neighbours to the east and those to the south of the EU, and some EU members have suggested that it be divided accordingly, although the individualized nature of the present policy gives no logical reason for such

[66] Pew Global Attitudes Project, 'The great divide: how Westerners and Muslims view each other', Survey report, Washington, DC, 22 June 2006, URL <http://pewglobal.org/reports/display.php?ReportID=253>.

[67] Eurobarometer, 'Attitudes toward European Union enlargement', Special Eurobarometer no. 255, European Commission, Brussels, July 2006, URL <http://ec.europa.eu/public_opinion/archives/eb_special_en.htm>, p. 70.

[68] European Commission (note 63).

[69] Council of the European Union, '2770th Council Meeting, General Affairs and External Relations: general affairs', Press Release, Brussels, 11 Dec. 2006, URL <http://europa.eu/rapid/pressReleasesAction.do?reference=PRES/06/352>.

[70] The European Neighbourhood Policy was first developed in detail in 2004 in European Commission, 'European Neighbourhood Policy', Strategy paper, Brussels, 12 May 2004, URL <http://ec.europa.eu/world/enp/documents_en.htm>.

[71] Torreblanca, J., quoted in Moravcsik, A., 'Open the doors', *Newsweek* (international edn), 2 Oct. 2006.

[72] E.g. the preliminary EU–Ukraine agreements in Oct. 2006 on visa facilitation and readmission is intended to be followed by the same arrangement with Moldova. Ukraine closely monitors developments in the EU–Russian relationship for the same reason.

differentiation. One author has argued (in the context of rethinking enlargement) that an 'enhanced neighbourhood policy should be tried out first in the east and later applied in the south'.[73]

By the end of 2006 the EU had agreed ENP action plans with 11 neighbours and the geographical framework (the 'list of neighbours') had been consolidated.[74] In December 2006 the European Commission put forward proposals for strengthening the ENP by seeking the conclusion of 'deep and comprehensive' free trade agreements (first with Ukraine), the facilitation of mobility and managed migration, and financial cooperation.[75] Financial assistance will be channelled under the new European Neighbourhood and Partnership Instrument (ENPI) starting in 2007.[76] The joint management of programmes under the instrument may provide the EU with more transparency and help the EU transfer its know-how to partners.

European security and defence

The failure to create a single staff and budget for the EU's Common Foreign and Security Policy (CFSP)—one consequence of the non-ratification of the 2003 Constitutional Treaty—has exacerbated the long-standing problems of institutional demarcation, bureaucracy and states' reluctance to cede powers or resources to the EU. The 2003 European Security Strategy has thus far worked poorly in generating coherent responses to specific crises and challenges around the world.[77] Lacking progress in its plans to create a 60 000-strong rapid reaction force, the EU continues to rely for the most part on its 'soft' policies and diplomacy. The Lebanon crisis in summer 2006, where EU countries made their troop contributions in a UN framework rather than to an EU operation, demonstrated the limits that the EU still faces in the 'hard' power context.[78] Unsurprisingly, initiatives by German and Polish politicians to revive the idea of a 'European army'—a German Social Democrat proposal concerning an EU army and Poland's incoherent suggestions on a 100 000-

[73] Grant, C., Europe's Blurred Boundaries: Rethinking Enlargement and Neighbourhood Policy (Centre for European Reform: London, 2006), p. 60. This has been reportedly contemplated by Germany.

[74] These action plans are available on the European Commission European Neighbourhood Policy website, URL <http://ec.europa.eu/world/enp/documents_en.htm>. A 12th, with Egypt, was adopted in Mar. 2007.

[75] European Commission, 'Strengthening the European Neighbourhood Policy', Communication to the Council and the European Parliament, Brussels, 4 Dec. 2006, URL <http://ec.europa.eu/world/enp/documents_en.htm>.

[76] The general provisions of the ENPI are laid down in European Parliament and Council Regulation (EC) no. 1638/2006 of 24 Oct. 2006, which is reproduced in *Official Journal of the European Union*, L310 (9 Nov. 2006), pp. 1–14.

[77] Council of the European Union, 'A secure Europe in a better world: European security strategy', Brussels, 12 Dec. 2003, URL <http://www.consilium.europa.eu/cms3_fo/showPage.ASP?id=266>. See also Grant, C. and Leonard, M., 'How to strengthen EU foreign policy', Policy brief, Centre for European Reform, London, 30 May 2006, URL <http://www.cer.org.uk/foreign_pol_new/index_foreign_pol_new.html>; and Bailes, A. J. K., *The European Security Strategy: An Evolutionary History*, SIPRI Policy Paper no. 10 (SIPRI: Stockholm, Feb. 2005), URL <http://www.sipri.org/>.

[78] On the events in Lebanon see chapter 2 in this volume.

strong EU–NATO force—proved to be non-starters.[79] In contrast, the cases of Iran and North Korea show that the EU states are able to adopt and pursue a concerted stance using their non-military instruments.[80]

The loss of the Constitutional Treaty also made it hard to focus instruments from different parts of the EU bureaucracy on members' shared internal security challenges of terrorism, organized crime and illegal immigration. The foiled terrorist plot of August 2006 in the UK to blow up civilian airliners, the unprecedented influx of illegal immigrants during the year and flourishing organized crime activities all underlined the need for decisive EU-wide measures—yet many justice and home affairs (JHA) decisions still have to be taken unanimously.[81] Attempts to allow more policy decisions to be agreed on a majority vote broke down at the informal meeting of JHA ministers at Tampere, Finland, in September. Nevertheless, plans are continuing for the adoption in 2007 of a broad programme leading to the creation of a joint coastal patrol network for the EU countries with coasts and other measures to fight illegal migration and human trafficking.[82]

As to external operations, crisis management remains the steadily evolving focus of the European Security and Defence Policy (ESDP). The ESDP's operative missions remain typically small but are broadening both in functional range and geographical terms (now in the Western Balkans, Eastern Europe and the Southern Caucasus, the Middle East, Africa and Asia). Seven of the eight EU crisis-management operations continuing at the end of 2006 were civilian.[83]

The Civil–Military Cell in the EU Military Staff officially reached full strength in 2006, although the need was recognized to do more for civil–military coordination.[84] Progress was made also in the 'systemic approach' to capability planning called for by the Headline Goal 2010, adopted in 2004.[85] Results included the preparation of the Force Catalogue 2006, which assessed EU states' pledges of forces and capabilities against required capabilities. The

[79] Dempsey, J. 'Germany proposes a European army', *International Herald Tribune*, 6 Nov. 2006; and Cienski, J. and Wagstyl, S., 'Poland proposes an EU army tied to Nato', *Financial Times*, 5 Nov. 2006.

[80] On both these nuclear-related problems see chapter 12 in this volume.

[81] Tigner, B., 'Europe's response to domestic security challenges snagged by constitution', *Defense News*, 2 Oct. 2006; and Bilefsky, D., 'EU fails to agree on policing role', *International Herald Tribune*, 22 Sep 2006.

[82] See, e.g., Associated Press, 'EU patrols off Africa due within a few weeks', *International Herald Tribune*, 25 July 2006; and Kanter, J., 'EU targets smuggling of Africans to Europe', *International Herald Tribune*, 30 Nov. 2006.

[83] The European Council also set up in Apr. 2006 the EU Planning Team for Kosovo (EUPT Kosovo) in preparation for a possible new EU mission in 2007. For full details of EU crisis-management operations in 2006 see appendix 3A in this volume.

[84] Council of the European Union, Council Conclusions on European Security and Defence Policy, 2761st External Relations Council meeting, Brussels, 13–14 Nov. 2006.

[85] Council of the European Union, 'Headline Goal 2010', annex 1 of 'ESDP presidency report', Brussels, 15 June 2004, URL <http://register.consilium.eu.int/pdf/en/04/st10/st10547.en04.pdf>.

catalogue will allow remaining EU shortfalls to be set out in a 'progress catalogue', due by the end of 2007.[86]

The continued migration of project groups of the former European Capabilities Action Plan (ECAP) to more integrated structures associated with the European Defence Agency (EDA) was noteworthy.[87] Further steps were taken towards creating a more competitive market for defence commodities in the EU.[88] With regard to capabilities, the EDA noted progress in the fields of command and control, strategic airlift and air-to-air refuelling.[89] In October the EDA presented a document called 'An initial long-term vision for European defence capability and capacity needs' (LTV) to EU defence ministers.[90] The aim of the LTV is to help EU defence planners identify and analyse the key trends shaping the future (for up to 20 years ahead) in the light of changes in military technology, the changing roles of armed forces and various other factors (financial, demographic, economic, legal etc.). The key desiderata for EU capabilities are defined as synergy, agility, selectivity and sustainability.[91] The EDA's work programme for 2007 builds in part on the LTV report. Major initiatives include establishing an ESDP capability development programme; developing a defence research and technology strategy to identify key defence technologies and find ways to 'spend more, spend better and spend more together'; elaborating the characteristics of the European defence technological and industrial base with the aim of increasing interdependence and specialization; and developing a 'cooperative armaments process', with initial focus on armoured fighting vehicles and the '21st century soldier' programme.[92]

Financial constraints limit the EDA's ambitions. Once again, EU ministers failed in November to agree on the EDA's three-year financial framework, although they adopted its budget for 2007.[93]

Battle groups are part of the EU's rapid response capacity.[94] From January 2007 the EU will have the capacity to undertake two 'nearly simultaneous'

---

[86] See EU Council Secretariat, 'Development of European military capabilities: the Force Catalogue 2006', Background, Brussels, Nov. 2006.

[87] The EDA became operational at the start of Jan. 2005, with the objectives of improving European defence capabilities, bringing about more efficient management of multinational arms cooperation, developing and integrating Europe's defence markets, and coordinating research and development.

[88] For more details see chapter 9 in this volume.

[89] The Strategic Airlift Interim Solution (SALIS) consortium was launched on 20 Oct. 2005. It includes 13 EU member states, Canada, Norway and Turkey and remains open to participation by other EU and NATO member states. SALIS is intended to serve as an example of solutions to overlapping capability shortfalls of the EU and NATO. Progress in air-to-air refuelling and strategic airlift was, however, assessed as insufficient owing to the inability of member states to significantly invest in these capabilities. European Defence Agency, 'Annual report by the Head of the European Defence Agency to the Council', Brussels, Nov. 2006, URL <http://www.eda.europa.eu/reference/reference.htm>.

[90] European Defence Agency (EDA), *An Initial Long-term Vision for European Defence Capability and Capacity Needs* (EDA: Brussels, 3 Oct. 2006), URL <http://www.eda.europa.eu/ltv/>.

[91] European Defence Agency (note 90). p. 6.

[92] European Defence Agency, 'EU defence ministers club together to research better protection for armed forces', Press release, Brussels, 13 Nov. 2006, URL <http://www.eda.europa.eu/news/news.htm>.

[93] 'EU/EDA/budget: ministers do not agree on EDA multiannual budget', *Atlantic News*, 14 Nov. 2006, p. 4.

battle group-sized operations. The required number of battle group packages for 2007–2009 has been decided, and the EU member states agreed to provide naval 'enablers' for the battle groups in the first half of 2007.[95]

IV. The North Atlantic Treaty Organization

Since the turn of the century NATO has continued moving away from the territorial defence of Europe towards out-of-area expeditionary tasks, plus limited non-military missions. However, this shift is not equally endorsed by all members,[96] and NATO is still searching for a strategy that would fend off charges of redundancy and consolidate its pertinence in the new, complex security environment. Its members, including the USA, are meanwhile tending to tackle their latest major security challenges outside, not through, the alliance framework. In this light, in order for NATO to preserve its relevance and find a new purpose, transformation has become an imperative. In 2006 Afghanistan, enlargement and transformation were the themes of NATO's effort to persuade publics and governments on both sides of the Atlantic of its continued pertinence to their security needs.

Out of area: focus on Afghanistan[97]

In 2006 NATO members provided more than 50 000 troops for a range of NATO-led actions that included missions in Kosovo and Bosnia and Herzegovina; training and helping to develop the officer corps in Iraq; supporting the African Union in the Darfur region of Sudan; and conducting counter-terrorism naval patrols in the Mediterranean.[98] Nonetheless, Afghanistan remains NATO's single largest external engagement and in 2006 became even more of a test case of its credibility and cohesion.

The NATO-led International Security Assistance Force (ISAF) has operated as a stabilizing presence in Kabul and in the north (the 2004 stage-1 deployment) and west (2005 stage-2 deployment) of the country. As NATO has moved into tougher areas of operation—stage 3 in southern Afghanistan from July 2006 and stage 4 in the east from October—and has taken over some roles from the separate US-led Operation Enduring Freedom counter-insurgency operation, more allies have become reluctant to provide troops at all or to let them move beyond certain areas and duties defined in national

---

[94] For discussion of battle groups in recent years see the previous editions of the Yearbook.

[95] EU Council Secretariat, 'EU battlegroups', Factsheet, Brussels, Nov. 2006; and EU Council Secretariat (note 86).

[96] In Nov. 2006 French President Jacques Chirac reaffirmed France's position that 'There was never any question of extending NATO to Asia. NATO is a military organization for North America and Europe.' 'NATO calls on Bosnia, Montenegro and Serbia to join Partnership for Peace', *Atlantic News*, 30 Nov. 2006, p. 1.

[97] For full treatment of the Afghanistan conflict see chapter 2 in this volume; the present chapter focuses on its relevance for NATO.

[98] On NATO troop contributions to missions in Afghanistan and Kosovo and the NATO Training Mission in Iraq see appendix 3A in this volume.

caveats. The year 2006 began with a difficult debate in the Netherlands over sending 1200 more troops, although the UK committed 4000 at the same time (and more later).[99] By September, the Supreme Allied Commander responsible for the operation, General James Jones, assessed that NATO forces were manned at only about 85 per cent of planned levels. During stage 4 some 12 000 US troops were reassigned from Operation Enduring Freedom to NATO command, bringing total allied forces to some 32 000 from 37 countries.[100]

At the NATO summit meeting at Riga in November 2006 the national caveats were the dominant issue, and significant progress was reported on eliminating or reducing them (especially for emergency situations).[101] NATO also announced its intention to start a gradual withdrawal from Afghanistan and to transfer responsibility for the country to Afghan security forces by 2008. The NATO Secretary General, Jaap de Hoop Scheffer, called for a broader and radical overhaul of military, civilian and development operations in Afghanistan, with the EU playing an expanding and vital role.[102] However, as Polish President Lech Kaczyński noted, 'The summit did not have the character of a major breakthrough' and the accompanying optimistic declarations about the mission in Afghanistan sounded less than fully convincing.[103]

Enlargement

Given its general political malaise and the burdens of Afghanistan, NATO continued to be unenthusiastic about expansion of the alliance following the latest 'big bang' enlargement of 2004. Albania, Croatia, the FYROM and Georgia met in mid-2006 in Dubrovnik, Croatia, in order to promote their membership aspirations and made clear that they hoped NATO would invite them to negotiate entry at the Riga summit meeting. The USA publicly supported the three Balkan countries, as expected, but went further by advocating the admission of Georgia and Ukraine as well.[104] While the Balkan candidates are now participants in NATO's Membership Action Plan and are formally well on the way to membership, Ukraine was evidently unprepared in political and practical terms for the USA's proposal, and Georgia remains handicapped by breakaway internal territories and unsettled border disputes. In September

---

[99] Associated Press, 'NATO nudges Dutch on Afghan mission', *International Herald Tribune*, 9 Jan 2006; and Associated Press, 'Britain to send 4,000 extra troops to Afghanistan', *International Herald Tribune*, 26 Jan. 2006.

[100] 8000 US troops remain active in Operation Enduring Freedom. On ISAF troop numbers and troop-contributing countries in 2006 see appendix 3A in this volume.

[101] North Atlantic Council, 'Riga summit declaration', NATO Press Release (2006)150, 29 Nov. 2006, URL <http://www.nato.int/docu/pr/2006/p06-150e.htm>. See also chapter 3 in this volume.

[102] 'There is no military solution . . . The answer is development, nation-building, building of roads, schools.' De Hoop Scheffer, J., quoted in Dempsey, J., 'NATO chief urges overhaul of Afghanistan effort', *International Herald Tribune*, 5 Nov. 2006.

[103] Ames, P., 'NATO can't agree on Afghan troop role', *Washington Post*, 29 Nov. 2006

[104] Wood, N., 'Four nations face barriers as they seek bids to join NATO', *New York Times*, 19 July 2006.

the NATO foreign ministers offered Georgia closer relations in the form of 'intensified dialogue'.[105]

Despite US support for Ukraine's participation in the Membership Action Plan and the qualified satisfaction expressed in June by NATO foreign ministers over the NATO–Ukraine intensified dialogue, the latter half of the year saw dwindling hopes for progress in the wake of Ukrainian domestic developments. The final blow came in September when the newly appointed Ukrainian Prime Minister, Viktor Yanukovich, declared that his country was not prepared for the Membership Action Plan and requested a pause in discussions on possible membership.[106]

In the run-up to the Riga summit meeting, NATO remained reluctant to offer membership of the Euro-Atlantic Partnership Council (EAPC), including the Partnership for Peace (PFP) programme, to Bosnia and Herzegovina, Montenegro, and Serbia, mainly because of the lack of satisfactory collaboration with the ICTY in The Hague. However, at US insistence, NATO reversed its position at the eleventh hour and agreed to invite all the three states to join the EAPC. The decision was officially justified by the desire not to isolate Serbia and its President Boris Tadić before the Serbian parliamentary elections in January 2007. In effect, the USA hoped that the NATO gesture would smooth the way for a compromise on Kosovo.[107]

At the Riga summit meeting, the NATO member states generally reaffirmed the organization's 'open door' policy for countries that meet NATO standards and indicated that they would extend further invitations at the next meeting in 2008.[108]

Transformation

Transformation is intended to be the engine for NATO's change and consolidation. It was planned that the November 2006 Riga summit meeting would provide new guidelines for it, thereby determining what NATO will do, with whom, where and how in the 21st century. However, during the year expectations were toned down and the Riga summit meeting was seen rather as a 'stepping stone' to future breakthroughs, probably at NATO's 60th anniversary meeting in 2009. This slow pace of progress carries some risk that the notion of transformation will be diluted to cover all types of ongoing change. One symptom is provided by the struggle of the Allied Command Transformation network—established after the 2002 Prague summit meeting to lead the

---

[105] North Atlantic Treaty Organization (NATO), 'NATO offers Intensified Dialogue to Georgia', NATO Update, 21 Sep. 2006. URL <http://www.nato.int/docu/update/>. Russia' reaction to this was sharp. It denounced NATO's decision and in the following weeks became embroiled in angry exchanges with Georgia—see section VI below.

[106] Socor, V., 'Yanukovych's nyet to NATO membership; painful, but not the final word', *Eurasia Daily Monitor*, 19 Sep. 2006.

[107] Dempsey, J., 'NATO to offer Serbia partnership', *International Herald Tribune*, 29 Nov. 2006. See also section V below.

[108] North Atlantic Council (note 101), para. 29.

military transformation of NATO forces and capabilities—to propagate its own vision in NATO.

In mid-2006, De Hoop Scheffer anticipated three 'baskets' of results from the Riga summit meeting.[109] The first was to cover operations such as Afghanistan and Kosovo and the second capabilities issues such as the NATO Response Force (NRF), strategic air lift and military spending. The third area for progress was political, including the question of NATO's partnership frameworks. In addition to strengthening existing links with the EU, the UN and countries in the Caucasus, Central Asia, the Gulf (under the Istanbul Cooperation Initiative) and the Mediterranean (under the Mediterranean Dialogue), the USA led the way in proposing that NATO should set up a 'global partnership' with interested countries such as Australia, New Zealand, South Korea and Japan, some of which were already operating with NATO in Afghanistan. The idea was that a new global partnership forum should include like-minded countries with a Western orientation, able to contribute to NATO's military missions around the world. As noted by an observer, the new forum would differ from the other partnership concepts in that its primary goal would not necessarily be to export democracy to the partnership regions but instead to import new security contributions to NATO. The emphasis on joint responses to new threats might lead to NATO admitting countries with dubious democratic credentials, such as Pakistan.[110] The proposal was viewed by some European countries, particularly Belgium, France and Greece, with suspicion as another variant of the USA's 'coalitions of the willing' concept, potentially weakening NATO as a collective defence organization. It was consequently deferred at the Riga summit meeting, although NATO did agree on practical improvements in consultations with non-NATO troop contributing countries and on a training cooperation initiative to share NATO training expertise with partners in the Istanbul Cooperation Initiative and the Mediterranean Dialogue.[111]

The largest policy achievement of the summit meeting was the endorsement at the highest political level of the Comprehensive Political Guidance (CPG) agreed in December 2005 by member states and endorsed by NATO defence ministers in June 2006.[112] The CPG sets out the framework and priorities for all of NATO's capability goals, planning disciplines and intelligence cooperation for the next 10–15 years. It analyses the range of threats in the probable future security environment and stresses that priority needs to be given to expeditionary forces and the capability to deploy and sustain them. Generally

[109] De Hoop Scheffer, J., 'Projecting stability', Speech at the Fundación para las Relaciones Internacionales y el Diálogo Exterior (FRIDE), Madrid, 10 July 2006, URL <http://www.nato.int/docu/speech/2006/s060710a.htm>.

[110] Kamp, K.-H., '"Global partnership": a new conflict within NATO?', Analysen und Argumente no. 29/2006, Konrad-Adenauer-Stiftung, Berlin, May 2006, URL <http://www.kas.de/proj/home/pub/9/1/year-2006/>.

[111] North Atlantic Council (note 101), para. 17.

[112] North Atlantic Council, 'Comprehensive Political Guidance', Riga, 29 Nov. 2006. URL <http://www.nato.int/docu/basictxt/b061129e.htm>.

speaking, the CPG supports NATO's 1999 Strategic Concept but does not replace it.[113]

In the area of military transformation, on 29 November the NATO Response Force was declared fully operational. The member states also announced agreement to share the costs of airlift for short-notice deployments of the NRF. The Riga summit meeting endorsed a set of initiatives designed to increase NATO force capacities, covering multinational joint expeditionary operations, strategic airlift, special operations forces, military support to stabilization operations and reconstruction endeavours, sharing information, data and intelligence in allied operations, further progress in the Alliance Ground Surveillance programme, and more.[114] The first major contract for a NATO ballistic missile defence system was signed during the summit meeting. This followed successful completion of a missile defence feasibility study, which confirmed that territorial missile defence of NATO population centres, forces and territory from the entire range of ballistic missile threats is technically feasible.[115]

At Riga, US Senator Richard Lugar called for NATO's role to be extended to the protection of energy security for member states.[116] This idea was warmly received by the Central and East European members, who feel most vulnerable to disruptions of the flow of oil and gas because of their heavy dependence on Russia. Ultimately, an anodyne statement calling for further study on energy security was placed in one of the last paragraphs of the Riga summit declaration.[117]

V. The Kosovo issue

The year 2006 was widely expected to be decisive for three key issues in the Western Balkans: the status of Kosovo, the relationship between Montenegro and Serbia, and the relationship between the entities and ethnic communities of Bosnia and Herzegovina.[118] By the year's end only the relationship between Serbia and Montenegro has been clarified. On 21 May 2006 Montenegro held a referendum on its independence. The EU had set a 55 per cent threshold for approval of the proposition: in the event a majority of 55.5 per cent voted in favour of independence, and 44.5 per cent against. With 86.5 per cent of the registered electorate voting, the result had substantial legitimacy.[119] The legal

[113] North Atlantic Council, 'The Alliance's Strategic Concept', Press Release NAC-S(99)65, Washington, DC, 24 Apr. 1999, URL <http://www.nato.int/docu/pr/1999/p99-065e.htm>.

[114] North Atlantic Council (note 101), para. 24.

[115] North Atlantic Treaty Organization (NATO), 'NATO on track for 2010 theatre missile defence', NATO Update, 28 Nov. 2006. URL <http://www.nato.int/docu/update/>.

[116] Lugar, R., 'Energy and NATO', Speech to the German Marshall Fund conference, 27 Nov. 2006, Riga, URL <http://lugar.senate.gov/energy/press/speech/riga.html>.

[117] North Atlantic Council (note 101), para. 45. On energy and security see chapter 6 in this volume.

[118] This third issue is not discussed in this chapter since there was no significant development in 2006.

[119] Organization for Security and Co-operation in Europe (OSCE), Office for Democratic Institutions and Human Rights (ODIHR), 'Republic of Montenegro referendum on state-status, 21 May 2006',

break-up of the former Yugoslavia of Josip Tito's times was thereby completed. Although a part of the Serbian establishment had expected a different outcome, rapid reconciliation between the two newly independent states followed. Tension recurred only when the Prime Minister of Kosovo visited his Montenegrin counterpart.[120] As Montenegro and Serbia had made a mutual commitment to respect each other's sovereignty and territorial integrity, Serbia's hostile reaction to Montenegro's offering such indirect recognition to Kosovo was understandable.

Otherwise, the main developments in 2006 in the Western Balkans were in the negotiations over Kosovo. The position of all parties on the province's future status became clearer, but there was no international agreement by the end of 2006, partly because the UN's special envoy for Kosovo—former Finnish President Martti Ahtisaari—deferred making his recommendations until 2007 in order not to interfere with the parliamentary elections in Serbia held on 21 January.

The starting positions of the two parties, Serbia and Kosovo, have been clear for a while: Serbia would consider solutions short of independence for Kosovo, whereas the Albanian Kosovars have excluded everything short of independence and sovereignty. Those who uphold Serbia's territorial integrity and believe that Kosovo should remain a province of Serbia refer to UN Security Council Resolution 1244 passed at the end of hostilities in 1999, which reaffirmed 'the commitment of all Member States to the sovereignty and territorial integrity of the Federal Republic of Yugoslavia'.[121] Those contesting it refer to the right to self-determination of peoples as well as other normative and practical considerations.[122]

The Serbian Government has sought to defer resolving Kosovo's status for as long as possible, in the hope that the conditions will change in Serbia's favour (e.g. as a result of violence by the Albanian community). Internally, the status of Kosovo is the only major issue on which the Serbian political class maintains some consensus, although there are differences in the stands of various political actors. The nationalist Serbian Radical Party has vehemently rejected the independence of Kosovo.[123] The Serbian Prime Minister, Vojislav Koštunica, reiterated many times during 2006 that 'Kosovo always was and always will be part of Serbia'.[124] However, Serbian President Tadić has

OSCE/ODIHR Referendum Observation Mission Final Report, Warsaw, 4 Aug. 2006, URL <http://www.osce.org/odihr-elections/18370.html>, p. 23.

[120] 'Kostunica: Montenegro require to respect Serbia's sovereignty and integrity—Tadic: unacceptable move by Podgorica', *V.I.P. Daily News Report*, 6 Nov. 2006, p. 1.

[121] UN Security Council Resolution 1244, 10 June 1999, URL <http://www.un.org/documents/scres.htm>. This position is officially reaffirmed in the 2006 Serbian constitution, which makes it an obligation for 'all state bodies to uphold and protect' Kosovo's existing provincial status. An English translation of the Constitution of the Republic of Serbia, which was adopted after a referendum on 28–29 Oct. 2006, is available at URL <http://www.srbija.sr.gov.yu/cinjenice_o_srbiji/ustav.php>.

[122] For developments until the end of 2005 see Dunay, P., 'Status and statehood in the Western Balkans', *SIPRI Yearbook 2006* (note 14), pp. 63–76.

[123] 'If radicals come to power', *V.I.P. Daily News Report*, 11 July 2006, p. 4.

[124] E.g. 'Serbia's PM vows to keep Kosovo', BBC News, 28 June 2006, URL <http://news.bbc.co.uk/2/5127464.stm>.

admitted that Kosovo is already 'closer to independence than to substantial autonomy',[125] and after meeting members of the US leadership in September he said he had 'the impression that the US Administration supports some kind of independence for Kosovo'.[126]

Kosovo for its part continued to give signs that, in spite of all doubts, it could act responsibly as an independent state. This was important given the earlier difficulties encountered by international bodies in seeking improvement in standards of Kosovar behaviour before Kosovo's status was settled ('standards before status'). After the eruption of violence in March 2004 it was deemed unwise to defer the discussion on status any longer, and it has been assessed that 'Kosovo Albanians have been under strict instructions from their political leadership to stay calm. It is argued that this will help ensure early independence.'[127] Although there have been some violent acts since then, they remained sporadic and limited.

An unresolved concern over potential Kosovo independence is how to provide for the rights of the Serb minority in Kosovo, in the hope that mass exodus from or secession by the Serb-inhabited area can be avoided. Current proposed solutions focus on decentralizing state power and establishing self-governing entities. According to the Serbian foreign minister, Vuk Drašković, adequate decentralization could guarantee that 95 percent of the Kosovo Serbs would live in municipalities with a Serb majority.[128] However, the Serbs in Kosovo remain mistrustful and under heavy international protection, while the Serbian Government claims that two-thirds of Kosovo's Serbs have been displaced to central Serbia.[129] Talks between the parties in Kosovo on minority protection ended in failure during the summer of 2006, and it remains likely that Kosovan independence would prompt further migration.

The key external actors in deciding Kosovo's future—the EU, the permanent members of the UN Security Council and the Contact Group[130]—look at the issue both against the broader background of stability and prosperity in the Western Balkans and in the light of their positions on other cases involving territorial integrity and the treatment of national minorities. The USA has clearly advocated an early decision on Kosovo's independence, followed by a much reduced US role in the Western Balkans. Nicholas Burns, US Deputy Secretary of State, declared in December that 'the Security Council will be requested to adopt a resolution on the status and we wish to see it happen very

[125] 'Bildt meets Kostunica, Draskovic and Dinkic for talks on Kosovo and Serbia's European prospects', V.I.P. Daily News Report, 17 Nov. 2006, p. 1.

[126] 'President Tadic: US administration supports independence for Kosovo', V.I.P. Daily News Report, 8 Sep. 2006, p. 1.

[127] King, I. and Mason, W., Peace at Any Price: How the World Failed Kosovo (Cornell University Press: Ithaca, N.Y., 2006), pp. 189–92; and 'Kosovo's future: decisions ahead', Strategic Comments, vol. 12, no. 6 (July 2006), p. 1.

[128] 'Draskovic: power to Albanians, integrity to Serbs', Kosovo Perspectives, no. 32 (15 Dec. 2006), p. 3.

[129] 'Independent Kosovo would destabilize Serbia, Macedonia and Montenegro', Kosovo Perspectives, no. 22 (29 Sep. 2006), p. 9.

[130] The Contact Group consists of France, Germany, Italy, Russia, the UK and the USA. Representatives of the EU and NATO also attend Contact Group meeting.

soon, let's say within a month after the [January 2007] vote in Serbia'.[131] One month previously, a US envoy indicated that the decision would be 'in keeping with the expectations of the majority in Kosovo, because these were the "legitimate aspirations" supported by the U.S.A.'.[132]

While the USA has long held these views, Russia's stance has evolved dramatically. It was long expected that Russia would be ready to strike a deal with the USA and others over Kosovo in the hope that the West would then accept the secession of the (Russian-backed) provinces of Abkhazia and South Ossetia from Georgia and Trans-Dniester from Moldova. During 2006, however, it became clear that Western powers were not ready to accept this implied trade-off and would continue to support the territorial integrity of Georgia and Moldova. This drove Russia back towards its more traditional policy of sympathy and cooperation with Serbia. Russia's representatives stated on a number of occasions that it might veto a decision in the Security Council 'if it should estimate that the resolution . . . was not in accordance with international law and Russian interests', and echoed Serbian arguments by calling for strict adherence (among other things) to UN Security Council Resolution 1244.[133] However, when Ahtisaari put forward his proposal in January 2007, Russia started to change its tone and no longer mentioned an eventual veto on the independence of Kosovo—a hint perhaps of renewed consideration being given to a quid pro quo.

Some EU member states have also taken a broader view: German Chancellor Angela Merkel stated that 'It is important that, on one side, the wish of the Kosovars for more independence be satisfied—but not at the price that we then have troubled situations in Serbia and democracy there is weakened'.[134] While the pro-independence majority in the EU might be able to handle Serbia's response, the question of precedent is ultimately trickier for other European states that face their own separatist challenges. For example, Spain—which faces such challenges in the Basque Country and Catalonia—is believed to have warned that Kosovo's independence could encourage other separatist movements in Western Europe and the Balkans.[135] The Spanish minister for the EU also claimed that an independent Kosovo 'would be con-

[131] United Nations Mission in Kosovo (UNMIK), Division of Public Information, 'Local media: media report', UNMIK Media Monitoring, 6 Dec. 2006. URL <http://www.unmikonline.org/dpi/localmed.nsf>.

[132] 'Wisner: There will be no more postponements', Kosovo Perspectives, no. 29 (17 Nov. 2006), p. 3.

[133] 'Spokesperson: Ahtisaari instructed by Contact Group to draft final status proposal', V.I.P. Daily News Report, 19 Sep. 2006, p. 1; and Russian Ministry of Foreign Affairs, 'Russian Minister of Foreign Affairs Sergey Lavrov meets with Serbian Minister of Foreign Affairs Vuk Draskovic', Press release, Moscow, 1 Nov. 2006, URL <http://www.mid.ru/brp_4.nsf/english/>.

[134] Associated Press, 'Merkel: Kosovo decision must reconcile autonomy with supporting Serbian democracy', International Herald Tribune, 7 Jan. 2007. Sweden has advocated a similarly balanced position since the autumn of 2006.

[135] Krasniqi, E., 'EU to cut Bosnia troops despite Kosovo worries', EUobserver, 14 Nov. 2006, URL <http://euobserver.com/15/22857/>.

trary to what EU aspires to, i.e. creation of multiethnic states'.[136] Romanian President Traian Basescu has said that 'solutions which grant collective rights to a national minority living on the territory of a sovereign and independent country should not be adopted'.[137]

In the event, Ahtisaari put forward his proposals on Kosovo to the Contact Group in late January 2007 and then presented them to the parties directly involved in Belgrade and Priština in early February.[138] His plan is much closer to the aspirations of Kosovo than those of Serbia. It offers all the main elements of sovereignty to Kosovo without naming it as a sovereign state. Internally, Kosovo is to adopt a constitution, have its own national symbols, and exercise authority with some exceptions over law enforcement, security, justice, public safety, intelligence, civil emergency response and border control. In its external relations Kosovo will have the right to negotiate and conclude international agreements, and to seek membership of international organizations. Refugees and internally displaced persons from Kosovo will have the right to return and reclaim their property. This de facto sovereignty will, at least temporarily, be limited by international civilian and military presences, while the EU will establish a rule-of-law mission in Kosovo. Further subtleties of the scenario include the possibility that Kosovo will declare complete independence without, however, rejecting the foreseen international presence and controls.

VI. The former Soviet area: security relations re-energized?

The year 2006 started and ended on the same note for the area of the former Soviet Union: energy issues are assuming a central position, both for the region's internal dynamics and its relations with the rest of Europe. Aside from this change, other security developments in the region showed a certain continuity.

Russia

In late 2006 a Russian politician offered a story of growing success and self-confidence in Russia's policy: '[Russia] has restored its sovereignty in the Chechen Republic and stopped separatist actions in other regions . . . the country has paid off much of its foreign debt . . . it has diversified its foreign policy and established mutually advantageous cooperation with the leading states of the world, including China and India [and] important measures have

---

[136] 'Navarro: Independent Kosovo contrary to EU's aspirations', *Kosovo Perspectives*, no. 31 (1 Dec. 2006), p. 2.

[137] 'Romania for Kosovo within Serbia', *Kosovo Perspectives*, no. 33 (22 Dec. 2006), p. 3.

[138] The Comprehensive Proposal for the Kosovo Status Settlement is available as an addendum to United Nations, Letter dated 26 March 2007 from the Secretary-General addressed to the President of the Security Council, UN document S/2007/168/Add.1, 26 Mar. 2007, URL <http://www.unosek.org/unosek/en/statusproposal.html>.

been taken to strengthen the country's defense capability'.[139] The Russian Foreign Minister, Sergei Lavrov, concluded that 'the role of the Russian factor in international affairs has considerably grown'.[140]

There is also another story to tell. Russia's recent economic upsurge has been based almost entirely on high oil and gas prices, rather than any general breakthrough in technology and competitiveness, and its (non-nuclear) armed forces continue to struggle with problems of quality and morale. Internationally, the events in Iran, Iraq and Kosovo have shown how hard it is for Russia to achieve more than a moderating or delaying influence over Western initiatives at the UN and elsewhere.[141] Perhaps most decisive for the tone of its external relations, the Russian leadership was increasingly castigated in 2006 for—as US Vice-President Cheney put it—'seeking to reverse the gains of the last decade' in democracy building and domestic reform, and for interfering with democratic movements in its neighbourhood.[142] Russian President Vladimir Putin has denied official responsibility for the most glaring occurrences such as the assassination of journalist Anna Politkovskaya in October 2006 and the poisoning of a former Russian agent, Alexander Litvinenko, in November 2006: but Russia's own investigations of these cases have produced no alternative explanation.

On all such points, President Putin shrugged off criticism and continued to play his cards—strong or weak—with characteristic vigour in 2006. In particular, his government developed the use of energy supply as an explicit weapon of Russian self-interest. The shock of the temporary shut-off of Russian gas supplies to and through Ukraine in January 2006, which caused severe difficulties in Germany and elsewhere, was followed by a similar action against Belarus—hitherto Russia's closest ally—in January 2007. While the ostensible agenda in each case was to bring neighbouring countries' payments closer to world prices for oil and gas, there was an undoubted subtext about Russia's wish to counter Ukraine's improving relationship with the West, as well as playing on vulnerabilities and divisions in the EU.[143] Even if the EU made a slow and unconvincing start on developing an energy policy— and was open to some criticism on market freedoms—Russia could not expect to emerge from such episodes without its intent and reliability as an energy supplier being questioned. The 2006 summit meeting of the Group of Eight

---

[139] Kokoshin, A., 'Real sovereignty and sovereign democracy', *Russia in Global Affairs*, no. 4/2006, (Oct.–Dec. 2006), URL <http://eng.globalaffairs.ru/numbers/17/1069.html>.

[140] Russian Ministry of Foreign Affairs, 'Transcript of remarks and replies to media questions by Russian Foreign Affairs Minister Sergey Lavrov at the press conference on the results of the activities of Russian diplomacy in 2006', Moscow, 20 Dec. 2006, URL <http://www.mid.ru/brp_4.nsf/english/>.

[141] Schröder, H.-H., 'Russia's position in a changing world', *Russian Analytical Digest*, no. 6 (19 Sep. 2006), URL <http://www.res.ethz.ch/analysis/rad/details.cfm?id=23103>, p. 2.

[142] The White House, 'Vice President's remarks at the 2006 Vilnius conference', Press release, Washington, DC, URL <http://www.whitehouse.gov/vicepresident/news-speeches/>.

[143] Some countries, notably in Central and Northern Europe, are already highly dependent on Russian oil and gas, and this is only part of the overall problem that within 20 years Europe will be drawing 90% of its energy imports from non-democratic regimes. Rahr, A., 'Konturen einer neuen Ostpolitik' [Contours of a new Ostpolitik], *GUSbarometer*, vol. 12, no. 41 (May 2006), p. 4. See also chapter 6 in this volume.

(G8) industrialized nations, which Russia hosted at St Petersburg, adopted fine-sounding principles on the mutual responsibility of energy producers, consumers and transit countries, and the importance of reliability and security in both demand and supply, but Russia itself evaded any specific new commitments and, notably, refused to ratify the 1994 Energy Charter Treaty.[144] A Russian analyst concluded in December 2006 that 'Moscow has managed to position itself as part of the energy security problem rather than part of the solution'.[145]

Meanwhile, President Putin intends to use part of Russia's financial windfall to step up the modernization of its armed forces—which has often been attempted since 1990, but never with such an economic foundation. Government pledges include putting more technologically advanced missiles, long-range aircraft and submarines into service, using fewer conscripts and raising wages, and increasing the number of units that are permanently combat ready. In terms of defence doctrine, Russia is preparing to 'fight in global, regional and—if necessary—also in several local conflicts'.[146]

Russia's actions presented a broad set of challenges for Europe in 2006. In reaction to the interruptions to gas supplies to Belarus and Ukraine, and hence to Western Europe through shared pipelines, the EU started its most serious discussions yet on a common energy policy while exposing major divisions between member countries.[147] Russia pressed ahead with the construction of a gas pipeline that would bypass Poland and thus allow Poland's supplies of Russian gas to be cut off without affecting Germany.[148]

Not surprisingly, political relations between Russia and EU members became chillier in 2006. German Chancellor Merkel proved a tougher counterpart for Russia than her predecessor, and relations with the UK were overshadowed by the Litvinenko affair. In November 2005 Russia banned the import of Polish meat, but this move eventually misfired by provoking Poland to block a new EU–Russia partnership agreement and by making the EU reflect on the need for a tougher stance.[149] Formal EU–Russian accords in

---

[144] G8 Summit 2006, 'Global energy security', St Petersburg, 16 July 2006, URL <http://en.g8russia.ru/docs/11.html>, para. 6. The Energy Charter Treaty, which was signed on 17 Dec. 1994, is available at URL <http://www.encharter.org/>.

[145] Zagorski, A., in Frolov, V. et al., 'Russia Profile weekly expert panel: 2006 in Russia's foreign policy', *Russia Profile*, 29 Dec. 2006.

[146] For this list of promises see Putin, V., 'Annual address to the Federal Assembly of the Russian Federation', Moscow, 10 May 2006, URL <http://www.kremlin.ru/eng/sdocs/speeches.shtml?type=70029>.

[147] The starting point for a common policy was proposed in a European Commission Green Paper in Mar. 2006, but some of its most basic tenets (including rationalization of the EU's internal energy market) remain highly controversial. European Commission, 'A European strategy for sustainable, competitive and secure energy', Green Paper, Brussels, 8 Mar. 2006, URL <http://ec.europa.eu/energy/green-paper-energy/index_en.htm>. See also Marcinkiewicz, K., 'Europe's energy musketeers must stand together', *Financial Times*, 9 Feb. 2006; and chapter 6 in this volume.

[148] For the Polish reaction see Petrovskaya, Yu., 'Pol'sha ne poterpit shantazha' [Poland does not stand blackmail], *Nezavisimaya gazeta*, 12 Oct. 2006, p. 9.

[149] It caused some difficulty for Russia to get out of the stalemate. In Jan. 2007 the Russian ambassador to the EU indicated that his country would resume meat import from Poland if experts were satis-

2006 were, consequently, confined to the visa facilitation and readmission agreements signed at the Sochi EU–Russia summit meeting in May 2006.[150]

From Belarus to Kyrgyzstan

In the Belarusian presidential election of March 2006, the incumbent, Alexander Lukashenko, won with 83 per cent of the votes and a turnout of 92.9 per cent. According to the Organization for Security and Co-operation in Europe (OSCE) the conduct of the election 'failed to meet OSCE commitments for democratic elections'.[151] According to Russia there were 'all the grounds to believe that the election was held in conformity with generally recognized standards, and the legitimacy of their results evokes no doubt'.[152] In late 2006, however, Russia emerged as a threat to Lukashenko by unilaterally imposing a large increase in prices for oil and gas deliveries to Belarus from January 2007. Belarus retaliated by introducing an oil transit tax, and after a few days—on 10 January—the dispute ended in a compromise.[153] According to one estimate, the new prices could lead to the collapse of one-quarter of all Belarusian companies;[154] and Lukashenko has certainly been given grounds to think twice about his policy of isolation from Europe with strategic cover from Russia alone.

Ukraine's parliamentary elections, also in March 2006, 'were conducted largely in line with OSCE commitments, Council of Europe commitments and other international standards for democratic elections'.[155] The Party of Regions

fied with their quality. Daly, J. C. K., 'Warsaw blocks EU–Russian negotiations on cooperation pact', *Eurasia Daily Monitor*, 18 Jan. 2007.

[150] The Agreement between the Russian Federation and the European Community on the Facilitation of the Issuance of Visas to the Citizens of the Russian Federation and the European Union and the Agreement between the Russian Federation and the European Community on Readmission were signed on 25 May 2006. They are available at URL <http://www.delrus.ec.europa.eu/en/p_242.htm>. The former agreement aims to facilitate interstate scientific and business relations. The latter guarantees that Russia will accept back, on expulsion by the EU, Russian citizens and citizens of other non-EU states and stateless persons who hold a valid Russian visa or residence permit, or who have unlawfully entered the territory of an EU member state directly from Russia. Russia for its part hailed the visa facilitation agreement as step in the direction of visa-free status for its citizens. Putin, V., 'Responses to questions from Russian journalists following the Russia–EU summit and press conference', Press release, Sochi, 25 May 2006, URL <http://www.kremlin.ru/eng/sdocs/speeches.shtml?type=82915>.

[151] Organization for Security and Co-operation in Europe (OSCE), Office for Democratic Institutions and Human Rights (ODIHR), 'Republic of Belarus presidential election, 19 March 2006', OSCE/ODIHR Election Observation Mission Report, Warsaw, 7 June 2006, URL <http://www.osce.org/odihr-elections/17955.html>, p. 3.

[152] Russian Ministry of Foreign Affairs, 'Statement by the Ministry of Foreign Affairs of the Russian Federation concerning Belarusian presidential election results', Moscow, 20 Mar. 2006, URL <http://www.mid.ru/brp_4.nsf/english/>.

[153] 'Russia–Belarus oil blockade ends', BBC News, 11 Jan. 2007, URL <http://news.bbc.co.uk/2/6248251.stm>.

[154] Lindner, R., 'Blockaden der »Freundschaft«: Der Russland-Belarus-Konflikt als Zeitenwende im postsowjetischen Raum' [Blockade of the 'friendship': the Russia–Belarus conflict as a turning point in the post-Soviet space], SWP-Aktuell no. 2007/A 03, Stiftung Wissenschaft und Politik, Berlin, Jan. 2007, URL <http://www.swp-berlin.org/de/produkte/swp_aktuell.php>, p. 1.

[155] Organization for Security and Co-operation in Europe (OSCE), Office for Democratic Institutions and Human Rights (ODIHR), 'Ukraine parliamentary elections, 26 March 2006', OSCE/ODIHR Elec-

gained most votes, further weakening the already embattled pro-reform leadership of President Viktor Yushchenko, and several months were spent on coalition talks that were more about personal status than policy differences.[156] Another complication was created by constitutional changes that attempted to remove some powers from the president while leaving him in command of the defence and foreign ministries—a system that has already been found ineffective and has reignited constitutional debate.[157]

Since taking over as Prime Minister, Yushchenko's more conservative rival Viktor Yanukovich has stated that when foreign policy decisions are made 'we have to think about preserving the country's unity'.[158] He was referring in particular to the issue of NATO accession, which he claims is supported by only one in five Ukrainians. The reduction in Ukraine's formal relations with NATO is noted above, while EU accession, although far less controversial in Ukraine, would mean surmounting currently impassable practical obstacles.

No other post-Soviet relationship caused so much anxiety in 2006 as that between Georgia and Russia. Long-standing disagreements include that over Russia's role in the conflicts in Abkhazia and South Ossetia and trade disputes. In May 2006, Russia added a ban on the import of Georgian mineral water to its 2005 ban on Georgian wine.[159] In late September, Georgia arrested four Russian soldiers, accusing them of spying. Even though they were handed over to the OSCE in early October for repatriation, Russia imposed punitive sanctions, cutting all air, road, rail, sea and postal communication between the two countries. This was followed by a crackdown on Georgian immigrants in Russia, hundreds of whom were expelled for alleged visa offences, threatening the vital flow of remittances to the Georgian economy.[160] In November the Russian gas supplier Gazprom announced that it would increase the price of gas supplied to Georgia from $110 to $235 per 1000 cubic metres, close to the price some West European customers pay.[161] The Georgian President fuelled

tion Observation Mission Report, 23 June 2006, URL <http://www.osce.org/odihr-elections/17714. html>, p. 1.

[156] Lindner, R., *Das Ende von Orange: Die Ukraine in der Transformationskrise* [The end of the orange [revolution]: Ukraine in the transformation crisis], SWP-Studie no. 2006/S 20 (Stiftung Wissenschaft und Politik: Berlin, Aug. 2006), URL <http://www.swp-berlin.org/de/produkte/swp_studien.php>

[157] Kozhukhar, I., 'V Kieve budet dva pravitel'stva i dve oppozitsii' [There will be two governments and two oppositions in Kyiv], *Nezavisimaya gazeta*, 18 Oct. 2006, p. 6.

[158] Center for Strategic and International Studies, 'Statesmen's forum with Viktor Yanukovych, Prime Minister of Ukraine', Transcript, Washington, DC, 4 Dec. 2006, URL <http://www.csis.org/component/option,com_csis_events/task,view/id,1151/>, pp. 7–8.

[159] 'Russia bans Georgia mineral water', BBC News, 5 May 2006, URL <http://news.bbc.co.uk/2/4976304.stm>.

[160] Parfitt, T., 'Russia escalates Georgia row despite release of "spies"', *The Guardian*, 3 Oct. 2006; and 'Georgia delays Russian expulsions', BBC News, 9 Oct. 2006, URL <http://news.bbc.co.uk/2/6034345.stm>. According to one analyst, the sanctions introduced were the toughest since the 1948 Berlin blockade. Jawad, P., 'Europas neue Nachbarschaft an der Schwelle zum Krieg' [Europe's new neighbourhood on the threshold of war], HSFK-Report, no. 7/2006 (Hessische Stiftung Friedens- und Konfliktforschung (HSFK): Frankfurt am Main, 2006), URL <http://www.hsfk.de/index php?id=9& detail=3451>, p. 2.

[161] Kramer, A. E., 'Gazprom of Russia to double natural gas prices for Georgia', *International Herald Tribune*, 22 Dec. 2006; and Socor, V., 'Gazprom's "pure commerce" in Georgia', *Eurasia Daily Monitor*, 9 Nov. 2006.

the fire in November by accusing Russia of ethnic cleansing in Abkhazia.[162] Whatever the rights and wrongs of the situation, these events made it more difficult for the EU or NATO to plan for strengthening their relations with Georgia.[163]

During 2006, a series of referendums were held by the de facto authorities in the disputed province of Nagorno-Karabakh in Azerbaijan, Georgia's breakaway territory of South Ossetia and Moldova's Trans-Dniester region. Even without general international recognition, the majority pro-autonomy votes were a signal of how difficult any eventual solution based on reintegration would be.[164]

Changes in Central Asia in 2006 were limited, although not without long-term significance. In Turkmenistan an opportunity for potential change arose with the death in December of President Saparmurad Niyazov, whose autocratic rule lasted for two decades (i.e. since Soviet times). In Kazakhstan there was some move away from a clearly presidential system—encouragingly, as the result of parliamentary pressure.[165] The lack of parallel progress in Kyrgyzstan, which had already prompted demonstrations in February 2005, led to a new wave of demonstrations against President Kurmanbek Bakiyev and his advisors in November 2006 and this time did result in constitutional change. Presidential powers were curtailed and those of the government and the parliament increased.[166] However, in January 2007 the President signed a new constitution that restored some of these powers.[167] This indicates a stalemate, with the prospect of future instability in Kyrgyzstan.

---

[162] Communications Office of the President of Georgia, 'Remarks H.E. the President of Georgia Mikheil Saakashvili European Parliament Strasbourg—14 November 2006', Tbilisi, 14 Nov. 2006, URL <http://www.president.gov.ge/?l=E&m=0&st=0&id=2071>.

[163] With the notable exception of Cyprus, the EU and NATO have expected candidate countries to solve any outstanding conflicts that may threaten security before membership is granted.

[164] Nagorno-Karabakh adopted its first constitution in a referendum on 10 Dec. 2006, with 83% of eligible voters in favour. Associated Press, 'Briefly: voters back sovereignty for Nagorno-Karabakh', *International Herald Tribune*, 11 Dec. 2006. In the 12 Nov. 2006 referendum in South Ossetia, 99% voted in favour of independence from Georgia. 'Russian MFA Information and Press Department commentary regarding a question from ITAR-TASS news agency about the results of the referendum and presidential elections in South Ossetia', URL <http://www.mid.ru/brp_4.nsf/english/>. In the 17 Sep. referendum in Trans-Dniester, 97.1% voters were in favour of independence from Moldova. Russian Ministry of Foreign Affairs, 'Russian MFA Information and Press Department commentary regarding media question about referendum in Transnistria', Moscow, 18 Sep. 2006 URL <http://www.mid.ru/brp_4.nsf/english/>.

[165] Panfilova, V., 'Sekvestr po-semeinomu: doch' Nursultana Nazarbayeva predlozhila ogranichit' polnomochiya ottsa' [Sequestration family-like: the daughter of Nursultan Nazarbayev initiated the curtailing of the sphere of authority of her father], *Nezavisimaya gazeta*, 12 Oct. 2006, p. 6.

[166] Gamova, S., 'Kirgiziyu snova likhoradit' [Kyrgyzstan has fever again], *Nezavisimaya gazeta*, 3 Nov. 2006, p. 6; and Peuch, J.-C., 'Kyrgyzstan: parliament adopts constitution curtailing presidential powers', Radio Free Europe/Radio Liberty, 8 Nov. 2006, URL <http://www.rferl.org/specials/central_asia/>.

[167] 'Bakiev signs the new version of the constitution', *Bishkek Observer*, 17 Jan. 2007, p. 1.

VII. Conclusions

The events of 11 September 2001 changed the focus of the Western world's security concerns, as the strategic ambiguity prevailing since the end of the cold war gave way to the imperative of fighting terrorism. Since then there has been a basic continuity in Western mainstream analysis, as evidenced by the US Administration's new strategic documents. The largest ongoing military operation, the fight against insurgency in Iraq, seems bound to create a lasting liability for the international community. It may soon become clearer that it is in the best interests of the campaign against terrorism to keep its major strands separate from the issues at stake in Iraq, rather than link them as closely as President Bush is still inclined to do.

Although transatlantic relations improved somewhat during 2006, the two main Euro-Atlantic security institutions remain in transition, still seeking ways to prove their respective relevance to the main new challenges. The European Union's foreign and security policies will remain handicapped for some time by the Union's constitutional crisis and, perhaps even more seriously, by enlargement fatigue. NATO has not done much better so far with its long-advertised transformation process. The continuing moderation of NATO's ambitions in 2006 suggests that NATO will continue to experience something of an interlude rather than a transformational breakthrough. Meanwhile, the fact that neither institution has reached a consensual 'grand vision' on global and European security also hinders closer EU–NATO cooperation.

Efforts to establish a lasting state structure in the Western Balkans continue to advance slowly with the separation of Serbia and Montenegro and the prospect of a new status for Kosovo. Kosovo also stands as a reminder that, despite newer agendas, ethnic composition and population trends can still influence international security. In the shorter term the focus will shift to Serbia's ability to make a productive adjustment, both internally and externally, to the emerging new realities.

Russia has recently modified the international security paradigm by reviving the perception that the security of oil and gas supply is a major strategic issue. Initial responses in the West risked a possible breakdown of European solidarity. During 2006, however, European states have at least accepted in principle the need to effectively coordinate their positions on this matter. It is possible that other aspects of Russia's current propensity for coming into collision with (most of) the Euro-Atlantic community might similarly bring West European actors closer to each other. From Russia's point of view, it has been using its new oil riches to recreate its pride, restore influence and maximize its power. It remains to be seen whether Russia's assumptions about its own relative independence of others' goodwill in the process make sense for the longer term. As long as the present course lasts, one consequence is the emergence of a—still not geographically precise—'soft division' between the new expanded West and the under-reformed, less integrated parts of Eastern Europe.

2. Major armed conflicts

SARA LINDBERG and NEIL J. MELVIN*

I. Introduction

In 2006 Africa, Asia and the Middle East were the principal geographical locations of armed conflicts, with events in Afghanistan, Iraq, Lebanon, Somalia and Sudan commanding much international attention. Elsewhere, long-standing, frozen and local conflicts continued to inflict a significant cost in terms of lives, suffering and economic damage. Section II examines three main features of the transnational aspects of collective armed violence, today considered vital for understanding the causes and progression of armed conflicts. Section III discusses three conflict areas that were active in 2006 and displayed striking transnational elements during the year: Afghanistan; Israel, the Palestinian territories and Lebanon; and Somalia. The conclusions are outlined in section IV.

Appendix 2A presents data on major armed conflicts in the 10-year period 1997–2006 based on the findings of the Uppsala Conflict Data Program (UCDP), and appendix 2B provides the definitions, sources and methods for the UCDP's data collection. Appendix 2C discusses forms of collective violence with elements beyond those of the standard definition of armed conflict and the availability of adequate conflict data.

II. Transnational dimensions of contemporary conflicts

Transnationalism has been identified as an important aspect of international relations for several decades.[1] The concept emerged as a way of understanding developments in the international order during the 1970s, partly in response to trends in global business and economics (the rise of transnational companies), which it was felt were calling into doubt the leading role of the state in some areas of the international system. Subsequently, the concept was developed in response to further work that explored the significance of state-based military capacities in the context of new global processes, the role of networks of non-

---

[1] Keohane, R. O. and Nye, J. S. (eds), *Transnational Relations and World Politics* (Harvard University Press: Cambridge, Mass., 1972). In this section, the term 'transnationalism' is used to denote a variety of cross-border interactions and connections between all types of actor, including both non-state and state actors, that go beyond interstate interactions, exchanges and links and which are facilitated by more open national borders. The term 'internationalization of conflict' is often used interchangeably with ideas about transnational aspects of conflict, although it generally implies the direct engagement of third-country state-based actors in conflicts rather than the diffuse groups of non-state and state actors that are understood to constitute transnational conflict networks.

* SIPRI intern Sebastian Merz assisted in compiling the data for section III.

state actors, the significance of diplomacy, multilateral institutions and ideas for effecting and limiting the power of the state in international relations.

Currently, the concept of transnationalism covers a broad range of phenomena and is based on a recognition that a set of interrelated developments—modern telecommunications and travel, multinational companies, global financial and commodities markets, increased levels and changed forms of population movement, and a reduced utility of state-based military forces—have posed significant challenges both to the primacy of states as international actors and to the concept of sovereignty. Collectively, such changes suggest that the nation-state model, which has provided the foundation of the modern international system, is being superseded by other types of governance and loyalty, frequently based on transnational affiliations.

Transnationalism has recently become a more important factor in the analysis of conflict as researchers have sought to supplement or supplant state-centric understandings of armed violence and its causes. The move to identify transnational aspects of conflict has further been linked to globalization and the growing role of non-state actors in collective violence.[2] In this way, transnationalism has provided explanations for and definitions of conflict that link local incidents of violence to broader social, political and economic developments in the world order.[3]

The evolution of thinking on the nature of transnationalism has also been accompanied by shifts in understandings of the appropriate policy response to the threats associated with transnational forces. Thus, the focus that emerged during the 1970s on strengthening multilateral institutions to manage global economic actors has been supplanted by a concern with building strong states. 'Failed' or 'failing' states have come to be viewed as not only creating problems for the populations in those states but also potentially posing threats to the international community as havens for transnational terrorist and criminal groups and as transit points for human trafficking and illegal migration.

The view that states are an inadequate frame of reference for analysing conflict causes and dynamics has been supported by research that begins from the observation that states and societies in particular regions are often linked together by networks of external relationships that play an important role in determining the prospects for peace or conflict.[4] This approach has been linked to notions of 'conflict diffusion' and 'contagion' and to research on the agents and relationships that foster the spread of intra-state conflict across state borders. Transnational 'conflict networks' consisting of a variety of social, economic and political connections, as well as state-based and non-

[2] Al-Rodhan, N. R. F., *The Geopolitical and Geosecurity Implications of Globalization* (Slatkine: Geneva, 2006).

[3] Duffield, M., *Global Governance and the New Wars: The Merging of Development and Security* (Zed Books: London, 2001); Robinson, W. I., *Transnational Conflicts: Central America, Social Change, and Globalization* (Verso: London, 2003); and Nordstrom, C., *Shadows of War: Violence, Power, and International Profiteering in the Twenty-First Century* (University of California Press: Berkeley, Calif., 2004).

[4] See appendix 2C; and Gleditsch, K. S., *All International Politics is Local: The Diffusion of Conflict, Integration, and Democratization* (University of Michigan Press: Ann Arbor, Mich., 2002).

state actors organized in relationships that reach far beyond the location of an intra-state conflict, have been identified as playing vital roles.[5]

The growing transnational character of global developments not only challenges states to develop responses through their own (global, multilateral and regional) cooperative groupings[6] but also opens up a way to address conflicts through transnational civil society organizations and movements.[7] These organizations range from the more traditional humanitarian actors, such as Oxfam and Médecins Sans Frontières, to non-governmental organizations that are ready to take on new generic functions, such as conflict mediation and post-conflict election monitoring.

Agreement is lacking on the exact nature of transnationalism and its overall importance for conflict. At the heart of the current debate is the issue of how much significance should be attached to the state in the context of transnational forces. Despite the relative decline of the state and the rise of non-state actors, some authors have recognized that states can also play important roles in transnational networks that include non-state actors.[8] The issue of the transnational challenge to state capacities and roles in conflict, notably the state monopoly on the use of violence, has been prominent in recent debates such as those on the shift in the character of armed conflicts from inter- to intra-state,[9] the importance of violent non-state actors, and the political significance of the aspects and forms of the privatization of security.[10]

An early effort by the US Department of Defense to identify transnational security threats noted as key factors terrorists, members of criminal groups, insurgents and opposing factions in civil wars that conduct operations outside their country of origin.[11] More recently, refugees and diaspora groups, militant Islamist networks and terrorism, legal and illegal economic networks, and

---

[5] Juma, L., 'The war in Congo: transnational conflict networks and the failure of internationalism', *Gonzaga Journal of International Law*, vol. 10, no. 2 (fall 2006), URL <http://www.gonzagajil.org/content/view/158/>, pp. 97–163.

[6] On new challenges for and developments in interstate regional security groups see Bailes, A. J. K. and Cottey, A., 'Regional security cooperation in the early 21st century', *SIPRI Yearbook 2006: Armaments, Disarmament and International Security* (Oxford University Press: Oxford, 2006), pp. 195–23; and chapter 4 in this volume. The roles of regional groups in modern-day peacekeeping are addressed in chapter 3 in this volume.

[7] Kaldor, M., *Global Civil Society: An Answer to War* (Polity: Cambridge, 2003), especially chapters 1, 5 and 6; and Tarrow, S., *The New Transnational Activism* (Cambridge University Press: Cambridge, 2005).

[8] Hveem, H., 'Explaining the regional phenomenon in an era of globalization', eds R. Stubbs and G. R. D. Underhill, *Political Economy and the Changing Global Order*, 2nd edn (Oxford University Press: Oxford, 2000), pp. 70–81; and Risse-Kappen, T., 'Structures of governance and transnational relations: what have we learned?', ed. T. Risse-Kappen, *Bringing Transnational Relations Back In: Non-State Actors, Domestic Structures and International Institutions* (Cambridge University Press: Cambridge, 2003), pp. 280–313.

[9] See also appendices 2A and 2C.

[10] See e.g. Bailes, A. J. K. and Frommelt, I. (eds), SIPRI, *Business and Security: Public–Private Sector Relationships in a New Security Environment* (Oxford University Press: Oxford, 2004); and Holmqvist, C., *Private Security Companies: The Case for Regulation*, SIPRI Policy Paper no. 9 (SIPRI: Stockholm, Jan. 2005), URL <http://www.sipri.org>.

[11] US Secretary of Defense, *Proliferation: Threat and Response* (US Government Printing Office: Washington, DC, 1996).

crime have been highlighted as playing prominent roles in conflicts.[12] Research has also drawn attention to the important role that transnational networks can play in peace-building and post-conflict reconstruction.[13]

Population displacement and diasporas

Previously, migration was predominantly a directed movement with specific points of departure and arrival. Today, however, more and more migrants have strong ties to more than one home country, blurring the coincidence of political, economic and geographic space.

Population movement as a result of conflict may be one of the key factors in conflict diffusion. Not only do refugees and displaced populations themselves suffer but they may also increase the risk of subsequent conflict in host and origin countries. For example, refugees may extend rebel networks to neighbouring countries. Although the vast majority of refugees do not engage in violence directly, refugee flows may facilitate the transnational spread of conflict-oriented ideologies, combatants and weapons, alter the ethnic composition of states and exacerbate the competition over resources.[14]

Diaspora and exile groups may play an important but sometimes also controversial role in conflicts and in political unrest in their countries of origin. This is by no means a new phenomenon, but the multiplication of diaspora communities playing such roles (especially since the end of the cold war), the prevalence of intra-state as opposed to interstate conflicts and the enhanced possibilities for transnational communication, mobilization and action have all led to a greater interest in examining this issue.[15]

Finally, conflict-generated diasporas—populations scattered to multiple locations as a result of violence—can play key roles in conflicts. A variety of types of role have been identified, including economic (providing funds for militant organizations, notably in Somalia) and political (lobbying) support.[16] Financial remittances from exile communities have been identified as of crucial importance for conflict economies—sometimes as the single most important source of income and means of survival for local populations. Other

[12] 'Transnationalism and conflict', *Internationale Politik*, vol. 7, no. 2 (spring 2006), pp. 8–48.

[13] A particular focus of work has been on the role of civil society—see e.g. Batliwala, S. and Brown, L. D. (eds), *Transnational Civil Society: An Introduction* (Kumarian Press: Bloomfield, Conn. 2006), especially chapters 9, 10 and 11—and of disapora communities—see e.g. Kent, G., 'Organised diaspora networks and homeland peacebuilding: the Bosnian world diaspora network as a potential development actor', *Conflict, Development and Security*, vol. 6, no. 3 (Oct. 2006), pp. 449–69.

[14] Salehyan I. and Gleditsch, K. S., 'Refugees and the spread of civil war', *International Organization*, vol. 60 (2006), pp. 335–66.

[15] See e.g. Diaspora, Development and Conflict, a research project conducted by the Danish Institute for International Studies (DIIS), on the DIIS website at URL <http://www.diis.dk/sw8952.asp>.

[16] Østergaard-Nielsen, E., *Diasporas and Conflict Resolution: Part of the Problem or Part of the Solution?*, DIIS Brief (Danish Institute for International Studies (DIIS): Copenhagen, Mar. 2006), pp. 5–7; von Hippel, K., *Counter Radicalization Development Assistance*, DIIS Working Paper no. 9 (DIIS: Copenhagen, Jan. 2006), URL <http://www.diis.dk/ sw19085.asp>; and Weiss Fagen, P. and Bump, M. N., *Remittances in Conflict and Crises: How Remittances Sustain Livelihoods in War, Crises and Transitions to Peace*, International Peace Academy Policy Paper (International Peace Academy: New York, N.Y., Feb. 2006).

recent examples include Sri Lanka and Kashmir, with populations scattered across the world but whose identity is tied to a symbolically important territory and who aspire to return to that territory. Diaspora communities often promote idealized visions of the homeland as part of their efforts to retain a distinctive cultural identity and may thereby foster radical nationalist sentiments or provide practical help to groups that are involved in conflict over territory. It has been suggested that diasporas can even prolong conflicts since they tend to be less willing to compromise:[17] the conflicts in the Balkans, for example, have been affected by the actions of diaspora communities that support radical nationalist forces by providing funds and often weapons and equipment.[18]

On the other hand, research has shown that disaporas are less often a source of conflict than was previously thought, reflecting the relative weight of other factors—strategic calculations, economic interests and the difficulty of mobilizing ethnic identities for political aims.[19] In fact, there have been efforts to use diasporas in conflict-resolution efforts, notably in the conflict between government forces and the Liberation Tigers of Tamil Eelam in Sri Lanka.[20]

Transnational conflict networks involving states

During the cold war, countries in both the East and the West supported armed groups outside the Euro-Atlantic region through so-called proxy wars. With the end of the two-bloc system, the leading military powers intervened more directly in conflicts. In recent years, however, the high cost of military interventions—notably the US-led interventions in Afghanistan and Iraq—coupled with the difficulty of resolving conflicts between weak states from outside and the political advantages of avoiding any close relations with armed groups have led renewed experimentation by large powers in what could be called proxy situations. In combination, notably with the rise of Islamist-inspired groups and networks, this has produced new conflict dynamics.

In 2006, the conflict in Lebanon contained strong elements of trans-nationalism. Hezbollah, in its confrontation with Israel, was in many respects arrogating the conventional sovereign state's right to make war or peace. Although it was a partner in the Lebanese Government, Hezbollah acted independently from key parts of the Lebanese state. The fact that Hezbollah is

[17] Lyons, T., 'Diasporas and homeland conflict', eds M. Kahler and B. F. Walter, *Territoriality and Conflict in an Era of Globalization* (Cambridge University Press: Cambridge, 2006).

[18] Sullivan, S., *Be not Afraid, for You Have Sons in America: How a Brooklyn Roofer Helped Lure the US into the Kosovo War* (St. Martin's Press: New York, N.Y., 2004); and Hockenos, P., *Homeland Calling: Exile Patriotism and the Balkan Wars* (Cornell University Press: Ithaca, N.Y., 2003).

[19] King, C. and Melvin, N. J., 'Diaspora politics: ethnic linkages, foreign policy, and security in Eurasia', *International Security*, vol. 24, no. 3 (winter 1999/2000), pp. 108–38.

[20] Zunzer, W., *Diaspora Communities and Civil Conflict Transformation*, Berghof Occasional Paper no. 26 (Berghof Research Center for Constructive Conflict Management: Berlin, Sep. 2004); Cheran, R., 'Diaspora circulation and transnationalism as agents for change in post conflict zones of Sri Lanka', Sep. 2003, URL <http://www.berghof-foundation.lk/scripts/DiasporaCirc.pdf>; and Østergaard-Nielsen (note 16).

widely believed to have received significant financial assistance and armaments from Iran and Syria highlights the way in which transnational linkages are working in the Middle East conflict.[21] Later in the year, in the conflict in Somalia, a number of countries in Africa and the Middle East aided armed Islamic militants who were trying to seize control of the country, while the United States and Ethiopia played key roles in supporting armed groups that challenged the Somali Union of Islamic Courts (UIC). This included the provision of support for the weak Transitional Federal Government (TFG), which eventually defeated the UIC. Both these cases illustrate models of cooperation between violent non-state actors and states with some motive for supporting them, with the net effect of undermining the viability, or at least the independence, of state structures in the target area.

International terrorism and crime

The recent rise in international terrorist threats, especially those associated with violent Islamist groups, has been linked closely with the issue of transnationalism. The creation of Islamist groups such as al-Qaeda, based on extended networks composed of cells of militants, has been seen as a potent challenge to a wide variety of states and societies. In particular, the ability of such groups to operate across great distances—using modern transportation and communications and often relying on dispersed networks based on family, clan or ethnicity—has challenged conventional security approaches and concepts of conflict.[22]

Islamist groups are regarded as archetypal transnational organizations because their mode of operation often transcends state boundaries and their ideology challenges the notion of the state. Thus, despite the important differences between groups—ranging from the Muslim Brotherhood in Egypt and the Islamic Action Front in Jordan to the militant Hezbollah and Hamas—they all criticize the state as artificial, illegitimate and rejected by populations. The declining popular acceptance of governing elites and their failure to protect human rights and guarantee the minimum requirements of a decent life have aided the rise of populist non-state Islamist opposition movements.

In addition to terrorism, transnational criminal networks have also emerged as a key element in conflict analysis and international security, notably in studies of the conflicts in the Balkans.[23] Analysis of the political economy of conflict has highlighted the importance of transnational, often illegal, eco-

---

[21] Hamzawy, A., 'Arab world: regional conflicts as moments of truth', *Arab Reform Bulletin*, Nov. 2006; Cody, E. and Moore, M., 'The best guerrilla force in the world', *Washington Post*, 14 Aug. 2006; and Integrated Regional Information Network, 'Lebanon: the many hands and faces of Hezbollah', 29 Mar. 2006, URL <http://www.irinnews.org/report.aspx?reportid=26242>. See also chapter 10 in this volume.

[22] Melvin, N. J., 'Islam, conflict and terrorism', *SIPRI Yearbook 2006* (note 6), pp. 123–38.

[23] Berdal, M. and Serrano, M., *Transnational Organized Crime and International Security: Business as Usual?* (Lynne Rienner: Boulder, Colo., 2002); and Gounev, P., 'Stabilizing Macedonia: conflict prevention, development, and organized crime', *Journal of International Affairs*, vol. 57, no. 1 (fall 2003), pp. 229–40.

nomic networks that connect non-state actors, ranging from organized crime groups to multinational companies. The struggle over natural resources in Africa, perhaps most notably 'conflict diamonds', has been widely viewed as a key element in the durability and complexity of conflicts such as those in Angola, the Democratic Republic of the Congo, Liberia and Sierra Leone.[24] Over the past decade, transnational criminal networks have also received growing attention as a result of their importance within the political economy of conflicts and especially since September 2001 due to connections with terrorist groups.[25] At the same time, the strong current focus of the international community on the transnational, even global, character of crime and terrorism may lead to undue attention being paid to the asymmetrical threats they pose to Western societies, when in fact crime and terrorism may have an even greater impact on conflicts in the developing world.

III. Transnationalism in armed conflicts in 2006

Three geographical locations of conflict that claimed international attention in 2006 most starkly demonstrate some of the transnational dimensions of modern conflict. The Afghanistan and Somalia conflicts and Israel's two-front war in the Palestinian territories and Lebanon were each derived from unique circumstances, yet they all serve to illustrate the limits of a state-centric understanding of the nature and origin of violence as a basis for conflict resolution. In each case, increasingly prominent non-state actors, underpinned by cross-border associations and networks, have filled a void owing to either the weakness or the perceived illegitimacy of the state.

Afghanistan

In 2006 Afghanistan suffered the highest levels of violence since the US-led invasion to oust the Taliban regime in 2001. The Taliban re-emerged from their defeat with an unexpected capacity to mount insurgency operations against the government and foreign security forces, especially in the south of the country. The main transnational element of the conflict was the Taliban's ability to operate from bases in neighbouring Pakistan—an allegation that has been contested by the Pakistani Government but is otherwise generally

---

[24] Collier, P., 'Natural resources and conflict in Africa', Crimes of War Project, War in Africa, Oct. 2004, URL <http://www.crimesofwar.org/africa-mag/afr_04_collier.html>.

[25] Woodward, S. L., *Balkan Tragedy: Chaos and Dissolution after the Cold War* (Brookings Institution Press: Washington, DC, 1995); United Nations, Final Report of the UN Panel of Experts on Violations of Security Council Sanctions against UNITA: The 'Fowler Report', in Letter dated 10 March from the chairman of the Security Council committee established pursuant to Resolution 864 (1993) concerning the situation in Angola addressed to the President of the Security Council, UN document S/2000/203, 10 Mar. 2000, URL <http://www.un.org/News/dh/latest/angolareport_eng.htm>, annex I; and Sanderson, T. M., 'Transnational terror and organized crime: blurring the lines', *SAIS Review of International Affairs*, vol. 24, no. 1 (winter/spring 2004), pp. 49–61.

accepted as fact—putting them beyond the reach of the coalition security forces.[26]

Violent acts in Afghanistan reached an unprecedented level in 2006, with the death of nearly 4000 people, a quarter of them civilians.[27] The escalation of violence was particularly sharp in the middle of the year as North Atlantic Treaty Organization (NATO) and US military commanders initiated operations to dislodge the Taliban from their strongholds in eastern and southern Afghanistan, mainly in Helmand, Kandahar and Oruzgan provinces. In several areas security problems brought reconstruction and development work to a halt. Concern that a still weak Afghan state would be incapable of containing other transnational militant terrorists remained a powerful motivator for continued international involvement in the country.

At the beginning of 2006, the international London Conference on Afghanistan—an initiative of the Afghan Government, the United Nations and international donors—resulted in the Afghanistan Compact, which built on full implementation of the 2001 Bonn Agreement.[28] The Afghan Government presented a five-year development plan to consolidate the state-building process under Afghan ownership, and international donors pledged $10 billion in reconstruction aid for the coming five years. However, the government's inability to extend its control and enforce order in large parts of the country obstructed efforts to develop democratic institutions. In the areas that it did control, inexperience, nepotism, corruption and lack of resources continued to hamper good governance.[29]

A surge in Taliban operations in the spring of 2006 led to a further deterioration of the security situation and testified to the Taliban's expanded capacity, confidence and resolve. The number of military confrontations and the increased levels of violence were also a manifestation of a strategic shift by the Operation Enduring Freedom (OEF) coalition forces, which were expanding their operations in the south of the country in preparation for handing over operational responsibility to the NATO-led International Security Assistance Force (ISAF).[30]

The perceived lack of improvement in the lives of many Afghans, especially those caught in the fighting, and the mounting civilian casualties, particularly from NATO air strikes, eroded popular support for the Afghan Government

---

[26] Rubin, B. R., 'Saving Afghanistan', *Foreign Affairs*, vol. 86, no. 1 (Jan./Feb. 2007); and Gall, C., 'Pakistan accused of backing Taliban', *International Herald Tribune*, 21 Jan. 2007.

[27] Zabuli, S., 'Afghanistan: NATO mission sees death toll zoom this year', Inter Press Service, 2 Dec. 2006, URL <http://ipsnews.net/print/asp?idnews=35690>. On the conflict in Afghanistan see also appendix 2A.

[28] The Afghanistan Compact, agreed at the London Conference on Afghanistan, 31 Jan.–1 Feb. 2006, URL <http://www.fco.gov.uk/Files/kfile/20060130 Afghanistan Compact Final Final,0.doc>.

[29] International Crisis Group, 'Countering Afghanistan's insurgency: no quick fixes', Asia Report no. 1223 (2 Nov. 2006).

[30] In 2004–2005 the Taliban extended their influence to large parts of southern Afghanistan, owing to the limited presence of international or Afghan security forces. Walsh, D., 'US troops to lead major attack on Taliban', *The Guardian*, 14 June 2006, URL <http://www.guardian.co.uk/afghanistan/story/0,, 1797387,00.html>. For more on ISAF see chapter 3 in this volume.

and the international military forces.[31] A shift in Taliban tactics could be discerned from the latter half of 2005, when they began to carry out suicide bombings—previously a rare occurrence in Afghanistan—on a regular basis.[32] According to a US military intelligence officer, a total of 139 suicide attacks were carried out in 2006—a substantial increase from the 27 attacks in 2005.[33] There was also a sharp increase in the number of roadside bombings. Both types of assault showed that Afghan insurgents had access to more sophisticated technology and better training. This tactical shift led some observers to note the similarity between the insurgency in Afghanistan and that in Iraq,[34] which may reflect the transnational spread of conflict patterns. While the Taliban have claimed to have had 'contacts with the mujahideen in Iraq'[35] and some analysts claim that the insurgents' use of tactics and technology is an indication that Iraqi militants participated in training or command, others suggest that tactics have migrated from Iraq either through human contacts or simply by the spread of information through the media.[36]

The United Nations Office on Drugs and Crime (UNODC) estimated that poppy cultivation in Afghanistan would increase by about 59 per cent in 2006, with the $2.7 billion drug trade amounting to one-third of Afghanistan's gross domestic product.[37] Despite a costly, two-year government eradication and crop-substitution programme, efforts to destroy poppy fields often exacerbated an already difficult economic situation for poor farmers and fuelled both general discontent and support for the insurgency.[38] Increasingly, links

---

[31] 'A survey of the Afghan people: Afghanistan in 2006', Asia Foundation, Nov. 2006, URL <http://www.asiafoundation.org/pdf/AG-survey06.pdf>; and Human Rights Watch, 'Afghanistan: NATO should do more to protect civilians', 30 Oct. 2006, URL <http://hrw.org/english/docs/2006/10/30/afghan 14475.htm>.

[32] Rahmani, W., 'Combating the ideology of suicide terrorism in Afghanistan', *Terrorism Monitor*, vol. 4, no. 21 (2 Nov. 2006), URL <http://www.jamestown.org/terrorism/news/article.php?articleid= 2370192>.

[33] Associated Press, 'Resurgent Taliban is focus of Gates' visit to Afghanistan', 16 Jan. 2007. In early Dec. 2006 NATO stated that suicide attacks had claimed the lives of 227 Afghans and 17 foreign troops during the year. 'Afghan suicide attack kills six', BBC News, 6 Dec. 2006, URL <http://news.bbc.co. uk/2/6212450.stm>.

[34] Rubin, B. R., *Afghanistan's Uncertain Transition from Turmoil to Normalcy*, Council on Foreign Relations, Center for Preventive Action, Council Special Report no. 12 (Council on Foreign Relations Press: New York, N.Y., Mar. 2006), URL <http://www.cfr.org/content/publications/attachments/ Afghanistan_CSR.pdf>, p. 7.

[35] Scheuer, M., 'History overtakes optimism in Afghanistan', *Terrorism Focus*, vol. 3, no. 6 (14 Feb. 2006), URL <http://www.jamestown.org/terrorism/news/article.php?articleid=2369902>.

[36] Karzai, H., 'Afghanistan and the globalisation of terror tactics', *IDSS Commentaries*, 4 Jan. 2006, URL <http://www.studies.agentura.ru/centres/idss/afghantactics.pdf>, pp. 1–2; Rohde, D. and Risen, J., 'CIA review highlights Afghan leader's woes', *New York Times*, 5 Nov. 2006; and Gall, C., 'Attacks in Afghanistan grow more frequent and lethal', *New York Times*, 27 Sep. 2006.

[37] Afghan Ministry of Counter Narcotics, Survey and Monitoring Directorate and United Nations Office on Drugs and Crime (UNODC), Illicit Crop Monitoring Programme, *Afghanistan Opium Survey 2006*, Executive Summary, Sep. 2006, URL <http://www.unodc.org/unodc/crop_monitoring. html>; and Buddenberg, D. and Byrd, W. A. (eds), UNODC and World Bank, Afghanistan's *Drug Industry: Structure, Functioning, Dynamics, and Implications for Counter-Narcotics Policy* (UNODC: New York, N.Y., Nov. 2006), URL <http://www.unodc. org/pdf/Afgh_drugindustry_Nov06.pdf>, section 2.

[38] The UNODC claimed that the increased cultivation in the south could be explained in part by the local strength of the insurgency, leaving considerable areas outside government control. Buddenberg and

between transnational organized crime and the drug trade in Afghanistan have come to be regarded as a major security concern.[39] Some US officials have claimed that criminal elements and illegally armed groups with links to the narcotics industry pose a greater threat than the Taliban to the future development of Afghanistan.[40]

The link between drug trafficking and the Taliban insurgency is complex, involving criminal networks of informants and various smuggling routes and systems of protection. The Taliban have reportedly charged transit fees for the safe passage of drug convoys through the border areas under their control,[41] a sharp contrast to their position at the end of their rule, when they sought to ban poppy cultivation altogether.[42]

In 2006 concern also grew over the alleged support underpinning the Afghan insurgency from militant elements in Pakistan, with which Afghanistan shares a long, porous border and a complicated history. Diplomatic relations between the President of Afghanistan, Hamid Karzai, and the President of Pakistan, Pervez Musharraf, became tense, with each leader blaming the other for failing to act against Taliban militants.[43] Musharraf was accused of failing to destroy training bases and sanctuaries for Taliban insurgents and al-Qaeda allies in the Federally Administrated Tribal Areas (FATA) of Pakistan.[44] In early 2007 the US Director of National Intelligence claimed that al-Qaeda and the Taliban maintain 'critical sanctuaries' in Pakistan, from where they can rebuild their strength.[45] Ethnic affinities among the Pashtun along the Afghan–Pakistani border, growing support for the Taliban insurgency and a growth of religious extremism have led to a reported 'Talibanization' of the

Byrd (note 37); UNODC (note 37); and 'UN warns of soaring Afghan opium', BBC News, 2 Sep. 2006, URL <http://news.bbc.co.uk/2/5308180.stm>.

[39] In general, the links between weak states and the rise of transnational organized crime began to emerge as a problem in the mid-1990s but this was not sufficiently recognized as a security problem, despite the apparent internal and cross-border security implications. Cornell, S., 'Narcotics, radicalism, and armed conflict in central Asia: the Islamic Movement of Uzbekistan', *Terrorism and Political Violence*, no. 17 (2005), pp. 577–97.

[40] Gallis, P., *NATO in Afghanistan: A Test of the Transatlantic Alliance*, Congressional Research Service (CRS) Report for Congress (US Library of Congress, CRS: Washington, DC, 22 Aug. 2006), p. 5.

[41] Wright, J., 'Afghanistan's opiate economy and terrorist financing', *Jane's Intelligence Review*, vol. 28, no. 3 (Mar. 2006), pp. 36–42; and Wright, J., 'The changing structure of the Afghan opium trade', *Jane's Intelligence Review*, vol. 18, no. 9 (Sep. 2006), pp. 6–14.

[42] After 2 decades of uninterrupted increase in opium poppy cultivation, the July 2000 ban by the Taliban led to an unprecedented (91%) reduction in poppy cultivation—from 82 172 hectares in 2000 to 7606 ha in 2001. United Nations International Drug Control Programme (UNDCP), *Afghanistan Annual Opium Poppy Survey 2001* (UNDCP: Islamabad, 2001), p. ii.

[43] Morarjee, R. and Bokhari, F., 'Dispute hits bid to tackle Taliban', *Financial Times*, 9–10 Dec. 2006, p. 5; and Gall, C., 'Pakistan's support for militants threatens region, Karzai says', *New York Times*, 13 Dec. 2006.

[44] The FATA are also thought to be bases for other types of crime, such as drug trafficking. On Afghanistan's cross-border relations see 'Afghanistan's regional diplomacy: starting from scratch', *Strategic Comments*, vol. 12, no. 5 (15 June 2006); and Saikal, A., 'Securing Afghanistan's border', *Survival*, vol. 48, no. 1 (spring 2006), pp. 129–42.

[45] 'Annual threat assessment of the Director of National Intelligence', Negroponte, J. D., Director of National Intelligence, 11 Jan. 2007, URL <http://intelligence.senate.gov/070111/negroponte.pdf>; and Walker, P., 'Al-Qaida rebuilding in Pakistan, US says', *The Guardian*, 12 Jan. 2007.

Pakistani FATA, areas over which government control has traditionally been very weak.[46]

Reports in 2006 suggested the possibility of more direct Pakistani assistance, implicating the Pakistani Inter-Services Intelligence (ISI) in facilitating the Taliban cause by 'turning a blind eye', but also through monetary support and assistance in coordinating cross-border activities.[47] Senior Afghan and NATO officials insist that Taliban fighters continue to be assisted by Pakistan, an allegation that has been vehemently refuted by Pakistani authorities.[48]

On 5 September 2006 Musharraf signalled a halt to his costly military campaign against extremists in the FATA by signing a controversial peace agreement with tribal elders in North Waziristan, which called for the cessation of fighting, the dismantling of border checkpoints that had been set up to find members of al-Qaeda and the Taliban, and the release of 132 Taliban fighters in Pakistani custody.[49] Sources soon reported a rise in cross-border infiltrations from these areas, with the Taliban and their supporters able to operate more freely and cross into Afghanistan: US and NATO sources claimed that there was a threefold increase in attacks in eastern Afghan provinces in the autumn.[50] Afghanistan's broader transformation appeared to hinge on its problematic relationship with Pakistan.

In early 2006, several people were killed by Afghan police during protests against the publication in September 2005 of a caricature of the Prophet Muhammad in a Danish newspaper.[51] The failure to subdue the protesters further testified to the significant weaknesses still extant within the Afghan regime. The inability to recruit, train and equip a capable police force in Afghanistan continued to exacerbate security problems during the year, particularly in the south of the country. In Kabul, violence occurred on a significant scale in May, when the fledgling police force could not contain demonstrations and looting incidents in which 12 people were killed.[52] A European Union police training mission was proposed for deployment in 2007 in order

---

[46] International Crisis Group, 'Pakistan's tribal areas: appeasing the militants', Asia Report no. 125 (11 Dec. 2006). For more on the Afghanistan–Pakistan connection and on Pashtun nationalism see Abou-Zahab, M. and Roy, O., *Islamist Networks: The Afghan–Pakistan Connection* (Columbia University Press: New York, N.Y., 2004).

[47] Rubin (note 26); and 'Afghanistan's regional diplomacy: starting from scratch' (note 44).

[48] See e.g. Gall, C., 'Pakistan accused of backing Taliban', *International Herald Tribune*, 21 Jan. 2007.

[49] International Crisis Group (note 46); and Niazi, T., 'Pakistan's peace deal with Taliban militants', *Terrorism Monitor*, vol. 4, no. 19 (5 Oct. 2006), URL <http://www.jamestown.org/terrorism/news/article.php?articleid=2370153>. A similar deal was struck with South Waziristan in Apr. 2005.

[50] United Nations, Report of the Security Council mission to Afghanistan, 11 to 16 November 2006, UN document S/2006/935, 4 Dec. 2006; Rubin (note 26), p. 71; and 'Pakistan deals "aiding Taleban"', BBC News, 11 Dec. 2006, URL <http://news.bbc.co.uk/2/619355.stm>.

[51] Witte, G. and Nakashima, E., 'Cartoon protests stoke anti-American mood', *Washington Post*, 7 Feb. 2006.

[52] The violence was triggered by a traffic incident in Kabul that, according to a US colonel, killed 1 person, caused by a US military convoy suffering technical problems. 'NATO/Afghanistan: great wave of violence in Afghanistan: ISAF extracts EU delegation staff from Kabul', *Atlantic News*, no. 3781 (1 June 2006), pp. 1–2.

to strengthen the Afghan police force.[53] The many challenges facing inter-national state-building efforts in Afghanistan continue to raise questions about the effectiveness of applying the Western state model to a country with little historical experience of a central state system.

Israel, the Palestinian territories and Lebanon

Israel was involved in two concurrent conflicts in 2006: with Hamas in the Palestinian territories and with Hezbollah in Lebanon. The former constituted an escalation of the long-running and seemingly intractable conflict between Israel and the Palestinians. Both conflicts exhibited the greater role of regional and transnational conflict networks and the link between state and non-state actors, as both Hamas and Hezbollah were strengthened by political, ideo-logical and practical support from states such as Iran and Syria.[54] With such broad involvement, any escalation like the Israeli military operation in Lebanon risked causing a significant geographical expansion of the conflict. In the broader regional context, Iran's support for Hezbollah, coupled with Iran's growing influence in the Middle East and the rise to power of the Shia community in Iraq, highlighted the potential transnational role that the Shia factor can play in regional politics.

In January 2006 Ehud Olmert replaced Ariel Sharon as Israeli Prime Min-ister, when Sharon was incapacitated by illness. In the same month Hamas won a landslide victory in the second election to the Palestinian Legislative Council (PLC), the parliamentary branch of the Palestinian Authority (PA), thus bringing to an end Fatah's long-standing political domination of the PA. The democratic election of Hamas brought to power a government that rejected negotiations on a two-state solution to the conflict with Israel, all but destroying any prospect for cooperation between the PA and Israel or other international actors.

Key international stakeholders such as the EU and the USA were sceptical about whether Hamas, which they classified as a terrorist organization, would be a dependable political partner.[55] The elections left the PA increasingly iso-lated, with the main international donor countries (led by the USA) refusing to support Hamas in its new capacity. Israel immediately stopped the transfer of tax revenues collected on behalf of the PA, an income that in 2005 represented around 35 per cent of the PA's budget.[56] In March 2006 the EU and the USA

[53] The EU approved the training mission on 13 Feb. 2007.

[54] Jones, C., 'Israeli offensive may not meet long-term objectives', *Jane's Intelligence Review*, vol. 18, no. 9 (Sep. 2006); and Salhani, C. and Saoud, D., 'Analysis: Iran, Syria use Lebanese militia', UPI International Intelligence, 12 July 2006.

[55] The US State Department listed Hamas as a Foreign Terrorist Organization in Nov. 2001, and the EU followed suit in Sep. 2003. US Department of State, 'Foreign Terrorist Organizations (FTOs)', 11 Oct. 2005, URL <http://www.state.gov/s/ct/rls/fs/37191.htm>; and Council of the European Union, 'Council Common Position 2003/651/CFSP of 12 Sep. 2003, updating Common Position 2001/931/CFSP on the application of specific measures to combat terrorism and repealing Common Position 2003/482/CFSP', *Official Journal of the European Communities*, L 229 (13 Sep. 2003), pp. 42–45.

[56] 'A dilemma over Hamas and its cash?', *The Economist*, 18 Feb. 2006, p. 35; and Brown, N. J., *Living with Palestinian Democracy*, Carnegie Endowment for International Peace Policy Brief no. 46 (Car-

suspended their financial assistance to the new PA administration and its agencies.[57] A US-imposed business ban restricted financial support from other donors by limiting bank transfers.[58] The PA was unable to pay its employees' salaries, which support about 30 per cent of the Palestinian population.[59] In spite of the fact that some aid was provided—a result of the diplomatic efforts of the Middle East Quartet (the EU, the UN, Russia and the USA) to find a mechanism to funnel aid directly to the Palestinian population—conditions in the Palestinian territories remained dire, with only limited provision of social services.[60]

Political fragmentation, coupled with severe financial challenges, led to a further deterioration of the security situation.[61] The armed forces and police split into Fatah and Hamas factions, and gunfights and kidnappings by both parties ensued in the Gaza Strip and the West Bank.[62] In May Hamas formed a shadow security force comprising 3000 members of aligned militant groups to complement the largely Fatah-loyal security forces, sparking another political crisis.[63] A general increase in violence could be discerned as poverty, in combination with an abundance of weapons, drove up crime rates.[64]

While Palestinian rivalries led to domestic instability, the search for peaceful resolution of the enduring conflict between Israel and the Palestinians remained at a standstill. Israel's parliamentary elections in March showed that the electorate favoured more unilateral Israeli action and, together with the election of Hamas, signaled a clear shift away from negotiations.[65] As Hamas

negie Endowment for International Peace: Washington, DC, June 2006), URL <http://www.carnegie endowment.org/files/pb46_Brown_final.pdf>, p. 6.

[57] 'EU suspends aid to Palestinians', BBC News, 7 Apr. 2006, URL <http://news.bbc.co.uk/2/4887226.stm>.

[58] Myre, G., 'In new problem for Palestinians, banks reject transfers', New York Times, 4 May 2006.

[59] World Bank, 'The impending Palestinian fiscal crisis, potential remedies', 7 May 2006, URL <http://siteresources.worldbank.org/INTWESTBANKGAZA/Resources/PalestinianFiscalCrisis,Potential RemediesMay7.pdf>.

[60] On 17 June the Quartet announced a Temporary International Mechanism for channelling aid through health services and social allowances, which appeared to work well. Middle East Quartet Statement, Washington, DC, 17 June 2006, S163/06, URL <http://www.state.gov/p/nea/rls/72900.htm>; International Institute for Strategic Studies (IISS), Strategic Survey 2006: The IISS Annual Review of World Affairs (Taylor & Francis: London, 2006), p. 230; European Commission, '40,000 Palestinian families to benefit from EU social allowances at the start of Ramadan', Press release IP/06/1251, 25 Sep. 2006; Morris, H., 'Pain of Hamas boycott worse than expected', Financial Times, 9 May 2006; and Erlanger, S., 'As Gazans wait for aid, their situation is dire', New York Times, 11 May 2006.

[61] 'Testing time as Hamas goes it alone', BBC News, 19 Mar. 2006, URL <http://news.bbc.co.uk/2/4823602.stm>. Hamas had held talks with Fatah on forming a unity government, but they failed and Hamas alone formed the government.

[62] IISS (note 60), p. 229; Myre, G., 'After shootout, Palestinians try to calm infighting', New York Times, 9 May 2006; and Morris, H., 'Further clashes in Gaza despite appeals for calm', Financial Times, 9 May 2006.

[63] 'Hamas, Syria, Iran coordinate strategy to gain control of Palestinian Authority', 28 May 2006, World News Connection, National Technical Information Service (NTIS), US Department of Commerce.

[64] International Crisis Group, 'The Arab–Israeli conflict: to reach a lasting peace', Middle East Report no. 58 (5 Oct. 2006).

[65] Olmert's victorious Kadima Party campaigned on a unilateral approach to disengagement from the occupied territories initiated by Ariel Sharon with the 2005 unilateral withdrawal from the Gaza Strip. 'Shutting itself in, hoping for the best', The Economist, 23 Mar. 2006.

did not recognize Israel and refused to call for an end to violence as a means of resistance, the two elections effectively brought the peace process to a halt.[66]

Violent skirmishes between Israel and Palestinians continued, with intermittent peaks in raids against suspected militants in the Palestinian territories. Attacks with Qassam rockets launched from the Gaza Strip and the West Bank and suicide attacks perpetrated by the Fatah-affiliated al-Aqsa Brigades and the Palestinian Islamic Jihad (PIJ) led to a continuation of Israeli air strikes in April and May, claiming Palestinian civilian casualties.[67] An alleged Israeli attack in which eight Palestinian civilians were killed in the Gaza Strip and a rocket attack on Israel from the Gaza Strip by Hamas's armed wing, the Izz ad-Din al-Qassam Brigades, effectively ended the informal truce that had been agreed in February 2005.[68]

The violence escalated on 25 June, when the Izz ad-Din al-Qassam Brigades, the Popular Resistance Committees (PRC) and a previously unknown group called the Army of Islam attacked an Israeli Army post near the Gaza Strip border: two Israeli soldiers were killed and one was abducted.[69] Israel responded by conducting a major military operation, moving into the Gaza Strip only hours after the ambush—the first major Israeli military incursion since the 2005 withdrawal from Gaza.[70] Around 60 Hamas officials, including several ministers, were taken into custody in an Israeli operation in the West Bank.[71] Rocket attacks and air strikes followed, and by mid-July about 65 Palestinians and 1 Israeli had been killed.[72]

On 12 July the Hezbollah Shiite group and its militant Islamic Resistance wing, based in Lebanon, kidnapped two Israeli soldiers in a cross-border raid near an Israeli Army base and killed several others.[73] Israel declared that Hezbollah's role as a political actor with representation in the Lebanese Gov-

---

[66] In addition, the Palestinians' deteriorating political and economic situation left no capable, willing political group to engage in effective negotiations with Israel. 'Moderating hand needed to guide Hamas and Israel to peace table', *Jane's Intelligence Review*, vol. 12, no. 6 (June 2006), pp. 28–30; and International Crisis Group (note 64), p. 2.

[67] International Crisis Group, *CrisisWatch*, no. 33 (1 May 2006), p. 10; *CrisisWatch*, no. 34 (1 June 2006), p. 11; 'Bomber strikes Israeli settlement', BBC News, 31 Mar. 2006, URL <http://news.bbc.co.uk/2/4863022.stm>; and 'Israel blames Hamas for bombing', BBC News, 19 Apr. 2006, URL <http://news.bbc.co.uk/2/4917704.stm>.

[68] 'Hamas breaks truce with rockets', BBC News, 10 June 2006, URL <http://news.bbc.co.uk/2/5066768.stm>.

[69] 'Israeli soldier 'seized' in raid', BBC News, 25 June 2006, URL <http://news.bbc.co.uk/2/5115092.stm>.

[70] 'Israeli soldiers push into Gaza', BBC News, 28 June 2006, URL <http://news.bbc.co.uk/2/5123640.stm>. On the 2005 withdrawal from the Gaza Strip see Holmqvist, C., 'Major armed conflicts', *SIPRI Yearbook 2006* (note 6), pp. 80–83.

[71] 'Might something good come out of it this time?', *The Economist*, 1 July 2006, p. 39. The Palestinian Prime Minister, Ismail Haniyeh, denied having any knowledge of the attack, which suggested that there might be a split in the organization. Rais, F. R., 'Hamas: the present stage', *Strategic Studies*, vol. 26, no. 3 (2006), pp. 82.

[72] al-Mughrabi, N., 'Israel kills 18 in Gaza as fighting intensifies', Reuters, 6 July 2006; and 'Deaths mount in attacks on Gaza', BBC News, 12 July 2006, URL <http://news.bbc.co.uk/2/5171148.stm>.

[73] Hardy, R., 'Hezbollah capture marks new escalation', BBC News, 12 July 2006, URL <http://news.bbc.co.uk/2/5172760.stm>.

ernment made the attack not an act of terrorism but an attack by the state of Lebanon. Israel refused to negotiate any offers of a prisoner exchange and responded to the perceived provocation by carrying out a military offensive against the Hezbollah stronghold in the south.[74]

Israeli forces launched heavy air strikes and moved 30 000 troops into Lebanon, the first time Israel had sent troops to the country since their withdrawal in 2000. Hezbollah responded by launching rockets against Israeli troops and towns in northern Israel. Both sides extended their military operations to include civilian targets. In an attempt to prevent the kidnapped Israeli soldiers from being relocated, and to interrupt weapon deliveries from abroad to Hezbollah, Israel attacked infrastructure across Lebanon, including the civilian airport and the single road connection to Syria, and announced an air and sea blockade against the country.[75]

The 34-day conflict ended in August, when Israel, Hezbollah and the Lebanese Government agreed to the ceasefire set out in UN Security Council Resolution 1701, and Israel began a gradual withdrawal from Lebanon.[76] By then the fighting had cost the lives of an estimated 1191 Lebanese and 162 Israelis, displaced scores of people from both countries, demolished thousands of homes (the vast majority Lebanese) and countless buildings and vital infrastructure, and caused billions of dollars worth of damage in both countries.[77]

The conflict ended inconclusively for both Israel and Hezbollah. Israel had neither recovered the kidnapped soldiers nor succeeded in its broader aim of subduing the threat that it perceived Hezbollah posed to its borders. The fighting revealed the military shortcomings of Israel, and its operation was criticized domestically for being poorly coordinated and weak, which strained Olmert's Government.[78] Hezbollah's capacity, with elaborate bunker systems and a level of arms build-up that Israeli intelligence had failed to recognize, surprised some observers.[79] Although Hezbollah suffered heavy casualties and a severely depleted weapon arsenal, the war boosted its support in Lebanon and elsewhere in the Middle East and made it a symbol of opposition to

---

[74] Myre, G. and Erlanger, S., 'Clashes spread to Lebanon as Hezbollah raids Israel', *New York Times*, 13 July 2006. The fierce Israeli retaliation is thought to have surprised the Hezbollah leadership, which had had previous successes in exchanging abducted Israelis for imprisoned members and allies. Susser, A., 'The war in Lebanon and the new Middle East', *RUSI Journal*, vol. 15, no. 4 (Aug. 2006), p. 36.

[75] Jones (note 54); and Salhani and Saoud (note 54). See also chapter 10 in this volume.

[76] UN Security Council Resolution 1701, 11 Aug. 2006. For this and other UN Security Council resolutions see URL <http://www.un.org/documents/scres.htm>. On the reinforced UN Interim Force in Lebanon, tasked with monitoring the ceasefire, see chapter 3 in this volume.

[77] See Lebanese Presidency of the Council of Ministers, Higher Relief Council, 'Lebanon under siege', URL <http://www.lebanonundersiege.gov.lb/english/F/Main/index.asp?>; Israeli Ministry of Foreign Affairs, 'Israel–Hizbullah conflict: victims of rocket attacks and IDF casualties', 12 July 2006, URL <http://www.mfa.gov.il/MFA/Terrorism-+Obstacle+to+Peace/Terrorism+from+Lebanon-+Hizbullah/Israel-Hizbullah+conflict-+Victims+of+rocket+attacks+and+IDF+casualties+July-Aug+2006. htm>; and 'Lebanon falters over truce detail', BBC News, 14 Aug. 2006, URL <http://news.bbc.co.uk/2/4789083. stm>. Figures are difficult to verify and highly contested; see appendix 2A.

[78] 'Israel's military chief resigns', BBC News, 17 Jan. 2007, URL <http://news.bbc.co.uk/2/6269353. stm>; van Creveld, M., 'Israel's Lebanese war', *RUSI Journal*, vol. 151, no. 5 (Oct. 2006), pp. 40–43; and Myre, G., 'Israel forms committee to investigate Lebanon war', *New York Times*, 18 Sep. 2006.

[79] Blanford, N., 'Deconstructing Hizbullah's surprise military prowess', *Jane's Intelligence Review*, vol. 18, no. 11 (Nov. 2006).

Israel.[80] Strengthened by its self-proclaimed military prowess and 'divine victory', Hezbollah publicly offered Hamas much-needed financial support.[81] After the ceasefire Hezbollah quickly took the lead in the reconstruction work. With monetary support from the wealthy Lebanese diaspora as well as external states (including Iran), Hezbollah promised to rebuild within a year the 15 000 homes that were destroyed and offered $12 000 to each family in need of replacement housing.[82]

Domestic politics in Lebanon were tainted by the polarizing effects of Hezbollah's unilateral decision to launch an attack on Israel. Despite the terms of UN Security Council Resolution 1701, Hezbollah refused to be disarmed, and the government expressed its reluctance to forcibly disarm the group.[83] In the second half of the year, Hezbollah called for a new government of unity because it was dissatisfied with the parties' political representation in the Western-backed coalition government led by Prime Minister Fouad Siniora. Hezbollah also aimed to obtain a veto position in the government, according to some observers in order to obstruct the impending trials of Syrian officials who were implicated in the assassinations of several leading Lebanese political figures, including former Prime Minister Rafiq al-Hariri.[84] In this and other ways Syria was seen as continuing to influence developments in Lebanon for its own ends, notwithstanding its military withdrawal following the non-violent Cedar Revolution of 2005.[85] With its demands for greater power in the cabinet unmet, Hezbollah and its allies pulled their ministers out of the government in November 2006.[86] Each side in the government called on its supporters to take part in demonstrations to show their support.

In the Palestinian territories, sustained Israeli attacks and intermittent factional clashes continued during the latter half of the year. Particularly severe clashes took place in the Gaza Strip between Hamas's auxiliary forces, then formally part of the police force, and members of the Fatah-dominated security forces demonstrating over unpaid wages. This raised fears of the outbreak

[80] Slackman, M., 'Lebanon throng hails Hezbollah chief, who calls militia stronger', *New York Times*, 23 Sep. 2006.

[81] Smith, C. S., 'Lebanon's future: bending toward Hezbollah or leaning to the West', *New York Times*, 22 Sep. 2006.

[82] Kifner, J., 'Hezbollah leads work to rebuild, gaining stature', *New York Times*, 16 Aug. 2006; and Integrated Regional Information Network, 'Lebanon: 3,000 displaced remain as rebuilding starts', 24 Aug. 2006.

[83] England, A., 'Hizbollah stages show of strength with huge rally', *Financial Times*, 23/24 Sep. 2006, p. 5.

[84] International Crisis Group, 'Lebanon at a tripwire', Middle East Briefing no. 20 (21 Dec. 2006). A UN investigation found 'Syrian involvement in this terrorist act'. See the Report of the International Independent Investigation Commission pursuant to Security Council Resolution 1595 (2005) in United Nations, Letter dated 20 October 2005 from the Secretary-General addressed to the President of the Security Council, UN document S/2005/662, 20 Oct. 2005, URL <http://www.un.org/news/dh/docs/mehlisreport/>. On 21 Nov. the anti-Syrian Lebanese Minister of Industry Pierre Gemayel was assassinated—the 16th violent attack on opponents of Syria in 2 years. 'Who's the assassin?', *The Economist*, 25 Nov. 2006, pp. 46–47.

[85] The withdrawal of Syrian troops and intelligence personnel was completed on 26 Apr. 2005, following massive public protests after the assassination of Hariri and in accordance with UN Security Council Resolution 1559, 2 Sep. 2004. IISS (note 60), p. 230.

[86] Slackman, M., 'Lebanon talks collapse as Shiites vacate cabinet', *New York Times*, 12 Nov. 2006.

of civil war.[87] Israeli raids in the Gaza Strip included a one-week operation in Beit Hanun, which killed more than 50 Palestinians, and massive shelling, which killed 18 civilians, purportedly by mistake.[88] In response, Hamas threatened to resume its suicide attacks in Israel, which could mark a reversal of its transformation from a militant group to a political party.[89]

The attempts by Hamas to overcome the political stalemate and end the international financial boycott of the group by creating a national unity government foundered as it affirmed that it would never recognize Israel.[90] Diplomatic efforts were further complicated by different lines taken by the Hamas leadership in the Palestinian Authority and the more hard-line exiled faction in Syria. Broader efforts to open a dialogue were obstructed by the reluctance of the USA and other states to give legitimacy to non-state actors that they consider to be involved in terrorist activities.[91]

In early 2007 prospects for prompt resolution of the separate but interlinked crises in the Middle East looked dim. In Lebanon, Hezbollah called for strikes, which turned violent and further strained the elected government.[92] Meanwhile, international donors gathered at a conference in Paris, where they confirmed their support for the Siniora Government with pledges of monetary assistance. In turn, Sheikh Hassan Nasrallah, the leader of Hezbollah, called for a Lebanese state free from foreign influences, promoting the belief that Israel acted in the war as a proxy of the USA to further the latter's interests in the region.[93]

It appears unlikely that progress can be achieved in the conflict in Lebanon unless the destabilizing influences of regional actors are replaced by impartial and constructive international involvement.[94] Although the ceasefire set out in UN Security Council Resolution 1701 remains largely intact, the underlying tensions in Lebanon have still not been addressed.[95] Israel's inability to prevent the kidnapping of its soldiers, defeat Hezbollah through force and stop rocket attacks on Israel from the Gaza Strip appeared to have eroded its power

---

[87] Erlanger, S., 'Fatal clashes in Gaza over unpaid salaries', *New York Times*, 2 Oct. 2006.

[88] Morris, H., 'Israelis vow to press on with Gaza offensive', *Financial Times*, 6 Nov. 2006, p. 3; and Morris, H., 'Israel's attacks on Gaza are bringing factions together, say Palestinians', *Financial Times*, 11–12 Nov. 2006, p. 6.

[89] Fisher, I., 'Palestinians mourn civilians killed by Israel', *New York Times*, 10 Nov. 2006; and Devi, S. and Morris, H., 'Talks resume on government as Gaza buries its dead', *Financial Times*, 10 Nov. 2006, p. 6.

[90] Myre, G., '"We will not recognise Israel", Palestinian premier affirms', *New York Times*, 7 Oct. 2006; and 'Hamas: no recognition of Israel', BBC News, 14 Nov. 2006, URL <http://news.bbc.co.uk/2/6146968.stm>.

[91] Neumann, P. R., 'Negotiating with terrorists', *Foreign Affairs*, vol. 86, no. 1 (Jan./Feb. 2007), pp. 128–38.

[92] Bakri, N. and Fattah, H. M., 'Clash pits Hezbollah against rule in Lebanon', *New York Times*, 24 Jan. 2007.

[93] Siegman, H., 'How Bush's backing imperils Israel', *Financial Times*, 15 Sep. 2006, p. 11; and 'Hezbollah leader urges defiance', BBC News, 7 Dec. 2006, URL <http://news.bbc.co.uk/2/6219732.stm>.

[94] Berkovich, D., 'Political deterioration in Lebanon: domestic crisis, regional problem', *Insight*, no. 1 (3 Dec. 2006).

[95] International Crisis Group, 'Israel/Hizbollah/Lebanon: avoiding renewed conflict', Middle East Report no. 59 (1 Nov. 2006).

of deterrence[96] and raised questions about its longer-term strategy to ensure national security in the region.

In 2006 the negative transnational influences appear to have greatly outweighed any positive impacts. Hamas and Hezbollah both benefited, at the very least, from political and material support from Iran and Syria. Recognition was given to the interlinked nature of the conflicts in the Middle East by British Prime Minister Tony Blair in his call for a 'Whole Middle East Strategy' to resolve the problems of the region.[97] Such a strategy, however, requires an exploration of new ways to engage with armed non-state actors with broad-based popular support that have assumed state functions.

Somalia

In 2006 violent battles and humanitarian crises in Somalia claimed scores of civilian casualties and led to widespread population displacement. The inability of the Transitional Federal Government to extend its control throughout the country enabled the Union of Islamic Courts to broaden its influence, at first challenged only by a US-supported constellation of Mogadishu warlords. As inter-communal strife had brought about further societal disintegration, there was greater transnational involvement in Somalia, which served as a proxy battleground for regional interests and as a focal point in the USA's 'global war on terrorism'.[98]

Since the fall of Muhammad Siyad Barre's dictatorial regime in 1991, Somalia has experienced 16 years of warlordism and internal violence. Devoid of any state authority to impose internal order and to counter destructive external influences, Somalia provided a base where transnational criminal and terrorist interests could intersect. Crime is rife in Somalia: fighting has commonly been clan-based and motivated more by opportunities for economic exploitation, including systems of 'taxation' at roadside checkpoints and through rampant weapons trading, than by political goals.[99] Somali ports and waters have been used for smuggling, illegal fishing and waste disposal, and by notorious pirate networks.[100] The Somali diaspora around the world con-

---

[96] Susser, A., 'The war in Lebanon and the new Middle East', *RUSI Journal*, vol. 15, no. 4 (Aug. 2006), p. 36.

[97] 'Prime Minister Tony Blair's speech on a "Whole Middle East Strategy"', London, 13 Nov. 2006, *The Times*, URL <http://www.timesonline.co.uk/tol/news/world/middle_east/article636380.ece>.

[98] On the Somali conflict see also Wiharta, S. and Anthony, I., 'Major armed conflicts', *SIPRI Yearbook 2003: Armaments, Disarmament and International Security* (Oxford University Press: Oxford, 2003), pp. 87–108.

[99] Vinci, A., 'An analysis and comparison of armed groups in Somalia', *African Security*, vol. 15, no. 1 (2006), pp. 84, 88.

[100] Integrated Regional Information Network for the Horn of Africa, 'Somalia: opening Mogadishu port', 31 Oct. 2006. The UN Monitoring Group detailed the sophisticated operations of contemporary transnationally linked pirate networks off the coast of Somalia, representing a risk beyond the most immediate region. United Nations, Letter dated 4 May 2006 from the Chairman of the Security Council Committee established pursuant to Resolution 751 (1992) concerning Somalia, addressed to the President of the Security Council, transmitting the report of the Monitoring Group on Somalia, UN document S/2006/229, 4 May 2006, pp. 25–30, URL <http://www.un.org/Docs/sc/committees/Somalia/Somalia

tinues to affect the conflict in various ways, and large Somali refugee populations outside the country may also be a destabilizing factor.

Of further concern to countries outside the region—not least the USA—were reports that terrorist training camps and members of al-Qaeda cells were in Somalia, described by al-Qaeda deputy Ayman al-Zawahiri as 'the southern garrison of Islam'.[101] Concern grew in 2006 that conditions were optimal in the failed state of Somalia for international terrorists to use it as a safe haven and breeding ground for the spread of radical Islam in Africa.[102]

In 2006 Somalia descended into further turmoil as three internally fragmented and externally sponsored armed groups vied for power. In addition, the country suffered the worst drought it had had for 10 years, compounding a dire humanitarian situation and aggravating clan fighting over grazing land.[103] In the early part of the year there was a rise in the influence and popularity of the UIC, which at first operated mainly in Mogadishu,[104] largely because of their efforts to re-establish law and order after years of anarchy.[105] As the armed wing of the Council of Somali Islamic Courts (CSIC), the UIC is an umbrella organization for 11 aligned but autonomous Sharia courts, formed in 1996 with the support of local businessmen who opposed the mismanagement of past regimes. CSIC Chairman Sheikh Hassan Dahir Aweys is listed by the USA as a terrorist suspect because of his previous affiliation with the al-Ittihad al-Islami, believed to have assisted al-Qaeda in the 1998 bombings of the US embassies in Kenya and Tanzania.[106]

SelEng.htm>; and United Nations, 'Somalia tells UN debate Islamic Courts' actions are threatening peace negotiations', UN News press release, 26 Sep. 2006.

[101] Recording of Ayman al-Zawahiri, disseminated by Al Jazeera on 20 Dec. 2006; a partial transcript is available at URL <http://ict.org.il/apage/printv/8215.php>. The US Assistant Secretary of State for African Affairs, Jendayi Frazer, conceded that the 'core interest' of the USA in Somalia is terrorism. 'Islamist takeover', *Africa Confidential*, vol. 47, no. 13 (23 June 2006), p. 6; Grono, N., 'Somalia: nation on the cusp of chaos or resurrection', *The Australian*, 8 Jan. 2007; and Reynolds, P., 'Twin US aims in Somalia', BBC News, 9 Jan. 2007, URL <http://news.bbc.co.uk/2/ 6244097.stm>.

[102] Frazer, J. E., Assistant Secretary for African Affairs, 'Somalia: US government policy and challenges', Remarks before the Senate Committee on Foreign Relations Subcommittee on African Affairs, 11 July, 2006; and Corey, C. W., 'State's Frazer cites danger of Somalia attracting terrorists', 23 June 2006, URL <http://usinfo.state.gov/xarchives/display.html?p=washfile-english&y=2006&m=June&x= 20060623120544WCyeroC0.1820185>. Other analysts questioned the credibility of such arguments, warranting a level of international involvement. Ken Menkhaus argues that the very degree of lawlessness in Somalia makes it inhospitable for terrorists who prefer to operate from 'quasi-states' that are governed, albeit poorly. Menkhaus, K., International Institute for Strategic Studies, *Somalia: State Collapse and the Threat of Terrorism*, Adelphi Paper no. 364 (Taylor & Francis: London, Mar. 2004), especially pp. 71–84.

[103] United Nations Office for the Coordination of Humanitarian Affairs (OCHA), 'Somalia: security vacuum compounding effects of drought', URL <http://www.un.org/events/tenstories_2006/story.asp?storyID=2500>; and International Relations and Security Network (ISN), 'Somalia suffering worst drought in decade', *ISN Security Watch*, 20 Jan. 2006, URL <http://www.isn.ethz.ch/news/sw/details.cfm?ID=14459>.

[104] The UIC is also referred to as the Islamic Courts Union (ICU). On 24 June 2006 the UIC changed its name to the Somali Supreme Islamic Courts Council, but in the remainder of this chapter the group is referred to as the UIC.

[105] 'Islamic courts take Somali politics in a new direction', *Business Monitor International*, 3 July 2006; and Gettleman, J., 'Islamists calm Somali capital with restraint', *New York Times*, 24 Sep. 2006.

[106] US Department of State, Office of the Coordinator for Counterterrorism, 'Executive Order 13224', Fact sheet, 23 Sep. 2001, URL <http://state.gov/s/ct/rls/fs/ 2002/16181.htm>; 'Islamic courts

In February 2006 Mogadishu's main warlords formed the Alliance for the Restoration of Peace and Counter-Terrorism (ARPCT) to counteract the rise of the UIC, with the stated intention of capturing alleged foreign al-Qaeda operatives operating under the protection of the UIC.[107] The US State Department declared its support for the objectives of the ARPCT, while denying reports that it was breaking the UN arms embargo against Somalia.[108]

Scattered clashes between the UIC and the ARPTC over control of Mogadishu peaked in the late spring of 2006, claiming some 330 lives before the Islamists gained control of the city on 5 June.[109] The ARPTC then virtually disintegrated, with some of its members opting to join the UIC, revealing the mutability of Somalia's conflict allegiances.[110] With minimal force the UIC extended its authority throughout much of southern and central Somalia and seized the strategic port of Kismayo in September, which the UIC considered to be a potential base from which foreign troops crossing the border from Kenya could be repulsed.[111]

Meanwhile, the internationally recognized Transitional Federal Government, led by interim president and former warlord Abdullahi Yusuf Ahmed, remained dysfunctional, domestically unpopular and unable to extend its influence beyond its temporary seat in Baydhabo, in western Somalia.[112] A controversy over whether to engage in peace talks with the UIC sparked mass

take Somali politics in a new direction' (note 105); and 'Roadblock', *Africa Confidential*, vol. 46, no. 18 (9 Sep. 2005), pp. 6–7. The USA further froze the assets of Al-Barakaat, the largest Somali company for telecommunications and money transfers, limiting remittances from worldwide supporters and the Somali diaspora, which are thought to have contributed greatly to the UIC's military build-up. United Nations, Letter dated 21 November 2006 from the Chairman of the Security Council Committee established pursuant to Resolution 751 (1992) addressed to the President of the Security Council, transmitting the final report of the Monitoring Group, UN document S/2006/913, 22 Nov. 2006, pp. 34–38, URL <http://www.un.org/Docs/sc/committees/Somalia/Somalia SelEng.htm>.

[107] A video recording in mid-2006 purports to show Somali Islamist fighters training and preparing for battle in Mogadishu alongside men of non-Somali descent. Tomlinson, C., 'Video shows Arabs fighting in Somalia', Associated Press, 5 July 2006, URL <http://www.somalilandtimes.net/sl/2005/233/3. shtml>.

[108] UN Security Council Resolution 733, 23 Jan. 1992; UN Security Council Resolution 1425, 22 Jan. 2002; and 'US denies funding Somalia warlords', *Daily Nation*, 11 May 2006, URL <http://www.xignite.com/xWorldNews.aspx?articleid=AFP20060511950011>. The USA was reported to be supporting the ARPCT financially as an extension of its 'global war on terrorism', and US Government officials have reportedly privately admitted this to be true. 'Terror in Mogadishu', *Africa Confidential*, vol. 47, no. 11 (26 May 2006), p. 3. The UIC continued to deny that it had links with al-Qaeda.

[109] 'Islamists claim Mogadishu victory', BBC News, 5 June 2006, URL <http://news.bbc.co.uk/2/5047766.stm>. The International Committee of the Red Cross (ICRC) estimated that the UIC–ARPCT conflict killed more than 300 people and injured 1500 in the first 5 months of 2006. ICRC, 'Somalia: ICRC alarmed by number of civilian casualties', Press release 06/52, 26 May 2006, URL <http://www.icrc.org/eng/news>.

[110] 'Embattled Somali warlord pulls out of vanquished anti-terror alliance', HornAfrik website, 15 June 2006, Translation from Somali, World News Connection, National Technical Information Service (NTIS), US Department of Commerce; and 'Warlord joins Somalia's Islamists', BBC News, 3 July 2006, URL <http://news.bbc.co.uk/2/5140182.stm>.

[111] Gettleman, J., 'Demonstrations become clashes after Islamists take Somali city', *New York Times*, 26 Sep. 2006; and 'Shooting at captured Somali port', BBC News, 25 Sep. 2006, <http://news.bbc.co.uk/2/5377626.stm>.

[112] The TFG was formed in 2004 as part of the Kenya-based Somali peace process in an attempt to forge unity between rival clan-based warlords. The TFG moved to Somalia in early 2006.

resignations by government ministers in July and the dissolution of the cabinet, dealing an additional blow to the already weakened TFG.[113]

In mid-2006 there were reports of Ethiopian troops crossing clandestinely into Somalia, threatening to defeat the Islamists if the latter approached Baydhabo, but Ethiopia admitted only to sending military advisers in support of the TFG.[114] As the UIC was not deterred from extending its de facto control over much of the country, the prospect of a military confrontation between the Islamists and the marginalized government loomed large, risking drawing in neighbouring states and the otherwise peaceful, semi-autonomous regions of Somaliland and Puntland in the north of Somalia. A September suicide attack on the Somali president's car convoy in Baydhabo, for which the UIC was blamed, sparked new violent tactics in Somalia's conflict; this was attributed by some—including the president himself—to al-Qaeda involvement.[115]

The support that the UIC gained for restoring order and ousting the warlords appeared to be gradually weakened by its strict enforcement of sharia law.[116] An attempt by the UIC to outlaw the widely used stimulant khat on the basis that it encouraged immorality prompted protests, leading to a violent response by Islamist fighters.[117]

Multiple rounds of talks in Khartoum, sponsored by the Arab League,[118] were held between the UIC and the TFG in the second half of 2006, but they failed to make any substantial progress. The UIC's refusal to negotiate while Ethiopian troops remained on Somali soil was countered by the TFG's rejection of what it deemed illegitimate territorial expansionism by the UIC.[119] Instead, both parties sought to strengthen their positions and build up military capacity with a strong influx of arms, in contravention of the 1992 UN arms embargo.[120] Reflecting the growing involvement of external actors, the United Nations Monitoring Group's November 2006 report implicated Ethiopia, Uganda and Yemen in violations of the arms embargo in support of the TFG, while the UIC reportedly received arms and training from Djibouti, Eritrea,

---

[113] 'Somalia's leaders sack government', BBC News, 7 Aug. 2006, URL <http://news.bbc.co.uk/2/5252602.stm>.

[114] 'Ethiopian troops on Somali soil', BBC News, 20 July 2006, URL <http://news.bbc.co.uk/2/5198338.stm>.

[115] 'Heading for the beach', *The Economist*, 30 Sep. 2006, p. 54; Integrated Regional Information Network, 'Somalia: probe continues as death toll rises in assassination bid', 19–20 Sep. 2006; Gettleman, J., 'Somali president survives suicide bomb; 8 others are killed', *New York Times*, 19 Sep. 2006; and 'Tight security after Somali blast', BBC News, 19 Sep. 2006, URL <http://news.bbc.co.uk/2/5360114.stm>.

[116] 'Unveiling Somalia's Islamists', BBC News, 6 Oct. 2006, URL <http://news.bbc.co.uk/2/5381826.stm>.

[117] 'Somali khat protester shot dead', BBC News, 16 Nov. 2006, URL <http://news.bbc.co.uk/2/6155796.stm>. A town under Islamic control in southern Somalia, Bulo Burto, made public an edict by which any residents discovered neglecting to pray 5 times a day would be beheaded. Associated Press, *Somaliland Times*, 6 Dec. 2006, URL <http://www.somalilandtimes.net/sl/2006/255/09.shtml>.

[118] On the Arab League and for a list of its members see the glossary in this volume.

[119] Integrated Regional Information Network, 'Hardline positions delay talks between rival groups', 1 Nov. 2006; and United Nations (note 100).

[120] See chapter 10 in this volume.

Iran, Libya, Saudi Arabia, Syria and the Gulf states.[121] Thousands of Eritrean and Ethiopian troops were reported to be in Somalia, ready to back the TFG and the UIC, respectively, creating the risk of regional war.[122] Ethiopia's involvement was seen as motivated partly by the possibility of a spillover of Islamist activity and attacks from Somalia, threatening to radicalize its 40 per cent Muslim population, and partly by the need to contain irredentist groups of Somali descent among the population of Ethiopia's south-eastern Ogaden region, advocating a 'Greater Somalia'.[123] The UIC publicly announced its pan-Somali aspirations and underlined them by carrying out cross-border military cooperation with rebel groups.[124] Meanwhile, Eritrea, caught in a stand-off with Ethiopia since their 1998–2000 border war, allegedly supplied the UIC with materials and troops, triggering concerns that the Eritrean–Ethiopian conflict might restart with Somalia as a proxy stage.[125]

In December 2006 the UN, in Security Council Resolution 1725, partially lifted its arms embargo to authorize the deployment of an 8000-strong peacekeeping mission led by the Intergovernmental Authority on Development (IGAD)—the IGAD Peace Support Mission to Somalia (IGASOM)—and to enable the strengthening of TFG security forces.[126] The UIC opposed the prospect of a military intervention and announced a jihad against all foreign 'infidels'. However, the rapidly deteriorating security situation and IGAD's inability to mount the mission postponed the deployment of IGASOM. The talks collapsed and, following clashes between the UIC and the TFG, backed by Ethiopian forces near Baydhabo,[127] the Islamist fighters were forced to retreat, with Sheikh Aweys calling on Muslims worldwide to join the UIC's jihad against Ethiopia.[128] Mogadishu fell without violent confrontation

[121] United Nations (note 106). Many of the implicated parties immediately rejected the report's findings. 'Islamists dismiss reports of foreign arms', *International Herald Tribune*, 16 Nov. 2006, p. 8; and 'Powers "stoking Somalia conflict"', BBC News, 15 Nov. 2006, URL <http://news.bbc.co.uk/2/6149276.stm>.

[122] United Nations (note 106); and Tomlinson, C., 'UN: regional war possible in Somalia', *Washington Post*, 27 Oct. 2006.

[123] Rosenthal, B., Agence France-Presse, ' Ethiopia shows its hand in Somalia crisis', ReliefWeb, 23 Mar. 2001, URL <http://www.reliefweb.int/rw/rwb.nsf/AllDocsByUNID/d545bf44072de9f7c1256a18004c3c7a>; Gettleman, J., 'US official offers a bleak assessment of Somalia', *New York Times*, 11 Nov. 2006; International Crisis Group, 'Somalia: the tough part is ahead', Crisis Group Africa Briefing no. 45 (26 Jan. 2007), especially pp. 4–6; and 'Islamic courts take Somali politics in a new direction' (note 105).

[124] Associated Press, 'Regions in Ethiopia, Kenya should be part of Somalia—Islamist', *Sudan Tribune*, 18 Nov. 2006, URL <http://www.sudantribune.com/spip.php?article18770>; and 'A threat to the Horn and beyond', *Africa Confidential*, vol. 47, no. 18 (8 Sep. 2006), pp. 1–2. On cross-border rebel groups and their links with the UIC see International Crisis Group (note 123), pp. 5–6.

[125] 'Threat of regional conflict over Somalia', BBC News, 16 Nov. 2006, URL <http://news.bbc.co.uk/2/6154690.stm>. During the war Ethiopia and Eritrea waged a small proxy war in southern Somalia, leaving substantial stocks of armaments behind. International Crisis Group (note 123), p. 6.

[126] UN Security Council Resolution 1725, 6 Dec. 2006. The International Crisis Group criticized the move, *inter alia*, as more likely to provoke a full-on military confrontation. Bryden, M., 'Storm clouds over Somalia as rivals prepare for battle', *The Nation*, 8 Dec. 2006, URL <http://www.crisisgroup.org/home/index.cfm?id=4569>. For the members of IGAD see the glossary in this volume.

[127] Agence France-Presse, 'Islamists and Somali troops exchange fire', *New York Times*, 9 Dec. 2006.

[128] Estimates of the number of foreign Islamist fighters in Somalia ranged from several hundred to thousands, including young radicals of the Somali diaspora. International Crisis Group (note 123), p. 4;

at the end of the year, followed by the fall of Kismayo. The remaining Islamists were driven to seek refuge in the dense forests along Somalia's porous border with Kenya. There they mixed with the tens of thousands of Somali refugees who had fled from the violent effects of the year's Islamist advance.[129]

The fighting in December 2006 caused a fresh influx of refugees to Kenya, adding pressure on camps that already housed 130 000 Somali refugees from the 1991 crisis. Massive flooding in Kenya's Dadaab region further compounded the crisis. To curb infiltrations by combatants, the border was closed and the US Navy began to patrol the adjacent waters.[130] By the end of 2006 the TFG, buttressed by Ethiopian troops, had established formal control of all of Somalia. The shattered Islamists came under additional pressure when the US Special Forces Command launched air strikes in the southern border regions, acting on 'credible intelligence' that foreign al-Qaeda operatives were hiding in the area.[131] Retreating Islamist fighters vowed to launch guerrilla-style attacks, mirroring the violent protracted conflicts in Afghanistan and Iraq.[132] Somali officials estimated that 3500 Islamists remained in the area of Mogadishu and were likely to seek to destabilize the city.[133] However, with its main leadership having fled to Kenya and Yemen, and its remaining troops in Somalia forced underground, it is uncertain how serious a threat the UIC presents from either within or outside Somali territory.

By early 2007 instability had returned to Mogadishu despite the stabilizing presence of Ethiopian and TFG troops, who were targeted by insurgents in recurrent hit-and-run attacks. The TFG's continuing intrinsic weaknesses have led to concern that there may be a re-emergence of the same violent clan-based warlordism and criminality that the UIC managed to suppress.[134] The long-standing lack of an effective central government in Somalia is likely to pose considerable challenges to state building. A political process that excludes powerful actors in the country, such as remaining Islamist elements,

---

and 'Somalia Islamists call for help', BBC News, 23 Dec. 2006, URL <http://news.bbc.co.uk/2/6206081.stm>.

[129] Integrated Regional Information Network, 'Kenya–Somalia: refugee camps expanded as more Somalis arrive', 10 Oct. 2006.

[130] Gettleman, J., 'Kenya closes border but denies turning back refugees', New York Times, 4 Jan. 2007; and 'US Navy patrols Somalia's coast', BBC News, 4 Jan. 2007, URL <http://news.bbc.co.uk/2/6229697.stm>.

[131] Garamone, J., 'Aircraft attack al Qaeda haven, Ike moves off Somalia', American Forces Press Service, 9 Jan. 2007; and 'US "targets al-Qaeda" in Somalia', BBC News, 9 Jan. 2007, URL <http://news.bbc.co.uk/2/6245943.stm>. The strikes appear to have missed their main targets (the 3 foreign al-Qaeda operatives thought to have been involved in terrorist attacks against US interests) but were reported to have killed others with close ties to the terrorist group. The reports on civilian casualties are highly contradictory but commonly estimate that about 20 were killed. Associated Press, 'Raid killed Somali allies of al-Qaeda, US says', New York Times, 12 Jan. 2007.

[132] 'Somalia's sudden shift in power', BBC News, 1 Jan. 2007, URL <http://news.bbc.co.uk/2/6222681.stm>.

[133] Associated Press, 'Somali official says 3,500 Islamists remain near Mogadishu', New York Times, 4 Jan. 2007.

[134] Hassan, M. O., 'Fears stalk Somalia's capital once again', BBC News, 11 Jan. 2007, URL <http://news.bbc.co.uk/2/6252359.stm>.

signals the prospect of further political fragmentation.[135] A protracted Ethiopian presence in Somalia is likely to add to the tensions but, with a peace mission not yet deployed and given the difficulties involved in reaching agreement on troops and funding, the TFG is likely to remain reliant on Ethiopian forces for a considerable time.

IV. Conclusions

Developments in armed conflicts in 2006 continued to reflect the broad trends that have emerged in recent years, one of the most important of which is the fact that conflicts are no longer fought directly between states. Rather, there has been a rise in the number of conflicts involving a mix of state-based and non-state actors, usually operating in extensive transnational conflict networks. Notable in this respect were the conflicts between state-based political and military groups, principally the US-led coalition of forces, and violent non-state actors claiming to be motivated by militant Islamist ideas. An intensification of violence in Afghanistan, the Middle East and the Horn of Africa pointed to the surge of militant Islamist groups following the launch of the 'global war on terrorism' after the September 2001 attacks on the USA. However, the complex nature of these conflicts suggests that caution should be exercised in ascribing narrow causes—for example international terrorism, transnationalist threats or geopolitical challenges—to many of the contemporary conflicts. As noted in appendix 2C, with a lack of consensus about the nature of collective violence in the world today, one set of perceptions of insecurity, formed by a set of strong states and their populations in response to a 'new' transnational vision of threats such as terrorism, is in many cases playing a disproportionate role in shaping security policy.

While many of the conflicts in 2006 involved transnational elements, with impacts and connections far beyond the principal sites of conflict, local populations in the developing world continued to suffer disproportionately as a result of conflict in comparison to people in the developed world. This, together with recognition of the complexity of contemporary conflicts and the key role of both states and non-state actors in transnational conflict networks, suggests that further research is required to clarify the character, impact and significance of transnationalism and conflict. A growing awareness of the transnational character of security issues in 2006, the urgent need to counter the negative aspects of this phenomenon, and the potential for making positive use of transnational actors and influences to promote conflict resolution and peace-building all suggest that, in the future, finding ways to address transnational aspects of conflict effectively will be high on the international policy agenda.

---

[135] 'Parliament sacks Somali speaker', BBC News, 17 Jan. 2007, URL <http://news.bbc.co.uk/2/6270661.stm>.

Appendix 2A. Patterns of major armed conflicts, 1997–2006

LOTTA HARBOM and PETER WALLENSTEEN*

I. Global patterns

In 2006, 17 major armed conflicts were active in 16 locations throughout the world.[1] Over the past 10 years the number of conflicts has fluctuated, starting at 19 in 1997 and then climbing to 26 in the peak year 1998. The figure declined steadily between 1999 and 2005, and then remained constant in 2006. It is notable that the same conflicts that were active in 2005 remained active in 2006.

For the third year running, no interstate conflict was recorded. In fact, during the entire period 1997–2006 only three conflicts were fought between states: Eritrea–Ethiopia (1998–2000); India–Pakistan (1997–2003); and Iraq versus the USA and its allies (2003). The remaining 31 major armed conflicts recorded for this period were fought within states and concerned either governmental power (21) or territory (10). Conflicts over government outnumbered those over territory in all 10 years.

In 2006, three intra-state conflicts were categorized as internationalized—that is, they included troops from a state that was external to the basic conflict, aiding one of the parties: the conflict between the Afghan Government and the Taliban; the conflict between the Iraqi Government and the numerous insurgency groups operating there; and the conflict between the US Government and al-Qaeda.[2] It is noteworthy that all these conflicts are linked to the US-led 'global war on terrorism'. In all three cases the external state contributed troops to the government side of the conflict.[3]

---

[1] The Uppsala Conflict Data Program (UCDP) defines a major armed conflict as a contested incompatibility concerning government and/or territory over which the use of armed force between the military forces of 2 parties—of which at least 1 is the government of a state—has resulted in at least 1000 battle-related deaths in a single calendar year. For a definition of the separate elements see appendix 2B in this volume. Traditionally, the UCDP has provided data on trends from 1990 in editions of the SIPRI Yearbook. This year, the period for which conflicts are reported has been changed and will from now on focus only on the most recent 10-year period (i.e. 1997–2006 this year, and so on). However, data on major armed conflicts since 1990 constitute the basis for the information presented here. Thus, conflict dyads that were recorded as active at some time in the period 1990–96 are listed in table 2A.3 if fighting between the same parties resulted in at least 1 battle-related death in 2006. Data on the longer time series (since 1990) are available at URL <http://www.pcr.uu.se/research/UCDP/our_ data1.htm>.

[2] If it had exceeded the threshold of 1000 battle-related deaths, the conflict between the Government of Somalia and the Supreme Islamic Council of Somalia (SICS) would have been included as an internationalized conflict, with Ethiopia contributing troops to the government side. However, reliable data set the death toll for 2006 below 600. For more on this conflict see URL <http://www.pcr.uu.se/database/>.

[3] For the states contributing troops in these conflicts see table 2A.3. On the conflict between the USA and al-Qaeda and the complex issues affecting its coding in the database see Eriksson, M., Sollenberg,

* Uppsala Conflict Data Program (UCDP), Department of Peace and Conflict Research, Uppsala University. For table 2A.3, Johan Brosche was responsible for the conflict locations Russia, Sudan and Turkey; Kristine Eck for India and Nepal; Hanne Fjelde for Afghanistan and the USA; Helena Grusell for Colombia and Peru; Lotta Harbom for the Philippines, Sri Lanka and Uganda; Stina Högbladh and Frida Möller for Burundi; Joakim Kreutz for Iraq and Myanmar; and Ralph Sundberg for Israel.

Table 2A.1. Regional distribution, number and types of major armed conflict, 1997–2006

Region	1997		1998		1999		2000		2001		2002		2003		2004		2005		2006	
	G	T	G	T	G	T	G	T	G	T	G	T	G	T	G	T	G	T	G	T
Africa	4	1	9	2	9	2	7	2	7	1	6	1	5	1	5	1	3	0	3	0
Americas	2	0	2	0	2	0	2	0	3	0	3	0	3	0	3	0	3	0	3	0
Asia	3	5	3	5	2	5	2	5	2	5	2	5	2	5	2	4	3	4	3	4
Europe	0	0	0	1	0	2	0	1	0	1	0	1	0	1	0	1	0	1	0	1
Middle East	2	2	2	2	1	2	2	2	1	2	0	2	1	2	1	2	1	2	1	2
Total	**11**	**8**	**16**	**10**	**14**	**11**	**13**	**10**	**13**	**9**	**11**	**9**	**11**	**9**	**11**	**8**	**10**	**7**	**10**	**7**
Total	**19**		**26**		**25**		**23**		**22**		**20**		**20**		**19**		**17**		**17**	

G = Government and T = Territory, the two types of incompatibility

II. Regional patterns

In 2006 seven major armed conflicts were recorded for Asia, the region with the highest total figure. Three conflicts each were recorded for Africa, the Americas and the Middle East regions. Europe saw the lowest number of conflicts, with only one recorded for 2006. The regional distribution of conflicts and locations for the period 1997–2006 is shown in tables 2A.1 and 2A.2, respectively. Figure 2A.1 presents the regional distribution and total number of conflicts for each year in this period.

In the 10-year period 1997–2006, 14 major armed conflicts were recorded for *Africa*.[4] Apart from 1997, in the first half of the period the highest number of conflicts was fought in this region, with the figure ranging from 11 (1998 and 1999) to 8 (2001). The number of conflicts then decreased from 2002 until 2005, and it remained constant in 2006. Of the 14 conflicts recorded for the period, all but one (Ethiopia–Eritrea) were fought within states. As many as seven of the intra-state conflicts were at some point internationalized in character, which distinguishes Africa from the other regions. A vast majority (12) of the 14 conflicts were fought over governmental power.

The Americas accounted for three major armed conflicts during the period.[5] The annual number of conflicts was steady throughout the period, with two conflicts recorded for 1997–2000 and three for each of the remaining years. All three conflicts in the region concerned governmental power.

M. and Wallensteen, P., 'Patterns of major armed conflict, 1990–2001', *SIPRI Yearbook 2002: Armaments, Disarmament and International Security* (Oxford University Press: Oxford, 2002), pp. 67–68.

[4] The 14 major armed conflicts recorded for Africa for the period 1997–2006 are Algeria, Angola, Burundi, the Democratic Republic of the Congo (formerly Zaire), the Republic of the Congo, Eritrea–Ethiopia, Guinea-Bissau, Liberia, Rwanda, Sierra Leone, Somalia, Sudan, Sudan (southern Sudan) and Uganda. Note that when only the name of a country is given, this indicates a conflict over government. When an intra-state conflict is over territory, the name of the contested territory appears after the country name in parentheses.

[5] The 3 major armed conflicts recorded for the Americas for the period 1997–2006 are Colombia, Peru and the USA (the conflict between the US Government and al-Qaeda).

Table 2A.2. Regional distribution of locations with at least one major armed conflict, 1997–2006

Region	1997	1998	1999	2000	2001	2002	2003	2004	2005	2006
Africa	5	11	11	9	8	7	5	5	3	3
Americas	2	2	2	2	3	3	3	3	3	3
Asia	8	8	7	6	6	6	6	5	6	6
Europe	0	1	2	1	1	1	1	1	1	1
Middle East	4	4	3	4	3	2	3	3	3	3
Total	**19**	**26**	**25**	**22**	**21**	**19**	**18**	**17**	**16**	**16**

Asia was the scene of 10 major armed conflicts in 1997–2006.[6] The annual numbers of conflicts in the region have been fairly constant, ranging between six (2004) and eight (1997 and 1998). In 1997, 2003, 2005 and 2006, the highest number for any region was recorded for Asia.[7] Four of the Asian conflicts recorded for 2006 were active in all 10 years of the period: India (Kashmir), Myanmar (Karen State), Sri Lanka ('Tamil Eelam')[8] and the Philippines. Of the 10 conflicts in Asia, one (India–Pakistan) was fought between states. Four of the intra-state conflicts concerned government, while five were fought over territory.

Only two of the major armed conflicts in the period 1997–2006 were located in *Europe*,[9] making it the region with the lowest total number of conflicts. In addition, on an annual basis Europe experienced the lowest number of conflicts in all years of the period.[10] In fact, at the outset of the period, in 1997, no major armed conflict was recorded for the region. One conflict was recorded for 1998 and yet another in 1999, which was the peak year for the period. Since 2000 the only conflict that has been active in Europe is that between the Russian Government and the separatist actors in Chechnya. Both conflicts in Europe were fought within states and concerned territory.

The Middle East accounted for a total of five major armed conflicts in the period.[11] Four conflicts were recorded for 1997 and the number has remained fairly stable since then, ranging between two (2002) and four (1997, 1998 and 2000). In each of the four years 2003–2006 there were three conflicts, and the same conflicts were active in the three years 2004–2006: the conflict in Iraq, Israel (Palestinian territories) and Turkey (Kurdistan). In fact, the latter two conflicts were active in all years of the period 1997–2006. One of the major armed conflicts in the region was fought

---

[6] The 10 major armed conflicts recorded for Asia for the period 1997–2006 were Afghanistan, Cambodia, India (Kashmir), India–Pakistan, Indonesia (East Timor), Myanmar (Karen State), Nepal, the Philippines, the Philippines (Mindanao) and Sri Lanka ('Tamil Eelam').

[7] In 2004 an equally high number was recorded for Africa.

[8] 'Tamil Eelam' (Tamil homeland) is the name given by Tamil separatists to the area in the north-eastern part of Sri Lanka for which they claim self-determination.

[9] The 2 major armed conflicts recorded for Europe for the period 1997–2006 are Russia (Chechnya) and Yugoslavia (Kosovo).

[10] In 1999 the figure for the Americas was as low as that for Europe.

[11] The 5 major armed conflicts registered for the Middle East for the period 1997–2006 are Iran, Iraq, Israel (Palestinian territories), Turkey (Kurdistan), and USA and its allies–Iraq.

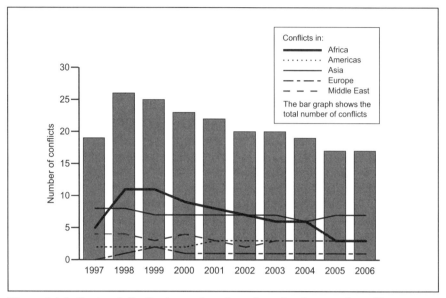

Figure 2A.1. Regional distribution and total number of major armed conflicts, 1997–2006

between states: the conflict between the USA with its allies and Iraq. The remaining four conflicts were intra-state, two fought over government and two over territory.[12]

III. Changes in the table of conflicts for 2006

The conflicts in 2006 that are listed in table 2A.3 are the same as those recorded for 2005. However, many of the conflicts in 2006 exhibited significant changes in intensity—as measured by an increase or decrease in the number of deaths—with a majority of them decreasing markedly.

Changes in intensity of conflict

Six of the 17 major armed conflicts that were active in 2006 showed an increase in intensity, four by more than 50 per cent—the USA, Afghanistan, Sri Lanka ('Tamil Eelam') and Israel (Palestinians)—and two by less than 50 per cent—Myanmar

---

[12] On 12 July 2006 Hezbollah guerrillas carried out an attack across the Lebanese border into Israel, capturing 2 Israeli soldiers and killing several more under cover of intense rocket fire. Israel responded by launching heavy military action against Hezbollah. The ensuing war lasted until 14 Aug., when it ended through UN Security Council Resolution 1701. Assessing the number of deaths in the 2006 conflict is complicated, mainly due to the vast number of strikes carried out by the Israeli Army and the difficulty this creates for single-event-based coding, the lack of reliable sources on confirmed deaths in these strikes and the problem of unreliable sources for the deaths of Hezbollah fighters. In line with the UCDP's conservative policy regarding the reliability of sources and figures, no uncorroborated estimate of death tolls has been accepted. When employing the standard UCDP method (see appendix 2B) the estimated death toll falls below the threshold of 1000 battle-related deaths. This conflict is therefore not included in table 2A.3. On this conflict and those in Afghanistan and Somalia see also chapter 2.

(Karen State) and the Philippines. The conflict between the US Government and al-Qaeda resulted in noticeably more deaths in 2006 than the previous year. As in 2005, the fighting took place mainly in Pakistan, but there were also some incidents in Afghanistan and Saudi Arabia.

In Afghanistan, 2006 was the most deadly year ever in the conflict between the government with its allies and the Taliban. The forces fighting on the government side conducted several large-scale operations during the year, but did not manage to uproot the rebels. The Taliban, for its part, changed tactics in 2006, markedly escalating its use of suicide bombings.

In Sri Lanka, sporadic ceasefire violations and tit-for-tat killings during the first months of the year quickly escalated into all-out warfare between the government and the Liberation Tigers of Tamil Eelam (LTTE) rebels. Aside from several government offensives, the year also saw maritime clashes and suicide bombings, the worst event involving suicide bombers driving a truck into buses full of sailors in the northeastern part of the country, killing over 100 people.[13]

The conflict between the Israeli Government and Palestinian insurgents escalated markedly in 2006. The ceasefire that was in place during much of 2005 was abandoned in January, when Hamas won the Palestinian elections. The year saw continued launching of rockets by Palestinian militants against Israeli cities and villages, with subsequent incursions by the Israeli Defence Forces (IDF) into the Gaza Strip and the West Bank in search of the militants who were responsible for the attacks. This grew into full-scale clashes following the capture and abduction of an IDF solider in a cross-border raid in late June. The IDF launched massive air and artillery strikes, coupled with infantry and tank incursions into the Gaza Strip. The Palestinians, both military and civilian, suffered heavy casualties in this fighting.

The protracted conflict between the Myanmar Government and the separatist Karen National Union (KNU) escalated somewhat during the year. However, the conflict pattern remained the same, with the rebels carrying our sporadic attacks on government troops, who are superior in both firepower and numbers, and the latter reciprocating by attacking Karen villages while purportedly looking for rebels.

In the long-running conflict between the Communist Party of the Philippines (CPP) rebel group and the Philippine Government, 2006 saw a slight increase in intensity. The rebels withdrew from negotiations in 2005 and in early 2006 they stepped up attacks. Escalating the conflict further, President Gloria Macapagal-Arroyo ordered the retraining and redeployment of troops to crush the communist insurgency in key regions around Manila within two years.

As many as 10 of the major armed conflicts exhibited a decrease in intensity compared to 2005, nine by more than 50 per cent: Burundi, Sudan, Uganda, Colombia, Peru, Nepal, Philippines (Mindanao), Russia (Chechnya) and Turkey (Kurdistan).

In Burundi, a peace process has been underway for over five years. At the start of 2006, the Parti pour la libération du people Hutu–Forces nationales de libération (Palipehutu-FNL, or the Party for the Liberation of the Hutu People–National Liberation Forces) was the only rebel group to remain outside the process, but in September a ceasefire agreement was signed. However, the parties remain far apart on critical political issues, and a more comprehensive agreement seems still to be some way off.

While the figures in table 2A.3 show a marked decrease in intensity in the conflict in Sudan, the situation in the Darfur region of the country continued to be grave in

---

[13] Agence France-Presse, 'Suicide bombing kills 103 in Sri Lanka', 16 Oct. 2006.

2006.[14] The Sudanese Government and the largest rebel group, the Sudan Liberation Movement/Army (SLM/A), signed the Darfur Peace Agreement on 5 May, after which the SLM/A leader, Minni Minawi, was granted the fourth highest position in the country's government. The agreement did not change the situation on the ground, which instead was characterized by continued violence against civilians and infighting among the rebels. The turmoil in Darfur also affected neighbouring Chad, which experienced large refugee flows and an armed conflict of its own.[15]

In Uganda, the marked decrease in the number of casualties is due to a landmark ceasefire agreement signed by the Ugandan Government and the Lord's Resistance Army (LRA) rebel group in August. The Government of Southern Sudan was instrumental in bringing the parties together and its vice-president, Riek Machar, acted as mediator. While the peace process has been painfully slow since August, there has been no fighting between the parties, apart from two alleged ceasefire violations. A major stumbling block is the indictments by the International Criminal Court (ICC) against five of the top commanders of the LRA, including Chairman Joseph Kony.

Two of the major armed conflicts registered for the Americas de-escalated in 2006. After the large government offensive in 2005, the situation was calmer in Colombia in 2006. In Peru, the last remnants of the Sendero Luminoso rebel group still operate in the Ayacucho region, south of Lima, but very few attacks are reported each year.

While fighting continued during the four first months of the year in Nepal, substantial political changes helped to reduce the conflict intensity and promote dialogue. In April King Gyanendra agreed to end direct rule and the parliament was reinstated. Subsequently, the Maoist rebels declared a ceasefire. Formal peace negotiations were initiated in May, and in November a peace agreement was signed, under which the rebels are to join a transitional government.

In the Philippines, a protracted conflict has been fought between the Moro Islamic Liberation Front (MILF) separatist group and the government. A ceasefire was signed in 2003, and since then negotiations on a comprehensive agreement have been conducted in Malaysia. While solutions to some key issues have yet to be found, such as the size of the ancestral domain claimed by the MILF, the ceasefire was largely respected in 2006 and the casualty figures are therefore low.

The conflict between the Russian Government and the self-proclaimed separatist Republic of Chechnya continued to de-escalate for the third year running. Despite decreasing intensity, fighting did occur both in Chechnya and in neighbouring regions, notably Dagestan and Ingushetia. The separatists experienced a great setback when one of their key leaders, Shamil Basayev, was killed in July.

---

[14] A note is warranted on the exceptionally low casualty figure for Sudan presented in table 2A.3. The reason is twofold: (*a*) information about the conflict is vague in the sense that reports often just use the term 'rebels', rarely stating which rebel group or faction is referred to; and (*b*) the SLM/A was severely weakened in late 2005, when a large faction left the movement. It was this breakaway faction as well as other groups that are not listed in the table that were involved in most of the fighting against the government in 2006. Furthermore, much of the violence in Darfur involves infighting between rebel and communal groups, as well as one-sided violence targeting civilians, neither of which is the focus of this appendix.

[15] Note that, since the fighting between the Chadian Government and any 1 rebel group did not reach the threshold of 1000 battle-related deaths, this conflict is not defined as a major armed conflict and is therefore not included here.

In Turkey, the protracted conflict between the government and the Partiya Karkeren Kurdistan (PKK, or the Kurdistan Workers' Party) continued, but on a markedly lower scale.

One conflict de-escalated by less than 50 per cent: that between the government of India and Kashmiri insurgents. The reduction brought the conflict below 1000 battle-related deaths for the first time since 1999 and points to the importance of improved relations between India and Pakistan for stability in the region.

Only one of the active conflicts displayed an unchanged, high rate of battle-related deaths: that between the Iraqi Government, supported by the US-led coalition, and Iraqi insurgents. It should be noted that the overall level of violence in Iraq actually increased in 2006 and that the stable death rate reported here reflects a distinct trend: the balance in the character of the violence changed, with a similar rate of battle-related deaths and an increase in clashes between Shia and Sunni groups as well as in incidents of death squads carrying out killings.

In three of the 17 major armed conflicts that were active in 2006, there were more than 1000 battle-related deaths: Iraq (over 5500), Afghanistan (over 3100) and Sri Lanka (over 1950).

Table 2A.3. Conflict locations with at least one major armed conflict in 2006

Location	Incompat- ibility[a]	Yr formed/ yr stated/ yr joined/ yr entered[b]	Warring parties[c]	Total deaths[d] (incl. 2006)	Deaths in 2006	Change from 2005[e]
Africa						
Burundi	Govt	1991/ 1991/1991/ ..	Govt of Burundi vs Palipehutu–FNL	<7 300	>100	– –

Palipehutu-FNL: Parti pour la libération du peuple Hutu–Forces nationales de libération (Party for the Liberation of the Hutu Peopele–National Liberation Forces)

Sudan	Govt	2003/ 2003/2003/ 2003	Govt of Sudan vs SLM/A	<4 500	25–100	– –

SLM/A: Sudan Liberation Movement/Army

Uganda	Govt	1987/ 1987/1988/ 1991	Govt of Uganda vs LRA*	<9 600	>200	– –

LRA: Lord's Resistance Army
* Note that in the early years of its existence the LRA used a number of different names, notably the Ugandan Christian Democratic Army (UCDA).

Americas						
Colombia	Govt	1964/ 1966/1966/ .. 1964/1965/ ..	Govt of Colombia vs FARC vs ELN	>44 800*	>500	– –

FARC: Fuerzas Armadas Revolucionarias de Colombia (Revolutionary Armed Forces of Colombia)
ELN: Ejército de Liberación Nationale (National Liberation Army)
* This figure includes deaths involving other parties than those listed above in the fighting since 1964, although a vast majority of the deaths can be attributed to FARC and, to a lesser extent, the ELN.

Peru	Govt	1980/ 1980/1980/ 1981	Govt of Peru vs Sendero Luminoso	>28 000	<25	– –

Sendero Luminoso: Shining Path

Location	Incompat-ibility[a]	Yr formed/ yr stated/ yr joined/ yr entered[b]	Warring parties[c]	Total deaths[d] (incl. 2006)	Deaths in 2006	Change from 2005[e]
USA*	Govt	2001/ 2001/2001/ 2001	Govt of USA, Multinational coalition** vs al-Qaeda	<2 900	<200	+ +

* Note that the 'Location' column refers to the government of the state that is being challenged by an opposition organization. Thus, location refers to the incompatibility and is not necessarily the geographical location of the fighting. For background and the origins of this intra-state conflict see *SIPRI Yearbook 2002*, pages 67–68.
** In 2006 the USA-led multinational coalition included troops from Australia, Belgium, Canada, Denmark, Estonia, France, Germany, Italy, the Netherlands, Norway, Pakistan, Poland, Portugal, Romania, Saudi Arabia, Spain and the UK.

Asia

Afghanistan	Govt	1990/ 1994/1994/ 2005	Govt of Afghanistan, Multinational coalition*, ISAF**, vs Taliban	..	>3 100	+ +

* In 2006 the USA-led multinational coalition included troops from Australia, Belgium, Canada, Denmark, Estonia, France, Germany, Italy, the Netherlands, Norway, Pakistan, Poland, Portugal, Romania, Spain and the UK. After a gradual takeover, the NATO-led International Security Assistance Force (ISAF) formally took full control over the international military presence in Afghanistan on 5 Oct. 2006.
** In 2006 the following countries contributed troops to ISAF: Albania, Australia, Austria, Azerbaijan, Belgium, Bulgaria, Canada, Croatia, Czech Republic, Denmark, Estonia, Finland, France, Germany, Greece, Hungary, Iceland, Ireland, Italy, Latvia, Lithuania, Luxembourg, Macedonia (Former Yugoslav Republic of), the Netherlands, New Zealand, Norway, Poland, Portugal, Romania, Slovakia, Slovenia, Spain, Sweden, Switzerland, Turkey, the UK and the USA. Note that, while all these countries sent troops to the ISAF force, not all had a mandate to fight. All the countries are listed here because information on the mandate of individual states' troops is often sensitive and hard to find.

India	Terr. (Kashmir)	1977/ 1977/1984/ 1990	Govt of India vs Kashmiri insurgents	>28 800	>700	–

Myanmar	Terr. (Karen State)	1948/ 1948/1948/ 1948	Govt of Myanmar vs KNU	>20 000	25–100	+

KNU: Karen National Union

Location	Incompat- ibility[a]	Yr formed/ yr stated/ yr joined/ yr entered[b]	Warring parties[c]	Total deaths[d] (incl. 2006)	Deaths in 2006	Change from 2005[e]
Nepal	Govt	1996/ 1996/1996/ 2002	Govt of Nepal vs CPN-M	<8 200	>400	– –

CPN-M: Communist Party of Nepal–Maoist

Location	Incompat- ibility[a]	Yr formed/ yr stated/ yr joined/ yr entered[b]	Warring parties[c]	Total deaths[d] (incl. 2006)	Deaths in 2006	Change from 2005[e]
Philippines	Govt	1968/ 1968/1969/ 1982	Govt of the Philippines vs CPP	20 000 – 27 000	>300	+
	Terr. (Mindanao)	1968/ 1981/1986/ 2000	vs MILF	<37 600	<25	– –

CPP: Communist Party of the Philippines
MILF: Moro Islamic Liberation Front

Location	Incompat- ibility[a]	Yr formed/ yr stated/ yr joined/ yr entered[b]	Warring parties[c]	Total deaths[d] (incl. 2006)	Deaths in 2006	Change from 2005[e]
Sri Lanka	Terr. ('Tamil Eelam')	1976 1976/1975/ 1989	Govt of Sri Lanka vs LTTE	>61 950	>1 950	+ +

LTTE: Liberation Tigers of Tamil Eelam

Europe

Location	Incompat- ibility[a]	Yr formed/ yr stated/ yr joined/ yr entered[b]	Warring parties[c]	Total deaths[d] (incl. 2006)	Deaths in 2006	Change from 2005[e]
Russia	Terr. (Chechnya)	1991/ 1991/1991/ 1995	Govt of Russia vs Republic of Chechnya	40 000– 70 000	<300	– –

Middle East

Location	Incompat- ibility[a]	Yr formed/ yr stated/ yr joined/ yr entered[b]	Warring parties[c]	Total deaths[d] (incl. 2006)	Deaths in 2006	Change from 2005[e]
Iraq	Govt	2003/ 2003/2003/ 2004	Govt of Iraq, Multinational coalition* vs Iraqi insurgents**	>18 600	>5 500	0

* The US-led multinational coalition in Iraq included combat troops from Albania, Armenia, Australia, Azerbaijan, Bosnia and Herzegovina, Bulgaria, the Czech Republic, Denmark, El Salvador, Estonia, Georgia, Italy, Japan, Kazakhstan, South Korea, Latvia, Lithuania, Macedonia (Former Yugoslav Republic of), Moldova, Mongolia, Poland, Romania, Slovakia, the UK and the USA.
** These included e.g. Tanzim Qa'idat al-Jihad fi Bilad al-Rafidayn (Organization of Jihad's Base in the Country of the Two Rivers), the Jaish Ansar al-Sunna (Army of Ansar al-Sunna) and al Jaysh al-Islami fi Iraq (Islamic Army of Iraq).

Location	Incompat- ibility[a]	Yr formed/ yr stated/ yr joined/ yr entered[b]	Warring parties[c]	Total deaths[d] (incl. 2006)	Deaths in 2006	Change from 2005[e]
Israel	Terr. (Palestinian territories)	1964/ 1964/1964/ ..	Govt of Israel vs Palestinian organizations*	>14 800	>500	+ +

* These included Fatah (Movement for the National Liberation of Palestine), Hamas (Islamic Resistance Movement), Palestinian Islamic Jihad (Jihad) and Popular Resistance Committees.

Location	Incompat- ibility[a]	Yr formed/ yr stated/ yr joined/ yr entered[b]	Warring parties[c]	Total deaths[d] (incl. 2006)	Deaths in 2006	Change from 2005[e]
Turkey	Terr. (Kurdistan)	1974/ 1974/1984/ 1992	Govt of Turkey vs PKK*	<30 600	>200	− −

PKK: Partiya Karkeren Kurdistan: Kurdistan Workers' Party

* Note that the PKK has changed names three times in as many years: in 2002 to Kadek (Kurdish Freedom and Democracy Congress), in Nov. 2003 to the Conference of the People's Congress of Kurdistan (KONGRA-GEL), and in Apr. 2005 the group to its previous name, the PKK.

Note that, although some countries are also the location of minor armed conflicts, the table lists only the major armed conflicts in those countries. For the definitions, methods and sources used see appendix 2B.

The conflicts in table 2A.3 are listed by location, in alphabetical order, within 5 geographical regions: Africa—excluding Egypt; the Americas—including North, Central and South America and the Caribbean; Asia—including Oceania, Australia and New Zealand; Europe—including the Caucasus; and the Middle East—Egypt, Iran, Iraq, Israel, Jordan, Kuwait, Lebanon, Syria, Turkey and the states of the Arabian peninsula.

[a] The stated general incompatible positions—'Govt' and 'Terr.'—refer to contested incompatibilities concerning *government* (type of political system or a change of central government or its composition) and *territory* (control of territory, secession or autonomy), respectively. Each location may have 1 or more incompatibilities over territory, if the disputed territories are different entities. There can be only 1 incompatibility over government in each location as, by definition, there can be only 1 government in each location.

[b] 'Year formed' is the year in which the original party in a major armed conflict—in conflicts where several parties have fought over the same incompatibility—first stated the incompatibility. 'Year stated' is the year in which *the active group* stated its incompatibility. 'Year joined' is the year in which the use of armed force began in the conflict between the active warring parties. 'Year entered' is the year in which the fighting between the government and the warring party for the first time reached the threshold of 1000 battle-related deaths in a single calendar year and was therefore entered in the database. In connection with the major data revision carried out by the UCDP (see appendix 2B, *SIPRI Yearbook 2005*), it became evident that the years listed in the tables for the early and mid-1990s sometimes referred to the start of the entire conflict and sometimes referred to the year in which the active group had stated its incompatibility. Although these years are often the same, there are also instances in which they are not. Therefore, in order to code this variable more stringently, 'Year formed' now refers to the start of the armed conflict itself, while the other 3 years listed in the table ('Year stated', 'Year joined' and 'Year entered') refer to the active warring party.

^c An opposition organization is any non-governmental group which has publicly announced a name for the group as well as its political goals and has used armed force to achieve its goals. Only those parties and alliances which were active during 2006 are listed in this column. Alliances are indicated by a comma between the names of warring parties.

^d The figures for total battle-related deaths refer to those deaths caused by the warring parties which can be directly connected to the incompatibility since the start of the conflict. This figure thus relates to the 'Year formed' variable. In the instance of intra-state conflicts, it should be noted that the figures include only battle-related deaths that can be attributed to fighting between the government and parties which were at some point listed in the table (i.e. groups that have crossed the threshold of 1000 battle-related deaths in a year). Information which covers a calendar year is necessarily more tentative for the last months of the year. Experience has also shown that the reliability of figures improves over time; they are therefore revised each year.

^e Numbers over 100 are as far as possible rounded to the nearest hundred. Thus, figures ranging between 101 and 150 are presented as >100, while figures ranging between 151 and 199 are presented as <200. Figures between 1 and 24 are presented as <25, while those between 25 and 100 are presented as 25–100.

^f The 'change from 2005' is measured as the increase or decrease in the number of battle-related deaths in 2006 compared with the number of battle-related deaths in 2005. Although the symbols are based on data that cannot be considered totally reliable, they represent the following changes:

++   increase in battle deaths of >50%

+   increase in battle deaths of >10–50%

0   stable rate of battle deaths ($\pm 10\%$)

–   decrease in battle deaths of >10–50%

– –   decrease in battle deaths of >50%

n.a.   not applicable, since the major armed conflict was not recorded for 2005.

Appendix 2B. Definitions, sources and methods for the conflict data

UPPSALA CONFLICT DATA PROGRAM

This appendix clarifies the definitions and methods used in the compilation of data on major armed conflicts and explains the treatment of the sources consulted. The armed conflict records presented in appendix 2A are compiled by the Uppsala Conflict Data Program (UCDP) of the Department of Peace and Conflict Research, Uppsala University.[1]

I. Definitions

The UCDP defines a major armed conflict as a contested incompatibility concerning government or territory over which the use of armed force between the military forces of two parties, of which at least one is the government of a state, has resulted in at least 1000 battle-related deaths in a single calendar year.[2] The separate elements are defined as follows:

1. *Incompatibility that concerns government or territory.* This refers to the stated generally incompatible positions of the parties to the conflict. An *incompatibility that concerns government* refers to incompatible positions regarding the state's type of political system or the composition of the government. It may also involve an aim to replace the current government. An *incompatibility that concerns territory* refers to incompatible positions regarding the status of a territory and may involve demands for secession or autonomy (intra-state conflict) or aims to change the state in control of a certain territory (interstate conflict).

2. *Use of armed force.* This refers to the use of armed force by the military forces of the parties to the conflict in order to promote the parties' general position in the conflict. Arms are defined as any material means of combat, including anything from manufactured weapons to sticks, stones, fire, water, and so on.

3. *Party.* This refers to the government of a state or an opposition organization or alliance of opposition organizations. The *government of a state* is the party which is generally regarded as being in central control, even by those organizations seeking to seize power. If this criterion is not applicable, the party controlling the capital of the state is regarded as the government. In most cases these two criteria coincide. An *opposition organization* is any non-governmental group which has announced a name for the group as well as its political goals and which has used armed force to achieve them. It should be noted that opposition organizations operating from bases in neighbouring states are listed as parties to the conflict in the location (country) where the

---

[1] See the UCDP Internet site at URL <http://www.pcr.uu.se/research/UCDP>.

[2] This definition of a major armed conflict differs slightly from that used by the UCDP in *SIPRI Yearbooks 1988–1999* (Oxford University Press: Oxford, 1988–99). The requirement that a conflict must cause at least 1000 battle-related deaths in a single year, rather than over the entire course of the conflict, ensures that only conflicts which reach a high level of intensity, as measured by the number of battle-related deaths, are included. Tables 2A.1 and 2A.2 have been retroactively revised accordingly.

government is challenged. Apart from these primary parties to the conflict, one other type of actor may be included in the table: a state or a multinational organization that supports one of the primary parties with regular troops. In order to be listed in the table, this secondary party must share the position of one of the warring parties. In contrast, a traditional peacekeeping operation is not considered to be a party to the conflict but is rather seen as an impartial part of a consensual peace process.

4. *State*. A state is an internationally recognized sovereign government controlling a specific territory or an internationally non-recognized government controlling a specific territory whose sovereignty is not disputed by an internationally recognized sovereign state which previously controlled the territory in question.

5. *Battle-related deaths*. This refers to the deaths caused by the warring parties that can be directly related to combat over the contested incompatibility. Once a conflict has reached the threshold of 1000 battle-related deaths in a year, it continues to appear in the annual table of major armed conflicts until the contested incompatibility has been resolved or until there is no recorded use of armed force resulting in at least one battle-related death between the same parties and concerning the same incompatibility during a year. The same conflict may reappear in subsequent years if there is renewed use of armed force between the same warring parties, resulting in at least one battle-related death and concerning the same incompatibility. The focus is thus not on political violence per se but on incompatibilities that are contested by the use of armed force. The UCDP registers one major type of political violence—battle-related deaths—which serves as a measure of the magnitude of a conflict. Other types of political violence are excluded, such as the unilateral use of armed force (e.g. massacres), unorganized or spontaneous public violence (e.g. communal violence) and violence that is not directed at the state (e.g. rebel groups fighting each other). These categories of political violence are expressions of phenomena that are distinct from armed conflict as defined here.

It should be noted that the period analysed in appendix 2A covers the years 1997–2006, but the conflicts included in the annual table have reached the required threshold in at least one calendar year since 1946.

II. Sources

The data presented in appendix 2A are based on information taken from a wide selection of publicly available sources, printed as well as electronic. The sources include news agencies, newspapers, academic journals, research reports, and documents from international and multinational organizations and non-governmental organizations (NGOs). In order to collect information on the aims and goals of the parties to the conflict, documents of the warring parties (governments and opposition organizations) and, for example, the Internet sites of rebel groups are often consulted.

Independent news sources, carefully selected over a number of years, constitute the basis of the data collection. The Factiva news database (previously known as the Reuters Business Briefing) is indispensable for the collection of general news reports. It contains 8000 sources in 22 languages from 118 countries and thus provides sources from all three crucial levels of the news media: international (e.g. Reuters and Agence France-Presse), regional and local. However, it is worth noting that the availability of regional and national news sources varies. This means that for some countries several sources are consulted, whereas for other countries and regions only a few high-quality region- or country-specific sources are used.

The UCDP regularly scrutinizes and revises the selection and combination of sources in order to maintain a high level of reliability and comparability between regions and countries. One important priority is to arrive at a balanced combination of sources of different origin with a view to avoiding bias. The reliability of the sources is judged using the expertise within the UCDP together with advice from a global network of experts (academics and policymakers). Both the independence of the source and the transparency of its origins are crucial. The latter is important because most sources are secondary, which means that the primary source also needs to be analysed in order to establish the reliability of a report. Each source is judged in relation to the context in which it is published. The potential interest of either the primary or secondary source to misrepresent an event is taken into account, as are the general climate and extent of media censorship. Reports from NGOs and international organizations are particularly useful in this context, to complement media reporting and facilitate cross-checking. The criterion that a source should be independent does not, of course, apply to those sources that are consulted precisely because they *are* biased, such as government documents or rebel groups' Internet sites. The UCDP is aware of the high level of scrutiny required and makes great effort to ensure the authenticity of the material used.

III. Methods

The data on major armed conflicts are compiled by calendar year. They include data on conflict location, type of incompatibility, onset of the armed conflict, warring parties, total number of battle-related deaths, number of battle-related deaths in a given year and change in battle-related deaths from the previous year.[3]

The data on battle-related deaths are given the most attention in the process of coding for the conflict database. Information on, for example, the date, news source, primary source, location and death toll is recorded for every event. Ideally, these individual events and figures are corroborated by two or more independent sources. The figures are then aggregated for the entire year of each conflict. The aggregated figures are compared to total figures given in official documents, in special reports or in the news media. Regional experts, such as researchers, diplomats and journalists, are often consulted during the data-collection process. Their role is mainly to clarify the contexts in which the events occur, thus facilitating proper interpretation of the reporting in published sources.

Because very little precise information is publicly available on death figures in armed conflicts, the numbers presented by the UCDP are best viewed as estimates. Rather than always providing exact numbers, ranges are sometimes given. The UCDP is generally conservative when estimating the number of battle-related deaths. Experience shows that, as more in-depth information on an armed conflict becomes available, the conservative, event-based estimates often prove more correct than others widely cited in the news media. If no figures are available or if the numbers given are unreliable, the UCDP does not provide a figure. Figures are revised retroactively each year as new information becomes available.

---

[3] See also the notes for table 2A.3 in appendix 2A.

Appendix 2C. Collective violence beyond the standard definition of armed conflict

MICHAEL BRZOSKA

I. Introduction

The major collections of data on armed conflicts are in agreement that the number of armed conflicts today is significantly lower than in the early 1990s. However, there is a widespread reluctance to accept these numbers as evidence of an increase in global peace and security. An example of this was the sceptical reception in some quarters of the *Human Security Report 2005*, which had the decline in warfare as its main message.[1] The data in that report are based on the same source—the database of the Uppsala Conflict Data Program (UCDP) of the Uppsala University Department of Peace and Conflict Studies—as the data reported in appendix 2A of this volume.[2]

Are the quantitative data on armed conflicts that are reported in this Yearbook and elsewhere a good measure of the trends in war and peace, insecurity and security, or are they representative of a specific class of collective violence with a declining relevance for peace and security policies?[3] Answers to this type of question have a high degree of policy relevance. For instance, if current quantitative data on armed conflicts are a good measure, the trend would signal a major success of the international community in reducing collective violence worldwide; if they measure only a certain class of collective violence, no such conclusion would be possible on the basis of these figures alone. Additional data would become vital.

Other figures, beyond data on the elements of the standard definition of armed conflict, are in fact available. The question is whether they are adequate to allow an extension of the findings based on the standard definition of armed conflict to broader concerns about collective violence. Section II of this appendix reviews the core features and limitations of the standard definition of armed conflict. There has been much controversy in the past over the relationship between violence, peace and security, but one view of what constitutes an armed conflict—with the elements of battle, political objectives and government participation at its core—has until recently dominated in both academic and policy circles.[4] Nonetheless, there are indications

---

[1] Human Security Centre, University of British Columbia, *Human Security Report 2005: War and Peace in the 21st Century* (Oxford University Press: New York, N.Y., 2005), URL <http://www.human securityreport.info>. For sceptical remarks and other conflict data see e.g. Leitenberg, M., *Deaths in Wars and Conflicts in the 20th Century*, Occasional Paper no. 29, 3rd edn (Cornell University, Peace Studies Program: Ithaca, N.Y., Aug. 2006), URL <http://www.clingendael.nl/publications/2006/20060800_cdsp_occ_leitenberg.pdf>, p. 8.

[2] UCDP data are available on the programme's website at URL <http://www.pcr.uu.se/research/UCDP/>.

[3] For the definition of collective violence see section II below.

[4] In peace research the issue of the relevant fields of analysis of violence has been heatedly debated at various times. One such debate ensued over Johan Galtung's distinction between 'positive' and 'negative' peace. See Galtung, J., 'Violence, peace and peace research', *Journal of Peace Research*, vol. 6 (1969), pp. 167–91. Interestingly, discussions among security experts in the 1990s on broadening the

that such a view is too narrow to facilitate an understanding of the trends in peace and security or to serve as a basis for formulating relevant policies.

Section III discusses recent responses to these challenges by those who have constructed additional data sets on aspects of collective violence, including the Human Security Centre. Section IV takes a more conceptual approach to the challenge of the declining relevance of the standard definition of armed conflict. Data requirements are sketched for two broad understandings of peace and security that are important in current policy debates—one on the victims of violence and the other on security risks to the fabric of societies.

The purpose of this appendix is to stimulate discussion on the correspondence between data requirements and alternative conceptions of peace and security—a traditional conception linked to armed conflict, and two linked to broader understandings of peace and security (see section IV). It does not attempt to provide workable definitions for the collection of additional data, still less the ready-to-use data themselves. For this to be done in a professional way, additional research and resources would be required. This appendix should therefore not be read as a criticism of the available data collections but rather as a contribution to the ongoing debates on what data should be collected for what purposes and how. As noted by Taylor Seybolt, data collectors have to seek a balance between the reliability and the validity of their data: 'that is, between accuracy in recording information and appropriateness of the information for addressing theoretical concepts of interest'.[5]

II. Limitations of the standard definition of armed conflict

The standard definition of armed conflict reflects a conception that was expressed perfectly in Carl von Clausewitz's dictum that 'war is the continuation of politics by other means'.[6] The conception of armed conflict as an extension of politics has shaped the efforts of data collectors, even though they may use slightly different definitions.[7]

This conception of armed conflict has five constituent elements: (a) deliberate violence by collectives, (b) the use of arms, (c) the battle, (d) political objectives and (e) a government as an actor on at least one side of a conflict. Various definitions may have additional data requirements, but in standard definitions of armed conflict these five elements need to be in evidence. The types of collective violence without battles (including violence carried out by both non-state actors and governments), such as massacres or terrorist acts carried out against civilians, are outside the realm of this conception.[8] This also applies to armed conflicts where the clash (or incompat-

concept of security beyond military security to include e.g. environmental change to some extent mirrored that earlier debate.

[5] Seybolt, T. B., 'Measuring violence: an introduction to conflict data sets', *SIPRI Yearbook 2002: Armaments, Disarmament and International Security* (Oxford University Press: Oxford, 2002), p. 96.

[6] The concepts 'armed conflict' and 'war' are not differentiated in this text: the usage corresponds to the praxis in various sources and strands of literature referred to in this appendix. Armed conflict is generally defined as the broader of the 2 categories when such a distinction is made in statistics.

[7] See Seybolt (note 5); and Eck, K., *A Beginner's Guide to Conflict Data: Finding and Using the Right Dataset*, UCDP Paper no. 1 (Uppsala Conflict Data Program (UCDP): Uppsala, 2005), URL <http://www.pcr.uu.se/publications/UCDP_pub/UCDP_paper1.pdf>.

[8] The data on battle-related deaths presented in appendix 2A only partly take into account cases of violence against civilians. Bombings, sniper attacks and urban warfare (bombs, explosions and assassinations) are recorded as acts of war if the targets of the attacks are military forces or recognized rep-

ibility[9]) is not about ruling a country or parts of its territory but, for instance, personal economic gain. The requirement that at least one of the parties to the conflict is a government reinforces the political dimension of armed conflicts.

Two of the five elements of the definition have gone unchallenged in recent debates about what constitutes an armed conflict: collective violence and the use of arms. The term *collective violence* means that the infliction of violence must be deliberately carried out by actors who are, or perceive themselves to be, part of a group with a common purpose beyond the immediate act of violence. Individual acts of violence, violent crime and general disorder are thus not included. Collective violence results from clashes that cause significant levels of destruction and death, for which various data sets have different thresholds. The second element, *the use of arms*, is generally defined rather widely to include the active use of any instrument or material to inflict violence but not, for instance, killing people by failing to cure illness.

The other three elements of the definition, however, have been heatedly debated for a number of years and are discussed below. Authors have claimed that since the end of the cold war there have been fundamental changes in how collective violence is used. Some argue that 'new wars' have become the dominant type of armed conflict,[10] a claim that others refute.[11] New wars are said to be marked by characteristics that call into question the validity of the standard political definition of a war, such as the avoidance of battle, the deliberate killing of civilians, the crucial role of economic motives in warfare and a fluidity of actors.[12]

The battle. One of the hypotheses of the new-wars literature is that the battle is not as central to warfare as it was both before and during the cold war, while a specific type of asymmetric warfare—marked by the strategic use of the deliberate killing of civilians—has become more frequent in recent armed conflicts.[13] Deliberate killing of civilians in massacres and terrorist acts has been a tactic in many armed conflicts, including those carried out during the cold war, but the new-war thesis argues that it has attained strategic importance for inferior fighting parties and can even be their

resentatives of the groups in conflict. In such cases, deaths of civilians 'caught in the crossfire' are also considered as battle-related deaths. The data exclude, however, death and devastation resulting from the targeting of civilians, even if such killing is deliberate. Uppsala Conflict Data Program, 'Definitions, sources and methods for Uppsala Conflict Data Program battle-death estimates', URL <http://www.pcr. uu.se/publications/UCDP_pub/UCDP Battle-deaths – definitions sources methods.pdf>. An example is helpful to illustrate the difference between civilian deaths that are recorded as battle-related violence by the UCDP and those that are not: for 1994, the UCDP reports fewer than 1000 battle victims for Rwanda, whereas the number of all victims of violence, mostly carried out by militia groups against civilians, is generally estimated at 800 000. See Human Security Centre (note 1), p. 41. For further comparisons of estimates of battle-related and total deaths in select wars see e.g. Leitenberg (note 1); and Gleditsch, N. P. and Lacina, B., 'Monitoring trends in global combat: a new dataset of battle deaths', *European Journal of Population*, vol. 21, nos 2–3 (2005), pp. 145–65.

[9] See appendix 2B in this volume for the UCDP's definition and use of this term.

[10] The concept was first introduced in Kaldor, M. and Vashee, B. (eds), *Restructuring the Global Military Sector*, vol. 1, *New Wars* (Pinter: London, 1997).

[11] See e.g. Kalyvas, S. N., '"New" and "old" civil wars: a valid distinction?', *World Politics*, vol. 54, no. 1 (2001), pp. 99–118.

[12] See Holmqvist, C., 'Major armed conflicts', *SIPRI Yearbook 2006: Armaments, Disarmament and International Security* (Oxford University Press: Oxford, 2006), pp. 77–107; and Krahmann, E., *New Threats and New Actors in International Security* (Palgrave Macmillan: New York, N.Y., 2005).

[13] This hypothesis is disputed, however, and does not have strong empirical support because the data on civilian victims of war are so thin. See e.g. Kalyvas (note 11); and Human Security Centre (note 1), pp. 70–76.

dominant method of warfare, as in the current conflict in Iraq. The purported recent change in the scale and significance of the deliberate killing of civilians in warfare challenges the reliability of the standard definition of armed conflict as a measure of collective violence. The deliberate killing of civilians who are not involved in battles, for instance those killed in massacres or terrorist acts, is not covered by this definition. This omission may make a crucial difference to whether a conflict is classified as 'major' in quantitative approaches. Such problems are well illustrated by the conflict in southern Lebanon and the north of Israel in the summer of 2006. This was widely perceived as an armed conflict of major consequence. According to the Lebanese and Israeli governments, over 2000 people were killed.[14] Many of them were civilians, although it is difficult to distinguish specifically civilian casualties in cases where a guerrilla force such as Hezbollah is fighting. It is even more difficult to judge whether death was directly related to combat, as required by the standard definition of 'battle death', or occurred outside of combat situations.

Political objectives. Debates on recent cases of collective violence have highlighted the difficulty of disentangling political, economic and ideological objectives. Warring parties will not necessarily reveal their intentions, and what look like economic motives to one observer may seem political to another. Armed groups generally stress political objectives in their public pronouncements, but they may in fact be primarily and ultimately interested in private economic gain. Armed groups that have economic or ideological objectives may not seek control of government or territory but may instead want to influence the way in which societies operate or may simply be interested in private gain. This presents major empirical problems for use of the standard definition of armed conflict, which requires the data compiler to decide whether the conflict is about political issues or not. Furthermore, why privilege objectives that relate to government and territory as definers of armed conflict and exclude all others? To return to the example of the armed conflict that took place in Lebanon in the summer of 2006, there were objectives, such as the release of hostages, the intimidation of populations and the weakening of Hezbollah. While these could be regarded as political objectives, neither side aimed at taking over a government or gaining control over a territory.

A government as an actor. The discussions about the changing nature of conflict are embedded in broader debates about the effects of globalization and the changing post-cold war international order on the power of governments, or rather their lack of such power, to control violence in their territories. Fighting without government involvement has become frequent. In a number of recent cases of violent conflict, such as the Democratic Republic of the Congo, it has even become difficult to determine who is the government.

What the challenges to all five criteria have in common is that they question the boundaries of the standard definition of armed conflict and aim to extend them to include other forms of collective violence. While this presents problems for data collectors, it reflects a more general broadening of concerns regarding peace and

---

[14] The Lebanese Government reported 1191 dead and the Israeli Government 162 dead. See Lebanese Presidency of the Council of Ministers, Higher Relief Council, 'Lebanon under siege' website, URL <http://www.lebanonundersiege.gov.lb/>; and Israeli Ministry of Foreign Affairs, 'Israel–Hizbullah conflict: victims of rocket attacks and IDF casualties', 12 July 2006, URL <http://www.mfa.gov.il/MFA/Terrorism-+Obstacle+to+Peace/Terrorism+from+Lebanon-+Hizbullah/Israel-Hizbullah+conflict-+Victims+of+rocket+attacks+and+IDF+casualties+July-Aug+2006.htm>.

security. Additional issues related to collective violence have become important subjects of peace and security politics.

III. Data beyond elements of the standard definition of armed conflict

Collectors of data on armed conflicts have responded to these challenges in different ways. For example, the Arbeitsgemeinschaft Kriegsursachenforschung (AKUF), in Hamburg, Germany, has dropped from its definition of armed conflict the requirement that one of the parties must be a government.[15] Data on mass killings of people of different political persuasion, ethnic background or societal position have received renewed attention. The updated data collection of Milton Leitenberg, of the University of Maryland, for instance, includes any available estimates of the total number of victims and, in a separate list, victims of massacres and other forms of one-sided violence.[16]

The best-organized effort to address broader concerns about collective violence is that of the UCDP. With support from the Human Security Centre, the UCDP has begun to compile two additional data sets on collective violence—one on non-state conflicts and one on one-sided violence—that are not restricted by the standard definition of armed conflict.

A non-state conflict is defined by the UCDP as the use of armed force between two organized groups, neither of which is the government of a state, which results in at least 25 battle-related deaths per year and per warring dyad.[17] One-sided violence is defined as the use of armed force by the government of a state or by a formally organized group against civilians which results in at least 25 deaths per year.[18] Both of these new data sets establish minimum thresholds for the number of victims, but each relaxes major elements of the standard definition of armed conflict. On the one hand, for the data on non-state conflicts the battle remains a requirement while the criteria of participation of a government and a political objective are dropped. One-sided violence, on the other hand, is included with no restrictions on the objectives of the use of such violence nor the collective actor, and no requirement for a battle. One-sided violence is thus close in conception to other data sets on genocides and massacres.[19]

These UCDP data sets have been developed to achieve 'a better understanding of the full range of threats to human security posed by collective violence'.[20] They have been used extensively in the publications of the Human Security Centre. Its first

---

[15] On AKUF data see URL <http://www.sozialwiss.uni-hamburg.de/publish/Ipw/Akuf/> (in German).

[16] Leitenberg (note 1).

[17] Kreutz, J. and Eck, K., 'UCDP non-state conflict codebook', UCDP, Sep. 2005, URL <http://www.pcr.uu.se/publications/UCDP_pub/Non-state conflict Dataset Codebook.pdf>, p. 1.

[18] Extrajudicial killing of people in custody is excluded from the definition. Kreutz, J. and Eck, K., 'UCDP one-sided violence codebook', UCDP, 28 Sep. 2005, URL <http://www.pcr.uu.se/publications/UCDP_pub/One-sided violence Dataset Codebook.pdf>, p. 1.

[19] References to and discussions of such data sets can be found in Leitenberg (note 1); and Human Security Centre, University of British Columbia, *Human Security Brief 2006*, URL <http://www.humansecuritybrief.info/>, chapter 2. The latter updates the core trend data on political violence that were published in the *Human Security Report 2005* and analyses key findings of data sets that track these changes.

[20] See the UCDP project description at URL <http://www.pcr.uu.se/research/UCDP/HumSec_index.htm>.

major publication, the *Human Security Report 2005*, presented data on 'violent threats to individuals', described as the focus of a preferred narrow definition of human security.[21] The report's team of authors, led by Andrew Mack, make a distinction between 'political violence' and 'criminal violence'. For them, in addition to the armed conflicts listed by the UCDP, political violence includes one-sided violence and non-state conflict as well as genocide and 'politicide'. The report includes data from a collection developed in the 1990s and maintained by Barbara Harff;[22] data on international terrorist incidents recorded since the early 1990s from the US Department of State;[23] and data on political repression from the Political Terror Scale (PTS), originally developed more than 20 years ago at the University of Purdue and now maintained by the University of North Carolina at Asheville.[24] The report also uses data from the Political Stability and Absence of Violence index of the World Bank, which measures the likelihood of destabilization of a government *inter alia* by domestic violence and terrorism and is one of the six dimensions of its Worldwide Indicators of Governance.[25]

In addition to political violence, the *Human Security Report 2005* covers criminal violence as a major concern for its human security audit. The report argues that this is necessary because 'In most states, most of the time, far more people are killed or injured by criminal violence than by warfare'.[26] Its authors warn, however, that only a few countries produce timely and comprehensive data on crime. Quantifying criminal violence thus runs into major data problems, particularly in those countries where human security is poor. There is also a major overlap with the data on genocides: the 1994 Rwanda genocide produces a spike in the global homicide statistics. The report contains global data on homicides and rape from Interpol, based on estimates for many regions.[27] However, the authors are sceptical about both the possibility and usefulness of combining such data in a single data set or even a single grading for each country in a 'human security index'. They argue that the available data, particularly on criminal violence—which in their view must be included in any composite index on human security—are not sufficiently comprehensive. Moreover,

---

[21] Human Security Centre (note 1), p. VIII.

[22] See Harff, B., 'Genocide', Background paper for the *Human Security Report 2005*, 17 July 2003, URL <http://www.humansecurityreport.info/background/Harff_Genocide.pdf>; and Harff, B., 'Genocide, politicide', University of Maryland, Integrated Network for Societal Conflict Research, 18 May 2004, URL <http://www.cidcm.umd.edu/inscr/genocide/>. In the latter publication Harff defines the difference between genocide and 'politicide': 'In genocides the victimized groups are defined by their perpetrators primarily in terms of their communal characteristics. In politicides, in contrast, groups are defined primarily in terms of their political opposition to the regime and dominant groups. In [both types of violence] killings are never accidental, nor are they acts of individuals . . . [but] are carried out at the explicit or tacit direction of state authorities, or those who claim state authority.'

[23] US Department of State, 'Country reports on terrorism', URL <http://www.state.gov/s/ct/rls/crt/>.

[24] Cornett, L. and Gibney, M., 'Tracking terror: the Political Terror Scale 1980–2001', Background paper for the *Human Security Report 2005*, 3 Aug. 2003, URL <http://www.humansecurityreport.info/background/Cornett-Gibney_Political_Terror_Scale_1980-2001.pdf>; and University of North Carolina at Asheville, Political Science Department, 'Political Terror Scale 1980–2005', URL <http://www.unca.edu/politicalscience/images/Colloquium/faculty-staff/gibney.html>.

[25] World Bank, 'Worldwide governance indicators: 1996–2005', Sep. 2006, URL <http://www.worldbank.org/wbi/governance/govdata/>.

[26] Human Security Centre (note 1), p. 64.

[27] See Newman, G. R., 'Human security: a world view of homicide and rape', Background paper for the *Human Security Report 2005*, [n.d.], URL <http://www.humansecurityreport.info/background/Newman_Homicide_and_Rape.pdf>, p. 3.

combining the data in an over-simplified, single indicator might conceal more information than it would convey.[28]

The *Human Security Brief 2006* takes a somewhat different approach to human security: its core message is that human security 'is about protecting individuals and communities from *any* form of political violence'.[29] While it also states that human security is about 'violent threats to individuals', no data on criminal violence or forms of violence other than political violence are presented or discussed. Political violence covers largely the same phenomena that were the subject of the 2005 report: UCDP-listed armed conflicts, one-sided violence and non-state conflict, with additional data on genocides and 'politicides' as well as on international terrorism.[30] In addition, data are included on terrorism incidents, presented by national location. These data are taken from the Terrorism Knowledge Base of the Memorial Institute for the Prevention of Terrorism (MIPT),[31] which integrates a number of major data sets on terrorism, most importantly that of the RAND Corporation.[32] The effort is funded by the US Department of Homeland Security.

The *Human Security Brief 2006* presents a narrower concept of human security than that of the *Human Security Report 2005*. The latter's broader concept encompasses all types of violent threat to individuals while the former focuses on a smaller set of forms of collective violence, for which the Human Security Cenetre uses the term political violence. While not explicitly defined other than through the data sets that are included, this concept neatly fits the centre's major policy message: that the incidences of most forms of political violence are declining and that 'many of these changes could be attributed to an explosion of international activism, spearheaded by the UN, that sought to stop ongoing wars, help negotiate peace settlements, support post-conflict reconstruction, and prevent old wars from starting again'.[33] The data-driven approach to support this message has added to the scepticism in many quarters, mentioned above, about the centre's findings.

Both the report and the brief contain discussion of concepts—for instance, the importance of data on the total number of victims, direct and indirect, of political violence—but they lack a comprehensive discussion of what data should be available for the preferred definition of human security.[34] Combined with the opaqueness of the definition of human security, this nourishes suspicion that the major findings of the Human Security Centre may reflect a bias in the selection of data towards proving the success of international activism. The centre could easily counter any such suspicion by taking a more conceptual, less data-driven approach.

IV. Data for broader concerns of peace and security policy

The standard definition of armed conflict corresponds to a specific view of the objective of peace and security policy: to prevent or to contain and end armed conflicts between states as well as those between states and rebel groups. While this

---

[28] Human Security Centre (note 1), pp. 90–91.

[29] Human Security Centre (note 19), p. 31.

[30] On the term 'politicide' see note 22.

[31] On the MIPT Terrorism Knowledge Base see URL <http://www.tkb.org/>.

[32] See the RAND–MIPT Terrorism Incident Database Project website at URL <http://www.rand.org/ise/projects/terrorismdatabase/>.

[33] Human Security Centre (note 19), p. 1.

[34] Human Security Centre (note 1), p. 91 and (note 19), p. 17.

view is important, it does not cover the full gamut of policy-relevant peace and security issues—in the perspective not just of non-governmental organizations (NGOs) and experts, but also of many governments and international organizations.

Two examples of broader concerns regarding peace and security are highlighted in this section. One is a variant of the concept of human security, discussed above. The other is related to the objective of preventing new types of threat to peace and security. There are other possible objectives of peace and security policy, such as one based on an understanding of human security that includes all serious threats to the life, health and livelihood of individuals and communities.[35] The discussion here does not aim to establish whether data requirements for such objectives can be met.

Concerns related to human security, particularly in the extreme cases of humanitarian emergencies, have received increasing attention in international politics. International attention to victims of collective violence has grown, through media coverage and the activities of international NGOs. This has put pressure on governments, particularly in the industrialized world, to do more to prevent or curtail collective violence. An important political expression of the growing attention to victims is the adoption of resolutions by the United Nations Security Council on the protection of civilians in armed conflict. The most recent one endorses the ultimate humanitarian principle of the 'responsibility to protect' with special reference to victims of war.[36]

There are several ways to define human security even within a relatively narrow focus (leaving, for instance, 'economic security' aside), but what they have in common is a focus on the victims of physical violence, regardless of the cause of their plight. From the perspective of humanitarian emergencies, an appropriate definition of human security would include all types of collective violence that threaten the life, health and livelihood of individuals and communities. It is intellectually defensible to also include individual violence without political objectives, such as murder and gang killings, or to limit the definition to the victims of political violence, as is done in the *Human Security Brief 2006*. A middle position is adopted here. Human security is thus defined as covering all types of collective violence, as itemized in table 2C.1.

The humanitarian turn in international politics has been mirrored by a broadening of national security concerns, particularly in the industrialized countries. This appendix argues that all types of collective violence can become a security concern if they are of sufficient magnitude to threaten the fabric of societies.[37] Documents such as the US National Security Strategies of 2002 and 2006 and the European Security Strategy of 2003 emphasize the current range of transnational threats to societies, such as international terrorism, the spread of weapons of mass destruction to non-state actors and transnational crime networks.[38] The actors involved seek to use violence to shape, or exercise control over, the will and behaviour of people in a particular society. Very low levels of violence can have such effects, as has been shown by recent terrorist attacks. With the exception of the attack on the New York World

[35] See chapter 7 in this volume.

[36] United Nations, 'Protection of civilians in armed conflict', UN Security Council Resolution 1674, 28 Apr. 2006, URL <http://www.un.org/Docs/sc/unsc_resolutions06.htm>.

[37] See also the Introduction and chapter 7 in this volume.

[38] The White House, 'The National Security Strategy of the United States of America', Washington, DC, Mar. 2006, URL <http://www.whitehouse.gov/nsc/nss/2006>; and Council of the European Union, 'A secure Europe in a better world: the European Security Strategy', Brussels, 12 Dec. 2003, URL <http://consilium.europa.eu/cms3_fo/showPage.ASP?id= 266>. See also chapter 2 in this volume.

Table 2C.1. Types of collective violence and availability of data

	Objectives	Infliction of violence	Opponents	Examples	Data coverage: incidents	Data coverage: direct victims	Data coverage: indirect victims[a]
A. Interstate conflict	Political control (territory, rule)	Battle	State–State	Eritrea–Ethiopia, 1998–2000	Armed conflict data	Battlefield deaths	No single consistent source
B. Conventional intra-state conflict	Political control (territory, rule)	Battle	Non-state group–State	Biafra, 1967–70	Armed conflict data	Battlefield deaths	No single consistent source
C. Guerrilla intra-state conflict	Political control (territory, rule)	Battle/one-sided violence	Non-state group–State	Mozambique, 1962–74	Armed conflict data	Battlefield deaths	No single consistent source
D. Riots	Political control (territory, rule)	Battle	Non-state group–State	Bangladesh, 2006	Non-state conflict data	Battlefield deaths	No single consistent source
E. Intra-territorial conflict	Political control (territory, rule)	Battle	Non-state group–Non-state group	Somalia, 1992–	Non-state conflict data	Battlefield deaths	No single consistent source
F. Communal conflict	Cultural dominance	Battle/one-sided violence	Local group–Local group	Northern Nigeria, 1992–	Non-state conflict data if battle; in genocide data if above high threshold	Battlefield deaths; in genocide data if above high threshold	In genocide data if above high threshold
G. Massacres/ genocides	Elimination of targeted group	One-sided violence	State–Non-state group	Rwanda, 1994	One-sided violence data, genocide data	One-sided death data, genocide data	No single consistent source
H. Non-state ethnic cleansing/pogroms	Elimination of targeted group	One-sided violence	Non-state group–Non-state group	Attacks on indigenous people, in many countries	In genocide data, if above high threshold	In genocide data, if above high threshold	No single consistent source
I. Non-state terrorism	Political gain	One-sided violence against government	Non-state group–State and population	al-Qaeda attack on New York, 2001	Terrorist incidents	Victims of terrorist incidents	No single consistent source

J. Organized crime	Economic gain	Battle/one-sided violence	Non-state group–State	Brazilian 'prison war', 2006	No good data	No good data	No good data	No good data
K. Gang fighting	Economic gain	Battle	Non-state group–Non-state group	Russian gang wars, 1995–98	Non-state conflict data if battle; data on genocide if above threshold	Battlefield deaths	No good data	
L. Violent evictions	Economic gain	One-sided violence	Non-state group–Non-state group	Evictions of illegal squatters by landlords, in many countries	No single consistent source	No single consistent source	No single consistent source	No single consistent source

[a] These are victims of the follow-on effects of the application of violence, e.g. lack of food, epidemics or the degradation of the local health system.

Trade Center in 2001, terrorist attacks typically cause far fewer casualties than armed conflicts, as traditionally defined. However, terrorist attacks are now commonly seen by people and governments alike as first-order threats and have the power to bring about major changes in behaviour or damage to the social fabric—on a scale almost comparable to major international wars of the past. An example of this (explicit or implicit) equation with war is the counterterrorist 'mobilization' in many countries after the 11 September 2001 attacks on the USA.

One reason for the shift in interest away from armed conflicts and towards humanitarian emergencies and threats to the fabric of societies is the relative incidence of various types of collective violence. While war between states with political objectives is not obsolete, it has become a rare phenomenon of only intermittent international importance, such as the case of the 2003 invasion of Iraq. The number of internal armed conflicts recorded in appendix 2A and in other statistical sources is also declining. At the same time, transnational threats to societies seem to be on the rise, judging by the (albeit scant) data available to substantiate such impressions. The MIPT database, for instance, records an increase in the incidence of terrorism over the past decade. Data for the main indicator of a humanitarian conception of peace and security—the total number of victims—are currently not available. Thus, while the data that are available clearly point in this direction,[39] it is still not possible to say with certainty whether the overall number of people dying from collective violence has or has not decreased over the past few years.

The discussion of the data required for broad conceptions of peace and security comes back to much the same issues as those raised in the discussion in section II on the definition of armed conflict. The use of arms and deliberate violence by collective actors remain constitutive elements of all conceptions, but the other three traditional criteria of conflict—a political purpose, a battle and a government as an actor—apply only to certain forms of collective violence. Table 2C.1 sets out 10 different forms of such violence, which vary both as regards the relevance of the five classic criteria and in terms of the interaction among actors—that is, who is using violence against whom. The 10 forms are not exclusive; in fact they partially overlap and there will often be overlapping forms of collective violence. The main purpose of the table is to illustrate the breadth of data needed for different conceptions of peace and security.

The standard, narrow definition of armed conflict is reflected in the types A–D in table 2C.1. Good data are available on the incidence of such events, such as the UCDP data on armed conflicts, which cover the full range of types—from interstate war to riots—as long as thresholds for the number of victims in 'battle' are crossed. The UCDP and other sources also provide data on battle-related deaths for these types of collective violence. However, there are no consistent, complete data on victims who are not on a battlefield, whether deliberately targeted or indirect victims.[40]

For a broader understanding of peace and security, all types of collective violence may be relevant. The issue is not whether one or all of the criteria of the standard definition of armed conflict are met, but whether there is a threat to human security that is sufficient to produce a humanitarian emergency or a threat to the fabric of a society.

---

[39] See e.g. Human Security Centre (note 19).
[40] On collective violence as an indirect cause of death see also chapter 7 in this volume.

New data sets, such as those of the UCDP and the Human Security Centre, cover additional forms of violence that go well beyond the traditional definition of armed conflict. Fairly good data are now available on both the incidence and the number of direct victims of all types of collective violence where the objectives are clearly political—including the elimination of ethnic, cultural or social groups (types E–I in table 2C.1, in addition to types A–D).[41] There is a lack of comprehensive data on collective violence driven by other, particularly economic, objectives. Data on crime are weak for many countries, and the UCDP non-state conflict data set, which in theory should also include fighting among gangs, in practice seems to pick up few such cases, partly because of a lack of information and partly because of the threshold requirement of 25 battle-related deaths per year.[42]

Most problematic is the lack of comprehensive data on all victims, including indirect victims of violence. The first challenge that needs to be tackled before such data can be collected is to define categories of indirect victims; the next task is to collect data corresponding to such definitions. Case studies have revealed the potential of various methods as well as the costs in time and resources of collecting such data.[43]

V. Conclusions: broad perceptions, narrow data

The data on major armed conflicts presented in the SIPRI Yearbook represent important, but not all, aspects of collective violence. Statements about the broader trends in peace and security that are made on the basis of data on armed conflicts alone are therefore hazardous. International peace and security policy has moved on to broader conceptions of what is important, as reflected in an approach that focuses on human security and humanitarian catastrophe and another that stresses threats to the fabric of society.

The limitations of the standard definition of armed conflict combined with broader conceptions of peace and security have stimulated some changes in definitions and new efforts to collect data. While the latter have produced important new data on aspects of collective violence, more needs to be done before either of the two broader conceptions of peace and security can be comprehensively discussed in quantitative terms. The most important gap is data on all types of victim of collective violence, although efforts are under way to improve such data. The Human Security Centre has announced that its *Human Security Report 2007* will focus on two major themes— 'The Hidden Costs of War' and 'The Causes of Peace'.[44] Another important gap is data on crime.

---

[41] Uppsala Conflict Data Program, 'UCDP non-state conflict dataset v.1.1 2002–2005' and 'UCDP one-sided violence dataset v.1.2 1989–2005', Dec. 2006, URL <http://www.pcr.uu.se/research/UCDP/our_data 1.htm>.

[42] Uppsala Conflict Data Program (note 41).

[43] See e.g. Restrepo, J., Vargas, J. F. and Spagat, M., 'The dynamics of the Colombian civil conflict: a new data set', *Homo Oeconomicus*, vol. 21, no. 2 (2004), pp. 396–428; Burnham, G. et al., 'Mortality after the 2003 invasion of Iraq: a cross-sectional cluster sample survey', *The Lancet*, vol. 368, no. 9545 (21 Oct. 2006), pp. 1421–28; Coghlan, B. et al., 'Mortality in the Democratic Republic of Congo: a nationwide survey', *The Lancet*, vol. 367, no. 9504 (7–13 Jan. 2006), pp. 44–51; and Research and Documentation Center (RDC) Sarajevo, 'Population losses in Bosnia and Herzegovina 92–95', URL <http://www.idc.org.ba/project/populationlosses.html>.

[44] Human Security Centre (note 19), p. 1.

Any analysis of trends can only be exact for those empirical phenomena that are covered in the definitions. Currently, definitions and data exist for only some types of collective violence. Until such time as additional data, with adequate definitions, are available, analysis of the broader trends in collective violence has to rely mainly on inferences made from data collected for a particular conflict or on partial observations that are not based on comprehensive data. Much, but not all, of the data that have become available on additional types of collective violence—the only exception being data beyond armed conflicts—support the contention of a downward trend in collective violence: but more comprehensive sets of statistics, including those on the total number of victims of collective violence and of crime, are needed in order to convince the sceptics.

3. Peacekeeping: keeping pace with changes in conflict

SHARON WIHARTA

I. Introduction

As 2006 began, it promised a continuation of the heightened international political commitment to peacekeeping[1] that had characterized the 'banner year' of 2005.[2] In April 2006 the United Nations Security Council reaffirmed its commitment to 'a responsibility to protect populations from genocide, war crimes, ethnic cleansing and crimes against humanity';[3] and the newly established United Nations Peacebuilding Commission took on its first two country cases, Burundi and Sierra Leone.[4] Illustrating the widespread recognition of the primary role of the United Nations in peacekeeping, some 70 per cent of Nepal's population reportedly wanted the UN to become involved in the country's peace process. In January 2007 both the Nepalese Government and the Communist Party of Nepal (Maoist) formally requested that the UN support the implementation of the peace agreement reached between them by assisting in the disarmament and demobilization of former combatants, among other tasks.[5] The UN and a number of regional security organizations took several steps to enhance their operational effectiveness in carrying out peace missions. For example, the UN embarked on an ambitious reform agenda aimed at professionalizing the conduct of UN peacekeeping.

However, unforeseen political and strategic developments in mid-2006 created severe problems for a number of peace missions and served to dampen the earlier optimism. Among others, conflict in Lebanon and mounting violence in Afghanistan necessitated major expansions of the international missions in those countries. The need to replace the small UN Office in Timor-Leste (UNOTIL) with a considerably larger integrated and multidimensional

---

[1] The term 'peacekeeping' is used in this chapter to cover all peace operations intended to facilitate the implementation of peace agreements already in place, to support a peace process, or to assist conflict prevention or peacebuilding efforts. On definitions see also appendix 3A.

[2] United Nations Department of Public Information, Peace and Security Section, *United Nations Peace Operations: Year in Review 2005* (United Nations: New York, N.Y., 2006), URL <http://www.un.org/Depts/dpko/dpko/pub/year_review05/introduction.htm>, p. 1.

[3] UN Security Council Resolution 1674, 28 Apr. 2006. The texts of UN Security Council resolutions can be accessed at URL <http://www.un.org/Docs/sc/>.

[4] The UN Peacebuilding Commission was created in Dec. 2005 and held its first session on 23 June 2006. On the Peacebuilding Commission see Wiharta, S., 'Peace-building: the new international focus on Africa', *SIPRI Yearbook 2006: Armaments, Disarmament and International Security* (Oxford University Press: Oxford, 2006), pp. 139–57.

[5] Martin, I., UN Special Representative for Nepal, quoted in Leopold, E., 'UN organizes mission to help peace pact in Nepal', Reuters AlertNet, 11 Jan. 2007, URL<http://www.alertnet.org/thenews/newsdesk/N11360879.htm>.

mission, the UN Mission in Timor (UNMIT), sparked new debate about the shortcomings of past international peacebuilding efforts. This discussion focused in particular on the growing complexity and increasing number of functional tasks given to peace missions, and the multiplicity of actors involved in conducting them. The apparent failure in Timor-Leste also clearly demonstrated the crucial importance of the emerging principle of local owner-ship in peacebuilding.[6]

Some long-standing core principles of peacekeeping, such as consent, impartiality, neutrality and the use of force only in self-defence, also came to the fore in policy discussions and severely tested in their practical implemen-tation. After the UN Operation in Burundi (ONUB) successfully oversaw a constitutional referendum and elections in that country, the new government accused the mission of favouring the opposition and requested that it be withdrawn ahead of schedule. Although sporadic violence continued in the country, the UN had little choice but to comply.[7] Similar political resistance emerged in Côte d'Ivoire: in September the chief of the Ivorian Army accused the international community of 'sickening partiality' and President Laurent Gbagbo urged UN and French peacekeepers to leave the country, saying that the UN-facilitated peace process had failed and that he intended instead to approach the African Union (AU) for assistance.[8] Following the decision by the European Union (EU) to include the Liberation Tigers of Tamil Eelam (LTTE) in its list of international terrorist organizations,[9] the LTTE demanded that EU monitors be expelled from the Norwegian-led Sri Lanka Monitoring Mission (SLMM), arguing that the mission was no longer either impartial or neutral.[10]

Thus in 2006 the UN and other multilateral security organizations were obliged to address recurring political and operational dilemmas in peace-

---

[6] 'Local ownership' here refers to full acceptance of the institutions and processes for upholding the rule of law by the people who will live under it and, in the long term, uphold it. This generally occurs only where the local stakeholders (government and population) have been centrally involved in defining those institutions and processes.

[7] ONUB was succeeded by a smaller political mission in 2007. Gowan, R., 'The UN and peace-keeping: taking the strain?', *Signal*, autumn 2006, pp. 44–51.

[8] Integrated Regional Information Networks (IRIN), 'Gbagbo snubs UN, New York meeting', 15 Sep. 2006, URL <http://www.irinnews.org/Report.aspx?ReportId=61094>; and IRIN, 'President says peace-keepers can leave', 20 Sep. 2006, URL <http://www.irinnews.org/Report.aspx?ReportId=61136>. The United Nations Operation in Côte d'Ivoire (UNOCI) and French peacekeeping forces (in Operation Licorne) remained in the country.

[9] The EU list of international terrorist organizations and persons linked to terrorist activities was established by Council Common Position of 27 December 2001 on the application of specific measures to combat terrorism, 2001/931/CFSP, *Official Journal of the European Communities*, L344 (28 Dec. 2001), pp. 93–96, and has been updated several times since then. The LTTE was added to the list by Council Common Position 2006/380/CFSP of 29 May 2006, *Official Journal of the European Union*, L144 (30 May 2006), pp. 25–29.

[10] In Jan. 2006 Norway announced that it would no longer align itself with the EU terrorist list because to continue to do so 'could cause difficulties for Norway in its role as neutral facilitator in certain peace processes'. Norwegian Ministry of Foreign Affairs, 'Norway's cooperation with the EU on the fight against terrorism', Press release no. 02/06, 4 Jan. 2006, URL <http://www.regjeringen.no/en/dep/ud/Press-Contacts/News/2006.html?id=419923>.

keeping and to re-evaluate the role of peacekeeping in the resolution of contemporary conflicts.

Section II of this chapter discusses recent efforts to enhance the efficacy and efficiency of peacekeeping. It also examines current paradigms of peacekeeping and questions whether they are still appropriate to address contemporary challenges. Section III illustrates some of the issues with developments during the year related to peacekeeping operations in four important theatres: Lebanon, Afghanistan, Timor-Leste and the Darfur region of Sudan. Section IV offers conclusions. Appendix 3A presents extensive data on the multilateral peace missions that were active for all or part of 2006.

II. Rethinking peacekeeping

Both the number and the scale of international peace operations reached unprecedented levels in 2006: over 148 000 military personnel and approximately 19 000 civilian police and civilian staff from 114 countries were deployed in 60 multilateral peace operations.[11] The continued surge in demand for deployable personnel and the difficulties experienced by states and by multilateral security organizations and alliances in meeting this demand warrant a close re-examination of the concept of peacekeeping—what it is, what it should aim to achieve and how it can best achieve those aims.

Peacekeeping has proved its effectiveness—and even necessity—in assisting conflict-ridden countries to establish lasting peace by creating an environment in which respect for human rights can be restored and democratization and sustainable development can take place. While there has been a dramatic rise in the number and intensity of intra-state conflicts since the early 1990s—these are now the dominant type of conflict and no interstate major armed conflict has been active in the past three years—the total number of conflicts around the world has declined dramatically in the same period. The *Human Security Report 2005* showed a strong correlation between this decline and the increase in international engagement, especially in the deployment of peace operations.[12]

The shift from inter- to intra-state conflict has been reflected in peacekeeping efforts. Prior to 1989, only two large-scale UN peace missions were deployed in the wake of an intra-state armed conflicts—in the Democratic Republic of the Congo and in Cyprus.[13] Since that time, only one major UN mission—the UN Mission in Ethiopia and Eritrea (UNMEE)—has been established in response to an interstate armed conflict.

[11] Figures are as of 31 Dec. 2006. As a statistical outlier, the 155 000 troops of the Multinational Force in Iraq are not included in the 2006 totals. The operation is, however, included in the total number of operations and listed in appendix 3A. On SIPRI's sources and methods see appendix 3A.

[12] Human Security Centre, University of British Columbia, *Human Security Report 2005: War and Peace in the 21st Century* (Oxford University Press: New York, N.Y., 2005), URL <http://www.humansecurityreport.info/>, p. 17.

[13] These were the UN Operation in the Congo (ONUC, 1960–64) and the UN Peacekeeping Force in Cyprus (UNFICYP, 1964–present).

A new phase in peacekeeping

The end of the cold war and the emergence of what have been called 'new wars'—predominantly intra-state conflicts characterized by, among other things, asymmetry between combatants, the avoidance of conventional battle, the deliberate targeting of civilians, the crucial role of economic motives and a fluidity of actors (global and local, state and non-state)—ushered in a new phase in the evolution of peacekeeping.[14] The frequency with which peace-keeping missions are now deployed in weak or failed states where the 'lingering forces of war and violence'[15] are still present after years of protracted civil conflict has led to significant developments in the conceptualization of peace-keeping, the articulation of mission mandates and the way in which those mandates are carried out.

Peace operations were traditionally mandated simply to monitor ceasefires, interpose between conflict parties and maintain buffer zones, and were bound by the principles of neutrality, impartiality, intervention only with the consent of the conflict parties and use of force only in self-defence. While peace-keepers are still fulfilling such a traditional mandate in theatres such as Cyprus, the Golan Heights and Kashmir, the early 1990s saw the launch of a second generation of UN operations in Angola, Cambodia and El Salvador. The range of tasks given to these new, multidimensional operations included, among many others, the disarmament, demobilization and reintegration (DDR) of combatants; justice and security sector reform; support for the extension of state authority and control; electoral assistance; and support to the protection of human rights. Many of these tasks are now common elements in the mandates of multidimensional peace operations.

While the established principles of peacekeeping have withstood the test of time, they have undergone considerable reinterpretation in the light of the new mandated tasks. For example, the recent trend towards more robust peace-keeping shows that positions on the use of force are evolving. At its meeting in February 2006, the UN Special Committee on Peacekeeping Operations endorsed the use of force in 'defence of the mandate' as well as in self-defence, and identified a need for 'an appropriately strong military and civilian police presence . . . in order to deter spoilers and establish the credibility of the United Nations'.[16] Similarly, the 2005 World Summit outcome document states that peacekeeping operations should have 'adequate capacity to counter

---

[14] Kaldor, M., *New and Old Wars: Organized Violence in a Global Era*, 2nd edn (Polity Press: Cambridge, 2006). See also appendix 2C in this volume.

[15] United Nations, Report of the Panel on United Nations Peace Operations, UN document A/55/305, 21 Aug. 2000.

[16] United Nations, Report of the Special Committee on Peacekeeping Operation and its Working Group at the 2004 Substantive Session, UN General Assembly document A/58/19, 26 Apr. 2004, URL <http://www.un.org/Depts/dpko/dpko/ctte/CTTEE.htm>; and United Nations, Report of the Special Committee on Peacekeeping and its Working Group: 2005 substantive session (New York, 31 January–25 February 2005), 2005 resumed session (New York, 4–8 April 2005), UN document A/59/19/Rev.1, undated, URL <http://www.un.org/Depts/dpko/dpko/ctte/5919rev.pdf>, paras 30 and 46.

hostilities and fulfil effectively their mandates'.[17] The shift away from limiting the use of force to self-defence is more pronounced in current national peacekeeping doctrines, such as those of the United Kingdom and the United States, which acknowledge the existence of a grey area between traditional peacekeeping and war fighting, and refer instead to the 'minimum necessary' or 'proportionate' use of force.[18]

More recent norms and concepts such as 'the responsibility to protect', human security and the rule of law are now ubiquitous in peace mission mandates.[19] This demonstrates, on the one hand, a palpable shift in the conception of sovereignty and, on the other, changes in the nature of conflicts themselves and in how the international community understands and seeks to resolve them.[20]

A debate of growing importance is whether the role of peacekeeping is merely to prevent the resumption of conflict by making it more difficult for spoilers to disrupt the peace or if it is also, and above all, to help rebuild states after conflict—what some observers have described as imposing a 'liberal peace'.[21] This entails a broader discussion of the political and moral implications of peace operations. It has also been argued that current peace operations often respond more to the concerns of the interveners to prevent insecurity and instability spilling over from failed states than to the needs of the country in conflict.[22] Afghanistan and Iraq provide the most extreme examples of a new dilemma in peace operations: how to balance the original interveners' counterterrorist aims with that of rebuilding the host state,[23] especially when elements of violence pitting local forces against the interveners continue. The initial post-invasion prioritization of counterterrorism by the US-led Multinational Force in Iraq (MNF-I) has clearly undermined rebuilding efforts in the

[17] United Nations, '2005 World Summit outcome', UN General Assembly document A/RES/60/1, 24 Oct. 2005, URL <http://www.un.org/summit2005/documents.html>, para. 92.

[18] Workshop on the Fundamental Principles of UN Peacekeeping, Saltsjöbaden, Sweden, 26–28 Sep. 2006; and Findlay, T., SIPRI, *The Use of Force in UN Peace Operations* (Oxford University Press: Oxford, 2002).

[19] E.g. the mandates of the United Nations Stabilization Mission in Haiti (MINUSTAH) and the United Nations Mission in Liberia (UNMIL). See appendix 3A.

[20] See Seybolt, T., SIPRI, *Humanitarian Military Intervention: The Conditions for Success and Failure* (Oxford University Press: Oxford, 2007); Holt, V. K. and Berkman, T. C., *The Impossible Mandate? Military Preparedness: The Responsibility to Protect and Modern Peace Operations* (Henry L. Stimson Center: Washington, DC, Sep. 2006); and Blocq, D. S., 'The fog of UN peacekeeping: ethical issues regarding the use of force to protect civilians in UN operations', *Journal of Military Ethics*, vol. 5, no. 3 (Nov 2006), pp. 201–13.

[21] Chandler, D., 'The responsibility to protect: imposing the liberal peace?', *International Peacekeeping*, vol. 11, no. 1 (spring 2004), pp. 59–81; and Doyle, M. W. and Sambanis, N., *Making War and Building Peace: United Nations Peace Operations* (Princeton University Press: Princeton, N.J., 2006).

[22] Tardy, T., 'Peace operations: reflections of, responses to, and victims of, globalization', Geneva Centre for Security Policy (GCSP) Policy Brief no. 4, 22 June 2006, URL <http://www.gcsp.ch/e/publications/Globalisation/Publications/>; and Bellamy, A., 'The "next stage" in peace operations theory?', *International Peacekeeping*, vol. 11, no. 1 (spring 2004), pp. 17–38.

[23] Edelstein, D. M., 'Foreign military forces and state-building: the dilemmas of providing security in post-conflict environments', Draft working paper for the Research Partnership on Postwar State-Building, University of Ottawa, Ottawa, 2006, URL <http://www.state-building.org/resources/Edelstein_RPPS_October2006.pdf>.

country. The situation in Iraq also clearly attests to the fact that, while a military force may be necessary to stabilize a country, a political resolution is still essential for sustainable peacebuilding. Finally, the role and status of the Multinational Force—which is legally sanctioned by the UN—have increasingly been called into question, particularly the way in which they have arguably blurred the line between peacekeeping and war fighting.

In recent years there has also been recognition that international peacekeeping and peacebuilding efforts that neglect the principle of local ownership are neither viable nor sustainable.[24] Meaningful consultation local stakeholders and their full participation in establishing objectives and priorities and assessing progress are needed if substantial political and popular support is to take root, as was clearly illustrated by the crisis in Timor-Leste in 2006 (see below).

Evolving attitudes and practices

The growth in the scale, scope and complexity of contemporary peacekeeping operations over the past decade suggests that the future of peacekeeping as a mechanism to assist countries in the transition from conflict to peace is assured. However, there is a growing recognition that understanding the conditions under which peacekeeping works best and the types of situation in which peacekeepers should or should not be deployed is crucial in order to avoid a repetition of the failures that occurred in the mid-1990s and to increase the efficacy and efficiency of peacekeeping.[25]

The establishment of ambitious mandates may be seen as evidence of growing international political commitment to peacekeeping, but this has created new operational dilemmas. These mandates often require technical and other capacity that is untested or not readily available.[26] The landmark 2000 *Report of the Panel on United Nations Peace Operations* (the Brahimi Report) proposed groundbreaking reform initiatives to improve the way in which peacekeeping operations are carried out.[27] Since then, much of the discourse about peacekeeping, as well as practical efforts to improve it, have focused on addressing the operational challenges of peacekeeping operations.[28] Both the UN and regional organizations and alliances such as the AU, the EU and the North Atlantic Treaty Organization (NATO) have taken steps to enhance their peacekeeping capacities. These steps have included undertaking substantial

---

[24] See e.g. Pouligny, B., *Peace Operations Seen from Below: UN Missions and Local People* (Hurst & Company: London, 2006); and Tschirgi, N., *Post-conflict Peacebuilding Revisited: Achievements, Limitations, Challenges* (International Peace Academy: New York, N.Y., 2004).

[25] Such failures occurred in e.g. Bosnia and Herzegovina, Rwanda and Somalia. See Findlay (note 18); and Seybolt (note 20).

[26] Center on International Cooperation, *Annual Review of Global Peace Operations 2007* (Lynne Rienner: Boulder, Colo., 2007).

[27] United Nations (note 15).

[28] See Durch, W. J. and Berkmanm T. C., *Who Should Keep the Peace? Providing Security for Twenty-First-Century Peace Operations* (Henry L. Stimson Center: Washington, DC, Sep. 2006).

organizational reforms, developing rapidly deployable forces, and building up expertise in areas such as civilian policing and the rule of law.

Although the UN and other organizations have made remarkable progress in building their capacities to conduct peace missions, merely possessing these capacities does not automatically mean that operations will be established when they are needed or guarantee that countries will participate in such operations. The moral imperative of peacekeeping may be universally accepted at the conceptual level, but a country's decision to participate is more likely to be based on self-interest. Ultimately, decisions about whether to set up or participate in a peace operation must take into account political dimensions and intra-regional divisions (if any) and are increasingly framed within the new 'risk' paradigm.[29] In the past, countries have attempted to mitigate risk by only sending their forces to UN-led peace operations. However, as UN operations have taken on more responsibilities, states have started to seek more control over the operations to which they contribute, for example by imposing strict conditions on the deployment of their forces or deploying their forces to non-UN missions in which they have greater influence.

The risk paradigm also entails the possibility of flawed risk assessments, which can have serious repercussions—as illustrated by the case of Afghanistan. Common security concerns may have brought NATO members together for the International Security Assistance Force (ISAF) mission, but the prospect of possible failure has caused divisions in the alliance.[30] Other factors influencing a country's participation in peacekeeping operations include the pressure placed on it by other members of the international community to conform to an agreed set of norms.[31] For example, Indonesia's offer to deploy peacekeepers to Lebanon in 2006 (see below) was in large part motivated by the Indonesian Government's desire to improve its image and standing in the international community. Conversely, domestic misgivings have greatly influenced countries' willingness, and in some cases ability, to participate in peace missions—particularly missions that have robust rules of engagement or are perceived as risky, morally unjustified or illegal. As the situation has deteriorated in Iraq since the 2003 invasion, many countries, bowing to domestic public pressure, have pulled out of the MNF-I. Spain is perhaps the highest-profile example. The sitting Popular Party government suffered electoral defeat in 2004 in what was widely interpreted as a reaction against its decision to commit soldiers to the MNF-I in the face of popular opposition.[32] Many

---

[29] See the Introduction in this volume for a discussion of 'risk' and 'threat' paradigms; and Chandler, D., *Empire in Denial: The Politics of State-Building* (Pluto Press: London, 2006).

[30] Coker, C., 'Between Iraq and a hard place: multinational co-operation, Afghanistan and strategic culture', *RUSI Journal*, vol. 151, no. 5 (Oct. 2006).

[31] Ladnier, J., 'National attitudes and motivations', eds D. Daniel, S. Wiharta, P. Taft and J. Ladnier, *Prospects for Peace Operations: Regional and National Dimensions* (Georgetown University Press: Washington, DC, forthcoming 2007).

[32] Also thought to have contributed significantly to the government's defeat in the 14 Mar. election were the bombings on trains in Madrid three days earlier and the government's initial decision to blame Basque separatists for the attack, which was ostensibly claimed by al-Qaeda as retaliation for Spain's involvement in Iraq. Ladnier (note 31).

countries have responded to domestic pressure by placing caveats on deployment of their forces in Afghanistan. These national caveats, even when they are imposed for legal and moral reasons, suggest the potential start of a worrying trend whereby the demands of participating countries may hinder the effective conduct of peace operations.

Recognizing that even the best set-up mission can be undermined by an unclear, inappropriate or unrealistic mandate, countries contributing to peace missions are increasingly calling for clear principles and guidelines, particularly when they are themselves subject to greater scrutiny and demands for accountability. In an effort to enhance both the efficacy and the efficiency of UN peacekeeping, the UN Department of Peacekeeping Operations (DPKO) embarked in 2006 on a major reform initiative, Peace Operations 2010.[33] One of the key objectives of Peace Operations 2010 is the development of a high-level doctrine document that states clearly the fundamental principles that apply, the major lessons learned and the factors that enable success in modern peace missions, along with the core functions of UN peace operations.

The missions surveyed in the next section illustrate how the principles and current practice of peacekeeping were tested by the conflicts in 2006.

III. Peace missions in practice in 2006

Lebanon: new tasks for UNIFIL

The new outbreak of hostilities between Israel and Lebanon's Hezbollah militia in July 2006 was largely unanticipated. The fighting was the most intense in the region in recent years: in the course of 34 days an estimated 1191 Lebanese and 162 Israelis were killed, 900 000 Lebanese civilians were displaced, and damage was inflicted on Lebanon's infrastructure that has been valued at an estimated $7–10 billion.[34]

In multiple and protracted negotiations on a resolution to the crisis, it was agreed that a sizeable multinational force would be needed to buttress a ceasefire. However, no agreement could be reached on what shape this force would take. On 26 July 2006 the Lebanese Government put forward a seven-point plan for resolving the conflict.[35] Elements of this plan were subsequently incorporated into UN Security Council Resolution 1701, which was adopted in

---

[33] For the latest draft of the main policy document see UN Department of Peacekeeping Operations, 'Capstone doctrine for United Nations peacekeeping operations: draft 2', 7 Sep. 2006, URL <http://www.challengesproject.net/roach/UN_Doctrine.do?pageId=96>.

[34] Lebanese Presidency of the Council of Ministers, Higher Relief Council, 'Lebanon under siege' website, URL <http://www.mfa.gov.il/MFA/Terrorism-+Obstacle+to+Peace/Terrorism+from+Lebanon-+Hizbullah/Israel-Hizbullah+conflict-+Victims+of+rocket+attacks+and+IDF+casualties+July-Aug+2006.htm>. On this conflict see chapter 2 in this volume; and International Crisis Group (ICG), *Israel/Palestine/Lebanon: Climbing Out of the Abyss,* Middle East Report no. 57 (ICG: Brussels, 25 July 2006), URL <http://www.crisisgroup.org/library/documents/asia/timor/120_resolving_timor_lestes_crisis.pdf>.

[35] 'Full text: Lebanon's seven-point proposal', BBC News, 8 Aug 2006, URL<http://news.bbc.co.uk/2/5256936.stm>.

August.[36] Resolution 1701 called for an immediate end to hostilities and the gradual withdrawal of Israeli forces from Lebanese territory. It authorized an increase in the mission strength of the UN Interim Force in Lebanon (UNIFIL, established in 1978) to 15 000 troops—nearly eight times its previous authorized mission strength. The reinforced UNIFIL was given a more proactive role, supporting the Lebanese Government's assertion of state control in southern Lebanon by ensuring that a 20 kilometre-wide buffer zone between the Litani River and the Blue Line (the UN-demarcated border between Israel and Lebanon) remain free of foreign armed personnel, assets and arms; assisting the government in securing its borders; and assisting in the implementation of the 1989 Taif Agreement, which calls for the disarmament of militias.[37] While UNIFIL was given robust rules of engagement, Resolution 1701 did not grant it powers under Chapter VII of the UN Charter and limited its use of force to 'areas of deployment of [UNIFIL] forces and as it deems within its capabilities'.[38] Israel had demanded that UNIFIL peacekeepers be gradually deployed alongside Lebanese forces in the buffer zone, to ensure that Hezbollah forces would not reoccupy territory there, as a precondition for withdrawing its 30 000 troops. It was hoped that the enlargement of UNIFIL and the presence of the Lebanese Army in the south of the country for the first time in decades would serve as strong confidence-building measures for the conflict parties, create space for political talks on a permanent and lasting ceasefire and, most importantly, improve security in the settlements that were affected.[39]

The UN and the Lebanese and Israeli governments agreed that the Israeli withdrawal should be completed by 1 October, and the corresponding staggered deployment of UN and Lebanese forces should be completed by 4 November.[40] However, when the ceasefire came into effect on 14 August,[41] it was still not clear when the expanded UNIFIL force would be ready for deployment nor was there agreement about which countries would contribute to the mission. Countries that were approached to contribute forces hesitated to make firm commitments until the mandate and the rules of engagement had been clarified. Also, something of a competition developed between different

[36] UN Security Council Resolution 1701, 11 Aug. 2006.

[37] The Taif Agreement, signed by the Lebanese Parliament on 22 Oct. 1989 at Taif, Saudi Arabia, was designed to end the civil war in Lebanon. For the full text of the agreement see URL<http://www.monde-diplomatique.fr/cahier/proche-orient/region-liban-taef-en>.

[38] United Nations Security Council Resolution 1701, para. 12. Chapter VII of the UN Charter authorizes the Security Council to use enforcement powers, including the use of force, to maintain or restore international peace and security in situations where the Security Council has determined the existence of 'any threat to the peace, breach of the peace or act of aggression'. The text of the Charter of the United Nations is available at URL <http://www.un.org/aboutun/charter>.

[39] England, A., 'Challenging times for Lebanon and Unifil', *Financial Times*, 18 Sep. 2006.

[40] United Nations, Report of the Secretary-General on the implementation of Resolution 1701 (2006) (for the period 11 to 17 August 2006), UN document S/2006/670, 18 Aug. 2006, URL <http://daccess-ods.un.org/TMP/2125790.html>.

[41] No formal ceasefire agreement was signed between the conflict parties, but the Lebanese Government and Hezbollah signalled their acceptance of Resolution 1701 on 12 Aug. 2006, and the Israeli Government followed suit on 13 Aug.

UN missions and between the UN and NATO in seeking contributions of personnel. Some troops and police originally earmarked for Afghanistan and Darfur were now diverted to UNIFIL.[42] The short timeline meant that the UN had to use a rolling deployment, including a vanguard of 3500 troops in mechanized battalions. Few countries have the capability to deploy mech-anized battalions rapidly, and thus it fell on European countries to assume responsibility for this advance deployment. Given UNIFIL's mandate and France's prominent role in securing Resolution 1701, France and other European countries were also expected to contribute significantly beyond the advance deployment. European countries now account for about half of UNIFIL's troop strength, making it the most sizeable European deployment under UN command since the early 1990s, but the commitments were only given after protracted negotiations. France, the lead nation for UNIFIL before the renewed hostilities, was initially slow to commit a large additional troop contingent to UNIFIL and to confirm that it would continue to lead the mis-sion. Finally, Italy committed 2500–3000 troops and France another 2000. China became the third largest contributor, with 1000 troops.[43]

The need for rapid deployment also obliged the UN Secretariat to innovate with regard to pre-mission planning—for example, making administrative pro-cesses more flexible by waiving the requirement for pre-inspection of troop contingents, and seconding a limited number of personnel without the usual two-month notification of member states. In spite of all of these efforts on the part of the UN, UNIFIL remained below its mandated strength at the end of 2006, with only 11 500 troops.[44]

Another important innovation related to the expansion of UNIFIL was the creation of a Strategic Military Cell at the UN specifically for strategic military command of the mission, which liaises directly with the UNIFIL Force Commander and reports directly to the UN Under-Secretary-General for Peacekeeping Operations. Strategic command of UN peace missions has previously been given to the DPKO. The new cell is comprised military officers from the troop-contributing countries and one officer from each of the permanent members of the Security Council.[45] The creation of the cell was one of the key conditions for European participation in the expanded UNIFIL.

The experience of UNIFIL in 2006 also underscored the fact that the principle of impartiality remains crucial in peacekeeping. Even though other Middle Eastern countries possessed armed forces that met the UN's require-ments for participation in the expanded UNIFIL, they were considered to be too closely linked to the conflict to be viable contributors. Similarly, Israel blocked early offers of troops from three Muslim countries, Bangladesh,

[42] 'The UN and Lebanon: robustly complicated', *The Economist*, 17 Aug. 2006.

[43] 'China ups Lebanon force to 1,000', BBC News, 18 Sep. 2006, URL <http://news.bbc.co.uk/2/5355128.stm>.

[44] United Nations, Department of Information, Peace and Security Section, 'United Nations peace-keeping operations', Background note, 31 Dec. 2006, URL <http://www.un.org/Depts/dpko/dpko/archive/2006/bn1206e.pdf>.

[45] Center on International Cooperation (note 26).

Indonesia and Malaysia, none of whose governments formally recognizes Israel.[46]-While UNIFIL now comprises troops from highly developed armed forces and has its own military command centre, it is vulnerable because of a lack of clarity over how to respond to breaches of Resolution 1701.[47] In its earlier incarnation, UNIFIL had failed to deter Israeli occupation and the actions of Palestinian guerrillas and Hezbollah,[48] and Resolution 1701 is strikingly similar to the Security Council resolutions that established UNIFIL's original mandate: resolutions 425 and 426.[49] Some observers have expressed doubts about the conflict parties' commitment to abiding by Resolution 1701, even after UNIFIL reaches its full complement of 15 000 soldiers.

Afghanistan: extending the boundaries of peacekeeping?

The outlook for Afghanistan was bleak at the end of 2006. Early optimism that the Afghanistan Compact would help the country to consolidate the gains made through the 2001 Bonn Agreement was quickly dissipated by a new wave of attacks by Taliban and other insurgent forces in the south of the country.[50] In 2006 the NATO-led International Security Assistance Force completed the phased expansion of its remit to all regions of Afghanistan by setting up regional commands—and taking over some of the role of the US-led counterterrorist Operation Enduring Freedom (OEF)—in the southern and eastern regions of the country, where resistance to coalition forces has been strongest. The first two stages of ISAF's expansion, in 2004 and 2005, had taken it into the north and west of the country, respectively, from its original base of operations in the Afghan capital, Kabul.

The core of the ISAF expansion strategy is establishing civil–military provincial reconstruction teams (PRTs) or taking over command of existing nationally led PRTs.[51] It was hoped that consolidating the different elements of ISAF under a single chain of command would reduce some of the confusion and

[46] Deen, T., Inter Press Service, 'U.N. force looks more European, less multinational', *Asian Tribune*, 30 Aug. 2006, URL <http://www.asiantribune.com/index.php?q=node/1775>.

[47] Barton, R. and Irvine, M., 'A new direction for Lebanon', *Transatlantic Security Notes & Comment*, vol. 1, no. 5 (Sep. 2006), URL <http://www.csis.org/media/csis/pubs/tsnc_0906.pdf>.

[48] Fattah, H. M. and Hoge, W., 'U.N. force in Lebanon offers harsh realities and lessons', *New York Times*, 17 July 2006.

[49] UN Security Council resolutions 425 and 426, 19 Mar. 1978.

[50] The Afghanistan Compact, which was launched on 31 Jan. 2006 at the London Conference on Afghanistan, is a 5-year framework for cooperation between the Afghan Government and the international community. The Agreement on Provisional Arrangements in Afghanistan pending the Reestablishment of Permanent Government Institutions (the Bonn Agreement), contained in United Nations, Letter dated 5 Dec. 2001 from the Secretary-General addressed to the President of the Security Council, UN document S/2001/1154, 5 Dec. 2001, URL <http://www.uno.de/frieden/afghanistan/talks/agreement. htm>. For more on the conflict in Afghanistan see chapter 2 in this volume.

[51] For the background to ISAF and PRTs see Jakobsen, P. V., *PRTs in Afghanistan: Successful but Not Sufficient*, Danish Institute for International Studies (DIIS), Report no. 6 (DIIS: Copenhagen, Feb. 2005), URL <http://www.diis.dk/graphics/Publications/Reports2005/pvj_prts_afghanistan.pdf>; and Cottey, A., 'Afghanistan and the new dynamics of intervention: counter-terrorism and nation building', *SIPRI Yearbook 2003: Armaments, Disarmament and International Security* (Oxford University Press: Oxford, 2003), pp. 167–94.

incoherence that had resulted when different regions were operating under separate national commands. In stage 3 of the expansion, which ended in July 2006, ISAF took over command of the four PRTs—led by Canada, the Netherlands, the UK and the USA—in the south of the country. In stage 4, completed in October 2006, the mission took over command of the eastern region, where US forces were concentrated. Discussions about ISAF's expansion had previously been driven in part by the US Government's desire to reduce the number of US troops participating in OEF. However, the increasing violence did not permit a US drawdown in 2006. Instead, the expansion into the eastern region largely involved 're-hatting' (redesignating as NATO forces) 12 000 US troops who were already in place.[52] By the end of the year, ISAF comprised 32 000 troops and was present in 19 provinces through 25 PRTs, making it the largest ground operation ever mounted by NATO.[53]

In 2006 NATO introduced a new strategy of establishing and maintaining secure zones, so-called ink spots, allowing development initiatives to take root in areas that had been relatively untouched by reconstruction efforts since the overthrow of the Taliban in 2001.[54] However, ISAF's ability to implement such measures in the south and east of Afghanistan was significantly hampered during the summer by fierce resistance from the Taliban insurgents and their supporters. The expansion into these areas necessitated a change in ISAF's role and its rules of engagement. NATO had announced new, more robust rules of engagement in 2005, reportedly permitting pre-emptive military strikes against perceived security threats.[55] In addition, in 2003 ISAF had outlined clear arrangements to enhance coordination and reduce conflict between its stabilization mission and OEF's counterterrorism mission.

In response to an upsurge of Taliban resistance in the southern provinces, ISAF launched Operation Medusa, a massive counter-insurgency offensive, in September 2006.[56] The two-week operation reportedly claimed the lives of hundreds of Taliban insurgents and five NATO soldiers.[57] ISAF personnel subsequently became the targets of insurgent attacks and between September and December the mission suffered the highest number of fatalities in any four-month period in its five-year history.[58]

ISAF's leadership has repeatedly emphasized that ISAF is distinct from OEF, but the growing number of direct military confrontations between ISAF and Taliban forces has reduced this distinction in the eyes of the local popula-

---

[52] Another 8000 US soldiers are deployed under OEF.

[53] 'NATO/Afghanistan: since expanding southward, ISAF has entered into direct confrontation with Taliban—results of one month of fighting', *Atlantic News*, 31 Aug. 2006.

[54] On the 'ink spot', or 'oil stain', strategy see Mills, G., 'Calibrating ink spots: filling Afghanistan's ungoverned spaces', *RUSI Journal*, vol. 15, no. 4 (Aug. 2006), pp. 16–25.

[55] Fox, D., 'NATO seeks stronger Afghan "rules of engagement"', Reuters AlertNet, 4 Aug 2005, URL <http://www.alertnet.org/thenews/newsdesk/SP58526.htm>; and Synovitz, R., 'Afghanistan: NATO troops apply "robust" new rules of engagement', Radio Free Europe/Radio Liberty, 7 Feb. 2006, URL <http://www.rferl.org/featuresarticle/2006/02/9749f7cd-a622-40ab-b636-a95744977452.html>.

[56] 'The challenges in Afghanistan', *Washington Times*, 25 Sep. 2006.

[57] Gall, C., 'New assault takes big toll on Taliban, NATO says', *New York Times*, 4 Sep. 2006.

[58] ISAF suffered 30 deaths between Sep. and Dec. 2006, and a total of 60 fatalities in 2006.

tion and even in ISAF's internal structure. Also, ISAF will in 2007 be, for the first time, under the command of a US four-star general, which may raise further concerns about the relationship between ISAF and OEF. British troops who had been stationed in the southern province of Helmand in early 2006 as part of OEF were re-hatted on 31 July as ISAF forces but continued to conduct counterterrorist operations.[59] Often such changes are not adequately communicated to the local population. The blurring of the line between a peace operation and a counterterrorist operation has concrete implications on the ground. The local population may not appreciate this nuanced technical difference and may perceive ISAF now to be only a combat operation. This could mean ultimately that ISAF forces in other parts of the country face more resistance.

In 2006 NATO, like the EU and the UN, had to overcome both logistical problems and difficulties in force generation. In September 2006 NATO intensified its efforts to obtain an extra 2500 troops for ISAF, including a 'hard-hitting' reserve battalion of 1000 soldiers that could be rapidly deployed wherever needed—first requested in early 2005—and another 1500 air support staff.[60] After nearly a month of negotiations, Poland announced that it would contribute 900 soldiers, who would arrive in early 2007; Romania pledged another 200 soldiers, to arrive at the end of 2006; and Canada and the UK together pledged another 900. These contributions came with conditions—for example, Poland preferred that most of its troops go to eastern Afghanistan, not to the south where they are most needed.[61]

Only a handful of NATO members are prepared to send their troops to southern and eastern Afghanistan. The most significant contingents have come from Canada, Denmark, the Netherlands, Romania and the UK along with NATO partner Australia. Other NATO members, including France, Germany, Italy, Spain and Turkey, have opted to send their personnel to calmer duty stations in the north and west. Even there, stringent national caveats on force protection—operating procedures that ensure maximum safety for personnel—have hampered the troops' ability to carry out their mandates. NATO's Riga summit of 28–29 November 2006 sought to address the issue of caveats and their impact on cohesion and interoperability of forces in Afghanistan. It yielded at least partial gains in lifting the national caveats, with several countries agreeing (in principle) to allow their troops to be deployed anywhere in the country as required.[62]

Questions were raised in 2006 about the relationship between the Afghan police and the ISAF mission. A report by the US departments of State and Defense criticized US efforts to train the Afghan police forces and the Afghan

[59] Leithead, A., 'Tough task ahead for Nato troops', BBC News, 31 July 2006, URL <http://news.bbc.co.uk/2/5232766.stm>.

[60] Morajee, R. and Dombey, D., 'Nato call for troops "unheeded for 18 months"', Financial Times, 12 Sep. 2006.

[61] Cooper, H., 'NATO Chief says more troops are needed in Afghanistan', New York Times, 22 Sep. 2006, section A, p. 10; and 'The challenges in Afghanistan' (note 56).

[62] Smith, J., 'Riga Summit delivers modest results despite tensions over Afghanistan', Transatlantic Security Notes & Comment, vol. 2, no. 1 (Jan. 2007), URL <http://www.csis.org/media/csis/pubs/tsnc_0107.pdf>. See also chapter 1 in this volume.

Army.[63] The report concluded that the USA had made some of the same mistakes in training police forces in Afghanistan that it made in Iraq, such as providing insufficient field training, tracking equipment poorly and relying on private contractors to conduct the training. The failure to create viable police forces to maintain law and order, the report alleged, had been pivotal in under-mining international efforts to stabilize both countries. Efforts to respond to some of the problems that the report identified are already under way. A pro-gramme that aims to hire 11 200 auxiliary police officers, primarily in the southern and eastern regions, has been established. The need for such a pro-gramme was highlighted by the fact that several local governors in these regions began hiring their own close protection personnel after being exposed to frequent attacks by the Taliban. Observers have argued that the hastily created programme—which provides only two weeks' training, while regular police officers are trained for eight weeks—could exacerbate the security situ-ation by placing poorly trained officers in the field and potentially allowing insurgents and criminals to infiltrate the force.

The reluctance of NATO member states to contribute their forces to ISAF and internal and public debates over such issues as command structures, policy harmonization, national caveats and the appropriateness of including counter-insurgency in ISAF's mandate in 2006 put NATO's solidarity and international image as an effective military alliance to the severest test. The outcome of ISAF, NATO's first mission outside the Euro-Atlantic zone, is perceived as vital not just to Afghanistan but also to the alliance itself. In the words of one Western diplomat, 'if NATO fails in Afghanistan, NATO fails'.[64]

Timor-Leste: back to the drawing board

Events in Timor-Leste in 2006, which led to the return of a relatively sub-stantial international engagement in the country and the deployment of an Australian-led military force, were perhaps the international community's biggest surprise—and a bitter pill to swallow. Just a year earlier, Timor-Leste was being heralded as one of the UN's biggest successes in peace and state building.

The UN presence in Timor-Leste dates back to 1999, when the Transitional Administration in East Timor (UNTAET) was established to provide security and assist the transition to independence after a referendum in favour of East Timor's secession from Indonesia.[65] UNTAET assumed executive functions

[63] US Department of State and US Department of Defense, Offices of Inspector General, *Interagency Assessment of Afghanistan Police Training and Readiness* (Departments of State and Defense: Washington, DC, Nov. 2006), URL <http://oig.state.gov/>. See also Glanz, J. and Rohde, D., 'Panel faults US-trained Afghan police', *New York Times*, 4 Dec. 2006.

[64] 'A senior Western diplomat' quoted in International Crisis Group (ICG), *Countering Afghanistan's Insurgency: No Quick Fixes*, Asia Report no. 123 (ICG: Brussels, 2 Nov. 2006), URL <http://www.crisisgroup.org/library/documents/asia/south_asia/123_countering_afghanistans_insurgency.pdf>.

[65] Dwan, R., 'Armed conflict prevention, management and resolution', *SIPRI Yearbook 2000: Armaments, Disarmament and International Security* (Oxford University Press: Oxford, 2000), pp. 117–18.

until the country's formal independence in May 2002. It was succeeded by two smaller peacebuilding missions that supported the country's efforts to build new state institutions.[66]

The UN was scheduled to withdraw from Timor-Leste entirely in May 2006, but its mandate was extended after a new outbreak of violence in the capital, Dili. In February around 400 members of the East Timorese armed forces (Falintil–Forças Armadas de Defesa de Timor-Leste, F-FDTL) demonstrated publicly to demand action from President Xanana Gusmão regarding alleged discrimination within the military against soldiers from the west of the country.[67] A government offer to set up a commission of inquiry was met with scepticism and about 200 more soldiers subsequently joined the strike. In March the commander of the F-FDTL, Brigadier General Taur Matan Ruak, dismissed all 594 striking soldiers, who constituted almost 40 per cent of the F-FDTL force.[68] The dismissed soldiers and their supporters continued to hold demonstrations in Dili and on 28 April the situation escalated into a breakdown of law and order, with widespread looting and arson attacks carried out by and between gangs of people from the eastern and western regions of Timor-Leste.[69] The national police force, the Polícia Nacional de Timor-Leste (PNTL), was unable to bring the situation under control. Prime Minister Marí Bim Amude Alkatiri, without consultating Gusmão, mobilized the army to restore order. The decision to use F-FDTL troops, who had no experience in riot control, to contain a volatile situation at the centre of which was a large group of former soldiers and their supporters, was widely criticized and its legality challenged.[70]

The violence stirred up latent social divisions. Although it claimed only 15 lives, it displaced 50 000 people and caused considerable damage to property.[71] It also led to conflict between various factions of the police and military services. As the situation threatened to escalate into civil war, the government declared a state of emergency on 24 May and requested international assistance in stabilizing the security situation.[72] The unrest also exacerbated tensions between Gusmão and Alkatiri. Gusmão subsequently requested Alkatiri's resignation, citing his mishandling of the security crisis as well as alle-

---

[66] These were the UN Mission of Support in Timor-Leste (May 2002–May 2005) and the UN Office in Timor-Leste (May 2005–Aug. 2006).

[67] United Nations, End of mandate report of the Secretary-General on the United Nations Office in Timor-Leste (for the period from 14 January to 12 April 2006), UN document to S/2006/251, 20 Apr. 2006.

[68] International Crisis Group (ICG), *Resolving Timor-Leste's Crisis*, Asia Report no. 120 (ICG: Brussels, 10 Oct. 2006), URL<http://www.crisisgroup.org/library/documents/asia/timor/120_resolving_timor_lestes_crisis.pdf>.

[69] 'Violence erupts at E Timor rally', BBC News, 28 Apr. 2006, URL <http://news.bbc.co.uk/2/4953574.stm>; and 'Emergency rule for E Timor leader', BBC News, 30 May 2006, URL <http://news.bbc.co.uk/2/5029794.stm>.

[70] At this point, a state of emergency had not yet been declared and the prime minister has no constitutional authority to mobilize the army. International Crisis Group (note 68).

[71] Tjahjadi, V., 'Hundreds of additional international troops land in East Timor 28 May', Agence France-Presse, 28 May 2006, Translated by National Technical Information Service (NTIS), US Department of Commerce.

[72] 'Emergency rule for E Timor leader' (note 69).

gations that he had authorized the distribution of arms to fuel the violence.[73] On 26 May, on the basis of a bilateral agreement, Australia deployed the 1300-strong International Security Forces (also known as Operation Astute and Joint Task Force) to disarm the armed groups and restore order in Timor-Leste.[74] The Timorese Government also asked the UN to remain in the country with a strengthened follow-on mission. Based on the recommendations of a multidisciplinary team dispatched by UN Secretary-General Kofi Annan in June to assess the situation,[75] the UN Security Council determined that an integrated multidimensional mission with a strong civilian policing component was needed. A controversial proposal by Timor-Leste that the International Security Forces should come under the command of the UN mission was eventually abandoned after vigorous opposition from Australia, the UK and the USA.[76]

UN Security Council Resolution 1704, adopted in August, authorized the establishment of the UN Integrated Mission in Timor-Leste (UNMIT), mandated to support the Timorese Government in 'consolidating stability, enhancing a culture of democratic governance, and facilitating political dialogue among Timorese stakeholders, in their efforts to bring about a process of national reconciliation and to foster social cohesion'. The mission is to consist of 'an appropriate civilian component, including up to 1608 police personnel, and an initial component of up to 34 military liaison and staff'.[77] Notably, it was decided in December 2006 that the police component of the mission would become the interim law enforcement agency. This will be the first time that the UN has assumed executive policing functions in a sovereign state.[78]

The events in Timor-Leste in 2006 demand a rigorous reassessment of the UN's earlier engagement there. Both the origin of the crisis and its escalation have been attributed to the international community's lack of sustained political and financial commitment to peacebuilding in the country and its desire for early withdrawal.[79] Rushed UN-led processes to establish the F-FDTL and the PNTL security forces created a defence force consisting of poorly integrated former resistance fighters, operating under a questionably delineated

---

[73] Agence France-Presse, 'East Timor rebels promise to turn in more weapons to Australian Forces: FM', 17 June 2006, Translated by National Technical Information Service (NTIS), US Department of Commerce.

[74] Agence France-Presse, 'Australia, East Timor agree on terms for military deployment', 25 May 2006, Translated by National Technical Information Service (NTIS), US Department of Commerce.

[75] United Nations, Report of the Secretary-General on Timor-Leste pursuant to Security Council resolution 1690 (2006), UN document S/2006/628, 8 Aug. 2006, URL <http://www.un.org/Docs/sc/sgrep06.htm>.

[76] UN Security Council Report, 'Timor-Leste', Security Council Report Monthly Forecast, Aug. 2006, pp. 10–13; and Security Council Report, 'Timor-Leste', Update Report no. 3, 17 Aug. 2006, URL <http://www.securitycouncilreport.org/>.

[77] UN Security Council Resolution 1704, 25 Aug. 2006.

[78] UN News Service, 'UN fully takes over policing role in Timor Leste after agreement with government', UN Daily News, no. DH/4786, 1 Dec. 2006, URL <http://www.un.org/news/dh/pdf/english/2006/01122006.pdf>. On the concept of executive policing see Dwan, R. (ed.), *Executive Policing: Enforcing the Law in Peace Operations*, SIPRI Research Report no. 16 (Oxford University Press: Oxford, 2002).

[79] See e.g. United Nations (note 75).

mandate, and a factious police force—many of whose officers had served in the Indonesian National Police before independence—which lacked the human and institutional capacity to control the unrest effectively.[80]

Although real progress was made in the operational aspects of East Timorese policing capacity after 2002, the institutional framework of the PNTL remains weak. At the heart of the problem is the failure to establish respect for the rule of law firmly within the PNTL's organizational culture. As this case illustrates, such normative change requires sustained and constant reinforcement and cannot easily be achieved through technical instruction. The report of the UN assessment mission also made clear that, because the UN had failed to find an inclusive approach and foster local ownership when building the rule of law, the relative stability and order that prevailed until April 2006 was inevitably fragile.

In the past, those conducting international operations have generally proved unwilling to engage in serious self-examination, and even incapable of doing so, owing both to time pressure in the mission and to political pressure from donors. In the case of rule of law missions, when self-assessments are made they often focus on quantitative factors, such as the numbers of officers trained and deployed or of command positions and police stations transferred into local hands. Both premature and overdue handovers can undermine long-term local ownership.[81] It is clear from the problems in Timor-Leste that the mission's progress and the local authorities' ability to uphold the rule of law unaided were misjudged. Developing a system for setting objectives and benchmarks and for measuring progress is complex and time consuming, but it could yield significant benefits in areas such as the timing of handovers of responsibility and ensuring that in future, lessons are learned and applied.

The United Nations–African Union hybrid mission in Darfur

At the end of 2005 discussions between the UN and the AU were under way about the possibility and viability of the UN taking over peacekeeping responsibilities in Darfur from the AU. The AU had been struggling to keep the AU Mission in Sudan (AMIS) operational with only half of the logistical capacity and funds necessary. The proposed handover would have involved subsuming AMIS into the existing UN Mission in Sudan (UNMIS), which was at that time tasked with assisting in the implementation of the Comprehensive Peace Agreement between the Sudanese Government and Sudan's People's Liberation Movement/Army (SPLM/A).

It was generally hoped that enlargement of UNMIS—with reliable funding and a robust renewed mandate backed up by well-trained and well-equipped forces and by civilian personnel from UN agencies—would improve the chances of tackling the complex challenges in Darfur. For several months the

---

[80] Lindberg, S. 'Case study: Timor-Leste', eds A. S. Hansen and S. Wiharta, SIPRI, *Local Ownership and the Rule of Law after Conflict* (Oxford University Press: Oxford, forthcoming 2007).

[81] Hansen, A. S. and Wiharta, S., *The Transition to a Just Order: Establishing Local Ownership after Conflict*, Policy report (Folke Bernadotte Academy Publications: Stockholm, Apr. 2007).

UN sought, on an informal basis, to obtain the agreement of troop-contributing countries to provide military personnel for a new mission. However, the countries approached expressed deep concern that not even a robust UN operation would fare any better than AMIS, given the lack of a strong commitment from the conflict parties to a peace process.[82] To complicate matters, Sudan was not in favour of the UN taking over responsibilities in Darfur and instead softened its earlier hostile stance towards AMIS.[83]

The Darfur Peace Agreement (DPA) was reached in May 2006 between the Sudanese Government and the main opposition group in Darfur, the faction of the Sudanese Liberation Movement/Army (SLM/A) led by Minni Minawi, following two years of intense and difficult negotiations brokered by the AU.[84] The DPA was intended to end a conflict that had claimed 200 000 lives or more and displaced 2 million people since 2003.[85] However, two parties to the negotiations—the SLM/A faction led by Abdel Wahid Mohamed Nur and the Justice and Equality Movement (JEM)—refused to subscribe to the accord.

The DPA sets out principles for sharing power and wealth in the region along with ceasefire and security arrangements. It also provides the framework for 'Darfur–Darfur Dialogue and Consultation': 'a conference in which representatives of all Darfurian stakeholders can meet to discuss the challenges of restoring peace to their land, overcoming the divisions between communities, and resolving the existing problems to build a common future'.[86] The DPA calls for the disarmament and demobilization of the pro-government Janjaweed militia by mid-October 2006 and the scaling down of the paramilitary Popular Defense Forces. The AU is charged with verifying the disarmament process. The DPA also calls for the reintegration of approximately 5000 former combatants into the Sudanese Armed Forces and the police forces, while another 3000 are to be supported through education and training programmes. Critically, the DPA details measures to increase security for internally displaced persons and humanitarian supply routes, specifically the establishment of buffer zones around the camps and the humanitarian assistance corridor. The parties also agreed to create a commission to work with the UN to help refugees and internally displaced persons to return to their homes.[87] However, the DPA conspicuously lacks any reference to the UN taking over peacekeeping responsibilities.

[82] Turner, M. and England, A., 'UN looks out of Africa for help in ending Sudan's cycle of violence', *Financial Times*, 18 Jan. 2006.

[83] Fisher, J., 'Darfur's doomed peacekeeping mission', BBC News, 9 Mar. 2006, URL <http://news.bbc.co.uk/2/4790822.stm>

[84] The Darfur Peace Agreement was signed at Abuja, Nigeria, on 5 May 2006. For the text of the agreement see URL <http://www.cfr.org/publication/11020/>. On the agreement see International Crisis Group (ICG), *Darfur's Fragile Peace Agreement*, Africa Briefing no. 39 (ICG: Brusssels, 20 June 2006), URL <http://www.crisisgroup.org/library/documents/africa/horn_of_africa/b039_darfur_s_fragile_peace_agreement.pdf>.

[85] 'Main parties sign Darfur accord', BBC News, 5 May 2006, URL <http://news.bbc.co.uk/2/4978668.stm>.

[86] Darfur Peace Agreement (note 84), article 31.

[87] United Nations, Report of the Secretary-General on Darfur, UN document S/2006/591, 28 July 2006.

The political provisions of the DPA include the establishment of a new body, the Transitional Darfur Regional Authority (TDRA), to administer the three states of the Darfur region. The TDRA is given responsibility for implementation of the DPA. The rebel factions are guaranteed a majority position in the TDRA but are not granted the national vice-presidency they had sought. Under the terms of the DPA, a popular referendum will be held in 2010 to decide whether to establish Darfur as a unitary region with a single government.

In the face of persistent, profound objections from the Sudanese Government to a UN-commanded operation in Darfur, in August 2006 the UN Security Council adopted Resolution 1706, which expanded the operational and geographical mandate of UNMIS to include Darfur.[88] Implementation of Resolution 1706 would have brought the total strength of UNMIS to 30 000 military and civilian personnel—in part because AMIS would be subsumed into the UN mission—making it the largest operation conducted in the UN's history.[89] The adoption of the resolution was welcomed by many as a significant step that moved the fragile peace process forward and finally paved the way for putting in place a UN operation and effectively addressing the dire humanitarian situation in the region.

However, the Government of Sudan strongly opposed Resolution 1706, threatening to expel AU personnel from its territory upon the expiration of AMIS's mandate on 30 September 2006 if the UN were to take over the mission.[90] The AU was forced to extend the mandate of AMIS for a further three months, while negotiations about the UN takeover continued. The AU and the UN proposed an emergency $21 million 'light support' package of resources to enable AMIS to fulfil its expanded mandate. This included the provision of 105 UN military staff, 33 police advisers and 25 civilian staff, along with logistical and material support.[91] Although the Sudanese Government agreed in principle to the support package, it granted access to only nine military staff and nine police advisers.

In November, the AU and the UN intensified their negotiations with the Sudanese Government, pushing for full implementation of the light support package and for a longer-term 'heavy support' package that would include substantial air assets and significant military capacity, police advisers and other civilian staff.[92] More importantly, a proposed alternative to a fully fledged UN mission—a UN–AU 'hybrid mission'—was agreed to in principle by the Sudanese Government. The hybrid mission will retain a predominantly

---

[88] UN Security Council Resolution 1706, 31 Aug. 2006.

[89] The resolution authorized increasing the size of the mission by 17 000 military personnel, 3300 civilian police (including 16 formed police units) and an appropriate civilian component in order to support implementation of the DPA. For further details about the elements of the proposed expansion of UNMIS see United Nations (note 87); and UN Security Council Resolution 1706.

[90] Green, M., 'Sudan threatens to expel peacekeepers from Darfur', *Financial Times*, 6 Sep. 2006.

[91] United Nations, Letter dated 28 Sep. 2006 from the Secretary-General addressed to the President of the Security Council, UN document S/2006/779, 29 Sep. 2006.

[92] United Nations, Monthly report of the Secretary-General on Darfur, UN document S/2006/1041, 28 Dec. 2006.

African character but will benefit from UN command-and-control structures and could be funded from the UN's peacekeeping assessment budget. It will be the first mission in which two organizations have joint command over a single operation. The Special Representative, the head of the mission, will be jointly appointed by the AU and the UN, while the Force Commander and the Deputy Force Commander will be appointed by the AU in consultation with the UN Secretary-General. The structure and mandated tasks of the hybrid mission will resemble those of the proposed UN mission. A joint technical assessment team and a further 25 police officers were sent to Darfur at the end of December 2006, but little further headway has been made to operationalize the new mission.

Although it was born out of political compromise, from an operational perspective the UN–AU hybrid mission is an important development in peacekeeping. The interaction between UN peace missions and those conducted by regional organizations or ad hoc coalitions has developed significantly in recent years. First, the previous norm of successive missions (either non-UN followed by UN or vice versa) is being replaced by a trend for simultaneous implementation of two or more missions in a given country.[93] Although they may be co-located and cooperate closely, the simultaneous missions are deployed and commanded separately and perform different functions according to the comparative advantages of the respective organizations conducting them. For example, the Operation in Côte d'Ivoire (UNOCI) is supported by the French military deployment Operation Licorne; in the Democratic Republic of the Congo, the EU's policing and civilian security sector reform missions (EUPOL Kinshasa and EUSEC DR Congo, respectively) supplement the extensive mandate of the UN Organization Mission in the Democratic Republic of the Congo (MONUC). The EU's military operation (EUFOR RD Congo) supported MONUC to enhance security during the election period. In Darfur, the EU, NATO and the UN collaborated to provide substantial support to the AU mission. The EU contributed military advisers who assisted the AU in establishing the command-and-control structure of AMIS and, more importantly, has provided most of the mission's budget. NATO provided crucial strategic airlift resources, and the UN has provided assistance with mission planning since AMIS's inception.[94]

The difficulties that the international community has experienced in establishing an effective peacekeeping mission in Darfur are a vivid reminder that the consent of the host government is crucial for the success of peace operations carried out by the UN or by other organizations or even coalitions of the willing (something the US-led Multinational Force in Iraq also felt keenly in

---

[93] E.g. the AU's African Mission in Burundi was succeeded by the much larger UN Operation in Burundi, which also had more responsibilities.

[94] European Union, 'Factsheet: EU support to the African Union Mission in Darfur–AMIS', document no. AMIS II/05, Oct. 2006, URL <http://www.consilium.europa.eu/uedocs/cmsUpload/0610 17factsheet5AMISII.doc.pdf>; and North Atlantic Treaty Organization, 'NATO's assistance to the African Union for Darfur', 24 Nov. 2006, URL <http://www.nato.int/issues/darfur/practice.html>.

2006).[95] Whether the hybrid mission will be fully deployed in 2007 in the shape in which it was originally conceived remains to be seen.

IV. Conclusions

Europe's difficulties in raising sufficient troops for both ISAF and UNIFIL raise serious questions about the EU's ability and commitment to serve as a global security actor. They also underline the fact that issues of force generation are not merely technical but deeply political. Domestic concerns in the European capitals about putting troops in harm's way certainly accounted in large part for the reluctance to commit substantial troops to either operation, not least because ISAF was already becoming in part a combat operation and UNIFIL seemed likely to develop along the same lines. Aside from that, both operations suffered from continuing political tensions between Washington and Brussels over the USA's policy on its 'global war on terrorism' and associated policies towards the Middle East.

Even so, as the missions reviewed in this chapter illustrate, peacekeeping overall has managed to adapt operationally to changes in the nature of conflict. There is a broad spectrum of operations deployed, ranging from small training missions to large-scale multidimensional operations. The UN was able to deploy quickly the crucial first wave of reinforcement for UNIFIL; NATO was ultimately able to reach its desired mission strength in ISAF; and Australia also rapidly responded to the unrest in Timor-Leste. At the same time, the crises that provided the contexts for these efforts underscored the fact that, while the international security environment is rapidly changing and peacekeeping needs to adapt in new ways, respecting established principles—such as consent from the host government and the local population, impartiality, and political will from the conflict parties and the wider community—remains essential. Concomitantly, the peacebuilding efforts in Timor-Leste and Afghanistan highlight the difficulties of coordinating interrelated complex functions which are often assumed by a multitude of actors on the ground. Further, failures in Timor-Leste and Afghanistan attest to the fact that there is no alternative to implementing the principle of local ownership.

However, any discussion about the prospects for peacekeeping must ultimately examine the fundamental question of what peacekeeping should be trying to achieve and for whom. The international community has proved capable of ensuring that the 'hardware' of peace operations is put in place, and of establishing missions that effectively carry out the main elements of their mandates. However, developments such as Timor-Leste's relapse into violence and Israel's military incursion into Lebanon in 2006 cast doubt on whether this is enough to justify calling the missions effective or successful: both crises occurred in places where an existing mission was deployed. This

---

[95] 'Stalemate over UN's Darfur force', BBC News, 6 June 2006, URL <http://news.bbc.co.uk/2/5050910.stm>.

suggests that evaluation of peace operations must take into account, and even focus on, the impact they have on the host countries.

In its attempts to keep pace with the changes in conflict, the international community has, over the past 16 years, placed strong emphasis on the efficiency of peace operations—sometimes at the expense of their efficacy. A more refined conceptualization of peacekeeping is now needed. One step forward could be the introduction of a 'demand-driven' approach, in which peace operations are conceived, planned and evaluated based on critical analysis of the underlying obstacles to peace and the broader human security needs of the host country—offering the possibility of more lasting change.

As the primary actor in maintaining international peace and security, it is the UN that will have the greatest influence on the future of peacekeeping. It is to be hoped that through Peace Operations 2010, the UN will set a new agenda that meets the many conceptual and practical challenges of peacekeeping today.

Appendix 3A. Multilateral peace missions in 2006

SHARON WIHARTA and KIRSTEN SODER

I. Global trends

A total of 60 peace missions were conducted in 2006, deploying 148 412 military and 19 154 civilian personnel.[1] The number of multilateral peace missions conducted each year has risen steadily since 2002, coinciding with several conflicts reaching negotiated settlements.[2] While the overall increase in the number of missions has been relatively small (from 48 in 2002), the number of personnel deployed has increased dramatically in the same period (see figure 3A.1).

In 2006, 167 566 personnel were deployed to peace missions, a higher number than in any previous year and an increase of over 36 000 personnel—or 28 per cent—since 2005. United Nations missions accounted for just over half of personnel deployments in 2006, although regional organizations and alliances have together conducted more missions than the UN in recent years.[3] With 73 505 troops and military observers and 14 061 civilian police and staff in 20 missions, the UN remains the single largest actor in peace operations, and in 2006 it deployed more than twice as many personnel as it did in 2000. Because of expansion of the International Security Assistance Force (ISAF) mission in Afghanistan, the North Atlantic Treaty Organization (NATO) deployed a total of 49 260 personnel to peace missions in 2006, its highest level of deployment since 2002 but lower than the 66 000 forces it deployed to the Balkans in 1999. Similarly, the African Union (AU) and the European Union (EU) have quadrupled their troop deployments since 2003 but still contribute relatively few troops. Of the 60 missions conducted in 2006, 10 had over 5000 personnel, twice the number of missions of this size in 2000, highlighting a trend towards larger peace missions. With personnel deployments to peace missions expected to increase further in 2007, the international community will almost certainly face critical problems finding the necessary personnel to keep missions operating at their approved full capacity.

The increase in the number of peace missions is also pushing the issue of financing to the fore in policy discussions. The combined known cost of multilateral peace operations in 2006 reached the unprecedented level of $5.5 billion (at constant (2005)

---

[1] Figures are as of 31 Dec. 2006. As a statistical outlier, the 155 200 troops of the Multinational Force in Iraq are not included in the 2006 totals nor are they included in calculation of the trend series. The Iraq operation is, however, included in the total number of operations and appears in table 3A.2. On SIPRI's sources and methods see section III.

[2] It should not be assumed that there is a direct inverse causal link between the number of armed conflicts and the number of peace operations.

[3] The regional organizations and alliances deploying peace missions in 2006 were the African Union (AU), the Economic and Monetary Community of Central African States (CEMAC), the Commonwealth of Independent States (CIS), the European Union (EU), the North Atlantic Treaty Organization (NATO), the Organization of American States (OAS) and the Organization for Security and Co-operation in Europe (OSCE). Non-standing (ad hoc) coalitions are counted separately.

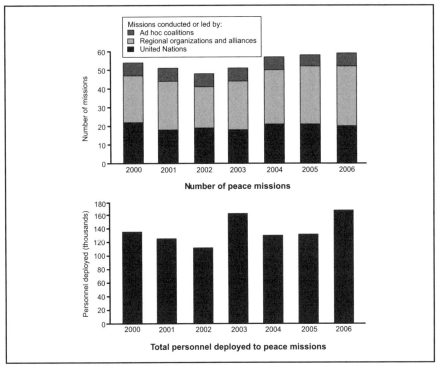

Figure 3A.1. Number of peace missions and number of personnel deployed to peace missions (excluding the Multinational Force in Iraq), 2000–2006

Source: SIPRI Multilateral Peace Operations Database, URL <http://conflict.sipri.org/>.

prices and exchange rates), continuing a steady rise since 2002.[4] If the costs associated with personnel deployment were included in EU and NATO budgets, then the total cost of peace missions for 2006 would be significantly higher. The UN accounts for the vast majority of the total cost and in 2006 spent 75 per cent more on peace operations than it did in 2000 (see figure 3A.2). The EU's expenditure on peace operations in 2006 was 40 times greater than in 2000, a reflection of its growing involvement in international security matters.

Seven new multilateral peace missions were established in 2006. The UN Integrated Office in Sierra Leone (UNIOSIL) opened following the departure of the multidimensional UN Mission in Sierra Leone (UNAMSIL). The international community sustained its commitment to the consolidation of peace in Timor-Leste with the launch of the fifth UN mission to the country—the UN Integrated Mission in Timor-Leste (UNMIT)—and the deployment of the Australian-led International Security Forces (ISF).[5] The AU launched the AU Mission for Support to the Elections in the Comoros (AMISEC). The EU launched the EU Police Mission for the Palestinian Territories (EUPOL COPPS) and the military operation EUFOR RD Congo in support of the United Nations Organisation Mission in the Democratic Republic of the Congo (MONUC) during the election process there. Following the

---

[4] This is the sum of the cost of operations carried out by the EU, NATO and the UN.
[5] The ISF is also known as Operation Astute and Joint Task Force.

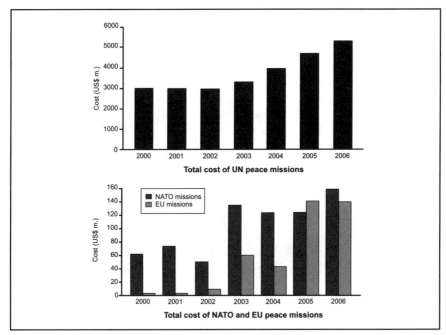

Figure 3A.2. Costs of United Nations, North Atlantic Treaty Organization and European Union peace missions, 2000–2006

Note: Figures for UN missions are for core operational costs, including the costs of deploying personnel. Figures for EU and NATO missions are for common costs and exclude, among other things, deployment costs.

Source: SIPRI Multilateral Peace Operations Database, URL <http://conflict.sipri.org/>.

May 2006 referendum in favour of Montenegrin independence, the Organization for Security and Co-operation in Europe (OSCE) opened a new mission in Montenegro, tasked with assisting the government in institution and capacity building in the rule of law. Two of the new missions, AMISEC and EUFOR RD Congo, terminated during the course of the year, having been deployed to assist during national elections.

The number of new peace mission launched each year has been decreasing since 2003 (see figure 3A.3), but was still higher in 2006 than during 2000–2002, which partly explains the near constant number of operational missions during the period 2000–2006. A majority of the new missions launched since 2001 have been follow-on missions and only two of the seven new missions in 2006 were located in new theatres. This fact reflects the international community's continued faith in international engagement as means to restore and build peace, but, as discussed in chapter 3, events in 2006 also raised questions about the effectiveness of past operations in establishing durable peace.

Six missions terminated in 2006: the UN Operation in Burundi (ONUB), the UN Office in Timor-Leste (UNOTIL), AMISEC, the EU's Aceh Monitoring Mission (AMM), the EU Police Advisory Team in the Former Yugoslav Republic of Macedonia (EUPAT) and EUFOR RD Congo.

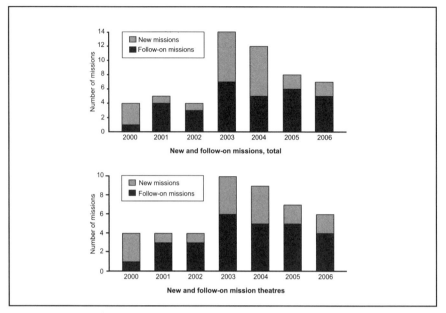

Figure 3A.3. Number of new and follow-on peace missions and number of theatres of new and follow-on peace missions, 2000–2006

Source: SIPRI Multilateral Peace Operations Database, URL <http://conflict.sipri.org/>.

II. Regional trends and developments

There were 15 peace missions in Africa in 2006 (see table 3A.1), one more than in 2005. Africa continues to be the region with the highest number of large, multidimensional peace operations and the one on which the UN, with eight missions, has focused its attention. Regional organizations were also strongly engaged, increasing the number of peace missions they conducted in Africa from four to six in 2006. Europe is the region with the highest number of peace missions, with a total of 22. Of these, 19—most of them civilian, institution-building missions—were carried out by regional organizations. Europe and Africa are the only regions where regional organizations have a strong presence.

With only nine peace missions deployed in 2006, Asia was the region with the second lowest number of peace missions. Of these, three were conducted by non-standing coalitions of states. Asia and the Middle East were the regions with the most missions led by non-standing coalitions. The launch of EUPOL COPPS brings the total number of peace missions in the Middle East to 11. The region has been the location of several long-standing traditional peacekeeping missions, but in the past two years has been the new geographic focus of EU civilian peace missions. The Americas was the region with the lowest number of peace missions in 2006.

Some significant missions that are not highlighted in chapter 3 are briefly discussed below.

Africa

The AU conducted two missions in 2006: the African Union Mission in Sudan (AMIS), which is discussed in chapter 3, and AMISEC in the Comoros. AMISEC was mandated to help create a secure environment for free and fair elections in May 2006 and in particular to ensure that the Comoran security forces did not interfere in the electoral process. The mission underlined the AU's sustained engagement in the Comoran peace process. A fragile power-sharing agreement, brokered in 2001 by the AU's predecessor, the Organization of African Unity, gave the individual islands of Grande Comore, Anjouan and Mohéli their own semi-autonomous governments and presidents, with a rotating national presidency.[6] AMISEC, which comprised nearly 500 soldiers and police officers under South African leadership, was deployed promptly after AU authorization. The mission terminated in June 2006 having executed its mandate successfully.

Asia

Although they were somewhat overshadowed by the crisis in Timor-Leste and the ambiguity of the situation in the Solomon Islands, there were quiet successes in the field of peace operations in Asia. The EU-led Aceh Monitoring Mission, established in 2005, was given the task of monitoring the disarmament, demobilization and reintegration of Free Aceh Movement (Gerakan Aceh Merdeka, GAM) troops and the withdrawal of Indonesian military and police forces. The AMM was also the first peace mission in which the Association of South East Asian Nations (ASEAN) has participated. This represents a groundbreaking shift away from the organization's long-standing principle of non-interference in the activities of member states. The presence of ASEAN and EU monitors contributed significantly to confidence building between the conflict parties and for this reason the mission's mandate was extended three times at the request of both. The mission closed after elections were conducted successfully in December 2006.

The Australian-led Regional Assistance Mission to Solomon Islands (RAMSI) was established in 2003 to restore law and order and assist the Solomon Islands Government in institution and capacity building in the rule of law. The mission, which had previously been seen as a success and a model of cooperative intervention, suffered setbacks in 2006 when riots erupted after parliamentary elections in April. Australia, Fiji, New Zealand and Papua New Guinea, the countries contributing to RAMSI, reinforced their presence with an additional 389 troops and 75 police officers to restore order. Subsequently, RAMSI was openly criticized for failing to foresee the riots, failing to address underlying problems of economic inequality and rural development in the Solomon Islands, and other perceived shortcomings.[7] The new prime minister of the Solomon Islands, Manasseh Sogavare, accused Australia of using RAMSI to interfere in the country's domestic affairs and of neo-colonialism.[8]

---

[6] The All-Party Framework Agreement (Fomboni Agreement) was signed by representatives of all 3 islands as well as the opposition parties on 17 Feb. 2001.

[7] Moore, C., 'Helpem fren: the Solomon Islands and RAMSI, 2003–2006', Paper presented at the National President's Forum, Australian Institute of International Affairs, Sydney, 14 July 2006, URL <http://operationspaix.net/Helpem-Fren-The-Solomon-Islands>.

[8] 'Solomon PM accuses Australia', BBC News, 18 Sep. 2006, URL <http://news.bbc.co.uk/2/5355220.stm>

Table 3A.1. Number of peace missions conducted by the United Nations, regional organizations and alliances, and ad hoc coalitions by region, 2006

Conducting organization	Africa	Americas	Asia	Europe	Middle East	World
United Nations[a]	8	1	4	3	4	20
Regional organizations or alliances	6	2	2	19	4	33
Non-standing coalitions	1	–	3	–	3	7
Total	**15**	**3**	**9**	**22**	**11**	**60**

[a] These figures include both peace missions led by the UN Department of Peacekeeping Operations and those led by the UN Department of Political Affairs.

Source: SIPRI Multilateral Peace Operations Database, URL <http://conflict.sipri.org/>.

The already tense situation worsened when Australia's high commissioner was expelled in September for allegedly interfering in the enquiry into the April riots and when Australian peacekeeping troops raided the prime minister's offices searching for evidence in an extradition dispute between Australia and the Solomon Islands.[9] At the end of the year, the uneasy and increasingly hostile relationship between the host government and RAMSI remained unresolved, suggesting that the mission has a challenging year ahead.

Middle East

The EU launched two missions within two months to support the Palestinian Authority (PA) with institution and capacity building in the rule of law: the EU Border Assistance Mission for the Rafah Crossing Point (EU BAM Rafah) in November 2005 and EUPOL COPPS in January 2006. Both missions are under the unified command of the EU Special Representative for the Middle East Peace Process. The framework for EU BAM Rafah's establishment was provided by the Agreement on Movement and Access signed between the Israeli Government and the PA on 15 November 2005 to allow reopening of the Rafah crossing point.[10] The mission was authorized to monitor, verify and evaluate the performance of PA border control, security and customs officials; to support the PA's capacity building in border control; and to support liaison between the PA, the Israeli Government and Egypt. Movement through the crossing point was once again severely restricted at Israel's insistence following an attack by Palestinian militants on an Israeli Army outpost on 25 June 2006 and a subsequent outbreak of violence. Of the approximately 340 000 people who used the Rafah crossing point between November 2005 and January 2007, only 80 000 did so after 25 June 2006.[11]

---

[9] The Solomon Islands Government refused to extradite Julian Moti, an Australian lawyer appointed Attorney General of the Solomon Islands, to Australia to face criminal charges. 'Solomon Islands "hiding fugitive"', BBC News, 2 Oct. 2006, URL <http://news.bbc.co.uk/2/5398684.stm>.

[10] The Agreement on Movement and Access and the Agreed Principles for Rafah Crossing, finalized on 15 Nov. 2005, are available at URL <http://www.met.gov.ps/pdf/rafahag.pdf>.

[11] United Press International, 'EU criticizes Rafah crossing closures', 18 Jan. 2007, URL <http://www.upi.com/InternationalIntelligence/view.php?StoryID=20070118-033712-2384r>.

Israel and EU BAM Rafah mission personnel accused the Palestinians of smuggling arms and money through the Rafah crossing into the Gaza Strip.[12] The victory of Hamas in Palestinian parliamentary elections in January 2006 also complicated matters, as the Israeli Government refused to allow Hamas ministers to cross the Egypt–Gaza Strip border.[13]

EUPOL COPPS was launched on 1 January 2006 to assist in building the capacity of the Palestinian police and criminal justice officials through implementation of the Palestinian Civil Police Development Plan, mentoring the Palestinian Civil Police, coordinating donor assistance for the Palestinian Civil Police Development Programme Trust Fund and advising on police-related criminal justice matters. The mission's three-year mandate reflects the long-term commitment of the EU to security sector reform in the Middle East. However, political developments, particularly the Hamas election victory and the decision of the Middle East Quartet—the EU, the UN, the USA and Russia—to reduce financial aid to the Palestinian territories, hampered the mission. EUPOL COPPS has neither reached its full strength of 33 civilian personnel nor been able to implement in full its assigned tasks.[14]

III. Sources and methods

Table 3A.2 provides data on the 60 multilateral peace missions that were ongoing or terminated in 2006. The table lists those missions that were conducted under the authority of the UN and operations conducted by regional organizations and alliances or by non-standing (ad hoc) coalitions of states that were sanctioned by the UN or authorized by a UN Security Council resolution, with the stated intention to: (*a*) serve as an instrument to facilitate the implementation of peace agreements already in place, (*b*) support a peace process, or (*c*) assist conflict-prevention or peacebuilding efforts.

SIPRI uses the UN Department of Peacekeeping Operations (DPKO) description of peacekeeping as a mechanism to assist conflict-ridden countries to create conditions for sustainable peace—which may include monitoring and observing ceasefire agreements; serving as confidence-building measures; protecting the delivery of humanitarian assistance; assisting with the demobilization and reintegration processes; strengthening institutional capacities in the areas of judiciary and the rule of law (including penal institutions), policing, and human rights; electoral support; and economic and social development. The table thus covers a broad range of peace missions to reflect the growing complexity of mandates of such missions and the potential for missions to change over the course of their mandate. The table does not include good offices, fact-finding or electoral assistance missions, nor does it include peace missions comprising non-resident individuals or teams of negotiators, or missions not sanctioned by the UN.[15]

---

[12] Palestine Media Centre, 'EU monitors to close Rafah crossing due to alleged smuggling, B'Tselem: Gaza power plant attack is a war crime', 28 Sep. 2006, URL <http://www.palestine-pmc.com/details.asp?cat=1&id=1190>.

[13] Pirozzi, N., 'Building security in the Palestinian territories', European Security Review no. 28, ISIS Europe, Brussels, 28 Feb. 2006, URL <http://www.isis-europe.org/>.

[14] On events in Israel, Lebanon and the Palestinian territories in 2006 see chapter 2 in this volume.

[15] E.g. in their capacity as mediators in the conflicts in the Philippines and Sri Lanka, Malaysia and Norway, respectively, have led observer missions to monitor the ceasefire agreements between the warring parties since 2003.

The missions are grouped by organization and listed chronologically within these groups. The first group, covering UN operations, is divided into two sections: 16 operations run by the DPKO and 4 operations that are defined as special political missions and peacebuilding missions. The next seven groups cover operations conducted or led by regional organizations or alliances: 2 by the AU, 1 by the Economic and Monetary Community of Central African States (Communauté Economique et Monétaire d'Afrique Centrale, CEMAC); 3 by the Commonwealth of Independent States (CIS), including 2 missions carried out by Russia under bilateral arrangements; 11 by the EU; 3 by NATO; 2 by the Organization of American States (OAS); and 11 by the OSCE. The final group lists 7 UN-sanctioned operations led by ad hoc coalitions of states.

Missions that were initiated in 2006 and new states joining an existing mission are shown in bold type. Operations and individual state participation that ended in 2006 are shown in italic type, and designated lead states (those that either have operational control or contribute the most personnel) in missions with a military component are underlined.

Legal instruments underlying the establishment of an operation—UN Security Council resolutions or formal decisions by regional organizations—and the start dates for the operations (by which SIPRI refers to dates of first deployments) are given in the first column.

The figures for approved personnel numbers, particularly for UN operations, are the most recently authorized staffing levels. Detailed breakdowns of personnel numbers by main contributing country and the number of local support staff are not included in the table but, where available, are provided in the notes. Data on national breakdowns of civilian staff are not available for UN missions. Complete information on national contributions to the missions can be found in the SIPRI Multilateral Peace Operations Database.[16]

Mission fatalities since the beginning of the mission and in 2006 are reported. Cause of death—whether accidental, by hostile act or through illness—as reported during 2006 is also recorded. Not all deaths in 2006 have had their cause reported, so the three figures do not always add up to the total number of deaths in 2006.

Budget figures are given in millions of US dollars at current prices. Beginning this year budget figures are presented on a calendar year rather than financial year basis to allow comparison of each mission over time.[17] Calendar-year data are calculated on the assumption of an even rate of spending throughout the financial year. Budgets set in currencies other than the US dollar are converted based on the aggregated market exchange rates for 2006 of the International Monetary Fund (IMF).[18]

Budget figures presented for UN missions refer to core operational costs, which among other things include the cost of deploying personnel, per diems for deployed personnel and direct non-field support costs (e.g. requirements for the support account for peacekeeping operations and the UN logistics base in Brindisi, Italy). The cost of UN peacekeeping missions is shared by all UN member states through a specially derived scale of assessed contributions that takes no account of their partici-

---

[16] The database can be accessed at URL <http://conflict.sipri.org/>. The database also gives full lists of mandated tasks, heads of missions and details of documentation relevant to individual missions.

[17] The conversion to a calendar year basis also allows suitable comparison with other SIPRI data sets presented in this volume.

[18] For further information on the budgets of peace missions see the SIPRI Multilateral Peace Operations Database.

pation in the missions. Political and peacebuilding missions are funded through regular budget assessments. UN peacekeeping budgets do not cover programmatic costs, such as those for disarmament, demobilization and reintegration, which are financed by voluntary contributions.

In contrast, budget figures for missions conducted by regional organizations and alliances, such as the EU and NATO, refer only to common costs. These include mainly the running costs of the EU and NATO headquarters (i.e. costs for civilian personnel and operations and maintenance) and investments in the infrastructure necessary to support the mission. The costs of deploying personnel are borne by individual contributing states and do not appear in the budget figures given here. Most EU missions are financed in one of two ways, depending on whether they are civilian or military missions. Civilian missions are funded through the Community Budget, while military missions or missions with military components are funded through the Athena mechanism, to which only the participating member states contribute.[19] For CIS missions there is no designated common budget and countries participating in the missions bear the cost of troop deployments.

In missions conducted or led by other organizations, such as the OAS Special Mission for Strengthening Democracy in Haiti and those led by ad hoc coalitions, budget figures for missions may include programme implementation.

For all these reasons, budget figures presented in this table should be viewed as estimates and the budgets for different missions should not be compared.

Unless otherwise stated, all figures are as of 31 December 2006 or, in the case of missions that were terminated in 2006, the date on which the mission closed.

Data on multilateral peace missions are obtained from the following categories of open source: (a) official information provided by the secretariat of the organization concerned; (b) information provided by missions themselves, either in official publications or in written responses to annual SIPRI questionnaires; and (c) information from national governments contributing to the mission in question.[20] These primary sources are supplemented with a wide selection of publicly available secondary sources consisting of specialist journals; research reports; news agencies; and international, regional and local newspapers.

---

[19] The Athena mechanism is an instrument for the administration of costs that are defined as common costs. The mechanism was agreed in European Union Council Decision 2004/197/CFSP of 23 Feb. 2004 establishing a mechanism to administer the financing of the common costs of European Union operations having military or defence implications, which appears in *Official Journal of the European Union*, L63 (28 Feb. 2004), pp. 68–83.

[20] In some instances, additional information on the mission is obtained through telephone interviews by SIPRI staff.

Table 3A.1. Multilateral peace missions, 2006

Acronym/ (Legal instrument)/ Start date	Name/ Location	Countries contributing troops, military observers (Mil. obs), civilian police (Civ. pol.) or civilian staff (Civ. staff) in 2006 (**bold text** = new in 2006; *italic* text = ended in 2006; underlined text = designated lead states)	Troops/ Military observers/ Civilian police/ Civilian staff		Total deaths: to date/in 2006/ (due to hostilities, accidents, illness)	Cost ($ m.): 2006/ Unpaid
			Approved	Actual		
United Nations						
Total: 16 missions		**114 contributing countries**	80 044 / 2 810 / 10 971 / 6 212	70 580 / 2 659 / 8 601 / 4 627	900 / 91	4 977.5 / 1 788.1
UNTSO (SCR 50)[1] June 1948	UN Truce Supervision Organization Egypt, Israel, Lebanon, Syria	Mil. obs: Argentina, Australia, Austria, **Belgium**, Canada, Chile, China, Denmark, Estonia, Finland, France, Ireland, Italy, Nepal, Netherlands, New Zealand, Norway, Russia, Slovakia, Slovenia, Sweden, Switzerland, USA	– / – / – / 125	– / 150 / – / 108[2]	48 / 4 (4, –, –)	30.0 / –
UNMOGIP (SCR 91)[3] Jan. 1949	UN Military Observer Group in India and Pakistan India, Pakistan (Kashmir)	Mil. obs: Chile, Croatia, Denmark, Finland, Italy, Korea (South), Sweden, Uruguay	– / 45 / – / 24	– / 41 / – / 23[4]	11 / –	7.9 / –
UNFICYP (SCR 186)[5] Mar. 1964	UN Peacekeeping Force in Cyprus Cyprus	Troops: Argentina, Austria, Brazil, Canada, Chile, Croatia, Hungary, Paraguay, Peru, Slovakia, UK Civ. pol.: Argentina, Australia, *Bosnia and Herzegovina*, Croatia, El Salvador, India, Ireland, Italy, Netherlands	860 / – / 62 / 42	854 / – / 64 / 38[6]	176 / 1 (–, –, 1)	46.6 / 23.5
UNDOF (SCR 350)[7] June 1974	UN Disengagement Observer Force Syria (Golan Heights)	Troops: Austria, Canada, **India**, Japan, Nepal, Poland, Slovakia	1 047 / – / – / 43	1 048 / – / – / 40[8]	42 / 1 (–, –, 1)	42.6 / 30.2

Mission (legal authority, start)	Name / Location	Contributing countries	Approved	Actual	Deaths	Cost ($ m.)
UNIFIL (SCR 425 and 426)[9] Mar. 1978	UN Interim Force in Lebanon, Lebanon	Troops: Belgium, China, Denmark, Finland, France, Germany, Ghana, Greece, Guatemala, Hungary, India, Indonesia, Ireland, Italy, Luxembourg, Malaysia, Nepal, Netherlands, Norway, Poland, Portugal, Qatar, Slovenia, Spain, Sweden, Turkey, Ukraine	15 000	11 563	258	98.4
			–	–	1	71.0
			266	125[10]	(1, –, –)	
MINURSO (SCR 690)[11] Sep. 1991	UN Mission for the Referendum in Western Sahara, Western Sahara	Troops: Denmark, Ghana, Korea (South), Malaysia	27	31	14	46.2
		Mil. obs: Argentina, Austria, Bangladesh, China, Croatia, Denmark, Egypt, El Salvador, France, Ghana, Greece, Guinea, Honduras, Hungary, Ireland, Italy, Kenya, Malaysia, Mongolia, Nigeria, Pakistan, Poland, Russia, Sri Lanka, Uruguay	203	183	–	49.6
			8	4		
		Civ. pol.: Egypt, El Salvador	115	102[12]		
UNOMIG (SCR 849 and 858)[13] Aug. 1993	UN Observer Mission to Georgia, Georgia (Abkhazia)	Mil. obs: Albania, Austria, Bangladesh, Croatia, Czech Rep., Denmark, Egypt, France, Germany, Greece, Hungary, Indonesia, Jordan, Korea (South), Pakistan, Poland, Romania, Russia, Sweden, Switzerland, Turkey, UK, Ukraine, Uruguay, USA	135	127	11	35.6
			18	12	1	13.6
		Civ. pol.: Germany, Ghana, Hungary, India, Poland, Russia, Switzerland	118	99[14]	(–, 1, –)	
UNMIK (SCR 1244)[15] June 1999	UN Interim Administration Mission in Kosovo, Serbia (Kosovo)	Mil. obs: Argentina, Bangladesh, Bolivia, Bulgaria, Chile, Czech Rep., Denmark, Finland, Hungary, Ireland, Italy, Jordan, Kenya, Malawi, Malaysia, Nepal, New Zealand, Norway, Pakistan, Poland, Portugal, Romania, Russia, Spain, UK, Ukraine, Zambia	38	37	46	240.0
			2 938	1 960	1	126.0
		Civ. pol.: Argentina, Austria, Bangladesh, Brazil, Bulgaria, China, Croatia, Czech Rep., Denmark, Egypt, Fiji, Finland, France, Germany, Ghana, Greece, Hungary, India, Italy, Jordan, Kenya, Kyrgyzstan, Lithuania, Malawi, Malaysia, Nepal, Netherlands, Nigeria, Norway, Pakistan, Philippines, Poland, Portugal, Romania, Russia, Slovenia, Spain, Sweden, Switzerland, Timor-Leste, Turkey, UK, Ukraine, USA, Zambia, Zimbabwe	621	508[16]	(–, –, 1)	

Acronym/ (Legal instrument/ Start date	Name/ Location	Countries contributing troops, military observers (Mil. obs), civilian police (Civ. pol.) or civilian staff (Civ. staff) in 2006 (**bold** text = new in 2006; *italic* text = ended in 2006; underlined text = designated lead states)	Troops/ Military observers/ Civilian police/ Civilian staff		Total deaths: to date/in 2006/ (due to hostilities, accidents, illness)	Cost ($ m.): 2006/ Unpaid
			Approved	Actual		
MONUC (SCR 1279)[17] Oct. 1999	UN Organization Mission in the Democratic Republic of the Congo Democratic Republic of the Congo	Troops: Bangladesh, **Benin**, Bolivia, China, Ghana, Guatemala, India, Indonesia, **Jordan**, *Kenya*, Malawi, Morocco, Nepal, *Netherlands*, Pakistan, Senegal, Serbia, South Africa, Tunisia, Uruguay Mil. obs: Algeria, Bangladesh, Belgium, Benin, Bolivia, Bosnia and Herzegovina, Burkina Faso, *Cameroon*, Canada, China, Czech Rep., Denmark, Egypt, France, Ghana, Guatemala, India, Indonesia, Ireland, Jordan, Kenya, Malawi, Malaysia, Mali, Mongolia, Morocco, *Mozambique*, Nepal, Netherlands, Niger, Nigeria, Pakistan, Paraguay, Peru, Poland, Romania, Russia, Senegal, South Africa, Spain, Sri Lanka, Sweden, Switzerland, Tunisia, UK, Ukraine, Uruguay, **Yemen**, Zambia Civ. pol.: Argentina, Bangladesh, Benin, Burkina Faso, Cameroon, Central African Republic, Chad, Côte d'Ivoire, Egypt, France, Guinea, India, Jordan, Madagascar, Mali, Niger, *Nigeria*, Romania, Russia, Senegal, Sweden, Turkey, **Ukraine**, Vanuatu, Yemen	15 815 760 1 141 1 165	16 487 734 1 075 9381[8]	98 21 (9, 1, 10)	1 146.2 160.4
UNMEE (SCR 1312)[19] July 2000	UN Mission in Ethiopia and Eritrea Eritrea, Ethiopia	Troops: *Austria*, Bangladesh, *Bulgaria*, *France*, Gambia, Ghana, India, Jordan, Kenya, Malaysia, Namibia, Nigeria, *Spain*, Tanzania, Tunisia, Uruguay, Zambia Mil. obs: Algeria, Austria, Bangladesh, **Bolivia**, Bosnia and Herzegovina, **Brazil**, Bulgaria, China, Croatia, Czech Rep., Denmark, Finland, **France**, Gambia, Germany, Ghana, Greece, Guatemala, India, Iran, Jordan, Kenya, **Kyrgyzstan**, Malaysia, **Mongolia**, Namibia, Nepal, Nigeria, Norway, **Pakistan**, Paraguay, Peru, Poland, Romania, Russia, South Africa, Spain, Sweden, Switzerland, Tanzania, Tunisia, Ukraine, Uruguay, USA, Zambia	2 070 230 – 233	2 063 222 – 151[20]	17 4 (–, 1, 3)	184.1 64.8

		Authorized	Actual		Cost
UNMIL (SCR 1509)[21] Nov. 2003	UN Mission in Liberia / Liberia	14 660	13 613	87	753.1
		215	188	17	251.6
		1 240	1 097	(–, 1, 14)	
		598	514[22]		

Troops: Bangladesh, Benin, Bolivia, Brazil, China, Croatia, Ecuador, Ethiopia, Finland, France, Germany, Ghana, Ireland, Jordan, Kenya, Korea (South), Malawi, *Mali*, Moldova, Mongolia, Namibia, Nepal, Nigeria, Pakistan, *Paraguay*, *Peru*, Philippines, Senegal, Sweden, Togo, UK, Ukraine, USA

Mil. obs: Bangladesh, Benin, Bolivia, Bulgaria, China, Czech Rep., Denmark, Ecuador, Egypt, El Salvador, Ethiopia, Gambia, Ghana, Indonesia, Jordan, Kenya, Korea (South), Kyrgyzstan, Malaysia, Mali, Moldova, Montenegro, Namibia, Nepal, Niger, Nigeria, Pakistan, Paraguay, Peru, *Philippines*, Poland, *Romania*, Russia, Senegal, Serbia, Togo, Ukraine, USA, Zambia

Civ. pol.: Argentina, Bangladesh, Bosnia and Herzegovina, China, Czech Rep., El Salvador, Fiji, Gambia, Germany, Ghana, Jamaica, Jordan, Kenya, Kyrgyzstan, **Macedonia**, Malawi, Namibia, Nepal, *Niger*, Nigeria, Norway, Pakistan, Philippines, **Poland**, *Portugal*, Russia, **Rwanda**, Samoa, *Senegal*, Serbia, Sri Lanka, Sweden, Turkey, Uganda, Ukraine, Uruguay, USA, Yemen, Zambia, Zimbabwe

		Authorized	Actual		Cost
UNOCI (SCR 1528)[23] Apr. 2004	UN Operation in Côte d'Ivoire / Côte d'Ivoire	7 915	7 847	27	438.3
		200	190	12	186.6
		1 200	992	(–, 8, 4)	
		467	362[24]		

Troops: Bangladesh, Benin, Brazil, France, *Gambia*, Ghana, Jordan, Kenya, Morocco, Niger, Pakistan, Paraguay, Philippines, Senegal, **Tanzania**, Togo, Tunisia, Uganda, Uruguay

Mil. obs: Bangladesh, Benin, Bolivia, Brazil, Chad, China, Congo (Rep. of), Croatia, Dominican Republic, Ecuador, El Salvador, **Ethiopia**, France, Gambia, Ghana, Guatemala, Guinea, India, Ireland, Jordan, Kenya, Moldova, Morocco, Namibia, Nepal, Niger, Nigeria, Pakistan, Paraguay, Peru, Philippines, Poland, Romania, Russia, Senegal, Serbia, **Tanzania**, Togo, Tunisia, Uganda, Uruguay, Yemen, Zambia, **Zimbabwe**

Civ. pol.: **Argentina**, Bangladesh, Benin, Cameroon, Canada, Central African Republic, Chad, Djibouti, *El Salvador*, France, *Ghana*, India, Jordan, *Lebanon*, Madagascar, Niger, Nigeria, **Pakistan**, Philippines, **Rwanda**, Senegal, **Switzerland**, Togo, Turkey, Uruguay, Vanuatu, Yemen

Acronym/ (Legal instrument)/ Start date	Name/ Location	Countries contributing troops, military observers (Mil. obs), civilian police (Civ. pol.) or civilian staff (Civ. staff) in 2006 (**bold text** = new in 2006; *italic text* = ended in 2006; underlined text = designated lead states)	Troops/ Military observers/ Civilian police/ Civilian staff		Total deaths: to date/in 2006/ (due to hostilities, accidents, illness)	Cost ($ m.): 2006/ Unpaid
			Approved	Actual		
ONUB (SCR 1545)[25] June 2004	UN Operation in Burundi / Burundi	*Troops: Algeria, Belgium, Burkina Faso, Ethiopia, Guatemala, India, Jordan, Kenya, Mali, Mozambique, Nepal, Nigeria, Pakistan, Russia, Senegal, South Africa, Thailand, Togo, Tunisia*	5 450 200 120 341	1 656[26] 75 14 245[27]	24 2 (1, 1, –)	236.2 91.3
		Mil. obs: Algeria, Bangladesh, Belgium, Benin, Bolivia, Burkina Faso, Chad, China, Egypt, Ethiopia, Gambia, Ghana, Guatemala, Guinea, India, Jordan, Kenya, Korea (South), Kyrgyzstan, Malawi, Malaysia, Mali, Mozambique, Namibia, Nepal, Niger, Nigeria, Pakistan, Paraguay, Peru, Philippines, Portugal, Romania, Russia, Senegal, Serbia, South Africa, Sri Lanka, Thailand, Togo, Tunisia, Uruguay, Yemen, Zambia				
		Civ. pol.: Benin, Burkina Faso, Cameroon, Chad, Guinea, Madagascar, Mali, Niger, Nigeria				
MINUSTAH (SCR 1542)[28] June 2004	UN Stabilization Mission in Haiti / Haiti	*Troops: Argentina, Bolivia, Brazil, Canada, Chile, Croatia, Ecuador, France, Guatemala, Jordan, Malaysia, Morocco, Nepal, **Pakistan**, Paraguay, Peru, Philippines, Spain, Sri Lanka, Uruguay, USA, Yemen*	7 200 – 1 951 522	6 684 – 1 692 433[29]	24 11 (5, 1, 1)	525.8 195.5
		*Civ. pol.: **Argentina**, Benin, Bosnia and Herzegovina, Brazil, Burkina Faso, Cameroon, Canada, Chad, Chile, China, **Colombia**, Egypt, El Salvador, France, Ghana, Guinea, Jordan, **Madagascar**, Mali, **Mauritius**, Nepal, Niger, Nigeria, Pakistan, Philippines, Romania, Russia, **Rwanda**, Senegal, Sierra Leone, Spain, Togo, Turkey, Uruguay, USA, Vanuatu, Yemen, Zambia*				
UNMIS (SCR 1590)[30] Mar. 2005	UN Mission in Sudan / Sudan	*Troops: Australia, Austria, Bangladesh, **Cambodia**, Canada, China, Croatia, Denmark, Egypt, Finland, Germany, Greece, India, Jordan, Kenya, **Malawi**, Malaysia, Nepal, **Netherlands**, New Zealand, **Nigeria**, Norway, Pakistan, **Russia**, Rwanda, **South Africa**, **Sweden**, Switzerland, **Tanzania**, Turkey, UK, Zambia, **Zimbabwe***	10 000[31] 750 685 1 187	8 734 680 592 812[32]	16 14 (1, 2, 10)	1 047.9 524.0

Mil. obs: Australia, Bangladesh, Belgium, Benin, Bolivia, **Botswana**, Brazil, **Burkina Faso**, Cambodia, Canada, China, **Denmark**, Ecuador, Egypt, El Salvador, Fiji, Gabon, <u>Germany</u>, Greece, Guatemala, Guinea, India, Indonesia, *Italy*, Jordan, Kenya, Korea (South), Kyrgyzstan, Malawi, Malaysia, **Mali**, Moldova, Mongolia, Mozambique, Namibia, Nepal, **Netherlands**, New Zealand, Nigeria, Norway, Pakistan, Paraguay, Peru, Philippines, Poland, Romania, Russia, Rwanda, *Sri Lanka*, Sweden, Tanzania, **Thailand**, Uganda, Ukraine, Yemen, Zambia, Zimbabwe

Civ. pol.: Argentina, **Australia**, Bangladesh, **Bosnia and Herzegovina**, Brazil, **Canada**, China, **Denmark**, **Egypt**, El Salvador, Fiji, Finland, **Gambia**, **Germany**, Ghana, India, Jamaica, Jordan, Kenya, **Kyrgyzstan**, Malaysia, Namibia, Nepal, **Netherlands**, Nigeria, Norway, Pakistan, Philippines, Russia, **Rwanda**, Samoa, Sri Lanka, Sweden, Tanzania, Turkey, Uganda, Ukraine, **Uruguay**, USA, **Vanuatu**, **Yemen**, Zambia, Zimbabwe

UNMIT (SCR 1704)[33] Aug. 2006	UN Integrated Mission in Timor-Leste	Timor-Leste						

Mil. obs: **Australia, Bangladesh, Brazil, China, Fiji, Malaysia, New Zealand, Pakistan, Philippines, Portugal, Singapore** — 34 — 1 — 98.6

Civ. pol.: **Australia,** <u>Bangladesh,</u> **Brazil, Canada, Croatia, El Salvador, Gambia, Jordan, Korea (South), Malaysia, Nepal, New Zealand, Pakistan, Philippines, Portugal, Romania, Russia, Samoa, Singapore, Spain, Sri Lanka, Sweden, Thailand, Turkey, Uruguay, USA, Vanuatu, Yemen, Zimbabwe** — 1 608 — 1 099 — 1 — (–, 1, –)

345 — 1293[4] — –

Acronym/ (Legal instrument)ᵃ/ Start date	Name/ Location	Countries contributing troops, military observers (Mil. obs), civilian police (Civ. pol.) or civilian staff (Civ. staff) in 2006; (**bold text** = new in 2006; *italic text* = ended in 2006; <u>underlined text</u> = designated lead states)	Troops/ Military observers/ Civilian police/ Civilian staff		Total deaths: to date/in 2006/ (due to hostilities, accidents, illness)	Cost ($ m.): 2006/ Unpaid
			Approved	Actual		
United Nations special political and peace-building missions						
Total: 4 missions		**96 contributing countries**	**294** **50** **93** **865**	**223** **43** **46** **787**	**10** **4**	**206.2** –
UNAMA (SCR 1401)³⁵ Mar. 2002	UN Assistance Mission in Afghanistan Afghanistan	Mil. obs: Australia, Austria, Bangladesh, Denmark, Germany, Korea (South), New Zealand, Poland, Romania, Uruguay Civ. pol.: *Canada, China, Denmark,* **Nepal**, Nigeria, Philippines, *Sweden* Civ. staff: **Argentina**, Australia, Austria, Bangladesh, *Belarus, Belgium,* Bosnia and Herzegovina, Brazil, **Bulgaria**, *Burundi,* Canada, China, **Congo (Dem. Rep. of)**, Croatia, **Czech Rep.**, **Denmark**, **Egypt**, El Salvador, *Ethiopia,* Fiji, Finland, France, Germany, Ghana, Guatemala, Honduras, *Hungary,* India, Iran, Iraq, Ireland, Italy, Jamaica, Japan, Jordan, Kenya, Korea (South), Kyrgyzstan, **Laos**, Liberia, Macedonia, Malaysia, Myanmar, **Nepal**, Netherlands, New Zealand, **Norway**, Pakistan, Peru, Philippines, Poland, *Portugal,* Romania, Russia, Rwanda, **Serbia and Montenegro**, Sierra Leone, South Africa, Spain, Sri Lanka, Sudan, Sweden, *Switzerland, Syria,* Tajikistan, Thailand, Trinidad and Tobago, Tunisia, **Uganda**, UK, Ukraine, USA, Uzbekistan, Zimbabwe	– 13 4 277	– 11 3 217³⁶	4 –	62.4 –
UNAMI (SCR 1500)³⁷ Aug. 2003	UN Assistance Mission in Iraq Iraq	Troops: **Fiji** Mil. obs: **Australia**, **Canada**, **Denmark**, **New Zealand**, UK Civ. staff: Afghanistan, **Australia**, Austria, Bangladesh, Barbados, Bosnia and Herzegovina, *Brazil,* Canada, Congo (Dem. Rep. of), Croatia, Czech Rep., Denmark, Ecuador, Egypt, Estonia, Ethiopia, Fiji, Finland, France, Germany, Ghana, Greece, India, Iran, Ireland, Italy,	294 8 – 406	223 11 – 396³⁸	4 2 (–, –, 2)	102.9 –

Jamaica, Japan, Jordan, Kenya, Korea (South), **Kuwait, Kyrgyzstan,** Lebanon, Macedonia, *Malta,* Morocco, Myanmar, **Nepal,** Netherlands, New Zealand, Nigeria, Pakistan, **Palestinian Territory,** Peru, Philippines, **Poland,** *Portugal,* Russia, **Senegal, Sierra Leone, Singapore, Somalia,** South Africa, Spain, Sri Lanka, Sudan, Sweden, Syria, Tajikistan, **Tanzania,** Thailand, Trinidad and Tobago, **Tunisia,** Uganda, UK, Uruguay, USA

Mission	Name	Location				
UNOTIL *(SCR 1599)*[39] *May 2005*	UN Office in Timor-Leste	*Timor-Leste*				18.6 —
		Mil. obs: *Australia, Bangladesh, Brazil, Malaysia,* **Mali***, New Zealand, Pakistan, Philippines, Portugal*	15	—		
		Civ. pol.: *Australia, Bangladesh, Brazil, China, Croatia, Jordan, Malaysia, Pakistan, Palau, Philippines, Portugal, Russia, Samoa, Spain, Sri Lanka, Turkey, USA*	60	12		
		Civ. staff: *Angola, Australia, Austria, Bangladesh, Belgium, Bosnia and Herzegovina, Brazil, Cambodia, Canada, Cape Verde,Chile, Colombia, Croatia, Ethiopia, Fiji, Finland, France, Germany, Guatemala, Guinea, Honduras, India, Indonesia, Ireland, Italy, Jamaica, Japan, Kenya, Liberia, Malaysia,* **Mexico***, Mozambique, Nepal, Netherlands,* **Norway***, New Zealand, Pakistan,* **Peru***, Philippines, Poland, Portugal, Sierra Leone, Singapore, Spain, Sri Lanka, St Vincent and the Grenadines, Switzerland, Tanzania, Thailand, Uganda, UK, USA, Zambia, Zimbabwe*	100	26	103[40]	
UNIOSIL **(SCR** **1620)**[41] **Jan. 2006**	**UN Integrated Office in Sierra Leone**	**Sierra Leone**				22.3 —
		Mil. obs: **Bangladesh, Ghana, Kenya, Nepal, Nigeria, Pakistan, Russia, UK, Zambia**	14	—		2
		Civ. pol.: **Gambia, Ghana, India, Kenya, Malaysia, Nepal, Nigeria, Norway, Portugal, Sweden, Turkey, UK**	29	9		2
		Civ. staff: **Afghanistan, Angola, Barbados, Bhutan, Bulgaria, Burundi, Cameroon, Canada, China, Congo (Dem. Rep. of), Croatia, Egypt, Ethiopia, Fiji, Finland, Germany, Ghana, Honduras, India, Italy, Jamaica, Japan, Kenya, Liberia, Macedonia, Malawi, Nepal, Nigeria, Pakistan, Palestinian Territory, Philippines, Poland, Portugal, Rwanda, Senegal, Sudan, Swaziland, Sweden, Trinidad and Tobago, Uganda, UK, USA, Zimbabwe**	82	17	71[42]	(–, –, 2)

Acronym/ (Legal instrument, Authorization date)/ Start date	Name/ Location	Countries contributing troops, military observers (Mil. obs), civilian police (Civ. pol.) or civilian staff (Civ. staff) in 2006 (**bold** text = new in 2006; *italic* text = ended in 2006; underlined text = designated lead states)	Troops/ Military observers/ Civilian police/ Civilian staff — Approved	Actual	Total deaths: to date/in 2006/ (due to hostilities, accidents, illness)	Cost ($ m.): 2006/ Unpaid
African Union (AU)						
Total: 2 missions		**30 contributing countries**	**6 603** / **450** / **1 590** / –	**5 381** / **632** / **1 376** / **1 029**	**13** / **5**	**296.6** / –
AMIS (AU, 28 May 2004)[43] June 2004	African Union Mission in Sudan, Sudan	Troops: Chad, Gambia, **Kenya**, Nigeria, Rwanda, Senegal, South Africa Mil. obs: Algeria, Benin, Botswana, Burkina Faso, **Burundi**, Cameroon, Chad, Congo (Rep. of), Egypt, Gabon, Gambia, Ghana, Kenya, Lesotho, Libya, Madagascar, Malawi, Mali, Mauritania, Mozambique, Namibia, Nigeria, Rwanda, Senegal, South Africa, Togo, **Uganda**, Zambia Civ. pol.: Botswana, **Burkina Faso**, Cameroon, Egypt, Gambia, Ghana, Kenya, **Lesotho**, Madagascar, Mali, Mauritania, **Niger**, Nigeria, Rwanda, Senegal, South Africa, Uganda, Zambia	6 171 / 450 / 1 560 / –	4 980 / 60[44] / 1 346 / 1 029	13 / 5 (2, 1, 2)	277.9[45] / ..
AMISEC[46] Mar. 2006	AU Mission for Support to the Elections in the Comoros, Comoros	Troops: *Rwanda, South Africa* Mil. obs: *Congo (Rep. of), Egypt, Mozambique, Nigeria* Civ. pol.: *Madagascar, Mauritius*[47]	432 / – / 30 / –	401[48] / 31 / 30 / –	– / –	18.8[49] / –
Economic and Monetary Community of Central African States (CEMAC)						
Total: 1 missions		**3 contributing countries**	350 / – / – / –	380 / – / – / –	8 / 2	9.4 / –

FOMUC (Libreville Summit, 2 Oct. 2002)[50] Jan. 2003	CEMAC Multinational Force in the Central African Republic Central African Republic	Troops: Chad, Congo (Rep. of), <u>Gabon</u>	350 — —	380[51] — —	8 2 (2, –, –)	9.4[52] —

Commonwealth of Independent States (CIS)

Total: 3 missions	**3 contributing countries**		**6 000** — — —	**4 619** — — —	**144** —	**. [53]** ::
– (Bilateral, 21 July 1992)[54] July 1992	Joint Control Commission Peacekeeping Force Moldova (Trans-Dniester)	Troops: Moldova, Russia, (Trans-Dniester)	1 500 — —	1 199 — —	32[55] :	:: ::
– (Bilateral, 24 June 1992)[56] July 1992	South Ossetia Joint Force Georgia (South Ossetia)	Troops: Georgia, Russia, (South Ossetia)	1 500 — —	1 420 — —	19 :	:: ::
– (CIS, 15 Oct. 1994)[57] June 1994	CIS Peacekeeping Forces in Georgia Georgia (Abkhazia)	Troops: Russia	3 000 — —	2 000 — —	125 :	:: ::

Acronym/ (Legal instrument, Authorization date)/ Start date	Name/ Location	Countries contributing troops, military observers (Mil. obs), civilian police (Civ. pol.) or civilian staff (Civ. staff) in 2006 (**bold** text = new in 2006; *italic* text = ended in 2006; underlined text = designated lead states)	Troops/ Military observers/ Civilian police/ Civilian staff		Total deaths: to date/in 2006/ (due to hostilities, accidents, illness)	Cost ($ m.): 2006/ Unpaid
			Approved	Actual		
European Union (EU)						
Total: 11 missions	**45 contributing countries**		**8 300** **156** **158** **18**[58]	**8 210** **95** **315** **199**	**20** **4**	**139.7** **–**
EUMM (Brioni Agreement)[59] July 1991	EU Monitoring Mission Western Balkans	Mil. obs: Austria, *Belgium, Denmark,* **Estonia,** Finland, France, Germany, Greece, Ireland, *Italy,* Netherlands, Norway, Slovakia, Spain, Sweden, UK	120 – –	– 59 –[60]	11 –	2.2 –
EUPM (CJA 2002/ 210/CFSP)[61] Jan. 2003	EU Police Mission in Bosnia and Herzegovina Bosnia and Herzegovina	Civ. pol.: Austria, Belgium, Bulgaria, Canada, Cyprus, Czech Rep., Denmark, Estonia, Finland, France, Germany, *Greece,* Hungary, *Iceland,* Ireland, Italy, Latvia, Lithuania, Luxembourg, Malta, Netherlands, Norway, Poland, Portugal, Romania, *Russia,* Slovakia, Slovenia, Spain, Sweden, Switzerland, Turkey, UK, Ukraine Civ. staff: *Austria,* Belgium, Bulgaria, *Finland,* France, Germany, Ireland, Italy, Netherlands, Norway, Portugal, Spain, Turkey, UK, Ukraine	– – –	– 173 286[62]	3 –	15.0 –
EUFOR ALTHEA (CJA 2004/ 570/CFSP)[63] Dec. 2004	EU Military Operation in Bosnia and Herzegovina Bosnia and Herzegovina	Troops: Albania, *Argentina,* Austria, Belgium, Bulgaria, Canada, Chile, Czech Rep., Estonia, Finland, France, Germany, Greece, Hungary, Ireland, Italy, Latvia, Lithuania, Luxembourg, **Macedonia,** Morocco, Netherlands, New Zealand, Norway, Poland, Portugal, Romania, Slovakia, Slovenia, Spain, Sweden, Switzerland, Turkey, *UK*	6 000 – –	5 935[64] – 85[65]	5 3 (–, 1, –)	44.4 –

Name / legal basis / start date	Location	Participating countries				Cost ($ m.)
EUPOL Kinshasa (CJA 2004/847/CFSP)[66] Apr. 2005	Democratic Republic of the Congo	Civ. pol.: **Angola**, *Belgium*, Canada, **Denmark**, France, Italy, **Mali**, *Netherlands*, Portugal, **Romania**, Sweden, Turkey, *UK* Civ. staff: **Belgium, France, Portugal**	30	50 467	—	5.6
EUSEC DR CONGO (CJA 2005/355/CFSP)[68] June 2005	Democratic Republic of the Congo	Civ. staff: Belgium, France, **Germany**, Hungary, **Luxembourg, Netherlands**, Portugal, **Sweden**, UK	8	32[69]	—	4.3
EUJUST LEX (CJA 2005/190/CFSP)[70] July 2005	Iraq	Civ. staff: *Belgium*, **Denmark**, France, Germany, **Italy, Lithuania, Netherlands, Poland, Portugal**, Spain, UK[71]	—	26	—	10.1
AMM EU Aceh Monitoring Mission (CJA 2005/643/CFSP)[72] Aug. 2005	*Indonesia (Aceh)*	Mil. obs: *Austria, Brunei Darussalam, Denmark, Finland, France, Germany, Ireland, Italy, Lithuania, Malaysia, Netherlands, Norway, Philippines, Singapore, Spain, Sweden, Switzerland, Thailand, UK*	36	367[73]	1 1 (–, 1, –)	14.5
EU BAM Rafah EU Border Assistance Mission for the Rafah Crossing Point (CJA 2005/889/CFSP)[74] Nov. 2005	Rafah Crossing Point	Civ. pol.: *Austria*, **Belgium, Denmark**, *Estonia*, **Finland, France, Germany**, Greece, **Italy**, Luxembourg, **Netherlands, Portugal, Romania, Spain, Sweden** Civ. staff: *Austria, Denmark*, **Estonia**, *Finland, France, Germany*, Italy, **Lithuania**, *Luxembourg, Portugal, Romania, Slovenia, Spain, UK*	75	63 87[75]	—	13.4

Acronym/ (Legal instrument, Authorization date)/ Start date	Name/ Location	Countries contributing troops, military observers (Mil. obs), civilian police (Civ. pol.) or civilian staff (Civ. staff) in 2006 (**bold text** = new in 2006; *italic text* = ended in 2006; underlined text = designated lead states)	Troops/ Military observers/ Civilian police/ Civilian staff		Total deaths: to date/in 2006/ (due to hostilities, accidents, illness)	Cost ($ m.): 2006/ Unpaid
			Approved	Actual		
EUPAT (*CJA 2005/ 826/CFSP*)[76] Dec. 2005	*EU Police Advisory Team in the Former Yugoslav Republic of Macedonia* *Former Yugoslav Republic of Macedonia*	Civ. pol.: *Austria, Belgium, Cyprus, Denmark, Finland, France, Germany,* ***Greece****, Hungary, Italy, Latvia,* **Netherlands***, Slovakia, Slovenia, Spain,* *Sweden, UK* Civ. staff: **Belgium****,* **Denmark***, France, Germany,* **Ireland***, Italy,* ***Portugal****,* **Sweden***, UK*	– 20 10	– 20 12[77]	– –	1.7 –
EUPOL COPPS (**CJA 2005/ 797/CFSP**)[78] **Jan. 2006**	**EU Police Mission for the Palestinian Territories** **Palestinian Territory**	Civ. pol.: *Austria,* **Belgium, Denmark, Finland, France, Germany, Ireland, Italy,** *Spain,* **Sweden, UK** Civ. staff: **Austria, Sweden, UK**	– 33 –	– 9 4[79]	– –	7.6 –
EUFOR DR Congo (*CJA 2006/ 319/CFSP*)[80] *July 2006*	*EUFOR DR Congo* *Democratic Republic of the Congo*	Troops: *Austria, Belgium, Cyprus,* **Finland***, France,* <u>*Germany*</u>*, Greece, Ireland, Italy, Luxembourg, Netherlands,* **Poland***, Portugal, Slovenia, Spain, Sweden, Turkey*	2 300 – –	2 275[81] – –	– –	20.9 –

North Atlantic Treaty Organization (NATO) and NATO-led

Total: 3 missions	**43 contributing countries**		**17 300** – –	**49 260** – –	**266** **66**	**155.7** –

Mission (SCR/Res.) Date	Name / Location	Contributing countries				
KFOR (SCR 1244)[82] June 1999	NATO Kosovo Force Serbia (Kosovo)	Troops: Argentina, Armenia, Austria, Azerbaijan, Belgium, Bulgaria, *Canada*, Czech Rep., Denmark, Estonia, Finland, France, Georgia, Germany, Greece, Hungary, Ireland, Italy, Latvia, Lithuania, Luxembourg, **Mongolia**, Morocco, **Netherlands**, Norway, Poland, **Portugal**, Romania, Slovakia, Slovenia, Spain, Sweden, Switzerland, Turkey, UK, *Ukraine*, USA	17 000	15 600[83] – –	96 6 (–, 1, –)	31.0 –
ISAF (SCR 1386)[84] Dec. 2001	International Security Assistance Force Afghanistan	Troops: Albania, **Australia**, Austria, Azerbaijan, Belgium, Bulgaria, Canada, Croatia, Czech Rep., Denmark, Estonia, Finland, France, Germany, Greece, Hungary, Iceland, Ireland, Italy, Latvia, Lithuania, Luxembourg, Macedonia, Netherlands, New Zealand, Norway, Poland, Portugal, Romania, Slovakia, Slovenia, Spain, Sweden, Switzerland, Turkey, UK, USA	– – –	33 460[85] – –	170 60 (48, –, –)	107.8 –
NTM-I (SCR 1546)[86] Aug. 2004	NATO Training Mission in Iraq Iraq	Troops: Bulgaria, Czech Rep., Denmark, Estonia, Hungary, Iceland, Italy, Lithuania, Netherlands, Norway, Poland, Portugal, Romania, Slovakia, **Slovenia**, Turkey, UK, **Ukraine**, USA[87]	300 – –	200 – –	– –	17.1 –
Organization of American States (OAS)						
Total: 2 missions	**12 contributing countries**		22 6	23 2	1 –	**18.5** –
MAPP/OEA (CP/RES. 859)[88] Feb. 2004	Mission to Support the Peace Process in Colombia Colombia	Civ. staff: *Argentina, Costa Rica*, Guatemala, **Mexico**, *Nicaragua, Norway, Peru*, Sweden, *Uruguay*	– – –	– – 5[89]	– –	5.5 –
— (CP/RES. 806)[90] June 2004	OAS Special Mission for Strengthening Democracy in Haiti Haiti	Civ. pol.: **Benin**, France Civ. staff: Argentina, ***Barbados***, **Benin**, **Bolivia**, Canada, *Colombia*, Dominica, Ecuador, **France**, Grenada, *Guatemala*, Mexico, Peru	22 6	18[91] 2	1 –	13.092 –

Organization for Security and Cooperation in Europe (OSCE)

Acronym/ (Legal instrument, Authorization date)/ Start date	Name/ Location	Countries contributing troops, military observers (Mil. obs), civilian police (Civ. pol.) or civilian staff (Civ. staff) in 2006 (**bold text** = new in 2006; *italic text* = ended in 2006; underlined text = designated lead states)	Troops/ Military observers/ Civilian police/ Civilian staff		Total deaths: to date/in 2006/ (due to hostilities, accidents, illness)	Cost ($ m.): 2006/ Unpaid
			Approved	Actual		
Total: 11 missions		**45 contributing countries**	– – 290	– – 536	7 3	127.0 –
— (CSO, 18 Sep. 1992)[93] Sep. 1992	OSCE Spillover Monitor Mission to Skopje, Former Yugoslav Republic of Macedonia	Civ. staff: Austria, Azerbaijan, Belarus, **Belgium**, *Bosnia and Herzegovina*, Croatia, *Estonia, Finland*, France, Georgia, Germany, Hungary, Ireland, Italy, Japan, *Netherlands*, Norway, Poland, *Portugal*, Romania, *Russia*, Slovenia, Spain, Sweden, *Switzerland, Tajikistan*, Turkey, UK, Ukraine, USA	– – 92	– – 69[94]	– –	12.8 –
— (CSO, 6 Nov. 1992)[95] Dec. 1992	OSCE Mission to Georgia, Georgia	Civ. staff: Austria, *Belgium, Bosnia and Herzegovina*, Bulgaria, Canada, Czech Rep., Estonia, Finland, France, Germany, Hungary, Ireland, Lithuania, Macedonia, *Moldova*, Poland, Romania, Russia, Slovakia, Turkey, UK, Ukraine, USA	– – 64	– – 48[96]	– –	14.8 –
— (CSO, 4 Feb. 1993)[97] Apr. 1993	OSCE Mission to Moldova, Moldova	Civ. staff: Belarus, France, Germany, **Italy**, Norway, Poland, Slovakia, UK, USA	– – 10	– – 11[98]	– –	2.0 –

Establishment	Operation/location	Contributing states	Intl. staff			Local staff		Cost	
(Rome Ministerial Council Decision no. 4.1, 1 Dec. 1993)[99] Feb. 1994	OSCE Centre in Dushanbe, Tajikistan	Civ. staff: Belarus, Bulgaria, **Denmark**, *France*, **Germany**, *Hungary*, Italy, *Latvia*, Lithuania, *Netherlands*, Norway, *Romania, Russia, Sweden*, **UK, Ukraine**, USA	14	–	–	12[100]	–	4.9	–
(10 Aug. 1995)[101] Aug. 1995	Personal Representative of the Chairman-in-Office on the Conflict Dealt with by the OSCE Minsk Conference, Azerbaijan (Nagorno–Karabakh)	Civ. staff: Czech Rep., *Finland*, **Germany**, Hungary, **Kazakhstan**, Poland, UK, *Ukraine*	6	–	–	6[102]	–	1.0	–
(Ministerial Council, 8 Dec. 1995)[103] Dec. 1995	OSCE Mission to Bosnia and Herzegovina	Civ. staff: *Albania*, **Armenia**, Austria, Azerbaijan, Belgium, Bulgaria, Canada, **Croatia**, Czech Rep., Finland, France, *Georgia*, Germany, **Greece**, Hungary, Ireland, **Italy**, *Japan*, **Kyrgyzstan**, *Latvia, Lithuania, Moldova*, Netherlands, Norway, *Portugal*, **Romania**, Russia, **Slovakia**, Slovenia, Spain, Sweden, Switzerland, Tajikistan, Turkey, UK, USA	–	–	–	93[104]	–	21.4	–
(PC/DEC 112, 18 Apr. 1996)[105] July 1996	OSCE Mission to Croatia	Civ. staff: Austria, Czech Rep., Estonia, *Finland*, France, *Georgia*, Germany, Greece, Italy, Lithuania, Moldova, Netherlands, Poland, Romania, Slovakia, Spain, Sweden, UK, USA, Uzbekistan	67	–	–	35[106]	–	10.5	–

Acronym/ (Legal instrument, Authorization date)/ Start date	Name/ Location	Countries contributing troops, military observers (Mil. obs), civilian police (Civ. pol.) or civilian staff (Civ. staff) in 2006 (**bold text** = new in 2006; *italic text* = ended in 2006; underlined text = designated lead states)	Troops/ Military observers/ Civilian police/ Civilian staff		Total deaths: to date/in 2006 (due to hostilities, accidents, illness)	Cost ($ m.): 2006/ Unpaid
			Approved	Actual		
(PC/DEC 160, 27 Mar. 1997)[107] Apr. 1997	OSCE Presence in Albania Albania	Civ. staff: Austria, *Belarus*, Bulgaria, Czech Rep., Finland, France, *Germany*, Ireland, **Italy**, Latvia, **Lithuania**, Netherlands, **Romania**, *Sweden*, **Turkey**, UK, USA	– – –	– – 29[108]	– –	4.8 –
OMIK (PC/DEC 305, 1 July 1999)[109] July 1999	OSCE Mission in Kosovo Serbia (Kosovo)	Civ. staff: *Albania*, Armenia, Austria, Azerbaijan, Belgium, Bosnia and Herzegovina, Bulgaria, Canada, **Croatia**, Czech Rep., Denmark, *Estonia*, *Finland*, France, Georgia, Germany, Greece, Hungary, Ireland, Italy, **Japan**, **Lithuania**, *Moldova*, Netherlands, Norway, Poland, Portugal, Romania, Russia, **Slovakia**, *Slovenia*, Spain, Sweden, Tajikistan, Turkey, UK, USA, Uzbekistan	– – –	– – 177[110]	7 3 (–, 1, 2)	42.8 –
(PC/DEC 401, 11 Jan. 2001)[111] Mar. 2001	OSCE Mission to Serbia Serbia	Civ. staff: Belgium, Bosnia and Herzegovina, Bulgaria, Canada, **Croatia**, **Czech Rep.**, **Denmark**, Estonia, *Finland*, *France*, **Georgia**, Germany, *Greece*, **Hungary**, Ireland, Italy, *Latvia*, Netherlands, *Moldova*, Norway, Portugal, *Romania*, **Slovakia**, Sweden, Turkey, UK, USA	– 3?	– – 41[112]	– –	9.5[113] –
(PC/DEC 732, 29 June 2006)[114] **June 2006**	**OSCE Mission to Montenegro Montenegro**	Civ. staff: **Bulgaria, Bosnia and Herzegovina, Germany, Ireland, Italy, Netherlands, Norway, Romania, Sweden, Turkey, UK, USA**	– – –	– – 15[115]	– –	2.5 –

Ad hoc coalitions

Total: 7 missions		57 contributing countries				
			4 950 / 2 000 / – / 15	159 830 / 1 700 / 1 407 / 206	2 936 / 872 / – / –	89 572.3 / –
NNSC (Armistice Agreement)[116] July 1953	Neutral Nations Supervisory Commission, North Korea, South Korea	Mil. obs: Sweden, Switzerland	– / – / – / –	– / 10 / – / –	– / –	1.9 / –
MFO (Protocol to Treaty of Peace)[117] Apr. 1982	Multinational Force and Observers, Egypt (Sinai)	Mil. obs: Australia, Canada, Colombia, Fiji, France, Hungary, Italy, New Zealand, Norway, Uruguay, USA. Civ. staff: USA	– / 2 000 / – / 15	– / 1 687 / – / 15[118]	49 / –	61.2 / –
TIPH 2 (Hebron Protocol)[119] Jan. 1997	Temporary International Presence in Hebron (Hebron)	Mil. obs: Turkey. Civ. pol.: Denmark, Italy, Norway. Civ. staff: Denmark, *Italy*, Norway, Sweden, Switzerland, *Turkey*	– / – / – / –	– / 3 / 18 / 32[120]	2 / –	2.5 / –
— (SCR 1464)[121] Feb. 2003	Operation Licorne, Côte d'Ivoire	Troops: France	4 000 / – / – / –	3 500[122] / – / – / –	23 / 3 / (–, 1, 1)	319.8 / –
RAMSI (Biketawa Declaration)[123] July 2003	Regional Assistance Mission in the Solomon Islands, Solomon Islands	Troops: Australia, Fiji, New Zealand, Papua New Guinea, Tonga. Civ. pol.: Australia, Cook Islands, Fiji, Kiribati, **Marshall Islands, Micronesia**, Nauru, New Zealand, **Palau**, Papua New Guinea, Samoa, Tonga, Tuvalu, Vanuatu. Civ. staff: Australia, Fiji, New Zealand, Papua New Guinea, *Samoa*, Tonga	– / – / – / –	200 / – / 389[124] / 159[125]	2 / –	101.5[126] / –

Acronym/ (Legal instrument/ Authorization date)/ Start date	Name/ Location	Countries contributing troops, military observers (Mil. obs), civilian police (Civ. pol.) or civilian staff (Civ. staff) in 2006 (**bold** text = new in 2006; *italic* text = ended in 2006; <u>underlined</u> text = designated lead states)	Troops/ Military observers/ Civilian police/ Civilian staff		Total deaths: to date/in 2006/ (due to hostilities, accidents, illness)	Cost ($ m.): 2006/ Unpaid
			Approved	Actual		
MNF-I (SCR 1511)[127] Nov. 2003	Multinational Force in Iraq Iraq	Troops: Albania, Armenia, <u>Australia</u>, Azerbaijan, Bosnia and Herzegovina, **Bulgaria**, Czech Rep., Denmark, El Salvador, Estonia, Georgia, Japan, Kazakhstan, Korea (South), Latvia, Lithuania, Macedonia, Moldova, Mongolia, Poland, *Portugal*, Romania, Singapore, Slovakia, <u>UK</u>, <u>USA</u> Civ. pol: **El Salvador**, **Italy**, UK, USA	– – – –	155 200 – 1 000[128] –	2 860 869 (746, 74, 11)[129]	89 033.0[130] –
ISF **(25 May 2006 and** **SCR** **1690)**[131] **May 2006**	**International Security Forces** **Timor-Leste**	Troops: <u>Australia</u>, **New Zealand** Civ. pol.: *Australia, Malaysia, New Zealand, Portugal*	950 – – –	930[132] – – –	– –	52.4 –

Notes: CEMAC = Economic and Monetary Union of Central African States; CIS = Commonwealth of Independent States; CJA = EU Council Joint Action; CP/RES. = OAS Permanent Council resolution; CSO = OSCE Committee of Senior Officials (now the Senior Council); DDR = disarmament, demobilization and reintegration; EU = European Union; MOU = Memorandum of Understanding; NATO = North Atlantic Treaty Organization; OAS = Organization of American States; OSCE = Organization for Security and Co-operation in Europe; PC/DEC = OSCE Permanent Council Decision; SC = UN Security Council; SCR = UN Security Council Resolution; SSR = security sector reform; UNV = UN volunteer.

[1] UNTSO was established by SCR 50 (29 May 1948) and mandated to assist the Mediator and the Truce Commission in supervising the truce in Palestine after the 1948 Arab–Israeli War. In the following years it also assisted in observing the General Armistice Agreement of 1949 and the ceasefires in the aftermath of the 1967 Six-Day Arab–Israeli War. UNTSO cooperates closely with UNDOF and UNIFIL. The mandate was maintained during 2006. A positive decision by the UN Security Council (SC) is required to terminate the mission.

[2] The mission is supported by 120 locally recruited staff.

[3] UNMOGIP was established by SCR 91 (30 Mar. 1951) to replace the UN Commission for India and Pakistan. It is mandated to supervise the ceasefire in Kashmir under the Karachi Agreement (July 1949). A positive decision by the SC is required to terminate the mission.

[4] The mission is supported by 49 locally recruited staff.

5 UNFICYP was established by SCR 186 (4 Mar. 1964), and mandated to prevent fighting between the Greek Cypriot and Turkish Cypriot communities and to contribute to the maintenance and restoration of law and order. Since the end of hostilities in 1974, the mandate has included monitoring the de facto ceasefire (Aug. 1974) and maintaining a buffer zone between the two sides. SCR 1728 (15 Dec. 2006) extended the mandate until 15 June 2007.

6 The mission is supported by 104 locally recruited staff.

7 UNDOF was established by SCR 350 (31 May 1974), in the wake of the 1973 Middle East War, in accordance with the Agreement on Disengagement. It is mandated to observe the ceasefire and the disengagement of Israeli and Syrian forces as well as to maintain an area of limitation and separation. SCR 1729 (15 Dec. 2006) extended the mandate until 30 June 2007.

8 The mission is supported by 107 locally recruited staff.

9 UNIFIL was established by SCR 425 and SCR 426 (19 Mar. 1978), with a mandate to confirm the withdrawal of Israeli forces from southern Lebanon and to assist the Government of Lebanon in ensuring the return of its effective authority in the area. Following the conflict between Hezbollah and Israel in July 2006, SCR 1701 (11 Aug. 2006) strengthened the mandate and authorized an increase of the military personnel to 15 000 and the extension of the mandate until 31 Aug. 2007.

10 The mission is supported by 304 locally recruited staff.

11 MINURSO was established by SCR 690 (29 Apr. 1991) to monitor the ceasefire between the Frente Polisario and the Moroccan Government, to observe the integration of Western Sahara into Morocco. The mandate was renewed until 30 Apr. 2007 by SCR 1720 (31 Oct. 2006). troops and to prepare for a referendum concerning the integration of Western Sahara into Morocco. The mandate was renewed until 30 Apr. 2007 by SCR 1720 (31 Oct. 2006).

12 The mission is supported by 138 locally recruited staff and 22 UN volunteers (UNVs).

13 UNOMIG was established by SCR 849 (9 July 1993) and SCR 858 (24 Aug. 1993). Its mandate of verifying the ceasefire between the Georgian Government and the Abkhazian authorities was invalidated by resumed fighting in Sep. 1993. It was given an interim mandate to maintain contacts with both sides to the conflict and with the Russian military contingents and to monitor and report on the situation. Following the signing of the 1994 Agreement on a Ceasefire and Separation of Forces, its mandate was expanded to include monitoring and verification of the implementation of the agreement by SCR 937 (27 July 1994). The present mandate was renewed until 15 Apr. 2007 by SCR 1716 (13 Oct. 2006).

14 The mission is supported by 181 locally recruited staff and 1 UNV.

15 UNMIK was established by SCR 1244 (10 June 1999). Its mandate includes, among others, promoting the establishment of substantial autonomy and self-government in Kosovo, performing civilian administrative functions, maintaining law and order, promoting human rights, and ensuring the safe return of all refugees and displaced persons. It cooperates with the EU and the OSCE, which are responsible for the 'reconstruction and economic development' and 'democratization and institution building' pillars, respectively. A positive decision by the SC is required to terminate the mission.

16 The mission is supported by 2040 locally recruited staff and 152 UNVs.

17 MONUC was established by SCR 1279 (30 Nov. 1999). It was mandated by SCR 1291 (24 Feb. 2000) to monitor the implementation of the Ceasefire Agreement between the DR Congo, Angola, Namibia, Rwanda, Uganda and Zimbabwe, to supervise and verify the disengagement of forces, to monitor human rights violations, and to facilitate the provision of humanitarian assistance. The mission was given UN Charter Chapter VII powers by SCR 1493 (28 July 2003) and revised by SCR 1565 (1 Oct. 2004) to include deploying and maintaining a presence in key areas of potential volatility; cooperating with ONUB to monitor and prevent the movement of combatants and arms across shared borders; ensuring the protection of civilians; facilitating the disarmament, demobilization and reintegration (DDR) process; and assisting in the successful completion of the electoral process. During the election period in 2006 MONUC was supported by EUFOR RD Congo. SCR 1711 (29 Sep. 2006) extended the mandate until 15 Feb. 2007 and authorized an increase in military personnel and civilian police.

18 The mission is supported by 2092 locally recruited staff and 665 UNVs.

19 UNMEE was established by SCR 1320 (15 Sep. 2000). It was expanded by SCR 1312 (31 July 2000) and mandated to monitor the ceasefire; to repatriate Ethiopian troops and supervise the position of Ethiopian and Eritrean troops outside a 25-km temporary security zone; to chair the Military Coordination Commission of the UN and the AU; and

to assist in mine clearance. SCR 1741 (30 Jan. 2007) extended the mandate until 31 July 2007, which was necessitated by delays in the demarcation process for the Eritrea–Ethiopia border.

20 The mission is supported by 194 locally recruited staff and 65 UNVs.

21 UNMIL was established by SCR 1509 (19 Sep. 2003) under UN Charter Chapter VII. It is mandated to support the implementation of the 2003 Comprehensive Peace Agreement, to provide assistance in matters of humanitarian and human rights, to assist in security sector reform (SSR), and to protect civilians. It cooperates with UNOCI and UNOSIL. SCR 1712 (29 Sep. 2006) renewed the current mandate until 31 Mar. 2007.

22 The mission is supported by 940 locally recruited staff and 263 UNVs.

23 UNOCI was established by SCR 1528 (27 Feb. 2004) under UN Charter Chapter VII. It is mandated to monitor the ceasefire agreement, support the interim Government of National Reconciliation in extending state control, to maintain law and order, to implement a DDR programme, to facilitate humanitarian assistance, to protect and promote human rights, and to assist in holding free elections. It cooperates with UNMIL and Operation Licorne. SCR 1739 (10 Jan. 2007) extended the mandate until 30 June 2007.

24 The mission is supported by 526 locally recruited staff and 209 UNVs.

25 ONUB was established by SCR 1545 (21 May 2004) under UN Charter Chapter VII. It was mandated to ensure respect of the 2000 Arusha Peace and Reconciliation Agreement, facilitate a DDR programme, assist in the successful completion of the electoral process, carry out institutional reforms and protect civilians. In carrying out its mandate, ONUB cooperated with MONUC. The mission closed on 31 Dec. 2006.

26 During 2006 the military component was gradually drawn down from the 5726 deployed in Jan. 2006.

27 The mission is supported by 308 locally recruited staff and 98 UNVs.

28 MINUSTAH was established by SCR 1542 (30 Apr. 2004) under UN Charter Chapter VII and mandated to maintain a secure and stable environment to ensure that the peace process is carried forward; to assist the Haitian Government's efforts in SSR, including a comprehensive DDR programme, building the capacity of the national police and re-establishing the rule of law; to assist the government in preparation for free elections; to support humanitarian and human rights activities; and to protect civilians. SCR 1702 (15 Aug. 2006) extended the mandate until 15 Feb. 2007.

29 The mission is supported by 642 locally recruited staff and 191 UNVs.

30 UNMIS was established by SCR 1590 (24 Mar. 2005) following the 2005 Comprehensive Peace Agreement. It is mandated to monitor the implementation of the peace agreement, to protect and promote human rights, and to facilitate the DDR process. SCR 1706 (31 Aug. 2006) expanded the mandate to include deployment to the Darfur region, where UNMIS is tasked to monitor implementation of the 2006 Darfur Peace Agreement and the 2006 N'Djamena Agreement on Humanitarian Cease-fire on the Conflict in Darfur, to maintain a presence in key areas, to monitor border activities, to protect civilians, and to promote and protect human rights. SCR 1714 (6 Oct. 2006) extended the mandate until 30 Apr. 2007.

31 These figures do not include the staffing level for Darfur authorized by SCR 1706 (31 Aug. 2006).

32 The mission is supported by 2234 locally recruited staff and 185 UNVs.

33 UNMIT was established by SCR 1704 (25 Aug. 2006) following the outbreak of violence in May 2006. It is mandated to support the Government of Timor-Leste in post-conflict peacebuilding; in capacity building, support and training of the East Timorese national police; and in the organization and holding of presidential and parliamentary elections in 2007. SCR 1745 (22 Feb. 2007) extended the mandate until 26 Feb 2008.

34 The mission is supported by 320 locally recruited staff and 100 UNVs.

35 UNAMA was established by SCR 1401 (28 Mar. 2002). It is mandated to promote national reconciliation; to fulfil the tasks and responsibilities entrusted to the UN in the 2001 Bonn Agreement, including those related to human rights, the rule of law and gender issues; and to manage all UN humanitarian, relief, recovery and reconstruction activities in Afghanistan in coordination with the Afghan Government. It cooperates with ISAF in carrying out its mandate. SRC 1662 (23 Mar. 2006) extended the mandate until 23 Mar. 2007.

36 The mission is supported by 843 locally recruited staff and 34 UNVs.

37 UNAMI was established by SCR 1500 (14 Aug. 2003). It is currently mandated to assist the Iraqi Government in the process of political and economic development, to coordinate reconstruction and humanitarian assistance, to promote human rights and national reconciliation, and to strengthen the rule of law. In carrying out its mandate, UNAMI cooperates with MNF-I, NTM-I and EUJUST LEX. SCR 1700 (10 Aug. 2006) extended the current mandate until 10 Aug. 2007.

38 The mission is supported by 189 locally recruited staff.

39 UNOTIL was established by SCR 1599 (28 Apr. 2005). It was mandated to support the capacity development of state institutions, including the National Police (PNTL) and Border Patrol Unit, and provide training in the area of human rights. The mission closed on 25 Aug. 2006 and was succeeded by UNMIT.

40 The mission was supported by 221 locally recruited staff and 34 UNVs.

41 UNIOSIL was established by SCR 1620 (31 Aug. 2005) to assist the Government of Sierra Leone in capacity building of state institutions, democratization, good governance, rule of law, human rights promotion, strengthening the security sector, and preparation for free and fair elections in 2007; to monitor security; to address cross-border challenges; and to coordinate with the Special Court for Sierra Leone. SCR 1734 (22 Dec. 2006) extended the mandate until 31 Dec. 2007.

42 The mission is supported by 176 locally recruited staff and 29 UNVs.

43 AMIS was initially established as an observer mission by the Agreement with the Sudanese Parties on the Modalities for the Establishment of the Ceasefire Commission and the Deployment of Observers in the Darfur on 28 May 2004 and was endorsed by SCR 1556 (30 July 2004) under UN Charter Chapter VII. Its mandate was expanded pursuant to a decision adopted at the 17th Meeting of the AU's Peace and Security Council (AU PSC/PR/Comm.(XVII), 20 Oct. 2004) and now includes monitoring the N'Djamena ceasefire agreement, assisting in confidence building between the parties and contributing to a secure environment in Darfur. AU PSC/AHG/Comm.(LXVI) (30 Nov. 2006) extended the mandate until 30 June 2007.

44 Contributors of additional military observers were listed by the AU as 'EU/USA' (23), 'Government of Sudan' (34), 'Justice and Equality Movement' (34) and 'Sudan Liberation Movement/Army' (34).

45 The budget is projected for 1 year based on the AMIS budget for Apr.–Dec. 2006.

46 AMISEC was established by the AU Peace and Security Council (AU, PSC/PR/Comm.1(XLVII), 21 Mar. 2006). It was mandated to provide a secure environment conducive to credible, free and fair elections taking place in May 2006. The mission closed on 9 June 2006.

47 France, Norway and the UK contributed logistical support and equipment.

48 A reinforcement contingent of 675 South African soldiers was deployed from 11 to 19 May 2006.

49 One-third of AMISEC's budget was funded by the EU.

50 FOMUC was established by a decision of the CEMAC Libreville Summit (2 Oct. 2002) to secure the border between Chad and the Central African Republic (CAR) and to guarantee the safety of former President Patassé. Following the 15 Mar. 2003 coup, its mandate was expanded by a decision of the Libreville Summit (21 Mar. 2003) to include contributing to the overall security environment, assisting in the restructuring of CAR's armed forces and supporting the transition process. The current mandate runs until 30 Jun. 2007.

51 FOMUC is supported by and co-located with a detachment of 225 French soldiers. In addition, there are 58 locally recruited staff.

52 79% of CEMAC's budget is funded by the EU and the remaining 21% by annual contributions of CEMAC member states.

53 While complete data are not available on all participating countries' costs for CIS missions, Russia's expenditure for CIS missions in 2006 was $1 883 226, including upkeep of coordinating structures in the CIS and spending related to the Collective Security Treaty. The Russian general contribution to CIS collective security and peacekeeping was $3 794 705 in 2006.

54 The Joint Control Commission Peacekeeping Force was established by the Agreement on the Principles Governing the Peaceful Settlement of the Armed Conflict in the Trans-Dniester region (21 July 1992). A monitoring commission with representatives from Moldova, Russia and the Trans-Dniester authorities coordinates the activities of the

joint peacekeeping contingent. The participation of parties to a conflict in peace operations is typically not included in the table; however, the substantial involvement of the parties to the conflict in this operation is a distinctive feature of CIS operations and of the peace agreement, which is the basis for the establishment of the operation.

55 This figure only includes Moldovan and Russian fatalities. The deaths were caused by accidents and illness.

56 The South Ossetia Joint Force was established by the Agreement on the Principles Governing the Peaceful Settlement of the Conflict in South Ossetia (24 June 1992). A joint Monitoring Commission with representatives of Russia, Georgia, and the North and South Ossetia authorities was established to oversee implementation of the agreement. On inclusion of participation of conflicting parties in the table see note 54.

57 The CIS Peacekeeping Forces in Georgia mission was established by the Georgian–Abkhazian Agreement on a Ceasefire and Separation of Forces (14 May 1994). The operation's mandate was approved by heads of state of the members of the CIS Council of Collective Security (21 Oct. 1994) and endorsed by the UN through SCR 937 (21 July 1994). Its mandate was extended indefinitely from Jan. 2004.

58 EU Council Joint Actions do not provide specific authorized personnel numbers. Instead they request that staff levels are consistent with the objectives and structures of each mission. The numbers listed for these EU missions are those agreed by the EU.

59 The EUMM was established by the Brioni Agreement (7 July 1991) between representatives of the European Community (EC) and the 6 republics of the former Yugoslavia. MOUs were signed with the governments of Albania in 1997 and Croatia in 1998. It is mandated to monitor political and security developments, borders, inter-ethnic issues and refugee returns; to contribute to the early warning mechanism of the European Council; and to contribute to confidence building and stabilization in the region (CJA 2000/811/CFSP, 23 Dec. 2000). CJA 2005/807/CFSP (21 Nov. 2005) amended the mission's geographical mandate to focus on Kosovo and Serbia and Montenegro. CJA 2006/867/CFSP (30 Nov. 2006) extended the mandate until 31 Dec. 2007.

60 The mission is supported by 64 locally recruited staff.

61 The EUPM was established by CJA 2002/210/CFSP (11 Mar. 2002) to ensure sustainable policing arrangements in Bosnia and Herzegovina under Bosnian ownership, in accordance with European and international standards. It is mandated to monitor, mentor and inspect locally recruited police force management. At the request of the Bosnian authorities, the EU modified the mandate (including the size) of the mission and extended it to the end of 2007 (CJA 2005/824/CFSP, 24. Nov. 2005).

62 The mission is supported by 215 locally recruited staff.

63 EUFOR ALTHEA was established by CJA 2004/570/CFSP (12 July 2004) and was endorsed and given UN Charter Chapter VII powers by SCR 1551 (9 July 2004). It is mandated to maintain a secure environment for the implementation of the 1995 Dayton Agreement, to assist in the strengthening of local capacity, and to support Bosnia and Herzegovina's progress towards EU integration. The contingents are grouped into 3 Multinational Task Forces (MNTFs): MNTF North (Tuzla), MNTF Southeast (Mostar) and MNTF Northwest (Banja Luka)—for which Austria, France and the UK, respectively, are the framework nations. SCR 1722 (21 Nov. 2006) extended the mandate until Nov. 2007.

64 In the spring of 2007, EUFOR ALTHEA will undergo a drawdown in its troop strength from 6000 to approximately 2500.

65 The mission is supported by 200 international contracted staff, who work for both EUFOR ALTHEA and NATO Headquarters.

66 EUPOL Kinshasa was established by CJA 2004/847/CFSP (9 Dec. 2004) and is mandated to monitor, mentor and advise the Congolese police force. EUPOL Kinshasa collaborates with EUSEC DR Congo. The mandate runs until 30 June 2007.

67 The mission is supported by 9 locally recruited staff.

68 EUSEC DR Congo was established by CJA 2005/355/CFSP (2 May 2005) to complement EUPOL Kinshasa. It is mandated to advise and assist the Congolese authorities on security matters, ensuring that policies are congruent with international humanitarian law, the standards of democratic governance and the principles of rule of law. In carrying out its activities, EUSEC also operates in close coordination with MONUC.

69 Of this figure, 21 are based in Kinshasa while 11 are located in the eastern parts of the DR Congo. The majority are military advisers. The mission is supported by c. 30 locally recruited staff.

70 EUJUST LEX was established by CJA 2005/190/CFSP (7 Mar. 2005) and was endorsed and given UN Charter Chapter VII powers by SCR 1546 (8 June 2004) as an integrated civilian rule-of-law mission to strengthen Iraq's criminal justice system through the training of police officers and magistrates. It will complement NTM-I and UNAMI. CJA 13171/06 (17 Oct. 2006) extended the mandate until 31 Dec. 2007.

71 Listed are the 10 states providing the training in 2006. Financial support also comes from Austria, Belgium, Egypt, Finland, Hungary, Luxembourg, Sweden and the USA.

72 AMM was established by CJA 2005/643/CFSP (9 Sep. 2005) to monitor implementation of the peace agreement set out in the 2005 MOU signed by the Government of Indonesia and the Free Aceh Movement (GAM). Its mandate includes monitoring the ceasefire; DDR of GAM fighters; assisting in the withdrawal of Indonesian military and police forces; and monitoring the human rights situation. During 2006, it underwent a reduction from the initial 230 to 36 staff and its district and sub-district offices closed on 7 Sep. 2006. The mission closed entirely on 15 Dec. 2006.

73 These are civilian observers. The mission was supported by 45 locally recruited staff.

74 EU BAM Rafah was established pursuant to CJA 2005/889/CFSP (12 Dec. 2005) and on the basis of the Agreement on Movement and Access between Israel and the Palestinian Authority (15 Nov. 2005). It is mandated to monitor, verify and evaluate the performance of Palestinian Authority border control, security and customs officials at the Rafah Crossing Point with regard to the 2005 Agreed Principles for Rafah Crossing; and support the Palestinian Authority's capacity building in the field of border control. The mandate runs until 24 May 2007.

75 The mission is supported by 11 locally recruited staff.

76 EUPAT was established by CJA 2005/826/CFSP (24 Nov. 2005). It was mandated to support the development of a national police service, monitoring and mentoring the police in the fields of border policing, public peace and order, accountability, and combating corruption and organized crime. The mission closed on 14 June 2006.

77 The mission is supported by 20 locally recruited staff.

78 EUPOL COPPS was established by CJA 2005/797/CFSP (14 Nov. 2005). It is mandated to provide a framework for and advise Palestinian criminal justice and police officials and coordinate EU aid to the Palestinian Authority. The mission's 3-year mandate runs until 31 Dec. 2008.

79 The mission is supported by 4 locally recruited staff.

80 EUFOR RD Congo was established by CJA 2006/319/CFSP (27 Apr. 2006) and mandated to support MONUC during the election process in the DR Congo. It was endorsed and given UN Charter Chapter VII powers by UN SCR1671 (24 Apr. 2006). The mission closed on 30 Nov. 2006.

81 Of these troops, 1075 were based in Kinshasa and 1200 were stationed in Libreville, Gabon, as a reserve force. The figure does not include a further strategic reserve of 1500 troops stationed in France.

82 KFOR was established by SCR 1244 (10 June 1999). Its mandated tasks include deterring renewed hostilities, establishing a secure environment, supporting UNMIK and monitoring borders. Along with KFOR Headquarters in Priština, KFOR contingents are grouped into 6 multinational task forces (MNTFs): MNTF Centre (Lipljan) led by Finland; MNTF North (Novo Selo), led by France; MNTF South (Prizren), led by Germany; MNTF West (Pec), led by Italy; and MNTF East (Urosevac), led by the USA. A Multinational Specialized Unit (Priština) is led by Italy.

83 Partner countries contribute 16% of these troops.

84 ISAF was established by SCR 1386 (20 Dec. 2001) under UN Charter Chapter VII as a multinational force mandated to assist the Afghan Interim Authority to maintain security, as envisaged in Annex 1 of the 2001 Bonn Agreement. NATO took on command and control of ISAF in Aug. 2003. Stages 3 and 4 of ISAF's expansion into southern and eastern Afghanistan were completed in July and Oct. 2006, respectively. ISAF also has control of all 24 provincial reconstruction teams (PRTs). ISAF divides Afghanistan into five areas of responsibility: Regional Command (RC) Centre (Kabul), led by France; RC North (Mazar-i-Sharif), led by Germany; RC West (Herat), led by Italy; RC South (Kandahar), led by the Netherlands; and RC East (Bagram), led by the USA. SCR 1707 (12 Sep. 2006) extended the mandate until 12 Oct. 2007.

85 This includes personnel serving in the PRTs from the following countries: Australia, Belgium, Canada, Czech Rep., Denmark, Estonia, Finland, France, Germany, Hungary, Iceland, Italy, Lithuania, the Netherlands, Norway, Romania, Spain, Sweden, Switzerland, the UK and the USA.

86 NTM-I was established pursuant to SCR 1546 (8 June 2004) and approved by the North Atlantic Council on 17 Nov. 2004. It is mandated to assist in the development of Iraq's security institutions through training and equipment of, in particular, middle- and senior-level personnel from the Iraqi security forces.

87 No data on national breakdown were available and therefore no lead nation could be identified.

88 MAPP/OEA was established by OAS Permanent Council (PC) resolution CP/RES 859 (1397/04) of 6 Feb. 2004 to support the efforts of the Colombian Government to engage in a political dialogue with the National Liberation Army (ELN). It is mandated to facilitate the DDR process.

89 The mission is supported by 32 international contracted staff, 15 national professionals and 53 locally recruited staff.

90 The OAS Special Mission for Strengthening Democracy in Haiti was established by OAS PC resolution CP/RES. 806 (1303/02) of 16 Jan. 2002. It is mandated to contribute to resolution of the political crisis in Haiti, including by assisting the Government of Haiti to strengthen its democratic processes and institutions. OAS General Assembly Resolution A/RES 2058 (XXXIV-O/04) of 8 June 2004 amended the mandate to include assistance in the holding of elections, promoting and protecting human rights, and the professionalization of the Haitian National Police.

91 The mission is supported by 103 locally recruited staff.

92 The figure is for the period 1 Oct. 2005–31 Sep. 2006

93 The OSCE Spillover Monitor Mission to Skopje was established following a decision of the 16th meeting of the OSCE Committee of Senior Officials (CSO) (18 Sep. 1993). It was authorized by the FYROM Government through Articles of Understanding agreed by an exchange of letters on 7 Nov. 1992. Its tasks include monitoring, police training, development and other activities related to the 1992 Ohrid Framework Agreement. PC.DEC/764 (14 Dec. 2006) extended the mandate until 31 Dec. 2007.

94 The mission is supported by 5 international contracted staff and 188 locally recruited staff.

95 The OSCE Mission to Georgia was established at the 17th CSO meeting (6 Nov. 1992). It was authorized by the Government of Georgia through an MOU on 23 Jan. 1993 and by South Ossetia's leaders through an exchange of letters on 1 Mar. 1993. Its initial objective was to promote negotiations between the conflicting parties. The mandate was expanded at the 14th PC Meeting (29 Mar. 1994) to include monitoring the Joint Peacekeeping Forces in South Ossetia. PC.DEC/450 (13 Dec. 1999) expanded the mandate to include monitoring Georgia's borders with Russian Republic of Ingushetia. PC.DEC/522, 19 Dec. 2002 expanded the mandate to include observing and reporting on cross-border movement between Georgia and the Russian Republic of Dagestan. PC.DEC/766 (14 Dec. 2006) extended the mandate until 31 Dec. 2007.

96 The mission is supported by 6 international contracted staff and 132 locally recruited staff.

97 The OSCE Mission to Moldova was established at the 19th CSO meeting (4 Feb. 1993) and authorized by the Government of Moldova through an MOU (7 May 1993). Its tasks include assisting the conflicting parties in pursuing negotiations on a lasting political settlement and gathering and providing information on the situation. PC.DEC/763 (14 Dec. 2006) extended the mandate until 31 Dec. 2007.

98 The mission is supported by 4 international contracted staff and 32 locally recruited staff.

99 The OSCE Centre in Dushanbe was established by a decision taken at the 4th meeting of the OSCE Ministerial Council, CSCE/4-C/Dec. 1, Decision I.4 (1 Dec. 1993). No bilateral MOU has been signed. The mission's mandate includes facilitating dialogue, promoting human rights and informing the OSCE about further developments. This was expanded in 2002 to include an economic and environmental dimension. PC.DEC/754 (23 Nov. 2006) extended the mandate until 31 Dec. 2007.

100 The mission is supported by 3 international contracted staff and 68 locally recruited staff.

101 A Personal Representative (PR) on the Conflict Dealt with by the OSCE Minsk Conference was appointed by the OSCE Chairman-in-Office (CIO) on 10 Aug. 1995. The Minsk Conference seeks a peaceful settlement to the Nagorno-Karabakh conflict. The PR's mandate consists of assisting the CIO in planning possible peacekeeping operations, assisting the parties in confidence-building measures and in humanitarian matters, and monitoring the ceasefire between the parties. The PR has 5 field assistants. A positive decision is required to terminate the mission.

102 The mission is supported by 11 locally recruited staff.

103 The OSCE Mission to Bosnia and Herzegovina was established by a decision of the 5th meeting of the Ministerial Council (MC(5).DEC/1, 8 Dec. 1995), in accordance with Annex 6 of the 1995 Dayton Agreement. The mission is mandated to assist the parties in regional stabilization measures and democracy building. PC.DEC/747 (23 Nov. 2006) extended the mandate until 31 Dec. 2007.

104 The mission is supported by 558 locally recruited staff.

105 The OSCE Mission to Croatia was established by PC.DEC/112 (18 Apr. 1996), PC.DEC/176 (26 June 1997) and C/DEC/239 (25 June 1998) revised its mandate. Its mandate includes assisting and monitoring the return of refugees and displaced persons and protecting national minorities.

106 The mission is supported by 144 locally recruited staff.

107 The OSCE Presence in Albania was established by PC.DEC/160 (27 Mar. 1997). PC.DEC/206 (11 Dec. 1997) established the current mandate. PC.DEC/750 (23 Nov. 2006) extended the mandate until 31 Dec. 2007.

108 The mission is supported by 93 locally recruited staff.

109 The OSCE Mission in Kosovo was established by the PC.DEC/305 (1 July 1999). Its mandate includes training police, judicial personnel and civil administrators and monitoring and promoting human rights. The mission is a component (pillar III) of UNMIK. Its headquarters are in Priština and 5 regional centres are sited throughout Kosovo, each covering 5 to 9 municipalities. 30 municipal teams, supervising the work of locally recruited authorities, were deployed to all municipalities. PC.DEC/765 (14 Dec. 2006) extended the mandate until 31 Dec. 2007.

110 The mission is supported by 62 international contracted staff and 749 locally recruited staff.

111 The OSCE Mission to Serbia is the new name given to the OSCE Mission to Serbia and Montenegro in June 2006. The mission was originally established by PC.DEC/401 (11 Jan. 2001) as the OSCE Mission to the Federal Republic of Yugoslavia. Its mandate is to advise on the implementation of laws and monitor the proper functioning and development of democratic institutions and processes in Serbia. It assists in the training and restructuring of law enforcement bodies and the judiciary. The latest change of name followed the declaration of independence by Montenegro (3 June 2006). PC.DEC/749 (23 Nov. 2006) extended the mandate until 31 Dec. 2007

112 The mission is supported by 2 international contracted staff and 138 locally recruited staff.

113 This figure covers the budget for the first month of deployment of the OSCE Mission to Montenegro as well as the budget of the OSCE Mission to Serbia.

114 The OSCE Mission to Montenegro was established by PC.DEC/732 (29 June 2006) following the declaration of independence by Montenegro (June 2006). Prior to independence, the current mission was part of the OSCE Mission to Serbia and Montenegro (see note 111). Its mandate is to assist in institution building and reform of law enforcement bodies and the judiciary and to support local and central governance structures. PC.DEC/751 (23 Nov. 2006) extended the mandate until 31 Dec. 2007.

115 The mission is supported by 30 locally recruited staff.

116 The NNSC was established by the agreement concerning a military armistice in Korea signed at Panmunjom (27 July 1953). It is mandated with the functions of supervision, observation, inspection and investigation implementation of the armistice agreement.

117 The MFO was established on 3 Aug. 1981 by the Protocol to the Treaty of Peace between Egypt and Israel, signed 26 Mar. 1979. Deployment began on 20 Mar. 1982 following the withdrawal of Israeli forces from the Sinai but the mission was not operational until 25 Apr. 1982, the day that Israel returned the Sinai to Egyptian sovereignty.

118 A large part of the MFO's basic mission in the Sinai is performed by the Civilian Observer Unit (COU). The COU has its origins in the US Sinai Field Mission, which came into existence with the Sinai II Agreement (4 Sep. 1975). The COU currently has 15 personnel, all US nationals.

119 TIPH 2 was established by the Protocol Concerning the Redeployment in Hebron (17 Jan. 1997) and the Agreement on the Temporary International Presence in Hebron (21 Jan. 1997). Its mandate is to provide by its presence a secure and stable environment. Following the attack on its headquarters on 8 Feb. 2006, TIPH 2 was temporarily withdrawn from Hebron and reduced in strength. On May 2006 TIPH 2 returned to conduct daytime patrols on a regular basis, but was stationed in Bethlehem. On 24 Oct. 2006 the mission returned to Hebron and since then operates on a normal basis. The mandate is renewed every 3 months pending approval from the Israeli and Palestinian sides.

120 The mission is supported by 8 locally recruited staff.

121 Operation Licorne, consisting entirely of French troops, was deployed under the authority of SCR 1464 (4 Feb. 2003), under UN Charter Chapter VII and in accordance with UN Charter Chapter VIII, to support the ECOWAS mission in contributing to a secure environment and, in particular, to facilitate implementation of the 2003 Linas–Marcoussis Agreement. SCR 1528 (27 Feb. 2004) provides its current authorization and revised the mandate to working in support of UNOCI. SCR 1739 (10 Jan. 2007) expanded the mandate and extended it until 30 June 2007.

122 The troops deployed in Côte d'Ivoire are supported by further troops based in Togo (100 personnel per air unit).

123 RAMSI was established under the framework of the 2000 Biketawa Declaration in which members of the Pacific Islands Forum agreed to mount a collective response to crises, usually at the request of the host government. It is mandated to assist the Solomon Islands Government in restoring law and order and in building up the capacity of the police force.

124 Civilian police numbers provided ranged from 308 to 389. In Apr. 2006 approximately 389 additional troops and 75 police were deployed in response to riots after parliamentary elections.

125 The figure does not include personnel assigned to the Office of the Special Coordinator. The mission is supported by 51 locally recruited staff.

126 This figure represents the Australian contribution to RAMSI for financial year 2006/2007.

127 The MNF-I was authorized by SCR 1511 (16 Oct. 2003) to contribute to the maintenance of security and stability in Iraq, including for the purpose of ensuring necessary conditions for the implementation of UNAMIS's mandated tasks. The mandate of MNF-I was reaffirmed by SCR 1546 (8 June 2004) following the dissolution of the Coalition Provisional Authority and the subsequent transfer of sovereignty to the Interim Government of Iraq. For MNF-I purposes, the territory of Iraq is divided into 5 areas covered by the following units: MNF North, Multinational Division (MND) Baghdad and MND West, for which the USA is the lead nation; MND Central South, maintained by Poland; and MND Southeast, maintained by Australia and the UK. SCR 1723 (28 Nov. 2006) extended the mandate until 31 Dec. 2007.

128 The figure for civilian police is approximate and includes 110 personnel drawn from coalition military forces.

129 The figure for total deaths to date only includes fatalities after the SC authorization. It is revised based on information received. Of the 869 deaths in 2006, 820 were suffered by the USA, 29 by the UK and the remaining 20 by other countries. The figure also includes 38 deaths owing to other causes.

130 This figure is the sum of British and US contributions. Contributing countries bear the costs for their own personnel. The estimated US contribution for financial year 2005/2006 (1 Oct. 2005–30 Sep. 2006) was $87 billion, which included emergency supplemental appropriations approved by the US Congress in June 2006. The British contribution for the period 1 Oct. 2005–30 Sep. 2006 is estimated at $1.1 billion. This was the amount requested from the British Ministry of Defence.

131 The ISF, also known as Operation Astute and Joint Task Force, was deployed at the request of the Government of Timor-Leste to assist in stabilizing the security environment in the county and endorsed by SCR 1690 (20 June 2006). The ISF cooperates closely with UNMIT.

132 In the first months of deployment there were up to 1300 Australian and 200 New Zealand troops on the ground. At the end of Sep. 2006 the deployed civilian police units of ISF were subsumed under UNMIT.

4. Regional security cooperation in the former Soviet area

ALYSON J. K. BAILES, VLADIMIR BARANOVSKY and
PÁL DUNAY

I. Introduction

The use of regional organizations for purposes of security cooperation has increased worldwide since the end of the cold war.[1] Traditionally devoted to avoiding conflict and limiting military tensions between neighbours or to combining their forces in other forms of positive cooperation, such communities have had to address a further range of new threats after the terrorist attacks on the United States on 11 September 2001. Aside from several overlapping organizations in the wider Europe, the tendency for such groups both to multiply and to elaborate their agendas has been plain in Africa, South-East Asia and Latin America (at both regional and subregional level). Analysts and policymakers have also increasingly noted that the regions generating the sharpest security problems—including dangers of the proliferation of weapons of mass destruction—are those that lack such structures for cooperation or where neighbouring states are linked only by negative dynamics.[2]

A chapter in the *SIPRI Yearbook 2006* proposed some universal criteria for judging the efficiency and legitimacy of security-oriented regional mechanisms.[3] The authors identified four broad types of role—not mutually exclusive—that regional organizations could play in the context of security: (*a*) avoiding, containing and resolving conflict within the region; (*b*) pursuing practical military cooperation, including in non-zero-sum contexts such as international peace missions; (*c*) promoting reform, democracy and good governance in the defence and security field or more generally; and (*d*) tackling

---

[1] For details and for a fuller explanation of the assumptions and definitions underlying this chapter see Bailes, A. J. K. and Cottey, A., 'Regional security cooperation in the early 21st century', *SIPRI Yearbook 2006: Armaments, Disarmament and International Security* (Oxford University Press: Oxford, 2006), pp. 195–223.

[2] E.g. the current US National Security Strategy argues specifically that the USA's relations with other 'centres of global power' must be supported by 'appropriate institutions, regional and global, to make cooperation more permanent, effective, and wide-reaching'. It states that 'this regional approach has particular application to Israeli–Palestinian issues, the conflicts in the Great Lakes region of Africa, and the conflict within Nepal'. The White House, 'The National Security Strategy of the United States of America', Washington, DC, Mar. 2006, URL <http://www.whitehouse.gov/nsc/nss/2006>, pp. 36 and 16, respectively.

[3] Bailes and Cottey (note 1).

* The assistance of Ivan Danilin (Institute of World Economy and International Relations, IMEMO) in the preparation of working materials for sections II–IV of this chapter is gratefully acknowledged.

functional issues, including the so-called new threats and other challenges arising in the borderland between security and economics. They suggested the following tests for legitimacy and effectiveness, based on observation and actual policy discourse rather than theory: '(*a*) whether cooperation is coerced and hegemonic; (*b*) whether it posits a zero-sum relationship with the outside world; (*c*) whether it is rigid or static (or adaptable and capable of growth); (*d*) whether it is artificial and superficial; and (*e*) whether it is efficient in terms of management and resource use'.[4] Tests based on the type of structure or degree of institutionalization were deliberately avoided, since these features should be adapted to regions' specific needs. SIPRI has examined a number of regional structures and evaluated them from these standpoints.[5]

This chapter applies this new analytical approach to three explicitly security-related constructs existing in the former Soviet space—the Commonwealth of Independent States (CIS), the Collective Security Treaty Organization (CSTO), and the grouping of Georgia, Ukraine, Azerbaijan and Moldova called the Organization for Democracy and Economic Development–GUAM (hereafter referred to as GUAM)—together with the Shanghai Cooperation Organization (SCO), which links some members of those groups with China (see table 4.1 in section II, below). All these groups tend to be poorly known outside their region and are often exposed to normative criticism both outside and in some parts of that region. The three Russia-led groups (the CIS, the CSTO and the SCO) are often seen in the West as aiming at a kind of neo-Soviet hegemony, implying coercion and undemocratic practices;[6] their opposition to terrorism and insurgency is interpreted as a common agenda of isolating and crushing minority elements; and strategically, they are viewed as an essentially zero-sum effort to balance Western groupings or to obstruct US and Western influence. It is widely assumed that all four groups suffer from rigid, artificial forms of governance and low levels of efficiency and output. The present account explores such judgements and normative questions, to which these organizations deserve to be subjected as much as any others. The answers are sought in a historical perspective and in the light of factual, dispassionate reporting and analysis.

The next section of this chapter provides the historical element by sketching the background to the emergence of the first post-Soviet regional grouping, the CIS, and the subsequent development of the CSTO, GUAM and the SCO. Sections III–VI evaluate the CIS, the CSTO, GUAM and the SCO, respect-

[4] Bailes and Cottey (note 1), p. 215.

[5] See Adisa, J., 'The African Union: the vision, programmes, policies and challenges', *SIPRI Yearbook 2003: Armaments, Disarmament and International Security* (Oxford University Press: Oxford, 2003), pp. 79–85; Hollis, R., 'The greater Middle East', and Rosas, M. C., 'Latin America and the Caribbean: security and defence in the post-cold war era', *SIPRI Yearbook 2005: Armaments, Disarmament and International Security* (Oxford University Press: Oxford, 2005), pp. 223–82; and Bailes, A. J. K. et al., *Regionalism in South Asian Diplomacy*, SIPRI Policy Paper no. 15 (SIPRI: Stockholm, Feb. 2007), URL <http://www.sipri.org>.

[6] In June 2006 US Secretary of Defense Donald Rumsfeld also called the SCO's security values into question by accusing the members of considering the accession of Iran as a full member at a time when it was causing proliferation- and terrorism-related concerns. Dyer, G. and Yeh, A., 'Iranian president to cause a stir at security summit', *Financial Times*, 14 June 2006, p. 3. See also section V below.

ively, against the five criteria proposed above. The conclusions are presented in section VII.

II. Background: basic realities of the former Soviet area

The break-up of the Soviet Union was neither adequately prepared nor seriously negotiated. Most of the political actors that were directly involved had very vague ideas (if any) of what would take the place of a single state that had covered one-sixth of the globe. Against such a background, it is not surprising that the emerging picture of regional security cooperation has its chaotic and controversial features. It has, in fact, developed in multiple formats that are set out and compared in table 4.1. The main factors shaping the evolution of security cooperation in the post-Soviet area since 1990 may be summarized as follows.

Force of inertia. For a certain period after the collapse of the Soviet Union, the inertial effect of a former common security space continued to influence the newly independent states, despite their formal independence. When the CIS was hastily proclaimed at the end of 1991 to replace the Soviet Union,[7] the idea of maintaining common armed forces and a joint military potential was considered workable. The same inertia—underpinned by economic, historical, societal, cultural and psychological factors—persisted well into the 1990s and beyond, but it could not indefinitely provide a driving force for promoting regional security cooperation in fast changing conditions.

'Former Soviet Union minus the Baltics'. The post-Soviet space was from the beginning divided into two areas. Estonia, Latvia and Lithuania, the three Baltic states, disengaged from the rest of the post-Soviet territory in a more radical way than any others, as clearly seen in their non-membership of the CIS. Conversely, they set their sights on joining the North Atlantic Treaty Organization (NATO) far earlier than, for instance, Georgia or Ukraine and were duly admitted as members of both NATO and the European Union (EU) in 2004.

Cooperation between antagonists. In some cases, the prospects for regional security cooperation were blocked or seriously undermined by disputes inherited from Soviet or pre-Soviet times, with the potential to cause open conflict—notably in the case of the dispute between Armenia and Azerbaijan over the autonomous region of Nagorno-Karabakh in south-western Azerbaijan. Sometimes, political and military interference in conflict areas by Russia in the early 1990s technically contributed to 'freezing them', but this was hardly perceived as neutral by Azerbaijan, Georgia or Moldova, shaping the understanding of and attitudes towards Russia's regional leadership (see also section V below). All this affected the membership of such security-

---

[7] The CIS was founded in Dec. 1991 to replace the dissolved Soviet Union. Today Armenia, Azerbaijan, Belarus, Georgia, Kazakhstan, Kyrgyzstan, Moldova, Russia, Tajikistan, Ukraine and Uzbekistan are CIS members (Turkmenistan withdrew its membership and became an associate member in Aug. 2005). On the group see URL <http://www.cis.minsk.by>. See also section III of this chapter.

related groupings as were created: thus the antagonists Armenia and Azerbaijan could participate in the group that developed out of the 1992 Collective Security Treaty (Tashkent Treaty)[8] only so long as this structure had little practical meaning. It started to be consolidated after 2002, when Azerbaijan decided to discontinue its membership. Similarly, Azerbaijan's participation in the GUAM grouping precludes Armenia's membership. The fact that both Armenia and Azerbaijan have continued to participate in the CIS says much about how weak this organization is in the security area.

A strategically heterogeneous space. The heterogeneous character of the former Soviet area not only undermines region-wide security cooperation but also promotes the development of smaller and cross-cutting groupings that may overlap or directly conflict with each other. The resulting scope for dissipation of effort may be illustrated by the fact that Russia and the Central Asian states are committed to cooperating against terrorism within three different frameworks: the CIS, the CSTO and the SCO.

Russia's predominance. The predominance of Russia in the former Soviet area (even if it is eroding) represents the most powerful independent variable within the post-Soviet space. Not only is Russia by far the strongest state in terms of size, military forces and economic potential, but it also has the strategic character of a 'hub' to which former Soviet states are joined by a more strategically significant relationship than any pair of such states can have with each other. The practical implications of these facts for regionalism are, however, neither straightforward nor predetermined: some neighbours accept or even seek Russia's 'paternalistic' lead, while others defy it almost on principle (see '*Politics first*' below).

The search for self-identification. In the slow but steady process of defining their separate identities, the former Soviet republics have often realized that their new state security agendas are dissimilar, perhaps conflicting, and becoming more so over time. Even a grouping as relatively tight as the CSTO embraces countries with such different geopolitical and security environments as Belarus, on the one hand, and Tajikistan and Uzbekistan, on the other. Different needs are of course compatible with cooperation, but they will gradually erode any structure that does not effectively recognize and accommodate them.

Politics first. The former Soviet area consists of a number of recently formed and still self-shaping states where security decisions may often reflect volatile political circumstances rather than sober analysis and experience. Russia's own strategic thinking, for example, is shaped by three broader political motives: (*a*) to ensure the country's sustainability as a sovereign political entity, (*b*) to neutralize possible hostile developments in adjacent territories

---

[8] The Collective Security Treaty was signed at Tashkent in 1992—initially by 6 states, which were later joined by 3 others. It entered into force in 1994. For the treaty see URL <http://dkb.gov.ru/start/> (in Russian). In 1999 Azerbaijan, Georgia and Uzbekistan refrained from prolonging the treaty, which thus retained 6 participants (Armenia, Belarus, Kazakhstan, Kyrgyzstan, Russia and Tajikistan). In 2002–2003 these states decided to institutionalize their cooperation on the basis of the treaty and establish the Collective Security Treaty Organization. Uzbekistan joined the CSTO in 2006.

and (c) to promote its broader international role (even if in a considerably reduced format compared with the Soviet Union). Russia's political reading of these imperatives affects its attitude to regional security options at any given time. For instance, the vision of the CIS as a vehicle for consolidating Russia's 'zone of influence' has provided a strong incentive for developing it further; but any suspicion that other partners are only using the group cynically to gain access to Russia's resources and military assistance on the cheap will drive Moscow towards limiting its investment. In practice, Russia has a persistent tendency to relapse into bilateralism when handling either friends (e.g. Belarus) or particularly tough opponents, thereby further complicating and undercutting the significance of the regional groups to which it belongs.

Other former Soviet states seem to prioritize political considerations in a similar way. For instance, the leaders of the Central Asian states supported the 'new breath of life' given to the Collective Security Treaty in the early 21st century partly for the political motive of stopping the syndrome of 'colour revolutions' (non-violent protests against governments with a specific colour as their symbol) spreading further. Overall, a vicious circle may develop whereby a lack of concrete security substance in regional cooperation increases the temptation to sacrifice utility to politics, which in turn keeps the whole phenomenon of regional security cooperation in the former Soviet area at a largely superficial level. At any moment, changing political circumstances could force a 'correction' of present relationships in one direction or another. (It is fair to note that this syndrome of a high declaratory stance combined with limited and fragile practical underpinning is a pattern that can be traced in multilateral activities in the Eastern bloc far back in the communist period.)

Ongoing reconfiguration. Patterns of cooperation among the former Soviet states have also been unstable over time for more substantial reasons, as the security perceptions (and self-perceptions) of actors continue to evolve. By 2006 Russia had basically overcome its economic, political and psychological post-imperial traumas, with high energy prices currently playing heavily into its hands. The leadership in Moscow has become much more self-confident and expects other international actors to recognize Russia's centrality within the former Soviet area. There are at least three factors, however, operating in the opposite direction: (a) the continuing different circumstances of the states in the area make it harder to establish a permanent and efficient form of cooperation; (b) some former Soviet states see Russia's reviving power as damaging their interests and are trying to find ways of counterbalancing it; and (c) influences from outside the former Soviet area seem set to become more significant than in the first decade after the collapse of the Soviet Union. Paradoxically, therefore, even as Russia sees an upswing in its power, it has to face more serious challenges from states in its neighborhood than it did only a few years ago. For other CIS states the corresponding challenge is how to maintain a delicate balance in the relationships that they need to develop with Russia, among themselves and in a broader geopolitical context.

Table 4.1. Membership of security-related groups involving the post-Soviet area, as of January 2007

	CIS	CSTO	GUAM	SCO[a]	NATO/EU[b]
Established	1991	2003	1997	2001	1949/1951
No. of members	12	7	4	6	26/27
Russia	x	x	–	x	–
Europe					
Belarus	x	x	–	–	–
Moldova	x	–	x	–	–
Ukraine	x	–	x	–	–
South Caucasus					
Armenia	x	x	–	–	–
Azerbaijan	x	–	x	–	–
Georgia	x	–	x	–	–
Central Asia					
Kazakhstan	x	x	–	x	–
Kyrgyzstan	x	x	–	x	–
Tajikistan	x	x	–	x	–
Turkmenistan	x	–	–	–	–
Uzbekistan	x	x	–	x	–
Baltic states					
Estonia	–	–	–	–	x
Latvia	–	–	–	–	x
Lithuania	–	–	–	–	x

CIS = Commonwealth of Independent States; CSTO = Collective Security Treaty Organization; GUAM = Organization for Democracy and Economic Development–GUAM (Georgia–Ukraine–Azerbaijan–Moldova); SCO = Shanghai Cooperation Organization; NATO = North Atlantic Treaty Organization; EU = European Union.

[a] China is the 6th member of the SCO.
[b] For the full membership of the EU and NATO see the glossary in this volume.

External factors. External factors play a considerable role in motivating, organizing and structuring post-Soviet regional security cooperation. To mention only a few: Russia's anti-NATO sentiments have been central to much of Russian policy thinking and policymaking in this area. Second, Russia's real, perceived or anticipated hegemony within the CIS has triggered attempts to establish alternative structures, such as GUAM, that may be oriented towards other international poles of power. Third, the motives bound up with a new 'great game' in Central Asia are not entirely absent from developments in the CSTO and the SCO. As the post-Soviet area becomes more interdependent with and exposed to other actors and influences, this trend can be expected to become even more prominent.

III. The Commonwealth of Independent States

The CIS emerged in December 1991 in the context of the demise of the Soviet Union and still brings together 12 of the 15 post-Soviet states. While its primary usefulness originally lay in easing the process of the dissolution of the Soviet Union, it was also expected to promote the new states' eventual positive integration. The former aim was basically successful, but the latter has been much less so—at least, at the pan-CIS level.

Institutional structure[9]

In the CIS institutional structure, the Council of Ministers of Defence (CMD) is the key body focusing on security issues. It was established in February 1992 as the tool of the CIS Council of Head of States to address issues of military policy and cooperation. Its sessions are held as need arises, normally at least once every four months.[10] CMD activities were intended to be supported by two institutions: a Secretariat for bureaucratic needs and a Headquarters for coordination of military cooperation of the CIS member states. The latter was supposed to bring together top military representatives and attain a formal status that was equal to, or higher than, the status of the General Staff of the host country (Russia). In the event, only some CIS countries took part in the activities of the Headquarters, with Ukraine as the most notable absentee. When Kazakhstan called for the abolition of the Headquarters in 2004, Russia reluctantly supported the proposal.[11]

Some elements of security-related multilateralism at the CIS level have survived, however: for example, functional bodies under the auspices of the CMD such as the Military–Technical Committee, the Military–Scientific Council, and the Coordination Committee on air defence issues and others. In practice, the influence of the Russian Ministry of Defence is predominant in all these bodies and most of the staff of the Secretariat, especially at top levels, are Russian military personnel. The same is true of the CMD, where Russian chairmanship was accepted as the only realistic solution.

United air defence

The most important remaining functional element of CIS military–political activity is the United Air Defence System (UnADS), with 10 of the 12 CIS

[9] On the structure of the CIS see URL <http://www.cis.minsk.by/>.

[10] E.g. the CMD meeting in Nov. 2006 considered 15 questions touching on a common (joint) communications system for the armed forces, peacekeeping, united air defence, social protection of the military, topography and hydro-meteorology services, etc. See Russian Ministry of Defence, 'Soobscheniye ob itogakh zasedaniya Soveta ministrov oborony gosudarstv-uchastnikov Sodruzhestva Nezavisimykh Gosudarstv v gorode Breste 23 noyabrya 2006 goda' [Notification of results of the meeting of the Council of Ministers of Defence of states participants of the CIS in Brest on 23 November 2006], 29 Dec. 2006, URL <http://www.mil.ru/info/1069/details/index.shtml?id=19944>.

[11] The Headquarters in fact ceased to exist at the end of 2005; many of its functions had been transferred in practice to the CSTO and others were absorbed by the CMD Secretariat.

members.[12] For 2006, for example, 292.6 million roubles (about $10.8 million) were allocated by the CIS Council of the Heads of Governments for these purposes.[13] Large-scale UnADS exercises have been organized every two years since 2001. The most recent exercise, held in 2005, was carried out for the first time under a unified command. As an example of a lower-scale exercise, a training event in October 2006 involved the command systems of eight countries and over 100 aircraft and helicopters.[14]

The effectiveness of the CIS UnADS is, however, tending to decline. From the late 1990s Georgia and Turkmenistan have ceased to participate in practice; some others, such as Ukraine and Uzbekistan, prefer to interact directly with Russia's Main Air Force Headquarters. Kazakhstan competes with Russia by offering Ukraine and other CIS member states its own training fields for launching air defence missiles and holding exercises also in non-CIS contexts. Ukraine's participation in the UnADS is also being downscaled as it could represent a complication in the context of Kyiv's growing, if still cautious, cooperation with NATO. So long as Russian radars remain on Ukrainian soil, Ukraine is demanding more money from Russia for services rendered.[15]

Russia continues to try to maintain the viability of the UnADS. In June 2005 the CMD debated the next five years of its development and agreed to set up three regional sub-groups with headquarters at Astana (Kazakhstan), Minsk (Belarus) and Rostov-on-Don (Russia). However, the scheme continues to suffer from competing forums for cooperation. The CSTO offers a prima facie more viable context for air defence cooperation given its smaller membership; and there are significant bilateral links between member countries, as in the case of Russia's supply of S-300PM air defence systems to Belarus in the context of plans for the two countries to create a joint air defence.[16]

---

[12] Formally, only 2 CIS states—Azerbaijan and Moldova—do not participate in the UnADS. 'Sostoyanie i perspektivy razvitiya ob'edinennoi sistemy PVO gosudarstv-uchastnikov SNG' [Current state and perspectives of development of the joint air defence system of CIS member states], URL <http://old.mil.ru/articles/article12935.shtml>.

[13] 'Resheniye o vydelenii assignovanii na sozdaniye i razvitiye obyedinyonnoi sistemy protivovozdushnoi oborony gosudarstvuchastnikov sodruzhestva nezavisimyh gosudarstv v 2006 godu' [Decision to allocate funds for the creation and development of the United Air Defence System of members of the Commonwealth of Independent States], 25 Nov. 2005, URL <http://www.pravoby.info/megdoc/part0/megd0097.htm>.

[14] 'Zavershilas komandno-shtabnaya trenirovka organov upravlenia i dezhurnikh sil ob'edinennoy systemy PVO gosudarstv SNG, v kotoroy bili zadeistvovany bolee 100 samoletov i vertoletov' [Command and staff training of control bodies and duty forces of United Air Defence System of CIS countries, in which over 100 aircraft and helicopters were used, completed], Rossiyskaya Gazeta, 19 Oct. 2006, URL <http://www.rg.ru/2006/10/19/ucheniy-anons.html>.

[15] ITAR-TASS (Kyiv), 'Ukraine: defense minister says Russia not paying enough for radar sites in Crimea', World News Connection, International Security and Counter Terrorism Reference Center, US Department of Commerce, 23 Dec. 2005.

[16] 'ODKB sostoyalas kak mezhdunarodnaya organizatsia, zayavil Lukashenko' [CSTO succeeded as an international organization, says Lukashenko], RIA Novosti, 23 June 2006, URL <http://rian.ru/politics/cis/20060623/49956051.html>.

Peace-support missions[17]

In the 1990s, the prospect of CIS peacekeeping activities was discussed widely in political and analytical circles. Today, the only extant peace-support mission is the CIS Peacekeeping Forces in Georgia.[18] The mandate of this mission to the secessionist republic of Abkhazia, composed solely of Russian military personnel, is endorsed by the United Nations. For the Government of Georgia, the CIS label on these forces is only a fig leaf for Russian involvement; for Russia, it is a legitimate point of reference in any discussion of the region's future. When Georgia calls for the withdrawal of Russian forces, Russia replies that the CIS presence could only be ended by a CIS decision (which requires unanimity, giving Russia a veto). CIS involvement in this instance has thus become an important political shibboleth for both Georgia and Russia and has the potential to further aggravate their relations.

Overall, the direct relevance of the CIS to maintaining security in its region has little obvious logic today. Future political or peacekeeping ventures in the name of the CIS are not inconceivable, but they would depend first and foremost—in the Georgian and other cases—on a transformation of political relations with Moscow, as well as on the CIS offering comparative practical advantages that are hard to identify at present.

The anti-terrorism agenda

The CIS started to develop a role in anti-terrorism, both on a political level and in terms of coordinating efforts, even before 11 September 2001. In June 1999 the members signed the Treaty on Cooperation among the States Members of the Commonwealth of Independent States in Combating Terrorism;[19] in 2000 they adopted the first CIS Programme for Combating International Terrorism, and further documents were approved at later summits (in 2001, 2003 and 2004).[20] The CIS members coordinate their efforts regarding accession to and implementation of basic UN anti-terrorist instruments and incorporate their provisions in national legislation.

In 2000 the CIS Anti-Terrorist Centre was created, with a special branch in Bishkek, Kyrgyzstan, that is designed to focus on anti-terrorism activities in Central Asia. It conducts anti-terrorism exercises, analyses and monitors terrorist threats, and trains anti-terrorism unit instructors. The August 2005 CIS summit meeting adopted a Concept and a new Programme of Cooperation for Combating Terrorism and other Extremist Activities.[21] In particular, an

---

[17] The Russian word 'mirotvorchestvo' does not differentiate between peacekeeping, peace-support and peace-enforcement operations (unless specific modifiers are added).

[18] Two other missions are operated by CIS members on a bilateral basis; see appendix 3A in this volume.

[19] For the treaty see URL <http://untreaty.un.org/English/Terrorism/csi_e.pdf.>.

[20] All the essential documents and agreements (from 2000) on CIS counterterrorism activities are available at URL <http://www.cis.minsk.by/main.aspx?uid=7216>.

[21] On the Concept see URL <http://cis.minsk.by/main.aspx?uid=4294> and on the Programme see URL <http://cis.minsk.by/main.aspx?uid=4006>.

agreement is foreseen on information exchange in the area of fighting terrorism and a treaty on combating terrorist and other extremist activities. The CIS Interparliamentary Assembly is working on a model penal code for these issues.[22]

Overall assessment

The CIS has a remarkable output in terms of documents but a much less impressive practical impact. The organization's overall political weakness may also doom its security dimension to a decline in the medium term. Applying the five evaluative criteria set out in section I, one may arrive at the following judgements.

First, Russia's hegemony is a basic fact in the CIS, also because of the lack of any significant counterbalance. However, it is noteworthy that Russia's hegemony in most cases cannot be translated into coercion with respect to its partners. They can escape by the common practice of non-participation in CIS decisions. This raises the more general question of whether Russia's policy fits the 21st century understanding of productive, 'everybody wins' security cooperation or whether it leaves open only the alternatives of dominance and inefficiency. Second, the CIS's weakness makes it hard to ascribe to it a zero-sum relationship with the outside world, but it does not achieve productive interactions either, whether as an institution or for its member states. Third, as regards adaptability, it is remarkable that the CIS has survived so long in spite of the serious political controversies among its members. However, its practical response to new challenges must be considered disappointing. Whether or not to call it artificial—the fourth criterion—is less simple. The objective grounds for CIS-wide security cooperation do exist, but the organization is unable to mobilize this potential. As a result it shows exactly the features attributed to 'hollow' groupings by the generic analysis referred to above: uneven levels of enthusiasm, rapid tailing-off in activities, failure to engage with outside actors, and so on. Lastly, the efficiency of CIS management is commensurate with its declining political significance.

IV. The Collective Security Treaty Organization

The CSTO has a very similar security agenda to that of the CIS but currently looks more sustainable and efficient, in effect becoming both the successor to and a 'hard core' within the latter, older group. The Collective Security Treaty was signed by six states on 15 May 1992, with a clause on mutual assistance in case of external aggression as its central element. Initially, it lacked practical substance and some parties dropped out when a protocol on continuation of the treaty was adopted in 1999. The decision for a 'new start' was taken at

---

[22] Brief information (in Russian) on different versions of the model penal code on fighting terrorism is available on the CIS Interparliamentary Assembly website at URL <http://www.iacis.ru/html/?id=66&nid=8>.

the 10th anniversary of the treaty, in May 2002, by its six remaining participants (Armenia, Belarus, Kazakhstan, Kyrgyzstan, Russia and Tajikistan), which became the founders of a new structure, the Collective Security Treaty Organization.[23] The statute of the CSTO entered into force in September 2003.

To a certain extent, the project of the CSTO seems to have been inspired by the NATO experience, as reflected even in their similar names but more importantly in aspects of their development and structure (a mutual assistance treaty, followed by an open-ended process of building 'hardware' infrastructures around it). Like NATO, the CSTO is governed by a system of political and military institutions. The political branch includes the Council of Ministers of Defence (CMD), as in the CIS; the Council of Ministers for Foreign Affairs; and the Committee of Secretaries of Security Councils. The top military body is the Joint Headquarters, headed on a rotation basis by the Chiefs of General Staff or analogous national bodies. The entire structure is headed by the Collective Security Council (CSC), at the level of heads of state of member countries. The practical management of the organization is carried out by the CSTO Secretary-General.[24] While such mirror-imaging says little about the CSTO's real significance compared with that of NATO, it does seem that the main lines of military cooperation between Russia and its post-Soviet partners are being reoriented from the CIS framework towards the CSTO.

Areas of cooperation

The decision to create Collective Rapid Deployment Forces (CRDF) was taken by the parties to the Collective Security Treaty as early as in May 2001 because of the menacing situation in Central Asia, linked with developments in neighbouring Afghanistan. By 1999–2000 anti-government fighters had penetrated into Kyrgyzstan and Tajikistan and challenged the regimes of those countries. Standing forces were mooted in that context to allow effective action against eventual external or domestic threats to security. At present, the CSTO is reported to be planning for the deployment of two groups of forces in case of war—in the East European Strategic Directorate (comprising national units of Belarus and Russia) and in the Caucasus (Armenia and Russia).[25] No information is available on whether this is supported by operational planning, training, and so forth. In June 2005 the decision was taken to develop the CRDF further, notably by establishing a Central Asian force group. This would strengthen CSTO military potential in the region, raising total CRDF strength in Central Asia from the current level of 4000 personnel to about

---

[23] See note 8.

[24] This position has been held by Nikolai Bordiuzha, former Secretary of the Security Council of the Russian Federation, since Apr. 2003.

[25] See e.g. 'Nikolai Bordiuzha: ODKB perehodit v kachestvenno novuyu fazu svoego razvitia' [Nikolai Bordiuzha: CSTO goes to a qualitative new phase of its development], ANN, 18 Sep. 2006, URL <http://www.annews.ru/news/detail.php?ID=26235.html>.

11 000.[26] The 4000 CRDF personnel serve in 10 battalions, with Russia and Tajikistan providing three battalions and Kazakhstan and Kyrgyzstan two battalions each. The air force component of the CRDF is deployed at the Russian base in Kant (Kyrgyzstan), which was designated as a CSTO installation in 2003.[27] The CSTO has developed further plans to strengthen military cooperation 'up to 2010 and beyond'.[28]

Politically, the real and perhaps increasing significance of these plans still lies in the context of regimes' concerns about possible colour revolutions in Central Asia. All the CSTO member states seem to agree that both tasks—outward-oriented defence and inward-oriented stability—will be best served by developing interoperability, increasing power-projection capabilities, and the like.

In June 2004 the CSC adopted a conceptual document on the peace-support activities of the CSTO. Preparation of a formal agreement on peace-support activities is reportedly nearly complete.[29]

Collective air defence activities seem to be gradually being transferred from the CIS to the CSTO framework, although the practical difference this makes is limited. The creation of a united air defence system is part of the CSTO 'coordination plans'. These also include the development of a joint system for identifying threats related to biological and chemical weapons. For this purpose, the CMD has established a Coordination Committee of commanders of chemical, biological and radiation protection forces and services. The CSTO also holds military exercises on a regular basis.

Military–technical cooperation is perhaps the most efficient tool for con-solidating the CSTO, since it is based on low-price deliveries of weaponry and military equipment by Russia to other member states. Initially, this principle was applied only to deliveries for units ascribed to collective rapid deployment forces, but since early 2005 it has been extended to all supplies destined for CSTO countries. Russia also uses this tool in its relations with its CIS partners in general, but the CSTO member states enjoy priority treatment. Russia has reportedly decided to be even more responsive to their demands in the case of emergencies and urgent requests.[30] In November 2004 the CSTO announced its intention to move military–technical cooperation to a qualitatively higher level, and in June 2005 the member states started to form an interstate commission for the purpose—in effect superseding an earlier CIS commission

[26] Panfilova, V., 'S uchetom strategicheskogo znachenia' [Taking into account strategic significance], *Nezavisimaya Gazeta*, 25 Sep. 2006, URL <http://www.ng.ru/courier/2006-09-25/17_strategy.html>.

[27] 'Russian Air Force chief to inspect Kant airbase', 14 Feb. 2006, World News Connection, National Technical Information Service (NTIS), US Department of Commerce; and Lachowski, Z., *Foreign Military Bases in Eurasia*, SIPRI Policy Paper no. 18 (SIPRI: Stockholm, June 2007), URL <http://www.sipri.org>.

[28] Interfax-AVN (Moscow), 'CSTO military commanders convene in Moscow', 2 Nov. 2006, World News Connection, National Technical Information Service (NTIS), US Department of Commerce.

[29] See e.g. 'Post-Soviet collective security group to be transformed-sec-gen', RIA Novosti, 24 May, 2006, URL <http://en.rian.ru/russia/20060524/48573945.html>.

[30] Interfax (Brest), 'Russia to supply CSTO states with arms—defense minister', 22 Nov. 2006, World News Connection, National Technical Information Service (NTIS), US Department of Commerce.

that had been abolished for its ineffectiveness. The new commission is further tasked with coordination of national research and development as well as the organization and financing of the joint development of weapons and military equipment.

The CSTO seems to have done more than the CIS to combat illegal drug trafficking, thanks partly to its smaller group of members, half of which lie directly across major drug routes. The CSTO's efforts are focused on the areas adjacent to Afghanistan, above all in Tajikistan. A large-scale multilateral operation aimed at intersecting drug-traffic routes was carried out in November 2004. In 2004 a special structure—the Coordinating Council on Psychotropic and Narcotic Substances Circulation Control—was established within the CSTO to deal with the illegal circulation of drugs, and a working group on Afghanistan was set up in 2005. There are also plans to create some further anti-narcotic structures and a special counterterrorism organ.[31]

The CSTO has become more active in developing counterterrorism measures. In April 2004 it endorsed the establishment of an international anti-terrorist media forum as a non-governmental structure dealing with informational support for the struggle against international terrorism. In June 2005 it was decided to prepare a CSTO list of terrorist and extremist organizations.[32] In August 2006 the CSTO conducted its 'Rubezh-2006' exercise (an annual exercise that this time was held in Kazakhstan), with a scenario tailored to anti-terrorist requirements, and in September the CSTO task force took part in a joint command and staff exercise, 'Atom–Antiterror', in Armenia that was organized by the CIS Anti-Terrorist Centre.[33]

Political positioning

The CSTO is taking steps to promote its international visibility. In December 2004 it became an observer at the UN General Assembly. For some time, Russia has promoted the idea of 'direct working contacts' between the CSTO and NATO, suggesting that this would be a convenient format for discussing the problems of the post-Soviet geopolitical space.[34] Afghanistan has been suggested as another possible focus for joint CSTO–NATO efforts, and Russia

---

[31] 'Nikolai Bordiuzha: ODKB perehodit v kachestvenno novuyu fazu svoego razvitia' (note 25). On plans for the creation of a counterterrorist structure see 'ODKB planiruet sozdat Anteterroristicheskiy komitet—Nikolay Bordiuzha' ['CSTO plans to create an Antiterrorist Committee—Nikolai Bordiuzha'], RIA Novosti, 13 Feb. 2007, URL <http://www.rian.ru/defense_safety/20070213/60659625.html>.

[32] 'V "terroristicheskie spiski" ODKB popala 21 organizatsia' [21 organizations are in CSTO 'terrorist lists'], REGNUM, 22 June 2006, URL <http:// www.regnum.ru/news/661766.html>.

[33] See e.g. Dmitriyev, O., '"Rubezh-2006": "Krasnyie", "siniye" i "korichnevyie"' ['Rubvesh-2006': the 'reds', the 'blues' and the 'brown'], RIA-Novosti, 23 Aug. 2006, URL <http://www.rian.ru/analytics/2006082353040763.html>; and Interview with then head of the CIS Counter-Terrorist Centre Boris Mylnikov, '"Atom–Antiterror": garantiya bezopasnosti' ['Atom–Antiterror': a security guarantee], *Krasnaya Zvezda*, 26 Sep 2006, URL <http://www.redstar.ru/2006/09/26_09/1_01.html>.

[34] 'Russia: Lavrov terms direct working contacts between CSTO, NATO promising', Tashkent, 21 Oct. 2005, World News Connection, National Technical Information Service (NTIS), US Department of Commerce.

has offered to develop a joint programme for training the staff of anti-narcotics bodies. On NATO's side, however, these ideas have failed to provoke an enthusiastic reaction. The explanation seems to relate to overall trends in Russia's relations with the West, as well as Westerners' understanding of the political functions of the CSTO. The CSTO is viewed not only as a tool in the hands of Moscow, but also as a means of consolidating the autocratic regimes in member states.[35]

Overall assessment

Those post-Soviet states that are interested, for various reasons, in regional security cooperation seem to prioritize the CSTO for this purpose. The CSTO has a more compact composition (now 7 member states, as against 12 in the CIS) and is more homogeneous politically, due to the non-participation of such 'Western-oriented' countries as Georgia and Ukraine. Again, the Collective Security Treaty as the basic instrument of the CSTO is by definition concentrated on security issues, whereas the CIS is a general-purpose structure. As an institution that is only five years old, the CSTO shows fewer symptoms of erosion and fatigue than the CIS does at present. Finally and perhaps decisively, Russia as a key player in both frameworks seems to have made a choice in favour of the CSTO. It is worth the effort for Russia to try to turn the CSTO into a more efficient organization, given its more loyal and controllable nature. The CIS can be held in reserve, but with minimal cost and political effort.

According to the five evaluative criteria, the CSTO could be characterized as a structure with a huge predominance of one country but also with a clear predisposition among the smaller participants' regimes to accept a certain security paternalism on the part of Russia. In other words, hegemonic cooperation is welcomed rather than imposed in the CSTO. Defining the CSTO's relations with its external environment in zero- or non-zero-sum terms has little meaning, especially since the CSTO's efforts towards international positioning have basically failed. The CSTO's adaptability has not been tested, but it looks capable both of growth and of moving into new spheres of activity. An attempt to bring together the security agendas of such countries as Armenia, Belarus and Tajikistan may seem artificial, but Russia's centrality as security provider (whatever security might mean in this context) operates here as a consolidating factor. CSTO efficiency has not yet been tested in the field.

---

[35] Tellingly, Uzbekistan joined the CSTO in 2006—after President Islam Karimov's forceful suppression of Uzbek opposition (including the 2005 Andijon incident), the spectacular cooling of his relations with the West and his reorientation towards Russia.

V. GUAM

In 1997 four states that had strained or remote relations with Russia—Georgia, Ukraine, Azerbaijan and Moldova—formed the GUAM group.[36] In the beginning it was a routine diplomatic tool for ad hoc rapprochement of its members' positions in a broader multilateral framework—for example at the Organization for Security and Co-operation in Europe (OSCE). The group's evolution towards more regular consultations was crowned in 2001 with its Charter, adopted in Yalta, Ukraine,[37] which upgraded the status of the group by defining goals and spheres of cooperation and setting up its institutional structure.

The colour revolutions that took place in Georgia (2003) and Ukraine (2004–2005) provided the impetus for relaunching GUAM as a framework linking the new political regimes. At the May 2006 Kyiv GUAM summit meeting, the participants formally transformed the existing framework into the Organization for Democracy and Economic Development–GUAM and adopted a new Charter.[38] In the new organization, the top level is formed by the Council, operating in various formats. Summit meetings are held every year, and the foreign ministers meet at least twice a year.[39] The Committee of National Coordinators is a working body that meets, on average, every four months. Seven working groups have been set up to promote cooperation in various areas: economy, trade, transport and information technology, among others. Other structures have been established, such as a Business Council and Parliamentary Assembly. The functions of a future secretariat are fulfilled by the GUAM information office in Kyiv.

Russia as a point of reference

What made the GUAM group special from the outset was that four of the CIS countries for the first time founded a security structure that would operate independently of Russia, potentially challenging the latter's overwhelming preponderance in the region. GUAM may not proclaim an anti-Russian orientation, but it looks essentially inspired by the idea of forging an alternative to Russia in the CIS area. Pointers in this direction include the fact that all the GUAM countries have foreign policies that diverge from

---

[36] An informal alignment of Azerbaijan, Georgia and Ukraine existed from late 1996, with Moldova moving closer to it. An unofficial 'group of four' emerged in May 1997 in the course of discussions on redefinition of the flank zone of the Treaty on Conventional Armed Forces in Europe. Lachowski, Z., 'Conventional arms control', *SIPRI Yearbook 1998: Armaments, Disarmament and International Security* (Oxford University Press: Oxford, 1998), pp. 501–17. GUAM's formal structure was established in Oct. 1997, when the presidents of the 4 states held a meeting during the summit of the Council of Europe: see URL <http://www.guam.org.ua>. In 1999 Uzbekistan joined the group, making it the GUUAM, but it left in 2005.

[37] For the 2001 GUUAM Charter see URL <http://www.guam.org.ua/224.472.1.0.1.0.phtml>.

[38] See the Kyiv Declaration on Establishment of the Organization for Democracy and Economic Development–GUAM and the Charter (Annex 6 to the Protocol of the CNC GUAM), 23 May 2006, at URL <http://www.mfa.gov.az/az/guam/2006_CNC_0426_protocol_attach08_Kyiv Declaration_last_Eng.pdf>.

[39] About 20 meetings (in various formats) took place in the 7-year period 2000–2006.

Russia's, and Russia views them with growing suspicion, the more so as Moscow's relations with the West become increasingly strained. The positions coordinated among GUAM members openly contradict Russia's approaches, notably on the 'frozen conflicts' in the former Soviet area where there is scope for a real diplomatic confrontation between GUAM and Russia. In addition, the cycles and trends of domestic political developments in Russia and in most of the GUAM countries do not coincide. Uzbekistan joined GUAM and withdrew from the Collective Security Treaty as its alienation from Russia deepened in the 1990s; it returned to the CSTO when it moved back politically towards Russia in 2005.

GUAM's attempt to escape Russia's political zone of gravity has been underlined by symbolic actions linked with West-led events: for instance, the April 1999 GUAM summit was held in Washington, DC, at the same time as the NATO summit there. Indeed, GUAM has been supported by the USA and the EU, a fact that can readily be interpreted by Russia as part of their attempts to penetrate into the CIS area and to challenge Russia's influence there. For Russia, all these factors confirm the 'original sin' of GUAM, its anti-Russian political orientation and the corresponding motives of its external supporters (or, as Moscow may see them, its instigators). On the converse logic, this is the precise advantage of GUAM for its participants, which can thereby operate more independently in the international arena.

Policies. The security-related agenda of GUAM has two major focuses: (*a*) conflict settlement and stability promotion, and (*b*) counterterrorism and anti-crime activities. To address the problems in these areas, GUAM member states have tried a number of options: making common assessments (as a rule, in the form of joint statements), coordinating approaches within broader multi-lateral structures, and developing—tentatively—common tools. The attention paid by GUAM to conflict settlement is natural since all its member states are either actual or potential parties to separatist conflicts in the former Soviet area. Georgia faces breakaway provinces in Abkhazia and South Ossetia, Azerbaijan has its frozen conflict of Nagorno-Karabakh, Moldova cannot exercise sovereignty over its Trans-Dniester region, and Ukraine faces a latent separatist tendency in the Crimea. Not surprisingly, appeals for the political settlement of unresolved conflicts have been the most regular component of joint statements adopted by GUAM from its early days; and the idea of establishing GUAM peacekeeping forces has been under discussion since 1999.

In 2005 it was decided to concentrate GUAM's conflict-settlement efforts on the Trans-Dniester region. While this was clearly in Moldova's interests, the leading role in revitalizing the issue was played by Ukraine. The new Ukrainian leadership, born of the Orange Revolution of 2004–2005, saw here an attractive opportunity to raise the country's international profile and to con-solidate its position as a leader of GUAM. The resulting 2005 Yushchenko Plan for resolving the Trans-Dniester problem was not formally launched under the auspices of GUAM, but was clearly associated with the group of like-minded GUAM states.[40] Similarly, it was in the spirit of GUAM (and with the noteworthy political support of the EU and the USA) that Moldova and Ukraine tightened their customs controls around the Trans-Dniester region in March 2006. There were some suggestions of breaking Russia's monopoly on peacekeeping in the region by deploying Ukrainian peacekeepers there and involving the OSCE in monitoring the border regime. Discussions on the establishment of a peacekeeping battalion and special GUAM police forces began in the spring of 2006; the idea was approved by the GUAM defence ministers in August 2006, and the political decision was taken at a meeting of the ministers of foreign affairs in September 2006.[41]

In a broader sense, GUAM seeks to change the format of conflict settlement hitherto prevailing in the former Soviet area, and it implicitly or openly blames Russia for the lack of progress. According to GUAM's logic, such efforts should aim at re-establishing the territorial integrity of concerned countries rather than maintaining the status quo of fragmentation. GUAM members also want the process to include a more international element that would include the EU and the USA. The political push for GUAM peacekeeping in conflict zones has yet, however, to bear practical fruit, so the GUAM countries' most visible (and politically relevant) achievement is the common diplomatic position they have been able to maintain, notably at the OSCE[42] and the UN.[43]

Counterterrorism policies at the level of GUAM are rather limited—mainly because of the hitherto relatively low level of terrorist activity in the GUAM states. The general framework is the Agreement on Cooperation among the Governments of GUUAM Participating States in the Field of Combat against Terrorism, Organized Crime and Other Dangerous Types of Crimes, signed in 2002.[44] In September 2006 the GUAM member states organized the first special meeting of counterterrorism experts in Baku; it was announced that such consultations and other forms of practical counterterrorism cooperation would be carried out regularly. Promoting interstate coordination and informa-

---

[40] The plan was put forward in May 2005 by Ukrainian President Viktor Yushchenko, but it was not accepted by Russia or Trans-Dniester. Russia was reported to have had its own plan for resolution of the Moldova problem. 'The plan of victory over Moldova', *Kommersant Daily*, 8 June 2005.

[41] ITAR-TASS (Kyiv), 'Ukraine suggests setting up GUAM peacekeeping unit', 30 May 2006, World News Connection, National Technical Information Service (NTIS), US Department of Commerce.

[42] E.g. the GUAM states presented a united front at the OSCE Ministerial Council meeting of Dec. 2005 in Ljubljana, Slovenia, in discussions on the withdrawal of Russian forces from Georgia and Moldova in accordance with the Istanbul summit decisions of 1999 (see chapter 14 in this volume). Moldova spoke as the chair of GUAM as well as a directly involved country.

[43] In 2006 the GUAM countries managed to get the issue of frozen conflicts in the former Soviet area on the agenda of the 61st session of the UN General Assembly—in spite of Russia's opposition. This was considered as a diplomatic defeat for Russia as well as a manifestation of GUAM's growing political solidity. During the session, the foreign ministers of the 4 countries held a meeting to discuss frozen conflicts (significantly, in the presence of a US State Department official and without any Russian representative).

[44] The agreement is available at URL <http://www.mfa.gov.ge/index.php?lang_id=ENG&sec_id=130&info_id=1927>. The background to the acronym GUUAM is given in note 36.

tion exchange has been defined as a goal.[45] To ensure better information exchange, the GUAM member states have decided to develop an International Information and Analytical System that will be operated by the GUAM Virtual Center for fighting terrorism, organized crime and narcotics trafficking. The launch of a national branch in Kyiv in May 2006 by the Security Service of Ukraine was promoted by the GUAM–US Framework Program of Trade and Transport Facilitation, Ensuring Border and Customs Control, Combating Terrorism, Organized Crime and Drug Trafficking, in effect from 6 December 2002.[46]

Overall assessment

The record of GUAM is controversial above all because of its clear political and—in practice—oppositional rationale, which may be a strong driving force for the development of the group but at the same time raises the most serious obstacles to success. For example, Uzbekistan's hasty moves into and out of GUAM[47] demonstrate not only Uzbekistan's own volatility, but also the reasons for doubt about the solidity and permanence of GUAM's political base. Even GUAM's four core members by no means constitute a homogeneous political, economic or strategic space: the members' territorial location, geopolitical challenges, opportunities and priorities all differ. Domestic trends are also dissimilar, and prospects for practical integration are bleak.

Since the commonality of the participants is so vague, GUAM may easily be superseded (and overshadowed) by broader political alignments. A case in point is the Community of Democratic Choice, which was set up in December 2005, when Kyiv became a meeting place for leaders and top officials from Estonia, Georgia, Latvia, Lithuania, Macedonia, Moldova, Slovenia, Romania, and Ukraine (member states) and Azerbaijan, Bulgaria, the Czech Republic, Hungary, Poland, the EU, the OSCE and the USA (observers).[48] This new group could compete with GUAM if it manages to pursue its ambitious self-assigned task of promoting the interaction of democratic regimes within the Baltic–Black–Caspian seas area, with a hidden subtext of counterbalancing

[45] Javadova, E., 'First meeting of experts of Special Service and law-enforcement bodies of GUAM countries for fight with terrorism held in Baku', Trend, 18 Sep. 2006, URL <http://www.trend.az/index.php?mod=shownews&news=27821&lang=en>.

[46] Attempts to tighten border security among post-Soviet states face difficulties arising from the former internal character of these borders. They are often still neither clearly marked nor defended. The security stakes are, however, high, as shown by the fact that significant interceptions of smuggled nuclear material were made on the Georgian border in 2003 and again in 2006. On the GUAM Virtual Center and the GUAM–US Framework Program see URL <http://www.guam.org.ua/221.492.1.1.1.0.phtml>.

[47] See note 36.

[48] This constellation could be described as a 'GUAM plus' formula because it is bigger than the core group and includes many—but not all—of the Baltic, Central European and Balkan states. On the Community see Peuch, J.-C., 'Ukraine: regional leaders set up Community of Democratic Choice', Radio Free Europe/Radio Liberty, 2 Dec. 2005, URL <http://www.rferl.org/featuresarticle/2005/12/045ad9d6-04ea-41ac-9c8e-6501191f1cd8.html>.

Russia.[49] Finding common mission statements of a very general character seems to be considerably easier, however, than coordinating concrete actions.

A persistent obstacle to turning words into deeds is the fact that national concerns and interests tend to prevail over the common cause, even when facing such a clear common challenge as Russia. Noteworthy in this regard is the low-profile way in which GUAM has reacted to specific cases of Russia's assertiveness towards some of its members—recently including the stand-off with Ukraine over gas supplies and restrictions on imports from Georgia and Moldova. All four GUAM states have different dynamics in their own relations with Russia, and this seems to outweigh the incentives for a common approach. As a result, it is possible to make only cautious predictions about GUAM's future. The group's efforts at international positioning will most probably continue along current lines, focusing on likeminded neighbouring states,[50] the USA[51] and the Euro-Atlantic institutions. For GUAM, there would be some logic in counterbalancing this orientation by opening channels to Russia, but it is unclear what could be Moscow's motive to reciprocate. The chances of operationalizing GUAM's role in conflict settlement within the former Soviet area are not promising, although such a development cannot be excluded. Russia's opposition and the resistance of separatist regimes are the most serious obstacles. Lastly, it seems feasible for GUAM to get involved in debates and policymaking on energy security (prices, pipelines, stabilization measures, investments and so on) only as a secondary player.

On the basis of the five evaluative criteria, the following final assessment of GUAM may be offered. The group is by definition non-hegemonic, since it emerged as an antithesis to the Russia-dominated CIS. Its internal configuration is more balanced and its modus operandi is non-coercive. Second, in GUAM's relations with external partners, Russia would seem to be the object of a zero-sum policy. Third, the group's agenda is relatively vague, but by the same token not rigid: there is scope for adaptation and changes, albeit probably at the price of distinctiveness. Fourth, the group lacks strong unifying factors, apart from those related to Russia, which makes it relatively superficial. Finally, applying any criteria of efficiency seems inappropriate given GUAM's lack of tangible results.

VI. The Shanghai Cooperation Organization

The SCO was established by a declaration issued in Shanghai on 15 June 2001 by six states: China, Kazakhstan, Kyrgyzstan, Russia, Tajikistan and Uzbeki-

---

[49] According to a Georgian participant in the Dec. 2005 meeting of the Community of Democratic Choice, 1 of its main objectives was to 'build an axis of democratic nations that do not want to remain within Russia's zone of influence'. Torbakov, I., 'Kremlin uses energy to teach ex-Soviet neighbors a lesson in geopolitical loyalty', *Eurasia Daily Monitor*, 2 Dec. 2005.

[50] E.g. the presidents of Bulgaria, Lithuania, Poland and Romania were either guests or observers at the GUAM summits of 2005 and 2006.

[51] The USA is the only external partner with which GUAM interacts in a special programme.

stan.[52] India, Iran, Mongolia and Pakistan have since become observer states with a right to attend high-level SCO meetings. Despite its relative youth, the group has maintained a fast tempo of action and development. On the world scene it has attracted both criticism and suspicion—notably from US quarters—and interest in the affiliation of additional countries such as Afghanistan. At the same time it is one of the least transparent and probably least well understood of the regional organizations with functions in the field of security. This section considers its distinctive characteristics, origins, structure, agenda and activities before assessing its performance from the point of view of both effectiveness and legitimacy.[53]

Characteristics and origins

The SCO distinguishes itself most clearly from other intergovernmental groups in the former Soviet area by the fact that it includes a large external power, China, and because potential new members also lie outside the former Soviet area. It covers one of the largest geographical areas of any regional organization, from the Polish border to Vladivostok and from the White Sea to the South China Sea and the border of Myanmar. Its six member and four observer states collectively possess 17.5 per cent of the world's proven oil reserves, 47–50 per cent of known natural gas reserves and some 45 per cent of the world's population.[54]

The group's origins go back to the long period of tension between China and the Soviet Union over their shared border, which became a multilateral issue with the independence of the Soviet Central Asian republics in 1992. In 1996 China, Russia and the three Central Asian states bordering on China—Kazakhstan, Kyrgyzstan and Tajikistan—signed the Shanghai Agreement on Confidence Building in the Military Field in the Border Area, followed in 1997 by the Agreement on Mutual Reductions of Armed Forces in Border Areas.[55] These agreements set out substantial, detailed measures of military restraint and transparency along China's borders with the other four countries. This shared security regime formed the first multilateral bond between what came to be called the Shanghai Five, but the countries' relations were further stabilized by a series of bilateral agreements on frontier delineation, trade and

---

[52] Declaration on the Establishment of Shanghai Cooperation Organization, 15 June 2001, URL <http://www.sectsco.org>, Archive 2001.

[53] For a fuller study of the SCO, including perspectives from key participating countries see Bailes, A. J. K. et al., *The Shanghai Cooperation Organization*, SIPRI Policy Paper no. 17 (SIPRI: Stockholm, May 2007), URL <http://www.sipri.org>.

[54] For figures on oil and natural gas see US Department of Energy, Energy Information Administration, World Proved Crude Oil Reserves, 1 Jan. 1980–1 Jan. 2006 Estimates, URL <http://www.eia. doc.gov/pub/international/iealf/cruideoilreserves.xls>, and World Crude Oil and Natural Gas Reserves, 1 Jan. 2005, URL <http://www.eia.dc.gov/pub/international/iea2004/tble81.xls>; and for population data see US Central Intelligence Agency (CIA), *The CIA World Factbook 2007*, URL <https://www.cia.gov/cia/publications/factbook/rankorder/2119rank.html>.

[55] On the agreements see Trofimov, D., 'Arms control in Central Asia', Bailes, A. J. K. et al., *Armament and Disarmament in the Caucasus and Central Asia*, SIPRI Policy Paper no. 3 (SIPRI: Stockholm, July 2003), URL <http://www.sipri.org>, pp. 47–55.

cooperation. In June 2001 the same five countries plus Uzbekistan (which does not have a border with China) further institutionalized their relations by setting up the SCO, with the declared objectives of 'strengthening mutual trust and good neighbourly friendship among the member states; in political, economic and trade, scientific and technological, cultural, educational, energy, communications, environment and other fields; devoting themselves jointly to preserving and safeguarding regional peace, security and stability; and establishing a democratic, fair and rational new international political and economic order'.[56] The SCO's founding documents signalled the special interest of the member states in fighting what they defined as 'terrorism, separatism and extremism'.[57]

Structure

The SCO was designed essentially as an intergovernmental network driven by annual summits and by regular meetings of the heads of governments, foreign ministers and other high officials. Most observer states (except India) send persons of equivalent rank to high-level meetings. The most frequent working-level meetings are in security-relevant areas, today including, for example, information security experts, secretaries of national security councils and heads of supreme courts.[58] There are also some signs of a wish to bring together other sectoral representatives, such as speakers of parliaments (who met in May 2006 for the first time). Central institutions are sparse and small, consisting of a Secretariat set up in Beijing in 2004 with a permanent staff of 30 and an initial budget of $2.6 million, and the Regional Anti-Terrorist Structure (RATS). For 2005 the budget of the SCO was increased to $3.8 million.[59] Chinese Ambassador Zhang Deguang was the first head of the SCO Secretariat and was succeeded on 1 January 2007 by Bolat Nurgaliev of Kazakhstan, who will hold the post until 2009 with the new title of Secretary-General.[60] The remainder of the SCO budget is allocated to RATS, formally launched in 2004 and established in Tashkent after years of discussion among

[56] Declaration on the Establishment of Shanghai Cooperation Organization (note 52).

[57] These terms are found in the preamble of the Shanghai Convention on Combating Terrorism, Separatism and Extremism, adopted in June 2001 and available at URL <http://www.sectsco.org/html/00093.html>. Terrorism, separatism and extremism are called 'the three evils' by the Chinese leaders, as mentioned by Russian President Vladimir Putin. See e.g. the speech by President Putin 'SCO—a new model of successful international cooperation', 14 June 2006, available at URL <http://www.kremlin.ru/eng/text/speeches2006/0614/0014_type104017_107007.shtml>.

[58] 'The Heads of States support the initiative of Republic of Uzbekistan on holding regular meetings of National Security Council Secretaries of member states of the Organisation'. Tashkent Declaration of Heads of Member States of Shanghai Cooperation Organization, 17 June 2004, URL <http://www.sectsco.org/html/00119.html>. For the announcement see URL <http://www.sectsco.org/html/01108.html>.

[59] Lukin, A. V. and Mochulskiy, A. F., 'Shanhaiskaia organizatsiia sotrudnichestva: strukturnoye oformleniye i perspektivy razvitiia [Shanghai Cooperation Organization: structural formation and perspectives of development], *Analiticheskiye zapiski MGIMO*, vol. 2, no. 4 (Feb. 2005), p. 25.

[60] Joint Communiqué of the Meeting of the Council of Heads of Member States of the Shanghai Cooperation Organization, Shanghai, 15 June 2006, URL <http://www.sectsco.org/news_detail.asp?id=938&Language ID=2>.

the countries involved.[61] RATS is responsible for information exchange and analytical work among the security services of SCO members. Its staff of 30 consists of seven each from China and Russia, six from Kazakhstan, five from Uzbekistan, three from Kyrgyzstan and two from Tajikistan.[62] One report has suggested that Russia has offered to contribute $0.5 billion to strengthen this aspect of the SCO organization, possibly with more elements of a military infrastructure.[63] The SCO's structure, staff and procedures are subject to a general, ongoing review.

More recently, the institutional structure has reflected a growing emphasis on economic cooperation, especially in the fields of energy and infrastructure. In October 2005 the members established the SCO Inter-Bank Association[64] and in 2006 the SCO Business Council, with an inaugural meeting drawing together 500 business people.[65]

Agenda

While the SCO's main *raison d'être* has been in the security field, it has not characterized itself (or acted in practice) as a military alliance comparable to NATO.[66] Russian President Vladimir Putin has 'publicly excluded any possibility of military operations conducted under the auspices of the SCO',[67] and it is significant that the first meeting of SCO defence ministers was not held until April 2006. The principal security agenda of the group is in fact twofold: the original Shanghai Five goal of mutual confidence building, stabilization and conflict avoidance (reflected in the continuing mutual inspections of border forces); and the countering of non-traditional threats such as transnational terrorism but also internal insurgency and dissent. Scope for confusion arises, however, from the fact that all members have a distinctly militarized approach to combating 'new threats' and that some of the SCO's most-reported activities have involved exercises using military forces in anti-terrorist or similar scenarios. These have included a China–Kyrgyzstan joint exercise in 2002, a multilateral exercise with all the members except Uzbeki-

---

[61] On RATS see Maksutov, R., 'The Shanghai Cooperation Organization: a Central Asian perspective', SIPRI Project Paper, URL <http://www.sipri.org/contents/worldsec/eurosec.html>, p. 11. See also China–Eurasia Forum (CEF), *CEF Monthly*, Jan. 2004, URL <http://www.silkroadstudies.org/new/docs/CEF/CEF_January.pdf>; and Huasheng, Z., 'The SCO in the last year', *CEF Quarterly*, July 2005, URL <http://www.chinaeurasia.org/Newsletter.html>, p. 10.

[62] 'The Shanghai Cooperation Organisation: internal contradictions', *IISS Strategic Comments*, vol. 12, no. 6 (July 2006), URL <http://www.iiss.org/stratcom>.

[63] Sysoev, G., 'ShOS v. NATO' [SCO v. NATO], *Kommersant*, 15 June 2006, URL <http://www.kommersant.com/doc.aspo?idr=520&id=682211>.

[64] The signing of the Agreement on SCO Interbank Cooperation was welcomed in the Joint Communiqué of the Moscow Meeting of the Council of Heads of Government of SCO Member States, Oct. 2005; see URL <http://www.sectsco.org/html/00648.html>.

[65] Wei, Y., 'Summit ascent: Shanghai Cooperation Organization charts its future', *Beijing Review*, vol. 49, no. 26 (29 June 2006), URL <http://www.bjreview.com.cn/06-26-e/w-1.htm>.

[66] Weitz, R., 'Shanghai summit fails to yield NATO-style defence agreement', *Jane's Intelligence Review*, vol. 18, no. 8 (Aug. 2006), pp. 40–43.

[67] Trenin, D., 'Russia and the Shanghai Cooperation Organization: a difficult match', *CEF Quarterly*, July 2005, p. 26.

stan in 2003, a large Chinese–Russian exercise in August 2005 that was observed by other SCO member states,[68] and a multilateral exercise hosted by Uzbekistan in 2006 that focused on the role of special forces and law enforcement agencies.[69] Russia will host another major anti-terrorist exercise close to its border with Kazakhstan in 2007. The SCO Convention on Combating Terrorism, Separatism and Extremism—adopted as one of the group's basic texts in 2001—provides, however, for multilateral cooperation in many different modes, starting with the pooling of relevant intelligence through RATS.[70] Given the less visible nature of such activities it is difficult for outsiders to judge how far they may have gone beyond a formalistic mode or whether bilateralism still prevails for really important purposes.

The other main area of SCO competence is economic, and here China has made the running, driven by an interest both in exploiting the regional market for exports and in securing new oil and gas supplies (plus reliable infrastructure to deliver them). In late 2003 Chinese Premier Wen Jiabao proposed to set up an SCO free trade area, and while this is currently a non-starter for the smaller members (which fear that Chinese goods will flood their markets) there is now an agreed objective of creating a zone favourable for the free movement of products, capital, technology and services by 2020.[71] An SCO forum for investment and development in the energy sector was set up in 2002, and in 2004 four working groups were established: on electronic trade, customs, inspection of goods and unification of standards, and investment cooperation. At the Shanghai summit of 2006, the SCO and the Eurasian Economic Community signed a memorandum of understanding on the improvement of energy and transport cooperation with the aim of facilitating regional trade.[72] On the face of it, the areas for cooperation that are most likely to satisfy all sides' economic interests are Chinese investment in the poorer parts of the region and the common financing of new energy and transport routes, but signs of tangible progress on either front are so far wanting. While some observers have expressed fear that the SCO will be used to create an exclusive energy cartel, observation of the tactics used by both Kazakhstan and Russia (by far the largest energy exporters) to play different clients off against one another makes this an improbable scenario for the near term, even if SCO structures could sustain such a large executive role. The reality remains that all the SCO members together are still not self-sufficient in the technology, investment resources or market potential needed to sustain the high growth rates that these essentially underdeveloped economies need.

---

[68] For details see de Haas, M., 'Russian–Chinese military exercises and their wider perspective: power play in Central Asia', Clingendael Institute, Conflict Studies Research Centre, Russian Series 05/51 (Defence Academy of the United Kingdom: Swindon, Oct. 2005), URL <http://www.defac. ac.uk/colleges/csrc/documentlistings/russian/05(51)MDH3.pdf>.

[69] Weitz (note 66), p. 42.

[70] See note 57.

[71] Lukin and Mochulskiy (note 59), pp. 21–22.

[72] The Eurasian Economic Community was created in Oct. 2000 by Belarus, Kazakhstan, Kyrgyzstan, Russia and Tajikistan and in 2006 joined by Uzbekistan. See URL <http://www.evrazes.com/>.

Overall assessment

Many assessments of the SCO go to the extremes either of painting the group as a malignant 'anti-NATO' one or of dismissing it as mere window dressing. Applying the evaluative criteria would lead to the more mundane conclusion that this group has its strengths and weaknesses, like any other. At the macro-level of security, the SCO (like the preceding Shanghai process) may have played its part in allowing the new China and Russia to coexist and manage their relations with the Central Asian states without open conflict. The SCO has not carried out active conflict management in Central Asia's own hot spots, nor promoted general defence reform, but it has apparently achieved some degree of coordination and interoperability among its members' forces and security services in regard to potential anti-terrorism deployments. It has developed joint policies in the related fields of homeland and functional security and has broached topics that are highly relevant to economic security, such as energy cooperation and infrastructure. The SCO's record is weakest, or downright negative, in respect to good governance and democracy building. All its members are authoritarian regimes, ranging from 'managed democracy' to dictatorship. The policies and tools developed in the name of SCO anti-terrorism policy could easily be used for suppression of all kinds (including the containment and persecution of elements claiming local autonomy). There is no chance in practice for the broader public of the member states to influence SCO proceedings or even, for the most part, to learn about them. As one writer concludes, 'the SCO is not a normative organization, and with an explicit focus on non-interference in domestic issues it is particularly appealing to the authoritarian regimes of the region'.[73]

Applying more detailed criteria of legitimacy and effectiveness, it is hard to say that membership of the SCO is coerced or that its style of operation is hegemonic. The power of China and Russia within the group constitutes a diarchy not dissimilar to patterns of cooperation in, for example, Europe and South America, although with the advantage steadily tipping towards China. Most of the current observer states have expressed interest in full membership and are held back only by the lack of consensus within the group on the merits of enlargement.[74] The Central Asian members are *demandeurs* in every dimension (except for Kazakhstan's oil and gas), but the SCO gives them symbolic recognition and equality and may actually help in their global policy of 'balancing'. The story of US bases in the area is instructive: the July 2005 Astana SCO summit demanded a timetable for the withdrawal of US forces and facilities set up in Central Asia for the first phase of the Afghanistan

[73] White, A., 'Guiding the "near abroad"—Russia and the Shanghai Cooperation Organization', *CEF Quarterly*, July 2005, URL <http://www.chinaeurasia.org/files/CEF_Quarterly_August_2005.pdf>, p. 29.

[74] Despite US warnings and complaints before the 2006 Shanghai summit that the SCO might grant membership to Iran, the member states agreed there to leave the situation as it was *sine die*. The Central Asian states are against letting others in to share the possible economic benefits (and to complicate the agenda), while Russia will not admit China's favourite candidate, Mongolia, without progress on Iran.

conflict.[75] When Uzbekistan soon thereafter gave the USA notice of termination of its basing rights it looked like a story of cause and effect.[76] Yet Kyrgyzstan allowed the US base at Manas (not far from the Kyrgyz capital, Bishkek) to remain and eventually made clear that it was interested mainly in exacting a higher price.[77] It is arguable that Central Asian elites that want to develop their Western links in a balanced way are actually freer to do so as long as SCO membership demonstrates their 'loyalty' to partners closer by.[78] In all events, nothing further was said about the 'Astana principle' on foreign basing at the Shanghai SCO summit of 2006.

This last point is also relevant to a judgement on whether the SCO is zero-sum in its strategic relationship with the rest of the world. Chinese President Hu Jintao said that 'the SCO was designed to boost regional stability rather than oppose the US',[79] and given the reality of Russia's and China's fears both about each other and about risks of chaos in Central Asia and Afghanistan this reading should not be dismissed out of hand. What is clear is that it is the SCO's official and collective policy to oppose any 'monopoly and domination in international affairs'.[80] Its two largest members wish to maintain their own independence from the USA, to present themselves as alternative regional leaders and (to some extent) global powers, and to limit the manifestations or at least the consequences of a US strategic presence in their own backyard. At the same time, China and Russia have continued to seek accommodation with the USA in other contexts, such as solidarity against terrorism. The SCO has not in practice closed the way to extending the roles of the OSCE, NATO's Euro-Atlantic Partnership and the EU in Central Asia: all these are held back at present mainly by their own limitations and hesitations. The most clearly negative aspect of the SCO's relations with the world lies in the group's lack of cooperative relations with most other regional institutions (or with individual Western states).[81]

The SCO has shown flexibility by its rapid growth and creation of new networks and mechanisms. The issues still emerging on its agenda (such as energy and economic development in general) and the keenness of more states to join it suggest that its profile will continue to rise, while it is hard to see a conjuncture that would destroy it. If such a risk exists it lies in the general fragility of SCO members' efforts to contain changes and threats through repression and manipulation. The incident at Andijon, Uzbekistan, in May

[75] See Declaration of Heads of Member States of Shanghai Cooperation Organization, Astana, 5 July 2005, URL <http://english.scosummit2006.org/en_bjzl/2006-04/21/content_145.htm>, section II.

[76] For details see Lachowski (note 27).

[77] The opening bid of Kyrgyzstan was to increase the rent from $2 million to as much as $207 million. Agreement was reached on $150 million 'in total assistance and compensation'. Sands, D. R., 'U.S., Kyrgyzstan reach deal on air base payment', *Washington Times*, 15 July 2006, URL <http://www.washingtontimes.com/world/20060714-100731-3908r.htm>.

[78] Maksutov (note 61), pp. 12–13.

[79] Dyer, G., 'Iran leader hits at intrusion in region', *Financial Times*, 16 June 2006, p. 4.

[80] Declaration of Heads of Member States of Shanghai Cooperation Organization (note 75).

[81] The SCO has concluded memoranda of understanding with the Association of South East Asian Nations and the CIS, and has received official observer status at the UN General Assembly.

2005 was just one reminder that such tactics increase the odds of a larger implosion in the long run, with broader regional repercussions.[82] For the SCO to play a more positive role vis-à-vis this most basic of Central Asian challenges it would need to mutate into an organization representing more than just its members' elites and helping to open the region for vital outside influences rather than blocking or profiteering from the latter. It would take an optimist to suggest today that the organization's flexibility extends that far.

The SCO fulfils its primary aim of conflict avoidance and peaceful dialogue among its members just by existing. On the same grounds, the input–output balance of the SCO as an institution can be seen as positive. What is holding it back, if anything, is its larger members' caution about depositing any substantial funds or other resources for the group's activities, plus the rudimentary nature of its central institutions.

VII. Conclusions

In many parts of the world, regional security cooperation among clusters of small and medium-size states has flourished. The regions around China and India have run into problems, conversely, because of one over-large state that has an antagonistic or hegemonic intent towards at least some of its neighbours. The success of several groupings that include the largest contemporary power of all, the USA, can be explained by special factors—the democratic and consensual nature of NATO, the North American Free Trade Agreement and the Organization of American States, and the existence of powerful balancers such as China in such Pacific-region frameworks as the Asia–Pacific Economic Cooperation group.

In this perspective, the three security-related groupings in the former Soviet area, and the SCO linking China with this region, form a unique set. They have survived with at least minimum levels of efficiency despite the highly asymmetric weight of Russia—although it is no coincidence that the SCO, where China balances Russia, is the most vigorous—and despite, or even because of, the non-democratic or imperfectly democratic nature of the regimes of its member states. These aberrations make it tempting for contemporary analysis to dismiss all four of the groups surveyed in this chapter as serving no real purpose, or only a negative one. It would also be easy to class all except GUAM as old-style ventures closest to cold war models such as the Warsaw Treaty Organization or the short-lived Sino-Soviet alignment after 1945.

It is easy to diagnose such views as superficial but harder to challenge them with confidence due to the lack of independent, especially Western, research on these four groups and to their own opaqueness. Nonetheless, the analysis in this chapter goes far enough to suggest that matters are more complicated. In

---

[82] On this incident, in which Uzbek security forces fired on demonstrators in Andijon, see e.g. Tarzi, A., 'Afghanistan: inconsistencies in the state of the war on terrorism', Radio Free Europe/Radio Liberty, URL <http://www.rferl.org/featuresarticle/2005/07/ef308e31-84dd-478d-a2c8-fb6440433939.html>.

the first place, any simple diagnosis of Russian coercion is undermined by the fact that the CSTO has a consensual character, that Russia's own lapses into bilateralism or selfishness are a major limiting factor, that increasingly pro-Western states such as Georgia and Ukraine have stayed in the CIS, and that the anti-Russia GUAM grouping is the most lacking in concrete results of all. Second, while only GUAM is in any sense pro-Western, defining any of the other groups simply as 'anti-NATO' would be misleading because important parts of their motives and agendas are basically self-regarding: notably, stabilizing Sino-Russian relations, avoiding open war between Russia and its former Soviet neighbours, formally recognizing the latter as sovereign and giving a framework for Central Asian balancing acts. These are not all bad things, either, for international peace and security.

Where the CIS, the CSTO and the SCO clearly deviate from Western expectations is in placing stability above considerations of democracy, openness or human rights and even treating respect for human rights as a threat to security. On the other hand, this has not prevented them from having elements of a characteristically 21st century security agenda, notably in the fields of counterterrorism and the drugs trade, while the SCO takes a well-conceived— if self-interested and barely consensual—approach to economic development. None of the groups has an impressive ratio of output to input, but the balance might be corrected by reflecting on problems that they may be avoiding by their mere existence. In that light, it would be too hasty to set limits to their survival or even to pick winners among them. At present they mark a kind of organizational frontier (even if soft and fluctuating) between the sphere of full Western institutional control and a differently run East Eurasian space. It cannot be ruled out that their leaders' skills will be equal to maintain that state of affairs for some time to come: or even—although it would take an optimist to bet on it—that inner political transformations could convert at least some of the groupings into instruments for more benign and non-zero-sum ends. The remaining alternatives would seem to be either the gradual extension of West-based institutions' authority across Central Asia or a period of renewed lack of structure or actual disorder, perhaps with Russia–China accommodation surviving on a narrower bilateral basis.

Of course, no full judgement can be made on such groups except by considering their interaction with the wider world of security. Thus far, the CIS, the CSTO and the SCO have deviated from global norms by having no ties, or only a relation of rivalry and distrust, with other regional communities. At bottom this only symptomizes the lack of a clear, stable and positive security accommodation between China and Russia themselves and with the Euro-Atlantic community, or indeed between them and their non-Western neighbours in West, South and South-East Asia. If these four groups were really strong there could be concern that they might stand in the way of resolving this question, but precisely because of their state-driven and politically contingent natures they can hardly be counted as a major hindrance. Perhaps the best thing that can be said about all four organizations is that, just as hypocrisy can be seen as the homage that vice pays to virtue (François de La Rochefoucauld), they have given some of the world community's less democratic states an opportunity to learn about the multinational and integrative methods that offer the best hope of mastering the world's security problems in future.

5. Democratic accountability of intelligence services

HANS BORN and IAN LEIGH*

I. Introduction[1]

While spying is said to be the second oldest profession, intelligence account-ability is a recent phenomenon. Until the mid-1970s, intelligence—with any oversight it might require—was considered to be a matter for the executive in nearly all democracies, let alone in dictatorships.[2] Prior to that, parliamentar-ians had hardly any information on or influence over the intelligence services.

Before the 1970s, the intelligence services of many countries, such as the United Kingdom, functioned on the basis of executive decrees, and there was thus no legal need to obtain parliament's approval of the structure and special powers of the services.[3] This situation started to change in the United States in the mid-1970s when, shocked by scandals involving domestic spying on anti-Viet Nam War protesters and revelations about illegal covert operations car-ried out by the Central Intelligence Agency (CIA), the US Congress enacted far-reaching legislation that created a key intelligence oversight role for the Congress and other oversight mechanisms. Reforms in Australia and Canada followed and the process gained momentum in the 1980s. After the end of the cold war, the third phase of intelligence oversight began in the post-Communist states, many of which—with Western encouragement and help—

[1] This chapter draws on Born, H. and Leigh, I., *Making Intelligence Accountable: Legal Standards and Best Practice for Oversight of Intelligence Agencies* (Publishing House of the Norwegian Parlia-ment: Oslo, 2005); and Born, H., Johnson, L. K. and Leigh, I. (eds), *Who's Watching the Spies? Establishing Intelligence Service Accountability* (Potomac Publishers: Dulles, Va., 2005). Both publica-tions are part of a wider research project, Making Intelligence Accountable, being carried out by the Geneva Centre for the Democratic Control of Armed Forces (DCAF) and the Human Rights Centre of the University of Durham and supported by the Norwegian Parliamentary Intelligence Oversight Com-mittee. On the project see URL <http://www.dcaf.ch/handbook_intelligence/>.

[2] Exceptions confirm the rule: the Netherlands and Germany started their parliamentary oversight earlier, in 1953 and 1956, respectively.

[3] Concerning the UK's security and intelligence services, until 1989 the only officially published details of their work was the so-called Maxwell-Fyfe directive, named after the Home Secretary who issued it in 1952. See *Lord Denning's Report*, Command Paper 2151 (Her Majesty's Stationery Office: London, Sep. 1963).

* The authors are grateful for the constructive comments of SIPRI's researchers and editors; Thorsten Wetzling, researcher at the Graduate Institute for International Relations, Geneva; and Fairlie Jensen, Research Assistant at the Geneva Centre for the Democratic Control of Armed Forces (DCAF).

Table 5.1. A legislative framework for the control of security and intelligence services

Elements of control
Subordination of the security and intelligence services to the executive (e.g. cabinet ministers, inspectors general and high-level coordinating bodies), including safeguards against possible ministerial abuse of the services
The authority of the parliament, specifically of its special parliamentary intelligence oversight committee
Authorization and appropriation of public funds
Permanent mandates of relevant agencies and their field(s) of operation
Internal control and direction within the services
Control over politically sensitive issues, such as covert operations and international cooperation
Reporting mechanisms to the executive, the parliament and the wider public
The process of appointing and dismissing the directors of the services
Any special powers or exemptions the services enjoy
The role of independent bodies such as the financial audit office and the courts and complaint mechanisms such as ombudsmen, tribunals, review boards and data protection officers

Source: These elements derive from the Geneva Centre for the Democratic Control of Armed Forces (DCAF) project Making Intelligence Accountable. See Born, H. and Leigh, I., *Making Intelligence Accountable: Legal Standards and Best Practice for Oversight of Intelligence Agencies* (Publishing House of the Norwegian Parliament: Oslo, 2005), pp. 121–29.

reformed their intelligence services by putting them for the first time on a statutory footing, supervised by both the executive and the parliament.[4]

Why did these various states successively change their old habits of keeping the intelligence services beyond public accountability? In many states, scandals provided the main impetus for change in the governance of intelligence services. This was the case in Australia, Canada, Norway and the USA, where legislative and public investigatory committees exposed human rights abuses and pushed for strengthened intelligence oversight systems.[5] Constitutional reform (e.g. in South Africa), transition to democracy (e.g. in Argentina, South Korea and Poland) and legal challenges brought by citizens (e.g. in the Netherlands, Romania and the UK) were all reasons why governments began to impose public accountability on their intelligence services. As of 2006, democratic parliamentary oversight of intelligence services on a statutory basis has become the international norm in democratic states and has received the backing of international bodies such as the parliamentary assemblies of the Council of Europe and the Western European Union.[6]

[4] Leigh, I., 'More closely watching the spies: three decades of experiences', eds Born, Johnson and Leigh (note 1), pp. 3–4.

[5] Leigh (note 4), pp. 3–5.

[6] Parliamentary Assembly of the Council of Europe, Recommendation 1713/2005, 23 June 2005, URL <http://assembly.coe.int/Main.asp?link=/Documents/AdoptedText/ta05/EREC1713.htm>; and Western European Union Assembly, Resolution 113, 4 Dec. 2002, URL <http://www.assembly-weu.org/en/documents/sessions_ordinaires/pv/2002/pv09.php#P225_15553>.

In the wake of the terrorist attacks on the USA of 11 September 2001, however, a number of new or renewed concerns have been raised, regarding both the professional adequacy of the Western world's intelligence services and the risk of their role and findings being distorted by political measures.[7] Various countries have carried out public and parliamentary special investigations into claims of failings or misconduct by intelligence services related, notably, to the preparation for and conduct of the conflicts in Afghanistan and Iraq. Prominent examples include the Congress-appointed 9/11 Commission in the USA; the Hutton Inquiry in the UK; the Arar Commission in Canada; the German special parliamentary inquest; and the Dutch Parliament's request to investigate the alleged torture practices of the Dutch Military Intelligence and Security Service in Iraq.[8] These special inquiries are proof that political leaders are no longer convinced that internal investigations are sufficient and are ready to meet the demand for greater public accountability.

Based on a comparative research project on intelligence accountability, this chapter focuses on how selected states have implemented democratic oversight of their intelligence services.[9] The states analysed are all democracies whose legislatures have adopted intelligence laws that put the functioning of their intelligence services on a legal footing and provide for oversight of intelligence. The sample of states includes Argentina, Bosnia and Herzegovina, Canada, Germany, Hungary, the Netherlands, Norway, Poland, South Africa, the UK and the USA.

Two further comments on scope and definitions are in order here. First, and as implied above, the initial step towards good oversight is a legislative framework adopted by a legitimate representative institution that sets out in clear and open terms such basic points as those listed in table 5.1. This chapter

---

[7] See Dunay, P. and Lachowski, Z., 'Euro-Atlantic security and institutions', and Guthrie, R., Hart, J. and Kuhlau, F., 'Chemical and biological warfare developments and arms control', *SIPRI Yearbook 2006: Armaments, Disarmament and International Security* (Oxford University Press: Oxford, 2006), pp. 33–62, and pp. 707–31; and Dunay, P. and Lachowski, Z., 'Euro-Atlantic security and institutions', and Guthrie, R., Hart, J. and Kuhlau, F., 'Chemical and biological warfare developments and arms control', *SIPRI Yearbook 2005: Armaments, Disarmament and International Security* (Oxford University Press: Oxford, 2005), pp. 43–75, and pp. 603–28.

[8] The National Commission on Terrorist Attacks upon the United States, also know as the Kean Commission, investigated the circumstances that led to the attacks as well as national preparedness for and immediate responses to the attacks; see URL <http://www.9-11commission.gov/>. The Investigation into the Circumstances Surrounding the Death of Dr David Kelly (also known as the Hutton Inquiry) investigated the circumstances surrounding Dr Kelly's death in the context of the controversy and debate over whether the British Government dossier on Iraq's alleged possession of weapons of mass destruction was of sufficient scope and quality to justify the government declaration that Saddam Hussein posed a national security threat to the UK; see URL <http://www.the-hutton-inquiry.org.uk/>. See also the website of the Commission of Inquiry into the Actions of Canadian Officials in Relation to Maher Arar at URL <http://www.ararcommission.ca/>. The mandate of the German Parliament's Committee of Inquiry of 7 Apr. 2006 is available at URL <http://www.bundestag.de/ausschuesse/ua/1_ua/auftrag/auftrag_engl.pdf>. The Dutch public inquiry followed press revelations that the Dutch Military Intelligence and Security Service used interrogation methods against Iraqi suspects (in Iraq) that amount to torture. See Hoedeman, J. and Koelé, T., 'Kabinet gelast onderzoek ontsporingen in Irak' [Cabinet requests investigation into derailments in Iraq], *De Volkskrant*, 19 Nov. 2006.

[9] See note 1.

generally assumes the existence of such frameworks and moves on to review the aspects of implementation that are especially important for oversight.[10]

Second, and especially in modern conditions where governments and societies face multiple risks arising in different dimensions, a widening range of authorities other than the intelligence services collect, analyse and use material that fits the definition of intelligence for their own specific purposes.[11] Defence intelligence is a well-known special field (and not uncommonly, a competitor with civilian agencies), and 'commercial intelligence' has its own and rather different meaning. Additionally, police, customs, immigration, transport security and even social security authorities are all increasingly involved in intelligence-like operations. For reasons of space this wider phenomenon is not covered in this chapter, but it raises obvious questions about the adequacy, consistency and coherence of democratic norms and oversight governing these different actors and activities: an important subject for further research and debate.

The major challenges of oversight are the focus of section II. In sections III, IV and V the three main pillars of oversight are described and analysed: executive oversight, parliamentary oversight and oversight by independent bodies. In this analysis, the concept of oversight is seen as a means of ensuring the accountability of the decisions and actions of security and intelligence agencies. The conclusions are presented in section VI.

II. The challenge of oversight

The need for intelligence is a fact of life for modern governments. Few states take the view that they can dispense with a foreign intelligence service and none is sufficiently immune from terrorism or the inquisitiveness of its neighbours to forgo an internal security service. Two basic patterns exist for organizing security and intelligence. In the first there is a single agency for domestic and foreign intelligence (e.g. in Bosnia and Herzegovina, the Netherlands, Spain and Turkey). In the second there are distinct agencies for domestic security and external intelligence, with either separate or overlapping territorial competences (as in Germany, Hungary, Poland, the UK and the USA). Despite these variations in the organizational structure or governmental setting, security and intelligence pose a common set of challenges for accountability the world over.

The need for secrecy versus the need for transparency

The fundamental difficulty that intelligence oversight poses is the conundrum of how to provide democratic control of a governmental function and institu-

---

[10] The relevant legislation for the countries discussed here is available for reference online. See the specific references to such legislation in the following discussion of individual countries.

[11] On governments' and societies' assessment of risk see the Introduction in this volume.

tions which are essential to the survival and flourishing of the state, but which must operate to a certain extent in justifiable secrecy.

In the case of security and intelligence, and in contrast to many other areas of governmental activity, it is widely accepted that official communications and operations can only be transparent to a limited extent, otherwise the relevant operations, sources and assets will be compromised. This suggests that the prevailing pattern of oversight for other governmental activities needs to be adapted for the circumstances of security and intelligence, yet that the need for rigorous control is greater, not less, than in the case of more mundane activities such as education or welfare.

The necessary secrecy surrounding security and intelligence runs the risk of encouraging and providing cover for illegal and ethically dubious practices on the part of the agencies involved. The democratic process itself may be subverted by the infiltration of political parties, trade unions or civil society groups in the name of security and intelligence. The privacy of countless individuals may be interfered with by the collection, storage and dissemination of personal data, whether accurate or flawed. Inefficiency and corruption may go unchecked. Since September 2001, because of increasingly multilateral intelligence cooperation in combating global terrorism, the risk has grown also of sharing information with regimes that may put it to discreditable use—an issue explored further in section III. Last but not least, human rights abuses or breaches of international law committed by a given country's intelligence services abroad may both harm the country's international standing and invite damaging retaliation. Furthermore, information about clandestine operations that becomes public may harm relations with the countries in which the operations are conducted or which are targeted by them.

The temptation for politicians

In modern states the security and intelligence agencies play a vital role in the support of government in its domestic, defence and foreign policies by supplying and analysing relevant intelligence and countering specified threats. It is essential that the agencies and officials who carry out these roles are under democratic supervision by elected politicians, rather than accountable only to themselves. However, there is a real danger that politicians will be tempted to use the agencies' resources of information (about political opponents) or exceptional powers (e.g. of covert entry and bugging) to serve a domestic party political agenda. This possibility of gathering information to discredit or influence domestic political figures and movements must be guarded against. Well-calibrated accountability structures therefore attempt to insulate security and intelligence agencies from political abuse without isolating them from executive control. In general, the solutions adopted by democratic states deal with this paradox in two ways: first, by balancing rights and responsibilities between the agencies and their political masters; and second, by creating checking mechanisms outside the executive branch (see sections IV and V on parliamentary oversight and independent bodies, respectively).

The challenges of intelligence oversight in new democracies

A great challenge is faced by countries that have recently made the transition to democracy from authoritarian regimes. In the past, the main task of internal security and intelligence services in such countries was to protect authoritarian leaders from their own people rather than to protect the state or the constitutional order. Primarily, the security and intelligence services fulfilled a repressive function. An enormous effort is required to reform the old security services into modern democratic services, and the process of turning them from a tool of repression into a modern tool of security policy requires careful monitoring by the executive and the parliament. In Europe the challenge is often exacerbated by the arrival of a new post-1989 generation of politicians with no particular knowledge of intelligence services—a problem that also applies to some politicians in older democracies. It is difficult to lead or to reform intelligence services from a position of ignorance or inexperience.

Since 1989 many former Communist states in Central and Eastern Europe have set up a double-headed constitutional arrangement for leading intelligence and security services, in which the president is responsible for some important functions (e.g. appointing a director) and the prime minister deals with day-to-day issues. Such an arrangement can perhaps be explained by a concern that no executive leader should have the monopoly on the use of intelligence services. However, intelligence services in the Czech Republic, Estonia, Latvia, Lithuania, Romania and Slovakia have misused this dual structure to play off the prime minister against the president or sometimes to escape oversight altogether.[12]

III. Executive oversight: addressing politically sensitive intelligence issues

The executive branch plays a major, if not the most important, role in controlling (tasking, steering and monitoring of) intelligence services. Three issues are addressed in this section: (*a*) the role of the executive in overseeing intelligence agencies; (*b*) the oversight of international intelligence cooperation; and (*c*) the structures to ensure that executive control does not lead to ministerial abuse of the services.

---

[12] Oxford Analytica, 'CEE: Security problems are not just structural', Daily Brief Services, Oxford, 24 Oct. 2006.

The role of the executive

The ultimate authority and legitimacy of intelligence agencies rests on legislative approval of their powers, operations and expenditure. However, for practical reasons and because of the sensitive nature as well as the urgency of the subject matter, effective external control of these agencies must rest with the government—the executive. There is no intrinsic conflict between effective executive control and parliamentary oversight. On the contrary, the latter depends on the former. Parliaments can only reliably call ministers to account for the actions of the intelligence agencies if the ministers have real powers of control and adequate information about the actions taken in their name. Where this is lacking, the only democratic alternative is for a parliamentary body or official to attempt to fill the vacuum. This, however, is a poor substitute because, while legislative bodies can effectively review the use of powers and expenditure *ex post facto*, they are not equipped to direct and manage these matters in real time in the same way as governmental structures are.

The cabinet ministers who are responsible for intelligence services need two types of power in order to discharge their responsibilities: a sufficient degree of control over intelligence agencies and the right to demand information from them. Ministers are entitled to expect total loyalty from the agencies in implementing the policies of the government in the country's interests. They also need to have adequate control and information to be able to account to the parliament for the agencies' use of their legal powers and their expenditure.

Effective control by the executive does not, however, imply direct managerial responsibility for security and intelligence operations. In many countries, both to prevent abuse and as a prerequisite of effective control, the respective competences of the responsible ministers and the agency directors are set out in legal provisions. In the interest of effectiveness they should be distinct but complementary. If ministers are too closely involved in day-to-day matters, it will be impossible for them to act as a source of external control and the basis of democratic oversight will be undermined. The precise dividing line between the respective responsibilities of ministers and the agency heads is difficult to draw. One useful model, however, is the 1984 Canadian Security Intelligence Service (CSIS) Act, which defines the director of the service as having 'the *control and management* of the Service', '*under the direction*' of the responsible minister.[13] The Polish intelligence legislation contains a provision that clearly distinguishes between the competencies of the prime minister (giving direction) and the heads of the agencies (drawing up plans of action and reporting to parliament and the public).[14] Particularly in societies in democratic transition, where the dividing line between civilian government and the intelligence services has previously been blurred, it may be necessary to provide detailed prohibitions to prevent future abuses. For

---

[13] Canada, Canadian Security Intelligence Service Act, 1984, section 6(1); the act, as amended, is available at URL <http://laws.justice.gc.ca/en/C-23> (emphasis added).

[14] Poland, Internal Security Agency and Foreign Intelligence Agency Act, 24 May 2002, URL <http://www.aw.gov.pl/eng/akty-prawne/akty-prawne.html>, article 7 (in Polish).

instance, in Bosnia and Herzegovina's 2004 legislation, the Chair of the Council of Ministers has a number of detailed policy and review functions but is expressly prevented from assuming 'in whole or in part' the rights and responsibilities of the director-general or deputy director-general of intelligence.[15]

International intelligence cooperation

Developing and maintaining international and cross-agency intelligence cooperation has become imperative in today's security environment. If the new perceived threats (i.e. militants and terrorists) operate in constantly changing cross-border structures (benefiting from creations of the information age such as mobile phones and the Internet), then the intelligence operatives and services trying to track them down must respond by operating in similarly dynamic cross-border style. Despite the manifold difficulties of intelligence sharing between states, intelligence agencies of different states cooperate in a number of ways: pooling resources, trading information, drawing up common threat assessments and, unfortunately, sometimes conspiring to circumvent domestic law.[16]

There are two concerns related to international intelligence cooperation that underline the need for strict and balanced executive control. The first is the temptation for intelligence services seeking information on pressing issues to disregard the original method used by a possibly less scrupulous overseas partner for obtaining the information. International law clearly prevents the use, for example in a terrorist prosecution or in deportation proceedings, of information obtained in another state through torture.[17] Under Article 15 of the 1984 Convention against Torture and Other Cruel, Inhuman or Degrading Treatment or Punishment,[18] any statement made as a result of torture is inadmissible in evidence in 'any proceedings', except in proceedings against the alleged torturer. It can be argued, although international law is not so specific here, that the same considerations apply even to the mediated use of information obtained by another state's security services through torture. As the British Judge David Neuberger commented in a relevant case: 'by using torture, or even by adopting the fruits of torture, a democratic state is weakening its case against terrorists, by adopting their methods, thereby losing the moral high ground an open democratic society enjoys'.[19]

[15] Bosnia and Herzegovina, Law on the Intelligence and Security Agency, 2004, URL <http://www.legislationline.org/upload/old/35d065b27c243a9098a01793763f1b86.pdf>, articles 8–10.

[16] Wetzling, T., 'Actors, activities and dimensions: understanding European counter-terrorism intelligence liaisons', eds S. Farson et al., *Handbook of Global Security and Intelligence: National Approaches* (Greenwood Publishing Group: Westport, Conn., forthcoming).

[17] Born and Leigh (note 1), pp. 66.

[18] The Convention against Torture and Other Cruel, Inhuman or Degrading Treatment or Punishment was opened for signature on 10 Dec. 1984 and entered into force on 26 June 1987. The text of the convention is available at URL <http://www.unhchr.ch/html/menu3/b/h_cat39.htm>.

[19] Lord Justice Neuberger (dissenting), *A. and others v. Secretary of State for the Home Department*, Court of Appeal (Civil Division), [2004] EWCA Civ. 1123, URL <http://www.bailii.org/ew/cases/EWCA/Civ/2004/1123.html>. Ultimately, the House of Lords found against the use of such material if it

A second reason for concern is that international intelligence cooperation may entail transferring information on national citizens to foreign intelligence services. Many countries have introduced legal safeguards and controls to avoid personal data on their citizens being supplied to other countries in breach of domestic law.[20] The issue goes wider than concern for the originating state's citizens. Since intelligence shared with foreign intelligence services is no longer under the control of the provider, inappropriate or careless use by the recipient may harm the intelligence activities of the supplier. More importantly, the intelligence provided to a foreign entity may be used or even be essential for supporting policies counter to the interests or objectives or against the ethical standards of the providers.[21] For these and other reasons, it is essential that international intelligence cooperation should be properly authorized by ministers and should be subject to a necessary minimum of safeguards to ensure compliance with domestic law and international legal obligations. At the least, international cooperation should be based on agreements or frameworks which have been subject to ministerial approval.

Safeguards against ministerial abuse of intelligence services

As noted above, executive control of the security sector carries potential risks which require additional safeguards. First, if there is excessive secrecy, the government in effect treats information acquired by public servants as its own property. The executive may attempt to withhold information about security accountability or procedures that are legitimate matters of public debate with the purported excuse of national security. Second, the executive may be tempted to use security agencies or their capacities to gather information in order to strengthen its position. Safeguards allowing officials to refuse unreasonable government instructions in the latter context are highly desirable.

There is a delicate balance between ensuring proper democratic control of the security sector and the distortion of intelligence findings to support a particular political option. The legislation governing security and intelligence agencies should contain clear arrangements for political direction and, in the case of internal agencies, political independence, to ensure that matters of policy are determined by politicians accountable to the public.

Various forms of safeguard may be used to prevent the misuse of agencies by the executive. In Australia, Canada and Hungary there is a requirement that

---

was clear that it had been obtained by torture. See *A. (FC) v. Secretary of State for the Home Department*, [2005] UKHL 71, URL <http://www.bailii.org/uk/cases/UKHL/2005/71.html>.

[20] See e.g. German Bundesverfassungsschutzgesetz [Federal Constitution protection law], Nov. 2002, URL <http://www.fas.org/irp/world/germany/docs/bverfg.htm>, article 19 (3), (unofficial English translation).

[21] See e.g. Fava, C., 'Draft report on the alleged use of European countries by the CIA for the transport and illegal detention of prisoners', 2006/2200 (INI), European Parliament, Temporary Committee on the Alleged Use of European Countries by the CIA for the Transport and Illegal Detention of Prisoners, 24 Nov. 2006, URL <http://www.europarl.europa.eu/comparl/tempcom/tdip/default_en.htm>.

ministerial instructions be put in writing.[22] Such instructions may also be required to be disclosed outside the agency. The Canadian act, for example, requires that they be given to the responsible review committee,[23] and Australian law requires them to be given to the independent Inspector-General of Intelligence and Security as soon as practicable after the instruction is issued.[24] A second type of group of safeguards aims at promoting the political neutrality and bipartisan use of the intelligence services. For example, the Australian intelligence legislation gives the director-general a duty to brief the leader of the opposition.[25] A bipartisan approach to security and intelligence is more likely to be maintained if leading opposition parliamentarians do not feel that they have been wholly excluded from the 'ring of secrecy'. The Australian example is drawn from a Westminster-style parliamentary democracy, albeit a federation. In a more complex federal presidential state there may be a range of actors who should be briefed on a 'need to know' basis. In Bosnia and Herzegovina[26] and the UK, for example, intelligence laws include clear provisions that the intelligence and security services shall not allow their impartiality to be undermined—be it by furthering the interests of certain political parties or by weakening the credibility of legitimate political movements in the country.[27] A third type of safeguard is the so-called open-door policy by which the agency head is granted the right of access to the prime minister or president in order, among other things, to express any politically related concerns. In the UK, the heads of the domestic (Security Service) and foreign (Secret Intelligence Service and Government Communications Headquarters) security agencies, although responsible to the home and foreign secretaries, respectively, have the right of direct access to the prime minister.[28] A fourth group of safeguards against ministerial abuse exists within the agency: for example, legal limits on what an agency can be asked to do; legal safeguards concerning the appointment and dismissal of the agency head; and independent mechanisms for dealing with suspected illegal activities (so-called whistle-blower or grievance procedures).

[22] E.g. Hungary, Act on the National Security Services, 19 Dec. 1995, URL <http://www.dcaf.ch/info/legal/countries/Hungary/Sec_Service_Act.pdf>, section 11.

[23] See e.g. Canada (note 13), section 6(2), requiring written instruction issued by the minister to the director of the service to be given to the Security Intelligence Review Committee.

[24] Australia, Inspector-General of Intelligence and Security Act, 1986; the act, as amended, is available at URL <http://www.austlii.edu.au/au/legis/cth/consol_act/ioiasa1986436.txt>, section 32B.

[25] Australia, Intelligence Services Act, 2001, URL <http://scaleplus.law.gov.au/html/pasteact/3/3483/pdf/IntelligServ2001.pdf>, section 19.

[26] See Bosnia and Herzegovina (note 15), article 6.

[27] Bosnia and Herzegovina (note 15), article 39; and United Kingdom, Security Service Act, 27 Apr. 1989, URL <http://www.opsi.gov.uk/ACTS/acts1989/Ukpga_19890005_en_2.htm#mdiv2>, section 2.

[28] United Kingdom (note 27), section 2(4); United Kingdom, Intelligence Service Act 1994, 26 May 1994, URL <http://www.opsi.gov.uk/acts/acts1994/Ukpga_19940013_en_2.htm>, sections 2(4), 4(4).

IV. Parliamentary oversight: inside or outside the ring of secrecy?

Oversight or scrutiny of the security sector cannot remain the preserve of the government alone without inviting potential abuse. Aside from their role in setting the legal framework, it is commonplace for parliaments to scrutinize governmental activity. In most democracies it is accepted that all areas of state activity should be open for investigation by the parliament, including the security and intelligence sector. Parliamentary involvement gives legitimacy and democratic accountability. It can help to ensure that security and intelligence organizations are serving the state as a whole and protecting the constitution, rather than narrower political or sectoral interests. However, there are corresponding risks to be avoided, including undue politicization of intelligence issues and irresponsible behaviour by parliamentarians in debate. This section elaborates on the role of the parliament in the oversight of intelligence services, including the sensitive issue of parliamentarians' access to classified information.

The role of the parliament

The international norm is for the parliament to establish a specialized body which is mandated to provide oversight of the intelligence services.[29] Without such a specialized committee, it is hard if not impossible for the parliament to exercise systematic and focused oversight of the intelligence services. Table 5.2 presents an overview of different parliamentary intelligence oversight committee systems in selected European countries.

The scope of the mandate of the parliamentary intelligence oversight committee is crucial for its success. One option is for the mandate to be comprehensive and include both policy and operations (e.g. as in Germany and the USA).[30] A parliamentary oversight body that deals with operations may have greater credibility and may be given greater powers, such as powers of subpoena. However, it will face inevitable restrictions on how it conducts its investigations and on what can be reported to the parliament or the public. It will operate in effect within a ring of secrecy and that will create a barrier between it and the remainder of the parliament. Provided that it establishes a reputation for independence and thoroughness, this need not affect its legitimacy. However, the parliament and the public will have to take it on trust to a certain degree that proper oversight of operational matters is taking place without supporting evidence being available. Another danger is that such an

[29] France is one of the rare liberal democracies where the parliament does not have a specialized committee dedicated to the oversight of intelligence services.

[30] US Senate Select Committee on Intelligence, 'Rules of the US Senate Select Committee on Intelligence', section 13; and Act Governing the Parliamentary Control of Intelligence Activities by the German Federation, Parliamentary Control Panel Act (PKGrG), Apr. 1978, section 2, 2a. See the discussion in Born and Leigh (note 1), pp. 77–102.

Table 5.2. Types of parliamentary intelligence oversight committees in democracies

Type of intelligence oversight committee	Examples of use
No parliamentary intelligence oversight committee	France
No parliamentary intelligence oversight committee but the parliament has at its disposal an independent committee of experts to ensure oversight of the intelligence services; members are appointed by the parliament; committee reports to the parliament	Norway
Parliamentary intelligence oversight committee and the parliament also has at its disposal an independent committee of experts, appointed by the parliament, which reports to the parliament	Belgium
Parliamentary intelligence oversight committee in combination with an independent committee of experts, appointed by the government and reporting to the government	Netherlands
Parliamentary intelligence oversight committee with expert staff	Germany, USA
Not one but several parliamentary intelligence oversight committees for domestic, foreign and military intelligence	Romania
Ad hoc investigative committees to investigate the role of government and intelligence services	German Parliament, Committee of Inquiry

oversight body gets too close to the agencies it is responsible for overseeing. For example, although a legal requirement that the oversight body be notified in advance of certain actions by the agency may appear to strengthen control, it could also protect that body from later criticism of these operations. This is a danger, for example, in the USA, where congressional intelligence oversight committees must be notified about special intelligence operations in advance.[31] The alternative approach is to limit the mandate of the parliamentary oversight committee to matters of policy and finance only (as in the UK) or human rights and the rule of law (as in Norway).[32] These aspects can be more readily examined in the public arena with fewer restrictions on disclosure—although the publication of precise budgetary details may be prejudicial to national security. The difficulty of the latter approach, however, is that it detracts from one of the key tasks of parliamentary scrutiny: to ensure that government policy in a given field is carried out effectively and within the boundaries of the law. Without access to some operational detail, an oversight body can have or give no assurance about the efficiency or the legality of the intelligence services.

[31] Such activities are regulated in the 1974 Hughes–Ryan Act; the 1980 Oversight Act, and the 1991 Intelligence Authorization Act. On congressional involvement in authorizing covert operations see Johnson, L. K., 'Governing in the absence of angels: on the practice of intelligence accountability in the United States', eds Born, Johnson and Leigh (note 1), pp. 64–66.

[32] Norway, Act Relating to the Monitoring of Intelligence, Surveillance and Security Services, Act no. 7, 3 Feb, 1995, URL <http://www.dcaf.ch/info/legal/countries/Norway/Law/IntelligenceAct.pdf>, section 2.

Access to secret information

As mentioned above, effective scrutiny of security and intelligence is pain-staking and unglamorous work for politicians, conducted almost entirely behind the scenes. Sensitive parliamentary investigations require in effect a parallel secure environment in the parliament for witnesses and papers. The preservation of necessary secrecy may create a barrier between the few parlia-mentarians involved and the remainder, causing those within the ring of secrecy to be envied or distrusted by colleagues. It is therefore essential that a cross section of parliamentarians who can command widespread trust and pub-lic credibility are involved—for example, senior politicians and leaders of par-liamentary factions. The parliament, and particularly the oversight body, must have sufficient power to obtain information and documents from the govern-ment and intelligence services. The precise extent to which a parliamentary oversight body requires access to security and intelligence information and the type of information concerned depends on its mandate. An oversight body that has functions which include reviewing operations and effectiveness will require access to more specific information than one with a remit solely cover-ing policy. Clearly, however, an oversight body should have unlimited access to the information necessary for discharging its duties.

Oversight is not only a matter of having access to information, but also of being informed about matters which are important but on which information is not available to the parliament as a whole. The US Congress has acknow-ledged this problem and has passed laws requiring that the executive keeps the congressional intelligence oversight committee completely and currently informed of the intelligence activities of all agencies, including covert actions.[33] Inevitably, for reasons of national security, there is a limit to what this committee can report to the rest of the Congress or the public. Different approaches are followed by various countries. In Australia, for example, the committee is not allowed to disclose in a report to the parliament the identity of, or more general information about, intelligence employees and other oper-ationally sensitive information.[34] In the UK, the Intelligence and Security Committee (ISC)—a committee of parliamentarians from both houses—is required by law to produce at minimum one annual report to the parliament. The report, however, is first submitted to the prime minister who can unilat-erally delete text from it, although in all cases to date changes have been agreed by consultation. The ISC's annual reports have contained many such deleted passages (marked by asterisks) in recent years. Additionally, the prime minister decides about the timing of the publication of the ISC's report, which may permit him or her to dampen its impact by delaying release until public interest in the relevant events has waned, or to synchronize the date of publi-cation with the government's prepared response. Members of the ISC have

---

[33] Johnson (note 31), pp. 64–66.
[34] Australia (note 25), schedule 1, part 1, clause 7.1.

complained about unnecessary delay in releasing their findings.[35] The danger of the British system is that the executive could use such procedural powers to interfere with and limit the parliamentary accountability of the intelligence services.

A last, but not unimportant, issue is whether parliamentarians are capable of keeping secrets. Research into the functioning of parliamentary intelligence oversight committees has indicated that parliaments rarely leak classified information.[36] This is not strange because parliamentarians are aware that, if they leak, they will lose the trust of the intelligence services and the government as well as the public. Furthermore, unless parliamentarians have immunity in such cases, leaking officially classified information is illegal. In many countries members of parliamentary intelligence oversight committees are screened and vetted before they are allowed to take a seat on the committee.[37] Vetting of parliamentarians is, however, a delicate subject. It can be argued that legislators should be immune from vetting (as they are in Argentina, the UK and the USA) because it creates inequality between parliamentarians and because the legislative mandate of parliamentarians should automatically imply access to classified information. Again, if parliamentarians are vetted (as for example in Poland and South Africa), the problem arises of their being dependent for security clearance on the same service that they are supposed to oversee. To avoid a conflict of interests and responsibilities in countries with such a procedure, the ultimate decision about appointing a parliamentarian to the intelligence committee is reserved for the leadership of the parliament alone. The intelligence services therefore play an advisory, not a deciding, role in the security clearance of parliamentarians for oversight work.[38]

The possibility of having access to information does not necessarily mean that members of the parliament will make use of that possibility. Parliamentarians may fear that their independence and freedom of speech will be compromised if they have knowledge of classified matters. In the Netherlands, for example, Socialist Party parliamentarians refused to become members of the parliamentary intelligence oversight committee for this reason. In the USA only 12 members of the House of Representatives made use of the right to read the 2006 classified intelligence bill (which passed in a vote of 327 to 96 in April 2006), and thus the great majority of members voted in favour of the bill without knowing its contents. The reason why so many members chose not to read the bill is that they would not be allowed to disclose any classified

[35] Leigh, I. 'Accountability of security and intelligence in the United Kingdom', eds Born, Johnson and Leigh (note 1), pp. 88–89.

[36] Born, H. and Johnson, L. K., 'Balancing operational efficiency and democratic legitimacy', eds Born, Johnson and Leigh (note 1). pp. 225–39.

[37] Vetting is a process by which an individual's personal background and political affiliation is examined to assesses his or her suitability for a position that may involve national security concerns. See Born and Leigh (note 1), p. 88.

[38] Born, H. and Johnson, L. K., 'Balancing operational efficiency and democratic legitimacy', eds Born, Johnson and Leigh (note 1). pp. 225–39.

information drawn from it during plenary debates in the Congress, even if the media had already reported on the matters concerned.[39]

V. Non-political oversight: the role of courts and independent bodies

The previous sections described the importance of the executive and of the parliament in relation to the accountability of intelligence and security agencies. The third branch of the state—the judiciary—also has a role to play, both as the ultimate guardian of the constitution and the law and through various review functions.

The role of the judiciary

It would be misleading to describe the judiciary as routinely involved in oversight. Intelligence-related cases that reach court are sporadic, and judges generally do not see it as their task to supervise the exercise of governmental functions but rather to review their constitutionality, legality or compliance with human rights standards as necessary. Nevertheless, because of the centrality of the rule of law as a source of control on arbitrary power in modern democracies, judicial practice is important. Judges are the final arbiters of the statutory powers that security and intelligence agencies possess.

There are both strengths and dangers in judicial scrutiny of intelligence matters. On the positive side, in most liberal states judges are perceived to be independent of the government; their presumably detached view lends credibility to the system of oversight in the eyes of the public. Traditionally, the courts have been perceived as guardians of individual rights and, arguably, judges are well suited to oversight tasks that involve the interests of individuals—for example the scrutiny of surveillance. There are, however, also problems that in part arise from the necessary tensions and limitations in judicial review of any governmental function, and in part are specific to the field of security.[40] Court procedures necessitate sensitive data being disclosed beyond the controlled environment of the security sector itself. Even if legal proceedings take place in camera, the judge, court staff and lawyers may be required to read or handle the information. This raises the difficult question of security vetting. In some countries judges are vetted or access to the handling of this category of cases is restricted to a small group. This may, however, raise questions about pre-vetted judges' impartiality in such proceedings, since the effect of the vetting requirement is to make them acceptable to one party in the case. In other countries vetting would be constitutionally unacceptable and the

---

[39] Not all of the 2006 intelligence bill is classified, but it contains classified provisions and sections. 'Classified intelligence bills often unread: secret process can discourage House debate', *Boston Globe*, 6 Aug. 2006, p. A1.

[40] Lustgarten, L. and Leigh, I., *In From the Cold: National Security and Parliamentary Democracy*, (Oxford University Press: Oxford, 1994), pp. 320–59.

seniority and reputation of the judges involved is taken as sufficient guarantee that they can be trusted with secret information.

The more general danger is that over intrusive control by the judges risks involving them in the tasks of the executive and blurs the separation of powers between these two branches of the state. The politicization of the judiciary may also result from the use of judges to conduct inquiries with a security dimension. Their wider credibility and legitimacy may be at risk of being undermined. Judicial scrutiny should be sparing and suitably modest in areas of government policy where judges have no special competence, for example, in assessing whether intelligence justified a decision to take a particular military action or whether it established an imminent threat to the state. Legal control by the courts proper can only operate effectively within the limited range of issues where a person's rights are affected by security decisions. Much security work, however, eludes this criterion since it does not affect a person's recognized legal rights (e.g. gathering information on individuals from public sources, or surveillance in public places). Even if individuals are affected, in many instances they are unlikely to bring legal challenges because the role of the agencies concerned will not be apparent to them (e.g. the targets of surveillance in some countries will never learn that they have been targeted). Challenges by an affected individual are most likely where there are legal procedures against that individual, such as prosecution or deportation, based on intelligence material. Much other security work is not directed towards immediate legal procedures in this way (e.g. long-term intelligence gathering) and is therefore likely to remain unchecked by legal challenge. State interests may be protected also by specific bars on the use of intelligence material in evidence for reasons of public policy. Examples include the common law concepts of public interest immunity or executive privilege and the current statutory bar on admissibility in court of evidence obtained from telephone tapping under the UK's 2000 Regulation of Investigatory Powers Act.[41] This act not only deprives prosecutors of potentially valuable evidence but also immunizes warrants for phone tapping from judicial challenge.

In several countries there are judicial procedures that have been specially adapted to a security context: thus, in Canada designated Federal Court judges hear surveillance applications from the CSIS and deal with immigration and freedom of information cases with a security dimension.[42]

The US 1978 Foreign Intelligence Surveillance Act (FISA) has operated for more than two decades.[43] It created a special court of judges for overseeing surveillance warrants issued by federal police agencies against suspected foreign intelligence agents inside the USA. According to FISA, the electronic surveillance of telephone calls between the USA and foreign countries needs the authorization of the FISA special court. In December 2005 *The New York*

[41] United Kingdom, Regulation of Investigatory Powers Act, 2000, URL <http://www.opsi.gov.uk/Acts/acts2000/20000023.htm>.

[42] Leigh, I., 'Secret proceedings in Canada', *Osgoode Hall Law Journal*, vol. 34 (1996) pp. 113–73.

[43] United States, Foreign Intelligence Surveillance Act (FISA), 1978, URL <http://caselaw.lp.findlaw.com/casecode/uscodes/50/chapters/36/toc.html>.

Times revealed that President George W. Bush had secretly authorized in 2002 the National Security Agency (NSA) 'terrorist surveillance program' to monitor calls between the USA and foreign countries without court authorization.[44] President Bush claimed that the NSA programme was both legal and necessary in the 'global war against terrorism'.[45] The American Civil Liberties Union (ACLU), however, contested the legality of the NSA programme in court and a federal judge ruled in August 2006 that it was illegal.[46] The Democratic Party gained control of the US Congress in the November 2006 elections, and the NSA Oversight Act bill was introduced in the House of Representatives in January 2007.[47] If passed, it would reaffirm that the FISA court authorization is the sole legal basis for wiretaps.

Similarly, in the UK designated judicial commissioners deal with some forms of authorization of surveillance—although not in court—under the 2000 Regulation of Investigatory Powers Act; other judicial commissioners review the system and check on the warrants and authorizations granted to the security and intelligence services by ministers. Even in cases such as this, where judges are used in order to safeguard the rights of individuals, there is the danger that familiarity and acclimatization to security material will gradually undermine their qualities of independence and external perspective. If judges become case hardened through overexposure to security techniques, information and assessments as revealed in intelligence-based warrant applications, then they may become less effective in practice at protecting individuals' rights. Evidence from countries that require prior judicial approval of surveillance warrants, such as Canada and the USA, does not suggest high rates of refusal. This casts into doubt whether such judges are really bringing an independent perspective to the process: ultimately, there may be little difference in outcome between this procedure and a system of approval within the agency itself or by a government minister.

One solution to the difficulties of handling intelligence as source material in court proceedings is the use of special, security-cleared legal representatives in deportation, employment and (increasingly) criminal cases.[48] Initially adapted from Canadian procedure, this system aims to balance so-called open justice with the state's security interests.[49] It allows a vetted lawyer to test the

[44] Risen, J. and Lichtblau, E., 'Bush lets U.S. spy on callers without courts', *New York Times*, 16 Dec. 2005.

[45] Lichtblau, E., 'Bush defends spy program and denies misleading public', *New York Times*, 2 Jan. 2006.

[46] *ACLU v. NSA*, Detroit District Court, 17 Aug. 2006; and Cable News Network, 'NSA eavesdropping program ruled unconstitutional', 17 Aug. 2006, URL <http://www.cnn.com/2006/POLITICS/08/17/domesticspying.lawsuit/>.

[47] Broache, A., 'Congress off to slow start with tech', *New York Times*, 9 Jan. 2007; and US House of Representatives, NSA Oversight Act, H.R. 11, 4 Jan. 2007, URL <http://thomas.loc.gov/cgi-bin/query/z?c110:H.R.11:>.

[48] British Treasury Solicitor, *Special Advocates: a Guide to the Role of Special Advocates* (Stationery Office: London, 2005).

[49] In the UK the Special Immigration Appeals Commission (SIAC) was established by the Special Immigration Appeals Commission Act 1997, following the ruling of the European Court of Human Rights in the Chahal case. *Chahal v. the United Kingdom*, 22414/93 [1996] ECHR 54, 15 Nov. 1996,

strength of the government's case and to challenge the evidence even where the complainant and his or her lawyer are excluded from parts of the legal process on security grounds. The European Court of Human Rights has advocated such procedural innovations as a means of satisfying Article 6 of the European Convention on Human Rights (the right to a fair and public trial),[50] even in security cases.[51] The UK's use of such special advocates has been criticized, however, by some of those who have undertaken the role and by a parliamentary select committee.[52]

Complaint systems

More generally, as explained above, the courts are inherently flawed as a means of accountability for or redress against security and intelligence agencies There is a clear need for alternative avenues of redress for individuals who claim to have been adversely affected by the exceptional powers often wielded by security and intelligence agencies. A proper complaint system can also bolster accountability by highlighting administrative failings and lessons to be learned, leading to improved performance. At the same time, the system should not help those who are legitimately targeted by a security or intelligence agency to find out about the agency's work. A complaint system should be independent, robust and fair to the complainant on the one hand, but sensitive to security needs on the other. For European states, the European Convention on Human Rights also has a bearing because of the rights it establishes to a fair trial by an independent and impartial tribunal, to respect for private life and to the availability of an effective remedy.[53]

An oversight system may handle complaints in a variety of ways. An independent official, such as an ombudsman, may have the power to investigate and report on a complaint against an agency—as in the Netherlands.[54] Other countries give jurisdiction to deal with complaints against the services as part

URL <http://www.worldlii.org/eu/cases/ECHR/1996/54.html>. The SIAC is able to receive intelligence information in closed hearings and without the presence of the appellant and through use of Special Advocates. Its initial jurisdiction was in cases of deportation on grounds of national security. However, the 2001 Anti-Terrorism Crime and Security Act extended the jurisdiction to include review of detention following a ministerial certificate that a non-national was a security threat; the latter provisions were, however, superseded with the introduction of 'control orders' under the 2005 Prevention of Terrorism Act, URL <http://www.opsi.gov.uk/ACTS/acts2005/20050002.htm>.

[50] On the right to a fair trial see *Edward and Lewis v. the United Kingdom*, [2003] 15 BHRC 189, 22 July 2003, URL <http://worldlii.org/eu/cases/ECHR/2003/381.html>. See also the European Convention on Human Rights, Rome, 4 Nov.1950, URL <http://www.hri.org/docs/ECHR50.html>.

[51] *Chahal v. the United Kingdom* (note 49).

[52] British House of Commons, Constitutional Affairs Select Committee, Seventh Report of Session 2004–5, the operation of the Special Immigration Appeals Commission (SIAC) and the use of Special Advocates, HC 323-I, 3 Apr. 2005, URL <http://www.publications.parliament.uk/pa/cm200405/cmselect/cmconst/323/323i.pdf>.

[53] Cameron, I., *National Security and the European Convention on Human Rights* (Iustus Forlag: Uppsala, 2000); and Cameron, I., 'Beyond the nation state: the influence of the European Court of Human Rights on intelligence accountability', eds Born, Johnson, and Leigh (note 1), pp. 34–53.

[54] Netherlands, Act of 7 February 2002, providing for rules relating to the intelligence and security services and amendment of several acts (Intelligence and Security Services Act 2002), URL <http://www.aivd.nl/contents/pages/4704/IntelligenceandSecurityServicesAct2002.pdf >, article 83.

of an independent inspector general of security and intelligence's general oversight role. New Zealand's Office of the Inspector-General of Intelligence and Security (established in 1996) and South Africa's Office of the Inspector-General of Intelligence are examples of this approach (see below for more on inspectors general).[55] Commissioners appointed under freedom of information or data protection legislation may also be able to investigate complaints in these fields against the agencies. These various ombudsman-type systems each stress the importance of an investigation by an independent official on behalf of the complainant. Their primary focus may be administrative failure rather than a legal error as such, and they give less emphasis to the complainant's own participation in the process and to transparency. The conclusion is usually a report, rather than a judgement or formal remedies, and (if the complaint is upheld) a recommendation for making amends and preventing recurrence of the mistake.

A less common approach is to deal with the complaints and grievances of citizens through a parliamentary intelligence oversight committee, as in Germany and Norway.[56] Such a procedure may be a good way to gain insight into potential executive shortcomings—of policy, legality and efficiency. The individual complainant may, however, feel that the complaint process is insufficiently independent—especially if the oversight body is too closely identified with the agencies it oversees or operates within the ring of secrecy. The disadvantages of having a single body handle complaints and oversight can be alleviated by maintaining distinct legal procedures for these different roles. A better option, however, is to give the two functions to different bodies, while ensuring that the oversight body can be alerted to the broader implications of specific complaints. Members of the services, as well as the public, are permitted in some countries to bring service-related issues to the attention of an ombudsman or parliamentary oversight body. In South Africa, for example, members of the service may complain to the Inspector-General, and in Germany officials may raise issues with the Parliamentary Control Panel.[57]

Complaints may also be handled by a specialist tribunal, established to deal with complaints either against a particular agency or over the use of specific powers. The UK has examples of both—the Intelligence Services Commissioner and the Commissioner for the Interception of Communications. Alternatively, a specialist oversight body may handle complaints through a tribunal-type procedure: this is one of the roles given to the Security Intelligence Review Committee (SIRC) in Canada. Tribunals have advantages over regular courts in handling security- and intelligence-related complaints: they can develop a distinct expertise tailored specifically to sensitive information.

[55] The South African office was created pursuant to section 210b of the South African Constitution. Constitution of the Republic of South Africa 1996, 8 May 1996 (amended 11 Oct. 1996), URL <http://www.polity.org.za/html/govdocs/constitution/saconst.html?rebookmark=1>.

[56] Sejersted, F., 'Intelligence and accountability in a state without enemies: the case of Norway', eds Born, Johnson, and Leigh (note 1), pp. 119–41.

[57] German Bundestag, Secretariat of the Parliamentary Control Commission, *Parliamentary Control of the Intelligence Services in Germany* (Bundespresseamt: Berlin, 2001), pp. 19–20.

Such processes are unlikely to involve a full public legal hearing. Complainants nevertheless face major hurdles: even if granted a hearing, they are likely to have severe practical difficulties in proving a case, in obtaining access to relevant evidence or in challenging the agency's version of events. To combat some of these problems, special security-cleared counsel have been introduced in Canada and in the UK to assist the tribunal reach a more objective assessment of the evidence and the arguments, even if full details cannot be disclosed to the complainant.

Inspectors general and auditing

A number of countries have created independent offices such as inspectors general, judicial commissioners or auditors to check on the activities of the security sector, with statutory powers of access to information and staff.[58] These offices provide impartial verification and assurance for the government that secret agencies are acting in accord with its policies, effectively and with propriety. They may also give redress for complaints. The concept of the inspector general derives from the US intelligence community, which now has a dozen or so officers of this kind, independent of the agencies they oversee. Some are statutory officials (e.g. the inspectors general for the CIA and the Department of Defense); others are derived from administrative arrangements established by the relevant minister (e.g. with regard to the Defense Intelligence Agency and the National Reconnaissance Office); and some report to the Congress as well as to the executive branch. A number of these inspectors general examine agency efficiency and the avoidance of waste and perform audit functions, in addition to looking at legality and policy compliance.

Usually inspectors general function within the ring of secrecy: their primary function is to strengthen accountability to the executive, rather than providing public assurance about accountability in Canada. The Inspector-General of the CSIS is an example: he or she has full access to information in the hands of the service in order to discharge this role.[59] Similarly, under legislation in Bosnia and Herzegovina the Inspector General exercises 'an internal control function' and may review the agency's activities; investigate complaints; initiate inspections, audits and investigations; and issue recommendations.[60] The Inspector General has a duty to report at least every six months to the SIRC and to keep the relevant ministers informed of developments on a regular and timely basis. The Inspector General's powers include questioning agency employees and obtaining access to agency premises and data. In South Africa, in contrast, the Inspector-General's role is to report to the parliament. In effect the office breaches the ring of secrecy and provides public assurance, in its report to the parliament, that an independent person with access to the

[58] United Kingdom, Cabinet Office, Intelligence and Security Committee Annual Report 2001–2002, URL <http://www.cabinetoffice.gov.uk/publications/reports/intelligence/Intelligence.pdf>, appendix 3.

[59] Canada (note 13), c. 21, sections 33.2 and 33.3.

[60] Bosnia Herzegovina (note 15), article 32.

relevant material has examined the activities of the security or intelligence agency. Not surprisingly, the Inspector-General is not allowed to publish much of the material on which an assessment of the agency's work is made, although it may be shared with other oversight bodies. Other types of inspectors general who report to the executive may also maintain an informal working relationship with parliamentary bodies; this is the case in Australia, and a number of the US inspectors general report periodically to the Congress.

Regardless of whether an inspector general reports to the legislature, the executive or the courts, careful legal delineation of the office's jurisdiction, independence and powers are vital. Independent officials may be asked to review an agency's performance against one or more of several standards: efficiency, compliance with government policies or targets, propriety or legality. In every case, in order to make a reliable assessment, the office will need unrestricted access to files and personnel. An independent official is unlikely in practice to be able to examine more than a fraction of the work of an agency. Consequently, some inspectors general operate by 'sampling' the work and files of the agencies overseen, in the hope that this will produce a ripple effect inducing the agency to establish more widespread procedures. Some also have jurisdiction to deal with individual complaints (as in Australia[61]).

The auditing of financial propriety is another independent function.[62] Both the executive and the legislature have a legitimate interest in ensuring that budgets voted for intelligence are spent lawfully and effectively. However, as with the handling of complaints, it requires some ingenuity to devise systems for protecting secrecy while ensuring that auditors have the wide access to classified information necessary to let them certify whether the services have used government funds within the law. Restrictions designed to protect the identities of certain sources of information and the details of particularly sensitive operations may be imposed on the access granted to an auditor general. What distinguishes the auditing of security and intelligence services from regular audits of other public bodies, however, is the nature of the reporting mechanisms. In order to protect the continuity of operations and the methods and sources of the services, special reporting mechanisms are in place in many countries. For example, in the UK only the chairmen of the parliament's Public Accounts Committee and the Intelligence and Security Committee are fully briefed about the outcome of the financial audit. These briefings may include reports on the legality and efficiency of expenditure, on possible irregularities and on whether the services have operated within or have exceeded the budget. In many countries, the public annual reports of the security and intelligence service (e.g. in the Netherlands) or of the parliamentary oversight body (e.g. in the UK) include statements about the outcome of the financial audits.

---

[61] Australia (note 24), sections 10–12.
[62] Born and Leigh (note 1), pp. 113–19.

VI. Conclusions

Democratic oversight of the intelligence services, including oversight by executive, parliamentary and independent bodies, has become even more essential against the background of the post-September 2001 fight against terrorism for at least four reasons. First, many services have been granted increased personnel numbers and higher budgets, creating a need for parliamentary oversight in order to ensure that taxpayers' money is effectively spent. Second, in various countries the special powers of intelligence services have significantly increased, which in turn increases the need for civil liberty supervision, especially by judges but also through other independent complaint mechanisms. [63] Third, higher levels of international cooperation have increased the need for effective executive control, as elaborated in this chapter. Finally, although intelligence services were always politicized to a certain extent (as shown, for example, by the Watergate scandal of the early 1970s and the missile gap discussion in the 1960s in the USA) the war in Iraq and the fight against terrorism have strengthened the apparent trend towards politicization of intelligence, creating an urgent need to insulate the services from political manipulation.

It should be underlined that democratic intelligence oversight systems have come into operation only comparatively recently (i.e. mostly since the mid-1970s and in many states only since the 1990s). This development represents a move away from a guardian state, in which important issues are left to the discretion of professionals, towards a democratic state in which important issues are subjected to normal democratic decision-making procedures. On the one hand, this can be regarded as a positive development in any democratic polity because it leads to a better system of checks and balances covering the intelligence services among other things. On the other hand, the submission of intelligence services to public accountability means that their role and work become increasingly part of public debate. The danger exists that political actors in these debates will use the control of the services to promote their party interests. In other words, democratic accountability of intelligence services is designed to limit the risk of politicization but also carries a danger of heightening that risk. These and other challenges can be addressed, for example, through more substantial oversight of international cooperation and increased access to classified information by elected office holders. It remains to be seen how the fledgling intelligence oversight systems reviewed in this chapter will cope with the full challenge of overseeing the secret intelligence community in the years to come.

---

[63] See e.g. the 2001 Uniting and Strengthening America by Providing Appropriate Tools Required to Intercept and Obstruct Terrorism Act (USA Patriot Act). US, USA Patriot Act, H.R. 3162, 24 Oct. 2001, available at URL <http://www.epic.org/privacy/terrorism/hr3162.html>. On the act see Public Broadcasting Service (PBS), 'Background report: the US Patriot Act', Online Newshour PBS, 27 Mar. 2006, URL <http://www.pbs.org/newshour/indepth_coverage/terrorism/homeland/patriotact.html>.

6. Energy and security: regional and global dimensions

KAMILA PRONIŃSKA

I. Introduction

The recent surge of debate about energy security and its place in international strategy and politics has often been compared to the impact of the first oil crisis in the 1970s. In reality, it has a different and more varied set of origins. Since the 1970s there have been changes in the structure of the energy market, the nature of energy security and the challenges to it, and the geopolitical environment. These changes all affect the understanding of what energy security is and what are the best national, regional and global methods of ensuring it. At the same time, states differ in their starting positions regarding energy security, and their energy strategies and policies are chosen under the influence of broader economic, geopolitical and ideological calculations than was the case in the 1970s. This leads some of them to take a nationalistic approach to energy security, often including a readiness to use force (military or economic) to protect their energy interests. Other countries show more understanding of the need for collective, institutional measures to ensure energy security.

All these factors shape contemporary international relations in ways that go beyond the direct strategic and geopolitical dimensions of energy security as such. On the one hand, they may lead to new strategic alliances and cooperation between states that are major energy market players; on the other hand, they provide sources of international tension and conflict. Such conflicts in turn may include 'resource conflicts', where the ownership and supply of energy is itself the key factor, or they may be conflicts in which resources provide one of many catalysts without taking the central role. Only during the two world wars of the 20th century did these diverse links between energy and the traditional or military security agenda become as obvious and visible as they are today. They are now illustrated not only by the military presence of major energy consumers in the regions abundant in oil and gas, but also by terrorist attacks on the energy sector and by the growing concern with providing military protection for energy infrastructure around the world.

This chapter concentrates primarily on one small aspect of the energy security conundrum—the link between energy and the traditional security agenda. It focuses for the most part on concerns related to the production, use and supply of oil and gas, and on the external dimensions of energy policy. Energy security clearly cannot be reduced to oil and gas: the use of other energy sources such as coal, nuclear energy or renewable sources[1] is equally relevant to enhancing a country's energy security, and may also trigger energy security concerns. Nevertheless, the significance of oil and gas to the world economy and the fact that they are traded over long distances from a few major production centres to consumers scattered literally worldwide make them the main source of security-relevant competition, tensions, policy dilemmas and even conflicts.

Section II of this chapter clarifies the meaning of energy security and the main components and processes that have affected analytical and political visions of the link between energy and security at different times. Section III looks in more detail at the evolving structure of, and trends within, the world market for oil and gas. Section IV considers the links between energy and international conflict, and section V reviews policy responses to energy security challenges that have been considered by states, groups of states and international organizations up to the present. The conclusions are presented in section VI.

II. A geostrategic approach to the security of energy supply

Energy security—the availability of energy in sufficient quantities and at affordable prices at all times—is a complex issue. It brings together a variety of economic, geopolitical, geological, ecological and institutional factors, but also breaks down into multiple (global, regional, national and individual consumer) levels of reference and analysis. Analysts' attempts to define energy security, and governments' anxiety to ensure it, are both made more difficult as a result. In addition, one's perspective on energy security depends on one's position in the energy supply chain. For exporters the most important part of the concept is security of demand for their energy resources or, in other words, security of revenues from the energy market. Earning petrodollars is very often a prerequisite for producers' economic security—and hence also for their own energy security. Most consumers, in contrast, focus their security concerns on the challenge of import dependency and the risk of supply disruption. In major energy-consuming countries, accordingly, the key security issues debated include diversity of supply, access to energy resources (often entailing competition with other major energy consumers), stable oil prices, security margins for emergencies and the introduction of alternative energy sources. Other elements of the energy supply chain also interpret energy security differently: for commercial companies a main component of security is a stable legal investment regime in producer countries.

Furthermore, the perception of energy security is in constant flux depending on the structure of the energy market, the state of consumer–producer rela-

---

[1] Renewable sources of energy are those that can regenerate over time or cannot be physically depleted. Most renewable energy is ultimately obtained from the sun, either directly or indirectly in the form of wind power, hydropower or photosynthetic energy stored in biomass, known as a bioenergy or biofuel. Non-solar renewable energy is geothermal power generated from the earth's heat.

tions, demand and supply trends, technological changes, and—not least—the fact or fear of energy crises, supply disruptions or price shocks. In practice, changes in perception can significantly affect both theoretical and practical approaches to energy security. Thus, energy analysts have not always perceived the significance of the geostrategic component in the same way.[2] For example, during the 1970s the concept of energy security focused on geostrategic aspects—reducing import dependency and the vulnerability of imported supplies to disruption—and was narrowly viewed through the prism of high dependency on Middle East oil suppliers and the threat of supply disruptions. In contrast, in the 1990s, when suppliers did not use energy as a weapon and oil supplies were plentiful at moderate prices, consuming countries became more confident about oil and gas abundance and more aware of their own strength as consumers. Since the 1980s importers have felt able, for instance, to impose sanctions on some oil-exporting countries and to build multilateral response mechanisms for energy crisis situations. Analysts have turned accordingly to other aspects of energy security. Prime issues have included, first, ensuring greater economic efficiency through liberalization and deregulation in the gas and electricity sectors, and second, enhancing the protection of the environment against threats generated by the production and use of energy, such as carbon dioxide emissions.

At state policy level, changes in the content of the energy security agenda have also been reflected in changes in its relative priority among national and international concerns. The decisions taken by the Organization of the Petroleum Exporting Countries (OPEC) in 1973—to impose an oil embargo on those consumer countries that favoured Israel and to raise oil prices drastically—provide perhaps the most spectacular example of an incident that lifted energy security to the top of political agendas.[3] These steps had a truly shocking impact on Western countries that were highly dependent on hitherto relatively cheap and easily obtainable imported oil. On the one hand, they showed the vulnerability of the importers' economies to disruption of physical oil supplies and to rapid price increases; on the other hand, the political character of the Arab countries' decisions crystallized the notion of energy as a weapon, with its potentially asymmetrical impact on highly developed economies. One result was to force major importers to consider multilateral measures to safeguard the future security of supply. For the first time in modern history energy security became an important issue of international debate, with results that included the creation of the International Energy Agency (IEA) and of multilateral response mechanisms to deal with potentially serious energy supply

[2] For further discussion on this see Skinner, R. and Arnott, R., *The Oil Supply and Demand Context for Security of Oil Supply to the EU from the GCC Countries*, Working Paper/Monograph no. 29 (Oxford Institute for Energy Studies: Oxford, 2 Apr. 2005), URL <http://www.oxfordenergy.org/books. php>, pp. 22–31; and Skinner, R., 'Energy security and producer–consumer dialogue: avoiding a Maginot mentality', Background Paper for Government of Canada Energy Symposium, Ottawa, 28 Oct. 2005, URL <http://www.oxfordenergy.org/presentations.php?1#>.

[3] OPEC was established in 1960. Its members are Algeria, Angola (since Dec. 2006), Indonesia, Iran, Iraq, Kuwait, Libya, Nigeria, Qatar, Saudi Arabia, the United Arab Emirates and Venezuela.

disruptions.[4] In the long-term perspective, the events of the 1970s gave a certain advantage to consumer countries by enriching their knowledge of how to protect themselves against similar future threats, and by prompting them to develop a wide range of methods and strategies to strengthen energy security at both the national and multilateral levels.

Nonetheless, the origins of strategic thinking about the security of energy supplies go back at least to World War I. One pivotal point for the emergence of energy security as an issue of national strategy was the decision of Winston Churchill, as cabinet minister responsible for the British Navy in the run-up to World War I, to switch from using indigenous coal to imported oil as fuel.[5] During World War II the significance of the energy factor was even more apparent. As the war effort was totally dependent on liquid fuels, both sides had two major strategic objectives—to defend their own sources and routes of oil supply, and to attack those of the enemy.[6]

Both these older and the more recent historical examples highlight the centrality of the issue of import dependency, which arises at two levels: the dependency of individual economies on energy, particularly on oil, and the dependency of highly developed countries on foreign producers. The second type of dependency results both from developed countries' larger appetites for energy and from the fact that energy resources (above all, oil and gas) are unevenly distributed across the world. In both contexts, the security of supply becomes one of the most important terms to be used in identifying and solving energy security challenges.

Richard Ullman, in an article which became a classic study on redefinition of security, distinguishes two types of constraints on energy resource supplies.[7] The first is when a non-renewable resource is becoming scarce through normal depletion; the second is when supplies are constrained through artificial government efforts to restrict supplies by means of boycotts, embargoes or cartel agreements. Paul Horsnell makes further distinctions between energy supply constraints.[8] He distinguishes between swings in oil prices that arise from 'policy discontinuity'—that is, changes in the producers' policy—and those caused by 'fundamental discontinuity', when the available supply within

[4] The IEA was established in 1974. Its members are Australia, Austria, Belgium, Canada, the Czech Republic, Denmark, Finland, France, Germany, Greece, Hungary, Ireland, Italy, Japan, South Korea, Luxembourg, the Netherlands, New Zealand, Norway, Portugal, Spain, Sweden, Switzerland, Turkey, the United Kingdom and the United States. The European Commission also participates in the IEA's work. The IEA's emergency response mechanisms were set up under the Agreement on an International Energy Program, signed on 18 Nov. 1974. The text of the agreement is available at URL <http://www.iea.org/Textbase/about/>.

[5] Yergin, D., 'Ensuring energy security', *Foreign Affairs*, vol. 85, no. 2 (Mar./Apr. 2006), p. 69.

[6] For more on this subject see Jensen, W. G., 'The importance of energy in the First and Second World Wars', *Historical Journal*, vol. 11, no. 3 (1968), pp. 538–54; Spaight, J. M., 'The war of oil', *Military Affairs*, vol. 13, no. 3 (autumn 1949), pp. 138–41; and Kinnear, J., 'Oil and the military: the challenge of leadership', *Vital Speeches of the Day*, vol. 59. no. 14 (1993), pp. 429–33.

[7] Ullman, R. H., 'Redefining security', *International Security*, vol. 8, no. 1 (summer 1983), p. 144.

[8] Horsnell, P., 'The probability of oil market disruption: with an emphasis on the Middle East', Prepared for the study Japanese Energy Security and Changing Global Energy Markets, Rice University, James Baker Institute for Public Policy, May 2000, URL <http://www.rice.edu/energy/publications/japaneseenergysecurity.html>.

the system is unable to meet the aggregate demand. He further identifies three types of sudden disruption of supply: '*force majeure* disruption' is the inability of a producer to export resources owing to internal or external conditions, such as war; 'export restriction disruption' arises when a producer or group of producers decides to restrict export for political or strategic reasons; and 'embargo disruption' occurs when a consuming country blocks imports from certain exporters.[9]

Regardless of the source of disruption, if the shock to supply cannot be immediately accommodated by the market, the energy (and economic) security of states can be at risk. Different countries, however, will be differently damaged as a function of the flexibility of their particular energy system. This makes it a matter of primary importance for policymakers to increase their own country's potential for flexible response and thereby decrease their vulnerability to disruptions. In general, as vulnerability decreases, energy security increases;[10] and only a country that can safeguard the supply of energy to its economy and citizens in a time of crisis can feel real energy security.

Today's anxieties about this issue are driven by a more complicated set of factors than in the 1970s. Key elements of these concerns have included: (*a*) a drastic increase in global energy demand; (*b*) the tight oil market and high oil prices; (*c*) an increase in the average level of national and regional import dependencies; (*d*) technical problems with electric power supply resulting in several temporary power blackouts; (*e*) weaknesses in the energy infrastructure along the whole supply chain; and (*f*) the liberalization and deregulation of internal energy markets. Non-economic factors leading to more or less significant disruptions in the oil market have included the impact of hurricanes in the Gulf of Mexico, terrorist attacks on strategic energy infrastructure in the Middle East, the ups and downs of the Iraq conflict following the US-led invasion of March 2003, and other conflicts and instabilities in some oil-producing countries and regions.

The concern about terrorist attacks deserves special mention as an addition to the traditional links between energy and traditional security. The terrorist attacks on the United States of 11 September 2001 underlined first and foremost that the developed world offers many appealing targets to terrorists, and the energy infrastructure may well be among them. In the aftermath of the attacks most countries moved their energy installations to a higher state of alert. Since the 2003 invasion of Iraq, the world has seen an increasing number of direct terrorist attacks on the energy sector in the world's major zone of production—the Middle East. Energy may now become not only an instrument of war (as in the oil embargo of 1973), but also its direct target, and the vulnerability of the whole energy sector can be described as the Achilles heel of the developed world. Terrorist attacks (including cyber-attacks) could be aimed not just at infrastructural elements in the oil and gas supply chain, such

[9] Horsnell (note 8), p. 6.
[10] Ullman (note 7), p. 146.

as terminals, tankers or long-distance pipelines, but also at installations in consuming countries, such as generating plants, energy grids or refineries. The difficulty of providing military-style protection or even surveillance for all of these is evident, but the physical security of the energy infrastructure is now more universally recognized as an important part of the energy security concept.

III. Patterns of energy supply and demand

The world energy balance and trends in the energy market

From the economic perspective, trends in energy supply and demand are the key factors influencing perceptions of energy security. Present security concerns owe much to the fact that demand for energy from all sources has steadily risen through the past decade. The fact that world production of oil and gas has also increased has not been enough to dispose of the problem. One significant factor has been the high rate of economic growth in the developing world, especially in China and India.

The latest projections from agencies monitoring energy data—the US Energy Information Administration (EIA) and the International Energy Agency—indicate continued strong growth in world energy consumption. For instance, the EIA forecasts that between 2003 and 2030 energy demand will grow by 71 per cent (see table 6.1). As to particular energy resources, worldwide oil demand will increase by 48 per cent over the same period. Natural gas and coal will be the fastest growing energy sources—gas use will grow by 92 per cent and coal use by 96 per cent. Higher fossil fuel prices, especially for oil and gas, are expected to promote the wider use of nuclear energy, which the EIA expects to rise by 31 per cent up to 2030, and of renewable sources, which is expected to grow at a rate similar to those for natural gas and coal.[11]

The rise in demand would not in itself have far-reaching implications for energy security if it were not for the increasingly tight supply situation in the oil market. A few elements are of key importance here. More than half of the extra oil output that has helped meet increasing demand during the past few years has come from Russia, which managed an impressive boost in output thanks to the recovery of its oil industry in the late 1990s.[12] At the same time some OPEC members were constrained from building spare capacity, initially by low oil prices and later—when prices went up—by other factors. Political conflicts in producing countries such as Nigeria and Venezuela not only made it impossible to expand production but also disrupted significant proportions of the oil supply to the world market. A similar effect on US production and

[11] US Energy Information Administration (EIA), *International Energy Outlook 2006* (EIA: Washington, DC, June 2006), URL <http://www.eia.doe.gov/oiaf/ieo/>, pp. 7–10.

[12] See e.g. Leijonhielm, J. and Larsson, R. L., 'Russia's strategic commodities: energy and metals as security levers', Swedish Defence Research Agency (FOI) User Report FOI-R--1346--SE, Stockholm, Nov. 2004, URL <http://www.foi.se/FOI/templates/Page____4356.aspx>, pp. 33–35.

supplies was caused by the impact of hurricanes in 2005 in the Gulf of Mexico and from instability in Iraq, including terrorist attacks on its energy infrastructure. In addition, a significant role in constraining growth in production was played by regulatory factors such as statutory restrictions on exploration in environmentally sensitive areas, investment sanctions, the taxation policies of producing countries, obstacles placed in the way of access to transport, refinery or storage facilities, unrealistically tight oil product specifications, and not least by market speculation.[13]

Given the expected strong rise in worldwide demand and the general drop in spare oil production capacity, developing additional oil production capacity in all the major producing regions will be one of the biggest challenges for the future. The Russian oil sector cannot carry as much of this burden as it has in the past. According to data from the oil company BP, OPEC countries accounted for nearly all of the net increase in global production in 2005.[14] Russian production is likely to be constrained in the future because investment in the country's energy sector is far below the required levels. Such underinvestment is a real risk in all producer countries. The IEA estimates that governments and companies need to invest more than $20 trillion in energy infrastructure over the next 25 years to meet demand.[15] Since most of these investment needs are in developing countries, it is, unfortunately, far from certain that all of them will be met.

As a consequence of the tight oil market and its increased vulnerability to problems in producing regions, there has been a gradual rise in oil prices since 2003. From the economic viewpoint a dramatic sudden increase in the price of crude oil can have more serious consequences than a slow increase, to which economies can adjust over time.[16] However, in either case the higher price will hit oil-intensive sectors and may also have an impact on a country's macroeconomic indexes. Expensive oil may raise inflation, increase the trade deficit and harm economic growth in importing countries. As noted above, however, importing countries' vulnerability varies markedly. In present conditions higher oil prices are generally more harmful for oil-importing developing countries, which use more than twice as much oil to produce a unit of economic output as member countries of the Organisation for Economic Co-operation and Development (OECD).[17]

[13] World Economic Forum and Cambridge Energy Research Associates, 'The new energy security paradigm', *Energy Vision Update*, spring 2006, URL <http://www.weforum.org/en/initiatives/energy/>, p. 25. 'Product specifications' are the quality requirements of oil products such as petrol, gas oil, diesel or jet fuel. The quality standards differ across the world, although a general trend for tightening quality specifications can be observed. Product specifications influence choices of crude oils processed by regional refineries and, if tight, they can significantly limit import abilities, affecting oil supply security and final oil product prices.

[14] BP, *Quantifying Energy: BP Statistical Review of World Energy June 2006* (BP plc: London, 2006), URL <http://www.bp.com/statisticalreview/>, p. 8.

[15] International Energy Agency (IEA), *World Energy Outlook 2006* (Organisation for Economic Co-operation and Development/IEA: Paris, 2006), pp. 75–77.

[16] 'Oil in troubled waters: a survey of oil', Supplement, *The Economist*, 30 Apr. 2005, p. 4.

[17] International Energy Agency, 'Analysis of the impact of high oil prices on the global economy', Paris, May 2004, URL <http://www.iea.org/textbase/publications/>, p. 2.

Table 6.1. World primary energy source and demand, 2003 and predictions for 2030

Energy source	Demand		Proportion of total demand (%)	
	2003	2030	2003	2030
Oil	80 mbd (4.0 b. tonnes)	118 mbd (5.9 b. tonnes)	*38*	*33*
Gas	2.7 tr. m³	5.2 tr. m³	*24*	*26*
Coal	4.9 b. tonnes	9.6 b. tonnes	*24*	*27*
Renewable sources	..	..	*8*	*9*
Total	**444 EJ**	**762 EJ**		

EJ = exajoule (10^{18} joules); mbd = million barrels per day.

Source: US Energy Information Administration (EIA), *International Energy Outlook 2006* (EIA: Washington, DC, 2006), URL <http://www.eia.doe.gov/oiaf/ieo/>, pp. 7–10, 37, 51.

Oil is the world's single largest energy source and is expected to keep this position, although its share in world primary energy consumption in 2003 will reduce (see table 6.1). Together, the three fossil fuels make up 86 per cent of total world energy consumption. As a more environmentally attractive energy source, world consumption of natural gas is projected to almost double by 2030.[18] As use of natural gas increases and spreads, its geopolitical significance and influence on international relations will further increase.

Structural changes in the world oil and gas market

Over more than a decade the structure of the world oil and gas market has changed significantly. One factor is the increasing number of major oil and gas exporters. The collapse of the Soviet Union enabled Russia, Azerbaijan and the Central Asian countries to break the stagnation of oil and gas exports to world markets, while at the same time South American and West African countries were building new oil production capabilities. Simultaneously, there has been a wider diversification of world consuming centres.

Russia is now the world's second largest oil producer, after Saudi Arabia, and the largest gas producer and exporter.[19] Its opening up to the world economy has brought significant changes to the oil and gas supply structure. After the collapse of the Soviet Union, a long period of decreasing production began for Russia's oil industry. It was therefore a surprise for OPEC when Russia's annual oil output started to increase steadily in the late 1990s; all the more so when, from 2000, Russian oil output grew at a rate of nearly half a million barrels a day—the single largest increase in world oil production at the time.[20] This spectacular growth has been reflected in Russia's oil exports, which in

[18] US Energy Information Administration (note 11), pp. 8, 37, 51.

[19] BP (note 14), pp. 8, 24.

[20] Morse, E. L. and Richard, J., 'The battle for energy dominance', *Foreign Affairs*, vol. 81, no. 2 (Mar./Apr. 2002), pp. 16–17. For Russian oil production data from 1995 to 2005 see BP (note 14), p. 8.

2000 began to rise for the first time since the Soviet era: from 2.9 mbd (145 million tonnes per year) in 2000 (a similar figure to that for 1992) to 3.8 mbd (187 million tonnes per year) in 2003.[21] For OPEC this signalled the entry of a new serious rival into a market that the OPEC cartel thought was rightfully its.[22] The element of paradox, as noted by Fadhil Chalabi, was that the 'driving force behind the spectacular increase since 2000 in Russian oil production and exports has been OPEC's high price policies'.[23]

OPEC's share of the oil market has decreased from 55 per cent in 1973 to 43 per cent in 2005.[24] Nevertheless, with 75 per cent of total world proved oil reserves, OPEC countries are and will continue to be the single most significant force in the oil market.[25] The Middle East and its leading producer— Saudi Arabia—play a pivotal role in world supply of oil and gas. The extraordinarily low oil production costs in the Middle East and the high quality and great abundance of its oil and gas—the region has 62 per cent of world proved oil reserves, expected to last for nearly 80 years, and 40 per cent of world proved gas reserves[26]—make the region unique and ensure that it will remain one of the most important factors in the contemporary energy market. While the economic arguments for the continuing reliance of the market as a whole and of consuming countries on supplies from the Middle East are understood, when the geostrategic aspects are taken into account the costs of such a dependency are high. The Middle East is one of the most politically unstable regions in the world, and its oil and gas infrastructure is particularly vulnerable to disruption. In practice, any kind of terrorist, political or military action in the region or even elsewhere is liable to disrupt Middle East supplies. Such disruption, if serious, could destabilize not only the world energy market but also the world economy as a whole.

Any producing region can be a source of energy supply disruptions. Recent events in Venezuela and Nigeria—the second and third most important OPEC producers outside the Middle East, respectively—disrupted oil flows to the market, and the Russian–Ukrainian gas crisis affected gas deliveries to the European Union (EU) in early 2006.[27] Over-reliance on any single foreign producer or region is, thus, unwise. In this context non-OPEC production in the Americas, the North Sea, Russia and the Caspian Sea region, and West Africa offers a chance for diversification of world oil supplies whose significance cannot be overestimated. The same applies *mutatis mutandis* to structural

[21] Leijonhielm and Larsson (note 12), table 3, p. 32. See also Chalabi, F., 'Russian oil and OPEC price policies', *Middle East Economic Survey*, vol. 47, no. 12 (Mar. 2004).

[22] Morse and Richard (note 20), p. 29.

[23] Chalabi (note 21).

[24] Organization of the Petroleum Exporting Countries (OPEC), *Annual Statistical Bulletin 2005* (OPEC: Vienna, 2006), URL <http://www.opec.org/library/Annual Statistical Bulletin/ASB2005.htm>, p. 24.

[25] BP (note 14), p. 6. The oil reserves figure is for the end of 2005.

[26] BP (note 14), pp. 6, 22.

[27] See e.g. 'Striking Venezuelan oil workers sacked', BBC News, 29 Jan. 2003, URL <http://news.bbc.co.uk/2/2705281.stm>; 'Militants claim Nigeria oil raid', BBC News, 8 Dec. 2006, URL <http://news.bbc.co.uk/2/6220562.stm>; and '"Lessons" for EU from gas crisis', BBC News, 4 Jan. 2006, URL <http://news.bbc.co.uk/2/4582652.stm>.

Figure 6.1. Current and projected oil and gas pipelines in Central Asia

Source: Based on a map by Wojciech Mankowski in Falkowski, M., *Russia's Policy in the Southern Caucasus and Central Asia*, Centre for Eastern Studies (CES) Studies no. 23 (CES: Warsaw, June 2006), URL <http://osw.waw.pl/en/epub/eprace/23/01.htm>, map 3, p. 83.

changes in world natural gas supplies that are tending to make the gas market more international, more flexible and in consequence more diversified.

Russia and four countries on or near the Caspian Sea—Azerbaijan, Kazakhstan, Turkmenistan and Uzbekistan—play the key role in the group of non-OPEC energy suppliers. Together they hold around 10 per cent of world oil reserves and over 32 per cent of natural gas reserves. Their shares in current world production are around 9 per cent for oil and 28 per cent for natural gas.[28] Russia's oil production is expected to increase by around 2–3 per cent per year, far below growth rates in previous years.[29] In the gas market Russia will remain a dominant exporter, but in the future it will be an increasingly important supplier in pipeline transport to Asia and its significance in the liquefied natural gas (LNG) market may rise.[30] However, lack of investment—today most of Russia's production comes from mature fields—may constrain production growth rates in both the oil and gas sectors. As to the Caspian Sea region, although its vast reserves are well known, it has only just begun to develop into a significant oil- and gas-exporting area. The reason is that most pipelines in the region were designed to supply the Soviet Union and after its collapse Russia maintained a monopoly over the transport of Caspian energy resources. The Baku–Tbilisi–Ceyhan pipeline, the first to free the Caspian

[28] BP (note 14), pp. 6, 8, 22, 24.

[29] Between 2003 and 2004 production rose by around 9%. BP (note 14), p. 8.

[30] LNG is a liquid obtained by cooling natural gas to –163°C. As a liquid it can be transported in ships before being returned to a gaseous state at 'regasification' terminals.

exporters from the monopoly of Russian state-owned gas company Gazprom, entered into operation quite recently, in 2005. (Figure 6.1 shows current and proposed oil and gas pipelines in Central Asia.)

Among other non-OPEC oil suppliers, sub-Saharan Africa deserves special mention. The region is expected to expand oil output hugely in the coming years. For example, Angola became a million-barrel-per-day producer in 2004 (and in December 2006 became an OPEC member), while other western African producers with offshore oil tracts are expected to increase production by up to 1.1 mbd by 2030. Significant oil production increases are projected also in Canada, Mexico and South America (in Argentina and Brazil, but also in Colombia and Ecuador with their difficult political situations). Some increase is also expected in Asia–Pacific countries such as Australia, Bangladesh, India, Myanmar and Viet Nam. At the same time prospects for one of the most important European sources of oil supply—the North Sea—are not encouraging. Norwegian oil output is projected to decrease from a peak of 3.6 mbd (179 million tonnes per year) in 2006 to 2.5 mbd (124 million tonnes per year) in 2030 and the United Kingdom's from 2.2 mbd (110 million tonnes per year) in 2010 to 1.4 mbd (70 million tonnes per year) in 2030.[31]

The above projections by the US EIA do not anticipate world oil production to peak until 2030. It is important to note, however, that they are based on proved reserves and on economic assumptions about future oil prices, rates of growth and the levels of investment. They do not take into account possible disruptions of any kind—caused by war, terrorism, political turmoil or weather. The analysts who stress the prospect of supplies peaking earlier argue that, first, both OPEC and non-OPEC countries are producing over 2 barrels of oil for every new barrel they find; second, reserves in many producing countries have been depleted by up to 50 per cent; third, companies have problems in finding new large oil fields; and finally, in recent years virtually all of the spare production capacity has been in the Middle East.[32]

All the major producers of natural gas are expected to increase their output by 2030, yet the two regions with the world's largest natural gas reserves—the Middle East and Russia and the Caspian Sea region, which account for more than two-thirds of proved reserves—will together account for only 47 per cent of increases in global output. In fact, the fastest growth rates in natural gas production will come from African producers (with an annual average growth rate of 4.9 per cent between 2003 and 2030). OECD countries will see their dependency on imported gas rise, since the projected growth in their natural gas production (averaging 0.5 per cent per year) will not match the projected rise in their demand of 1.5 per cent per year.[33]

The most significant structural change in the natural gas market is that this fuel of choice has been transformed from a marginal energy resource consumed in regionally distinct markets to a fuel traded internationally and trans-

[31] US Energy Information Administration (note 11), pp. 31–32.

[32] For more discussion on this subject see 2005 Global Oil and Gas Forum, *The New Energy Security* (Aspen Institute: Washington, DC, 2006), URL <http://www.aspeninstitute.org/ee/globalenergy/>.

[33] US Energy Information Administration (note 11), pp. 39–40.

ported across great distances.[34] Technological improvements that have low-
ered the cost of LNG have facilitated the development of an international gas
market and the spot gas trade. In 2004 only 12 countries produced LNG—
Algeria, Australia, Brunei, Indonesia, Libya, Malaysia, Nigeria, Oman, Qatar,
Trinidad and Tobago, the United Arab Emirates (UAE) and the USA—but
Russia and Egypt joined the LNG business in 2005 and others, including Iran
(and perhaps Saudi Arabia), are expected to follow suit from the next decade
onwards.[35] Similarly, more countries are acquiring LNG regasification terminals so that they can import LNG. The LNG trade has potentially far-
reaching implications for energy security: it gives a chance to diversify the
sources of natural gas imports and makes the gas market overall more flexible.
Through trade in LNG, what used to be three separate regional trading zones
for gas—the Americas, the Asia–Pacific region and Europe—are becoming
more linked, which also means that disruption of supplies in one producing
region can affect the others. Finally, the increasing importance of natural gas
suppliers together with the new LNG trade have raised concerns over the
potential for a gas cartel.[36] In reality, the question of whether the gas market
could become a global market similar to that of oil is still open.

The structural changes of the past decades have been even more significant
on the energy demand side. In the 1970s the OECD accounted for 70 per cent
of global oil consumption, and North America alone consumed twice as much
oil as Asia's countries. Today these proportions look quite different: the
OECD's share of global oil demand decreased to around 60 per cent in 2005
and Asia's oil consumption is very close to that of North America. Demand
for oil and other primary energy sources in developing countries has mush-
roomed as a consequence of their economic and demographic growth, industrial activity and expanding transport use. The most spectacular examples are
provided by two of the fastest growing Asian countries—China and India.
China's oil consumption rose from 6.1 mbd (285 million tonnes per year) in
2003 to 7.1 mbd (334 million tonnes per year) in 2004, an increase of 17 per
cent. Its oil consumption has more than doubled since 1993 when it first
became a net oil importer. By 2005 it was dependent on imports for 50 per
cent of its oil needs and this proportion is increasing rapidly. As to India, its
domestic oil consumption has risen steadily—by 57 per cent between 1995
and 2005—while its effective oil import dependency increased to over 68 per
cent. In both these countries, statistics for primary energy use and natural gas
consumption are telling. China's demand for natural gas rose over the decade

[34] Soligo, R. and Jaffe, A. M., 'Market structure in the new gas economy: is cartelization possible?',
Paper prepared for the Geopolitics of Natural Gas Study of the Stanford University Program on Energy
and Sustainable Development and the Rice University James A. Baker III Institute for Public Policy,
May 2004, URL <http://pesd.stanford.edu/publications/>, p. 8.

[35] US Energy Information Administration (note 11), p. 40.

[36] See Soligo and Jaffe (note 34); Daniel, P. D., 'Natural gas in North America: a global commodity
with an exciting—but uncertain—future', Paper presented at the Ziff North American Gas Strategies
Conference, Calgary, Alberta, 3 Nov. 2003, URL <http://www.enbridge.com/about/commentary.php>;
and Yergin, D. and Stoppard, M., 'The next prize', *Foreign Affairs*, vol. 82, no. 6 (Nov./Dec. 2003),
pp. 103–14.

1996–2005 by more than 163 per cent and India's by 78 per cent. Total primary energy use during the past decade rose in China by 61 per cent and in India by 43 per cent.[37]

Emerging economies now account for nearly two-thirds of the present increase in world energy use.[38] Looking ahead, energy market structure on the demand side will be further transformed. The EIA projects that the aggregate energy demand from countries outside the OECD will by 2030 exceed energy use within the OECD by 34 per cent—meaning that natural gas and oil consumption in non-OECD countries will grow three times as fast as OECD consumption.[39] The largest share of this non-OECD growth will take place in Asia, notably in China and India, while in the OECD North American consumption will grow fastest. Energy demand in non-OECD countries is expected to more than double by 2030. However, the OECD will remain a major natural gas consumer, although its share of world gas demand will decline from over 50 per cent to nearer 40 per cent.[40]

Such sweeping changes in the demand and supply structure of the energy market create both opportunities and challenges. As Anoush Ehteshami and Sven Behrendt note, these changes will increase the bargaining power of suppliers 'as they find hungry new customers for their processed and unprocessed hydrocarbon resource', but on the other hand 'consumers will for the first time in decades, have the opportunity to negotiate alternative deals with a number of suppliers that operate outside of the OPEC-pricing mechanism'.[41] Overall, strong and increasing dependence on imported oil and natural gas—which will become a feature of both OECD and non-OECD economies—will heighten the world's vulnerability to disruption of oil and natural gas supplies. Together with the tight supply situation in the oil market, this is bound to further intensify energy security concerns, with consequences that will influence international relations and help to shape the future global energy security system.

IV. Energy security concerns as a source of conflict

States' activities aimed at ensuring energy security are an important element in their foreign policy and foreign relations. However, many features of the international environment—the stability of producing regions, market supply and demand and price trends, the state of consumer–producer relations, consciousness of potential challenges and threats to energy security, and so on—influence national energy strategies and lead states to adopt different policies and use different tools at different times. Countries' efforts to assure access to natural resources affect security dynamics particularly in those parts of the

---

[37] BP (note 14), pp. 8, 11, 12, 27, 40.

[38] BP (note 14), p. 40.

[39] US Energy Information Administration (note 11), pp. 7–8.

[40] US Energy Information Administration (note 11), p. 37.

[41] Ehteshami, A. and Behrendt, S., 'Perspective: geopolitical transformations and the shifting energy markets', *Energy Vision Update*, spring 2006, URL <http://www.weforum.org/en/initiatives/energy/>, p. 21.

world that are crucial for global energy security, and may lead both to regional alliances and to conflicts between major energy-consuming and energy-producing countries. Thus, contemporary structural changes in the energy market have serious geopolitical implications.

When considering the role of energy security concerns in generating tension or even conflict between states, it is important to emphasize that most states would regard actual armed conflict as an extreme measure for the purpose. Indeed, energy codependency between states, like other factors of inter-dependence, may help to reduce the likelihood of military conflict between them.[42] The distinction should be kept clear between, on the one hand, an increase in tension between major energy market players that leads to rivalry rather than direct armed confrontation, and on the other, actual conflict over energy and other occurrences of the use of force in regions abundant in oil and gas.

Competition for resources is not new or characteristic of our times. Together with competition for territory, it lies at the root of most violent conflicts in history. The thesis of an increasing number of conflicts over energy resource has become popular lately, yet analysts were forecasting this trend more than three decades ago. For instance, Richard Ullman in the early 1980s noticed a drop in the incidences of conflict over territory and predicted that 'as demand for some essential commodities increases and supplies appear more precarious', more conflicts over resources, oil in particular, would arise. He prophesied that such struggles 'will often take the form of overt military confrontations whose violent phases will more likely be short, sharp shocks rather then pro-tracted wars', and that they would occur between neighbouring states above all.[43]

Indeed, the militarization of energy policy—that is, employing military means to guarantee stability in oil- and gas-producing regions[44]—has been a phenomenon in international affairs for some time. A striking example from 1980 is the Carter Doctrine in which, responding to the 1979 Soviet invasion of Afghanistan, US President Jimmy Carter stated that the USA would use 'any means necessary', including military force, to defend its vital interests in the Persian Gulf, including the flow of oil.[45] Since the end of World War II, one of the fundamental guarantees of secure oil supplies from the Middle East to the world market—in times of peace and of war—has been the combination of US policies designed to bolster the Saudi Arabian monarchy. This commitment, dating back to the meeting of President Franklin D. Roosevelt and King Ibn Saud in February 1945, has involved direct US military engagement in the region, for instance during the 1980–1988 Iraq–Iran War or after Iraq's 1990 invasion of Kuwait.

---

[42] Kemp, G., 'Scarcity and strategy', *Foreign Affairs*, vol. 56, no. 2 (Jan. 1978), p. 396.

[43] Ullman (note 7), pp. 139–40.

[44] Klare, M. T., 'Oil wars: transforming the American military into a global oil-protection service', TomDispatch.com, 7 Oct. 2004, URL <http://www.tomdispatch.com/index.mhtml?pid=1888>.

[45] Carter, J., State of the Union Address, Washington, DC, 23 Jan. 1980, URL <http://www.jimmy carterlibrary.org/documents/speeches/>.

In a typical 'resource conflict', the energy factor predominates. However, there are also conflicts in which energy resources are just one of many elements or catalysts. There are, thus, three basic ways in which energy resources and armed conflicts interconnect. The first and most obvious is when energy resources are the proximate cause of a conflict; the second is when they play the role of an instrument, target or any other secondary element of war; and the third is when profits from the sale of energy resources help to finance armed conflicts.[46]

In the traditional regions of great-power rivalry—the Middle East and Central Asia—the abundance of oil and gas reserves led to competition between states over access to these resources and also, as in the case of the landlocked Caspian Sea basin, over pipeline routes. Both local and outside powers may maintain a military presence in order to protect drilling rigs, pipelines, refineries and other oil and gas facilities, as well as to ensure the stability of producing or transit regions. Usually, foreign troops are stationed with the clear aim of protecting the flow of oil and gas—typical examples are the different types of US presence in Colombia and the Persian Gulf region. Sometimes, a wider military campaign—like Russia's in Chechnya or the USA's in Iraq—is also seen by many observers as having an energy component because, even if it has other prima facie motives, it takes place in an area of great significance for regional and (in the case of Iraq) global energy security.

The 2003 US-led invasion of Iraq aimed to create a new, Western-friendly Iraq as the first building block of a more democratic and stable Middle East that would, among other things, ensure Western access to the region's energy resources. Paradoxically, the operation and post-war US military presence in Iraq have not only failed to stabilize the region or to increase the security of oil supplies, but have also opened the door to new threats. Today, the increasing terrorist activity in the Middle East includes frequent attacks on oil facilities in Iraq, yet there are many other tempting oil-related targets for terrorists in the region. The Strait of Hormuz is the world's most important oil chokepoint, with 17 million barrels (2.3 million tonnes) of oil passing through it each day, about 20 per cent of the global supply.[47] Just one supertanker on fire in the narrow strait could block the passage for other shipping and seriously disrupt supplies to the global oil market for weeks.

Another, and perhaps the most disturbing, factor that may shape the future security dynamics of the region is the continuing expansion of Iran's influence. Iran could at any moment try to block the Strait of Hormuz. More generally, the Persian Gulf abounds in major unresolved territorial disputes between its states, for example between Iran and the UAE, between Saudi Arabia and Qatar, and between Qatar and Bahrain. All these factors and more—including developments involving Israel—could destabilize the Middle East political

[46] On this subject see Klare, M. T., *Resource Wars: The New Landscape of Global Conflict* (Metropolitan Books: New York, N.Y., 2001); Renner, M., *The Anatomy of Resource Wars*, Worldwatch Paper no. 162 (Worldwatch Institute: Washington, DC, Oct. 2002); and Kemp (note 42).

[47] US Energy Information Administration, 'World oil transit chokepoints', Country Analysis Briefs, Nov. 2005, URL <http://www.eia.doe.gov/cabs/World_Oil_Transit_Chokepoints/Full.html>.

scene and thus threaten oil supplies. This makes them also a potential source of armed conflict or military intervention.

Fierce territorial disputes over oil and gas deposits occur also in other geostrategically important regions, primarily Central Asia and the South China Sea. Relative to the South China Sea, disputes in Central Asia between Caspian Sea littoral states have a more peaceful and diplomatic character and are only one aspect of a wider international rivalry that started after the Soviet Union's collapse and the opening up of the region's oil and gas fields to Western companies. The key issues include access to Caspian Sea energy resources for foreign companies, and rival pipeline schemes to ensure (for each particular state) the most profitable route for exports to world markets. The construction of new export facilities, especially large-diameter pipelines, to transport increasing volumes of Caspian oil and gas to world markets has become the most important field of international competition in the region. However, other geopolitical interests are also at stake in the local rivalry between China, Iran, Russia, the USA and other powers. Future threats to security in Central Asia are, on balance, more likely to flow from ethnic conflicts, separatist movements and unstable political regimes and economic systems than from a 'great game' of competition over oil and gas transport routes.

In the South China Sea, prolonged international quarrels and disputes over the boundaries of exclusive economic zones and the ownership of islands seem to be the main destabilizing factors in the region, which is not only believed to hold substantial oil and gas deposits but is also the chief route for seaborne oil and gas supplies to Asian countries. Tensions and military activity date back to the 1970s, around the time of China's 1974 invasion of the Paracel Islands. Soon after the discovery of large oil deposits in the Spratly Islands in 1976, several littoral countries began production there. Territorial disputes over the Spratly Islands have involved six states: Brunei Darussalam, China, Malaysia, the Philippines, Taiwan and Viet Nam. All have built up their military presence in the region, so that today up to 65 islets, reefs and rocks in the South China Sea are occupied by military troops from various countries.[48] Since the late 1980s there have been recurrent naval clashes in the South China Sea. In its 1992 Law on the Territorial Sea and the Contiguous Zone, China claimed sovereignty over the whole Spratly and Paracel archipelagos and authorized itself to use force in the event of any attempt at occupation by another country.[49] These and other ongoing disputes—China and Viet Nam are locked in a similar dispute over the Gulf of Tonkin, Malaysia and the Philippines over the areas east of Borneo, and Malaysia and Viet Nam

---

[48] Kiesow, I., 'China's quest for energy: impact upon foreign and security policy', Swedish Defence Research Agency (FOI) User Report FOI-R--1371--SE, Stockholm, Nov. 2004, URL <http://www.foi.se/FOI/templates/Page____4531.aspx>, p. 25.

[49] The Law on the Territorial Sea and the Contiguous Zone of the People's Republic of China was adopted on 25 Feb. 1992. An English translation of the law is available at URL <http://www.un.org/Depts/los/LEGISLATIONANDTREATIES/STATEFILES/CHN.htm>. See also e.g. Buszyński, L., 'ASEAN security dilemmas', *Survival*, vol. 34, no. 4 (winter 1992/93), pp. 90–107; and Burgess, J. P., 'The politics of the South China Sea: territoriality and international law', *Security Dialogue*, vol. 34, no. 1 (Mar. 2003), pp. 7–10.

over the maritime boundary in the Gulf of Thailand—destabilize the situation in South-East Asia and could indirectly threaten the energy security of other Asian states, like Japan or South Korea. Although China has often been seen as the prime mover in regional conflicts, in more recent years the Chinese Government has shown some tendency to try to resolve territorial problems through more diplomatic measures.[50] A telling example is the 2002 code of conduct in the South China Sea, the first political document concluded between China and the Association of South East Asian Nations (ASEAN) over the disputed region.[51] The code of conduct stresses the need for peaceful settlement of territorial and jurisdictional disputes in the region and obliges the parties to avoid any activity that could 'complicate or escalate disputes and affect peace and stability', including action to inhabit currently uninhabited islands and other features.

An equally problematic issue in the South China Sea is control over its energy arteries, particularly the sea lanes from the Persian Gulf region and the approaches to the Strait of Malacca, through which 11.7 million barrels (1.6 million tonnes) of oil and two-thirds of global LNG deliveries pass daily, bound for China, Japan, South Korea and other Pacific Rim countries.[52] China, India, the USA and some other states feel entitled to use their own military sources to protect these sea lanes against piracy or terrorist attacks and ensure free passage for their ships and tankers, yet they are also suspicious of each other. India and Japan see Chinese naval expansion as a bid for dominance in the region and a threat to their own security. For the USA, China's leading military position in the South China Sea appears to challenge its own military role in the Western Pacific, as well as threatening Taiwan. At the same time, China regards US plans for military presence in the Strait of Malacca as a threat to its national interests in the South China Sea, while Indonesia and Malaysia also reject the idea of US patrols in the strait.

The strategic engagements of the USA in the Persian Gulf, China in the South China Sea and Russia in Central Asia underline that these are the primary potential zones of interstate rivalry in the energy context. Within this 'strategic triangle'[53] the world's largest oil and natural gas deposits are to be found, national frontiers have for years been disputed and the security interests of various states collide. Even so, for the most part it is rather difficult to imagine that these rivalries could turn into armed conflict—too many states have too much to lose. Armed conflict with an energy resource dimension is in practice more likely to take place outside the strategic triangle, particularly in Africa.

---

[50] See Gill, B., 'China's new security multilateralism and its implications for the Asia–Pacific region', *SIPRI Yearbook 2004: Armaments, Disarmament and International Security* (Oxford University Press: Oxford, 2004), pp. 207–30.

[51] The Declaration on the Conduct of Parties in the South China Sea was signed on 4 Nov. 2002. Its text is available at URL <http://www.aseansec.org/13163.htm>.

[52] US Energy Information Administration (note 47); and BP (note 14), map, p. 31.

[53] Klare (note 46), p. 49.

The structural conditions of many African countries—authoritarian governments, weak and corrupt political elites, poverty and economic inequality within societies, the unbalanced distribution of revenues from energy resources, and so on—make them prone to internal armed conflicts that have a resource dimension. The pillaging of energy resources is often a factor that prolongs an armed conflict even if it was triggered by other reasons. In Angola, oil revenues—which account for 90 per cent of government income[54]—fuelled arms purchases during the 1974–2002 civil war; oil money has been an increasingly important issue in the ongoing conflicts in Sudan, at first in the south of the country and currently in Darfur. It is telling that during these civil conflicts oil companies from Canada, China, France, Kuwait, Malaysia, Russia, Sweden and the USA among others have bought oil concessions and begun to develop oil facilities in Sudan.[55] Today, the situation in Nigeria is also evolving towards increased volatility and conflict. Instead of giving the country a chance to be one of the wealthiest in Africa, oil has enriched a tiny minority of Nigerians and led to environmental and health problems as well as impoverishing the oil-producing regions' inhabitants. This finally led to open conflict in the Niger Delta region.

V. Responses to energy security challenges: consumer and producer policies

As stressed above, the rapidly rising demand for energy has led to more competition in the world energy market. At the same time, both consumer and producer countries have become more aware lately of the many new challenges and threats to their energy security in the near future. The complexity of these problems requires all states to develop equally sophisticated energy policies on two fronts—internal and external. The internal dimension of energy security policy focuses primarily on such issues as (*a*) the choice of energy sources, which should include diversifying and optimizing the national energy structure as well as promoting environmental protection; (*b*) the security of state energy infrastructure—energy grids, refineries, pipelines, power stations and so on; (*c*) energy demand management; (*d*) energy efficiency; and (*e*) liberalization and deregulation of the energy sector. The development and promotion of alternatives to fossil fuel energy sources—renewable sources and nuclear energy—can play an important role in this dimension of energy policy. External energy policy is more about the security of import supplies, access to oil and gas fields, diversification among foreign suppliers, and the variety and safety of transport routes. International cooperation with exporters and transit countries, and with other importers, can make an important contribution to this policy. Yet, as discussed above, countries may also use less

[54] US Energy Information Administration, 'Angola', Country Analysis Briefs, Jan. 2006, URL <http://www.eia.doe.gov/cabs/Angola/Full.html>.

[55] On the oil factor in the Sudanese conflicts see Human Rights Watch, *Sudan, Oil, and Human Rights* (Human Rights Watch: Brussels, 2003), URL <http://www.hrw.org/reports/2003/sudan1103/>.

peaceful means to secure their interests in the energy sphere—armed force, sanctions, embargoes or the manipulation of energy as a weapon.

For all countries, energy resources represent more than just traded commodities. They are strategic goods par excellence. Accordingly, states' decisions on almost every dimension of both internal and external energy policy are based not just on economic, but in a large measure also on geopolitical and security calculations. For instance, European countries' decisions in the 1970s to begin oil production in the North Sea—one of the costliest regions in the world for drilling—and Russia's recent, very costly and technologically advanced oil and gas pipeline developments (such as the Blue Stream and Nord Stream gas pipelines[56]) were dictated above all by security and geopolitical calculations.

Today it is clear that some aspects of energy security, which has traditionally been regarded as a purely national or internal matter, are best addressed collectively on a multilateral basis. The reason is that one country's energy policy choices may have significant impacts on other countries' choices. Rising demand in one region—often as an effect of low energy efficiency and weak, demand-oriented policies—aggravates international competition over access to energy resources and to the supply system. If producers adopt a nationalistic policy and close their energy sector to foreign direct investments, they are in effect reducing their chances of developing new exploration programmes, production and transport capabilities in the region. In the long term this will also prejudice the supply situation in the world energy market. Finally, problems such as high carbon dioxide emissions generated by the energy sector, old, unsafe nuclear plants, and the transport and storage of radioactive waste materials, even if they are treated as national policy matters, generate risks and dangers that have a transnational character and are of concern to the whole international community.

Nevertheless, countries' readings of the energy security concept often lead them to make policy choices that disregard the energy interests and needs of other market players. Robert Skinner notes that 'Energy security's banality is due in large measure to its having been so leveraged as a pretext for all manner of policy, from imperialism to isolationism, from expansionism to protectionism, from communism to economic liberalism'.[57] In effect, countries' approaches to energy security range from the extremely self-centred and nationalistic to the consistently cooperative. The former approach is more or less characteristic of some of the major energy importers and exporters like China, India, Iran, Russia, Venezuela and the USA, while most European

---

[56] The Blue Stream gas pipeline links Russia and Turkey under the Black Sea, providing an alternative to gas deliveries through Ukraine, Moldova, Romania and Bulgaria. Supply of natural gas through the pipeline began in Feb. 2003. See the Gazprom website at URL <http://www.gazprom.com/eng/articles/article8895.shtml>. The Nord Stream pipeline is also an offshore project, running through the Baltic Sea, aimed at avoiding transit states in deliveries of Russian gas to West European countries. The pipeline is expected to begin operation in 2010 and carry around 55 billion m³ a year. The minimum total investment cost is estimated at €5 billion. See the Nord Stream website at URL <http://www.nord-stream.com/> and note 65 below.

[57] Skinner (note 2), p. 3.

countries represent the latter approach. Naturally, in some fields of energy security and in certain circumstances, countries categorized as having a nationalistic vision of energy policy can also act cooperatively. The USA was the initiator of the 1974 Washington conference that established the International Energy Agency, and US strategic reserves are one of the key elements of the present global energy security system. Russia is an active participant in the Energy Charter Conference and Transit Protocol negotiations.[58] It also maintains an energy dialogue with the EU and initiates international debates on energy security matters, as at the July 2006 St Petersburg Summit of the Group of Eight industrialized nations (G8).[59] At the same time, these countries consciously avoid legally binding international agreements—Russia has not ratified the Energy Charter Treaty nor the USA the Kyoto Protocol.[60] On the other side, a rise in protectionism and nationalism in energy policy can be observed in some European countries. France and Spain intervened in 2006 in cross-border takeovers of their national energy companies in a way that brought both countries into conflict with the European Commission.[61] These are not isolated incidents, since many other EU members have not opened their national energy sectors to foreign competition.

A nationalistic approach to energy policy in countries with more or less autocratic regimes such as China, Iran, Russia or Venezuela is simply a continuation of their wider economic policy course. Placing national economic and strategic interests first, they want to participate in the world economic system but on their own terms.[62] The USA, for its part, acts as a superpower in all security-related spheres, including energy. Symptoms of the nationalistic approach generally include a readiness to resort to the extreme instrument of a military presence or use of force to secure national interests in the regions abundant in energy resources—for example, China's behaviour in the South China Sea or the USA's armed interventions and military presence in the Middle East, as discussed above. A nationalistic energy policy also manifests

[58] The Energy Charter Conference governs the operation of the Energy Charter Treaty, which was signed on 17 Dec. 1994. The treaty contains provisions regulating 5 broad areas: trade, investment, competition, transit and environmental issues. The proposed Transit Protocol aims to develop operational rules governing energy transit flows on the basis of the treaty's provisions for non-discriminatory transit. The protocol has been under negotiation since 2000. At the end of 2002 multilateral negotiations were provisionally concluded, although a few issues remained to be resolved in bilateral consultations between Russia and the EU. For the text of the treaty, the members of the conference and the draft text of the protocol see URL <http://www.encharter.org/>.

[59] See G8 Summit 2006, 'Chair's summary', St Petersburg, 17 July 2006, URL <http://en.g8russia.ru/docs/25.html>; and G8 Summit 2006, 'Global energy security', St Petersburg, 16 July 2006, URL <http://en.g8russia.ru/docs/11.html>. The summit meeting was preceded by an international conference on energy security on 13–14 Mar. 2006.

[60] The Kyoto Protocol to the United Nations Framework Convention on Climate Change was signed on 18 Dec. 1997 and entered into force on 16 Feb. 2005. The text of the protocol is available at URL <http://unfccc.int/>.

[61] See e.g. Gow, D., 'Spain illegally blocking E.ON's Endesa bid', *The Guardian*, 25 Sep. 2006, URL <http://business.guardian.co.uk/story/0,,1880637,00.html>; and 'To the barricades', *The Economist*, 2 Mar. 2006, URL <http://www.economist.com/background/displaystory.cfm?story_id=5578849>.

[62] Linde, C. van der, 'Energy in a changing world', Clingendael Energy Papers no. 11, Netherlands Institute of International Relations, Clingendael, Dec. 2005, URL <http://www.clingendael.nl/ciep/publications/?id=6123>, p. 13.

itself, however, in economic terms through producers' determination to keep the profits of oil and gas production and the large cash flows generated by the oil and gas companies within their own countries. Such governments accordingly maintain strong state control over the energy sector, including seeking to control foreign investment activity and, if necessary, blocking all access by foreign investors to the energy sector or using them only when they serve the national interest. The most radical option is the nationalization of the energy sector. Some spectacular examples of such a policy have occurred recently in several producing countries. In May 2006 Bolivia nationalized its natural gas sector and increased taxes on foreign energy companies. In Russia, Mikhail Khodorkovsky, the independent owner of the Yukos oil corporation, was prosecuted and dispossessed; the oil company Sibneft was bought in October 2005 by Gazprom; and changes have been made in the law providing access to licences and oil export taxes have been increased—these last both complicating the situation of foreign investors. In Venezuela the government has taken steps to enhance its control by reducing the autonomy of Petróleos de Venezuela SA (PDVSA), increasing the royalties paid by private companies under the 2001 Hydrocarbons Law,[63] and changing the structure of the oil industry—converting operating service agreements with foreign companies into joint ventures with PDVSA, which is in turn changing the nature of foreign participation in the country's energy sector.

A nationalistic policy by energy producers leads inevitably to tensions with consumer countries, as seen in the traditionally close but now strained US–Venezuelan relations. It also raises concerns over future global energy security, since—as noted above—such a policy tends to discourage foreign companies from investing in exploration and production, with negative effects on future supplies. It can also happen, however, that such methods help to strengthen cooperation and a common front among consumer countries. Russia's action in January 2006 to interrupt gas supplies to Ukraine has renewed fears of the use of energy as a weapon in Europe and directly prompted the most intensive and comprehensive discussion yet on a common EU energy policy. In a Green Paper presented two months after the gas crisis, the European Commission urged that the fragmented approach to energy be abandoned and a common policy on both internal and external aspects be developed.[64] Such a policy could enable the 25 member countries to speak with one voice on energy security-related issues in global and other international forums, and give the EU greater clout in negotiations with key energy suppliers. Nonetheless, producers may also play consumer countries against each other—Russia might refuse a compromise to EU negotiators in the framework of collective dialogue and yet strike bargains with particular

[63] The Ley orgánica de hidrocarburos [Hydrocarbons Law], Decree no. 1510, 2 Nov. 2001, came into effect on 1 Jan. 2002. The text of the law, in Spanish and in English, is available at URL <http://www.leydehidrocarburos.gov.ve/>.

[64] European Commission, 'A European strategy for sustainable, competitive and secure energy', Green Paper, Brussels, 8 Mar. 2006, URL <http://ec.europa.eu/energy/green-paper-energy/index_en.htm>.

member states on the same key energy issues in bilateral relations. In effect, Germany has been strengthening its energy links with Russia and protecting its own national interest, regardless of the other EU members' energy (or general security) concerns.[65]

Taking into account the present tight oil market and consumers' concerns over supply security, the nationalistic energy policy maintained by major energy importers may have more serious geopolitical implications. China's increasing demand for energy made it a net oil importer in 1993. Since then its external energy strategy has been aimed at diversifying oil supplies through investments. The China National Petroleum Corporation (CNPC) is buying licences for oil and gas production across the world, from the Asia–Pacific region through the Middle East and Africa to South America; taking over foreign oil companies; and looking for pipeline solutions for transporting energy resources from Russia and Central Asia.[66] India, the world's second fastest growing economy, has been developing a similar strategy in recent years. The quests of both countries for energy and for a larger investment stake bring them closer to each other, yet at the same time exacerbate the energy security concerns of other major importers.

China has clashed with Japan and the USA over energy issues several times. As well as their disputes over oil and gas resources in the East China Sea, China and Japan have competed in particular to host the pipeline route from Russia's East Siberia oil fields and for a stake in oil and gas production on the island of Sakhalin. The USA for its part sees China's energy strategy as creating new economic and strategic challenges that alter the whole geopolitical scene. China has not only been investing its capital in all major world producing regions but also attempted to purchase one of the largest US oil companies, Unocal,[67] and has been cultivating good relations with producers, like Venezuela, that have recently been on bad terms with the USA.[68] The CNPC is investing in oil drillings in Sudan while the USA has imposed sanctions on that country, including a prohibition on US citizens and companies investing

---

[65] Former German Chancellor Gerhard Schröder was instrumental in concluding the agreement between German companies and Gazprom on construction of the Nord Stream gas pipeline that was signed 8 Sep. 2005, shortly before he left office, and his government guaranteed a credit of €1.2 billion for the project. Schröder was appointed to the board of Gazprom 2 weeks after leaving office. The agreement will make Germany the main redistributor of additional future Russian gas supplies in the EU member countries of Central and Eastern Europe since the pipeline excludes them as transit states. Poland and the 3 Baltic states are therefore suspicious about the project, which, from their point of view, may threaten their future energy security. 'Schroeder govt guaranteed credit for Russia's Gazprom, report confirmed', *MosNews*, 2 Apr. 2006, URL <http://www.mosnews.com/news/2006/04/02/>; and Cohen, A., 'The north European gas pipeline threatens Europe's energy security', Backgrounder no. 1980, Heritage Foundation, Washington, DC, 26 Oct. 2006, URL <http://www.heritage.org/Research/Europe/bg1980.cfm>.

[66] Zweig, D. and Bi Jianhai, 'China's global hunt for energy', *Foreign Affairs*, vol. 84, no. 5 (Sep./Oct. 2005), pp. 25–38.

[67] Unocal was eventually bought by the US company Chevron in Aug. 2005.

[68] See e.g. Associated Press, 'China to invest US$5b on oil projects in Venezuela', *China Daily*, 29 Aug. 2006, URL <http://www.chinadaily.com.cn/china/2006-08/29/content_676248.htm>.

there.[69] Although the USA's own policies can be seen as driven by national interest, US Government analysts make a clear distinction between these policies and those of China: 'Whereas the United States has shifted from an oil import strategy that was based upon controlling the oil at its source to one that is based on global market supply and pricing, the Chinese strategy is still focused on owning the import oil at the production point.'[70]

In reality, looking only at China's external measures distorts the picture of the country's activities in the energy field. The real long-term policy goal of China is to base its tremendous economic growth on domestic resources. It therefore seeks to enhance energy efficiency through shifting its economy from energy-intensive industries and introducing high energy-efficiency standards; to build strategic stocks; to develop alternative energy resources; perhaps also to increase its proportional reliance on coal; and to invest in oil and gas exploration on its own territory. Moreover, as some analysts note, China is not acting very differently from other countries in its investments in oil fields and pipelines.[71] Overall, China's increasing import dependency and its investment activity ought to help to increase future oil supplies in the energy market, and it could also eventually lead to cooperation with the USA and other major consumers in protecting vital sea lanes and promoting stability in oil- and gas-producing regions.

The oil crisis of the 1970s put national governments under pressure to find ways of assuring energy supplies in times of crisis. They saw the need in extreme circumstances to work together and coordinate their responses. The OECD member countries of the time formed a common front vis-à-vis OPEC and established the IEA, with its focus on crisis management policies. Today, the emergency arrangements among IEA members are still one of the most important pillars of the energy security system. The most general requirement is that IEA countries must hold oil stocks in three categories—company, government and agency stocks—that are used in response to any oil supply emergency. The last time emergency stocks were released was in 2005 after natural disasters in the Gulf of Mexico disrupted oil production. The example of cooperation within the IEA illustrates that consumers can work together not only in their own national interest but also for a wider international good, that is, for global energy security. On the other hand, a major weakness of the IEA system is that two of the greatest emerging powers in the energy market—China and India—are not members. If 'old' and 'new' major energy importers could find a way to cooperate for the mutual defence of supplies, this should create mutual confidence that in turn would be important for other aspects of cooperation in the energy market, including the positive involvement of all the

---

[69] US Department of the Treasury, Office of Foreign Assets Control, 'Sudan: what you need to know about U.S. sanctions', Washington, DC, 27 Apr. 2006, URL <http://www.treas.gov/offices/enforcement/ofac/programs/>.

[70] US–China Economic and Security Review Commission, *2004 Report to Congress of the U.S.–China Economic and Security Review Commission* (US Government Printing Office: Washington, DC, June 2004), URL <http://www.uscc.gov/annual_report/04_annual_report.htm>, p. 165. On the implications of China's energy policy see Kiesow (note 48).

[71] Kiesow (note 48), p. 49.

major importers in securing future oil and gas supplies. Given the strategic as well as economic benefits of such multilateral cooperation in the energy security field, it should be a high priority for international diplomacy to explore possible routes towards it.

Individual market players will always have divergent energy interests and will compete with each other in the energy market. Nevertheless, they also have many common or parallel objectives—reducing the vulnerability of the market and of their own economy to disruption, ensuring the physical security of energy infrastructure and the safety of supply routes, enhancing political and economic stability in producing regions, and constructing a transparent legal framework for investment. These issues should become fields for wider cooperation involving both consuming and producing countries. Some attempts at such cooperation have already been made at the regional level. For instance, in the framework of the EU–Russia Energy Dialogue, launched in October 2000, both sides have initiated cooperation on the safety of energy transport networks;[72] and in Asia in 2004 China proposed the launch of an energy cooperation initiative and the creation of a common Asian energy policy designed especially to prevent terrorism and piracy against shipping in the Strait of Malacca.[73] It is worth noting that the North Atlantic Treaty Organization (NATO) has embarked on a study of how to promote energy security.[74]

Another factor that could play a significant role in enhancing links and interdependencies between states is their shared need for advanced, appropriate and affordable technologies. An energy strategy needs to be multifaceted: it should diversify supplies, diversify energy mix (e.g. through enhancing the use of renewables or nuclear energy), conserve energy resources by increasing fuel efficiency, maximize indigenous domestic production and open the way for the use of next-generation energy sources. Advanced energy technologies and large-scale investments are necessary to achieve most of these goals, and technological cooperation between states can give them the best chance of securing their future energy needs in a cost-effective way. The outstanding example in the field of next-generation technologies is the cooperation between the EU and the USA: the 2003 Fuel Cell Amendment to the 2001 Non-Nuclear Energy Cooperation Agreement enables the two sides to conduct joint research on the use of hydrogen as an alternative fuel source.[75] One of the

[72] On the EU–Russia Energy Dialogue see the European Commission Directorate-General for Energy and Transport website, URL <http://ec.europa.eu/energy/russia/overview/index_en.htm>.

[73] The Qingdao Initiative on energy cooperation was launched at the Asia Cooperation Dialogue (ACD) foreign ministers' meeting in Qingdao, China, on 22 June 2004. It covers 11 areas of regional energy cooperation between ACD members, including: construction of new energy infrastructure; ensuring safe transport along vital energy shipping routes; exchanges of information on energy issues; cooperation on exploration and exploitation; energy efficiency, renewable energy and environmental protection; and enhancing rural electrification. The ACD Energy Forum was established as a follow-up, its first meeting taking place on 26–28 Sep. 2005 on Bali. For the text of the Qingdao Initiative see URL <http://www.acddialogue.com/web/35.php> and for the Joint Declaration of the 1st ACD Energy Forum see URL <http://www.acddialogue.com/web/36.php?id=48>.

[74] North Atlantic Council, Riga Summit Declaration, NATO Press Release (2006)150, 29 Nov. 2006, URL <http://www.nato.int/docu/pr/2006/p06-150e.htm>, para. 45.

[75] The Amendment to the Implementing Agreement between the Department of Energy of the United States of America and the European Commission for Non-Nuclear Energy Scientific and Technological

few tangible achievements thus far of the EU–Russia Energy Dialogue has been in precisely the field of technology cooperation. Since 2002 both sides have been developing cooperation in the sphere of advanced energy technologies through the EU–Russia Energy Dialogue Technology Centre, based in Moscow. A more controversial recent example is the Indian–US Civil Nuclear Cooperation Initiative, launched in 2005, which gives India access to US civil nuclear technology.[76]

VI. Conclusions

Energy security is one of the highest-ranking issues in both national and international debates. The focus on it is determined by several factors. Trends in the world energy market are important, including the rising global demand for energy, a tight oil market, high oil prices, rising import dependencies and the prospect of future scarcity of oil and gas. Concerns are also intensified by external events such as terrorist attacks on energy infrastructure, power blackouts, hurricanes in the Gulf of Mexico and instability in some producing countries.

The growing importance of energy security issues will have many geostrategic repercussions. The struggle for access to and control over energy resources is likely to exacerbate tensions among the main global energy market players, which may even lead to conflicts. The three basic sources of such tension are: (*a*) the divergent energy interests of consumer countries and greater competition between them in world energy markets; (*b*) consumer–producer relations and fears of the use of energy as a weapon; and (*c*) unsolved territorial disputes over ownership of energy resources. Apart from international tensions, intra-state conflicts with an energy resource dimension are likely to occur, particularly in Africa. On the whole, the worldwide focus on energy security will significantly raise the strategic importance of all geographical areas with rich oil and gas reserves. This means that not only the Middle East but also Africa, Central Asia, South America and South-East Asia will attract continuous attention as areas of potential tension and conflict over the upcoming decades.

At the same time, however, while the nature of states' concerns has been similar to those already apparent in the 20th century—the rise in import dependencies, security of oil and gas supplies, the unstable political situation in producer regions, and fears that oil or gas may be used as a political weapon—the perception of how to deal with challenges to energy security has been changing. Both national and international approaches to energy security need to be further rethought. Nationalistic approaches to energy security, such

Cooperation relating to Cooperation in the Area of Fuel Cells was signed on 16 June 2003. The texts of the amendment and of the original agreement, signed on 14 May 2001, are available at URL <http://ec.europa.eu/research/energy/gp/gp_ef/article_1098_en.htm>.

[76] See Ahlström, C. 'Legal aspects of the Indian–US Civil Nuclear Cooperation Initiative', *SIPRI Yearbook 2006: Armaments, Disarmament and International Security* (Oxford University Press: Oxford, 2006), pp. 669–85.

as can be seen in many consumer and producer countries today, are not a good recipe for handling global energy security needs even leaving aside the risk of their leading to conflict. Wider international cooperation could build more trust and release tensions between major market players, thus improving the future security of oil and gas supply for all.

It is important to stress that in a field like energy, international cooperation is not opposed to or incompatible with competition. At present it is impossible to say which of these forces will prevail in the energy market in future. They could, of course, coexist, but would then need to be better balanced. As an example, the present IEA response mechanism that excludes China and India and provides for international responses only to oil disruption is inadequate to deal with the present energy market structure and with the wide range of new challenges to energy security that need a collective answer. Future international cooperation, responding to such imperatives, is likely to transform the present institutional energy market order. New institutions and cooperation mechanisms may be established by consumers themselves, or together with producers (as happens today in bilateral or multilateral consumer–producer dialogues). There is also a possibility that major gas producers will try to create a cartel similar to OPEC.

Finally, it is worth noting that only a breakthrough in the development of alternative energy sources, and particularly in alternative fuels for transport, could significantly change parts of the above forecast. Growing environmental concerns combined with increased risks of disruption to future oil and gas supplies may result in greater attention being given to the issues of development of nuclear energy, renewable energy sources and biofuel production. Progress in these fields, too, will depend not only on national energy policies but also on international cooperation, especially in the sphere of know-how exchange. However, the development of alternative energy sources—nuclear energy in particular—will create new security concerns even while it reduces present energy security risks.[77]

---

[77] On the perceived risks to security posed by civil uses of nuclear energy see chapter 12 in this volume.

Part II. Military spending and armaments, 2006

Chapter 7. Analysing risks to human lives

Chapter 8. Military expenditure

Chapter 9. Arms production

Chapter 10. International arms transfers

7. Analysing risks to human lives

ELISABETH SKÖNS*

I. Introduction

During 2006, world governments spent roughly $1200 billion on the military sector. This spending generates significant business for the arms industry, with the 100 largest arms-producing companies making domestic and foreign arms sales worth $290 billion and global arms exports amounting to $39–56 billion in 2005.[1] An important question is whether this spending achieves the stated purpose—the provision of security. The answer depends on many factors, including the definition of security and the means that are most cost-effective in attaining this security.

If the ultimate objective of security is to save human beings from preventable premature death and disability, then the appropriate security policy would focus on prevention instruments and risk-reduction strategies for their causes. Furthermore, if it is assumed that the pattern of causes of premature death and disability will not change significantly in the near future, then the historic pattern can be used to identify principal causes and risk factors as well as to develop strategies of prevention and risk reduction.

While collective violence causes a great many premature deaths and disabilities, other types of injury cause an even greater number. Moreover, the major cause of premature death and disability is a range of diseases that could be prevented relatively easily (see table 7.2 below). There are also linkages between different causes of death and between their respective risk factors. Thus, the impact of collective violence on humans is not limited to the number of deaths that it causes but extends to the poverty and ill health that it brings. Equally, poverty and ill health create the circumstances in which violence is likely to break out.

In this chapter the risks to human lives are reviewed in a concrete way, by focusing on the actual causes of death and disability worldwide. Particular attention is paid to low-income countries, where mortality rates and premature deaths are well above the world average, and where a great proportion of these deaths could be prevented at relatively low cost. This review is based on studies conducted in the fields of epidemiology and public health economics, which analyse actual risks to human lives with a view to identifying measures for their prevention and the costs of such measures.

---

[1] See chapters 8–10 in this volume. The figure of $290 billion refers to the combined arms sales of the SIPRI Top 100 arms-producing companies in the world excluding China.

* The author is grateful to Sissela Bok, Michael Brzoska and Thomas Ohlson as well as to SIPRI colleagues for comments on earlier versions of this text.

This section continues with a discussion of the much contested definition of security. Section II provides an overview of actual causes of death and disability and the associated risk factors, along with recommended preventive interventions or risk-reduction strategies. The links between risks to human lives from disease and from collective violence are discussed in section III, with a view to assessing their implications for security analysis and policy and, therefore, also for resource allocation. The conclusions are presented in section IV.

Conceptions of security

Security is a contested concept. Traditionally, security has been thought of in terms of external military threats or risks posed to a state by another state or by internal armed threats from non-state actors. Changes in the contemporary security environment have resulted in a plethora of attempts to define and conceptualize—both politically and theoretically—these changes and their implications for states, societies and individuals. The traditional conception of security has been joined by others which both broaden the nature of possible threats (adding to armed threats such threats as terrorism, organized crime and disease, which are associated with risk factors in the economic, political, societal and environmental domains) and deepen the objects that are being threatened (to include global security, sub-national groups and individuals).[2]

The reconceptualizations of security that involve the broadening of state security to include new risks and threats beyond attack by military force have given birth to such concepts as homeland security, functional security and environmental security. The deeper concepts of security which relate to the protection of human individuals from threats to their security as individuals require the building of a social framework in which humans can live free from both fear and want.[3] The broader concepts of security also require that the diverse threats are addressed in a comprehensive manner, which necessitates examination of the interlinkages among those threats from a human perspective.[4]

---

[2] Sköns, E., 'Financing security in a global context', *SIPRI Yearbook 2005: Armaments, Disarmament and International Security* (Oxford University Press: Oxford, 2005), pp. 285–306.

[3] This perspective was embodied in the UN Millennium Declaration of Sep. 2000 and first spelled out by UN Secretary-General Kofi Annan in May 2000. United Nations, 'United Nations Millennium Declaration', UN General Assembly Resolution 55/2, 8 Sep. 2000, URL <http://www.un.org/millennium goals/>; and United Nations, 'Secretary-General salutes international workshop on human security in Mongolia', Press Release SG/SM/7382, 8 May 2000, URL <http://www.un.org/News/Press/docs/2000/20000508.sgsm7382.doc.html>. For a critical discussion of this perspective, which is one way of conceptualizing 'human security', see Owen, T., 'Conspicuously absent? Why the Secretary-General used human security in all but name', *St Anthony's International Review*, vol. 1, no. 2 (Nov. 2005), pp. 37–42; and Paris, R., 'Human security: paradigm shift or hot air?', *International Security*, vol. 26, no. 2 (fall 2001), pp. 87–102.

[4] Owada, H., 'The United Nations and the maintenance of international peace and security: the current debate in the light of reform proposals', Keynote speech at the Research Forum on International Law, European Society of International Law and Graduate Institute of International Studies, Geneva, 26 May 2005, URL <http://www.esil-sedi.eu/english/forum2005.html>.

The result is that there is no longer a universally accepted definition, in theory or in practice, of security. Different theoretical perspectives stress different values and there is always an element of subjectivity in interpretations of what an objective definition of security should entail. Realist theories focus on international problems and stress conflict; transnational corporate-globalist views emphasize economic aspects and the preservation of the existing international economic system; and the emerging human security perspectives focus on the conditions of individuals and the planet.[5] In addition, risk analysis is emerging as a complementary way of addressing security problems in order to overcome the contradiction between different types of security concepts.[6] Table 7.1 lists the security threats and risks covered in five recent studies as an illustration of the different security analyses that result from different theoretical approaches.

Different conceptions of security can be represented in a matrix with the rows representing the different types of threat to security and the columns the various referent objects of security. One representation of such a security matrix is shown in figure 7.1. However, the rows and columns of any such matrix are not fixed and the choice of threats and referent objects made in the figure is by no means the only one possible when thinking about new security concepts. Perceived security threats include not only military threats, but also a number of additional phenomena that have been 'securitized', including political, economic, societal, environmental and ecological threats.[7] The referent object of security is who or what is threatened and needs protection; it ranges from global and collective security via national, state and regime security and sub-national security linked to class, religion or ethnicity to the security of the individual. In recent years, the security of the individual has been emphasized over national security, as can be observed, for example, in the notion of the 'responsibility to protect' as a norm guiding international humanitarian interventions.[8]

Different concepts of security are represented by the different cells in this matrix, which represent different choices of threat and referent and thus also require different instruments or interventions to address security threats and risks. The choice between different security concepts has often been seen as a zero-sum game, in which the enhancement of security for one type of actor—for example, the state or regime—from one type of threat decreases the secur-

---

[5] Alternative values in the main theories are set out in Gurtov, M., *Global Politics in the Human Interest*, 4th edn (Lynne Rienner: Boulder, Colo., 1999), pp. 25–26. See also Rojas Aravena, F., 'Human security: emerging concept of security in the twenty-first century', *Disarmament Forum*, no. 2, 2002, pp. 5–14.

[6] E.g. 'reflexive security studies' is a risk-based research strand within international security studies that applies sociological theories on 'risk society' to understand contemporary security problems. See the Introduction in this volume.

[7] Buzan, B., Wæver, O. and de Wilde, J., *Security: A New Framework for Analysis* (Lynne Rienner: Boulder, Colo., 1998).

[8] International Commission on Intervention and State Sovereignty, *The Responsibility to Protect* (International Development Research Centre: Ottawa, Dec. 2001), URL <http://www.iciss.ca/report-en.asp>.

Table 7.1. Select studies of security threats and risks, 2004–2006

Security object/ Purpose of study	Major threats and risks identified
United Nations High-level Panel, 'A more secure world: our shared responsibility', 2004	
Collective security	Economic and social: poverty; infectious disease; environmental degradation
To suggest collective	Interstate conflict
approaches to meet	Internal conflict: civil war; genocide; other large-scale atrocities
the challenges of	Nuclear, radiological, chemical and biological weapons
global, national,	Terrorism
regional and human	Transnational organized crime
security threats	
US National Intelligence Council, *Mapping the Global Future*, 2004	
US national security	*Insecurity trends*: international terrorism; intensifying internal conflicts: rising powers (e.g. China); weapons of mass destruction
To analyse	*Non-security trends*:
developments up	Globalization: an expanding and integrating global economy; the
to 2030 which	technological revolution; lingering social inequalities;
might warrant US	Changing geopolitical landscape: rising Asia and other rising states;
policy action	the ageing powers; growing energy demands; the duration of US unipolarity
	New challenges to governance: halting progress of democratization
Human Security Centre, *The Human Security Report 2005*, 2005	
Human security	Armed conflicts
	Genocides and 'politicides'
To examine major	Refugee flows
trends in global	Military coups
political violence,	Human rights abuse
and their	International terrorism
consequences	
World Economic Forum, *Global Risks 2006*, 2006	
Corporate security	Economic: energy supply, indebtedness, the US dollar, China, critical infrastructure
To assess systemic	Societal: regulations, corporate governance, intellectual property
risks to global	rights, organized crime, global pandemics, chronic disease in
business and their	industrial countries, epidemic disease in developing countries
likely effects on	Environmental: tropical cyclones, earthquakes, climate change
markets and	Technological: technological convergence, nanotechnology,
industries	electromagnetic fields, ubiquitous computing
	Geopolitical: terrorism, European dislocation, hotspots
European Union Institute for Security Studies, *The New Global Puzzle*, 2006	
State and human	Demographic trends
security	Economic trends
	Energy trends
To analyse relevant	Environmental trends
trends for future	Science and technology
EU security policy	

Sources: United Nations, 'A more secure world: our shared responsibility', Report of the High-level Panel on Threats, Challenges and Change, UN document A/59/565 and Corr. 1, 4 Dec. 2004, URL <http://www.un.org/secureworld/>; US National Intelligence Council (NIC), *Mapping the Global Future*, Report of the NIC's 2020 Project (Government Printing Office: Washington, DC, Dec. 2004), URL <http://www.dni.gov/nic/NIC_globaltrend2020.html>; University of British Columbia, Human Security Centre, *Human Security Report 2005: War and Peace in the 21st Century* (Oxford University Press: New York, N.Y., 2005), URL <http://www.humansecurityreport.info/>; World Economic Forum, *Global Risks 2006* (World Economic Forum: Geneva, 2006), URL <http://www.weforum.org/en/initiatives/globalrisk/>; and EU Institute for Security Studies (EU-ISS), *The New Global Puzzle: What World for the EU in 2025?* (EU-ISS: Paris, 2006), URL <http://www.iss-eu.org/public/content/bookse. html>.

ity of another actor at another level—for example, a religious or ethnic minority in that state or even all or some of its citizens. In the contemporary security environment, security at the human and other sub-national levels is increasingly becoming a major concern in the international system at the expense of national security and additional perceived threats are continuously emerging. In this environment, traditional security analysis is insufficient to correctly address security problems, largely because it cannot deal with the dangers of zero-sum thinking that seem to invariably result from such analysis.

The potential to mitigate the seemingly zero-sum results that traditional security theory often generates may be offered by applying a risk analysis across the cells of the security matrix. The basic rationale of this chapter is to argue that a risk-based approach in combination with cost–benefit analysis of the methods of risk reduction and prevention—in this case at the level of the individual—is a useful complement to traditional security analysis. Such an approach opens up the potential for an improved trade-off between security concerns at different levels, allowing for a win–win outcome. It also makes it necessary to explore the interlinkages between different types of security, threats and risk factors in order to identify such trade-offs.

This chapter's focus on threats and risks to human lives that have traditionally not been classified as security threats has two major implications. First, it suggests that the opportunity costs of military spending are very high. This is especially the case in terms of regime security lost through lack of social investments—such investment would increase individual security and thus gain the regime higher levels of legitimacy from both citizens and the international community. Second, this type of evidence may lead not only to normative and well-intentioned recommendations at the level of individual and human security but might also be interpreted as strengthening security at several levels and in several dimensions simultaneously—that is, it would also have a realist, rational-choice based appeal.

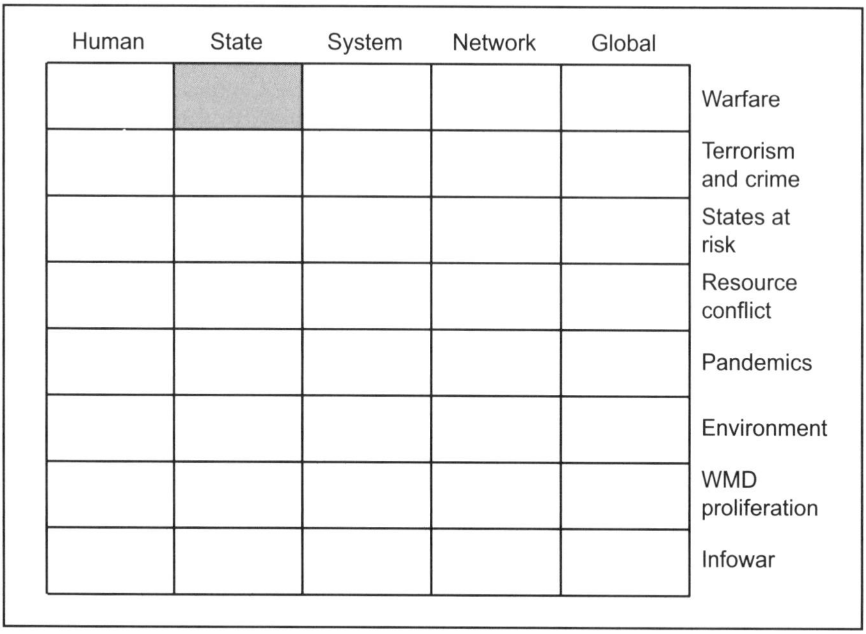

Human	State	System	Network	Global	
					Warfare
					Terrorism and crime
					States at risk
					Resource conflict
					Pandemics
					Environment
					WMD proliferation
					Infowar

Figure 7.1. A representation of the security matrix

The shaded cell represents the traditional concept of state security.

Source: Brown University, Watson Institute for International Studies, Global Security Matrix website, URL <http://www.globalsecuritymatrix.org/>.

II. Major risks to human lives

In its most generic form, risk refers to a potential negative impact on an asset or some characteristic of value that may arise from some present process or future event. Assessments of risks to human lives are made in the discipline of epidemiology, a branch of medicine that studies the causes, distribution, and control of disease in populations and serves as the foundation for preventive interventions. The concept of risk used in epidemiological studies is based on the actual outcome of disease in a population during a given time period, such as mortality (annual number of deaths in a certain number of population at risk) or, more recently, years of healthy life lost owing to premature death and disability related to a given disease, condition or injury.[9]

Global patterns of death and disability, risk factors underlying them and recommended prevention strategies are reviewed in this section. This review is based on official statistics on reported causes of death and disability and on major studies of risk factors and related prevention strategies.

[9] Rothman, K. J. and Greenland, S. (eds), *Modern Epidemiology*, 2nd edn (Lippincott–Raven: Philadelphia, Pa., 1998).

World Health Organization data on causes of death and disability

The patterns of death and disability described in this section are based on statistics of the World Health Organization (WHO). Three types of indicators are used: numbers of death, rates of mortality and numbers of disability-adjusted life years (DALYs). The DALY is a measure developed in order to quantify the global burden of disease and injury. It combines in a single indicator years of life lost due to premature death and years of healthy life lost as a result of disability.

Problems with the data

While providing a rough assessment of the causes of death and disability, the WHO statistics suffer from several weaknesses. First, complete death registration data are available for only one-third of those who die. Some information on another third is available through the urban death registration systems and national sample registration systems of China and India. For the remaining one-third, only partial information is available from epidemiological studies, disease registers and surveillance systems.[10] These problems are worst for data on death and disability from violence, and in particular from collective violence, for which no accurate data exist. Therefore, a number of estimation methods are employed in producing these statistics. Second, the accuracy of the diagnoses of the cause of death is often questionable for several reasons, including death registration without medical opinion, underreporting of causes of death of a sensitive nature, misinterpretation of the rules for selecting underlying causes and difficulties of identifying a single cause of death.[11] Third, the selection of factors used as the ultimate causes of death and disability in the WHO data appear somewhat arbitrary. In principle, the cause of death should refer to factors inherent in the human body, while factors external to it are generally regarded as risk factors. However, the dividing line between these two is difficult to define. While nutritional deficiency is among the causes of death and disability in WHO data, hunger is not; and while traffic accidents and collective violence are considered to be causes of death, disasters are not. The problem can be illustrated by a question posed by two researchers on food security: 'What, for example, is the "cause" of death of a starving person, caught in a civil war, who ends up in a refugee camp, and then dies of measles?'[12] As mentioned above, the inclusion of unintentional and intentional injury (i.e. accidents and violence) as causes of death also involves severe difficulties in obtaining reliable data, a problem that is discussed in more detail in section III.

---

[10] Mathers, C. D., Lopez, A. D. and Murray, C. J. L., 'The burden of disease and mortality by condition: data, methods, and results for 2001', eds A. D. Lopez et al., World Bank, *Global Burden of Disease and Risk Factors* (Oxford University Press: New York, N.Y., Apr. 2006), URL <http://www.dcp2.org/pubs/GBD/>, p. 51.

[11] Mathers, Lopez and Murray (note 10), pp. 53–55.

[12] Falcon, W. P. and Naylor, R. L., 'Rethinking food security for the twenty-first century', *American Journal of Agricultural Economics*, vol. 87, no. 5 (Nov. 2005), p. 1114.

Table 7.2. Causes of death and disability, worldwide and by income group, 2005

| Cause | Deaths (th.) | Mortality rates (deaths/100 000) by country income group | | | | | Burden of disease (m. DALYs) |
		World	High	Upper middle	Lower middle	Low	
Communicable diseases	17 258	268	57	91	110	509	566
Infectious/parasitic	10 262	159	16	41	65	312	325
Tuberculosis	1 411	22	1	5	16	37	31
HIV/AIDS	2 830	44	2	16	29	76	83
Diarrhoeal diseases	1 682	26	1	5	8	55	58
Malaria	888	14	0	0	0	32	34
Respiratory infections	3 757	58	37	22	23	103	87
Perinatal conditions	2 331	36	3	21	18	66	93
Maternal conditions	460	7	0	1	1	16	30
Nutritional deficiencies	448	7	2	6	2	13	31
Non-communicable diseases/conditions	35 367	549	752	517	583	456	720
Cardiovascular diseases	17 528	272	325	242	292	242	153
Cancers	7 586	118	225	117	126	73	79
Respiratory diseases	4 027	63	55	39	85	51	58
Digestive diseases	1 995	31	37	37	30	29	46
Neuropsychiatric conditions	1 167	18	43	14	11	16	198
Diabetes	1 118	17	25	36	13	15	18
Other	1 946	30	42	33	26	29	168
Injuries	5 403	84	50	67	86	97	184
Unintentional (accidents)	3 700	57	34	41	57	69	134
Road traffic accidents	1 313	20	12	17	22	22	42
Other unintentional	2 387	37	22	24	35	47	92
Intentional (violence)	1 703	26	16	27	29	28	50
Self-inflicted violence	912	14	13	8	18	12	21
Interpersonal violence	593	9	2	18	9	10	22
Collective violence	184	3	0	0	2	5	7
Total	**58 028**	**901**	**859**	**675**	**778**	**1 062**	**1 471**

DALY = Disability-adjusted life year.

Source: World Health Organization, 'Projections of mortality and burden of disease 2006: projected deaths by income group, age, sex and cause for the years 2005, 2015 and 2030', Spreadsheet, Nov. 2006; and World Health Organization, 'Projections of mortality and burden of disease 2006: projected DALYs by income group, age, sex and cause for the years 2005, 2015 and 2030', Spreadsheet, Nov. 2006—both available at URL <http://www.who.int/health info/statistics/bodprojections2030/en/>.

Assessing the global burden of disease and injury (i.e. the years lost due to premature death and disability) is even more problematic, since it involves at least two additional estimation methodologies: identifying the number of disabled, and relating death and disability to an estimated length of healthy life in the absence of death and disability.[13] Finally, WHO also makes projections into the future. While the most recent year for which original data on mortality and the burden of disease have been produced is 2002, projections have been made for 2005, 2015 and 2030. These projections are highly uncertain, in particular for 2015 and 2030, because of the uncertainties associated with the assumptions underlying the projections.[14] Thus, while these data provide rough indications of causes of death and disability, the interpretation of these data should consider their weaknesses.[15]

While all these difficulties have an impact on the accuracy of the data, the data nevertheless indicate the rough magnitude and pattern of different causes of death. Since this type of data is essential for any analysis of the pattern of risk factors and for the identification of prevention strategies that mitigate both freedom from want and freedom from fear, more investment in its production is needed.

Patterns in WHO data on causes of death and disability

According to WHO estimates, around 58 million people died in 2005, of whom 9.6 million were children younger than five and 35.7 million were younger than 70.[16] Of the total number of deaths, roughly 35 million died from non-communicable diseases, 17 million from communicable diseases, and 5 million from injuries (see table 7.2).

The global burden of disease and injury amounted to an estimated 1471 million DALYs in 2005, almost half of which were caused by non-communicable diseases, while communicable diseases accounted for 38 per cent and injuries for 13 per cent. The mortality rates differ significantly between country income groups. In high-income countries non-communicable diseases account for a 13-times higher mortality rate than communicable diseases, a difference which is to a great extent due to high mortality from cardiovascular diseases and cancer. In low-income countries communicable diseases generate slightly higher mortality than non-communicable diseases, with very high death rates from infectious diseases—most profoundly from HIV/AIDS, but also from

[13] The DALY indicator uses the same life expectancy 'ideal' standard for specifying years of life lost for all population subgroups, whether or not their current life expectancy is lower than that of other groups. Similarly, premature death is defined as all deaths earlier than the standard life expectancy. The techniques used in calculating DALYs are described and discussed in Mathers, Lopez and Murray (note 10).

[14] The models used to project future health trends are 'based largely on projection of economic and social development', 'using the historically observed relationships of these with cause-specific mortality rates'. Mathers, C. D. and Loncar, D., 'Projections of global mortality and burden of disease from 2002 to 2030', *PLoS Medicine*, vol. 3, no. 11 (Nov. 2006), pp. 2011–30.

[15] One criticism of the WHO projections is that they are too optimistic because they cannot take into account unpredictable new developments. Another issue is the uncertainty of the socio-economic forecast of the World Bank, on which they are based, and a third source of uncertainty is whether socio-economic developments will have the same impact on disease and injury in all countries. 'Disease plans must expect the unexpected', *New Scientist*, 2 Dec. 2006, p. 3.

[16] World Health Organization (WHO), 'Projections of mortality and burden of disease 2006: projected deaths by WHO region, age, sex and cause for the years 2005, 2015 and 2030', Spreadsheet, Nov. 2006, URL <http://www.who.int/healthinfo/statistics/bodprojections2030/en/>.

diarrhoeal diseases, tuberculosis and malaria—respiratory infections and peri-
natal conditions.

Risk factors

The key to prevention is identification of risk factors. WHO has identified
10 leading risk factors behind the global burden of disease. These are (in order
of importance): being underweight, unsafe sex, high blood pressure, tobacco
consumption, alcohol consumption, unsafe water, sanitation and hygiene, iron
deficiency, indoor smoke from solid fuels, high cholesterol, and being overweight and obesity.[17] Together, these risk factors account for more than one-
third of all deaths worldwide.

The importance of different risk factors varies significantly between poor
and rich countries. In the developed countries, almost half of all the disease
burden is caused by tobacco (12.2 per cent), blood pressure (10.9 per cent),
alcohol (9.2 per cent), cholesterol (7.6 per cent) and being overweight (7.4 per
cent). In high-mortality developing countries, mainly located in sub-Saharan
Africa and South-East Asia, one-third of the disease burden results from four
risk factors: being underweight (14.9 per cent), unsafe sex (10.2 per cent),
unsafe water, sanitation and hygiene (5.5 per cent), and indoor smoke from
solid fuels (3.7 per cent).[18] There is a strong concentration of risks in high-
mortality developing countries, which represent roughly two-fifths of the
world's population. In these countries, the rates of disease and injury are particularly high and these are largely caused by a few risk factors. Being underweight and micronutrient (vitamin and mineral) deficiencies together account
for about one-quarter of the disease burden in these countries. The disease
burden in high-mortality developing countries resulting from these risks is
close to the total disease and injury burden in developed countries.[19]

The chain of events leading to death and disability includes both proximal
and distal factors, where proximal factors act directly to cause disease and
injury, while distal factors are further back in the causal chain and act via a
number of intermediaries. Thus, it is important to consider the entire causal
chain in the assessment of risks to health. Furthermore, many risks cannot be
considered separately because they do not act in isolation from other risks.[20] In
fact, the complex, multi-causal nature of disease may often mean that different
preventive strategies are possible, and thus that parallel actions can potentially
bring reinforced benefits.

Among the 10 leading global risk factors identified for high-mortality
developing countries, four are related to undernourishment—being underweight and zinc, iron and vitamin A deficiencies—and two are related to the
physical environment—unsafe water, sanitation and hygiene and indoor

[17] WHO, *The World Health Report 2002: Reducing Risks, Promoting Healthy Life* (WHO: Geneva,
2002), URL <http://www.who.int/whr/2002/en/>, Overview, p. 7.
[18] WHO (note 17), table 5.1, p. 102.
[19] WHO (note 17), pp. 82–83.
[20] WHO (note 17), pp. 13–14, 26–27.

smoke from solid fuels.[21] While different types of undernutrition and environmental factor are major proximal causes, poverty is a distal cause.

Hunger as a risk factor

Hunger is a major risk factor for disease. Underweight children are at increased risk of mortality from infectious illnesses, such as diarrhoea and pneumonia. An estimated 50–70 per cent of the burden of diarrhoeal diseases, measles, malaria and lower respiratory infections in childhood is attributable to childhood undernutrition. Being underweight was estimated to have caused 3.7 million deaths in 2000, accounting for about 1 in 15 deaths. Since deaths from undernutrition occur almost exclusively among young children, the share in the loss of healthy life years is even higher: about 9.5 per cent of global DALYs were attributed to being underweight.[22]

The high number of lives that are threatened by hunger has led to the state of hunger being termed as 'food insecurity'.[23] The Food and Agricultural Organization (FAO) has estimated that 10 million people die every year of hunger and hunger-related diseases.[24] In developing countries, more than 20 million low-birthweight children are born every year, and almost one-third of all children in developing countries are stunted, with heights in the range that suggests chronic undernutrition. According to the FAO, more than 5 million children die from hunger-related causes every year.[25]

The most recent estimates by the FAO show that in 2001–2003 there were 854 million undernourished people worldwide, of whom 820 million were in developing countries, 25 million in transition countries and 9 million in industrialized countries.[26] The agreed goals of halving the number of undernourished people by 2015 (the 1996 World Food Summit target) and halving their proportion of population by 2015 (one of the Millennium Development Goals, MDGs) are still far from being achieved, in particular for African countries.[27] Hunger occurs in three different forms: acute, chronic and hidden.

[21] WHO (note 17), table 5.1, p. 102.

[22] WHO (note 17), pp. 53–54.

[23] Following the literature on hunger, the term 'hunger' is used here to mean undernourishment. Undernourished persons are defined as those 'whose food intake falls below the minimum requirement or food intake that is insufficient to meet dietary energy requirements continuously'. United Nations Statistics Divisions, Common Database, URL <http://unstats.un.org/unsd/cdb/cdb_dict_xrxx.asp?def_code=433>. Precise definitions in terms of calorie intake are contested. See Mason, J. B., 'Measuring hunger and malnutrition', Keynote Paper presented at the International Scientific Symposium on Measurement and Assessment of Food Deprivation and Undernutrition, Food and Agricultural Organization, Rome, 26–28 June 2002, URL <http://www.fao.org/docrep/005/y4249e/y4249e0d.htm>.

[24] World Food Programme (WFP), 'Faces of the hungry', WFP website, 2007, URL <http://www.wfp.org/aboutwfp/introduction/hunger_who.asp>.

[25] FAO, *The State of Food Insecurity in the World 2004: Monitoring Progress towards the World Food Summit and Millennium Development Goals* (FAO: Rome, 2004), URL <http://www.fao.org/docrep/007/y5650e/y5650e00.htm>, p. 8.

[26] FAO, *The State of Food Insecurity in the World 2006: Eradicating World Hunger—Taking Stock Ten Years after the World Food Summit* (FAO: Rome, 2006), URL <http://www.fao.org/docrep/009/a0750e/a0750e00.htm>, p. 8.

[27] FAO (note 26), pp. 8–12. See also the UN Millennium Developments Goals website, URL <http://www.un.org/millenniumgoals/>.

While those suffering from acute hunger are those most visible through reports on famines and disasters, acute hunger accounts for only about 10 per cent of the total number of hungry people. The chronically undernourished are the great majority (90 per cent) of the hungry.[28]

While hunger is a risk factor for disease, it also has its own risk factors. Chronic hunger is caused by a constant or recurrent lack of access to food. However, there is more than enough food available to feed the world population of 6.54 billion people. Thus, the cause of hunger is that the hungry do not have the money to buy food or the means to produce it. The reasons for this constitute the risk factors for hunger. The World Food Programme identifies five such factors: poverty, the agricultural infrastructure, overexploitation of the environment, natural disasters and armed conflicts.[29] The United Nations Millennium Project points to overlapping, although slightly different, risk factors: poverty, low food production, mothers' lack of education, poor water, sanitation and health facilities, and climatic shocks. It adds to this a number of identified vulnerabilities to crises, such as disasters and wars, and other hazards, such as insecure rights to land, lack of proper agricultural technology, inability to store produce after harvest, weather variations, environmental degradation, poor health, food shortages and lack of income-earning opportunities.[30]

Since 1992, the proportion of food crises that can be attributed mainly to human causes, such as violent conflict and economic failures, has increased from around 15 per cent to more than 35 per cent, and the number of food crises requiring emergency assistance has also been rising, from an average of 15 per year during the 1980s to more than 30 per year since 2000.[31] Most of the specific crises as well as the increase were concentrated in Africa. Natural and human-induced factors tend to reinforce each other, producing complex crises. Nevertheless, only 8 per cent of the 10 million people who die from hunger and hunger-related diseases each year are the victims of major disasters and wars.[32]

While poverty is a major risk factor for hunger, historical trends show that undernourishment does not decrease at the same rate as poverty. Although the reasons for the slower rate of decline in hunger are not clear, the FAO suggests that an important factor may be that hunger itself acts as a barrier to escaping poverty—the 'hunger trap'.[33] Thus, hunger is not only a consequence, but also a cause of poverty.

[28] Sanchez, P. et al., UN Millennium Project, Task Force on Hunger, *Halving Hunger: It Can be Done* (Earthscan: London, 2005), URL <http://www.unmillenniumproject.org/reports/tf_hunger.htm>, p. 2. Another 2 billion people experience hidden hunger, caused by a lack of essential micronutrients, although they consume adequate amounts of calories and protein.

[29] World Food Programme (WFP), 'Why does hunger exist?', WFP website, 2007, URL <http://www.wfp.org/aboutwfp/introduction/hunger_causes.asp>.

[30] Sanchez et al. (note 28), p. 5.

[31] FAO (note 25), p. 16.

[32] World Food Programme (note 24).

[33] FAO (note 26), p. 13.

Paradoxically, being a farmer reportedly constitutes a major risk factor for hunger. Three-quarters of the hungry live in rural areas, mainly in the villages of Asia and Africa. About half of the hungry are smallholder family households unable either to grow or to buy enough food to meet the family's requirements, and another 20 per cent are landless rural people.[34]

Environmental risk factors

Environmental conditions constitute important risk factors, particularly in developing countries, playing a major role in more than 80 per cent of the diseases regularly reported by WHO. Globally, an estimated 24 per cent of the disease burden and 23 per cent of all deaths can be attributed to environmental factors.[35] In some areas these figures are much higher; for example, in sub-Saharan Africa such factors accounted for nearly 35 per cent of the disease burden.[36]

The leading environmental risk factor is unsafe water, poor sanitation and hygiene, accounting for about 3 per cent of all deaths (1.7 million) and 3.7 per cent of all DALYs. Indoor smoke from solid fuels causes another 1.6 million deaths per year, and accounts for 2.7 per cent of all DALYs. Nearly half the world's population cooks with solid fuels. Several diseases are strongly related to indoor use of solid fuels, which is estimated to cause 36 per cent of lower respiratory infections. Urban air pollution, generated by motor vehicles, industries and energy production, causes about 5 per cent of tracheal, bronchial and lung cancer globally, causing about 1.4 per cent of all deaths (0.8 million) and 0.8 per cent of all DALYs. Climate change has been estimated to have been responsible in 2000 for 6 per cent of malaria in some middle-income countries and approximately 2.4 per cent of worldwide diarrhoea. Globally, it was estimated to account for 0.3 per cent of all deaths (154 000) and 0.4 per cent of all DALYs. Other environmental factors include excessive exposure to toxic chemicals and pesticides (0.35 million deaths). There are thus important links between disease and environmental factors.[37]

Poverty as a risk factor

Poverty is a third major risk factor for disease. Furthermore, both hunger and environmental risk factors for disease are also strongly associated with absolute poverty.

The greatest burden of disease and injury is borne by the poor countries and by the disadvantaged in all societies. The vast majority of threats to health are more commonly found among poor people, particularly those with little

---

[34] Sanchez et al. (note 28), pp. 3–4; and World Food Programme (note 24).

[35] Prüss-Üstün, A. and Corvalán, C., *Preventing Disease through Healthy Environments: Towards an Estimate of the Environmental Burden of Disease* (WHO: Geneva, 2006), URL <http://www.who.int/quantifying_ehimpacts/publications/preventingdisease/en/>, p. 9.

[36] WHO and UN Environment Programme, Health and Environment Linkages Initiative (HELI), 'Priority risks: the human toll', HELI website, URL <http://www.who.int/heli/risks/en/>.

[37] WHO (note 17), pp. 67–73.

formal education and with low-status occupations. This is the case because poverty, while being a key determinant of health status in itself, is also an underlying risk factor of several proximal risk factors. Thus, there is a strong relationship between underweight children and absolute poverty. People living on less than $1 per day are generally at a 2–3 times higher risk of having underweight children compared with people living on more than $2 per day.[38] Unsafe water, sanitation and hygiene and indoor air pollution are also strongly related with absolute poverty.

Thus, the links between poverty and disease are well established. Poverty not only increases the risk of becoming ill, but poor people are also at higher risk of dying from their illness than are wealthier people. The impact of poverty on health was summarized in the 2001 report of the Commission on Macroeconomics and Health (CMH), according to which poor people have a disproportionate burden of avoidable deaths; they are more susceptible to diseases because of malnutrition, inadequate sanitation and lack of clean water; they are less likely to have access to medical care; and they are less reached by existing life-saving interventions, including preventive measures and access to essential medicines.[39]

Prevention

Preventive interventions can be categorized according to when in a negative development they take place: (*a*) primary interventions are those aiming to prevent an event before it occurs; (*b*) secondary interventions consist of emergency measures providing an immediate response to the negative impact of an event; and (*c*) tertiary intervention involve long-term treatment of the effects of an event or processes.

Effective health interventions to either prevent or cure the diseases which have the highest premature death and disability outcomes have already been identified. What is lacking is investment and institutional reforms to implement them adequately. In its 2001 report the CMH estimated the costs involved in reducing deaths from the most common causes in low-income countries and among the poor in middle-income countries, which have far lower life expectancies and far higher age-adjusted mortality rates than the rest of the world. It estimated that by 2010 around 8 million lives could be saved each year by a set of essential health interventions against infectious diseases—HIV/AIDS, malaria, tuberculosis and childhood infectious diseases—and nutritional deficiencies. The recommended programme for prevention and cure was estimated to require an increase of $57 billion (at constant 2002 prices) in annual health outlays by 2007 for this group of countries. Given the

---

[38] WHO (note 17), p. 50.

[39] Commission on Macroeconomics and Health (CMH), *Macroeconomics and Health: Investing in Health for Economic Development* (WHO: Geneva, 2001), URL <http://www.cmhealth.org/>; and WHO, CMH Support Unit, 'Investing in health: a summary of the findings of the Commission on Macroeconomics and Health', Geneva, 2003, URL <http://www.emro.who.int/cbi/cmh-documents. htm>, p. 10.

low income in these countries, domestic resource mobilization would fall short of need, thus requiring also increased donor financing for health. According to the proposed burden-sharing concept, the national governments in the targeted countries would need to increase their annual domestic spending on health by 1 per cent of their gross national product (GNP) by 2007 and by 2 per cent of GNP by 2015, resulting in domestically financed additional health spending of $35 billion in 2007 and $63 billion by 2015, while the annual external aid required would be $22 billion in 2007 and $31 billion in 2015 in the form of country-level programmes. In addition, allocations to the development of 'global public goods' were recommended ($5 billion in 2007 and $7 billion in 2015) to be spent on research and development focused on the health needs of the poor (e.g. new affordable drugs and vaccines) and on epidemiological data collection and analysis and surveillance of infectious diseases at the international level.[40] Five years after the publication of the report some progress had been made towards these goals.[41]

Similarly, WHO has examined the extent to which the global disease burden could be eased over a 20-year period if the most important risk factors to human lives could be reduced. Data on the costs and effectiveness of a set of interventions targeting different risk factors were developed for different regions and subregions, with the aim of helping policymakers identify which interventions should be selected for given levels of resource availability if the goal were to minimize the burden of disease. The conclusion was that 'Very substantial health gains can be made for relatively modest expenditures on interventions to reduce risks'.[42] For example, in Africa, one of the regions with the highest mortality rates and highest burden of disease, a number of recommended interventions could reduce the burden of disease by over 140 million DALYs, at an annual cost of about I$6.8 billion.[43] These include interventions to prevent HIV and the provision of vitamin, iron and zinc supplements in combination with treatment for diarrhoea and pneumonia in children. Another example, based on cross-country research on neonatal mortality, is a set of interventions that could reduce death rates by 59 per cent in 75 high-mortality countries, saving 2.3 million lives, at a cost of $4 billion.[44]

---

[40] Commission on Macroeconomics and Health (note 39), pp. 6, 11; and WHO (note 39), p. 20. On 'global public goods' see the websites of the Global Network on Global Public Goods, URL <http://www.sdnp.undp.org/gpgn/>, and the International Task Force on Global Public Goods, URL <http://www.gpgtaskforce.org/>.

[41] A 2006 follow-up to the CMH report showed that external funding for health was increasing and that, although health expenditure as a share of GDP and of general government expenditure had increased in several of the countries with CMH follow-up programmes, many countries were progressing too slowly to reach their national health spending targets by 2015. WHO, *Tough Choices: Investing in Health for Development—Experiences from National Follow-up to the Commission on Macroeconomics and Health* (WHO: Geneva, 2006), URL <http://www.emro.who.int/cbi/cmh-documents.htm>, pp. 26–28.

[42] WHO (note 17), p. 137.

[43] I$ means international dollar, which is the US dollar value of a local currency figure converted at the purchasing power parity rate.

[44] United Nations Development Programme (UNDP), *Human Development Report 2005: International Cooperation at a Crossroads—Aid, Trade and Security in an Unequal World* (UNDP: New York, N.Y., 2005), URL <http://hdr.undp.org/reports/global/2005/>, p. 33.

Provision of health services can be seen as a tertiary form of prevention. The number and quality of health workers are positively correlated with immunization coverage, outreach of primary care, and infant, child and maternal survival. At least 1.3 billion people worldwide lack access to the most basic health care, often because there are no health workers. Shortages are most severe in sub-Saharan Africa, which has 11 per cent of the world population and 24 per cent of the global burden of disease but only 3 per cent of the world's health workers. While there are a total of 59 million full-time paid health workers worldwide, there is a serious shortage of health workers in 57 developing countries, where an estimated 4.3 million additional doctors, nurses, midwives and other public health workers are needed. For these countries to build up such health workforces, an annual increase in health budgets corresponding to at least $20 per person would be needed.[45]

Hunger

Approaches to preventing hunger include tertiary interventions, such as specific nutrition measures, secondary interventions, such as food emergency aid in crises, and primary interventions, aiming at preventing hunger itself.

In the short term, food aid can help break the cycle of hunger and poverty. Nutrition interventions such as breastfeeding and providing vitamin A and zinc supplements are important tertiary prevention measures which have the potential to reduce child mortality significantly at a low cost.[46] Food aid can also help to slow down the impact of HIV/AIDS, since without sufficient food and nutrition the infected lack one of the main defences against HIV and other AIDS-related infections, such as tuberculosis. The effectiveness of drug treatment and the body's drug tolerance are greatly improved by good nutrition.[47]

The hunger trap suggests that per capita income growth is not always sufficient to eradicate hunger, and thus that poverty reduction does not benefit proportionately those among the poor who are also undernourished. The concentration of hunger in rural areas suggests that no sustained reduction in hunger is possible without special emphasis on agricultural and rural development. Agricultural growth appears to be critical for hunger reduction, since reportedly over 70 per cent of the poor in developing countries live in rural areas and depend on agriculture for their livelihoods, directly or indirectly. Particularly in the countries with the least food security, agriculture is crucial for income and employment generation. According to the FAO, improved technology can also contribute to agricultural growth if it is adapted to local conditions that favour small-scale farmers, increases their incomes and reduces food prices. Similarly, trade can contribute to hunger reduction. How-

---

[45] WHO, *The World Health Report 2006: Working Together for Health* (WHO: Geneva, 2006), URL <http://www.who.int/whr/2006/en/>, pp. xv, 8, 12–15.

[46] FAO (note 25), p. 9. In the 42 countries where more than 90% of child deaths occur, these relatively inexpensive and effective nutrition interventions could reduce child mortality by 25% and save the lives of 2.4 million children each year.

[47] World Food Programme (note 29), p. 5.

ever, trade gains are neither automatic nor universal but need to be coupled with measures to improve market infrastructure, local institutions and safety nets.[48]

In outlining a strategy for hunger reduction, the FAO recommends a twin-track approach, combining longer-term interventions to enhance productive potential and rural development (primary prevention) with programmes and policies that respond to the immediate needs of poor and food-insecure people (tertiary prevention).[49] The FAO recommends that the former should focus on agricultural and rural development, creating employment and ensuring access by the poor to productive assets—physical, human and financial. The latter interventions, for tertiary prevention, may include social safety nets, cash transfers, health interventions and food and nutrition programmes. Promoting agricultural growth would require public investment in infrastructure, agricultural research and education. It would also benefit from more targeting of foreign development assistance to agriculture and rural development and greater focus on the countries with high levels of undernourishment.

Environmental factors

Public and preventive health strategies based on environmental interventions have been found to be cost-effective and can also yield benefits for the overall well-being of communities, according to a 2006 WHO report.[50] One of the key UN Millennium Development Goals is to halve the proportion of people without sustainable access to safe drinking water and sanitation by 2015. The global economic benefits of investments in meeting this target have been estimated to outweigh costs by a ratio of 8:1.[51] These benefits include gains in economic productivity, as well as savings in health care costs and in healthy life years lost. Reducing the disease burden of environmental risk factors would also contribute significantly to many of the other MDGs.

Poverty

While the standard criterion for defining poverty is level of income, it can also be defined as the deprivation of basic capabilities.[52] This perspective does not deny the fact that low income is one of the major aspects of poverty, but rather argues that lack of income can be a principal reason for capability deprivation. Furthermore, adherents of this perspective also argue that improvement of capability is likely to be a determinant of greater earning power, since enhanced capabilities would tend to expand a person's ability to be more productive and earn a higher income. This is of particular importance for the removal of income poverty. While improved education and health care can

---

[48] FAO (note 26), pp. 13, 29.
[49] FAO (note 26), p. 29.
[50] Prüss-Üstün and Corvalán (note 35).
[51] Prüss-Üstün and Corvalán (note 35), p. 67.
[52] Sen, A., *Development as Freedom* (Oxford University Press: Oxford, 1999), p. 87.

improve the quality of life directly, they can also increase a person's ability to earn an income.[53] Thus, in this perspective, the provision of education, health care and other entitlements has a more direct impact on poverty.

The poverty-reduction strategies of the Organisation for Economic Co-operation and Development (OECD) focus on broad-based growth and improved access to social services. Reduction of inequalities is also seen as important, since increased inequalities is the main reason why the number of poor people does not decrease in spite of economic growth in developing countries.[54] The OECD poverty-reduction strategy rests on the perception that poverty is caused by economic structures and availability and access to resources. The main policy interventions thus fall into three categories: pro-poor economic growth; empowerment, rights and pro-poor governance; and basic social services for human development. The goal of these interventions is to generate economic, political, human and social capabilities.[55]

Interdependence in preventive interventions

The above review shows that there is a significant overlap and interdependence between three major risk factors for death and disability—hunger, environment and poverty—and therefore also great synergies between the risk-reduction and prevention strategies for addressing these factors. This is apparent also in the Millennium Development Goals, which cover several of the interventions recommended for the reduction and prevention of these three risk factors: reduction of poverty, hunger, mortality rates for children under five, the incidence of major diseases (including HIV/AIDS and malaria), and the number of people without access to safe drinking water and sanitation, as well as increased environmental sustainability.[56] The annual cost of attaining these goals by 2015 for a typical low-income country has been estimated as $70–80 per capita in 2006, rising to $120–160 per capita in 2015.[57] While part of the required investment is expected to be financed through domestic resource mobilization, part will need to be financed through official development assistance (ODA) from foreign governments. This would require an increase in total global ODA for direct MDG support from $16 billion in 2002 to $73 billion in 2006 and $135 billion by 2015 (in constant 2003 dollars).[58]

[53] Sen (note 52), p. 90.

[54] Organisation for Economic Co-operation and Development (OECD), Development Assistance Committee, *The DAC Guidelines: Poverty Reduction* (OECD: Paris, 2001), URL <http://www.oecd.org/dac/guidelines/>, p. 31.

[55] Organisation for Economic Co-operation and Development (note 54), pp. 50–51.

[56] UN Millennium Development Goals (note 27).

[57] UN Millennium Project, *Investing in Development: A Practical Plan to Achieve the Millennium Development Goals* (Earthscan: London, 2005), URL <http://www.unmillenniumproject.org/reports/>, pp. 239–40.

[58] While total ODA has increased from $58.3 billion in 2002 to $106.8 billion in 2005 (at current prices and exchange rates), ODA for direct support of the MDGs fell short of the target according to the UN. For ODA data for 1996–2005 see Manning, R., *Development Co-operation Report 2006* (Organisation for Economic Co-operation and Development: Paris, 2007), URL <http://www.sourceoecd.org/developmentreport/>, 'Statistical annex', table 8, p. 146. For an evaluation of the progress towards the

This is a small investment compared with military expenditure, which was $1200 billion in 2006. Furthermore, this type of investment may also have an impact on the incidence of collective violence and on the consequences of violence.

III. The links between disease and violence prevention

Having established the synergies between different interventions to reduce the risk factors for death and disability from disease, the remaining question to address is the links between these and the prevention of death and disability from violence. This section provides an account of data and reports on violence from a public health perspective.

Violence as a cause of death and disability

According to WHO projections for 2005, 5.4 million deaths were caused by injuries (see table 7.2). Of these, unintentional injuries (accidents) accounted for 3.7 million deaths, the main cause being road traffic accidents, while intentional injuries (violence) accounted for 1.7 million deaths. Suicides accounted for slightly more than half of violence-related deaths, murder for roughly one-third and collective violence for about one-fifth.[59]

The WHO data show that most of the reported overall violence-related deaths occur in low-income countries (45 per cent in 2005) and lower-middle-income countries (38 per cent), while less than 10 per cent of all violence-related deaths occur in high-income countries.[60] Country income group has no strong influence on suicide rates, while murder rates are much lower in high-income countries than in low- and middle-income countries (see table 7.2). Comparing regions, the highest suicide rates are found in the Western Pacific and European regions, where suicides accounted for around 20 deaths per 100 000 people in 2005. The rates of murder show great variation between regions with very high rates for the African and American regions (20 and 18 deaths per 100 000, respectively) compared with all other regions, which all have fewer than 10 murders per 100 000 people.[61] Deaths caused by collective violence are concentrated in low-income countries. WHO pro-

---

MDGs, including analysis of the ODA, see United Nations, *The Millennium Development Goals Report 2006* (UN: New York, N.Y., 2006), URL <http://mdgs.un.org/unsd/mdg/>.

[59] Collective violence is defined by WHO as 'the instrumental use of violence by people who identify themselves as members of a group—whether this group is transitory or has a more permanent identity—against another group or set of individuals, in order to achieve political, economic or social objectives'. WHO, 'Collective violence', Fact sheet, Geneva, 2002, URL <http://www.who.int/violence_injury_prevention/violence/world_report/factsheets/en/>. On definitions of armed conflict and collective violence see appendix 2C in this volume.

[60] WHO, 'Projections of mortality and burden of disease 2006: projected deaths by income group, age, sex and cause for the years 2005, 2015 and 2030', Spreadsheet, Nov. 2006, URL <http://www.who.int/healthinfo/statistics/bodprojections2030/en/>.

[61] WHO (note 16).

jections for 2005 show that low-income countries account for 78 per cent of all deaths caused by collective violence.[62]

Data on violence-related deaths are highly uncertain for several reasons.[63] While deaths from self-inflicted and interpersonal violence are at least reported in official statistics on causes of death, the WHO data on deaths caused by collective violence are based on a variety of other sources.[64] The latter data have been criticized as being too high compared with estimates of deaths from armed conflicts in other sources.[65] Data on deaths from armed conflict and wars are compiled by researchers, are based on reports in the media and are selected according to definitions developed for this purpose.[66] However, the WHO data on collective violence have a broader coverage than just armed conflict in that they cover any form of instrumental use of violence by one group against another, including genocide.[67]

Nevertheless, it is likely that WHO underestimates the overall mortality caused by collective violence, owing to the linkages between violent conflict and health. The increased mortality rates of civilians during violent conflict, as mapped in a major study on violence and health, are usually caused by (*a*) injuries, (*b*) decreased access to food, leading to poor nutrition, (*c*) increased risk of communicable diseases, (*d*) diminished access to health services, (*e*) reduced health services, (*f*) reduced public health programmes, (*g*) poor environmental conditions and (*h*) psychosocial distress.[68] Thus, the impact of collective violence on death can be great in terms of mortality, morbidity and disability.

These linkages have been demonstrated in a major study on the impact of the war in Iraq on mortality rates. In a cooperative effort between Iraqi and US public health researchers and medical doctors, mortality rates were compared

---

[62] WHO (note 60).

[63] Krug, E. G. et al. (eds), *World Report on Violence and Health* (WHO: Geneva, 2002), URL <http://www.who.int/violence_injury_prevention/violence/world_report/en/>, p. 9.

[64] The WHO statistics uses country-specific estimates of war deaths from a variety of published and unpublished databases, primarily data from Project Ploughshares's *Armed Conflicts Report*, as cross-checked against historical and current estimates by other research groups. Mathers, Lopez and Murray (note 10), pp. 56, 65–66; and Mathers, C. D. and Loncar, D., 'Updated projections of global mortality and burden of disease, 2002–2030: data sources, methods and results', Working Paper, WHO, Geneva, Oct. 2005, revised Nov. 2006, URL <http://www.who.int/healthinfo/statistics/bodprojections2030/en/>.

[65] The basis for this criticism is that the WHO figures are 2–9 times higher than those reported in other data sets on armed conflicts and WHO has not provided a credible explanation for this difference. University of British Columbia, Human Security Centre, *Human Security Report 2005: War and Peace in the 21st Century* (Oxford University Press: New York, N.Y., 2005), URL <http://www.humansecurityreport.info/>, p. 30.

[66] On the availability of data on armed conflict see appendix 2C in this volume; and Melander, E., Öberg, M. and Hall, J., *The 'New Wars' Debate Revisited: An Empirical Evaluation of the Atrociousness of 'New Wars'*, Uppsala Peace Research Papers no. 9 (Uppsala University, Department of Peace and Conflict Research: Uppsala, 2006). An example of a data set on armed conflicts is that of the Uppsala Conflict Data Program, from which the data reported in appendix 2A in this volume are drawn. See the Uppsala Conflict Data Program website at URL <http://www.pcr.uu.se/research/UCDP/>.

[67] WHO (note 17), p. 79.

[68] Krug et al. (note 63), p. 225.

before and after the US-led coalition invasion in March 2003.[69] Significantly, by taking a public health approach this study shows the strong impact of violent conflict on overall mortality. It found that during the period March 2003–June 2006 about 655 000 more Iraqi people died than would be expected in a non-conflict situation. About 601 000 of these excess deaths had violent causes. These were distributed as follows: 56 per cent gunshots, 13 per cent car bombs, 14 per cent other explosives/ordnance, 13 per cent air strikes, and 4 per cent unknown and accidents. This study showed much higher casualties caused by the conflict than those reported through passive surveillance measures, such as the Iraq Body Count, which by October 2006 had recorded a range of 43 937–48 783 media-reported civilian deaths in Iraq resulting from the military intervention by the US-led coalition in March 2003.[70] In December 2005, US President George W. Bush said that approximately 30 000 Iraqis had died during the invasion and in the violence since.[71]

Violence: risk factors and instruments of prevention

Identification of risk factors for collective violence is an extremely complex task. While WHO has undertaken to do this, based on studies by researchers in the field, the resulting list of risk factors should be regarded as a preliminary contribution. These are: (a) a lack of democratic processes and unequal access to power; (b) social inequality marked by grossly unequal distribution of, and access to, resources; (c) control by a single group of valuable natural resources, such as diamonds, oil, timber and drugs; and (d) rapid demographic change that outstrips the capacity of the state to provide essential services and job opportunities.[72] Based on these risk factors, WHO's recommended measures to prevent collective violence and lessen its impacts include: (a) reducing poverty, both in absolute and relative terms, and ensuring that development assistance is targeted so as to make the greatest possible impact on poverty; (b) reducing inequality between groups in society; (c) reducing access to weapons; and (d) ensuring that promotion and application of internationally agreed treaties, including those relating to human rights. More specific measures include investing in health development. This is based on the assessment that a strong emphasis on social services can help maintain social cohesion and stability and that early manifestations of situations that can lead to conflicts can often be detected in the health sector.[73]

---

[69] Burnham, G. et al., 'Mortality after the 2003 invasion of Iraq: a cross-sectional cluster sample survey', *The Lancet*, vol. 368, no. 9545 (21 Oct. 2006), pp. 1421–28.

[70] Thieren, M., 'Deaths in Iraq: how many, and why it matters', Open Democracy, 18 Oct. 2006, URL <http://www.opendemocracy.net/conflict-iraq/iraq_deaths_4011.jsp>. See also the Iraq Body Count website at URL <http://www.iraqbodycount.org/>.

[71] The White House, 'President discusses war on terror and upcoming Iraqi elections', Press release, Washington, DC, 12 Dec. 2005, URL <http://www.whitehouse.gov/news/releases/2005/12/>. See also King, N., 'Iraqi death toll exceeds 600,000, study estimates', *Wall Street Journal*, 11 Oct. 2006, p. A4.

[72] Krug et al. (note 63), p. 220.

[73] Krug et al. (note 63), pp. 228–29.

The risk factors and recommended prevention instruments for collective violence identified by WHO are confirmed by studies on armed conflicts. There is general agreement that such violence is related to both socio-economic factors—local as well as global—and political factors, such as local governance and the global world order. This conclusion is independent of the perspective—such as the 'new wars' paradigm or more locally rooted per-spectives[74]—from which the new dynamics of internal collective violence in Africa and elsewhere are studied. Furthermore, armed conflict has a strongly detrimental impact on the economy and on development, which increases the risk of renewed violent conflict, catching affected countries in a 'conflict trap'.[75]

Implications for security assessments

Some of these risk factors for collective violence and armed conflict and the recommended prevention strategies overlap with those for disease. Collective violence also has an indirect impact on death and disability through its effects on disease, access to health services and food security. Thus, the relative util-ity of devoting resources directly to reduce human vulnerability to disease, by investment in measures to reduce hunger, bad environment and poverty, is potentially doubled: it limits unnecessary deaths from disease while giving populations a better chance of survival when exposed to the consequences of violent conflict. Because of this double utility, potential belligerents in an intra-state conflict, such as the government or rebels, might find themselves less prone to seek violent solutions to internal issues because the popular legitimacy of the regime will be heightened, and so it will be more difficult to mobilize people to fight against it.

More generally, the strong interlinkages between and within risk factors and prevention strategies suggest that there is potentially great scope for security policies that cover a broader spectrum of threats. Such broad policies, extend-ing beyond the normal bounds of what is traditionally considered security policy, may also bring reinforced benefits for traditional security concerns. This is where economists can contribute to the design of security policy, at least in the selection of its constituent elements and the balance between them. Such contributions, which include discussion of trade-offs over a broad range of security objects and threats, are already beginning to emerge.[76] However,

[74] On the new-wars paradigm see Kaldor, M., *New and Old Wars: Organized Violence in a Global Era* (Polity Press: Cambridge, 1999); and Duffield, M., *Global Governance and the New Wars: the Merging of Development and Security* (Zed Books: London, 2001). For a more locally rooted per-spective see Mkandawire, T., 'The terrible toll of post-colonial "rebel movements" in Africa: towards an explanation of the violence against the peasantry', *Journal of Modern African Studies*, vol. 40, no. 2 (June 2002), pp. 181–215.

[75] Stewart, F. and Fitzgerald, V. (eds), *War and Underdevelopment*, vol. 1, *The Economic and Social Consequences of Conflict* (Oxford University Press: Oxford, 2001); and Collier, P. et al., *Breaking the Conflict Trap: Civil War and Development Policy*, World Bank Policy Research Report (Oxford University Press: New York, N.Y., June 2003), URL <http://econ.worldbank.org/prr/>.

[76] See e.g. Brück, T., 'An economic analysis of security policies', *Defence and Peace Economics*, vol. 16, no. 5 (Oct. 2005), pp. 375–89.

for cost–benefit analysis of this cross-cutting type to become a reality, much better data are required, as well as an expansion of risk analysis of the type conducted for and by WHO to all important areas of security concern.

IV. Conclusions

This chapter reviews risks to human lives based on epidemiological studies and according to a public health perspective, in which risk factors are identified based on observed historical patterns. By focusing on actual outcomes in terms of death and disability, high-probability negative impacts on human lives are brought into focus, while low-probability future events are neglected. The advantage of using this type of analysis is that it is based on data on what actually kills and disables people today, and the risk factors behind these deaths and disabilities. Its major disadvantage, in particular when related to security problems, is that it does not include potential future risks and threats to human lives which, although they have had a low incidence in the past or may even have a very low probability in the future, are still associated with grave potential outcomes if they occur. This applies to a wide range of security threats, such as attacks by weapons of mass destruction, terrorist incidents, large-scale conventional war, major disasters and incremental climate change. While it is not argued that this type of risk analysis can replace security analysis based on subjective expert assessments of future threats and risks, it is nonetheless one important tool among others for assessing risks to human lives.

The data and risk assessments reported on here inspire two major observations. The first is the simple observation that most of the risks to human life reviewed in this chapter cannot be reduced by the use of weapons—or military expenditure generally. Most risks to human lives identified in this chapter require non-military preventive interventions. The big risks to human lives include hunger, environmental factors and poverty. Few of these risks can be prevented or managed using military means. From this it can be deduced that, if a global security policy existed, and if the objective of that policy were to save lives globally, then a cost-effective approach would include the implementation of the type of recommended health interventions cited in this chapter. For an overall annual investment of around $57 billion in health interventions, an estimated 8 million lives could be saved each year, many of which would be those of children. The cost of attaining the Millennium Development Goals has been estimated at $135 billion in annual official development assistance for direct MDG support by 2015. These levels of investment are small in comparison with the level of military expenditure, amounting to $1200 billion in 2006.

This point can be regarded as wishful thinking or a normative statement, but there are other reasons for shifting priorities in resource allocation for security objectives, which is the second observation that arises from this review. The synergies between risk factors and prevention strategies for disease and for collective violence suggest that there is an overlap in the agendas of freedom from want and freedom from fear. These synergies have theoretical implications for different conceptions of security. The overlaps between the risk factors in different areas open up the possibility of trade-offs between different types of security strategies. In addressing one type of security threat, other types of security threat can be considered, so that one way of addressing the threats does not have a negative impact on another type. Finally, there is an economic dimension to this line of reasoning, since it also has implications for resource allocation. Risk analysis in combination with cost–benefit analysis can help decision makers to develop more cost-efficient security strategies by exploiting some of these trade-offs and the dual utility offered by some risk-reduction and prevention instruments.

While economic scarcity and competition for resources are potential sources of conflict and violence,[77] using the world's resources constructively to address the kind of issues set out in the MDGs—including by transfers from the richer to those more in need—is an inherently cooperative activity that is likely to improve human survival directly as well as strengthen international security indirectly.

---

[77] On the potential for conflicts over sources of energy see chapter 6 in this volume.

8. Military expenditure

PETTER STÅLENHEIM, CATALINA PERDOMO and
ELISABETH SKÖNS

I. Introduction

World military expenditure in 2006 is estimated to have totalled $1204 billion
in current prices.[1] This represents an increase of 3.5 per cent in real terms
since 2005 and has raised average spending per capita from $173 to $177 in
constant (2005) prices and exchange rates and to $184 in current prices.[2] Mili-
tary spending amounted to 2.5 per cent of world gross domestic product
(GDP).[3]

This chapter analyses military expenditure in 2006 and sets it in the context
of the main developments during the past decade. Section II analyses trends in
military expenditure by region and in the 15 countries with the highest military expenditure. Section III looks at priorities in government spending and
compares allocations for education, health care and the military. Section IV
analyses military expenditure in the United States, assesses its economic
impact and describes some alternative ways of viewing US security spending
as a whole. Section V reviews recent developments region by region and sets
each region's military expenditure in an economic and security context.
Section VI contains brief conclusions.

Appendix 8A presents SIPRI data on military expenditure for 167 countries
for the 10-year period 1997–2006. World and regional totals in constant
(2005) US dollars are provided in table 8A.1. Data for individual countries are
provided in three formats: in local currency at current prices (table 8A.2); in
constant (2005) US dollars (table 8A.3); and as a share of GDP (table 8A.4).
Appendix 8B presents spending by members of the North Atlantic Treaty
Organization (NATO) for the period 2000–2006, disaggregated into spending
on equipment and personnel. Appendix 8C describes the sources and methods

---

[1] This equals $1158 billion in constant (2005) prices and exchange rates. Unless otherwise stated,
military expenditure figures in this chapter are given in US dollars at constant (2005) prices and
exchange rates. In *SIPRI Yearbook 2006*, 2003 was used as the base year for comparison of data across
years. Owing to a sharp fall in the value of the US dollar between 2003 and 2005, the change of base
year has caused a change in world ranking of military spenders and in their shares of total world military
expenditure. The effects of this change of base years are discussed further in appendix 8C.

[2] These per capita averages are based on estimated total world populations of 6540 million in 2006
and 6465 million in 2005. United Nations Population Fund (UNFPA), *State of the World Population
2006* (UNFPA: New York, N.Y., 2006); and United Nations Population Fund (UNFPA), *State of the
World Population 2005* (UNFPA: New York, N.Y., 2005)—both available at URL <http://www.unfpa.
org/swp/>.

[3] This share of GDP is based on a projected figure for world GDP in 2006 of $47 767 billion at
market exchange rates. International Monetary Fund (IMF), *World Economic Outlook, September 2006:
Financial Systems and Economic Cycles* (IMF: Washington, DC, 2006), URL <http://www.imf.org/
external/pubs/ft/weo/2006/02/>, Statistical appendix, table 1, 'Summary of world output', p. 189.

Table 8.1. World and regional military expenditure estimates, 1997–2006

Figures are in US$ b., at constant (2005) prices and exchange rates. Figures in italics are percentages. Figures do not always add up to totals because of the conventions of rounding.

Region[a]	1997	1998	1999	2000	2001	2002	2003	2004	2005	2006	Change 97–06
Africa	**10.3**	**11.1**	**12.3**	**13.0**	**13.2**	**14.4**	**14.0**	**14.8**	**15.3**	**(15.5)**	**(+51)**
North	4.4	4.6	4.6	5.0	5.2	5.6	5.7	6.2	6.5	6.5	+47
Sub-Saharan	5.8	6.5	7.7	8.0	8.0	8.9	8.3	8.6	8.8	9.0	+55
Americas	**375**	**367**	**368**	**381**	**387**	**431**	**481**	**522**	**549**	**575**	**+53**
Caribbean	..	..	..	..	..	..	..	..	..	..	..
Central	3.7	3.6	3.8	3.9	3.9	3.7	3.8	3.5	3.5	3.5	−5
North	347	340	341	354	357	399	453	493	518	542	+56
South	24.1	23.2	22.5	23.3	26.3	27.4	24.5	25.1	27.4	29.1	+21
Asia, Oceania	**131**	**132**	**136**	**139**	**146**	**153**	**160**	**167**	**176**	**185**	**+41**
Central	0.6	(0.6)	0.6	..	(0.7)	(0.7)	(0.8)	(0.9)	(1.0)	(1.1)	(+73)
East	99.6	100	100	103	109	116	121	126	131	138	+39
Oceania	10.9	11.4	11.9	11.8	12.2	12.7	13.2	13.8	14.3	15.0	+37
South	19.6	20.2	22.6	23.4	24.2	24.3	25.0	25.8	29.0	30.7	+57
Europe	**283**	**275**	**280**	**287**	**287**	**294**	**302**	**306**	**309**	**310**	**+10**
Central	14.8	14.7	14.4	14.4	14.9	15.2	15.7	15.7	16.0	16.7	+13
Eastern	23.7	15.6	15.9	21.4	23.4	25.8	27.6	28.9	34.2	38.3	+61
Western	244	245	249	251	249	253	259	262	258	255	+5
Middle East	**46.1**	**49.3**	**48.9**	**55.8**	**58.4**	**55.9**	**58.0**	**62.8**	**70.5**	**72.5**	**+57**
World	**844**	**834**	**844**	**876**	**892**	**948**	**1016**	**1072**	**1119**	**1158**	**+37**
Change (%)		−1.2	1.2	3.8	1.9	6.2	7.2	5.5	4.4	3.5	

( ) = Total based on country data accounting for less than 90 per cent of the regional total; . . = Available data account for less than 60 per cent of the regional total.

[a] For the country coverage of the regions see appendix 8A, table 8A.1. Some countries are excluded because of lack of data or of consistent time series data—Africa excludes Angola, Benin, Equatorial Guinea and Somalia; Americas excludes Cuba, Guyana, Haiti and Trinidad and Tobago; Asia excludes North Korea, Myanmar (Burma) and Viet Nam; and the Middle East excludes Qatar. World totals exclude all these countries.

Source: Appendix 8A, tables 8A.1 and 8A.3.

for SIPRI's military expenditure data, and appendix 8D provides statistics on governments' reporting of their military expenditure to SIPRI and the United Nations.

II. Regional trends and major spenders

SIPRI estimates of military expenditure presented here are likely to be under-estimates. There are two basic reasons for this: (*a*) the estimates of world and regional totals do not include data for all countries, due to lack of consistent data; and (*b*) the country data reflect official information as reported by governments, which sometimes understate their actual level of military spend-ing. In addition to the prevalent practice of governments concealing smaller or larger parts of their military outlays, military spending sometimes takes place outside the control of the government. This can be because the armed forces

themselves have income from non-government sources to use at their own discretion or because of significant military spending by non-state actors, such as
rebel groups.

The world military expenditure in 2006 of $1158 billion (at constant 2005
prices and exchange rates) represents an increase in real terms of 3.5 per cent
compared to 2005 and of 37 per cent over the 10-year period 1997–2006 (see
table 8.1). The trend in world military expenditure is highly influenced by US
military expenditure. In 2006 the $24 billion real-terms increase in US spend-
ing accounted for 62 per cent of the $39 billion total increase in world military
expenditure.

The region where military expenditure increased the most in relative terms
in 2006 was Eastern Europe, with a 12 per cent increase. In two regions military expenditure decreased in 2006: these were Western Europe, with a
decrease of 1.5 per cent, and Central America, with a decrease of 0.7 per cent.

Over the 10-year period 1997–2006, Central Asia, with its 73 per cent
increase, had by far the highest increase among world regions. The estimate of
total Central Asian military expenditure is somewhat unreliable because of
lack of data for certain countries and also because of the lack of detail in the
data that are available. Military spending in Eastern Europe and the Middle
East also increased greatly over the decade, by 61 and 57 per cent, respectively. Central America was the only region where military spending decreased
over this 10-year period, with a fall of 5 per cent.

Table 8.2 lists the 15 countries with the highest military spending in 2006 as
measured in 2005 prices and exchange rates.[4] These 15 countries account for
83 per cent of total world military spending, while the top 5 countries alone
account for 63 per cent. With its 46 per cent share of total world military
expenditure, the USA is by far the biggest spender, followed at a distance by
the United Kingdom, France, China and Japan, which each account for
4–5 per cent.[5] Military expenditure per capita varies greatly between states.
While some rich states with an abundance of resources and relatively small
populations can afford to spend more than $1500 per inhabitant, poorer coun-
tries and more populous ones often spend less then $50 per capita. However,
the economic burden of spending on the military relative to what a country can
afford is better captured by expressing military expenditure as a share of GDP,
as presented in table 8A.4 in appendix 8A.

Table 8.2 also provides a ranking of countries based on military spending in
dollars converted using gross national product-level purchasing power parity
(PPP) rates. This ranking is presented as an illustration of a major problem

---

[4] The change in base year from 2003 to 2005 has affected the relative world rankings. See note 1 and
appendix 8C.

[5] When (as in *SIPRI Yearbook 2006*) military expenditure is calculated using 2003 as the base year,
US military expenditure in 2005 accounts for 48% of the world total. Calculated using 2005 prices and
exchange rates, US spending in 2005 accounts for only 45% of the total. This difference is due to the
depreciation of the relative value of the US dollar between the two base years.

Table 8.2. The 15 countries with the highest military expenditure in 2006 in market exchange rate terms and purchasing power parity terms

Spending figures are in US$, at constant (2005) prices and exchange rates.

Military expenditure in MER dollar terms					Military expenditure in PPP dollar terms[a]		
		Spending ($ b.)	Spending per capita ($)	World share (%)			Spending ($ b.)
Rank	Country			Spending	Popul.	Rank	Country	
1	USA	528.7	1 756	46	5	1	USA	528.7
2	UK	59.2	990	5	1	2	China	[188.2]
3	France	53.1	875	5	1	3	India	114.3
4	China	[49.5]	[37]	[4]	20	4	Russia	[82.8]
5	Japan	43.7	341	4	2	5	UK	51.4
Sub-total top 5		**734.2**		**63**	**29**	**Sub-total top 5**		**965.5**
6	Germany	37.0	447	3	1	6	France	46.6
7	Russia	[34.7]	[244]	[3]	2	7	Saudi Arabia[b, c]	36.4
8	Italy	29.9	514	3	1	8	Japan	35.2
9	Saudi Arabia[b, c]	29.0	1 152	3	–	9	Brazil	32.0
10	India	23.9	21	2	17	10	Germany	31.2
Sub-total top 10		**888.7**		**77**	**50**	**Sub-total top 10**		**1 147.0**
11	Korea, South	21.9	455	2	1	11	South Korea	30.1
12	Australia[c]	13.8	676	1	–	12	Iran[b]	28.6
13	Canada[c]	13.5	414	1	–	13	Italy	28.6
14	Brazil	13.4	71	1	3	14	Turkey	20.2
15	Spain	12.3	284	1	1	15	Pakistan	15.6
Sub-total top 15		**963.7**		**83**	**56**	**Sub-total top 15**		**1 270.2**
World		**1 158**	**177**	**100**	**100**	**World**		..

MER = market exchange rate; PPP = purchasing power parity; [ ] = estimated figure.

[a] The figures in PPP dollar terms are converted at PPP rates (for 2005), calculated by the World Bank, based on comparisons of gross national product.

[b] Data for Iran and Saudi Arabia include expenditure for public order and safety and might be slight overestimates.

[c] The populations of Australia, Canada and Saudi Arabia each constitute less than 0.5% of the total world population.

Sources: **Military expenditure**: Appendix 8A; **PPP rates**: World Bank, *World Development Report 2006: Equity and Development* (World Bank: Washington, DC, 2005), URL <http://econ.worldbank.org/wdr/>, table 1, pp. 292–93, and table 5, p. 300; **2006 population**: United Nations Population Fund (UNFPA), *State of the World Population 2006* (UNFPA: New York, N.Y., 2006), URL <http://unfpa.org/swp/>.

encountered in international comparison of economic data—the choice of conversion method has a major impact on the figures.[6]

---

[6] On the use of PPP rates in international comparisons of military expenditure see Ward, M., 'International comparisons of military expenditures: issues and challenges of using purchasing power parities', *SIPRI Yearbook 2006: Armaments, Disarmament and International Security* (Oxford University Press: Oxford, 2006), pp. 369–86.

III. Military and social budget priorities

Data on military and social expenditures and comparisons between them are often used in order to assess how governments prioritize military and social goals. Such data are used in domestic policy debates in order to assess government policies and the use of taxpayers' money, and by individuals and groups interested in assessing how their government addresses their security and social needs. The latter has become more relevant with the emergence of security concepts that focus on the security of the individual, rather than on the security of the state.[7]

National and international actors also use data on a country's military and social expenditures for various types of decisions. For example, some donor countries continue to use military expenditure data as a basis for their assessments of recipient countries' commitment to development when granting economic aid.[8] Nevertheless, the Development Assistance Committee of the Organisation for Economic Co-operation and Development (OECD) recommends that donor states focus less on levels of military spending and instead assess the process by which that level is decided.[9] Another example is when licensing authorities in arms exporting countries use data on social expenditure as one of several criteria for their decisions. According to criterion 8 of the European Union (EU) Code of Conduct on Arms Exports, EU member states should consider the recipient country's relative levels of military and social expenditures in order to establish whether a proposed export of arms could 'seriously hamper the sustainable development of the recipient country'.[10]

This section looks at the data on government spending on the military, education and health sectors that are available in sources of international statistics. Although most users of these data look at figures for individual countries, it is also interesting to aggregate the data by country income groups since this allows spending by a specific country to be compared with the average for its income group. This section presents available data on average military and social expenditures as shares of GDP for low-, middle- and high-income countries. It continues by describing some of the considerations that should be taken into account when using figures on military and social expenditures.

---

[7] See chapter 7 in this volume.

[8] See Omitoogun, W. and Sköns, E., 'Military expenditure data: a 40-year overview', *SIPRI Yearbook 2006* (note 6), p. 290.

[9] Organisation for Economic Co-operation and Development (OECD), Development Assistance Committee (DAC), *Security System Reform and Governance*, DAC Guidelines and Reference Series (OECD: Paris, 2005), URL <http://www.oecd.org/dac/conflict/ssr/>, p. 37.

[10] The European Union Code of Conduct on Arms Exports was adopted at the Brussels European Council on 5 June 1998 and is available at URL <http://consilium.europa.eu/uedocs/cmsUpload/08675r2 en8.pdf>. See also Bauer, S and Bromley, M., *The European Union Code of Conduct on Arms Exports: Improving the Annual Report*, SIPRI Policy Paper no. 8 (SIPRI: Stockholm, 2004), URL <http://www. sipri.org/>.

Table 8.3. Military and social expenditure priorities, select countries, 1999–2003[a]

Figures are averages of the percentage of each country's gross domestic product devoted to each sector

Income group/ Sector[b]	1999	2000	2001	2002	2003	Average, 1999–2003
Low-income countries						
Military	2.7	2.7	2.5	2.5	2.3	2.5
Education	3.4	3.5	3.8	4.0	4.0	3.8
Health	1.8	2.0	2.0	2.2	2.2	2.1
Middle-income countries						
Military	1.9	1.9	2.0	1.9	1.9	1.9
Education	4.8	4.5	4.7	4.6	4.7	4.7
Health	3.3	3.3	3.4	3.4	3.4	3.4
High-income countries						
Military	2.1	2.0	2.0	2.0	2.0	2.0
Education	5.5	5.4	5.6	5.7	5.9	5.6
Health	5.8	5.8	6.1	6.2	6.4	6.1

[a] The countries covered are those for which data are available for at least 2 of the 3 sectors throughout the 5-year period, totalling 82 of the 167 countries in the SIPRI Military Expenditure Database. The coverage is uneven between income groups: 24 high-income countries out of 37 countries; 45 middle-income countries out of 81; and 13 low-income countries out of 49 countries in the SIPRI database. In addition, although data were available for Eritrea (a low-income country), it has nevertheless been excluded as a statistical outlier.

[b] The data on education and health expenditures refer to general government expenditure, including central, regional and local government. Data on health expenditure include social security contributions and funding from external resources.

Sources: **Military expenditure**: Appendix 8A; **Education expenditure**: UNESCO Institute for Statistics (UIS), UIS Global Education Database, accessed 18 Jan. 2006, URL <http://stats.uis.unesco.org/>; **Health expenditure**: World Health Organization (WHO), *The World Health Report* 2004–2006 (WHO: Geneva, 2004–2006), URL <http://www.who.int/whr/en/>.

Data on military and social expenditures

A national budgeting process involves the allocation of public funds to various categories of public spending, subject to the constraints of the size of the total budget and the size of the national economy.[11] Two of the main areas competing for resources are the military and social sectors.

The purpose of military spending is to provide the military defence of, principally, a country's national security (both its state interest and territory) and, ultimately, security of its citizens. The purpose of social expenditure is to provide social services to the citizens of a country. This often involves significant redistribution of resources between income groups and generations in order to

[11] In the standard neoclassical model, nation states are represented as rational agents which maximize a welfare function for their citizens depending on the security and economic situations and subject to budget constraint. Smith, R., 'The demand for military expenditure', eds K. Hartley and T. Sandler, *Handbook of Defense Economics*, vol. 1 (North-Holland: Amsterdam, 1995), p. 71.

attain government social policy goals. Social expenditure is a broad category, covering support for education, health care, institutional care for the elderly and disabled, retirement pensions, as well as other types of state subsidy.[12] Only two types of social expenditure are considered here—for the education and health sectors. This is common practice since these are the categories of spending for which it is possible to find roughly comparable data for a large number of countries.[13] Moreover, providing education and health care are two of the most basic requirements when attending to social needs.[14]

Table 8.3 presents data on the average proportion of national GDP spent by governments on the military, education and health sectors by country income group. Spending as a proportion of national GDP is used to show the relative burden of the expenditure on the national economy. The table covers the period 1999–2003, which is the most recent five-year period for which such data are available. Data are organized into three country income groups in order to illustrate the pattern for and differences between these three types of countries. Data are not available for all countries in each income group. In particular, data are available for a higher proportion of high-income countries than low- and middle-income countries, and thus the figures for the former group are more representative than those for the latter groups. Caution should therefore be exercised when using these figures since the averages could differ if data for more countries were available.

Three main observations arise from table 8.3. First, the high- and middle-income countries prioritized spending on education and health care over military expenditure during the five-year period 1999–2003, both on average for the period and for each year in the period. In contrast, the low-income group prioritized spending on the military over health expenditure but prioritized expenditure on education over both. Second, the higher the level of income, the higher the proportion of GDP devoted to social spending. While low-income countries spent on average 5.9 per cent of GDP on health care and education, middle- and high-income countries spent 8.1 per cent and 11.7 per cent, respectively. Finally, the share of GDP spent on the military remained roughly constant at around 2 per cent in both high- and middle-income countries during the five-year period, while in low-income countries it declined somewhat. At the same time spending on education and health care as a share

---

[12] Organisation for Economic Co-operation and Development (OECD), '1980–1998, 20 years of social expenditure: the OECD database', Paris, URL <http://www.oecd.org/dataoecd/3/63/2084281.pdf>.

[13] See Gupta, S. et al., *Review of Social Issues in IMF-Supported Programs*, International Monetary Fund (IMF) Occasional Paper no. 191 (IMF: Washington, DC, Jan. 2000); Baqir, R., 'Social sector spending in a panel of countries', IMF Working Paper no. WP/02/35, IMF, Washington, DC, Feb. 2002, URL <http://www.imf.org/external/pubs/cat/longres.cfm?sk=15564>; and Martin, R. and Segura-Ubiergo, A., 'Social spending in IMF-supported programs', Independent Evaluation Office (IEO) Background Paper no. BP/04/1, International Monetary Fund, Washington, DC, Apr. 2004, URL <http://www.imf.org/external/np/ieo/pap.asp>.

[14] United Nations Development Programme (UNDP), *Human Development Report 2005: International Cooperation at a Crossroads—Aid, Trade and Security in an Unequal World* (UNDP: New York, N.Y., 2005), URL <http://hdr.undp.org/reports/global/2005/>, pp. 18–19. See also the definition of social opportunities in Sen, A., *Development as Freedom* (Oxford University Press: Oxford, 1999), pp. 11, 295.

of GDP increased in high- and low-income countries but remained relatively stable in middle-income countries.

These average figures offer a rough picture of typical national relative priorities between military and social expenditures and could be used to compare the spending of a specific country with the average for its income group. This must be done with due consideration of the weaknesses in the data related to the limited sample of countries and other factors described below.

The utility of the expenditure data

Spending figures are useful only if their limitations are considered and if they are put into a broader context. Three limitations are considered here.

Principally, data on military and social expenditure are only a measure of input and do not necessarily indicate the level of output, in this case military capability and standards of education and health, since the output also depends on a range of other factors. What the spending figures do indicate are government priorities. However, such priorities need to be analysed in their political, social and economic contexts in order to establish their popular legitimacy and if they correspond to the relative needs of these sectors.

Second, if the main purpose of the data is to assess government expenditure priorities, in principle only public expenditure is relevant, and not private expenditure. However, the level of private expenditure may have an impact on the level of public expenditure. In some countries there is a significant amount of private expenditure on social services.[15] Such large private provision of social services can be caused by, for example, shortcomings in public sector provision of services or the interest of the private sector in offering broader choices of services such as religious or elite schools.[16] In some countries, funding from the private and public sectors has become increasingly mixed, with some public resources being allocated to finance the provision of services by the private sector and with some private funding of public social services.[17] Similarly, even though the military sector is often perceived as belonging exclusively to the public sector, non-state groups also have significant armed forces, which are thus financed by non-government sources.

A third complication is that, while data-collecting organizations strive to obtain data which conform as closely as possible to their definitions, in practice countries report data compiled according to their own definitions. In many cases, these national definitions differ widely from the definitions of the data-collecting organizations, as well as between countries. It is therefore difficult for governments to fill in standardized questionnaires such as SIPRI's on military expenditure, UNESCO's on education expenditure and the World

---

[15] E.g. in Chile, China and Paraguay private expenditure constitutes as much as 40% of total education expenditure. UNESCO and Organisation for Economic Co-operation and Development (OECD), World Education Indicators Programme, *Financing Education: Investments and Returns*, Analysis of the World Education Indicators, 2002 edn (OECD: Paris, 2003), URL <http://www.uis.unesco.org/ev.php?ID=5245_201&ID2=DO_TOPIC>, p. 102.

[16] UNESCO and Organisation for Economic Co-operation and Development (note 15), pp. 95–96.

[17] UNESCO and Organisation for Economic Co-operation and Development (note 15), p. 94.

Health Organization's on health expenditure. Furthermore, lack of sufficient information means that these organizations cannot make their own calculations in accordance with their standardized definitions, and so problems with the comparability of the data also need to be considered.

IV. The United States

Military expenditure trends

US military expenditure has increased significantly since 2001, when the post-September 2001 'global war on terrorism' was launched by the US Administration of President George W. Bush. Between financial years (FYs) 2001 and 2006, outlays by the US Department of Defense (DOD) increased by 53 per cent in real terms, while the increase in outlays for national defence (a functional category that includes non-DOD defence-related activities) was 49 per cent (see table 8.4).[18] These increases are the result primarily of the massive supplemental appropriations made under the heading 'global war on terrorism', mostly to fund military operations in Afghanistan, Iraq and elsewhere.

The largest relative increase was in outlays for research, development, test and evaluation (RDT&E), rising by 58 per cent in real terms between FYs 2001 and 2006, while the increases in funding for operations and maintenance and for procurement were both 47 per cent. Military construction, military personnel and family housing received below average increases.

Appropriations for the 'global war on terrorism'

Between September 2001 and June 2006, the US Government provided a total of $432 billion in annual and supplemental appropriations under the heading 'global war on terrorism' (see table 8.5).[19] Of this, $381 billion was provided for military operations—$254 billion for the operation in Iraq and $128 billion for those in Afghanistan, the Philippines, the Horn of Africa and elsewhere. Of this, the total already obligated (i.e. commissioned to particular projects) by June 2006 amounted to about $287 billion for foreign operations (excluding classified activities),[20] of which $227 billion was for military operations in Iraq and $60 billion for operations in Afghanistan and elsewhere; an additional

---

[18] According to SIPRI data, US military expenditure increased by 53% in real terms between 2001 and 2006. This is higher than the rate of increase reported in official US data because of the method of conversion into constant dollars. While SIPRI uses the consumer price index (CPI) for price conversion for all countries, the US official figures are converted using military-specific deflators. Thus, the SIPRI data show the trend in the purchasing power of the military budget had it instead been spent on typical consumer goods and services, while the US official data show the trend in its purchasing power for military goods and services. The nominal change is the same for the two series.

[19] In US Government documents the heading used is 'Global War on Terror'.

[20] Funding of classified 'global war on terrorism' activities is not included in the DOD reports. It has been estimated by the US Congressional Budget Office to be at least $25 billion. US Government Accountability Office (GAO), *Global War on Terrorism*, Report GAO-07-76 (GAO: Washington, DC, Nov. 2006), URL <http://www.gao.gov/docdblite/details.php?rptno=GAO-07-76>, p. 10.

Table 8.4. Trends in US military expenditure, financial years 2001–2006

Figures are in US$ b. and are for financial years (running for 12 months from 1 Oct. of the previous year).

	2001	2002	2003	2004	2005	2006[a]	Change, 2001–2006 (%)
Outlays in constant (FY 2007) prices							
DOD outlays[b]							
Military personnel	91.8	101.6	120.6	124.2	134.8	119.5	*30*
O&M	133.9	152.3	173.0	192.0	199.5	197.4	*47*
Procurement	61.5	69.4	74.6	82.1	86.2	90.7	*47*
RDT&E	45.7	49.5	58.5	65.5	68.8	72.3	*58*
Military construction	5.6	5.7	6.4	6.8	5.6	7.5	*34*
Family housing	3.9	4.2	4.2	4.2	3.9	3.9	*0*
Other	1.2	0.7	1.6	1.8	1.6	2.4	*100*
Sub-total[b]	**343.6**	**382.0**	**435.7**	**476.6**	**500.4**	**493.7**	*44*
Anticipated supplemental appropriations[c]	..	..	..	..	..	30.8	
Total DOD outlays	**343.6**	**382.0**	**435.7**	**476.6**	**500.4**	**524.5**	*53*
Outlays in constant (FY 2000) prices							
National defence[d]	297.2	329.4	365.3	397.3	419.8	443.1	*49*
Outlays in current prices[d]							
DOD, military	290.3	332.0	387.3	436.5	474.2	512.1	
DOE, military	12.9	14.8	16.0	16.6	18.0	18.7	
Other military-related	1.6	1.8	1.6	2.8	3.1	5.1	
Total national defence	**304.9**	**348.6**	**404.9**	**455.9**	**495.3**	**535.9**	

DOD = Department of Defense; DOE = Department of Energy; FY = financial year; O&M = operations and maintenance; RDT&E = research, development, test and evaluation.

[a] Figures for 2006 are for budgeted, not actual, expenditure. These are estimated figures, based on requests for budget authority.

[b] Figures for DOD outlays are from data released by the DOD in Mar. 2006 which do not include future emergency funding for FY 2006.

[c] This figure is based on data from the US Office of Management and Budget (OMB), which include anticipated funding for the 'global war on terrorism' for FY 2006.

[d] This data series from the OMB includes outlays from 'anticipated funding for the global war on terrorism' for FY 2006.

Sources: **DOD outlays**: US Department of Defense (DOD), Office of the Under Secretary of Defense (Comptroller), *National Defense Budget Estimates for FY 2007* (DOD: Washington, DC, Mar. 2006), URL <http://www.defenselink.mil/comptroller/defbudget/fy2007/>, table 6-11, p. 133; **Supplemental appropriations and national defence outlays**: US Office of Management and Budget, *Historical Tables: Budget of the United States Government, Fiscal Year 2007* (Government Printing Office: Washington, DC, 2006), URL <http://www.whitehouse.gov/omb/budget/fy2007/>, tables 3.2, 6.1.

$27.7 billion was obligated for US homeland defence activities.[21] Most of this funding was provided through supplemental appropriations outside the annual defence budget.

Total 'global war on terrorism' funding for FY 2006 was approximately $114.4 billion, of which $15.9 billion was for military personnel, $55.9 billion for operations and maintenance, $21.5 billion for procurement, and $21.1 billion for RDT&E and military construction.[22]

The US Congressional Budget Office has projected the costs of military and diplomatic operations in Iraq for the period FYs 2007–2016 under two scenarios specified by the US House of Representatives Budget Committee.[23] In the first scenario, assuming the removal of all US troops from Iraq by the end of 2009, the total cost over this 10-year period was projected as being $166 billion for the US military (in addition to the $254 billion already appropriated for the period FYs 2003–2006) and $36 billion for the US costs for diplomatic operations, Iraqi security forces, foreign aid and ex-combatants' programmes (in addition to $37 billion for the period FYs 2003–2006). This would bring the total cost for the period 2003–16 to $493 billion. In the second scenario, assuming a reduction in the number of US troops in Iraq to 40 000 by 2010, the cost for military operations in 2007–16 is projected to be $368 billion, with other costs of $38 billion, bringing the total cost for US military and other operations in Iraq to $697 billion from the beginning of the war in March 2003 to the end of FY 2016.

Future spending

The Bush Administration's budget request in February 2006 to the US Congress for FY 2007 included $441 billion in budget authority for the DOD, an increase of 8 per cent over the enacted funding level for FY 2006 in nominal terms.[24] However, this FY 2006 figure does not include supplemental 'global war on terrorism' appropriation requests after February 2006. Adding the subsequent supplements requested during 2006—$70 billion for FY 2006 and $50 billion for FY 2007—the overall budget authority requested for the DOD totalled $538 billion in FY 2006 and $491 billion for FY 2007.[25]

---

[21] US Government Accountability Office (note 20), p. 10.

[22] US Government Accountability Office (note 20), p. 8.

[23] US Congress, Congressional Budget Office (CBO), 'Estimated costs of U.S. operations in Iraq under two specified scenarios', Washington, DC, 13 July 2006, URL <http://www.cbo.gov/showdoc.cfm?index=7393>.

[24] US Department of Defense (DOD), Office of the Under Secretary of Defense (Comptroller), *National Defense Budget Estimates for FY 2007* (DOD: Washington, DC, Mar. 2006), URL <http://www.defenselink.mil/comptroller/defbudget/fy2007/>, table 1-1, p. 4. In US budget terminology, budget authority is the authority to spend in the current as well as future years and actual expenditure during the year is called outlays. This figure of $441 billion is slightly higher than the original figure of $439.3 billion presented by President Bush in his budget request on 6 Feb. 2006. US Department of Defense, 'Fiscal 2007 Department of Defense budget is released', Press release no. 104-06, Washington, DC, 6 Feb. 2006, URL <http://www.defenselink.mil/Releases/Release.aspx?ReleaseID=9287>.

[25] Kosiak, S., 'Historical and projected funding for defense: presentation of the FY 2007 request in tables and charts', Center for Strategic and Budgetary Assessments, Washington, DC, 7 Apr. 2006, URL <http://www.csbaonline.org/2006-1/2.DefenseBudget/Topline.shtml>, table 1.

Table 8.5. US appropriations for the 'global war on terrorism', financial years 2001–2006

Figures are for budget authority, in US$ b. Years are financial years (running for 12 months from 1 Oct. of the previous year). Figures do not always add up because of the conventions of rounding.

	2001	2002	2003	2004	2005	2006	Total 2001–2006
Military operations	14	18	80	88	70	111	381
Iraq[a]	0	0	46	68	53	87	254
Afghanistan and other[b]	14	18	34	21	18	24	128
Indigenous security forces[c]	0	0	0	5	7	5	17
Iraq	0	0	0	5	6	3	14
Afghanistan	0	0	0	0	1	2	3
Diplomatic operations and foreign aid	<0.5	2	8	17	3	4	34
Iraq	0	0	3	15	1	3	22
Other	<0.5	2	5	2	2	1	12
Total	**14**	**19**	**88**	**111**	**81**	**120**	**432**

[a] This is funding for Operation Iraqi Freedom.

[b] This includes funding for Operation Enduring Freedom (in and around Afghanistan), Operation Noble Eagle (homeland security missions), restructuring of army and Marine Corps units and classified activities other than those funded through the Iraq Freedom Fund. It excludes funds for Operation Noble Eagle for 2005 and 2006 because these have been included in annual DOD appropriations and cannot be identified separately.

[c] Funding for indigenous security forces is for training and equipping local military and police units in Afghanistan and Iraq.

Sources: US Congress, Congressional Budget Office (CBO), *The Budget and Economic Outlook: An Update* (CBO: Washington, DC, Aug. 2006), URL <http://www.cbo.gov/showdoc.cfm?index=7492>, box 1-1, p. 9.

According to the Future Year Defense Plan for FYs 2007–2011, budget authority for national defence was projected to increase in real terms from $463 billion in FY 2007 to $482 billion in FY 2009 and then fall to $477.2 billion in FY 2011 (all at constant FY 2007 prices), not including estimated future spending for wars.[26] According to the US Army, Navy and Air Force, this will lead to a substantial gap between their funding and the costs of their planned future activities. During the 2006 congressional budget process of the FY 2007 defence budget, the Army Chief of Staff, General Peter Schoomaker, testified that the US Army had a funding shortfall of $17 billion caused by the need to replace equipment that had been worn out or destroyed in combat in Afghanistan and Iraq and he projected an annual shortfall of $12 billion for each of FYs 2008 and 2009. Similarly, US Air Force officials argued that they faced a budget shortfall of $8 billion in FYs 2008–2013 to pay for personnel, equipment and operational costs. According to the US Navy, its shortfall will

[26] US Department of Defense, Office of the Under Secretary of Defense (Comptroller) (note 24), table 1-2, p. 5.

be $3–4 billion annually compared with the projected costs of achieving its goal of building a 313-ship fleet. To save money, both the air force and the navy are cutting their forces, by roughly 40 000 personnel each. However, according to the Senate Budget Committee, this would not be nearly enough to close the gap between force planning and budget plans, to allow the services to afford all the weapon programmes in their acquisition plans.[27]

While these budget shortfalls are partly related to costs incurred for the wars in Afghanistan and Iraq—for example, for repairs and replacement of equipment damaged or destroyed in combat—another factor is the increased costs of weapon programmes initiated before the wars. The post-September 2001 period has been associated with substantial increases in the cost of weapon systems. The USA's weapon system acquisition plan has increased from 71 major weapon programmes with a combined cost of $790 billion in FY 2001 to 85 programmes with a cost of $1585 billion by December 2005.[28] This is the result both of an increasing number of major weapon programmes and of increasing unit programme costs. This trend is unlikely to be changed, at least in the short term, owing to the character of the weapon acquisition process, including the contractual arrangements and 'pork barrel' politics. Thus, according to a 2006 report by the Republican Party staff on the Senate Budget Committee, it would be difficult for the Congress to stem these cost increases by cancelling some ongoing weapon acquisition programmes because of the contractual arrangements and the employment implications, which have historically been an important political barrier to the cancellation of arms production programmes.[29]

Overall, the paradox of the dynamics of US military spending by the end of 2006 was that, in spite of the strong increase in US military expenditure during the period FYs 2001–2006 and a level of military spending nearly as high as the combined military expenditure of all other countries in the world, the funding is nevertheless insufficient for the defence plans of the US armed forces.

Alternative strategies and spending

The USA's post-September 2001 policies have not only incurred great costs. By the end of 2006 it had been demonstrated in a number of assessments that

[27] Matthews, W., 'Worldwide defense spending forecast: leading the pack', *Defense News*, 11 Sep. 2006.

[28] US Senate, Budget Committee, Republican Staff, 'Informed budgeteer', *Budget Bulletin*, 28 July 2006, URL <http://www.senate.gov/~budget/republican/NewBB.htm>. By the end of FY 2006, the acquisition plan had reached 87 programmes at a total cost of $1613 billion. US Department of Defense, 'Selected Acquisition Report (SAR) summary tables as of date: September 30, 2006', Washington, DC, 14 Nov. 2006, URL <http://www.acq.osd.mil/ara/am/sar/>.

[29] US Senate (note 28). According to the Senate Budget Committee, DOD contracts contain a termination liability clause to indemnify the contractor if the government prematurely ends the contract for reasons other than default by the contractor, and the termination liability payment is often larger than the amount the government would have to pay to continue production.

Table 8.6. The proposals of the Task Force on a Unified Security Budget for the United States, 2007

Figures are in US$ b. and are the proposed changes from the US Administration's budget request for financial year 2007

Item	Proposed change
Combat aircraft (in F-22 and F-35 programmes)	−5.3
Future combat systems	−2.7
Ships (Virginia Class submarines and DD(X) destroyer)	−5.6
Nuclear warheads, weapons and missiles	−14.0
National missile defence	−8.0
Military forces and personnel (air force and navy)	−7.2
Research and development	−5.0
Waste in procurement and business operations	5.0
Other	−8.7
Total proposed cuts in military spending	**−61.5**
Homeland security (public health, first responders, public transport security)	23.75
Economic development assistance	10.00
Alternative energy sources	8.80
Non-proliferation (focusing on dismantling and securing nuclear weapons)	4.60
Diplomatic operations	1.80
Contributions to international organizations, peace missions, etc.	2.79
Total proposed increases in non-military spending	**51.74**

Source: Korb, L. and Pemberton, M., *Report of the Task Force on a Unified Security Budget for the United States, 2007* (Foreign Policy in Focus and the Center for Defense Information: Washington, DC, May 2006), URL <http://www.fpif.org/fpiftxt/3253/>, pp. 16, 22.

these policies had not achieved their aims.[30] These are two important factors behind the emergence of a number of alternative security strategies and spending options by the domestic political opposition during 2006.

A proposal from the Democratic Party in early 2006 included a number of non-military (e.g. homeland, energy and diplomatic) strategies to protect US territory, communication systems, chemical and nuclear plants and critical infrastructure from terrorist attacks, to reduce US dependence on foreign oil and to restore confidence in the ability of the US Government to respond to an attack or natural disaster.[31] However, it did not imply cuts in US military spending, since it also included a plan to rebuild the military forces. Similarly, a set of proposals for reforming US military strategy by a think tank associated with the Democratic Party included a number of suggestions for defensive

---

[30] For a brief summary see Gold, D., 'Is the war on terror "worth it"?', Security Policy Working Group, Proteus Fund, New York, N.Y., Sep. 2006, URL <http://www.proteusfund.org/spwg/collab/>. For a broader review of the domestic critique during 2006 of US defence policy, both as regards the war in Iraq and the design and requirements of future US armed forces, see chapter 1 in this volume.

[31] US Democratic Party, 'Real security: the Democratic plan to protect America and restore our leadership in the world', Washington, DC, 29 Mar. 2006, URL <http://www.democrats.gov/BK.html>.

measures, expanding non-military forms of engagement and raising taxes, while also calling for a 'bigger and better military'.[32]

A third set of proposals is contained in the third version of the Unified Security Budget, which is the work of a group of non-governmental policy analysts that includes former government officials who have served in the US DOD, Congress and armed forces.[33] Based on a broad conception of security, the Unified Security Budget's analysis covered both military and non-military expenditure items for promoting security and identified $62 billion in cuts to the defence budget, 'mostly to weapon systems that have scant relevance to the threats we face', and suggested $52 billion for additional non-military measures for defence and prevention.[34] These proposals are summarized in table 8.6.

Economic impact

The massive increase in US military spending is taking place in a period of rising budget deficits, increasing US Government debt and increasing outlays on servicing that debt. It has also been one of the factors contributing to the deterioration of these economic indicators. According to the US Office of Management and Budget, the slowdown in the US economy that began in 2001 was exacerbated by the terrorist attacks of 11 September 2001. The deterioration in the performance of the economy, together with reduction in income tax and additional spending in response to the terrorist attacks, produced a fall in the US Government's budget surplus to $128 billion in 2001 and a return to deficits in 2002.[35] By FY 2006, the deficit was $423 billion, corresponding to 3.2 per cent of GDP. During the period FYs 2001–2006 the US Government's debt increased by $2.84 trillion and in FY 2006 corresponded to 66.1 per cent of GDP, while net interest payments to service the debt increased from $206 billion to $220 billion (see table 8.7).

In the long term there will be greater competition for funds from the US budget because of the increased cost of servicing the debt caused by the rising budget deficit and the costly demands of the ageing baby boom generation. People born in the post-World War II baby boom period will begin to retire in FY 2008 and to do so in great numbers from FY 2011, which will result in dramatic increases in US Government spending on retirement and health programmes. According to the US Government Accountability Office, in the

---

[32] Marshall, W. (ed.), Progressive Policy Institute, *With All Our Might: A Progressive Strategy for Defeating Jihadism and Defending Liberty* (Routledge: London, 2006). See also Hartung, W. D., 'Fighting the "good fight": an alternative to current Democratic proposals for a new national security strategy', Security Policy Working Group, Proteus Fund, New York, N.Y., Sep. 2006, URL <http://www.proteus fund.org/spwg/collab/>.

[33] Korb, L. and Pemberton, M., *Report of the Task Force on a Unified Security Budget for the United States, 2007* (Foreign Policy in Focus and the Center for Defense Information: Washington, DC, May 2006), URL <http://www.fpif.org/fpiftxt/3253/>.

[34] Korb and Pemberton (note 33), p. i.

[35] US Office of Management and Budget, *Historical Tables: Budget of the United States Government, Fiscal Year 2007* (Government Printing Office: Washington, DC, 2006), URL <http://www.whitehouse. gov/omb/budget/fy2007/>, pp. 5–6.

Table 8.7. US budget surplus or deficit, government debt and net interest payments, financial years 2000–2007

Years are financial years (running for 12 months from 1 Oct. of the previous year).

	2000	2001	2002	2003	2004	2005	2006[a]	2007[a]
Figures in current prices ($ b.)								
Surplus/deficit	+236	+128	−158	−378	−413	−318	−423	−354
Debt	5 629	5 770	6 198	6 760	7 355	7 905	8 611	9 295
Net interest payments	223	206	171	153	160	184	220	247
Figures as a share of gross domestic product (%)								
Surplus/deficit	+2.4	+1.3	−1.5	−3.5	−3.6	−2.6	−3.2	−2.6
Debt	58.0	57.4	59.7	62.6	63.7	64.3	66.1	67.5
Net interest payments	2.3	2.0	1.6	1.4	1.4	1.5	1.7	1.8

[a] Figures for financial years 2006 and 2007 are estimates, based on requested budget authority.

Source: US Office of Management and Budget, *Historical Tables: Budget of the United States Government, Fiscal Year 2007* (Government Printing Office: Washington, DC, 2006), URL <http://www.whitehouse.gov/omb/budget/fy2007/>, tables 1.3, 7.1, 8.1, 8.4.

absence of policy changes, the currently growing imbalance between expected US Government spending and tax revenues will mean 'ultimately unsustainable federal deficits and debt that serve to threaten [the USA's] future national security as well as the standard of living for the American people'.[36]

In addition, the US military operations in Afghanistan, Iraq and elsewhere will have a long-term economic impact far beyond the direct effect of military expenditure. The indirect costs of armed conflict include a range of costs to the warring parties themselves, as well as to neighbouring countries, and the negative macroeconomic impact of disturbances caused by the conflict.[37] Among the indirect costs to the parties are the lives lost, the treatment of the wounded, the destruction of infrastructure, productive capacity and other capital, and the lack of investment in the country of conflict. Some of these may incur further budgetary costs (e.g. for the provision of care for injured soldiers), while others affect the national economy. In addition, major armed conflicts often have global macroeconomic implications, in the case of the conflict in Iraq primarily due to the impact on the oil market.

When these factors are taken into account, the costs to the USA of the war in Iraq become much higher than the increased level of military expenditure. In an assessment produced in late 2006 by Linda Bilmes and Joseph Stiglitz, current and future budgetary costs for military operations, demobilization and

[36] US Government Accountability Office (GAO), *21st Century Challenges: Reexamining the Base of the Federal Government*, GAO-05-325SP (GAO: Washington, DC, Feb. 2005), URL <http://www.gao.gov/21stcentury.html>, p. 5.

[37] See e.g. Hartley, K., 'Iraq and the costs of conflict', *Socialist Review*, July 2006; and Sköns, E., 'The costs of armed conflict', International Task Force on Global Public Goods, *Peace and Security*, Expert Paper Series no. 5 (Secretariat of the International Task Force on Global Public Goods: Stockholm, 2006), URL <http://www.gpgtaskforce.org/bazment.aspx?page_id=265>, pp. 169–90.

ex-combatants' health care and disability compensation were estimated to total $1012 billion for the period up to 2016.[38] In addition, the economic impact of lives lost, jobs interrupted and increased oil prices as a result of political uncertainty in the Middle East was estimated at $1255 billion, resulting in a total cost of $2267 billion.[39]

Thus, even for a power such as the USA, a major war like that in Iraq involves a significant economic burden, with severe future economic and political implications.

V. Regional survey[40]

Africa

In 2006 military expenditure in Africa amounted to $15.5 billion in constant (2005) dollars (see table 8.1). This represents an increase in real terms of 1.3 per cent since 2005. The rate of increase was significantly lower than in the previous two years: 5.3 per cent in 2004 and 3.5 per cent in 2005. Over the 10-year period 1997–2006, total military spending in the region increased by 51 per cent in real terms. As in previous years, North Africa, and in particular Algeria, accounted for the bulk of the increase. Sub-Saharan Africa, with 46 of the 50 African states, only accounts for 58 per cent of the region's military expenditure, the rest being spent by the four North African countries.

Algeria was responsible for 46 per cent of North African military expenditure in 2006 and was the second highest spender in Africa. Algeria's ambitions to replace or upgrade ageing weapon systems have led it to approach both France and the USA for arms purchases.[41] However, in 2006 Russia stepped in to meet Algeria's requests. Under the terms of contracts signed between December 2005 and March 2006, Algeria will purchase arms from Russia worth $10.5 billion and Russia will in return write off Algeria's remaining $4.74 billion Soviet-era debt.[42] Morocco increased its military expenditure only marginally in 2006, while Libya and Tunisia decreased theirs, in Tunisia's case by 16 per cent.

Even if military expenditure in sub-Saharan Africa is not high in absolute terms compared to that of other regions, the economic burden that it represents is considerable. In 2005 the military burdens of Angola and Burundi—as

[38] Bilmes. L. and Stiglitz, J. E., 'Encore: Iraq hemorrhage', *Milken Institute Review*, no. 4/2006 (Dec. 2006), pp. 76–83. This study is based on the 2 scenarios used in the Congressional Budget Office report to the US Congress (note 23).

[39] This was an upward revision of the same authors' earlier estimates of $1026–2239 billion. Bilmes, L. and Stiglitz, J, E., 'The economic costs of the Iraq war: an appraisal three years after the beginning of the conflict', National Bureau of Economic Research (NBER) Working Paper no. 12054, Cambridge, Mass., Feb. 2006, available at URL <http://www2.gsb.columbia.edu/faculty/jstiglitz/papers.cfm>.

[40] For the country coverage of the regions discussed in this section see appendix 8A, table 8A.1

[41] Daoud, A., 'North Africa's own defense buildup: regional risk or legitimate decision?', *North Africa Journal*, 18 Apr. 2006.

[42] Anderson, G. and Novichkov, N., 'Algeria signs for Russian arms', *Jane's Defence Weekly*, 22 Mar. 2006, p. 19; and Abdullaev, N., 'Russia eyes debt-for-deals strategy', *Defense News*, 20 Mar. 2006. For more on Russia's deals with Algeria see chapter 10 in this volume.

measured by military spending as a share of GDP—were among the highest in the world, at 5.7 and 6.2 per cent of GDP, respectively. At the same time, these two countries were among those with the lowest human development indices.[43] Both countries are recovering from war and are re-establishing government institutions and, as in many other poor countries, there is constant debate over priorities in the allocation of their scarce resources (as discussed in section III). While such countries need to keep their armed forces satisfied in order to maintain the military's support for civilian government, they also need to provide for the social needs of their populations. According to a 2006 report, one of the main causes of military mutinies against civilian rule in Africa is inefficient military expenditure as a result of problems such as corruption.[44]

South Africa is one of the few countries in the region that has made progress towards more efficient military expenditure. Although South Africa has the largest military budget in Africa ($3.6 billion in 2006), it represents a moderate and stable economic burden of 1.5 per cent of GDP. The stability and efficiency of the South African military budget is the result of a transformation process that was undertaken in the decade after the transition to democracy in order to make the military sector accountable to civil authorities.[45] Key guidelines for the control of the military have been created as part of the transformation process. Those guiding the military budget are contained in the 1996 White Paper on Defence, the 1998 Defence Review, the 1999 Public Finance Management Act and the 2002 Defence Act.[46]

Several other sub-Saharan countries are in the process of reforming their military sectors. During such reform processes there can be apparent increases in military expenditure, at least in the short term.[47] In post-conflict countries these reforms can include demobilization or the integration of former rebel combatants into national armies as well as the rebuilding of military infrastructure damaged during the war.[48] For example, in the Democratic Republic

[43] United Nations Development Programme (UNDP), *Human Development Report 2006: Beyond Scarcity—Power, Poverty and the Global Water Crisis* (UNDP: New York, N.Y., 2006), URL <http://hdr.undp.org/hdr2006/>, p. 413

[44] Reeve, R., 'Inadequate military funding puts African countries at risk of coup', *Jane's Intelligence Review*, Apr. 2006, pp. 6–10.

[45] Le Roux, L., 'South Africa', eds W. Omitoogun and E. Hutchful, SIPRI, *Budgeting for the Military Sector in Africa: The Processes and Mechanisms of Control* (Oxford University Press: Oxford, 2006), p. 197.

[46] South African Department of Defence (DOD), *Defence in a Democracy: White Paper on National Defence for the Republic of South Africa* (DOD: Pretoria, May 1996); and South African Department of Defence, *South African Defence Review* (DOD: Pretoria, 1998). The Public Finance Management Act, Act no. 1 of 1999 (as amended by Act no. 29 of 1999), was assented to on 2 Mar. 1999 and took effect on 1 Apr. 2000. The Defence Act, Act no. 42 of 2002, was assented to on 12 Feb. 2003 and took effect on 23 May 2003. These documents are available at URL <http://www.dod.mil.za/documents/documents.htm>. See also South African National Treasury, *Estimates of National Expenditure 2006* (National Treasury: Pretoria, Feb. 2006), URL <http://www.treasury.gov.za/documents/budget/2006/ene/>, p. 462.

[47] Omitoogun, W., 'Introduction', eds Omitoogun and Hutchful (note 45), p. 3.

[48] Omitoogun and Sköns (note 8), p. 283. On military expenditure in post-conflict states see also Collier, C. and Hoeffler, A., 'Military expenditure in post-conflict societies', Centre for the Study of African Economies Working Paper no. 2004-13, Oxford University, Oxford, 8 Apr. 2004, URL <http://www.csae.ox.ac.uk/workingpapers/wps-list.html>.

of the Congo (DRC), after the transitional government had been established in 2003 according to the 2002 Global and All-Inclusive Agreement, military expenditure increased by 56 per cent in 2004 over 2003.[49] Since then military spending has decreased by 27 per cent. However, these are figures for government spending on the military and do not include the spending by rebels and other non-governmental actors. If this non-governmental spending were included, the overall trend in military spending would most likely be a greater decrease since the end of the conflict.

Latin America

Military expenditure in Latin America (i.e. South and Central America) amounted to $32.7 billion in constant (2005) dollars in 2006. This represents an increase of 5 per cent in real terms since 2005, considerably lower than the 8 per cent increase in the previous year. Over the 10-year period 1997–2006 military spending in this region rose by 18 per cent in real terms.

Increases in the military expenditure of Latin American countries have been levelling off following the end of the rule of the last military dictatorship in 1990.[50] Since 1993, the post-1990 year with the highest annual rate of increase in the region's military expenditure (18 per cent), spending levels have increased more slowly. The high rate of increase in the years immediately after the end of the dictatorships can be explained by pressure from strong military lobbies on the new civilian governments.[51] However, in some of these countries democratic government has become well rooted, making military reforms possible, including modernization processes. Such reforms intensified in the aftermath of the September 2001 terrorist attacks on the USA, following pressure from the USA to make security institutions more effective, and with the end of the economic crises of the late 1990s.[52]

However, the characteristics of the reforms differ within the region. Two Central American countries—Costa Rica and Panama—have no defence forces, having disbanded them and replaced them with paramilitary forces—in 1948 and 1990, respectively. Other countries, following peace agreements in the 1980s, have focused on shifting resources from the military sector to

---

[49] The Global and All-Inclusive Agreement on Transition in the Democratic Republic of the Congo was signed at Pretoria on 17 Dec. 2002. Among other objectives agreed was the formation of a restructured and integrated national army. The text of the agreement is available at URL <http://www.relief web.int/rw/RWB.NSF/db900SID/MHII-65G8B8>. See also UN General Assembly Resolution A/RES/59/207, 17 Mar. 2005, URL <http://www.un.org/ga/59/>, Article 6.

[50] There was a military-backed government in Venezuela for a short time in 2002.

[51] Robledo Hoecker, M., 'Instituciones, intereses y cultura política en las relaciones entre civiles y militares en Chile: 1990–2004' [Institutions, interest and political culture in the civil–military relations in Chile: 1990–2004], eds J. S. Tulchin, R. Benítez Manaut and R. Diamint, *El rompecabezas: Conformando la seguridad hemisférica en el siglo XXI* [The puzzle: creating hemispheric security in the 21st century] (Prometeo Libros: Buenos Aires, 2006), pp. 475–78.

[52] Martín, F. E., 'The Latin American military in the new millennium', *Hemisphere*, vol. 16 (spring 2006), p. 3.

internal security.[53] The latter trend continued during the 10-year period 1997–2006, with military expenditure in Central America decreasing by 5 per cent in real terms. This represents the only regional decrease in military spending globally over this period. However, in a few countries, such as Guatemala, the police force's lack of capabilities has led to the military taking over some policing functions, blurring the line between the roles of the police and the military.[54]

While South American countries have internal security concerns similar to those in Central America, the approach to reforming the armed forces is different.[55] There is currently a focus in South America on modernization of equipment. Chile and Venezuela have both pursued large programmes for the modernization of their military capabilities and many other South American states have done so on a smaller scale. These countries have made two types of political argument to justify their acquisitions of up-to-date armaments. One group of countries argues that these arms purchases are the routine replacement of old equipment and the acquisition of capabilities for a more active role in international peace operations. Countries in the other group argue that their acquisitions of equipment are in response to a perceived military threat. Of course, both of these arguments can be used simultaneously, while other tacit motives—such as support of the local arms industry, as in Brazil—are not aired in the political discourse.

The first group includes Argentina, Brazil, Chile and Uruguay. The modernization of the Brazilian military has focused on the air force, with the acquisition of Mirage 2000 combat aircraft and a number of helicopters. The main Brazilian replacement programme in 2006 was the purchase of 62 transport aircraft for $64 million. The modernized fleet is part of the Brazilian Government's ongoing prioritization of control over the Amazon through the Amazon Surveillance System (Sistema de Vigilância da Amazônia, SIVAM).[56] The F-X next-generation combat aircraft programme, which Brazil cancelled in 2005 to redirect funds to the 'Fome Zero' (zero hunger) plan, was revived in 2006.[57] Brazil's procurement programme is part of its efforts to maintain its

[53] Córdova Macías, R. and Pérez, O. J., 'La agenda de seguridad en centroamérica hacias el siglo XXI' [The security agenda in Central America towards the XXI century], eds Tulchin, Benítez Manaut and Diamint (note 51), pp. 226–30.

[54] 'Army to patrol streets for another two terms', *Latin American Weekly Report*, 3 Oct. 2006, p. 12; and 'Civilians and soldiers: roles and outlooks', *Latin American Security and Strategic Review*, Oct. 2006, pp. 4–5.

[55] Bruneau, T. C. and Goetze, R. B., 'Civilian–military relations in Latin America', *Military Review*, Sep./Oct. 2006, p. 68.

[56] SIPRI Arms Transfers Database, URL <http://www.sipri.org/contents/armstrad/>; 'CASA delivers first 12 Brazilians C-295s', *International Air Letter*, 27 Oct. 2006, p. 5; and Brazilian Ministry of Defence, 'Política de defesa nacional' [National defence policy], Decree no. 5484 of 30 June 2005, URL <https://www.planalto.gov.br/ccivil_03/_Ato2004-2006/2005/Decreto/D5484.htm>, section 7.1.

[57] Baranauskas, T., 'Brazil appears ready for major aircraft buys', Government & Industry Group, Forecast International, Newtown, Conn., 18 Dec. 2006, URL <http://emarketalerts.forecast1.com/mic/eabstract.cfm?recno=131002>. See also Sköns, E. et al., 'Military expenditure', *SIPRI Yearbook 2004: Armaments, Disarmament and International Security* (Oxford University Press: Oxford, 2004), pp. 335–37.

role as a major regional power and to gain support for a permanent seat on the UN Security Council.[58]

The second group of countries, whose modernization programmes are in response to a perceived military threat, includes Bolivia, Colombia and Venezuela. Bolivia has expressed concern about neighbouring Chile's modernization programmes.[59] As part of its own plan's to divert resources to the modernization of its armed forces, in 2006 it was proposed that 2–3 per cent of the profit from the country's gas sales be invested in the military.[60]

Colombia's military spending is driven mostly by its four-decade-long war against insurgent groups and the fight against the drug trade. In the past decade the Colombian Government has pursued a number of strategies to end the conflict. Plan Colombia, which aimed to restart the peace process with the rebels, generate employment and intensify counter-narcotics activities, has been complemented since 2003 by the Plan Patriota military strategic programme, which aims for the reoccupation of areas under rebel control.[61] One of the advantages that the Colombian military has over the rebels is air power, hence the need to maintain a capable air force.[62] In 2006 the Colombian Congress approved a new law securing funds for modernization programmes, starting in 2007.[63] However, most of the funds will finance an upgrade of 20 combat aircraft bought in the 1970s for conventional defence purposes. This contradicts the previous preference of the Colombian Government for counter-insurgency equipment over conventional war weaponry.[64]

For the second consecutive year, in 2006 Venezuela had the highest rate of increase in military spending in South America: 20 per cent in real terms, resulting in a 35 per cent increase since 2004. Venezuela thereby overtook Argentina to become the fourth biggest spender in Latin America. While Venezuela's arms acquisitions are part of a modernization strategy, they are also in response to a perceived major regional threat. Arguing that Venezuela needs to be prepared for an eventual invasion from the USA, the government of President Hugo Chávez is acquiring heavy equipment—such as SU-30 combat aircraft—as well as production licences for AK-47 (Kalashnikov)

---

[58] Bitencourt, L., '¿Liderazgo brasileño en seguridad hemisférica?' [Brazilian leadership in hemispheric security?], eds Tulchin, Benítez Manaut and Diamint (note 51), p. 388.

[59] E.g. 'El Ejecutivo renovará el armamento de las FFAA' [The government will renew the armament of the armed forces], *La Razón* (La Paz), 13 Feb. 2007; and 'Bolivian military to modernize force structure', Forecast International, Newtown, Conn., 21 Feb. 2007, URL <http://emarketalerts.forecast1.com/mic/eabstract.cfm?recno=132732>.

[60] Baranauskas, T., 'Bolivian military to get additional funding to finance revitalization', Forecast International, Newtown, Conn., 7 Dec. 2006, URL <http://emarketalerts.forecast1.com/mic/eabstract.cfm?recno=130742>; and Associated Press, 'Bolivia: recursos del gas para las FFAA' [Bolivia: gas resources for the armed forces], *La República* (Lima), 15 Nov. 2006.

[61] On Plan Patriota see Veillette, C., *Plan Colombia: A Progress Report*, US Library of Congress, Congressional Research Service (CRS) Report for Congress RL32774 (CRS: Washington, DC, 22 June 2005), URL <http://fpc.state.gov/c13800.htm>, p. 9.

[62] McDermott, J., 'No end in sight', *Jane's Defence Weekly*, 26 July 2006, pp. 28–29.

[63] The law, Ley de reforma tributaria [Tributary reform law], Law 1111 of 27 Dec. 2006, is available at URL <http://www.presidencia.gov.co/prensa_new/leyes/> (in Spanish).

[64] 'Más plata para la guerra' [More money for war], *Semana* (Bogotá), 28 Oct. 2006, URL <http://www.semana.com/wf_InfoArticulo.aspx?IdArt=97836>.

rifles.[65] Another reason for the purchases is to reduce the country's dependence on the USA as a provider of military equipment.[66]

Asia and Oceania

In 2006 military expenditure in Asia and Oceania increased by $9 billion, or 5 per cent in real terms, reaching $185 billion in constant (2005) dollars. This represents a continuation of a long-term regional trend of rapidly increasing military expenditure, only slightly moderated by the Asian financial crisis in 1997–98. Since 1997 the region's military expenditure has increased by $54 billion or 41 per cent.

China and India together account for 40 per cent of the region's total spending, and their high rates of increase—China's military expenditure grew by 12 per cent in 2006 and India's by 7 per cent—also dictate the overall trend of regional spending. This effect on the regional trend is somewhat offset by the stability of Japan's military spending, which is the second largest in the region after China's. South Korea and Australia also increased their military spending significantly in 2006, by $1520 million (or 7 per cent) and $672 million (or 5 per cent), respectively. Only a few countries in the region reduced their military spending to any considerable extent in 2006, including three countries—Japan, Taiwan and Malaysia—that decreased their spending by more than $100 million—by $464 million, $389 million and $124 million, respectively.

In Japan, the level of military expenditure—specifically, the appropriate share of GDP to spend on the military—has become an increasingly contested issue in the past few years. This is partly a consequence of external pressure for Japanese participation in international humanitarian operations and partly owing to the perceived increased threat from China and North Korea. Following North Korea's missile tests in July 2006 and its nuclear test in October, some in Japan called for a more typical role for their country in the international community.[67] The new Japanese prime minister, Shinzo Abe, reinforced the efforts of his predecessor, Junichiro Koizumi, to revise the constitution to allow Japan to possess armed forces and to regain the right to use force to solve international disputes.[68] The constitution currently allows the use of force only in response to an attack on the country. North Korea's mis-

---

[65] See chapter 10 in this volume.

[66] Malamud, C. and García Encina, C., '¿Rearme o renovación del equipamiento militar en América Latina?' [Rearmament or renovation of military equipment in Latin America?], Working Paper no. 31/2006, Real Instituto Elcano, Madrid, 15 Dec. 2006, URL <http://www.realinstitutoelcano.org/docu mentos/278.asp>.

[67] On North Korea's missile and nuclear tests see chapter 12 and appendix 12B in this volume.

[68] Kyodo News, 'Abe vows bold departure from postwar Japan's constitution, education', Tokyo, 26 Jan. 2007, URL <http://www.findarticles.com/p/articles/mi_m0XPQ/is_2007_Jan_29/ai_n17156 594>; and Pilling, D., 'Japan gives defence agency ministry status', *Financial Times*, 9 Jan. 2007, p. 5. The Japanese Constitution, promulgated on 3 Nov. 1946, is available in English translation at URL <http://www.sangiin.go.jp/eng/law/>. It was largely drafted by US officials during the post-World War II occupation of Japan and is commonly referred to as the 'peace constitution' because of its renunciation of 'war as a sovereign right of the nation and the threat or use of force as means of settling international disputes' (Article 9).

sile and nuclear tests also sparked a media debate over whether Japan should acquire nuclear weapons and capabilities for offensive strikes. Before being elected prime minister, Abe was quite frank about his view that Japan needs an offensive strike capability,[69] but he has recently denied that Japan has any nuclear ambitions.[70] In a strong indication of changing sentiments within the Japanese leadership, on 9 January 2007 the Japan Defense Agency, a part of the prime minister's office, was promoted to full ministry status.[71]

Although Japan's military spending has traditionally been capped at 1 per cent of GDP (excluding military pensions), its economy is so large that the country's military expenditure was the biggest in Asia and Oceania and the fourth largest in the world for many years. The large absolute level of Japanese military expenditure, together with a very capable arms industry, has been of concern for many of Japan's neighbours, in spite of the constitutional limitations. With a large and growing public debt, an ageing population and large costs expected to arise from the realignment of US forces in Japan, the Japanese Government has reduced military spending since 2003 by 2.5 per cent in real terms.[72] This reduction has occurred at the same time as the government expects the self-defence forces to take on new and more demanding tasks.[73] One priority for 2007 is the development and deployment of a ballistic missile defence system, which received a 30 per cent nominal increase in spending in the draft budget for 2007, while total military spending is proposed to decrease by 0.2 per cent in nominal terms.[74]

For the first time, China's military expenditure exceeded that of Japan in 2006, with the result that China became the biggest spender in the region and the fourth largest in the world. The precise level of Chinese military expenditure is disputed, with estimates ranging from the official Chinese figure of $35 billion, via SIPRI's estimate of $49.5 billion to the US Defense Intelligence Agency's estimate of $80–115 billion.[75] What is undisputed is the very rapid increasing trend in Chinese military expenditure, with an increase of

[69] Matsumura, M., 'Prudence and realism in Japan's nuclear options', Brookings Institution, Washington, DC, 10 Nov. 2006, URL <http://www.brookings.edu/views/op-ed/fellows/matsumura2006 1110.htm>; and Blumenthal, D., 'America and Japan approach a rising China', Asian Outlook no. 4, American Enterprise Institute, Washington, DC, 11 Dec. 2006, URL <http://www.aei.org/publications/ pubID.25257,filter.foreign/pub_detail.asp>.

[70] Abe, S., Policy speech to the 166th Session of the Diet, Tokyo, 26 Jan. 2007, URL <http://www. kantei.go.jp/foreign/abespeech/2007/01/26speech_e.html>.

[71] Pilling (note 68).

[72] Agence France-Presse, 'Japan considering further cut in foreign aid, defense spending: report', Defense News, 22 May 2006. On US basing policy in Japan and elsewhere in Eurasia see Lachowski, Z., Foreign Military Bases in Eurasia, SIPRI Policy Paper no. 18 (SIPRI: Stockholm, June 2007), URL <http://www.sipri.org/>

[73] Minnick, W. and Masaki, H., 'Japan's military copes with larger role, smaller budget', Defense News, 2 Jan. 2007.

[74] Japanese Ministry of Defense, [(Proposed) national defence budget: 2007 budget summary], URL <http://www.mod.go.jp/j/library/archives/yosan/2007/yosan.pdf>, pp. 4–5; Abe (note 70); and Fish, T., 'China increases hi-tech capabilities whilst Japan increases its missile defence budget', Asia–Pacific Defence Reporter, vol. 32, no. 7 (Sep. 2006), p. 8.

[75] Maples, M. D., 'Current and projected national security threats to the United States', Statement for the record, US Senate Select Committee on Intelligence, Washington, DC, 11 Jan. 2007, URL <http:// www.dia.mil/publicaffairs/Testimonies/statement26.html>.

195 per cent over the decade 1997–2006. There are several reasons for the large increase. The most frequently offered official explanation is that military salaries have needed to rise to stay in line with non-military pay levels, and this is certainly one contributing factor to the increasing trend. Military spending is also said to be increasing as improved economic conditions allow the People's Liberation Army (PLA) to be compensated for the years in the 1980s when spending was cut.[76]

On 29 December 2006 China released its biennial Defence White Paper.[77] This document does not make any secret of the fact that major procurement programmes are also a cause of the increased military expenditure. It explicitly names 'opposing and containing the separatist forces for "Taiwan independence" and their activities' as one of the aims of these acquisitions but also expresses a wish to keep abreast with the 'revolution in military affairs' including an ambition to 'informationize' the PLA (i.e. improve its network capabilities).[78] The White Paper reports extensively on what the Chinese leadership perceives as the main threats against the country, but few facts and figures are provided.[79] Nor is there any serious discussion on how military plans relate to the assessed threats. In spite of this, the White Paper is a clear improvement in transparency compared to earlier editions.[80]

Ongoing programmes for modernization and transformation of the armed forces in several Asian countries point towards continued increases in military expenditure in Asia and Oceania in the coming years.[81] This trend might be exacerbated by renewed fighting in Sri Lanka between the government and the Liberation Tigers of Tamil Eelam as well as a clear ambition from the interim military government in Thailand to increase military spending.[82]

As in many other regions, military expenditure in Asia is sensitive to the general economic situation. Before the Asian financial crisis in 1997–98, the military expenditure of Asian countries was increasing rapidly, following and even surpassing the high growth rates of the national economies. The financial crisis changed this and forced many Asian countries to reduce military spending and to cancel or postpone major procurement deals. Spending started to increase faster again after 2000 and many countries resumed procurement plans that had been cancelled or deferred.[83] Some countries remained cautious,

---

[76] Chinese State Council, *China's National Defence in 2006* (Information Office of the State Council of the People's Republic of China: Beijing, Dec. 2006), URL <http://www.china.org.cn/english/features/book/194421.htm>, chapters IV and IX.

[77] Chinese State Council (note 76).

[78] Chinese State Council (note 76), chapter II.

[79] Chinese State Council (note 76), chapter I.

[80] The defence white papers of July 1998, Oct. 2000, Dec. 2002 and Dec. 2004 are available in English at URL <http://www.china.org.cn/e-white/>.

[81] The armed forces of Australia, China, India, Indonesia, South Korea and Taiwan are all going through major modernization or transformation programmes involving costly procurement of military equipment. Ratnam, G., 'Asia is top arms destination', *Defense News*, 12 Sep. 2005.

[82] Associated Press, 'Sri Lanka expands military in "marked shift"', LankaNewspapers.com, 17 Nov. 2006, URL <http://www.lankanewspapers.com/news/2006/11/9355.html>; and 'Winai: military budget may be given big boost', *Asian Defence Journal*, Dec. 2006, p. 41.

[83] 'Asia's land forces equipment requirements', *Asian Defence Yearbook 2006* (Syed Hussain Publications: Kuala Lumpur, 2006), p. 5.

however. Indonesia, for example, has only slowly resumed the procurement of combat aircraft that was cancelled in 1999.[84] Malaysia reactivated shelved procurement plans in its 2001–2005 Eighth Malaysia Plan. It was more conservative, however, when drafting the subsequent Ninth Malaysia Plan, for 2006–2010, reducing planned military spending by almost a quarter from what was requested.[85] At the end of the Eighth Plan, about half of the procurement budget was accounted for by equipment orders carried over from the previous plan. The Ninth Plan focuses more on internal security and the police than on the military.[86]

In Oceania, Australia has committed itself to annual real-terms increases in military expenditure of 3 per cent each year until 2016. This major commitment is part of the Defence Capability Plan 2006–2016 in which all branches of the armed forces are to receive new and upgraded equipment, with the aim of achieving network-centric warfare capabilities.[87] This drive for modernization and increased capabilities is explained partly by Australia's perception of itself as a major regional power with responsibility for maintaining order and upholding humanitarian values, primarily in South-East Asia, and partly by the long-standing economic growth which allows for extra allocations to the military.[88]

Europe

Military expenditure in Europe rose by $1.5 billion or 0.5 per cent in 2006, continuing an unbroken regional trend of slowly increasing military spending since 1998 (see table 8.1). This small overall increase was the net result of large increases in Russia, in particular, and also in Spain and Turkey together with decreases in Germany, Italy and the UK. Azerbaijan and Belarus, with increases of 82 and 56 per cent, respectively, stand out as the countries with the world's highest relative increases in military expenditure in 2006. Five other countries—Croatia, Estonia, Latvia, Slovenia and Russia—also increased their military expenditure by more than 10 per cent. Two coun-

[84] 'News briefs', *Air Forces Monthly*, Feb. 2006, p. 25; and 'Indonesia's Sukhois: promise or problem', *Asia–Pacific Defence Reporter*, vol. 32, no. 1 (Feb. 2006), pp. 26–27.

[85] 'Budget pressures slow Malaysian spending', *Asia–Pacific Defence Reporter*, vol. 32, no. 4 (May 2006), p. 13; and Malaysian Prime Minister's Department, Economic Planning Unit, *Ninth Malaysia Plan 2006–2010* (Prime Minister's Department: Putrajaya, 2006), URL <http://www.epu.jpm.my/rm9/html/english.htm>.

[86] Mahmud, B., 'The Malaysian Army: adapting to new concepts and technologies', *Asian Defence Journal*, Mar. 2006, pp. 10–15; and Mahmud, B., 'Overview of the Ninth Malaysia Plan', *Asian Defence Journal*, Apr. 2006, pp. 12–17.

[87] La Franchi, P., 'Australia increases defence spending for another five years' and '53 percent growth in defence capital spend to 2016', *Asia–Pacific Defence Reporter*, vol. 32, no. 4 (May 2006), pp. 6, 20–21; 'Australia', *Asian Defence Yearbook 2006* (note 83), pp. 36–37; and Australian Department of Defence, *Defence Capability Plan 2006–2016: Public Version* (Defence Materiel Organisation: Canberra, 2006), URL <http://www.defence.gov.au/dmo/id/dcp/dcp.cfm>.

[88] Australian Department of Defence (DOD), *Australia's National Security: A Defence Update 2005* (DOD: Canberra, 15 Dec. 2005), URL <http://www.defence.gov.au/update2005/>; and Ferguson, G. and Lee-Frampton, N., 'Australian defense budget grows, New Zealand meets program goals', *Defense News*, 11 May 2006.

tries—Hungary and Italy—decreased their military spending by more than 10 per cent.

Over the 10-year period 1997–2006, European military expenditure has increased by $28 billion or almost 10 per cent. In absolute terms, Russia and the UK are the two countries that increased their military expenditure most over the decade—by $13.4 billion and $10.9 billion, respectively. Germany and Turkey are the two states that have decreased their military spending most, by $3.9 and $2.4 billion, respectively. In relative terms, the three former-Soviet states Azerbaijan, Latvia and Georgia stand out with increases of 537, 487 and 316 per cent, respectively, over the decade. Croatia, Cyprus and Moldova all decreased their military spending by more than half over the same period.

NATO Europe and the European Union

The annual reiteration by NATO Secretary General Jaap de Hoop Scheffer that there is a need for increased military spending in Europe received a rebuff in 2006. His predecessor in the post, Javier Solana, now High Representative for the EU's Common Foreign and Security Policy, said in June that current spending would be enough to cover EU member states' defence needs if it were better allocated and more efficiently spent.[89] Indeed, the idea behind the EU's creation in 2004 of the European Defence Agency (EDA) was to coordinate military procurement and research and development efforts in order to reduce duplication and to bring economies of scale.[90]

Four main interacting factors lie behind the trends in the military expenditure of the European members of NATO, the members of the EU and states aspiring to join either of these organizations. The first factor is foreign military operations. Many of the countries contributing troops to NATO or EU military operations in, for example, Afghanistan, Bosnia and Herzegovina, Iraq and Kosovo cover the cost of these operations from the ordinary defence budget. Thus, as a result of participation in such missions, either total military expenditure has to be increased or, as is the case in Germany, spending on routine military activities and procurement has to be reduced.[91] In other countries, such as Italy, the cost of foreign operations is not included in the annual defence budget but is instead funded through extra allocations or from a contingency fund.[92] The SIPRI figures for 2006 for these countries include data on such spending as far as they are known.

The second factor, which affects all European NATO members, EU members and aspirant members, is the transformation of the armed forces to

---

[89] Solana, J., 'Europa profitiert vom neuen Markt für Verteidigungsgüter' [Europe profits from the new market for defence goods], *Handelsblatt*, 30 June 2006, p. 7. See also Agence France-Presse, 'EU defense spending poorly allocated: Solana', *Defense News*, 30 June 2006. For De Hoop Scheffer's calls for increased spending see e.g. Agence France-Presse, 'NATO chief embarrassed by low defense spending', *Defense News*, 29 Sep. 2006.

[90] On recent developments in the EDA see chapters 1 and 9 in this volume.

[91] Agence France-Presse, 'German military will not get more money because of Lebanon: minister', *Defense News*, 19 Sep. 2006.

[92] Kington, T., 'Italy may cut international military exercises by half', *Defence News*, 27 Feb. 2006.

enable them to address new security threats.[93] The aim is to convert part or all of the traditional territorial defence forces into forces able to cooperate with partners in foreign military operations such as peacekeeping and humanitarian military intervention. For many countries, transformation has meant increasing military expenditure. In France, for example, the 2003 Law on Military Planning provides for annual increases in military spending until 2008 in order to have a fully professional force able to take the lead in extra-European operations.[94] In advance of the elections of April–June 2007, the French defence minister, Michèle Alliot-Marie, has pushed major procurement projects beyond the point where they can be cancelled.[95] In other countries, such as Germany and Italy, transformation has been funded within a declining military budget and priority has been given to keeping debt and budget deficits within the rules of the EU Stability and Growth Pact.[96]

The third factor driving European military expenditure is NATO's enlargement of its membership and the pressure for increased spending that the alliance has put on all aspiring and new members. In individual membership action plans, the required minimum military expenditure is set at 2 per cent of GDP, a level that very few of the current member states reach.[97] Only five of the pre-1999 NATO member states—France, Greece, Portugal, Turkey and the UK—meet the requirement and only two of the new member states—Bulgaria and Romania. De Hoop Scheffer has even said that he feels ashamed by this contrast.[98] In spite of this pressure to spend a certain amount on the military, the absolute level of military spending or its share of GDP is not a good measure of a state's military capability or of its willingness to contribute to an alliance's common security and operations. Italy is a clear example of a NATO member state that contributes considerably to the alliance's activities while spending less than the 2 per cent threshold. According to NATO figures, Italy decreased its military spending from 2.0 per cent of its GDP in 2004 to only 1.7 per cent in 2006.[99] Yet it contributes to, and takes a leading role in, many EU and NATO operations and has over 10 000 troops stationed abroad.[100]

[93] See Sköns, E., 'Financing security in a global context', *SIPRI Yearbook 2005: Armaments, Disarmament and International Security* (Oxford University Press: Oxford, 2005), pp. 285–306.

[94] The text of Loi relative à la programmation militaire pour les années 2003 à 2008 [Law on military planning for the years 2003 to 2008], Law no. 2003-73 of 27 Jan. 2003, is available at URL <http://www.legifrance.gouv.fr/WAspad/UnTexteDeJorf?numjo=DEFX0200133L> (in French).

[95] Tran, P., 'French industry offers plan for aircraft carrier', *Defense News*, 2 Jan. 2007; and Tran, P., 'French defense minister: maintain modernization momentum', *Defense News*, 29 Sep. 2006.

[96] The Stability and Growth Pact was adopted in July 1997 to ensure budgetary discipline by the EU member states participating in Economic and Monetary Union. See the website of the EU Directorate General for Economic and Financial Affairs, URL <http://europa.eu.int/comm/economy_finance/about/activities/sgp/sgp_en.htm>.

[97] Agence France-Presse, 'NATO chief embarrassed by low defense spending' (note 89).

[98] Agence France-Presse, 'NATO chief embarrassed by low defense spending' (note 89).

[99] North Atlantic Treaty Organization (NATO), 'NATO–Russia compendium of financial and economic data relating to defence', Press release (2006)159, 18 Dec. 2006, URL <http://www.nato.int/docu/pr/2006/p06-159e.htm>, table 3.

[100] Valpolini, P., 'More budget cuts hit Italy's forces', *Jane's Defence Weekly*, 15 Feb. 2006, p. 14.

A major reason for Italy not adhering to the NATO level of military spending is the problem of financial balances and controlling budget deficits, which is the fourth factor affecting European military expenditure. Germany has also chosen to prioritize abiding by the rules of the EU Stability and Growth Pact rather than trying to attain the 2 per cent military spending level. In 2005 Germany allocated 1.4 per cent of its GDP to the military and in 2006 its spending decreased by 2.8 per cent, continuing a trend that started in 2002.[101] Hungary and Slovakia have also stated that sound state finances have a higher priority than reaching the 2 per cent military expenditure level, with the Slovak defence minister expecting no increase in his country's military expenditure before 2016.[102]

Russia and Eastern Europe

Russian military expenditure in 2006 is estimated to have been $34.7 billion in constant (2005) dollars. Russia was the fourth largest spender in Europe and accounted for 11 per cent of total European military spending. Russian military spending increased by almost 12 per cent in 2006, following on from a 19 per cent increase in 2005. Since the start of this increasing trend in 1998, Russia's spending has increased by 155 per cent, but, because there have been several changes in Russia's budgetary system during this period, it is not possible to follow the exact movements in this trend.[103] According to the Russian Defence Minister, Sergei Ivanov, spending on national defence should be kept at about 2.6–2.9 per cent of GDP in order not to repeat the mistakes of overspending made by the Soviet Union during the cold war arms race.[104]

Many of the other states of Eastern Europe (that is, the European members of the Commonwealth of Independent States) have followed Russia's example of increasing military expenditure. In the past two years some of the highest rates of increase in military expenditure have been in countries in Eastern Europe. In 2005 Georgia increased its spending by 185 per cent and in 2006 Azerbaijan increased its spending by 82 per cent. Armenia and Belarus also increased their spending at a considerable rate in 2006, with increases of 17 and 56 per cent, respectively.

---

[101] According to NATO figures, Germany spent 1.3% of its GDP on the military in 2006. North Atlantic Treaty Organization (note 99).

[102] Hungarian News Agency (MTI), 'Defence minister's talks in Brussels', Hungarian Ministry of Defence, Budapest, 17 July 2006, URL <http://www.honvedelem.hu/news/defence_minister8217s_talks _in_brussels>; and Czech News Agency (CTK), 'Slovak military budget frozen for nine years: minister', Prague, 16 May 2006.

[103] On the changes in the Russian budgetary system introduced in 2004 see Cooper, J., 'Military expenditure in the 2005 and 2006 federal budgets of the Russian Federation', Research note, SIPRI, Stockholm, Jan. 2006, URL <http://www.sipri.org/contents/milap/cooper_russia_20060130>.

[104] Agence France-Presse, 'Russian military spending to remain steady: minister', *Defense News*, 11 May 2006.

The Middle East

Military expenditure in the Middle East increased by 2.8 per cent in real terms in 2006, amounting to $72.5 billion in constant (2005) dollars. Saudi Arabia continued to have the largest annual increase in the region, with a 14 per cent rise in 2006. However, the impact of Saudi Arabia's increase on the regional trend was offset by decreases in other countries.

Military spending in the Middle East increased by 57 per cent in real terms over the 10-year period 1997–2006. The trend in military spending during this decade does not correlate with security needs and instead tends to follow the fluctuations in oil revenue.[105] For instance, in 2005 high oil prices were mirrored in increases in the military expenditure of most Middle Eastern countries and an increase in the regional total of 12 per cent. In 2006 the increase in military spending was more moderate. Oil prices—and thus the income of many Middle Eastern governments—fell in the second half of the year, partly as a result of the drop in the value of the US dollar.[106]

The Middle East has the highest military expenditure burden in the world, and in 2005 it remained at the 1997–2005 average of 6 per cent of GDP. High military spending in the Middle East goes hand in hand with a lack of transparency and accountability in military budgets.

Israel is one of the few democracies in the region, but even there military expenditure remains for the most part secret. International organizations together with the State Comptroller's office and public opinion have demanded greater transparency in the Israeli military budgeting processes.[107] In 2006 Israel for the first time published a public report on its military expenditure, giving information on plans for 2007. However, the report only gives details for 2 per cent of the approved budget while providing an aggregated figure for defence spending and stating that details of the rest of the expenditure remain secret.[108] Detailed information is given for the costs of constructing the barrier between the Palestinian territories and Israel and for civil defence, and welfare outlays such as pensions. The Israeli Ministry of Defence explained that these specific accounts were chosen in order to reveal the contribution that military spending makes to social welfare.[109] Security strategy, force structure and modernization plans are not described.

[105] Omitoogun, W., 'Military expenditure in the Middle East after the Iraq war', *SIPRI Yearbook 2004* (note 57), p. 381.

[106] 'Oil price dips below $62 a barrel', BBC News, 11 Dec. 2006, URL <http://news.bbc.co.uk/2/6169629.stm>; and 'Oil in biggest fall in two years', BBC News, 2 Jan. 2007, URL <http://news.bbc.co.uk/2/6231879.stm>.

[107] E.g. International Monetary Fund (IMF), *Israel: Report on Observance of Standards and Codes—Fiscal Transparency Module*, Country Report no. 04/112 (IMF: Washington, DC, Apr. 2004), URL <http://www.imf.org/external/pubs/cat/longres.cfm?sk=17344>; and Korin-Lieber, S., 'Taming the defense budget', *Globes online*, 31 Aug. 2006, URL <http://www.globes.co.il/serveen/globes/DocView.asp?did=1000128681>.

[108] Israeli Ministry of Defence (MOD), [Proposed security budget financial year 2007: subjects not categorized] (MOD: Jerusalem, 30 Oct. 2006). See also Opall-Rome, B., 'Israel MoD inches toward budget transparency', *Defense News*, 13 Nov. 2006.

[109] Opall-Rome (note 108).

The availability of detailed information on military expenditure is even poorer in other states in the region. In the member states of the Gulf Cooperation Council (GCC) in particular, most defence-related decisions are made by members of the royal families.[110] The distribution of power between Shiite and Sunni communities within the region and its countries often influences political choices.[111] The potential Shiite threat to the established Sunni monarchies of the GCC states has been one reason for the GCC governments' maintaining high levels of military expenditure since the 1980s. The establishment of a Shiite-dominated government in Iraq and the growing influence of Iranian supported Shiite groups there and in Lebanon has revived this argument.[112] In order to counter Iran's influence in the region, Saudi Arabia has changed its defence doctrine since 2005.[113]

Since 2002 Saudi Arabia has maintained an increasing trend in military expenditure. Not only is this country the biggest spender in the Middle East by far, with 40 per cent of the region's total military spending in 2006, but it is also the world's largest oil exporter. The country's decision to prioritize spending on the military has been influenced by the emergence of new threats. These threats include the porous northern border with Iraq, domestic terrorism and the potential non-conventional warfare capabilities of Iran and Syria.[114] In addition, the country feels the need to build a defence capability independent of the USA since, following the attacks of September 2001, there has been a cooling and growing complexity in US–Saudi realtions.[115] With this in mind, the Saudi Government continues to modernize military equipment and aims to increase troop numbers by around 25 per cent.[116]

Access to military expenditure data from other countries in the Middle East is even more limited or entirely impossible. Qatar is an example of a country that does not make military expenditure data publicly available. Iran does give limited access to, and thus the opportunity to evaluate, military spending information. It was the region's third biggest spender in 2006, after Saudi Arabia and Israel. This follows a decade in which Iran increased its military spending by 231 per cent, which represents by far the largest increase in the region (followed by Saudi Arabia with an increase of 64 per cent in 1997–2006). In the past few years, Iran has focused on expanding its defence capabilities to bolster its national security in a volatile regional environment.[117] The Iranian

[110] On the GCC see the glossary in this volume. The members of the GCC are Bahrain, Kuwait, Oman, Qatar, Saudi Arabia and the United Arab Emirates.

[111] Hasbani, N., 'The geopolitics of weapons procurement in the Gulf states', *Defense & Security Analysis*, vol. 22, no. 1 (Mar. 2006), pp. 73–88.

[112] Nasr, V., 'When the Shiites rise', *Foreign Affairs*, vol. 85, no. 4 (July/Aug. 2006), pp. 66–67.

[113] 'Saudi military spending rising', *International Air Letter*, 27 July 2006, p. 5; and Susser, A., 'The war in Lebanon and the new Middle East', *RUSI Journal*, vol. 151, no. 4 (Aug. 2006), p. 34.

[114] Susser (note 113), p. 35.

[115] Hasbani (note 111), p. 85.

[116] 'Saudi military spending rising' (note 113); and Kahwaji, R., 'More arms deals seen in turbulent Middle East', *Defense News*, 12 Nov. 2006.

[117] See e.g. Islamic Republic News Agency (IRNA), 'Iranian daily calls for increased military spending', Tehran, 4 Apr. 2006. See also chapter 10 in this volume.

threat perception is affected by the presence of US troops in the region and the tension with the international community over its nuclear programme.[118]

For the first time in decades data are available on military expenditure in Iraq. The available figures are for salaries and pensions for both defence and interior forces. The extent to which US allocations for the restructuring of Iraqi armed forces are included is unknown.

VI. Conclusions

World military expenditure continued to increase during 2006. This upward trend is attributable primarily to the USA, which accounted for 62 per cent of the total increase in world military expenditure and 46 per cent of total world military spending in 2006. The increase in US military expenditure has to a large extent been driven by supplemental allocations for those operations and policies associated with the 'global war on terrorism'. In Europe total military expenditure has been relatively stable in recent years. In both East Asia and the Middle East, increasing financial resources has been decisive in driving military expenditure upwards. China is the prime example of a country where a booming economy, amongst other factors, has allowed a steep rise in military expenditure. In both South America and Eastern Europe, military expenditure has been increasing partly because of modernization and re-equipment of the armed forces.

Government policymakers will always have to choose how to allocate their scarce resources and whether to prioritize security or social goals. At least in the short term, however, there seems to be little chance of there being a rapid decline in world military expenditure, which could allow governments to give higher priority to social expenditure. A decline in military expenditure is a possibility in some regions, but the data presented in this chapter show a strong upward trend in the world total, which is unlikely to be reversed while the world's largest military spender remains at war. The world trend is likely to be driven for the foreseeable future by the defence and security choices and polices pursued by the USA.

[118] Hafezi, P., 'Iran says it needs strong army to deter aggressors', *Defense News*, 20 Sep. 2006. For more on nuclear issues see chapter 12 in this volume.

Appendix 8A. Tables of military expenditure

PETTER STÅLENHEIM, CATALINA PERDOMO and
ELISABETH SKÖNS*

Table 8A.1 presents military expenditure by region, by certain international organizations and by income group for the period 1997–2006 in US dollars at constant 2005 prices and exchange rates, and also for 2006 in current US dollars. Military expenditure by individual countries is presented in table 8A.2 in local currency and at current prices for the period 1997–2006 and in table 8A.3 in US dollars at constant 2005 prices and exchange rates for the period 1997–2006 and for 2006 in current US dollars. Table 8A.4 presents military expenditure for the period 1997–2005 as a percentage of countries' gross domestic product (GDP). Sources and methods are explained in appendix 8C. Notes and explanations of the conventions used appear below table 8A.4.

Military expenditure data from different editions of the SIPRI Yearbook should not be combined because of data revision between editions. Revisions can be significant; for example, when a better time series becomes available the entire SIPRI series is revised accordingly. Revisions in constant dollar series can also originate in significant revisions in the economic statistics of the International Monetary Fund that are used for these calculations. When data are presented in local currency (in table 8A.2) but not in US dollars or as a share of GDP (in tables 8A.3 and 8A.4), this is owing to a lack of economic data.

* Contribution of military expenditure data, estimates and advice are gratefully acknowledged from Julian Cooper (Centre for Russian and East European Studies, University of Birmingham), David Darchiashvili (Center for Civil–Military Relations and Security Studies, Tbilisi), Dimitar Dimitrov (University of National and World Economy, Sofia), Paul Dunne (University of the West of England, Bristol), Nazir Kamal (United Nations, New York), Armen Kouyoumdjian (Country Risk Strategist, Valparaiso), Pavan Nair (Jagruti Seva Sanstha, Pune), Elina Noor (Institute of Strategic and International Studies, Kuala Lumpur), Pere Ortega (Centre d'Estudis per la Pau J. M. Delàs, Barcelona), Tamara Pataraia (Caucasus Institute for Peace, Democracy and Development, Tbilisi), Sam Perlo-Freeman (University of the West of England, Bristol), Jamie Polanco (Ministry of National Defence, Bogotá), Thomas Scheetz (Lincoln University College, Buenos Aires), Ron Smith (Birkbeck College, London) and Ozren Zunec (University of Zagreb).

Table 8A.1. Military expenditure by region, by international organization and by income group, in constant US dollars for 1997–2006 and current US dollars for 2006

Figures are in US $b., at constant 2005 prices and exchange rates except in the right-most column, marked *, where they are in current US$ b. Figures do not always add up to totals because of the conventions of rounding.

	1997	1998	1999	2000	2001	2002	2003	2004	2005	2006	2006*
World total	**844**	**834**	**844**	**876**	**892**	**948**	**1 016**	**1 072**	**1 119**	**1 158**	**1 204**
Geographical regions											
Africa	10.3	11.1	12.3	13.0	13.2	14.4	14.0	14.8	15.3	(15.5)	(16.1)
North Africa	4.4	4.6	4.6	5.0	5.2	5.6	5.7	6.2	6.5	6.5	6.7
Sub-Saharan Africa	5.8	6.5	7.7	8.0	8.0	8.9	8.3	8.6	8.8	9.0	9.4
Americas	375	367	368	381	387	431	481	522	549	575	597
Caribbean	..	..	..	..	..	..	..	..	..	..	..
Central America	3.7	3.6	3.8	3.9	3.9	3.7	3.8	3.5	3.5	3.5	3.5
North America	347	340	341	354	357	399	453	493	518	542	561
South America	24.1	23.2	22.5	23.3	26.3	27.4	24.5	25.1	27.4	29.1	32.0
Asia and Oceania	131	132	136	139	146	153	160	167	176	185	190
Central Asia	0.6	(0.6)	0.6	..	(0.7)	(0.7)	(0.8)	(0.9)	(1.0)	(1.1)	(1.2)
East Asia	99.6	100	100	103	109	116	121	126	131	138	142
Oceania	10.9	11.4	11.9	11.8	12.2	12.7	13.2	13.8	14.3	15.0	15.2
South Asia	19.6	20.2	22.6	23.4	24.2	24.3	25.0	25.8	29.0	30.7	31.2
Europe	283	275	280	287	287	294	302	306	309	310	325
Central Europe	14.8	14.7	14.4	14.4	14.9	15.2	15.7	15.7	16.0	16.7	17.8
Eastern Europe	23.7	15.6	15.9	21.4	23.4	25.8	27.6	28.9	34.2	38.3	43.8
Western Europe	244	245	249	251	249	253	259	262	258	255	264
Middle East	46.1	49.3	48.9	55.8	58.4	55.9	58.0	62.8	70.5	72.5	75.9

	1997	1998	1999	2000	2001	2002	2003	2004	2005	2006	2006*
Organizations											
ASEAN	12.9	11.7	11.7	11.8	12.5	13.2	14.8	14.9	15.3	15.9	17.6
CIS	24.3	16.2	16.5	22.0	24.0	26.5	28.4	29.8	35.2	39.4	45.0
EU	222	221	225	227	226	230	238	254	252	248	257
NATO	574	568	583	596	598	645	705	753	775	797	825
NATO Europe	228	228	242	242	241	246	252	260	257	255	264
OECD	672	666	673	689	691	739	801	845	868	891	920
OPEC	34.5	36.4	35.3	40.6	43.4	39.9	41.7	45.9	51.8	56.9	60.2
OSCE	629	615	621	641	644	694	756	800	827	853	887
Income group (by 2005 gross national income per capita)											
Low (≤$875)	22.3	23.7	27.5	28.1	28.6	29.5	29.7	30.5	34.0	35.8	36.9
Lower middle ($876–$3465)	61.3	62.5	64.6	73.3	80.9	86.9	90.9	96.8	103	110	119
Upper middle ($3466–$10 725)	65.7	57.2	59.6	64.5	67.6	69.4	71.1	72.4	79.2	84.3	91.1
High (≥$10 726)	695	691	692	710	715	762	825	873	903	927	957

( ) = Total based on country data accounting for less than 90% of the regional total; . . = Available data account for less than 60% of the regional total; ASEAN = Association of South East Asian Nations; CIS = Commonwealth of Independent States; NATO = North Atlantic Treaty Organization; OECD = Organisation for Economic Co-operation and Development; OPEC = Organization of the Petroleum Exporting Countries; OSCE = Organization for Security and Co-operation in Europe.

Notes: The world total and the totals for regions, organizations and income groups in table 8A.1 are estimates, based on data in table 8A.3. When military expenditure data for a country are missing for a few years, estimates are made, most often on the assumption that the rate of change in that country's military expenditure is the same as that for the region to which it belongs. When no estimates can be made, countries are excluded from the totals. The countries excluded from all totals in table 8A.1 are Angola, Benin, Cuba, Equatorial Guinea, Guyana, Haiti, Iraq, North Korea, Myanmar (Burma), Qatar, Somalia, Trinidad and Tobago and Viet Nam.

Totals for geographical regions add up to the world total and sub-regional totals add up to regional totals. Totals for regions and income groups cover the same groups of countries for all years, while totals for organizations cover only the member countries in the year given.

The country coverage of income groups is based on figures of 2005 gross national income (GNI) per capita as calculated in World Bank, *World Development Report 2007: Development and the Next Generation* (World Bank: Washington, DC, 2006), URL <http://econ.worldbank.org/wdr/>.

Africa: Algeria, Angola, Benin, Botswana, Burkina Faso, Burundi, Cameroon, Cape Verde, Central African Republic, Chad, Congo (Republic of the), Congo (Democratic Republic of, the DRC), Côte d'Ivoire, Djibouti, Equatorial Guinea, Eritrea, Ethiopia, Gabon, Gambia, Ghana, Guinea, Guinea-Bissau, Kenya, Lesotho, Liberia, Libya, Madagascar, Malawi, Mali, Mauritania, Mauritius, Morocco, Mozambique, Namibia, Niger, Nigeria, Rwanda, Senegal, Seychelles, Sierra Leone, Somalia, South Africa, Sudan, Swaziland, Tanzania, Togo, Tunisia, Uganda, Zambia, Zimbabwe. *North Africa:* Algeria, Libya, Morocco, Tunisia. *Sub-Saharan Africa:* Angola, Benin, Botswana, Burkina Faso, Burundi, Cameroon, Cape Verde, Central African Republic, Chad, Congo (Republic of the), Congo (Democratic Republic of the, DRC), Côte d'Ivoire, Djibouti, Equatorial Guinea, Eritrea, Ethiopia, Gabon, Gambia, Ghana, Guinea, Guinea-Bissau, Kenya, Lesotho, Liberia, Madagascar, Malawi, Mali, Mauritania, Mauritius, Mozambique, Namibia, Niger, Nigeria, Rwanda, Senegal, Seychelles, Sierra Leone, Somalia, South Africa, Sudan, Swaziland, Tanzania, Togo, Uganda, Zambia, Zimbabwe.

Americas: Argentina, Bahamas, Barbados, Belize, Bolivia, Brazil, Canada, Chile, Colombia, Costa Rica, Cuba, Dominican Republic, Ecuador, El Salvador, Guatemala, Guyana, Haiti, Honduras, Jamaica, Mexico, Nicaragua, Panama, Paraguay, Peru, Trinidad and Tobago, Uruguay, USA, Venezuela. *Caribbean:* Bahamas, Barbados, Cuba, Dominican Republic, Haiti, Jamaica and Trinidad and Tobago. *Central America:* Belize, Costa Rica, El Salvador, Guatemala, Honduras, Mexico, Nicaragua, Panama. *North America:* Canada, USA. *South America:* Argentina, Bolivia, Brazil, Chile, Colombia, Ecuador, Guyana, Paraguay, Peru, Uruguay, Venezuela.

Asia and Oceania: Afghanistan, Australia, Bangladesh, Brunei, Cambodia, China, Fiji, India, Indonesia, Japan, Kazakhstan, New Zealand, North Korea, South Korea, Kyrgyzstan, Laos, Malaysia, Mongolia, Myanmar (Burma), Nepal, Pakistan, Papua New Guinea, Philippines, Singapore, Sri Lanka, Taiwan, Tajikistan, Thailand, Tonga, Turkmenistan, Uzbekistan, Viet Nam. *Central Asia:* Kazakhstan, Kyrgyzstan, Tajikistan, Turkmenistan, Uzbekistan. *East Asia:* Brunei, Cambodia, China, Indonesia, Japan, North Korea, South Korea, Laos, Malaysia, Mongolia, Myanmar (Burma), Philippines, Singapore, Taiwan, Thailand, Viet Nam. *South Asia:* Afghanistan, Bangladesh, India, Nepal, Pakistan, Sri Lanka. *Oceania:* Australia, Fiji, New Zealand, Papua New Guinea, Tonga.

Europe: Albania, Armenia, Austria, Azerbaijan, Belarus, Belgium, Bosnia and Herzegovina, Bulgaria, Croatia, Cyprus, Czech Republic, Denmark, Estonia, Finland, France, Georgia, Germany, Greece, Hungary, Iceland, Ireland, Italy, Latvia, Lithuania, Luxembourg, Macedonia (Former Yugoslav Republic of, FYROM), Malta, Moldova, Netherlands, Norway, Poland, Portugal, Romania, Russia, Serbia and Montenegro, Slovakia, Slovenia, Spain, Sweden, Switzerland, Turkey, UK, Ukraine. *Central Europe:* Albania, Bosnia and Herzegovina, Bulgaria, Croatia, Czech Republic, Estonia, Hungary, Latvia, Lithuania, Macedonia (Former Yugoslav Republic of, FYROM), Poland, Romania, Serbia and Montenegro, Slovakia, Slovenia. *Eastern Europe:* Armenia, Azerbaijan, Belarus, Georgia, Moldova, Russia, Ukraine. *Western Europe:* Austria, Belgium, Cyprus, Denmark, Finland, France, Germany, Greece, Iceland, Ireland, Italy, Luxembourg, Malta, Netherlands, Norway, Portugal, Spain, Sweden, Switzerland, Turkey, UK.

Middle East: Bahrain, Egypt, Iran, Iraq, Israel, Jordan, Kuwait, Lebanon, Oman, Qatar, Saudi Arabia, Syria, United Arab Emirates, Yemen.

ASEAN: Brunei, Cambodia (1999–), Indonesia, Laos (1997–), Malaysia, Myanmar (Burma) (1997–), Philippines, Singapore, Thailand, Viet Nam.

CIS: Armenia, Azerbaijan, Belarus, Georgia, Kazakhstan, Kyrgyzstan, Moldova, Russia, Tajikistan, Turkmenistan (associate member since Aug. 2005), Ukraine, Uzbekistan.

European Union: Austria, Belgium, Cyprus (2004–), Czech Republic (2004–), Denmark, Estonia (2004–), Finland, France, Germany, Greece, Hungary (2004–), Ireland, Italy, Latvia (2004–), Lithuania (2004–), Luxembourg, Malta (2004–), Netherlands, Poland (2004–), Portugal, Slovakia (2004–), Slovenia (2004–), Spain, Sweden, UK.

NATO: Belgium, Bulgaria (2004–), Canada, Czech Republic (1999–), Denmark, Estonia (2004–), France, Germany, Greece, Hungary (1999–), Iceland, Italy, Latvia (2004–), Lithuania (2004–), Luxembourg, Netherlands, Norway, Poland (1999–), Portugal, Romania (2004–), Slovakia (2004–), Slovenia (2004–), Spain, Turkey, UK, USA. *NATO Europe:* Belgium, Bulgaria (2004–), Czech Republic (1999–), Denmark, Estonia (2004–), France, Germany, Greece, Hungary (1999–), Iceland, Italy, Latvia (2004–), Lithuania (2004–), Luxembourg, Netherlands, Norway, Poland (1999–), Portugal, Romania (2004–), Slovakia (2004–), Slovenia (2004–), Spain, Turkey, UK.

OECD: Australia, Austria, Belgium, Canada, Czech Republic, Denmark, Finland, France, Germany, Greece, Hungary, Iceland, Ireland, Italy, Japan, South Korea, Luxembourg, Mexico, Netherlands, New Zealand, Norway, Poland, Portugal, Slovakia (2000–), Spain, Sweden, Switzerland, Turkey, UK, USA.

OPEC: Algeria, Indonesia, Iran, Iraq, Kuwait, Libya, Nigeria, Qatar, Saudi Arabia, United Arab Emirates, Venezuela.

OSCE: Albania, Armenia, Austria, Azerbaijan, Belarus, Belgium, Bosnia and Herzegovina, Bulgaria, Canada, Croatia, Cyprus, Czech Republic, Denmark, Estonia, Finland, France, Georgia, Germany, Greece, Hungary, Iceland, Ireland, Italy, Kazakhstan, Kyrgyzstan, Latvia, Lithuania, Luxembourg, Macedonia (Former Yugoslav Republic of, FYROM), Malta, Moldova, Netherlands, Norway, Poland, Portugal, Romania, Russia, Serbia and Montenegro (2000–), Slovakia, Slovenia, Spain, Sweden, Switzerland, Tajikistan, Turkey, Turkmenistan, UK, Ukraine, USA, Uzbekistan.

Low-income countries (GNI/capita ≤$875 in 2005): Afghanistan, Bangladesh, Benin, Burkina Faso, Burundi, Cambodia, Central African Republic, Chad, Congo (Democratic Republic of the, DRC), Côte d'Ivoire, Eritrea, Ethiopia, Gambia, Ghana, Guinea, Guinea-Bissau, Haiti, India, Kenya, North Korea, Kyrgyzstan, Laos, Liberia, Madagascar, Malawi, Mali, Mauritania, Mongolia, Mozambique, Myanmar (Burma), Nepal, Niger, Nigeria, Pakistan, Papua New Guinea, Rwanda, Senegal, Sierra Leone, Somalia, Sudan, Tajikistan, Togo, Uganda, Uzbekistan, Viet Nam, Yemen, Zambia, Zimbabwe.

Lower-middle income countries (GNI/capita $876–$3465 in 2005): Albania, Algeria, Angola, Armenia, Azerbaijan, Belarus, Bolivia, Bosnia and Herzegovina, Brazil, Bulgaria, Cameroon, Cape Verde, China, Colombia, Congo (Republic of the), Cuba, Djibouti, Dominican Republic, Ecuador, Egypt, El Salvador, Fiji, Georgia, Guatemala, Guyana, Honduras, Indonesia, Iran, Iraq, Jamaica, Jordan, Kazakhstan, Lesotho, Macedonia (Former Yugoslav Republic of, FYROM), Moldova, Morocco, Namibia, Nicaragua, Paraguay, Peru, Philippines, Serbia and Montenegro, Sri Lanka, Swaziland, Syria, Thailand, Tonga, Trinidad and Tobago, Turkmenistan, Tunisia, Ukraine.

Upper-middle income countries (GNI/capita $3466–$10 725 in 2005): Argentina, Barbados, Belize, Botswana, Chile, Costa Rica, Croatia, Czech Republic, Equatorial Guinea, Estonia, Gabon, Hungary, Latvia, Lebanon, Lithuania, Libya, Malaysia, Mauritius, Mexico, Oman, Panama, Poland, Romania, Russia, Seychelles, Slovakia, South Africa, Turkey, Uruguay, Venezuela.

High-income countries (GNI/capita ≤$10 726 in 2005): Australia, Austria, Bahamas, Bahrain, Belgium, Brunei, Canada, Cyprus, Denmark, Finland, France, Germany, Greece, Iceland, Ireland, Israel, Italy, Japan, South Korea, Kuwait, Luxembourg, Malta, Netherlands, New Zealand, Norway, Portugal, Qatar, Saudi Arabia, Singapore, Slovenia, Spain, Sweden, Switzerland, Taiwan, United Arab Emirates, UK, USA.

Table 8A.2. Military expenditure by country, in local currency, 1997–2006

Figures are in local currency at current prices and are for calendar years, unless otherwise stated.

Country	Currency	1997	1998	1999	2000	2001	2002	2003	2004	2005	2006
Africa											
North Africa											
Algeria§1	m. dinars	101 126	112 248	121 597	141 576	149 468	167 000	170 764	201 929	214 320	224 767
Libya	m. dinars	577	675	535	556	496	575	700	894	981	1 000
Morocco2	m. dirhams	15 643	16 102	16 492	16 685	18 543	19 414	19 976	20 133	20 506	21 075
Tunisia	m. dinars	396	417	424	456	483	491	525	554	608	574
Sub-Saharan Africa											
Angola3	b. kwanzas	[0.2]	[0.1]	[1.7]	[2.0]	[2.8]	[7.5]	[22.2]	[68.4]	144	..
Benin	m. CFA francs	..	..	..	..	..	..	..	..	..	24 464
Botswana	m. pula	586	765	784	942	1 229	1 415	1 560	[1 728]	[1 602]	..
Burkina Faso	m. CFA francs	22 500	23 300	25 700	26 100	27 000	33 400	31 960	34 700	40 173	[44 501]
Burundi	b. francs	21.8	26.3	28.5	30.5	44.2	41.8	47.0	49.4	53.5	50.7
Cameroon§	m. CFA francs	69 288	80 969	89 095	87 598	91 118	101 500	109 556	116 808	117 670	134 345
Cape Verde	m. escudos	382	443	518	814	572	530	554	586	..	..
Central Afr. Rep.‡4	m. CFA francs	..	..	..	..	..	7 445	8 729	7 979	8 121	..
Chad	b. CFA francs	12.0	11.8	16.0	18.8	22.5	23.9	23.8	26.7	29.3	30.9
Congo, Republic of	m. CFA francs	..	..	..	..	28 374	35 035	39 916	40 050	41 400	44 070
Congo, DRC5	m./b. francs	110	42.8	600	2 901	..	..	48.0	78.0	71.0	(76.0)
Côte d'Ivoire	b. CFA francs	54.6	..	..	..	..	..	124	..	..	..
Djibouti	m. francs	4 019	4 042	4 053	3 979	4 045	4 500	..	..	..	..
Equatorial Guinea	m. CFA francs	..	..	..	..	..	..	..	..	..	..
Eritrea6	m. nakfa	634	1 936	2 225	2 220	1 884	2 104	2 520	..	..	..
Ethiopia7	m. birr	1 512	3 263	5 589	5 075	3 154	2 671	2 397	2 686	2 960	3 000
Gabon	b. CFA francs	..	..	..	65.0	60.0	66.0	63.0	65.0	58.0	60.0
Gambia‡	m. dalasis	42.6	43.1	40.1	42.5	38.5	48.6	51.1	57.9	..	..
Ghana8	m. cedis	93 148	132 812	158 060	277 269	231 740	297 800	439 200	636 097	726 111	827 595

Country	Currency	1997	1998	1999	2000	2001	2002	2003	2004	2005	2006
Guinea[9]	b. francs	48.6	55.7	76.6	80.3	171	194	167	182	..	..
Guinea-Bissau[10]	m. CFA francs	1 061	1 711	..	6 786	4 533	4 435	4 362	..	6 391	..
Kenya	m. shillings	10 327	10 381	10 684	12 614	15 349	16 844	18 676	20 570	23 936	27 087
Lesotho	m. maloti	132	154	208	212	201	206	207	203	214	..
Liberia	m. dollars	..	..	..	..	(1 990)	(2 590)	..	..	..	..
Madagascar[11]	b. ariary	53.5	54.9	56.6	63.9	85.7	78.9	89.8	102	108	116
Malawi	m. kwacha	434	450	635	698	916	1 136	1 276	..	..	..
Mali	b. CFA francs	31.3	32.2	36.0	41.4	43.8	45.8	51.6	54.5	63.2	68.9
Mauritania[12]	b. ouguiyas	5.2	6.3	4.8	6.7	9.0	13.3	9.9	16.4	18.6	17.7
Mauritius	m. rupees	206	203	228	246	262	285	304	319	363	..
Mozambique[13]	m. new meticais	[485]	[585]	722	843	1 048	1 267	1 422	1 753	1 436	1 459
Namibia[14]	m. dollars	386	436	646	641	833	928	979	1 079	1 192	1 306
Niger	b. CFA francs	10.1	13.0	14.5	14.3	18.2	14.4	14.3	17.2	..	..
Nigeria[15]	m. naira	17 920	25 162	45 400	37 490	63 472	108 148	75 913	65 400	88 506	101 452
Rwanda[16]	b. francs	23.3	27.2	27.0	23.9	25.2	24.3	23.0	24.7	34.3	37.7
Senegal¶[17]	m. CFA francs	41 324	44 300	48 200	44 400	50 500	51 829	56 293	56 819	65 469	77 528
Seychelles	m. rupees	57.3	55.5	59.3	59.0	64.8	64.1	66.1	87.6	69.0	77.0
Sierra Leone[18]	m. leones	(9 315)	..	..	[55 000]	37 868	33 371	40 774	35 243	34 041	41 859
Somalia	shillings										
South Africa	m. rand	11 131	10 716	10 678	13 128	15 516	18 616	20 247	20 277	22 687	23 752
Sudan[19]	b. dinars	15.4	52.2	109	151	100	128	104	..	..	..
Swaziland	m. emalangeni	[137]	[163]	[180]	[186]	[184]	[223]	[261]	[298]	..	..
Tanzania	b. shillings	72.6	89.3	95.7	108	132	136	130	139	152	179
Togo	m. CFA francs										
Uganda‡	b. shillings	139	181	212	[202]	[215]	[230]	[270]	325	350	360
Zambia[20]	b. kwacha	57.0	85.0	134	..	100	..	..	585	..	..
Zimbabwe[21]	m. new dollars	3.4	3.7	10.1	15.4	15.8	37.3	136	1 292	2 942	..

Americas

Caribbean											
Bahamas	m. dollars	[33.6]	33.4	34.1	28.6	28.1	30.2	32.9	34.9	39.2	48.3
Barbados	m. dollars	33.0	37.9	40.4	43.6	47.0	47.2	46.9	46.9	..	..
Cuba	m. pesos	..	..	..	..	..	..	..	..	..	..
Dominican Rep.	m. pesos	1 682	1 818	2 005	2 872	3 742	4 440	3 578	4 093	5 336	[5 392]
Haiti	gourdes	..	..	..	..	..	..	..	..	..	..
Jamaica‡	m. dollars	1 951	1 741	1 762	1 873	2 133	2 755	3 167	3 311	3 469	3 689
Trinidad & Tobago	dollars	..	..	..	..	..	..	..	..	..	..
Central America											
Belize	th. dollars	18 790	..	..	..	..	..	..	..	..	..
Costa Rica[22]	m. colones	..	..	..	..	..	..	..	..	..	..
El Salvador	m. dollar	97.5	96.3	99.8	112	109	109	106	106	108	109
Guatemala	m. quetzales	801	894	914	1 225	1 546	1 239	1 420	913	798	1 111
Honduras† § [23]	m. lempiras	..	..	..	516	646	898	919	928	933	1 041
Mexico† §	m. new pesos	18 306	20 950	25 825	29 228	30 884	31 083	33 404	32 690	34 800	35 196
Nicaragua[24]	m. córdobas	286	278	318	390	389	501	537	505	565	613
Panama[25]	m. balboas	118	104	112	..	..	..	..	..	..	..
North America											
Canada	m. dollars	11 001	11 495	12 199	12 326	12 972	13 332	13 952	14 749	15 739	16 677
USA[26]	m. dollars	276 324	274 278	280 969	301 697	312 743	356 720	415 223	464 676	504 638	546 018
South America											
Argentina	m. pesos	3 769	3 782	3 852	3 739	3 638	3 784	4 433	4 803	5 553	[5 897]
Bolivia[27]	m. bolivianos	797	1 002	848	869	1 104	1 064	1 161	1 171	[1 232]	[1 298]
Brazil	m. reais	[17 440]	[16 960]	[16 408]	18 617	23 062	28 620	25 590	25 620	30 450	[34 043]
Chile§ [28]	b. pesos	1 114	1 249	1 367	1 502	1 615	1 765	1 743	2 216	2 463	2 809
Colombia[29]	b. pesos	3 537	4 356	5 372	5 935	7 228	7 405	[8 823]	[9 790]	[10 588]	[11 120]
Ecuador[30]	m. US dollars	499	549	296	266	384	505	739	710	887	[934]
Guyana	m. dollars	..	..	..	..	..	..	..	..	..	..
Paraguay	b. guaranies	[284]	[294]	[266]	[283]	284	296	345	310	341	[425]

Country	Currency	1997	1998	1999	2000	2001	2002	2003	2004	2005	2006
Peru[31]	m. nuevos soles	2 224	2 671	2 773	3 228	3 486	2 709	3 066	3 178	3 585	3 653
Uruguay	m. pesos	[3 812]	[4 114]	4 501	4 009	4 375	4 330	4 755	5 009	5 349	5 442
Venezuela	b. bolivares	753	716	927	1 030	1 524	1 388	1 706	2 571	3 357	4 475
Asia and Oceania											
Central Asia											
Kazakhstan[32]	b. tenge	17.9	19.0	17.2	20.4	32.5	37.7	47.5	58.0	78.7	[93.2]
Kyrgyzstan[32]	m. soms	955	912	1 267	1 864	1 734	2 055	2 408	2 688	3 100	[3 483]
Tajikistan[32]	th. somoni	10 713	17 562	18 723	21 496	29 577	70 700	106 500	134 000	..	..
Turkmenistan[32 33]	b. manats	440	436	582	..	..	..	..	..	..	..
Uzbekistan[32 34]	m. sum	[13 700]	..	34 860	..	41 115	..	53 018	..	..	..
East Asia											
Brunei	m. dollars	548	492	438	421	390	405	424	(337)	(414)	449
Cambodia[35]	b. riel	447	481	474	455	417	407	411	423	451	498
China, P. R.[36]	b. yuan	[131]	[149]	[165]	[182]	[216]	[253]	[283]	[324]	[363]	[411]
Indonesia	b. rupiahs	8 336	10 349	10 254	13 945	16 416	19 291	27 446	[32 111]	[33 091]	[40 491]
Japan[† § 37]	b. yen	4 922	4 942	4 934	4 935	4 950	4 956	4 954	4 916	4 868	4 824
Korea, North[38]	b. won	..	(2.9)	(2.9)	(3.0)	(3.1)	(3.3)	(3.9)	(4.2)	(5.0)	..
Korea, South[† ¶ 39]	b. won	13 102	13 594	13 337	14 477	15 497	16 364	17 515	18 941	20 823	22 863
Laos	b. kip	53.0	66.5	224	278	325	..	..	..	..	..
Malaysia	m. ringgits	5 877	4 547	6 321	5 826	7 351	8 504	10 950	10 728	11 817	11 734
Mongolia	m. tugriks	14 767	16 750	18 416	26 126	25 384	28 071	27 899	32 891	35 940	..
Myanmar[40]	b. kyats	29.8	37.3	43.7	58.8	63.9	73.1	..	..	..	..
Philippines	m. pesos	29 212	31 512	32 959	36 208	35 977	38 907	44 440	43 847	47 634	52 657
Singapore	m. dollars	6 618	7 475	7 616	7 466	7 721	8 108	8 230	8 525	9 099	9 849
Taiwan	b. dollars	302	299	258	243	248	225	228	249	250	241
Thailand	m. baht	98 172	86 133	74 809	71 268	75 413	76 724	77 774	77 067	81 171	85 936
Viet Nam	b. dong	..	..	..	..	..	..	..	..	..	..

South Asia											
Afghanistan	m. afghani	..	..	..	..	..	..	29 376	33 958	36 042	..
Bangladesh	m. taka	25 863	28 436	31 277	33 377	34 020	34 105	36 150	39 630	43 005	46 950
India[41]	b. rupees	416	492	598	642	689	717	761	812	982	1 102
Nepal[¶][42]	m. rupees	2 471	2 789	3 239	3 648	4 837	6 621	7 951	9 756	12 488	12 171
Pakistan	b. rupees	132	140	147	154	170	188	210	240	270	[290]
Sri Lanka[†][43]	b. rupees	37.1	42.5	40.1	56.9	54.2	49.2	47.0	[56.3]	61.5	68.4
Oceania											
Australia	m. dollars	10 207	10 799	11 496	11 975	12 995	14 077	14 965	16 119	17 184	18 694
Fiji	m. dollars	47.0	48.0	49.0	73.0	86.0	71.0	[70.0]	[55.0]	..	..
New Zealand	m. dollars	1 344	1 363	1 380	1 422	1 428	1 411	1 468	1 524	1 563	1 612
Papua New Guinea	m. kina	92.6	86.0	80.0	85.0	85.5	66.3	68.8	78.7	94.2	89.5
Tonga	th. pa'anga	3 623	3 693	3 535	3 837	4 211	4 319	4 314	4 121	..	..
Europe											
Albania[¶][44]	m. leks	4 442	5 067	5 891	6 519	7 638	8 220	9 279	10 574	11 730	14 168
Armenia[†][45]	b. drams	31.4	33.7	36.5	36.7	36.8	36.8	44.3	52.3	61.0	74.1
Austria	m. euros	[1 920]	[1 943]	[1 994]	[2 090]	[1 999]	1 999	2 111	2 158	2 160	2 181
Azerbaijan[46]	m. new manat	[73.4]	[83.0]	[99.1]	[107]	[123]	[136]	[173]	[224]	297	587
Belarus[†][¶]	b. roubles	6.0	10.0	39.0	115	247	366	475	679	793	[1 334]
Belgium	m. euros	3 267	3 297	3 378	3 463	3 393	3 344	3 434	3 449	3 385	3 542
Bosnia–Herzegov.[47]	m. marka	..	..	..	..	..	501	351	316	274	..
Bulgaria[†]	m. leva	372	512	595	677	805	859	895	930	1 006	1 116
Croatia[†][48]	m. kunas	7 000	7 500	6 084	4 510	4 336	4 355	4 089	3 585	3 649	4 081
Cyprus[†]	m. pounds	185	169	106	118	142	100	101	107	109	114
Czech Republic	m. koruny	31 328	37 643	41 688	44 670	44 978	48 924	53 194	52 481	52 953	55 694
Denmark	m. kroner	18 521	19 071	19 428	19 339	21 017	21 269	21 075	21 441	20 800	23 026
Estonia	m. krooni	736	843	1 083	1 329	1 640	2 028	2 376	2 581	2 576	2 950
Finland	m. euros	1 700	1 761	1 552	1 691	1 653	1 712	2 006	2 131	2 206	2 274
France[49]	m. euros	36 756	36 012	36 510	36 702	37 187	38 681	40 684	42 690	42 545	43 202
Georgia[50]	m. lari	[57.1]	[57.1]	[52.4]	[37.2]	[49.4]	74.6	91.5	135	417	427

Country	Currency	1997	1998	1999	2000	2001	2002	2003	2004	2005	2006
Germany	m. euros	29 451	29 822	30 603	30 554	30 648	31 168	31 060	30 610	30 600	30 220
Greece	m. euros	4 433	5 061	5 439	5 921	5 986	6 085	6 309	[6 565]	[7 426]	[7 972]
Hungary	m. forint	146 820	151 215	191 485	226 041	272 426	279 569	314 380	310 731	318 552	277 804
Iceland	krónur	0	0	0	0	0	0	0	0	0	0
Ireland	m. euros	623	644	677	734	835	841	848	850	917	932
Italy[51]	m. euros	19 987	21 052	22 240	24 325	24 592	25 887	26 795	27 476	26 959	24 508
Latvia[52]	m. lats	22.1	24.8	33.1	42.4	54.6	91.0	108	124	155	184
Lithuania[53]	m. litai	[245]	[448]	[388]	[644]	[652]	715	816	864	852	961
Luxembourg	m. euros	119	129	132	139	179	192	205	[213]	[238]	[263]
Macedonia, FYR[54]	m. denar	4 163	4 302	3 769	4 602	15 397	6 841	6 292	6 683	6 259	6 149
Malta[†]	th. liri	12 020	11 297	11 164	11 109	12 205	12 317	12 874	13 948	14 121	13 930
Moldova[†¶][55]	m. lei	80.5	57.0	63.0	63.3	76.7	94.7	109	113	127	126
Netherlands	m. euros	6 056	6 154	6 595	6 482	6 929	7 149	7 404	7 552	7 693	7 923
Norway	m. kroner	23 010	25 087	25 809	25 722	26 669	32 461	31 985	32 945	31 471	32 143
Poland	m. zlotys	[10 489]	12 133	12 800	13 763	14 864	15 400	16 249	17 793	19 023	20 677
Portugal	m. euros	2 089	2 098	2 259	2 393	2 598	2 765	2 792	[3 051]	[3 363]	[3 279]
Romania[56]	m. new lei	[770]	[1 113]	1 465	2 031	2 864	3 491	4 151	4 994	5 675	6 506
Russia[57]	b. roubles	[105]	[85.6]	[165]	[271]	[365]	[470]	[568]	[656]	[880]	[1 076]
Serbia–Monten.[58]	m. dinars	[5 406]	6 441	8 600	21 292	33 060	43 695	42 070	43 154	41 996	45 738
Slovakia[†¶]	m. korunas	16 792	14 009	13 532	15 760	19 051	19 947	22 965	22 944	25 550	28 245
Slovenia	m. tolars	46 434	50 030	49 958	49 518	65 903	78 552	86 346	94 873	99 085	120 221
Spain	m. euros	6 750	6 756	7 092	7 599	7 972	8 414	8 587	9 132	9 508	10 243
Sweden[59]	m. kronor	39 726	40 801	42 541	44 542	42 639	42 401	42 903	40 527	41 240	39 823
Switzerland[†¶]	m. francs	4 634	4 532	4 416	4 503	4 476	4 461	4 437	4 381	4 344	4 284
Turkey[60]	m. new lira	1 183	2 289	4 168	6 248	8 844	12 108	13 553	13 386	13 840	16 451
UK[61]	m. pounds	21 792	22 261	22 530	23 301	24 217	25 718	29 845	32 217	33 042	33 440
Ukraine[§][62]	m. hryvnias	3 851	3 442	3 890	6 184	5 848	6 266	7 615	8 963	[10 244]	[11 336]

Middle East

Bahrain[63]	m. dinars	109	111	123	121	126	126	176	180	182	177
Egypt	m. pounds	8 503	9 439	9 881	10 847	11 859	12 741	13 948	14 684	15 213	16 476
Iran[64]	b. rials	8 540	10 624	17 757	31 113	38 310	35 362	48 291	63 073	81 183	95 879
Iraq[65]	b. dinars	. .	. .	. .	. .	. .	. .	. .	. .	(2 213)	(3 574)
Israel[66]	b. new shekels	31.4	34.3	37.4	39.5	40.6	47.4	44.7	45.8	56.2	52.3
Jordan	m. dinars	[324]	[312]	[322]	[330]	[329]	[407]	[480]	458	477	492
Kuwait	m. dinars	745	696	696	827	824	858	933	1 032	1 142	1 147
Lebanon	b. pounds	[1 044]	1 052	1 251	1 102	1 445	1 368	1 392	1 439	1 510	1 417
Oman‡[67]	m. rials	760	676	687	809	933	958	1 010	1 144	1 404	1 245
Qatar	m. riyals	. .	. .	. .	. .	. .	. .	. .	. .	. .	. .
Saudi Arabia[68]	m. rials	67 975	78 231	68 700	74 866	78 850	69 382	70 303	78 414	95 146	110 779
Syria	b. pounds	[37.6]	[40.4]	39.5	49.9	47.6	47.9	59.0	74.7	68.9	65.5
UAE[69]	m. dirhams	8 629	8 712	8 790	8 688	8 796	9 139	9 244	8 943	9 399	. .
Yemen	b. riyals	51.3	52.2	61.5	76.6	[91.1]	130	148	136	193	. .

Table 8A.3. Military expenditure by country, in constant US dollars for 1997–2006 and current US dollars for 2006

Figures are in US$ m. at constant 2005 prices and exchange rates except in the right-most column, marked *, where they are in current US$ m. Figures are for calendar years unless otherwise stated.

Current	1997	1998	1999	2000	2001	2002	2003	2004	2005	2006	2006*
Africa											
North Africa											
Algeria§1	1 703	1 801	1 900	2 205	2 234	2 461	2 453	2 801	2 925	3 014	3 089
Libya	367	414	320	342	335	431	536	699	749	741	763
Morocco2	1 994	1 997	2 032	2 017	2 228	2 269	2 308	2 292	2 312	2 314	2 406
Tunisia	379	386	382	400	415	411	428	436	469	395	432
Sub-Saharan Africa											
Angola3	[1 186]	[423]	[1 546]	[436]	[224]	[304]	[456]	[973]	1 654	:	:
Benin	:	:	:	:	:	:	:	:	:	44.7	47.0
Botswana	209	256	243	269	329	351	355	[367]	[313]	:	:
Burkina Faso	51.3	50.6	56.4	57.4	56.6	68.4	64.2	70.0	76.2	[82.2]	[85.5]
Burundi	42.6	45.7	47.9	41.2	54.7	52.4	54.6	51.9	49.5	46.0	49.2
Cameroon§	154	175	189	183	183	198	212	226	223	243	258
Cape Verde	4.9	5.5	6.1	9.9	6.7	6.1	6.3	6.8	:	:	:
Central African Republic‡4	:	:	:	:	:	14.8	16.7	15.6	15.4	:	:
Chad	26.9	25.3	37.4	42.3	45.0	45.5	46.1	54.6	55.5	55.3	59.4
Congo, Republic of	:	:	:	:	58.9	69.7	79.9	78.3	78.5	79.2	84.7
Congo, DRC5	61.1	18.4	67.0	49.8	:	:	128	200	150	(146)	(169)
Côte d'Ivoire	131	:	:	:	:	:	247	247	:	:	:
Djibouti	26.1	25.7	25.7	24.9	24.8	27.5	:	:	:	:	:
Equatorial Guinea	:	:	:	:	:	:	:	:	:	:	:
Eritrea6	135	378	400	333	247	236	230	:	:	:	:
Ethiopia7	246	518	822	741	502	418	319	346	341	316	345
Gabon	:	:	:	129	117	129	120	123	110	112	115
Gambia‡	2.5	2.4	2.2	2.3	2.0	2.3	2.1	2.1	:	:	:

Ghana[8]	41.5	51.6	54.7	76.6	48.2	53.9	62.8	80.7	80.0	83.1	90.2
Guinea[9]	28.4	31.0	40.7	40.0	80.9	89.0	68.0	63.0	..	..	..
Guinea-Bissau[10]	2.5	3.8	..	13.8	8.9	8.5	8.6	8.6	12.1	..	..
Kenya	247	233	227	243	280	301	304	300	317	315	372
Lesotho	35.3	38.1	48.7	46.7	49.1	37.6	35.4	33.0	33.6	..	..
Liberia	..	..	..	..	(48.6)	(55.4)	..	..	..	..	..
Madagascar[11]	57.7	55.8	52.3	52.7	66.1	52.5	60.5	60.2	54.0	52.9	53.5
Malawi	17.7	14.1	13.8	11.7	12.5	13.5	13.9	..	..	..	..
Mali	68.2	67.5	76.3	88.4	88.9	88.5	101	110	120	130	132
Mauritania[12]	32.2	36.1	26.4	35.7	45.8	65.2	46.1	69.3	70.0	62.9	65.9
Mauritius	10.7	9.8	10.3	10.7	10.8	11.0	11.3	11.3	12.3	..	..
Mozambique[13]	[43.2]	[51.3]	61.6	63.8	72.7	75.3	74.4	81.3	62.3	55.4	57.2
Namibia[14]	106	113	154	140	166	166	164	173	187	197	191
Niger	22.8	28.1	32.1	30.8	37.6	29.0	29.3	35.2	..	..	..
Nigeria[15]	356	454	781	593	845	1 274	784	566	674	724	798
Rwanda[16]	62.3	68.5	69.6	59.1	60.5	57.1	50.4	48.3	61.5	63.2	68.3
Senegal¶[17]	86.7	91.9	99.1	90.6	100	100	109	110	124	145	479
Seychelles	13.8	13.0	13.1	12.2	12.7	12.5	12.5	15.9	12.5	14.0	14.0
Sierra Leone[18]	(7.8)	..	..	[25.5]	17.2	15.7	17.8	12.0	11.8	13.2	14.1
Somalia	..	..	..	..	..	..	..	..	..	..	..
South Africa	2 654	2 391	2 265	2 644	2 957	3 249	3 338	3 297	3 568	3 610	3 467
Sudan[19]	132	381	684	900	565	663	502	..	..	..	..
Swaziland	[37.9]	[41.8]	[43.5]	[40.1]	[37.5]	[40.5]	[44.2]	[48.8]	..	..	..
Tanzania	99.1	108	107	114	133	136	125	134	135	149	141
Togo	..	..	..	..	..	..	34.1	33.9	33.2	..	..
Uganda‡	104	136	150	[139]	[145]	[156]	[169]	197	197	..	..
Zambia[20]	63.9	76.5	95.1	46.4	..	..	..	..	197	191	195
Zimbabwe[21]	150	123	211	207	120	118	92.4	132	132	..	..

Current	1997	1998	1999	2000	2001	2002	2003	2004	2005	2006	2006*
Americas											
Caribbean											
Bahamas	[38.4]	37.5	37.8	31.4	30.0	31.9	33.5	35.4	39.2	47.3	48.3
Barbados	19.0	22.2	23.2	24.5	25.7	25.8	25.2	24.9	:	:	:
Cuba	:										
Dominican Republic	153	158	164	218	261	294	186	140	175	[165]	[165]
Haiti	:										
Jamaica†	64.6	53.1	50.7	49.8	53.0	64.0	66.7	61.4	55.7	54.8	56.1
Trinidad and Tobago	:										
Central America											
Belize	8.9										
Costa Rica[22]	:										
El Salvador	121	117	121	132	124	122	116	111	108	105	109
Guatemala	178	186	181	229	269	199	217	130	105	137	146
Honduras†§[23]	:	:	:	41.0	46.8	60.4	57.4	53.6	49.6	52.6	55.1
Mexico†§	3 160	3 120	3 298	3 409	3 388	3 246	3 336	3 119	3 193	3 136	3 201
Nicaragua[24]	33.4	28.7	29.5	32.5	30.2	37.4	38.1	33.0	33.8	33.5	34.9
Panama[25]	128	112	119	:							
North America											
Canada	10 748	11 122	11 603	11 412	11 709	11 771	11 984	12 441	12 986	13 507	14 837
USA[26]	336 185	328 611	329 421	342 172	344 932	387 303	440 813	480 451	504 638	528 692	546 018
South America											
Argentina	2 074	2 062	2 125	2 082	2 048	1 692	1 748	1 813	1 912	[1 847]	[1 927]
Bolivia[27]	133	155	128	126	157	150	158	153	[153]	[155]	[162]
Brazil	[12 569]	[11 845]	[10 928]	11 583	13 428	15 369	11 979	11 250	12 510	[13 446]	[15 638]
Chile§[28]	2 551	2 719	2 879	3 048	3 164	3 374	3 241	4 077	4 397	4 858	5 256
Colombia[29]	2 997	3 111	3 460	3 500	3 948	3 803	[4 229]	[4 431]	[4 562]	[4 609]	[4 595]
Ecuador[30]	696	688	353	317	439	578	778	727	887	[908]	[934]

Guyana	:	:	:	:	:	:	:	:	:	:	:
Paraguay	[90.0]	[83.5]	[70.8]	[69.1]	64.7	61.0	62.2	53.6	55.2	[63.5]	[76.1]
Peru[31]	855	958	961	1 078	1 141	885	980	980	1 088	1 086	1 118
Uruguay	[310]	[302]	313	266	278	241	222	214	219	210	227
Venezuela	1 791	1 254	1 314	1 257	1 654	1 229	1 152	1 427	1 606	1 924	2 084
Asia and Oceania											
Central Asia											
Kazakhstan[32]	248	246	206	215	317	347	411	470	592	[650]	[768]
Kyrgyzstan[32]	51.1	44.2	44.8	55.5	48.3	56.1	63.8	68.4	75.6	[80.5]	[86.7]
Tajikistan[32]	17.3	19.8	16.6	14.3	14.2	30.3	39.2	46.0	:	:	:
Turkmenistan[32 33]	198	168	182	:	:	:	:	:	:	:	:
Uzbekistan[32 34]	[115]	:	173	:	92.5	:	72.0	:	:	:	:
East Asia											
Brunei	334	301	269	254	234	249	260	(205)	(249)	268	283
Cambodia[35]	147	138	131	127	117	110	110	109	110	114	121
China, P. R.[36]	[16 800]	[19 300]	[21 600]	[23 800]	[28 000]	[33 100]	[36 600]	[40 300]	[44 300]	[49 500]	[51 400]
Indonesia	2 653	2 079	1 710	2 242	2 367	2 486	3 319	[3 655]	[3 410]	[3 695]	[4 430]
Japan[† § 37]	43 521	43 405	43 483	43 802	44 275	44 725	44 814	44 473	44 165	43 701	41702
Korea, North[38]	:	:	:	:	:	:	:	:	:	:	:
Korea, South[† ¶ 39]	16 706	16 127	15 689	16 652	17 120	17 605	18 197	19 000	20 333	21 853	23 928
Laos	44.3	29.1	42.9	42.5	46.1	:	:	:	:	:	:
Malaysia	1 858	1 365	1 847	1 677	2 087	2 370	3 020	2 917	3 120	2 996	3 200
Mongolia	20.2	21.3	21.0	28.1	27.0	28.4	26.1	29.7	29.8	:	:
Myanmar[40]	27 571	22 722	22 505	30 349	27 201	19 809	:	:	:	:	:
Philippines	828	818	807	853	794	833	920	857	865	901	1 019
Singapore	4 153	4 703	4 791	4 634	4 745	5 002	5 051	5 147	5 468	5 868	6 194
Taiwan	9 487	9 247	7 966	7 389	7 539	6 871	6 966	7 494	7 352	6 963	7 380
Thailand	3 006	2 440	2 113	1 982	2 063	2 087	2 077	2 003	2 018	2 045	2 265
Viet Nam	:	:	:	:	:	:	:	:	:	:	:

Current	1997	1998	1999	2000	2001	2002	2003	2004	2005	2006	2006*
South Asia											
Afghanistan	..	..	..	..	..	..	834	777	728	:	:
Bangladesh	615	624	647	675	675	655	657	659	669	692	678
India[41]	14 144	14 757	17 150	17 697	18 313	18 256	18 664	19 204	22 273	23 933	24 014
Nepal¶[42]	52.1	52.9	57.1	62.8	81.1	108	122	146	175	161	165
Pakistan	3 285	3 281	3 311	3 320	3 553	3 819	4 138	4 399	4 534	[4 572]	[4 818]
Sri Lanka†[43]	716	751	676	904	755	625	562	[626]	612	616	664
Oceania											
Australia	9 675	10 150	10 648	10 617	11 037	11 608	12 008	12 639	13 122	13 794	14 075
Fiji	34.9	33.7	33.8	49.7	56.2	46.1	[43.6]	[33.3]	:	:	:
New Zealand	1 110	1 112	1 127	1 132	1 107	1 066	1 090	1 106	1 101	1 094	1 022
Papua New Guinea	65.6	53.6	43.4	39.9	36.7	25.5	23.0	25.8	30.4	27.9	29.0
Tonga	3.4	3.4	3.1	3.2	3.2	3.0	2.7	2.3	:	:	:
Europe											
Albania¶[44]	63.0	59.6	69.0	76.3	86.7	86.6	97.3	108	117	139	146
Armenia†[45]	86.8	85.6	87.4	90.4	88.1	89.7	105	115	133	156	177
Austria	[2 743]	[2 751]	[2 808]	[2 875]	[2 679]	2 632	2 741	2 746	2 687	2 676	2 751
Azerbaijan[46]	[89.6]	[102]	[133]	[141]	[160]	[172]	[215]	[260]	314	571	657
Belarus†¶	196	189	187	205	274	284	287	348	368	[574]	[622]
Belgium	4 723	4 722	4 783	4 783	4 573	4 434	4 482	4 409	4 210	4 331	4 465
Bosnia and Herzegovina[47]	..	..	..	..	..	328	228	205	174	:	:
Bulgaria†	412	478	542	559	619	624	637	622	641	665	720
Croatia†[48]	1 559	1 570	1 231	867	795	785	737	623	613	684	705
Cyprus†	494	441	273	291	344	235	228	237	234	239	307
Czech Republic	1 715	1 862	2 019	2 082	2 003	2 140	2 325	2 231	2 210	2 264	2 474
Denmark	3 655	3 695	3 673	3 553	3 774	3 728	3 618	3 638	3 467	3 770	3 890
Estonia	80.9	85.6	106	126	147	175	202	213	204	225	238
Finland	2 381	2 434	2 120	2 234	2 129	2 171	2 521	2 673	2 744	2 791	2 878

France[49]	51 926	50 535	50 979	50 395	50 225	51 257	52 643	54 018	52 917	53 091	54 686
Georgia[50]	[53.6]	[51.7]	[39.8]	[27.2]	[34.5]	49.3	57.7	80.6	230	223	239
Germany	40 854	40 993	41 822	41 147	40 474	40 604	40 044	38 816	38 060	36 984	38 108
Greece	7 228	7 876	8 246	8 701	8 508	8 350	8 361	[8 456]	[9 236]	[9 642]	[10 091]
Hungary	1 350	1 217	1 401	1 507	1 662	1 621	1 742	1 612	1 596	1 353	1 295
Iceland	0	0	0	0	0	0	0	0	0	0	0
Ireland	1 012	1 022	1 057	1 085	1 177	1 133	1 104	1 083	1 141	1 121	1 180
Italy[51]	29 781	30 763	31 969	34 102	33 543	34 459	34 739	34 853	33 531	29 891	30 905
Latvia[52]	52.5	56.2	73.3	91.6	115	188	217	234	274	308	330
Lithuania[53]	[98.2]	[171]	[147]	[242]	[242]	264	305	319	308	335	351
Luxembourg	174	187	190	194	243	256	267	[272]	[296]	[319]	[333]
Macedonia, FYR[54]	97.2	101	88.8	102	325	142	129	136	127	121	127
Malta†	42.0	38.5	37.3	36.2	38.7	38.2	39.4	41.6	40.8	39.2	41.0
Moldova†¶[55]	50.5	33.2	26.4	20.2	22.3	26.9	27.0	24.7	24.6	22.4	..
Netherlands	9 147	9 114	9 557	9 116	9 352	9 344	9 479	9 549	9 568	9 751	10 029
Norway	4 203	4 482	4 506	4 358	4 385	5 269	5 066	5 194	4 887	4 891	5 070
Poland	[4 900]	5 073	4 989	4 874	4 990	5 073	5 311	5 615	5 880	6 330	6 627
Portugal[56]	3 282	3 210	3 378	3 479	3 617	3 719	3 636	[3 882]	[4 183]	[3 980]	[4 135]
Romania[56]	[2 069]	1 696	1 696	1 614	1 693	1 684	1 737	1 868	1 948	2 100	2 323
Russia[57]	[21 300]	[13 600]	[14 000]	[19 100]	[21 300]	[23 600]	[25 100]	[26 100]	[31 100]	[34 700]	[39 800]
Serbia and Montenegro[58]	[781]	715	671	970	772	854	749	692	580	562	678
Slovakia†¶	952	744	650	676	761	771	818	760	824	873	943
Slovenia	393	392	369	336	412	457	476	505	514	610	632
Spain	10 599	10 418	10 690	11 073	11 214	11 483	11 374	11 741	11 826	12 328	12 966
Sweden[59]	5 780	5 954	6 178	6 411	5 993	5 833	5 791	5 450	5 521	5 271	5 418
Switzerland†¶	3 976	3 888	3 757	3 773	3 714	3 678	3 635	3 560	3 489	3 405	3 438
Turkey[60]	13 684	14 339	15 832	15 322	14 046	13 265	11 851	10 778	10 301	11 291	11 248
UK[61]	48 276	47 691	47 529	47 778	48 760	50 949	57 452	60 234	60 076	59 213	61 925
Ukraine§[62]	1 918	1 551	1 429	1 772	1 497	1 592	1 839	1 985	[1 999]	[2 023]	[2 245]

Current	1997	1998	1999	2000	2001	2002	2003	2004	2005	2006	2006*
Middle East											
Bahrain[63]	297	304	340	337	356	357	491	491	483	458	470
Egypt	2 073	2 215	2 249	2 404	2 570	2 688	2 816	2 664	2 632	2 710	2 868
Iran[64]	2 977	3 142	4 374	6 695	7 408	5 981	7 013	7 982	9 057	9 849	10 453
Iraq[65]	:	:	:	:	:	:	:	:	(1 503)	(1 641)	(2 407)
Israel[66]	8 519	8 827	9 149	9 553	9 712	10 735	10 050	10 339	12 522	11 373	11 737
Jordan	[538]	[502]	[515]	[524]	[514]	[624]	[724]	669	673	659	694
Kuwait	2 933	2 735	2 658	3 082	3 029	3 126	3 369	3 679	3 909	3 836	3 953
Lebanon	[735]	708	840	743	978	911	914	957	1 002	899	940
Oman‡[67]	1 934	1 735	1 757	2 091	2 439	2 520	2 667	3 011	3 652	3 091	3 238
Qatar	:	:	:	:	:	:	:	:	:	:	:
Saudi Arabia[68]	17 749	20 500	18 248	20 112	21 421	18 805	18 944	21 060	25 372	29 032	29 541
Syria	[3 789]	[4 104]	4 167	5 474	5 070	5 053	5 883	7 134	6 138	5 526	5 835
UAE[69]	3 067	3 036	2 999	2 925	2 882	2 909	2 853	2 629	2 559	:	:
Yemen	565	543	589	700	[744]	943	973	793	1 009	:	:

Table 8A.4. Military expenditure by country as percentage of gross domestic product, 1997–2005

Country	1997	1998	1999	2000	2001	2002	2003	2004	2005
Africa									
North Africa									
Algeria§[1]	3.6	4.0	3.8	3.5	3.5	3.7	3.3	3.4	2.9
Libya	4.1	5.3	3.8	3.1	2.7	2.4	2.3	2.4	2.0
Morocco[2]	4.9	4.7	4.8	4.7	4.8	4.9	4.8	4.5	4.5
Tunisia	1.9	1.8	1.7	1.7	1.7	1.6	1.6	1.6	1.6
Sub-Saharan Africa									
Angola[3]	[10.3]	[5.2]	[9.9]	[2.2]	[1.4]	[1.8]	[2.2]	[4.0]	5.7
Benin	..	..	..	..	..	..	..	..	..
Botswana	3.1	3.7	3.2	3.0	3.5	3.8	3.9	[3.8]	[3.0]
Burkina Faso	1.4	1.3	1.4	1.4	1.3	1.5	1.3	1.3	1.3
Burundi	6.4	6.6	6.3	6.0	8.0	7.2	7.3	6.6	6.2
Cameroon§	1.3	1.5	1.5	1.3	1.3	1.3	1.4	1.4	1.3
Cape Verde	0.8	0.9	0.8	1.3	0.8	0.7	0.7	0.7	..
Central African Republic‡[4]	1.3	..	..	..	..	1.1	1.3	1.2	1.1
Chad	1.3	1.2	1.7	1.9	1.8	1.7	1.5	1.1	1.0
Congo, Republic of	1.4	0.4	1.2	1.0	1.4	1.7	1.9	1.7	1.4
Congo, DRC[5]	0.8	..	..	..	..	..	2.1	3.0	2.4
Côte d'Ivoire	4.5	4.4	4.2	4.0	3.9	4.2	1.5	..	..
Djibouti	12.8	35.3	37.4	36.2	24.7	23.7	..	..	..
Equatorial Guinea	3.4	6.7	10.7	9.6	5.0	3.9	24.1	..	..
Eritrea[6]	1.0	1.0	0.8	1.9	1.9	1.9	2.9	2.8	2.6
Ethiopia[7]	0.7	0.8	0.8	0.8	0.6	0.7	1.8	1.7	1.5
Gabon	1.2	1.3	1.6	1.0	0.6	0.6	0.5	0.5	..
Gambia‡									
Ghana[8]				1.5	2.9	3.1	0.7	0.8	0.7
Guinea[9]							2.3	2.0	..

Country	1997	1998	1999	2000	2001	2002	2003	2004	2005
Guinea-Bissau[10]	0.7	1.4	..	4.4	3.1	3.1	3.1	..	4.0
Kenya	1.3	1.2	1.2	1.3	1.5	1.6	1.6	1.6	1.7
Lesotho	2.8	3.1	3.7	3.6	3.1	2.8	2.6	2.3	2.3
Liberia	..	..	..	..	(8.0)	(7.7)	..	..	..
Madagascar[11]	1.5	1.3	1.2	1.2	1.4	1.3	1.3	1.2	1.1
Malawi	1.0	0.8	0.8	0.7	0.7	0.8	0.7		
Mali	2.0	1.9	2.0	2.2	2.0	2.0	2.1	2.2	2.3
Mauritania[12]	3.2	3.4	2.4	3.0	3.6	5.0	2.8	4.0	3.6
Mauritius	0.2	0.2	0.2	0.2	0.2	0.2	0.2	0.2	0.2
Mozambique[13]	[1.2]	[1.2]	1.4	1.5	1.4	1.3	1.2	1.3	0.9
Namibia[14]	2.3	2.3	3.1	2.8	3.1	2.9	3.0	3.0	3.2
Niger	0.9	1.1	1.2	1.2	1.4	1.0	1.0	1.2	..
Nigeria[15]	0.6	0.9	1.4	0.8	1.3	1.9	1.1	0.8	0.7
Rwanda[16]	4.2	4.4	4.2	3.4	3.3	2.9	2.5	2.3	2.9
Senegal¶[17]	1.5	1.5	1.5	1.3	1.4	1.4	1.4	1.4	1.5
Seychelles	2.0	1.7	1.8	1.7	1.8	1.7	1.7	2.3	1.8
Sierra Leone[18]	(1.1)	..	..	[4.1]	2.4	1.7	1.8	1.2	1.0
Somalia									
South Africa	1.6	1.4	1.3	1.4	1.5	1.6	1.6	1.5	1.5
Sudan[19]	1.0	2.4	4.1	4.8	2.9	3.2	2.3	..	..
Swaziland	[1.9]	[2.1]	[2.0]	[1.8]	[1.6]	[1.7]	[1.7]	[1.8]	..
Tanzania	1.5	1.6	1.5	1.5	1.6	1.4	1.2	1.1	1.1
Togo	..	..	..	..	..	..	1.6	1.6	1.5
Uganda‡	1.9	2.3	2.4	[2.1]	[2.1]	[2.1]	[2.1]	2.6	2.3
Zambia[20]	1.1	1.4	1.8	..	0.8	..	..	2.3	..
Zimbabwe[21]	3.4	2.6	4.4	4.7	2.2	2.2	2.5	5.4	2.3

Americas

Caribbean									
Bahamas	[0.9]	0.8	0.7	0.6	0.5	0.6	0.6	0.6	0.7
Barbados	0.8	0.8	0.8	0.9	0.9	1.0	0.9	0.8	:
Cuba	:	:	:	:	:	:	:	:	:
Dominican Republic	0.6	0.6	0.6	0.7	0.9	1.0	0.6	0.4	0.5
Haiti	:	:	:	:	:	:	:	:	:
Jamaica[‡]	0.7	0.6	0.6	0.6	0.6	0.7	0.7	0.6	0.6
Trinidad and Tobago	:	:	:	:	:	:	:	:	:
Central America									
Belize	1.4	:	:	:	:	:	:	:	:
Costa Rica[22]	0.0	0.0	0.0	0.0	0.0	0.0	0.0	0.0	0.0
El Salvador	0.9	0.8	0.8	0.9	0.8	0.8	0.7	0.7	0.6
Guatemala	0.7	0.7	0.7	0.8	0.9	0.7	0.7	0.4	0.3
Honduras[†][§][23]	:	:	:	0.6	0.7	0.8	0.8	0.7	0.6
Mexico[†][§]	0.6	0.5	0.6	0.5	0.5	0.5	0.5	0.4	0.4
Nicaragua[24]	0.9	0.7	0.7	0.8	0.7	0.9	0.9	0.7	0.7
Panama[25]	1.2	1.0	1.0	:	:	:	:	:	:
North America									
Canada	1.2	1.3	1.2	1.1	1.2	1.2	1.1	1.1	1.1
USA[26]	3.4	3.2	3.1	3.1	3.1	3.4	3.8	4.0	4.1
South America									
Argentina	1.3	1.3	1.4	1.3	1.4	1.2	1.2	1.1	1.0
Bolivia[27]	1.9	2.1	1.8	1.7	2.1	1.9	1.9	1.7	[1.6]
Brazil	[2.0]	[1.9]	[1.7]	1.7	1.9	2.1	1.6	1.5	1.6
Chile[§][28]	3.2	3.4	3.7	3.7	3.7	3.8	3.4	3.8	3.8
Colombia[29]	2.9	3.1	3.5	3.4	3.8	3.6	[3.9]	[3.8]	[3.7]
Ecuador[30]	2.1	2.4	1.8	1.7	1.8	2.1	2.7	2.3	2.6
Guyana	:	:	:	:	:	:	:	:	:
Paraguay	[1.4]	[1.3]	[1.1]	[1.1]	1.0	0.9	0.9	0.7	0.7

Country	1997	1998	1999	2000	2001	2002	2003	2004	2005
Peru[31]	1.4	1.6	1.6	1.7	1.9	1.4	1.4	1.3	1.4
Uruguay	[1.9]	[1.8]	1.9	1.6	1.8	1.7	1.5	1.3	1.3
Venezuela	1.8	1.4	1.6	1.3	1.7	1.3	1.3	1.2	1.2
Asia and Oceania									
Central Asia									
Kazakhstan[32]	1.1	1.1	0.8	0.8	1.0	1.1	1.1	1.0	1.1
Kyrgyzstan[32]	3.1	2.7	2.6	2.9	2.3	2.7	2.9	2.8	3.1
Tajikistan[32]	1.7	1.7	1.4	1.2	1.2	2.1	2.2	2.2	..
Turkmenistan[32 33]	4.0	3.1	2.9	..	..	..	..	..	..
Uzbekistan[32 34]	[1.4]	..	1.6	..	0.8	..	0.5	..	..
East Asia									
Brunei	7.2	7.5	6.1	5.7	5.2	5.3	5.1	(3.6)	(3.9)
Cambodia[35]	4.4	4.1	3.5	3.2	2.7	2.4	2.3	2.0	1.8
China, P. R.[36]	[1.7]	[1.9]	[2.0]	[2.0]	[2.2]	[2.3]	[2.3]	[2.0]	[2.0]
Indonesia	1.3	1.1	0.9	1.0	1.0	1.0	1.3	[1.4]	[1.2]
Japan[† § 37]	1.0	1.0	1.0	1.0	1.0	1.0	1.0	1.0	1.0
Korea, North[38]	..	..	..	..	..	..	..	..	..
Korea, South[† ¶ 39]	2.7	2.8	2.5	2.5	2.5	2.4	2.4	2.4	2.6
Laos	2.4	1.6	2.2	2.0	2.1	..	..	..	..
Malaysia	2.1	1.6	2.1	1.7	2.2	2.3	2.8	2.4	2.4
Mongolia	1.6	1.9	1.8	2.4	2.0	2.1	1.8	1.7	1.6
Myanmar[40]	2.7	2.3	2.0	2.3	1.8	1.3	..	..	..
Philippines	1.2	1.2	1.1	1.1	1.0	1.0	1.0	0.9	0.9
Singapore	4.7	5.4	5.4	4.7	5.0	5.1	5.1	4.7	4.7
Taiwan	3.5	3.2	2.7	2.4	2.5	2.2	2.2	2.3	2.2
Thailand	2.1	1.9	1.6	1.4	1.5	1.4	1.3	1.2	1.1
Viet Nam	..	..	..	..	..	..	..	..	..

South Asia									
Afghanistan	: :	: :	: :	: :	: :	: :	13.0	11.9	9.9
Bangladesh	1.3	1.3	1.3	1.3	1.2	1.1	1.1	1.1	1.0
India[41]	2.7	2.8	3.1	3.1	3.0	2.9	2.8	2.6	2.8
Nepal[¶42]	0.8	0.8	0.9	0.9	1.1	1.5	1.6	1.8	2.1
Pakistan	4.9	4.8	3.9	3.7	3.9	3.9	3.7	3.6	3.5
Sri Lanka[‡43]	4.2	4.1	3.6	4.5	3.9	3.1	2.7	[2.8]	2.6
Oceania									
Australia	1.8	1.8	1.8	1.8	1.8	1.8	1.9	1.9	1.8
Fiji	1.6	1.5	1.3	2.0	2.3	1.8	[1.6]	[1.2]	: :
New Zealand	1.4	1.3	1.3	1.3	1.2	1.1	1.1	1.1	1.0
Papua New Guinea	1.3	1.1	0.9	0.9	0.8	0.6	0.5	0.6	0.6
Tonga	1.6	1.5	1.4	1.4	1.4	1.2	1.2	1.0	: :
Europe									
Albania[¶44]	1.4	1.2	1.2	1.2	1.3	1.3	1.4	1.4	1.4
Armenia[†45]	3.9	3.5	3.7	3.6	3.1	2.7	2.7	2.7	2.7
Austria	[1.1]	[1.0]	[1.0]	[1.0]	[0.9]	0.9	0.9	0.9	0.9
Azerbaijan[46]	[2.3]	[2.4]	[2.6]	[2.3]	[2.3]	[2.2]	[2.4]	[2.6]	2.5
Belarus[†¶]	1.6	1.4	1.3	1.3	1.4	1.4	1.3	1.4	1.2
Belgium	1.5	1.5	1.4	1.4	1.3	1.3	1.2	1.2	1.1
Bosnia and Herzegovina[47]	: :	: :	: :	: :	: :	4.3	2.8	2.3	1.9
Bulgaria[†]	2.1	2.3	2.5	2.5	2.7	2.7	2.8	2.4	2.4
Croatia[†48]	5.7	5.5	4.3	3.0	2.6	2.7	2.6	2.4	1.6
Cyprus[†]	4.1	3.5	2.0	2.1	2.3	2.4	2.1	1.7	1.4
Czech Republic	1.7	1.9	2.0	2.0	1.9	1.6	1.5	1.5	1.4
Denmark	1.6	1.6	1.6	1.5	1.6	1.5	1.5	1.5	1.8
Estonia	1.1	1.1	1.3	1.4	1.5	1.5	1.8	1.8	1.5
Finland	1.6	1.5	1.3	1.3	1.2	1.7	1.4	1.4	1.4
France[49]	2.9	2.7	2.7	2.5	2.5	2.5	2.6	2.6	2.5
Georgia[50]	[1.3]	[1.1]	[0.9]	[0.6]	[0.7]	1.0	1.1	1.4	3.5
Germany	1.5	1.5	1.5	1.5	1.5	1.5	1.4	1.4	1.4

Country	1997	1998	1999	2000	2001	2002	2003	2004	2005
Greece	4.5	4.7	4.8	4.7	4.4	4.2	4.0	[3.9]	[4.1]
Hungary	1.7	1.5	1.7	1.7	1.8	1.7	1.7	1.5	1.5
Iceland	0.0	0.0	0.0	0.0	0.0	0.0	0.0	0.0	0.0
Ireland	1.0	0.9	0.8	0.8	0.8	0.7	0.7	0.6	0.6
Italy[51]	1.9	1.9	2.0	2.0	2.0	2.0	2.0	2.0	1.9
Latvia[52]	0.6	0.6	0.8	0.9	1.0	1.6	1.7	1.7	1.7
Lithuania[53]	[0.6]	[1.0]	[0.9]	[1.4]	[1.3]	1.4	1.4	1.4	1.2
Luxembourg	0.7	0.7	0.7	0.6	0.8	0.8	0.8	[0.8]	[0.8]
Macedonia, FYR[54]	2.2	2.2	1.8	1.9	6.6	2.8	2.5	2.5	2.2
Malta†	0.8	0.7	0.7	0.6	0.7	0.7	0.7	0.7	0.7
Moldova†¶[55]	0.9	0.6	0.5	0.4	0.4	0.4	0.4	0.4	0.3
Netherlands	1.8	1.7	1.7	1.6	1.5	1.5	1.6	1.5	1.5
Norway	2.1	2.2	2.1	1.8	1.7	2.1	2.0	1.9	1.7
Poland	[2.0]	2.0	1.9	1.8	1.9	1.9	1.9	1.9	1.9
Portugal	2.3	2.2	2.0	2.0	2.0	2.0	2.0	[2.1]	[2.3]
Romania[56]	[3.0]	[3.0]	2.7	2.5	2.5	2.3	2.1	2.0	2.0
Russia[57]	[4.5]	[3.3]	[3.4]	[3.7]	[4.1]	[4.3]	[4.3]	[3.9]	[4.1]
Serbia and Montenegro[58]	[4.8]	4.4	4.5	6.0	4.7	4.8	3.8	3.3	2.6
Slovakia†¶	2.4	1.8	1.6	1.7	1.9	1.8	1.9	1.7	1.7
Slovenia	1.5	1.4	1.3	1.2	1.4	1.5	1.5	1.5	1.5
Spain	1.3	1.3	1.2	1.2	1.2	1.2	1.1	1.1	1.1
Sweden[59]	2.1	2.1	2.0	2.0	1.9	1.8	1.7	1.6	1.5
Switzerland†¶	1.2	1.2	1.1	1.1	1.1	1.0	1.0	1.0	1.0
Turkey[60]	4.1	4.4	5.4	5.0	5.0	4.4	3.8	3.1	2.8
UK[61]	2.7	2.6	2.5	2.4	2.4	2.5	2.7	2.7	2.7
Ukraine§[62]	4.1	3.4	3.0	3.6	2.9	2.8	2.8	2.6	[2.4]

Middle East

Bahrain[63]	4.6	4.8	4.9	4.0	4.2	4.0	4.9	4.4	3.6
Egypt	3.3	3.3	3.2	3.2	3.3	3.4	3.3	3.0	2.8
Iran[64]	2.9	3.2	4.1	5.4	5.7	3.8	4.4	4.5	5.8
Iraq[65]	..	..	..	..	..	..	..	..	..
Israel[66]	8.5	8.4	8.3	8.0	8.1	9.2	8.5	8.3	9.7
Jordan	[6.3]	[5.6]	[5.6]	[5.5]	[5.2]	[6.0]	[6.7]	5.7	5.3
Kuwait	8.1	8.8	7.6	7.2	7.7	7.4	6.5	5.9	4.8
Lebanon	[4.3]	4.1	4.9	4.4	5.6	4.9	4.6	4.4	4.5
Oman‡[67]	12.5	12.5	11.4	10.6	12.2	12.3	12.1	12.0	11.9
Qatar	11.0	..	..	..	..	..	..	..	..
Saudi Arabia[68]	[5.0]	14.3	11.4	10.6	11.5	9.8	8.7	8.4	8.2
Syria	4.8	[5.1]	4.8	5.5	5.0	4.7	5.6	6.4	5.1
UAE[69]	4.8	5.1	4.3	3.4	3.4	3.3	2.8	2.3	2.0
Yemen	5.8	6.2	5.2	5.0	[5.6]	7.2	7.1	5.7	7.0

( ) = uncertain figure; [ ] = SIPRI estimate; | = change of multiple of currency; † = figures for these countries do not include military pensions; ‡ = figures for these countries are for current spending only; § = figures for the adopted budget, rather than actual expenditure; ¶ = figures for these countries do not include spending on paramilitary forces.

1 The figures for Algeria are budget figures for operational expenditure only. In July 2006 the Algerian Government issued supplementary budgets increasing the total expenditure by 35%. It is not clear if any of these extra funds were allocated to the military.

2 The figures for Morocco for 1998–2006 are for the adopted budget, rather than actual expenditure.

3 The figures for Angola should be seen in the context of highly uncertain economic statistics due to the impact of war on the Angolan economy. Figures are for defence, public order and security.

4 The figures for the Central African Republic are for current expenditure only. Investment expenditure for 2005 amounted to 775 000 CFA francs.

5 The figures for the Democratic Republic of the Congo (DRC) in 2006 are forward estimates by the International Monetary Fund (IMF) and are probably an underestimate owing to the country's high rate of inflation. Until 1997 the DRC was know as Zaire.

6 The figures for Eritrea in 1995 include expenditure for demobilization. Eritrea changed its currency during the period. All figures have been converted to the most recent currency.

7 The figures for Ethiopia in 1999 include an allocation of 1 billion birr in addition to the original defence budget.

8 The figures for Ghana for 2001 onwards are for the adopted budget.

[9] The figures for Guinea might be an underestimate as the IMF reports large extra-budgetary spending for the military.

[10] An armed conflict broke out in Guinea-Bissau in 1998, which led to a substantial increase in military expenditure, especially in 2000. According to the IMF, the increase was financed by a credit from the banking system, as well as by promissory notes. Due to the conflict, no data are available for 1999 and the consistency of figures before and after this year is uncertain. Guinea-Bissau changed its currency during the period. All figures have been converted to the most recent currency.

[11] The figures for Madagascar include expenditure for the gendarmerie and the national police. Madagascar changed its currency during the period. All figures have been converted to the most recent currency.

[12] The figures for Mauritania are for operating expenditure only.

[13] The figures for Mozambique include expenditure for the demobilization of government and RENAMO soldiers and the formation of a new unified army. The domobilization process ended in 1998/99. Mozambique changed its currency during the period. All figures have been converted to the most recent currency.

[14] The figures for Namibia in 1999 refer to the budget of the Ministry of Defence only. In addition to this, the 1999 budget of the Ministry of Finance includes a contingency provision of N$104 million for the Namibian military presence in the Democratic Republic of the Congo. The figures for 2002 include a supplementary allocation of N$78.5 million.

[15] The figures for Nigeria before 1999 are understated because of the military's use of a favourable specific dollar exchange rate.

[16] The figures for Rwanda for 1998 are the official defence budget. According to the IMF there are additional sources of funding for military activities, both within the budget and extra-budgetary. Figures for 2005 and 2006 include allocations for African Union peacekeeping missions.

[17] The figures for Senegal do not include expenditure for paramilitary forces, which in 1998 amounted to 21 100 million CFA francs.

[18] The figures for Sierra Leone in 1998 and 1999 are not available due to the coup d'état and subsequent civil war.

[19] Sudan changed its currency during the period. All figures have been converted to the most recent currency.

[20] The figures for Zambia are uncertain, especially those in constant dollars and shares of GDP, because of very high inflation and several changes of currency.

[21] The figures for Zimbabwe should be used with caution due to the extreme level of inflation in the country. Zimbabwe changed its currency during the period. All figures have been converted to the most recent currency. The figures for 1999 include a supplementary allocation of NewZ$1.8 million.

[22] Costa Rica has no armed forces. Expenditure for paramilitary forces, border guard, and maritime and air surveillance is less than 0.05% of GDP.

[23] The figures for Honduras exclude arms import as well as military pensions. In 2005 spending on military pensions was budgeted at 58.9 million lempiras.

[24] The figures for Nicaragua include military aid from the USA and Taiwan. For 2004–2006 this amounted to 7–13 million córdobas. The figures for 2002–2006 are for the adopted budget, rather than actual expenditure.

[25] The Panamanian Defence Forces were abolished in 1990 and replaced by a paramilitary force consisting of the national police, and air and maritime services.

[26] The figures for the USA are for financial years (1 Oct.–30 Sep.) rather than calendar years.

[27] The figures for Bolivia include some expenditure for civil defence.

[28] The figures for Chile include direct transfers from the state-owned copper company Corporacion Nacional del Cobre (CODELCO) for military purchases. Since 2005 these transfers have increased rapidly owing to rising copper prices.

[29] The figures for Colombia in 2002–2004 include a special allocation of 2.6 billion pesos from a war tax decree of 12 Aug. 2002.

[30] Ecuador changed its currency from the sucre to the US dollar on 13 Mar. 2000, at a rate of $1 to 25 000 sucres. Current price figures for 1997–2000 represent the dollar value of military expenditure at the market exchange rate for that year.

[31] The figures for Peru from 2005 do not include the transfer of 20% of gas production revenues from the state-owned company CAMISEA for the armed forces and national police.

[32] For the Central Asian countries purchasing power parity (PPP) rates were used for conversion to constant dollars up to and including *SIPRI Yearbook 2002*.

[33] The coverage of the series for Turkmenistan varies over time due to classification changes in the Turkmen system of public accounts.

[34] The figures for Uzbekistan expressed in constant US dollars should be seen in the light of the considerable difference between the official and the unofficial exchange rate values of the sum.

[35] The figures for Cambodia are for defence and security, including the regular police force.

[36] The figures for China are for estimated total military expenditure. On the estimates in local currency and share of GDP for the period 1989–98, see Wang, S., 'The military expenditure of China, 1989–98', *SIPRI Yearbook 1999: Armaments, Disarmament and International Security* (Oxford University Press: Oxford, 1999), pp. 334–49. The estimates for the years 1999–2002 are based on the percentage change in official military expenditure and on the assumption of a gradual decrease in the commercial earnings of the People's Liberation Army (PLA).

[37] The figures for Japan include the Special Action Committee on Okinawa (SACO).

[38] The figures for North Korea are as reported by North Korean authorities and are heavily contested. Owing to the lack of a credible exchange rate between the North Korean won and the US dollar no dollar estimates can be provided.

[39] The figures for South Korea exclude arms imports as well as military pensions and paramilitary forces.

[40] The figures for Myanmar are not presented in US dollar terms owing to the extreme variation in stated exchange rate between the kyat and the US dollar.

[41] The figures for India include expenditure on paramilitary forces from the Border Security Force, Central Reserve Police Force, Assam Rifles and Indo-Tibetan Border Police, but exclude spending for military nuclear activities.

[42] The figures for Nepal do not include expenditure on paramilitary forces, which in FY 1998/99 amounted to 3315 million rupees.

[43] Since the figures for Sri Lanka are for current expenditure only, a special allocation in 2000 of 28 billion rupees for war-related expenditure is not fully reflected in the official figure.

[44] The figures for Albania from 2001 onwards are for budgeted rather than actual expenditure. The figures do not include expenditure for paramilitary forces and before 2006 pensions are not fully included.

[45] The figures for Armenia do not include military pensions. For 2004–2006 these amounted to 9979, 1113 and 12440 b. drams, respectively

[46] Azerbaijan changed its currency during the period. All figures have been converted to the most recent currency.

[47] The figures for Bosnia and Herzegovina from 2005 onwards are for the Armed Forces of Bosnia and Herzegovina, which was founded in 2005 from the Croat–Bosniak Army of the Federation of Bosnia and Herzegovina and the Bosnian Serb Army of Republika Srpska. The figures for Bosnia and Herzegovina prior to 2005 include expenditure for both the Army of the Federation of Bosnia and Herzegovina and the Army of Republika Srpska.

[48] If the figures for Croatia included military pensions, total military expenditure would be *c.* 10–15% higher.

[49] The figures for France for 2006 are calculated with a new methodology due to a change in the French budgetary system and financial law.

[50] The figures for Georgia from 2002 are for the budgeted expenditure. The budget figures for 2003 are believed to be an underestimation of actual spending because of the political turmoil during the year.

[51] The figures for Italy include spending on civil defence, which typically accounts for about 4.5% of the total.

[52] The figures for Latvia do not include allocations for military pensions paid by Russia, which averaged 27 million lats per year over the 3 years 1996–1998.

[53] The figures for Lithuania exclude most expenditure on paramilitary forces.

[54] The definition of military expenditure for the FYROM changed in 2006. Border troops were transferred from the Ministry of Defence to the Ministry of Interior Affairs and part of the military pensions, previously entirely excluded, are now included.

[55] The figures for Moldova exclude expenditure on military pensions and paramilitary forces. Adding all military items in the budget would give total military expenditure for 2003 of 361 million lei instead of 109 million lei and 432 million lei instead of 113 million lei in 2004.

[56] Romania changed its currency during the period. All figures have been converted to the most recent currency.

[57] For sources and methods of the military expenditure figures for Russia see Cooper, J., 'The military expenditure of the USSR and the Russian Federation, 1987–97', *SIPRI Yearbook 1998: Armaments, Disarmament and International Security* (Oxford University Press: Oxford, 1998), pp. 243–59. Up to and including *SIPRI Yearbook 2002*, PPP rates were used for Russia for converting local currency figures to constant dollars.

[58] Montenegro seceded from the State Union of Serbia and Montenegro on 3 June 2006.

[59] Sweden changed its accounting system in 2001, giving rise to a series break between 2000 and 2001. This break means that the decrease in military expenditure between 2000 and 2001 is overestimated by 1.4 percentage points.

[60] The figures for Turkey are in new Turkish lira. The Turkish lira was redenominated in 2005 at the rate of 1 new Turkish lira = 1 million Turkish lira.

[61] The series for the UK has a break between 2000 and 2001, because in 2001 the UK changed its accounting system for military expenditure from a 'cash basis' to a 'resource basis'. It is not clear what impact this change had on the trend in British military expenditure.

[62] The figures for Ukraine are for the adopted budget for the Ministry of Defence, military pensions and paramilitary forces. Actual expenditure was reportedly 95–99% of that budgeted for 1996–99.

[63] The figures for Bahrain include current and project expenditure by the Ministry of Defence. For 2005–2006 figures for project expenditure, which in previous years accounted for about 5% of the total, were not reported.

[64] The figures for Iran include expenditure on public order and safety but exclude spending on paramilitary forces such as the Revolutionary Guards.

[65] The figures for Iraq are for the salaries and pensions of the defence and interior forces. The data should be seen in the light of the unstable security situation and high rate of inflation.

[66] The figures for Israel include military aid from the USA of approximately US$2 billion annually.

[67] The figures for Oman are for current expenditure on defence and national security.

[68] The figures for Saudi Arabia are for defence and security.

[69] The figures for the UAE exclude the local military expenditure of its 7 constituent emirates. If this spending were included, the UAE's total military expenditure would be considerably higher.

Appendix 8B. NATO military expenditure by category

PETTER STÅLENHEIM

Table 8B.1. NATO military expenditure on personnel and equipment, 2000–2006

Figures are in US$ m. at 2005 prices and exchange rates. Years are financial years for Canada, the UK and the USA and calendar years for all other countries. Figures in italics are percentage changes from the previous year.

Country	Item	2000	2001	2002	2003	2004	2005	2006
North America								
Canada	Personnel	5 000	5 103	5 329	5 458	5 785	6 103	6 119
	Personnel change		*2.1*	*4.4*	*2.4*	*6.0*	*5.5*	*0.3*
	Equipment	1 413	1 320	1 642	1 651	1 732	1 563	1 779
	Equipment change		*-6.5*	*24.4*	*0.6*	*4.9*	*-9.7*	*13.8*
USA	Personnel	129 085	124 894	139 629	159 029	165 465	175 384	157 089
	Personnel change		*-3.2*	*11.8*	*13.9*	*4.0*	*6.0*	*-10.4*
	Equipment	74 988	88 547	106 232	108 017	118 266	123 491	128 932
	Equipment change		*18.1*	*20.0*	*1.7*	*9.5*	*4.4*	*4.4*
Europe								
Belgium	Personnel	3 148	3 144	3 169	3 262	3 291	3 160	3 265
	Personnel change		*-0.1*	*0.8*	*2.9*	*0.9*	*-4.0*	*3.3*
	Equipment	277	327	314	239	228	268	234
	Equipment change		*17.9*	*-3.8*	*-24.0*	*-4.4*	*17.2*	*-12.6*
Bulgaria	Personnel					392	336	344
	Personnel change						*-14.4*	*2.5*
	Equipment					58.4	111	94.0
	Equipment change						*89.9*	*-15.3*

Czech Republic	Personnel	884	928	965	958	1 044	1 108	1 040
	Personnel change		4.9	4.0	-0.7	9.0	6.1	-6.2
	Equipment	464	410	370	450	385	258	248
	Equipment change		-11.6	-9.7	21.6	-14.6	-32.9	-3.8
Denmark	Personnel	1 939	1 974	1 939	1 864	1 944	1 905	1 837
	Personnel change		1.8	-1.8	-3.9	4.3	-2.0	-3.5
	Equipment	525	633	503	583	698	388	585
	Equipment change		20.6	-20.6	15.9	19.8	-44.5	50.9
Estonia	Personnel					62.4	59.5	58.4
	Personnel change						-4.6	-1.8
	Equipment					24.0	24.3	32.6
	Equipment change						1.3	33.9
France	Personnel	30 434	30 406	31 121	31 022	30 997	30 708	29 873
	Personnel change		-0.1	2.3	-0.3	-0.1	-0.9	-2.7
	Equipment	9 503	9 738	9 800	10 803	11 315	11 285	12 556
	Equipment change		2.5	0.6	10.2	4.7	-0.3	11.3
Germany	Personnel	24 963	24 412	24 130	24 069	23 010	22 172	21 630
	Personnel change		-2.2	-1.2	-0.3	-4.4	-3.6	-2.4
	Equipment	5 560	5 677	5 707	5 506	5 744	5 396	5 550
	Equipment change		2.1	0.5	-3.5	4.3	-6.1	2.9
Greece	Personnel	5 502	5 507	4 494	4 211	4 782	5 006	5 205
	Personnel change		0.1	-18.4	-6.3	13.5	4.7	4.0
	Equipment	1 569	1 308	870	603	454	1 032	1 050
	Equipment change		-16.6	-33.5	-30.6	-24.8	127.4	1.8
Hungary	Personnel	736	796	798	849	797	768	705
	Personnel change		8.2	0.2	6.4	-6.2	-3.6	-8.3
	Equipment	187	175	180	179	191	135	127
	Equipment change		-6.6	3.1	-0.4	6.6	-29.6	-5.5

Country	Item	2000	2001	2002	2003	2004	2005	2006
Italy	Personnel	24 338	24 266	25 504	25 254	26 254	25 853	25 429
	Personnel change		-0.3	5.1	-1.0	3.9	-1.5	-1.6
	Equipment	4 890	3 460	4 268	4 490	4 076	3 049	2 350
	Equipment change		-29.3	23.4	5.2	-9.2	-25.2	-22.9
Latvia	Personnel					78.5	102	113
	Personnel change						29.4	11.8
	Equipment					13.3	17.6	35.9
	Equipment change						32.3	103.9
Lithuania	Personnel					163	178	185
	Personnel change						8.7	4.3
	Equipment					39.2	46.6	59.0
	Equipment change						18.8	26.5
Luxembourg	Personnel	147	166	173	180	187	184	188
	Personnel change		12.9	3.9	4.3	3.9	-1.8	2.4
	Equipment	9.0	29.4	14.7	16.8	19.7	27.9	21.4
	Equipment change		226.6	-50.1	14.7	16.8	41.9	-23.4
Netherlands	Personnel	4 635	4 491	4 788	4 990	4 753	4 831	5 050
	Personnel change		-3.1	6.6	4.2	-4.7	1.6	4.5
	Equipment	1 554	1 559	1 484	1 416	1 561	1 528	1 770
	Equipment change		0.4	-4.9	-4.5	10.2	-2.1	15.9
Norway	Personnel	1 777	1 713	1 997	2 039	2 145	2 093	2 046
	Personnel change		-3.6	16.6	2.1	5.2	-2.4	-2.3
	Equipment	847	928	1 249	1 105	1 188	1 029	1 169
	Equipment change		9.7	34.5	-11.5	7.5	-13.4	13.6

Poland							
Personnel	2 959	3 121	3 119	3 258	3 233	3 173	3 394
Personnel change		5.5	-0.1	4.5	-0.8	-1.9	7.0
Equipment	416	428	534	624	776	808	1 063
Equipment change		3.0	24.7	16.9	24.4	4.0	31.6
Portugal							
Personnel	2 846	2 924	2 356	2 144	2 165	2 381	2 184
Personnel change		2.7	-19.4	-9.0	1.0	9.9	-8.3
Equipment	223	192	115	202	222	280	378
Equipment change		-13.8	-40.0	74.9	10.0	25.9	35.2
Romania							
Personnel					944	1 126	1 189
Personnel change						19.2	5.6
Equipment					477	394	468
Equipment change						-17.4	18.5
Slovakia							
Personnel					384	384	426
Personnel change						0.1	10.9
Equipment					89.9	122	134
Equipment change						35.2	10.1
Slovenia							
Personnel					311	329	357
Personnel change						5.9	8.4
Equipment					93.4	48.6	70.4
Equipment change						-48.0	44.8
Spain							
Personnel	7 079	7 112	7 168	7 062	7 065	7 125	7 389
Personnel change		0.5	0.8	-1.5	0.0	0.9	3.7
Equipment	1 433	1 419	3 035	2 815	2 994	2 880	3 255
Equipment change		-1.0	113.9	-7.3	6.3	-3.8	13.0
Turkey							
Personnel	6 908	6 274	6 082	5 407	5 355	5 374	5 486
Personnel change		-9.2	-3.1	-11.1	-1.0	0.3	2.1
Equipment	4 335	4 628	4 179	4 533	3 541	3 074	3 901
Equipment change		6.8	-9.7	8.5	-21.9	-13.2	26.9

Country	Item	2000	2001	2002	2003	2004	2005	2006
UK	Personnel	18 436	19 408	19 866	20 127	20 133	23 519	22 339
	Personnel change		5.3	2.4	1.3	0.0	16.8	−5.0
	Equipment	12 416	11 871	11 797	11 505	11 555	11 149	11 859
	Equipment change		−4.4	−0.6	−2.5	0.4	−3.5	6.4
NATO Europe	Personnel	136 732	136 643	137 669	136 697	139 482	141 874	139 734
	Personnel change		−0.1	0.8	−0.7	2.0	1.7	−1.5
	Equipment	44 208	42 784	44 422	45 072	45 743	43 350	47 010
	Equipment change		−3.2	3.8	1.5	1.5	−5.2	8.4
NATO Europe (16 countries)	Personnel	136 732	136 643	137 669	136 697	137 146	139 360	137 061
	Personnel change		−0.1	0.8	−0.7	0.3	1.6	−1.6
	Equipment	44 208	42 784	44 422	45 072	44 947	42 585	46 117
	Equipment change		−3.2	3.8	1.5	−0.3	−5.3	8.3
NATO total	Personnel	270 816	266 640	282 627	301 183	310 732	323 360	302 942
	Personnel change		−1.5	6.0	6.6	3.2	4.1	−6.3
	Equipment	120 609	132 651	152 296	154 740	165 741	168 404	177 721
	Equipment change		10.0	14.8	1.6	7.1	1.6	5.5
NATO total (18 countries)	Personnel	270 816	266 640	282 627	301 183	308 396	320 847	300 269
	Personnel change		−1.5	6.0	6.6	2.4	4.0	−6.4
	Equipment	120 609	132 651	152 296	154 740	164 945	167 640	176 828
	Equipment change		10.0	14.8	1.6	6.6	1.6	5.5

Notes: The figures in this table were calculated, based on NATO statistics on the distribution of total military expenditure by category, by applying the shares for personnel and equipment to the figures for total military expenditure at converted to constant 2005 US dollars using consumer price indices (CPI) from the International Monetary Fund publication *International Financial Statistics*. Data are included in the NATO Europe and NATO total from the year of accession, which was 2004 for Bulgaria, Estonia, Latvia, Lithuania, Slovakia and Slovenia. An additional series is provided for totals of only those states that were members throughout the period 2000–2006 (16 countries in NATO Europe and 18 in NATO total), in order to show the trend for a consistent group of countries.

In 2004 the NATO member states agreed on a change in the definition of military expenditure. For all countries except France, Italy, Luxembourg and the Netherlands, figures from 2002 are reported according to the new definition, excluding 'Other Forces' not 'realistically deployable'. Data reported by France, Italy, Luxembourg and the Netherlands do not entirely conform with the new definition. For Greece, Hungary, Portugal and Turkey the change in definitions has made a big difference. All data are reported according to the old definition up to and including 2002 and for personnel shares up to 2003 creating two breaks in all series except for the countries that have yet not changed definitions (France, Italy, Luxembourg and the Netherlands)—one between 2001 and 2002 and one between 2002 and 2003.

Sources: NATO, 'NATO–Russia compendium of financial and economic data relating to defence', Press release (2005)161, 9 Dec. 2005, URL <http://www.nato.int/docu/pr/2005/p05-161e.htm>; and NATO, 'NATO–Russia compendium of financial and economic data relating to defence', Press release (2006)159, 18 Dec. 2006, URL <http://www.nato.int/docu/pr/2006/p06-159e.htm>.

Appendix 8C. Sources and methods for military expenditure data

PETTER STÅLENHEIM

I. Introduction

This appendix describes the sources and methods for the SIPRI military expenditure data provided in the tables in chapter 8 and appendices 8A and 8B, and on the SIPRI website, URL <http://www.sipri.org/contents/milap/>. For a more comprehensive overview of the conceptual problems and sources of uncertainty involved in all sets of military expenditure data, the reader is referred to other sources.[1] The data in this edition of the Yearbook should not be linked with the SIPRI military expenditure series in earlier editions because data are continuously revised and updated. This is true in particular for the most recent years as data for budget allocations are replaced by data for actual expenditure. In some cases entire series are revised as new and better data become available. Consistent series dating back to 1988 are available on the SIPRI website and on request from SIPRI. These series cannot always be combined with the SIPRI series for the earlier years, 1950–87, since SIPRI conducted a major review of the data for many countries for the period beginning in 1988. Changes in base years and method of currency conversion also hinder comparison between editions of the SIPRI Yearbook. In this edition, the base year for the constant dollar series (table 8A.3) is 2005. Conversion to constant US dollars has been made using market exchange rates (MERs) for all countries (see section IV).

II. The purpose of the data

The main purpose of the data on military expenditure is to provide an easily identifiable measure of the scale of resources absorbed by the military. Military expenditure is an input measure which is not directly related to the 'output' of military activities, such as military capability or military security.[2] Long-term trends in military expenditure and sudden changes in trend may be signs of a change in military output, but such an interpretation should be made with caution.

Military expenditure data as measured in constant dollars (table 8A.3) are an indicator of the trend in the volume of resources used for military activities with the purpose of allowing comparisons over time for individual countries and comparisons between countries. Military expenditure as a share of gross domestic product (GDP) (table 8A.4) is an indicator of the proportion of a country's resources used for military activities, and therefore of the economic burden imposed on the national economy.

---

[1] Such overviews include Brzoska, M., 'World military expenditures', eds K. Hartley and T. Sandler, *Handbook of Defense Economics*, vol. 1 (Elsevier: Amsterdam, 1995); Ball, N., 'Measuring third world security expenditure: a research note', *World Development*, vol. 12, no. 2 (1984), pp. 157–64; and Omitoogun, W., *Military Expenditure Data in Africa: A Survey of Cameroon, Ethiopia, Ghana, Kenya, Nigeria and Uganda*, SIPRI Research Report no. 17 (Oxford University Press: Oxford, 2003).

[2] See Hagelin, B. and Sköns, E., 'The military sector in a changing context', *SIPRI Yearbook 2003: Armaments, Disarmament and International Security* (Oxford University Press: Oxford, 2003), pp. 282–300.

III. The coverage of the data

The military expenditure tables in appendix 8A cover 167 countries. This edition of the Yearbook covers the 10-year period 1997–2006.

Total military expenditure figures are calculated for three country groupings—by geographical region, by membership of international organizations and by income per capita. The coverage of each of these groupings is provided in the notes to table 8A.1.

The definition of military expenditure

The definition of military expenditure adopted by SIPRI is used as a guideline. Where possible, SIPRI military expenditure data include all current and capital expenditure on: (*a*) the armed forces, including peacekeeping forces; (*b*) defence ministries and other government agencies engaged in defence projects; (*c*) paramilitary forces, when judged to be trained and equipped for military operations; and (*d*) military space activities. Such expenditure should include: (*a*) military and civil personnel, including retirement pensions of military personnel and social services for personnel; (*b*) operations and maintenance; (*c*) procurement; (*d*) military research and development; and (*e*) military aid (in the military expenditure of the donor country). Civil defence and current expenditure for past military activities, such as for veterans' benefits, demobilization, conversion and weapon destruction, are excluded.

In practice it is not possible to apply this definition to all countries, since this would require more detailed information than is available about what is included in military budgets and about off-budget military expenditure items. In many cases SIPRI has to use the national data provided, regardless of definition. Priority is then given to the choice of a uniform time series for each country to achieve consistency over time, rather than to adjusting the figures for individual years according to a common definition. In cases where it is impossible to use the same source and definition for all years, the percentage change between years in the deviant source is applied to the existing series in order to make the trend as correct as possible. Such figures are shown in square brackets in the tables. In the light of these difficulties, military expenditure data are not suitable for accurate comparison between countries and are more appropriately used for comparisons over time.

IV. Methods

Estimation

SIPRI data reflect the official data reported by governments. As a general rule, SIPRI assumes national data to be accurate until there is evidence to the contrary. Estimates are predominantly made either when the coverage of official data does not correspond to the SIPRI definition or when there is no consistent time series available. In the first case, estimates are made on the basis of an analysis of official government budget and expenditure accounts. The most comprehensive estimates of this type, those for China and Russia, have been presented in detail in previous editions of the Yearbook.[3] In the second case, differing time series are linked together. In order not to

---

[3] Cooper, J., 'The military expenditure of the USSR and the Russian Federation, 1987–97', *SIPRI Yearbook 1998: Armaments, Disarmament and International Security* (Oxford University Press: Oxford,

introduce assumptions or extrapolations into the military expenditure statistics, estimates are always based on empirical evidence. Thus, no estimates are made for countries that do not release any official data, and no figures are displayed for these countries. SIPRI estimates are presented in square brackets in the tables—this most often occurs when two different series are linked together. Round brackets are used when data are uncertain for other reasons, such as the reliability of the source or the economic context.

Data for the most recent years include two types of estimate, which apply to all countries. First, figures for the most recent year or years are for adopted budget, budget estimates or revised estimates, the majority of which are revised in subsequent years. Second, in table 8A.3, the deflator used for the final year in the series is an estimate based on part of a year or as provided by the International Monetary Fund (IMF). Unless exceptional uncertainty is involved, these estimates are not bracketed.

The totals for the world, regions, organizations and income groups in table 8A.1 are estimates because data are not available for all countries in all years. These estimates are most often made on the assumption that the rate of change in an individual country for which data are missing is the same as the average in the region to which it belongs. When no estimate can be made, countries are excluded from the totals.

Calculations

The SIPRI military expenditure figures are presented on a calendar-year basis with one exception. For the USA, SIPRI follows the reporting format of the source—a financial-year basis. In order to calculate calendar-year data for the USA, data for the final financial year would have to be collected from sources not comparable to the North Atlantic Treaty Organization (NATO) statistics used for earlier years. Calendar-year data for other countries are calculated on the assumption of an even rate of expenditure throughout the financial year.

The original data are provided in local currency at current prices (table 8A.2). In order to enable comparisons between countries and over time, these are converted to US dollars at constant prices (table 8A.3). The *deflator* used for conversion from current to constant prices is the consumer price index of the country concerned. This choice of deflator is connected to the purpose of the SIPRI data—it should be an indicator of resource use on an opportunity-cost basis.[4] In order to better facilitate comparison to other current economic measures, often expressed in current dollar terms, the right-most column in tables 8A.1 and 8A.3 also provides military expenditure for 2006 in current US dollars.

Conversion to dollars is done for all countries using the annual average MER. If purchasing power parity (PPP) conversion rate were used instead of MERs, there would be a significant increase in the reported level of military spending in many countries.[5] For example, Russian military expenditure converted using PPP rates

1998), pp. 243–59; and Wang, S., 'The military expenditure of China, 1989–98', *SIPRI Yearbook 1999: Armaments, Disarmament and International Security* (Oxford University Press: Oxford, 1999), pp. 334–49.

[4] A military-specific deflator would be a more appropriate choice if the objective were to measure purchasing power in terms of the amount of military personnel, goods and services that could be bought for the monetary allocations for military purposes.

[5] The PPP dollar rate of a country's currency is defined as 'the number of units of a country's currency required to buy the same amount of goods and services in the domestic market as a U.S. dollar would buy in the United States'. World Bank, *World Development Indicators 2003* (World Bank:

($82.8 million in 2006) is 2.4 times higher than in MER dollars ($34.7 million in 2006). In the most extreme cases, conversion using PPPs instead of the MER can result in a tenfold increase in the dollar value of a country's military expenditure.[6]

The PPP rate is in many ways a more appropriate conversion factor than the MER for international comparison of national economic data, especially for countries in transition and developing countries. Considering opportunity cost, the ideal approach would be to use PPP rates for all countries. However, this is not possible since currently available PPP data are not sufficiently reliable for all countries in the SIPRI database. Therefore, for the sake of consistency and simplicity, MERs will be used for all countries until more reliable, regularly updated PPP data become available.[7]

The choice of base year—the year in whose prices the data are expressed—also has a significant impact on cross-country comparisons of expenditure data because different national currencies vary against the dollar in different ways. Beginning in this edition of the SIPRI Yearbook, the base year has been changed to 2005, having previously been 2003. The most salient effect of this change is the decrease in the USA's share of 2005 total world military expenditure from 48 per cent using 2003 as the base year to 46 per cent when expressed in 2005 prices and exchange rates. The change of base year and the decline in the value of the US dollar in relation to other currencies over recent years also have an impact on the regional shares of total world military expenditure. For Europe, the region where currencies gained most against the dollar, the shift in base year from 2003 to 2005 has resulted in an increase of approximately 2.1 percentage points in the region's share of world military spending.

Each country's ratio of military expenditure to GDP (table 8A.4) is calculated in domestic currency at current prices and for calendar years.

V. The limitations of the data

A number of limitations are associated with the data on military expenditure. They are of three main types: reliability, validity and comparability.

The main problems of reliability are due to the limited and varying definitions of expenditure. The coverage of official data on military expenditure varies significantly between countries and over time for the same country. In many countries the official data cover only a part of total military expenditure. Important items can be hidden under non-military budget headings or can even be financed entirely outside the government budget. Many such off-budget mechanisms are employed in practice.[8]

Washington, DC, 2003), p. 285. On the problems of international comparison of military expenditure and currency conversion see Ward, M., 'International comparisons of military expenditures: issues and challenges of using purchasing power parities', *SIPRI Yearbook 2006: Armaments, Disarmament and International Security* (Oxford University Press: Oxford, 2006), pp. 369–86. For a methodological description of the problems see 'Sources and methods for military expenditure data', *SIPRI Yearbook 1999* (note 3), pp. 327–33.

[6] Table 8.2 in chapter 8 shows the impact of using PPP rates rather than MERs on the level of military expenditure in dollar terms for the 15 countries with the highest military expenditure in 2006.

[7] The World Bank started a new round of benchmark surveys of price levels used for producing PPP rates in 2003. The ambition is that this will produce more reliable PPP rates.

[8] For an overview of such mechanisms see Hendrickson, D. and Ball, N., 'Off-budget military expenditure and revenue: issues and policy perspectives for donors', Conflict, Security and Development Group (CSDG) Occasional Papers no. 1, CSDG, King's College London, Jan. 2002, URL <http://www.dfid.gov.uk/pubs/files/offbudget-military-exp.pdf>.

Furthermore, in some countries actual expenditure may be different from budgeted expenditure—it is most often higher, but in some cases it may be significantly lower.

The expenditure data's validity is limited by its very nature: the fact that the data are only an input measure limits their utility as an indicator of military strength or capability. While military expenditure does have an impact on military capability, so do many other factors such as the technological level of military equipment, the state of maintenance and repair, and so on. The most appropriate use of military expenditure data, even when reliably measured and reported, is therefore as an indicator of the economic resources consumed for military purposes.

The comparability of the data is complicated by the method used for conversion into a common currency, usually the US dollar. As illustrated above, the choice of conversion factor makes a great difference in cross-country comparisons of military expenditure. This is a general problem in international comparisons of economic data, which is not specific to military expenditure. Nonetheless, it does represent a major limitation, and it should be borne in mind when using military expenditure data converted by different types of conversion rate.

VI. Sources

The sources for military expenditure data are, in order of priority: (*a*) primary sources, that is, official data provided by national governments, either in their official publications or in response to questionnaires; (*b*) secondary sources which quote primary data; and (*c*) other secondary sources.

The first category consists of national budget documents, defence White Papers and public finance statistics as well as responses to a SIPRI questionnaire which is sent out annually to the finance and defence ministries, central banks, and national statistical offices of the countries in the SIPRI database (see appendix 8D). It also includes government responses to questionnaires about military expenditure sent out by the United Nations and, if made available by the countries themselves, the Organization for Security and Co-operation in Europe.

The second category includes international statistics, such as those of NATO and the IMF. Data for the 16 pre-1999 NATO member states have traditionally been taken from NATO military expenditure statistics published in a number of NATO sources. The introduction of a new definition in 2005 by NATO has made it necessary to rely on other sources for some NATO countries for the most recent years. Data for many developing countries are taken from the IMF's *Government Finance Statistics Yearbook*, which provides a defence heading for most IMF member countries, and from Country Reports by IMF staff. This category also includes publications of other organizations that provide proper references to the primary sources used, such as the Country Reports of the Economist Intelligence Unit.

The third category of sources consists of specialist journals and newspapers.

The main sources for economic data are the publications of the IMF: International *Financial Statistics*, *World Economic Outlook* and Country Reports by IMF staff. The source for PPP rates is the World Bank's *World Development Report 2006*.

Appendix 8D. The reporting of military expenditure data

CATALINA PERDOMO and ÅSA BLOMSTRÖM

I. Introduction

The United Nations asserts that 'a better flow of objective information on military matters can help to relieve international tension and is therefore an important contribution to conflict prevention' and that transparency in military issues is an essential element for building trust among countries.[1] Obtaining primary and comparable data on official military expenditure is an important task for both SIPRI and the United Nations Department of Disarmament Affairs (DDA). The systems through which countries can report their military expenditure to the UN and SIPRI are described in section II of this appendix. The levels of reporting to the UN and SIPRI in 2006 are given in section III and the trends for the period 2001–2006 in section IV.

II. The reporting systems

The United Nations reporting system

The UN Secretary-General every year invites all member states (currently 192) through a *note verbale* to report their military expenditure for the most recent financial year. The basis for this request is UN General Assembly Resolution 35/142 B, 'Reduction of military budgets', adopted in 1980.[2] Successive biennial General Assembly resolutions have called for the continued reporting of military expenditure by member states.[3]

Countries are requested to report, preferably (and to the extent possible) using the reporting instrument developed for this purpose—the UN Standardized Instrument for Reporting Military Expenditures—or in any other format for reporting military expenditure developed by other international or regional organizations. The instrument is in the form of a matrix with fields for the reporting of disaggregated data by function—aggregate personnel, operations and maintenance, procurement, construction, and research and development—and by military service—air force, army, navy and so on—as well as aggregated totals. Since it was believed that some countries found this matrix too complicated, since 2003 the United Nations has provided an alternative, simplified reporting form with a view to encourage reporting by an increased number of countries.[4] The reported data are included in an annual report by

---

[1] UN General Assembly Resolution A/RES/60/44, 8 Dec. 2005. UN General Assembly resolutions are available at URL <http://www.un.org/documents/resga.htm>.

[2] UN General Assembly Resolution A/RES/35/142 B, 12 Dec. 1980.

[3] The most recent such resolution is UN General Assembly Resolution A/RES/60/44 (note 1).

[4] United Nations, Department for Disarmament Affairs, *Transparency in Armaments: United Nations Instrument for Reporting Military Expenditures, Global and Regional Participation 1981–2002* (United Nations: New York, N.Y., 2003), URL <http://disarmament2.un.org/cab/milex.html>, p. 3. The UN's standardized instrument and simplified form are reproduced on pp. 12–14.

Table 8D.1. Reporting of military expenditure data to SIPRI and the United Nations, by region, 2006

Figures are numbers of countries.

Region/subregion[a]	Reporting to SIPRI			Reporting to the UN				Total SIPRI and UN reports[d]
	Requests	Countries reporting data	Total	Requests	Countries reporting data	Nil reports[b]	Total[c]	
Africa	49[e]	Mauritius, Namibia, Seychelles, South Africa	4	50	Burkina Faso, Mauritius, Namibia[f], Zambia[f]	(0)	4	6
Americas								
North America	2	Canada, USA	2	2	Canada, USA	(0)	2	2
Central America	7	Belize, El Salvador, Guatemala, Honduras, Mexico	5	7	Mexico, Nicaragua[f]	(0)	2	6
South America	11	Colombia, Ecuador, Uruguay	3	11	Argentina, Bolivia, Brazil, Chile[f], Ecuador, Paraguay	(0)	6	8
Caribbean	8	–	0	8	Jamaica[f], Suriname[f], Trinidad and Tobago[f]	(0)	3	3
Asia and Oceania								
Central Asia	5	Kazakhstan	1	5	Kazakhstan, Kyrgyzstan, Tajikistan[f]	(0)	3	3
East Asia	16	Japan, South Korea, Taiwan, Thailand	4	17	Cambodia, Indonesia, Japan, South Korea[f], Mongolia, Thailand[f]	(0)	6	7
South Asia	6	–	0	6	Bangladesh, Nepal	(0)	2	2
Oceania	4	Australia	1	4	New Zealand	(0)	1	2
Europe								
West Europe	21	Austria, Belgium, Cyprus, Denmark, Finland, France, Germany, Greece, Ireland, Italy, Luxembourg, Malta, Norway, Portugal, Spain, Sweden, Switzerland, Turkey	18	21	Belgium, Cyprus, Denmark, Finland, Germany, Greece, Ireland[f], Italy, Luxembourg, Malta, Netherlands, Norway, Spain, Sweden, Switzerland, Turkey, UK	(1)	18	20
Central Europe	16	Albania, Bosnia and Herzegovina,	15	16	Albania, Bosnia and Herzegovina,	(0)	14	16

Eastern Europe	Bulgaria, Croatia, Czech Republic, Estonia, Hungary, Latvia, Lithuania, FYROM, Montenegro, Poland, Romania, Slovenia, Serbia	7	Armenia, Georgia, Moldova, Russia, Ukraine	5	7	Bulgaria, Croatia, Czech Republic, Estonia, Hungary, Latvia, Lithuania, FYROM, Poland, Romania, Slovakia, Slovenia	(0)	Armenia[f], Belarus, Georgia, Moldova, Russia	5	6
Middle East		14	Jordan, Lebanon	2	14		(0)	Israel[f], Lebanon[f]	2	3
Small states[g]	–	0		0	24		(10)	San Marino[f]	11	1
Total		**166**		**60**	**192**		**(11)**		**79**	**85**

FYROM = Former Yugoslav Republic of Macedonia.

[a] In order to make the SIPRI and UN reporting systems comparable, countries are grouped according to the geographical regions in the SIPRI Military Expenditure Database. See appendix 8A in this volume.

[b] 11 UN member states submitted nil reports: Andorra, Costa Rica, Iceland, Liechtenstein, Marshall Islands, Monaco, Nauru, Saint Lucia, Saint Vincent and the Grenadines, Solomon Islands and Vanuatu. In addition, 2 non-UN members submitted nil reports: Cook Islands and Holy See.

[c] The total number of UN reports includes countries reporting data and those submitting nil reports.

[d] This column shows the total number of countries that submitted reports with military expenditure data to either SIPRI or the UN (excluding the nil reports). Totals may be smaller than the sums of reports to the UN and SIPRI because the same country may report to both organizations.

[e] There are 50 African countries in the SIPRI database, but SIPRI is unable to send requests to Rwanda because of a lack of contact details.

[f] These 15 countries reported their data using a simplified UN form.

[g] These are very small UN member states with no or only minimal defence forces.

Sources: Submitted filled-in SIPRI questionnaires; and United Nations, 'Objective information on military matters, including transparency of military expenditures', Report of the UN Secretary-General, UN document A/61/133, 26 July 2006; A/61/133/Add. 1, 6 Oct. 2006; and A/61/133/Add. 2, 4 Jan. 2007, URL <http://disarmament2.un.org/cab/milex.html>.

Table 8D.2. Number of countries reporting their military expenditure to SIPRI and the United Nations, 2001–2006

	2001	2002	2003	2004	2005	2006
UN reporting system[a]						
Standardized reports (incl. nil reports)	61	81	65	64	67	64
Nil reports[b]	5	11	11	10	12	11
Simplified reports	..	..	10	14	7	15
Total reporting (incl. nil reports)	61	81	75	78	74	79
Total number of UN requests	189	191	191	191	191	192
SIPRI reporting system						
Reports[c]	63	61	64	62	67	60
Total number of SIPRI requests	158	158	158	159	167	166

[a] The figures for 2001–2003 and 2005 include some late submissions of data to the UN and are therefore slightly higher than those presented in previous editions of the SIPRI Yearbook. The data for 2006 include late submissions up to 31 Jan. 2007, but some countries may yet report. All figures exclude non-UN member states that submitted reports.

[b] These figures exclude nil reports by non-UN members.

[c] A revised counting system means that the figures for responses to SIPRI in 2001 and 2002 are higher than those published in previous editions of the SIPRI Yearbook.

Sources: Submitted filled-in SIPRI questionnaires; and United Nations, 'Objective information on military matters, including transparency of military expenditures', Reports of the Secretary-General, various dates, 2001–2007, URL <http://disarmament.un.org/cab/milex.html>.

the UN Secretary-General to the General Assembly and are published in appropriate UN media.[5]

The SIPRI reporting system

SIPRI has been sending requests for data on military expenditure to governments on a regular basis since 1993. Such requests are sent to all countries that are included in the SIPRI Military Expenditure Database (currently 167 countries).[6] Every year SIPRI sends questionnaires to various national government offices and embassies of the respective countries. The SIPRI questionnaire is a simplified version of the UN instrument, with fields for data on spending on military and civilian personnel, operations and maintenance, procurement, military construction, military research and development, and paramilitary forces. Data are requested for the five most recent years in order to ensure consistency over time. The reported data are one of the sources of information used in preparing SIPRI's tables of military expenditure,

---

[5] United Nations, Department for Disarmament Affairs, *Transparency in Armaments: United Nations Standardized Instrument for Reporting Military Expenditures—Guidelines* (United Nations: New York, N.Y., [n.d.]), p. 1; and UN General Assembly Resolution A/RES/60/44 (note 1).

[6] There is 1 exception: SIPRI is unable to send requests to Rwanda because of a lack of contact details.

which are published in the SIPRI Yearbook, are available in the online SIPRI Military Expenditure Database and on request from SIPRI.[7]

III. Reporting of military expenditure data in 2006

In 2006 a total of 85 countries reported data on military spending to either the UN or SIPRI (see table 8D.1). Including 'nil reports' to the UN, the total number of countries reporting data was 96.[8]

In 2006 the number of reports received by SIPRI was 60. This was a decrease from the 67 countries that reported in 2005 and represents a response rate of 36 per cent in 2006 against 39 per cent in 2005.

The number of countries reporting data to the UN increased to 68 in 2006 from 62 in 2005. These data reports represent a response rate of 35 per cent of the member states in 2006, up from 32 per cent in 2005. Including nil reports, the total number of reports to the UN increased from 74 in 2005 to 79 in 2006.

On a regional basis, the best response in 2006 was from Europe and the Americas, where most countries submitted reports to both SIPRI and the UN. In Western Europe 20 out of 21 counties reported to either SIPRI or the UN (excluding the nil report from Iceland). In Central Europe all of the 16 countries covered by SIPRI and the UN reported data, including newly independent Montenegro. Of the seven Eastern European states (the European members of the Commonwealth of Independent States), six reported to either SIPRI or the UN. Both North American countries, six of the seven Central American countries and eight of the 11 South American countries reported data to either SIPRI or the UN. No Caribbean country responded to SIPRI, but three reported to the UN.

In Africa and the Middle East the response rate was very low in 2006, as it has been in previous years. In Africa six of a total of 50 states submitted data to SIPRI or the UN, while in the Middle East three out of 14 states did. Furthermore, only two of the six South Asian countries reported to the UN and none to SIPRI. In contrast, reporting by Central Asian countries improved in 2006—three of the six countries reported, compared to only one in 2005.

IV. Trends in reporting of military expenditure, 2001–2006

In spite of the DDA's efforts to enhance participation in the UN Standardized Instrument for Reporting Military Expenditures, there has been no significant increase in participation in recent years (see table 8D.2). In fact, the number of countries reporting to the UN in 2006 (79 countries) is lower than in 2002 (81). Thus, it appears that the simplified report introduced in 2002 has not delivered the intended result of an increased level of reporting. Instead, countries that previously reported with the standardized instrument have changed to the simplified form.[9]

---

[7] See appendix 8A. The SIPRI Military Expenditure Database is available at URL <http://www.sipri.org/contents/milap/milex/mex_database1.html>.

[8] A nil report is a questionnaire returned to the UN with no data entered, submitted by a country with no or very small defence forces.

[9] E.g. in 2005 Thailand reported using the standardized instrument and in 2006 it used the simplified form.

The regions with low reporting rates—Africa and the Middle East—have maintained low reporting rates over time.[10] Furthermore, countries in these low-reporting regions consistently fail to report data, rather than reporting intermittently as in other regions.[11] However, the total number of countries participating in the UN reporting system at least once during the period 2001–2006 has increased.

The total number of requests sent by SIPRI has increased from 158 requests in 2001 to 166 in 2006. However, the number of countries reporting to SIPRI has varied little over the period: in 2001 the number was 63 compared to 60 in 2006. As a consequence, the rate of response to SIPRI has decreased over this period, from 40 per cent to 36 per cent.

[10] United Nations (note 4), pp. 8–11.
[11] United Nations (note 4), p. 3.

9. Arms production

ELISABETH SKÖNS and EAMON SURRY

I. Introduction

Arms sales by the 100 largest arms-producing companies (the 'SIPRI Top 100') continued to increase in 2005, although the increase was smaller than in 2004. Companies in the United States and Western Europe dominate the list, together accounting for 92 per cent of the arms sales of the Top 100 in 2005. At the same time, the concentration of the arms industry continued, resulting in further growth of the large companies at the top of the list and a declining number of competitors. This raises the issue of monopolistic tendencies in arms production, which presents governments with the challenge of how to maintain control over costs and production schedules in arms procurement.

The concentration process is partly a response to the high and rising fixed costs of advanced weapon systems. This has been a major factor behind the developments in the arms industry since the end of World War II and continues to shape the industry.[1] Mergers and acquisitions allow companies to achieve economies of scale but also lead to reduced competition, and therefore fewer incentives to keep prices down and innovation up. This tension between the benefits of scale and of competition has been the central dilemma for governments in arms procurement and defence industrial policy for the past 40 years.[2]

Rather than trying to stem the increase in sophistication of weapon systems, government strategies to deal with this economic dilemma include international collaboration and arms exports to extend production runs, increasing use of commercial technology in weapon systems, as well as outsourcing, privatization and partnerships with the private sector. However, rising unit costs continue to drive developments in arms procurement, resulting in a long-term decline in the number of weapons that can be purchased. The implication is that choices have to be made in defence policies and arms procurement with

---

[1] This was expressed in its sharpest form by Norman Augustine, who predicted in the 1970s that the cost growth in major weapon systems would eventually lead to a situation in which even the major military spenders could only afford 'one plane, one tank, one ship'. Augustine, N. R., 'One plane, one tank, one ship: trend for the future?', *Defense Management Journal*, vol. 11, no, 2 (Apr. 1975), pp. 34–40.

[2] The main trends and drivers in the arms industry during the past 40 years are described in Dunne, J. P. and Surry, E., 'Arms production', *SIPRI Yearbook 2006: Armaments, Disarmament and International Security* (Oxford University Press: Oxford, 2006), pp. 387–418; and Dunne, P., 'Sector futures: defence industry', European Foundation for the Improvement of Living and Working Conditions, European Monitoring Centre on Change (EMCC), May 2006, URL <http://eurofound.europa.eu/emcc/content/source/eu06019a.html>.

inevitable consequences in terms of further consolidation and downsizing of the arms industry.

Simultaneously, ongoing transformation of the armed forces—to adapt to current military requirements and to meet future uncertainties—has important implications for the arms industry. While the ultimate goals, as well as the economic and political limitations, of military transformation differ between countries—including between the USA and European countries—the transformation processes are associated with the same type of technological developments in information and communications technology. Current transformation processes focus on enabling the supply of detailed, accurate and real-time data to all participants in complex military operations, a basic idea variously expressed as 'network-centric warfare', 'network-generated capabilities', 'network-enabled capabilities', 'networked operations' and 'network-based defence'. These developments may involve less emphasis on major platforms and more emphasis on their networking capabilities. However, the squeeze between rising costs and budget constraints looks set to continue and governments will still need to choose which indigenous industrial capabilities to keep, while relying on imports for the capabilities not retained.

In 2006 the need for military transformation became a political issue in the USA, whose high level of weapon procurements to a large extent drives developments in the global arms industry. One main objective of the 2006 Quadrennial Defense Review was to speed up military transformation towards small, high-technology forces and to be prepared for effective network-centric warfare.[3] However, the review also reflected experience from the war in Iraq in that it emphasized the need for more capabilities for asymmetric warfare, with more emphasis on military manpower and less on high-tech systems. This suggests that, rather than focusing on one type of strategy and military technology, these two agendas will exist side by side.

While the arms industry is adapting to shifts in military requirements, it is also seeing opportunities in the expanding demand for domestic, or homeland, security systems. As a result, many military electronics companies are diversifying into homeland security markets and some arms-producing companies are being transformed into 'defence and security' companies.

Section II of this chapter describes the level of and trends in the arms sales of the SIPRI Top 100 companies in 2005. It identifies the companies that experienced the largest increases in their arms sales in 2005 and the reasons for these increases. Section III describes some of the developments in the US arms industry, outlining the pattern of domestic acquisitions in 2006, the impact of the US Administration's post-September 2001 policies, and the implementation of US Department of Defense (DOD) policy to shape the US defence industrial base. Section IV describes some of the developments in the West European arms industry, similarly outlining the pattern of intra-European and transatlantic acquisitions during 2006. It also reviews the debate

---

[3] US Department of Defense, 'Quadrennial Defense Review Report', Washington, DC, 6 Feb. 2006, URL <http://www.defenselink.mil/qdr/>. For an analysis of the review see chapter 1 in this volume.

during 2006 in the United Kingdom on its new defence industrial strategy, which aims to provide tools for the implementation of the British defence industrial policy, and summarizes developments in 2006 in European Union-wide policies and policy implementation affecting the European arms industry. Section V presents the conclusions. Appendices 9A and 9B include tables of the Top 100 arms-producing companies in 2005 and major acquisitions in the North American and West European arms industry in 2006.

II. The SIPRI Top 100 arms-producing companies

The value of the combined arms sales of the 100 largest arms-producing companies in the world apart from China in 2005 was $290 billion, compared with $266 billion for the same companies in 2004 (see table 9.1).[4] The SIPRI Top 100 is dominated by companies based in the USA, with 40 US companies making 63 per cent of the Top 100's arms sales in 2005, while 32 West European companies accounted for 29 per cent and 9 Russian companies for 2 per cent. Companies based in Japan, Israel and India, in that order, accounted for most of the remaining 6 per cent.

The companies in the Top 100 for 2005 increased their combined arms sales by 9 per cent in nominal terms and 6 per cent in real terms over the previous year. Compared with the arms sales of the companies in the Top 100 for 2004, the increase was smaller—6 per cent in nominal terms and 3 per cent in real terms (see table 9.2). Over the period 2002–2005, the arms sales of the Top 100 for each year have increased by 38 per cent in nominal terms and by 18 per cent in real terms.

Companies that increased their arms sales the most in 2005

Some companies continue to have tremendous increases in arms sales. While in 1995 there was only one company with an annual arms sales increase of more than $1 billion and 11 companies with increases of more than 30 per cent,[5] in 2005 there were 6 companies in the first category and 19 companies in the second category (see table 9.3). Most of these high increases were the result of acquisitions rather than of organic growth.

The six companies with an increase in arms sales in 2005 greater than $1 billion are all in the top 10 of the Top 100 for 2005. The other four companies in the top 10 group are Boeing, Lockheed Martin, EADS and Thales. After a number of setbacks in the early 2000s,[6] Boeing increased its arms sales in 2005 by $550 million and in 2006 had a backlog of $80 billion in military

[4] Chinese companies are not included because comparable data do not exist.

[5] Sköns, E. and Cooper, J., 'Arms production', *SIPRI Yearbook 1997: Armaments, Disarmament and International Security* (Oxford University Press: Oxford, 1997), table 8.2, p. 241.

[6] In 2001 Boeing lost the competition for the Joint Strike Fighter contract, with potential revenues of $200 billion, and in 2004 the US Air Force cancelled its plan to lease 100 tanker aircraft from Boeing. Sköns, E. et al., 'Military expenditure', *SIPRI Yearbook 2004: Armaments, Disarmament and International Security* (Oxford University Press: Oxford, 2004), pp. 317–19.

Table 9.1. Regional and national shares of arms sales for the SIPRI Top 100 arms-producing companies in the world excluding China,[a] 2005 compared to 2004

Arms sales figures are in US$ b., at current prices and exchange rates. Figures do not always add up to totals because of the conventions of rounding.

Number of companies	Region/ country	Arms sales[b] ($ b.)		Change in arms sales, 2004–05 (%)		Share of total Top 100 arms sales, 2005 (%)
		2004[c]	2005	Nominal[d]	Real[e]	
41	**North America**	**167.3**	**183.0**	*9*	*6*	*63.1*
40	USA	166.8	182.5	*9*	*6*	*62.9*
1	Canada	0.5	0.4	*–4*	*–13*	*0.2*
32	**Western Europe**	**78.4**	**85.3**	*9*	*7*	*29.4*
10	UK	31.7	34.2	*8*	*6*	*11.8*
6	France	18.8	19.9	*6*	*4*	*6.9*
1	Trans-European[f]	9.5	9.6	*1*	*–1*	*3.3*
3	Italy	8.3	10.9	*33*	*30*	*3.8*
7	Germany	5.6	6.0	*8*	*6*	*2.1*
1	Sweden	1.9	2.1	*9*	*11*	*0.7*
2	Spain	1.7	1.6	*–4*	*–7*	*0.6*
1	Switzerland	0.6	0.6	*–6*	*–7*	*0.2*
1	Norway	0.4	0.4	*–8*	*–13*	*0.1*
9	**Eastern Europe**	**4.6**	**5.4**	*18*	*3*	*1.9*
9	Russia[g]	4.6	5.4	*18*	*3*	*1.9*
9	**Other OECD**	**7.8**	**8.3**	*6*	*5*	*2.9*
6	Japan[h]	6.1	6.2	*2*	*4*	*2.1*
2	Korea, South[i]	1.3	1.6	*25*	*9*	*0.6*
1	Australia	0.4	0.5	*14*	*7*	*0.2*
9	**Other non-OECD**	**7.4**	**8.0**	*9*	*4*	*2.8*
4	Israel	3.5	3.7	*7*	*6*	*1.3*
3	India	2.7	3.0	*10*	*3*	*1.0*
1	Singapore	0.9	0.9	*9*	*7*	*0.3*
1	Brazil	0.4	0.4	*8*	*–16*	*0.1*
100	**Total**	**265.5**	**290.1**	*9*	*6*	*100.0*

OECD = Organisation for Economic Co-operation and Development.

[a] Chinese companies are not included because comparable data do not exist. Other countries that could possibly have companies that are large enough to appear in the SIPRI Top 100 list had data been available include Kazakhstan, Pakistan and Ukraine.

[b] Arms sales include all company arms sales, both domestic and export.

[c] Arms sales figures for 2004 refer to companies in the SIPRI Top 100 for 2005, and not to companies in the Top 100 for 2004.

[d] This column gives the change in arms sales 2004–2005 in current dollars.

[e] This column gives the change in arms sales 2004–2005 in constant (2005) dollars. In some cases, although the national economy experienced inflation in 2004–2005, the movement in exchange rates means that the real change is higher than the nominal change after conversion to US dollars.

[f] The company classified as trans-European is EADS, which is based in three countries— France, Germany and Spain—and registered in the Netherlands.

g The figure for the combined arms sales of the 9 Russian companies in 2004 includes a rough estimate for 1 of these.

h Arms sales data for Japanese companies represent new military contracts awarded by the Japan Defense Agency, rather than actual arms sales for the year.

i Figures for South Korean companies are uncertain.

Source: Appendix 9A, table 9A.1.

contracts.[7] The other three companies had roughly constant arms sales in 2005 but have had significant increases in recent years.

The $2.7 billion increase in arms sales by Finmeccanica is attributable primarily to a number of acquisitions. Most significantly, in a deal worth €1.5 billion ($2.0 billion) at the end of 2004, the company acquired GKN's 50 per cent share in the previous joint venture AgustaWestland, one of the largest producers of helicopters in the world.[8] During 2005 Finmeccanica completed two other major transactions. First, as part of the deal dissolving AMS, a previous joint venture in defence electronics with BAE Systems, Finmeccanica resumed full control of AMS's Italian assets (renamed Selex Sistemi Integrati), acquired BAE Systems' secure communications operations (renamed Selex Communications), and obtained a 75 per cent share in AMS's avionics business (renamed Selex Sensors and Airborne Systems). All of these were integrated into Finmeccanica's defence electronics division.[9] Second, the company acquired a 52.7 per cent stake in Datamat, an Italian information technology company with a substantial defence and space division.[10] These acquisitions, accounting for $3.5 billion in annual revenues, represented a major phase in Finmeccanica's restructuring plan to focus its activities on aerospace, defence and security while reducing its civil activities in response to political pressure.[11] In March 2006 the company completed its stock market flotation of Ansaldo STS, its signalling, railway and subway operation, although it retained a 40 per cent stake. This transaction gave Finmeccanica €520 million ($625 million) to help fund further acquisitions and investments in the aerospace and defence sector, primarily in the USA.[12]

Many of the other companies that appear in table 9.3 are Russian and many are information technology (IT) companies.

[7] Ratnam, G., 'Turbulent flight for Boeing: analysts question setbacks in high-profile programs', *Defense News*, 10 July 2006.

[8] Finmeccanica, 'Finmeccanica: closing with GKN of the acquisition of 100% of AgustaWestland', Press release, Rome, 30 Nov. 2004, URL <http://www.finmeccanica.it/Holding/EN/Corporate/Sala_stampa/Comunicati_stampa/>.

[9] Finmeccanica, 'Selex venture boosts Finmeccanica's defence electronics business', Press release, Rome, 18 May 2005, URL <http://www.finmeccanica.it/Holding/EN/Corporate/Sala_stampa/Comunicati_stampa/>.

[10] Anderson, G., 'Finmeccanica acquisitions prompt upswing in orders and revenues', *Jane's Defence Industry*, Nov. 2005, p. 12.

[11] Nativi, A., 'Finmeccanica remains hungry for growth through acquisitions', *Aviation Week and Space Technology*, 11 Apr. 2005; and Kington, T., 'Divestiture difficulties: political shackles complicate moves by Italy's Finmeccanica', *Defense News*, 1 Aug. 2005.

[12] Kington, T., 'Finmeccanica shifts 520M euros to A&D', *Defense News*, 3 Apr. 2006.

Table 9.2. Trends in arms sales of companies in the SIPRI Top 100 arms-producing companies in the world excluding China, 2002–2005

	2002	2003	2004	2005	2002–2005
Arms sales at current prices and exchange rates					
Total ($ b.)	210.1	234.2	272.6	290.1	
Change (%)		*11.5*	*16.4*	*6.4*	*38.1*
Arms sales at constant (2005) prices and exchange rates					
Total ($ b.)	246.0	256.7	280.9	290.1	
Change (%)		*4.4*	*9.5*	*3.2*	*17.9*

Note: The data in this table refer to the companies in the SIPRI Top 100 in each year, which means that they refer to a different set of companies each year, as ranked from a consistent set of data. The figure for 2004 is thus different from the figure for 2004 in table 9.1.

Source: Appendix 9A.

Russian companies

Four Russian companies were among those that increased their arms sales by more than 30 per cent in 2005: Admiralteiskie Verfi, Almaz-Antei, Severnaya Verf and TRV Corporation.[13] Russian companies have only been included in the SIPRI Top 100 list since 2002, when data availability first allowed it.[14] However, the estimates based on this information are somewhat uncertain and it is difficult to find information explaining the level and trend in Russian companies' arms sales.[15]

The increase in the arms sales of Almaz-Antei, which makes it the Russian company with the largest arms sales in 2005, can be partly attributed to domestic sales of up to $530 million and the export of missile systems to China and Viet Nam.[16] The company, which develops and manufactures air defence systems, was formed in 2002 as part of the Russian military industrial strategy to form large integrated structures in leading industry sectors.[17] In October 2005 it obtained the right to independently—that is, without going through the state export company Rosoboronexport—export spare parts and provide maintenance services for Russian military equipment used by foreign

---

[13] TRV (Takticheskoe Raketnoe Vooruzhenie, tactical missile armament) Corporation is also known in English as the Tactical Missiles Corporation.

[14] On transparency in the Russian arms industry see Surry, E., *Transparency in the Arms Industry*, SIPRI Policy Paper no. 12 (SIPRI: Stockholm, Jan. 2006), URL <http://www.sipri.org/>.

[15] SIPRI estimates the arms sales of most Russian companies on the basis of data on their total sales, a proportion of which is then attributed to arms sales based on data published by the Centre for Analysis of Strategies and Technologies, Moscow.

[16] Makienko, K., '2005 rating of Russia's largest defence companies', *Moscow Defense Brief*, no. 6 (2006); and Vasiliev, D., 'Russia's arms trade with foreign states in 2005', *Moscow Defense Brief*, no. 5 (2006).

[17] See e.g. Cooper, J., 'Developments in the Russian arms industry', *SIPRI Yearbook 2006* (note 2), pp. 431–48.

customers.[18] There is a high demand for Russian air defence systems: in 2006 the value of Rosoboronexport orders for air defence systems amounted to $3.5 billion.[19]

The increase in arms sales for the two Russian shipbuilding companies in table 9.3 was the result primarily of the export in 2005 to China of three Kilo Class (Project 636M) conventional submarines by Admiralteiskie Verfi and one Sovremenny Class (Project 956EM) destroyer by Severnaya Verf.[20] A second such destroyer was delivered by Severnaya Verf in 2006.[21] A complete picture of Admiralteiskie Verfi's activities is difficult to obtain because it makes little information publicly available, citing state secrecy as the justification.[22] More information is available on Severnaya Verf. In addition to exports, Severnaya Verf also has a major domestic order for four 20380 series corvettes, the first of which was launched in 2005, while two more are under construction.[23] In late 2005 the company also won a domestic contract for a new class of frigates to be completed over a 15-year period.[24] In August 2005 Severnaya Verf was merged with Baltiysky Zavod under the control of United Industrial Corporation, after Mezhprombank (International Industrial Bank) became the majority shareholder in both shipyards. These two shipyards, both located in St Petersburg, are among the largest and most technically advanced in the Russian naval shipbuilding sector. In the long term, Rosprom, the Russian federal agency for industry, plans to concentrate the naval shipbuilding industry into two state-controlled management companies: the Centre for Subsurface Shipbuilding and the Centre for Surface Shipbuilding. However, further consolidation of the Russian shipbuilding industry is expected to be complicated, since some of these shipyards are privately owned.[25]

Overall, the Russian shipbuilding companies experienced a marked rise in total sales as well as in arms sales in 2005, making them the leading sector in the Russian arms industry for the first time since systematic data on Russian arms-producing companies became available, in 2001. While one of the main

---

[18] Interfax–AVN, 'Almaz-Antei granted right to conduct foreign economic activity', Moscow, 5 Oct. 2005. Systems manufactured by Almaz-Antei are in service with *c.* 50 armed forces abroad. Interfax–AVN, 'Almaz-Antei consortium's air defense system exports to total $5–6 billion in near future', Moscow, 9 Dec. 2005.

[19] Abdullaev, N., 'Orders flood some Russian arms makers', *Defense News*, 24 July 2006. See also chapter 10 in this volume.

[20] In addition, Krasnoye Sormovo exported 1 and Sevmash 2 Kilo Class submarines to China. Lantratov, K., 'Russia shares state secret with UN', *Kommersant*, 20 June 2006, URL <http://www.kommersant.com/p683546/>.

[21] Novichkov, N., 'China accepts final Sovremenny', *Jane's Defence Weekly*, 11 Oct. 2006, p. 16; and Abdullaev, N., 'Russia sends 4th destroyer to China', *Defense News*, 9 Oct. 2006. See also chapter 10 in this volume.

[22] Pronini, L., 'Russian firms to display upgrades, training gear', *Defense News*, 13 June 2005.

[23] Severnaya Verf, 'The keel-laying of the corvette for Russian Navy took place at JCS Shipbuilding plant «Severnaya Verf»', News item, 10 Nov. 2006, URL <http://www.nordsy.spb.ru/sv2/news_eng.php?id=46>; and 'Russia launches new ship', *Defense News*, 22 May 2006.

[24] Scott, R., 'Severnaya Verf secures Russian frigate contract', *Jane's Defence Weekly*, 2 Nov. 2005, p. 12.

[25] Makienko, K., 'Consolidation and restructuring of the Russian shipbuilding sector during 2005', *Moscow Defense Brief*, no. 5 (2006).

Table 9.3. Companies in the SIPRI Top 100 with the largest increase in arms sales in 2005

Figures are in US$ m., at current prices and exchange rates. Figures in italics are percentages.

Rank 2005	Company	Country	Sector[a]	Arms sales ($ m.) 2004	Arms sales ($ m.) 2005	Change 2004–05 $ m.	Change 2004–05 %
Companies with the largest absolute increase in arms sales (by more than $1 b.)							
4	BAE Systems	UK	A Ac El Mi MV SA/A Sh	19 840	23 230	3 390	*17*
9	L-3 Communications	USA	El	5 970	8 970	3 000	*50*
7	Finmeccanica	Italy	A Ac El Mi SA/A	7 130	9 800	2 670	*37*
5	Raytheon	USA	El Mi	17 150	19 800	2 650	*16*
2	Northrop Grumman	USA	Ac El Mi Sh	25 970	27 590	1 620	*6*
6	General Dynamics	USA	A El MV Sh	15 150	16 570	1 420	*9*
Companies with the largest relative increase in arms sales (by more than 30 %)							
91	Severnaya Verf[b]	Russia	Sh	20	440	420	*2 100*
97	Universal Shipbuilding Corp.[b, c]	Japan	Sh	100	360	260	*260*
40	Armor Holdings	USA	Comp (MV Oth)	610	1 190	580	*95*
98	TRV Corporation	Russia	Mi	220	350	180	*95*
65	Admiralteiskie Verfi[b]	Russia	Sh	340	660	320	*94*
32	EDS	USA	Comp (Oth)	990	1 570	580	*59*
41	CACI International	USA	Comp (Oth)	770	1 190	420	*55*
49	AM General	USA	MV	690	1 050	360	*52*
9	L-3 Communications	USA	El	5 970	8 970	3 000	*50*
27	Textron	USA	Ac El Eng MV	1 300	1 800	500	*39*
47	Oshkosh Truck	USA	MV	770	1 060	290	*38*
7	Finmeccanica	Italy	A Ac El Mi SA/A	7 130	9 800	2 670	*37*
31	Almaz-Antei	Russia	Mi	1 190	1 590	400	*34*
39	Thyssen Krupp[b]	Germany	Sh	930	1 240	310	*33*
86	United Industrial	USA	Ac	360	480	120	*33*
16	ITT Industries	USA	El	2 410	3 190	780	*32*
21	Dassault Aviation	France	Ac	1 670	2 210	540	*32*
30	DRS Technologies	USA	El	1 280	1 680	400	*31*
48	Samsung[d]	S. Korea	A MV SA/A	800	1 050	250	*31*

[a] A = artillery, Ac = aircraft, El = electronics, Eng = engines, Mi = missiles, MV = military vehicles, SA/A = small arms/ammunition, Sh = ships and Oth = other. Comp (. . .) = components, services or anything less than final systems in the sectors in the parentheses.

[b] Shipbuilding companies often have bulky arms sales that do not accurately reflect the continuous activities of the company and may therefore be misleading.

[c] Arms sales data for Japanese companies represent new military contracts awarded by the Japan Defense Agency rather than actual arms sales for the year.

[d] Data for Samsung arms sales are uncertain. The SIPRI figure is the sum of an estimated approximate arms sales figure for Samsung Techwin and 50% of the 2004 arms sales of Samsung Thales.

Source: Appendix 9A.

characteristics of the Russian arms industry continues to be its export orient-ation,[26] exports as a share of total sales declined to 62 per cent in 2005, com-pared with 68 per cent in 2004, as a result of increased domestic procure-ment.[27] The decision in January 2007 that Rosoboronexport, the Russian state export corporation, will once more have the monopoly on export sales of final systems is likely to have an impact on the Russian arms industry in 2007.[28]

The increase in the arms sales of TRV Corporation is a consequence of the government programme to reform and develop the Russian arms industry during the period 2002–2006. TRV was established in 2002 by combining six companies specializing in tactical missiles, as one of the sectors to be inte-grated into larger structures. In 2004 a presidential decree was signed aiming at further development of TRV, and since then eight arms-producing com-panies have been added.[29]

Although these four Russian companies have made significant increases in their arms sales in 2005, the general assessment is that further contraction of the Russian arms industry is almost inevitable because it lacks resources and has structural problems.[30]

Information technology companies

Several of the large increases in arms sales in 2005 were as a result of increased sales of information technology and services, such as development of advanced communications networks, integration of technology systems and analytical services. Companies that increased their arms sales in these areas in 2005 include EDS, CACI International, L-3 Communications, ITT Industries and DRS Technologies (see table 9.3).

EDS is an example of the type of primarily civil-focused IT company with-out which governments would be unable to go to war or modernize their armed forces. EDS provides IT services and solutions to a broad range of clients, and its arms sales, primarily by its business segment Defence Industry Solutions, accounted for only 8 per cent of its total revenues in 2005. Like many other companies that specialize in IT services, EDS has positioned itself as a supplier of network-centric capabilities and as a way for governments to outsource the modernization of a variety of military support functions.[31] In

---

[26] Makienko, K., 'Evolution of Russia's defense industry in 2005', *Moscow Defense Brief*, no. 5 (2006). See also Cooper (note 17).

[27] Lantratov, K. and Safronov, I., 'Shipbuilding overtakes aviation', *Kommersant*, 13 June 2006, URL <http://kommersant.com/page.asp?id=681459>.

[28] The Presidential Decree on several issues concerning military-technical cooperation between the Russian Federation and foreign states, Decree no. 54, was signed on 18 Jan. 2007. The text of the decree is available at URL <http://document.kremlin.ru/doc.asp?ID=037563> (in Russian). See also chapter 10 in this volume.

[29] TRV Corporation, 'Tactical Missiles Corporation JSC history', URL <http://eng.ktrv.ru/about_eng/history_eng/>, p. 10.

[30] Cooper (note 17).

[31] EDS also argues that it seeks to capitalize on financial pressures on governments to do 'more with less' with their military forces: 'Defense departments worldwide are seeking to deliver greater military capability with lower expenditure. EDS . . . can help these departments manage and exploit information to meet their military objectives with reduced costs.' EDS, 'Defense', EDS website, URL <http://www.

2000 the company signed a contract worth $7 billion to build the world's largest intranet for the US Navy. Despite public criticism of the company's implementation of the project, in 2006 the contract was extended for 3 years and by $3 billion, making it the company's largest ever military contract.[32] Not withstanding the controversies, in March 2005 the British Ministry of Defence (MOD) awarded EDS (as consortium leader) a contract worth £2.3 billion ($4 billion) over 10 years to consolidate defence information networks under the MOD's Defence Information Infrastructure (Future) project.[33] Revenues from this project can partly account for the company's greatly increased arms sales in 2005.[34] Through its British subsidiary, EDS is also seeking more military work of this type in Western Europe by exploiting the relationships it has built through its extensive non-defence work for governments.[35]

The increase in the 2005 arms sales of CACI International, a company that provides IT solutions and services to the US Department of Defense, is a result of acquisitions.[36] The company bought four companies during 2004, including American Management Systems' Defence and Intelligence Group.[37] The proportion of its annual revenues from US DOD contracts increased markedly, from 67 per cent in financial year (FY) 2004 to 73 per cent in FY 2005.[38]

The increase in the arms sales of L-3 Communications is also primarily attributable to a long series of acquisitions,[39] but according to the company there has also been some organic growth.[40] L-3 has had a clear strategy in recent years of acquiring small- to medium-sized companies that specialize in

eds.com/industries/defense/>. On the broader trend towards outsourcing of military services and functions by contracting to the private sector see Sköns, E. and Weidacher, R., 'Arms production', *SIPRI Yearbook 2002: Armaments, Disarmament and International Security* (Oxford University Press: Oxford, 2002), pp. 341–46.

[32] E.g. Onley, D., 'Hanlon on NMCI: "EDS was not prepared"', *Government Computer News*, 22 June 2004; and Webb, C. L., 'Navy–Marine Corps intranet project takes fresh flak', *Washington Post*, 24 June 2004. On the contract extension see EDS, 'EDS signs NMCI contract extension to 2010', News release, Plano, Tex., 24 Mar. 2006, URL <http://www.eds.com/news/releases/2905/>.

[33] EDS, 'EDS-Led consortium signs contract with UK Ministry of Defence for Defence Information Infrastructure project: approximately $4 billion contract is largest win since 2002', News release, Plano, Tex., 22 Mar. 2005, URL <http://www.eds.com/news/releases/2282/>.

[34] EDS, *2005 Annual Report* (EDS: Plano, Tex., 2006), URL <http://www.eds.com/investor/annual/2005/>, p. AR-11.

[35] Felstead, P., 'EDS looks to strengthen its presence in European defence markets', *Jane's Defence Weekly*, 14 Sep. 2005.

[36] CACI conducted interrogations for the US Army in Iraq in 2003–2005. After one of its employees was implicated in the Abu Ghraib prison abuse scandal, the company decided to withdraw from the interrogation business when the contract expired in Sep. 2005. McCarthy, E., 'CACI plans to drop interrogation work; firm was entangled in Abu Ghraib', *Washington Post*, 15 Sep. 2005, p. D04.

[37] See Surry, E., 'Table of acquisitions, 2005', *SIPRI Yearbook 2006* (note 2), pp. 428–30.

[38] CACI International, 'Form 10-K annual report under Section 13 or 15(d) of the Securities Exchange Act of 1934 for the fiscal year ended June 30, 2005', Arlington, Va., 13 Sep. 2005, URL <http://www.sec.gov/edgar.shtml>.

[39] See e.g. appendix 9B; Surry (note 37); and Surry, E., 'Table of acquisitions, 2004', *SIPRI Yearbook 2005: Armaments, Disarmament and International Security* (Oxford University Press: Oxford, 2005), pp. 414–16.

[40] Ratnam, G., 'Frank Lanza, Chairman, Chief Executive, L-3 Communications', *Defense News*, 16 Jan. 2006.

the provision of high-tech products and services to the US DOD and other—primarily intelligence—government agencies. In 2005 L-3 acquired the Titan Corporation for $2.65 billion.[41] L-3 is one of several companies in the arms industry that seek to exploit their expertise in the growing market for domestic (homeland) security products and services (see section III below).[42]

ITT Industries and DRS Technologies both provide military electronics, communications and technology support services to the US DOD and have recently made acquisitions that augment their defence operations.[43] These companies operate in the niche market for highly specialized dual-use goods in which products and services have been in high demand in recent years.[44] For example, ITT manufactures global positioning system (GPS) satellite navigation equipment which is bought by both military and commercial customers.[45] Such IT and services companies frequently perform work that may not always be classified as military, but it is clear that armed forces cannot operate or service their highly complex systems without them.

The increases in the military sales of these IT companies is a continuation of the trend for the nature of the arms industry to change.[46] This takes place both as a result of a new type of company moving into the arms industry, as some of the above examples illustrate, and of major arms-producing companies buying IT companies, as illustrated by some of the acquisitions that took place in 2006 (see appendix 9B).

III. The United States

In the United States, the wisdom of spending large sums of money on network-centric warfare capabilities was increasingly questioned in 2006, and advocates of low-technology warfare made some progress. There were two

---

[41] L-3 Communications, 'L-3 announces agreement to acquire the Titan Corporation', Press release, New York, N.Y., 3 June 2005, URL <http://www.l-3com.com/news-events/pressrelease.aspx>.

[42] Murphy, J., 'L-3 outlines avenues for growth', *Jane's Defence Industry*, June 2006, p. 12; and L-3 Communications, 'L-3 Communications acquires two leaders in threat detection for military and homeland security applications', Press release, New York, N.Y., 21 Mar. 2006, URL <http://www.l-3com.com/news-events/pressreleases.aspx>.

[43] In 2004 ITT Industries bought the Remote Sensing Systems unit of Eastman Kodak for $725 million. ITT Industries, 'ITT Industries to acquire Kodak's Remote Sensing Systems (RSS)', Press release, White Plains, N.Y., 9 Feb. 2004. In Jan. 2006 DRS Technologies completed the acquisition of Engineered Support Systems for $1.97 billion. DRS Technologies, 'DRS Technologies completes acquisition of Engineered Support Systems', Press release, Parsippany, N.J., 31 Jan. 2006, URL <http://www.drs.com/press/archivelist.cfm>.

[44] DRS Technologies focuses on 'several key areas of importance to the U.S. [DOD], such as intelligence, surveillance, reconnaissance, power management, advanced communications and network systems'. DRS Technologies, 'Form 10-k annual report pursuant to Section 13 or 15(d) of the Securities Exchange Act of 1934 for the fiscal year ended March 31, 2006', Parsippany, N.J.,, 12 June 2006, URL <http://www.sec.gov/edgar.shtml>.

[45] Ratnam, G., 'Diverse ITT holds onto defense', *Defense News*, 17 May 2005. Approximately 44% of the sales in ITT's Defense Electronics and Services division are generated through contracts for technical and support services which the company provides for the military and other government agencies. ITT, 'Business & products: Defense Electronics & Services', ITT website, URL <http://www.itt.com/business/prof-defn.asp>.

[46] Dunne and Surry (note 2), pp. 412–13.

main reasons: scepticism over whether stated transformation policies were achieving their goals,[47] and budgetary pressures arising partly from the need to prioritize the repair and replacement of military equipment used in the wars in Afghanistan and Iraq.[48] The Quadrennial Defense Review spelled out some success for the 'traditionalists', in that it argued that not only high-tech systems but also military manpower mattered. In November 2006 Donald Rumsfeld, who was seen as a major driving force behind the idea of transformation, left the post of Secretary of Defense. However, early statements from his successor, Robert Gates, indicated that there might be no significant change in the military transformation project.[49]

This section provides an overview of mergers and acquisitions in the US arms industry, the impact of post-September 2001 US policies on the arms industry and developments in US defence industrial policy.

Mergers and acquisitions

After a period of intensive consolidation in the US arms industry between 1993 and 1998, the underlying dynamics and financial magnitude of mergers and acquisitions have been less dramatic. In particular, there have been fewer large-scale mergers. While there is no indication of a decline in the number of mergers and acquisitions, there is clear evidence of a gradual decline in average transaction values. Consolidation continues primarily at the subcontractor level and in particular in the IT and military services sectors.

Because of several years of record profits and an unusually high level of surplus cash, some analysts anticipated that there could be more large-scale acquisitions in 2006.[50] However, there was only one deal with a value in excess of $1 billion in 2006, as compared to three in 2005.[51] This was Boeing's $1.7 billion purchase of Aviall, one of the largest providers of new aviation parts and services in the aerospace industry.[52]

---

[47] According to Loren Thompson, director of defence studies at the Lexington Institute: 'The [Quadrennial Defense Review] has failed to institutionalize the concepts of transformation that [Defense Secretary Donald] Rumsfeld and his advisers have espoused for the last four years . . . That's partly because of political resistance, but it's partly because of their own incompetence'. Bruno, M., 'Experts: 2005 QDR fails to deliver transformation', *Aviation Week*, 19 Dec. 2005. Another analyst, Richard Aboulafia of the Teal Group, argued that: 'Transformation is basically dead [for] Three reasons: strategic irrelevance, marketing overhype and budgetary impossibility'. Rigby, B., 'US military "transformation" is dead: analysts', *Defense News*, 7 Dec. 2006. See also chapter 1 in this volume.

[48] See chapter 8 in this volume.

[49] US Senate, Armed Services Committee, 'Advance policy questions for Dr. Robert M. Gates, nominee to be Secretary of Defense', 5 Dec. 2006, URL <http://armed-services.senate.gov/testimony.cfm?wit_id=5850&id=2446>.

[50] Wayne, L., 'Cash puts U.S. military contractors in bind', *International Herald Tribune*, 13 May 2005; and Ratnam, G., 'Industry's full pockets: surplus cash, tight U.S. budgets may mean wave of acquisitions', *Defense News*, 16 May 2005. See also Koch, A., 'Acquisition and mergers market looks to remain hot in 2006', *Jane's Defence Weekly*, 4 Jan. 2006, p. 19.

[51] See appendix 9B; and Surry (note 37).

[52] Boeing, 'Boeing to acquire Aviall to enhance its growing services business', Press release, Chicago, Ill., 1 May 2006, URL <http://www.boeing.com/news/releases/>.

Also during 2006, Halliburton began the process of divesting its subsidiary KBR by staging an initial public offering (IPO) of 17 per cent of its shares and announced plans to sell the rest of the company by April 2007.[53] KBR has attracted criticism from the US Congress, watchdog organizations and others, in particular for its work in Iraq.[54] The IPO took place despite British national security concerns arising from KBR's majority stake in the Devonport naval shipyard.[55]

Intra-US acquisitions during 2006 focused on providers with capabilities that companies anticipate will be in great demand in the near future, particularly IT products and services and other types of military services (see appendix 9B). Some of the small companies currently being acquired are highly specialized and operate in niche markets. In particular, as governments try to cut costs by keeping existing equipment in service longer, there is a trend towards the acquisition of companies that provide maintenance and upgrades to existing technology. Acquisitions of small companies are also made for the purpose of entering the expanding homeland security sector. In 2006 L-3 Communications purchased four small US companies, Lockheed Martin five and SAIC four. Raytheon, General Dynamics, EDO and CACI International each made two such acquisitions. The values of these transactions are not always disclosed by the companies involved, but none of these deals was large.

Two examples that typify this trend are L-3 Communications' acquisition of Nova Engineering, which produces communications systems for network-centric warfare and works on several large programmes, including the DOD's Joint Tactical Radio System,[56] and Raytheon's purchase of Houston Associates, a company which develops 'mission-critical networks and network-centric command and control infrastructure applications'.[57]

According to one report, acquisitions of companies that provide systems engineering and technical assistance have more than doubled from 47 in 2001 to 98 in 2005 and the share of services sales in the revenues of the 100 companies with the largest value of contracts with the DOD has increased from 30 per cent in 2000 to 34 per cent in 2005.[58]

Profits in the US defence and aerospace industries are high and growing. The growth in these industries' operating profits exceeded that of the Standard

---

[53] Halliburton, 'KBR announces pricing of its initial public offering', Press release, Houston, Tex., 15 Nov. 2006, URL <http://www.halliburton.com/news/>; Witte, G., 'KBR shares up 22% on 1st day of trading', *Washington Post*, 17 Nov. 2006, p. D03; and Merle, R., 'Minority stake in KBR will be sold', *Washington Post*, 28 Jan. 2006, p. D01.

[54] For an account of this criticism see the company's entry on the Windfalls of War website at URL <http://www.publicintegrity.org/wow/bio.aspx?act=pro&ddlC=31>; and the Halliburton Watch website, URL <http://www.halliburtonwatch.org/>.

[55] Boxell, J., 'UK demands Halliburton drop KBR float', *Financial Times*, 14 Nov. 2006.

[56] Butterfield, E., 'L-3 gets net-centric with Nova Engineering buy', *Washington Technology*, 14 Aug. 2006, URL <http://www.washingtontechnology.com/news/1_1/29122-1.html>.

[57] Raytheon, 'Raytheon acquires Houston Associates, Inc.', News release, McKinney, Tex., 24 Jan. 2006, URL <http://www.raytheon.com/newsroom/>.

[58] Ratnam, G., 'For DOD, merger decisions get tougher', *Defense News*, 9 Oct. 2006.

& Poor's 500 companies in five of the nine years 1996–2004.[59] As measured by return on invested capital during the period 2002–2004, the profitability of major defence and aerospace companies was greater than in comparable non-defence companies. The combined net profits of the five largest US arms-producing companies in the SIPRI Top 100 for 2005 increased from $5.9 billion in 2004 to $8.1 billion in 2005, an increase of 39 per cent.[60] Not only have the companies benefited from the wars in Afghanistan and Iraq, but so have the chief executive officers (CEOs) of large defence contractors. A 2006 study surveyed the earnings of the CEOs of all publicly listed US companies among the 100 largest defence contractors that derived at least 10 per cent of their revenues from arms sales. It showed that the combined earnings since September 2001 of the 34 highest-earning CEOs amounted to almost $1 billion.[61]

The impact of US post-September 2001 policies on the defence and security industries

Two ways in which the USA's post-September 2001 policies have had an impact on the US arms industry are directly through increased US DOD spending on equipment and services used for the military operations in Afghanistan and Iraq, and indirectly through the impact on arms exports. There has also been an impact on sectors outside the arms industry, through spending by the DOD and other government agencies on security services and reconstruction in Afghanistan and Iraq. Beyond the foreign military operations, post-September 2001 policies have also caused a surge in the demand for goods and services for US homeland security requirements.

Impact on the arms industry

The US arms industry has benefited greatly from the expansion in US spending on arms procurement and research, development, test and evaluation (RDT&E). As a result of the massive funding for military operations in Afghanistan and Iraq,[62] US expenditure on arms procurement has increased in real terms from $62 billion in FY 2001 to $91 billion in FY 2006 and RDT&E expenditure from $46 billion in FY 2001 to $72 billion in FY 2006 (in con-

---

[59] US Department of Defense (DOD), Office of Under Secretary of Defense Acquisition, Technology & Logistics Industrial Policy, *Annual Industrial Capabilities Report to Congress* (DOD: Washington, DC, Feb. 2006), URL <http://www.acq.osd.mil/ip/ip_products.html>, p. 5. The Standard & Poor's (S&P) 500 are the 500 large publicly listed US companies. Their stocks comprise the S&P 500 Index, which is designed to be an indicator of US equity values.

[60] These companies are Lockheed Martin, General Dynamics, Northrop Grumman, Raytheon and Boeing. Profits are for net income after taxes, as provided in their annual reports.

[61] Anderson, S. et al., *Executive Excess: Defense and Oil Executives Cash in on Conflict*, 13th Annual CEO Compensation Survey (Institute for Policy Studies and United for a Fair Economy: Washington, DC, Aug. 2006), URL <http://www.faireconomy.org/>.

[62] See chapter 8 in this volume.

stant FY 2007 prices).[63] This rate of increase would not have taken place without appropriations under the heading 'global war on terrorism'. However, it is difficult to know the details of how this money has been spent. While information is available on individual DOD contract awards, it requires a major effort to identify and process the information required to form a coherent picture.[64] Another difficulty in tracing the impact of the 'global war on terrorism' on the industry is that war replacement orders are often included in larger contracts.

The war in Iraq has had an impact on the arms sales of several companies in the SIPRI Top 100. At least three companies with major increases in arms sales during 2005 (see table 9.3) have benefited greatly: AM General, Armor Holdings and Oshkosh Truck. These companies provide military vehicles and their upgrades and repair. In mid-2003 the US DOD began a major programme to provide additional armour for light vehicles and trucks in Iraq.[65] AM General is the sole supplier of M-1151 and M-1152 High Mobility Multipurpose Wheeled Vehicles (HMMWV or Humvees), which have been used in great numbers in Iraq, and has on-going contracts totalling $191.9 million for such vehicles.[66] Armor Holdings specializes in fitting armour to a variety of military vehicles, but in particular to HMMWVs, and in 2005 supplied 6684 HMMWVs to US forces abroad and Iraqi forces, in addition to 3945 vehicles in 2004.[67] Oshkosh Truck has received several types of contract related to the war in Iraq, including for high-mobility trucks—such as the Medium Tactical Vehicle Replacement (MTVR)—which support troops in Iraq. However, the main reason for the increase in Oshkosh's arms sales is its provision of logistics services, including maintenance and support functions, with services facilities in Iraq and Kuwait.[68] Some of these increases are likely to be temporary, since they are due to improvements to a stock of vehicles.

The wars in Afghanistan and Iraq have also reinforced the tendency, which emerged well before their start, for outsourcing traditional military functions, such as the maintenance, servicing and repair of military equipment, to the private sector, Thus, in addition to the impact on the traditional arms industry, these wars have also resulted in a flow of contracts to companies in other sectors, primarily those providing security services. However, not all companies gain. The cost of military operations abroad imposes pressure on

[63] US Department of Defense (DOD), Office of the Under Secretary of Defense (Comptroller), *National Defense Budget Estimates for FY 2007* (DOD: Washington, DC, Mar. 2006), URL <http://www.defenselink.mil/comptroller/defbudget/fy2007/>, table 6 11, p. 133.

[64] A comprehensive list of companies awarded US DOD contracts for work in Iraq has been compiled by the Center for Public Integrity for the period Jan. 2002–June 2004. See the Windfalls of War website at URL <http://www.publicintegrity.org/wow/>. A list of the companies that received most of these contracts is reproduced in Sköns, E. and Surry, E., 'Arms production', *SIPRI Yearbook 2005* (note 39), p. 392.

[65] Goure, D., 'Rolling thunder', *Armed Forces Journal*, May 2005, pp. 24–27.

[66] '$191.9M more to AM General for M1151 & M1152 Humvee Jeeps', *Defense Industry Daily*, 23 Mar. 2006, URL <http://www.defenseindustrydaily.com/2006/03/23/>.

[67] Armor Holdings, *05 Annual Report: Protecting the Future* (Armor Holdings: Jacksonville, Fla., n.d.), p. 10. See also Ratnam, G., 'War in Iraq keeps armor firm busy', *Defense News*, 22 Nov. 2004.

[68] Much, M., 'War in Iraq keeps truck manufacturer busy', *Investor's Business Daily*, 2 May 2005.

Table 9.4. The 10 largest recipients of homeland security contracts from the US Government, 2001–2006

Company (parent company)	DHS contracts 2001–2006 ($ b.)	Type of DHS contract
1. InVision Technologies (General Electric)	15.90	Explosive-detection machines for the TSA
2. IBM	15.50	Digitization of antiquated paper trails used by the CBPA to track US trade information
3. Apptis	9.70	Updating of IT systems infrastructure for the the OCIS and the CBPA
4. L-3 Communications	5.42	Airport bomb screening devices for the TSA
5. Apogen Technologies (QinetiQ)	4.29	IT systems for secret electronic information sharing
6. SAIC	4.06	Infrared scanners for detection of hazardous materials
7. EADS North America	3.60	Helicopters and maintenance services for the Coast Guard and the CBPA
8. Honeywell	2.78	Engineering, communications and surveillance support; special fibres for protection
9. Integrated Coast (Lockheed Martin/ Northrop Grumman)	2.26	Updating of aircraft fleet of the Coast Guard
10. ITS	2.20	IT systems infrastructure for the CBPA and the OCIS
Total, top 10	**61.42**	
Total, all contracts	**130**	

CBPA = Customs and Border Protection Agency; DHS = Department of Homeland Security; IT = Information technology; OCIS = Office of Citizenship and Immigration Services; TSA = Transportation Security Administration.

Note: Contracts are those awarded by the DHS since its formation in 2003 and by the 22 agencies from which it was formed for 2001–2002

Source: Monahan, R. and Beaumont, E. H., 'Big time security', *Forbes*, 3 Aug. 2006, URL <http://www.forbes.com/home/business/2006/08/02/homeland-security-contracts-cx_rm_0803 homeland.html>.

procurement in other areas and some companies may lose out because of the shift in procurement spending from long-term programmes to more immediately needed war-fighting capabilities.[69]

The arms industry has also profited more generally from US Government post-September 2001 policies through arms exports.[70] The most significant example of this is the $5.1 billion sale to Pakistan of F-16 combat aircraft,

---

[69] 'Collateral damage', *The Economist*, 24 Aug. 2006.

[70] Myerscough, R. and Stohl, R., 'Update: U.S. post-Sept. 11 arms trade policy', Center for Defense Information, Washington, DC, 3 Jan. 2007, URL <http://www.cdi.org/program/index.cfm?programid= 73>.

which was concluded in September 2006. This transaction has been justified by the US Administration as necessary in the 'global war against terrorism'.[71]

A more indirect impact on export sales comes through the increased attractiveness on the global arms market of weapon systems that have been demonstrated in wars. A war acts as a window display for weapons to potential customers, a fact openly acknowledged by industry as well as governments.[72]

Impact on the homeland security industry

US post-September 2001 policies also cover homeland (i.e. domestic) security, in particular border security and transportation security. For that purpose the US Department of Homeland Security (DHS) was created in January 2003 by bringing together 22 relevant agencies. According to a report by *Forbes*, in FY 2006 the DHS budget amounted to $40.3 billion, an increase from a combined FY 2003 budget of $28.2 billion for the 22 individual agencies.[73] Sales to the DHS have increased greatly since it was formed. According to *Forbes*, the number of companies with contracts from the DHS has increased from 3512 in 2003 to 33 890 in 2005. Since September 2001 the value of contracts awarded by the DHS—and before 2003 the 22 agencies that later joined to form the DHS—to private contractors totals at least $130 billion, of which half has gone to the 10 biggest companies in that industry.[74]

Table 9.4 shows the 10 companies which received the most revenues from US homeland security contracts in the period 2001–2006. Seven of these are, or are owned by, companies in the SIPRI Top 100 arms-producing companies. Although the dynamics of the arms and homeland security industries may be different, this overlap between large companies in the two industries and the trend for companies that started out in the arms industry to win domestic security contracts blur the line between the two industries.[75]

Defence industrial policy

The objective of DOD policies on research, development and procurement and associated policies is to guide and influence the transformation of the US arms industry by spreading market demand across a broad spectrum of industry segments to meet emerging DOD requirements. While the size and type of

---

[71] Myerscough, R., 'Update: United States and Pakistan break F-16 stalemate, finalizing $5 billion sale', Center for Defense Information, Washington, DC, 4 Oct. 2006, URL <http://www.cdi.org/program/issue/index.cfm?ProgramID=73&issueid=84>. See also chapter 10 in this volume.

[72] International Relations and Security Network, 'War is good for arms business', Center for Security Studies, Zurich, 2 Apr. 2003, URL <http://www.isn.ethz.ch/news/sw/details.cfm?ID=6229>.

[73] Monahan, R. and Beaumont, E. H., 'Big time security', *Forbes*, 3 Aug. 2006, URL <http://www.forbes.com/home/business/2006/08/02/homeland-security-contracts-cx_rm_0803homeland.html>.

[74] Monahan and Beaumont (note 73).

[75] There are many other examples of this trend. E.g. in 2006 Boeing was awarded a contract by the DHS to build a security fence on the US–Mexico border. US Department of Homeland Security, 'DHS announces SBInet contract award to Boeing', Press release, Washington, DC, 21 Sep. 2006, URL <http://www.dhs.gov/xnews/releases/pr_1158876536376.shtm>.

DOD contracts for research, development and procurement shape the technological and programmatic focus of the industry, its decisions on mergers and acquisitions in the arms industry shape the financial and competitive structure of the industry. The DOD incorporates policies on the industrial base into its acquisition regulations and strategies in order to promote competition and innovation, and in specific cases to preserve critical defence industrial capabilities and technologies. This section outlines DOD policies in three areas of concern to the DOD: its dependence on commercial markets for IT, the consolidation of the industry and the impact of foreign acquisitions of companies of importance to the US defence industrial base. This account is based primarily on the 2006 edition of the US DOD *Annual Industrial Capabilities Report to Congress*, which describes the situation in the US defence industrial base and the policy measures the DOD has taken to address concerns regarding technological and industrial capabilities.[76]

Policy on commercial markets

A main concern of the DOD is its increasing reliance on commercial markets, in particular for IT products, since the influence of the DOD over such markets is limited. The 2006 report describes how commercial IT products offer a number of benefits to the DOD: they are the most advanced available; they often offer better performance and are less expensive than technology procured solely for DOD applications, since their development costs are amortized over the broader commercial business base; and there are many competitive suppliers. Therefore, to the extent that the DOD can use commercial IT, it does so.[77]

The reason for DOD concerns is that the IT industry is a global one and so non-US suppliers may offer the best products for certain functions. In a global market, the DOD has limited ability to influence the strategic direction of the market, faces security of supply risks and has to consider the possibility that the product has been tampered with. While US military spending accounts for almost half of global military expenditure,[78] US military spending on IT accounts for only about 1 per cent of the world IT market, according to the DOD.[79] Thus, the US Government's methods for influencing the military market are unlikely to have the same effect in the commercial IT market.

In addition, the DOD argues, the potential exists for more strategic problems, such as a possible loss of intellectual capability in the USA, particularly in microelectronics, as research, development and design work threatens to follow production work to lower-cost foreign facilities. The DOD plans to assess the potential impact of these issues on sensitive military applications in more detail.[80]

---

[76] US Department of Defense (note 59).
[77] US Department of Defense (note 59), p. 3.
[78] See chapter 8 in this volume.
[79] US Department of Defense (note 59), p. 3.
[80] US Department of Defense (note 59), p. 3.

Policy on mergers and acquisitions

One of the DOD's tasks is to take action to preserve endangered US industrial capabilities. Before any intervention in the defence industrial base, the DOD must 'verify the warfighting utility of the industrial capability, that the industrial capability is unique and at risk, that there are no acceptable alternatives, and that the proposed action is the most cost- and mission-effective'.[81]

US defence industrial policy is based on the view that the competitive pressures of the marketplace are the best mechanism to shape an industrial environment that supports future military strategies. Therefore, the DOD intervenes in the marketplace only when necessary to maintain appropriate competition and develop or preserve industrial and technological capabilities essential to the DOD. It acknowledges the need for companies to merge to create industrial capabilities essential for future warfare. The DOD believes that such flexibility is essential 'if the DOD is to capitalize on the revolutionary technologies of tomorrow'.[82] Overall, the US DOD has no blanket policy on mergers and acquisition but evaluates each proposed transaction on its particular merits in the context of the specific market and the changing dynamics of that market.

The DOD has become increasingly sensitive to the innovative capabilities of small firms and is concerned that acquisitions should neither threaten that innovative value for the military nor lead to future consolidations that would be detrimental to the DOD. The DOD therefore will seek to develop instruments to protect and promote innovation and may seek regulatory support for this.[83]

The DOD's interventions on mergers and acquisitions in the defence industrial base are regulated by several frameworks. The provisions of the 1976 Hart–Scott–Rodino Antitrust Improvement Act allow the DOD to review—as part of the overall merger and acquisition reviews by anti-monopoly agencies—transactions valued at more than $50 million as regards their impacts on national security and defence industrial capabilities.[84] In 2005 the DOD reviewed 23 merger transactions of this type. Of these, only one—BAE Systems' acquisition of United Defense, the only foreign transaction reviewed—was deemed to require a consent order to protect continued competition.[85]

In 2006 the DOD reviewed five cases of mergers liable to produce a monopoly that were being considered by the Federal Trade Commission.[86] One of these was the plan by Boeing and Lockheed to form a joint venture, the United Launch Alliance (ULA), combining Boeing's Delta 4 and Lockheed Martin's Atlas 5 launch operations into a company with annual revenues of the order of

---

[81] US Department of Defense (note 59), p. 4.

[82] US Department of Defense (note 59), p. 7.

[83] US Department of Defense (note 59), p. 9.

[84] The 1976 Antitrust Improvements Act, US Public Law 94-435, was signed into law on 30 Sep. 1976.

[85] US Department of Defense (note 59), p. 10.

[86] Ratnam (note 58).

$1 billion. While this deal would create a near-monopoly in rocket launches, it was nevertheless supported by the DOD on the basis that the disadvantages were outweighed by its positive effects in ensuring the survival of two options to launch military satellites.[87] This deal shows that monopoly power has become acceptable under some circumstances. Other problematic mergers in 2006 included deals that might produce conflicts of interests or vertically integrated firms that control the assembly, production and distribution of their products. This type of issue is becoming particularly problematic in regard to the acquisition of service companies, a great number of which are now being bought by the large arms-producing companies. One such case was the acquisition by General Dynamics of Anteon, an IT and services company, which had been contracted by the DOD to supervise some of the DOD's contracts with General Dynamics. The deal was only approved after Anteon agreed to sell its programme management division.[88]

Policy on foreign acquisitions

Acquisitions of or mergers with US-based firms by foreign companies are reviewed by the inter-agency Committee on Foreign Investment in the United States (CFIUS), which includes representatives of the DOD. Reviews are made on the basis of the Exon–Florio provisions of the 1988 Omnibus Trade and Competitiveness Act, which amended Section 721 of the 1950 Defense Production Act.[89] The Exon–Florio provisions allow the suspension or blocking of a foreign acquisition of US-based firms when it poses a credible threat to national security.[90]

The objectives of the DOD in assessing foreign acquisitions are to (*a*) 'protect the reliability of supply of goods and services to the Department'; (*b*) 'minimize the risks of unauthorized transfer of classified information and military and dual-use technologies'; and (*c*) ensure that there is 'congruence of strategic interests between the acquiring firm and the DOD'. At the same time, the DOD 'strives to facilitate the development of an integrated defense industrial base among U.S. allies and trading partners in order to increase interoperability in coalition warfare and reduce DOD acquisition costs'. The intelligence community also prepares for the DOD a risk assessment of the acquiring company and country which evaluates: (*a*) their compliance with US and international export control laws and other international regimes which seek to control proliferation of weapons of mass destruction; (*b*) their potential

---

[87] Lockheed Martin, 'FTC gives clearance to United Launch Alliance', Press release, Bethesda, Md., 3 Oct. 2006, URL <http://www.lockheedmartin.com/wms/findPage.do?dsp=fec&ci=17936&rsbci=0>.

[88] Merle, R., 'General Dynamics wins clearance to buy Anteon', *Washington Post*, 8 June 2006, p. D04.

[89] The 1950 Defense Production Act, US Public Law 81-774, was signed into law on 8 Sep. 1950. Since then it has been regularly reauthorized and amended. The 1988 Omnibus Trade and Competitiveness Act, US Public Law 100-418, was signed into law on 23 Aug. 1988. The Exon–Florio provisions are contained in Section 5021 of the 1988 act, which amended Section 721 of the 1950 act.

[90] US Department of Defense (note 59), p. 11.

reliability as suppliers; and (c) their support in fighting international terrorism.[91]

During 2005, 65 CFIUS cases were filed, with a total value of $29.7 billion, of which 12 per cent involved US firms deemed to possess critical technologies and 17 per cent involved US firms that were deemed to be otherwise important to the defence industrial base. In 23 cases the DOD remedied concerns about foreign ownership, control and influence by imposing risk-mitigation measures on the acquiring firms.[92]

IV. Western Europe

In Western Europe, the armed forces and the arms industry have not benefited from the same increase in military expenditure as in the United States.[93] European governments are therefore under greater pressure to cut costs, transform their armed forces and make adjustments to their arms industries. In addition, the continuing development of the European Security and Defence Policy (ESDP) of the European Union (EU) has involved continuing modification of national defence and security policies. There has been a shift in emphasis from territorial defence to military operations outside Europe and transformation of the armed forces to enable them to join multinational operations. The rising costs of equipment as well as of transformation, combined with budget constraints, mean that the number of weapon systems bought will have to decline. Governments have to make decisions about which defence industrial capabilities to retain and which to abandon, while industry has to adapt to a declining and changing domestic market. Under these circumstances, many arms-producing companies in Western Europe are looking towards foreign arms markets, in particular in the USA, while at the same time the European Commission is pressing for greater competition in the arms industry and European companies are being acquired by foreign companies. Different strategies are developed by governments and industry to achieve synergies through the establishment of an open European defence market and integration of the industry. In this context, in 2005–2006 the UK reviewed the implementation of its defence industrial policy.

This section provides an overview of the mergers and acquisitions in the West European arms industry in 2006, reviews the debate in the UK during 2006 following the adoption by its government of a new defence industrial strategy and describes the work of the European Defence Agency (EDA) aimed at strengthening the European defence industrial base.

---

[91] US Department of Defense (note 59), p. 12.
[92] US Department of Defense (note 59), p. 12.
[93] See chapter 8 in this volume.

Mergers and acquisitions

During 2006 there was no significant case of cross-border integration of the West European arms industry (see appendix 9B). The only major acquisition was a deal between two investment companies: the European investment group Cinven acquired Avio, an Italian engine producer, from the US Carlyle Group for €2.57 billion ($3.4 billion).[94] When Carlyle and Finmeccanica bought Avio in 2003 the purchase price was €1.5 billion ($1.7 billion),[95] illustrating how investment companies use the buying and selling of arms-producing companies to make large profits. Avio is likely to be used once more in this way by its new owner.[96]

Several US investment firms, primarily private equity firms, have acquired West European arms companies in recent years. Such deals include the purchases of MTU Aero Engines (Germany) by Kohlberg Kravis Roberts & Co. (USA) in 2003 for $1.4 billion, Thales Acoustics (UK) by J. F. Lehman (USA) in 2004 and NP Aerospace (UK) by the Carlyle Group in 2005.[97] All three of these US firms already have close connections with the US DOD and are now developing close relations with government officials in Europe as a means of obtaining insight and influence in the European arms industry. The most controversial deal of this type has been Carlyle's acquisition in 2003 of a one-third share and 51 per cent voting rights in QinetiQ, then the main research laboratory of the British Ministry of Defence. After the company was listed on the London stock exchange in February 2006, Carlyle sold stocks worth $281 million, earning four times its initial investment while retaining ownership of stock worth nearly $300 million.[98]

Some European governments, including France and Germany, are trying to legislate to protect their military-related firms from hostile foreign takeovers. In August 2005 the French industry ministry announced a policy of blocking takeover bids—assessed on a case-by-case basis—in 10 key strategic sectors, including armaments and dual civil–military technology, to avoid such assets and technologies falling into foreign hands.[99] However, this policy may be examined by the European Commission. In October 2006 the Commission formally asked France to modify its Decree 2005-1739 of December 2005, establishing an 'authorization procedure for foreign investments in certain sectors of activities that could affect public policy, public security or national

---

[94] Carlyle Group, 'The Carlyle Group and Finmeccanica agree to sell Avio to Cinven for €2.57 billion', News release, Milan, 7 Aug. 2006, URL <http://www.thecarlylegroup.com/eng/news/>.

[95] Carlyle Group, 'The Carlyle Group and Finmeccanica: agreement for the acquisition of FiatAvio's aerospace business', News release, Milan, 2 July 2003, URL <http://www.thecarlylegroup.com/eng/news/>.

[96] Cinven describes itself as a company 'renowned for [its] exit capabilities'. Cinven, 'Creating value', Cinven website, URL <http://www.cinven.com/firstlevel3.asp?pageid=5>.

[97] See Surry, E. and Baumann, H., 'Table of acquisitions, 2003', *SIPRI Yearbook 2004* (note 6), pp. 429–30; Surry (note 37); and Surry (note 39).

[98] O'Hara, T., 'Carlyle shows it's still tops in defense', *Washington Post*, 13 Feb. 2006, p. D01.

[99] Lewis, J. A. C., 'France moves to protect defence firms', *Jane's Defence Weekly*, 17 Sep. 2005, p. 23.

defence'.[100] The Commission was concerned that some of the provisions of this decree could discourage investment from other EU member states, contradicting EU treaty rules on the free movement of capital and the right of establishment.

The general policy of the French Government is focused on two objectives: to reintroduce the notion of an industrial policy that guarantees the preservation of key defence competencies and to support the development of the defence industrial and technological base at the national as well as European levels.[101] This policy is based on a principle of 'competitive autonomy' of the industrial and technological base, where autonomy refers to security of supply, unrestricted use of procured equipment and the possibility of exporting arms to friendly states and allies. As part of the process of promoting competitiveness in the arms industry as well as European consolidation, the French Government's policy is to proceed with the controlled sale of its holdings in arms-producing companies. Another aim is to develop close ties with the arms industry in order to support French arms-producing companies in the world marketplace, indicating a strong focus on arms exports.[102]

Similarly, in September 2005, the German Cabinet approved a change in the foreign trade law that allows the government to veto a foreign acquisition of a domestic firm 'if it is necessary to safeguard essential security interests'.[103] This was an expansion of the veto rights introduced in 2003 and was in response to the Carlyle Group's interest in buying MTU Friedrichshafen, although the latter was eventually sold to the Swedish investment company EQT in late 2005.

During 2006, the main US acquisitions in the West European arms industry were made by one company, L-3 Communications, which announced its acquisition of four European companies (three in the UK and one in Germany). At the same time, European arms-producing companies continued to seek access to the large US market through the acquisition of US-based companies. However, as in previous years, it was primarily British companies that

---

[100] European Union, 'Free movement of capital: Commission calls on France to modify its legislation establishing an authorisation procedure for foreign investments in certain sectors of activity', Press Release IP/06/1353, Brussels, 12 Oct. 2006, URL <http://europa.eu/rapid/pressReleasesAction.do?reference=IP/06/1353>. The text of Décret no. 2005-1739 du 30 décembre 2005 réglementant les relations financières avec l'étranger et portant application de l'article L. 151-3 du code monétaire et financier [Decree no. 2005-1739 of 30 December 2005 regulating financial relations with foreign countries and concerning the application of article L. 151-3 of the monetary and financial code] is available at URL <http://www.legifrance.gouv.fr/WAspad/UnTexteDeJorf?numjo=ECOX0508949D> (in French). Previously, in June 2002 the European Court of Justice had restricted government efforts to keep control of privatized industries when it outlawed a golden share that allowed the French Government to veto foreign takeovers of the oil company Elf Aquitaine. The court judged such a veto to be a serious impairment of the fundamental principle of the free movement of capital. *Commission of the European Communities v. French Republic*, Case C-483/99, European Court of Justice, Judgment of the Court of 4 June 2002.

[101] French Ministry of Defence, 'For a competitive autonomy in Europe: the defence procurement policy', Paris, July 2004, URL <http://www.defense.gouv.fr/defense/overview/the_ministry_of_defence/an_introduction_to_french_defence/the_french_defence_policy>, p. VI.

[102] French Ministry of Defence (note 101), p. VII.

[103] Aguera, M., 'Germany tightens rules on foreign ownership', *Defense News*, 19 Sep. 2005.

succeeded in doing so. In 2006 the British companies Rolls Royce, GKN and Meggitt all made small acquisitions in the US arms industry.[104]

Within Europe, there were few cross-border acquisitions in 2006 and most large acquisitions were domestic. These included the acquisition by Thales of the satellite unit of Alcatel (France); Saab's acquisition of the defence operations of Ericsson (Sweden), whereby Ericsson effectively left the arms industry;[105] and the acquisition by VT Group of Lex Vehicle Solutions, a supplier of vehicles and services to the British MOD.

The main event with Europe-wide significance was the sale by BAE Systems of its 20 per cent stake in Airbus, with the result that EADS became the sole owner of that company. This sale reflected BAE Systems' strategy of focusing on its defence operations.[106]

The debate on the British defence industrial strategy

The ongoing debate in the UK following the publication in December 2005 of a new defence industrial strategy provides a good illustration of the challenges confronting the European arms industry. Arms-producing companies face a dilemma arising from changing threat perceptions, technological developments and budget constraints under conditions of rising costs and the simultaneous internationalization of the private arms industry.

In its 2005 Defence Industrial Strategy White Paper, the British MOD provides information about its future military requirements, clarifies its defence industrial policy and identifies those industrial capabilities that it wants to be retained in the UK for defence reasons.[107] It also recognizes that the implementation of this strategy will require changes on the part of both industry and the government and in state–industry relations.

Acknowledging that 'no country outside the US can afford to have a full cradle to grave industry in every sector', the White Paper states that industry will have to adjust to lower production levels once the current major equipment projects have been completed, while retaining the specialist skills and systems engineering capabilities required to manage military capability through the life cycle of weapon systems.[108] This means abandoning indigenous capabilities for the manufacture of basic platforms and instead concentrating on the maintenance and upgrading of platforms in use.[109] According to

[104] See appendix 9B; and Scott, R. et al., 'No pain no gain', *Jane's Defence Weekly*, 5 Apr. 2006, pp. 24–29.

[105] Ericsson, 'Ericsson agrees to sell its defense business to Saab', Press release, 12 Jun. 2006, URL <http://www.ericsson.com/ericsson/press/releases/>.

[106] 'BAE confirms possible Airbus sale', BBC News, 7 Apr. 2006, URL <http://news.bbc.co.uk/2/4886154.stm>.

[107] British Ministry of Defence (MOD), *Defence Industrial Strategy: Defence White Paper*, Cm 6697 (MOD: London, Dec. 2005), URL <http://www.mod.uk/DefenceInternet/AboutDefence/CorporatePublications/PolicyStrategyandPlanning/DefenceIndustrialStrategyDefenceWhitePapercm6697.htm>.

[108] British Ministry of Defence (note 107), pp. 2, 7.

[109] Scott et al. (note 104); and Cook, N., 'Preserving innovation', *Jane's Defence Weekly*, 4 Jan. 2006, p. 11.

the White Paper, the criteria to be used in selecting which defence industrial capabilities should be retained are: (*a*) appropriate sovereignty, including operational independence and security of supply; (*b*) through-life cycle capability management, partly through increased military outsourcing; (*c*) maintaining key industrial capabilities; and (*d*) maintaining close customer–supplier relationships.[110]

Sectors to be downsized include warships, fixed-wing manned aircraft, helicopters, missiles and torpedoes. The sectors and capabilities to be retained in the UK include system engineering, submarines, a through-life capability to maintain and upgrade armoured fighting vehicles and fixed-wing aircraft, general munitions, and a few specific industrial C⁴ISTAR (command, control, communication and computers, intelligence, surveillance, target acquisition and reconnaissance) capabilities.[111]

One of the reasons for the need for greater clarity from the MOD on future defence planning was the fact that private arms-producing companies 'now have more choice than ever before about which markets to enter, which secure the best return for shareholders, and where to base their operations'. Thus, the White Paper notes that if the government does not make clear which capabilities need to be retained, industry will make independent decisions and necessary indigenous capabilities may disappear.[112]

The reactions to the White Paper during 2006 were mixed.[113] Industry, which had influenced the proposals in the White Paper, was mostly positive, although BAE Systems continued to argue that industry would go where the market is, and that the USA clearly is the most important market for defence research, technology and procurement.[114] From those outside industry, concerns were raised that the use of partnering arrangements could make the MOD too reliant on monopoly suppliers, in particular on BAE Systems.[115] According to a more fundamental critique, the White Paper showed that the MOD was continuing the drive for ever more sophisticated and expensive military platforms, including a massively costly replacement of the Trident system of submarines, missiles and nuclear warheads, rather than addressing a

[110] British Ministry of Defence (note 107), pp. 17–18.

[111] British Ministry of Defence (note 107), pp. 7–10, 59–127.

[112] British Ministry of Defence (note 107), p. 6. See also Murphy, J., 'Key DIS architect explains timing', *Jane's Defence Weekly*, 5 Apr. 2006, pp. 16, 26–29.

[113] Reactions of the defence industry, trade unions, academics and government officials are presented in British House of Commons, Defence Committee, *The Defence Industrial Strategy*, Seventh Report of Session 2005–06 (Stationery Office: London, May 2006), URL <http://www.parliament.uk/parliament ary_committees/defence_committee.cfm>. For a debate on the inexorable rise of defence equipment costs see Pugh, P. et al., 'Our unaffordable defence policy: what now?', *RUSI Defence Systems*, vol. 9, no. 2 (autumn 2006), pp. 12–17.

[114] Turner, M., BAE Systems Chief Executive, Oral evidence taken before the Defence Committee, 28 Feb. 2006, British House of Commons (note 113), p. Ev 47. See also Scott et al. (note 104).

[115] Chuter, A., 'U.K. MoD, industry await effects of White Paper', *Defense News*, 2 Jan. 2006; and Murphy, J., 'MoD and industry need to "sex up" relationship, says Drayson', *Jane's Defence Weekly*, 15 Feb. 2006, p. 28.

broader global security context and the role that the British manufacturing and technology base could play within it.[116]

The implications of the defence economics problem—that is, rising costs of research and development under budget constraints—and of the White Paper's criteria for selecting those defence industrial capabilities that should be retained were analysed in evidence submitted by Professor Keith Hartley of York University during the parliamentary hearings on the defence industrial strategy.[117] He noted that in the area of procurement policy, the White Paper's commitment to retaining key defence industrial capabilities might mean that competition will not always be possible, and that this was one of the reasons why the White Paper, while continuing to support a competitive procurement policy, also includes a shift towards alternative approaches, especially partnering. However, while offering companies guaranteed markets, partnering agreements will not necessarily lead to cost-efficient outcomes, since firms have little incentive to economize and minimize costs unless there are strong pressures for them to do so.[118] Hartley also observed that the option to use noncompetitive contracts and the White Paper's reference to the need to provide industry with adequate incentives to stay in the market present a challenge for the British Defence Procurement Agency (DPA). The DPA will have to formulate appropriate contracts that offer adequate profit incentives to reward risk and innovation in non-competitive markets, while at the same time delivering value for money to the British armed forces and taxpayers.[119]

In the field of industrial policy, Hartley argued that the defence industrial strategy will result in increased MOD dependence on domestic monopolies and in high costs, compared with importing, since industry will require a minimum acceptable return to induce it to remain in the British market. Hartley raised particular concerns about the implications of partnering agreements with BAE Systems, considering its dominance of the British arms industry, which raises the possibility that the company may be able to influence government policy in its favour. In view of this, Hartley suggested that 'consideration might be given to treating BAE as a regulated firm in the same way as the UK regulates its privatised utilities', since there might be lessons to be drawn on pricing, incentives and profitability rules.[120]

---

[116] Schofield, S., 'The UK defence industrial strategy and alternative approaches', British American Security Information Council (BASIC), BASIC Papers no. 50, Mar. 2006, URL <http://www.basicint.org/pubs/Papers/BP50.htm>. On the replacement of Trident see appendix 12A in this volume.

[117] Hartley, K., Memorandum to the Defence Committee, 2 Feb. 2006, British House of Commons (note 113), pp. Ev 102–105. See also Hartley, K., 'The defence industrial strategy: an economists view', University of York, Centre for Defence Economics, May 2006, URL <http://www.york.ac.uk/depts/econ/research/associated/>.

[118] Hartley, Memorandum (note 117), pp. Ev 102–103.

[119] Hartley, Memorandum (note 117), p. Ev 103.

[120] Hartley, Memorandum (note 117), p. Ev 104.

European Union developments

The process of internationalization of the European arms industry has been driven by industry, while developments at the government level have been slower. With the establishment by the EU of the European Defence Agency in July 2004,[121] political developments have gained some momentum. The tasks of the EDA are closely linked to the implementation of the ESDP and focus in particular on enhancing military capabilities in the sphere of crisis management. The EDA has four directorates with different functions which work towards that goal.[122] The Capabilities Directorate has the task of translating the ESDP's strategic military objectives and politico-military requirements into actual capabilities. The Armaments Directorate promotes European armaments collaboration, based in particular on early identification of common needs, in order to harmonize requirements before national armaments programmes have already assumed a specific shape. It currently focuses on cooperation in two fields: the A-400M transport aircraft and armoured fighting vehicles. The Research and Technology (R&T) Directorate promotes European collaboration in R&T and the development of policies and strategies to strengthen military technology in Europe, for example by establishing agreed European R&T priorities and increasing synergies between military and security research.

A major task of the Industry and Market Directorate is to promote the development of a European defence equipment market through efforts to harmonize existing rules and regulations on arms procurement. During 2006 the EDA introduced measures designed to encourage competition and transparency in European arms procurement. A new voluntary mechanism, based on the 2005 Code of Conduct for Defence Procurement, was implemented on 1 July 2006.[123] The mechanism calls on member states to open up their defence procurement to cross-border competition and covers contracts with a value greater than €1 million. A new publicly accessible electronic bulletin

---

[121] Council of the European Union, Joint Action 2004/551/CFSP of 12 July 2004 on the establishment of the European Defence Agency, Brussels, 12 July 2004, URL <http://europa.eu/scadplus/leg/en/lvb/r00002.htm>. For the states participating in the EDA see the glossary in this volume.

[122] European Defence Agency, 'Background', EDA website, 20 Dec. 2006, URL <http://www.eda.europa.eu/background.htm>.

[123] The text of the Code of Conduct on Defence Procurement of the EU Member States Participating in the European Defence Agency, approved on 21 Nov. 2005, is available at <http://www.eda.europa.eu/reference/eda/EDA - Code of Conduct - European Defence Equipment Market.htm>. See also European Defence Agency, 'EU governments agree voluntary code for cross-border competition in defence equipment market', Press release, Brussels, 21 Nov. 2005, URL <http://www.eda.europa.eu/news/2005-11-21-1.htm>. Hungary and Spain did not commit themselves to the Code of Conduct, while Denmark does not participate in the EDA. The new mechanism is underpinned by the Code of Best Practice in the Supply Chain, agreed on 15 May 2006, the text of which is available at URL <http://www.eda.europa.eu/reference/eda/eda - code of best practice in the supply chain - european defence equipment market.htm>. See also European Defence Agency, 'Birth of European defence equipment market with launch of code of conduct', Press release, Brussels, 30 June 2006, URL <http://www.eda.europa.eu/news/2006-06-30-0.htm>.

board was also established, allowing tender information to be made available online.[124]

In parallel with the activities of the EDA, in December 2006 the European Commission issued its interpretation of how Article 296 of the Treaty of Rome should be applied by member states, in order 'to prevent possible mis-interpretation and misuse'.[125] It mentions in particular the controversial issue of offsets in the arms trade, stating that Article 296 should not allow member states to derogate from EU rules on public procurement regarding the use of indirect non-military offsets, since these serve economic interests with no direct link to the imported equipment nor national security interests.[126]

While the EDA's work is based on a stated recognition that European defence budgets will not increase significantly in the near future, concerns have nevertheless been raised, especially among non-governmental organizations, that current developments in the ESDP signal a return to a renewed build-up of military forces and armaments, and the development of a European military–industrial complex or even security–industrial complex, in a manner that will not be conducive to the EU's declared security strategy.[127] These concerns have been reinforced by the role of the arms industry in the EU policy development process and its lobbying for stronger government support to make European companies competitive relative to the US arms industry. One of the questions raised is whether peace missions under the ESDP require the same type of advanced networking military technologies as war-fighting operations under the US national security doctrine.[128]

V. Conclusions

The trend of increasing arms sales in the SIPRI Top 100 arms-producing companies continued during 2005, spurred in particular by the growth in the arms

---

[124] The EDA's Electronic Bulletin Board is at URL <http://www.eda.europa.eu/ebbweb/>. See also Tigner, B., 'Inching toward a common market: electronic tender form is first step for EDA, EU', *Defense News*, 6 Feb. 2006.

[125] European Commission, 'Interpretative Communication on the application of Article 296 of the Treaty in the field of defence procurement', COM(2006) 779 final, Brussels, 7 Dec. 2006, URL <http://ec.europa.eu/internal_market/publicprocurement/dpp_en.htm>. Article 296 of the 1957 Treaty Establishing the European Community (Treaty of Rome, as amended by the 1997 Treaty of Amsterdam) permits EU member states to derogate from the rules of the single market in the case of public procurement when this is necessary for the protection of their 'essential security interests'. The text of the current version of the Treaty of Rome is available at URL <http://europa.eu.int/eur-lex/en/treaties/dat/EC_consol.html>.

[126] On offsets in the arms trade see Brauer, J. and Dunne, J. P. (eds), *Arms Trade and Economic Development: Theory, Policy and Cases in Arms Trade Offsets* (Routledge: London, 2004).

[127] Slijper, F., *The Emerging EU Military–Industrial Complex: Arms Industry Lobbying in Brussels*, TNI Briefing Series no. 2005/1 (Transnational Institute: Amsterdam, May 2005), URL <http://www.tni.org/reports/militarism/eumilitary.htm>; and Hayes, B., *Arming Big Brother: The EU's Security Research Programme*, TNI Briefing Series no. 1/2006 (Transnational Institute: Amsterdam, Apr. 2006), URL <http://www.tni.org/reports/militarism/bigbrother.htm>.

[128] Broek, M. and de Vries, W., *The Arms Industry and the EU Constitution* (European Network Against Arms Trade: London, Jan. 2006), URL <http://www.enaat.org/publications/>.

sales of US companies, which account for a major share—63 per cent—of the Top 100 companies' arms sales.

Six companies increased their arms sales by more than $1 billion in 2005: two European companies—BAE Systems and Finmeccanica—and four US companies—L-3 Communications, Raytheon, Northrop Grumman and General Dynamics. Four Russian companies were among the companies with the largest relative increases in arms sales—by 30 per cent or more—reflecting their increased export sales and in one case the consolidation of several companies into one. Also among the companies with the largest relative increases were several with increased sales in information technology and services. This growth was achieved primarily through acquisitions of smaller companies or units. Some of these acquiring companies are traditional, large arms-producers, while others are relatively new entrants in the Top 100 list. This phenomenon contributed to the continuing process of concentration in both the West European and the US arms industries, although at a slower rate than in previous years.

Two ways in which the United States' post-September 2001 policies have affected the US arms industry are through the increase in demand from the DOD generated by the massive increase in military expenditure to finance the military operations in Afghanistan and Iraq, and through their impact on arms exports. These policies have also led to a strong growth in expenditure on homeland security, thereby increasing demand in the broader security industry.

In Western Europe there has not been a strong increase in the demand for military equipment. The West European governments have therefore been under pressure to achieve cost savings, one of the main tasks of the European Defence Agency. The EDA is trying to achieve this primarily by promoting European collaboration in arms production and research as well as by developing joint policies to strengthen military technology in Europe. However, although it is assumed that the development of the ESDP will not require increased European military expenditure, there are concerns that current developments in the European Security and Defence Policy and the armaments required for that purpose will involve a renewed military build-up in the European Union.

Appendix 9A. The 100 largest arms-producing companies, 2005

EAMON SURRY and THE SIPRI ARMS INDUSTRY NETWORK*

I. Selection criteria and sources of data

Table 9A.1 lists the world's 100 largest arms-producing companies (excluding Chinese companies), ranked by their arms sales in 2005. The table contains information on the companies' arms sales in 2004 and 2005 and their total sales, profit and employment in 2005. It includes public and private companies, but excludes manufacturing or maintenance units of the armed services. Only companies with manufacturing activities in the field of military goods and services are listed, not holding or investment companies. Chinese companies are excluded because of the lack of data. Companies from other countries might also have been included at the lower end of the list had sufficient data been available.

Publicly available information on arms sales and other financial and employment data on the arms industry worldwide are limited. The sources of data for table 9A.1 include: company annual reports and websites, a SIPRI questionnaire, and news published in the business sections of newspapers, in military journals and by Internet news services specializing in military matters. Press releases, marketing reports, government publications of prime contract awards and country surveys were also consulted. Where no data are available from these sources, estimates have been made by SIPRI. The scope of the data and the geographical coverage are largely determined by the availability of information. All data are continuously revised and updated and may change between different editions of the SIPRI Yearbook.

The source for the dollar exchange rates is the International Monetary Fund (IMF), as provided in its *International Financial Statistics*.

II. Definitions

Arms sales. Arms sales are defined by SIPRI as sales of military goods and services to military customers, including both sales for domestic procurement and sales for export. Military goods and services are those which are designed specifically for military purposes and the technologies related to such goods and services. They exclude sales of general-purpose goods (e.g. oil, electricity, office computers, cleaning services, uniforms and boots). They include all revenue related to the sale of military equipment, that is, not only for the manufacture but also for the research and development, maintenance, servicing and repair of the equipment. This definition serves as a

* Participants in the network for 2005 were: Julian Cooper (Centre for Russian and East European Studies, University of Birmingham), Ken Epps (Project Ploughshares, Waterloo, Ontario), Gülay Günlük-Senesen (Istanbul University), Giovanni Gasparini (Istituto Affari Internazionali, Rome), Jean-Paul Hébert (Centre Interdisciplinaire de Recherches sur la Paix et d'Études Stratégiques, Paris) and Reuven Pedatzur (Tel Aviv University).

guideline; in practice it is difficult to apply. Nor is there any good alternative, since no generally agreed standard definition of 'arms sales' exists. The data on arms sales in table 9A.1 often reflect only what each company considers to be the defence share of its total sales. The comparability of company arms sales in table 9A.1 is therefore limited.

Total sales, profit and employment. Data on total sales, profit and employment are for entire companies, not for arms-producing divisions alone. All data are for consolidated sales, including those of national and foreign subsidiaries. The profit data represent profit after taxes. Employment data are year-end figures, except for those companies which publish only a yearly average. All data are presented on the financial year basis reported by the company in its annual report.

III. Calculations

Arms sales are sometimes estimated by SIPRI. In some cases SIPRI uses the figure for the total sales of a 'defence' division, although the division may also have some, unspecified, civil sales. When the company does not report a sales figure for a defence division or similar entity, estimates can sometimes be made based on data on contract awards, information on the company's current arms production programmes and figures provided by company officials in media or other reports.

The data for arms sales are used as an approximation of the annual value of arms production. For most companies this is realistic. The main exception is shipbuilding companies. For these companies there is a significant discrepancy between the value of annual production and annual sales because of the long lead (production) time of ships and the low production run (number). Some shipbuilding companies provide estimates of the value of their annual production. These data are then used by SIPRI for those companies.

All data are collected in local currency and at current prices. For conversion from local currencies to US dollars, SIPRI uses the IMF annual average of market exchange rates. The data in table 9A.1 are provided in current dollars. Changes between years in these data are difficult to interpret because the change in dollar values is made up of several components: the change in arms sales, the rate of inflation and, for sales conducted in local currency, fluctuations in the exchange rate. Sales on the international arms market are often conducted in dollars. Fluctuations in exchange rates then do not have an impact on the dollar values but affect instead the value in local currency. If the value of the dollar declines, then the company's revenue in local currency falls and, if its production inputs are paid for in local currency—which most often is the case—this has a negative impact on the company's profit margins. Calculations in constant dollar terms are difficult to interpret for the same reasons. Without knowing the relative shares of arms sales derived from domestic procurement and from arms exports, it is impossible to interpret the exact meaning and implications of the arms sales data. These data should therefore be used with caution. This is particularly true for countries with strongly fluctuating exchange rates.

Table 9A.1. The 100 largest arms-producing companies in the world (excluding China), 2005

Figures for sales and profits are in US$ m., at current prices and exchange rates.

Rank[a] 2005	Rank[a] 2004	Company (parent company)	Country/region	Sector[b]	Arms sales 2005	Arms sales 2004	Total sales, 2005	Arms sales as % of total sales, 2005	Profit, 2005	Employment, 2005
1	1	Boeing	USA	Ac El Mi Sp	28 050	27 500	54 845	51	2 572	153 000
2	3	Northrop Grumman	USA	Ac El Mi Sh Sp	27 590	26 210	30 721	90	1 400	123 600
3	2	Lockheed Martin	USA	Ac El Mi Sp	26 460	26 400	37 213	71	1 825	135 000
4	4	BAE Systems[c]	UK	A Ac El MV Mi SA/A Sh	23 230	19 840	28 020	83	1 060	100 000
5	5	Raytheon	USA	El Mi	19 800	17 150	21 894	90	871	80 000
6	6	General Dynamics	USA	A El MV Sh	16 570	15 150	21 244	78	1 461	72 200
7	9	Finmeccanica	Italy	A Ac El MV Mi SA/A	9 800	7 130	14 265	69	493	56 600
8	7	EADS[d]	Europe	Ac El Mi Sp	9 580	9 470	42 545	23	2 085	113 210
9	11	L-3 Communications[e]	USA	El	8 970	5 970	9 445	95	509	59 500
10	8	Thales	France	El Mi SA/A	8 940	8 950	12 765	70	415	53 370
11	10	United Technologies Corp., UTC	USA	El Eng	6 840	6 740	42 725	16	3 069	222 200
12	12	SAIC	USA	Comp (Oth)	5 060	4 670	7 792	65	927	42 500
S	S	MBDA (BAE Systems, UK/ EADS, Europe/ Finmeccanica, Italy)	Europe	Mi	4 080	3 850	4 080	100	..	10 600
13	15	DCN	France	Sh	3 520	3 240	3 524	100	340	12 200
14	14	Rolls Royce	UK	Eng	3 470	3 310	12 005	29	631	36 200
15	13	Computer Sciences Corp.	USA	Comp (Oth)	3 400	4 330	14 616	23	634	79 000
S	S	Pratt & Whitney (UTC)	USA	Eng	3 280	2 990	9 295	35	..	38 500
16	21	ITT Industries	USA	El	3 190	2 410	7 430	43	360	41 000
17	17	General Electric	USA	Eng	3 000	3 000	149 702	2	16 353	316 000
18	18	Honeywell International	USA	El	2 940	2 810	27 653	11	1 655	116 000
S	S	AgustaWestland (Finmeccanica)[f]	Italy	Ac	2 850	..	3 097	92	182	8 530

19	16	Halliburton	USA	Comp (Oth)	2 720	3 100	20 994	*13*	2 358	106 000
S	S	KBR (Halliburton)[g]	USA	Comp (Oth)	2 720	3 100	10 894	*25*	. .	. .
20	19	SAFRAN[h]	France	Comp (Ac El Eng)	2 630	2 510	13 155	*20*	623	58 000
S	23	United Defense (BAE Systems, UK)	USA	MV	. .	. .	. .	*. .*	. .	. .
21	29	Dassault Aviation Groupe	France	Ac	2 210	1 670	4 264	*52*	379	12 080
22	20	Mitsubishi Heavy Industries[i]	Japan	Ac MV Mi Sh	2 190	2 500	25 333	*9*	271	62 210
S	S	Eurocopter Group (EADS)	Europe	Ac	2 120	1 620	3 994	*53*	. .	12 790
23	25	Saab	Sweden	Ac El Mi	2 110	1 930	2 585	*82*	160	12 830
24	26	Alliant Techsystems	USA	SA/A	2 060	1 740	3 217	*64*	154	15 200
S	24	Snecma (SAFRAN)[h]	France	Eng	. .	. .	. .	*. .*	. .	. .
25	30	Harris	USA	El	1 870	1 550	3 001	*62*	202	12 600
26	31	Rockwell Collins	USA	El	1 810	1 540	3 445	*53*	396	17 000
27	37	Textron	USA	Ac El Eng MV	1 800	1 300	10 043	*18*	203	37 000
28	27	Rheinmetall	Germany	A El MV SA/A	1 740	1 720	4 296	*41*	147	18 550
29	28	CEA	France	Oth	1 710	1 720	3 993	*43*	−167	15 010
30	39	DRS Technologies	USA	El	1 680	1 280	1 736	*97*	82	9 800
31	41	Almaz-Antei[j]	Russia	Mi	1 590	1 190	1 770	*90*	64	87 500
32	48	EDS	USA	Comp (Oth)	1 570	990	19 757	*8*	150	117 000
33	34	QinetiQ	UK	Comp (Oth)	1 550	1 390	1 912	*81*	165	11 450
S	S	Sikorsky (UTC)	USA	Ac	1 550	1 690	2 802	*55*	. .	9 640
34	35	Israel Aircraft Industries	Israel	Ac El Mi	1 520	1 370	2 340	*65*	25	15 000
35	33	Goodrich	USA	Comp (Ac)	1 510	1 420	5 397	*28*	264	22 000
36	40	Smiths	UK	El	1 450	1 240	5 485	*26*	402	30 000
37	43	URS Corp.	USA	El	1 410	1 150	3 918	*36*	82	29 200
S	S	Selex Sensors & Airborne Systems (Finmeccanica)	Italy	Comp (El)	1 380	560	1 841	*75*	85	7 170
38	44	Anteon	USA	Comp (Oth)	1 310	1 130	1 493	*88*	79	9 500
39	51	ThyssenKrupp[k]	Germany	Sh	1 240	930	52 318	*2*	1 267	187 220
40	70	Armor Holdings	USA	Comp (MV Oth)	1 190	610	1 637	*73*	133	4 940
41	57	CACI International	USA	Comp (Oth)	1 190	770	1 623	*73*	85	10 400

Rank[a]		Company (parent company)	Country/region	Sector[b]	Arms sales		Total sales, 2005	Arms sales as % of total sales, 2005	Profit, 2005	Employment, 2005
2005	2004				2005	2004				
42	36	Kawasaki Heavy Industries[i]	Japan	Ac Eng Mi Sh	1 180	1 320	11 999	10	149	28 920
43	47	VT Group	UK	Sh	1 170	1 040	1 540	76	76	9 920
44	42	Ordnance Factories	India	A SA/A	1 150	1 150	1 371	84	..	118 640
S	S	Alenia Aeronautica (Finmeccanica)	Italy	Ac	1 120	1 030	1 418	79	..	7 340
45	52	Hindustan Aeronautics	India	Ac Mi	1 100	900	1 219	90	151	29 100
S	46	Sagem (SAFRAN)[h]	France	El	..	..	..	..	..	..
46	50	Elbit Systems	Israel	El	1 070	940	1 070	100	32	6 340
47	59	Oshkosh Truck	USA	MV	1 060	770	2 959	36	160	7 960
48	56	Samsung[l]	S. Korea	A El MV Mi Sh	1 050	800	141 033	1	9 452	222 000
49	64	AM General[m]	USA	MV	1 050	690	..	..	..	..
50	49	Mitsubishi Electric[i]	Japan	El Mi	1 040	950	32 701	3	868	99 440
51	53	Cobham	UK	Comp (Ac El)	1 010	900	1 982	51	216	10 720
52	54	NEC[i]	Japan	El	980	840	43 776	2	110	154 180
53	45	Navantia[n]	Spain	Sh	970	1 090	1 211	80	−124	5 560
54	55	Engineered Support Systems	USA	El	970	840	1 018	95	87	3 670
S	S	EADS Space (EADS, Europe)	France	Sp	960	..	3 356	29	..	10 980
55	S	ST Engineering[o]	Singapore	Ac El MV SA/A Sh	940	860	2 034	46	241	13 100
56	58	ManTech International	USA	Comp (Oth)	930	770	980	95	44	6 000
57	62	GIAT Industries	France	A MV SA/A	910	730	909	100	15	..
58	S	Dyncorp[p]	USA	Comp (Oth)	870	940	1 967	44	7	14 400
S	S	Samsung Techwin (Samsung)	S. Korea	A El Eng MV	850	620	2 335	36	82	4 400
59	60	Rafael	Israel	Ac Mi SA/A Oth	800	760	846	95	..	5 000
S	S	Devonport Management (KBR)[q]	UK	Sh	800	700	849	94	40	5 100
60	61	Krauss-Maffei Wegmann[r]	Germany	MV	750	750	746	100	..	2 700
61	22	GKN[s]	UK	Ac	740	2 400	6 633	11	107	36 500
62	65	Diehl	Germany	Mi SA/A	720	650	2 052	35	..	10 300

		Company	Country	Sector						
63	67	Bharat Electronics	India	El	700	620	807	87	132	12 260
S	–	Selex Communications (Finmeccanica)	Italy	Comp (El Oth)	680	..	846	80	32	4 480
64	69	Indra	Spain	El	670	610	1 495	45	129	7 580
65	–	Admiralteiskie Verfi[j]	Russia	Sh	650	340	689	95	..	..
66	74	Stewart & Stevenson	USA	MV	630	550	726	87	26	1 250
67	79	EDO	USA	El	620	480	648	95	26	3 000
68	66	MTU Aero Engines	Germany	Eng	610	620	2 672	23	41	6 750
69	73	Fincantieri	Italy	Sh	610	560	2 822	21	64	9 380
70	63	Babcock International Group	UK	Sh	610	700	1 521	40	54	8 760
71	71	Irkut[j]	Russia	Ac	600	570	712	84	84	15 420
72	76	Korea Aerospace Industries	S. Korea	Ac	590	510	661	89	1	2 730
73	68	RUAG	Switzerland	A Ac Eng SA/A	580	620	959	61	–15	5 640
74	77	Aerospace Corp.[t]	USA	Comp (Oth)	580	510	664	87	..	3 500
75	78	Curtiss-Wright	USA	Comp (Ac)	570	480	1 131	50	75	5 890
76	–	Sevmash[j]	Russia	Sh	540	..	677	79	73	26 300
77	85	Cubic	USA	Comp (El Oth)	540	450	804	68	12	6 000
78	72	Avio	Italy	Eng	530	560	1 593	33	–136	4 800
S	S	United States Marine Repair (BAE Systems, UK)	USA	Comp (Sh)	..	530	..	..	..	..
79	32	Sukhoi[j]	Russia	Ac	520	1 470	562	93	–	27 000
80	86	Tenix	Australia	El SA/A Sh	500	440	777	64	..	4 000
81	87	DaimlerChrysler, DC[u]	Germany	Eng	500	440	186 289	–	3 540	382 720
82	82	Mitre[v]	USA	Oth	500	460	962	51	..	5 750
S	S	ADI (Transfield Group/ Thales, France)	Australia	El SA/A Sh	500	440	558	90	..	2 500
S	S	MTU Friedrichshafen (DC)	Germany	Eng	500	440	1 904	26	..	5 780
83	84	Ultra Electronics	UK	El	490	450	623	78	53	2 880
84	96	Jacobs Engineering Group[w]	USA	Comp (Oth)	480	390	5 635	8	151	27 200
85	90	Moog	USA	Comp (El Mi)	480	430	1 051	46	65	6 660
86	100	United Industrial	USA	Ac	480	360	517	93	41	2 000

Rank 2005	Rank 2004	Company (parent company)	Country/region	Sector[b]	Arms sales 2005	Arms sales 2004	Total sales, 2005	Arms sales as % of total sales, 2005	Profit, 2005	Employment, 2005
S	–	Selex Sistemi Integrati (Finmeccanica)	Italy	Comp (El)	470	..	728	65	72	3 100
87	88	MAN	Germany	MV Sh	460	440	18 248	3	587	60 780
88	95	Meggitt	UK	Oth	460	390	1 121	41	120	5 680
89	97	Toshiba[i]	Japan	El Mi	450	380	57 554	1	709	172 000
90	80	CAE	Canada	El	440	460	914	48	54	5 000
91	–	Severnaya Verf[j,x]	Russia	Sh	440	20	453	98	9	3 500
S	S	General Dynamics Land Systems Canada (General Dynamics, USA)	Canada	MV	420	..	..	..	..	..
S	94	SMA (SAFRAN)	France	Comp (Ac)	..	..	..	..	..	..
S	–	MBDA Italia (MBDA, Europe)	Italy	Mi	410	..	409	100	–39	1 480
92	89	Aerokosmicheskoe Oborudovanie[j]	Russia	El	400	440	585	69	48	38 900
S	–	BAE Systems Australia (BAE Systems, UK)	Australia	Comp (El)	400	..	..	..	..	2 600
S	S	Samsung Thales (Thales, France/Samsung)	S. Korea	El	400	360	400	100	27	1 000
93	99	Embraer	Brazil	Ac	390	360	3 752	10	291	16 950
94	–	Teledyne Technologies	USA	El	390	340	1 207	32	64	7 270
S	S	Oto Melara (Finmeccanica)	Italy	A MV Mi	390	390	392	100	7	1 350
95	98	Orbital Sciences Corp.	USA	Sp	380	370	703	54	28	2 600
S	S	Areva (CEA)	France	Eng Oth	380	390	12 593	3	1 305	..
96	93	Kongsberg Gruppen	Norway	El Mi SA/A	370	400	885	42	41	3 370
97	–	Universal Shipbuilding Corp.[i,y]	Japan	Sh	360	100	..	..	..	..
98	–	TRV Corp.[j,z]	Russia	Mi	350	220	374	95	7	22 260
99	–	MMPP Salyut[j]	Russia	Comp (Ac)	350	310	403	87	5	13 520
100	92	Israel Military Industries	Israel	A MV SA/A	340	400	379	90	..	2 720

[a] Companies are ranked according to the value of their arms sales in 2005. Companies with the designation S in the rank columns are subsidiaries. A dash (–) in place of a rank for 2004 indicates either that the company did not make arms sales in 2004 or that it did not rank among the 100 largest companies in 2004. Company names and structures are listed as they were on 31 Dec. 2005. Information about subsequent changes is provided in these notes. The 2004 ranks may differ from those published in *SIPRI Yearbook 2006* owing to the continual revision of data, most often because of changes reported by the company itself and sometimes because of improved estimations. Major revisions are explained in these footnotes.

[b] Key to abbreviations: A = artillery, Ac = aircraft, El = electronics, Eng = engines, Mi = missiles, MV = military vehicles, SA/A = small arms/ammunition, Sh = ships, Sp = space and Oth = other. Comp (. . .) = components, services or anything less than final systems in the sectors within the parentheses; it is used only for companies that do not produce final systems.

[c] Figures for BAE Systems arms sales are obtained by subtracting sales by its Commercial Aerospace division from total sales. The sales by its Commercial Aerospace business group were primarily accounted for by its 20% stake in Airbus. In addition, BAE Systems' arms sales include an estimate of $1146 million for the arms sales of United Defense in the first 6 months of the year. United Defense was acquired by BAE Systems in June 2005. As part of this acquisition BAE Systems also acquired United States Marine Repair.

[d] EADS (the European Aeronautic Defence and Space Company) is 22.32% owned by DaimlerChrysler (Germany), 29.75% by SOGEADE (whose share capital is held by Lagardère and the French State) and 5.44% by SEPI, a Spanish state holding company. EADS is registered in the Netherlands.

[e] Data for L-3 Communications arms sales in 2005 include an estimate of $750 million for the arms sales of the Titan Corporation in the first 7 months of that year. L-3 Communications completed its acquisition of the Titan Corporation on 29 July 2005.

[f] In Nov. 2004 Finmeccanica (Italy) completed the acquisition of GKN's (UK) 50% share in the helicopter company AgustaWestland, which had previously been a joint venture.

[g] Figures for KBR arms sales are estimates based on one-third of its 'Government and Infrastructure' division sales. During 2004 and 2005 the company performed services and support work for the US Army under a Logistics Civil Augmentation Program (LOGCAP) contract awarded in 2001. During 2006 the US Army announced that KBR's contract would not be renewed. Also during 2006 KBR's parent company Halliburton initiated a public offering of KBR shares.

[h] In May 2005 Snecma merged with Sagem to form SAFRAN. To enable a comparison of the finances of SAFRAN in 2004 and 2005, the company reported pro forma data in which the merger was presumed to have taken place on 1 Jan. 2004. During 2005 SAFRAN also obtained 100% of the shares of SMA, which had previously been held by Snecma, EADS and Renault.

[i] For Japanese companies figures in the arms sales column represent new military contracts rather than arms sales.

[j] This is the fourth year that Russian companies have been covered by the SIPRI Top 100. There may be other Russian companies that should be in the list, but insufficient data are available. The situation in the Russian arms industry is still very fluid, and company names are likely to change as they are restructured. Irkut and Sukhoi provide detailed financial information on their websites. For Irkut, all data are from its own consolidated financial statements. For Sukhoi, consolidated revenue data was provided on special request to the Centre for Analysis of Strategies and Technologies (CAST). Data for Admiralteiskie Verfi and MMPP Salyut total sales and arms sales are from CAST. For all other Russian companies in the list, figures for total sales and profits in 2005 are from Expert RA, the Russian rating agency, while figures for arms sales share estimates and employment are from CAST.

[k] Figures for ThyssenKrupp arms sales are estimates. The company acquired German submarine maker Howaldtswerke-Deutsche Werft (HDW) in Jan. 2005.

[l] Data for Samsung arms sales are uncertain. The figure is the sum of estimated arms sales for Samsung Techwin and 50% of the 2004 sales of Samsung Thales (2005 data were not available).

[m] Limited financial data are publicly available for AM General. The SIPRI estimate of arms sales is based on a 3-year average of US Department of Defense prime contract awards plus an estimate of its exports.

[n] The military shipbuilding activities of Izar were transferred to a new company, 'New Izar', on 31 Dec. 2004. The company was subsequently launched with the name Navantia on 2 Mar. 2005. The Spanish state holding company SEPI is the sole shareholder. Data for 2005 are based on available data for 2004.

[o] ST Engineering was previously a subsidiary of Singapore Technologies Pte Ltd, which was dissolved on 31 Dec. 2004. As of 1 Jan. 2005, all companies that were under the control of Singapore Technologies Pte Ltd, including ST Engineering, came under the direct control of Temasek Holdings, an investment holding company of the Singaporean Government.

[p] Computer Sciences Corporation completed its sale of Dyncorp International to Veritas Capital in Feb. 2005.

[q] Devonport Management Limited is owned by Halliburton KBR (51%), Balfour Beatty (24.5%) and the Weir Group (24.5%).

[r] Figures for Krauss-Maffei Wegmann were provided on special request from the company.

[s] GKN's arms sales declined markedly in 2005 due to the 2004 sale of its 50% stake in AgustaWestland.

[t] The Aerospace Corporation operates a Federally Funded Research and Development Center for the US Air Force.

[u] Figures for DaimlerChrysler arms sales are for the arms-producing activities of MTU Friedrichshafen and exclude DaimlerChrysler's 22.32% share in EADS. With the sales of MTU Aero Engines in late 2003 and MTU Friedrichshafen in late 2005, DaimlerChrysler has now divested itself of all its major arms-producing activities other than its share in EADS.

[v] Mitre operates 3 Federally Funded Research and Development Centers for the US Department of Defense.

[w] Figures for Jacobs Engineering Group arms sales represent US Department of Defense prime contracts awarded.

[x] Severnaya Verf's 2004 arms sales are based on the 2005 arms sales share estimate.

[y] Universal Shipbuilding Corporation was established in Oct. 2002 when NKK Corporation and Hitachi Zosen Corporation integrated their shipbuilding operations. NKK and Kawasaki Steel Corporation subsequently merged to form JFE Holdings. During 2005, therefore, Universal Shipbuilding Corporation was jointly owned by JFE Holdings (50%) and Hitachi Zosen Corporation (50%). In Nov. 2006 JFE was in talks to take full control of the joint venture.

[z] TRV (Takticheskoe Raketnoe Vooruzhenie, tactical missile armament) Corporation is translated in the English language version of the CAST list as the Tactical Missiles Corporation.

Appendix 9B. Major arms industry acquisitions, 2006

EAMON SURRY

Table 9B.1 lists major acquisitions in the North American and West European arms industry that were announced or completed between 1 January and 31 December 2006. It is not an exhaustive list of all acquisition activity but gives a general overview of strategically significant and financially noteworthy transactions.

Table 9B.1. Major acquisitions in the North American and West European arms industry, 2006

Figures are in US$ m., rounded to the nearest million, at current prices.

Buyer company (country)	Acquired company (country)	Seller company (country)[a]	Deal value[b] ($ m.)
Within North America (between US-based companies unless indicated otherwise)			
Armor Holdings	Stewart & Stevenson Services	..	755
Armor Holdings	Integrated Textile Systems	..	..
Boeing	Aviall	..	1 700
CACI International	AlphaInsight	Privately held	..
CACI International	Information Systems Support	..	..
Curtiss-Wright	Swantech	..	4
EDO	CAS	..	176
EDO	Impact Science & Technology	..	124
General Dynamics	CMC Scranton division	Duchossois Industries	..
General Dynamics	SNC Technologies	SNC-Lavalin Group	275
L-3 Communications	CyTerra	..	..
L-3 Communications	Nova Engineering	..	45
L-3 Communications	SafeView	..	..
L-3 Communications	SSG Precision Optronics	..	..
Lockheed Martin	Aspen Systems	Employee owned	..
Lockheed Martin	ISX	Privately held	..
Lockheed Martin	Management Systems Designers	Employee owned	..
Lockheed Martin	Pacific Architects and Engineers	..	..
Lockheed Martin	Savi Technology	Infolink Systems	..
Northrop Grumman	Essex	..	580
Raytheon	Houston Associates	Privately held	..
Raytheon	Virtual Technology	..	..
Rockwell Collins	Anzus	Privately held	..
Rockwell Collins	IP Unwired (Canada)	..	..
SAIC	Applied Ordnance Technology	..	..

Buyer company (country)	Acquired company (country)	Seller company (country)[a]	Deal value[b] ($ m.)
SAIC	Applied Marine Technology	..	..
SAIC	bd Systems	..	..
SAIC	Cornerstone Industry	..	..
Teledyne Technologies[c]	Assets of KM Microwave	..	..
Teledyne Technologies[c]	CollaborX	..	18
Teledyne Technologies[c]	Ocean Design	..	30
United Industrial Corp.	McTurbine	..	31
United Industrial Corp.	Symtx	..	34
Within Western Europe			
Cinven (W. Europe)[d]	Avio (Italy)	Carlyle Group (USA)	3 400
Kongsberg (Norway)	Navtek (Norway)	..	..
Norwegian Government and Patria (Finland)[e]	Nammo (Norway)	Saab (Sweden)	..
Saab (Sweden)	Ericsson Microwave Systems (Sweden)	Ericsson (Sweden)	550
Thales (France)	Alcatel's satellite unit (France)	Alcatel (France)	825
VT Group (UK)	Hotel and Catering Training Company (UK)	ECI Partners (UK)	18
VT Group (UK)	Lex Vehicle Solutions (UK)	RAC (UK)	156
QinetiQ (UK)	Graphics Research (UK)	..	2
Transatlantic: West European acquisitions of companies based in North America			
BAE Systems (UK)	National Sensor Systems (USA)	..	9
GKN (UK)	Stellex Aerostructures (USA)	Carlyle Group (USA)	..
Meggitt (UK)[f]	Firearms Training Systems (USA)	..	..
Rolls Royce (UK)[g]	Data Systems & Solutions (USA)	SAIC (USA)	59
ThyssenKrupp Services (Germany)	Alcoa's Aerospace Service Business (USA)	..	..
Transatlantic: North American acquisitions of West European-based companies			
Esterline Technologies (USA)	Wallop Defence Systems (UK)	Cobham (UK)	59
Lockheed Martin (USA)[h]	HMT Vehicles (UK)	Privately held	..
L-3 Communications (USA)	Advanced System Architectures (UK)	..	..
L-3 Communications (USA)	Magnet-Motor (Germany)	..	..
L-3 Communications (USA)	Nautronix Defence Group (UK)	Nautronix Holdings (UK)	65
L-3 Communications (USA)	TRL Electronics (UK)	..	169

[a] In the 'Seller company' column, '. .' indicates that the ownership of the acquired company was not specified in available sources. The company may have been either privately held or publicly listed.

[b] In cases where the deal value was not available in US dollars, currency conversion was made using the International Monetary Fund average exchange rate for the calendar month in which the transaction was made. Companies do not always disclose the value of transactions.

[c] Teledyne Technologies completed the acquisition of assets of KM Microwave, CollaborX and Ocean Design through its subsidiaries Teledyne Wireless, Teledyne Brown Engineering and Teledyne Instruments, respectively.

[d] Cinven is an investment firm with offices in London, Frankfurt, Milan and Paris. Prior to this acquisition, Avio was jointly owned by the Carlyle Group (70%) and Finmeccanica (30%). As part of the transaction, Finmeccanica agreed to reinvest in Avio, maintaining a 15% stake with an option to increase this to 30%.

[e] Saab transferred its 27.5% share in Nammo to the Norwegian Government and Patria. This increased the share owned by the Norwegian Government from 45% to 50% and the share owned by Patria from 27.5% to 50%.

[f] Meggitt completed the acquisition of Firearms Training Systems through its US subsidiary Meggitt USA.

[g] Data Systems and Solutions, headquartered in the USA, was established in 1999 as a joint venture between SAIC and Rolls Royce. Rolls Royce acquired SAIC's 50% share of their former joint venture in Mar. 2006.

[h] HMT Vehicles was acquired by Lockheed Martin UK Holdings, a subsidiary of Lockheed Martin.

Source: The SIPRI Arms Industry Files on mergers and acquisitions.

10. International arms transfers

SIEMON T. WEZEMAN, MARK BROMLEY,
DAMIEN FRUCHART, PAUL HOLTOM and
PIETER D. WEZEMAN

I. Introduction

The recent global trend in transfers of major conventional weapons shows clear signs of change.[1] Since 2003–2004 there has been a consistent upward trend of the level of arms transfers. This is markedly different from the trend between 1986 and 2003, when there was a near consistent downward trend. However, the current level of arms transfers is still just half of that in the mid-1980s at the height of the cold war.

The SIPRI Arms Transfers Project collects data on international transfers of major conventional weapons. These data form the basis of the analysis presented in section II of this chapter. Section II also presents an estimate of the financial value of the global arms trade and focuses particularly on transfers to the Middle East, including acquisitions of long-range strike weapons. Section III examines how countries cope with the fact that modern weapons have become too costly for individual countries to develop, leading to dependency on imported weapons and technology. Section IV discusses arms transfers to non-state actors such as rebel forces, an issue highlighted in 2006 by the supply of arms to Hezbollah and to the different factions in Somalia. Section V gives an overview of developments in transparency in arms transfers. Section VI presents the conclusions.

Appendix 10B outlines the methodology of the data collection and the SIPRI trend indicator value (TIV) calculation. As part of an ongoing review process, several limited changes have been made to the methodology: for example, a greater number of components and some smaller weapons have been added to the SIPRI Arms Transfers Database. In previous editions of the SIPRI Yearbook, data on specific deals were included as an appendix to this chapter. These data are now available on the SIPRI website in two formats: a

---

[1] SIPRI data on arms transfers refer to actual deliveries of major conventional weapons. To allow comparison between the data on deliveries of different weapons and identification of general trends, SIPRI uses a *trend-indicator value* (TIV). These data are only an indicator of the volume of international arms transfers and not of the actual financial values of such transfers. The method used to calculate the TIV is described in appendix 10C and a more detailed description is available on the SIPRI Arms Transfers Project website at URL <http://www.sipri.org/contents/armstrad/atmethods.html>. The figures in this chapter may differ from those in previous editions of the SIPRI Yearbook because the Arms Transfers database is constantly updated.

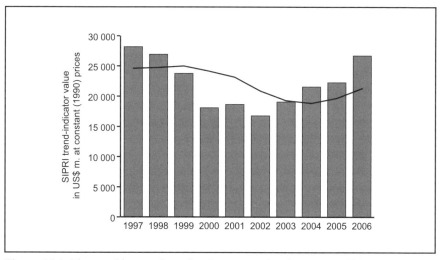

Figure 10.1. The trend in transfers of major conventional weapons, 1997–2006

Note: The bar graph shows annual totals and the line graph shows the five-year moving average. Five-year averages are plotted at the last year of each five-year period.

register of the data used for the analysis presented in this chapter, and a more flexible, searchable database with the most recent data.[2]

Appendix 10C discusses a proposal for a global, legally binding arms trade treaty that was introduced in the United Nations General Assembly only months after the UN small arms and light weapons (SALW) control process suffered a major setback in mid-2006.

II. International arms transfers 2002–2006

SIPRI measures trends in transfers of major conventional weapons in two ways. First, it identifies the volume of transfers using a unique methodology resulting in a unique SIPRI TIV. The TIV is the main analytical tool used in this chapter to describe trends. Second, for several years SIPRI has used the information that is available on the financial value of the arms trade to provide an additional statistical overview. Although these two data sets measure arms transfers in contrasting ways, both reveal a similar picture of an upward trend (see figure 10.1).

The trend in arms transfers

As figure 10.1 shows, the upward trend in arms transfers since 2003 continued in 2006. In 2002 transfers reached their lowest level since 1960. In 2006 they were almost 50 per cent higher than in 2002. Five-year averages also show a

---

[2] The data in the register are valid as of 19 Feb. 2007. SIPRI's online database is continually updated. See the SIPRI Arms Transfers Project website, URL <http://www.sipri.org/contents/armstrad/>.

consistent upward trend of the level of arms transfers since 2004.[3] After the United States and Russia (by far the largest exporters), Germany, France and the United Kingdom were the largest exporters of major conventional weapons. Since 1950 these countries have been the five main global arms exporters. In terms of imports more fluctuation is evident, but even here the list of the largest recipients remained more or less stable, with China being by far the largest importer, followed by India, Greece and the United Arab Emirates (UAE) (see tables 10A.1 and 10A.2 in appendix 10A). This fairly static major exporter ranking and more fluid major importer ranking has been the normal picture for as long as SIPRI has analysed international arms transfers. However, what is far more meaningful than ranking is the often changing relations between suppliers and recipients, as well as the impact of arms deliveries on regional stability, economies and countries' internal politics.

The financial value of the international arms trade

As noted above, the SIPRI TIV was not developed to assess economic aspects of the arms trade. In order to make such assessments data are needed on the financial value of weapon sales. By combining national data on the value of arms exports, generally released by supplier governments in reports or public statements, it is possible to give a rough estimate of the financial value of the arms trade (see table 10A.3 in appendix 10A for the aggregated data from each report). The value in 2005, the most recent year for which data are available, is estimated at $39–56 billion.[4] This is a slight change from 2004 when the estimate was $42–55 billion. In 2004 this accounted for 0.5–0.6 per cent of total world trade and for 2005 for 0.4–0.5 per cent.[5] The financial data are incomplete and do not provide an answer to most research questions; thus, the TIV is the main analytical tool used in this chapter to describe trends.[6]

Significant arms transfers

The USA was the largest exporter of major conventional weapons in the period 2002–2006. It accounted for 30 per cent of total transfers of major conven-

---

[3] Because yearly delivery schedules may vary, a single year period is often too short for reliable conclusions. To reduce short-term fluctuations, SIPRI calculates a 5-year-average trend indicator value.

[4] SIPRI estimates that the countries that produce national export data account for over 90% of total arms exports. Because some governments present several sets of data, the estimate is presented as a range between the aggregate of the lowest and the aggregate of the highest reported values. It should be noted that official arms export data are not entirely reliable or comparable between years. See the SIPRI Arms Transfers Project website, URL <http://www.sipri.org/contents/armstrad/at_gov_ind_data.html>.

[5] Total world trade in 2004 and 2005 amounted to $9085 and $10 354 billion, respectively. International Monetary Fund, International Financial Statistics online, URL <http://ifs.apdi.net/imf/>.

[6] For more on the usefulness of different types of data see Wezeman, S., *The Future of the United Nations Register of Conventional Arms*, SIPRI Policy Paper no. 4 (SIPRI: Stockholm, Aug. 2003); Bauer, S. and Bromley, M., *The European Union Code of Conduct on Arms Exports*, SIPRI Policy Paper no. 8 (SIPRI: Stockholm, Nov. 2004)—all SIPRI Policy Papers are available at URL <http://www.sipri.org/>; and Hagelin, B. et al., 'Transparency in the arms life cycle', *SIPRI Yearbook 2006: Armaments, Disarmament and International Security* (Oxford University Press: Oxford, 2006), pp. 245–67.

tional weapons and delivered to 68 countries. Almost 39 per cent of these deliveries went to the Middle East (including Turkey), 26 per cent to the Asia–Pacific region and 26 per cent to Europe (almost all to other members of the North Atlantic Treaty Organization, NATO).

The heightened tension in North-East Asia owing to the North Korean nuclear test on 9 October 2006 is likely to lead to increased arms acquisitions by South Korea and Japan, much—but certainly not all—of which will come from the USA.[7] Soon after the test Japan stated that it would accelerate the deployment of an anti-ballistic missile (ABM) system estimated to cost up to $9.3 billion that consists mainly of PAC-3 and SM-3 missiles from the USA. The first PAC-3 missiles were delivered in 2006.[8] In mid-2006 Japan agreed to export components and technology for ABM systems to the USA as part of a joint programme to further develop the PAC-3 and SM-3.[9]

The US decision to sign agreements with other countries for the final development and pre-production (production, sustainment and follow-on development, PSFD) phase of the Joint Strike Fighter (JSF, also called the F-35) combat aircraft was probably of greater significance in 2006 than actual deliveries of weapons. The JSF programme has major implications for Euro-Atlantic relations and the global market for combat aircraft. In recent years the programme has been heavily criticized by its European partners,[10] and in early-2006 some of these partners still had serious doubts over whether they should remain committed to the JSF or find (European) alternatives. The main problems remained the restrictions that the US Administration of George W. Bush imposed on access to JSF technology, the low level of involvement of non-US industries and the increasing cost. The technology transfer restrictions would make it hard or impossible for non-US users to modify the aircraft (and especially its software) to use non-US weapons and other non-US equipment. However, by mid-2006 the USA had become more flexible and seemed to have agreed to full transfer of technology.[11] On the issue of industry involvement, several countries remained sceptical but in general, non-US companies seemed satisfied they would get a fair chance to compete for work.[12]

---

[7] On North Korea's nuclear test see appendix 12B in this volume.

[8] Grevatt, J., 'Japan considers missile options in face of North Korean threat', *Jane's Defence Industry*, vol. 23, no. 11 (Nov. 2006), p. 11.

[9] In principle agreement had already been reached in 2004. See Japanese Ministry of Foreign Affairs, 'Exchange of notes concerning the transfer of arms and military technologies to the United States of America', Press release, 23 June 2006, URL <http://www.mofa.go.jp/announce/announce/2006/6/0623-2.html>.

[10] European countries involved in the JSF are Denmark, Italy, the Netherlands, Norway, Turkey and the UK. See Sköns, E., Bauer, S. and Surry, E., 'Arms production', *SIPRI Yearbook 2004: Armaments, Disarmament and International Security* (Oxford University Press: Oxford, 2004), p. 414, note 107.

[11] 'UK signs up to herald next phase of the JSF', *Preview*, Jan. 2007, pp. 1–2; 'US–UK JSF dispute resolved', *Air Forces Monthly*, no. 220 (July 2006), p. 6; and 'Australia wins technology transfer assurances on JSF', *Asian Defence Journal*, Sep. 2006, p. 52.

[12] Except for BAE Systems (UK), non-US company participation in the JSF programme is not based on fixed shares but on 'best value for money', with companies in partner countries bidding for selected parts of the JSF work. Lake, J., 'Joint Strike Fighter and the UK', *Air Forces Monthly*, no. 227 (Feb. 2007), pp. 28–29.

At the end of 2006 there were still unresolved financial problems. The eventual cost of the programme largely depends on how many JSF aircraft are actually bought, in particular by the USA. However, not uncommonly for large arms programmes, the original cost estimates have already more than doubled.[13] Since the development costs as well as the total production run are still not clear, costs are likely to increase even more.

Despite this uncertainty, by the end of 2006 most partner countries had signed up for the PSFD phase, starting from 2007, in which a few JSF will be ordered for final evaluation. The decision to actually order operational aircraft will not be made before 2008 or 2009, and full production is expected to start in 2013.[14] While it is generally accepted that the JSF is technologically a low-risk project,[15] most JSF partners remain uneasy about the issues of access to technology and cost, and in some cases have a 'plan B' in case the JSF does not work out politically or financially.[16] However, countries signing up for the PSFD phase will have probably invested too much to withdraw from the final acquisition.

Comprising some 4500 aircraft and worth an estimated $500 billion, the JSF project is often reported to be the largest-ever arms deal and is expected to take a major part of the global combat aircraft market for the coming 25 years.[17] This swallows a significant part of the procurement budget of the countries buying the JSF, partly committing them to a specific type of force structure for many years to come.[18] It also gives smaller producers of combat

[13] The current cost estimate for the JSF aircraft programme is based on plans for 4500 aircraft. In 2002 the estimate was based on 6000, and this number could be reduced still further. In 2002 the unit cost of 3000 JSF aircraft for the UK and the USA was expected to be $37–48 million, with the price of the simplest, most numerous version of the JSF, the F-35A, estimated at $37 million. Current US procurement plans include 2443 JSF aircraft at just over $110 million each. An Oct. 2006 Dutch audit report estimated that the F-35A aircraft would cost $81 million each against a 1999 estimate of $43 million. Merret, N., 'F-35 moves into production mode', *Asia–Pacific Defence Reporter*, vol. 32, no. 8 (Oct. 2006), p. 22; 'Netherlands concerned over spiralling JSF costs', *Air Forces Monthly*, no. 225 (Dec. 2006), p. 11; Dutch General Accounting Office, 'Monitoring verwerving Joint Strike Fighter' [Dutch], 11 Oct. 2006, URL <http://www.rekenkamer.nl/>; Fabey, M., 'High initial JSF costs to drop after 2014', *Defense News*, 12 June 2006. The JSF project illustrates that the costs (and economic or technical 'spin-offs') of large weapon acquisition programmes are hard to determine, partly because the process of calculating the costs is often not transparent. See Hagelin et al. (note 6), pp. 245–67.

[14] Australia, Canada, the Netherlands, Turkey and the UK had signed by the end of 2006. Denmark, Italy and Norway signed in early 2007. 'F-35 Joint Strike Fighter: events and contracts 2007', *Defense Industry Daily*, 18 Apr. 2007, URL <http://www.defenseindustrydaily.com/2007/04/f35-joint-strike-fighter-events-contracts-2007-updated/>; Merret, N., 'Australia's commitment to JSF programme deepens', *Asia–Pacific Defence Reporter*, vol. 32, no. 10 (Dec. 2006/Jan. 2007), p. 12; and Lake (note 12), p. 30.

[15] Merret (note 13). However, from early 2006 to early 2007 the US Government Accountability Office (GAO) produced 3 reports concluding that technological risks did still exist because final development of the JSF would overlap with the start of production, thus increasing the price. It advised that production should be delayed until the design was mature. GAO, *Joint Strike Fighter: Progress Made and Challenges Remain*, GAO-07-360 (GAO: Washington DC, Mar. 2007) URL <http://www.gao.gov/docsearch/>; and Lake, J., 'Facing a "bomber gap"', *Air Forces Monthly*, no. 217 (Apr. 2006), p. 32.

[16] Lake (note 12), p. 28.

[17] Fabey, M., 'High initial JSF costs to drop after 2014', *Defense News*, 12 June 2006,.

[18] Niccoli, R., 'One fighter or two?', *Air Forces Monthly*, no. 227 (Feb. 2007), pp. 33–36. Combat aircraft are one of the largest procurement costs for countries. The JSF will consume some 90% of the

Table 10.1. Local consumption of conventional arms compared with exports of conventional arms in the five largest arms-exporting countries, 2002–2006.

The first figure for each country represents units ordered for local use, the second represents units exported. Figures are approximate and refer only to newly produced equipment.

	Country					
System	USA	Russia	Germany	France	UK	EU[a]
Combat aircraft	260/301	3/293	45/0	55/57	55/16	260/58
ASW/combat helicopter	5/148	1/45	0/0	17/23	7/0	45/23
Large surface ship	19/0	2/5	3/10	3/3	3/0	20/11
Submarine	3/0	1/8	4/8	1/2	0/0	8/9
Tank	0/330	50/630	0/124	110/49	10/0	275/56
Armoured vehicle	750/747	20/827	0/8	0/5	0/84	1750/350
SAM system	20/6	5/72	3/0	0/52	0/10	6/62

ASW = anti-submarine warfare; SAM = surface-to-air missile.

[a] The EU is included as a distinct entity to show its position if it were a single exporter. 'Local use' figures for the EU include intra-EU transfers; export figures from the EU are exports from all EU members to non-EU members.

Sources: SIPRI Arms Transfers Database and archives.

aircraft (e.g. France and India) little room for exports, leaving them without an economy of scale.

In the period 2002–2006 *Russia* was the second largest exporter of major conventional weapons, with 28 per cent of total transfers and exporting to 46 countries. Despite repeated plans for more acquisitions by the Russian armed forces, the Russian arms industry has remained largely dependent on exports: many more units of major conventional weapons are exported than are bought for the Russian armed forces. While export dependency can be seen as normal for all major arms producers, Russia's export dependency is unusually high and without exports there would be little left of its arms industry (see table 10.1). Russian has plans for massive acquisitions from its own industry (e.g. over 1000 new aircraft between 2007 and 2015[19]), but it remains to be seen how many of these plans will be realized.

In 2002–2006 China and India remained the main customers for Russian weapons, accounting for 45 and 25 per cent, respectively, of total Russian deliveries, and they are expected to remain among Russia's biggest arms markets in the near future. Both countries have in recent years emphasized their regional power status and are interested in acquiring equipment for power projection, such as aircraft carriers; long-range strike, tanker and transport aircraft; and ship-launched land-attack missiles. The Chinese and

total US budget for combat aircraft from around 2012. Fabey (note 17); Government Accountability Office (note 15).

[19] Silent, J., 'Russian procurement 2007–2015', *Air Forces Monthly*, no. 221 (Aug. 2006), p. 27.

Indian arms industries are still unable to produce most of these systems, but Russia has been keen to fill the gap.

In 2005 China ordered 38 Il-76 long-range transport aircraft and Il-78 tanker–transport aircraft from Russia. Originally it was planned that these would be produced in Uzbekistan (with many major components produced in Russia), but in late 2006 Russia decided to set up a new production line within its borders and supply the majority of the aircraft itself. This was done not only because Russia felt that the Uzbek factory was unreliable and because Russian industry would benefit more from the sale and the almost certain new orders from China and other buyers, but also in order to possess a complete Russian production line for large military transport aircraft.[20]

China also showed strong interest in acquiring weapons and technology linked to aircraft carriers. At the end of 2006 China was close to signing an order for two Russian Su-33 aircraft with an option to buy up to 48 more.[21] Russia is also reportedly helping China to complete construction of an aircraft carrier acquired in 2000 from Ukraine (from which the Su-33 can be operated), and with the production of three Chinese-designed aircraft carriers.[22] In 2006 Russia finished the latest Chinese orders of complete major combat ships: eight Project-636 (Kilo Class[23]) submarines and two Sovremenny Class destroyers. However, in December 2006 the President of China, Hu Jintao, again strongly underlined China's need for a strong and modern navy.[24] While China has during the last decade developed its own major combat ships, these are often equipped with air-defence systems and other key equipment supplied by Russia.[25] There have also been new reports about plans for additional orders of ships from Russia.[26]

[20] Abdullaev, N., 'Russia transfers work on China's Ilyushins', *Defense News*, 15 Jan. 2007, p. 10. After the break-up of the Soviet Union the two Soviet production lines for large military transport aircraft were located outside Russia in Ukraine and Uzbekistan. Efforts to develop and produce the An-70 in cooperation with Ukraine have been delayed, leaving the Soviet-era Il-76 as the only large military transport aircraft available for Russian use.

[21] 'Chinese Navy to buy up to 50 Su-33', *Air Forces Monthly*, no. 225 (Dec. 2006), p. 5. Buying Su-33 aircraft for land-based operations would not make sense because the only difference from the Su-30 combat aircraft already used by China is their specific equipment for carrier operations.

[22] Construction of the aircraft carrier *Varyag* was started by the Soviet Union. The ship was inherited by Ukraine, which in 2000 sold it unfinished to a Hong Kong-based company for use as a floating casino in Macau. However, in late 2005 it was reported that the vessel was at a naval shipyard in Dalian, China. In 2005 Chinese delegations toured Russian and Ukrainian producers of aircraft carriers, carrier equipment and carrier aircraft. 'Chinese Navy to buy up to 50 Su-33', *Air Forces Monthly*, no 225 (Dec. 2006), p. 5; Butowski, P., 'Porte-avions chinois' [Chinese aircraft carrier], *Air & Cosmos*, no. 1996 (9 Sep. 2005), p. 9; and Farrer, M., 'PLA(N) training carrier on way?', *Asia–Pacific Defence Reporter*, vol. 31, no. 6 (July/Aug. 2005), pp. 44–46.

[23] Soviet and Russian weapons often have a Western (NATO and/or US) as well as a Russian designation. In this chapter the Russian designation is primarily used. Western designations are given in parentheses.

[24] 'Chinese president calls for strengthened, modernized navy', *People's Daily*, 27 Dec. 2006, URL <http://english.people.com.cn/200612/27/eng20061227_336273.html>.

[25] Saunders, S. (ed.), *Jane's Fighting Ships 2006–2007* (Jane's Information Group: Coulsdon, 2006), pp. 126–29.

[26] Fong, K., 'Asian submarine force development update', *Asian Defence Journal*, 9 Sep. 2006, p. 26.

India bought additional Su-30MKI combat aircraft and a large number of T-90S tanks from Russia. However, European and US companies are very active in the Indian market and issues like diversification of suppliers, access to advanced technology, offsets and especially Indian co-production of weapons may lead to a stronger interest from India in non-Russian weapons.

The extensive dependency on the somewhat uncertain Chinese and Indian markets makes Russia anxious to diversify and it is actively seeking other markets, often in countries to which Western companies are unwilling to deliver.[27] For example, an order from Venezuela was signed despite strong US opposition. The deal is politically significant since it clearly shows how difficult it is even for a superpower like the USA to restrict arms transfers to recipients that it does not favour, even in a region considered by many as a US 'backyard'. Aside from blocking any direct sale of US military technology to Venezuela, since 2005 the USA has also blocked sales of non-US military equipment containing US components and has made clear that even sales of weapons without a US component to Venezuela may have repercussions for the companies involved. European and other countries are willing to sell equipment, but most of their weapons have US components and many non-US companies have more to lose on the US market than to gain in Venezuela.[28] An order signed by Venezuela with Spain in 2005 for transport and maritime patrol aircraft was cancelled in 2006 because the aircraft contained US technology. Similarly, planned orders for combat aircraft from Brazil and modernization of Venezuela's F-16 combat aircraft by Israel were abandoned.[29] This has left Venezuela with few sources of military equipment, but Russia has stepped into the gap by selling $3.4 billion worth of arms to the country, including 24 Su-30 combat aircraft for around $1 billion as well as transport and combat helicopters. Venezuela is also interested in Russian air-defence systems, submarines and other weapons worth a further $3 billion.[30] However, while portrayed by the US Government and sections of the US

---

[27] There have been recent signs that China is more interested in technology from Russia and elsewhere than in Russian weapons. Its main non-Russian source would be European, most likely France, which has long favoured ending the EU arms embargo on China, holding adoption of the new legally binding version of the EU Code of Conduct on Arms Exports hostage to lifting the embargo. In 2006 Greece and Italy joined France in advocating an end to the ban. 'Greece to continue working for lifting EU arms embargo against China', *People's Daily*, 20 Jan. 2006, <http://english.people.com.cn/200601/20/eng20060120_236856.html>; 'Italy prone to lift arms sales ban against China', *People's Daily*, 19 Sep. 2006, URL <http://english.people.com.cn/200609/18/eng20060918_303851.html>; Rettman, A., 'France blocking plan for EU Code on arms exports', *EUObserver*, 18 Jan. 2007, URL <http://euobserver.com/9/23296>; and Yu-li, L. and Wu, S., Overseas Office Republic of China (Taiwan), 'EU not to tackle issues regarding lifting of China arms ban', Press release, Taipei, 24 Mar. 2006, URL <http://www.roc-taiwan.org/fp.asp?xItem=10686&ctNode=463&mp=1>.

[28] The Swedish company Saab, which has much to lose on the US market, cancelled all its contracts with Venezuela, even for systems without US components such as RBS-70 surface-to-air missile systems. See 'Saab stops Venezuela arms sales', BBC News, 3 Aug. 2006, URL <http://news.bbc.co.uk/2/5243880.stm>.

[29] Higuera, J., 'Spain seals Venezuela deal in face of opposition', *Jane's Defence Weekly*, 7 Dec. 2005, p. 4; and 'Love on the rocks: CASA's $600m Venezuelan plane sale in heavy turbulence', *Defense Industry Daily*, 14 Feb. 2006, URL <http://www.defenseindustrydaily.com/2006/02/love-on-the-rocks-casas-600m-venezuelan-plane-sale-in-heavy-turbulence/index.php>.

[30] Gentile, C., 'Venezuela bolsters military against US', *Washington Times*, 19 Feb. 2007.

media as destabilizing, and while relatively large for Latin America, these deals are not of exceptional size, especially when it is understood that Venezuela probably has to replace most of its inventory with new weapons that do not contain any US components.

In 2006 the largest single deal signed for Russian weapons since the break-up of the Soviet Union was agreed with Algeria.[31] With a value of up to $10.5 billion, it includes mainly weapons for inter-state use, such as combat aircraft, tanks and air-defence systems. At the same time, Russia is selling weapons to Morocco (the country most likely to feel threatened by the Russia–Algeria deal) and offering to sell more.[32]

Russia has started to offer potential customers credits to pay for weaponry bought from Russia. While this is a common arms export-promoting measure for Western countries and was also common for the Soviet Union, it had not been used by Russia until 2006.[33] This new policy may partly be the result of Russia finally having the financial room to offer credits instead of insisting on payment before or on delivery.[34]

In January 2007 President Vladimir Putin, who at first opposed the idea, issued a decree making Rosoberonexport Russia's only arms export agency from March 2007, stripping four companies—accounting for some 10 per cent of Russia's total exports—of their right to independently export complete systems.[35] Officially, this was done to prevent Russian companies from competing with each other on foreign markets. However, it will also increase the income of Rosoberonexport, and thus of the Russian state, since companies that use it pay between 5 and 15 per cent of the contract price for its services.[36] The decree also stipulates that Rosoberonexport's profits are to be used for research and development (R&D), thus ensuring greater state control over R&D as well as over exports generally. In general, Russia's use of—often insecure—credits, its willingness to ignore US pressure and the better coordination of its marketing efforts underline that the global arms market is a buyers' market, with strong competition among suppliers to win orders. It also

---

[31] However, as 'reward' Russia had to cancel some $4.5 billion in debt that Algeria still owed from the Soviet period. 'Russian–Algerian deal', *Military Technology*, vol. 30, no. 1 (2006), p. 248; and Vatanka, A. and Weitz, R., 'Russian roulette', *Jane's Intelligence Review*, Jan. 2007, p. 39.

[32] Vatanka and Weitz (note 31).

[33] Credits of up $1 billion were also offered to Indonesia. See Guerin, B., 'Indonesia–Russia: arms, atoms and oil', *Asia Times*, 1 Dec. 2006, URL <http://www.atimes.com/atimes/Southeast_Asia/HL12 Ae02.html>. For more on export credits see Evans, P. C., 'The financing factor in arms sales: the role of official export credits and guarantees', *SIPRI Yearbook 2003: Armaments, Disarmament and International Security* (Oxford University Press: Oxford, 2003), pp. 539–60.

[34] In Soviet times credits were used to promote exports. However, several large credits (now inherited by Russia) are still outstanding. Russia recently wrote off a large part of the debts Algeria and Syria had as a result of Soviet credit arrangements linked to arms deals.

[35] The Presidential Decree on several issues concerning military-technical cooperation between the Russian Federation and foreign states, Decree no. 54, was signed on 18 Jan. 2007. The text of the decree is available at URL <http://document.kremlin.ru/doc.asp?ID=037563> (in Russian). See also chapter 9 in this volume.

[36] Internal Russian power politics probably also influenced the decree. 'Sergey Chemezov scores a monopoly', *Kommersant*, 15 Dec. 2006, URL <http://www.kommersant.com/p730496/r_529/Rosoboro-noexport_Arms_Exporter/>.

shows the eagerness or even desperation with which Russia is trying to diversify its major customers.

The member states of *the European Union* (EU) combined accounted for 31 per cent of global arms transfers in the period 2002–2006.[37] While some of the EU exporters are very dependent on markets outside the EU, a significant proportion of the transfers take place between EU countries. Exports by EU members to non-EU recipients accounted for some 68 per cent of the combined total exports of EU members, making the EU the third largest exporter of major conventional weapons.[38] Six EU members—Germany, France, the UK, the Netherlands, Italy and Sweden (in order of quantity of exports)—were among the top 10 suppliers of major conventional weapons in 2002–2006. Among the most important developments in 2006 were the memoranda of understanding (MOU) signed by the UK and France with Saudi Arabia for major deals (see below), demonstrating the renewed importance of the Middle East as a market. These events also illustrate the competitiveness of European products in sensitive markets, or rather of European export policies, which are less restrictive and less prone to change than US policies.

Supplying the Middle East

The international tension related to suspicion that Iran intends to develop nuclear weapons,[39] the armed conflict between Israel and Hezbollah (with Iranian and Syrian involvement), and the war in Iraq were the major security concerns in the Middle East in 2006. Arms transfers played an important role in all these issues.[40]

The Middle East (including Egypt and Turkey) has long been one of the most important destinations for arms exports, having accounted for almost a quarter of all imports between 1950 and 2006. Since 1967 it has repeatedly had the dubious distinction of being the region with the world's largest arms imports. In the early and mid-1990s the Middle East's level of arms imports decreased, but in recent years most countries in the region have again pursued large arms acquisitions, almost all from abroad. Although most of the countries in the region have tried to develop an indigenous arms production capability, only Israel has significant development and production capabilities and none has achieved anything close to self-sufficiency. Iranian claims of major progress in its production of a range of advanced weapons have been given ample media attention worldwide. However, most systems that are labelled as made in Iran are actually Chinese, Russian, or North Korean

---

[37] This figure includes the combined deliveries of all 25 EU members (by 31 Dec. 2006; not including Romania and Bulgaria, which joined on 1 Jan. 2007) for the 5-year period 2002–2006.

[38] The intra-EU market may hold some surprises in the near future. Pressure is increasing to open up the EU arms market for intra-EU competion and some preliminary agreements have been reached. See chapter 9 in this volume.

[39] On Iran and its nuclear programme see chapter 12 in this volume.

[40] On arms transfers to Iraq since 2003 see Hagelin, B., Bromley, M. and Wezeman, S., 'International arms transfers', *SIPRI Yearbook 2006* (note 6), pp. 465–68.

designs and rely heavily on imported components. The few entirely local products use simple technology or are only produced in small numbers, probably for propaganda use.[41]

Much attention has recently been given to arms imports by Iran. Russia has supplied substantial amounts of arms, the bulk of which consist of armoured vehicles of older designs such as T-72 tanks and BMP-2 infantry fighting vehicles (IFVs).[42] Only Belarus, China, North Korea and Ukraine have in the past 10 years delivered more than a handful of weapons to Iran, but these are relatively simple (e.g. some small combat ships from China). In 2006 the USA objected to Russia's agreement to sell 29 Tor-M1 (SA-15) air-defence systems to Iran, one of the small number of truly advanced weapons it has managed to obtain in many years. Discussions are also ongoing between Russia and Iran on the sale of S-300 (SA-10) air-defence systems.[43] These systems would form one of the few effective military obstacles to air attacks on sites where the USA suspects Iran is developing a nuclear weapon capacity. While the sale of Tor-M1 systems took place prior to the December 2006 UN embargo, when trading arms with Iran was legal, for most suppliers Iran is not a legitimate recipient of weapons.[44]

The USA has put strong pressure on foreign companies not to sell military equipment to Iran. In 2006, for example, it placed an embargo on dealings between US entities and Rosoboronexport because of an alleged connection with suspected Iranian nuclear weapon activities.[45]

However, Iranian imports were dwarfed by acquisitions by the Gulf Cooperation Council (GCC) members and Israel (see table 10.2),[46] and this disparity is unlikely to change in the near future. Saudi Arabia, the UAE and Israel have major ongoing or new arms acquisition programmes while Iran and Syria have almost none. Unlike Iran, the GCC countries are seen as legitimate and attractive clients by a great diversity of suppliers and the GCC countries have been able to obtain more and better weapons. For example, the 80 F-16E combat

[41] Johnson, R., 'Iran strives for self-suffiency in conventional weapons', *Jane's Intelligence Review*, Dec. 2006, p. 44–46

[42] For more data on Iranian arms imports see the SIPRI Arms Transfers Project website (note 2). The T-72 in particular has been outclassed by more modern tanks—such as the US M-1 tank used by Saudi Arabia and Kuwait and the French Leclerc used by the United Arab Emirates—since the 1991 Gulf War.

[43] Grimmett, R. F., *Conventional Arms Transfers to Developing Nations, 1998–2005*, US Library of Congress, Congressional Research Service (CRS) Report for Congress RL33696 (CRS: Washington, DC, Aug. 2006), updated annually, available at URL <http://opencrs.cdt.org/>; US Department of State, Daily press briefing, Washington, DC, 16 Jan. 2007, URL <http:// www.state.gov/r/pa/prs/dpb/2007/78707. htm>; and 'USA may impose against Russia for selling 29 Tor-M1 complexes to Iran', *Pravda*, 25 Jan. 2007, URL <http://english.pravda.ru/world/americas/25-01-2007/86770-TorM1-0>.

[44] Even before the UN embargo EU countries did not generally sell weapons to Iran, but no law prevented it, as Austria's sale of anti-materiel rifles in 2004 showed. APA–OTS, 'Steyr Mannlicher wehrt sich gegen US-verdächtigungen' [Steyr Mannlicher defends itself against US accusations], 13 Feb. 2007, URL <http://www.ots.at/presseaussendung.php?schluessel=OTS_20070213_OTS0156&ch=wirtschaft>. Discussions on a general EU arms embargo on Iran had by mid-Jan. 2007 led to no more than a reaffirmation of the EU's opposition to selling arms to Iran. Dombey, D. and Fidelius, S., 'Germany proposes wider Iran sanctions', *Financial Times*, 18 Jan. 2007.

[45] Baev, P. K., 'Moscow outraged by US sanctions against two Russian companies', *Eurasia Daily Monitor*, 7 Aug. 2006, URL <http://www.jamestown.org/edm/>.

[46] The GCC members are Bahrain, Kuwait, Oman, Qatar, Saudi Arabia and the UAE.

Table 10.2. Transfers of major conventional weapons by supplier to Iraq, Iran, Israel, Syria and the countries of the Gulf Cooperation Council, 1997–2006

Data are SIPRI trend-indicator values expressed in US$m. at constant (1990) prices.

Recipient	Supplier					Total
	USA	Russia	China	EU	Others	
Iraq	63	68	0	131	135	**397**
Iran	0	3 437	840	10	237	**4 524**
Israel	5 503	0	0	1 121	0	**6 624**
Syria	0	512	0	0	92	**604**
GCC countries[a]	9 972	404	89	10 576	496	**21 537**
Saudi Arabia	5 253	0	0	3 274	108	**8 635**
United Arab Emirates	3 220	310	0	5 519	314	**9 363**
Other GCC	1 499	94	89	1 783	74	**3 539**

Note: The SIPRI data on arms transfers relate to actual deliveries of major conventional weapons. To permit comparison between the data on such deliveries of different weapons and identification of general trends, SIPRI uses a *trend-indicator value*. The SIPRI values are only an indicator of the volume of international arms transfers and not the actual money values of such transfers, Thus they are not comparable to economic statistics such as gross domestic product or export/import figures.

[a] The member states of the Gulf Cooperation Council (GCC) are Bahrain, Kuwait, Oman, Qatar, Saudi Arabia and the United Arab Emirates.

Source: SIPRI Arms Transfers Database.

aircraft that the UAE has received from the USA and the 72 Eurofighter Typhoon combat aircraft that Saudi Arabia is about to order from the UK are not only several times superior in number to Iranian aircraft, but are among the most advanced combat aircraft available.

Within the GCC the UAE and Saudi Arabia are by far the largest arms importers. The UAE in particular has acquired large numbers of naval, air and land weapons over the past 10 years. Saudi Arabia's arms imports were high in the 1990s but have been more limited in the past five years due to financial problems. However, since 2005 Saudi Arabia has been gaining financial strength, partly because of increased oil revenues, and orders for arms worth at least $50 billion are being negotiated.[47] In late 2005 Saudi Arabia signed a £10 billion ($19 billion) MOU with the UK, which included 72 Eurofighter Typhoon combat aircraft and long-range air-to-surface missiles (ASM).[48]

[47] On Saudi military expenditure see chapter 8 in this volume.

[48] The deal was controversial because of the willingness of the British Government to stop an ongoing investigation for bribery connected to earlier arms deals with Saudi Arabia. The government claimed the investigation was cancelled for reasons of national security since it would 'damage the intelligence relation' with Saudi Arabia. However, the British intelligence services denied such damage would be likely. The Organisation for Economic Cooperation in Development (OECD) criticized the UK for breaking the OECD anti-corruption rules that it had agreed to. Peel, M., 'People could die: how the inquiry into BAE's Saudi deals was brought to earth', *Financial Times*, 26 Feb. 2006, p. 13. The deal also has military implications for the UK since the Saudi aircraft would partly come from Typhoon

Another deal, potentially worth up to $10 billion, was agreed with France for a border protection system including combat and transport helicopters and other weapons. Requests to purchase arms worth over $8.7 billion were made to the USA, including 373 tanks and 724 armoured vehicles.[49] As with earlier major Saudi agreements, it remains to be seen how many of the MOUs and requests will be turned into actual orders. However, even if only a proportion similar to earlier MOUs lead to deliveries, Saudi Arabia will in a few years become the largest arms importer in the region.

Saudi Arabia carefully balances its purchases between suppliers and seeks to buy what it cannot get from one supplier from another source. For example, since 1992 the USA has repeatedly refused to supply the country with long-range ASMs for its 72 US-supplied F-15S long-range combat aircraft, but the UK has been a willing supplier of such weapons (to be used on UK-supplied Tornado combat aircraft). Since the early 1990s the UAE has diversified its sources of supply even more than its neighbour, for example buying combat aircraft from both France and the USA and Pantzyr-S1 surface-to-air missiles (SAMs) from Russia.

Supplying long-range strike systems to the Middle East

Of the several armed conflicts in the Middle East in modern times most have been ground wars and proved to be expensive, relatively futile affairs resulting in stalemates. Recent battlefield experience seems to have demonstrated the capacity of air power to deliver quicker, comparatively cheap and more decisive results. The delivery of long-range strike systems is giving several Middle Eastern states a capability to attack 'strategic' targets (e.g. oil instal-lations, waterworks or nuclear installations) over a long distance; a new and potentially much more dangerous phenomenon than earlier supplies of large numbers of tanks and other equipment for ground war.

While much attention is focused on the Iranian missile acquisitions, many other Middle Eastern countries have acquired long-range strike systems (see table 10.3). Next to its aspiration to be a regional power, Iran's suspected nuclear weapon ambitions may be rooted in a perception of its own vulner-ability caused in part by its poorly equipped conventional armed forces. Since 1979 Iran has not been able to procure enough new and advanced equipment to replace or modernize its largely outdated military equipment, which leaves it at a considerable disadvantage in defensive and offensive capabilities vis-à-vis its potential adversaries: the USA, Israel and the Gulf states. Although Iran has not been able to obtain a modern conventional capability, it appears to have been more successful in alarming its likely adversaries by obtaining an

production earmarked for the UK. This would leave the UK with a combat aircraft gap for several years. Lake, J., 'Facing a "bomber gap"', *Air Forces Monthly*, no. 217 (Apr. 2006), p. 32; and 'Saudi shopping spree: Eurofighter flying off with $10b Saudi contract (updated)', *Defense Industry Daily*, 18 Dec. 2006, URL <http://www.defenseindustrydaily.com/>.

[49] 'Saudi shopping spree' (note 48).

Table 10.3. Long-range strike systems delivered to the Middle East, 1997–2006

Table includes systems with a range of 300 km or more, delivered or ordered after 1997. Data in italics are not certain.

Country	Designation	Type	No.	Range	Source
Iran	Scud Mod-C	SSM	..	500	North Korea (produced in Iran as Shahab-1)
	Scud Mod-D	SSM	..	700	North Korea (produced in Iran as Shahab-2)
	No-dong	SSM	..	1300+	North Korea (produced in Iran as Shahab-3)
	BM-25	*SSM*	*18*	*2000+*	*North Korea*
	SS-N-27 (Club)	*SSM*	*..*	*300*	*Russia, for use on Project-877 (Kilo) submarines; on order*
	Zelzal-3	*SSM*	*..*	*400*	*Local design and production*
Israel	F-15I	Aircraft	25	..	USA (1998–99)
	F-16I	Aircraft	102	..	USA (from 2004)
	Jericho-3	*SSM*	*..*	*3 500*	*Local design and production; on order (with nuclear warhead)*
	STAR-1	*ASM*	*..*	*400*	*Local design and production*
	Gabriel-4LR	*SSM*	*..*	*..*	*Local design and production (possibly for use on Dolphin submarines)*
Saudi Arabia	F-15S	Aircraft	72	..	USA (1995–99)
	Tornado	Aircraft	100	..	Modernization of Saudi aircraft by UK (on order)
	Typhoon	*Aircraft*	*72*	*..*	*UK (on order)*
	Black Shaheen	ASM	..	300	UK (on order)
Syria	Scud Mod-C	SSM	..	500	North Korea and Iran
	Scud Mod-D	*SSM*	*..*	*700*	*North Korea and Iran*
UAE	Black Shaheen	ASM	*600*	300	France (from 2003)
	Mirage-2000-5	Aircraft	62	..	France (from 2003)
	ATACMS-ER	SSM	202	300	USA; on order
	F-16E	Aircraft	80	..	USA (2004–2006)

ASM = air-to-surface missile; SSM = surface-to-surface missile; UAE = United Arab Emirates.

[a] Ranges for aircraft are not given since they depend on a range of factors such as fuel and weapons carried, flight altitude etc. All aircraft listed have an in-flight refuelling capability that extends ranges to several 1000 km at least.

Source: SIPRI Arms Transfers Database and archives.

unknown but limited number of ballistic missiles. The types of missile acquired are too inaccurate to be of significant use with conventional warheads, so it is widely suspected that the missiles are evidence of Iran's nuclear weapon ambitions. However, Iran may have acquired the missiles for reasons of regional and international prestige, as the only credible (if poor quality) option available for hitting long distance targets, or for their internal propaganda value. The exact range of the most capable of these missiles, called the Shahab-3 in Iran, is not known precisely, but it is estimated to be up to 2500 kilometres.[50] Iran claims it builds the Shahab-3 indigenously, but it is generally accepted that it is no more than a version of the North Korean Nodong, and that Iran's missile programme is dependent on technology and components from North Korea and possibly elsewhere.[51]

In 2006 it was reported that Iran had obtained from North Korea 18 ballistic missiles of a new type, referred to as BM-25, with an estimated range of over 2000 km.[52] Iran also has a small number of long-range strike aircraft, most notably the Su-24. An order for modernization has been placed with Russian companies and the aircraft have been used more actively in training for long-range attack and air-to-air refuelling.[53] Supplying Iran with ballistic missiles or other potential delivery systems for nuclear weapons was banned by the December 2006 UN Security Council Resolution 1737, which as well as establishing sanctions against Iran, banned both export to and import from the country of items and technology potentially related to nuclear weapons.[54] While conventional arms are not explicitly included, technologies that can be used in both conventional and nuclear military applications are covered, as are goods and technology that could contribute to the development of nuclear weapon delivery systems. Missiles are specifically mentioned as such goods.

It is disturbing that, while many suppliers acknowledged after the August 1990 Iraqi invasion of Kuwait that the Middle East was a region exceptionally prone to destabilizing build-ups of weapons,[55] some of these same suppliers have since shown little restraint in delivering new and potentially even more destabilizing long-range strike weapons. The export constraints aimed at preventing an uncontrolled arms race in the region seem to be undermined by supplier competition. The main capability the USA did not want to include in the F-16E deal with the UAE was, as with Saudi Arabia, long-range ASMs. The UAE subsequently turned to France, which supplied a package of 62 Mirage-2000-5 combat aircraft equipped with Black Shaheen missiles with a range of 300 km.

Israel has received a steady supply of advanced weapons, predominantly from—and partly financed by—the USA.[56] Israel is largely dependent on US supplies for major platforms, which are usually customized by Israel with

---

[50] *Jane's Strategic Weapon Systems*, no. 45 (Jane's Information Group: Coulsdon, July 2006), pp. 68–71. The missile has until now only been tested to a range of 1200–1300 km.

[51] See Wezeman, S., 'Suppliers of ballistic missile technology', *SIPRI Yearbook 2004: Armaments, Disarmament and International Security* (Oxford University Press: Oxford, 2004), pp. 544–56. Further deliveries of any ballistic missile components or technologies are banned by the UN Security Council.

[52] Ben-David, A., 'EROS-B1 boosts Israeli surveillance capability', *Jane's Defence Weekly*, 3 May 2006, p. 6; and Ben-David, A.,'Iran acquires ballistic missiles from DPRK', *Jane's Defence Weekly*, 4 Jan 2006, p. 5.

[53] Hughes, R., 'Iran eyes long-range air strike capability', *Jane's Defence Weekly*, 7 Feb. 2007, p. 11.

[54] UN Security Council Resolution 1737, 23 Dec. 2006. All UN resolutions in this chapter can be found at URL <http://www.un.org/documents/>. On the background to the sanctions see chapter 15 in this volume.

[55] The UN Register of Conventional Arms was set up mainly to prevent new build-ups of weapons in the Middle East.

[56] In 2006 the USA provided Israel with at least $2.3 billion in aid for arms procurement. Since 1992 the USA has given over $40 billion to Israel in such aid. Murphy, J., 'US reveals FMF packages', *Jane's Defence Weekly*, 7 Dec. 2005.

local electronics and armaments. Currently, Israel's most significant arms imports are F-16I combat aircraft from the USA. These aircraft increase the already substantial long-range strike capabilities which Israel has built up over many years and which feature in repeated speculation about possible pre-emptive attacks on Iranian nuclear facilities.[57]

Despite Syria being a major actor in the conflict in Lebanon and having serious ongoing problems with Israel,[58] its arms imports have been modest in the past 15 years compared with the major arms recipients in the region. As in the case of Iran, its main long-range strike procurement was an unknown quantity of Scud Mod-D ballistic missiles from North Korea, with a range of about 700 km. There are no indications that Syria could develop nuclear weapons in the near future, but the USA maintains that Syria has both chemical and biological weapon programmes linked to missile delivery systems.[59]

The GCC and Israel have built up extensive and well-equipped conventional forces with imported weapons, including long-range strike systems, while Iran and Syria have been less successful. As a result, the qualitative and quantitative gap between Iranian and Syrian conventional military equipment and that of other major actors in the region is growing. Israel and several of the GCC members have acquired a capability to attack targets at long range with much more precision than the surface-to-surface missiles (SSMs) or any other weapon that Iran (or Syria) possesses. This could well put pressure on countries like Iran and Syria to seek counterbalancing capabilities. These could take the form of advanced defensive measures (e.g. air defence systems) that are generally—but not widely—available to both countries; conventional but asymmetic options; or (despite existing obligations not to acquire them) weapons of mass destruction (WMD).

III. Import dependency or import substitution

The process of developing technologically complex major conventional weapons and integrating them into a military system or network has become a major challenge, demanding substantial financial resources and a highly skilled workforce. This has created a situation where few states are able to develop even a limited range of weapons on their own, let alone develop the complete range that is sought. With the possible exceptions of Russia and the USA, all countries are dependent on imports of foreign weapon technology for indigenously developed weapons. Often such dependency is extensive and deepening, and there is a serious possibility that the USA will soon become

[57] In 1982 Israel used an earlier F-16 version to attack Iraq's near-complete Osirak nuclear reactor.

[58] To put these problems in the context of Israel's long-range strike capabilities: Israeli aircraft have repeatedly violated Syrian airspace, attacked a Palestinian camp in Syria in 2003 and flew low over the summer residence of the Syrian President in June 2006, all with impunity. Federman, J., 'Home fly-by sends message to Syrian leader', Associated Press, 28 June 2006.

[59] Statement by Lieutenant General Michael D. Maples, US Army Director, Defense Intelligence Agency, before the US Senate Select Committee on Intelligence, Current and Projected National Security Threats to the United States, 11 Jan. 2007, URL <http://www.dia.mil/publicaffairs/Testimonies/statement26.html>.

the only country able to fund development of advanced weapons and technologies on its own, creating a US monopoly of key technologies.

While some countries may accept dependency, others may find it politically embarrassing, economically disadvantageous or militarily threatening. As a remedy for one-sided dependency, countries launch cooperative weapon development programmes creating not only a larger market and pool of R&D funds and technological resources, but also interdependence. Such interdependence seems to work best when there is an existing cultural and political affinity, as between European states, or military and economic interdependence, as in NATO or the European Communities. Alternatively, countries may develop niche technology that, while not included in cooperative programmes, still creates interdependence. The third option, self-sufficiency, involves substituting imports for local development and production of weapons.

Since 1945 both dependency and self-sufficiency have been practised by European countries. While most NATO countries produced their own weapons, most also accepted a high level of dependency on the USA. However, some countries—either out of national pride or extensive national responsibilities that were not fully compatible with US policies (as with France) or in the framework of neutrality (as with Sweden and Switzerland)—tried to develop self-sufficiency. Only France came close to achieving it, and even today it is able to provide many of its weapons needs on its own. Switzerland and Sweden quickly found that they were not able to develop all their weapon requirements unaided, and were often dependent on imports of complete weapons and even more so on the import of major components such as engines and electronics.

By the 1960s it had become apparent to European countries that pan-European cooperative programmes would be the solution to coping with the escalating costs of major weapons, particularly aircraft. Today many major European weapons are the result of European cooperation and it is certain that this trend will increase in the future. However, increased US–European cooperation and interdependence may be much slower in coming. The recent troubles over access to US technology in the JSF programme (see above) have reinforced the concern that some European countries have expressed about being dependent on the USA. The fact that the European Defence Agency is specifically trying to fill equipment-capability gaps with products from the European arms industry (and not by import from non-EU producers) may indicate a desire to remain independent.

Three 'regional powers' outside Europe—Japan, South Korea and Australia—have long accepted dependence on the USA. However, in recent times they have tried to decrease this one-sided dependence, or to modify it to interdependence through cooperation with the USA or the supply of niche products. For all three countries, the existence of close security ties with the superpower has provided a secure basis for dependency and for a US willingness to become partly dependent on them.

Japan has made some attempts to reduce its dependency on the USA through small acquisitions from Europe and several more extensive local weapon-development programmes. On the one hand, these programmes have generally been of limited success, and the most ambitious of them, the F-2 (or FSX) combat aircraft, was terminated in 2004 for technical and financial reasons.[60] On the other hand, Japan's electronics industry produces cutting-edge military and dual-use products. The USA has for some time been keen to access these products for military use, but Japan's constitution limits its military exports. However, this has recently begun to change and it is now willing to export military technology to the USA, starting with technology for advanced anti-ballistic missile systems.[61] Japan is still largely dependent on US weapons, but the advanced—and in some cases probably unique—Japanese technology to be used in cooperative systems is likely to make the dependency two-sided, perhaps irreversibly so.

South Korea has been more direct in its attempts to reduce dependency on the USA by acquiring European weapons and developing indigenous systems based on European, Russian, US and local technology.[62] Unlike Japan, South Korea actively markets its weapons abroad.[63] South Korea has a highly advanced arms industry and its access to the European and US markets means it does not need to export elsewhere: most recently it has been discussing sales of advanced trainer aircraft to the USA and of tanks to Turkey.[64] South Korean designs are still dependent on imported components, however.

The Chinese military build-up, reductions in the US presence in South Korea and Japan, and North Korea's nuclear test and continued development of ballistic missiles, may combine to increase Japanese and South Korean interest in developing indigenous weapons. South Korea has already reacted to the July 2006 North Korean missile tests by announcing the development of a long-range cruise missile, and in Japan the acquisition of offensive missile capabilities has been hotly debated.[65]

In most parts of the world a dependable regional cooperative environment is generally either underdeveloped or completely lacking. Thus, cooperation in development of arms is not yet an option for most non-European states. *Russia* has largely maintained the self-sufficiency of the Soviet era, but there are serious doubts as to whether this is sustainable. While it has inherited the key parts of the Soviet arms industrial base it has spent little on R&D since 1990,

---

[60] 'Japan to end F2 production early', *Air Forces Monthly*, no. 199 (Oct. 2004), p. 14; and Global Security.org, 'F-2 support fighter/FSX', 14 Nov. 2006, URL <http://www.globalsecurity.org/military/world/japan/f-2.htm>.

[61] Japanese Ministry of Foreign Affairs (note 9).

[62] South Korea has a long-term plan for the development of a high-tech arms industry and in 2006 budgeted some $30 billion for R&D over the next 5 years. The entire $150 billion is to 'establish a more advanced domestic defence industrial capability'. 'ROK increases spending', *Asia–Pacific Defence Reporter*, vol. 32, no. 6 (July/Aug. 2006), p. 12.

[63] 'South Korea responds', *Asia–Pacific Defence Reporter*, vol. 32, no. 6 (July/Aug. 2006), p. 12.

[64] 'South Korea responds' (note 63).

[65] 'Japanese missiles', *Asia–Pacific Defence Reporter*, vol. 32, no. 6 (July/Aug. 2006), p. 12. See also chapter 8 in this volume, pp. 290–91

leaving its technology trailing behind that of other major arms producers. However, Russia is unwilling to accept dependence on imports or even cooperation on weapons. Instead it remains committed to national development and production of the full spectrum of weapons and has set up facilities to replace those lost to former Soviet republics with the break-up of the Soviet Union (e.g. for large transport aircraft; see above). The Russian solution for now is to keep the inherited industrial base and development skills as intact as possible by ordering 'silver bullets' (one-off prototypes or operational systems). Since Russia has limited funds for R&D it is under pressure—but also willing—to sell as many weapons as possible abroad, using the income to pay for R&D and to keep the production line 'warm'. Such sales are sometimes described as cooperative or joint projects, but in general these terms mean only that the so-called partner country pays for complete development of weapons in Russia, by Russian companies.[66]

Other countries also feel dependency to be a problem. Most Arab states and China, Israel, India, Iran and Pakistan, have all at one point stated an aim to be self-sufficient. *Israel* has a unique relationship with the USA that includes a strategic–military element, and while it produces many weapon designs locally it generally accepts dependency on the USA.[67] Despite being one of the largest markets for military equipment and having ample funds to support an arms industry, the efforts of *Arab states* in the 1960s and 1970s to organize a pan-Arab arms industry have failed. Only Egypt has established a rudimentary arms industry. The arms industries of *Iran* and *Pakistan* have developed somewhat in parallel. Both have recently undergone expansion but are far from self-sufficient and, despite propaganda to the contrary, largely rely on foreign designs and components. *China* is working hard to develop its arms industry. Having learned from and partly absorbed the foreign technology it has acquired in the past two decades—mainly from Russia, but also from European, Israeli and US systems—China seems confident that it can soon develop and produce most weapons on its own.

India is probably the best documented case of a country trying to achieve military self-sufficiency. It provides a good illustration of the problems inherent in attaining it. Since the 1950s India has had the goal of establishing an arms industry capable of fulfilling most of its military requirements. However, while it has succeeded in building a large military–industrial base, India has failed to achieve self-sufficiency: its designs depend largely on imported components and most of its arms are imported, including almost all major weapons.

In recent years India has tried to further involve its arms industry in producing for the Indian armed forces and for export. A 2005 report by the Kelkar Committee, an independent body set up in May 2004 to provide ideas

---

[66] Normal direct arms sales are now called 'military-technical cooperation' in Russia.

[67] Part of the reason for this dependency is that the Israeli procurement budget consists in large part of US aid, which the USA stipulates should generally only be used to buy US-produced weapons. Israel maintains self-sufficiency in development and production of nuclear weapons and some related delivery systems. See appendix 12A in this volume on Israel's nuclear capability.

for improving Indian industrial performance, presented a 15-year arms acquisition plan. It was highly critical of the state-owned arms production facilities and included suggestions for an offset policy, greater private industry involvement and more arms exports. Critics of the report claimed that the suggestions were not new, and that the entrenched powers (i.e. the state-owned arms producers) at the Indian Ministry of Defence would probably block most of its proposals.[68] Despite this, the Indian Government remains committed to the goal of procuring 70 per cent of its military equipment from Indian sources by 2010.[69]

However, because many indigenous projects have faced technical difficulties and been delayed or even cancelled, India has repeatedly been forced to buy foreign equipment, including frigates, submarines, tanks, surface-to-air systems, combat aircraft, and engines for tanks and combat aircraft.[70] India has often tried to involve its own industry in such foreign acquisitions, mainly through licensed production, but it has encountered serious problems in the process. Official Indian reports are often highly critical of industrial performance. A May 2006 report on the Indian production of 140 Su-30MKI combat aircraft bought from Russia (the largest current Indian arms programme), criticized the fact that deliveries are delayed and aircraft are delivered without several 'critical' systems. It also pointed out that the projected cost of the deal had increased by some 90 per cent, from $4.9 billion when ordered in 2000 to $8.6 billion by mid-2005 when production was still barely underway. Cost increases are more the rule than the exception in arms production, and in this case it made the aircraft so much more expensive than if it were imported directly that by late-2006 India had given up the goal of producing large parts of the Su-30 aircraft locally and chose instead to import them from Russia as near-complete kits.[71] India has also abandoned some of the flagships of its arms industry after many years of trial and a good deal of error. The Arjun tank programme has been replaced by licensed production of up to 1000 Russian T-90 tanks, but somewhat optimistically India still plans to produce 75–95 per cent of the components itself (except for the first 640 tanks, which will be delivered complete or as kits for assembly in India). The domestically produced rifle has been scrapped; the Trishul SAM system has been at least

---

[68] Bedi, R., 'Report urges kick-start to Indian defence sector', *Jane's Defence Weekly*, 20 Apr. 2005, p. 21.

[69] Suman, M., 'Defence offsets and technology transfer', *Indian Defence Review*, vol. 21, no. 3 (July–Sep. 2006), pp. 57–61.

[70] Anderson, G., 'India may purchase globally in order to "counter security threats"', *Defence Industry*, July 2005, p. 5; and Anderson, G., 'India faces calls to reduce military imports', *Defence Industry*, Aug. 2005, p. 11.

[71] In addition to lowering the price this will also speed up production. The last of the 140 aircraft is now scheduled to be finished in 2014, instead of 2017 as was earlier planned. 'Costs and time kill full SU-30MKI production in India', *Defense Industry Daily*, 26 Sep. 2006, URL <http://www. defenseindustrydaily.com/>; Raghuvanshi, V., 'India's Su-30 costs double', *Defense News*, 28 Aug. 2006; and 'Indian Su-30MKI production costs escalate', *Air Forces Monthly*, no. 220 (July 2006), p. 22.

temporarily replaced by the Israeli Barak; and India's light combat aircraft has been partly replaced by the MiG-29 and other acquisitions from abroad.[72]

In mid-2006 the Indian Government introduced new procurement rules for military equipment. These rules demand a 30 per cent offset worth over 3 billion Indian rupees (about $65 million) from any foreign supplier of military equipment.[73] While the offsets do not have to be specifically military, it is hoped that they will include military technology transfers, orders from Indian arms producers (directly, involving the production of the acquired product, and, indirectly, as counter-trade) and foreign investment in the Indian arms industry, which in 2001 was opened to private investment.[74] India intends that its offsets policy will promote self-reliance by increasing the content of Indian-developed technology in weapons acquired from abroad and by providing Indian private industry with better opportunities to compete with the much-criticized state-owned producers.[75] However, critics point out that—as with most offset policies—the new rules will make arms acquisitions more complicated and unclear unless the offsets are limited to direct involvement in the production of the weapons acquired.[76]

Two possible problems can follow from the pursuit of self-sufficiency in the production of advanced conventional weapons: a failure to achieve it, leading to a search for non-conventional alternatives; or a strong need to export. To a large extent a policy of self-sufficiency stands or falls by having adequate finances to back it. A big internal market (e.g. the USA) or strong economy (e.g. the USA, the EU, or Japan) can bear R&D costs without resorting to exports to establish economies of scale. Exports are therefore optional and can, at least potentially, be governed by moral considerations. Other states have to export. Russia and China are clear examples of countries without the internal market or the financial resources to sustain the necessary R&D: therefore they must rely on income from exports. Such a situation can force countries to supply weapons to controversial destinations.

If the example of India is a yardstick, efforts to achieve self-sufficiency are doomed to failure. Realistically, most countries can aspire only to inter-dependence.[77] However, if they are unwilling to accept dependency, and

---

[72] 'Tanks for India', *Asia–Pacific Defence Reporter*, vol. 36, no. 6 (July/Aug. 2006), p. 12; and Novichkov, N., 'Russia signs new contract with India for MBTs', *Jane's Defence Weekly*, 18 Oct. 2006, p. 6.

[73] Offsets are arrangements whereby purchasers, instead of just paying cash for a product, offset some of the cost through counter-trade (barter) or by being directly involved in production. Offsets may also take the form of technology transfers that can be used in development of indigenous products.

[74] Suman (note 71), pp. 57–61.

[75] Bedi, R., 'India revises procurement procedures', *Jane's Defence Weekly*, 6 Sep. 2006, p. 20.

[76] Suman (note 71).

[77] It is claimed that the much discussed 'revolution in military affairs' offers countries the chance to bypass 1970s and 1980s 'legacy' technologies. While 'piggybacking' on concepts and technologies developed elsewhere (as China does) provides the potential to advance more quickly and with less risk, countries must still acquire large quantities of legacy materiel to meet their military aims. Fish, T., 'Insurgents apply NCW concepts faster than the West', *Asia–Pacific Defence Reporter*, vol. 32, no. 7 (Sep. 2006), p. 18. *Asia–Pacific Defence Reporter*, vol. 32, no. 5 (June 2006), p. 11; and Gompert, D., Lachow, I. and Perkins, J., *Battle-Wise* (National Defense University Press: Washington, DC, 2006), URL <http://www.ndu.edu/ctnsp/battlewise.htm>, p. 44.

interdependence is unattainable, they may pursue alternative weapons (e.g. WMD, even when generally accepted as prohibited) or strategies (e.g. asymmetric strategies like terrorism, guerrilla tactics and cyber-warfare) that provide independence as well as a major military impact.

IV. State supplies of arms to rebels

The war between Israel and Hezbollah in Lebanon, the civil war in Somalia and the discussions in the UN on small arms and light weapons and an arms trade treaty all underline the important role that rebel forces play as combatants and as recipients of weapons. SIPRI has for many years recorded supplies of major conventional weapons to rebels and has consistently found that such supplies are marginal in volume or value.[78] Transfers of SALW to rebels have probably been more extensive but are nevertheless marginal in volume and value in a global, or even regional, context. However, as many past and ongoing conflicts prove, even limited supplies to rebels can have a major impact on local and regional security.[79] The repeated and often gross violations of mandatory UN arms embargoes show how difficult the issue is to solve.

The supply of arms (and other support) to rebels is not a new phenomenon. It has taken place for as long as there have been arms transfers and played an important role in the proxy wars fought between East and West during the cold war (e.g. US supplies in the 1980s to the mujahedin in Afghanistan and the Contras in Nicaragua, or Soviet deliveries in the 1960s and 1970s to the Vietcong in South Viet Nam).

As with supplies to state recipients, governments often have political or ideological reasons for delivering weapons to rebels, although the prospect of long-term economic gain (e.g. after the rebels gain power) play a role too. However, private suppliers (known as brokers or arms dealers) and some countries mainly have a more immediate profit motive.

The Liberation Tigers of Tamil Eelam in Sri Lanka and many of the rebel forces in West Africa clearly get most of their weapons from unscrupulous private dealers on the 'open market' (paid in some cases with money from private supporters around the world). In some cases rebels get their supplies from a mix of political supporters and profit-seeking brokers. The two most obvious cases of arms supplies to rebels in 2006—to Hezbollah and in Somalia—mainly involved states as suppliers.

The legal status of supplying rebel groups with weapons is debated. Obviously from the point of view of the government against which a rebel group operates, supplies to those groups are illegal. However, the fact that the UN Security Council establishes specific arms embargoes against rebel groups

---

[78] Between 1950 and 2006 SIPRI identified 39 rebel groups as recipients. Such transfers accounted for less than 0.1% of all transfers in that period, but are often badly documented in open sources.

[79] There are also major economic effects. To deal with the rather limited, mainly foreign-supplied inventory of Hezbollah, Israel had to launch an expensive military operation costing an estimated $6.6 billion, while the cost of disruption of the Israeli economy was estimated to be $5.5 billion. Ben-David, A., 'Israel revives plan for anti-rocket laser system', *Jane's Defence Weekly*, 6 Sep. 2006, p. 18.

(7 out of 12 UN embargoes in force by 31 December 2006 were specifically against non-state actors) implies that such supplies are not outlawed by default.[80]

Supplying Hezbollah

One of the biggest surprises of the war between Israel and Hezbollah in southern Lebanon in July and August of 2006 was that Hezbollah had over the years built up a much better-armed conventional force than was previously thought.[81] Most of the weapons appear to have been supplied by Iran and Syria. It is argued that Iran supplies Hezbollah because it is in Iran's interest to fight a war by proxy against Israel; either to keep Israel busy, or to be true to the goals of the Islamic Revolution. Iran might also wish to play the role of leader of the Islamic world, either by showing how to deal with the 'Israeli problem' or by standing up for victims of Israeli 'aggression'.[82]

The 1989 Taif Agreement and several subsequent UN Security Council resolutions have tried to prevent the flow of arms to Hezbollah and other non-governmental forces in Lebanon. However, these were not precisely worded and left room to allow transfers to Hezbollah. For example, in September 2004 the UN Security Council called for the 'disbanding and disarmament of all Lebanese and non-Lebanese militias'.[83] Iran, Syria and several Lebanese ministers claimed that Hezbollah was not a 'militia' and that arms transfers to it were therefore not prohibited.[84] Table 10.4 lists the suppliers of Hezbollah's weapons.

Hezbollah built up its arsenal with systems (mainly rockets) that could be used to attack Israel indiscriminately, and with weapons such as anti-tank missiles and man portable air defence systems (MANPADS)[85] to deal with the inevitable Israeli counter-attack.[86] According to Israeli sources, Hezbollah fired 4228 unguided rockets from single- or multiple-rocket launchers against Israel between 12 July and 14 August 2006. Of these, almost 4000 were 122-millimetre rockets with a range of 20–35 km (often called Katyusha) and some 250 larger and longer-range rockets, mostly 220-mm and 320-mm rockets produced in Syria (but probably based on or copies of Russian/Soviet and Chinese designs). The 122-mm rockets could have come from a number

---

[80] For a list of United Nations and other internationally agreed embargoes see the SIPRI Arms Transfers Project website (note 2). The issue of legality played a prominent role in UN discussions on small arms and light weapons and the arms trade treaty initiative. See appendix 10C.

[81] For more on this conflict see chapter 2 in this volume.

[82] Fish, T., 'The long arm of Tehran stirs trouble in Lebanon', *Asia–Pacific Defence Reporter*, vol. 32, no. 6 (July/Aug 2006), p. 5.

[83] UN Security Council Resolution 1559, 2 Sep. 2004.

[84] Schiff, Z., 'Lebanon admits it approved weapons transfer to Hezbollah', *Haaretz*, 26 Feb. 2006.

[85] For more on MANPADS see appendix 14A in this volume.

[86] Sand, B., 'After Lebanon, Israel learns new and old lessons', *Asia–Pacific Defence Reporter*, vol. 32, no. 7 (Sep. 2006), pp. 14–16.

Table 10.4. Origin of major conventional weapons used by Hezbollah in 2006

Supplier	Designation	Type	Number	Comment
Iran	C-802	AShM	Few	
	BGM-71 TOW	ATM	. .	Including Iranian-produced version
	QW-1	Portable SAM	Few	Iranian-produced Misagh-1 version
	SA-7	Portable SAM	Few	
	SA-14	Portable SAM	Few	
	SA-16	Portable SAM	Few	
	BM-21	Rocket	±4000 used	
	Fajr-3	Rocket	. .	
	Fajr-5	Rocket	. .	
	Zelzal-2	SSM	. .	
	Mirsad-1	UAV	Few	Mohajer-4 or Ababil; used in armed role as cruise missile
Iran/Syria	Metis/AT-13	ATM	100s	
	Konkurs/AT-5	ATM	100s	Including Iranian-produced Towsan-1 version
Syria	AT-3	ATM	100s	Iranian-produced Ra'ad version
	Fagot/AT-4	ATM	100s	
	Kornet/AT-14	ATM	100s	
	. .	Rocket (220 mm)	. .	Called Ra'ad by Hezbollah; probably a copy or based on the Russian BM-22 (Uragan)
	. .	Rocket (302 mm)	. .	Called Khaibar-1 by Hezbollah; probably a copy or based on the Chinese WS-1
Unknown	Milan	ATM	Few	

ATM = anti-tank missile; AShM = anti-ship missile; SAM = surface-to-air missile; SSM = surface-to-surface missile; UAV = unmanned aerial vehicle.

Sources: SIPRI Arms Transfers Database and archive.

of suppliers since it is probably the most used and produced artillery rocket worldwide. Despite earlier reports of major deliveries of Iranian rockets to Hezbollah, Israel claims that only one Iranian Fajr-3 rocket could be identified. However, it came as a surprise—not least to the Israeli Navy—when Hezbollah fired what were almost certainly C-802 anti-ship missiles against Israeli naval ships off the Lebanese coast.[87]

There has long been a fear that non-state actors could acquire long-range missiles or other 'strike' systems, allowing them to threaten 'strategic' targets.

---

[87] 'Hezbollah'stic examination' [English], *Kommersant*, 23 Aug. 2006, URL <http://www.kommersant.com/ page.asp?id=698954>; Darling, D., 'Hezbollah's arsenal', *Weekly Standard*, 31 July 2006, URL <http:// www.weeklystandard.com/Content/Public/Articles/000/000/012/481ydesv.asp>; and Gambill, G., 'Hezbollah's strategic rocket arsenal', *Middle East Intelligence Bulletin*, Nov./Dec. 2002, URL <http://www.meib.org/articles/0211_l2.htm>.

In 2006 Hezbollah tried to use several long-range strike systems capable of reaching almost every part of Israel, but these proved militarily ineffective (although they may have had propaganda value). Hezbollah claimed it was in possession of (Iranian delivered) Zelzal-2 surface-to-surface missiles with a range of 300 km, and this was certainly a matter of concern to Israelis living in possible target areas, but only one was reported as used.[88] Before the conflict Israel had shot down several Hezbollah reconnaissance unmanned aerial vehicles (UAV), and during the conflict Israel claimed to have shot down an armed UAV 'en route to a strategic target'.[89] However, it only carried an insignificant 10 kilogram explosive warhead, making it a fairly ineffectual weapon.[90]

The USA singled out China for criticism because several of the weapons that Hezbollah received from Iran are produced in China (e.g. the C-802). Some of the equipment that Hezbollah received from Iran and Syria was only recently delivered to these countries, and included Kornet and RPG-29 anti-tank weapons delivered in 1990–1999 by Russia to Syria, and British night-vision equipment supplied in 2003 to Iran for anti-narcotic-smuggling operations.[91] Such diversions of equipment highlight the difficulties in properly administering export controls when post-delivery controls and sanctions for diversion are apparently weak or non-existent.[92]

During and after the fighting in mid-2006 Iran is reported to have continued supplying weapons to Hezbollah, including portable SAMs.[93] However, UN Security Council Resolution 1701 established an embargo on arms transfers to all non-government or non-UN groups in Lebanon, making it illegal to supply Hezbollah.[94] The embargo forms part of a set of measures to help the Lebanese Government extend full sovereignty over its territory following the conflict in 2006. Disarming Hezbollah and establishing Lebanese Government control over Hezbollah-controlled areas was one of the key Israeli conditions for agreeing to a ceasefire and withdrawal from Lebanon.

Syria has committed itself to curbing the flow of arms over the Lebanon–Syria border to the rebel group.[95] However, the Lebanese Government, the UN, the USA and other states claim that arms continue to cross the border; charges that Hezbollah admits to be true.[96]

---

[88] Blanford, N., 'Hizbullah set for long-term operation', *Jane's Defence Weekly*, 2 Aug. 2006, p. 5.

[89] 'Accident report updates', *Air Forces Monthly*, no. 224 (Nov. 2006), p. 77.

[90] Another UAV may have carried a (still insignificant) warhead of up to 50 kg, but it exploded on launch. Opall-Rome, B., 'Israeli missiles down armed Hizbollah UAVs', *Defense News*, 2 Oct. 2006, p. 6.

[91] Sand (note 88), p. 16; King, O. and Sturcke, J., 'Pressure on Beckett over Hizbullah's "British equipment"', *The Guardian*, 21 Aug. 2006.

[92] On export controls see chapter 15 in this volume.

[93] Hughes, R., 'Iran answers Hizbullah call for SAM systems', *Jane's Defence Weekly*, 9 Aug. 2006.

[94] UN Security Council Resolution 1701, 11 Aug. 2006.

[95] Williamson, H. and Peel, Q., 'EU to debate arms control call', *Financial Times*, 15 Sep. 2006, p. 5; and UN News Service, 'Syria agrees to help enforce arms embargo on its border with Lebanon, says Annan', 1 Sep. 2006, URL <http://www.un.org/apps/news/story.asp?NewsID=19697&Cr=Leban&Cr1#>.

[96] 'Bolton: Syria, Iran arming Hizbullah', *Jerusalem Post*, 31 Oct. 2006; Gresh, A., 'Reconcontre avec Hassan Nasrallah' [Meeting with Hassan Nasrallah], *Carnets du Diplo* (Le Monde Diplomatique blog), 7 Apr. 2007, URL <http://blog.mondediplo.net/2007-04-07-Rencontre-avec-Hassan-Nasrallah>;

Breaking the Somalia embargo

Prior to December 2006 Somalia was under a complete UN arms embargo. However, there were repeated reports of states supplying weapons to one or more of the Somali factions and all factions also managing to buy supplies on the black market. UN reports from May and November 2006 suggested that these supplies had increased.[97] The November report alleged that Eritrea, Iran, Libya, Saudi Arabia and Syria, had supplied the Islamic Courts Union (ICU) with arms, while the Transitional Federal Government (TFG) was receiving arms from Ethiopia, Uganda and Yemen. The report noted increases in the number of suppliers, the volume of weapons transferred, and the sophistication of the equipment involved. Transfers from Eritrea, Iran and Syria to the ICU were alleged to include MANPADS; 122-mm, 130-mm and 152-mm artillery systems; anti-aircraft guns; guided anti-tank weapons; and even sophisticated SA-6 SAMs. Not surprisingly, all accused countries denied involvement in any embargo violation.[98]

Other reports claimed large-scale breaches of the embargo and also accused the USA of providing support to the Alliance for the Restoration of Peace and Counter-Terrorism (ARPCT), a loose coalition of warlords formed in February 2006 to counter the growing strength of the ICU.[99] The USA denied the allegations, but US officials reportedly admitted to providing financial support to the ARPCT, and this may have been used to buy arms.[100] The President of Somalia, Abdullahi Yusuf Ahmed, who is head of the TFG, boasted that despite the embargo he was able to procure weapons for his forces to attack some of the warlords. Moreover, Ethiopian forces have moved into Somalia to support the TFG.[101]

On 6 December 2006, under pressure from certain regional states,[102] the UN Security Council partially lifted the 1992 UN arms embargo on Somalia to allow for the deployment of a regional intervention force to protect the TFG and for the arming and training of the TFG security forces.[103] The matter became urgent at the end of 2006 when the ICU had taken control of most of Somalia and seemed poised to overrun even the last strongholds of the TFG. At the same time the USA accused the ICU of harbouring al-Qaeda members.

---

and Khoury, J., 'Nasrallah admits Iran supplies Hezbollah with arms', *Haaretz*, 4 Feb. 2007 URL <http://www.haaretz.com/hasen/spages/821548.html>.

[97] United Nations, Report of the Monitoring Group on Somalia pursuant to Security Council Resolution 1676 (2006), S/2006/913, 22 Nov. 2006; and Report of the Monitoring Group on Somalia persuant to Security Council Resolution 1630 (2005), S/2006/229, 4 May 2006. UN documents on the Somali embargo are available at URL <http://www.un.org/sc/committees/751/index.shtml>.

[98] The Nov. 2006 report has been criticized because it depends too much on unidentfied 'intelligence sources'. It also includes named weapons such as '2nd generation IR-guided anti-tank weapons' that do not exist.

[99] Wax, E. and DeYoung, K., 'US secretly backing warlords in Somalia', *Washington Post*, 17 May 2006; and 'Terror in Mogadishu', *Africa Confidential*, vol. 47, no. 11 (26 May 2006), pp. 3–4

[100] 'Terror in Mogadishu' (note 102).

[101] On the conflict in Somalia in 2006 see chapter 2 in this volume.

[102] 'Somalia: a threat to the Horn and beyond', *Africa Confidential*, vol. 47, no. 18 (8 Sep. 2006).

[103] UN Security Council Resolution 1725, 6 Dec. 2006.

By that time Ethiopian troops had already moved into Somalia to support the TFG. The partial lifting of the embargo legalized this presence and allowed US armed actions against the ICU from late-2006. The Arab League as well as a number of non-governmental organizations (NGOs) criticized the move. They argued that the Security Council, by taking the side of the TFG, was prolonging the conflict and damaging the chance of a negotiated settlement (TFG–ICU peace talks had already been scheduled for mid-December 2006), and possibly even causing the conflict to spread to other countries in the region.[104]

V. Official arms transfer transparency[105]

Official and publicly accessible data on arms transfers are important for assessing the policies of exporters and importers and for holding to account those who are responsible for those policies. However, making data on arms sales and acquisitions publicly available is a sensitive point for nearly all states. Several global and regional mechanisms for the reporting arms sales and arms acquisitions have been in force since the early 1990s, but transparency remains limited.

The UN Register of Conventional Arms

The UN Register of Conventional Arms (UNROCA) remains the key international mechanism of official transparency on arms transfers,[106] and in 2006 there was little change in terms of reporting.[107] As in previous years about 120 countries responded, and substantial information gaps remained in those regions where destabilizing build-ups of weapons through imports might be expected: Africa, the Middle East (where almost all countries never report) and North-East Asia (where China has not reported since 1998, North Korea has never reported and Taiwan is not asked to report). Discrepancies between exporter and importer reports remained as large as ever, while some reports, even from prominent advocates of transparency (e.g. the USA), continued to

---

[104] Associated Press, 'UN Security Council OKs Somalia forces', 6 Dec. 2006, URL; and Shabelle Media Network, 'Arab League warns the US-backed draft resolution will spark civil war', 5 Dec. 2006, URL <http://www.shabelle.net/news/ne1815.htm>.

[105] This section covers official reports on arms transfers available to the public. On intergovernmental exchanges of information, such as occur within the Organization for Security and Co-operation in Europe, the Organization of American States, the Economic Community of West African States and the Wassenaar Arrangement see chapters 14 and 15 in this volume.

[106] The only other global public reporting mechanism where arms transfers are reported to any degree is the UN Commodity Trade Statistics Database (UN Comtrade).

[107] Data reported to UNROCA since 1992 is available at URL <http://disarmament.un.org/cab/register.html>. Interestingly, especially with regard to the discrepancies in reporting resulting from the unclearly defined 7 UNROCA categories, the UNROCA was used to define the scope of the UN arms embargo against North Korea, established on 14 Oct. 2006. This embargo covers only UNROCA-defined major conventional weapons, unlike previous embargoes that cover all weapons and equipment intended for use by the military. UN Security Council Resolution 1718, 14 Oct. 2006. On the embargo on North Korea see chapter 15 in this volume.

be sloppy. Nonetheless, the Register again revealed significant information, mainly on countries where official or unofficial open source information is hard to come by. For example, most of the data reported by Ukraine in 2006 was not available in unofficial sources.

The future of the UNROCA was once again discussed by a group of government experts, the fifth review since its inception. As before it was agreed that countries should provide more detailed reports and that more categories of weapons and support systems should be added, as well as acquisitions from national production and data on holdings. However, as with the earlier reviews, reaching consensus on significant changes was held hostage to discussions on the status of WMD in the UNROCA.

The final recommendations were limited, but included changing the weight threshold at which ships must be reported from 750 to 500 tonnes.[108] The fifth review also decided to provide a separate standardized form for SALW reporting,[109] whereas previously countries were simply encouraged to supply data. Lastly, it was agreed that only transfers to or from other UN members should be reported. This should encourage China to resume reporting: since 1998 it has used US reporting of transfers to Taiwan as a justification for not reporting.

The EU Annual Report

In October 2006 the EU published its eighth annual report on the implementation of the EU Code of Conduct on Arms Exports.[110] Published on 16 October 2006, the eighth annual report arrived more than two months earlier than previous editions.[111] In another boost to transparency, information on transfers to countries under an EU arms embargo were placed in a separate section with specific explanations of why exports were approved to these destinations. A table was also provided showing the number of consultations carried out per destination country.[112]

EU member states have agreed to submit data to the EU annual report on the value of licences granted, and on actual exports broken down by destination

---

[108] The original threshold proposed in 1991 was 500 tonnes, but was amended to 750 tonnes in the final resolution that established the UNROCA.

[109] This report, and earlier reports, are available at URL <http://disarmament.un.org/cab/register. html#item3>. For a broader discussion of the problems related to improving UNROCA reporting see Wezeman (note 6), p. 5.

[110] Council of the European Union, 'Eighth annual report according to operative provision 8 of the European Union Code of Conduct on Arms Exports', *Official Journal of the European Union*, C250 (16 Oct. 2006), p. 3.

[111] The previous 2 reports were published on 21 Dec. 2004 and 23 Dec. 2005, respectively. All EU annual reports are available at URL <http://www.sipri.org/contents/armstrad/atlinks_gov.html>.

[112] Consultations occur when a member state is considering granting an export licence for a transaction which is 'essentially similar' to one which has been blocked by another EU member in the past 3 years. In such cases, the member state which is considering the licence is obliged to consult with the member state that blocked the earlier deal and obtain information about their reasons for doing so.

and EU Military List category.[113] The number of states submitting these data continues to increase. While only five states submitted these data to the sixth annual report (2004), 18 states submitted such data to the 2006 report. Older EU member states (including some with a record of pushing for greater transparency) continue to submit incomplete data. For example, Belgium, Italy, Sweden and the UK all failed to submit data on either export licences or actual exports disaggregated by the categories of the EU Military List. In contrast, all 10 states that joined the EU in 2004 managed to submitted these data. This is mainly because the newer member states have recently updated their systems of export control and data collection to comply with the demands of EU accession.

In an effort to harmonize methodologies in the collection and processing of data submitted to the EU annual report, a confidential survey was conducted among member states of current national practices in this area.[114] Increases in the amount of data submitted to the annual report represent a significant improvement to the comprehensiveness and comparability of data. Nonetheless, questions remain about the usefulness of financial data for assessing how states are interpreting and applying the criteria of the EU Code of Conduct, the initial rationale behind the annual report.[115]

Developments in national transparency

Individual reports or official statements from states are another significant source of public information on arms transfers.[116] In 2006 28 states produced such reports or statements, including three countries that did so for the first time.

EU membership continues to act as an important driver for increased arms export transparency at the national level. In March 2006, *Slovenia*, a new member of the EU, published its first annual report on arms exports. The report gives information on export and import licences for military equipment, detailing the category of goods involved, the number of items exported, their financial value and their destination. *Bulgaria* published its first report on arms transfers in February 2007 after its accession to the EU in January. The report covers activities in 2005 and provides information on the number of export and import licences granted and used, their financial value, and the categories of equipment covered, broken down by recipient or supplier country. The aspiration of future EU membership also encourages greater transparency. *The Former Yugoslav Republic of Macedonia* (FYROM) published its first annual report on arms exports in June 2006. It contains detailed

---

[113] 'Common Military List of the European Union (equipment covered by the European Union Code of Conduct on Arms Exports) adopted by the Council on 27 February 2006', *Official Journal of the European Union*, C66 (17 Mar. 2006), pp. 1–28.

[114] Council of the European Union (note 114), p. 3.

[115] See Bauer and Bromley (note 6).

[116] All publicly available national reports on arms transfers are available at URL <http://www.sipri.org/contents/armstrad/atlinks_gov.html>.

information on all arms export and transit licences, including a description of exported goods, the number of units exported, the recipients and the type of end-user.

Aside from EU member states, few countries produce national reports on their arms exports. In 2006 Australia published its first such report since February 2003, providing arms export data for the period July 2002 to June 2004. However, Canada and South Africa again failed to release arms export reports, meaning that for both states the most recent available data covers arms exports during 2002.

VI. Conclusions

The trend of increasing transfers of major conventional weapons first visible in the early 2000s continued in 2006. Despite this growing demand, the market remains a buyers' market where importers are able to play-off different suppliers against one another, not only to get better financial arrangements but, more significantly, to obtain advanced weapons and technology. This seems to undermine efforts to prevent the spread of certain types of weapons that are viewed as more 'aggressive' and destabilizing.

European–US arms trade relations took a turn for the better with the resolution of technology transfer issues related to the JSF. The US agreed in principle to share with all JSF partners much or all of the advanced US technology involved, taking the sting out of a heated European–US debate and boosting trust in Euro-Atlantic cooperation and interdependence.

Russia managed—despite continuing doubts over its ability to develop new generations of weapons—to land several large contracts in new and existing markets. However, in general these were still based on technology and designs from the cold war period. Russia's willingness to supply arms to Iran and Venezuela despite strong US pressure not to do so should also be noted.

Several states in the Middle East have during the past ten years imported large amounts of weapons, including many long-range strike weapons. Oil-producing countries, in particular in the Middle East, could—thanks to continuing high oil and gas prices—afford the luxury of additional major equipment acquisitions.

While much attention has been given to Russian arms sales to Iran and Syria, the Gulf states and Israel have imported much more, and Saudi Arabia has signed major deals with France, the UK and the USA, dwarfing Russian sales. All this weaponry is once more accumulating in a region considered to be extremely volatile.

At the global level, public transparency on arms transfers is still patchy and inconsistent. Many recipient states in areas of conflict or tension are not transparent to any degree about their arms acquisitions. Reports or statements on arms transfers or acquisitions still come mainly from Western states. However, most of these focus on financial data and often do not provide information on the types of equipment or weapons transferred, meaning that they are not the most useful data when analysing the impact of arms transfers. Transparency is, however, slowly on the increase and may benefit from discussions on an arms trade treaty.[117]

---

[117] See appendix 10C.

Appendix 10A. The suppliers and recipients of major conventional weapons

THE SIPRI ARMS TRANSFERS PROJECT

Table 10A.1 The recipients of major conventional weapons, 2002–2006

The table includes all countries and non-state actors with imports of major conventional weapons in the five-year period 2002–2006. Ranking is according to the 2002–2006 aggregate imports. Figures are SIPRI trend-indicator values expressed in US\$ m. at constant (1990) prices. Figures may not add up because of the conventions of rounding.

Rank order 2002–2006	2001–2005[a]	Recipient	2002	2003	2004	2005	2006	2002–2006
1	1	China	2 636	2 068	2 853	3 791	3 261	14 609
2	2	India	1 659	2 928	2 476	1 417	1 672	10 152
3	3	Greece	484	2 226	1 984	1 097	1 452	7 243
4	4	UAE	208	734	1 348	2 319	2 439	7 048
5	7	South Korea	336	599	1 030	627	1 292	3 884
6	5	Australia	711	864	558	560	768	3 461
7	10	Israel	280	291	845	1 047	994	3 457
8	6	Egypt	656	575	542	740	526	3 039
9	9	Turkey	887	585	174	845	454	2 945
10	12	Iran	538	439	377	327	891	2 572
11	11	USA	394	511	510	444	417	2 276
12	15	Taiwan	314	116	341	775	624	2 170
13	8	UK	715	789	137	28	462	2 131
14	13	Pakistan	528	592	373	236	309	2 038
15	14	Japan	426	465	412	305	400	2 008
16	16	Saudi Arabia	549	159	941	148	148	1 945
17	17	Italy	165	516	435	129	697	1 942
18	30	Chile	62	175	50	470	1 125	1 882
19	22	Spain	246	110	271	323	378	1 328
20	19	Singapore	235	70	384	552	54	1 295
21	21	Yemen	592	40	314	308	–	1 254
22	23	Poland	286	405	229	97	224	1 241
23	49	South Africa	4	2	2	315	862	1 185
24	31	Germany	64	50	222	222	529	1 087
25	25	Romania	24	25	288	594	131	1 062
26	18	Canada	395	139	308	97	100	1 039
27	45	Malaysia	139	137	81	16	654	1 027
28	20	Algeria	233	197	272	152	173	1 027
29	26	Netherlands	317	172	151	121	171	932
30	42	Portugal	–	57	43	391	431	922
31	28	Viet Nam	129	32	259	308	179	907
32	27	Czech Republic	47	104	7	622	65	845
33	24	Brazil	165	71	124	143	323	826
34	35	Peru	5	22	47	368	365	807

Rank order

2002– 2006	2001– 2005[a]	Recipient	2002	2003	2004	2005	2006	2002– 2006
35	29	Jordan	122	300	199	32	117	770
36	33	Indonesia	66	358	155	21	54	654
37	62	Norway	92	4	6	3	501	606
38	55	Oman	31	23	41	100	406	601
39	63	Venezuela	45	13	13	27	498	596
40	36	Denmark	38	46	229	117	133	563
41	32	Sudan	57	102	270	81	48	558
42	39	Switzerland	53	91	175	159	72	550
43	38	Eritrea	2	–	202	276	70	550
44	34	Thailand	156	153	117	58	47	531
45	44	Finland	16	232	76	76	84	484
46	41	Mexico	79	31	247	25	68	450
47	58	Iraq	–	–	47	154	195	396
48	47	Ethiopia	20	193	162	–	–	375
49	43	Sweden	75	63	48	63	122	371
50	40	Myanmar (Burma)	250	70	11	25	7	363
51	101	Hungary	–	–	3	13	337	353
52	37	Colombia	163	115	11	8	33	330
53	52	Morocco	167	7	–	96	49	319
54	50	Kazakhstan	83	62	46	72	53	316
55	57	France	38	57	93	–	121	309
56	51	Bangladesh	39	9	25	27	208	308
57	122	Belarus	–	–	–	6	254	260
58	53	Tunisia	75	–	–	168	16	259
59	60	Argentina	16	12	162	4	53	247
60	48	Libya	–	145	74	–	5	224
61	69	Kuwait	18	49	–	21	107	195
62	66	Bulgaria	–	2	12	158	20	192
63	54	New Zealand	17	108	50	8	8	191
64	67	Bahrain	58	6	10	53	60	187
65	59	Austria	66	43	55	21	–	185
66	64	Azerbaijan	128	–	3	45	–	176
67	68	Armenia	–	–	151	–	–	151
68	81	Nigeria	6	52	10	–	72	140
69	73	Côte d'Ivoire	32	68	14	–	–	114
70	77	Lithuania	7	1	55	12	33	108
71	82	Philippines	5	8	37	14	43	107
72	74	Syria	19	46	19	7	9	100
73	65	Georgia	–	1	45	49	–	95
74	61	Sri Lanka	11	12	26	18	20	87
75	72	Belgium	36	27	18	–	4	85
76	79	Uganda	22	19	26	13	–	80
77	80	Afghanistan	33	17	–	28	–	78
78	124	Gabon	–	–	5	–	63	68
79	76	Ireland	23	–	28	4	11	66
80	88	Zimbabwe	–	23	–	20	20	63
81	83	Latvia	8	28	15	7	4	62

Rank order

2002–2006	2001–2005[a]	Recipient	2002	2003	2004	2005	2006	2002–2006
82	87	Tanzania	–	56	–	–	–	56
83	78	Congo, DRC	14	15	–	14	13	56
84	46	Angola	24	2	8	22	–	56
85	85	Nepal	8	9	32	4	–	53
86	89	Ecuador	1	–	19	33	–	53
87	70	Cyprus	11	8	–	–	26	45
88	90	Albania	–	2	–	42	–	44
89	95	Estonia	1	15	5	12	8	41
90	86	North Korea	10	10	9	5	5	39
91	97	Uruguay	11	–	–	20	7	38
92	112	Jamaica	–	–	–	13	25	38
93	84	Slovenia	2	15	15	2	2	36
94	117	Bolivia	–	–	1	9	26	36
95	92	Ghana	1	6	27	–	–	34
96	75	Croatia	2	24	8	–	–	34
97	98	Slovakia	27	–	–	4	–	31
98	100	Turkmenistan	–	20	10	–	–	30
99	99	Dominican Republic	–	3	27	–	–	30
100	103	El Salvador	16	9	–	–	–	25
101	104	Kenya	–	–	–	25	–	25
102	94	Qatar	12	12	–	–	–	24
103	91	Namibia	11	–	13	–	–	24
104	105	Burkina Faso	–	–	–	19	–	19
105	106	Malta	–	–	–	18	–	18
106	107	Kyrgyzstan	–	9	5	3	1	18
107	96	Botswana	1	7	9	–	–	17
108	129	Zambia	1	–	–	–	15	16
109	126	Lebanon/Hezbollah[b]	3	–	1	–	11	15
110	109	Mauritania	15	–	–	–	–	15
111	111	Mali	1	–	–	13	–	14
112	137	Tajikistan	–	–	–	–	13	13
113	113	Cameroon	6	–	–	5	–	11
114	116	Djibouti	2	–	–	8	–	10
115	140	Central African Republic	–	–	–	–	9	9
116	108	Equatorial Guinea	–	–	8	–	–	8
117	120	Gambia	–	–	7	–	–	7
118	123	Benin	6	–	–	–	–	6
119	115	Uzbekistan	5	–	–	–	–	5
120	114	Paraguay	–	–	4	1	–	5
121	138	Russia	–	–	–	–	4	4
122	93	Laos	–	–	–	4	–	4
123	127	Congo (Republic of)	–	–	–	4	–	4
124	128	Brunei	–	–	–	1	3	4
125	125	Burundi	4	–	–	–	–	4
126	110	Chad	–	–	–	–	2	2
127	132	Mozambique	–	1	–	–	–	1
128	133	Luxembourg	–	1	–	–	–	1

Rank order

2002–2006	2001–2005[a]	Recipient	2002	2003	2004	2005	2006	2002–2006
129	118	Lesotho	–	–	1	–	–	1
130	134	Lebanon	–	–	–	1	–	1
131	121	Guinea	–	1	–	–	–	1
132	135	Uganda/LRA[b]	–	–	–	–	–	–
133	136	Macedonia/NLA[b]	–	–	–	–	–	–
134	56	Afghanistan/NA[b]	–	–	–	–	–	–
135	130	Trinidad and Tobago	–	–	–	–	–	–
136	131	Swaziland	–	–	–	–	–	–
137	102	Serbia and Montenegro	–	–	–	–	–	–
138	139	Panama	–	–	–	–	–	–
139	71	Macedonia	–	–	–	–	–	–
140	119	Guyana	–	–	–	–	–	–
141	141	Bhutan	–	–	–	–	–	–
n.a.	n.a.	Unknown country[c]	–	–	3	–	–	3
n.a.	n.a.	Unknown rebel group[c]	–	–	–	–	–	–
		Total	**16 796**	**19 086**	**21 591**	**22 305**	**26 765**	**10 6543**

– = between 0 and 0.5.

[a] The rank order for recipients in 2001–2005 differs from that published in *SIPRI Yearbook 2006* (pp. 477–80) because of subsequent revision of figures for these years.

[b] Non-state actor/rebel group: LRA = Lord's Resistance Army; NA = Northern Alliance (UFSA, United Islamic Front for the Salvation of Afghanistan); NLA = National Liberation Army.

[c] One or more unknown recipient(s).

Note: The SIPRI data on arms transfers relate to actual deliveries of major conventional weapons. To permit comparison between the data on such deliveries of different weapons and to identify general trends, SIPRI uses a *trend-indicator value*. This value is only an indicator of the volume of international arms transfers and not of the financial values of such transfers. Thus, it is not comparable to economic statistics such as gross domestic product or export/import figures. The method for calculating the trend-indicator value is described in appendix 10B and on the SIPRI Arms Transfers Project website, URL <http://www.sipri.org/contents/armstrad/atmethods.html>.

Source: SIPRI Arms Transfers Database.

Table 10A.2. The suppliers of major conventional weapons, 2002–2006

The list includes all countries and non-state actors with exports of major conventional weapons in the five-year period 2002–2006. Ranking is according to the 2002–2006 aggregate exports. Figures are SIPRI trend-indicator values expressed in US$ m. at constant (1990) prices. Figures may not add up because of the conventions of rounding.

Rank order								
2002–2006	2001–2005[a]	Supplier	2002	2003	2004	2005	2006	2002–2006
1	1	USA	4 949	5 586	6 639	7 066	7 888	32 128
2	2	Russia	5 655	5 442	6 485	6 449	6 733	30 764
3	4	Germany	899	1 881	1 001	1 533	3 850	9 164
4	3	France	1 312	1 282	2 687	2 050	1 557	8 888
5	5	UK	742	680	1 083	912	1 071	4 488
6	10	Netherlands	243	343	271	877	1 481	3 215
7	9	Italy	407	321	216	787	860	2 591
8	7	China	544	532	271	223	564	2 134
9	6	Sweden	127	468	306	587	472	1 960
10	11	Israel	365	309	535	240	224	1 673
11	8	Ukraine	210	456	427	308	133	1 534
12	16	Spain	120	158	73	116	803	1 270
13	12	Canada	182	279	305	193	227	1 186
14	13	Switzerland	109	139	201	166	144	759
15	14	Uzbekistan	73	340	170	–	–	583
16	17	Poland	36	70	65	103	169	443
17	19	Belgium	34	15	47	185	50	331
18	20	Norway	91	83	79	12	2	267
19	18	South Korea	–	114	20	39	89	262
20	24	South Africa	16	42	62	23	115	258
21	21	Denmark	6	61	173	–	3	243
22	15	Belarus	54	80	50	24	–	208
23	22	Czech Republic	58	65	0	23	56	202
24	29	Turkey	23	38	10	47	45	163
25	30	Austria	82	3	3	3	61	152
26	27	Brazil	26	–	56	61	1	144
27	25	Australia	30	40	2	50	4	126
28	23	Slovakia	44	–	79	–	–	123
29	31	Finland	18	23	21	25	31	118
30	28	Georgia	108	–	7	–	–	115
31	33	Kyrgyzstan	–	92	–	–	–	92
32	32	Indonesia	49	–	25	8	8	90
33	34	Bulgaria	32	48	–	–	–	80
34	38	Greece	–	8	32	13	23	76
35	39	Libya	11	38	–	–	24	73
36	35	Singapore	2	–	66	3	–	71
37	26	North Korea	45	13	13	–	–	71
38	37	Jordan	–	–	42	15	13	70
39	36	Hungary	–	–	–	68	–	68

Rank order								
2002–2006	2001–2005[a]	Supplier	2002	2003	2004	2005	2006	2002–2006
40	40	Lebanon	45	–	–	–	–	45
41	44	India	–	4	22	4	11	41
42	42	Saudi Arabia	–	–	–	36	–	36
43	45	UAE	–	–	2	25	7	34
44	43	Pakistan	9	9	7	9	–	34
45	46	Romania	–	24	–	–	–	24
46	54	Iran	3	–	1	–	9	13
47	49	Thailand	–	5	5	–	–	10
48	50	Malta	–	–	10	–	–	10
49	48	Serbia and Montenegro	–	–	4	–	5	9
50	61	Venezuela	–	–	1	–	6	7
51	51	Peru	–	–	5	–	–	5
52	47	Kazakhstan	–	–	5	–	–	5
53	52	Moldova	–	–	–	4	–	4
54	55	Bosnia and Herzegovina	4	–	–	–	–	4
55	64	Syria	–	–	–	–	3	3
56	57	Lithuania	3	–	–	–	–	3
57	58	New Zealand	1	–	1	–	–	2
58	59	Chile	2	–	–	–	–	2
59	62	Oman	–	–	–	1	–	1
60	63	Angola	1	–	–	–	–	1
61	53	Taiwan	–	–	–	–	–	–
62	41	Egypt	–	–	–	–	–	–
63	60	Bahrain	–	–	–	–	–	–
64	56	Argentina	–	–	–	–	–	–
n.a.	n.a.	Unknown country[b]	30	–	4	14	18	66
		Total	**16 796**	**19 086**	**21 591**	**22 305**	**26 765**	**106 543**

– = between 0 and 0.5.

[a] The rank order for suppliers in 2001–2005 differs from that published in *SIPRI Yearbook 2006* (pp. 481–82) because of subsequent revision of figures for these years.

[b] One or more unknown supplier(s).

Note: The SIPRI data on arms transfers relate to actual deliveries of major conventional weapons. To permit comparison between the data on such deliveries of different weapons and to identify general trends, SIPRI uses a *trend-indicator value*. This value is only an indicator of the volume of international arms transfers and not of the financial values of such transfers. Thus, it is not comparable to economic statistics such as gross domestic product or export/import figures. The method for calculating the trend-indicator value is described in appendix 10B and on the SIPRI Arms Transfers Project website, URL <http://www.sipri.org/contents/armstrad/atmethods.html>.

Source: SIPRI Arms Transfers Database.

Table 10A.3. The financial value of global arms exports according to national government and industry sources, 1998–2005

Figures are in US$ m. at constant (2005) prices.

	1998	1999	2000	2001	2002	2003	2004	2005	Stated data coverage
World total[a]	45 054– 49 783	40 570– 42 916	36 033– 37 413	27 944– 35 985	30 749– 37 450	36 547– 46 408	41 913– 54 805	39 042– 55 964	
National figures									
Australia	11	390	24	56	268	408	..	..	Arms exports (figure for 2003 from 1 July 2003 to 30 June 2004)
Austria	278	493	588	381	240	295	21	318	Licences for arms exports
Belgium	866	777	814	838	1 174	798	699	318	Licences for arms exports
Brazil	84	468	203	320	181	52	295	285	Arms exports
Canada	340	343	365	422	469	..	..	..	Arms exports (excludes exports to the USA)
Czech Republic	122	112	91	59	79	99	116	110	Arms exports
Denmark	..	..	..	75	116	96	131	109	Licences for arms exports
Finland	41	50	25	39	55	59	54	128	Arms exports
France	7 712	4 634	2 776	3 065	4 434	5 046	9 010	4 744	Arms exports
Germany	911	1 816	711	362	326	1 597	1 450	2 027	Arms exports (only covers exports of 'weapons of war')
Greece	..	54	22	50	53	134	19	36	Licences for arms exports
Hungary	..	..	19	10	8	13	12	15	Arms exports
India	40	20	..	..	51	100	73	57	Arms exports (figure for 2005 from 1 Apr. 2005 to 31 Mar. 2006)
Ireland	27	75	32	53	37	42	35	37	Licences for arms exports
Israel	2 251	1 883	2 001	2 206	2 171	2 495	2 688	2 600	Arms exports
Italy	139	1 107	631	546	499	755	617	1 034	Arms exports
Korea, South	176	231	62	221	..	255	434	..	Arms exports
Netherlands	575	457	436	643	461	1 379	802	1 461	Licences for arms exports
Norway	165	184	137	197	312	453	309	382	Arms exports
Pakistan	..	35	45	88	109	106	103	..	Arms exports
Poland	..	..	45	55	87	219	338	361	Licences for arms exports

Portugal	20	14	14	11	6	30	15	9	Arms exports
Romania	67	79	43	28	48	74	43	36	Arms exports
Russia	3 115	3 975	4 174	4 086	5 233	5 733	5 976	6 126	Arms exports
Slovakia	43	65	50	103	34	46	84	62	Arms exports
South Africa	140	210	226	223	264	435	. .	. .	Licences for arms exports
Spain	218	176	144	228	282	459	522	521	Arms exports
Sweden	530	519	541	327	384	851	1 026	1 155	Arms exports
	668	553	707	534	732	1 254	1 455	1 416	Arms exports (including other equipment, services and software to military users)
Switzerland	176	181	144	169	194	299	240	207	Arms exports
Turkey	96	98	140	148	269	351	203	337	Arms exports
UK	3 905	1 861	2 953	2 434	1 533	1 720	2 633	2 527	Arms exports
	11 965	8 064	7 561	6 694	6 706	7 878	9 772	12 986	Arms exports (including aerospace equipment and services)
Ukraine	359	. .	567	551	543	531	. .	. .	Arms exports
USA	18 664	19 949	14 344	9 952	10 692	11 172	11 828	11 552	Arms exports
	18 240	20 569	12 376	14 142	11 488	12 785	18 920	. .	Arms exports (foreign military sales added to commercial exports)

. . = No data available.

Note: Conversion to constant (2005) US$ is made using the market exchange rates of the reporting year and the US consumer price index (CPI). The countries included in this table are those that provide official financial data on their arms exports for at least 4 of the 8 years covered. SIPRI estimates that together they account for over 90% of exports of conventional arms. By totalling the financial value of these exports it is possible to estimate the value of the global arms trade. The national arms export data in this table are not entirely reliable or comparable between years. For certain countries, data on the value of arms export licences have been used because these are the only figures available.

[a] Totals are based on data provided annually by each country. Where data is unavailable totals include estimates based on the average rate of change in the sample as a whole. Because some governments present more than one set of data, the totals are presented as a range between the aggregate of the lowest and the aggregate of the highest reported values. When calculating annual totals national figures are converted to calendar years, assuming equal distribution over the range of years.

Sources: Data are based on published information or direct communication with governments or official industry bodies. For a full list of sources and all available financial data on arms exports see URL <http://www.sipri.org/contents/armstrad/at_gov_ind_data.html>.

Appendix 10B. Sources and methods for arms transfers data

THE SIPRI ARMS TRANSFERS PROJECT

The SIPRI Arms Transfers Project reports on international flows of conventional weapons. Since publicly available information is inadequate for the tracking of all weapons and other military equipment, SIPRI covers only what it terms *major conventional weapons*. Data are collected from open sources for the SIPRI Arms Transfers Database and presented in a register that identifies the suppliers, recipients and weapons delivered,[1] and in tables that provide a measure of the trends in the total flow of major weapons and its geographical pattern. SIPRI has developed a unique trend-indicator value (TIV) system. This value is not comparable to financial data such as gross domestic product, public expenditure or export/import figures.

The database covers the period from 1950. Data collection and analysis are continuous processes. As new data become available the database is updated for all years included in the database.[2]

I. Revision of methods in 2006

New published information on arms transfers often includes new delivery data. This is also true for data on individual systems, which may necessitate a new calculation of their TIV. From time to time, however, more significant and generic modifications are introduced to reflect the changing reality of arms transfers or to make use of new sources of information. In the 1980s, for example, radar systems were added to the database. In 2006 several changes were introduced into the coverage of the database, while the calculation of the SIPRI TIV for production under licence was reviewed and modified. These changes have been made retroactively for the entire database in order to preserve a meaningful time series from 1950.

Revisions to the range of coverage

In 2006 the coverage of the database was expanded to include: (*a*) turrets with guns of at least 20-millimetre calibre for tanks and other armoured vehicles; and (*b*) turrets with guns of at least 57-mm calibre (or with several guns with a 57-mm combined calibre) for ships. Generally, these are not stand-alone systems but are subsystems of

---

[1] This register of transfers of major conventional weapons appeared in previous editions of the SIPRI Yearbook, but is now available on the SIPRI website in 2 formats: a register with the data used for the analysis presented in this chapter, and a more flexible searchable database with the most recent data. SIPRI's online database is continually updated. See URL <http://www.sipri.org/contents/armstrad/>.

[2] Thus, data from several editions of the SIPRI Yearbook or other SIPRI publications cannot be combined or compared. Readers who require time-series TIV data for periods before the years covered in this volume should contact the the SIPRI Arms Transfers Project via URL <http://www.sipri.org/contents/armstrad/>.

platforms classified by SIPRI as 'major weapons'. In this respect they are similar to many of the radar systems added to the coverage in the 1980s.

These subsystems are only included when they are supplied from a country other than the supplier of the platform on which they are mounted. They are also included when used for the modernization of existing platforms. Generally, the number of items is derived from the number of platforms, but where available, exact numbers of ordered and delivered items are used. These subsystems are included because: they provide a more complete picture of arms transfer relations between suppliers and recipients; they are for the most part technically advanced systems and as such important (and often export controlled); and because major platforms are becoming more and more dependent on such components supplied from other countries. It also makes it possible to capture at least part of the trend for 'cooperative' weapons. They can be included because they are discrete items that can be identified from open sources as a specific 'measurable' component.

With regard to SIPRI's register, this means that additional information is available on some of the major components of conventional weapons. For the TIV tables the value of the platform would be reduced by the value of the components, and the TIV of the components would appear as coming from a supplier different to the supplier of the platform. Alternatively, in cases of components supplied for indigenous platforms, the TIV of the component would be listed where previously nothing would have been listed.

Revisions to the SIPRI trend-indicator value

The SIPRI TIV for weapons produced under licence has been reviewed. While weapons are still listed separately in the register when the recipient is involved in their production, this involvement no longer affects the calculation of the TIV. The previous calculation of the percentage of input from the licenser was problematic and margins of error large, especially in cases with a high input.

II. Selection criteria and coverage

Selection criteria

SIPRI uses the term 'arms transfer' rather than 'arms trade' because the latter is usually associated with 'sale'. SIPRI covers not only sales of weapons, including manufacturing licences, but also other forms of weapon supply, such as aid and gifts.

The weapons transferred must be destined for the armed forces, paramilitary forces or intelligence agencies of another country. Weapons supplied to or from rebel forces in an armed conflict are included as deliveries to or from the individual rebel forces, identified under separate 'recipient' or 'supplier' headings. Supplies to or from international organizations are also included and categorized in the same fashion. In cases where deliveries are identified but it is not possible to identify either the supplier or the recipient with an acceptable degree of certainty, transfers are registered as coming from 'unknown' suppliers or going to 'unknown' recipients. Suppliers are termed 'multiple' only if there is a transfer agreement for weapons produced by two or more cooperating countries and if it is not clear which country will make the delivery.

Weapons must be transferred voluntarily by the supplier. This includes weapons delivered illegally—without proper authorization by the government of the supplier or the recipient country—but excludes captured weapons and weapons obtained from defectors. Finally, the weapons must have a military purpose. Systems such as aircraft used mainly for other branches of government but registered with and operated by the armed forces are excluded. Weapons supplied for technical or arms procurement evaluation purposes only are not included.

Major conventional weapons: the coverage

SIPRI covers only what it terms *major conventional weapons*, defined as:

1. *Aircraft*: all fixed-wing aircraft and helicopters, including unmanned reconnaissance/surveillance aircraft, with the exception of microlight aircraft, powered and unpowered gliders and target drones.

2. *Armoured vehicles*: all vehicles with integral armour protection, including all types of tank, tank destroyer, armoured car, armoured personnel carrier, armoured support vehicle and infantry fighting vehicle. Only vehicles with very light armour protection (such as trucks with an integral but lightly armoured cabin) are excluded.

3. *Artillery*: naval, fixed, self-propelled and towed guns, howitzers, multiple rocket launchers and mortars, with a calibre equal to or above 100 mm.

4. *Sensors*: (*a*) all land-, aircraft- and ship-based active (radar) and passive (e.g. electro-optical) surveillance systems with a range of at least 25 kilometres, with the exception of navigation and weather radars, (*b*) all fire-control radars, with the exception of range-only radars, and (*c*) Anti-submarine warfare and anti-ship sonar systems for ships and helicopters. In cases where the system is fitted on a platform (vehicle, aircraft or ship), the register only notes those systems that come from a different supplier from that of the platform.

5. *Air defence systems*: (*a*) all land-based surface-to-air missile (SAM) systems, and (*b*) all anti-aircraft guns with a calibre of more than 40 mm. This includes self-propelled systems on armoured or unarmoured chassis.

6. *Missiles*: all powered, guided missiles and torpedoes with conventional warheads. Unguided rockets, guided but unpowered shells and bombs, free-fall aerial munitions, anti-submarine rockets and target drones are excluded.

7. *Ships*: (*a*) all ships with a standard tonnage of 100 tonnes or more, and (*b*) all ships armed with artillery of 100-mm calibre or more, torpedoes or guided missiles, with the exception of most survey ships, tugs and some transport ships.

8. *Engines*: (*a*) engines for military aircraft, for example, combat-capable aircraft, larger military transport and support aircraft, including helicopters; (*b*) engines for combat ships, such as fast attack craft, corvettes, frigates, destroyers, cruisers, aircraft carriers and submarines; (*c*) engines for most armoured vehicles—generally engines of more than 200 horsepower output. In cases where the system is fitted on a platform (vehicle, aircraft or ship), the register only notes those systems that come from a different supplier from the supplier of the platform.

9. *Other*: (*a*) all turrets for armoured vehicles fitted with a gun of at least 20-mm calibre or with guided anti-tank missiles, (*b*) all turrets for ships fitted with a gun of at least 57-mm calibre, and (*c*) all turrets for ships fitted with multiple guns with a combined calibre of at least 57 mm. In cases where the system is fitted on a platform

(vehicle or ship), the register only notes those systems that come from a different supplier from the supplier of the platform.

The statistics presented refer to transfers of weapons in these nine categories only. Transfers of other military equipment—such as small arms and light weapons, trucks, artillery under 100-mm calibre, ammunition, support equipment and components, as well as services or technology transfers—are not included.

III. The SIPRI trend indicator

The SIPRI system for the valuation of arms transfers is designed as a trend-measuring device. It allows the measurement of changes in the total flow of major weapons and its geographical pattern. The trends presented in the tables of SIPRI trend-indicator values are based only on actual deliveries during the year or years covered in the relevant tables and figures, not on orders signed in a year.

The TIV system, in which similar weapons have similar values, shows both the quantity and quality of the weapons transferred—in other words, it describes the transfer of military resources. It does not reflect the financial value of (or payments for) weapons transferred. This is impossible for three reasons. First, in many cases no reliable data on the value of a transfer are available. Second, even if the value of a transfer is known, in almost every case it is the total value of a deal, which may include not only the weapons themselves but also other items related to these weapons (e.g. spare parts, armament or ammunition) as well as support systems (e.g. specialized vehicles) and items related to the integration of the weapon in the armed forces (e.g. training, or software changes to existing systems). Third, even if the value of a transfer is known, important details about the financial arrangements of the transfer (e.g. credit or loan conditions and discounts) are often unavailable.[3]

Measuring the military implications of transfers would require a concentration on the value of the weapons as a military resource. Again, this could be done from the actual money values of the weapons transferred, assuming that these values generally reflect the military capability of the weapon. However, the problems listed above would still apply (e.g. a very expensive weapon may be transferred as aid at a 'zero' price, and therefore not show up in financial statistics, but still be a significant transfer of military resources). The SIPRI solution is a system in which military resources are measured by including an evaluation of the technical parameters of weapons. The purpose and performance of a weapon are evaluated, and it is assigned a value in an index that reflects its value as a military resource in relation to other weapons. This can be done under the condition that a number of benchmarks or reference points are established by assigning some weapons a fixed place in the index, thus forming its core. All other weapons are compared to these core weapons.

In short, the process of calculating the SIPRI TIV for individual weapons is as follows. For a number of weapon types it is possible to find the average unit acquisition price in open sources. It is assumed that such real prices roughly reflect the military resource value of a system. For example, a combat aircraft bought for $10 million may be assumed to be a resource twice as great as one bought for

---

[3] It is possible to present a very rough idea of the economic factors from the financial statistics now available from most arms-exporting countries. However, most of these statistics lack sufficient detail.

$5 million, and a submarine bought for $100 million may be assumed to be 10 times the resource a $10 million combat aircraft would represent. Weapons with a real price are used as the core weapons of the valuation. Weapons for which a price is not known are compared with core weapons in the following steps.

1. The description of a weapon is compared with the description of the core weapon. In cases where no core weapon exactly matches the description of the weapon for which a price is to be found, the closest match is sought.

2. Standard characteristics of size and performance (weight, speed, range and pay-load) are compared with those of a core weapon of a similar description. For example, a 15 000-kilogram combat aircraft would be compared with a combat air-craft of similar size.

3. Other characteristics, such as the type of electronics, loading or unloading arrangements, engine, tracks or wheels, armament and materials, are compared.

4. Weapons are compared with a core weapon from the same period.

Weapons in a 'used' condition are given a value 40 per cent of that of a new weapon. Used weapons that have been significantly refurbished or modified by the supplier before delivery (and have thereby become a greater military resource) are given a value of 66 per cent of the value when new. In reality there may be huge differences in the military resource value of a used weapon depending on its condition and the modifications during the years of use.

The SIPRI trend indicator does not take into account the conditions under which a weapon is operated (e.g. an F-16 combat aircraft operated by well-balanced, well-trained and well-integrated armed forces has a much greater military value than the same aircraft operated by a developing country; the resource is the same but the effect is very different). The trend indicator also accepts the prices of the core weapons as genuine rather than reflecting costs that, even if officially part of the programme, are not exclusively related to the weapon itself. For example, funds that appear to be allocated to a particular weapon programme could be related to optional add-ons and armament or to the development of basic technology that will be included (free of cost) in other programmes. Such funds could also act, in effect, as government subsidies to keep industry in business by paying more than the weapon is worth.

IV. Sources

The Arms Transfers Project uses a variety of sources to collect data: newspapers; periodicals and journals; books, monographs and annual reference works; and official national and international documents. The common criterion for all these sources is that they are open, that is, published and available to the public.

Such open information cannot, however, provide a comprehensive picture of world arms transfers. Published reports often provide only partial information, and substantial disagreement between them is common. Order and delivery dates and exact numbers (or even types) of weapons ordered and delivered, or the identity of suppliers or recipients, may not always be clear. Exercising judgement and making informed estimates are therefore important elements in compiling the SIPRI Arms Transfers Database. Estimates are conservative and may very well be underestimates.

All sources of data as well as calculations of estimates, while not published by SIPRI, are documented in the SIPRI database.

Appendix 10C. Towards an arms trade treaty?

PAUL HOLTOM and SIEMON T. WEZEMAN

I. Introduction

The most significant developments for conventional arms control in 2006 were the agreement reached in the United Nations General Assembly on the principle of a legally binding and universal arms trade treaty (ATT), and the establishment of a group of governmental experts to examine the issue. These achievements contrasted with the lack of progress at the review conference for the UN Programme of Action (POA) on small arms and light weapons (SALW).[1]

The issue of global guidelines for the control of conventional arms has been on the international agenda for a long time. In 1925 the League of Nations produced a draft Convention on the Arms Trade that was never adopted. Disarmament is an element of the UN Charter and the question of conventional arms control has been frequently discussed in the General Assembly's annual deliberations on armaments. In contrast to chemical, biological and nuclear weapons, which are governed by global conventions prohibiting their transfer, there are no global conventions or treaties prohibiting or restricting transfers of conventional weapons.[2]

During the cold war the two blocs, and individual countries, used conventional weapon transfers with little restraint to establish or maintain spheres of influence. In the early to mid-1990s issues relating to conventional weapon proliferation began to attract more attention, and several sets of guidelines or principles on arms transfers were agreed by groups of countries, which included some of the largest arms exporters.[3] In 1991 the UN Register of Conventional Arms (UNROCA) was established to promote transparency in the conventional arms trade.

In the mid-1990s the global focus shifted towards SALW (leading to the 2001 UN SALW Conference), which were regarded as the most destabilizing conventional weapons.[4] However, by 2006 attention had moved back to conventional weapons as a whole, and the principle of an ATT was agreed by the UN. As with the SALW process, the ATT initiative emerged from a civil society campaign, pioneered by a group

---

[1] The United Nations Programme of Action to Prevent, Combat and Eradicate the Illicit Trade in Small Arms and Light Weapons in All Its Aspects (POA). In this appendix SALW are defined in accordance with the definition agreed within the UN.

[2] On chemical and biological weapon control see chapter 13 in this volume and on nuclear weapon control see chapter 12.

[3] These include the principles of the Organization for Security and Co-operation in Europe, United Nations guidelines, the guidelines of the 5 permanent members of the UN Security Council and European Union criteria. See Goldblat, J., SIPRI and International Peace Research Institute Oslo, *Arms Control: The New Guide to Negotiations and Agreements* (Sage Publications: London, 2002), pp. 241–46.

[4] See UN General Assembly Resolution A/RES/50/70, 15 Jan. 1996. UN resolutions, draft resolutions and other official UN documents are available at UN documentation service web page at URL <http://www.un.org/documents/>. UN press releases are available at URL <http://www.un.org/News/Press/archives.htm>. On the 2001 UN Conference on The Illicit Trade in Small Arms and Light Weapons in All Its Aspects and the 2006 review conference see URL <http://disarmament.un.org/cab/salw.html>.

of Nobel Peace Prize Laureates, which was later taken up by governments and brought within the UN framework.

Section II of this appendix briefly analyses the failure of the 2006 review conference. Section III focuses on the evolution of the ATT initiative, and section IV examines the key issues that must be addressed if a meaningful ATT is to be achieved. Section V presents the conclusions.

II. The breakdown of the small arms and light weapons process

By 2001 there was a global consensus that SALW posed serious problems for peace, security and stability. However, there was disagreement on the extent of the problem and, more importantly, on how it should be resolved. Ultimately, the 2001 UN SALW conference focused narrowly on 'illicit' trade. Its key outcome was the POA, which tasked governments with several measures to combat the illicit SALW trade.[5] In addition to biennial reviews, it was agreed that after five years the POA would be assessed, modified if necessary, and that efforts would be made to reach agreement on new issues to be addressed within the POA framework. The first clear signs that the review conference would not meet this goal were evident in the preparatory meeting in January 2006. A lack of consensus—mainly on the issues of ammunition possession, prohibitions on transfers to non-state actors and global guidelines for SALW transfers[6]—prevented the adoption of an official agenda for the conference.[7] At the review conference in New York in July 2006, opposition from a number of states on the same issues ensured that the conference concluded without agreement on a final document and failed to provide 'either a mandate to conduct a further review in five years, or guidance on future implementation'.[8]

The difficulty of achieving consensus within the UN system is regarded as one of the reasons for conference's lack of success.[9] It has been argued that it was the 'tyranny of the minority'—China, Cuba, Egypt, India, Iran, Israel, Pakistan, Russia and the United States—and its calls for a narrow interpretation of the conference agenda, that obstructed the POA process.[10] This minority is largely formed of the same countries that have consistently blocked attempts to broaden the process since the 2001 SALW conference. The inclusion of global principles governing SALW transfers were initially blocked by Cuba, Iran, Pakistan and the USA (although Cuba, Iran and Pakistan reportedly withdrew their opposition to the final conference

---

[5] For an overall assessment of developments relating to the POA see *Reviewing Action on Small Arms 2006: Assessing the First Five Years of the UN Programme of Action by Biting the Bullet* (Biting the Bullet: Bradford, 2006).

[6] See United Nations, 'Press conference by president-designate of conference on small arms, light weapons', Press release, New York, 21 June 2006.

[7] See the draft provisional agenda. United Nations, 'Preparatory committee for review conference on illicit small arms trade concludes session without agreement on draft final document', Press release, UN document DC/3011, 20 Jan 2006.

[8] United Nations, 'United Nations conference aimed at strengthening global effort against illicit small arms trade ends without agreement on final document', Press release, UN document DC/3037, 7 July 2006. For a non-governmental perspective on the review conference see Stohl, R., 'UN conference on tackling small arms ends in deadlock', *Jane's Intelligence Review*, Sep. 2006, pp. 44–46; and 'UN small arms conference deadlocks', *Arms Control Today*, vol. 36, no. 7 (Sep. 2006), pp. 46–47.

[9] Stohl (note 8), p. 45.

[10] Peters, R., 'Small arms and light weapons: making the UN Programme of Action work', *Disarmament Diplomacy*, no. 82 (spring 2006), URL <http//www.acronym.org.uk/dd/dd82/82rp.htm>.

document, while the USA remained opposed).[11] The USA also made clear that it would not compromise on the 'redlines' it laid down in 2001 on transfers to non-state actors, the development of legally binding agreements and the domestic implications of monitoring and restricting arms transfers.[12] Sierra Leone's representative at the review conference expressed the frustration of the majority: 'we shall not depend on this concept of consensus, which, in my view, has been used as a weapon to destroy the work we have done, the work that you have done, and all that we have put in'.[13]

Six years after the 2001 UN SALW conference, the USA's lack of support is still the main barrier to an effective global regime for controlling SALW transfers. Nevertheless, two positive results emerged from the review conference. First, the global community remains committed to the POA as a framework for global and national action to combat the illicit trade in SALW. For example, Canada suggested an informal intersessional meeting of states in 2007 to discuss measures to accelerate implementation of the existing POA and the potential for development outside the UN SALW process,[14] and a biennial meeting of states is still scheduled for 2008.[15] Second, several countries used the conference to sound out opinions on an ATT. While the issue was not discussed at length, there was enough feedback to convince those governments in favour to propose a draft resolution in the General Assembly in late 2006.

III. Evolution of the arms trade treaty initiative

The current proposal for an ATT draws on the principles of the Nobel Peace Laureates' International Code of Conduct on Arms Transfers and Draft Framework Convention on International Arms Transfers.[16] These documents call on governments to adhere to their commitments on international human rights and humanitarian law when considering applications for export licences. The Draft Framework Convention also calls for a universal, legally binding agreement governing international arms transfers. It was first circulated at the 2001 UN SALW Conference; an early example of how the campaigns for improving SALW controls and the ATT initiative have converged.

In October 2003, the non-governmental organizations (NGOs) Amnesty International, Oxfam and the International Action Network on Small Arms (IANSA) launched the Control Arms campaign, the main purpose of which was to promote an

---

[11] Stohl (note 8), p. 45.

[12] Opening statement by Joseph, R., US Undersecretary of State for Arms Control and International Security, quoted in Stohl (note 8), pp. 45–46. The US National Rifle Association mobilized its members to send over 100 000 letters of protest to the UN. Prior to the review conference UN Secretary General Kofi Annan felt 'forced' to issue a statement stating that there would be no attempt to impose a ban on the legal trade and use of arms. He also felt obliged to deny there were plans to hold a conference session on 4 July 2006, US Independence Day. United Nations, 'UN not negotiating "global gun ban", nor is there intention to deny law-abiding citizens right to bear arms', Press release, UN document DC/3031, 26 June 2006; and United Nations (note 6).

[13] United Nations, 'Conference aimed at strengthening global effort against illicit small arms trade ends without agreement on final document', Press release, UN document DC/3037, 7 July, 2006.

[14] United Nations (note 13).

[15] United Nations General Assembly, Revised draft resolution, 'The illicit trade in small arms and light weapons in all its aspects', UN document A/C.1/61/L.15/REV.1, 19 Oct. 2006.

[16] Both documents are available at the Arms Trade Treaty website, URL <http://www.armstrade treaty.com/>.

ATT.[17] The campaign seeks harmonization of the criteria, standards, interpretations and implementation of national arms transfer controls as a means of preventing 'irresponsible' transfers. It proposes a set of legally binding principles that clearly define the international legal commitments and responsibilities of states and calls for compliance with these principles to be monitored and verified, and for sanctions against transgressors. It also recommends what governments should consider with regard to end-use and end-users when authorizing arms transfers.[18]

As with the NGO-led campaigns against anti-personnel mines and for tighter controls on the transfer, use and disposal of SALW,[19] the Control Arms campaign persuaded a large number of states to promote, and lobby other states to support, the ATT initiative.[20] In September 2004, the UK became the first permanent member of the UN Security Council to back the initiative.[21] The European Union (EU) issued a statement of support the following autumn.[22] On 24 July 2006 the governments of Argentina, Australia, Costa Rica, Finland, Japan, Kenya and the UK circulated a draft resolution, 'Towards an Arms Trade Treaty', among the members of the UN General Assembly First Committee. By 10 October 2006, the number of co-sponsors had reached 77.[23]

The draft resolution acknowledged the right of states to manufacture and trade conventional arms for self-defence and security, but also stated that the 'absence of common international standards on the import, export and transfer of conventional arms is a contributory factor to conflict, the displacement of people, crime and terrorism'.[24] It was emphasized that a legally binding instrument should be 'negotiated on a non-discriminatory, transparent and multilateral basis' to establish common global transfer control standards. On 26 October 2006 the draft resolution was adopted in the UN General Assembly First Committee with the support of 139 governments. The USA voted against and there were 24 abstentions. In the General Assembly vote on 6 December, 14 more governments voted in favour, with no change in the number of abstaining and opposing states.[25] In 2007 the UN Secretary-General will publish a report on the views of member states before establishing a group of governmental experts (GGE) in 2008 to examine 'the feasibility, scope and

[17] See the website of the Control Arms campaign, URL <http://www.controlarms.org>.

[18] See Control Arms, *Compilation of Global Principles for Arms Transfers* (Control Arms: London, 9 Aug. 2006).

[19] On the International Campaign to Ban Landmines see URL <http://www.icbl.org/>. For a comparison of the development of the NGO initiatives see Brem, S. and Rutherford, K., 'Walking together or a divided agenda? Comparing landmines and small arms campaigns', *Security Dialogue*, vol. 32, no. 2 (2001), pp. 169–86.

[20] In 2003 Cambodia, Costa Rica, Finland, Iceland, and Mali announced their support for an ATT.

[21] 'Britain backs arms treaty calls', BBC News, 30 Sep. 2004, URL <http://news.bbc.co.uk/2/3704322.stm>; and Straw, J., British Foreign Secretary, 'Securing a global arms trade treaty', Speech given at the Institute of Civil Engineers, London, 15 Mar. 2005, URL <http://www.fco.gov.uk/>.

[22] Council of the European Union, 'EU Council conclusions on an international treaty on the arms trade', 2678th General Affairs Council meeting, Luxembourg 3 Oct. 2005, URL <http://www.europa-eu-un.org/articles/en/article_5080_en.htm>.

[23] For the text of the draft and a full list of co-sponsors see United Nations, 'Towards an arms trade treaty: establishing common international standards for the import, export and transfer of conventional arms', Draft resolution, UN document A/C.1/61/L.55, 12 Oct 2006.

[24] United Nations (note 23).

[25] On both occasions, the USA was the sole 'no' vote. Of the 24 countries that abstained on 26 Oct. 2006, Cuba and Djibouti voted for the resolution on 7 Dec. 2006, while Somalia was absent from the vote. Laos, the Marshall Islands and Zimbabwe were absent from the 26 Oct. vote but abstained on 7 Dec. 2006. United Nations (note 23); UN General Assembly Resolution A/RES/61/89, 18 Dec. 2006.

draft parameters for a comprehensive, legally binding instrument establishing common international standards for the import, export and transfer of conventional arms'.[26]

IV. Key issues for an arms trade treaty

Proposals for an ATT have been kept deliberately vague in the hope of encouraging frank, open, non-judgemental, multilateral talks. A number of issues will need to be addressed by the GGE, including the scope in terms of transfers and actors; the development of global legally binding guidelines; monitoring, verification and sanctions mechanisms; and the balancing of supplier and recipient political and economic interests.

Scope

Despite calls for the ATT's coverage to be 'comprehensive in scope', its range has not yet been elaborated. The experience of negotiating the UNROCA suggests that agreement on the types of conventional arms that an ATT would cover could be difficult to achieve.[27] Although the expanded categories of the UNROCA could serve as a model, other options exist to help set the scope of the ATT, for example, the control lists developed, respectively, by the Organization for Security and Co-operation in Europe (OSCE) and the Wassenaar Arrangement on Export Controls for Conventional Arms and Dual-use Goods (WA).[28] It is also necessary to decide if an ATT will apply to transfers of spare parts, components, upgrade kits, arms-making equipment and dual-use goods, as well as other technology transfers and licensed production. Transit and trans-shipment controls should also be addressed, as well as the issue of periodic reviews and updates.

Defining the range of actors covered by an ATT will also pose problems. Although international organizations and transfer control regimes have produced best practice guidelines on brokering in recent years,[29] it took five years to establish a GGE to explore 'steps to enhance international cooperation in preventing, combating and eradicating illicit brokering'.[30] Such protracted progress suggests that achieving global agreement on brokering will be a challenge.

The issue of rebel groups as recipients is also likely to be problematic. Some sub-Saharan African states have argued for a global prohibition on SALW transfers to

---

[26] UN General Assembly Resolution A/RES/61/89 (note 25).

[27] Laurance, E. J., Wezeman, S. T. and Wulf, H., *Arms Watch: SIPRI Report on the First Year of the UN Register of Conventional Arms*, SIPRI Research Report no. 6 (Oxford University Press: Oxford, 1993), pp. 10–13.

[28] See the SIPRI Arms Transfers Project website for the OSCE and WA control lists, URL <http://www.sipri.org/contents/armstrad/>. On the WA see see chapter 15 in this volume.

[29] E.g. 'Council Common Position 2003/468/CFSP on the control of arms brokering', 23 June 2003, *Official Journal of the European Union*, L 156/79 (25 June 2003); OSCE, 'National control of brokering activities', *Handbook of Best Practices on Small Arms and Light Weapons* (OSCE: Vienna, 2003), URL <http://www.osce.org/fsc/item_11_13550.html>; and Wassenaar Arrangement, 'Elements for effective legislation on arms brokering', Dec. 2003, URL, <http://www.wassenaar.org/publicdocuments/2003_effectivelegislation.html>.

[30] See UN General Assembly Resolution A/RES/60/81, 11 Jan. 2006.

such groups due to their destabilizing impact.[31] In contrast, the USA is opposed to a complete ban on arms transfers to rebel groups since this would remove the option of providing military support to 'pro-democratic' rebels in 'totalitarian countries'. Despite opposing a blanket ban, the USA has been the leading advocate for prohibiting transfers of man-portable air defence systems (MANPADS) to rebel groups, as well as accepting UN Security Council arms embargoes that specifically target certain rebel groups.[32] It remains to be seen whether a nuanced position on non-state actors as recipients can be forged and adopted within the framework of an ATT.

Global, legally binding guidelines

Despite the lack of a legally binding treaty on conventional arms exports, groups of supplier and recipient states have sought to develop common minimum standards and guidelines for controlling arms transfers. Although in some cases these ad hoc political approaches have proved effective, there have also been efforts to make guidelines legally binding, such as the recent discussion within the EU on its Code of Conduct on Arms Transfers.[33]

In contrast, US officials are reportedly concerned that 'the only way for a global arms trade treaty to work is to have everyone agree on a standard. . . . For us, that standard would be so far below what we are already required to do under US law that we had to vote against it in order to maintain our higher standards'.[34] This position seems to conflict with the 1999 US Congress International Arms Sales Code of Conduct, which required the USA to begin negotiations 'to establish an international regime . . . to limit, restrict, or prohibit arms transfers to countries that do not observe certain fundamental values of human liberty, peace, and international stability'.[35]

Russian officials have also expressed doubts that legally binding criteria can be achieved because of the potentially 'subjective' nature of criteria-based assessments.[36] In this regard, the EU Code of Conduct illustrates the challenges of reaching agreement on how to interpret and implement a set of agreed common standards among (supposedly) like-minded states. Disagreements in the WA show the difficulties in achieving similar objectives when the group is composed of states that hold very different opinions on what constitutes a responsible 'end-user'.

At present, UN Security Council arms embargoes are the only global, legally binding prohibitions on arms transfers. However, as sanctions committees and panels

---

[31] E.g. Nigerian representatives pushed for a ban on SALW transfers to non-state actors at the 2006 SALW Review Conference, arguing that arms transfers should only be allowed for legitimate national defence and security needs or for peacekeeping. United Nations, 'Security Council debates global progress against illicit small arms trade', Press release, UN document SC/8667, 20 Mar. 2006; and United Nations, 'International arms trade treaty aim of draft resolution approved by disarmament committee', Press release, 26 Oct. 2006, UN document GA/DIS/3335.

[32] On non-state actors and embargoes see chapter 10; on MANPADS see appendix 14A in this volume.

[33] On the EU Code of Conduct see chapter 15 in this volume.

[34] Dent, J., 'Britain welcomes UN arms control vote', *The Guardian*, 27 Oct. 2006.

[35] International Arms Sales Code of Conduct Act of 1999, Part of HR 3194, Consolidated Appropriations Act, 106th Congress, 1st session, <http://www.fas.org/asmp/campaigns/code/intlcodetext.html>.

[36] See United Nations, 'International arms trade treaty aim of draft resolution approved by disarmament committee', Press release, UN document GA/DIS/3335, 26 Oct 2006 URL <http://www.un.org/News/Press/>; and Kozyulin, V., 'Istoria mezhdunarodnykh initsiativ po sozdaniyu dogovora o torgovle oruzheiem' [History of the international initiative to create a treaty on the arms trade'], *Eksport vooruzhenii*, July–Aug. 2006, pp. 25–26.

of experts monitoring these embargoes report, not all UN members comply with arms embargo demands.

Monitoring, verification and sanction mechanisms

One of the most innovative proposals of the ATT initiative (although not detailed in the draft ATT resolution) is for mechanisms to monitor and verify compliance as well as to impose sanctions for non-compliance. If implemented, these measures would remedy one of the major shortcomings of existing transfer control arrangements, and under such conditions compulsory reporting to UNROCA could be realistically considered. However, such levels of public transparency may not be acceptable to all UN members.[37] For example, Pyotr Litavrin, head of the Russian Ministry of Foreign Affairs Department for Questions of Security and Disarmament, reportedly asked how 'it is possible to operate a mechanism for monitoring and controlling [compliance with] an ATT, as well as a mechanism for comparing and verifying [data] that is received'.[38]

There are examples of prohibitive arms control treaties that include elaborate verification apparata, compliance mechanisms and non-compliance measures.[39] However, it is unlikely that such intrusive mechanisms could be established to verify compliance with an ATT. One alternative is a permanent international sanctions committee, which would collect national reports on transfers and cases of concern to be investigated in a manner comparable to UN sanctions committees. However, such a body would be unlikely to avoid the problems these committees face in sanctioning arms embargo violators.

Balancing the interests of suppliers and importers

The ATT initiative is notable for the role played by states that are not major arms producers or suppliers. Because of its non-discriminatory nature the initiative has attracted strong support among states in sub-Saharan Africa and Latin America, unlike 'exclusive' international supplier groups such as the WA. The initiative has also provided a framework for African and Latin American countries to discuss global principles for international arms transfers with European states.[40] However, Cuba, Israel and Libya have expressed fears that ATT guidelines could be used for political ends to block arms transfers to countries that are merely attempting to meet their legitimate defence needs.[41] There are also concerns that an ATT could lead to the establishment of yet another 'supplier cartel' for conventional arms.[42] States from

---

[37] Laurance, Wezeman and Wolf (note 27).

[38] Kozyulin (note 36).

[39] E.g the Treaty on the Elimination of Intermediate-range and Shorter-range Missiles, and the Chemical Weapons Convention. For a discussion of these mechanisms see Anthony, I., 'Reflections on continuity and change in arms control', *SIPRI Yearbook 2006: Armaments, Disarmament and International Security* (Oxford University Press: Oxford, 2006), p. 601.

[40] E.g see the Finland–Tanzania-led International Workshop on Global Principles for Arms Transfers, Dar es Salaam, Tanzania, 20–22 Feb. 2005, URL <http://www.saferafrica.org/DocumentsCentre/Conferences/SaferAfrica/Continental/TanzaniaFeb2005/Content.php>.

[41] United Nations, 'International arms trade treaty aim of draft resolution approved by Disarmament Committee', Press release, UN document GA/DIS/3335, 26 Oct. 2006.

[42] 'UN initiates arms trade agreement', BBC News, 27 Oct. 2006, URL <http://www.bbc.co.uk/2/6088200.stm>.

the developing world have already expressed dissatisfaction with current arms control regimes in these terms.[43]

Supplier states not only want to preserve their ability to use transfer controls as a foreign policy tool (to deny arms to foes and supply allies), but also to protect their commercial and economic interests. Therefore, support for the ATT initiative by the British Defence Manufacturers Association could be viewed as a sign that the British Government does not foresee that an ATT would significantly affect transfer controls or arms sales.[44] It remains to be seen whether other national arms industries can be similarly reassured. For example, because the Russian arms industry is particularly export dependent and some of its recipients are not universally regarded as responsible end-users, Russian concerns and demands could be especially hard to overcome.[45] While France has expressed support for an ATT, China and the USA remain unconvinced of its value. For an ATT to succeed, it seems clear that differences of opinion between the permanent members of the UN Security Council need to be dealt with, not least because 'these five countries alone are responsible for the majority of the global arms trade'.[46]

Although the ATT initiative offers an opportunity for the suppliers and recipients to discuss their positions, needs and concerns, this does not mean that each side will understand or accept the other's position. The fact that a number of states are verbally committed to an ATT does not mean that the initiative will overcome the lack of political will or the strategic and commercial interests that make most 'supplier-based export controls little more than acts of tokenism'.[47]

V. Conclusions

Both the SALW and ATT processes have their roots in civil society campaigns. In both cases it was mainly civil society groups, organized on a global level, that offered suggestions to governments and pressured them to act, much as the Pugwash movement did in its campaign for nuclear arms control.[48]

Since its arrival on the UN agenda, the SALW control process has faced a number of daunting obstacles. Although no state wants to be seen as being in favour of 'illicit transfers', it has proven difficult to achieve agreement on definitions of 'illicit' and 'legal' transfers within the UN framework. One of the biggest stumbling blocks has been the complexity of the approach to the illicit trade in SALW, in which three connected but very different issues are conflated: the stability of countries, crime (both national and international), and private gun ownership. A small minority of states—

[43] On recipient concern about supplier control regimes see Mallik, A., *Technology and Security in the 21st Century: A Demand-side Perspective*, SIPRI Research Report no. 26 (Oxford University Press: Oxford, 2004).

[44] 'Arms trade treaty', *Defence Manufacturers Association News*, no. 35 (Jan. 2006), p. 4.

[45] On the current state of the Russian arms industry see chapter 10 and Cooper, J., 'Developments in the Russian arms industry', *SIPRI Yearbook 2006* (note 39), pp. 431–48.

[46] Stohl, R., Center for Defense Information, 'United Nations to consider arms trade treaty—US opposes', 15 Nov. 2006, URL <http://www.cdi.org/>. On the arms trade of China, France, Russia, the UK and the USA see also chapter 10 in this volume

[47] Cooper, N., 'What's the point of arms transfer controls?', *Contemporary Security Policy*, vol 27, no. 1 (Apr. 2006), p. 131.

[48] The Pugwash Conferences on Science and World Affairs is an international organization of scholars and public figures that seeks to limit armed conflict and find solutions to global security threats. It was founded in 1957 by Joseph Rotblat and Bertrand Russell in Pugwash, Nova Scotia.

the USA in particular—view the latter as a purely domestic issue and therefore a subject that should be kept off the agenda of global discussions.

The ATT initiative developed in parallel with the SALW process but now has the greater momentum. It attempts to establish a global framework in which legal definitions of a 'transfer', a 'weapon' and—most importantly—'situations in which transfers are to be restricted or prohibited' are clearly defined. Because it is broader in scope than the SALW process (in terms of types of weapons and transfers), it is likely to face greater challenges. None of the existing principles or guidelines on arms transfers has had a significant impact on controlling transfers to conflict zones and conflict-prone areas or to unstable states or regimes that are recognized as dictatorial or abusers of human-rights. However, while the ATT initiative draws on these existing mechanisms, it addresses past failures with its proposal for an effective verification and sanctions mechanism.

A number of states have already obstructed efforts to agree on clear legal definitions of what constitutes 'illicit' and 'legal' transfers in the SALW process, as well as blocking intrusive verification mechanisms as part of, for example, efforts to mark and trace weapons and ammunition. Furthermore, many countries already have difficulties in complying with the UNROCA, a relatively basic transparency mechanism. It is unlikely that these problems will be overcome in the near future, and some doubt that an effective, legally binding verification and sanctions mechanism is possible. In the short term, either a voluntary ATT or a legally binding but vague and weak ATT seem more realistic aims.

However, any such outcome would provide the potential for incremental improvements and, despite considerable challenges, the ATT initiative remains the most significant global development in conventional arms control for many years. It has put the issue firmly back on the UN agenda, which in recent times has focused perhaps too heavily on issues of weapons of mass destruction.

Part III. Non-proliferation, arms control and disarmament, 2006

11. Reducing security risks by controlling possession and use of civil materials

IAN ANTHONY

I. Introduction

In recent years the need to complement the traditional framework for arms control with other measures in order to adapt it to new security challenges has increasingly been recognized. In a number of cases initiatives have been taken to supplement the multi- and bilateral agreements that have traditionally been perceived as the core of arms control efforts.

The existing arms control agreements were designed to help manage the risk of attacks being mounted by the armed forces of states. As part of the effort to address that problem, bi- and multilateral arms control agreements referred to state behaviour when defining what would be subject to control. In a number of cases these agreements went further by identifying parts of the military establishment of states when defining the scope of controls and by developing detailed lists of objects to which restraint measures or reductions would apply.

Since the 11 September 2001 terrorist attacks on the United States there has been a much greater focus on how to block access to weapons by non-state actors and in particular by groups planning acts of mass-impact terrorism.[1] The effort to supplement the arms control framework to take into account the risks that non-state actors present has been stimulated by assessments that emphasize the potential threat that is posed by the possibility that such groups could succeed in acquiring weapons. In a 2006 speech the Director General of the United Kingdom's Security Service speculated that 'today we see the use of home-made improvised explosive devices; tomorrow's threat may include the use of chemicals, bacteriological agents, radioactive materials and even nuclear technology'.[2]

Efforts are needed to augment arms control with new measures tailored to current conditions. However, a number of observers have pointed out that in future, given the changing nature of the threats perceived in a number of countries and regions, it will be necessary to look even wider to identify the full range of threat-reduction tools that will be required. Soon after the 11 September attacks Jayantha Dhanapala, then the Undersecretary-General for Disarmament Affairs at the United Nations, noted that there are extremist groups in all regions that are prepared to use 'unthinkable methods to bring about the crash

---

[1] See appendix 11A.

[2] Manningham-Buller, E., 'The international terrorist threat to the UK', Speech at Queen Mary's College, London, 9 Nov. 2006, URL <http://www.mi5.gov.uk/output/Page568.html>.

of civilization in its entirety' and pointed to the need for a multidimensional response, including 'diverse, synergistic contributions'.[3] The focus on new, non-state groups is one key element of this multidimensional response. Another is the attempt to develop new and advanced international standards to manage and control a range of potentially dangerous materials that go beyond the lists of items traditionally associated with nuclear, biological and chemical weapons.

Section II of this chapter identifies and briefly describes some of the recent initiatives to develop security-related standards for materials not normally thought of as weapons. Section III briefly examines how the European Union (EU) has approached this issue in a region where civil goods move freely within a single market. The development of this approach is particularly complicated in Europe because in the areas discussed in this chapter it can be argued that control measures cut horizontally across the three 'pillars' on which the EU organizes its activities.[4]

Section IV examines efforts to engage with the private sector of industry as part of the overall security-building effort. A key part of this effort to develop and promote control standards is to enlist the support of a different group of non-state actors (in particular the private sector and the specialized research community) that are the custodians of many of the relevant materials, items and technologies. Engagement with these actors is at an early stage and will certainly be a complicated new challenge. The effort will probably include the incorporation of new standards in legislation and regulations that will make the non-governmental sector the target of security controls. However, it is also likely to include efforts to encourage that sector to develop voluntary standards and apply them, perhaps as part of the system of quality management.[5]

Some tentative conclusions are offered in the final section of the chapter. UN Security Council Resolution 1540 is discussed in appendix 11A, and the resolution is reproduced in appendix 11B.

II. Recent developments

Traditionally, arms control has mainly addressed the control of items that are specially designed, developed or adapted for military use, but there have been some efforts to deal with what are usually referred to as dual-use items. This term has been employed to classify items that were not specially designed, developed or adapted for military use but that could nevertheless be used by a state's armed forces in military programmes. One example of such an item is a chemical that has legitimate industrial applications but is also the direct precursor of a chemical weapon. Another example is a lathe that can be equipped

---

[3] Dhanapala, J., 'The impact of September 11 on multilateral arms control', *Arms Control Today*, Mar. 2002, URL <http://www.armscontrol.org/act/2002_03/dhanapalamarch02.asp>.

[4] On the 3 EU pillars see the glossary in this volume and section III below.

[5] According to the International Organization for Standardization (ISO) definition, total quality management consists of the coordinated activities to direct and control an organization with regard to quality, where quality is the degree to which a set of inherent characteristics fulfil stated requirements.

with numerical controls (software that determines the actions of the machine) and can work in more than two axes that can be coordinated simultaneously.

Such dual-use items are of interest to arms controllers because of their military potential. Interest in such items increased in the 1990s in the light of proof that some countries (notably, Iraq) had made the acquisition of dual-use items a central element of their arms procurement strategy. The dual-use issue remains an important part of the arms control discussion. However, this chapter focuses on items that are purely civil in their origin and technical specifications—but that could be put to harmful use—rather than on items that are dual-use in the sense that they have military applications.

A topical example can be used by way of illustration. Liquefied natural gas (LNG) is not a material of interest to any organized military force for battlefield use, nor can it be turned into a battlefield weapon.[6] However, if released, LNG will evaporate and the resulting vapour cloud can explode and burn when combined with air. In 2003 the US Government drew attention to the potential risk of a successful terrorist attack on the energy infrastructure of a country, including on LNG during storage or transport.[7] In future the quantity of LNG being produced and transported as well as the number and frequency of cargo movements are expected to rise significantly as this fuel plays an increasingly important part in energy strategy. Although in this case it was the USA that highlighted the issue, there is no Western monopoly of concern over security risks associated with LNG: the most important producers and exporters include several non-Western countries with a recent history of attacks that were carried out by non-state groups (including Algeria, Egypt, Indonesia, Nigeria, Qatar, Russia and the United Arab Emirates).[8]

The example of LNG illustrates another feature of the discussion about risks that emanate from the civil sector—the relationship between safety and security. In January 2004 an accident involving a train carrying LNG caused a major explosion and fire at the Sonatrach LNG facility at Skikda, Algeria.[9] Where there are inherent dangers associated with particular materials or processes there is a need to reduce the risk that lack of competence, negligence or the use of inappropriate or outdated equipment and methods will cause damaging accidents. The process of reducing this risk is normally referred to in different sectors as safety. Safety measures do not usually assume that individuals or groups with malicious intent are taking deliberate actions to cause damage.

---

[6] On additional security-related issues surrounding the use of LNG see chapter 6 in this volume.

[7] US Department of Homeland Security, 'The national strategy for the physical protection of critical infrastructure and key assets', Feb. 2003, URL <http://www.dhs.gov/xprevprot/publications/publication_0017.shtm>, p. 52.

[8] US Department of Energy, Energy Information Administration, 'The global liquefied natural gas market: status and outlook', Report no. DOE/EIA-0637, Dec. 2003, URL <http://www.eia.doe.gov/oiaf/analysispaper/global/>.

[9] Hightower, M. et al., Sandia National Laboratories, 'Guidance on risk analysis and safety implications of a large liquefied natural gas (LNG) spill over water', Sandia report SAND2004-6258, Dec. 2004, URL <http://www.fossil.energy.gov/programs/oilgas/storage/lng/sandia_lng_1204.pdf>, pp. 159–60.

In relation to bio-safety and bio-security, good safety practices create a sound platform for enhanced security. With bio-safety as a basis, additional measures that have been adapted to meet particular security threats can be identified and implemented so that bio-safety and bio-security measures are managed together. The World Health Organization (WHO) produced a laboratory bio-security guidance document in September 2006 in which bio-safety is defined as 'the containment principles, technologies and practices that are implemented to prevent the *unintentional* exposure to pathogens and toxins, or their accidental release'. Laboratory bio-security is defined as 'the protection, control and accountability for valuable biological materials . . . within laboratories, in order to prevent *their unauthorized access, loss, theft, misuse, diversion or intentional release*'.[10]

Other analyses have pointed to potential conflicts between security measures and safety measures in particular conditions. In the field of nuclear safety and security Igor Khripunov has taken note of the argument that 'Proponents of safety typically call for building increased redundancy into at-risk systems, while proponents of security point out that greater redundancy might . . . create a situation in which there are more components and equipment than can affordably be secured against malicious acts—making security costlier and more elusive than it already is.'[11] However, after analysing the relationship between safety and security Khripunov concludes that 'Notwithstanding the tension between the two concepts, the characteristics of a good security culture would likely result in improved safety, quality, and productivity within the organization, since closer attention to personnel performance tends to produce better results in every area.'[12]

The discussion of how to enhance security by controlling civil materials has taken place against the background of transnational interdependence, including in the economic sphere.[13] In this context a number of recent intergovernmental discussions have pointed to the fact that any major disruption in the global supply chain could have serious consequences for the sustainable growth and development of many economies. For example, at the 2006 Symposium on Total Supply Chain Security, organized under the auspices of the Asia–Pacific Economic Cooperation (APEC) group, delegates pointed to the need for an approach to supply-chain security based on 'greater consistency of

---

[10] World Health Organization (WHO), 'Biorisk management: laboratory biosecurity guidance', WHO document WHO/CDS/EPR/2006.6, Sep. 2006, URL <http://www.who.int/csr/resources/publications/biosafety/WHO_CDS_EPR_2006_6/en/> (emphasis added). Issues related to bio-security are addressed in greater detail in chapter 13 in this volume. See also Roffey, R. and Kuhlau, F., 'Enhancing bio-security: the need for a global strategy', *SIPRI Yearbook 2006: Armaments, Disarmament and International Security* (Oxford University Press: Oxford, 2006), pp. 732–48.

[11] Khripunov, I., 'Nuclear security: attitude check', *Bulletin of the Atomic Scientists*, vol. 61, no. 1 (Jan./Feb. 2005), pp. 58–64. The need to account for and secure nuclear material is discussed further in appendix 12C in this volume.

[12] Khripunov (note 11), p. 62.

[13] See also the Introduction and chapter 7 in this volume.

principles, guidelines and standards of security across and between the various nodes in the supply chain'.[14]

As a further example, in the maritime parts of the supply chain, the International Maritime Organization (IMO) has been trying to establish a comprehensive set of standards through a combination of legal and political agreements among states. The political momentum generated in the immediate aftermath of the terrorist attacks on the USA meant that by December 2002 'a comprehensive series of measures designed to prevent and suppress acts of terrorism against shipping and in port facilities had been developed'.[15]

These enhanced security standards were formalized in the Code of Conduct for International Ship and Port Facility Security (ISPS Code), which amended the 1974 International Convention for the Safety of Life at Sea (SOLAS Convention).[16] Under the ISPS Code the relevant authorities are required to draw up security plans for ports and other land facilities as well as for ships. The ship and port security plans, which must receive formal government approval, define security measures for a range of conditions. The authorities are required to appoint dedicated security officers to implement these plans on ships, in shipping companies and at ports.

The ISPS Code and the associated SOLAS amendments that were adopted in 2002 entered into force in 2004, and port authorities and operators, shipowners and operators as well as relevant national authorities now face the task of implementing them. This process of implementation depends for its success on cooperation from many actors in the private sector and the approach to engaging with the private sector is discussed further below. However, it is broadly true that the benefits of strengthened security can only be achieved if established standards are translated into practical measures that are applied by the relevant actors at relevant facilities. As an example of this synergy between standards and practical measures, the International Organization for Standardization (ISO) published a publicly available standard (PAS), ISO/PAS 20858, at the same time as the ISPS Code came into force to help

[14] Asia–Pacific Economic Cooperation (APEC), Symposium on Total Supply Chain Security, 'Factsheet on total supply chain security', Singapore, 6–7 July 2006, URL <http://app.mot.gov.sg/data/ fs_06_07_03c.htm>. The APEC members are listed in the glossary in this volume.

[15] Mitropoulos, E. E., Secretary-General of the International Maritime Organization, 'Security of the international container supply chain: threats, challenges and solutions', Speech to the Ministry of Foreign Affairs, Berlin, 18 Jan. 2005, URL <http://www.imo.org/InfoResource/mainframe.asp?topic_id= 1028&doc_id=4650 >.

[16] International Maritime Organization (IMO), 'IMO adopts comprehensive maritime security measures', Conference of Contracting Governments to the International Convention for the Safety of Life at Sea, 1974, 9–13 Dec. 2002. The International Convention for the Safety of Life at Sea opened for signature on 1 Nov. 1974 and entered into force on 25 May 1980. It is reproduced at URL <http://www.imo. org/Conventions/contents.asp?topic_id=257&doc_id=647>. On SOLAS see Ahlström, C., 'The Proliferation Security Initiative: international laws aspects of the Statement of Interdiction Principles', *SIPRI Yearbook 2005: Armaments, Disarmament and International Security* (Oxford University Press: Oxford, 2005), p. 764. The ISPS Code is available on the IMO website at URL <http://www.imo.org>.

with its implementation.[17] This coordinated response was possible because of the long-standing cooperation between the IMO and the ISO.

The recent efforts to strengthen nuclear security illustrate another approach to implementing agreed standards, namely the important role that a specialized agency—the International Atomic Energy Agency (IAEA)—can play in providing both a framework in which to agree standards and a technical resource to help states implement them. The fact that fissile materials are indispensable elements of a nuclear weapon has led to the development of elaborate security provisions to safeguard against the diversion of such material to military use. After analysing the potential utility of radiological (as opposed to nuclear) weapons, military forces concluded long ago that there was no operational reason for developing such weapons. However, a number of other nuclear activities contain potential safety and security risks, although they have no military component.

On 11 September 2001 the IAEA Board of Governors, which was meeting in Vienna, considered the question of whether additional measures were needed to improve the security of nuclear materials and other radioactive materials. The board had before it the report of an expert group that had previously discussed whether there was a need to revise the 1980 Convention on the Physical Protection of Nuclear Material (CPPNM) which was, at that time, the only international legally binding undertaking in the area of physical protection of nuclear material.[18] The CPPNM was developed in the 1970s, when the main concern of the drafters was to ensure the safe and secure transport of nuclear material given environmental concerns about the performance of the nuclear power industry and the growing activism of groups and individuals opposed to international nuclear shipments. However, the CPPNM did not address the security and protection of nuclear facilities, although the IAEA did develop technical documents and policy guidelines to address this issue.

In 2001 the draft report from a Group of Legal and Technical Experts (Group of Experts) convened by the IAEA Director General to prepare draft amendments to strengthen the CPPNM found that:

although responsibility for establishing and operating a comprehensive physical protection system for nuclear materials and facilities within a State rests entirely with the Government of that State, the need for international co-operation becomes particularly evident in situations where the effectiveness of physical protection in one State depends on other States taking, as appropriate, adequate measures to deter or defeat

---

[17] International Organization for Standardization (ISO), 'ISO/PAS 20858:2004, Ships and marine technology: maritime port facility security assessments and security plan development', 7 July 2004, URL <http://www.iso.org/>.

[18] The Convention on the Physical Protection of Nuclear Material opened for signature on 3 Mar. 1980 and entered into force on 8 Feb. 1987. The text of the amended CPPNM is available at URL <http://www.iaea.org/NewsCenter/Features/PhysicalProtection/>. For a brief summary and a list of signatories and parties to the convention see annex A in this volume. See also Kile, S. N., 'Nuclear arms control and non-proliferation', *SIPRI Yearbook 2006* (note 10), pp. 636–37.

hostile actions against nuclear facilities and materials when such materials are transported across national frontiers.[19]

In March 2003 the Group of Experts adopted its final report setting out
possible amendments to the CPPNM. Following discussion by IAEA member
states amendments to strengthen the security provisions of the convention
were adopted in July 2005 and the name of the convention was changed to the
Convention on the Physical Protection of Nuclear Material and Nuclear
Facilities. The amended convention obliges states parties to protect nuclear
facilities and material in peaceful domestic use, storage and transport. The
amended CPPNM establishes measures related to the prevention, detection
and punishment of domestic offences linked to nuclear material. The revised
convention also envisages expanded international cooperation in order to
speed up the location and recovery of stolen or smuggled nuclear material and
to reduce the impact of acts of sabotage.[20]

The amended CPPNM forms one part of a nuclear security framework that
also includes published technical standards that can be used by operators on a
voluntary basis and non-legally binding codes and guidelines that have been
endorsed by states. The fact that certain sources of radioactivity need to be
shielded because there may be harmful effects if they are exposed raises both a
safety issue (because of evidence of shortfalls in the procedures for accounting
for, storing and disposing of such sources) and a security issue (because such
sources may be open to malicious use). As the IAEA has expressed this, 'the
continuing incidents and accidents involving radiation sources and the new
concern about the possible malicious use of radioactive sources indicate a
clear need for a comprehensive set of standards and guidance documents to
support States in their effort to ensure an adequate level of both safety and
security of radioactive sources'.[21]

The Code of Conduct on the Safety and Security of Radioactive Sources
was approved by the IAEA Board of Governors on 8 September 2003.[22] It
contains safety and security standards as well as guidelines that indicate how
to meet some of these standards. Any state may apply the standards contained

---

[19] International Atomic Energy Agency, 'Measures to improve the security of nuclear materials and
other radioactive materials', IAEA document GC(45)/INF/14, 14 Sep. 2001, URL <http://www.iaea.
org/About/Policy/GC/GC45/Documents/gc45inf-14.pdf>.

[20] At the conference to consider amending the CPPNM, 89 states agreed to a set of amendments that
will enter into force when two-thirds of those 89 states deposit their ratification of the amended treaty.
As of 18 Sep. 2006, 6 states (Austria, Bulgaria, Croatia, Libya, Seychelles and Turkmenistan) had
ratified the amended CPPNM. For the text of the amendment see 'Nuclear security measures to protect
against nuclear terrorism: amendment to the Convention on the Physical Protection of Nuclear Material',
Report by the Director General to the Board of Governors General Conference, GOV/INF/2005/10-
GC(49)/INF/6, Vienna, 6 Sep. 2005, URL <http://www.iaea.org/About/Policy/GC/GC49/Documents/
gc49inf-6.pdf>. See also Kile (note 18), pp. 636–37.

[21] International Atomic Energy Agency, 'Developing guidance for the safety and security of radiation
sources', URL <http://www-ns.iaea.org/tech-areas/radiation-safety/source.htm>.

[22] See International Atomic Energy Agency, 'Code of Conduct on the Safety and Security of Radioactive Sources, and supplementary guidance on the import and export of radioactive sources', URL
<http://www-ns.iaea.org/tech-areas/radiation-safety/code-of-conduct.htm>.

in the Code of Conduct and its widespread use would promote consistent international approaches to radiation protection, safety and security.

In 2005 the International Convention for the Suppression of Acts of Nuclear Terrorism was adopted by the UN General Assembly and opened for signature. This convention identifies actions by individuals that are to be considered as criminal offences and requires states to develop the measures necessary to establish those offences under its national law and to make them 'punishable by appropriate penalties' that take into account their grave nature. The convention also requires states to ensure that the national authorities needed to investigate the offences exist and to ensure that they have the power and the resources needed to cooperate with one another in investigations and prosecutions.[23]

In addition to the development of the framework of laws, regulations and guidelines to promote nuclear safety and security, the IAEA has recruited a technical secretariat that is able to help (at the request of countries) with the development of national strategies or to advise on dealing with specific technical problems. As part of its work, the IAEA has also developed a number of action plans on different aspects of nuclear safety and security through which technical assistance financed by donors can be delivered.

III. The efforts of the European Union

The structure of the EU is often illustrated by three 'pillars'. The first pillar includes the single market—within which there should be free movement of people, goods, services and capital—and matters related to the environment and trade policy. In this pillar the institutions of the EU have the right to draw up legal instruments and introduce legislation. In the two other pillars the EU has agreed to strengthen cooperation between member states: in the second pillar external cooperation is coordinated within the scope of the Common Foreign and Security Policy; and in the third pillar cooperation on police matters and criminal law is organized in the areas of justice, liberty and security. In the third pillar the Council of the European Union can take framework decisions that harmonize national rules. The 1997 Treaty of Amsterdam

---

[23] The International Convention for the Suppression of Acts of Nuclear Terrorism is reproduced as an annex to United Nations, Measures to eliminate international terrorism: Report of the Ad Hoc Committee established by General Assembly Resolution 51/210 of 17 December 1996, UN General Assembly document A/59/766, 4 Apr. 2005. The convention was opened for signature on 14 Sep. 2005 and will enter into force 30 days after it is signed and ratified by at least 22 states. See also Kile (note 18), p. 637. The need to redouble efforts to prevent nuclear terrorism was underlined by the disclosure, in Feb. 2006, by Georgian authorities of the seizure of around 80 grams of uranium enriched to 89% in uranium-235. IAEA Staff Report, 'Georgian authorities report seized illicit nuclear material', 25 Jan. 2007, URL <http://www.iaea.org/NewsCenter/News/2007/georgia_material.html>. This material was seized from an alleged Russian citizen, who claimed that he could acquire additional quantities against payment. Georgian authorities were unable to verify this information because of alleged lack of cooperation by Russian authorities. Butler, D., 'Georgian sting seizes bomb grade uranium', ABC News online, 25 Jan. 2007, URL <http://abcnews.go.com/Politics/wireStory?id=2820902&page=1>.

strengthened the authority of the Court of Justice over matters belonging to this pillar.[24]

This structure means that the EU is necessarily deeply engaged in discussing measures that control the movement of civil goods because of the potential impact on the single market. The administrative structure of the EU and the various divisions of legal competence contain the risk that separate activities to address essentially the same common problem will be carried out in different EU pillars simultaneously. In a functional area that has both internal and external aspects and where the division of legal competence between the EU and its member states is unclear or where the areas of legal competence overlap, there may be separate proposals for internal action and external assistance from different parts of the EU as well as multiple member state initiatives. These various initiatives may or may not be coordinated with one another, and any given actor may simply be unaware of the actions being taken in a different part of the EU. In addition, the European Commission has drawn attention to the fact that in a changing international environment the internal and external policies of the EU are inextricably linked.[25] New policies for external action are now being debated in Europe, which could allow the EU to play a greater role in ensuring that vital transnational and trans-regional flows of goods and supplies are unimpeded by deliberate or accidental disruption. New instruments, such as the Stability Instrument, have been adopted to help finance activities that can help safeguard against such disruptions.[26] The external projection of internal policies is likely to become an important element of future EU external action in this functional area.

The EU is aware of the risk that a piecemeal approach might be adopted in a new and rapidly evolving security situation. In its 'Hague Programme' on freedom, security and justice the EU noted that 'in the field of security, the coordination and coherence between the internal and the external dimension has been growing in importance and needs to continue to be vigorously pursued'.[27] In an effort to produce this coherence, in May 2005 the European Commission published its five-year Action Plan for Freedom, Justice and Security containing detailed proposals on, among other things, terrorism. One element of the anti-terrorism component of the Action Plan was the protection

[24] The Treaty of Amsterdam amending the Treaty on European Union, the Treaties Establishing the European Communities and Certain Related Acts was opened for signature on 2 Oct. 1997 and entered into force on 1 May 1999. It is available at URL <http://europa.eu.int/eur-lex/en/treaties/dat/amsterdam.html>.

[25] Commission of the European Communities, 'Europe in the world: some practical proposals for greater coherence, effectiveness and visibility', Communication from the Commission to the European Council of June 2006, COM(2006) 278 final, Brussels, 8 June 2006, p. 4, URL <http://www.ec.europa.eu/comm/external_relations/euw_com06_278_en.pdf>.

[26] 'Regulation (EC) No. 1717/2006 of the European Parliament and of the Council of 15 November 2006 establishing an Instrument for Stability', *Official Journal of the European Union*, L327 (24 Nov. 2006), pp. 1–11. On the Instrument for Stability see International Security Information Service (ISIS), Europe, 'The Stability Instrument: defining the Commission's role in crisis response', ISIS Briefing, Brussels, 27 June 2005, available at URL <http://www.isis-europe.org/>.

[27] Council of the European Union, 'The Hague Programme: strengthening freedom, security and justice in the European Union', document 16054/04, Brussels, 13 Dec. 2004, URL <http://www.ec.europa.eu/justice_home/doc_centre/doc/hague_programme_en.pdf>.

of critical infrastructure, which was defined to include both transport (airports, sea ports, intermodal facilities where cargo or passengers can move between transport modes, railway and mass transit networks, and traffic control systems) and the production, storage and transport of dangerous goods (e.g. chemical, biological, radiological and nuclear materials).[28] To achieve its counterterrorism objectives in these areas the EU has engaged in a number of activities intended to produce the following outcomes: (*a*) ensure that the various actors have the proper skills and competences to perform essential security tasks; (*b*) make certain that items being stored or moved are screened and evaluated against security criteria; (*c*) increase the time available for screening items during transport by requiring advance notification of the contents of shipments; (*d*) guarantee the physical security of items in storage or in transit; and (*e*) inspect stored items or items in transit.

To bring about the necessary changes the EU has taken a mixed approach by combining regulations and directives in some areas with efforts to encourage or stimulate voluntary action in others. For example, the Commission has proposed measures to ensure greater security of explosives, detonators, bomb-making equipment and firearms aimed at improving the security of the storage and transport of explosives as well as at ensuring the traceability of industrial and chemical precursors. The proposed measures include legislation to bring elements from international agreements (such as the UN 2001 Protocol against the Illicit Manufacturing of and Trafficking in Firearms, their Parts and Components and Ammunition) into Community legislation as well as the elaboration of voluntary measures through a 'structured dialogue' with industry and other non-governmental bodies.[29] A somewhat similar approach is being adopted in regard to preventive and responsive measures such as bio-security, preparedness and response. [30]

Legal and administrative decisions have also been used on other occasions to translate emerging international standards into law and practice in a uniform way across the EU. For example, in April 2005 security amendments were made to the Customs Code contained in EC Regulation 648/2005, which establishes the legal basis for customs procedures in all EU member states. The elements introduced in the Customs Code were based on the 2005 Frame-

---

[28] Commission of the European Communities, 'Critical infrastructure protection in the fight against terrorism', Communication from the Commission to the Council and the European Parliament, COM(2004) 702 final, Brussels, 20 Oct. 2004.

[29] The Protocol against the Illicit Manufacturing of and Trafficking in Firearms, their Parts and Components and Ammunition, supplementing the United Nations Convention against Transnational Organized Crime was opened for signature on 31 May 2001 and entered into force on 3 July 2005, URL <http://www.unodc.org/pdf/crime/a_res_55/255e.pdf>. The approach and its elements are described in Commission of the European Communities, 'Communication from the Commission on measures to ensure greater security in explosives, detonators, bomb-making equipment and firearms', COM(2005) 329 final, Brussels, 18 July 2005, URL <http://www.eur-lex.europa.eu/LexUriServ/site/en/com/2005/com2005_0329en01.pdf>.

[30] The EU measures related to these activities are described in chapter 13 in this volume.

work of Standards to Secure and Facilitate Global Trade developed under the umbrella of the World Customs Organization (WCO).[31]

Voluntary standards, which are discussed further below, can support policy and regulatory initiatives of this kind. For example, technical standards are currently being developed for mechanical and electronic seals for freight containers. These standards will help manufacturers understand and incorporate security practices when making their products to ensure that the seals are suitable for securing freight containers for international commerce in the light of the anticipated future regulatory environment. The development of these standards is therefore being followed closely by the WCO, the EU and the United Nations Economic Commission for Europe.

Although the Hague Programme in effect set the objective of securing the entire supply chain for goods and services in the EU, the supply chain is not entirely contained within the boundaries of the European single market. The supply chain includes all of the actors associated with a particular transaction: the suppliers of unprocessed raw materials, all the intermediate actors engaged in processing and manufacturing, the service providers and the final customer. The supply chain links many companies, including those operating in the European single market.

The modifications to the Customs Code are part of an EU effort to promote integrated border management at the external perimeter of the single market. The new code creates the legal status of authorized economic operator (AEO), which enables companies to earn the right to use simplified customs procedures by putting in place and certifying internal procedures that enhance security in the supply chain. However, goods and services as well as people and capital move freely within the single market and are not subject to customs controls. These transactions can also pose a security risk.

In February 2006 the Commission Directorate-General for Energy and Transport (DG TREN) presented a proposal for a regulation on enhancing supply-chain security.[32] The draft regulation, which was discussed in advance with the officials who developed the modifications to the Customs Code, contains a voluntary scheme based on creating 'secure operators'. The characteristics of a secure operator are similar to those of an AEO in the customs area, and it is intended that a company which meets the minimum requirements to be an AEO will automatically qualify to be a secure operator. The secure-operator status is expected to be relevant mainly to specific groups such as coastal shippers, transport companies, freight forwarders, warehouse and storage operators, and inland terminal operators whose operations take place exclusively within the single market even if they work with goods that

[31] The changes to the Customs Code are described in Anthony, I. and Bauer, S., 'Transfer controls', *SIPRI Yearbook 2006* (note 10), pp. 775–97. Their implementation is discussed further in chapter 15 in this volume.

[32] Commission of the European Communities, Communication from the Commission to the Council, the European Parliament, the European Economic and Social Committee and the Committee of the Regions on enhancing supply chain security, COM(2006), 79, Brussels, 27 Feb. 2006, URL <http://www.ec.europa.eu/dgs/energy_transport/security/intermodal/doc/com_2006_0079_en.pdf>.

originate elsewhere or are later designated for export. The expectation is that the market will reward the secure operators by giving them certain advantages. It might be expected, for example, that companies elsewhere in the supply chain that are AEOs or secure operators would prefer to work with partners that hold the same or similar status, because this could strengthen their own security measures. It is also possible that there might be benefits in reduced insurance premiums for secure operators.

The European Commission has proposed that EU member states set up secure-operator schemes covering all types of packaging and all transport modes. It has proposed that these schemes be made compatible with the systems that are already being set up to designate AEOs for customs purposes. The Commission has also proposed that there should be mutual recognition between the AEO and secure-operator certification processes.[33]

The development of greater supply-chain security is inevitably a long-term process. The initiative is primarily aimed at actors in the supply chain that could be potential targets for mass-impact terrorism attacks, which narrows the scope of application somewhat. Nevertheless, the Commission estimates that this might include almost 1 million operators across the EU. Moreover, these are companies that work with purely civil items and whose personnel are familiar with the need for safety measures but generally have a low level of security awareness.

Not surprisingly, the initial reaction of industry to this proposal by the European Commission was somewhat negative, although the Commission had tried to anticipate the most likely criticisms during drafting. The European Small Business Alliance (ESBA) argued that the scheme would disadvantage small companies that are unable to meet the requirements of a secure operator 'without any clear benefits'.[34] The British Federation of Small Businesses estimated that introducing the secure-operator requirements might cost a small business an initial fee of €135 000 (c. $243 000) and an annual fee of €131 000 (c. $250 000).[35]

The complaint by industry that the EU was creating a 'forest of regulations' was a response to the fact that the EU made changes to the Customs Code and proposed the regulation on supply-chain security shortly after security regulations related to civil aviation and port security came into effect. After civil aircraft were used to mount attacks in the USA in September 2001, the EU rapidly developed EC Regulation 2320/2002 to lay down new aviation security provisions. The regulation was adopted on 16 December 2002 and entered

[33] Commission of the European Communities (note 32), p. 8.

[34] Sommer, T., President of the ESBA, quoted in 'Transport security proposal could "cripple" small businesses', Euractiv.com, 4 Sep. 2006, URL <http://www.euractiv.com/en/transport/transport-security-proposal-cripple-small-businesses/article-157458>.

[35] Cave, A., Federation of Small Businesses, 'Briefing note: European Commission's proposal on enhancing supply chain security', 9 Aug. 2006, URL <http://www.fsb.org.uk/data/default.asp?id=409&loc=policy>.

into force in January 2003.[36] It contains provisions related to many aspects of aviation security, including some that have a direct impact on the movement of air cargo. As well as establishing certain common minimum security standards, every EU member state is required to establish a national civil aviation security programme with corresponding quality-control and training programmes within three months of entry into force of the regulation. Member states are permitted to apply more stringent security measures at the national level according to need. Reviewing the implementation of the regulation after two years of operation, the Commission expressed the view that errors in drafting (owing largely to the speed of the process) needed to be corrected because the 25 national systems that had been put in place had created a potential distortion of competition that could undermine the single market. The Commission has argued for the greatest possible harmonization of security measures and procedures to facilitate the work of industry (including airlines, cargo shippers and freight forwarders as well as manufacturers of security equipment).[37]

In September 2005 the European Commission presented a new proposal that would require member states to undertake an assessment of the risk to aviation security and to justify national actions and security measures more stringent than those laid down in the January 2003 regulation if requested to do so by the Commission. This proposal was intended to address concerns that industry might be burdened with unnecessary security requirements, while preserving the right of member states to respond to threats with heightened security requirements. Particular attention was drawn to the security of air cargo, and the Commission suggested interlinking the security requirements for regulated agents and known shippers with the AEO concept developed in the Customs Code.[38]

The EU has taken a somewhat similar approach in regard to port security. The international standards developed in the SOLAS Convention and the ISPS Code have been incorporated in EU law through a regulation.[39] A subsequent directive establishes implementing measures to be taken by member states to try to ensure uniform implementation that does not distort the single market.[40]

---

[36] 'Regulation (EC) No. 2320/2002 of the European Parliament and of the Council of 16 December 2002 establishing common rules in the field of civil aviation security', *Official Journal of the European Communities*, L355 (30 Dec. 2002), pp. 1–21.

[37] European Commission, 'Proposal for a Regulation of the European Parliament and of the Council on common rules in the field of civil aviation security', COM(2005) 429 final, Brussels, 22 Sep. 2005, URL <http://eur-lex.europa.eu/en/dossier/dossier_06.htm>, p. 2.

[38] European Commission (note 37).

[39] 'Regulation (EC) No. 725/2004 of the European Parliament and of the Council of 31 March 2004 on enhancing ship and port facility security', *Official Journal of the European Union*, L129 (29 Apr. 2004), pp. 1–86.

[40] 'Directive 2005/65/EC of the European Parliament and of the Council of 26 October 2005 on enhancing port security', *Official Journal of the European Union*, no. L310 (25 Nov. 2005), pp. 1–12.

IV. The role of business and the private sector in securing sensitive civil items

The previous sections underline that the need to combat mass-impact terrorism is creating new sets of security regulations that apply directly to business. Business can readily share the objective of preventing mass-impact terrorism. Apart from protecting themselves from direct attack, the business community should recognize three other compelling reasons to put in place effective security systems. First, businesses have a legal duty to comply with the law and face the risk of punishment if they do not. Second, they have a moral obligation to their employees and to the societies that support their activities not to contribute to activities that undermine security. Third, they have a self-interest that stems from the potentially devastating economic consequences for their companies if they are connected in the public mind with mass-impact terrorism. Industry recognizes the need for regulation—on the condition that rules are clearly drafted, well publicized, do not disrupt day-to-day business practice, include checks on enforcement, and provided that punishments for non-compliance 'fit the crime'.

When multiple regulators take an interest in solving the same basic problem, however, it is understandable that business would become nervous. To take the European example, in the worst case (from the perspective of business), a business might face five sets of requirements under anti-terrorist legislation: a European supply-chain security regulation, European customs regulations, aviation security regulations, port security regulations and security regulations specific to the particular product. Even if the regulations offer the opportunity to earn the right to use simplified procedures, the detailed requirements to achieve the status of trusted partner might differ in each case. Moreover, this would be the situation for European regulations, but additional or different requirements could apply in other jurisdictions such as the USA.

This view was summarized in 2003 by a Swedish business association, which requested that new systems should avoid creating the need for new information technology systems that would require heavy investments. A concern was expressed that 'too many new initiatives are under way, at the same time, which will make coordination of the different projects more difficult and lead to fragmentation and non-compatible solutions'.[41] More recently, responding to the proposed EU regulation on the security of supply chains, the International Road Transport Union pointed to the risk that too many security initiatives would create confusion for operators.[42]

---

[41] Confederation of Swedish Enterprise and Swedish Chamber of Commerce, 'Reformation of the Community Customs Code: position paper on the Swedish business community's response to the European Commission's latest initiatives', Interinstitutional file 2003/167(COD), 2003, URL <http://www.swedfreight.se/sidor/transppol/EU%20_ccr_sw_com.pdf>.

[42] Dahlin, B., President of the International Road Transport Union Goods Transport Liaison Committee, quoted in 'Transport security proposal could "cripple" small businesses' (note 34).

The idea of forming a closer partnership between regulators and industry is being explored and an informal bargain seems to be emerging: a business that can demonstrate that it has internal mechanisms in place to ensure that its actions do not undermine security will be relieved of some regulatory requirements. What is now needed is common understanding of what business must do in order to take advantage of simplified procedures related to security regulations, and detailed work to elaborate the agreed elements. Particular attention is required in two areas—the need to understand the potential uses of civil items and knowledge about the background of persons with access to them.

To simplify and harmonize the task of industry, several initiatives are exploring the development of certified standards for business security systems that would become part of a company's quality-management system. A growing number of companies use a management approach based on documenting policies and procedures to improve and control the various processes that will ultimately lead to improved business performance.[43]

Although designing a management system probably has to be approached on a company-by-company basis, if there are too many variations and differences in approach by companies there may be less confidence in the effectiveness of such measures. In general, a set of standards will have to establish company policy at the highest level and must put in place an organizational structure to determine the authority and responsibility of different officers of the company. The system should offer guidance to partners along the supply chain and to subsidiaries of the company and affiliates, and it should create obligations on staff to carry out established duties with real and serious consequences for non-compliance. The standard would need to address issues of physical security, access controls, personnel security, documentation procedures, information security, and issues related to staff education, training and awareness. Several groups are exploring the development of voluntary security standards together with accreditation systems for them.[44]

Creating standards is a complicated process that requires administration, which can be provided by dedicated standards organizations, such as the ISO, a global body, and the European Committee for Standardization (Comité Européen de Normalisation, CEN), a European organization.[45] Where possible, standards should be developed at the international level to promote harmonization and to avoid creating technical barriers to trade.

---

[43] A number of such approaches have been developed, including SIX-SIGMA, Total Quality Management and the ISO 9000 series of standards.

[44] Standards are the specifications, contained in technical agreements, that provide the framework for compatible technology or a compatible approach to a particular issue or problem worldwide. Standards are voluntary, and businesses adopt them because they see a self-interest in knowing that they are using methods or technologies that are accepted internationally by both their customers and their competitors.

[45] The ISO is a network of the national standards institutes of 157 countries, with a Central Secretariat that coordinates the system. It is a non-governmental organization but many of its member institutes are government agencies or have some official status in their countries. See the ISO website, URL <http://www.iso.org>. The CEN is a committee of the national standards bodies of the EU and European Free Trade Association countries that has set itself the task of contributing to the development of standards in the European Economic Area. See the CEN website, URL <http://www.cen.eu>.

Although a standard can be said to be established once the specifications are agreed and published, it will normally have greater effect if implementation is validated in some way. The most common form of validation is an audit process. The company concerned is likely to conduct its own review of implementation and may publish a report on steps taken, but an audit to verify conformance with agreed criteria may have more credibility if it is carried out by an independent body. This audit can lead to certification—written assurance (the certificate) by the independent external body that has audited the system and verified that it conforms to the requirements specified in the standard.

The certification process could be carried out by a government agency or government-accredited organizations if the standard is related to security or linked to compliance with anti-terrorism laws, and there are precedents for this in other areas of regulation. The responsible government agencies can take advantage of certification guidelines prepared by international bodies.[46] Alternatively, the task of certification might be given to a trusted party that would probably need to be accredited—that is, recognized as competent to carry out certification in the particular business sector of concern.[47]

Standards bodies are now beginning to take security issues into the catalogue of standards being developed. A CEN working group is tasked with developing a standard for Protection and Security of the Citizen.[48] The mandate for the group was created in December 2003 and it has been meeting since March 2004. The working group is a network that brings CEN members together with representatives of relevant directorates-general from the European Commission, the Joint Research Centre within the Commission, the European Police Office (Europol) and a number of industry associations. It has established a number of expert groups that examine different issues to see whether there is an argument for producing a standard in that area. These groups are looking at a number of issues of relevance to the matters discussed in this chapter, including: (a) integrated border management, (b) critical infrastructure and energy supply, (c) security of the supply chain, (d) defence against terrorism, and (e) reduction of crime risks in products and services.

The ISO is also developing standards for the provision of protection against threats to people, physical assets, and infrastructure and information technology assets, including electronic networks and facilities. The ISO's Strategic Advisory Group on Security is working on initiatives such as a written guide to encourage all technical committees across the ISO system to take security

---

[46] E.g. the WCO sets guidelines for national customs administrations about how to certify the requirements for supply-chain security programmes that were recently agreed in the WCO framework. This facilitates the mutual recognition of certificates between countries. The EU is developing guidelines for certifying the status of an AEO, which was created in the revised Customs Code.

[47] The European Co-operation for Accreditation (EA) was established in 2000 through the merger of several accreditation bodies to create a network of nationally recognized accreditation bodies. The participants in the EA currently cover accreditation of certification bodies in laboratories, inspection agencies, quality-management systems and environmental-management systems.

[48] European Committee for Standardization, 'CEN BT/WG 161: "protection and security of the citizen"', URL <http://www.cen.eu/cenorm/businessdomains/businessdomains/security+and+defence/security/btwg161.asp>.

into account in a coordinated and logical way. The need for a number of new international standards has also been identified, such as standards for built infrastructure, personal identification, transport of goods and persons, and cyber-security. As part of the ISO's work to support the transport of goods, a specification has been developed for an ISO publicly available standard on security-management systems for the supply chain (ISO/PAS 28001).[49] Work to create ISO/PAS 28001 began at the end of 2005. The specification for ISO/PAS 28001 outlines the requirements to enable an organization to establish, implement, maintain and improve a security-management system, including financing, manufacturing, information management and the facilities for packing, storing and transferring goods between modes of transport and locations. This is part of a series of security standards that are published by the ISO, and others are being developed.

V. Conclusions

Much work is being done to create a framework for controlling items that represent a potential security risk but cannot be brought into the scope of arms control because of their purely civil nature. These efforts involve a wide range of actors that are not traditionally accustomed to thinking about security matters. Developing the process in a coherent manner is a formidable challenge.

It is premature to reach conclusions about the final outcome of efforts to put in place measures to strengthen security by controlling non-military items. There is currently no system for bringing together the different communities that are engaged in the process to exchange information and describe their activities to one another. An effort to coordinate initiatives as diverse as those described in this chapter or to seek a single framework in which to manage them would be unlikely to succeed. However, a regular opportunity for reporting and information exchange could be organized either on a regional basis or under the global umbrella provided by the United Nations.

Several processes already in place involve the business community directly, including some that address supply-chain security. In one way or another, these different processes all require the classification of items in the supply chain against a set of technical risk factors, the screening of transactions against problematic end-user and end-use information, the establishment of a comprehensive, electronic system for document archival and retrieval, the creation of an effective information system for collecting information and reporting it in different formats, and the development of an education and training programme. Moreover, all of these processes promote the idea that a business can be awarded the status of a trusted, secure operator and that certain benefits will flow from possessing that status.

---

[49] International Organization for Standardization, 'PAS 28001: Ships and marine technology: best practices for implementing supply chain security, assessments and plans', 4 Apr. 2006, URL <http://www.iso.org/>.

Appendix 11A. United Nations Security Council Resolution 1540: non-proliferation by means of international legislation

CHRISTER AHLSTRÖM

I. Introduction

The terrorist attacks in the United States on 11 September 2001 have brought about a significant change in the international efforts to combat the proliferation of weapons of mass destruction (WMD). The issue of proliferation involving non-state actors was not on the international agenda prior to September 2001—even if certain events had demonstrated its relevance (e.g. the 1995 attacks with nerve agents by the Aum Shinrikyo religious sect in Tokyo). After September 2001 it became obvious that non-proliferation efforts had to include non-state actors within their ambit as the nexus between terrorism and the capacity for mass destruction became evident. The non-proliferation agenda was also significantly affected by the revelation in 2003 of the existence of a private network of suppliers of sensitive nuclear technologies led by the Pakistani scientist Abdul Qadeer Khan. This widened the focus to non-state actors not only as recipients, but also as suppliers of sensitive goods and technologies.

The multilateral export control regimes have extended their coverage to include proliferation involving non-state actors.[1] The informal nature of these regimes meant that they could amend their guidelines quickly, but their membership is limited. The formal elements of the non-proliferation regimes, the multilateral treaties on non-proliferation—the 1968 Treaty on the Non-Proliferation of Nuclear Weapons (Non-Proliferation Treaty, NPT),[2] the 1972 Biological and Toxin Weapons Convention (BTWC),[3] and the 1993 Chemical Weapons Convention (CWC)[4]—have a broader reach because of their wider participation. However, they were drafted with the primary objective of preventing the proliferation of WMD among states and, with the possible exception of the CWC,[5] they are not equipped to deal with non-state actors.

---

[1] On multilateral export control regimes see section III below and chapter 15 in this volume.

[2] The Treaty on the Non-Proliferation of Nuclear Weapons was opened for signature on 1 July 1968 and entered into force on 5 Mar. 1970; the text is available in *United Nations Treaty Series*, vol. 729 (1970), p. 161 and at URL <http://www.un.org/Depts/dda/WMD/treaty/>.

[3] The Convention on the Prohibition of the Development, Production and Stockpiling of Bacteriological (Biological) and Toxin Weapons and on their Destruction was opened for signature on 10 Apr. 1972 and entered into force on 26 Mar. 1975. The text is available in *United Nations Treaty Series*, vol. 1015 (1976), p. 163 and on the SIPRI Chemical and Biological Warfare website, URL <http://www.sipri.org/contents/cbwarfare/>. On the BTWC see chapter 13 in this volume.

[4] The Convention on the Prohibition of the Development, Production, Stockpiling and Use of Chemical Weapons and on their Destruction (corrected version), 8 Aug. 1994 was opened for signature on 13 Jan. 1993 and entered into force on 29 Apr. 1997. The text is reproduced in *International Legal Materials*, vol. 32 (1993), p. 800 and on the SIPRI Chemical and Biological Warfare Programme website (note 3). On the CWC see chapter 13 in this volume.

[5] The CWC differs from the NPT in that it contains a detailed provision (Article VII) that obliges the parties to enact domestic legislation, including penal legislation, prohibiting individuals from acquiring or using chemical weapons. The BTWC contains a similar provision (Article IV) that obliges the states

From a policy perspective, the option of seeking formal amendments to the BTWC and the NPT, in particular, does not seem attractive because such efforts would run the risk of getting bogged down in protracted, politically complicated negotiations.

In a speech before the United Nations General Assembly on 23 September 2003, US President George W. Bush urged the UN Security Council to adopt a new 'anti-proliferation' resolution that would 'call on all Members of the United Nations to criminalize the proliferation of weapons of mass destruction, to enact strict export controls consistent with international standards and to secure any and all sensitive materials within their own borders'.[6] Subsequently, the USA set out to negotiate an anti-proliferation resolution among the permanent members of the Security Council. The negotiations were held within a small circle of member states, which caused some consternation among the other UN members. At the request of some members, the Security Council held a meeting on 22 April 2004 in order to provide an opportunity for all the members to present their views on the draft resolution. Several national delegations took the opportunity to speak.[7] While a majority of delegations agreed on the importance of the substance of the draft resolution, a majority also expressed reservations regarding the proposed procedure whereby the Security Council would be legislating (in the sense of adopting general obligations not limited to a specific situation) for the other UN members under Chapter VII of the UN Charter. After seven months of negotiation the Security Council adopted the resolution by consensus on 28 April 2004.[8]

The major controversy caused by the adoption of Resolution 1540 and, in 2001, of Resolution 1373[9]—relates to the question of the authority of the Security Council to impose general obligations on UN members by means of a binding resolution under Chapter VII of the UN Charter.[10] Previously, the Security Council had exercised its powers mainly under Chapter VII in relation to a more or less specific threat in a more or less specific situation. Is the Security Council exceeding its authority under

---

parties to take measures to prohibit and prevent the acquisition of biological weapons on their territories, but it is not as detailed as the corresponding provision of the CWC.

[6] See United Nations, Address by President George W. Bush to the 58th session of the General Assembly, UN document A/58/PV.7, 23 Sep. 2003, URL <http://www.un.org/ga/58/pv.html>, p. 11.

[7] See United Nations, Security Council meeting on non-proliferation of weapons of mass destruction, UN documents S/PV.4950 and S/PV.4950 (Resumption 1), 22 Apr. 2004, URL <http://www.un.org/Depts/dhl/resguide/scact2004.htm>.

[8] See UN Security Council Resolution 1540, 28 Apr. 2004; it is reproduced in appendix 11B. For this and other UN Security Council resolutions discussed in this chapter see URL <http://www.un.org/documents/scres.htm>. See also Bosch, O. and Ham, P. van (eds), *Global Non-Proliferation and Counter-Terrorism: The Impact of UNSCR 1540* (Brookings Institution Press: Washington, DC, 2005); and *International Lawyer* vol. 40, no. 2 (2006), pp. 490–93.

[9] UN Security Council Resolution 1373, 28 Sep. 2001. This resolution sets out certain mandatory measures to prevent and suppress international terrorism, including reporting to the UN Counter-Terrorism Committee on the actions taken in their respective legal systems. On the resolution's 'legislative' elements see e.g. Szasz, P. C., 'The Security Council starts legislating', *American Journal of International Law*, vol. 96 (2002), pp. 901–905; and Ward, C. A., 'Building capacity to combat international terrorism: the role of the United Nations Security Council', *Journal of Conflict & Security Law*, vol. 8, no. 2 (2003), pp. 289–305.

[10] Lavalle, R., 'A novel, if awkward, exercise in international law-making: Security Council Resolution 1540 (2004)', *Netherlands International Law Review*, vol. 51 (2004), pp. 411–37; Marschik, A., 'The Security Council as world legislator? Theory, practice and consequences of an expanding world power', IILJ Working Paper, no. 2005/18, Institute for International Law and Justice (IILJ), New York University School of Law, New York, N.Y., 2005, URL <http://www.iilj.org/papers/>; and Beyer, E., 'The Security Council and Resolution 1540: a law-maker above the law?', Unpublished LLM international law thesis, Uppsala University, Faculty of Law, 2006.

the Charter (i.e. acting ultra vires) when adopting resolutions of a more generic and 'legislative' kind? Some states and legal commentators have expressed concern that it may be. Without addressing the controversial question of whether the decisions of the Security Council are subject to judicial review,[11] it may be noted that the main indicator of the acceptance by member states of such an alleged ultra vires resolution would be the actual level of implementation.[12]

This appendix addresses three issues in relation to Resolution 1540. Section II discusses the authority of the Security Council to adopt binding resolutions that contain legislative elements under Chapter VII of the UN Charter. This is a controversial issue within international legal doctrine, but for reasons of space this appendix does not present a comprehensive treatment of the issue. Section III analyses the extent and character of the legal obligations that the resolution establishes. The implementation of Resolution 1540 is discussed in section IV, and a concluding observation on the use of legislative resolutions by the Security Council is presented in section V.

II. The powers of the Security Council under the United Nations Charter

As an organ of a global organization, the Security Council is entrusted with the powers that its Charter bestows on it. Articles 24–26 of the UN Charter establish the functions and powers of the Security Council. According to Article 24, the members of the organization 'confer on the Security Council primary responsibility for the maintenance of international peace and security, and agree that in carrying out its duties under this responsibility the Security Council acts on their behalf'. This assignment of primary responsibility is linked to the interest of ensuring 'prompt and effective action' by the UN. Yet Article 24 also establishes that the Security Council in discharging its duties shall 'act in accordance with the Purposes and Principles of the United Nations'.[13] As this formulation indicates, the powers of the Security Council are not unfettered.[14] It is also recognized that further 'specific powers' granted to the Security Council are laid down in Chapters VI, VII, VIII and XII.

Under Article 25 the members of the United Nations 'agree to accept and carry out the decisions of the Security Council in accordance with the present Charter'. A key term in this provision is 'decisions' because it is in relation to such acts of the Security Council that the member states have pledged their acceptance and execution. Article 25 can also be read as creating this duty for UN members—as a matter of law—only if the Security Council has acted 'in accordance with the present Charter'.

[11] See e.g. Martenczuk, B., 'The Security Council, the International Court and judicial review: what lessons from Lockerbie?', *European Journal of International Law*, vol. 10, no. 3 (1999), pp. 517–47; and Fassbender, B., '*Quis judicabit*? The Security Council, its powers and its legal control', *European Journal of International Law*, vol. 11, no. 1 (2000), pp. 219–32.

[12] It has been argued that an ultra vires resolution may be accepted by the subsequent practice of the members of the organization if this practice shows that the members are acting in accordance with the resolution. See Marschik (note 10), p. 7.

[13] The purposes and principles of the United Nations are laid down in Articles 1 and 2 of the Charter. Charter of the United Nations, URL <http://www.un.org/aboutun/charter/>. It should be noted that Article 2:7 states that 'nothing in the present Charter shall authorize the United Nations to intervene in matters which are essentially within the domestic jurisdiction of any state'. This proviso is, however, not applicable to enforcement measures under Chapter VII of the Charter.

[14] See Bowett, D. W., *The Law of International Institutions*, 4th edn (Stevens & Sons: London, 1982), p. 33.

In other words, members would be obliged to respect the Security Council's decisions only if it acted within its powers (i.e. intra vires). However, some international lawyers are not prepared to accept such an interpretation because it would give individual member states some leeway to decide whether or not a decision is intra vires.[15] Several key provisions of the UN Charter are vague and, consequently, it may be difficult in a concrete situation to determine whether the Security Council has acted within its powers. Yet if the Security Council were to take a decision on a matter that appears to be outside its powers it could be considered a moot point whether the member states would be under a legal obligation to comply with the decision.[16]

Resolution 1540 was adopted with reference to the specific powers of the Security Council under Chapter VII of the Charter. Chapter VII deals with 'action with respect to threats to the peace, breaches of the peace, and acts of aggression'. The first preambular paragraph of Resolution 1540 states that the 'proliferation of nuclear, chemical and biological weapons, as well as their means of delivery, constitutes a threat to international peace and security'. The explicit characterization of such proliferation as a threat to international peace and security is significant because it paves the way for measures under Chapter VII of the Charter (see below).[17] The formulation used is broad and covers any proliferation—not just proliferation involving non-state actors.

According to Article 39 of Chapter VII, the Security Council 'shall determine the existence of any threat to the peace, breach of the peace, or act of aggression and shall make recommendations, or decide what measures shall be taken in accordance with Articles 41 and 42, to maintain or restore international peace and security'. The first analytical question is thus whether the risk of proliferation of WMD involving non-state actors qualifies as 'a threat to international peace and security', and whether the adoption of a resolution establishing general obligations could be seen as a 'measure' in the terms of Article 39. The key terms in this provision are not defined in the UN Charter. The General Assembly subsequently defined the concept of aggression,[18] but the notions of 'threat to the peace' and 'breach of the peace' remain undefined.[19] It has therefore been recognized that the Security Council enjoys 'considerable discretion' when it comes to the designation of a particular situation as

---

[15] Delbrück, J., 'Article 25', eds B. Simma et al., *The Charter of the United Nations: A Commentary*, 2nd edn, vol. 1 (Oxford University Press: Oxford, 2002), p. 459.

[16] See *Prosecutor v. Tadic*, Appeal on Jurisdiction (ICTY, no. IT-94-1-AR72), section 43, 2 Oct. 1995; Nolte, G., 'The limits of the Security Council's powers and its functions in the international legal system: some reflections', ed. M. Byers, *The Role of Law in International Politics: Essays in International Relations and International Law* (Oxford University Press: Oxford, 2000), pp. 315–26; and Talmon, S., 'The Security Council as world legislator', *American Journal of International Law*, vol. 99 (2005), pp. 175–93.

[17] Resolution 1540 also 'reaffirms' the statement made by the President of the Security Council, adopted at its meeting at the level of heads of state and government on 31 Jan. 1992, declaring that the proliferation of WMD is a threat to international peace and security. See United Nations, Note by the President of the Security Council, UN document S/23500, 31 Jan. 1992, reprinted in *International Legal Materials*, vol. 31 (1992), p. 762. In Resolution 825, adopted on 11 May 1993 in relation to North Korea's withdrawal from the NPT, the Security Council noted the 'crucial contribution which progress in non-proliferation can make to the maintenance of international peace and security'. In Resolution 1172, adopted on 6 June 1998 as a reaction to the nuclear weapon tests carried out by India and Pakistan, the Security Council also declared that the 'proliferation of all weapons of mass destruction constitutes a threat to international peace and security'.

[18] See the annex to UN General Assembly Resolution 3314, 14 Dec. 1974, URL <http://www.un.org/documents/ga/res/29/ares29.htm>.

[19] See Österdahl, I., *Threat to the Peace: The Interpretation by the Security Council of Article 39 of the UN Charter* (Iustus Förlag: Uppsala, 1998).

a threat to the peace.[20] The Security Council has on at least three other occasions indicated that it considers the spread of WMD to be a threat to international peace and security. The logic of this reasoning is that the more states that possess such weapons, the greater the risk of use.[21] However, a difference between Resolution 1540 and the previous pronouncements of the Security Council is that the statement about a threat to the peace is made *in abstracto*—that is, not in relation to a specific situation threatening international peace and security as was previously the case. Some international lawyers argue that the powers of the Security Council under Chapter VII may only be exercised in relation to a specific situation,[22] but such a qualification would seem to follow from the Security Council's past practice rather than the wording of Article 39. Hence, it is dubious to argue that Resolution 1540 is ultra vires simply because of its focus on a generic rather than specific threat to the peace.

The subsequent question is whether the adoption of a resolution establishing general obligations could be seen as a 'measure' under Article 41, which deals with the measures not involving the use of armed force that the Security Council may decide on in order to give effect to its decisions. Article 41 lists examples of such measures (e.g. interruption of economic relations), but the list of measures is not intended to be exhaustive. The Security Council has also used its powers under Chapter VII in order to establish general obligations in other fields, and the International Criminal Tribunal for Former Yugoslavia, has found it to be in accordance with the UN Charter.[23] Hence, there would not seem to be any provision in the UN Charter that renders the adoption of Resolution 1540 manifestly ultra vires from a procedural and substantive perspective.[24] That said, whether the adoption of binding resolutions that contain general obligations that are not limited to a specific situation may be said to constitute an effective and legitimate method of addressing an international problem is an open question, addressed in section IV.

III. The substance of Resolution 1540

The preamble

The preambular paragraphs of a Security Council resolution are not designed to create specific legal obligations or to establish a cause for action by the UN member states, but they provide insight into the political rationale behind the adoption of the

---

[20] See Frowein, J. A. and Krisch, N., 'Article 39', eds Simma et al. (note 15), p. 719.

[21] On this view see Sagan, B. and Waltz, K. N., *The Spread of Nuclear Weapons: A Debate Renewed*, 2nd edn (W.W. Norton & Company: New York, N.Y., 2003).

[22] See e.g. Happold, M., 'Security Council Resolution 1373 and the constitution of the United Nations', *Leiden Journal of International Law*, vol. 16 (2003), pp. 593–610.

[23] *Prosecutor v. Tadic* (note 16), sections 35, 39.

[24] One argument against the constitutionality of Resolution 1540 relates to the general role of the UN in the field of armaments (including conventional and non-conventional weapons). Under the UN Charter, the General Assembly and the Security Council are both endowed only with a recommendatory role when it comes to the level and composition of the armaments of the member states (articles 11 and 26). It has been suggested in legal doctrine that attempts by the Security Council to regulate armaments in general—in contrast to specific situations such as the disarmament regime established for Iraq after the 1991 Gulf War—may amount to an ultra vires measure. See Frowein and Krisch (note 20), p. 726. The International Court of Justice (ICJ) has also stated that states are only bound by those limitations on armaments that they themselves have accepted. ICJ, *Military and Paramilitary Activities in and against Nicaragua* (Nicaragua v. United States of America), *ICJ Reports 1986*, URL <http://www.icj-cij.org/icjwww/icases/inus/inusframe.htm>, p. 14, para. 269.

resolution. Hence, preambular paragraphs may facilitate proper interpretation of the operative parts of a resolution. This is particularly true for Resolution 1540 which, in its preamble, defines the key concepts in the operative part.

Resolution 1540 is designed to reduce the risk of proliferation of WMD to non-state actors. The definition of this term is crucial because non-state actors constitute the personal field of application (*ratione personae*) of the resolution. The key element of this definition is that the individual or entity should not be legally authorized by any state to conduct the activities that fall under the resolution. The definition includes individuals or entities engaged in prohibited activities irrespective of the motivation—pecuniary (e.g. the A. Q. Khan network) or political (as in the case of a terrorist organization). The material field of application (*ratione materiae*) of Resolution 1540 is rather wide. The resolution contains definitions of the terms 'means of delivery' and 'related materials'. It is noteworthy that the 'traditional' parameters of range and payload used for other purposes of missile control are not included in the definition of means of delivery—hence, the definition covers any missile, rocket and other unmanned system capable of delivering WMD. However, the definition is limited by the formulation that missiles and the like should be 'specially' designed for the delivery of WMD. This could be perceived as an inconsistency because such delivery systems are already explicitly prohibited by Article I(2) of the BTWC and Article II of the CWC. Thus, with the exception of nuclear delivery vehicles, not many existing systems are included in the definition. The definition of related materials is very broad because it relates to materials, equipment and technology covered by 'relevant multilateral treaties' as well as 'arrangements'. Neither the 'relevant multilateral treaties' nor the 'arrangements' in question are identified in the resolution. Furthermore, the resolution does not specify which national control list would be relevant for determining the scope of the provisions. It is apparent that the definitions provided in the resolution may, in fact, give rise to more questions than answers.

In the fifth preambular paragraph of Resolution 1540 the Security Council affirms its support for the multilateral treaties that aim to eliminate or prevent the proliferation of nuclear, biological or chemical (NBC) weapons and stresses the importance of their full implementation by all parties in order to promote international stability. The full and effective implementation of existing non-proliferation treaties has become a leitmotif for much of the current work in the field of non-proliferation. There is a growing realization that a treaty entered into without corresponding national measures being taken in order to effectively implement its provisions may create opportunities for non-state and state actors to engage in proliferation activities. In the context of the multilateral treaties the preamble welcomes the efforts made by 'multilateral arrangements' which contribute to non-proliferation (i.e. the informal export control regimes that control the transfer of goods and technologies that may be used for the production of WMD). The work conducted in these informal arrangements has been viewed as controversial by non-participants because the arrangements have been alleged to put the interest of non-proliferation before the interest of the widest possible exchange of goods and technologies for peaceful purposes. A perennial issue within the multilateral treaty regimes has been the question of the removal of such alleged trade barriers, and the full membership of the treaty regimes has been reluctant to recognize the work carried out in the export control regimes. It is thus notable that the UN Security Council now welcomes the efforts of the export control regimes. Yet it also notes in the subsequent preambular paragraph that prevention of the proliferation of NBC weapons 'should not hamper international cooperation in materials, equipment and technology for peaceful purposes *while goals of peaceful utilization should not be used as a cover for proliferation*' (emphasis added). This formulation more or less restates the relevant provisions of the non-proliferation treaties with one important addition. While the treaties declare that the control efforts should not hamper international cooperation in goods and technologies for peaceful purposes, Resolution 1540 adds that peaceful use should not be a cover for proliferation. In other words, the formulation in the resolution qualifies the right to peaceful use in comparison with the similar provisions of the treaties.

While the Security Council recognizes that most states have 'undertaken binding legal obligations', or have made 'other commitments' aimed at preventing the proliferation of WMD, it is also recognized that there is a need for all states to take additional measures to prevent the proliferation of NBC weapons and their means of delivery. Against this backdrop the Security Council adopted the measures included in the operative part of the resolution.

The operative part

In five of the paragraphs of the operative part of the resolution the Security Council decides that the member states shall undertake a defined measure. As noted above, the paragraphs of a resolution in which the Security Council 'decides' are the ones that create an obligation under international law for the member states to take implementing action. The other paragraphs of the operative part are framed in the form of recommendations—outlining what member states are encouraged to do.

In operative paragraph 1 of Resolution 1540, the Security Council decides that states shall not provide support to non-state actors that attempt to develop, acquire, manufacture, possess, transport, transfer or use NBC weapons and their means of delivery. This provision corresponds to the main intent of the non-proliferation clauses of the, BTWC, the CWC and the NPT with the difference that it specifically applies to non-state actors. Its scope is wide because it covers 'any form of support'—which must be read to cover not only the weapons themselves, but also goods and technologies that may be used for the production of WMD, as well as financial support to a development programme. The provision is also broad in the sense that it covers all the stages in an acquisition process. In other words, the scope of Resolution 1540 is much wider than that of the non-proliferation treaties.

Operative paragraph 2 relates specifically to the domestic legal systems of the member states. Apart from the obligation on UN member states not to assist in the proliferation of WMD to non-state actors, they are also obliged to 'adopt and enforce' effective domestic legislation that would prohibit such activities under their jurisdictions. The provision specifically refers to 'laws'—which in most countries would imply the involvement of the legislature.[25]

Operative paragraph 3 lays down detailed obligations for the domestic control of goods and technologies that may be used to produce WMD. While the previous two

---

[25] This element of the resolution was criticized by some member states as an encroachment on the separation of powers in domestic constitutional law. It was argued that legislatures would find themselves under an international obligation to adopt laws conforming to the demands of the resolution, and that this international obligation would have been established before they could exercise their domestic constitutional functions in the making of international agreements. See UN documents S/PV.4950 and S/PV.4950 (Resumption 1) (note 7).

paragraphs specifically relate to non-state actors, paragraph 3 outlines more general obligations. It lists the specific controls that member states should establish over such weapons and 'related materials'.

Operative paragraph 3's obligations are extensive and potentially demanding in terms of resources. The member states are required to establish and maintain effective accounting systems, physical protection measures, border controls, law enforcement measures and national export controls that would also cover trans-shipments. For many developing countries these requirements could seem totally unrealistic because of a lack of resources. The Security Council recognizes that some states may require implementation assistance and invites states to offer such assistance.

Article 103 of the UN Charter establishes that in the event of a conflict between obligations owed under the Charter and obligations under any other international agreement the former will prevail. It anticipates the situation in which a member state may seek to avoid honouring decisions of the Security Council with the argument that doing so may conflict with existing treaty obligations. In this context it is interesting to note that in operative paragraph 5 of Resolution 1540 the Security Council decides that the obligations in the resolution are not to conflict with the BTWC, the CWC and the NPT or alter the responsibilities of the International Atomic Energy Agency or the Organization for the Prohibition of Chemical Weapons.

Operative paragraph 10 recommends that member states take cooperative action to prevent illicit trafficking in WMD, their means of delivery, and related materials. During the negotiation of the resolution, the USA sought to include a provision that would authorize the interdiction and seizure of WMD in transit. The *So San* incident in 2002 had demonstrated the limits set by international law to undertake such measures on the high seas,[26] and the policy objective of the US Government was to have an authorization by the UN Security Council in a binding resolution under Chapter VII to remedy this lack of legal authorization. However, this proposal was not accepted by the Security Council members and the provision in operative paragraph 10 makes clear that such cooperative actions should be consistent with existing international law.[27]

In operational paragraph 8 the Security Council calls on the UN members to ensure universality and full implementation of multilateral treaties in the field of non-proliferation of WMD. This paragraph is significant because it does not contain the other component found in the relevant treaties—disarmament by the existing possessors of such weapons. While the Security Council declares its intention 'to monitor closely' the implementation of Resolution 1540, there are no sanctions envisaged in the resolution for those member states that do not comply with its requirements.

Resolution 1540 imposes significant obligations on the UN member states and the new elements in these obligations are likely to be most significant for those states that are not participants in the export control regimes and that may not have enacted implementation legislation in relation to the non-proliferation treaties. Given the significant character of these obligations, it may be questioned how suitable the language of the resolution is as a guide for national implementation legislation. As noted above, some definitions give rise to uncertainties and, more importantly, at several points the resolution calls on the UN members to adopt 'appropriate' and 'effective'

[26] On the *So San* incident see Ahlström, C., 'The Proliferation Security Initiative: international law aspects of the Statement of Interdiction Principles', *SIPRI Yearbook 2005: Armaments, Disarmament and International Security* (Oxford University Press: Oxford, 2005), pp. 741–42.

[27] Ahlström (note 26), p. 763.

national legislation, but the resolution provides no further criteria for judging appropriateness and effectiveness. In the light of this it would essentially be up to the individual member state to decide, and this situation may in turn lead to differences in implementation between them. The procedures surrounding Resolution 1540 also did not produce any published *travaux preparatoires*—which in many instances serve as an important tool for the proper interpretation of ambiguous treaties, as well as other forms of legislation.

IV. The implementation of Resolution 1540

In the controversy over whether the Security Council has the power to adopt legislating resolutions it would be pertinent to assess the extent to which the member states have implemented Resolution 1540, as a practical indicator of how far they have been willing to conform to its provisions.

To monitor the implementation of the resolution, the Security Council established the 1540 Committee, consisting of all members of the Security Council, to sit for a maximum of two years. The member states were requested to report to the committee no later than six months after the adoption of the resolution (i.e. before 28 October 2004) on steps they had taken, or intended to take, in order to implement it—in other words, not necessarily on full and complete implementation. This procedure does not address the point that reporting in itself is no guarantee of compliance nor does it make clear the standards of compliance by which states would be assessed. A full check of national measures for compliance and adequacy with the range of international conventions would demand abundant resources. The 1540 Committee began its work in June 2004.[28] In August the committee adopted guidelines for the conduct of its work as well as for the preparation of national reports. Towards the end of 2004 the committee began to hire experts for the task of assessing the national reports.[29] The first experts began work in February 2005. However, no more than eight experts were involved at any time and the level of relevant knowledge in the states making up the Security Council at the time and the levels of expertise were uneven.

Out of a total UN membership of 191, 59 member states (and one non-member, the European Union) submitted their first national report by the deadline, on 28 October 2004.[30] As of 7 December 2004, the number of member states that had submitted reports increased to 87.[31] An overwhelming majority of the 104 non-submitting states were developing countries. As of 16 December 2005, the response rate had improved somewhat and 124 member states had submitted their initial reports, while 67 mem-

---

[28] United Nations, Letter dated 8 December 2004 from the Chairman of the Security Council Committee established pursuant to Resolution 1540 (2004) addressed to the President of the Security Council, UN document S/2004/958, 8 Dec. 2004.

[29] Most of the documents related to the work of the 1540 Committee are available on its website, URL <http://disarmament2.un.org/Committee1540/>.

[30] In comparison, 112 states had complied with the reporting requirement in Resolution 1373 by the end of 2001. See Stiles, K. W. and Thayne, A., 'Compliance with international law: international law on terrorism at the United Nations', *Cooperation and Conflict*, vol. 41, no. 2 (2006), pp. 153–76; and Stiles, K. W., 'The power of procedure and the procedures of the powerful: anti-terror law in the United Nations', *Journal of Peace Research*, vol. 43, no. 1 (2006), pp. 37–54.

[31] United Nations, Letter dated 8 December 2004 from the Chairman of the Security Council Committee established pursuant to Resolution 1540 (2004) addressed to the President of the Security Council, Corrigendum, UN document S/2004/958/Corr.1, 23 Dec. 2004.

ber states had yet to do so.[32] On 25 April 2006, two years after the adoption of the resolution and one and a half year after the expiry of the deadline, the committee submitted to the Security Council its third successive report, the first to make substantive comments on implementation. At this time, 62 UN member states had still not submitted a first report.[33] However, it should be emphasized that the countries that have submitted national reports account for the overwhelming majority of the trade in the relevant goods and technologies. Over half of the non-reporting states were in Africa, while another significant group consisted of small states in the Pacific region. Again, most were developing countries that were generally parties to the formal treaties on non-proliferation of WMD but not participants in the informal export control regimes. Reports from such countries would have revealed the need for them to take substantial additional measures to implement Resolution 1540, underlining that the work needed in order to implement the terms of the resolution is still greater than indicated in the third report of the 1540 Committee as it stands. Tellingly, the language of this report is generic, referring to the overall implementation level, rather than identifying what individual member states have done or have yet to do. More detailed information on the level of implementation in particular member states may be accessed in the legislative database that the 1540 Committee has made available on the Internet.[34]

With respect to the implementation of operative paragraph 1 of the resolution (the obligation to refrain from supporting non-state actors seeking to acquire or develop WMD and their means of delivery), the committee noted that a majority of the 62 states that had not submitted reports are parties to the treaties on non-proliferation of WMD. In light of this it concluded that 'these States should be in a position to report within a short period of time on steps they have taken to implement the obligations under those agreements in their national legislation'.[35] The assumption made about the role of the formal treaties in relation to the fulfilment of operative paragraph 1 seems too sweeping because the former do not, in general, relate to non-state actors in the first place.

The committee has identified several issues in relation to the implementation of operative paragraph 2. Several states have apparently reported that the implementation of this requirement would be met by means of their pre-existing legislation on export control, but the committee notes that the requirements of the resolution cannot be considered to be met just by such measures. Furthermore, some member states have also reported the measures they have undertaken to implement the BTWC, the CWC and the NPT as sufficient to meet the requirements of operative paragraph 2. The committee states, however, that these treaties 'deal primarily with State-to-State prohibited activities' and that they do not 'explicitly address non-State actors'.[36] The committee also notes that some member states have recently adopted anti-terrorism legislation that criminalizes the acquisition of WMD by terrorist organizations. In this context the committee cautions that the material field of application of Reso-

[32] United Nations, Letter dated 19 December 2005 from the Chairman of the Security Council Committee established pursuant to Resolution 1540 (2004) addressed to the President of the Security Council, UN document S/2005/799, 19 Dec. 2005.

[33] United Nations, Letter dated 25 April 2006 from the Chairman of the Security Council Committee established pursuant to Resolution 1540 (2004) addressed to the President of the Security Council, UN document S/2006/257, 25 Apr. 2006.

[34] See 1540 Committee, 'Legislative database', URL <http://disarmament2.un.org/Committee1540/legalDB.html>.

[35] United Nations (note 33), p. 10.

[36] United Nations (note 33), p. 11.

lution 1540 is wider because of its focus on all non-state actors, rather than terrorists alone. Looking at the different categories of WMD, the committee notes that the most 'promising' level of implementation is in the field of chemical weapons—at least as long as the material provisions of the resolution correspond to the provisions of the CWC.[37] A similar situation also exists with respect to biological and nuclear weapons. Several states have legislation that covers, and provisions that penalize violations of, the prohibition to manufacture and acquire biological weapons. However, with respect to the requirements in the resolution that have no correspondence in the BTWC, the situation is not as good. With regard to the means of delivery for WMD the committee notes that only 36 states have legislation in place that prohibits non-state actors from acquiring such means. The general conclusion drawn on operative paragraph 2 is that major variations exist in the domestic legislation of member states, and the committee concludes by expressing concern about the number of states that 'still have no legislation in place that prohibits and penalizes the possible use by non-State actors of their territory as a safe haven for activities related to weapons of mass destruction'. The committee recommends the Security Council to encourage states that have a legal framework already in place to revisit their legislation in order to fill gaps related to all aspects of operative paragraph 2. Hence, the report indicates that several UN members have reported national legislation that, on closer analysis, does not meet the requirements of the resolution.

As noted above, operative paragraph 3 is the most demanding provision of the resolution. In its review of the implementation of paragraphs 3(a) and 3(b)—accounting and effective physical protection measures—the committee notes that most of the measures reported relate to hazardous NBC weapon-related materials and the like that are used for permitted peaceful purposes. Only 14 member states have reported that they have taken such measures in relation to the means of delivery of WMD. A problem in connection with the measures reported under this provision is that they often serve other purposes than security—for example, occupational health and environmental protection. Hence, it cannot be taken for granted that such legislation covers all obligations under paragraphs 3(a) and (b). The committee also notes that some states might consider that there is no need for legislation on accounting and physical protection measures because they currently do not have any goods and technologies within their territories. Here the committee reiterates that Resolution 1540 establishes a 'direct and binding requirement' with which all states are meant to comply. Without uniform implementation there is a risk that some member states' territories may become 'proliferation pathways'.

Paragraphs 3(c) and 3(d) require the member states to develop and maintain effective border controls as well as export and trans-shipment controls. In relation to border controls, the committee notes that 77 states have reported that they have a national legal framework for the control of the flow of goods over their borders and that these controls also cover items related to WMD. While many of these states also have enforcement agencies for border control, there are apparently some instances where such enforcement agencies do not have a specific authority in relation to

---

[37] The higher level of national implementation in respect of the CWC can largely be credited to the focused work (in the framework of the Article VII Action Plan) that the Organisation for the Prohibition of Chemical Weapons has conducted in recent years in order to ensure full national implementation of the provisions of the treaty. See Guthrie, R., Hart, J. and Kuhlau, F., 'Chemical and biological warfare developments and arms control', *SIPRI Yearbook 2006: Armaments, Disarmament and International Security* (Oxford University Press: Oxford, 2006), p. 715.

WMD and their means of delivery. The general conclusion in relation to the requirement for border controls is: 'The Committee's findings concerning border control efforts raise concern that a large number of States might not have either the technical capacity or the equipment to implement the full range of border controls called for under resolution 1540 (2004)'.[38]

The establishment of a domestic export control system is a prerequisite for being able to differentiate between legitimate trade for peaceful purposes and illicit trafficking of dual-use goods (items that were not specially designed, developed or adapted for military use but that could nevertheless be used in military programmes). In this context the committee notes that 'effective measures of export control will facilitate legitimate and secure trade among States. Such controls can also reduce the incidence of theft or diversion, including the illicit acquisition and use of such items'.[39] Of the 129 UN member states that have submitted national reports, 80 report that they have some export controls in place that cover items related to WMD, while 69 report that they have penalties associated with export control legislation. It is mainly among the participants in the multilateral export control regimes that the implementation of the specific requirements of Resolution 1540 is found to be comprehensive.[40] Specifically in relation to the licensing of exports and imports of sensitive goods, 69 states report that they have such a system. Few participating states, however, have reported on the existence of any penalties for violating, or on the enforcement of, such licensing requirements.

While almost all UN member states that have export control legislation in place also have adopted national control lists, the committee notes that these vary: 59 include items for biological weapons, 66 cover goods and technologies for chemical weapons, 61 list nuclear items, and 55 include the means of delivery of WMD. It is also noted that some countries exercise control over goods and technologies not listed in any control list (so-called catch-all controls) and that 38 countries exercise control over intangible transfers of technology (i.e. where no goods physically cross any borders). The number of UN member states controlling the provision of financial services related to the export of items related to WMD stands at 16, while 9 member states report that they also control the provision of transport services. Finally, with respect to end-use controls, the committee notes that 49 states have reported that they exercise such controls. However, as far as control over the transfer, trans-shipment or re-export of dual-use items is concerned, the 1540 Committee notes that a limited number of member states exercise such control. In relation to this situation, the committee concludes that 'these findings outline another gap in the international system that could be exploited, particularly with the increase in the use of free-trade zones or similar territories'.[41]

In its conclusions, the committee notes that Resolution 1540 is an important and timely response to the threat of non-state actors, in particular terrorists, acquiring WMD. However, this response may only be effective if all UN members 'irrespective of whether they possess a potential associated with weapons of mass destruction and their mean of delivery implement fully the requirements laid down in the resolution

---

[38] United Nations (note 33), p. 20.

[39] United Nations (note 33), p. 21.

[40] For a list of the current membership of the multilateral export control regimes see table 11.1 in chapter 11.

[41] United Nations (note 33), p. 22.

and cooperate closely among themselves to this end'.[42] Examination of the national reports reveals that several member states intend to base their implementation of the provisions of Resolution 1540 on legislation that predated the adoption of the resolution. However, as noted above, most of this legislation was originally designed to comply with non-proliferation treaties that, at least in significant parts, do not address the threats posed by non-state actors. The committee notes that at least 'some' states have shown an interest in revisiting the existing legal framework in order to bring it in line with the new requirements established by Resolution 1540. The lack of sufficient information in many national reports coupled with the sizeable number of UN member states that still have to submit their first national reports leads the 1540 Committee to conclude that 'much needs to be done henceforth to fulfil the implementation obligations under resolution 1540 (2004) in a comprehensive manner'.[43] It is also obvious from the first substantive report of the 1540 Committee that the formal status of the resolution plays an important role for it. On several occasions the committee emphasizes its binding nature when discussing the lack of implementation of Resolution 1540.

On the basis of the 1540 Committee's report, the Security Council adopted Resolution 1673 on 27 April 2006, in which the Security Council notes that not all UN member states have submitted their first national reports on their implementation of Resolution 1540. It also notes that the full implementation of the resolution's requirements, including the adoption of national laws and measures, 'is a long term task that will require continuous efforts at national, regional and international levels'. Resolution 1673 is also adopted under Chapter VII of the UN Charter. In the resolution, the Security Council reiterates its decision on the adoption and the requirements of Resolution 1540 and emphasizes the importance of all states fully implementing the resolution. It calls on all states that have not yet submitted any reports to do so 'without delay' rather than setting any precise deadline. Interestingly, the operative paragraphs containing (legally binding) decisions by the Security Council are directed at the 1540 Committee, rather than at the recalcitrant member states. The Security Council decides to extend the mandate of the 1540 Committee for an additional two years (until 27 April 2008) and decides that the committee shall intensify its efforts to promote the full implementation of Resolution 1540. The latter, however, may be an empty expectation owing to the lack of funding, staff and so on.[44]

Given the relatively clear provision in Article 25 of the UN Charter that member states *shall* carry out the decisions of the Security Council it may seem out of the ordinary that the Security Council finds itself in the situation of having to reiterate a previous legally binding resolution. The implementation record thus far of Resolution 1540 has most probably led at least some members of the Security Council to realize that its adoption was not the quick fix they may originally have expected. The same understanding would explain why, although the 1540 Committee was originally envisaged to sit for only two years (Resolution 1540 provides no time frame for

---

[42] United Nations (note 33), p. 28. The General Assembly has called on its members to strengthen and coordinate their efforts to combat the proliferation of WMD to terrorists. See e. g. United Nations, The United Nations Global Counter-Terrorism Strategy, UN document A/RES/60/288, 8 Sep. 2006.

[43] United Nations (note 33), p. 28.

[44] Some countries and organizations have provided funding for regional meetings to support the implementation of Resolution 1540. See e.g. 'Council Joint Action 2006/419/CFSP of 12 June 2006 in support of the implementation of the United Nations Security Council Resolution 1540 (2004) and in the framework of the implementation of the EU Strategy against the Proliferation of Weapons of Mass Destruction', *Official Journal of the European Union*, L165 (17 June 2006), p. 30.

complete implementation), Resolution 1673 explicitly recognizes that full implementation is a 'long-term task'. On the other hand, there is information to suggest that countries which strongly supported Resolution 1540 never intended the UN to be the sole implementing organization. More effort is needed in the national and regional programmes of outreach to improve non-proliferation awareness and capacity—the results of which have not filtered back to the United Nations. It also remains to be seen whether the explicit recognition that the full implementation of Resolution 1540 is a long-term task may—as in the case of the UN Counter-Terrorism Committee—lead the 1540 Committee to adopt a conciliatory and non-confrontational posture, rather than relying mainly on the formal character of the obligations laid down in the resolution.

V. Conclusions

This appendix addresses the question of whether the actual implementation of a controversial UN Security Council resolution could be used as a measure of its acceptance by the UN members. If this were so, then the fact that about one-third of the UN member states have never reported under UN Security Council Resolution 1540 would seem to call such acceptance into question. However, there are other ways of reading the situation. Countries may have had practical or political reasons for not responding. This is all the more plausible because no clear penalty was defined in the resolution. That said, the implementation of Resolution 1540 thus far would seem to indicate that its acceptance is still far from universal and, hence, that it remains controversial. A substantial number of member states missed the deadline for reporting set by the resolution, and an equally significant number of member states have yet to submit their first national reports. Among those member states that have provided reports, there seems to be a tendency to refer to pre-existing national legislation as far as possible. The 1540 Committee has reported that only some UN members seem ready to take a fresh look at their national legislation in view of the new threat of weapons of mass destruction coming into the possession of non-state actors and to take action to remedy any deficiencies found in the national legislation.

The level of implementation of Resolution 1540 would also indicate that a legislative resolution under Chapter VII of the UN Charter need not necessarily imply a prompt answer to an urgent threat to international peace and security. Resolution 1540 will probably not be implemented by all UN member states for several years—despite the fact that its provisions are legally binding under the Charter of the United Nations. The main proponents of the resolution may also not have envisaged the UN as the sole implementing body.

In view of all these complexities, it is too early to tell if the UN Security Council has achieved the purpose of the resolution. This could only be determined if a direct survey of compliance and the reasons for non-compliance were to be carried out. After only two years of operation, it is not possible to determine whether the resolution has been a success.

Appendix 11B. United Nations Security Council Resolution 1540

Adopted by the Security Council at its 4956th meeting, on 28 April 2004

The Security Council,

Affirming that proliferation of nuclear, chemical and biological weapons, as well as their means of delivery* constitutes a threat to international peace and security,

Reaffirming, in this context, the Statement of its President adopted at the Council's meeting at the level of Heads of State and Government on 31 January 1992 (S/23500), including the need for all Member States to fulfil their obligations in relation to arms control and disarmament and to prevent proliferation in all its aspects of all weapons of mass destruction,

Recalling also that the Statement underlined the need for all Member States to resolve peacefully in accordance with the Charter any problems in that context threatening or disrupting the maintenance of regional and global stability,

Affirming its resolve to take appropriate and effective actions against any threat to international peace and security caused by the proliferation of nuclear, chemical and biological weapons and their means of delivery, in conformity with its primary responsibilities, as provided for in the United Nations Charter,

Affirming its support for the multilateral treaties whose aim is to eliminate or prevent the proliferation of nuclear, chemical or biological weapons and the importance for all States parties to these treaties to implement them fully in order to promote international stability,

Welcoming efforts in this context by multilateral arrangements which contribute to non-proliferation,

Affirming that prevention of proliferation of nuclear, chemical and biological weapons should not hamper international cooperation in materials, equipment and technology for peaceful purposes while goals of peaceful utilization should not be used as a cover for proliferation,

Gravely concerned by the threat of terrorism and the risk that non-State actors* such as those identified in the United Nations list established and maintained by the Committee established under Security Council resolution 1267 and those to whom resolution 1373 applies, may acquire, develop, traffic in or use nuclear, chemical and biological weapons and their means of delivery,

Gravely concerned by the threat of illicit trafficking in nuclear, chemical, or biological weapons and their means of delivery, and related materials,* which adds a new dimension to the issue of proliferation of such weapons and also poses a threat to international peace and security,

Recognizing the need to enhance coordination of efforts on national, subregional, regional and international levels in order to strengthen a global response to this serious challenge and threat to international security,

Recognizing that most States have undertaken binding legal obligations under treaties to which they are parties, or have made other commitments aimed at preventing the proliferation of nuclear, chemical or biological weapons, and have taken effective measures to account for, secure and physically protect sensitive materials, such as those required by the Convention on the Physical Protection of Nuclear Materials and those recommended by the IAEA Code of Conduct on the Safety and Security of Radioactive Sources,

---

* Definitions for the purpose of this resolution only:

Means of delivery: missiles, rockets and other unmanned systems capable of delivering nuclear, chemical, or biological weapons, that are specially designed for such use.

Non-State actor: individual or entity, not acting under the lawful authority of any State in conducting activities which come within the scope of this resolution.

Related materials: materials, equipment and technology covered by relevant multilateral treaties and arrangements, or included on national control lists, which could be used for the design, development, production or use of nuclear, chemical and biological weapons and their means of delivery.

Recognizing further the urgent need for all States to take additional effective measures to prevent the proliferation of nuclear, chemical or biological weapons and their means of delivery,

Encouraging all Member States to implement fully the disarmament treaties and agreements to which they are party,

Reaffirming the need to combat by all means, in accordance with the Charter of the United Nations, threats to international peace and security caused by terrorist acts,

Determined to facilitate henceforth an effective response to global threats in the area of non-proliferation,

Acting under Chapter VII of the Charter of the United Nations,

1. *Decides that* all States shall refrain from providing any form of support to non-State actors that attempt to develop, acquire, manufacture, possess, transport, transfer or use nuclear, chemical or biological weapons and their means of delivery;

2. *Decides also* that all States, in accordance with their national procedures, shall adopt and enforce appropriate effective laws which prohibit any non-State actor to manufacture, acquire, possess, develop, transport, transfer or use nuclear, chemical or biological weapons and their means of delivery, in particular for terrorist purposes, as well as attempts to engage in any of the foregoing activities, participate in them as an accomplice, assist or finance them;

3. *Decides also* that all States shall take and enforce effective measures to establish domestic controls to prevent the proliferation of nuclear, chemical, or biological weapons and their means of delivery, including by establishing appropriate controls over related materials and to this end shall:

(*a*) Develop and maintain appropriate effective measures to account for and secure such items in production, use, storage or transport;

(*b*) Develop and maintain appropriate effective physical protection measures;

(*c*) Develop and maintain appropriate effective border controls and law enforcement efforts to detect, deter, prevent and combat, including through international cooperation when necessary, the illicit trafficking and brokering in such items in accordance with their national legal authorities and legislation and consistent with international law;

(*d*) Establish, develop, review and maintain appropriate effective national export and trans-shipment controls over such items, including appropriate laws and regulations to control export, transit, trans-shipment and re-export and controls on providing funds and services related to such export and trans-shipment such as financing, and transporting that would contribute to proliferation, as well as establishing end-user controls; and establishing and enforcing appropriate criminal or civil penalties for violations of such export control laws and regulations;

4. *Decides* to establish, in accordance with rule 28 of its provisional rules of procedure, for a period of no longer than two years, a Committee of the Security Council, consisting of all members of the Council, which will, calling as appropriate on other expertise, report to the Security Council for its examination, on the implementation of this resolution, and to this end calls upon States to present a first report no later than six months from the adoption of this resolution to the Committee on steps they have taken or intend to take to implement this resolution;

5. *Decides* that none of the obligations set forth in this resolution shall be interpreted so as to conflict with or alter the rights and obligations of State Parties to the Nuclear Non-Proliferation Treaty, the Chemical Weapons Convention and the Biological and Toxin Weapons Convention or alter the responsibilities of the International Atomic Energy Agency or the Organization for the Prohibition of Chemical Weapons;

6. *Recognizes* the utility in implementing this resolution of effective national control lists and calls upon all Member States, when necessary, to pursue at the earliest opportunity the development of such lists;

7. *Recognizes* that some States may require assistance in implementing the provisions of this resolution within their territories and invites States in a position to do so to offer assistance as appropriate in response to specific requests to the States lacking the legal and regulatory infrastructure, implementation

experience and/or resources for fulfilling the above provisions;

8. *Calls upon* all States:

(*a*) To promote the universal adoption and full implementation, and, where necessary, strengthening of multilateral treaties to which they are parties, whose aim is to prevent the proliferation of nuclear, biological or chemical weapons;

(*b*) To adopt national rules and regulations, where it has not yet been done, to ensure compliance with their commitments under the key multilateral non-proliferation treaties;

(*c*) To renew and fulfil their commitment to multilateral cooperation, in particular within the framework of the International Atomic Energy Agency, the Organization for the Prohibition of Chemical Weapons and the Biological and Toxin Weapons Convention, as important means of pursuing and achieving their common objectives in the area of non-proliferation and of promoting international cooperation for peaceful purposes;

(*d*) To develop appropriate ways to work with and inform industry and the public regarding their obligations under such laws;

9. *Calls upon* all States to promote dialogue and cooperation on non-proliferation so as to address the threat posed by proliferation of nuclear, chemical, or biological weapons, and their means of delivery;

10. Further to counter that threat, *calls upon* all States, in accordance with their national legal authorities and legislation and consistent with international law, to take cooperative action to prevent illicit trafficking in nuclear, chemical or biological weapons, their means of delivery, and related materials;

11. *Expresses* its intention to monitor closely the implementation of this resolution and, at the appropriate level, to take further decisions which may be required to this end;

12. *Decides* to remain seized of the matter.

———

Source: United Nations website, URL <http://www.un.org/Docs/sc/unsc_resolutions04.html>.

12. Nuclear arms control and non-proliferation

SHANNON N. KILE

I. Introduction

In 2006 two long-running challenges to the nuclear non-proliferation regime moved again to centre stage at the United Nations Security Council. The first involves the nuclear weapon ambitions of the Democratic People's Republic of Korea (DPRK, or North Korea), which in October 2006 carried out a nuclear test explosion using technology and material that had been imported for peaceful purposes. The second involves the efforts of the International Atomic Energy Agency (IAEA) to clarify unresolved questions about the scope and nature of Iran's uranium enrichment and other sensitive nuclear fuel cycle activities. During the year the Security Council imposed sanctions on Iran and North Korea that targeted their activities of proliferation concern. Elsewhere, controversy continued over the Indian–US Civil Nuclear Cooperation Initiative (CNCI) and its proposed exemption for India from nuclear supplier restrictions. In Geneva, renewed but ultimately fruitless efforts were made at the Conference on Disarmament (CD) to open the long-delayed negotiations on a global fissile material cut-off treaty (FMCT). Russian President Vladimir Putin's proposal for a new strategic arms reduction treaty with the United States to succeed the 1991 Treaty on the Reduction and Limitation of Strategic Offensive Arms (START I Treaty)[1] drew a cautious response from the USA and a promise of further discussion. There was one modest bright note for nuclear non-proliferation efforts in 2006, when leaders from five Central Asian states signed a treaty creating a nuclear weapon-free zone in the region.[2]

This chapter reviews the main developments in nuclear arms control and non-proliferation in 2006. Section II describes the circumstances surrounding North Korea's nuclear test explosion and examines the Security Council's decisions to impose sanctions on North Korea. Section III summarizes developments in the confrontation between Iran and the Security Council over the latter's demand that Iran halt its uranium enrichment programme. Section IV examines the controversy over the Indian–US nuclear deal, focusing on the obstacles to its implementation. Section V summarizes international initiatives aimed at enhancing the safety and custodial security of nuclear

---

[1] The Treaty on the Reduction and Limitation of Strategic Offensive Arms (START I Treaty) was signed on 31 July 1991 by the Soviet Union and the USA and entered into force for Belarus, Kazakhstan Russia, Ukraine and the USA on 5 Dec. 1994. For a brief summary of the treaty see annex A in this volume.

[2] The Central Asian Nuclear Weapon-Free Zone Treaty was signed on 8 Sep. 2006 by Kazakhstan, Kyrgyzstan, Tajikistan, Turkmenistan and Uzbekistan. For a brief description of the treaty see annex A in this volume.

materials and facilities and preventing nuclear terrorism. Section VI describes the efforts at the CD to resolve the impasse that has blocked the opening of negotiations on an FMCT, while section VII presents the conclusions.

Appendix 12A provides tables of data on the nuclear forces of the United States, Russia, the United Kingdom, France, China, India, Pakistan, Israel and North Korea. Appendix 12B provides data on North Korea's nuclear test explosion and information about all previous nuclear tests known to have been conducted by other states. Appendix 12C provides an overview of global inventories of fissile material and efforts to dispose safely of the large quantities of material deemed to be in excess of national security requirements.

II. North Korea's nuclear programme and the Six-Party Talks

The international confrontation over North Korea's nuclear programme intensified in 2006. The dispute had entered its current phase in 2002, when a series of tit-for-tat moves by North Korea and the USA resulted in the collapse of the 1994 Agreed Framework and the expulsion of IAEA monitors from North Korea.[3] This was followed in April 2003 by North Korea's formal withdrawal from the 1968 Treaty on the Non-Proliferation of Nuclear Weapons (Non-Proliferation Treaty, NPT).[4] In February 2005 North Korea further raised the stakes in the crisis by declaring that it had developed nuclear weapons.[5]

The year 2006 opened against the background of a North Korean boycott of the Six-Party Talks—involving China, Japan, North Korea, South Korea, Russia and the USA—which aim at resolving the diplomatic impasse over North Korea's nuclear programme.[6] The talks had achieved an apparent breakthrough the previous year when, on 19 September 2005, the parties issued a Joint Statement on principles guiding future talks aimed at the 'verifiable denuclearization of the Korean Peninsula in a peaceful manner'.[7] Immediately after the Joint Statement was issued, however, the two main antagonists—North Korea and the USA—presented conflicting versions of what had

---

[3] International Atomic Energy Agency (IAEA), Agreed Framework between the United States of America and the Democratic People's Republic of Korea, 21 Oct. 1994, INFCIRC/457, 2 Nov. 1994. On the breakdown of the Agreed Framework see Kile, S. N., 'Nuclear arms control, non-proliferation and missile defence', *SIPRI Yearbook 2003: Armaments, Disarmament and International Security* (Oxford University Press: Oxford, 2003), pp. 578–92.

[4] The Treaty on the Non-Proliferation of Nuclear Weapons was opened for signature on 1 July 1968 and entered into force on 5 Mar. 1970. According to the NPT, only states that manufactured and exploded a nuclear device prior to 1 Jan. 1967 are legally recognized as nuclear weapon states. By this definition, China, France, Russia, the UK and the USA are the nuclear weapon states parties to the NPT. For a brief description of the NPT and a list of the signatories and parties to the treaty see annex A in this volume. North Korea acceded to the NPT as a non-nuclear weapon state party on 12 Dec. 1985. Its withdrawal from the treaty took effect on 10 Apr. 2003. North Korea's comprehensive safeguards agreement with the IAEA (INFCIRC/403) was considered also to have lapsed on that date.

[5] For an assessment of North Korea's nuclear weapon capabilities see appendix 12A.

[6] Prior to 2006, there had been 5 rounds of the Six-Party Talks: 27–29 Aug. 2003; 25–28 Feb. 2004; 23–26 June 2004; 26 July–7 Aug. and 13–19 Sep. 2005; and 9–11 Nov. 2005.

[7] US Department of State, 'Joint Statement of the fourth round of the Six-Party Talks', 19 Sep. 2005, Washington, DC, URL <http://www.state.gov/r/pa/prs/ps/2005/53490.htm>.

actually been agreed, especially with regard to the sequencing of a possible deal on dismantling North Korea's nuclear infrastructure.[8]

The prospects for resolving the disagreement were complicated by the USA's imposition, on 15 September 2005, of new restrictions on North Korea's trading and financial activities. According to the USA, the measures had been imposed in response to North Korea's suspected involvement in a number of illegal activities, including money laundering and currency counter-feiting.[9] The North Korean Government was reportedly hit especially hard by the Chinese-approved freezing of the accounts at a bank in Macao used by North Korean trading companies and individuals in the leadership.[10] North Korea denounced the measures as a US tactic to derail progress at the Six-Party Talks, pointing out that the announcement of the measures had coincided with that of the Joint Statement.[11] In December 2005 North Korea declared that it would not return to the talks until the USA lifted the banking and other financial sanctions against it.[12] During the first half of 2006 North Korean officials continued to blame the US sanctions for the breakdown of the Six-Party Talks.[13]

North Korea heightened international concern about its strategic aims when it announced on 20 June that it would no longer observe its self-imposed moratorium, dating from 1999, on the flight-testing of long-range missiles.[14] On 5 July 2006 the North Korean Army test-launched seven ballistic missiles. North Korea described the tests as 'routine military exercises' that fell under its sovereign right to self-defence and emphasized that they did not violate any treaty commitment or other international legal constraint.[15] The flight tests involved several types of missile. Six short- and medium-range Hwasŏng-6 (Scud Mod-C) and Nodong missiles were successfully launched from the test facility at Musudan-ri into the Sea of Japan.[16] The seventh missile tested was a multi-stage Taepodong-2. This missile, to which some sources have attributed

[8] For a description of the Joint Statement see Kile, S. N., 'Nuclear arms control and non-proliferation', *SIPRI Yearbook 2006: Armaments, Disarmament and International Security* (Oxford University Press: Oxford, 2006), pp. 632–33.

[9] US Department of State, Bureau of International Information Programs (USINFO), 'U.S. cites Banco Delta Asia for money laundering, other crimes', Current Issues, 15 Sep. 2005, URL <http://usinfo.state.gov/usinfo/products/washfile.html>.

[10] Lague, D. and Greenlees, D., 'Squeeze on Banco Delta Asia hit North Korea where it hurt', *International Herald Tribune*, 18 Jan. 2007.

[11] Korea Central News Agency, 'DPRK Foreign Ministry's spokesman urges U.S. to lift financial sanctions against DPRK', Pyongyang, 9 Jan. 2006, URL <http://www.kcna.co.jp/item/2006/200601/news01/10.htm>; and Korea Central News Agency, 'KCNA blasts U.S. gimmick to evade responsibility for deadlocked talks', Pyongyang, 11 Feb. 2006, URL <http://www.kcna.co.jp/item/2006/200602/news02/13.htm>.

[12] Korea Central News Agency, 'U.S. perfidy under fire', Pyongyang, 6 Dec. 2005, URL <http://www.kcna.co.jp/item/2005/200512/news12/07.htm>.

[13] Korea Central News Agency, 'DPRK Foreign Ministry: DPRK's stand on Six-Party Talks clarified', Pyongyang, 1 June 2006, URL <http://www.kcna.co.jp/item/2006/200606/news06/02.htm>.

[14] Cooper, H. and Gordon, M., 'North Korea disavows its moratorium on testing of long-range missiles', *New York Times*, 21 June 2006.

[15] Korea Central News Agency, 'DPRK Foreign Ministry spokesman on its missile launches', Pyongyang, 6 July 2006, URL <http://www.kcna.co.jp/item/2006/200607/news07/07.htm>.

[16] Priest, D. and Faiola, A., 'North Korea tests long-range missile', *Washington Post*, 6 July 2006.

a range in excess of 3500 kilometres, had not previously been flight-tested.[17] It crashed into the sea after its first-stage booster apparently failed less than one minute after launch. The long range of Taepodong-2 has made it of particular concern to the USA, which reportedly activated parts of its national missile defence system in anticipation of the test.[18] Some non-governmental analysts pointed out that, the highly publicized failure of the Taepodong aside, North Korea's older short- and medium-range ballistic missiles seemed to perform well. This underscored the threat that North Korea's conventionally armed missile force poses to its neighbours and served to enhance the country's reputation as a missile technology supplier.[19]

The missile tests provoked widespread condemnation. In July 2006 the United Nations Security Council unanimously adopted Resolution 1695, which demanded that North Korea immediately suspend its ballistic missile activities and re-establish its flight-testing moratorium.[20] The resolution also required all states to undertake to 'prevent missile and missile-related items, materials, goods and technology' from being transferred to North Korea's missile or weapons of mass destruction (WMD) programmes. In addition, Japan moved to tighten its restrictions on travel and remittances to North Korea, while indicating that it could consider taking pre-emptive military action against North Korean missile bases if these were deemed to pose an imminent threat to Japan.[21] South Korea suspended regular deliveries of rice and fertilizer to North Korea but warned that overreacting to the missile tests would needlessly heighten tensions in the region.[22]

North Korea's nuclear test explosion

On 9 October 2006 North Korea announced that its army had 'successfully conducted an underground nuclear test under secure conditions'.[23] The explosion was detected by seismic sensors around the world, but the small yield of the blast raised questions about whether it was nuclear in origin. On 16 October, US intelligence officials announced that air samples had detected telltale radioactive debris that confirmed that North Korea had detonated a plutonium-fuelled nuclear explosive device.[24]

---

[17] See US Air Force, National Air and Space Intelligence Center (NASIC), *Ballistic and Cruise Missile Threat*, NAIC-1031-0985-03 (NASIC: Wright-Patterson Air Force Base, Ohio, Aug. 2003), URL <http://www.nukestrat.com/us/afn/NAIC2003rev.pdf>, p. 17.

[18] Gertz, B., 'N. Korean threat activates shield', *Washington Times*, 20 June 2006.

[19] Sterngold, J., 'Missile failure masks success', *San Francisco Chronicle*, 6 July 2006.

[20] UN Security Council Resolution 1695, 15 July 2006. UN Security Council resolutions can be accessed at URL <http://www.un.org/documents/scres.htm>.

[21] 'Seoul slams Japan for pondering strikes on N. Korea', *Chosun Ilbo*, 11 July 2006; and Yamaguchi, M., Associated Press, 'Japan mulling action over N. Korea missiles', CBS News, 10 July 2006, URL <http://www.cbsnews.com/stories/2006/07/10/ap/world/mainD8IP0DUO0.shtml>.

[22] Onishi, N., 'Missile tests divide Seoul from Tokyo', *New York Times*, 11 July 2006.

[23] Korea Central News Agency, 'DPRK successfully conducts underground nuclear test', Pyongyang, 9 Oct. 2006, URL <http://www.kcna.co.jp/item/2006/200610/news10/10.htm>.

[24] Office of the Director of National Intelligence, 'Statement by the Office of the Director of National Intelligence on the North Korea nuclear test', News release, 16 Oct. 2006, URL <http://www.dni.gov/

The North Korean test was not unexpected outside the country. There had been media speculation, based on reports of conversations between North Korean leader Kim Jong Il and foreign diplomats, that North Korea might be planning to carry out a nuclear test.[25] There had also been indications from US intelligence sources during the summer of 2006 that North Korea was preparing an underground nuclear test site.[26] In addition, on 3 October 2006 North Korea had announced that it would conduct a nuclear test, although it did not say when this would occur.[27]

North Korea's official explanations for carrying out the test emphasized its defensive purpose. According to Kim Yong-nam, president of the Presidium of the North Korean Supreme People's Assembly, the test was a 'historic event'; it enhanced the credibility of North Korea's nuclear deterrent in the face of US threats and thereby contributed to stability in North-East Asia.[28] A North Korean Foreign Ministry statement offered a similar rationale, stating that the country had been 'compelled to substantially prove its possession of nukes to protect its sovereignty and right to existence from the daily increasing danger of war from the US'.[29] These statements suggested that the test was intended in part to dispel any doubt in the USA or elsewhere that North Korea had mastered the engineering and design skills needed to build a first-generation nuclear weapon.[30] However, the unexpectedly low yield of the explosion, which led many foreign experts to believe that it had been a fizzle (an inefficient detonation releasing less explosive energy than expected), served to reinforce doubt that North Korea could manufacture a reliable nuclear weapon.[31]

In the view of many foreign analysts, North Korea probably had a parallel political rationale for carrying out the test: to signal displeasure with the sanctions imposed against it, and to gain diplomatic leverage for wresting concessions from the USA and its allies. Kim Yong-nam appeared partly to confirm the latter view when he warned that North Korea would carry out further nuclear tests if the USA did not abandon its efforts to isolate and sanction it.[32]

announcements/20061016_release.pdf>. For further detail about the test and the methods used to determine whether a nuclear explosion had occurred see appendix 12B.

[25] Song-wu, P., 'Diplomats in N. Korea believe underground nuke test highly probable', *Korea Times*, 10 Sep. 2006, URL <http://times.hankooki.com/lpage/200609/kt2006091017222510440.htm>; and Fifeld, A., 'Pyongyang "likely to test nuclear bomb"', *Financial Times*, 26 Sep. 2006.

[26] Karl, J., 'N. Korea appears to be preparing for nuclear test', ABC News, 17 Aug. 2006, URL <http://abcnews.go.com/International/print?id=2326083>.

[27] Korea Central News Agency, 'DPRK Foreign Ministry clarifies stand on new measure to bolster war deterrent', Pyongyang, 3 Oct. 2006, URL <http://www.kcna.co.jp/item/2006/200610/news10/04.htm>.

[28] Yonhap News, 'Additional nuke tests hinge on U.S. said by Kim Young Nam', *Daily NK*, 11 Oct. 2006, URL <http://www.dailynk.com/english/read.php?cataId=nk09000&num=1203>.

[29] Korea Central News Agency, 'DPRK Foreign Ministry spokesman on U.S. moves concerning its nuclear test', Pyongyang, 12 Oct. 2006, URL <http://www.kcna.co.jp/item/2006/200610/news10/12.htm>.

[30] Reuters, 'US not certain North Korea has nuclear weapons', ABC News, 1 Mar. 2006, URL <http://abcnews.go.com/International/print?id=1671969>.

[31] Sanger, D. and Broad, W., 'Small blast, or "big deal"? U.S. experts look for clues', *New York Times*, 11 Oct. 2006.

[32] Yonhap News (note 28).

Some analysts speculated that the decision to carry out the test may have been pushed through by hard-line elements in the North Korean military, who believed that the USA would be compelled to deal with the regime on an equal basis once it had unequivocally demonstrated its status as a de facto nuclear weapon state.[33]

In response to North Korea's claim to have carried out a nuclear test, the UN Security Council convened in emergency session. The USA, backed by non-permanent member Japan, proposed a tough draft resolution that would among other things have prohibited all trade in military goods and equipment with North Korea. China and Russia demurred, proposing instead less stringent measures. They also insisted that any resolution be adopted under Article 41 of Chapter VII of the UN Charter, which permits economic and other measures to 'give effect' to Security Council decisions but precludes the use of military force.[34]

On 14 October Resolution 1718 was unanimously approved by the Security Council. Invoking Article 41, the resolution 'expressed the gravest concern' about North Korea's nuclear test. It declared that North Korea should 'abandon all nuclear weapons and existing nuclear programs' as well as 'all other existing weapon of mass destruction and ballistic missile programs' in a 'complete, verifiable and irreversible manner'. It also called on North Korea to 'return immediately to the Six-Party Talks without preconditions'. The resolution required all UN member states to take a variety of measures to restrict certain conventional weapon systems and dual-use goods and materials from entering North Korea.[35] Member states were also asked to take action, 'in accordance with their national authorities and legislation, and consistent with international law', to prevent the transfer of prohibited items to North Korea by inspecting cargo en route to and from the country. This requirement sparked controversy in South Korea, where the government of President Roo Moo-hyun had consistently ruled out joining efforts to interdict North Korean vessels as part of the US-led Proliferation Security Initiative (PSI).[36] China also expressed opposition to the practice of cargo inspections.[37]

[33] Kwanwoo, J., Agence France-Presse, 'North Korean hardline military behind nuclear test say analysts', Space War, 16 Oct. 2006, URL <http://www.spacewar.com/reports/North_Korean_Hardline_Mili tary_Behind_Nuclear_Test_Say_Analysts_999.html>.

[34] O'Neill, J. and Choe, S., 'U.S. softens proposal on North Korea at U.N.', New York Times, 12 Oct. 2006; and Kerr, P., 'North Korean test provokes widespread condemnation', Arms Control Today, vol. 36, no. 9 (Nov. 2006), URL <http://www.armscontrol.org/act/archived.asp>. Chapter VII of the UN Charter authorizes the Security Council to use enforcement powers to maintain or restore international peace and security in situations where the Security Council has determined the existence of 'any threat to the peace, breach of the peace or act of aggression'. Military force is permitted under Article 42. The text of the Charter of the United Nations is available at URL <http://www.un.org/aboutun/charter>.

[35] On these UN sanctions see chapter 15 in this volume.

[36] O'Neill and Choe (note 34). For an analysis of legal aspects of the PSI see Ahlström, C., 'The Proliferation Security Initiative: international law aspects of the Statement of Interdiction Principles', SIPRI Yearbook 2005· Armaments, Disarmament and International Security (Oxford University Press: Oxford, 2005), pp. 741–65.

[37] Permanent Mission of the People's Republic of China to the United Nations, 'Explanatory remarks by Ambassador Wang Guangya at the Security Council after taking vote on draft Resolution on DPRK nuclear test', New York, N.Y., 14 Oct. 2006, URL <http://www.china-un.org/eng/smhwj/2006/t276121. htm>.

The North Korean nuclear test provoked a particularly sharp reaction from China. It issued a strongly worded rebuke to its neighbour that condemned the test as a 'brazen' act of defiance of the international community.[38] China, which is North Korea's largest supplier of oil and food aid, had previously counselled caution in dealing with North Korea and had refused to support proposed economic sanctions against it. However, North Korea's decision to carry out the test in the face of Chinese opposition had reportedly angered China, prompting it to threaten sanctions of its own—including a reduction of oil shipments—if North Korea did not return to the Six-Party Talks.[39] This pressure was widely credited with inducing North Korea to announce, on 31 October 2006, that it was prepared to return to the talks.[40] China was also reported to have played an instrumental role in persuading the USA to agree to discuss the financial sanctions issue directly with North Korea as a way of enticing the latter back to the negotiating table.[41]

On 18 December 2006 the Six-Party Talks resumed in Beijing after a year-long hiatus.[42] During one of several bilateral meetings on the margins of the talks, the USA offered North Korea a package of economic and energy assistance measures on condition that North Korea agree to begin dismantling its nuclear infrastructure, as envisioned in the 19 September 2005 Joint Statement. For its part, North Korea continued to insist that the USA must first lift its banking and other financial sanctions before it would discuss nuclear disarmament. The talks adjourned on 22 December without any apparent progress and with no date set for the next round.[43]

III. Iran and nuclear proliferation concerns

In 2006 the international controversy over the scope and nature of Iran's nuclear programme intensified as Iran proceeded apace with its uranium enrichment and other sensitive nuclear fuel cycle activities.[44] The controversy emerged at the end of 2002 and centred on findings by the IAEA that Iran had

---

[38] 'Beijing "resolutely opposed" to DPRK nuclear test', *People's Daily*, 10 Oct. 2006.

[39] Kahn, J., 'China seems set to harden stance', *International Herald Tribune*, 20 Oct. 2006, pp. 1, 4; and McGregor, R., 'Failure of policy to restrain neighbour rankles with China', *Financial Times*, 9 Oct. 2006, pp. 1, 5.

[40] Korea Central News Agency, 'Spokesman for DPRK Foreign Ministry on resumption of Six-Party Talks', Pyongyang, 31 Oct. 2006, URL <http://www.kcna.co.jp/item/2006/200611/news11/02.htm>; and 'North Korea talks set to resume', BBC News, 31 Aug. 2006, URL <http://news.bbc.co.uk/2/6102092.stm>.

[41] Cooper, H., 'U.S. debates value of North Korea talks', *New York Times*, 2 Nov. 2006.

[42] Kerr, P. 'No progress at North Korea talks', *Arms Control Today*, vol. 37, no. 1 (Jan./Feb. 2007), URL <http://www.armscontrol.org/act/archived.asp>.

[43] The Six-Party Talks resumed on 8 Feb. 2007 and concluded with an agreement on a series of steps for implementing the Sep. 2005 Joint Statement, beginning with the 'disablement' of North Korea's heavy water reactor at Yongbyon. US Department of State, 'North Korea: denuclearization action plan', Media note, Washington, DC, 13 Feb. 2007, URL <http://www.state.gov/r/pa/prs/ps/2007/february/80479.htm>.

[44] For a description of the origins of the nuclear controversy see Kile, S. N., 'Nuclear arms control and non-proliferation', *SIPRI Yearbook 2004: Armaments, Disarmament and International Security* (Oxford University Press: Oxford, 2004), pp. 604–607.

failed, over a period of two decades, to declare important nuclear activities in contravention of its NPT-mandated comprehensive safeguards agreement with the agency.[45] It was heightened by revelations, in 2003, that Iran had procured nuclear technology and equipment through the smuggling network organized by the former head of Pakistan's nuclear weapon programme, Abdul Qadeer Khan.[46] Iran maintains that its nuclear programme is intended solely for peaceful purposes and that any safeguards violations were minor in nature, involving failures to report certain permitted activities to the IAEA.[47] However, in Europe, the USA and elsewhere, there is concern that Iran is attempting to put into place, under the cover of a civilian nuclear energy programme, the sensitive fuel cycle facilities needed to produce plutonium and highly enriched uranium (HEU) for nuclear weapons. Since October 2003, three European Union (EU) member states—France, Germany and the UK, known as the E3—have taken the lead in attempting to resolve the controversy through negotiations with Iran. These negotiations have also involved the participation of the High Representative for the EU's Common Foreign and Security Policy (CFSP), Javier Solana.[48]

Iran's resumption of uranium enrichment activities

At the beginning of 2006, Iran took steps to restart its uranium enrichment programme in the face of mounting international pressure to permanently halt the programme. On 3 January 2006 Iran informed the IAEA that it had decided to end the 'voluntary and non-legally binding suspension' of its enrichment programme and resume centrifuge research and development (R&D) activities.[49] The suspension had been in place since November 2004, when Iran pledged to halt all enrichment-related activities while talks were under way with the E3/EU about a broader package of measures aimed at addressing international concerns about the country's nuclear programme.[50] At the time, Iran categorically rejected E3/EU demands for a permanent cessation

[45] Iran acceded to the NPT as a non-nuclear weapon state on 2 Feb. 1970. Its comprehensive safeguards agreement with the IAEA (INFCIRC/214) entered into force on 15 May 1974.

[46] For further detail on the Khan network see Kile, S. N., 'Nuclear arms control and non-proliferation', *SIPRI Yearbook 2005* (note 36), pp. 552–55; and Clary, C., 'A. Q. Khan and the limits of the non-proliferation regime', *Disarmament Forum*, no. 4 (2004), URL <http://www.unidir.org/pdf/articles/pdf-art2188.pdf>.

[47] Iranian officials have also argued that the country had been compelled to carry out some civil nuclear activities in secrecy in order to evade US efforts, in contravention of its obligation under Article IV of the NPT, to block Iran's nuclear programme. See 'Statement by Ambassador Ali A. Soltanieh, Islamic Republic of Iran', IAEA Board of Governors meeting, Vienna, 12 Sep. 2003, URL <http://www.iaea.org/NewsCenter/Focus/IaeaIran/bog12092003_statement-iran.pdf>.

[48] For European and Iranian views on the nuclear issue see Kile, S. N. (ed.), *Europe and Iran: Perspectives on Non-Proliferation*, SIPRI Research Report No. 21 (Oxford University Press: Oxford, 2005).

[49] International Atomic Energy Agency (IAEA), 'Iran to resume nuclear research and development', Press release PR 2006/01, Vienna, 3 Jan. 2006, URL <http://www.iaea.org/NewsCenter/PressReleases/2006/prn200601.html>.

[50] The text of the agreement between France, Germany, Iran and the UK, signed in Paris on 15 Nov. 2004, is reproduced in IAEA, INFCIRC/637, 26 Nov. 2004, URL <http://www.iaea.org/Publications/Documents/Infcircs/2004/infcirc637.pdf>. For the background to these negotiations see Kile (note 48).

of its enrichment programme. In August 2005 Iran partially lifted the suspension when it restarted uranium conversion operations, under IAEA monitoring, at a facility near Esfahan.[51] That move led to the collapse of the negotiations with the E3/EU.

On 10 January 2006 Iran began removing IAEA seals from centrifuges and other equipment at the Pilot Fuel Enrichment Plant (PFEP) at Natanz and at two subsidiaries of the Atomic Energy Organization of Iran (AEOI).[52] In response, the E3 foreign ministers and Solana issued a statement that condemned Iran's decision as a 'clear rejection of the [negotiating] process'.[53] They noted that the IAEA Board of Governors had previously requested that Iran continue the suspension while the agency worked to resolve questions about Iran's past nuclear activities. Declaring that the time had come 'for the Security Council to become involved to reinforce the authority of IAEA Resolutions', they announced that the three governments would call for an 'Extraordinary IAEA Board meeting with a view for it to take the necessary action to that end'.

On 4 February 2006 the IAEA Board of Governors adopted a resolution requesting the Director General to 'report to the Security Council all IAEA reports and resolutions' relating to the Iranian nuclear issue.[54] The Board's decision to report Iran to the Security Council followed its adoption, on 24 September 2005, of a resolution stating that 'Iran's many failures and breaches of its obligations to comply' with its safeguards agreement 'constitute non-compliance in the context of Article XII.C of the Agency's Statute'.[55] In the new resolution, the Board expressed 'serious concern' that the IAEA was still 'not in a position to clarify some important issues relating to Iran's nuclear programme' and urged Iran to extend 'indispensable and overdue co-operation' to the agency. The resolution listed five steps that the Board required Iran to take in order to build confidence about the 'exclusively peaceful nature of its nuclear programme': (a) re-establish full and sustained suspension of all enrichment-related and reprocessing activities; (b) reconsider the construction at Arak of a 40-megawatt research reactor moderated by heavy water; (c) promptly ratify and implement in full the 2003 Additional

[51] IAEA, 'Iran starts feeding uranium ore concentrate at uranium conversion facility', Press release PR 2005/09, Vienna, 8 Aug. 2005, URL <http://www.iaea.org/NewsCenter/PressReleases/2005/prn2005 09.html>.

[52] IAEA, 'Iran begins removal of IAEA seals at enrichment-related locations', Press release PR 2006/02, Vienna, 10 Jan. 2006, URL <http://www.iaea.org/NewsCenter/PressReleases/2006/prn2006 02.html>. The AEOI subsidiaries were Farayand Technique and Pars Trash.

[53] 'E3/EU statement on the Iran nuclear issue', Berlin, 12 Jan. 2006, URL <http://www.diplomatie. gouv.fr/actu/bulletin.gb.asp?liste=20060113.gb.html>.

[54] IAEA, 'Implementation of the NPT safeguards agreement in the Islamic Republic of Iran', Resolution adopted by the IAEA Board of Governors, GOV/2006/14, Vienna, 4 Feb. 2006, URL <http:// www.iaea.org/Publications/Documents/Board/2006/gov2006-14.pdf>.

[55] IAEA, 'Implementation of the NPT safeguards agreement in the Islamic Republic of Iran', Resolution adopted by the IAEA Board of Governors, GOV/2005/77, Vienna, 24 Sep. 2005, URL <http:// www.iaea.org/Publications/Documents/Board/2005/gov2005-77.pdf>, p. 1. According to Article XII of the IAEA Statute, the 'Board shall call upon the recipient State or States to remedy forthwith any [safeguards] non-compliance which it finds to have occurred. The Board shall report the non-compliance to all members and to the Security Council and General Assembly of the United Nations.'

Protocol;[56] (*d*) continue to act in accordance with the provisions of the Additional Protocol pending its ratification; and (*e*) implement transparency measures, as requested by the Director General, which 'extend beyond the formal requirements of the Safeguards Agreement and Additional Protocol'. The latter measures would include granting inspectors unhindered access to key personnel, workshops and R&D sites as well as making available to them all original documentation related to the procurement of dual-use equipment.[57]

The Board approved the resolution by 27 votes to 3, with five abstentions.[58] Russia and China, two of the five permanent members (P5) of the Security Council, agreed to support the resolution after an agreement was reached with the other P5 states and Germany that the Security Council would not take any action until after the March 2006 meeting of the IAEA Board, when Director General Mohamad ElBaradei's next report on Iran's nuclear programme was due. The delay was intended to give Iran time to halt its enrichment activities and to improve cooperation with the IAEA.[59]

Iran reacted defiantly to the resolution, making good on its earlier threat to end voluntary cooperation with the IAEA if the Board reported Iran's nuclear file to the Security Council.[60] On 6 February Iran informed the IAEA that it would no longer act in accordance with the provisions of the Additional Protocol and would suspend as well all other non-legally binding transparency measures.[61] It also asked the IAEA to remove all containment and surveillance measures, such as seals and cameras, 'that were in place beyond the normal Agency safeguards measures'.[62] In addition, on 15 February Iran announced that it had begun small-scale 'enrichment tests' on a 10-centrifuge cascade at the PFEP at Natanz.[63]

The IAEA Director General's assessment of Iran's nuclear programme

On 27 February ElBaradei issued the latest in a series of reports to the IAEA Board on Iran's implementation of its safeguards agreement.[64] The report painted a mixed picture of the results achieved by IAEA inspections. It stated

---

[56] On 18 Dec. 2003 Iran signed an Additional Protocol to its comprehensive safeguards agreement. IAEA, 'Iran signs Additional Protocol on nuclear safeguards', IAEA News Center, 18 Dec. 2003, URL <http://www.iaea.org/NewsCenter/News/2003/iranap20031218. html>.

[57] IAEA (note 54).

[58] Kerr, P., 'IAEA reports Iran to UN Security Council', *Arms Control Today*, vol. 36, no. 2 (Mar. 2006), URL <http://www.armscontrol.org/act/archived.asp>.

[59] Weisman, S. R., 'China and Russia support sending Iran case to U.N.', *New York Times*, 31 Jan. 2006.

[60] Esfandiari, G, 'Tehran threatens to end nuclear cooperation if referred to UN', Radio Free Europe/Radio Liberty (RFE/RL), 13 Jan. 2006, URL <http://rfe.rferl.org/featuresarticle/2006/01/01726 b6f-65db-47ef-86ca-cbc59a21048a.html>.

[61] IAEA, 'Implementation of the NPT safeguards agreement in the Islamic Republic of Iran', Report by the Director General to the IAEA Board of Governors, GOV/2006/15, 27 Feb. 2006, URL <http://www.iaea.org/Publications/Documents/Board/2006/ gov2006-15.pdf>, p. 6; and Kerr (note 58).

[62] Kerr (note 58); IAEA (note 61); and Reuters, 'Iran tells nuclear watchdog to remove monitoring gear', ABC News, 7 Feb. 2006, URL <http://www.abc.net.au/news/newsitems/200602/s1563703.htm>.

[63] Kerr (note 58).

[64] IAEA (note 61).

that agency inspectors were able to verify that none of the declared nuclear materials inside Iran had been diverted to prohibited activities. However, because the agency was not satisfied that it could adequately reconstruct the history of Iran's previously undeclared nuclear activities, it was yet not in a position to conclude that there were no such activities under way, including activities that might have a military dimension.

ElBaradei's report stated that the IAEA had made little progress in the preceding months towards resolving a number of outstanding safeguards compliance issues, most of which had to do with Iranian activities in the 1980s and 1990s. The first of these involved determining the origins of low-enriched uranium (LEU) and HEU particles discovered in environmental samples taken at various centrifuge-related facilities and workshops in Iran. According to ElBaradei, the results of the environmental samples taken in Pakistan in December 2005, together with the results of earlier samples, 'tended, on balance, to support Iran's statement' attributing the presence of the enriched uranium particles to contamination from centrifuge components imported through 'foreign intermediaries', although the agency had yet to establish a definitive conclusion with respect to all of the contamination.[65] The second issue had to do with Iran's P-1 and P-2 centrifuge programmes; in particular, verifying Iranian statements about the procurement of centrifuge design information, components and related equipment through a network of foreign intermediaries; and determining the scope and timelines of Iran's centrifuge R&D activities.[66]

In addition to these issues, ElBaradei reported that the IAEA was continuing to assess other aspects of Iran's nuclear activities. These included the dates of plutonium separation experiments; the purpose of experiments involving the isotope polonium-210; and certain activities at the Gchine uranium mine. The IAEA also continued to press for expanded access to Lavisan-Shian, a site outside Tehran where undeclared nuclear weapon-related activities may have taken place at the Physics Research Centre previously located there.[67]

ElBaradei's report stated that the IAEA had not been able to shed further light on the origins of a 15-page document, discovered by inspectors the previous year, that 'related to the fabrication of nuclear weapon components'. The document described 'procedures for the reduction of [uranium hexafluoride] to uranium metal in small quantities, and for the casting of enriched and depleted uranium metal into hemispheres'.[68] The existence of the document has been a matter of concern, since the uranium metal hemispheres could

[65] IAEA (note 61), pp. 2–3. On the contamination issue see IAEA, 'Implementation of the NPT safeguards agreement in the Islamic Republic of Iran', Report by the Director General to the IAEA Board of Governors, GOV/2004/83, Vienna, 15 Nov. 2004, URL <http://www.iaea.org/Publications/Documents/Board/2004/gov2004-83.pdf>, pp. 8–10.

[66] IAEA (note 61), pp. 3–4, 10. On Iran's gas centrifuge enrichment programmes see International Institute for Strategic Studies (IISS), *Iran's Strategic Weapons Programme: A Net Assessment* (Routledge: Abingdon, 2005), pp. 45–56.

[67] IAEA (note 61). See also Shire, J. and Albright, D., 'Iran's NPT violations: numerous and possibly on-going?', Institute for Science and International Security (ISIS), ISIS Issue Analysis, 13 Sep. 2006, URL <http://www.isis-online.org/publications/iran/irannptviola tions.pdf>.

[68] IAEA (note 61), pp. 4–5.

be used to form the core of an implosion-type nuclear weapon.[69] ElBaradei's report noted that in January 2006 Iran had complied with an IAEA request to allow inspectors to re-examine the document but had insisted that it remain in Tehran under IAEA seal. During the visit, Iran had again told the agency that it had never requested the document, which had been provided by a foreign intermediary.[70]

The report also noted that the IAEA had made no headway in confirming information about a secretive Iranian project known as Green Salt.[71] It had been described the previous month in a written update on the IAEA's progress in verifying Iran's implementation of its safeguards agreement prepared by the Deputy Director General for Safeguards, Olli Heinonen.[72] The project allegedly involved work on the conversion of uranium dioxide into uranium tetrafluoride ('green salt'), as well as tests related to high explosives and the design of a missile re-entry vehicle.[73] ElBaradei's report stated that the IAEA was not able to substantiate whether Iran ever had such a project, but it noted that the purported activities 'appeared to have administrative connections'; the report did not repeat Heinonen's earlier statement that these activities 'could have a military nuclear dimension'.[74] In response to IAEA queries in February 2006, Iran had restated that the information about the alleged project was 'baseless'. Iran's denials notwithstanding, there was considerable media interest in the alleged Green Salt project, since it appeared to link Iran's nuclear fuel production activities to a military programme.[75]

Nuclear diplomacy at the Security Council

Following the conclusion of the IAEA Board of Governor's meeting on 8 March, the 15 members of the UN Security Council took up consideration of the Iranian nuclear file.[76] On 29 March the president of the Security Council issued a statement about Iran's nuclear programme expressing 'serious concern' about its resumption of enrichment-related activities and suspension of

[69] Jahn, G., 'Iran said to have nuclear warhead plans', Associated Press, 31 Jan. 2006, URL <http://www.breitbart.com/news/2006/01/31/D8FG37780.html>.

[70] IAEA (note 61), p. 5.

[71] This information was based at least in part on intelligence provided by the USA, which had come into possession of an allegedly stolen laptop computer containing a large number of documents describing the project's activities. Sciolino, E. and Broad, W. J., 'Atomic agency sees possible link of military to Iran nuclear work', New York Times, 1 Feb. 2006.

[72] IAEA, 'Developments in the implementation of the NPT safeguards agreement in the Islamic Republic of Iran and agency verification of Iran's suspension of enrichment-related and reprocessing activities', Update brief by the Deputy Director General for Safeguards, Vienna, 31 Jan. 2006, URL <http://www.iaea.org/NewsCenter/Statements/DDGs/2006/ heinonen31012006.pdf>.

[73] Some processes for enriching uranium involve an intermediate step in which uranium dioxide is converted to uranium tetrafluoride, a green crystalline compound commonly called 'green salt'. The compound is then converted to uranium hexafluoride (UF_6), a volatile gas used in isotopic separation (i.e. enrichment) processes to yield uranium-235.

[74] IAEA (note 61), p. 8; and IAEA (note 72), p. 3.

[75] Sciolino and Broad (note 71).

[76] Webb, G., 'Nuclear standoff with Iran moves to Security Council', Global Security Newswire, 8 Mar. 2006, URL <http://www.nti.org>.

cooperation with the IAEA under the Additional Protocol.[77] The presidential statement called on Iran to take the steps demanded by the IAEA Board's February resolution, including a return to the full suspension of its enrichment and related R&D activities.

In response to the Security Council statement, Iran emphasized that it was legally entitled, as a non-nuclear weapon state party to the NPT, to pursue the development of nuclear energy for peaceful purposes. On 11 April 2006 Iranian President Mahmoud Ahmadinejad announced that Iran had succeeded in enriching uranium to the 3.5 per cent level required for nuclear fuel.[78] Iranian nuclear officials explained that the uranium had been enriched in laboratory-scale quantities using a 164-centrifuge cascade at the PFEP. They added that Iran aimed to complete a 3000-centrifuge complex by March 2007 as the first stage in a planned commercial-scale, 54 000-centrifuge fuel production facility to be built underground at Natanz.[79] Ahmadinejad's theatrically staged announcement of the feat was greeted sceptically by many foreign experts, who speculated that it had less to do with a scientific breakthrough than with a political message to Europe and the United States that Iran's enrichment programme was unstoppable.[80] Subsequent reports indicated that the programme continued to be plagued by technical difficulties, especially with respect to the sustainability of centrifuge operations and the production of uranium hexafluoride (UF_6) for the centrifuges.[81]

Iran's defiance of the non-binding presidential statement led to protracted discussions at the Security Council about how to induce or compel Iran to comply with the Security Council's requests. In early May 2006 France, the UK and the USA put forward a draft resolution, under Chapter VII of the UN Charter, requiring Iran to stop all enrichment-related activities. At the insistence of China and Russia, the draft resolution did not set a deadline for compliance or specify the action to be taken should Iran fail to comply.[82] The E3/EU also put forward, with US support, a new offer of nuclear technology assistance to Iran in exchange for the latter's suspension of its enrichment programme.[83] The offer was rejected by President Ahmadinejad, who complained that by asking Iran to make a major concession without any guarantee that the

---

[77] UN Security Council, Statement by the president of the Security Council, S/PRST/2006/15, 29 Mar. 2006.

[78] 'Iran proclaims breakthrough in nuclear program', *Global Security Newswire*, 12 Apr. 2006, URL <http://www.nti.org>.

[79] See International Institute for Strategic Studies (note 66), pp. 48–51.

[80] Fathi, N., Sanger, D. E. and Broad, W. J., 'Iran reports big advance in enrichment of uranium', *New York Times*, 12 Apr. 2006.

[81] Fitzpatrick, M., 'Assessing Iran's nuclear programme', *Survival*, vol. 48, no. 3 (autumn 2006), pp. 18–21; and Marcus, J., 'Iran enrichment: a Chinese puzzle?', BBC News, 19 May 2006, URL <http://news.bbc.co.uk/2/4995350.stm>. Iran is believed to have achieved the 3.5% enrichment level announced by Ahmadinejad by using Chinese-supplied UF_6 rather than domestically produced UF_6, which was reportedly contaminated by metal particles that rendered it unsuitable for use as gas centrifuge feedstock. See Hibbs, M., 'Intelligence estimates vary widely on Iran's timeline to purify UF_6', *Nuclear Fuels*, vol. 30, no. 18 (29 Aug. 2005), p. 1.

[82] Sciolino, E., 'U.S., Britain and France draft U.N. resolution on Iran's nuclear ambitions', *New York Times*, 3 May 2006.

[83] Dombey, D., 'EU to offer Iran nuclear reactor', *Financial Times*, 17 May 2006.

promised benefits would materialize, the E3/EU were offering 'candy for gold'.[84]

With the discussions at the Security Council nearing an impasse, the United States moved to adjust its diplomatic strategy towards Iran. In a major shift in US policy, Secretary of State Condoleezza Rice announced on 31 May 2006 that the United States would join the E3/EU for direct talks with Iran if the latter 'immediately' suspended all enrichment and reprocessing activities and resumed cooperation with the IAEA under the Additional Protocol.[85] Rice said that the US offer was meant to 'give new energy' to European efforts to reach a deal with Iran. The announcement was widely seen as a recognition by the US Administration that it could not hope to assemble a coalition of states to enforce punitive sanctions—or to consider taking military action against Iran's nuclear facilities—unless it had first demonstrated its commitment to exhausting all diplomatic options by directly engaging the Iranian regime.[86] Officials in Tehran described the offer as being driven by the USA's diplomatic isolation rather than by a sincere desire to reach a deal with Iran. They emphasized that Iran would not agree to suspend its enrichment programme as a precondition for direct talks with the USA.[87]

The P5+1 proposal

On 6 June 2006 China, France, Germany, Russia, the UK and the USA (the 'P5+1 states') announced a new package of incentives on nuclear energy, technology cooperation, and political and security issues aimed at persuading Iran to suspend indefinitely its uranium enrichment.[88] The offer came as ElBaradei issued a report to the IAEA Board showing that Iran had stepped up its uranium enrichment activities, in disregard of the non-binding March UN Security Council presidential statement.[89] The P5+1 proposal set out what was in effect a negotiating agenda. However, it stipulated that before any negotiations could begin, Iran would have to take the following steps: commit to addressing all the outstanding safeguards compliance concerns through full cooperation with the IAEA; suspend all enrichment-related and reprocessing activities for the duration of the negotiations; and resume implementation of

[84] Mehr News Agency, 'EU incentives like candy for gold', Arak, 17 May 2006, URL <http://www.mehrnews.com/en/NewsDetail.aspx?NewsID=327636>.

[85] US Department of State, 'Statement by Secretary of State Condaleeza Rice', Washington, DC, 31 May 2006, URL <http://www.state.gov/secretary/rm/2006/67088.htm>.

[86] Sanger, D. E., 'Bush's realization on Iran: no good choice left except talks', *New York Times*, 1 June 2006.

[87] Mehr News Agency, 'Tehran rejects Washington's condition for nuclear negotiations, Tehran, 1 June 2006, URL <http://www.mehrnews.com/en/NewsDetail.aspx?NewsID=334472>; and Slackman, M., 'Tehran rebuffs U.S. on talks', *International Herald Tribune*, 2 June 2006.

[88] Kerr, P., 'U.S. allies await Iran's response to nuclear offer', *Arms Control Today*, vol. 36, no. 6 (July/Aug. 2006), URL <http://www.armscontrol.org/act/archived.asp>.

[89] IAEA, 'Implementation of the NPT safeguards agreement in the Islamic Republic of Iran', Report by the Director General to the IAEA Board of Governors, GOV/2006/38, 8 June 2006, URL <http://www.iaea.org/Publications/Documents/Board/2006/gov2006-38.pdf>.

the Additional Protocol.[90] In return for these commitments, the P5+1 states were prepared to discuss with Iran the package of nuclear and other incentives. The proposal warned that the UN Security Council would adopt unspecified 'proportionate measures if Iran refused to negotiate'.[91]

The proposal contained several nuclear-related provisions, including the setting up of a multilateral venture to provide Iran with a light-water reactor (LWR) for power generation, giving Iran part ownership of a Russian enrichment facility and creating a five-year 'buffer stock' of enriched uranium stored in Iran under IAEA supervision.[92] A number of these elements, such as the provision of the LWR, had been included in the E3/EU proposal made to Iran in August 2005. Significantly, the proposal left open the possibility that Iran could be allowed to domestically enrich uranium to produce nuclear fuel. However, US officials indicated that before this could happen Iran would have to restore international confidence that its nuclear activities were entirely for peaceful purposes—a task that would probably take many years.[93]

The P5+1 proposal set no deadline by which Iran had to respond. Despite repeated prompting by world leaders, officials in Tehran emphasized that they would take 'as long as necessary' before replying to the proposal.[94] Concerned that Iran was seeking to buy time for its enrichment programme, on 12 July 2006 the P5+1 states issued a statement declaring that 'Iran has failed to take the steps needed to allow negotiations to begin, specifically the suspension of all enrichment-related and reprocessing activities'.[95] As a result, they were compelled to return to the UN Security Council, where they would seek a resolution 'which would make the IAEA-required suspension mandatory'.

Resolution 1696

In July 2006 the UN Security Council passed Resolution 1696.[96] The resolution, which was adopted by 14 votes to 1 (Qatar was the sole dissenter), demanded that Iran suspend by 31 August all uranium enrichment-related and plutonium reprocessing activities, subject to verification by the IAEA. It stated that the enrichment suspension, as well as full Iranian compliance with the requirements of the IAEA Board of Governors, would contribute to a 'diplomatic, negotiated solution' that guaranteed Iran's nuclear programme was for exclusively peaceful purposes. The resolution warned that in the case of Iran-

---

[90] Iran Focus, 'Text of P5+1 package of nuclear incentives offered to Iran', London, 18 July 2006, URL <http://www.iranfocus.com/modules/news/article.php?storyid=7946>.

[91] Kerr (note 88).

[92] The package also promised support for Iran's membership in the World Trade Organization, the lifting of restrictions on the use of US technology in agriculture and the supply of US-manufactured spare parts for Iranian civilian aircraft.

[93] Cooper, H. and Sciolino, E., 'U.S. says plan offers Iran uranium option', *New York Times*, 8 June 2006.

[94] Islamic Republic News Agency, 'Larijani rejects any deadline for responding to P5+1 offer', Tehran, 29 June 2006, URL <http://www.irna.com/en/news/view/menu-234/0606292803093903.htm>.

[95] Douste-Blazy, P., French Foreign Minister, 'P5+1 statement: negotiations with Iran', Press statement, Paris, 12 July 2006, URL <http://www.state.gov/p/eur/rls/or/68910.htm>.

[96] UN Security Council Resolution 1696, 31 July 2006.

ian non-compliance the Security Council would be forced to adopt unspecified 'appropriate measures'.

Iran's chief nuclear negotiator, Ali Larijani, promptly denounced Resolution 1696 as 'illegal' and declared that Iran would continue its enrichment programme beyond the suspension deadline set by the Security Council.[97] Shortly before the Security Council deadline, Iran responded officially to the P5+1 proposal. Larijani described the lengthy document as offering a 'new formula' for resolving international concerns about its nuclear programme.[98] He also said that Iran was willing to hold 'serious talks' with the P5+1 states on all aspects of their proposal.[99] However, Larijani reiterated that Iran would not agree to suspend its enrichment programme as a precondition for those talks.[100]

Iran's decision to defy the Security Council's demand that it halt all enrichment-related activities was confirmed by a report from IAEA Director General ElBaradei on 31 August 2006.[101] The report stated that Iran appeared to be making modest progress in its enrichment programme. It was continuing to carry out tests of a 164-centrifuge cascade at the Natanz pilot plant, which involved feeding UF_6 gas into the centrifuges 'for very short periods of time', and was in the process of installing a second 164-centrifuge cascade there. Iran was also proceeding with a uranium conversion campaign begun in June 2006 at the Esfahan facility and as of 24 August had produced 26 tonnes of UF_6. In addition, Iran was continuing to build a heavy water-moderated reactor near Arak, despite the Security Council's call for the country to 'reconsider' the project. With regard to safeguards compliance, ElBaradei's report stated that the IAEA was asking Iran for information regarding HEU particles found in environmental samples taken at a waste storage facility.[102] The discovery, which had not previously been reported, raised the possibility that Iran might have either imported or produced undeclared enriched uranium.[103]

The autumn of 2006 was marked by protracted discussions among the P5+1 states over how to respond to Iran's defiance of Resolution 1696. While there was general agreement that the Security Council had to take action against

[97] Slackman, M., 'Iran says it will ignore U.N. deadline on uranium program', *New York Times*, 7 Aug. 2006.

[98] Shire, J. and Albright, D., 'Iran's response to the EU: confused but sporadically hopeful', Institute for Science and International Security (ISIS), ISIS Issue Analysis, 13 Sep. 2006, URL <http://www.isis-online.org/publications/iran/confusedbuthopeful.pdf>.

[99] Fars News Agency, 'Larijani calls for immediate talks with 5+1', Tehran, 22 Aug. 2006, URL <http://www.farsnews.com/English/newstext.php?nn=8505310280>.

[100] Slackman, M., 'Iran won't give promise to end uranium effort', *New York Times*, 23 Aug. 2006.

[101] IAEA, 'Implementation of the NPT safeguards agreement in the Islamic Republic of Iran', Report by the Director General to the IAEA Board of Governors, GOV/2006/53, 31 Aug. 2006, URL <http://www.iaea.org/Publications/Documents/Board/2006/gov2006-53.pdf>.

[102] IAEA (note 101), p. 4. The particles were found in containers that had been used to store depleted uranium targets used in plutonium separation experiments.

[103] Iran later informed the IAEA that the contamination may have resulted from the temporary storage of spent fuel from the Tehran Research Reactor in containers that were used at the Karaj facility. IAEA, 'Implementation of the NPT safeguards agreement in the Islamic Republic of Iran', Report by the Director General to the IAEA Board of Governors, GOV/2006/64, 14 Nov. 2006, URL <http://www.iaea.org/Publications/Documents/Board/2006/gov2006-64.pdf>, p. 3.

Iran, disagreements persisted over the type of measures to be included in a resolution. The USA called for the imposition of comprehensive trade and economic sanctions aimed at isolating Iran. In contrast, China, Russia and, to a lesser extent, the E3 favoured a more restricted series of low-level measures, at least as a first step towards reinforcing the Security Council's authority.[104] There were also disagreements on specific issues, such as Russia's insistence—over US objections—that any resolution exempt from sanctions the Russian-supplied Bushehr nuclear power plant.

Finally, on 23 December 2006, the Security Council unanimously adopted Resolution 1737 under Article 41 of Chapter VII of the UN Charter. The resolution, which was sponsored by the E3, was based on a draft that had been put forward in October and amended several times after objections from China and Russia.[105] The resolution expressed the Security Council's determination to 'persuade Iran to comply with Resolution 1696 and with the requirements of the IAEA, and also to constrain Iran's development of sensitive technologies in support of its nuclear and missile programmes'. It required UN member states to 'take the necessary measures to prevent the supply, sale or transfer directly or indirectly' of a variety of items that could 'contribute' to Iran's enrichment or heavy-water reactor programmes as well as the development of nuclear-weapon delivery systems, such as ballistic missiles. The relevant items were contained in several lists referenced by the resolution.[106]

Iran promptly rejected the UN resolution as 'invalid' and 'illegal'.[107] As 2006 ended, Iran announced that it would begin work on assembling and installing the initial 3000 uranium centrifuges at Natanz. It also vowed to take unspecified action to reduce its cooperation with the IAEA.

IV. The Indian–US Civil Nuclear Cooperation Initiative

In 2006 India and the United States took steps towards implementation of the controversial Civil Nuclear Cooperation Initiative.[108] The CNCI had been launched in July 2005 in a joint statement by US President George W. Bush and Indian Prime Minister Manmohan Singh. The initiative reflects the growing rapprochement between India and the USA and the two leaders'

---

[104] 'Security Council leaders move towards Iran sanctions', *Global Security Newswire*, 10 Oct. 2006, URL <http://www.nti.org>; and Dinmore, G. and Bozorgmehr, N., 'Rice fails to win support for Iran referral to Security Council', *Financial Times*, 17 Oct. 2006.

[105] 'UN passes Iran nuclear sanctions', BBC News, 23 Dec. 2006, URL <http://news.bbc.co.uk/2/6205295.stm>.

[106] On Security Council Resolution 1737 and the lists of sensitive items see chapter 15 in this volume.

[107] 'UN votes for Iran nuclear sanctions', AlJazeera, 23 Dec. 2006, URL <http://english.aljazeera.net/NR/exeres/A742D5DB-379A-4A0F-8DFA-40213800A37C.htm>; and Reuters, 'Iran defies UN nuclear sanctions', *Financial Times*, 24 Dec. 2006.

[108] For further information about the origins of the CNCI see Ahlström, C., 'Legal aspects of the Indian–US Civil Nuclear Cooperation Initiative', *SIPRI Yearbook 2006* (note 8), pp. 669–85.

commitment to transform Indian–US relations in the direction of a 'global partnership'.[109]

The goal of the CNCI is the resumption of 'full civil nuclear cooperation' between India and the USA. This represents a reversal of three decades of US non-proliferation policy, which had been aimed at preventing India from obtaining nuclear fuel and reactors from US and other suppliers following India's 'peaceful nuclear explosion' of 1974.[110] Alluding to this shift, President Bush declared in the joint statement that India, as a 'responsible state' with a demonstrated commitment to preventing the spread of WMD, 'should acquire the same benefits and advantages' as other such states with advanced nuclear technology. He promised to work to persuade the US Congress to amend legislation that currently prohibited most nuclear trade with India.[111] He also pledged to work to create an exemption in the Nuclear Suppliers Group (NSG) Guidelines that would allow India to have access to international markets for nuclear fuel and technology.[112]

In return, Singh pledged that India would assume the same 'responsibilities and practices' aimed at preventing nuclear weapon proliferation as other countries with advanced nuclear technology.[113] As part of this commitment, India would separate its civilian from its military nuclear facilities, voluntarily place the civilian facilities under IAEA safeguards, and sign and adhere to an Additional Protocol. Furthermore, Singh promised that India would continue its moratorium on nuclear testing, work with the United States for the conclusion of a global fissile material cut-off treaty, refrain from exporting uranium-enrichment and plutonium-separation technologies to countries that did not already have them, and harmonize its export control legislation with NSG and Missile Technology Control Regime (MTCR) guidelines.[114]

---

[109] The White House, 'Joint statement between US President George W. Bush and Indian Prime Minister Manmohan Singh', News release, Washington, DC, 18 July 2005, URL <http://www.white house.gov/news/releases/2005/07/20050718-6.html>; and Ahlström (note 108).

[110] The Indian nuclear explosive device was widely believed to have used US and other foreign-supplied nuclear technology provided for peaceful purposes. For a comprehensive history of India's nuclear programme see Perkovich, G., *India's Nuclear Bomb: the Impact on Global Proliferation* (University of California Press: Berkeley, Calif., 1999).

[111] The 1978 Nuclear Non-proliferation Act (NNPA), 10 Mar. 1978, US Public Law 95-242, reprinted in *Nuclear Regulatory Legislation*, NUREG-0980, vol. 1, no. 6 (US Nuclear Regulatory Commission, Office of the General Counsel: Washington, DC, June 2002), pp. 151–53. The NNPA requires non-nuclear weapon states to conclude with the IAEA a comprehensive or 'full scope' safeguards agreement (INFCIRC/153), covering all sources of special fissionable material on their territories, as a condition for peaceful nuclear cooperation with the USA. India is not a party to the NPT and is not legally recognized as a nuclear weapon state.

[112] The Nuclear Suppliers Group was created in 1975 in response to India's nuclear test explosion the previous year. On the NSG's composition and activities in 2006 see the glossary and chapter 15 in this volume. The latest version of the NSG Guidelines, as well as a statement on how they are to be applied, are available at URL <http://www.nuclearsuppliersgroup.org/guide.html>.

[113] The White House (note 109).

[114] The White House (note 109). On the MTCR see the glossary and chapter 15 in this volume. The MTCR Guidelines for Sensitive Missile-Relevant Transfers are available at URL <http://www.state.gov/www/global/arms/treaties/mtcr_anx.html>.

The Indian separation plan

One of the most controversial aspects of the CNCI had to do with India's commitment to separate its nuclear programme into civilian and military components. The July 2005 joint statement established a bilateral working group to discuss India's plan for doing so and to agree other legal and technical modalities for resuming nuclear commerce.[115]

Through the separation plan, India sought to demonstrate its commitment to non-proliferation and responsible nuclear stewardship practices, while preserving flexibility for pursuing its long-term nuclear energy development programme and for maintaining its military nuclear capability in accordance with perceived national security requirements.[116] As a way of balancing these goals, India initially indicated that it would only accept voluntary safeguards arrangements for civilian nuclear facilities of the type that the IAEA had in place in the five NPT-recognized nuclear weapon states.[117] The voluntary arrangements would allow India to add and remove at will facilities that were subject to IAEA facility-specific safeguards. This would keep open the possibility that a 'civilian' nuclear facility could be reassigned to the country's military programme. It would also help to overcome the reluctance of India's nuclear establishment to place more of the country's nuclear facilities under civilian safeguards.[118]

US officials called for a separation plan that was 'credible, transparent and defensible from a non-proliferation standpoint'.[119] They insisted that any future safeguards arrangements for India's civilian nuclear fuel cycle had to apply in perpetuity in order to give adequate assurance to supplier states that nuclear material and technology imported by India for peaceful purposes would not be diverted to military activities.[120] US officials also urged the Indian Government to take a 'comprehensive' approach in deciding which facilities would be designated as civilian and hence subject to permanent safeguards.[121] While declining to suggest specific criteria for doing so, they appeared to want India to designate as civilian facilities all its nuclear infrastructure not directly associated with nuclear weapon production. Some non-governmental experts suggested that a more feasible and cost-effective

[115] Squassoni, S., *India's Nuclear Separation Plan: Issues and Views*, US Library of Congress, Congressional Research Service (CRS) Report for Congress RL33292 (CRS: Washington, DC, 3 Mar. 2006), URL <http://www.opencrs.com/document/RL33292>, pp. 8–9; and 'U.S. says obstacles remain to U.S.–Indian agreement', *Global Security Newswire*, 23 Jan. 2006, URL <http://www.nti.org>.

[116] Varadarajan, S., 'Nuclear separation plan seeks fine balance', *The Hindu*, 8 Mar. 2006.

[117] Subramanian, T., 'Identifying a civilian nuclear facility is India's decision', *The Hindu*, 12 Aug. 2005.

[118] Balachandran, G., 'International nuclear control regimes and India's participation in civilian nuclear trade: key issues', *Strategic Analysis* (New Delhi), vol. 29, no. 4 (Oct.–Dec. 2005).

[119] Joseph, R., Under Secretary of State, 'The nonproliferation implications of the July 18, 2005 US–India joint statement', Prepared remarks before the US Senate Foreign Relations Committee, 2 Nov. 2005, URL <http://foreign.senate.gov/testimony/2005/JosephTestimony051102.pdf>.

[120] Squassoni (note 115), pp. 13–14. There was also concern that agreeing to voluntary offer safeguards arrangements of the type in place in the 5 nuclear weapon states would tacitly endorse India's claim to nuclear weapon state status.

[121] Joseph (note 119).

approach, given the extensive commingling of India's civil and military nuclear activities, would be to focus on placing under permanent safeguards particularly sensitive facilities and programmes, such as India's fast breeder reactors and associated spent-fuel reprocessing plants.[122]

At a summit meeting in New Delhi on 2 March 2006, President Bush and Prime Minister Singh announced that they had reached agreement on an Indian plan for separating its nuclear programme into civilian and military components.[123] In exchange for India's acceptance of permanent safeguards on its civilian facilities, the plan contained several measures aimed at guaranteeing foreign nuclear fuel supplies to India. These included the development by India of a nuclear fuel strategic reserve and a US commitment to help India find alternative sources of nuclear fuel in the event of a supply interruption.[124] Ensuring the reliability of fuel supplies has been a key Indian objective in implementation of the CNCI because of previous interruptions.[125] In the USA the fuel supply assurance was criticized since it appeared to mean that the USA would help India to find foreign sources of nuclear fuel even in the event that the latter resumed nuclear weapon testing.[126]

The main focus of the separation plan was on India's 22 nuclear power reactors, 15 of which were operational and 7 under construction. India offered to designate 14 of these reactors as civilian facilities and to place them permanently under 'India-specific' IAEA safeguards in a 'phased manner by 2014'.[127] This figure included six foreign-supplied power reactors that India had already agreed would be subject to IAEA facility-specific (INFCIRC/66) safeguards.[128] The eight remaining planned or completed power reactors, as well as all research reactors, would be designated as military facilities. According to Indian calculations, the 14 reactors to be placed under civilian safeguards would account for 65 per cent of India's total installed nuclear power capacity (measured in megawatts-electric, MW(e)), compared to the 19 per cent accounted for by the reactors currently operating under facility-specific safeguards.[129] In the separation plan, India pledged to place under

[122] Albright, D. and Basu, S., 'Separating Indian military and civilian nuclear facilities', Institute for Science and International Security (ISIS), ISIS Report, 19 Dec. 2005, URL <http://www.isis-online.org/publications/southasia/indiannuclearfacilities.pdf>.

[123] The White House, 'President, Prime Minister Singh discuss growing strategic partnership', News release, New Delhi, 2 Mar. 2006, URL <http://www.whitehouse.gov/news/releases/2006/03/20060302-9.html>.

[124] Indian Department of Atomic Energy, 'PM's Suo-Motu statement on discussions on civil nuclear energy cooperation with the US: implementation of India's separation plan', Press release, New Delhi, 7 Mar. 2006, URL <http://www.dae.gov.in/press/suopm0703.htm>; and Baruah, A., 'US, India clinch deal on nuclear separation', The Hindu, 3 Mar. 2006.

[125] The United States halted its supply of nuclear fuel to India's Tarapur reactors after India conducted its first nuclear test explosion, in 1974.

[126] Ruppe, D., 'U.S. would assure India fuel even if Delhi tests nuclear weapons', Global Security Newswire, 7 Apr. 2006, URL <http://www.nti.org>.

[127] Indian Department of Atomic Energy (note 124).

[128] Two of the 6 reactors—1000-MW(e) LWRs from Russia—are under construction at Kudankulam and are scheduled to be completed in 2007 and 2008, respectively.

[129] Indian Department of Atomic Energy (note 124). The 15 power reactors currently operated by India have an installed capacity of 3310 MW(e), which represents c. 3% of the country's total installed electricity generation capacity.

IAEA safeguards all future power reactors and breeder reactors designated as civilian facilities. Indian officials emphasized that India retained the sole right to determine which facilities would be so designated.[130]

India declined to include on the list of civilian nuclear facilities several reactors that had been subjects of international concern. The ageing CIRUS reactor, located at the Bhabha Atomic Research Centre (BARC) in Trombay, has been at the centre of a long-running Indian dispute with Canada and the United States over whether India had violated the original supply contracts with those countries by reportedly using plutonium produced at the reactor in its 1974 nuclear explosion.[131] Although CIRUS was not included in the list of civilian facilities, India announced that it would shut down the reactor in 2010. With regard to its fast-neutron breeder reactor programme, India rejected calls to place under safeguards the 500-MW(e) prototype fast breeder reactor (PFBR) under construction at Kalpakkam as well as the fast breeder test reactor there, which became operational in 1985. Singh and other Indian officials emphasized that a key principle guiding the separation process was that it not be prejudicial to the Indian Department of Atomic Energy's three-stage nuclear development plan, dating from the 1950s, which envisions a thorium-based closed fuel cycle.[132] Despite numerous technical problems, the fast breeder reactor programme remains integral to the second stage of that plan. In the United States, India's unwillingness to place its fast breeder reactors under civilian safeguards emerged as a major concern, since those reactors could be used to produce large amounts of plutonium that would enable India to expand its nuclear arsenal significantly.[133]

There were few details about which other facilities would be kept off the civilian list. An Indian Government document explaining the plan to the Indian Parliament indicated that civilian facilities located in 'larger hubs of strategic significance' would be excluded from the civilian list.[134] According to one Indian analyst, two such 'strategic hubs'—BARC and the Indira Gandhi Centre for Atomic Research in Kalpakkam—were considered to be too sensitive to permit outside inspections of any of the facilities they contain, including facilities not engaged in military-related activities.[135] The Rattehalli uranium enrichment facilities located at Mysore would similarly remain unsafeguarded. The separation plan postponed a decision about which of the plants located within the Nuclear Fuel Complex in Hyderabad would be offered for safeguards.

---

[130] Indian Department of Atomic Energy (note 124).

[131] Perkovich (note 110), pp. 183–87.

[132] Indian Department of Atomic Energy (note 124). For a description of the 3-stage plan see Perkovich (note 110), pp. 26–28.

[133] See Mian, Z. et al., 'Fissile materials in South Asia and the implications of the U.S.–Indian nuclear deal', Draft report for the International Panel on Fissile Materials, 11 July 2006, URL <http://www.armscontrol.org/pdf/20060711_IPFM-DraftReport-US-India-Deal.pdf>.

[134] Embassy of India, Washington, DC, 'Implementation of India–United States joint statement of July 18, 2005: India's separation plan', Press release, 7 Mar. 2006, URL <http://www.indianembassy.org/newsite/press_release/2006/Mar/sepplan.pdf>.

[135] Varadarajan, S., 'Nuclear separation plan seeks fine balance', The Hindu, 8 Mar. 2006.

US legislative action

In the autumn of 2005 the US Congress took up consideration of legislation that had been introduced by the Bush Administration amending the 1954 Atomic Energy Act (AEA) by specifically exempting India from certain of its provisions. Congress's approval of the legislation in December 2006 paved the way for negotiations to begin between India and the USA on a so-called 123 agreement specifying the terms governing the resumption of trade in nuclear materials and technology envisioned in the CNCI.[136] However, the resulting agreement will still have to be approved by a joint resolution of Congress before it can enter into force.

The hearings on the proposed legislation held by the US House of Representatives International Affairs Committee and the Senate Foreign Relations Committee reflected the wider public debate under way about the Indian–US nuclear deal. Proponents of the deal argued that the growing strategic importance of India, and its rapidly improving relations with the United States, warranted making a one-time exception to some non-proliferation rules and regulatory arrangements.[137] They also asserted that foreign nuclear fuel imports and technical cooperation would help India to expand energy production significantly while not meaningfully contributing to India's capacity to produce fissile material for nuclear weapons.[138] Furthermore, India's acceptance of safeguards on additional nuclear facilities, along with its accession to a future FMCT, would represent important gains for the non-proliferation regime and help to draw India into the regime.[139]

In contrast, many critics of the deal rejected the idea that its implementation was crucial for strengthening the India–US relationship, since those relations were already strong and, in the long run, would grow stronger regardless of whether Congress approved the deal.[140] Opponents of the deal also warned that it would implicitly endorse, if not actually assist, the further growth of India's

---

[136] McGoldrick, F., Bengelsdorf, H. and Scheinman, L., 'The U.S.–India nuclear deal: taking stock', *Arms Control Today*, vol. 35, no.8 (Oct. 2005), URL <http://www.armscontrol.org/act/archived.asp>. Section 123 of the 1954 Atomic Energy Act, US Public Law 42-2153, 30 Aug. 1954, requires the US Government to conclude an agreement containing a number of binding conditions and assurances, including full-scope safeguards, as a prerequisite for any significant peaceful nuclear cooperation with any state not legally recognized under the NPT as a nuclear weapon state.

[137] See e.g. Schaffer, T. and Mitra, P., 'The Bush visit and the nuclear deal', *South Asia Monitor*, no. 93 (6 Apr. 2006), URL <http://www.csis.org/saprog/sam_archives/>; and Spring, B., 'Nuclear energy cooperation with India will strengthen US–India ties', Heritage Foundation, Executive Memorandum no. 1007, 25 July 2006, URL <http://www.heritage.org/Research/AsiaandthePacific/em1007.cfm>.

[138] Tellis, A., *Atoms for War? U.S.–Indian Civilian Nuclear Cooperation and India's Nuclear Arsenal* (Carnegie Endowment for International Peace: Washington, DC, June 2006), URL <http://www.carnegieendowment.org/files/atomsforwarfinal4.pdf>.

[139] The White House, 'India civil nuclear cooperation: responding to critics', News release, Washington, DC, 8 Mar. 2006, URL <http://www.whitehouse.gov/news/releases2006/03/20060308-3.html>.

[140] Perkovich, G., 'Faulty promises: the US–India nuclear deal', Carnegie Endowment for International Peace, Policy Outlook no. 21, Sep. 2005, URL <http://www.carnegieendowment.org/files/PO21.Perkovich.pdf>.

nuclear arsenal, in contravention of US commitments under the NPT.[141] There was particular concern that, if India were allowed to resume imports of nuclear fuel, it could use its limited domestic uranium reserves to support fissile material production for weapon purposes.[142] In addition, critics argued that the proposed deal, by making a special exemption for a favoured US ally, would complicate efforts to enforce existing rules with states such as Iran and North Korea and to convince other states to accept tougher non-proliferation standards.[143] In doing so, it would undermine the non-proliferation regime, which was built on norms that apply universally, and damage important multilateral endeavours, including the NSG and the NPT regime itself. Finally, India's record on non-proliferation came under scrutiny, with some analysts identifying concerns related to India's nuclear procurement practices and its national export control system.[144]

In spite of the controversy surrounding the proposed nuclear deal with India, there was strong bipartisan support in the US Congress for amending the Atomic Energy Act to allow the deal to go forward. Many congressional leaders praised it as a step towards cementing the emerging strategic partnership between India and the United States, although some also expressed concern that the Bush Administration had not been sufficiently forthcoming in releasing classified information about India's compliance with its non-proliferation commitments and about its relations with Iran.[145] On 8–9 December 2006 the House of Representatives and the Senate approved by wide margins a final version of the legislation, which became known as the Henry Hyde United States–India Peaceful Atomic Energy Cooperation Act, or Hyde Act, after the bill's chief sponsor in the House of Representatives.[146] President Bush signed the bill into US law on 18 December 2006.[147]

---

[141] As a nuclear weapon state party to the NPT, the United Sates is obligated under Article I 'not to assist, encourage or induce any non-nuclear weapon State to manufacture or otherwise acquire nuclear weapons or other nuclear explosive devices'. For a legal analysis of the CNCI's implications for the obligations assumed by the USA under the NPT see Ahlström (note 108).

[142] Kimball, D., 'Civil, military separation plan not credible', *Asian Affairs*, Apr. 2006, URL <http://www.asianaffairs.com>.

[143] Motz, K. and Milhollin, G., 'Seventeen myths about the Indian nuclear deal: an analysis of nuclear cooperation with India', Wisconsin Project on Nuclear Arms Control, Washington, DC, 13 June 2006 <http://www.wisconsinproject.org/countries/india/Seventeen_Myths.htm>; and Kimball, D. J. and Cirincione, J., 'A nonproliferation disaster', Center for American Progress, Washington, DC, 11 Dec. 2006, URL <http://www.americanprogress.org/issues/2006/12/india_deal.html>.

[144] Albright, D. and Basu, S., 'Neither a determined proliferator nor a responsible nuclear state: India's record needs scrutiny', Institute for Science and International Security (ISIS), ISIS Report, 5 Apr. 2006, URL <http://www.isis-online.org/publications/southasia/indiacritique.pdf>.

[145] Sengupta, S., 'Pact transforms US–India ties', *International Herald Tribune*, 11 Dec. 2006, p. 4.

[146] US House of Representatives, 'United States and India Nuclear Cooperation Promotion Act of 2006: report and additional views', Report no. 109-590, part 1, 21 July 2006, URL <http://thomas.loc.gov/cgi-bin/cpquery/T?&report=hr590p1&dbname=109>. 'US approves Indian nuclear deal', BBC News, 9 Dec. 2006, <http://news.bbc.co.uk/2/6219998.stm>. The text of the 2006 Henry J. Hyde United States–India Peaceful Atomic Energy Act, US Public Law 109-401, 8 Dec. 2006, is available at URL <http://www.armscontrol.org/pdf/20061208_H5682CR_HSE.pdf>.

[147] The White House, 'President's statement on H.R. 5682, the "Henry J. Hyde United States–India Peaceful Atomic Energy Cooperation Act of 2006"', Press release, Washington, DC, 18 Dec. 2006, URL <http://www.whitehouse.gov/news/releases/2006/12/20061218-12.html>.

Indian reactions

With the US Congress's approval of the Hyde Act, the focus of efforts to implement the CNCI shifted to India, where the proposed deal has been the subject of considerable debate among scientific experts and policymakers.[148] Indian officials reacted cautiously to the US legislation. While welcoming it, Minister of External Affairs Pranab Mukherjee said that the legislation contained 'extraneous and prescriptive provisions' outside the scope of the July 2005 joint statement that potentially interfered with India's sovereign right to determine its foreign policy.[149] He also emphasized that India would not allow external scrutiny of, or interference with, its military nuclear programme.

A number of specific provisions in the US legislation were sharply criticized by leading figures in India's nuclear establishment, who urged that India should insist that they be eliminated when negotiating the 123 agreement.[150] Their main criticism was that the Hyde Act would limit India's nuclear options by imposing, 'through the back door', restrictions that in some cases went beyond those of the NPT. One specific objection was that the act called for a 'joint moratorium' by China, India and Pakistan on producing fissile material for nuclear weapons pending the conclusion of an FMCT.[151] A second objection was that the act required made India's continued adhere to its unilateral moratorium on nuclear testing a condition for US nuclear cooperation.[152] These provisions were seen as contradicting Prime Minister Singh's assurance to the Indian Parliament that the nuclear deal would not 'limit the options or compromise the integrity of [India's] strategic programme'.[153] The issue of nuclear testing was particularly important to many the leaders of India's nuclear establishment because they considered that tests might be necessary in the future in order to modernize India's nuclear arsenal in accordance with its perceived national security requirements.[154] The Hyde Act was seen as constraining this option because it stipulated not only that US nuclear cooperation would be terminated if India conducted tests but also that India would be required to return all equipment and materials of US origin that

---

[148] For Indian perspectives on the CNCI see Delhi Policy Group (DPG), *The Debate on Indo-US Nuclear Cooperation* (DPG: New Delhi, 2006).

[149] 'Text of the *suo motu* statement made by the Union Minister of External Affairs, Shri Pranab Mukherjee, on Indo–US Civil Nuclear Cooperation in the Lok Sabha, December 12, 2006', *The Hindu*, 17 Dec. 2006. There was particular concern in India that the Hyde Act, in Section 103, required the US president to report annually to the US Congress whether India was supporting US-backed efforts to 'sanction and contain' Iran for its alleged pursuit nuclear capabilities.

[150] 'Hyde Act and nuclear scientists' note', *The Hindu*, 16 Dec. 2006 .

[151] Srinivasan, M., 'India may lose control of its nuclear future', *The Hindu*, 14 Dec. 2006.

[152] 'Hyde Act and nuclear scientists' note' (note 150).

[153] Office of the Prime Minister of India, 'Statement of the PM in Rajya Sabha on the India–US nuclear agreement', New Delhi, 17 Aug. 2006, URL <http://pmindia.nic.in/parl/pcontent.asp?id=30>.

[154] 'India to keep option open on future N-test: Pranab', Rediff.com, 19 Dec. 2006, URL <http://www.rediff.com/news/2006/dec/19ndeal12.htm>.

it may have received under the deal as well as any material produced by India with these items.[155]

A second area of criticism was that the Hyde Act reneged on the 2 March 2006 agreement on fuel supply guarantees for the power reactors that India promised to place under permanent civilian safeguards.[156] These guarantees were understood in India as having been offered unconditionally by the USA.[157] However, the congressional conference report accompanying the Hyde Act clarified that the assurance of supply arrangements to which the USA had agreed covered only the disruption of fuel supplies 'due to market failures or similar reasons and not due to Indian actions that are inconsistent with the July 18, 2005 commitments, such as a nuclear explosive test'.[158]

A third area of Indian criticism was that the Hyde Act in effect denied India 'full cooperation' in civilian nuclear energy. Specifically, the legislation did not permit the transfer to India of reprocessing, enrichment and heavy water technology and equipment: the requests for such transfers would have to be approved by the US Congress on a case-by-case basis.[159] The legislation also did not give India the right to reprocess spent fuel produced from reactors or material imported from the United States. These restrictions had been added to the final version of the act to ensure that India, which had already developed these technologies, would not divert—even inadvertently—US-supplied technology and equipment to the unsafeguarded facilities associated with its military programme.[160]

Finally, the Hyde Act was criticized as an attempt by the USA to dictate the parameters of the safeguards agreement and Additional Protocol that India was supposed to sign with the IAEA.[161] The US legislation required that 'India and the IAEA [be] making substantial progress towards concluding an Additional Protocol consistent with IAEA standards and principles, practices and policies that would apply to India's civil nuclear programme' before the US Congress would remove restrictions on nuclear trade with India. It defined the Additional Protocol as one based on the IAEA's Model Additional Protocol (INFCIRC/540) rather than as an India-specific complementary access protocol to a safeguards agreement with the IAEA, as demanded by India. India has consistently ruled out accepting an intrusive inspections regime that is reserved for non-nuclear weapon states.

---

[155] Chari, P. R., 'Indo-US nuclear deal: unending drama in many acts', Institute of Peace and Conflict Studies (IPCS), IPCS Issue Brief no. 42, Jan. 2007, URL <http://www.ipcs.org/newIpcsPublications.jsp?status=publications&status1=issue&mod=d>, p. 3.

[156] Varadarajan, S., 'Lifetime fuel guarantee remains a sticking point in "123" talks with U.S.', *The Hindu*, 13 Dec. 2006.

[157] Varadarajan (note 156). Some Indian officials cited as a precedent the Kudankulam reactor deal with Russia, in which India had received sovereign and unqualified Russian guarantees for the lifetime supply of fuel for the reactors being imported from Russia.

[158] US House of Representatives (note 146), p. 10. For the 'July 18, 2005 commitments' see The White House (note 109).

[159] 'Hyde Act and nuclear scientists' note' (note 150).

[160] US House of Representatives (note 146), p. 21.

[161] Srinivasan (note 151).

Next steps and implications for nuclear supplier arrangements

While the US Congress's approval of the Hyde Act enabled the USA to open negotiations with India on the 123 agreement in 2007, the negative reaction in India suggests that these negotiations are likely to be difficult.[162] President Bush appeared to recognize this when he declared, in his signing statement for the act, that some of its provisions were 'advisory' rather than binding measures.[163]

The Indian–US nuclear deal is emerging as a contentious issue for the 45-member Nuclear Suppliers Group. At the NSG's annual meeting, held on 1–2 June 2006, the USA called on it to make an India-specific exception in its guidelines for nuclear transfers.[164] This would exempt India from the rule, adopted by the NSG in 1992, that prohibits nuclear exports to states that have not concluded a comprehensive safeguards agreement (INFCIRC/153) with the IAEA covering all of their nuclear facilities. The US proposal was supported by France, Russia and the UK, and China later said that it would not oppose it.[165] At the same time, the idea of making an exemption for India was sharply criticized by several member states, notably Ireland and Sweden. The NSG, which operates on the basis of the consensus principle, reportedly decided not to take up the US request until India has completed the parallel negotiations on the 123 agreement with the USA and the new safeguards agreement with the IAEA.[166] Because these negotiations are likely to be protracted, some senior NSG representatives have speculated that the NSG will not formally address the issue until 2008.[167] President Bush's December 2006 signing statement for the Hyde Act suggested that he might waive restrictions on the transfer of items covered by the NSG Guidelines without waiting for the NSG's approval.[168]

The US proposal for an India-specific exemption from the NSG Guidelines led to calls from other countries for similar treatment. In 2006 Israel reportedly sought an exemption from NSG transfer restrictions but was rebuffed by the USA.[169] In October 2006 Pakistan proposed a civil nuclear energy agree-

[162] 'Be wary of banking on 123 Agreement', *Business Line*, 3 Jan. 2006, URL <http://www.thehindu businessline.com/2007/01/03/stories/2007010300580900.htm>.

[163] The White House (note 147); and Varadarajan (note 156).

[164] Boese, W., 'Nuclear suppliers still split on U.S.–Indian deal', *Arms Control Today*, vol. 36, no. 6 (July/Aug. 2006), URL <http://www.armscontrol.org/act/archived.asp>.

[165] 'China not to oppose nuclear deal: US', *Dawn*, 20 Dec. 2006, URL <http://www.dawn.com/2006/12/20/int6.htm>.

[166] Hibbs, M., 'More delays loom over NSG trade sanctions and India', *Nuclear Fuel*, vol. 32, no. 1 (1 Jan. 2007), pp. 11–12.

[167] Hibbs (note 166). At the 1995 NPT Review Conference there was a consensus agreement among the states parties to establish the principle of comprehensive nuclear safeguards as a condition for nuclear supply that formed part of the bargain over the decision to indefinitely extend the NPT.

[168] The statement declared that the Hyde Act's prohibition, in Section 104(d)(2), on 'transferring or approving the transfer of an item to India contrary to Nuclear Suppliers Group transfer guidelines that may be in effect at the time of such future transfer' was not binding on the administration. The White House (note 147).

[169] Hibbs, M., 'US rebuffed Israeli request for exemption from NSG trade rule', *Nuclear Fuel*, vol. 32, no. 1 (1 Jan. 2007), pp. 1, 10.

ment with the USA, along the lines of the Indian–US deal.[170] It also urged the NSG to adopt a 'non-discriminatory' approach to regulating nuclear trade based on 'objective criteria' of responsible nuclear stewardship and non-proliferation practices, such as those being introduced in Pakistan's export control system.[171] China—which hopes to resume the sale of reactors to Pakistan—indicated that it would support Pakistan's proposal.[172]

The Indian–US nuclear deal stimulated other activities by nuclear suppliers. In March 2006 Russia agreed to supply a 'limited amount' of uranium fuel for India's two safeguarded nuclear reactors at Tarapur. Russia's decision to supply fuel at a time when the Tarapur reactors might have to shut down due to a fuel shortage was reportedly influenced by the 2 March 2006 agreement between Bush and Singh on implementing the CNCI.[173]

V. International cooperation to improve nuclear security[174]

In 2006 concern about the risk of nuclear materials falling into the hands of non-state actors who could use them in acts of terrorism led to continued investment in strengthening several countries' national measures for protecting nuclear materials and facilities. Investment in international non-proliferation and disarmament assistance (INDA) programmes remained at roughly the same level as in previous years and several new political initiatives were launched in 2006. In particular, the major INDA donor, the USA, budgeted $1.85 billion for the 2007 financial year (FY), only slightly less than the $1.86 billion it budgeted in FY 2006.[175] The 19 member states of the Group of Eight (G8) Global Partnership against the Spread of Weapons and Materials of Mass Destruction[176] reaffirmed in July 2006 their commitment to raise up to $20 billion by 2012 to support priority projects under the Global Partnership.[177] Some INDA programmes ended in 2006, either because they had accomplished their goals or because they were considered unnecessary in light of improvements in the Russian economy.

---

[170] Subramanian, N., 'Pakistan presses U.S. for civil nuclear energy pact', *The Hindu*, 26 Oct. 2006; and Akhtar, S., 'US nuclear policy in South Asia', *Dawn*, 31 Mar. 2006, URL <http://www.dawn.com/2006/03/31/ed.htm>.

[171] See e.g. Ul Haq, E., Chairman of the Pakistani Joint Chiefs of Staff Committee 'Pakistan's approach towards the challenges of non-proliferation and export controls', Keynote address to the annual conference of the South Asian Strategic Stability Institute (UK), Brussels, Belgium, 16 Nov. 2006, URL <http://www.sassu.org.uk/html/HomePG_topics/General Ehsan Ul-Haq speech.htm>.

[172] Hibbs (note 164); and Sappenfield, M. and Montero, D., 'China woos India and Pakistan with nuclear know-how', *Christian Science Monitor*, 21 Nov. 2006.

[173] 'Russia to provide fuel for Tarapur reactors', *Times of India*, 14 Mar. 2006. Russia invoked the 'safety exceptions' clause in the NSG Guidelines, as it had in 2001 when it supplied fuel to Tarapur.

[174] Vitaly Fedchenko, SIPRI Researcher, wrote this section of the chapter.

[175] Managing the Atom Project, Interactive Threat Reduction Budget database, accessed 16 Apr. 2007, URL <http://www.nti.org/e_research/cnwm/charts/cnm_funding_interactive.asp>.

[176] The G8 Global Partnership against the Spread of Weapons and Materials of Mass Destruction was established in 2002 at the G8 summit meeting in Kananaskis, Canada. Anthony, I., 'Arms control in the new security environment', *SIPRI Yearbook 2003* (note 3), pp. 567–70.

[177] G8 Summit 2006, 'Report on the G8 global partnership' and 'GPWG Annual Report 2006: consolidated report data, Annex A', St Petersburg, 16 July 2006, URL <http://g8russia.ru>.

Russian–US cooperation on nuclear security

In June 2006 Russia and the USA signed a protocol extending the 1992 Russia–USA Cooperative Threat Reduction (CTR) Umbrella Agreement for Russia for a further seven years.[178] The Umbrella Agreement provided the legal framework for activities in Russia under the CTR Program (also known as the Nunn–Lugar Program). This programme includes INDA programmes to the states of the former Soviet Union and, besides Russia, has also assisted Belarus, Kazakhstan and Ukraine to become free of nuclear weapons and their means of delivery and paved the way for the 2002 G8 Global Partnership.[179]

The operational launch of the Mayak Fissile Material Storage Facility in Ozyorsk, Chelyabinsk oblast, Russia, was announced on 11 July 2006.[180] Construction of the facility was completed in 2003 with Russian and US funds. Its purpose is to provide safe and secure storage for surplus Russian weapon-grade plutonium and HEU. Its maximum storage capacity was reported to be 50 tonnes of plutonium and 200 tonnes of HEU.[181] Russia currently plans to use about half of its plutonium storage capacity.[182]

On 15 September 2006 Russia and the USA formally concluded an agreement that they had reached in July 2005 on issues relating to liability for accidents in the bilateral plutonium disposition programme.[183] This programme had been stalled since 2003 while the two sides negotiated language to resolve the impasse.[184] The plutonium disposition programme was established under the 2000 Russia–USA Plutonium Management and Disposition Agreement (PMDA), in which the two countries agreed to eliminate 34 tonnes of surplus weapon-grade plutonium each.[185] The new liability agreement

---

[178] The Agreement between the Russian Federation and the United States of America concerning the Safe and Secure Transportation, Storage, and Destruction of Weapons and the Prevention of Weapons Proliferation, commonly known as the CTR Umbrella Agreement for Russia, was signed on 17 June 1992 at Washington, DC. On the extension of the Umbrella Agreement see The White House, 'Cooperative Threat Reduction Agreement with Russia extended', Press release, 19 June 2006, URL <http://www.whitehouse.gov/news/releases/2006/06/20060619-7.html>. The agreement had previously been extended in 1999.

[179] Office of Senator Richard G. Lugar, 'Progress made against roadblocks to the Nunn–Lugar program', Press release, Washington, DC, 19 June 2006, URL <http://lugar.senate.gov/pressapp/record.cfm?id=257390>.

[180] Tkachenko, Y., 'Fissile materials storage unit in S. Urals to guarantee n-security', ITAR-TASS, Moscow, 11 July 2006.

[181] US General Accounting Office, National Security and International Affairs Division, 'Weapons of mass destruction:effort to reduce Russian arsenals may cost more, achieve less than planned', Report to the Chairman and Ranking Minority Member, Committee on Armed Services, House of Representatives, Washington, DC, GAO/NSIAD-99-76, 13 Apr. 1999, URL <http://www.gao.gov/archive/1999/ns99076.pdf>.

[182] 'Rosatom: bomba sovsem ne strashnaya' [Rosatom: the bomb is not scary at all], Trud, 15 Nov. 2006, URL <http://www.trud.ru/issue/article.php?id=200611152110203>.

[183] US Department of Energy, 'U.S. and Russia sign liability protocol', Press release, Washington, DC, 15 Sep. 2006, URL <http://www.energy.gov/print/4160.htm>; and Hebert, H. J., 'US, Russia resolve plutonium dispute', Associated Press, 15 Sep. 2006, URL <http://www.partnershipforglobalsecurity.org/Publications/News/Nuclear News/index.asp>.

[184] On the liability issue see Kile (note 8), pp. 634–37.

[185] The Agreement between the Government of the United States of America and the Government of the Russian Federation Concerning the Management and Disposition of Plutonium Designated as No

underwent Russian inter-agency review in 2006 and was signed as a protocol to the Plutonium Management and Disposition Agreement.

The Nuclear Cities Initiative (NCI), funded by the US Department of Energy (DOE), expired on 22 September 2006. The NCI was established in 1998 to manage the economic conversion of 10 Russian closed nuclear cities that had manufactured nuclear weapons and their essential ingredients. A key aim of the NCI was to provide alternative employment to laid-off nuclear weapon specialists in order to prevent them offering their skills to 'states and organizations of proliferation concern'.[186] Because of Russia's rejection of a US demand for a blanket liability exemption for all US staff working in NCI projects, the NCI was not extended in 2003, although a three-year grace period was agreed to allow the completion of existing projects.[187]

The DOE reported in October 2006 that it had completed, two years ahead of schedule, a programme to install security enhancements designed to protect against terrorist attacks or unauthorized access at 50 Russian Navy nuclear sites. The programme was a part of a larger DOE-sponsored effort to upgrade the protection, control and accounting of nuclear materials in Russia. The DOE is also reportedly cooperating with the Russian Strategic Rocket Forces to install security upgrades at 25 sites, a task scheduled for completion by the end of 2007. In addition, the DOE started similar work at unidentified Russian military storage sites pursuant to an agreement reached at the 2005 Russia–US summit in Bratislava.[188]

The Global Initiative to Combat Nuclear Terrorism

At the July 2006 G8 summit meeting, President Bush and President Putin launched the Russian–US Global Initiative to Combat Nuclear Terrorism.[189] The initiative is designed to 'prevent the acquisition, transport, or use by terrorists of nuclear materials and radioactive substances or improvised explosive devices using such materials, as well as hostile actions against nuclear facilities'. It builds on the 2005 International Convention for the Suppression of Acts of Nuclear Terrorism.[190] It also complements the 1980 Convention on

---

Longer Required for Defense Purposes and Related Cooperation was signed on 1 Sep. 2000. The text of the agreement is available at URL <http://www.nnsa.doe.gov/na-20/docs/2000_Agreement.pdf>.

[186] US Department of Energy, Office of Nonproliferation and National Security, *Nuclear Cities Initiative Program Strategy* (Department of Energy: Washington, DC, Aug. 1999), URL <http://www.ransac.org/new-web-site/primary/transform/nci/ncibook.html>, p. 1.

[187] Harrington, C., 'U.S.–Russian nuclear program expires', *Arms Control Today*, vol. 36, no. 8 (Oct. 2006), URL <http://www.armscontrol.org/act/archived.asp>.

[188] US Department of Energy, National Nuclear Security Administration (NNSA), 'NNSA secures all Russian navy nuclear sites', Press release, 24 Oct. 2006, URL <http://www.nnsa.doe.gov/docs/news releases/2006/PR_ 2006-10-24_NA-06-39.pdf>. On the 2005 agreement see the White House, 'Joint statement by President Bush and President Putin on nuclear security cooperation', Press release, 24 Feb. 2005, URL <http://www.whitehouse.gov/news/releases/2005/02/20050224-8.html>.

[189] G8 Summit 2006, 'Joint statement by U.S. President George Bush and Russian Federation President V. V. Putin announcing the Global Initiative to Combat Nuclear Terrorism', St Petersburg, 15 July 2006, URL <http://en.g8russia.ru/docs/5.html>.

[190] Kile (note 8), p. 637.

the Physical Protection of Nuclear Material and Nuclear Facilities[191] and UN Security Council resolutions 1373 and 1540,[192] as well as relevant national legal instruments. The aims of the initiative are to improve protection, control and accounting of nuclear and radioactive materials; to detect and suppress illicit handling of such materials, especially for terrorist purposes; to improve preparedness for responding to acts of nuclear terrorism; to facilitate development of technical means to combat nuclear terrorism; and to improve law enforcement and national legal instruments for preventing and penalizing acts of terrorism. The initiative does not cover military stockpiles and facilities.

A meeting was held on 30–31 October 2006 in Rabat, Morocco, at which Russia, the USA and 11 'Global Initiative partner' states agreed a statement of principles for the Global Initiative.[193] The states also established terms of reference for facilitating provision of assistance for states requiring it in the framework of the initiative.[194]

VI. The fissile material cut-off treaty

In 2006 there were renewed, but ultimately unsuccessful, efforts at the Conference on Disarmament in Geneva to overcome the procedural impasse that has prevented the opening of negotiations on a fissile material cut-off treaty. The negotiations have been delayed since 1995, when the CD adopted a mandate (the so-called Shannon mandate, named after the Canadian ambassador to the CD, Gerald Shannon, who had been appointed special coordinator) to 'negotiate a non-discriminatory, multilateral and effectively verifiable treaty banning the production of fissile material for nuclear weapons or other nuclear explosive devices'.[195] The Shannon mandate left unresolved key differences over the scope of the proposed ban, but its adoption paved the way for the decision in 1998 to establish an ad hoc committee for negotiating an

---

[191] The Convention on the Physical Protection of Nuclear Material was opened for signature on 3 Mar. 1980 and entered into force on 8 Feb. 1987. In 2005 it was amended and renamed the Convention on the Physical Protection of Nuclear Material and Nuclear Facilities. The CPPNM is the only multilateral treaty in force that deals with physical protection issues. For a brief description and the parties to the convention see annex A. The 1980 text of the convention is available at URL <http://www.iaea.org/Publications/Documents/Conventions/cppnm.html>. For details of the 2005 amendments see IAEA Board of Governors General Conference, 'Nuclear security: measures to protect against nuclear terrorism: amendment to the Convention on the Physical Protection of Nuclear Material', Report by the Director General, GOV/INF/2005/10-GC(49)/INF/6, 6 Sep. 2005, URL <http://www.iaea.org/About/Policy/GC/GC49/Documents/gc49inf-6.pdf>.

[192] UN Security Council Resolution 1373, 28 Sep. 2001; and UN Security Council Resolution 1540, 28 Apr. 2004.

[193] McCormack, S., Spokesman, US Department of State, 'Statement of principles by participants in the Global Initiative to Combat Nuclear Terrorism', Press statement, Washington, DC, 31 Oct. 2006, URL <http://www.state.gov/r/pa/prs/ps/2006/75405.htm>.

[194] The 11 states were Australia, Canada, China, France, Germany, Italy, Japan, Kazakhstan, Morocco, Turkey and the UK. Porth, J. S., 'Nations meet in Morocco on how to counter nuclear terror threat', Current Issues, US Department of State, Bureau of International Information Programs (USINFO), 30 Oct. 2006, URL <http://usinfo.state.gov/usinfo/products/washfile.html>.

[195] Shannon, G. E., Report on consultations on the most appropriate arrangement to negotiate a treaty banning the production of fissile material for nuclear weapons or other nuclear explosive devices, CD/1299, 24 Mar. 1995, URL <http://www.reachingcriticalwill.org/political/cd/shannon.html>.

FMCT.[196] However, the CD has subsequently been unable to adopt a work programme—which is a prerequisite for convening the negotiating committee—because of a dispute over whether to establish negotiating committees for other items on its agenda.[197] Many member states and informal groups of states insist that progress towards an FMCT should be linked to simultaneous movement on issues of particular concern to them, notably nuclear disarmament, the prevention of an arms race in outer space (PAROS) and negative security assurances (NSAs).[198] All of these agenda items have been perennially divisive issues in the CD. This insistence on a 'balanced programme of work' has effectively stalled the FMCT negotiation process because the CD operates on the consensus principle.[199]

In recent years PAROS has become a top priority for both China and Russia, largely because of their concern that the USA may eventually deploy a space-based missile defence system that would threaten their strategic nuclear forces. Other states, in particular Canada, have warned that the deployment of space-based weapons might precipitate a destabilizing arms race in outer space. In 2006 China and Russia reiterated their view that the FMCT negotiations could not be the sole item on the CD's work programme and must be accompanied by the convening of a body to consider the PAROS issue.[200] China reaffirmed its position that such a body could have a discussion mandate rather than a negotiation mandate, as long as this were understood to be a step towards negotiating a new legal instrument governing the military uses of space.[201] However, the USA has resolutely rejected proposals for re-establishing an ad hoc committee on PAROS and has refused to discuss the issue.[202] The USA has also ruled out consideration of an international ban on space-based weapons, arguing that such a ban would be 'impossible to define in a way that

---

[196] Conference on Disarmament, 'Decision on the establishment of an ad hoc committee under item 1 of the agenda entitled "Cessation of the nuclear arms race and nuclear disarmament"', CD/1547, 11 Aug. 1998.

[197] The CD has a permanent agenda that was agreed in 1978 at the UN General Assembly's first Special Session on Disarmament. For more information on the CD see Center for Nonproliferation Studies, 'Conference on Disarmament (CD)', Inventory of International Nonproliferation Organizations and Regimes, URL <http://nti.org/e_research/official_docs/inventory/pdfs/cd.pdf>.

[198] NSAs are commitments by the 5 nuclear weapon states not to use, or threaten to use, nuclear weapons against non-nuclear weapon states parties to the NPT.

[199] There have been numerous proposals for revising the CD's rules of procedure, in particular the consensus principle, which has remained unchanged since the now 65-member body originated as the Ten Nation Committee on Disarmament in 1959. See e.g. Weapons of Mass Destruction Commission (the Blix Commission), *Weapons of Terror: Freeing the World of Nuclear, Biological and Chemical Weapons* (Weapons of Mass Destruction Commission: Stockholm, 2006), p. 180.

[200] Cheng, J., Ambassador for Disarmament Affairs of China, Statement on PAROS by at the plenary of the Conference on Disarmament, Geneva, 8 June 2006, URL <http://www.reachingcriticalwill.org/political/cd/speeches06/8JuneChina.pdf>; and Loshchinin, V., Permanent Representative of the Russian Federation to the Conference on Disarmament, 'PAROS: the importance of the issue', Statement to the Conference on Disarmament, Geneva, 8 June 2006, URL <http://www.reachingcriticalwill.org/political/cd/speeches06/8JuneRussia1.pdf>.

[201] Cheng (note 200). Prior to 2003 China had insisted on convening an ad hoc negotiating committee on PAROS.

[202] Between 1985 and 1995, the CD had a subsidiary committee on PAROS, which analyzed relevant issues and terminology but never conducted a negotiation.

excludes practical and important uses of space-based systems' for peaceful purposes.[203]

In addition to differences over which agenda items to include on the work programme, there have been two main substantive obstacles to opening negotiations on an FMCT. The first has to do with the linkage of an FMCT to progress towards nuclear disarmament. The Group of 21 (G-21) non-aligned states at the CD have long called for the establishment of an ad hoc committee on nuclear disarmament that would negotiate, in parallel with the FMCT ad hoc committee, a convention leading to the phased elimination of nuclear weapons within a specified period of time.[204] France, Russia, the UK and the USA have adamantly opposed the establishment of a committee on nuclear disarmament. The second obstacle has to do with questions about the scope of an FMCT: whether it should ban only the future production of fissile material for weapon purposes or should also prevent existing stocks of such material from being used to manufacture new weapons. Many non-aligned states, in particular Egypt and Pakistan, have demanded that the ban should go beyond mandating a cut-off of fissile material production and cover existing stocks. This idea has generated strong opposition from the P5 states, which continue to hold large inventories of fissile material for military purposes.[205] These states, along with India, argue that the mandate should apply only to the future production of fissile material.

The disputes over the treaty's scope and its relationship to nuclear disarmament reflect an underlying disagreement at the CD over the basic purpose of an FMCT. The P5 states tend to view it as an extension of existing non-proliferation arrangements and commitments. By banning the future production of fissile material for nuclear weapons after an agreed date, it would serve to make permanent the moratorium on producing such material that the P5 are already observing.[206] At the same time, it would cap the supply of weapon-usable material available to the de facto nuclear weapon states that have not joined the NPT—India, Israel, Pakistan and possibly North Korea—and promote their adherence to an emergent global norm.[207]

Most of the other member states have sought to forge an FMCT that would be a measure for nuclear disarmament as well as non-proliferation. Some G-21 states, among them Algeria, Brazil and South Africa, do not use the term 'fis-

[203] Delegation of the United States of America to the Conference on Disarmament, Statement at the Conference on Disarmament, Geneva, 13 June 2006, URL <http://www.reachingcriticalwill.org/political/cd/speeches06/13JuneUS.pdf>.

[204] al-Shibib, B., Permanent Representative of the Republic of Iraq, Statement on behalf of the Group of 21 at the Conference on Disarmament, Geneva, 28 Feb. 2006, URL <http://www.reachingcriticalwill.org/political/cd/speeches06/28FebG21.pdf>. See also Kile, S. N., 'Nuclear arms control', *SIPRI Yearbook 1998: Armaments, Disarmament and International Security* (Oxford University Press: Oxford, 1998), p. 431; and Kile, S. N., 'Nuclear arms control', *SIPRI Yearbook 1998: Armaments, Disarmament and International Security* (Oxford University Press: Oxford, 1999), p. 530. For a list of the current members of the G-21 see URL <http://www.reachingcriticalwill.org/political/cd/cdindex.html>.

[205] For an estimate of global inventories of fissile material see appendix 12C.

[206] France, Russia, the UK and the USA have publicly declared they no longer produce HEU and plutonium for nuclear weapons. China is also believed to have halted such production.

[207] Rissanen, J., 'Time for a fissban—or farewell?', *Disarmament Diplomacy*, no. 83 (winter 2006), URL <http://www.acronym.org.uk/dd/dd83/83fissban.htm>.

sile material cut-off treaty', since this implies only a ban on future production. They refer instead to a 'fissile material treaty' that would have a broader mandate covering existing stocks.[208] Under most proposals, these stocks would have to be declared and then placed under some form of international safeguards or supervision. In 2006 Pakistan renewed its call for a fissile material treaty that would impose upper limits, based on 'the principles of proportionality and sufficiency', on existing stocks so that all national holdings of fissile material for military purposes would be 'equalized at the lowest level possible'.[209] For Pakistan and some other countries, the inclusion of existing stocks has become a *sine qua non* for an FMCT, primarily because of regional security rivalries. Pakistan is concerned that a treaty banning only future production would perpetuate its perceived inferiority in holdings of weapon-usable fissile material vis-à-vis those of India. In the Middle East, Egypt and other Arab states see an FMCT as way to constrain and eventually reduce Israel's nuclear arsenal.[210]

The US draft treaty

On 18 May 2006 the USA put forward at the CD the draft text of an FMCT. In presenting the document, Acting Assistant Secretary of State Stephen Rademaker declared that the US objective was to set out, 'with no preconditions', the essential elements of an 'effective FMCT' that could be negotiated and opened for signature by the end of the year.[211] He emphasized that the United States saw 'no need at this time . . . for the negotiation of new multilateral agreements' apart from the FMCT, which was the only item on the CD's agenda that enjoyed consensus support. However, Rademaker added that the US delegation was prepared to discuss a range of 'new' and 'traditional' security issues in conjunction with the FMCT negotiations. The latter remark was welcomed at the CD, since it improved the prospects for reaching a deal on a work programme.[212]

---

[208] See e.g. Mtshali, G. J., Permanent Representative of the Republic of South Africa to the Conference on Disarmament, Statement of the Republic of South Africa on a fissile material treaty, Conference on Disarmament, Geneva, 17 May 2006, URL <http://www.reachingcriticalwill.org/political/cd/speeches 06/17MaySouthAfrica.pdf>.

[209] Khan, M., Permanent Representative of Pakistan to the Conference on Disarmament, Statement at the Conference on Disarmament, Geneva, 16 May 2006, URL <http://www.reachingcriticalwill.org/political/cd/speeches06/statements 16 may/16MayPakistan.pdf>.

[210] Rissanen (note 207).

[211] Rademaker, S. G., US Acting Assistant Secretary of State for International Security and Non-proliferation, 'Rising to the challenge of effective multilateralism', Remarks at the Conference on Disarmament, Geneva, 18 May 2006, URL <http://www.state.gov/t/isn/rls/rm/66419.htm>.

[212] A compromise work programme was proposed in 2003—the so-called Five Ambassadors Initiative or A5 proposal—envisioning the concurrent 'negotiation' of an FMCT and 'discussions' of negotiating mandates for the other 3 issues, appeared to win the support of most member states. Conference on Disarmament, 'Initiative of the ambassadors Dembri, Lint, Reyes, Salander and Vega: proposal of a program of work', CD/1693/Rev.1, 5 Sep. 2003, URL <http://www.reachingcriticalwill.org/political/cd/A5.pdf>.

Under the US draft treaty, the states parties would undertake not to produce fissile material for nuclear weapons or other nuclear explosive devices.[213] The draft's definition, in Article II, of the term 'fissile material' includes only those materials most likely to be used in nuclear weapons rather than a wider range of 'weapon-grade' or 'weapon-usable' materials, as has been proposed by some arms control advocates.[214] The text also defines the term 'produce fissile material', which is directly linked to the scope of the proposed treaty:[215] it states that 'the term "produce fissile material" does not include activities involving fissile material produced prior to entry into force of the Treaty'. This is consistent with the long-standing US position that existing stocks of fissile material would be unaffected by an FMCT. The draft treaty does not prohibit the production of fissile material for non-explosive purposes, such as HEU for naval propulsion reactors.

The most controversial feature of the US draft treaty is that it does not include any provisions for an international verification mechanism. According to Rademaker, the lack of a verification mechanism does not 'mean that compliance with the treaty would be unverified, but rather that the primary responsibility for verification would rest with the parties using their own national means and methods'.[216] This reflects the Bush Administration's position, announced in 2004, that an FMCT is not 'effectively verifiable'.[217] The administration's main justification was that, because an FMCT would allow the retention of existing stocks as well as the continued production of fissile material for civilian and non-explosive uses, inspectors would find it difficult to determine the purpose for which any suspect fissile material had been made and whether it had been manufactured before or after the treaty took effect.[218]

---

[213] US Mission to the United Nations in Geneva, 'US tables draft FMCT text at Conference on Disarmament', Press release, Geneva, 18 May 2006, URL <http://geneva.usmission.gov/Press2006/0518 DraftFMCT.html>.

[214] The US draft treaty defines 'fissile material' as: (a) plutonium, except plutonium whose isotopic composition includes 80% or greater plutonium-238; (b) uranium containing a 20% or greater enrichment in the isotopes uranium-233 or uranium-235, separately or in combination; or (c) any material that contains the material defined in a or b.

[215] The US draft treaty defines 'produce fissile material' as: (a) to separate any fissile material from fission products in irradiated nuclear material; (b) to enrich plutonium-239 in plutonium by any isotopic separation process; or (c) to enrich uranium-233 or uranium-235 in uranium to an enrichment of 20% or greater in those isotopes, separately or in combination, by any isotopic separation process.

[216] Rademaker (note 211).

[217] Sanders, J. W., Permanent Representative of the USA to the Conference on Disarmament and Special Representative of the President for the Nonproliferation of Nuclear Weapons, 'US proposals to the Conference on Disarmament', Remarks to the Conference on Disarmament, Geneva, 29 July 2004, URL <http://www.state.gov/t/ac/rls/rm/2004/34929.htm>; and Boese, W., 'Bush shifts fissile material ban policy', *Arms Control Today*, vol. 34, no. 7 (Sep. 2004), URL <http://www.armscontrol.org/act/archived.asp>.

[218] Nuclear forensic techniques exist that are designed to determine the 'age' of nuclear material (i.e. the time since the parent isotope was last chemically separated from its decay products). IAEA, *Nuclear Forensics Support*, Technical Guidance, Reference manual, IAEA Nuclear Security Series no. 2, STI/PUB/1241 (IAEA: Vienna, 2006), URL <http://www-pub.iaea.org/MTCD/publications/PDF/Pub1241_web.pdf>, p. 30; and Moody, K. J., Hutcheon, I. D. and Grant, P. M., *Nuclear Forensic Analysis* (CRC Press: Boca Raton, Fla., 2005), pp. 207–40. E.g. the method for determining the age of HEU is given in Moorthy, A. R. and Kato, W. Y., 'HEU age determination', BNL-52535, Formal report, Brookhaven National Laboratory, Department of Advanced Technology, Long Island, N.Y., 1 July 1997, URL <http://www.osti.gov/energycitations/purl.cover.jsp?purl=/534522-eS1Bs2/webviewable/>.

The US Administration concluded that even extensive verification measures might not be able to detect or deter a determined cheater. At the same time, such measures would provide a false sense of security for compliant parties while also intruding into the legitimate security affairs of some states.[219]

This position put the United States at odds with most other CD member states, which believed that an FMCT should include formal verification provisions, as was clearly envisioned in the Shannon mandate. There has been widespread support for the idea that a verification regime should be based on the system of comprehensive safeguards agreements already in place between the IAEA and non-nuclear weapon states parties to the NPT.[220] In practical terms, this would involve extending safeguards-based verification arrangements to the nuclear weapon states as well as to the states outside the NPT, leading to the eventual 'convergence' of the FMCT and NPT regimes.

While not endorsing the US draft treaty's lack of verification measures, Australia and several European states pointed out that this was not an obstacle to opening negotiations without preconditions. The talks could focus initially on reaching a framework agreement that would establish a norm regarding the cessation of fissile material production for nuclear weapons; measures to verify compliance could be left to subsequent, largely technical, negotiations.[221] However, many other member states were reluctant to embrace the idea of starting negotiations in which some of the parties might not be committed to an 'effectively verifiable' FMCT. India expressed concern that the omission of a verification mechanism might 'engender a lack of confidence in compliance with the treaty, encourage wilful non-compliance and lead to allegations and counter-allegations of non-compliance'.[222]

The reactions at the CD to the US draft treaty were generally reserved. The USA won plaudits for showing some flexibility regarding procedural roadblocks.[223] However, many observers noted that the US proposal would require a revision of the Shannon mandate—a task likely to be as divisive as adopting a work programme. There was also considerable speculation that the main factor driving the USA's submission of the draft treaty was the Bush Adminis-

---

[219] US Mission to the United Nations in Geneva, 'United States of America White Paper on a fissile material cutoff treaty', Geneva, 18 May 2006, URL <http://geneva.usmission.gov/Press2006/0518White Paper.html>.

[220] For a discussion of how IAEA safeguards arrangements and practices contribute to verifying an FMCT see Rauf, T., Head of Verification and Security Policy Coordination, IAEA, 'A cut-off of production of fissionable material: considerations, requirements and IAEA capabilities', Statement to the Conference on Disarmament, Geneva, 24 Aug. 2006, URL <http://www.reachingcriticalwill.org/political/cd/speeches06/24AugustIAEA.pdf>.

[221] Millar, C., Ambassador for Disarmament of Australia, 'Fissile material cut-off treaty', Statement to the Conference on Disarmament, Geneva, 17 May 2006, URL <http://www.reachingcriticalwill.org/political/cd/speeches06/17MayAustralia.doc>.

[222] Prasad, J., Ambassador and Permanent Representative of India to the Conference on Disarmament, Statement to the Conference on Disarmament, Geneva, 17 May 2006, URL <http://www.reachingcriticalwill.org/political/cd/speeches06/17MayIndia.pdf>.

[223] Crail, P., 'U.S. fissile material proposals stir cautious optimism', *WMD Insights*, July/Aug. 2006, URL <http://wmdinsights.com/17/17_G1_USFissileMaterial.htm>.

tration's desire to draw India into an FMCT and thereby improve the chances that the US Congress would approve the Indian–US nuclear deal.[224]

The CD ended its annual sessions for 2006 having failed, for the 11th consecutive year, to open negotiations on a treaty banning the production of fissile material for nuclear weapons. The frustration with procedural 'hostage-taking' and other dysfunctional features of the CD has led to a number of proposals for negotiating a fissile material treaty in an ad hoc forum of like-minded states outside that body.[225] To be effective, any resulting treaty would eventually have to include countries such as India, Israel and Pakistan, which either are producing fissile material for weapon purposes or, in the case of China, may be determined to keep open the option to do so in the future. While not publicly opposing an FMCT, none of these countries has shown enthusiasm for concluding a ban on the production of fissile materials in the short term.

VII. Conclusions

In 2006 the UN Security Council moved to the centre of the escalating confrontations over the nuclear programmes of Iran and North Korea. In a reflection of the depth of international concern about these programmes, the Security Council demanded that both countries halt their activities of proliferation concern—including non-proscribed activities such as ballistic missile flight-testing—and subsequently imposed sanctions on them for failing to heed its demands. The sanctions agreed to by the Security Council involved a set of limited financial and trade restrictions that were specifically aimed at denying Iran and North Korea access to the technology, equipment and expertise that could contribute to their nuclear and ballistic missile programmes. Together with punitive measures imposed by individual Security Council members, the selective sanctions seemed likely to have some effect in constraining the Iranian and North Korean programmes. They did not, however, appear to change the structure of incentives for Iran and North Korea to engage to pursue these programmes and may actually have reinforced Iran's commitment to developing sensitive nuclear fuel-cycle facilities. In this regard, the Security Council was largely ineffective in asserting its authority under the UN Charter to take action to preserve international peace and security.

It remains an open question whether a fractious and often fractured Security Council can summon the resolve and unity of purpose to take a more robust approach to dealing with tough proliferation cases such as Iran and North Korea. The diplomatic bargaining preceding the Security Council's resolutions on Iran and North Korea underscored the fact that for many states non-proliferation is only one objective among numerous—and often competing—commercial, economic and strategic objectives. The nuclear diplomacy at the Security Council also highlighted the difficulty of mobilizing international

---

[224] Krepon, M., 'The Bush Administration tables a draft "cutoff" treaty: analysis of key elements', Stimson Center, Washington, DC, 18 May 2006, URL <http://www.stimson.org/pub.cfm?id=293>.

[225] Rissanen (note 207).

support for a global non-proliferation regime that has come under increasingly sharp criticism, especially from the non-aligned states, for perpetuating a discriminatory division between those countries that have nuclear weapons and those that do not. This difficulty was compounded in 2006 by the widespread perception that, in the proposed nuclear deal with India, the US Administration was seeking to impose one set of rules for states that it deemed to be 'responsible' and another set for those deemed to be dangerous, based on whether the states were friends or potential adversaries of the USA. The growing discontent with the global non-proliferation regime raises the prospect that fewer and fewer states may be willing to defend its rules and regulatory restraints against alleged transgressors unless the normative legitimacy of the regime itself is strengthened. This will require, above all, a renewed commitment by all states to implement fully their non-proliferation and disarmament commitments within a framework of rules and norms that apply universally.

Appendix 12A. World nuclear forces, 2007

SHANNON N. KILE, VITALY FEDCHENKO and
HANS M. KRISTENSEN

I. Introduction

Eight nuclear weapon states possessed roughly 11 530 operational nuclear weapons as of January 2007 (see table 12A.1). Several thousand nuclear weapons are kept on high alert, ready to be launched within minutes. If all nuclear warheads are counted—operational warheads, spares, and those in both active and inactive storage—the United States, Russia, the United Kingdom, France, China, India, Pakistan and Israel together possessed an estimated total of more than 26 000 warheads.[1] A ninth state, the Democratic People's Republic of Korea (DPRK, or North Korea), demonstrated a nuclear weapon capability when it carried out a nuclear test explosion in 2006, but whether it has developed any operational nuclear weapons is not known.

All of the five legally recognized nuclear weapon states, as defined by the 1968 Treaty on the Non-proliferation of Nuclear Weapons (Non-Proliferation Treaty, NPT),[2] appear determined to remain nuclear weapon powers for the foreseeable future and are in the midst of or have plans for modernizing their nuclear forces. Russia and the USA are in the process of reducing their operational nuclear forces from cold war levels as a result of two bilateral treaties: the 1991 Treaty on the Reduction and Limitation of Strategic Offensive Arms (START I Treaty) and the 2002 Strategic Offensive Reductions Treaty (SORT).[3] The USA plans to reduce its total stockpile by almost half by 2012. It also intends to begin production of new nuclear warheads for the first time since the end of the cold war. Similarly, Russia has announced a plan to reduce its strategic forces—mainly by eliminating its inter-continental ballistic missiles (ICBMs)—but also to retain for another decade, rather than dismantling, its ICBMs equipped with multiple independently targetable re-entry vehicles (MIRVs). Russia is in the final phases of developing or has introduced a new ICBM, a new class of strategic submarines with a new submarine-launched ballistic missile (SLBM), and a new cruise missile. Tables 12A.2 and 12A.3 show the composition of the deployed nuclear forces of the USA and Russia, respectively.

---

[1] In this appendix 'stockpile' refers to the total inventory of nuclear warheads, and 'operational warheads' and 'arsenal' refer to that portion of the stockpile that is available for delivery by missiles and aircraft.

[2] The NPT was opened for signature on 1 July 1968 and entered into force on 5 Mar. 1970. According to the treaty, only states that manufactured and exploded a nuclear device prior to 1 Jan. 1967 are legally recognized as nuclear weapon states. By this definition, China, France, Russia, the UK and the USA are the nuclear weapon states parties to the NPT. For a brief description of the NPT and a list of the signatories and parties to the treaty see annex A in this volume.

[3] The START I Treaty was signed on 31 July 1991 by the USA and the USSR; it entered into force on 5 Dec. 1994 for Russia and the USA. Under the 1992 Lisbon Protocol, which also entered into force on 5 Dec. 1994, Belarus, Kazakhstan and Ukraine assumed the obligations of the former USSR under the treaty. For the text of the START I Treaty see URL <http://www.state.gov/www/global/arms/starthtm/start/toc.html>. SORT was signed by Russia and the USA on 24 May 2002 and entered into force on 1 June 2003. For the text of SORT see URL <http://www.state.gov/t/ac/trt/18016.htm>. For brief descriptions of both treaties see annex A in this volume. On the implications of SORT see 'Special section', *Arms Control Today*, vol. 32, no. 5 (June 2002), pp. 3–23.

Table 12A.1. World nuclear forces, by number of deployed warheads, January 2007

Country	Strategic warheads	Non-strategic warheads	Total number of warheads
USA	4 545	500	5 045[a]
Russia	3 284	2 330	5 614[b]
UK	~160	–	~160[c]
France	348	–	348
China	~145	?[d]	~145
India			~50[e]
Pakistan			~60[e]
Israel			≤100[e]
North Korea			~6[f]
Total			**~11 530**

[a] The total US stockpile, including reserves, contains c. 10 000 warheads.

[b] The total Russian stockpile contains c. 15 000 warheads, of which c. 9300 are in storage or awaiting dismantlement.

[c] The British deployed arsenal is said to consist of fewer than 160 warheads, but the UK probably also has a small number of spares for a total stockpile of about 195 warheads. Some warheads on British strategic submarines have sub-strategic missions.

[d] It is not certain whether China has non-strategic warheads.

[e] The stockpiles of India, Israel and Pakistan are thought to be only partly deployed.

[f] North Korea carried out a nuclear test explosion in Oct. 2006, but there is no public information to verify that it has weaponized its nuclear capability. The number shown is an estimate of the number of warheads that North Korea could produce based on calculations of its stockpile of separated plutonium.

The nuclear arsenals of the UK, France and China are considerably smaller than those of the USA and Russia, but all three states have plans to deploy new nuclear weapons or have announced their intention to do so. Data on their delivery vehicles and nuclear warhead stockpiles are presented in tables 12A.4, 12A.5 and 12A.6, respectively. China will soon deploy a new generation of strategic missiles and cruise missiles, but it remains unclear whether it intends to deploy a significantly larger strategic nuclear force or a more modern force of roughly the same size. France is currently engaged in developing and deploying a new generation of nuclear-powered ballistic missile submarines (SSBNs, from 'ship submersible ballistic nuclear'), SLBMs and air-launched nuclear weapons. The number of operational warheads may decrease somewhat with the introduction of the new SLBM around 2010. Unlike any of the other nuclear weapon states, France continues to deploy nuclear weapons on a surface ship in peacetime. The British nuclear weapon stockpile has levelled out at just under 200 warheads. In 2006 the British Government announced its intention to build a new class of strategic submarines to replace its Trident fleet but to make modest reductions in its operational nuclear weapons.

It is particularly difficult to find reliable public information about the operational status of the nuclear arsenals of the three states that are believed to possess nuclear weapons but are not parties to the NPT: India, Pakistan and Israel. What information is available is often contradictory or inaccurate. India and Pakistan are both thought to be expanding their nuclear strike capabilities, while Israel seems to be waiting to see how the situation in Iran develops. Tables 12A.7, 12A.8 and 12A.9 present information about the status of the Indian, Pakistani and Israeli nuclear arsenals, respectively. The figures in the tables are estimates based on public information and contain some uncertainties, as reflected in the notes.

II. US nuclear forces[4]

The USA maintains approximately 5045 operational nuclear warheads, of which roughly 4545 are strategic and 500 are non-strategic (see table 12A.2).[5] Another 260 warheads are held as spares. In addition to this operational arsenal, roughly 5000 warheads are in the responsive force or the inactive reserve or are awaiting dismantlement. Thus, the USA has a total stockpile of just over 10 000 warheads.

Of the current US stockpile, more than 4000 warheads are expected to be retired by 2012 for eventual dismantlement as a result of the 2004 Nuclear Weapons Stockpile Plan.[6] Most of these excess warheads will come from the large reserve of inactive warheads, while a smaller number will come from warheads removed from operational status as a result of the implementation of SORT. This will leave a stockpile of nearly 6000 warheads by 2012.

In 2006 the administration of President George W. Bush proposed a comprehensive plan to revitalize the US nuclear weapon production complex. The plan, known as Complex 2030, includes the resumption of nuclear warhead production for the first time since the cold war.[7] The new series of warheads will be known as Reliable Replacement Warheads (RRWs). The US Government has said that the RRWs will have wider performance margins, be simpler to maintain and be tailored for the type of deterrence missions envisioned for the 21st century. The design of the first warhead, known as the RRW-1, is based on a primary warhead (the SKUA-9, used to test secondary warheads during the cold war) and a secondary warhead, which were tested together four times in the 1980s. The RRW-1 will use insensitive high explosives, will have a fire-resistant pit and enhanced security features to prevent unauthorized use, and will be encased in the Mk-5 re-entry body, which is used for the W88 warhead (currently deployed on the Trident II (D-5) SLBM). Delivery of the first production unit is planned for 2012–14, when the RRW-1 will begin to replace W76 warheads on the Trident II (D-5). The intention appears to be to replace most or all types of warhead in the stockpile with RRWs.

In an effort to 'ensure that stockpile and infrastructure transformation is not misperceived by other nations as "restarting the arms race"', the Bush Administration

---

[4] This section draws heavily on information gathered by Hans M. Kristensen, director of the Nuclear Information Project at the Federation of American Scientists (FAS). See URL <http://www.nukestrat.com>.

[5] The 5045 warheads represent a reduction of nearly 500 compared with the estimate in *SIPRI Yearbook 2006*. The reduction is due to the downloading of some ICBMs, the temporary omission of 2 SSBNs from the count during their missile conversion and new information obtained about the composition of the arsenal.

[6] The classified Nuclear Weapons Stockpile Plan was submitted to the US Congress on 3 June 2004. US Department of Energy, National Nuclear Security Administration, 'Administration plans significant reduction in nuclear weapons stockpile', News release, Washington, DC, 3 June 2004, URL <http://www.nnsa.doe.gov/newsreleases.htm>.

[7] US Department of Energy (DOE), National Nuclear Security Administration, *Complex 2030: An Infrastructure Planning Scenario for a Nuclear Weapons Complex Able to Meet the Threat of the 21st Century*, DOE/NA-0013 (DOE: Washington, DC, Oct. 2006).

announced in 2006 that it would increase warhead dismantlements planned for financial year (FY) 2007 by nearly 50 per cent compared to FY 2006 and would increase the average annual warhead dismantlements at the Pantex Plant by 25 per cent.[8] However, since the rate of dismantlement at Pantex has been slow in recent years (100 or fewer warheads per year), increasing the average rate by 25 per cent would have only a limited effect on reducing the stockpile. In fact, the US Department of Energy (DOE) estimates that dismantlement of the current backlog and warheads retired as a result of the 2004 Nuclear Weapons Stockpile Plan will not be completed until 2023,[9] corresponding to the dismantlement of an average of approximately 250 warheads per year. Instead, the priority is to extend the life of the remaining nearly 6000 warheads indefinitely.

In parallel with these adjustments to the US nuclear forces, the Department of Defense (DOD) has upgraded its nuclear strike plans to reflect new presidential guidance and a transition in war planning from the Single Integrated Operational Plan (SIOP) of the cold war era to a set of smaller and more flexible strike plans. The new central strategic war plan is known as OPLAN (Operations Plan) 8044. General Richard B. Meyers, chairman of the Joint Chiefs of Staff, described some of the planning changes in congressional testimony in February 2005: '[US Strategic Command] has revised [the USA's] strategic deterrence and response plan that became effective in the fall of 2004. This revised, detailed plan provides more flexible options to assure allies, and dissuade, deter, and if necessary, defeat adversaries in a wider range of contingencies'.[10]

One example of these changes is CONPLAN (Concept Plan) 8022, a plan for the quick use of nuclear, conventional or information warfare capabilities to destroy—pre-emptively, if necessary—'time-urgent targets' anywhere in the world. Secretary of Defense Donald Rumsfeld issued an Alert Order in early 2004 that directed the US military to put CONPLAN 8022 into effect. As a result, the pre-emption policy of the Bush Administration is now operational for nuclear forces.

Land-based ballistic missiles

The US ICBM force is undergoing significant changes as part of the USA's implementation of SORT. It is estimated that approximately 900 warheads were deployed on 500 ICBMs as of January 2007, some 150 fewer warheads than the estimated number in 2006. This reduction was due to the downloading of Minuteman III missiles of the 341st Wing at Malmstrom Air Force Base (AFB), Montana, to a single re-entry vehicle (SRV) configuration. The download, which began in mid-2005, involves 150 of the wing's 200 missiles and is scheduled for completion in mid-2008. The 50 remaining missiles will be deactivated in 2007 to implement the decision set out in the 2006 Quadrennial Defense Review to reduce the US ICBM force from 500 to 450 missiles by 2008. The Minuteman III missiles of the 91st Wing

---

[8] D'Agostino, T. P., Deputy Administrator for Defense Programs, National Nuclear Security Administration, Statement before the House Armed Services Committee Subcommittee on Strategic Forces, 5 Apr. 2006, URL <http://www.nnsa.doe.gov/docs/congressional/2006/2006-04-05_HASC_Transformation_Hearing_Statement (DAgostino).pdf>, p. 10.

[9] D'Agostino (note 8), p. 8.

[10] Myers, R. B., US Air Force, Chairman of the Joint Chiefs of Staff, Posture statement before the Senate Armed Services Committee, URL <http://www.senate.gov/~armed_services/statemnt/2005/February/Myers 02-17-05.pdf>, 17 Feb. 2005, p. 32.

Table 12A.2. US nuclear forces, January 2007

Type	Designation	No. deployed	Year first deployed	Range (km)[a]	Warhead loading	No. of warheads
Strategic forces						
Bombers[b]						
B-52H	Stratofortress	85/56	1961	16 000	ALCM 5–150 kt	984[c]
					ACM 5–150 kt	400
B-2	Spirit	21/16	1994	11 000	Bombs	533[d]
Subtotal		*106/72*				*1 917*
ICBMs[e]						
LGM-30G	Minuteman III					
	Mk-12	50[f]	1970	13 000	3 x 170 kt	150
		150			1 x 170 kt	150
	Mk-12A	150	1979	13 000	2–3 x 335 kt	450
		100			1 x 335 kt	100
	Mk-21 SERV[g]	50	2006	13 000	1 x 300 kt	50
Subtotal		*500*				*900*
SSBNs/SLBMs[h]						
UGM-133A	Trident II (D-5)					
	Mk-4	?	1992	>7 400	6 x 100 kt	1 344
	Mk-5	?	1990	>7 400	6 x 475 kt	384
Subtotal		*288*				*1 728*
Total strategic forces						**4 545**
Non-strategic forces						
B61-3, -4 bombs		n.a.	1979	n.a.	0.3–170 kt	400[i]
Tomahawk SLCM		320	1984	2 500	1 x 5–150 kt	100[j]
Total non-strategic forces						**500**
Total						**5 045**[k]

ALCM = air-launched cruise missile; ACM = Advanced Cruise Missile; ICBM = intercontinental ballistic missile; kt = kiloton; n.a. = not applicable; SERV = security-enhanced re-entry vehicle; SLBM = submarine-launched ballistic missile; SLCM = sea-launched cruise missile; SSBN = nuclear-powered ballistic missile submarine; ? = unknown.

[a] Aircraft range is given for illustrative purposes only; actual mission range will vary according to flight profile and weapon loading.

[b] The first figure in the *No. deployed* column is the total number of B-52H bombers in the inventory, including those for training, testing and reserve. The second figure is for primary mission inventory aircraft, i.e. the number of operational aircraft assigned for nuclear and conventional wartime missions.

[c] Another 360 ALCM warheads are in reserve.

[d] Available for both the B-52H and B-2A bombers, but the B-2A is thought to be the main bomb-delivery vehicle.

[e] The 2006 Quadrennial Defense Review decided to reduce the ICBM force by 50 missiles to 450 by 2008. The download of most Minuteman ICBMs to a single warhead to meet the warhead ceiling mandated by the 2002 Strategic Offensive Reductions Treaty (SORT) is underway. The W62 (Mk-12) will be retired by 2009. The 450 missiles will carry a total of 500 warheads with hundreds more in reserve for upload if necessary.

[f] The 50 missiles of the 564th Missile Squadron at Malmstrom Air Force Base are scheduled for withdrawal from service in 2007.

g The SERV programme converts the W87/Mk-21 warhead previously deployed on the Peacekeeper ICBM for deployment on the Minuteman III ICBM.

h Two of 14 SSBNs are undergoing conversion from the C-4 missile.

i As many as 400 bombs (including possibly inactive weapons) are deployed in Europe.

j Another 190 W80-0 warheads are in inactive storage.

k Another 260 warheads are spares and roughly 5000 warheads are kept in the responsive force or inactive stockpile or are awaiting dismantlement, giving a total stockpile of just over 10 000 warheads. In addition, more than 12 000 plutonium pits are stored at the Pantex Plant in Texas.

Sources: US Department of Defense, various budget reports and press releases; US Department of Energy, various budget reports; US Department of State, START I Treaty Memoranda of Understanding, 1990–July 2006; US Department of Defense, various documents obtained under the Freedom of Information Act; US Air Force, US Navy and US Department of Energy, personal communications; 'NRDC Nuclear Notebook', *Bulletin of the Atomic Scientists*, various issues; US Naval Institute, *Proceedings*, various issues; and Authors' estimates.

at Minot AFB, North Dakota, will also begin downloading to meet the SORT limit. Once completed, the ICBM force will carry 500 warheads on 450 missiles with several hundred additional warheads held in reserve for potential upload in a crisis.

In October 2006 the US Air Force (USAF) began replacing 170-kiloton W62 warheads on the Minuteman III ICBMs at Warren AFB with the modified 300-kt W87/Mk-21 security-enhanced re-entry vehicle (SERV). The W87 warhead was previously deployed on the Peacekeeper (MX) ICBM until the missile was withdrawn from service in 2005. Each reconfigured Minuteman III will carry one W87 but can be equipped with up to two warheads. The greater explosive power of the W87 will broaden the range of hardened targets that can be held at risk with the Minuteman force. The last W62 warhead will be retired by 2009.

Work continued in 2006 on modernizing the guidance and propulsion systems of the Minuteman ICBM force. Four Minuteman III missile test launches were conducted in 2006 from Vandenberg AFB, California. The missiles test-launched on 16 February and 7 April each carried one unarmed re-entry vehicle; those test-launched on 14 June and 20 July each carried three unarmed re-entry vehicles. The missiles tested in February and June flew to the normal range of 7725 kilometres to Kwajalein atoll in the Marshall Islands. The missiles launched in July flew 6760 km, also to Kwajalein, but those launched in April flew to an 'extended range' of 8200 km. The purpose of the longer flight was to test the Minuteman III ICBM at a range more in line with actual strike plans. The February launch was the third and final verification flight of the W87/Mk-21 SERV warhead.

Work is continuing on the design of a new ICBM to begin replacing Minuteman III missiles from 2018. The Mission Need Statement (MNS) for the new ICBM states that nuclear weapons will 'continue to play a unique and indispensable role in US security policy' and that a credible and effective land-based nuclear deterrent force 'beyond 2020' will 'prepare the US for an uncertain future by maintaining US qualitative superiority in nuclear war-fighting capabilities in the 2020–2040 time frame'.[11]

---

[11] US Department of the Air Force, Headquarters, Air Force Space Command/Data Records Management, 'Final mission need statement (MNS), AFSPC 001-00: land-based strategic nuclear deterrent', Acquisition Category One (ACAT I), 18 Jan. 2002, p. 2.

Ballistic missile submarines

The USA continues to retrofit the two remaining SSBNs that carried the Trident I (C-4) SLBM with the longer-range and more accurate Trident II (D-5) missile, with the SSBNs USS *Henry M. Jackson* and USS *Alabama* scheduled to become operational in 2007 and 2008, respectively. The other 12 SSBNs carry 288 Trident II (D-5) SLBMs, each of which is estimated to carry an average of six warheads for a total of roughly 1728 warheads. With the completion of the Trident II (D-5) conversion of the *Henry M. Jackson* and the *Alabama*, the SLBM force will increase to 336 Trident II (D-5) missiles in the next two years.[12]

After moving five Atlantic Ocean-based SSBNs to the Pacific Ocean in 2002–2005, thereby boosting the US Pacific SSBN fleet to nine boats, the US Navy announced in 2006 that USS *Alaska* would be moved to Kings Bay, Georgia, in 2008.[13] In the future, eight SSBNs will patrol in the Pacific and six in the Atlantic, which means that the US sea-based deterrent will continue to be focused on China and other countries in the Pacific region.

Procurement of the Trident II (D-5) SLBM ended in 2006. In 2008 the US Navy will begin production of a modified Trident II (D-5) missile known as Trident II (D-5) Life-Extended (D5LE). A total of 108 missiles are to be built by 2011, at a cost of more than $4 billion, with initial deployment planned for 2013. The D5LE will arm the Ohio Class SSBNs for the rest of their service lives, which have been extended from 30 years to 44 years. The oldest ship is scheduled to be retired in 2029, at which point it is planned that a new SSBN class will become operational. The D5LE may also arm the UK's next class of SSBNs.

Four Trident II (D-5) missiles were flight-tested in 2006. On 9 May USS *Alaska* (SSBN-732) launched two Trident II (D-5) missiles towards Kwajalein from a position off the coast of California. USS *Maryland* (SSBN-738) launched two Trident II (D-5) missiles from the waters off Florida on 21 November, marking the 116th and 117th consecutive successful Trident II (D-5) launches conducted by the US Navy since the missile was deployed in 1990. The 21 November test included the third and final development test of the new arming, firing and fusing (AF&F) system for the W76-1 warhead, which is scheduled to begin deployment from September 2007.

The development of the AF&F system for the W76 warhead is part of a three-part upgrade (formally called a life extension) of the warhead. The new fuse will 'enable [the] W76 to take advantage of [the] higher accuracy of the D-5 missile' to hold at risk a wider range of targets, including hardened targets.[14] The increased accuracy of the W76-1 warhead may also permit a reduction of its explosive yield. Another upgrade involves the development of an 'accuracy adjunct' for the Mk-4 re-entry

---

[12] The USA will count only 12 of its 14 submarines as operational, because 2 are normally in dry dock for refit.

[13] 'Navy to move USS *Alaska* to Kings Bay', News4Georgia.com, 7 June 2006, URL <http://www.news4georgia.com/9334494/detail.html>.

[14] US Department of Energy (DOE), Office of Defense Programs, *Stockpile Stewardship and Management Plan: First Annual Update, October 1997* (DOE: Washington, DC, Oct. 2006), pp. 1–14. See also Nanos, G. P., Director, US Strategic Systems Program, 'Strategic systems update', *Submarine Review*, Apr. 1997, pp. 12–17.

vehicle to enhance the accuracy of the W76-1/Mk-4 and to enable deployment of conventional warheads on the Trident II (D-5) SLBM.[15]

Long-range bombers

The size of the US bomber force remained unchanged in 2006, but the aircraft and their nuclear weapons continued to be upgraded. Close to 2000 nuclear warheads are earmarked for delivery by B-52H and B-2 bombers, including W80-1 warheads for delivery on air-launched cruise missiles (ALCMs) and B61-7, B61-11, B83-0 and B83-1 gravity bombs.

The USAF has decided to retire the Advanced Cruise Missile (ACM), possibly as early as 2008.[16] The decision to retire the missile, which carried the W80 warhead, is part of a larger plan to reduce the number of W80 warheads. The life extension of the warhead has been put on hold (only design work will continue) and the inventory of ALCMs will be reduced to 528 by 2012.[17]

The ongoing Avionics Midlife Improvement (AMI) programme for the B-52H bomber—the only carrier of ALCMs and ACMs—to improve the aircraft's navigation and nuclear weapon delivery capabilities is expected to be completed in September 2008. The existing USAF satellite communications (AFSATCOM) radio will also be replaced by extremely high frequency (EHF) radio to improve communications in nuclear strike scenarios.

The USAF is studying options for a new long-range strike aircraft that would eventually replace the current US bomber force. It is also studying options for a new nuclear cruise missile.

Non-strategic nuclear weapons

As of January 2007 the USA retained approximately 500 active non-strategic nuclear warheads. Another 1155 non-strategic warheads were in inactive storage. Despite the significant numbers of warheads (Russia probably retains many more), neither the 2001 US Nuclear Posture Review nor SORT addresses non-strategic nuclear weapons.[18]

Up to 400 B61 bombs are deployed at eight airbases in six European NATO member states (Belgium, Germany, Italy, the Netherlands, Turkey and the UK). The aircraft of non-nuclear weapon NATO states that are assigned nuclear strike missions

---

[15] In the 2006 Quadrennial Defense Review the DOC indicated that it would replace nuclear warheads on 24 Trident II (D-5) missiles with 96 conventional warheads for deployment in 2008. However, The US Congress has been unwilling to fund the programme and instead asked the DOD to conduct a study on the implications for crisis stability of mixing nuclear and conventional ballistic missiles.

[16] Kristensen, H. M., 'US Air Force decides to retire advanced cruise missile', Federation of American Scientists Strategic Security blog, 7 Mar. 2007, URL <http://www.fas.org/blog/ssp/2007/03/us_air_force_decides_to_retire.php>.

[17] Burg, R., US Air Force, Strategic Security Directorate, 'ICBMs, helicopters, cruise missiles, bombers and warheads', Presentation to the US Senate Armed Services Committee Subcommittee on Strategic Forces, Washington, DC, 28 Mar. 2007.

[18] On the 2001 Nuclear Posture Review see US Department of Defense, 'Nuclear Posture Review [excerpts], submitted to Congress on 31 December 2001', 8 Jan. 2002, URL <http://www.globalsecurity.org/wmd/library/policy/dod/npr.htm>, p. 17; and Kristensen, H. M. and Kile, S. N., 'World nuclear forces', *SIPRI Yearbook 2003: Armaments, Disarmament and International Security* (Oxford University Press: Oxford, 2003), pp. 612–13.

with US nuclear weapons include Belgian and Dutch F-16 and German and Italian Tornado combat aircraft.[19] The US arsenal in Europe may include inactive bombs.

Only 100 W80-0 warheads for the Tomahawk cruise missile (TLAM/N, from Tomahawk land attack missile, nuclear) are active; another 190 are in inactive storage. The TLAM/N is earmarked for deployment on selected Los Angeles, Improved Los Angeles and Virginia Class nuclear-powered attack submarines (SSNs, from ship submersible nuclear). It is not deployed at sea under normal circumstances but can be redeployed within 30 days of a decision to do so. All TLAM/N missiles are stored at the strategic weapons facilities at Bangor, Washington, and Kings Bay, Georgia.

Nuclear warhead stockpile management and modernization

The US stockpile of just over 10 000 warheads is organized in two categories: active and inactive warheads. The active category includes intact warheads (with all the components) that are deployed on operational delivery systems, are part of the 'responsive force' of reserve warheads that can be deployed on operational delivery systems in a relatively short time or are spares. The inactive category includes warheads that are held in long-term storage as a reserve with their limited-life components (tritium) removed. As SORT and the 2004 Nuclear Weapons Stockpile Plan are implemented over the next five years, the 'responsive force' will gradually increase to contain roughly twice as many warheads as there are operationally deployed warheads. In addition to the approximately 10 000 active and inactive warheads, the USA keeps about 5000 plutonium cores (pits) in storage at the Pantex Plant as a strategic reserve. Approximately the same number of canned assemblies (thermonuclear secondaries) are kept at the Oak Ridge Y-12 Plant in Tennessee. Another 10 000 pits held at Pantex make up most of the 34 tonnes of weapon-grade plutonium previously declared in excess of military needs by the administration of President Bill Clinton. All of the nearly 15 000 pits at Pantex come from retired warheads. Production of plutonium pits has resumed at Los Alamos on a small scale and the current US Administration has proposed building a consolidated plutonium facility with the capacity to produce about 125 pits per year by 2013.

III. Russian nuclear forces

In 2006 Russia continued to reduce its strategic nuclear forces in accordance with its commitments under SORT and as part of a doctrinal shift away from a 'substantially redundant' (*suschestvenno izbytochnyi*) towards a 'minimally sufficient' (*garantirovanno dostatochnyi*) deterrence posture. At the same time, Russia reaffirmed that it would retain for the foreseeable future all three elements—ICBMs, SLBMs and strategic bombers—of its nuclear 'triad' (see table 12A.3). According to a senior Russian military planner, Russia's strategic nuclear forces can still guarantee 'minimally sufficient' deterrence until 2015–20 within the force ceilings imposed by SORT, even

---

[19] On the history and status of US nuclear weapons in Europe see Kristensen, H. M., *U.S. Nuclear Weapons in Europe: A Review of Post-Cold War Policy, Force Levels, and War Planning* (Natural Resources Defense Council: Washington, DC, Feb. 2005), URL <http://www.nrdc.org/nuclear/euro/contents.asp>.

if the USA develops a ballistic missile defence (BMD) system.[20] However, he said that qualitative upgrades would be needed to enhance the Russian nuclear triad's survivability and ability to penetrate missile defences. Accordingly, Russia would prioritize the procurement of the SS-27 Topol-M land-based and SS-NX-30 Bulava SLBM systems, while continuing efforts to extend the service lives of older missile systems as an interim measure.[21]

In early 2007 Russia announced plans to procure another 10 SS-N-23 Skiff SLBMs and 7 SS-27 Topol-M ICBMs, 3 of them road-mobile and 4 silo-based.[22]

There were unconfirmed reports in the Russian press that part of the A-135 anti-ballistic missile interceptor system around Moscow may have been withdrawn from service.[23] The system became operational in 1968 and was modernized in 1989. The long-range SH-11 Gorgon (51T6) interceptors may have been retired in full or in part, leaving only four (or possibly five) shorter-range SH-10 Gazelle (53T6) interceptor sites operational. An SH-10 Gazelle missile was test-launched at Sary-Shagan on 5 December 2006.[24]

Land-based ballistic missiles

The ICBMs assigned to the Russian Strategic Rocket Forces (SRF) have traditionally made up the largest element of the Soviet/Russian strategic nuclear forces. The SRF currently consists of three missile armies with 13 missile divisions: the 27th Guards Missile Army (headquarters in Vladimir, five divisions), the 31st Missile Army (Orenburg, three divisions) and the 33rd Guards Missile Army (Omsk, five divisions).[25]

Russia has on combat duty 76 SS-18 Satan (R-36M) heavy ICBMs in two versions: the R-36MUTTKh and the R-36M2 Voevoda, deployed in Dombarovsky and Uzhur.[26] The former was first deployed in 1979–83 and the latter in 1988–92. Both are silo-based, two-stage, liquid-propellant ICBMs.[27]

As of January 2007 Russia's roughly 40 remaining R-36MUTTKh missiles had been in service for approximately 25 years.[28] Russia is reportedly pursuing a technical programme, called Zaryad'ye, to extend the service life of both versions of the SS-18 ICBM. As part of this programme, some SS-18 ICBMs that have reached the end of their service life are refurbished as space launch vehicles (SLVs) and used to place

---

[20] Umnov, S., 'SYaS Rossii: naraschivaniye vozmozhnostey po preodoleniyu protivoraketnoy oborony' [Russia's SNF: building up ballistic missile defence penetration capacities], Interview with Lieutenant General Vladimir Vasilenko, head of the Fourth Central Scientific Research Institute of the Russian Ministry of Defence, *Voenno-Promyshlennyi Kur'er*, 8–14 Mar. 2006, URL <http://www.vpk-news.ru/article.asp?pr_sign=archive.2006.125.articles.conception_01>.

[21] Umnov (note 20).

[22] Khudoleev, V., 'Nash otvet: "Topol'-M"' [Our response: 'Topol-M'], *Krasnaya Zvezda*, 20 Feb. 2007, URL <http://www.redstar.ru/2007/02/20_02/1_01.html>.

[23] 'Raketu ispytali bez tseli' [Missile was tested without the target], *Kommersant*, 6 Dec. 2006, p. 4.

[24] 'Raketu ispytali bez tseli' (note 23).

[25] US Department of State, START I Treaty Memorandum of Understanding, Jan. 2007.

[26] US Department of State (note 25).

[27] Lennox, D. (ed.), *Jane's Strategic Weapon Systems* (Jane's Information Group: Coulsdon, July 2006), pp. 128–30.

[28] Interfax-AVN, 'Russian commander says "heavy" ICBMs to remain in service another decade', 12 Nov. 2006, Translation from Russian, World News Connection, National Technical Information Service (NTIS), US Department of Commerce.

Table 12A.3. Russian nuclear forces, January 2007

Type and Russian designation (NATO/US designation)	No. deployed	Year first deployed	Range (km)[a]	Warhead loading	No. of warheads
Strategic offensive forces					
Bombers					
Tu-95MS6 (Bear H-6)	32	1981	6 500–10 500	6 x AS-15A ALCMs, bombs	192
Tu-95MS16 (Bear-H16)	32	1981	6 500–10 500	16 x AS-15A ALCMs, bombs	512
Tu-160 (Blackjack)	14	1987	10 500–13 200	12 x AS-15B ALCMs or AS-16 SRAMs, bombs	168
Subtotal	*78*				*872*
ICBMs					
RS-20 B/V (SS-18 Satan)	76	1979	11 000–15 000	10 x 500–750 kt	760
RS-18 (SS-19 Stiletto)	123	1980	10 000	6 x 500–750 kt	738
RS-12M Topol (SS-25 Sickle)	243	1985	10 500	1 x 550 kt	243
RS-12M2 Topol-M (SS-27)	44	1997	10 500	1 x 550 kt	44
RS-12M1 Topol-M (SS-27)	3	2006	10 500	1 x 550 kt	3
Subtotal	*489*				*1 788*
SLBMs					
RSM-50 (SS-N-18 M1 Stingray)	80	1978	6 500	3 x 200 kt	252
RSM-54 Sineva (SS-N-23 Skiff)	96	1986	9 000	4 x 100 kt	384
Subtotal	*180*				*636*
Total strategic offensive forces	**743**				**3 284**
Strategic defensive forces					
ABMs[b]					
51T6 (SH-11 Gorgon)	32	1989		1 x 1000 kt	32
53T6 (SH-08 Gazelle)	68	1986		1 x 10 kt	68
Non-strategic forces					
Land-based non-strategic bombers					
Tu-22M (Backfire)	116	1974		2 x AS-4 ASMs, bombs	
Su-24 (Fencer)	371	1974		2 x bombs	
Subtotal	*487*				*974[c]*
Naval non-strategic attack aircraft					
Tu-22M (Backfire)	58	1974		2 x AS-4 ASMs, bombs	
Su-24 (Fencer)	58	1974		2 x bombs	
Subtotal	*116*				*232[c]*
SLCMs					
SS-N-12, SS-N-19, SS-N-21, SS-N-22					266
ASW and SAM weapons					
SS-N-15/16, torpedoes, SA-N-3/6					158
Total strategic defensive and non-strategic forces					**2 330**
Total					**5 614**

ABM = anti-ballistic missile; ALCM = air-launched cruise missile; ASM = air-to-surface missile; ASW = anti-submarine warfare; ICBM = intercontinental ballistic missile; kt = kiloton; NATO = North Atlantic Treaty Organization; SAM = surface-to-air missile; SLBM = submarine-launched ballistic missile; SLCM = sea-launched cruise missile; SRAM = short-range attack missile.

[a] Aircraft range is given for illustrative purposes only; actual mission range will vary according to flight profile and weapon loading.

[b] The Gorgon missile may have been retired. The SA-10 Grumble, SA-12A Gladiator, SA-12B Giant and S-400 Triumf may have some capability against some ballistic missiles. About 600 nuclear warheads may be associated with them.

[c] Figure includes warheads for all land-based and naval aircraft.

Sources: US Department of State, START I Treaty Memoranda of Understanding, 1990–Jan. 2007; US Air Force, National Air and Space Intelligence Center (NASIC), *Ballistic and Cruise Missile Threat* (NASIC: Wright-Patterson Air Force Base, Ohio, Mar. 2006), URL <http://www.nukestrat.com/us/afn/threat.htm>; US Central Intelligence Agency, National Intelligence Council, 'Foreign missile developments and the ballistic missile threat through 2015' (unclassified summary), Dec. 2001, URL <http://www.fas.org/spp/starwars/CIA-NIE. htm>; US Department of Defense, 'Proliferation: threat and response', Washington, DC, Jan. 2001, URL <http://www.fas.org/irp/threat/prolif00.pdf>; World News Connection, National Technical Information Service (NTIS), US Department of Commerce, various issues; 'Russia: general nuclear weapons developments', Nuclear Threat Initiative/Monterey Institute Center for Nonproliferation Studies, URL <http://www.nti.org/db/nisprofs/russia/weapons/gendevs. htm>; Russianforces.org; International Institute for Strategic Studies, *The Military Balance 2005–2006* (Routledge: London, 2005); Cochran, T. B. et al., *Nuclear Weapons Databook Volume IV: Soviet Nuclear Weapons* (Harper & Row: New York, N.Y., 1989); *Proceedings*, US Naval Institute, various issues; 'NRDC nuclear notebook', *Bulletin of the Atomic Scientists*, various issues; Safronov, I., 'Raketu ispytali bez tseli' [The rocket was tested without a target], *Kommersant*, 6 Dec. 2006, p. 4; and Authors' estimates.

commercial or military satellites into space.[29] On 12 July 2006 the SRF successfully launched a Dnepr SLV—a modified R-36MUTTKh missile—which put into orbit a US satellite, the Genesis 1.[30] The missile used had been on combat alert for 'over 20 years'.[31] On 26 July another Dnepr SLV, built from an R-36MUTTKh missile that had been on combat alert for 25 years, was launched from Baikonur, Kazakhstan. It was supposed to put into orbit 18 satellites but exploded shortly after lift-off.[32]

The service life of the newer R-36M2 Voevoda missile was originally set at 15 years but was extended to 20 years in 2006 after successful testing in the Zaryad'ye programme. On 21 December 2006 an R-36M2 missile that had been on combat alert for 19 years was successfully launched from Dombarovsky in Orenburg oblast. The simulated warheads reportedly reached their targets at the Kura test range in Kamchatka. Following the test, the SRF reiterated its intention to extend the mis-

---

[29] Safronov, I. and Lantratov, K., 'Ukrainskaya "Satana" razbilas' vmeste so sputnikami' [Ukrainian 'Satana' crashed along with satellites], *Kommersant*, 28 July 2006; and Umnov (note 20).

[30] Alekseev, V., 'Mirnyi naryad "Voevody"' [Peaceful guise of 'Voevoda'], *Nezavisimoe Voennoe Obozrenie*, 21 July 2006, URL <http://nvo.ng.ru/armament/2006-07-21/6_voevoda.html>.

[31] Interfax-AVN, 'Russia to keep RS-20 missile in service for at least another 10 years', 12 July 2006, Translation from Russian, World News Connection, National Technical Information Service (NTIS), US Department of Commerce.

[32] Safronov and Lantratov (note 29).

sile's service life to 25 years and to keep it on combat alert until 2016.[33] On 3 March 2006, Russia had signed an agreement with Ukraine on a joint programme to extend the service life of the R-36M2.[34]

Russia has 123 SS-19 Stiletto (RS-18) missiles deployed at Kozelsk and Tatischevo.[35] The SS-19 is a silo-based, two-stage, liquid-propellant ICBM capable of carrying up to six warheads. The SS-19 Stiletto is considered to be the most reliable of Russia's missiles. Of 159 test launches performed up to January 2007, only three are reported to have failed.[36] On 9 November 2006 an SS-19 missile was launched from Baikonur. A single dummy warhead was reported to have hit its target at the Kura range.[37] Based on the results of the test the SRF decided to extend the missile's service life to 30 years. Russia also has programmes to convert SS-19 missiles to Rokot and Strela SLVs.[38] A Rokot SLV was successfully launched on 28 July 2006 from the Plesetsk test site and put a satellite into orbit.[39]

Russia has 243 SS-25 Sickle (RS-12M) ICBMs deployed in nine missile divisions across the country.[40] The SS-25 is a road-mobile, three-stage solid-propellant ICBM that carries a single warhead. The missile was first deployed in 1985 and production ceased in 1994. According to Russian press reports, 144 SS-25s are expected to be in service in 2010.[41] The SRF intends to extend the SS-25 missile's original 10-year service life to 23 years or more, in which case it will remain operational until 2016–18. As part of the service life-extension programme, an SS-25 missile was successfully launched from the Plesetsk test site on 3 August 2006.[42]

The SS-27 Topol-M missile is a three-stage solid-propellant ICBM developed in both road-mobile (RS-12M1) and silo-based (RS-12M2) versions, which the missile's designers say use standardized and interoperable components.[43] As of January 2007 the SRF had deployed 47 Topol-M missiles of both versions.[44] The Russian Minister of Defence, Sergei Ivanov, has announced plans to procure 'tens of silo-based . . . and

[33] 'Pusk mezhkontinental'noy ballisticheskoy rakety RS-20V ("Voevoda")' [Launch of the intercontinental ballistic missile RS-20V ('Voevoda')], Information and Public Relations Service, Russian Strategic Rocket Forces, 21 Dec. 2006, URL <http://www.mil.ru/848/1045/1275/rvsn/19220/index.shtml?id=19753>.

[34] Matarykin, V., 'Ukraine, Russia sign contract to extend RS-20 service life', ITAR-TASS, 3 Mar. 2006, Translation from Russian, World News Connection, National Technical Information Service (NTIS), US Department of Commerce.

[35] US Department of State (note 25).

[36] 'Russian company to make ICBM into space rocket', ITAR-TASS, 10 Nov. 2006, Translation from Russian, World News Connection, National Technical Information Service (NTIS), US Department of Commerce.

[37] Interfax-AVN, 'Intercontinental ballistic missile successfully hits target at training range', 9 Nov. 2006, URL <http://www.interfax.ru/e/B/politics/28.html?id_issue=11 619144>.

[38] Zaytsev, Y., 'Kosmos: puti konversii' [Outer space: ways of conversion], RIA Novosti, 21 Nov. 2006, URL <http://www.rian.ru/analytics/20061121/55853307.html>.

[39] Russian Federal Space Agency, 'Kompsat-2 launch', 28 July 2006, URL <http://www.roscosmos.ru/Start1Show.asp?STARTID=611>.

[40] US Department of State (note 25).

[41] Safronov, I., 'Russian missiles will die of old age', *Kommersant*, 1 Apr. 2005.

[42] 'Raketa "Topol" porazila uslovnuyu tsel'' ['Topol' missile has hit a simulated target], Vesti.ru, 3 Aug. 2007, URL <http://www.vesti.ru/news.html?id=97109>.

[43] Pulin, G., 'Formiruetsya perspektivnyi oblik SYaS' [The future look of SNF is being shaped], *Voenno-Promyshlennyi Kur'er*, 5–11 Apr. 2006, URL <http://www.vpk-news.ru/article.asp?pr_sign=archive.2006.129.articles.army_02>.

[44] US Department of State (note 25).

more than 50 road-mobile Topol-M missiles between 2007 and 2015'.[45] The RS-12M2 was first deployed in 1997 with the 60th Missile Division in Tatischevo, Saratov oblast. In 2006 two additional missiles entered service there, bringing the total number deployed at Tatischevo to 44.[46] On 10 December 2006 Russia deployed for the first time three RS-12M1 missiles, which entered service at the 54th Missile Division in Teikovo, Ivanovo region.[47]

Russia is working to enhance the capability of the SS-27 ICBM's warheads to penetrate ballistic missile defences.[48] On 22 April 2006 the SRF successfully launched a K65M-R missile (a modification of the Kosmos-3M SLV) from the Kapustin Yar test site, Arkhangelsk oblast, to the Balkhash test range in Kazakhstan. According to press reports, the launch was a part of a programme to develop a new re-entry vehicle that would be mountable on both the SS-27 and SS-NX-30 ICBMs (see below). It is reported to be capable of manoeuvring in flight in order to penetrate missile defence systems.[49] In March 2006, options for equipping the SS-27 missile with three warheads, using the technology developed for the phased-out intermediate-range ballistic missile (IRBM) SS-20 Saber, were demonstrated for Ivanov by the Moscow Institute of Thermal Technology.[50]

Ballistic missile submarines

The Russian Navy operates 13 SSBNs in its Northern and Pacific fleets. Of these, six are Delta III Class (Project 667BDR Kalmar) submarines.[51] Some Russian experts have suggested that the ships of this class, which entered service in 1982, may be retired by 2010.[52] However, it was reported in November 2004 that the Russian Navy plans to have 208 SLBMs by 2010, which will not be possible if the Delta III Class is retired.[53] The Russian Navy also operates six Delta IV Class (Project 667BDRM Delfin) submarines, all of which are based in the Northern Fleet. Four of these—the *Bryansk*, the *Tula*, the *Verkhotur'e* and the *Yekaterinburg*—are currently in service, the *Bryansk* and the *Tula* having returned from overhaul in January and October

[45] Russian State Duma, Transcript of the Plenary Session, 7 Feb. 2007, URL <http://wbase.duma.gov.ru/steno/nph-sdb.exe> (Author's translation). See also Isachenkov, V., 'Russia plans new ICBMs, nuclear subs', *Washington Post*, 7 Feb. 2007.

[46] ARMS-TASS, 'RVSN budut poluchat' ezhegodno po 5–6 MBR "Topol'-M"' [SRF will be receiving 5–6 Topol-M ICBMs annually], 15 Dec. 2006, URL <http://armstass.su/?page=article&aid=34150&cid=25>.

[47] Babkin, S. and Kuznetsov, V., 'Russian strategic troops to get MIRVed missiles', ITAR-TASS, 15 Dec. 2006, Translation from Russian, World News Connection, National Technical Information Service (NTIS), US Department of Commerce.

[48] RIA Novosti, 'Russia to re-equip its new mobile ICBMs with multiple warheads -1', 15 Dec. 2006, URL <http://en.rian.ru/russia/20061215/56980585.html>.

[49] Safronov, I., 'Rossiya skreschivayet boegolovki' [Russia interbreeds warheads], *Kommersant*, 24 Apr. 2006. The new re-entry vehicle was first tested on 1 Nov. 2005.

[50] Safronov, I., 'Sergei Ivanov ukreplyaet raketno-yadernyi schit rodiny' [Sergei Ivanov strengthens nuclear missile shield], *Kommersant*, 15 Mar. 2006.

[51] The *Petropavlovsk-Kamchatskii*, *Svyatoi Georgii Pobedonosets*, *Zelenograd* and *Podol'sk* submarines are deployed with the Pacific Fleet, and the *Ryazan'* and *Borisoglebsk* are with the Northern Fleet.

[52] 'Iz-pod vody dostali' [Reached from under water], *Kommersant Business Guide*, 4 July 2006, URL <http://www.kommersant.ru/application.html?DocID=686179>.

[53] 'Mnogoletnie plany Miniborony' [Long-term plans of the Defence Ministry], *Kommersant*, 18 Nov. 2004, p. 3.

2006, respectively. In November 2006 two Delta IV Class submarines—the *Kareliya* and the *Novomoskovsk*—entered the Zvezdochka shipyard to undergo service life-extension overhauls and refitting with upgraded SS-N-23 Skiff missiles.[54] The six Delta IV Class submarines may remain in service until 2015–20.

The Russian Navy operates one Typhoon Class submarine, renamed the *Dmitrii Donskoi* following its overhaul and relaunch in June 2002, as a test platform for the new SS-NX-30 Bulava missile.[55] Russian military officials indicated in 2005 that this and the two remaining Typhoon Class submarines—the *Arkhangel'sk* and the *Severstal'*, which were laid up in 2004 for financial reasons—are to be upgraded by replacing their obsolete SS-N-20 Sturgeon SLBMs with the SS-NX-30.[56]

Russia is building three SSBNs of a new class, the Project 955 Borei, which does not yet have a NATO designation. The first submarine in the class, the *Yurii Dolgorukii*, was launched on 15 April 2007, 11 years after the keel was laid down. The second and third ships in the new class, the *Aleksandr Nevskii* and the *Vladimir Monomakh*, were laid down at the Sevmash shipyard in March 2004 (tentatively commissioned for 2009) and March 2006 (tentatively commissioned for 2011), respectively.[57] These SSBNs will be longer than the *Yurii Dolgorukii* and will be armed with 16 rather than 12 SS-NX-30 SLBMs.[58] The construction of the fourth Borei Class submarine is expected to begin in 2007.[59] According to Ivanov, the government plans to have eight Borei Class SSBNs by 2015.[60]

Russia's SLBM force currently consists of two types of missile. The SS-N-18 M1 Stingray (RSM-50) is deployed on Delta III Class submarines. It has two liquid-fuelled stages and carries three warheads.[61] On 10 September 2006 the Delta III Class SSBN the *Svyatoi Georgii Pobedonosets* launched a Stingray SLBM from waters off Simushir Island in the Pacific Ocean. The simulated warheads reportedly hit their target at the Chizha test range in north-western Russia.[62]

The SS-N-23 Skiff (RSM-54 Sineva) SLBM, a successor to the SS-N-18, was first test-launched in 1983. The missile underwent a modernization programme in 1996–2002, including the development of an improved warhead. The upgraded version of

---

[54] Interfax-AVN, 'SSBN *Kareliya* enters Zvezdochka yard for medium repair', 2 Nov. 2006, Translation from Russian, World News Connection, National Technical Information Service (NTIS), US Department of Commerce; 'Tula rejoins Russian Navy fleet after refit', *Jane's Missiles & Rockets*, vol. 10, no. 3 (Mar. 2006), p. 14; and Popov, A., '"Begemot" ego proslavil' ['Begemot' made him famous], *Severnyi Rabochii*, 30 Nov. 2006, URL <http://www.nworker.ru/article.phtml?id=4616>.

[55] The Soviet Union built 6 Typhoon Class (Project 941 Akula) SSBNs in 1976–89. Russia decommissioned 3 in 1996.

[56] Tul'ev, M., 'V interesah triady' [In the interest of the triad], *Voenno-Promyshlennyi Kur'ier*, 11 May 2005, URL <http://www.vpk-news.ru/article.asp?pr_sign=archive.2005.83.articles.army_03>; and Interfax-AVN, 'Russian defense minister on plans to equip new submarines with Bulava missiles', 28 Sep. 2005, Translation from Russian, World News Connection, National Technical Information Service (NTIS), US Department of Commerce.

[57] 'Iz-pod vody dostali' (note 52).

[58] 'Atomnyi podvodnyi kreiser "Yurii Dolgorukii" gotovitsya k spusku' [SSBN 'Yurii Dolgorukii' is being prepared for launch], Lenta.ru, 26 July 2006, URL <http://lenta.ru/news/2006/07/26/submarine/>.

[59] 'Novyye podvodnyye lodki' [New submarines], *Vzglyad*, 19 Mar. 2006, URL <http://www.vz.ru/society/2006/3/19/26532.html>; and Nikol'skii, A., 'Oruzhiya ne khvatit' [Coming short of weapons], *Vedomosti*, 7 Aug. 2006.

[60] Isachenkov (note 45).

[61] Lennox (note 27), pp. 149–50.

[62] Russian Federal Space Agency, 'Ob uspeshnykh ucheniyakh morskikh strategicheskikh yadernykh sil Rossii' [On successful manoeuvres of Russian sea-based strategic nuclear forces], 28 July 2006, URL <http://www.federalspace.ru/NewsDoSele.asp?NEWSID=1809>.

the missile, known in Russia as Sineva ('the Blue'), is being installed on Delta IV Class SSBNs undergoing overhaul. The Sineva missile has the same range as the SS-N-23 but can carry up to 10 warheads, according to the US Air Force.[63] Four Sineva SLBMs were delivered in 2006 and there are plans to procure another 10 in 2007.[64] The missile was test-launched three times in 2006. On 24 May 2006 an attempt to launch the Shtil SLV (a modified SS-N-23) from the *Yekaterinburg* SSBN at an underwater position in the Barents Sea was reportedly postponed due to a technical failure. A successful launch two days later put the COMPASS-2 satellite into orbit.[65] On 30 June 2006 a Delta IV Class SSBN identified in press reports as the *Tula* launched an SS-N-23 from an underwater position in the Barents Sea. A single simulated unarmed re-entry vehicle hit its target at the Kura range.[66] On 9 September 2006 the *Yekaterinburg* reportedly successfully fired an SS-N-23 SLBM from a position near the North Pole to the Chizha test range.[67]

Russia is giving high priority to the development of a new three-stage, solid-propellant SLBM, the SS-NX-30 (RSM-56 Bulava).[68] The missile will reportedly have a maximum range of 8300 km.[69] Russia has declared that the Bulava will be attributed under START counting rules as carrying six warheads.[70] All three test launches of the Bulava in 2006 ended in failure. On 7 September and 25 October 2006 the Typhoon Class SSBN the *Dmitrii Donskoi* launched Bulava missiles from submerged positions in the Barents Sea towards the Kura test range, but in both cases the missiles failed shortly after launch. On 24 December 2006 the *Dmitrii Donskoi* attempted to launch a Bulava missile from a surface location, but this time the third stage of the missile exploded before it reached the Kura test range.[71]

Prior to the 2006 failures, the Bulava test programme was scheduled to include 10 flight tests, which were to be completed by the end of 2007, in time for the launch of the first Borei Class SSBN.[72] The head of the Russian Space Agency, Anatolii Per-

---

[63] US Air Force, National Air and Space Intelligence Center (NASIC), *Ballistic and Cruise Missile Threat* (NASIC: Wright-Patterson Air Force Base, Ohio, Mar. 2006), URL <http://www.nukestrat.com/us/afn/threats.htm>.

[64] Khudoleev (note 22).

[65] Safronov, I., 'Severnyi flot pomog seismologam' [The Northern Fleet helped seismologists], *Kommersant*, 29 May 2006.

[66] ITAR-TASS, 'Nose cone of RSM-54 ballistic missile hits target on Kamchatka', 30 June 2006, Translation from Russian, World News Connection, National Technical Information Service (NTIS), US Department of Commerce; and RIA Novosti, 'Atomnyi raketonosets "Tula" sovershil pusk ballisticheskoi rakety' ['Tula' SSBN launched a ballistic missile], 30 June 2006, URL <http://www.rian.ru/defense_safety/weapons/20060630/50709481.html>.

[67] Russian Federal Space Agency (note 62).

[68] President Vladimir Putin declared in his 2006 Annual Address to the Federal Assembly that the Russian Navy would soon commission new SSBNs carrying strategic weapons for the first time since 1990, and that those submarines would be equipped with the 'new Bulava missile system, which together with the Topol-M system will form the backbone of our strategic deterrent force'. Putin, V., President of the Russian Federation, Annual Address to the Federal Assembly of the Russian Federation, 10 May 2006, URL <http://www.kremlin.ru/eng/sdocs/speeches.shtml>.

[69] Lennox (note 27), p. 166.

[70] US Department of State (note 25).

[71] '"Bulava" s plech' ['Bulava' off shoulders], *Kommersant*, 26 Dec. 2006; and '"Bulavu" razberut na dvukh komissiyakh' ['Bulava' to be examined by two commissions], *Kommersant*, 27 Dec. 2006. On previous tests see Kile, S. N., Fedchenko, V. and Kristensen, H. M., 'World nuclear forces, 2006', *SIPRI Yearbook 2006: Armaments, Disarmament and International Security* (Oxford University Press: Oxford, 2006), p. 652.

[72] 'Russia's Bulava undergoes fast-track test programme', *Jane's Missiles & Rockets*, vol. 10, no. 6 (June 2006).

minov, was quoted as saying after the third launch failure in 2006 that the Bulava would require 12–14 additional test launches, which would delay the operational deployment of the missile.[73]

Strategic aviation

Russia's strategic aviation units are grouped under the 37th Air Army of the Supreme High Command (Strategic) of the Russian Air Force. They include the 22nd Guards Heavy Bomber Division based in Engels and Ryazan, with 14 Tu-160 Blackjack, 17 Tu-95MS16 Bear-H16 and 7 Tu-95MS6 Bear-H6 aircraft; and the 326th Heavy Bomber Division, based in Ukrainka, Khabarovsk kray, with 15 Tu-95MS16 and 25 Tu-95MS6 aircraft.[74] The 37th Air Army also comprises four divisions of Tu-22M3 Backfire C bombers.[75] Ivanov announced in February 2007 that Russia plans to have a total of 50 Tu-160 and Tu-95MS bombers in service by 2015.[76]

In July 2006, one Tu-160 was returned to combat duty after modernization.[77] All remaining Tu-160s will undergo similar modernization.[78] The 2006 State Defense Order allocated funds for deployment of another Tu-160, but it did not enter service in 2006.[79]

In 2006 Russian strategic aviation participated in a number of military exercises. In March, 15 Tu-95MS bombers, accompanied by Il-78 Midas tanker aircraft and Su-27 Flanker support aircraft, took part in an exercise in northern Russia that reportedly included eight successful launches of cruise missiles.[80] On 14 April 2006 four Tu-95MS bombers from the 326th Heavy Bomber Division were joined at the Pemboy test range near Vorkuta by two Tu-160 and two Tu-95MS bombers of the 22nd Guards Heavy Bomber Division, with each aircraft successfully launching one cruise missile.[81] On 24 August 2006 two Tu-160 and two Tu-95MS bombers conducted training launches of cruise missiles during an exercise in northern Russia.[82] During the large-scale strategic aviation exercise held on 26–30 September 2006,

[73] ' "Bulavu" razberut na dvukh komissiyakh' (note 71).

[74] US Department of State (note 25).

[75] 'Strategic Aviation', Russian Nuclear Forces Project, 2 Nov. 2005, URL <http://www.russian forces.org/eng/aviation/>; and Khudoleev, V., '37-ya derzhit kurs' [37th Army is following the course], *Krasnaya Zvezda*, 23 Dec. 2005, URL <http://www.redstar.ru/2005/12/23_12/1_02.html>.

[76] State Duma of the Russian Federation, Transcript of plenary session, 7 Feb. 2007, URL <http://wbase.duma.gov.ru/steno/nph-sdb.exe> (in Russian).

[77] Khudoleev, V., '37-ya derzhit kurs' [37th Army is following the course], *Krasnaya Zvezda*, 23 Dec. 2005, URL <http://www.redstar.ru/2005/12/23_12/1_02.html>; and Gavrilov, Y., ' "Belyi aist" poluchaet imya' ['White stork' is given a name], *Rossiiskaya Gazeta*, 6 July 2006 .

[78] Pulin, G., 'Nam otvoditsya osnovnaya rol' v politike uprezhdeniya' [We are assigned to play a major role in the policy of pre-emption], *Voenno-Promyshlennyi Kur'ier*, 15 Feb. 2006, URL <http://www.vpk-news.ru/article.asp?pr_sign=archive.2006.122.articles.names_01>.

[79] 'Fradkov distributes defense order', *Kommersant*, 1 Dec. 2005.

[80] RIA Novosti, 'Russian bombers launch cruise missiles during exercises in Far North', 22 Mar. 2006, URL <http://en.rian.ru/russia/20060322/44647211.html>.

[81] ITAR-TASS, 'Eight strategic planes launch cruise missiles at targets near Vorkuta', 14 Apr. 2006, Translation from Russian, World News Connection, National Technical Information Service (NTIS), US Department of Commerce.

[82] RIA Novosti, 'Russian strategic bombers launch cruise missiles in exercises', 22 Mar. 2006, URL <http://en.rian.ru/russia/20060824/53088583.html>.

Tu-160 and Tu-95MS aircraft launched at least three ALCMs at the Pemboy test range.[83]

IV. British nuclear forces

The UK possesses an arsenal of about 160 warheads that are available for use by a fleet of four Vanguard Class Trident SSBNs (see table 12A.4). It leases 58 Trident II (D-5) SLBMs, including spares, from the US Navy. Under a system of 'mingled asset ownership', Trident II (D-5) missiles to be loaded onto British submarines are randomly selected from the stockpile at the US Navy's Trident facility in Kings Bay, Georgia. The submarines then go to the Royal Naval Armaments Depot at Coulport, near Faslane in Scotland, where the missiles are fitted with warheads designed and manufactured at the UK's Atomic Weapons Establishment, Aldermaston. Each SSBN is equipped with 16 Trident II (D-5) missiles carrying up to 48 warheads. The warhead is similar to the US W76 warhead and has an explosive yield of about 100 kt. It is believed that a number of the Trident II (D-5) missiles are deployed with only one warhead instead of three; this warhead may also have a greatly reduced explosive yield, possibly produced by the detonation of only the fission primary.[84] The reduced force loading is in accordance with the sub-strategic role given to the Trident fleet in the British Ministry of Defence's 1998 Strategic Defence Review.[85] A 2002 addendum to the Strategic Defence Review extended the role of nuclear weapons to include deterring 'leaders of states of concern and terrorist organizations'.[86]

In a posture known as Continuous At Sea Deterrence (CASD), one British SSBN is on patrol at all times. The second and third SSBNs can be put to sea fairly rapidly with similar loadings. There are not enough missiles in the British inventory to arm the fourth submarine. Since the end of the cold war, the SSBN on patrol has been kept at a level of reduced readiness with a 'notice to fire' measured in days and its missiles de-targeted. There are reports that some patrol coordination takes place with France. The 300th British deterrent patrol will be completed in 2007.

The four Vanguard Class SSBNs were each designed to operate for almost another 20 years before reaching the end of their nominal service lives, beginning in the early 2020s. In March 2007 the British Parliament approved the government's plan to replace the Vanguard SSBNs in order to maintain a 'minimum nuclear deterrent capability necessary to provide effective deterrence'.[87] The British Government had

---

[83] Russian Nuclear Forces Project, 'Large-scale bomber exercise', 29 Sep. 2006, URL <http://russian forces.org/blog/2006/09/largescale_bomber_exercise.shtml>.

[84] Quinlan, M., 'The future of United Kingdom nuclear weapons: shaping the debate', *International Affairs*, vol. 82, no. 4 (July 2006).

[85] The 1998 Strategic Defence Review stated that 'the credibility of deterrence also depends on retaining an option for a limited strike that would not automatically lead to a full scale nuclear exchange' as a means of demonstrating resolve or conveying a political message. British Ministry of Defence (MOD), '*The Strategic Defence Review: Modern Forces for the Modern World*, Cm 3999 (MOD: London, July 1998), URL <http://www.mod.uk/DefenceInternet/AboutDefence/CorporatePublications/PolicyStrategyandPlanning/StrategicDefenceReview.htm>, p. 63.

[86] British Ministry of Defence, *The Strategic Defence Review: A New Chapter*, Cm 5566, vol. 1 (Stationery Office: London, July 2002), URL <http://www.mod.uk/DefenceInternet/AboutDefence/CorporatePublications/PolicyStrategyandPlanning/StrategicDefenceReviewANewChaptercm5566.htm>, p. 12.

[87] British Ministry of Defence and British Foreign and Commonwealth Office, *The Future of the United Kingdom's Nuclear Deterrent*, CM 6994 (Stationery Office: London, Dec. 2006), URL <http://

Table 12A.4. British nuclear forces, January 2007

Type and designation	No. deployed	Year first deployed	Range (km)	Warhead loading	No. of warheads
SLBMs					
Trident II (D-5)	48	1994	>7 400	1–3 x 100 kt	~160[a]

kt = kiloton; SLBM = submarine-launched ballistic missile; SSBN = nuclear-powered ballistic missile submarine.

[a] Fewer than 160 warheads are operationally available, up to 144 to arm 48 missiles on 3 of 4 SSBNs. Only 1 submarine is on patrol at any time, with up to 48 warheads. The UK—like the other 4 nuclear weapon states—probably also has a small reserve of inactive warheads. The size of this reserve is unknown but might include enough warheads to arm 1 submarine. This would give a total stockpile of close to 200 warheads.

Sources: British Ministry of Defence (MOD), White Papers, press releases and the MOD website, URL <http://www.mod.uk/issues/sdr/>; British House of Commons, *Parliamentary Debates (Hansard)*; Omand, D., 'Nuclear deterrence in a changing world: the view from a UK perspective', *RUSI Journal*, June 1996, pp. 15–22; Norris, R. S. et al., *Nuclear Weapons Databook*, vol. 5, *British, French, and Chinese Nuclear Weapons* (Westview: Boulder, Colo., 1994), p. 9; 'NRDC Nuclear Notebook', *Bulletin of the Atomic Scientists*, various issues; and Authors' estimates.

concluded in its December 2006 White Paper, after 'an exhaustive review of possible future threats and deterrent options', that 'renewing the Trident system, by replacing the existing submarines and extending the life of the Trident missiles, is the best and most cost effective way to maintain our ability to deter future threats to the UK'.[88] Critics complained that the government had taken the decision to renew the Trident system without a public debate on whether the UK still needed a nuclear deterrent.[89]

In the 2006 White Paper, the government also proposed starting, in the near future, the design and construction work on a successor SSBN to the Vanguard Class that would enter service in the 2020s. It held out the possibility of purchasing three rather than four submarines but emphasized that this would not entail any change from the current CASD posture, which was deemed to be essential for 'invulnerability and assuredness' and to 'motivate the crews'.[90] The government proposed that the new SSBN might be equipped with the modified Trident II (D-5LE) SLBMs that the USA is building, thereby keeping the Trident II (D-5) missile in service until the early 2040s. To assuage concerns that the UK was not complying with its commitment under Article VI of the NPT to work in good faith towards nuclear disarmament, the government also proposed making a small reduction in its nuclear stockpile to 160

www.mod.uk/NR/rdonlyres/AC00DD79-76D6-4FE3-91A1-6A56B03C092F/0/DefenceWhitePaper2006_Cm6994.pdf>.

[88] British Ministry of Defence, 'Government announces intention to maintain the UK's nuclear deterrent', *Defence News*, 4 Dec. 2006, URL <http://www.mod.uk/DefenceInternet/DefenceNews/Defence PolicyAndBusiness/GovernmentAnnouncesIntentionToMaintainTheUksNuclearDeterrent.htm>.

[89] Johnson, R., 'The UK White Paper on renewing Trident: the wrong decision at the wrong time', *Disarmament Diplomacy*, no. 83 (winter 2006), URL <http://www.acronym.org.uk/dd/dd83/83uk.htm>; and British House of Commons, Defence Committee, *The Future of the UK's Strategic Nuclear Deterrent: The White Paper*, 2 vols (Stationery Office: London, 7 Mar. 2007), URL <http://www.publications. parliament.uk/pa/cm/cmdfence.htm>.

[90] British Ministry of Defence and British Foreign and Commonwealth Office (note 87).

warheads. Additional warheads may be held in reserve. The White Paper deferred a decision until the next parliament on whether to refurbish or replace the current warheads. In the meantime, the MOD is to conduct a review of the optimum service life of the existing stockpile and examine a range of replacement options.

According to the White Paper, the procurement costs of the new submarines and associated infrastructure would be about £15–20 billion ($28.5–38 billion), at 2006 prices, for a four-boat fleet. Most of this cost (*c.* £1 billion, or $1.9 billion, per annum) would be incurred during the period 2012–27.[91]

V. French nuclear forces

France continues to modernize and upgrade its nuclear forces. It maintains an operational arsenal of about 348 nuclear warheads for delivery by SLBMs, carrier-based strike aircraft and land-based aircraft (see table 12A.5).

The backbone of France's nuclear deterrent is the Force Océanique Stratégique (FOST), which consists of a fleet of four operational SSBNs, of which three are of the new Triomphant Class and one is of the L'Inflexible Class (formerly Redoutable Class). The last L'Inflexible Class SSBN will be retired when the fourth and final vessel of the Triomphant Class, *Le Terrible*, enters service in 2010. The French Navy's SSBNs are armed with 16 Aérospatiale M45 missiles carrying up to six TN-75 warheads.[92] In 2010–15, beginning with *Le Terrible*, Triomphant Class SSBNs will be retrofitted with the longer-range M51.1 SLBM. The new missile will be armed with up to six TN-75 nuclear warheads and have a maximum range of 8000 km.[93] On 9 November 2006 an unarmed M51.1 missile was test-launched for the first time from the Landes Missile Launch Test Centre at Biscarosse, Aquitaine, over the Bay of Biscay.[94] The first flight test of the M51.1 with an unarmed re-entry vehicle is scheduled for 2007, and simulated underwater test launches are due to start in late 2008 at Toulon, Provence-Alpes-Côte d'Azur. The first underwater launch from a submarine is planned for 2010. A total of 10 test launches are planned.[95] On 29 December 2006 the French Ministry of Defence signed a €270 million ($349.6 million) contract with EADS Astrium for a follow-on version, the M51.2, which will carry the new Tête Nucléaire Océanique (TNO) warhead.[96] The M51.2 is scheduled to replace the M51.1 in 2015–17. The M51 SLBM will remain in service until after 2030.

[91] British Ministry of Defence and British Foreign and Commonwealth Office (note 87).

[92] Norris, R. S. and Kristensen, H. M., 'French nuclear forces, 2005', *Bulletin of the Atomic Scientists*, vol. 61, No. 4 (July/Aug. 2005), pp. 73–75.

[93] 'France's nuclear-powered *Le Vigilant* prepares for patrol', *Jane's Missiles & Rockets*, vol. 9, no. 2 (Feb. 2005), p. 5.

[94] 'France tests strategic missile', Global Security Newswire, 10 Nov. 2006, URL <http://www.nti. org/d_newswire/issues/2006_11_10.html>; and Agence France-Presse, 'France tests ballistic missile for nuclear deployment', Spacewar.com, 9 Nov. 2006, URL <http://www.spacewar.com/reports/France_ Tests_Ballistic_Missile_For_Nuclear_Deployment_999.html>.

[95] Isby, D., 'M51 tests set to begin on schedule', *Jane's Missiles & Rockets*, vol. 10, no. 12 (Dec. 2006), p. 10.

[96] Tran, P., 'France inks missile, Link 16 contracts', *Defense News*, 19 Jan. 2007.

Table 12A.5. French nuclear forces, January 2007

Type	No. deployed	Year first deployed	Range (km)[a]	Warhead loading	No. of warheads
Land-based aircraft					
Mirage 2000N	60	1988	2 750	1 x 300 kt ASMP	50
Carrier-based aircraft					
Super Étendard	24	1978	650	1 x 300 kt ASMP	10
SLBMs[b]					
M45	48	1996	6 000[c]	6 x 100 kt	288
Total					**348**

ASMP = Air–Sol Moyenne Portée; kt = kiloton; SLBM = submarine-launched ballistic missile; SSBN = nuclear-powered ballistic missile submarine.

[a] Aircraft range is given for illustrative purposes only; actual mission range will vary according to flight profile and weapon loading.

[b] The fourth and final Triomphant Class SSBN, *Le Terrible*, will replace *L'Inflexible* in 2010 and be retrofitted with the longer-range M51.1 SLBM.

[c] The range of the M45 SLBM is listed as only 4000 km in a 2001 report from the National Defence Commission of the French National Assembly.

Sources: French Ministry of Defense website, URL <http://www.defense.gouv.fr/>, various policy papers, press releases and force profiles; French National Assembly, various defence bills and reports; Norris, R. S. et al., *Nuclear Weapons Databook*, vol. 5, *British, French, and Chinese Nuclear Weapons* (Westview: Boulder, Colo., 1994), p. 10; *Air Actualités*, various issues; *Aviation Week & Space Technology*, various issues; 'NRDC Nuclear Notebook', *Bulletin of the Atomic Scientists*, various issues; and Authors' estimates.

The air component of the French nuclear force consists of two types of aircraft: approximately 60 Mirage 2000N aircraft, which equip the three Air Force squadrons with nuclear strike roles; and about 24 Super Étendard aircraft deployed on the aircraft carrier *Charles de Gaulle*. Both types of aircraft carry the Air–Sol Moyenne Portée (ASMP) cruise missile. A total of 90 ASMP missiles have been produced, along with 80 TN81 300-kt warheads for them. It is estimated that France currently has about 60 operational ASMP missiles equipped with nuclear warheads, but additional missiles may be in inactive storage.[97] A new follow-on cruise missile, the ASMP-A (Air–Sol Moyenne Portée Améliorée), is under development by the company MBDA and will enter service in December 2008, one year later than originally expected. The nuclear-capable missile will initially equip one Mirage 2000N squadron and then a second squadron in September 2010. An Air Force Rafale F3 squadron is reportedly scheduled to receive the ASMP-A in December 2009, and the Navy's Rafale F3 combat aircraft will receive the missile in 2010.[98]

There has been a gradual evolution in France's nuclear doctrine since the end of the cold war. Although French officials continue to reject adoption of a no-first-use posture, they have emphasized the need for greater flexibility in meeting a widening range of plausible deterrence scenarios. On 19 January 2006 President Jacques Chirac

---

[97] Fiszer, M., 'French MoD to develop nuclear missile', *Journal of Electronic Defense*, vol. 26, no. 12 (Dec. 2003), p. 21.

[98] Isby (note 95).

delivered a speech at L'Ile-Longue nuclear submarine base setting out a new rationale for France's *force de frappe* (nuclear deterrent force).[99] In the speech he cited the dangers of regional instability, growing extremism and the proliferation of weapons of mass destruction (WMD) and said that France's nuclear deterrent remained the fundamental guarantor of its security. He threatened to retaliate with nuclear weapons against any state found to be supporting terrorism against France or considering the use of WMD. Chirac revealed that French nuclear forces had already been reconfigured to enable them to destroy the power centres of any state sponsoring a terrorist attack against France. This involved, among other measures, reducing the number of nuclear warheads on SLBMs to allow more precisely targeted strikes. He did not say whether France was prepared to carry out pre-emptive nuclear strikes against a country that it regarded as a threat. The doctrinal change announced by Chirac was similar to one made by the UK in 2002 and, to a lesser extent, the USA.

VI. Chinese nuclear forces

China is estimated to have an arsenal of approximately 145 operational nuclear weapons for delivery mainly by ballistic missiles and aircraft. Additional warheads may be in reserve, giving a total stockpile of some 200 warheads. The size of the Chinese nuclear stockpile is thought not to have changed significantly for many years. In February 2006 the director of the US Defense Intelligence Agency repeated an estimate that has been cited by various US government agencies since the mid-1990s that China has over 100 nuclear warheads operationally deployed on ballistic missiles and some additional warheads in storage.[100] Some non-governmental analysts have calculated that China's operational arsenal may be as small as 80 warheads.[101] In 2004 the Chinese Foreign Ministry stated that China possessed 'the smallest nuclear arsenal' of all the legally recognized nuclear weapon states.[102]

China has a long-term nuclear force modernization programme under way. According its 2006 Defence White Paper, China 'upholds the principles of counterattack in self-defense and limited development of nuclear weapons, and aims at building a lean and effective nuclear force' while pledging not to enter into a nuclear arms race with any other country.[103] It also reiterates that China 'remains firmly committed to the policy of no first use of nuclear weapons at any time and under any circumstances'.

[99] Chirac, J., 'Speech by Jacques Chirac, President of the French Republic, during his visit to the Strategic Air and Maritime Forces at Landivisiau/L'Ile Longue', 19 Jan. 2006, URL <http://www.elysee.fr/elysee/elysee.fr/anglais/speeches_and_documents/2006/speech_by_jacques_chirac_president_of_the_french_republic_during_his_visit_to_the_stategic_forces.38447.html>.

[100] Maples, M. D., Director, US Defense Intelligence Agency, 'Current and projected national security threats to the United States', Statement for the record, US Senate Armed Services Committee, 28 Feb. 2006, URL <http://www.dia.mil/publicaffairs/Testimonies/statement24.html>; and Kristensen, H. M., Norris, R. S. and McKinzie, M. G., *Chinese Nuclear Forces and U.S. Nuclear War Planning* (Federation of American Scientists and Natural Resources Defense Council: Washington, DC, Nov. 2006), URL <http://www.fas.org/nuke/guide/china/Book2006.pdf>, p. 37.

[101] Lewis, J., 'The ambiguous arsenal', *Bulletin of the Atomic Scientists*, vol. 61, no. 3 (May/June 2005), pp. 52–59.

[102] Chinese Ministry of Foreign Affairs, 'Fact sheet: China: nuclear disarmament and reduction of [nuclear weapons (?)]', Beijing, 27 Apr. 2004, URL <http://www.fmprc.gov.cn/eng/wjb/zzjg/jks/cjjk/2622/t93539.htm>.

[103] Chinese State Council, *China's National Defence in 2006* (Information Office of the State Council of the People's Republic of China: Beijing, Dec. 2006), URL <http://www.china.org.cn/english/features/book/194421.htm>.

Table 12A.6. Chinese nuclear forces, January 2007

Type and Chinese designation (US designation)	No. deployed	Year first deployed	Range (km)[a]	Warhead loading	No. of warheads
Strategic weapons					
Land-based missiles					
DF-3A (CSS-2)	16	1971	3 100[b]	1 x 3.3 Mt	16
DF-4 (CSS-3)	22	1980	>5 500	1 x 3.3 Mt	22
DF-5A (CSS-4)	20	1981	13 000	1 x 4–5 Mt	20
DF-21A (CSS-5)	35	1991	2 100[b]	1 x 200–300 kt	35
DF-31 (?)	0	(2007)	~7 250	1 x ?	0
DF-31A (?)	0	(2008–2010)	~11 270	1 x ?	0
Subtotal	*93*				*93*
SLBMs					
JL-1 (CSS-NX-3)[c]	12	1986	>1 770	1 x 200–300 kt	12
JL-2 (?)	0	(2008–2010)	>8 000	1 x ?	0
Subtotal	*12*				*12*
Aircraft[d]					
H-6 (B-6)	20	1965	3 100	1 x bomb	~20
Attack (Qian-5, others?)	?	1972–?	?	1 x bomb	~20
Subtotal	*>20*				*~40*
Total strategic weapons					**~145**
Non-strategic weapons[e]					
Short-range ballistic missiles (DF-15 and DF-11)					?
Total					**~145[f]**

kt = kiloton; Mt = Megaton; SLBM = submarine-launched ballistic missile; ? = unknown.

[a] Aircraft range is given for illustrative purposes only; actual mission range will vary according to flight profile and weapon loading.

[b] The range of the DF-3A and the DF-21A missiles may be longer than is normally reported.

[c] The JL-1 SLBM has never been fully operational.

[d] A small stockpile of bombs with yields between 10 kt and 3 Mt is thought to exist for delivery by aircraft. Chinese aircraft are not believed to have nuclear weapon delivery as a primary role. Figures for aircraft are for nuclear-configured versions only.

[e] The existence of tactical warheads is highly uncertain, but several low-yield nuclear tests in the 1970s and US Government statements in the 1980s and 1990s suggest that some tactical warheads may have been developed.

[f] Additional warheads are thought to be in storage. The total stockpile is believed to comprise *c.* 200 warheads.

Sources: Chinese Ministry of Foreign Affairs, various documents; US Department of Defense (DOD), Office of the Secretary of Defense, 'Military power of the People's Republic of China', Annual Report to Congress, various years, URL <http://www.defenselink.mil/pubs/china.html>; US Air Force, National Air and Space Intelligence Center (NASIC), various documents; US Central Intelligence Agency, various documents; US Department of Defense, 'Proliferation: threat and response', Washington, DC, Jan. 2001, URL <http://www.fas.org/irp/threat/prolif00.pdf>; Kristensen, H. M., Norris, R. S. and McKinzie, M. G., *Chinese Nuclear Forces and U.S. Nuclear War Planning* (Federation of American Scientists and Natural Resources Defense Council: Washington, DC, Nov. 2006), URL <http://www.fas.org/

nuke/guide/china/Book2006.pdf>; Norris, R. S. et al., *Nuclear Weapons Databook*, vol. 5, *British, French, and Chinese Nuclear Weapons* (Westview: Boulder, Colo., 1994); 'NRDC Nuclear Notebook', *Bulletin of the Atomic Scientists*, various issues; and Authors' estimates.

There continues to be considerable uncertainty in the US intelligence community and among non-governmental researchers about the scope and pace of China's nuclear modernization programme.[104] In particular, it is unclear whether China intends to expand its force of nuclear-armed ballistic missiles significantly or to deploy newer, more survivable missiles in a force of roughly the same size as it has today.

China's land-based ballistic missiles are operated by the People's Liberation Army's Second Artillery Corps (SAC). According to data published annually by the US DOD, in 2006 the SAC had two types of operationally deployed ICBM: the liquid-propellant, silo-based DF-5A (CSS-4) and the smaller, silo-based or transport-able DF-4 (CSS-3).[105] China is developing two solid-propellant, road/rail-mobile ICBMs: the DF-31 and the longer-range DF-31A. On 4 September 2006 a DF-31 missile was successfully test-launched from the Wuzhai launch site towards the Taklimakan desert.[106] The US DOD forecast that that the DF-31 would achieve initial operational capability in 2006, but the missile was still not operational in early 2007. The deployment of the longer-range DF-31A is not expected before 2008–2010.

China currently deploys as part of its nuclear forces one type of medium-range bal-listic missile (MRBM)[107]—the solid-propellant, road-mobile DF-21A (CSS-5)—and one type of IRBM—the liquid-propellant, surface-based DF-3A (CSS-2). In 2006 the US DOD increased its estimate of the size of the DF-21A stockpile.[108] The DF-21A supplements China's ageing DF-3A missiles.[109] The DF-3A and the DF-4 are expected to be completely replaced by the DF-31 once the latter enters service. The deployment of road-mobile ICBMs is intended to improve the survivability of China's long-range nuclear forces. The US intelligence community has stated that China might deploy multiple warheads on its DF-5A missiles to ensure the effective-ness of its deterrent against missile defence systems, but neither the DF-31 nor its variants are thought to be designed to carry multiple warheads.

The SAC celebrated its 40th anniversary in July 2006.[110] Shortly before this event Chinese President Hu Jintao announced a decision to 'carry out reforms and innov-ations' on the SAC, which would include improved military training and would focus

---

[104] Kristensen, Norris and McKinzie (note 100), p. 43; and Nuclear Threat Initiative, 'Expert study finds smaller Chinese nuclear arsenal', Global Security Newswire, 4 May 2006, URL <http://www.nti.org/
d_newswire/issues/2006_5_4.html>.

[105] US Department of Defense (DOD), Office of the Secretary of Defense, *Military Power of the People's Republic of China 2006*, Annual report to Congress (DOD: Washington, DC, 2006), p. 50. This and previous years' reports are available at URL <http://www.defenselink.mil/pubs/china.html>.

[106] ITAR-TASS, 'China test launches intercontinental ballistic missile', 5 Sep. 2006.

[107] Although China has its own system for defining missile ranges, the US DOD definitions are used here: short-range = <1100 km; medium-range = 1100–2750 km; intermediate-range = 2750–5500 km; and intercontinental range = >5500 km. See Kristensen, Norris and McKinzie (note 100), p. 218.

[108] US Department of Defense (note 105). See also table 12.A.6; and Kile, Fedchenko and Kristensen (note 71), p. 658.

[109] US Department of Defense (DOD), Office of the Secretary of Defense, *Military Power of the People's Republic of China 2004*, Annual report to Congress (DOD: Washington, DC, 2004), p. 37.

[110] Xinhua, 'Account of Party Central Committee's care and concern for the strategic missile units', 5 July 2006, Translation from Chinese, World News Connection, National Technical Information Ser-vice (NTIS), US Department of Commerce.

on increasing the force's effectiveness and survivability in modern, high-intensity, information-centric conflicts.[111] The 2006 White Paper states that the SAC 'aims at progressively improving its force structure of having both nuclear and conventional missiles, and raising its capabilities in strategic deterrence and conventional strike under conditions of informationization'.[112]

As of early 2007 the Chinese submarine force consisted of approximately 55 operational ships, including about 50 diesel-powered ships, 3–5 nuclear-powered Han Class attack submarines and a single Type 092 (Xia Class) SSBN armed with 12 intermediate-range solid-propellant, single-warhead JL-1 (CSS-N-3) SLBMs. The Type 092 SSBN has never conducted a deterrent patrol.[113] This may change in the future because, according to the 2006 White Paper, the Chinese Navy 'aims at gradual extension of the strategic depth for offshore defensive operations and enhancing its capabilities in integrated maritime operations and nuclear counterattacks'.[114] To this end, China is developing the Type 094 (Jin Class) SSBN. The Type 094 ship is not expected to enter service before 2011 at the earliest. It will carry the intercontinental-range JL-2 SLBM, which is a modified DF-31 ICBM with a range of more than 8000 km.[115] In 2005 China carried out a successful test-launch of the JL-2 from a submerged submarine in the Pacific Ocean near the Shandong Peninsula.[116]

It is generally thought that China has a small stockpile of nuclear bombs earmarked for delivery by aircraft. Although the Chinese Air Force was not believed to have units whose primary purpose was to deliver nuclear bombs, the US National Security Council asserted in 1993 that 'some units [of the Chinese Air Force] may be tasked for nuclear delivery as a contingency mission'.[117] The most likely aircraft to have a nuclear role today are the H-6 bomber and perhaps a fighter-bomber. China is also developing land-attack cruise missiles that may be for delivery by the H-6. In 2005 a US DOD report stated that, once developed, there 'are no technological bars to placing on these systems a nuclear payload'.[118] The cruise missiles in development include the DH-10 and the YJ-63; the latter is capable of delivering a 500-kg warhead within a range of 400–500 km.[119]

[111] Nuclear Threat Initiative, 'China announces strategic missile plans', Global Security Newswire, 4 May 2006, URL <http://www.nti.org/d_newswire/issues/2006_6_30.html>; 'PLA 2nd Artillery Corps focuses on survivability', *Jane's Missiles & Rockets*, vol. 10, no. 9 (Sep. 2006), p. 7; and [Editorial: vigorously promoting innovation and development of military training in the new century and new stage], *Jiefangjun Bao*, 28 June 2006, URL <http://www.chinamil.com.cn/site1/ztpd/2006-06/28/content_511633.htm>, quoted in Chase, M., 'China's Second Artillery Corps: new trends in force modernization, doctrine and training', *China Brief*, vol. 6, no. 25 (19 Dec. 2006), URL <http://jamestown.org/images/pdf/ cb_006_025.pdf>.

[112] Chinese State Council (note 103).

[113] Kristensen, Norris and McKinzie (note 100), pp. 77–80.

[114] Chinese State Council (note 103).

[115] Different estimates suggest that the Type 094 SSBN would carry either 12 or 16 SLBMs. Kristensen, Norris and McKinzie (note 100), p. 83.

[116] 'China test-fires new submarine-launched missile', *Daily Yomiuri*, 18 June 2005; and 'China test fires long-range missile from submarine', *Jane's Missiles and Rockets*, vol. 9, no. 8 (Aug. 2005), p. 4.

[117] US National Security Council, 'Report to Congress on status of China, India and Pakistan nuclear and ballistic missile programs', [28 July 1993], p. 2.

[118] US Department of Defense (DOD), Office of the Secretary of Defense, *Military Power of the People's Republic of China 2005*, Annual report to Congress (DOD: Washington, DC, 2005), p. 29.

[119] Kristensen, Norris and McKinzie (note 100), p. 104–106.

VII. Indian nuclear forces

On the basis of an upper-bound estimate of its inventory of weapon-grade pluto-nium—520 kg at the end of 2005[120]—India has the material capacity to build an arsenal of more than 100 nuclear weapons. The estimate presented here, that the Indian arsenal holds about 50 nuclear weapons, is conservative. It is based on the lower range of a widely cited estimate of India's military plutonium inventory as well as on unclassified assessments made by the US intelligence community.[121]

Most published estimates of the size of the Indian nuclear stockpile are based on calculations of the total amount of weapon-grade plutonium that India has produced. There are several factors that introduce uncertainty into these calculations. First, there are different assessments of the lifetime operating capacity (the reliability and efficiency) of the 100-megawatt-thermal (MW(t)) Dhruva reactor and the ageing 40-MW(t) CIRUS reactor, which are dedicated to producing plutonium for military use.[122] Second, it is not known whether India has used non-weapon-grade plutonium (either in the form of reactor-grade plutonium or a mix of isotopes closer to weapon-grade plutonium) to manufacture nuclear weapons. Finally, there are different views on how to calculate the losses of nuclear material that occur during production, pro-cessing and testing.

Estimates of the size of the Indian nuclear stockpile must also take into account the evidence that India is not seeking to build the largest nuclear arsenal that it can. Numerous media and government reports have suggested that India has not manu-factured as many nuclear weapons as it could given its material resources. Moreover, India appears to be separating less weapon-grade plutonium annually than it could, given the nominal capacities of its reprocessing plants.[123]

In 2006 there was considerable debate about the potential impact of the Indian–US Civil Nuclear Cooperation Initiative on India's nuclear weapon production capabilities.[124] Critics of the deal expressed concern about the unwillingness of the Indian Department of Atomic Energy to place the prototype fast breeder reactor (PFBR) under International Atomic Energy Agency (IAEA) safeguards as part of the plan to separate the country's nuclear programme into civilian and military com-ponents, pointing out that India's annual capacity to produce weapon-grade pluto-

---

[120] See appendix 12C, table 12C.2.

[121] Albright, D., 'India's military plutonium inventory, end of 2004', 7 May 2005, Institute for Sci-ence and International Security (ISIS), *Global Stocks of Nuclear Explosive Materials*, URL <http://www.isis-online.org/global_stocks/end2003/india_military_plutonium.pdf>. The estimate assumes that each warhead would require at least 5 kg of plutonium. See also US Defense Intelligence Agency, 'A primer on the future threat: the decades ahead: 1999–2020', July 1999, p. 38, reproduced in Scarborough, R., *Rumsfeld's War* (Regnery: Washington, DC, 2004), pp. 194–223.

[122] In 2006 India announced that it would shut down the CIRUS reactor in 2010. 'Implementation of India–United States Joint Statement of July 18, 2005: India's separation plan', Embassy of India, Press release, Washington, DC, 7 Mar. 2006, URL <http://www.indianembassy.org/newsite/press_release/2006/Mar/sepplan.pdf>.

[123] Tellis, A., *Atoms for War? U.S.–Indian Civilian Nuclear Cooperation and India's Nuclear Arsenal* (Carnegie Endowment for International Peace: Washington, DC, June 2006), URL <http://www.carnegie
endowment.org/files/atomsforwarfinal4.pdf>.

[124] On the CNCI see chapter 12; and Ahlström, C., 'Legal aspects of the Indian–US Civil Nuclear Cooperation Initiative', *SIPRI Yearbook 2006* (note 71), pp. 669–85.

Table 12A.7. Indian nuclear forces, January 2007

Type	Range (km)[a]	Payload (kg)	Status
Land-based ballistic missiles			
Prithvi I (P-I)	150	800	Entered service in 1994, widely believed to have a nuclear delivery role
Agni I[b]	>700	1 000	Inducted into Indian Army service in 2004
Agni II	>2 000	1 000	Inducted into Indian Army service in 2004[c]
Sea-based ballistic missiles[d]			
Dhanush	400	1 000	Inducted into service in 2006
Aircraft[e]			
Mirage 2000H Vajra	1 850	6 300	Aircraft has reportedly been certified for delivery of nuclear gravity bombs
Jaguar IS Shamsher	1 400	4 760	Some of the 4 squadrons may have nuclear delivery role

[a] Missile payloads may have to be reduced in order to achieve maximum range. Aircraft range is given for illustrative purposes only; actual mission range will vary according to flight profile and weapon loading.

[b] The original Agni I, now known as the Agni, was a technology demonstrator programme that ended in 1996.

[c] The US Air Force reported in Mar. 2006 that Agni II was 'not yet deployed'.

[d] The Indian Government stated in 2006 that it did not have a submarine-launched ballistic missile (the Sagarika) in development.

[e] Other aircraft in the Indian Air Force's inventory that are potentially suitable for a nuclear role are the MiG-27 (Bahadur) and the Su-30MKI. The Su-30MKI can be refuelled by the IL-78 aerial tanker.

Sources: Indian Ministry of Defence, annual reports and press releases; International Institute for Strategic Studies (IISS), *The Military Balance 2005–2006* (Routledge: Abingdon, 2005); US Air Force, National Air and Space Intelligence Center (NASIC), *Ballistic and Cruise Missile Threat* (NASIC: Wright-Patterson Air Force Base, Ohio, Mar. 2006), URL <http://www.nukestrat.com/us/afn/threats.htm>; US Central Intelligence Agency, 'Unclassified report to Congress on the acquisition of technology relating to weapons of mass destruction and advanced conventional munitions, 1 January through 30 June 2002', Apr. 2003, URL <http://www.fas.org/irp/threat/bian_apr_2003.htm>; US Central Intelligence Agency, National Intelligence Council, 'Foreign missile developments and the ballistic missile threat through 2015' (unclassified summary), Dec. 2001, URL <http://www.fas.org/spp/starwars/CIA_NIE.htm>; Lennox, D. (ed.), *Jane's Strategic Weapon Systems* (Jane's Information Group: Coulsdon, 2004); Bharat Rakshak consortium of Indian military websites, URL <http://www.bharat-rakshak.com>; Raghuvanshi, V., *Defense News*, various articles; and Authors' estimates.

nium will dramatically increase with the PFBR's scheduled completion in 2010.[125] Critics also claimed that, by allowing the sale to India of foreign nuclear fuel for power reactors designated as civilian facilities, the deal would free the country's limited domestic uranium supplies for military purposes. A study released in 2006

[125] Mian, Z. et al., *Fissile Materials in South Asia and the Implications of the U.S.–Indian Nuclear Deal*, Report for the International Panel on Fissile Materials, 11 July 2006, URL <http://www.armscontrol.org/pdf/20060711_IPFM-DraftReport-US-India-Deal.pdf>.

disputed this, based on calculations showing that India already has sufficient indigenous reserves of natural uranium to build the largest possible nuclear arsenal it might desire to build.[126]

It is not publicly known whether India has produced highly enriched uranium (HEU) for weapon purposes. It operates two gas centrifuge facilities: a pilot-scale plant at the Bhabha Atomic Research Centre (BARC) complex; and a larger plant, known as the Rare Materials Project (RMP), which has been operating since about 1990 near Mysore. The primary purpose of the RMP is believed to be production of HEU for an indigenous nuclear-powered submarine (Advanced Technology Vessel, ATV) that is currently in development. The Department of Atomic Energy reportedly plans to increase the RMP's capacity to produce enriched uranium in order to meet both civilian and military requirements.[127]

According to the draft document published in 1999 and subsequent statements, India's nuclear doctrine is 'based on the principle of a minimum credible deterrence and no-first-use'.[128] How the doctrine will evolve in the future remains to be seen, but there are already indications that the no-first-use principle is eroding. Additional guidelines published in January 2003 stated that India would use nuclear weapons to deter or retaliate against the use of chemical or biological weapons.[129] Such use would amount to first use of nuclear weapons. There have been no official statements specifying the size of the nuclear stockpile required for 'credible minimum deterrence' but, according to the Indian Ministry of Defence, it involves 'a mix of land-based, maritime and air capabilities'.[130] Most observers believe that India maintains a recessed nuclear posture—that is, nuclear warheads are not mated to their delivery vehicles, and some nuclear warheads may be stored in an unassembled or inactive form.

Strike aircraft

At present, aircraft are the core of India's nuclear strike capabilities. The Indian Air Force (IAF) has reportedly certified the Mirage 2000H Vajra ('Divine Thunder') multi-role aircraft for delivery of nuclear gravity bombs. The IAF deploys two squadrons of Mirage 2000H aircraft at the Gwalior Air Force Station in north-central India. In October 2006 the IAF was reportedly negotiating with France over the purchase of an unspecified number of Mirage 2000-5 aircraft.[131] These could potentially be used to augment the IAF's nuclear strike capability, although this has not been confirmed by reliable sources. In addition to the Mirage 2000H, some of the IAF's four

---

[126] Tellis (note 123).

[127] Albright, D. and Basu, S., 'India's gas centrifuge enrichment program: growing capacity for military purposes', Institute for Science and International Security (ISIS) Report, 18 Jan. 2007, URL <http://www.isis-online.org/publications/southasia/indiagrowingcapacity.pdf>.

[128] Indian Ministry of External Affairs (MEA), *Draft Report of National Security Advisory Board on Indian Nuclear Doctrine* (MEA: New Delhi, 17 Aug. 1999), URL <http://meaindia.nic.in/disarmament/dm17Aug99.htm>.

[129] Indian Ministry of External Affairs, 'Cabinet Committee on Security reviews operationalization of India's nuclear doctrine', Press release, 4 Jan. 2003, URL <http://meaindia.nic.in/pressrelease/2003/01/04pr01.htm>.

[130] Indian Ministry of Defence (MOD), *Annual Report 2004–05* (MOD: New Delhi, 2005), URL <http://mod.nic.in/reports/report05.htm>, p. 14.

[131] 'IAF mulls purchase of French Mirage fighters', *Tribune of India*, 5 Oct. 2006. In Aug. 2005 Qatar and India suspended negotiations on India's purchase of 12 secondhand Mirage 2000-5 aircraft.

squadrons of Jaguar IS Shamsher ('Sword') fighter-bombers may have a nuclear delivery role.[132] India's MiG-27 and u-30 MKI aircraft are also potentially suitable for a nuclear role.

Ballistic missiles

For many years the Prithvi ('Earth') was the only operational ballistic missile in India's arsenal and the first believed to have a nuclear capability. The Prithvi I (SS-150) is a single-stage, road-mobile ballistic missile capable of delivering a 1000-kg warhead to a maximum range of 150 km. The missile was first flight-tested in 1988 and entered service with the Indian Army in 1994. It is currently deployed with the Army's 333, 444 and 555 missile groups. On 11 June 2006 a Prithvi I missile was successfully test-launched at the Integrated Test Range (ITR) at Chandipur-on-Sea, Orissa, on the Bay of Bengal. Officials at India's Defence Research and Development Organisation (DRDO) described the test, which involved the Indian Army, as a 'user trial'.[133] A number of Prithvi I missiles are widely believed to have been modified to deliver nuclear warheads, although this has never been officially confirmed.

There are two newer versions of the Prithvi missile with improved range, accuracy and handling. The Prithvi II (SS-250), which has entered into service with the air force, can carry a 500–700-kg warhead to a maximum range of 250 km. It is nuclear capable but is not believed to be assigned a nuclear role. On 20 November 2006 India successfully test-fired a Prithvi II missile from the ITR into the Bay of Bengal.[134] The Prithvi III (SS-350), a two-stage solid-fuel missile designed to deliver a 1000-kg warhead to a range of up to 350 km, is in development.

Indian defence sources indicate that the family of longer-range Agni ('Fire') ballistic missiles, which are designed to provide short reaction time launch capability, has largely taken over the Prithvi's nuclear role.[135] The original Agni missile was a technology demonstrator that was flight-tested several times between 1989 and 1994 up to a range of 1500 km but was never operationally deployed. The short-range Agni I is a single-stage, solid-fuel missile that can deliver a 1000-kg warhead to a maximum range of 700–800 km. The two-stage Agni II can deliver a similar payload to a range of up to 2000–2500 km. The missiles are road- and rail-mobile and both can carry nuclear as well as conventional warheads. In 2004 the Agni I and Agni II were inducted into service with the Indian Army's 334 and 335 missile groups, respectively. The Indian Army is reported to believe that the DRDO's pre-induction testing of the Agni I and Agni II was inadequate.[136] Numerous Indian Government statements and press reports indicate that the Agni II missile has been deployed, but a March 2006 US Air Force report claimed that it had not.[137]

---

[132] Norris, R. and Kristensen, H., 'India's nuclear forces', *Bulletin of the Atomic Scientists*, vol. 61, no. 5 (Sep./ Oct. 2005), pp. 73–75.

[133] Press Trust of India, 'Prithvi test-fired', *The Hindu*, 12 June 2006.

[134] Press Trust of India, 'Prithvi-II test fired', *The Hindu*, 20 Nov. 2006.

[135] Vishwakarma, A., 'Prithvi SRBM', Bharat Rakshak consortium of Indian military websites, updated 28 Dec. 2005, URL <http://www.bharat-rakshak.com/MISSILES/Prithvi.html>.

[136] 'Panel reviews Agni III ballistic missile failure', *Jane's Missiles & Rockets*, vol. 11, no. 1 (Jan. 2007), p. 2.

[137] E.g. Press Trust of India, 'India begins deploying Agni missiles', *Express India*, 31 Aug. 2004; and US Air Force (note 63).

On 12 April 2007 the DRDO conducted the first successful flight test of the inter-mediate-range Agni III ballistic missile. The two-stage, solid-fuel missile was launched on a 15-minute trajectory into the Indian Ocean from a rail-mobile launcher system at the missile testing facility on Wheeler Island.[138] The Agni III has a range of 3000–3500 km and is capable of delivering a payload of up to 1.5 tonnes against targets in most of China, although Indian officials have denied that the Agni III was designed with China in mind. The Ministry of Defence press release on the launch does not mention a nuclear capability, but media reports widely accredited such a statement to the ministry.[139] An earlier launch attempt, on 9 July 2006, failed when the second stage did not separate, causing the missile to crash into the sea.

Shortly after the 2007 Agni III test, Indian newspapers quoted engineers as saying that India was capable of producing a long-range ballistic missile, possibly with a range of about 5000 km. According to some reports, India is working on an ICBM with a range of 9000–12 000 km. The missile might be a three-stage design, with the first two stages using solid propellant and the third stage using liquid propellant, and could have a range of 9000–12 000 km. It may carry two or three nuclear warheads with yields of 15–20 kt.[140] In any case, it is not expected to enter service until after 2015. This ICBM, known as the Surya ('Sun'), is believed to be based on India's Polar Space-Launch vehicle (PSLV).[141] In 2006 a former senior US official warned that 'unwise' US space cooperation with India would facilitate India's final steps towards developing an ICBM, which could destabilize international relations and potentially even threaten the USA.[142]

India continues to develop the naval component of its planned 'triad' of nuclear forces. The Indian Navy is acquiring a rudimentary nuclear capability with the Dha-nush ('Bow') ship-based launcher system. The system uses a modified version of the Prithvi II missile and will be capable of carrying both conventional and nuclear war-heads.[143] Western analysts had speculated that India was developing a more advanced sea-based nuclear strike capability in the form of an SLBM called the Sagarika ('Oceanic'), which has sometimes been reported to be a sea-launched cruise missile. However, in 2006 the Indian Ministry of Defence stated that 'There is no missile project of by name "Sagarika".'[144]

VIII. Pakistani nuclear forces

The estimate presented here—that Pakistan possesses approximately 60 nuclear weapons—is conservative. On the basis of recent estimates of the size of Pakistan's

[138] Indian Ministry of Defence, 'Agni III launched successfully', Press release, 12 Apr. 2007.

[139] See e.g. Naqvi, M., 'India test-fires nuclear-capable missile', *The Guardian*, 12 Apr. 2007; and Associated Press, 'India successfully test fires nuclear-capable missile', *Jerusalem Post*, 12 Apr. 2007.

[140] Madhuprasad, N., DH News Service, 'India to develop intercontinental ballistic missile', *Deccan Herald*, 25 Aug. 2005, URL <http://www.deccanherald.com>.

[141] 'Indian press reports potential for ICBM development', *Jane's Missiles & Rockets*, vol. 9, no. 10 (Oct. 2005), pp. 10–11.

[142] Speier, R., 'U.S. space aid to India: on a "glide path" to ICBM trouble?', *Arms Control Today*, vol. 36, no. 2 (Mar. 2006).

[143] Indian Ministry of Defence, 'Dhanush successfully test fired', Press release, New Delhi, 8 Nov. 2004, URL <http://mod.nic.in/pressreleases/content.asp?id=853>.

[144] Indian Ministry of Defence, 'Development and trials missiles', Press release, New Delhi, 2 Aug. 2006, URL <http://pib.nic.in/release/rel_print_page1.asp?relid=19395>.

military inventory of HEU and separated plutonium, the country could in theory produce 70–100 nuclear weapons.[145] However, Pakistan is believed to have used only part of this HEU and plutonium inventory to manufacture warheads, so it is likely to have produced fewer weapons than this. US intelligence sources estimate the size of the Pakistani nuclear arsenal to be 50–60 warheads.[146] Pakistani officials claim that the country has already produced more warheads than needed to satisfy its current 'minimum deterrence requirement' but note that this requirement is subject to review 'according to situation'.[147] Pakistani Prime Minister Shaukat Aziz asserted in January 2007 that, since the Indian–US CNCI could result in more fissile material becoming available for India's military stockpile, and since India has expressed interest in acquiring missile defences, Pakistan 'would need to take measures to ensure the credibility of our deterrence'.[148] Those measures may involve an expansion of the country's capabilities to produce fissile material for nuclear weapons.

Pakistan's current nuclear arsenal is based primarily on HEU, which is produced by a gas centrifuge uranium-enrichment facility at the Kahuta Research Laboratories (also called the A. Q. Khan Research Laboratories). There is evidence that Pakistan may be moving towards a plutonium-based arsenal.[149] Pakistan is currently operating the 50-MW(t) Khushab I reactor, which is capable of producing about 10–12 kg of weapon-grade plutonium per year.[150] In 2006 commercial satellite imagery showed the construction of a second heavy-water reactor inside the nuclear complex in the Khushab district of Punjab. According to one estimate by non-governmental experts, the new reactor, dubbed Khushab II, would be 'capable of operating in excess of 1000 megawatts-thermal' and 'could produce over 200 kilograms of weapon-grade plutonium per year'.[151] Both US and Pakistani officials confirmed that a plutonium-producing reactor was being built at that location but disputed this estimate as substantially overstating the reactor's power and production capacity.[152] A subsequent analysis produced by another non-governmental expert concluded that the reactor's

[145] As estimated in appendix 12C, Pakistan might have 1.3 ± 0.2 tonnes of HEU and about 64 kg of separated plutonium at the end of 2006. It is assumed that Pakistan's HEU weapons are of solid core, implosion-type designs requiring 15–20 kg of HEU each: plutonium weapons require at the very least $c.$ 4–5 kg of plutonium metal.

[146] Koch, A., 'Pakistan moves towards a plutonium-based arsenal', *Jane's Intelligence Review*, vol. 18, no. 9 (Sep. 2006), pp. 48–49. These weapons are thought to be stored in partially disassembled form, separately from their delivery systems.

[147] Interview with Gen. Ehsanul Haq, Chairman of Joint Chiefs of Staff Committee, *Today with Kamran Khan* TV programme, Karachi Geo News TV, 24 Nov. 2006, Translation from Urdu, World News Connection, National Technical Information Service (NTIS), US Department of Commerce.

[148] Press Trust of India, 'Pak apprehensive about Indo-US nuclear deal: Aziz', *Economic Times*, 31 Jan. 2007.

[149] To achieve the same yield, plutonium-based nuclear warheads are normally lighter and more compact than those using HEU. Plutonium warheads can be fitted into smaller missiles, possibly including cruise missiles, or can provide for longer ranges of already deployed ballistic missiles.

[150] Mian, Z. et. al., 'Fissile materials in South Asia: the implications of the U.S.–India nuclear deal', International Panel on Fissile Materials (IPFM) Research Report no. 1, Sep. 2006, URL <http://www.fissilematerials.org/ipfm/site_down/ipfmresearchreport01.pdf>.

[151] Albright, D. and Brannan, P., 'Commercial satellite imagery suggests Pakistan is building a second, much larger plutonium production reactor: is South Asia headed for a dramatic buildup in nuclear arsenals?', Institute for Science and International Security (ISIS) Report, 24 July 2006, URL <http://www.isis-online.org/publications/southasia/newkhushab.pdf >.

[152] Warrick, J., 'Pakistani reactor not as significant as was reported, administration says', *Washington Post*, 5 Aug. 2006. According to the US State Department, 'the reactor will be over ten times less capable' than the estimate by Albright and Brannan (note 151). Jillani, S., 'Pakistan nuclear report disputed', BBC News, 7 Aug. 2006, URL <http://news.bbc.co.uk/2/5251936.stm>.

'power level is more likely to be in the 40 to 100 MWt range'.[153] The new reactor would still allow Pakistan to increase its plutonium production at least two- or three-fold, provided that the country has sufficient spent fuel-reprocessing capacity.

According to Pakistani officials, the country's nuclear command and control organization has three layers. At the top is the National Command Authority (NCA), which was established in 2000. The NCA consists of the highest-level members of the government and is headed by the president, currently General Pervez Musharraf. The second layer is the NCA's secretariat, the Strategic Plans Division (SPD), which is 'in charge of developing and managing Pakistan's nuclear capability in all dimensions'.[154] The third layer consists of a Strategic Force Command in each of the army, the navy and the air force, which are responsible for planning, control and 'operational directives for nuclear weapons deployment and use'. While affiliated with their respective armed forces, the strategic force commands are subordinated to the NCA.[155]

In 2006 the Pakistani prime minister reaffirmed that the country subscribes 'to the doctrine of minimum credible deterrence and [is] opposed to any nuclear proliferation as well as an arms race in the region'.[156] Pakistan has consistently rejected a no-first-use nuclear policy because of its fears of being overrun by India's larger conventional forces in a military conflict. However, Pakistan has pledged that it will 'not use or threaten to use nuclear weapons against non-nuclear weapon states'.[157]

Ballistic and cruise missiles

Pakistan is working to increase and diversify its missile inventory. It is developing short- and medium-range ballistic missiles as well as cruise missiles, some of which are known to have a nuclear delivery role. Pakistani military officials denied in 2006 that they were seeking to develop long-range ballistic missiles that could strike targets outside the region.[158] In 2006 Pakistan carried out a number of ballistic missile flight tests. It notified India of its intention to carry out the tests, in accordance with an October 2005 bilateral agreement requiring each country to provide the other with at least 72 hours' notice before conducting a flight test of a surface-to-surface ballistic missiles launched from land or sea.[159]

[153] Cochran, T. B., 'What is the Size of Khushab II?', Natural Resources Defense Council, 8 Sep. 2006, URL <http://docs.nrdc.org/nuclear/nuc_06090801A.pdf>.

[154] Kidwai, K., Director-General of Pakistan's Strategic Plans Division, quoted in 'Pakistan's evolution as a nuclear weapons state', *Strategic Insights*, 1 Nov. 2006, URL <http://www.ccc.nps.navy.mil/news/kidwaiNov06.pdf>.

[155] Khan, S. and Tsuchiya, T., 'Pakistan sets up tri-command nuclear force: officials', Kyodo News, 10 Aug. 2006, URL <http://www.chugoku-np.co.jp/abom/2006e/kyodo/Ak06081001.html>.

[156] Aziz, S., Prime Minister of Pakistan, quoted in 'PM warns of arms race in South Asia', *The Dawn*, 25 Jan. 2006, URL <http://www.dawn.com/2006/01/25/top3.htm>.

[157] Khan, M., Pakistan's Permanent Representative to the UN, quoted in United Nations Office in Geneva, 'Conference on Disarmament starts debate on negative security assurances', Press Release, 3 Aug. 2006, URL <http://www.unog.ch/unog/website/news_media.nsf/(httpNewsByYear en)/B0B499E F402F3050C12571BF00332A50>.

[158] Haq, E., Chairman of Joint Chiefs of Staff Committee, Interview on *Today with Kamran Khan* TV programme, Karachi Geo News TV, 24 Nov. 2006, Translation from Urdu, World News Connection, National Technical Information Service (NTIS), US Department of Commerce.

[159] Creegan, E., 'India, Pakistan sign missile notification pact', *Arms Control Today*, Nov. 2005, URL <http://www.armscontrol.org/act/2005_11/NOV-IndiaPak.asp>. The text of the agreement is available at URL <http://www.stimson.org/?SN=SA20060207949>.

Table 12A.8. Pakistani nuclear forces, January 2007

Type	Range (km)^a	Payload (kg)	Status
Short-range ballistic missiles			
Abdali (Hatf-2)	180–200	250–450	Test-launched on 19 Feb. 2006
Ghaznavi (Hatf-3)	90^b	500–700	Entered service in 2004; fewer than 50 launchers have been deployed
Shaheen I (Hatf-4)	>450^c	750–1 000	Entered service in 2003; fewer than 50 launchers have been deployed
Medium-range ballistic missiles			
Ghauri I (Hatf-5)	~1 300	700–1 000	Entered service with the Pakistani Army in 2003. Fewer than 50 launchers deployed
Aircraft			
F-16A/B	1 600	4 500	34 aircraft, deployed in 3 squadrons; most likely aircraft to have a nuclear delivery role

^{a} Missile payloads may have to be reduced in order to achieve maximum range. Aircraft range is given for illustrative purposes only; actual mission range will vary according to flight profile and weapon loading.

^{b} The US National Air and Space Intelligence Center (NASIC) gives the maximum range as 400 km.

^{c} Some unofficial sources claim that the range is 600–1500 km.

Sources: US Air Force, National Air and Space Intelligence Center (NASIC), *Ballistic and Cruise Missile Threat* (NASIC: Wright-Patterson Air Force Base, Ohio, Mar. 2006), URL <http://www.nukestrat.com/us/afn/NASIC2006.pdf>; US Central Intelligence Agency, 'Unclassified report to Congress on the acquisition of technology relating to weapons of mass destruction and advanced conventional munitions, 1 January through 30 June 2002', Apr. 2003, URL <https://www.cia.gov/cia/reports/archive/reports_2002.html>; US Central Intelligence Agency, National Intelligence Council, 'Foreign missile developments and the ballistic missile threat through 2015' (unclassified summary), Dec. 2001, URL <http://www.fas.org/spp/starwars/CIA-NIE.htm>; Lennox, D. (ed.), *Jane's Strategic Weapon Systems* (Jane's Information Group: Coulsdon, 2007); Office of the Press Secretary to the President of Pakistan, 'Pakistan successfully test fire surface to surface Hatf-II Abdali missile', Press release, 19 Feb. 2006, URL <http://www.presidentofpakistan.gov.pk/NewsEventsDetail.aspx?News EventID=2960>: and Authors' estimates.

Pakistan is known to deploy two types of road-mobile, solid-propellant, single-warhead short-range ballistic missile (SRBM): the Ghaznavi (Hatf-3) and the Shaheen I (Hatf-4). A third SRBM, the Abdali (Hatf-2), may also have begun to be deployed in 2005. The Abdali programme was thought to have been cancelled due to technical problems, but on 19 February 2006 Pakistan conducted a test launch of the missile. A press release from President Musharraf's office stated that the Abdali can carry a nuclear warhead.[160] The Ghaznavi SRBM formally entered service with the

---

[160] Office of the Press Secretary to the President of Pakistan, 'Pakistan successfully test fire surface to surface Hatf-II Abdali missile', Press release, 19 Feb. 2006, URL <http://www.presidentofpakistan.gov. pk/NewsEventsDetail.aspx?NewsEventID=2960>.

Pakistani Army in 2004. It is believed to be a domestically produced copy of the Chinese M-11 missile. A Ghaznavi missile was successfully test-launched on 9 December 2006.[161] The Shaheen I SRBM, which has been declared to be nuclear capable, entered service with the Pakistani Army in 2003. A Shaheen I missile was test-launched on 29 November 2006.[162]

Pakistan's only MRBM currently in service is the Ghauri I (Hatf-5), a road-mobile, liquid-propellant, single-warhead ballistic missile. It has been declared by Pakistani defence officials to be nuclear capable. The Ghauri I is believed to be based on North Korea's Nodong 1/2 missile technology and was reportedly developed with extensive design and engineering assistance from North Korea. Pakistani defence sources indicate that limited production of the Ghauri I began in late 2002 and that it entered into service in January 2003, although it was still in development. A Ghauri I missile was successfully test-launched on 16 November 2006.[163] Pakistan is also developing the two-stage, road-mobile, solid-propellant Shaheen II (Hatf-6) MRBM. On 29 April 2006 it conducted the third test launch of this missile. Its reported range of 2000–2500 km means that it can reach targets across India.[164]

On 11 August 2005 Pakistan carried out the first test flight of a ground-launched cruise missile, designated the Babur (Hatf-7), at a new test range in Baluchistan.[165] Pakistani officials indicated that the Babur had a range of 500 km and was capable of carrying a nuclear warhead. A second successful test flight of the Babur was conducted on 21 March 2006. Both trials were made from a ground launcher, but Pakistan also plans to deploy the missile on surface ships and submarines.[166]

Strike aircraft

The aircraft of the Pakistani Air Force that is most likely to be used in the nuclear weapon delivery role is the F-16. Other aircraft, such as the Mirage V and the Chinese-produced A-5, could also be used. Pakistan currently maintains 32 F-16 aircraft in service, deployed in three squadrons. On 26 March 2005, the US Administration announced that it was notifying the US Congress of plans to sell 75 F-16s to Pakistan.[167] US officials said that the deal, which was intended to reward Pakistan for its cooperation in the 'global war on terrorism', would not affect the military balance in the region. In 2005 the USA gave Pakistan two additional F-16 aircraft as a

---

[161] 'Pakistan successfully test fires Hatf-III ballistic missile', *PakTribune,* 10 Dec. 2006, URL <http://www.paktribune.com/news/index.shtml?162642>.

[162] Office of the Press Secretary to the President of Pakistan, 'Pakistan successfully launches Shaheen-1 missile', Press release, 29 Nov. 2006, URL <http://www.presidentofpakistan.gov.pk/News EventsDetail.aspx?NewsEventID=3411>.

[163] 'Pakistan tests "nuclear" missile', BBC News, 16 Nov. 206, URL <http://news.bbc.co.uk/2/6153 242.stm>.

[164] Agence France-Presse, 'Pakistan "successfully" test fires long-range nuclear capable missile', 29 Apr. 2006, Translation from French, World News Connection, National Technical Information Service (NTIS), US Department of Commerce.

[165] Associated Press, 'Pakistan test fires nuclear-capable cruise missile', *International Herald Tribune,* 11 Aug 2005.

[166] 'Pakistan's Babur completes test firing', *Jane's Missiles and Rockets,* vol. 10, no. 5 (May 2006), p. 9.

[167] Baker, P., 'Bush: US to sell F-16s to Pakistan', *Washington Post,* 25 Mar. 2005.

Table 12A.9. Israeli nuclear forces, January 2007

Type	Range (km)[a]	Payload (kg)	Status
Aircraft[b]			
F-16A/B/C/ D/I Falcon	1 600	5 400	205 aircraft in the inventory; some are believed to be certified for nuclear weapon delivery
Ballistic missiles[c]			
Jericho II	1 500–1 800	750–1 000	c. 50 missiles; first deployed in 1990; test-launched 27 June 2001
Submarines			
Type 800 Dolphin			Rumoured to be equipped with nuclear-capable cruise missiles, but this is denied by Israeli officials

[a] Missile payloads may have to be reduced in order to achieve maximum range. Aircraft range is given for illustrative purposes only; actual mission range will vary according to flight profile and weapon loading.

[b] Some of Israel's 25 F-15I aircraft may also have a long-range nuclear delivery role.

[c] The Shavit space launch vehicle, if converted to a ballistic missile, could deliver a 775-kg payload a distance of 4000 km. The Jericho I, first deployed in 1973, is no longer thought to be operational.

Sources: Cohen, A. and Burr, W., 'Israel crosses the threshold', *Bulletin of the Atomic Scientists*, May/June 2006, pp. 22–30; Cohen, A., *Israel and the Bomb* (Columbia University Press: New York, N.Y., 1998); Albright, D., Berkhout, F. and Walker, W., SIPRI, *Plutonium and Highly Enriched Uranium 1996: World Inventories, Capabilities and Policies* (Oxford University Press: Oxford, 1997); Lennox, D. (ed.), *Jane's Strategic Weapon Systems* (Jane's Information Group: Coulsdon, 2007); Fetter, S., 'Israeli ballistic missile capabilities', *Physics and Society*, vol. 19, no. 3 (July 1990), pp. 3–4 (see 'Ballistic missile primer' (unpublished) for an updated analysis, URL <http://www.puaf.umd.edu/Fetter/1990-MissilePrimer.pdf>); 'NRDC Nuclear Notebook', *Bulletin of the Atomic Scientists*, various issues; and Authors' estimates.

goodwill gesture.[168] In 2006 Pakistan signed a deal with the USA to buy 18 Block 52 F-16C/D aircraft, with an option for 18 more. Under the terms of the agreement, the 32 F-16A/B aircraft already in Pakistani service are to receive a midlife update. Pakistan is also to receive 26 secondhand F-16 aircraft at a later date.[169]

IX. Israeli nuclear forces

The size of the Israeli nuclear weapon stockpile is unknown but is widely believed to consist of 100–200 plutonium warheads. According to one estimate, Israel possessed up to 0.56 tonnes of military plutonium as of December 2005,[170] or the equivalent of

[168] 'F-16 deal update', PakistaniDefence.com, Aug. 2005, URL <http://www.pakistanidefence.com/news/MonthlyNewsArchive/2005/August2005.htm>.

[169] Schanz, M. V., 'Aerospace World: US and Pakistan hammer out new F-16 deal', *Air Force Magazine*, Dec. 2006, p. 12.

[170] See appendix 12C, table 12C.2.

about 110 warheads, assuming that each contains 5 kg of plutonium. However, only part of this plutonium may have been used to produce warheads. The US Defense Intelligence Agency estimated in 1999 that Israel had assembled 60–80 nuclear warheads.[171] Many analysts believe that it has a recessed nuclear arsenal (one that is stored but not armed, requiring some preparation before use). If this is true, the warheads for Israel's purported nuclear weapon delivery systems may not actually be deployed. These delivery systems are believed to be strike aircraft, land-based ballistic missiles and possibly sea-launched cruise missiles (see table 12A.8). There has been speculation that Israel may have produced non-strategic nuclear weapons, including artillery shells and atomic demolition munitions.

On 6 July 2006 Israel signed a contract for the procurement of two Type 800 Dolphin Class diesel-electric attack submarines from Germany, with an option for a third. When the new submarines are delivered, after 2012, they will augment Israel's current fleet of three submarines of the same class. Germany's decision to sell the submarines to Israel has been controversial. Some reports suggest that Israel may have developed a nuclear-capable SLCM, based on the US-made Harpoon missile, and has modified the submarine's torpedo tubes to launch the missile.[172]

Israel continues to maintain its long-standing policy of nuclear ambiguity, neither officially confirming nor denying that it possesses nuclear weapons. However, in December 2006 Israeli Prime Minister Ehud Olmert made a statement that was widely interpreted as tacitly acknowledging that Israel possessed a nuclear arsenal. Speaking to German television, Olmert included Israel in a list of countries possessing nuclear weapons.[173] The remark was quickly disavowed by Olmert and other Israeli officials, who reiterated that Israel 'will not be the first country that introduces nuclear weapons to the Middle East'.[174]

X. North Korea's military nuclear capabilities

There is little publicly available information about North Korea's nuclear weapon programme. In February 2005 North Korea declared for the first time that it had produced nuclear weapons,[175] and in October 2006 it unambiguously demonstrated a nuclear weapon capability by carrying out an underground nuclear test explosion.[176] However, the unexpectedly low yield of the explosion led many foreign experts to believe that it ended in a 'fizzle'—an inefficient detonation releasing less explosive energy than expected. This has raised doubts about whether North Korea has

---

[171] US Defense Intelligence Agency (note 121). The US DOD predicted that the Israeli stockpile in 2020 would consist of 65–85 weapons, suggesting that the stockpile is not increasing in size.

[172] Ben-David, A., 'Israel orders two more Dolphin subs', *Jane's Defense Weekly*, 30 Aug. 2006, p. 5; and Katz, Y., 'Exclusive: Israel buys 2 German subs', *Jerusalem Post*, 22 Aug. 2006.

[173] 'Was Olmert über Atomwaffen sagte' [What Olmert said about nuclear weapons], N24 television channel, 12 Dec. 2006, URL <http://www.n24.de/politik/article.php?articleId=88274>.

[174] Boudreaux, R., 'Fallout rains on Israel's Olmert after nuclear remark', *Los Angeles Times*, 13 Dec. 2006.

[175] Korea Central News Agency, 'DPRK FM on its stand to suspend its participation in Six-Party Talks for indefinite period', 10 Feb. 2005, URL <http://www.kcna.co.jp/item/2005/200502/news02/11.htm>.

[176] On the North Korean explosion and the methods used to determine its nature see appendix 12B.

mastered the design and engineering skills needed to manufacture an operational nuclear weapon.[177]

North Korea is widely believed to have produced and separated enough plutonium from the spent fuel of its 5-megawatt-electric (MW(e)) graphite-moderated research reactor at Yongbyon to be able to build a small number of nuclear warheads.[178] One non-governmental expert has estimated that the Yongbyon reactor produces about 6 kg of weapon-grade plutonium per year and that, as of November 2006, North Korea possessed 40–50 kg of separated plutonium, with an additional 4–8 kg of plutonium contained in the nuclear fuel currently loaded into the reactor.[179] Other non-governmental experts have estimated that, as of February 2007, North Korea had a total plutonium stock of 46–64 kg of plutonium, of which about 28–50 kg was believed to be in separated form and usable in nuclear weapons.[180] Based on these estimates, North Korea could have produced about six nuclear explosive devices by the end of 2006, assuming that 8 kg of plutonium would be used to manufacture each device.[181]

Apart from the plutonium weapon programme, there have been allegations that North Korea is pursuing a clandestine gas centrifuge programme aimed at producing HEU for use in nuclear weapons. On 16 October 2002 the US State Department issued a statement declaring that North Korea had acknowledged that it had such a programme.[182] North Korea denied having done so, but the ensuing controversy led to the collapse of the 1994 Agreed Framework.[183] Pakistani President Musharraf acknowledged in September 2006 that the Abdul Qadeer Khan network had provided North Korea with 'nearly two dozen P-1 and P-2 centrifuges', other equipment and

[177] Sanger, D. and Broad, W., 'Small blast, or "big deal"? U.S. Experts look for clues', *New York Times*, 11 Oct. 2006.

[178] In addition to the 5-MW(e) reactor at Yongbyon, North Korea began work in the early 1990s on a 50-MW(e) reactor at Yongbyon and a 200-MW(e) reactor at Taechon, about 20 km from Yongbyon; both reactors remain unfinished and have reportedly been abandoned since 1994. Hecker, S., 'Report on North Korean nuclear program', Nautilus Institute, Policy Forum Online, 06-97A, 15 Nov. 2006, URL <http://www.nautilus.org/fora/security/0697Hecker.html>.

[179] Hecker (note 178).

[180] Albright, D. and Brannan, P., 'The North Korean plutonium stock, February 2007', Institute for Science and International Security (ISIS), 20 Feb. 2007, URL <http://www.isis-online.org/publications/dprk/DPRKplutoniumFEB.pdf>.

[181] The IAEA has established 8 kg as a 'significant quantity' of plutonium—i.e. 'the approximate amount of nuclear material for which the possibility of manufacturing a nuclear explosive device cannot be excluded'. International Atomic Energy Agency (IAEA), 'IAEA safeguards glossary: 2001 edition', International Nuclear Verification Series no. 3 (2001), URL <http://www-pub.iaea.org/MTCD/publications/PDF/nvs-3-cd/PDF/NVS3_prn.pdf>, p. 3. Some researchers suggest that the significant quantity should be considerably lower. Cochran, T. B. and Paine, C. E., *The Amount of Plutonium and Highly-Enriched Uranium Needed for Pure Fission Nuclear Weapons* (Natural Resources Defense Council: New York, N.Y., Apr. 1995), URL <http://www.nrdc.org/nuclear/fissionw/fissionweapons.pdf>.

[182] Boucher, R., Spokesman, US Department of State, Bureau of Public Affairs, 'North Korean nuclear program', Press statement, 16 Oct. 2002, URL <http://www.state.gov/r/pa/prs/ps/2002/14432.htm>. On uranium enrichment in North Korea see Kile, S. N., 'Nuclear arms control, non-proliferation and ballistic missile defence', *SIPRI Yearbook 2003* (note 18), pp. 583–85; and Niksch, L. A., *North Korea's Nuclear Weapons Program*, US Library of Congress, Congressional Research Service (CRS) Report for Congress RL33590 (CRS: Washington, DC, 5 Oct. 2006), URL <http://fpc.state.gov/documents/organization/74904.pdf>, pp. 11–12.

[183] IAEA, 'Agreed Framework between the United States of America and the Democratic People's Republic of Korea', 21 Oct. 1994, INFCIRC/457, 2 Nov. 1994. See Kile (note 182), pp. 578–92.

'coaching on centrifuge technology'.[184] There is no open-source evidence that North Korea has produced HEU, and in February 2007 US intelligence officials backed away from earlier claims that North Korea had a covert, production-scale uranium enrichment programme.[185]

North Korea deploys approximately 500–600 road-mobile SRBMs of three types— Hwasŏng-5 (Scud B), Hwasŏng-6 (Scud Mod-C) and Hwasŏng-7 (Scud Mod-D)— and 50–200 road-mobile Nodong MRBMs.[186] It is also developing the longer-range Taepodong-1 and the Taepodong-2 missiles. On 5 July 2006 North Korea test-launched seven missiles from the test facility at Musudan-ri into the Sea of Japan: three Hwasŏng-6s, three Nodongs and one Taepodong-2.[187] The launch of the Taepodong-2 ended in failure.[188] Most analysts consider it unlikely that North Korea has developed a nuclear warhead that is light and compact enough to fit onto a ballistic missile delivery system.[189]

[184] Musharraf, P., *In the Line of Fire: A Memoir* (Free Press: New York, N.Y., Sep. 2006), p. 296.

[185] Kessler, G., 'New doubts on nuclear efforts by North Korea', *Washington Post*, 1 Mar. 2007.

[186] US Air Force (note 63); Lennox (note 27), pp. 91–100; and Nuclear Threat Initiative, 'Missile capabilities', North Korea Profile, Dec. 2006, URL <http://www.nti.org/e_research/profiles/NK/Missile/62.html>.

[187] Priest, D. and Faiola, A., 'North Korea tests long-range missile', *Washington Post*, 6 July 2006.

[188] Richardson, D., 'Transonic buffeting may have doomed Taepo Dong-2', *Jane's Missiles & Rockets*, vol. 10, no. 9 (Sep. 2006), p. 8.

[189] See e.g. Hecker (note 178).

Appendix 12B. Nuclear explosions, 1945–2006

VITALY FEDCHENKO and RAGNHILD FERM HELLGREN*

I. Introduction

In October 2006 the Democratic People's Republic of Korea (DPRK, or North Korea) conducted a nuclear test explosion, the first nuclear explosion recorded since those conducted by India and Pakistan in 1998. This appendix presents a brief discussion of the North Korean explosion, in particular how international researchers have sought to determine its nature, location and yield based on the available data, and then presents data on all the nuclear explosions conducted since 1945.

II. The nuclear test in North Korea

On 9 October 2006 the Korean Central News Agency (KCNA) reported that North Korea had on that day successfully conducted an underground nuclear test explosion 'under secure conditions'.[1] North Korea had announced on 3 October its intention to conduct a nuclear test.[2] The Chinese Government was given 20 minutes' prior warning of the test and was informed that the explosion's yield would be 4 kilotons.[3]

Following the 9 October announcement, numerous measurements and studies were carried out by governmental and independent experts outside North Korea to determine whether there had been an explosion and, if so, its nature, location and actual yield. A seismic event was recorded by several monitoring networks at 01:35 UTC on 9 October 2006, originating 70 kilometres north of the city of Kimchaek in North Korea's North Hamgyong province. The wave patterns recorded at monitoring stations and the depth of the event (less than 1 km) indicate that it was an explosion rather than an earthquake. Data on the seismic magnitude of the event were used to estimate the yield of the explosion, although the lack of information on the geology of the test site affects the reliability of such estimates.[4] Based on the seismic data, the governments of France, South Korea and the United States, along with independent researchers, concluded with a high degree of certainty that there had been an explo-

---

[1] Korean Central News Agency, 'DPRK successfully conducts underground nuclear test', Pyongyang, 9 Oct. 2006, URL <http://www.kcna.co.jp/item/2006/200610/news10/10.htm>.

[2] Korean Central News Agency, 'DPRK foreign ministry clarifies stand on new measure to bolster war deterrent', Pyongyang, 3 Oct. 2006, URL <http://www.kcna.co.jp/item/2006/200610/news10/04.htm>.

[3] CNN, 'North Korea claims nuclear test', 9 Oct. 2006, URL <http://www.cnn.com/2006/WORLD/asiapcf/10/08/korea.nuclear.test/>; and Linzer, D., 'Low yield of blast surprises analysts', *Washington Post*, 10 Oct. 2006.

[4] US National Academy of Sciences, *Technical Issues Related to the Comprehensive Nuclear Test Ban Treaty* (National Academy Press: Washington, DC, 2002), URL <http://www.nap.edu/catalog/10471.html>, pp. 41–42.

* The authors are grateful to Jangnyeol Moon, visiting researcher at SIPRI, and Sukeyuki Ichimasa, Research Fellow at the Japan Institute of International Affairs Center for the Promotion of Disarmament, for their help in preparing this appendix.

sion and that its yield was well below 1 kt.[5] Different estimates of the time, location and size of the 9 October explosion are given in table 12B.1.

Seismic data alone are insufficient to confirm that an underground explosion is nuclear. Immediately after the 3 October announcement by North Korea, the USA deployed its WC-135W Constant Phoenix atmospheric collection aircraft,[6] which is normally used for collection of particulate and gaseous effluents and debris in support of the 1963 Partial Test-Ban Treaty.[7] Based on analysis of atmospheric radioactive debris collected by the aircraft, the US Government announced on 16 October that the event had been a nuclear explosion.[8] This was corroborated by the findings of South Korea and, later, the Comprehensive Nuclear-Test-Ban Treaty Organization (CTBTO).[9] Analysis of the debris also indicated that the test used plutonium, which was confirmed by North Korean officials.[10]

The extent to which the North Korean nuclear test was successful is uncertain. The discrepancy between the pre-announced yield of 4 kt and the estimated actual yield of less than 1 kt made some experts speculate that the test ended in a 'fizzle'—that is, an inefficient detonation releasing less explosive energy than expected. As reported in the South Korean press, a North Korean diplomat acknowledged that the test was 'smaller in scale than expected'.[11] However, even the predicted yield was several times smaller than that expected from a basic plutonium weapon design.

III. Estimated number of nuclear explosions, 1945–2006

Table 12B.2 lists the known nuclear explosions to date, including nuclear tests conducted in nuclear weapon test programmes, explosions carried out for peaceful purposes and the two nuclear bombs dropped on Hiroshima and Nagasaki in August

[5] Garwin, R. L. and von Hippel, F. N., 'A technical analysis of North Korea's Oct. 9 nuclear test', *Arms Control Today*, Nov. 2006. An early official Russian estimate that the yield was 5–15 kt was dismissed by US Government officials as inaccurate. It was identical to an estimate reportedly given to Russia by North Korea in the run-up to the test. Chanlett-Avery, E. and Squassoni, S., *North Korea's Nuclear Test: Motivations, Implications, and U.S. Options*, US Library of Congress, Congressional Research Service (CRS) Report for Congress RL33709 (CRS: Washington, DC, 4 Oct. 2006), URL <http://fpc.state.gov/fpc/75427.htm>; and Linzer (note 3).

[6] Chin, T., 'Seoul's intelligence capabilities "a total failure"', *Korea Herald*, 18 Oct. 2006.

[7] US Department of the Air Force, 'WC-135 Constant Phoenix', Fact sheet, Oct. 2005, URL <http://www.af.mil/factsheets/factsheet.asp?fsID=192>. The Treaty Banning Nuclear Weapon Tests in the Atmosphere, in Outer Space and Under Water (Partial Test-Ban Treaty) was opened for signature on 5 Aug. 1963 and entered into force on 10 Oct. 1963. For the text of the treaty see URL <http://www.state.gov/t/ac/trt/4797.htm>. For a description of the treaty and a list of the signatories and parties see annex A in this volume.

[8] Office of the Director of National Intelligence, 'Statement by the Office of the Director of National Intelligence on the North Korea nuclear test', News release, 16 Oct. 2006, URL <http://www.dni.gov/announcements/20061016_release.pdf>. Collection and analysis of atmospheric debris are not an entirely reliable way to establish that an underground nuclear explosion has occurred. On-site inspection would probably be needed to establish with absolute certainty that the North Korean test was nuclear.

[9] 'S. Korean gov't officially confirms N. Korea's nuclear test', *Yonhap News*, 25 Oct. 2006; 'ROK confirms radiation level normal following Pyongyang's nuke test', *Yonhap News*, 25 Oct. 2006; and US Defense Treaty Readiness Inspection Program, 'CTBTO observatory detects radioactive materials from DPRK nuclear test', *Weekly Treaty Review*, 5–11 Jan. 2007, URL <http://dtirp.dtra.mil/tic/WTR/wtr_11jan07.pdf>, p. 19.

[10] Shanker, T. and Sanger, D. E., 'North Korean fuel identified as plutonium', *New York Times*, 17 Oct. 2006; and Hecker, S. S., 'Report on North Korean nuclear program', Nautilus Institute, Policy Forum Online 06-97A, 15 Nov. 2006, URL <http://www.nautilus.org/fora/security/0697Hecker.html>.

[11] MacAskill, E., 'Diplomat says test was smaller than expected', *The Guardian*, 11 Oct. 2006.

Table 12B.1. Data on North Korea's nuclear explosion, 9 October 2006

Source[a]	Origin time (UTC)	Latitude (degrees)	Longitude (degrees)	Error margin[b]	Body wave magnitude[c]
IDC[d]	01:35.27.6	41.3119 N	129.0189 E	±20.6 km	4.1
NEIC	01:35.28	41.29 N	129.09 E	± 8.1 km	4.3
CEME	01:35.26.0	41.31 N	128.96 E	. .	4.0
KIGAM	01:35	40.81 N	129.10 E	. .	3.9

UTC = Coordinated Universal Time; . . = Data not available.

[a] Because of differences between estimates, particularly regarding the precise site of the explosion, data from 4 sources—1 internationally recognized body and 3 national bodies—are provided for comparison. IDC = Comprehensive Nuclear Test-Ban Treaty Organization (CTBTO) International Data Centre, Vienna; NEIC = US Geological Survey (USGS), National Earthquake Information Center, Denver, Colorado; CEME = Geophysical Service of the Russian Academy of Sciences, Central Experimental Methodical Expedition; KIGAM = Korea Institute of Geoscience and Mineral Resources (South Korea).

[b] The error margins listed here are horizontal location errors provided by the data sources. See USGS Earthquake Hazards Program, 'Recent earthquakes—glossary', URL <http://earthquake.usgs.gov/eq center/recenteqsus/ glossary.htm>.

[c] Body wave magnitude indicates the size of the event. In order to give a reasonably correct estimate of the yield of an underground explosion, detailed information is needed, e.g. on the geological conditions in the area where the explosion took place. Body wave magnitude is therefore an unambiguous way of giving the size of an explosion.

[d] The IDC was 'in a test and provisional operation mode only' and only 60% of the monitoring stations in the CTBTO's International Monitoring System were contributing data at the time of the event. 'North Korea: a real test for the CTBT verification system?', *CTBTO Spectrum*, no. 9 (Jan. 2007), pp. 24, 28, URL <http://www.ctbto.org/reference/outreach/140207_spectrum9_web_final.pdf>.

Sources: **IDC data**: Swedish Defence Research Agency (FOI), Swedish National Data Centre, Information provided to the authors, Feb. 2007; **NEIC data**: NEIC, 'Magnitude 4.3: North Korea', Preliminary Earthquake Report, 8 Nov. 2006, URL <http://earthquake.usgs.gov/eqcenter/eqinthenews/2006/ustqab/>; **CEME data**: CEME, 'Information message about underground nuclear explosion made by the Northern Korea on October 9, 2006', 9 Oct. 2006, URL <http://www.ceme.gsras.ru/cgi-bin/info_quakee.pl?mode=1&id=84>; **KIGAM data**: Lee, Y. W. and Ahn, J. H., [Seismic waves released: it is an explosion], *Chosun Ilbo*, 9 Oct. 2006, URL <http://www.chosun.com/national/news/200610/200610090665.html>; and Lee, J. N., Yonhap News, [KIGAM: 'official magnitude figure 3.58–3.7, no change'], *Hankyoreh*, 10 Oct. 2006.

1945. The totals also include tests for safety purposes carried out by France, the Soviet Union/Russia and the USA,[12] irrespective of the yield and of whether they caused a nuclear explosion. The tables do not include subcritical experiments. Simultaneous detonations, also called salvo explosions, were carried out by the USA (from 1963) and the Soviet Union (from 1965), mainly for economic reasons.[13] Of the Soviet tests, 20 per cent were salvo experiments, as were 6 per cent of the US tests.

[12] In a safety experiment, or a safety trial, more or less fully developed nuclear devices are subjected to simulated accident conditions. The nuclear weapon core is destroyed by conventional explosives with no or very small releases of fission energy. The UK also carried out numerous safety tests, but they are not included in table 12B.2 because of their high number.

[13] The Soviet Union conducted simultaneous tests including as many as 8 devices on 23 Aug. 1975 and on 24 Oct. 1990 (the last Soviet test).

Table 12B.2. Estimated number of nuclear explosions, 1945–2006

a = atmospheric (or in a few cases underwater); u = underground.

Year	USA[a] a	USA[a] u	USSR/Russia a	USSR/Russia u	UK[a] a	UK[a] u	France a	France u	China a	China u	India a	India u	Pakistan a	Pakistan u	North Korea a	North Korea u	Total
1945	3	–	–	–	–	–	–	–	–	–	–	–	–	–	–	–	3
1946	2[b]	–	–	–	–	–	–	–	–	–	–	–	–	–	–	–	2
1947	–	–	–	–	–	–	–	–	–	–	–	–	–	–	–	–	–
1948	3	–	–	–	–	–	–	–	–	–	–	–	–	–	–	–	3
1949	–	–	1	–	–	–	–	–	–	–	–	–	–	–	–	–	1
1950	–	–	–	–	–	–	–	–	–	–	–	–	–	–	–	–	–
1951	15	1	2	–	–	–	–	–	–	–	–	–	–	–	–	–	18
1952	10	–	–	–	1	–	–	–	–	–	–	–	–	–	–	–	11
1953	11	–	5	–	2	–	–	–	–	–	–	–	–	–	–	–	18
1954	6	–	10	–	–	–	–	–	–	–	–	–	–	–	–	–	16
1955	17[b]	1	6[b]	–	–	–	–	–	–	–	–	–	–	–	–	–	24
1956	18	–	9	–	6	–	–	–	–	–	–	–	–	–	–	–	33
1957	27	5	16[b]	–	7	–	–	–	–	–	–	–	–	–	–	–	55
1958[c]	62[d]	15	34	–	5	–	–	–	–	–	–	–	–	–	–	–	116
1959[c]	–	–	–	–	–	–	–	–	–	–	–	–	–	–	–	–	–
1960[c]	–	–	–	–	–	–	3	–	–	–	–	–	–	–	–	–	3
1961[c]	–	10	58[b]	1	–	–	1	1	–	–	–	–	–	–	–	–	71
1962	39[b]	57	78	1	–	2	–	1	–	–	–	–	–	–	–	–	178
1963[e]	4	43	–	–	–	–	–	3	–	–	–	–	–	–	–	–	50
1964	–	45	–	9	–	2	–	3	1	–	–	–	–	–	–	–	60
1965	–	38	–	14	–	1	–	4	1	–	–	–	–	–	–	–	58
1966	–	48	–	18	–	–	6	1	3	–	–	–	–	–	–	–	76
1967	–	42	–	17	–	–	3	–	2	–	–	–	–	–	–	–	64
1968	–	56	–	17	–	–	5	–	1	–	–	–	–	–	–	–	79
1969	–	46	–	19	–	–	–	–	1	1	–	–	–	–	–	–	67
1970	–	39	–	16	–	–	8	–	1	–	–	–	–	–	–	–	64
1971	–	24	–	23	–	–	5	–	1	–	–	–	–	–	–	–	53
1972	–	27	–	24	–	–	4	–	2	–	–	–	–	–	–	–	57
1973	–	24	–	17	–	–	6	–	1	–	–	–	–	–	–	–	48
1974	–	22	–	21	–	1	9	–	1	–	–	1	–	–	–	–	55
1975	–	22	–	19	–	–	–	2	–	1	–	–	–	–	–	–	44
1976	–	20	–	21	–	1	–	5	3	1	–	–	–	–	–	–	51
1977	–	20	–	24	–	–	–	9	1	–	–	–	–	–	–	–	54
1978	–	19	–	31	–	2	–	11	2	1	–	–	–	–	–	–	66
1979	–	15	–	31	–	1	–	10	1	–	–	–	–	–	–	–	58
1980	–	14	–	24	–	3	–	12	1	–	–	–	–	–	–	–	54
1981	–	16	–	21	–	1	–	12	–	–	–	–	–	–	–	–	50
1982	–	18	–	19	–	1	–	10	–	1	–	–	–	–	–	–	49
1983	–	18	–	25	–	1	–	9	–	2	–	–	–	–	–	–	55
1984	–	18	–	27	–	2	–	8	–	2	–	–	–	–	–	–	57
1985[f]	–	17	–	10	–	1	–	8	–	–	–	–	–	–	–	–	36
1986[f]	–	14	–	–	–	1	–	8	–	–	–	–	–	–	–	–	23
1987[f]	–	14	–	23	–	1	–	8	–	1	–	–	–	–	–	–	47
1988	–	15	–	16	–	–	–	8	–	1	–	–	–	–	–	–	40
1989	–	11	–	7	–	1	–	9	–	–	–	–	–	–	–	–	28
1990	–	8	–	1	–	1	–	6	–	2	–	–	–	–	–	–	18

Year	USA[a]		USSR/ Russia		UK[a]		France		China		India		Pakistan		North Korea		Total
	a	u	a	u	a	u	a	u	a	u	a	u	a	u	a	u	
1991[g]	−	7	−	−	−	1	−	6	−	−	−	−	−	−	−	−	14
1992[g]	−	6	−	−	−		−	−	−	2	−	−	−	−	−	−	8
1993[g]	−	−	−	−	−		−	−	−	1	−	−	−	−	−	−	1
1994[g]	−	−	−	−	−		−	−	−	2	−	−	−	−	−	−	2
1995[g]	−	−	−	−	−		−	5	−	2	−	−	−	−	−	−	7
1996[g]	−	−	−	−	−	−	−	1	−	2	−	−	−	−	−	−	3
1997	−	−	−	−	−	−	−	−	−	−	−	−	−	−	−	−	0
1998	−	−	−	−	−	−	−	−	−	−	2[h]	−	2[h]	−	−	−	4
1999	−	−	−	−	−	−	−	−	−	−	−	−	−	−	−	−	0
2000	−	−	−	−	−	−	−	−	−	−	−	−	−	−	−	−	0
2001	−	−	−	−	−	−	−	−	−	−	−	−	−	−	−	−	0
2002	−	−	−	−	−	−	−	−	−	−	−	−	−	−	−	−	0
2003	−	−	−	−	−	−	−	−	−	−	−	−	−	−	−	−	0
2004	−	−	−	−	−	−	−	−	−	−	−	−	−	−	−	−	0
2005	−	−	−	−	−	−	−	−	−	−	−	−	−	−	−	−	0
2006	−	−	−	−	−	−	−	−	−	−	−	−	−	−	−	1	1
Subtotal	217	815	219	496	21	24	50	160	23	22	−	3	−	2	−	1	2 053
Total	**1 032**		**715**		**45**		**210**		**45**		**3**		**2**		**1**		

Note: For the purposes of this table 'underground nuclear test' is defined according to Section I, para. 2 of the 1990 Protocol to the 1974 US–Soviet Treaty on the Limitation of Underground Nuclear Weapon Tests (Threshold Test Ban Treaty, TTBT): 'either a single underground nuclear explosion conducted at a test site, or two or more underground nuclear explosions conducted at a test site within an area delineated by a circle having a diameter of two kilometers and conducted within a total period of time of 0.1 second'. For the text of the TTBT and the Protocol see URL <http://www.state.gov/t/ac/trt/5204.htm>. 'Underground nuclear explosion' is defined according to the 1976 US–Soviet Treaty on Underground Nuclear Explosions for Peaceful Purposes (Peaceful Nuclear Explosions Treaty, PNET): 'any individual or group underground nuclear explosion for peaceful purposes' (Article II.a). 'Group explosion' is defined as 'two or more individual explosions for which the time interval between successive individual explosions does not exceed five seconds and for which the emplacement points of all explosives can be interconnected by straight line segments, each of which joins two emplacement points and each of which does not exceed 40 kilometers' (PNET, Article II.c). For the text of the PNET see URL <http://www.state.gov/t/ac/trt/5182.htm>. For brief descriptions of the TTBT and PNET see annex A in this volume.

[a] All British tests from 1962 were conducted jointly with the USA at the US Nevada Test Site but are listed only under 'UK' in this table. Thus, the number of US tests is higher than shown. Safety tests carried out by the UK are not included in the table.

[b] 1 of these tests was carried out under water.

[c] The UK, the Soviet Union and the USA observed a moratorium on testing from Nov. 1958 to Sep. 1961.

[d] 2 of these tests were carried out under water.

[e] On 5 Aug. 1963 the USSR, the UK and the USA signed the Partial Test-Ban Treaty (PTBT), prohibiting nuclear explosions in the atmosphere, in outer space and under water. It was subsequently opened for signature by all other states. For a description of the treaty and a list of the signatories and parties see annex A in this volume.

[f] The USSR observed a unilateral moratorium on testing between Aug. 1985 and Feb. 1987.

[g] The USSR and then Russia observed a moratorium on testing from Jan. 1991 and the USA from Oct. 1992, until they signed the Comprehensive Nuclear Test-Ban Treaty (CTBT);

France observed a similar moratorium from Apr. 1992 to Sep. 1995. The CTBT was opened for signature by all states on 24 Sep. 1996, and all 5 of the Non-Proliferation Treaty (NPT)-defined nuclear weapon states signed it on that day. It has not yet entered into force. For a brief description of the CTBT and lists of the states that have signed or ratified it see annex A in this volume.

[h] India's detonations on 11 and 13 May 1998 are listed as 1 test for each date. The 5 detonations by Pakistan on 28 May 1998 are also listed as 1 test.

Sources: Swedish Defence Research Agency (FOI), various estimates, including information from the CTBTO International Data Center; Reports from the Australian Seismological Centre, Australian Geological Survey Organisation, Canberra; US Department of Energy (DOE), *United States Nuclear Tests: July 1945 through September 1992* (DOE: Washington, DC, 1994); Norris, R. S., Burrows, A. S. and Fieldhouse, R. W., 'British, French and Chinese nuclear weapons', *Nuclear Weapons Databook, Vol. V* (Natural Resources Defense Council: Washington, DC, 1994); Direction des centres d'experimentations nucléaires (DIRCEN) and Commissariat à l'Énergie Atomique (CEA), *Assessment of French Nuclear Testing* (DIRCEN and CEA: Paris, 1998); Russian Ministry of Atomic Energy and Russian Ministry of Defense, *USSR Nuclear Weapons Tests and Peaceful Nuclear Explosions, 1949 through 1990* (All-Russian Research Institute of Experimental Physics, Russian Federal Nuclear Center (VNIIEF): Sarov, 1996); Natural Resources Defense Council, 'Archive of nuclear data', URL <http://www.nrdc.org/nuclear/nudb/datainx.asp>; and Swedish Defence Research Agency (FOI), Swedish National Data Centre, Information provided to the authors, Feb. 2007.

Appendix 12C. Fissile materials: global stocks, production and elimination

HAROLD FEIVESON, ALEXANDER GLASER, ZIA MIAN and
FRANK VON HIPPEL*

I. Introduction: fissile materials and nuclear weapons

Fissile materials can sustain an explosive fission chain reaction. They are essential for all types of nuclear explosives, from first-generation fission weapons to advanced thermonuclear weapons. The most common fissile materials are uranium enriched to more than 20 per cent in the chain-reacting isotope uranium-235 (U-235) and plutonium of almost any isotopic composition. The fission of 1 kilogram of fissile material—the approximate amount that fissioned in both the Hiroshima and Nagasaki bombs—releases energy equivalent to the explosion of about 18 kilotons of chemical high explosive.

Lack of access to fissile materials represents the main technical barrier to the acquisition of nuclear weapons. International monitoring of the production, use and disposition (i.e. management and disposal) of both military and civilian fissile materials is crucial for nuclear disarmament, for halting the proliferation of nuclear weapons and for ensuring that terrorists do not acquire them.

This section reviews some basic background information on fissile materials and their use in nuclear weapons. Section II discusses the need for better information on military and civilian holdings of highly enriched uranium (HEU) and separated plutonium and provides estimates for current global holdings of these materials. Section III describes the production of HEU by gas centrifuge, the creation of plutonium in nuclear reactors and its subsequent separation, and the current approaches to disposition of these materials. Section IV presents some conclusions.

Only 0.7 per cent of naturally occurring uranium is U-235. The remainder is almost entirely the non-chain-reacting isotope U-238. Although in principle uranium with an enrichment of U-235 as low as 6 per cent could sustain an explosive chain reaction, the critical mass of material required would be infinitely large. Enrichment to 20 per cent U-235 is generally taken to be the lowest concentration practicable for use in weapons. Uranium enriched to 20 per cent or higher is defined as HEU. The International Atomic Energy Agency (IAEA) considers such HEU a direct-use weapon material. In practice, however, in order to minimize the mass of the nuclear explosive, weapon-grade uranium is usually enriched to over 90 per cent in U-235.

Increasing the fraction of U-235 in uranium requires sophisticated isotope separation technology. Isotope separation on the scale required to produce nuclear weapons is not considered to be within the reach of terrorist groups.

Plutonium is produced in a nuclear reactor when U-238 absorbs a neutron and becomes U-239, which subsequently decays to plutonium-239 (Pu-239) via the inter-

---

* This appendix is based primarily on chapters 1, 2, 3 and 6 of International Panel on Fissile Materials (IPFM), Global Fissile Material Report 2006 (IPFM: Princeton, N.J., 2006), URL <http://www.fissilematerials.org/>. Many of the documents referred to in that book and in this appendix are archived on the IPFM website at URL <http://www.ipfmlibrary.org/>.

mediate, short-lived isotope neptunium-239. The longer an atom of Pu-239 stays in a reactor after it has been created, the greater the likelihood that it will absorb a second neutron and become Pu-240—or a third or fourth neutron and become Pu-241 or Pu-242. Plutonium therefore comes in a variety of isotopic mixtures. Weapon designers prefer to work with a mixture that is predominantly Pu-239 because of its relatively low rate of spontaneous emission of neutrons and gamma rays and low generation of radioactive heat. Weapon-grade plutonium contains more than 90 per cent of the isotope Pu-239. The plutonium in typical spent fuel from power reactors (reactor-grade plutonium) contains 50–60 per cent Pu-239 and about 25 per cent Pu-240.

For a time, many in the nuclear industry believed that the plutonium generated in power reactors could not be used for weapons. One reason was the belief (or hope) that the spontaneous emission of neutrons by Pu-240, which is typically four times more abundant in power-reactor spent fuel than in weapon-grade plutonium, would start the explosive chain reaction prematurely during the implosion of the plutonium core and sharply reduce the weapon's explosive yield. However, it is now understood that virtually any combination of plutonium isotopes can be used to make a nuclear weapon with a reliable yield of at least 1 kiloton, using technologies no more sophisticated than those used in the Nagasaki bomb.[1]

The amount of fissile material in a nuclear warhead depends on design details, including whether it is a pure fission weapon, such as the Hiroshima and Nagasaki bombs, or a two-stage, thermonuclear weapon. The Hiroshima bomb contained about 60 kg of uranium enriched to about 80 per cent in chain-reacting U-235. In this 'gun-type' weapon, one piece of HEU of less than a critical mass was fired into another to make a supercritical mass able to sustain an exponentially growing fission chain reaction. The Nagasaki bomb was an implosion device operated on a principle that has been incorporated into most modern weapons. Chemical explosives imploded a 6-kg mass of plutonium to a higher density. While 6 kg is normally less than critical mass, this implosion reduced the spaces between the atomic nuclei and resulted in less leakage of neutrons out of the mass, with the result that it became supercritical. In both designs, the chain reaction was initiated by releasing neutrons at the moment when the fissile material was most supercritical.

Gun-type weapons are simpler than implosion devices (although they can only be constructed using HEU, not plutonium, and require at least twice as much HEU as an implosion weapon), and those with the intent to make them do not need a high level of technical sophistication. Indeed, the US Department of Energy (DOE) has warned that it may be possible for intruders in a fissile-material storage facility to use nuclear materials for on-site assembly of an improvised nuclear device in the short time before guards could intervene.[2]

The IAEA defines a significant quantity of fissile material as 'the approximate amount of nuclear material for which the possibility of manufacturing a nuclear explosive device cannot be excluded'. This estimate is for a first-generation implosion

[1] Mark, J. C., 'Explosive properties of reactor-grade plutonium', *Science & Global Security*, vol. 4 (1993), p. 111; and US Department of Energy (DOE), *Nonproliferation and Arms Control Assessment of Weapons-Usable Fissile Material Storage and Excess Plutonium Disposition Alternatives*, DOE/NN-0007 (DOE: Washington, DC, Jan. 1997), URL <http://www.ipfmlibrary.org/doe97.pdf>, pp. 37–39.

[2] US Department of Energy (DOE), Office of Security Affairs, Office of Safeguards and Security, 'Protection and control planning', *Manual for Protection and Control of Safeguards and Security Interests*, DOE M 5632.1C-1 (DOE: Washington, DC, 15 July 1994).

bomb and includes production losses. The agency assumes a significant quantity to be 8 kg of plutonium or HEU containing 25 kg of U-235.[3]

In more advanced, modern fission weapons, the yield is typically boosted by an order of magnitude by introducing a mixture of deuterium and tritium, heavy isotopes of hydrogen, into the hollow shell of fissile material (the 'pit' of the weapon) just before it is imploded.[4] When the temperature of the fissioning material inside the pit reaches 100 million degrees Celsius, it can ignite the fusion of tritium with deuterium, which produces a burst of neutrons that increase the fraction of fissile material fissioned and thereby the power of the explosion.

Advanced fission weapons may contain significantly less material than the 6 kg of plutonium in the Nagasaki bomb. For example, the US Government has declassified the fact that 4 kg of plutonium is sufficient to make a nuclear explosive device.[5] Based on the critical mass ratios, it is plausible to assume that three times that amount of weapon-grade uranium (about 12 kg) would be sufficient if HEU were used in a similarly advanced design of a fission weapon.

In a modern thermonuclear weapon, a fission nuclear explosive generates X-rays that compress and ignite a second nuclear explosive, a 'secondary', containing both uranium and thermonuclear fuel. The energy released by the secondary is generated by both the fission of HEU and the fusion of deuterium and tritium. In the secondary, the tritium is produced during the explosion by neutron absorption in lithium-6. Modern warheads therefore typically contain both plutonium and HEU. It is assumed that the average modern nuclear warhead contains the equivalent of about 25 kg of HEU enriched to 90 per cent in the isotope U-235.[6]

II. Military and civilian fissile material stocks

During the cold war, the Soviet Union and the USA produced almost the entire current global stockpile of HEU for nuclear weapons and naval propulsion reactors and about half the global stockpile of separated plutonium for nuclear weapons. The other half of the plutonium stockpile derives from the reprocessing of civilian spent power-reactor fuel. The main contributors to military stockpiles of HEU and plutonium have ceased production, but the civilian stockpile of plutonium continues to grow at a significant rate.

---

[3] This can be plutonium of any composition, but less than 80% Pu-238. Plutonium containing more than 80% Pu-238 is considered unusable for nuclear weapons because of the large amount of heat generated by the relatively short (88-year) half-life of the isotope. The IAEA figure for HEU presumably corresponds to the amount required for 90% enriched uranium. For lower enrichments, more material would be required. International Atomic Energy Agency (IAEA), *Safeguards Glossary 2001 Edition*, International Nuclear Verification Series no. 3 (IAEA: Vienna, June 2002), URL <http://www-pub. iaea.org/MTCD/publications/PubDetails.asp?pubid=6570>, pp. 23, 24.

[4] Deuterium, a stable isotope of hydrogen with 1 neutron and 1 proton in the nucleus, occurs naturally. Tritium, which has 2 neutrons and 1 proton, has a half-life of 12 years and is made in nuclear reactors. The natural abundance of tritium is negligible.

[5] 'Hypothetically, a mass of 4 kilograms of plutonium or uranium-233 is sufficient for one nuclear explosive device.' US Department of Energy (DOE), Office of Declassification, 'Restricted data declassification decisions 1946 to the present', RDD-7, Washington, DC, 1 Jan. 2001, p. 26.

[6] E.g. the US Enrichment Corporation (USEC) uses this figure. The corporation purchases low-enriched uranium produced by blending down Russia's excess 90% enriched HEU as part of a Russia–USA agreement. The 25 kg figure is used to calculate the number of warheads equivalent to the quantity of HEU blended down. See the USEC US–Russian Megatons to Megawatts Program, URL <http://www.usec.com/v2001_02/html/megatons_fact.asp>.

Availability of information

Non-nuclear weapon states that are parties to the 1968 Treaty on the Non-proliferation of Nuclear Weapons (Non-Proliferation Treaty, NPT)[7] are required to declare to the IAEA, and update regularly, information on the locations and quantities of all nuclear materials on their territories. In the European Union (EU) the European Atomic Energy Community (Euratom), which shares monitoring responsiblities with the IAEA, provides such reports on behalf of the EU member states. The IAEA does not make this information available to other governments or the public; it publishes only the total quantities of fissile materials under its safeguards in all the non-nuclear weapon states. The NPT does not require any disclosure of fissile material stocks by the five nuclear weapon states—China, France, Russia, the United Kingdom and the USA—that are parties to the NPT.[8] Despite this, all five states have made public some information on their production and holdings of fissile material. Since 1998 these five states (plus Belgium, Germany, Japan and Switzerland) have each year publicly declared to the IAEA their holdings of civilian plutonium, and in some cases of civilian HEU.[9] The UK and the USA have each published details of their total stocks of military plutonium and HEU. All but China (which has made unofficial indications) have officially declared that they have ended or suspended their production of fissile materials for weapons.[10]

In 1994 the US Department of Energy made public the total quantity of HEU that it had produced, and in 1996 published a history of US plutonium production and use.[11] A much fuller history of US HEU production and disposition was completed in January 2001 but was only released five years later as a result of a series of appeals under the US Freedom of Information Act by the Federation of American Scientists.[12] In 1998 the UK made public its entire stocks of HEU and civilian and military plutonium.[13]

A 1993 United Nations General Assembly resolution proposed a fissile material cut-off treaty (FMCT), and a negotiating mandate was agreed in 1995 at the Conference

---

[7] For a description of the main provisions of the NPT and a list of the parties see annex A in this volume. The full text of the NPT is available at URL <http://disarmament.un.org/wmd/npt/npttext.html>.

[8] There are 3 confirmed nuclear weapon states (those that have openly tested nuclear weapons) that are not party to the NPT: India, North Korea and Pakistan. Israel is an unconfirmed but de facto nuclear weapon state not party to the NPT. On the nuclear forces of all 9 nuclear weapon states see appendix 12A.

[9] These declarations are published by the International Atomic Energy Agency (IAEA) as additions to INFCIRC/549. See IAEA, URL <http://www.iaea.org/Publications/Documents/Infcircs/>.

[10] Albright, D., Berkhout, F. and Walker, W., SIPRI, *Plutonium and Highly Enriched Uranium 1996: World Inventories, Capabilities, and Policies* (Oxford University Press: Oxford, 1997), pp. 38, 68, 76, 80.

[11] US Department of Energy, 'Declassification of the United States total production of highly enriched uranium', Fact sheet, Washington, DC, 27 June 1994; and US Department of Energy, 'Declassification of today's highly enriched uranium inventories at Department of Energy laboratories', Fact sheet, Washington, DC, 27 June 1994—both available at URL <http://www.osti.gov/opennet/forms. jsp?formurl=document/press/pcconten.html>; and US Department of Energy (DOE), *Plutonium—The First 50 Years: United States Plutonium Production, Acquisition, and Utilization from 1944 through 1994*, DOE/DP-0127 (DOE: Washington, DC, 1996).

[12] US Department of Energy (DOE), *Uranium—Striking a Balance: A Historical Report on the United States HEU Production, Acquisition, and Utilization Activities from 1945 through September 30, 1996* (DOE: Washington, DC, 2001).

[13] British Ministry of Defence, *Strategic Defence Review*, Cm 3999 (Stationery Office: London, 1998), URL <http://www.mod.uk/DefenceInternet/AboutDefence/CorporatePublications/PolicyStrategy andPlanning/StrategicDefenceReview.htm>, para. 72.

Table 12C.1. Global stocks of highly enriched uranium[a]

Country	National stockpiles (93% enriched equivalent, tonnes)	Production status	Comments
China	22 ± 5.5	Stopped 1987–89	
France	33 ± 6.6	Stopped early 1996	
India	0.2 ± 0.1	Continuing	
Pakistan[b]	1.3 ± 0.2	Continuing	
Russia[c]	770 ± 300	Stopped 1987 or 1988	Includes 100 tonnes assumed to be reserved for naval and other reactor fuel; does not include 215 tonnes to be blended down
UK[d]	23.4 (declared in 2002)	Stopped 1963	
USA[e]	495 (declared)	Stopped 1992	Includes 128 tonnes reserved for naval and other reactor fuel; Does not include 139 for blend-down, or for disposition as waste
Non-nuclear weapon states[f]	~10		
Total	**~1325 ± 310**		**Not including 354 tonnes to be blended down**

[a] Estimates are for the end of 2003 but the blending down of excess Russian and US weapon HEU up to late 2006 has been taken into account. Totals are rounded to nearest 5 tonnes.

[b] This figure assumes production at a rate of 0.1 tonnes per year between 2003 and 2006.

[c] As of 1 Oct. 2006, 285 tonnes of Russia's weapon-grade HEU had been blended down. The estimate shown for the Russian reserve for naval reactors is not based on any public information.

[d] This figure includes 21.9 tonnes of HEU as of 31 Mar. 2002, the average enrichments of which were not given. The UK declared 1.5 tonnes of civilian HEU to the IAEA as of the end of 2005.

[e] The amount of US HEU is given in actual tonnes, not 93% enriched equivalent. As of 30 Sep. 1996 the USA had an inventory of 740.7 tonnes of HEU containing 620.3 tonnes of U-235 and had declared 174 tonnes with approximately 70-per cent average enrichment to be excess. An additional 20 tonnes were declared excess in 2005, an amount that was increased to 52 tonnes in 2006. As of the end of 2006, the USA had blended down 87 tonnes of HEU.

[f] This figure does not include HEU originally enriched to 20–26% in spent fast-reactor fuel in Kazakhstan.

Sources: Institute for Science and International Security, 'Global stocks of nuclear explosive materials', Dec. 2003, URL <http://www.isisonline.org/global_stocks/end2003/tableof contents.html>; Albright, D., Berkhout, F. and Walker, W., SIPRI, *Plutonium and Highly Enriched Uranium 1996: World Inventories, Capabilities and Policies* (Oxford University Press: Oxford, 1997), p. 80, table 4.1; **Russia**: United States Enrichment Corporation, 'Megatons to megawatts', URL <http://www.usec.com>; **UK**: British Ministry of Defence, 'Historical accounting for UK defence highly enriched uranium', London, Mar. 2006, URL <http://www.mod.uk/DefenceInternet/AboutDefence/CorporatePublications/HealthandSafety Publications/Uranium>; International Atomic Energy Agency (IAEA), INFCIRC/549/Add.8/9,

15 Sep. 2006, URL <http://www.iaea.org/Publications/Documents/Infcircs/>; **USA**: US Department of Energy (DOE), *Highly Enriched Uranium, Striking a Balance: A Historical Report on the United States Highly Enriched Uranium Production, Acquisition, and Utilization Activities from 1945 through September 30, 1996* (DOE: Washington, DC, 2001); Presentation by Robert George and Dean Tousley, US Department of Energy, 'US Highly Enriched Uranium Disposition', to the Nuclear Energy Institute Fuel Supply Forum, 24 Jan. 2006—available at URL <http://www.pogo.org/m/hsp/Y12/appendix-F.pdf>; Statement by William Tobey, Deputy Administrator for Defence Nuclear Nonproliferation, National Nuclear Security Administration, US Department of Energy, before the House Government Reform Committee Subcommittee on National Security, Emerging Threats, and International Relations, 26 Sep. 2006—available at URL <http://www.gsinstitute.org/docs/SNS_Congressional_Transcript.pdf>; **Non-nuclear weapon states**: International Atomic Energy Agency (IAEA), *Annual Report 2005* (IAEA: Vienna, 2006), table A20.

on Disarmament.[14] One of the 13 steps agreed to by the NPT nuclear weapon states at the 2000 NPT Review Conference was to begin talks on a 'non-discriminatory, multilateral and international effectively verifiable treaty banning the production of fissile material for nuclear weapons' and reach agreement within five years.[15] If nuclear disarmament is ever to be carried towards completion, all states with nuclear weapons will eventually have to declare to the IAEA or some similar international institution their entire stocks of fissile material by amount, form and location. There are obvious benefits for a country to prepare such a declaration as soon as possible, not least for itself, because reconstruction of the history of its fissile-material production may be based on ephemeral and inadequate records, the interpretation of which will require the assistance of production workers who will become less available with time. A 2006 report on Britain's HEU stocks describes the problems that its authors encountered with original records:

This review has been conducted from an audit of annual accounts and the delivery/receipt records at sites. A major problem encountered in examining the records was that a considerable number had been destroyed for the early years of the programme. . . . Even where records have survived, other problems have been encountered, including: . . . [distinguishing] between new make and recycled HEU . . . some early records make no specific mention of waste and effluent disposals . . . [and for] some records . . . assessments had to be made to establish units. Other records do not identify quantities to decimal places and may have been rounded. . . . [and] in some cases no indication of enrichment value was available. Average figures were used, or knowledge of the process used to assure that the material was indeed HEU.[16]

The British and US precedents show that it is possible to make substantial declarations about fissile stocks without serious negative consequences. To date, however, none of the other nuclear weapon states has made comparable declarations. Published estimates of their stocks of fissile materials produced for weapons are made by independent non-governmental analysts and have substantial levels of uncertainty. The most complete compilation of publicly available data and estimates of global pro-

---

[14] On the FMCT see chapter 12.

[15] 2000 Review Conference of the Parties to the Treaty on the Non-Proliferation of Nuclear Weapons, Final document, New York, 19 May 2000, URL <http://disarmament2.un.org/wmd/npt/final doc.html>.

[16] British Ministry of Defence, 'Historical accounting for UK defence highly enriched uranium', London, Mar. 2006, URL <http://www.mod.uk/DefenceInternet/AboutDefence/CorporatePublications/HealthandSafetyPublications/Uranium>, p 5.

duction and consumption of fissile materials can be found in the 1996 SIPRI study by David Albright, Frans Berkhout and William Walker.[17] Albright and his colleagues at the Institute for Science and International Security have regularly updated this information.[18] The figures below are based largely on this work.

Highly enriched uranium

As of mid-2006, the global stockpiles of HEU totalled roughly 1025–1625 tonnes (see table 12C.1) plus about 350 tonnes of HEU excess to weapon requirements that will be blended down to low-enriched uranium (LEU).[19] More than 99 per cent of this material is in the possession of the five NPT-signatory nuclear weapon states. The only states believed to be currently producing HEU are Pakistan (for weapons) and India (for naval-reactor fuel). Their estimated production rates are approximately 100 kg per year each.[20] France, Russia, the UK and the USA use HEU to fuel submarine and ship- propulsion reactors, although France is transferring to LEU fuel for this purpose.[21] During the cold war, the Soviet Union and the USA each used more than 2 tonnes of HEU per year for this purpose,[22] and today, Russia and the USA annually use about 1 tonne and 2 tonnes of weapon-grade-equivalent HEU, respectively.[23] The Soviet Union and the USA have also used—and Russia still uses—HEU for other military purposes, including to fuel plutonium and tritium production reactors.

HEU is also used to fuel civilian research reactors as well as Russia's fleet of nine nuclear-powered civilian vessels—eight icebreakers and one transporter ship—that ply the country's northern seaways.[24] As part of the Atoms for Peace programme, the Soviet Union/Russia and the USA have been supplying HEU to many countries for civilian research reactors and medical-isotope production since the 1950s. Most civilian HEU is in the NPT-signatory nuclear weapon states, but more than 10 tonnes is in non-nuclear weapon states.[25] Roughly 50 tonnes of the HEU shown in table 12C.1 is

---

[17] Albright, Berkhout and Walker (note 10).

[18] Institute for Science and International Security (ISIS), 'Global stocks of nuclear explosive materials', Dec. 2003, URL <http://www.isis-online.org/global_stocks/end2003/tableofcontents.html>.

[19] LEU is uranium enriched in U-235 to less than 20%.

[20] Mian, Z. et al., *Fissile Materials in South Asia and the Implications of the US–India Nuclear Deal*, (Princeton University: Princeton, N.J., Sep. 2006), URL <http://www.fissilematerials.org/southasia.pdf>. Israel may also have been producing HEU using centrifuge technology since 1979 or 1980 and a laser-isotope enrichment process since 1981. Barnaby, F., *The Invisible Bomb: The Nuclear Arms Race in the Middle East* (IB Tauris: London, 1989), p. 40.

[21] Ma, C. Y. and von Hippel, F., 'Ending the production of HEU for naval reactors', *Nonproliferation Review*, vol. 8 no. 1 (spring 2001), pp. 86–107.

[22] Albright, Berkhout and Walker (note 10), pp. 88, 112.

[23] Most of Russia's nuclear submarines are believed to be fuelled by uranium enriched to 21–45%. Ma and von Hippel (note 20).

[24] See International Atomic Energy Agency, The National Report of the Russian Federation on Compliance with the Obligations of the Joint Convention on the Safety of Spent Fuel Management and the Safety of Radioactive Waste Management, Moscow, 2006, URL <http://www-ns.iaea.org/conventions/waste-jointconvention.htm>, p. 14. Sea trials of the newest Russian icebreaker, the *50 Let Pobedy* [50 Years of Victory], took place in Jan. 2007. See Novosti, 'Russia tests nuclear icebreaker on open sea', 23 Feb. 2007, URL <http://en.rian.ru/russia/20070131/59989100.html>.

[25] International Atomic Energy Agency (IAEA), *Annual Report 2005* (IAEA: Vienna, 2006). Table A20 shows that 19.4 tonnes of HEU are under IAEA safeguards in the non-nuclear weapon states. An unofficial breakdown by the Institute for Science and International Security shows that about 11 tonnes of this material was in Kazakhstan—mostly in fresh and spent fuel associated with the shut-down

in the fuel cycles of civilian research reactors worldwide and of Russia's nuclear-powered civilian vessels.[26] Even though this material currently represents only a small percentage of the global total, it would be sufficient for about 1000 gun-type nuclear weapons and more than twice as many implosion-type weapons. Also, this HEU is located at more than 100 sites, many of which are inherently difficult to secure. This civilian HEU is currently the object of a global clean-out campaign in which research reactors are being converted to LEU and excess civilian HEU is being blended down. This programme is, however, far from comprehensive.[27]

The global stock of HEU is shrinking. In 1993 Russia contracted for 500 tonnes of 90 per cent enriched uranium in redundant warheads to be blended down to LEU with 4–5 per cent U-235 to be sold to the USA for use as power-reactor fuel.[28] As of 31 December 2006, 292 tonnes had been blended down, the equivalent of almost 11 700 nuclear bombs.[29] In 1994 the USA similarly declared 174 tonnes of its weapon-grade HEU to be excess[30] and began to blend down most of it to LEU for use as fuel in US power reactors. As of July 2006, about 87 tonnes had been blended down.[31]

In late 2005 the USA declared an additional 200 tonnes of HEU to be excess. However, only 52 tonnes of this material will be blended down to LEU. Of the remainder, 128 tonnes of weapon-grade uranium will be reserved for British and US naval-reactor fuel, and 20 tonnes for space reactors and research reactors.[32] If Russia has similarly reserved the equivalent of 100 tonnes of weapon-grade uranium for future naval-reactor use, this would leave 370–970 tonnes of HEU in Russia's weapon stockpile and 320 tonnes in the US weapon stockpile.

If Russia and the USA reduced their stocks of nuclear warheads to 1000 each—as many analysts believe they could before expecting other countries to join them in similar disarmament measures[33]—then they would each only require about 30 tonnes

---

BN-350 fast-neutron power and desalination reactor whose fresh fuel was enriched to up to 26%. URL <http://www.isis-online.org/global_stocks/end2003/civil_heu_watch2005.pdf>; In 2005, the Nuclear Threat Initiative announced that the unused BN-350 fresh fuel (containing 2.9 tonnes of HEU) had been blended down. Nuclear Threat Initiative (NTI), 'Government of Kazakhstan and NTI mark success of HEU blend-down project', Press release, 8 Oct. 2005. The U-235 in the spent BN-350 fuel is probably mostly fissioned down to less than 20% enrichment.

[26] Glaser, A. and von Hippel, F., 'Global cleanout: reducing the threat of HEU-fueled nuclear terrorism', *Arms Control Today*, Jan./Feb. 2006, pp. 18–23.

[27] Glaser and von Hippel (note 25).

[28] Russian–US Agreement Concerning the Disposition of Highly Enriched Uranium Extracted from Nuclear Weapons, signed on 18 Feb. 1993 at Washington, DC.

[29] US Enrichment Corporation, 'Progress report: US–Russian megatons to megawatts program', 31 Dec. 2006, URL <http://www.usec.com/v2001_02/HTML/Megatons_status.asp>.

[30] In 2001 this number was revised to 178 tonnes, but more recent statements by the US Department of Energy (DOE) quote the earlier quantity of 174 tonnes. US DOE (note 12), p. 2.

[31] Tobey, W., Deputy Administrator for Defense Nuclear Nonproliferation, US National Nuclear Security Administration, testimony before the US House Government Reform Committee Subcommittee on National Security, Emerging Threats, and International Relations, 26 Sep. 2006.

[32] Presentation by Samuel Bodman, US Secretary of Energy, to the 2005 Carnegie International Non-proliferation Conference, 7–8 Nov. 2005, URL <http://www.carnegieendowment.org/static/npp/2005 conference/2005_conference.htm#Bodman/>. Bodman originally announced that 160 of the 200 tonnes would be reserved for naval-reactor fuel. However, 40 of the 160 tonnes was later found to be unsuitable for that use. Presentation by Robert George and Dean Tousley, US Department of Energy, 'US Highly Enriched Uranium Disposition', to the Nuclear Energy Institute Fuel Supply Forum, 24 Jan. 2006— available at URL <http://www.pogo.org/m/hsp/Y12/appendix-F.pdf>.

[33] Feiveson, H. (ed.), *The Nuclear Turning Point: A Blueprint for Deep Cuts and De-alerting of Nuclear Weapons* (Brookings: Washington, DC, 1999), pp. 136–37.

Table 12C.2. Global stocks of separated plutonium

Country	Military stocks, as of December 2005 (tonnes)	Military production status	Civilian stocks as of December 2005, unless indicated (tonnes)
Belgium	0		3.3 in Belgium + 0.4 abroad (end of 2004)
China	4 ± 2	Stopped in 1991	0
France	5 ± 1.25	Stopped in 1994	81.2 (includes 30 foreign owned)
Germany	0		20–25 in France, Germany and the UK
India[a]	0.52	Continuing	5.4
Israel	0.45 ± 0.11	Continuing	0
Japan	0		5.9 in Japan + a total of 38 in France and the UK
North Korea	0.035 ± 0.018	Continuing	0
Pakistan	0.064	Continuing	0
Russia[b]	145 ± 25 (34–50 declared excess)	Effectively stopped in 1997	41.2
Switzerland	0		Up to a total of 2 in France and the UK
UK	7.6 (4.4 declared excess)	Stopped in 1989	104.9 (includes 27 foreign owned and 1 abroad)
USA[c]	92 (45 declared excess)	Stopped in 1988	0
Totals	**~255 ± 28 (up to 100 declared excess)**		**~245**

[a] In 2005 US President George W. Bush and India's Prime Minister Mohanman Singh proposed that India separate its military and civilian nuclear activities and submit its civilian nuclear activities to IAEA monitoring in exchange for access to materials and technology in the international market to support its civilian nuclear programme. Consequently, India has proposed to include in the military sector much of the plutonium separated from India's spent power-reactor fuel that is labelled civilian here.

[b] The military plutonium holdings of the NPT-signatory nuclear weapon states were unchanged between 2003 and 2005, except for Russia, which is producing about 1.2 tonnes of weapon-grade plutonium annually in 3 production reactors that continue to operate because they also produce heat and electricity for nearby communities. Russia has committed not to use this material for weapons.

[c] In its IAEA INFCIRC/549 statement of 4 Nov. 2005, the USA declared as civilian stocks a total of 45 tonnes of material described as plutonium contained in unirradiated MOX fuel or other forms, and unirradiated separated plutonium held elsewhere.

Sources: Institute for Science and International Security (ISIS), 'Global stocks of nuclear explosive materials', Dec. 2003, URL <http://www.isis-online.org/global_stocks/end2003/tableofcontents.html>; Military production status: Albright, D., Berkhout, F. and Walker, W., SIPRI, *Plutonium and Highly Enriched Uranium 1996: World Inventories, Capabilities, and Policies* (Oxford University Press: Oxford, 1997); Civilian stocks (except for India): declarations by country to the International Atomic Energy Agency (IAEA) under INFCIRC/549, 31 Mar 1998, URL <http://www.iaea.org/Publications/Documents/Infcircs/index.html>; **India:** Estimate based on assuming 50% of India's accumulated heavy-water reactor spent fuel has been reprocessed. Mian, Z. et al., *Fissile Materials in South Asia and*

of HEU for weapons, including material used for research and development (R&D) and in working inventories. On this scale, the 250 or so tonnes of HEU that the USA and Russia have so far kept in reserve for naval-propulsion and other reactors is a huge amount. This suggests that the question of HEU-fuelled reactors will have to be dealt with before it can become politically feasible to make such deep cuts in the stockpiles of weapon-grade HEU.

Separated plutonium

The global stockpile of separated plutonium is a little over 500 tonnes. It is divided almost equally between weapon and civilian stocks, but it is all weapon-usable. It is held mostly in nuclear weapon states, but Japan and a few non-nuclear weapon states in Europe also have significant stocks (see table 12C.2).

France, the UK and the USA have officially announced that they have stopped producing and separating plutonium for use in weapons, and China has given unofficial indications to that effect. Russia continues to produce about 1.2 tonnes of separated weapon-grade plutonium per year as an unwanted by-product of the continued operation of three plutonium-production reactors, which supply heat and power to local populations. Russia and the USA are cooperating on a project to refurbish and build coal-fired district heating plants to make it possible to shut down these reactors.[34] To the best of the authors' knowledge, India, Israel, North Korea and Pakistan have not stopped their production of plutonium for weapons.

Russia and the USA own virtually all of the world's stock of military plutonium: 120–170 and 92 tonnes, respectively. Russia has declared 34–50 tonnes of weapon plutonium as excess, and the USA has declared as excess 45 tonnes of government-owned plutonium.[35] However, they could declare considerably more. Assuming that in the average Russian or US warhead there is 4 kg of plutonium, each country would require about 30 tonnes of weapon-grade plutonium to support the roughly 6000 warheads that they are each expected to retain up to 2012, including R&D and process inventories. Thus, Russia and the USA could declare as excess over half and about one-third, respectively, of their remaining stockpiles. If they reduced the number of

---

[34] Nuclear Threat Initiative (NTI), 'Plutonium production reactor shutdown,' URL <http://www.nti.org/e_research/cnwm/ending/plutonium.asp/>.

[35] At their 2 Sep. 1998 summit, US President Bill Clinton and Russian President Boris Yeltsin declared the intentions of the USA and Russia to 'remove by stages approximately 50 tonnes of plutonium from their nuclear weapons programs, and to convert this material so that it can never be used in nuclear weapons'. However, because only 34 tonnes of the US material declared excess was from its weapon programme, the US–Russian Plutonium Management and Disposition Agreement, signed at Moscow on 1 Sep. 2000, covered only 34 tonnes each. In its Nov. 2005 INFCIRC/549 statement to the International Atomic Energy Agency the USA declared as civilian stocks a total of 45 tonnes, described as 'plutonium contained in unirradiated MOX fuel or other forms' and 'unirradiated separated plutonium held elsewhere'. It also declared excess 7.5 tonnes of plutonium in government-owned spent fuel.

their nuclear weapons to 1000 each, Russia and the USA would require perhaps only 5 tonnes of weapon-grade plutonium each.[36]

Large quantities of plutonium have been separated from civilian spent fuel in reprocessing plants in a few countries. Some of this plutonium has been mixed with uranium and then fabricated into mixed-oxide (MOX) fuel and used in light-water reactors (LWRs).[37] However, most of it remains stockpiled in reprocessing plants at La Hague in France, Sellafield in the UK and at the Mayak plant in Ozersk, Russia. A similarly large stockpile is expected to build up at Japan's new Rokkasho Reprocessing Plant. The global total of separated civilian plutonium is about 250 tonnes, about as much as has been produced for weapons, and is still growing.

The fact that the amount of civilian separated plutonium already exceeds the amount of weapon plutonium that has not been declared excess could complicate future negotiations on nuclear arms reductions if the issue of eliminating additional excess weapon plutonium is confronted.

III. The production and disposition of fissile materials

The production of HEU and plutonium both start with natural uranium. HEU is produced by enriching natural uranium to increase the percentage of U-235. Plutonium is produced in nuclear reactors through the exposure of U-238 to neutron radiation and is subsequently separated in a reprocessing operation. The five nuclear weapon states party to the NPT have produced both weapon-grade uranium and plutonium. India, Israel and North Korea have produced mainly plutonium, and Pakistan mainly HEU. The potential for production of HEU and plutonium is also inherent in the civilian nuclear fuel cycle.

Highly enriched uranium production

Since natural uranium contains only about 0.7 per cent of the chain-reacting U-235 and about 99.3 per cent of the non-chain-reacting U-238, it has to be enriched in U-235 to be usable in nuclear weapons. Natural uranium must also be enriched in order to fuel LWRs, but only to 3–5 per cent U-235, which is not weapon-usable.

The isotopes U-235 and U-238 are chemically almost identical, differing in weight by only about 1 per cent, which means that they are very difficult to separate either chemically or physically. Only a small number of states possess the enrichment capacity to separate these isotopes from LWR fuel on a scale sufficient to make nuclear weapons. However, even a small enrichment plant such as the one that Iran proposes to build at Natanz, which is designed to fuel only a single 1000 megawatts-electric (MW(e)) power reactor, could make enough HEU for tens of nuclear bombs a year.[38]

---

[36] This estimate assumes 4 kg of plutonium per warhead and a working inventory and R&D stock of about 20%.

[37] LWRs use ordinary water to slow the neutrons in the nuclear reaction and to cool the reactor core.

[38] In any enrichment facility, the feed (e.g. natural uranium) is split into 2 streams: the product stream enriched in U-235, and the waste (or 'tails') stream depleted in U-235. The work required is measured in separative work units (SWU). Similarly, the capacity of enrichment facilities is commonly measured in SWU per year (SWU/yr). Thus, for example, if 0.2% of the U-235 is left in the depleted uranium, it takes about 150 tonnes of natural uranium feed and 130 000 SWU to produce 20 tonnes per year of uranium enriched to 4 % U-235, a typical annual fuel requirement for a 1000 MW(e) LWR reactor. For 0.3% U-235 in the depleted uranium, a plant with a separative capacity of 130 000 SWU/yr could use the

Thus, the uranium feed and the enrichment capacity required to sustain even a small civil nuclear power programme based on LWRs would offer a platform for a significant weapon programme.

There are several demonstrated methods for enriching uranium, but today the two main techniques that are used on a commercial scale are gaseous diffusion and gas centrifuges. France and the USA still operate gaseous diffusion plants but both countries plan to switch to more economical gas centrifuge enrichment technology. Table 12C.3 shows the current operational status of enrichment facilities worldwide.

In a modern gas centrifuge, uranium is fed into a rotor in gaseous form (uranium hexafluoride, UF_6) and is rotated at enormous speeds so that the UF_6 is pressed against the wall of the rotor with more than 100 000 times the force of gravity. The centrifugal force pushes the heavier U-238 closer to the wall than the lighter U-235. The gas closer to the wall becomes depleted in U-235, whereas the gas closer to the axis of the rotor is enriched in U-235. This effect is exploited to separate the two isotopes.

Both the throughput of material and the enrichment achieved by a single machine are very small, so the process is repeated tens of times in a system of hundreds or thousands of interconnected centrifuges (a 'cascade') to produce uranium enriched to the 3–5 per cent level used in most LWRs (the most common type of reactor). If the cascade is extended to three times as many stages, or the uranium is recycled through the cascade three or four times, then weapon-grade uranium can be produced.

From a non-proliferation perspective, centrifuge technology has two major disadvantages relative to gaseous diffusion technology. First, the inventory in a centrifuge plant is only tens of kilograms, while it is more than 1000 tonnes in a large gaseous diffusion plant. This means that it could take only days to reconfigure and refill a centrifuge cascade for HEU production, while it would take months in the case of a gaseous diffusion plant. This makes centrifuge plants more susceptible to a 'breakout' scenario, in which peaceful technology is quickly converted to weapon use.

Second, clandestine centrifuge facilities are virtually impossible to detect with remote sensing techniques. A centrifuge plant with a capacity to make enough HEU for a bomb or two per year could be small and indistinguishable from many other industrial facilities. Furthermore, unlike gaseous diffusion enrichment plants, which require huge amounts of electric power to operate, centrifuge plants have low power consumption and therefore no unusual thermal signatures compared to other types of factories with comparable floor areas. Leakage of UF_6 to the atmosphere from centrifuge facilities is also minimal (and therefore difficult to detect) because the gas in the pipes is below atmospheric pressure. Air therefore leaks into the centrifuges rather than the UF_6 leaking out.[39]

From a technical perspective, the disposal of HEU is simple and straightforward. The material can be blended down to LEU by mixing it with depleted, natural or slightly enriched uranium. As noted above, both Russia and the USA are blending down some of their excess weapon-grade uranium. This process cannot be reversed

---

same amount of natural uranium feed to produce about 650 kg/year of weapon-grade uranium (93% U-235). For an extensive technical overview of uranium enrichment and proliferation risks see Krass, A. S. et al., SIPRI, *Uranium Enrichment and Nuclear Weapon Proliferation* (Taylor & Francis: London, 1983), URL <http://www.sipri.org/contents/publications/Krass83.html>.

[39] A small amount of UF_6 does leak out when the containers are connected to and disconnected from the cascade.

Table 12C.3. Significant uranium enrichment facilities and capacity worldwide, as of December 2005

Country	Facility name/ location	Type	Status	Enrichment process[a]	Capacity (thousands SWU/yr)[b]
Brazil	Resende Enrichment	Civilian	Under construction	GC	120
China	Lanzhou 2	Civilian	Operational	GC	500
	Shaanxi Enrichment Plant	Civilian	Operational	GC	500
France	Eurodif (Georges Besse)	Civilian	Operational	GD	10 800
	Georges Besse II	Civilian	Planned	GC	7 500
Germany	Urenco[c] Deutschland	Civilian	Operational	GC	1 800/4 500
India	Rattehali	Military	Operational	GC	4–10
Iran	Natanz	Civilian	Under construction	GC	100–250
Japan	Rokkasho Enrichment Plant	Civilian	Operational	GC	1050
Netherlands	Urenco Nederland	Civilian	Operational	GC	2 500/3 500
Pakistan	Kahuta	Military	Operational	GC	15–20
Russia	Angarsk	Civilian	Operational	GC	2 350
	Novouralsk	Civilian	Operational	GC	12 160
	Seversk	Civilian	Operational	GC	3 550
	Zelenogorsk	Civilian	Operational	GC	7 210
UK	Capenhurst	Civilian	Operational	GC	4 000
USA	Paducah	Civilian	Operational	GD	11 300
	Piketon, Ohio	Civilian	Planned	GC	3 500
	Portsmouth	Civilian	Standby	GD	7 400
	Eunice, NM (LES/Urenco)	Civilian	Planned	GC	3 000

[a] GC = gas centrifuge; GD = gaseous diffusion. Apart from some laboratory facilities, all enrichment facilities today use the GD or GC process.

[b] SWU/yr = Separative work units per year: a SWU is a measure of the effort required in an enrichment facility to separate uranium of a given content of uranium-235 into 2 components, 1 with a higher and 1 with a lower percentage of uranium-235.

[c] Capacities for Urenco facilities also show scheduled expansions.

Sources: Except where indicated below, enrichment capacity data are based on International Atomic Energy Agency (IAEA), Nuclear Fuel Cycle Information System (NFCIS), Feb. 2006, URL <http://www-nfcis.iaea.org/Default.asp>; **China**: IAEA, *Country Nuclear Fuel Cycle Profiles*, 2nd edn, (IAEA: Vienna 2005); **India**: Ramana, M. V., 'An estimate of India's uranium enrichment capacity', *Science & Global Security*, vol. 12 (2004); **Iran**: Estimates for the Natanz facility assumes 50 000 machines with a capacity of 2–5 SWU/yr each. Hibbs, M., 'Current capacity at Natanz Plant about 2500 SWU/year, data suggest,' *Nuclear Fuel*, 31 Jan. 2005; **Pakistan**: Albright, D., Berkhout, F. and Walker, W., SIPRI, *Plutonium and Highly Enriched Uranium 1996: World Inventories, Capabilities and Policies* (Oxford University Press: Oxford, 1997); **Russia**: International Business Relations Corporation, *Russian Enrichment Industry, State & Prospects. Annual Report 2004* (Department of Nuclear Power & Nuclear Fuel Cycle: Moscow, 2005), Fig. 5.1 (data for 2000–10); **USA**: Estimates for planned facilities based on Nuclear Regulatory Commission, 'Gas centrifuge enrichment facility licensing', 25 Aug. 2006, URL <http://www.nrc.gov/materials/fuel-cycle-fac/gas-centrifuge.html>.

without re-enrichment. It is economically attractive since the product (LEU) can be sold for use as commercial reactor fuel at a price several times higher than the cost of the blending-down process.

Plutonium production

Plutonium is produced in nuclear reactors. Almost all reactors dedicated to the production of plutonium for weapons use natural uranium as fuel. In such reactors, about 0.9 grams of plutonium are produced per gram of U-235 fissioned or, almost equivalently, per megawatt-day. For example, India's CIRUS research reactor, which generates 40 MW(t), would—at 70 per cent capacity—produce about 9.2 kg of weapon-grade plutonium annually.[40]

Plutonium is also produced in civilian power reactors. In LWRs the net plutonium production is only 0.2–0.3 g of plutonium per megawatt-day, because most of the plutonium is fissioned *in situ* during its long residence in the reactor core. A 1000-MW(e) (3000-MW(t)) LWR, operating at 90 per cent of its capacity, produces about 250 kg of plutonium per year. Because the burn-up of the fuel is much higher than in production reactors, more than 40 per cent of the plutonium produced consists of heavier plutonium isotopes.

In heavy-water reactors (HWRs), which use water enriched in deuterium and are fuelled with natural uranium, production of plutonium per megawatt-day is about twice as high as in LWRs and the fraction of heavier isotopes in the plutonium is smaller—about 25 per cent. CANDU (Canadian Deuterium–Uranium) reactors, the dominant HWR type, are refuelled continuously, instead of every 18–24 months as in the case of LWRs. This means that international monitoring of the fuel is more costly.

Global civil nuclear capacity grew rapidly during the 1970s and 1980s. Later, public opposition, high costs, unresolved waste issues and the 1979 Three Mile Island and 1986 Chernobyl accidents led to a sharp decline in new orders for nuclear power plants worldwide. As of the end of 2006, the world nuclear capacity stood at about 370 gigawatts-electric (GW(e)), almost 90 per cent of which was in LWRs.[41]

The total spent fuel generated annually by the world's reactors is approximately 10 000 tonnes, containing about 75 tonnes of plutonium. Less than one-quarter of the spent fuel generated each year is reprocessed. The remainder is stored at reactor sites.

Several countries have produced prototype sodium-cooled reactors that, when fuelled by plutonium, can produce more fissile plutonium than they consume. When they are configured in this way, they are known as breeder reactors. The cores of such reactors are surrounded by natural or depleted uranium blankets. The plutonium that builds up in these blankets is weapon-grade, typically with a Pu-239 fraction of more than 95 per cent. Although the uranium-based spent fuel of all reactors contains substantial amounts of plutonium, as long as the plutonium remains embedded in the spent fuel along with the highly radioactive fission products, it is dilute and difficult to access. The fuel elements containing the spent fuel can only be handled remotely

---

[40] MW(t) refers to the total power that a reactor generates, while MW(e) refers to the electrical power that a reactor generates. Megawatt-day (MW-day) denotes the total energy that would be produced in a 24-hour period by a reactor producing power at a constant rate of 1 MW(t). The fission of 1 g of uranium or plutonium releases about 1 MW-day of energy.

[41] International Atomic Energy Agency (IAEA), IAEA Power Reactor Information System (PRIS), 19 Jan. 2007, URL <http://www.iaea.org/programmes/a2>.

Table 12C.4. Significant reprocessing facilities worldwide, as of December 2005

All facilities process light-water reactor (LWR) fuel, except where indicated.

Country	Facility name /location	Type	Status	Design capacity (tHM/yr)[a]
France	La Hague UP2	Civilian	Operational	1000
	La Hague UP3	Civilian	Operational	1000
India[b]	Trombay (HWR fuel)[c]	Military	Operational	50
	Tarapur (HWR fuel)	Unclear	Operational	100
	Kalpakkam (HWR fuel)	Unclear	Operational	100
Israel	Dimona (HWR fuel)	Military	Operational	40–100
Japan	JNC Tokai	Civilian	Operational	210
	Rokkasho	Civilian	Operational	800
Pakistan	Nilore (HWR fuel)	Military	Operational	10–20
Russia	Mayak RT-1, Ozersk (formerly Chelyabinsk-65)	Civilian	Operational	400
	Seversk (formerly Tomsk 7)	Military	Operational	6000
	Zheleznogorsk (formerly Krasnoyarsk-26)	Military	Operational	3500
UK	BNFL B205 Magnox, Sellafield (graphite-moderated reactor fuel)	Civilian	Operational	1500
	BNFL Thorp, Sellafield	Civilian	Shut down, future uncertain	900

HWR = Heavy water reactor.

[a] Design capacity refers to the highest amount of spent fuel the plant is designed to process and is measured in tonnes of heavy metal per year (tHM/yr), tHM being a measure of the amount of heavy metal—uranium in these cases—that is in the spent fuel. Actual throughput is often a small fraction of the design capacity. E.g. Russia's RT-1 plant has never reprocessed more than 130 tHM/yr and France, because of the non-renewal of its foreign contracts will soon only reprocess 850 tHM/yr. LWR spent fuel contains about 1% plutonium, and heavy-water- and graphite-moderated reactor fuel about 0.4%.

[b] As part of the 2005 Indian–US nuclear deal, India has decided that none of its reprocessing plants will be opened for IAEA safeguards inspections.

Sources: Except where indicated below, data on design capacity are based on International Atomic Energy Agency (IAEA), Nuclear Fuel Cycle Information System (NFCIS), Feb. 2006, URL <http://www-nfcis.iaea.org/>; **India**: Mian, Z. and Nayyar, A. H., 'An initial analysis of Kr-85 production and dispersion from reprocessing in India and Pakistan', *Science and Global Security*, vol. 10, no. 3 (2002) pp. 151–79; **Israel**: Estimate inferred from Albright, D., Berkhout, F. and Walker, W., SIPRI, *Plutonium and Highly Enriched Uranium 1996: World Inventories, Capabilities and Policies* (Oxford University Press: Oxford, 1997); **Pakistan**: Mian and Nayyar (above); **Russia**: Estimates for Seversk and Zheleznogorsk facilities are based on Bukharin, O. A., Cochran, T. and Norris R. S., *Making the Russian Bomb: From Stalin to Yeltsin* (Westview: Boulder, Colo., 1995), pp. 280, 291; Data for plutonium concentration in spent fuel are based on Gesh, C. J. et al., 'Summary of near-term options for Russian plutonium production reactors', Pacific Northwest National Laboratory, PNL-9982, July 1994, p. 9.

owing to the very intense radiation field generated by the fission products, which makes their theft a rather unrealistic scenario.[42] Separated plutonium emits very little penetrating radiation, however, and is directly weapon usable.

Reprocessing

Separation of plutonium is carried out in a reprocessing facility. With the method that is currently used—plutonium and uranium recovery by extraction (PUREX)—spent fuel is chopped into small pieces and dissolved in hot nitric acid. The plutonium is then extracted into an organic solvent, which is mixed with the nitric acid using blenders and pulse columns and then separated with centrifugal extractors. Because all of this has to be done behind heavy shielding and with remote handling, reprocessing requires both resources and expertise. However, detailed descriptions of the process have been available in the technical literature since the 1950s.

At present, France, India, Japan, Russia and the UK are carrying out large-scale reprocessing and recovery of plutonium from civilian spent fuel (see table 12C.4). This civilian separation of plutonium stemmed originally from the interest of the industrialized countries in commercializing plutonium breeder reactors. Interest peaked in the 1970s, driven by an expectation that the world's nuclear generating capacity would grow to thousands of gigawatts by the year 2000 and approach 10 000 GW(e) in 2020.[43] Such a huge capacity could not have been supported by known reserves of high-grade uranium ore.

Efforts to commercialize plutonium breeder reactors have failed, however, because of their high cost and technical difficulties.[44] A few countries in Western Europe are therefore using their separated plutonium mixed with uranium to make MOX fuel for conventional LWRs as a substitute for standard LEU fuel. This is not a particularly economically attractive strategy because MOX fuel fabrication is costly. Furthermore, one recycle reduces the amount of plutonium by only about one-third. The spent MOX is being stored. Reprocessing continues in France and Japan largely because of local resistance to both indefinite storage of spent fuel on reactor sites and to the siting of centralized interim or long-term storage facilities.[45] However, all the

---

[42] E.g. consider the dose rate from a pressurized water reactor (PWR) fuel assembly to an unshielded person. A typical PWR assembly contains about 500 kg of uranium. The fuel has a burn-up of up to 50 000 MW-days per tonne and contains about 6 kg of plutonium. Even after 15 years of cooling, a person 1 metre from such a fuel assembly would receive a lethal dose of radiation in a few minutes. A person 5 m away would receive a lethal dose in a couple of hours. Lloyd, W. R., Sheaffer, M. K. and Sutcliffe, W. G., 'Dose rate estimates from irradiated light-water-reactor fuel assemblies in air', Lawrence Livermore National Laboratory, 1994, URL <http://www.osti.gov/energycitations/product. biblio.jsp?osti_id=10137382>, p. 3. After the first decade from discharge, the dose rate declines by roughly a factor of 2 every 30 years.

[43] See e.g. US Atomic Energy Commission, 'Proposed final environmental statement on the liquid metal fast breeder reactor program', Washington, DC, 1974.

[44] A list of 11 shutdown and 8 operational fast-neutron reactors as of 1995 is given in Albright, Berkhout and Walker (note 10), p. 196. Since that time, 2 more reactors (Kazakhstan's BN-350 and France's Superphénix) have been shut down permanently, 1 (Japan's Monju) was shut down for more than a decade by a sodium fire, and France's Phénix is scheduled to be shut down. Russia's BN-600 has operated at an average of 74% of its capacity since 1980 but has been plagued with 15 sodium fires in 23 years. Bakanov, M. V., Oshkanov, N. N. and Potapov, O. A., 'Experience in operating the BN-600 unit at the Belyiyar nuclear power plant', *Atomic Energy 96*, no. 5 (2004), p. 315.

[45] See e.g. Katsuta, T. and Suzuki, T., *Japan's Spent Fuel and Plutonium Management Challenge* (International Panel on Fissile Materials: Princeton, N.J., Sep. 2006), URL <http://www.fissilematerials. org/ipfm/site_down/ipfmresearchreport02.pdf>.

foreign customers of the French, Russian and British reprocessing companies appear to be shifting to interim domestic spent fuel storage because of the high costs of reprocessing and the fact that interim storage must be found for the repatriated reprocessing waste in any case.

Russia and the UK are simply storing their separated plutonium, and Japan has delayed its plutonium-recycling programme by a decade because of local opposition, provoked in part by reports of accident cover-ups and falsified quality control information. As a result, the global stockpile of separated civilian plutonium has been growing steadily for decades. From 1996—when all countries with civilian separated plutonium stocks (except India) agreed to publicly declare their civilian plutonium holdings annually to the IAEA—to 2005, the global stockpile rose from 160 tonnes to 250 tonnes, not including the plutonium declared excess for weapons use by Russia and the USA.

Japan's new reprocessing plant began operation in 2006, meaning that the growth of the global stockpile of separated civilian plutonium will continue for some time even if the UK ends its reprocessing operations by 2012, as currently planned. The USA abandoned reprocessing in the late 1970s for economic and non-proliferation reasons. The US Administration of President George W. Bush has recently embraced reprocessing, however, as part of its proposed Global Nuclear Energy Partnership.[46] This initiative—like Japan's reprocessing—is also driven principally by pressures to begin removing spent fuel from power reactor sites.[47]

Plutonium disposition

The debate on the management and irreversible disposal of separated plutonium inventories has focused primarily on the weapon plutonium declared excess by both Russia and the USA. The options were laid out in the 1990s when the US National Academy of Sciences published two extensive studies on the subject.[48] Most of the considerations are equally applicable, however, to the disposition of civilian stocks of separated plutonium that are accumulating in Europe, Russia and—soon—Japan.

One option is to store excess inventories of separated plutonium indefinitely in high-security facilities, such as that built with US assistance near the Mayak reprocessing facility in Russia,[49] and the UK's Sellafield reprocessing plant. This approach is only as effective, however, as the institution responsible for security. In 1998, a report by the Royal Society of London expressed deep concern over the fact that at some stage the UK's very large stockpile of separated civilian (but weapon-usable)

---

[46] See the website of the US DOE's Global Nuclear Energy Partnership at URL <http://www.gnep.energy.gov/>.

[47] See e.g. von Hippel, F., *Management of Spent Fuel in the United States: The Illogic of Reprocessing* (International Panel on Fissile Materials: Princeton, N.J., Jan. 2007), URL <http://www.ipfmlibrary.org/ipfmresearchreport03.pdf>.

[48] National Academy of Sciences, *Management and Disposition of Excess Weapons Plutonium* (National Academy Press: Washington, DC, 1994); and National Academy of Sciences, *Management and Disposition of Excess Weapons Plutonium: Reactor-Related Options* (National Academy Press: Washington, DC, 1995). These studies built on analyses in an earlier article. See Berkhout, F. et al., 'Disposition of separated plutonium', *Science and Global Security*, vol. 3 (1993), pp. 161–213.

[49] See the discussion of the history of this facility, the construction of which was subsidized by the USA, in Bunn, M. and Weir, A., 'Securing nuclear warheads and materials', Nuclear Threat Initiative, Washington, DC, July 2006, URL <http://www.nti.org/e_research/cnwm/securing/mayak.asp>.

plutonium might be accessed for illicit weapon production.[50] If this is a concern in the UK, it should be a concern in any country with significant quantities of separated plutonium.

Aside from storage, all options under consideration for disposing of separated plutonium involve mixing it with fission products, either produced by neutron irradiation after fabrication into reactor fuel or through mixing with fission-product waste from reprocessing. The effectiveness of this approach is often measured by the spent-fuel standard, which was defined by the US National Academy of Sciences as the objective of making excess plutonium as inaccessible for weapon use as the much larger and growing stock of plutonium in spent fuel.[51]

One way to do this is by mixing the plutonium with uranium to make MOX fuel and then irradiating the fuel in power reactors. MOX fuel containing about 4–8 per cent plutonium mixed with depleted uranium can be used as an alternative to LEU fuel in a LWR.[52] In a second approach, the plutonium would be mixed with existing fission products in highly radioactive reprocessing waste, or with spent fuel, to create a radiological barrier.[53]

In the long term (after a century or so of cooling), the gamma-radiation field around spent fuel will die down to levels that are no longer dangerous enough to deter handling, and additional protective barriers such as deep underground storage would be required.

Russia and the USA each agreed in 2000 to eliminate 34 tonnes of weapon plutonium.[54] However, Russia agreed only on the conditions that its plutonium and most of the US plutonium be disposed of in MOX fuel and that the governments of the other members of the Group of Eight (G8) industrialized nations fund the building and operation of the necessary infrastructure in Russia to fabricate MOX fuel.[55] Implementation of the agreement was stalled for years by disputes between Russia and the USA with regard to immunity from liability of US contractors in Russia.[56] The governments of the G8 states have committed $800 million, but that is not enough to cover both the construction and operation of a MOX-fuel fabrication plant. The estimated cost of constructing the US MOX facility increased from less than $1 billion to $4.9 billion between 2002 and 2006.[57] In 2006 the US Congress began to reassess this

[50] Royal Society of London, *Management of Separated Plutonium* (Royal Society: London, 1 Feb. 1998), URL <http://www.royalsoc.ac.uk/document.asp?tip=1&id=1915>.

[51] National Academy of Sciences, *Management and Disposition of Excess Weapons Plutonium* (note 47), p. 34. The US Department of Energy put the standard in different but essentially equivalent words: 'A concept to make the plutonium as unattractive and inaccessible for retrieval and weapons use as the residual plutonium in the spent fuel from commercial reactors'. US Department of Energy (DOE), Office of Fissile Material Disposition, *Technical Summary Report for Surplus Weapons-Usable Plutonium Disposition*, DOE/MD-0003 Rev. 1 (DOE: Washington, DC, 1996), URL <http://www.fas.org/nuke/control/fmd/docs/PUD71996.htm>.

[52] Organisation for Economic Co-operation and Development (OECD) Nuclear Energy Agency, *Plutonium Fuel: An Assessment* (OECD: Paris, 1989), pp. 50–51.

[53] On the options for disposition with spent fuel see von Hippel, F. et al., 'Storage MOX: a third way for plutonium disposal?', *Science and Global Security*, vol. 10 (2002), p. 85.

[54] The US–Russian Plutonium Management and Disposition Agreement was signed at Moscow on 1 Sep. 2000.

[55] The members of the G8 are listed in the glossary in this volume.

[56] The issue was finally resolved in 2006—see chapter 12 in this volume; and US Department of Energy, Office of Public Affairs, 'US and Russia sign liability protocol', 15 Sep. 2006, URL <http://www.energy.gov/print/4160.htm>.

[57] US Department of Energy (DOE), Office of the Inspector General, Office of Audit Services, 'Status of the mixed oxide fuel fabrication facility', DOE/IG-173, Washington, DC, 21 Dec. 2005.

programme and considered the idea of decoupling the Russian and US plutonium disposition programmes and shifting the focus of the US programme to the option of immobilizing the plutonium with fission products.[58]

IV. Conclusions

At present, there are roughly 1700 tonnes of HEU and 500 tonnes of separated plutonium in the world, enough for more than 100 000 nuclear weapons. Virtually all the HEU and about half the plutonium are a legacy of the nuclear arms race of the cold war. Russia and the USA could reduce their stockpiles of weapon materials by about 90 per cent and still each have enough for 1000 nuclear warheads—roughly as many as the rest of the nuclear weapon states combined.

About 250 tonnes of plutonium has been separated from civilian spent nuclear power-reactor fuel, mostly in France, Russia and the UK. The growing stock of civilian separated plutonium will soon be significantly larger than the amount of weapon plutonium. This could complicate future negotiations on nuclear arms reductions if the issue of eliminating excess weapon plutonium is confronted.

Russia, the UK and the USA have reserved very large stocks of weapon-usable HEU for future use in their naval reactors. The USA alone has declared a naval reserve of weapon-grade uranium that is large enough to make approximately 5000 nuclear warheads. This suggests that the question of HEU-fuelled reactors will have to be dealt with before deep cuts in the stockpiles of weapon HEU become politically feasible.

There remain large uncertainties about the size of fissile material stockpiles held by various countries. Declarations of fissile material stocks and greater transparency about production histories and disposition would build confidence for further reductions in the stockpiles of weapon fissile materials and will be necessary if nuclear disarmament is to be achieved.

---

[58] 'House appropriators deliver blow to DOE's GNEP, MOX programs', *Nuclear Fuel*, 22 May 2006.

13. Chemical and biological weapon developments and arms control

JOHN HART and FRIDA KUHLAU

I. Introduction

The Sixth Review Conference of the States Parties to the 1972 Biological and Toxin Weapons Convention (BTWC), held on 20 November–8 December 2006, agreed to continue convening annual meetings in the period 2007–10.[1] A three-person convention implementation support unit (ISU) will be set up to receive and distribute information among the parties, partly to assist these inter-sessional meetings.

The 11th Conference of the States Parties (CSP) to the 1993 Chemical Weapons Convention (CWC), the principal international legal instrument against chemical weapons, met in December 2006.[2] It took mainly procedural decisions on implementation matters, but it also decided that representatives of the Executive Council of the Organisation for the Prohibition of Chemical Weapons (OPCW) should visit the CW facilities of parties that have requested extension of the CW destruction deadlines. The CWC mandates that all CW stockpiles must be destroyed no later than 29 April 2012, and these visits reflect the increased concern among the parties that the deadline will not be met by all of the states that possess chemical weapons.

Efforts continued in 2006 to achieve universal membership of the BTWC and the CWC and on ensuring that the states parties implement their convention obligations through effective national measures. Developments related to bio-security and bio-safety received attention in various frameworks and initiatives, including ad hoc arrangements and activities at the national and regional levels. Some of these efforts concentrate on improving disease surveillance and response, while others are devoted to international non-proliferation and disarmament assistance measures. Such decentralized and overlapping initiatives are partly a consequence of the BTWC's weak verifica-

---

[1] On the Sixth Review Conference see the United Nations 'Weapons of mass destruction' website, URL <http://disarmament2.un.org/wmd/bwc/>. The Convention on the Prohibition of the Development, Production and Stockpiling of Bacteriological (Biological) and Toxin Weapons and on their Destruction was signed on 10 Apr. 1972 and entered into force on 26 Mar. 1975. The text is reproduced on the SIPRI Chemical and Biological Warfare Programme website at URL <http://www.sipri.org/contents/cbwarfare/>. The site includes complete lists of parties, signatories and non-signatories to this convention. See also annex A in this volume.

[2] The Convention on the Prohibition of the Development, Production, Stockpiling and Use of Chemical Weapons and on their Destruction was signed on 13 Jan. 1993 and entered into force on 29 Apr. 1997. The text is available on the SIPRI Chemical and Biological Warfare Programme website (note 1), which includes complete lists of parties, signatories and non-signatories to this convention. See also annex A in this volume.

tion provisions. In 2006 allegations of the development or use of chemical and biological weapons (CBWs) continued to be made and more information became available about past CBW programmes.

Section II of this chapter discusses the outcome of the Sixth Review Conference of the BTWC. Developments related to the CWC are described in section III, and section IV examines allegations of CBW use and past CBW programmes. Developments in Iraq and the verification lessons learned in 2006 by the United Nations Monitoring, Verification and Inspection Commission (UNMOVIC) are discussed in section V. The prevention of bio-terrorism and remediation measures, including developments related to biological and chemical security, are addressed in section VI. Section VII presents the conclusions.

II. Biological weapon disarmament

The major biological weapon (BW) disarmament and arms control event in 2006 was the Sixth Review Conference of the States Parties to the Biological and Toxin Weapons Convention. As of December 2006, 155 states had ratified or acceded to the convention.[3] On 26–28 April a preparatory committee met in Geneva, adopted the provisional agenda and draft rules of procedure for the review conference, and requested the conference secretariat to prepare background reports.[4] Legal and political analysts also published briefing material and analyses to assist in preparation for the review conference.[5]

In the period preceding the review conference the Council of the European Union (EU) adopted a Joint Action that authorizes spending up to €867 000 ($1.1 million) and has a planned duration of 18 months. It will support the BTWC by promoting universal membership and national implementation of its provisions.[6] A key motivation among the parties for achieving universal

---

[3] The states that had signed but not ratified the BTWC were Burundi, Central African Republic, Egypt, Guyana, Haiti, Ivory Coast, Gabon, Liberia, Madagascar, Malawi, Myanmar (Burma), Nepal, Somalia, Syria, Tanzania and the United Arab Emirates. The states that had neither signed nor ratified the convention were Andorra, Angola, Cameron, Chad, Comoros, Cook Islands, Djibouti, Eritrea, Guinea, Israel, Kazakhstan, Kiribati, Marshall Islands, Mauritania, Micronesia, Montenegro, Mozambique, Namibia, Nauru, Niue, Samoa, Trinidad and Tobago, Tuvalu and Zambia.

[4] Preparatory Committee for the Sixth Review Conference of the States Parties to the Convention on the Prohibition of Development, Production and Stockpiling of Bacteriological (Biological) and Toxin Weapons and on their Destruction, 'Report of the Preparatory Committee', document BWC/CONF.VI/PC/2, 3 May 2006, para. 22, pp. 4–5. For background papers and review conference documents cited in this chapter see the UN Office at Geneva 'Disarmament' website, URL <http://www.unog.ch/>.

[5] E.g. British American Security Information Council (BASIC), the Harvard Sussex Program and the Verification Research, Training and Information Centre (VERTIC), *Briefing Book: BWC Sixth Review Conference 2006* (nbmedia: Geneva, Oct. 2006); and Zanders, J. P. and Nixdorff, K., *Enforcing Non-Proliferation: The European Union and the 2006 BTWC Review Conference*, Chaillot Paper no. 93 (European Union Institute for Security Studies: Paris, Nov. 2006).

[6] The Joint Action identifies 3 main types of provision that should be incorporated into the national implementation of the convention: (*a*) adoption of national legislation, including penal legislation, which encompasses the full scope of BTWC prohibitions; (*b*) effective regulations or legislation to control and monitor transfers of relevant dual-use technologies; and (*c*) effective implementation and enforcement to prevent violations and sanction breaches. 'Council Joint Action 2006/184/CFSP of 27 February 2006 in support of the Biological and Toxin Weapons Convention, in the framework of the EU Strategy against

membership of the BTWC and comprehensive implementation of its provisions is the recognition that such measures will raise barriers against possible bio-terrorism. Under the Joint Action regional workshops will be convened to explain the benefits of joining the convention to non-parties and to offer them EU technical assistance to join and implement it. A survey of national legislation and the extent to which the convention is effectively implemented will also be carried out. The Council of the European Union also adopted a Common Position stating that the BTWC is 'the cornerstone of efforts to prevent biological agents and toxins from ever being developed and used as weapons'.[7]

The Sixth Review Conference was focused and constructive. Masood Khan of Pakistan, the president of the conference, emphasized the importance of producing a 'concise and accessible' final document and that the parties should reaffirm the norms and core elements of the BTWC. Khan urged that synergies be sought between proposals and mechanisms—rather than viewing them as 'trade-offs'—and the avoidance of a 'lowest common denominator' outcome.[8] The UN Secretary-General, Kofi Annan, stated that the BTWC must be viewed as 'part of an interlinked array of tools . . . to deal with an interlinked array of problems', including public health requirements, terrorism and criminal activity by non-state actors.[9] General debate and the tabling of national papers were followed by an article-by-article review of the convention by the Committee of the Whole. Plenary sessions met periodically during the conference to consider cross-cutting issues and 'clusters' of delegations negotiated text for inclusion in the review conference's final statement.[10]

The parties discussed: (*a*) scientific and technological developments, (*b*) national implementation of the convention, (*c*) confidence-building measures (CBMs), (*d*) implementation support, (*e*) the modalities for possible meetings between the Sixth and Seventh Review Conferences, (*f*) bio-safety and bio-security, (*g*) scientific and technological cooperation, (*h*) compliance and verification, (*i*) coordination with other organizations, and (*j*) bio-terrorism. The ISU, which will be attached to the UN Department for Disarmament Affairs, among other things will help coordinate efforts by the BTWC parties to develop measures to promote effective implementation of the convention,

---

the Proliferation of Weapons of Mass Destruction', *Official Journal of the European Union*, L65 (7 Mar. 2006), pp. 51–55.

[7] 'Council Common Position 2006/242/CFSP of 20 March 2006 relating to the 2006 Review Conference of the Biological and Toxin Weapons Convention (BTWC)', *Official Journal of the European Union*, L88 (25 Mar. 2006), p. 65, para. 1.

[8] Sixth BTWC Review Conference, 'Opening statement by the President of the Sixth Review Conference of the Biological Weapons Convention, Ambassador Masood Khan (Pakistan)', Geneva, 20 Nov. 2006.

[9] Sixth BTWC Review Conference, 'The Secretary-General: remarks to the Sixth Review Conference of the Biological Weapons Convention', Geneva, 20 Nov. 2006.

[10] The BioWeapons Prevention Project (BWPP) produced daily briefing papers on the work of the conference. See the BWPP website at URL <http://www.bwpp.org>. Non-governmental organizations were also able to make presentations on a range of activities related to the BTWC during lunch breaks. See Center for Arms Control and Non-Proliferation, 'BWC observer', URL <http://www.bwc06.org/>; and the Biological and Toxin Weapons Convention website at URL <http://www.opbw.org>.

improve bio-safety and bio-security at biological facilities and enhance national capabilities for disease surveillance, detection and diagnosis.[11] The final document of the conference included an article-by-article review of the parties' understanding of the BTWC provisions and noted the results of the 2003–2005 inter-sessional process: meetings of experts and states parties that were conducted in accordance with a decision of the 2002 reconvened Fifth Review Conference of the States Parties to the BTWC.[12]

Verifying compliance with the convention was also considered: both with regard to specific cases of concern, and in terms of general procedures and mechanisms to ensure, for example, that the BTWC effectively covers scientific and technological developments.[13] The United States identified several mechanisms for addressing compliance concerns. It is developing guidelines and procedures that can be used in response to any disease outbreak to determine whether it is caused deliberately and, if so, the most suitable scientific and technological means to identity those responsible.[14]

During the review conference new groupings of mainly Western states and one of Latin American states emerged.[15] These groups took positions that differed from those of the Western Group[16] and the Group of the Non-Aligned Movement (NAM) and Other States, respectively.[17] Some developing states did not express or de-emphasized the past criticism that national export controls may conflict with Article X of the BTWC, which calls for the convention to be implemented in a manner that avoids hampering economic and technological development and preventing the exchange of information, material and equipment for peaceful purposes.[18] In addition, some members of the East European Group are now EU members and increasingly associate themselves with the work of the Western Group.

The conference considered action plans on universality, national implementation, Article X and comprehensive implementation of the BTWC. The proposed action plan on national implementation urged the parties to designate a national implementing body for the convention, enact legislation, review their national export control laws and submit periodic updates to the other parties.

---

[11] See UN Office at Geneva (note 4).

[12] On past BTWC review conferences see CBW chapters in previous editions of the SIPRI Yearbook.

[13] On suspected BW programmes see section IV.

[14] Sixth BTWC Review Conference, 'Confronting noncompliance with the Biological Weapons Convention', document BWC/CONF.VI/WP.27*(revised), 24 Nov. 2006.

[15] The mainly Western group was referred to as JACKSNNZ (Japan, Australia, Canada, Korea (South), Switzerland, Norway and New Zealand) or Jacksons 7. They were among the most active Western Group participants at the conference. The group of Latin American states were Argentina, Bolivia, Brazil, Chile, Colombia, Costa Rica, Ecuador, El Salvador, Guatemala, Mexico, Peru and Uruguay. This group prepared a number of joint working papers.

[16] The Western Group comprises mainly West European states as well as Australia, Canada, New Zealand and the USA.

[17] E.g. the positions differed in terms of the level of attention devoted to verification and compliance issues.

[18] Some developing states maintain that the implementation of export control regimes by mainly developed states impedes the full implementation of Article X. They also argue that the convention should be implemented so that it does not impede economic cooperation and development.

Agreement could not be reached on such an action plan, in part because of a late proposal by the NAM to adopt an action plan on the implementation of Article X.[19] Linking national implementation to Article X implementation was unacceptable to a number of parties, including the USA.

In 1986 the Second Review Conference of the States Parties to the BTWC agreed in its Final Declaration that the parties should submit annual data exchanges on activities of possible BW relevance to serve as a CBM.[20] However, some parties have failed to comply with this politically binding decision to provide information and, among those that have, some have done so irregularly. The quality and completeness of the information submitted have also periodically been questioned. In some cases this can be a positive development provided that other parties successfully seek informal clarification. Given their sensitive nature, such consultations are presumably carried out either bilaterally or among a limited number of parties. The nature and scope of such consultations that have occurred have not generally been published in detail and thus they tend to be poorly understood.[21] The extent to which CBMs adequately cover current bio-defence programmes and those that counter bio-terrorism (as opposed to traditional biological defence programmes) is also not clear and a matter of concern to many analysts because such programmes could serve as a cover for prohibited activities. Proposals have therefore been put forward to make the annual data exchanges legally binding, and to revise and expand the CBM formats,[22] although there is continued concern that sensitive national security and proprietary business information not be divulged. The shortcomings of the CBMs can be seen as reason to further develop them in the BTWC framework and as grounds for looking to other mechanisms to strengthen the international prohibition against BW. Such mechanisms could include national implementation of UN Security Council Resolution 1373— which deals with threats to international peace and security caused by terrorist acts—and the work of the 1540 Committee, a non-permanent body that assists with the implementation of UN Security Council Resolution 1540.[23]

[19] Pearson, G., 'The Biological Weapons Convention Sixth Review Conference', *CBW Conventions Bulletin*, no. 74 (Dec. 2006), p. 35.

[20] In 1991 the Third Review Conference agreed that information would be provided in other areas, including past offensive and defensive biological research and development programmes.

[21] For an account of consultations carried out in order to clarify the status of Soviet compliance with the BTWC see Kelly, D. C., 'The Trilateral Agreement: lessons for biological weapons verification', eds T. Findlay and O. Meier, Verification Research, Training and Information Centre (VERTIC), *Verification Yearbook 2002* (VERTIC: London, 2002), pp. 93–109.

[22] E.g. Hunger, I. and Isla, N., 'Confidence-building needs transparency: an analysis of the BTWC's confidence-building measures', *Disarmament Forum*, no. 3 (2006), pp. 27–36. See also the Hamburg Centre for Biological Arms Control website at URL <http://www.biological-arms-control.org/projects/CBM_en.htm>.

[23] UN Security Council Resolution 1373, 28 Sep. 2001; and UN Security Council Resolution 1540, 28 Apr. 2004. See the discussion of Resolution 1737 in chapter 15 and of Resolution 1540 in appendix 11A in this volume. Resolution 1540 is reproduced as appendix 11B in this volume. See also the 1540 Committee website at URL <http://disarmament2.un.org/Committee1540/>. These and other UN Security Council resolutions discussed in this chapter are available at URL <http://www.un.org/documents/scres.htm>.

As at the 1996 Fourth Review Conference of the BTWC, in 2006 Iran tabled a proposal to amend Article I of the convention to explicitly include a prohibition against the 'use' of BW and stated that it had requested the depositaries of the convention (Russia, the United Kingdom and the USA) to start the amendment process.[24] Iran argued that the amendment is necessary in part because the prohibition of use contained in the 1925 Geneva Protocol is insufficient since many of the parties to the protocol had or maintain reservations that leave open the possibility of using CBW.[25] The other delegations generally opposed amending the BTWC because this could open the door for other amendments. The final document of the Sixth Review Conference, like that of the Fourth Review Conference, states that the parties understand the prohibitions of Article I to include a ban on the use of BW.[26]

Russia proposed that the term 'biological weapon' should be more precisely defined on the basis of the type and quantity of biological agents that are allowed for non-prohibited purposes, but the proposal failed to gain support.[27] Concern continued that narrowing the definition would undermine the general purpose criterion embodied in the Article I prohibition against BW, which bans all 'microbial, other biological agents, or toxins whatever their origin or method of production' except for non-prohibited purposes.[28] The general purpose criterion is the principal mechanism for ensuring that the BTWC can be applied regardless of future scientific and technological developments.[29] There is also concern that an agreement on a quantitative declaration threshold could weaken the convention because large quantities of biological agents can be grown quickly from small initial feedstocks. The conference's final document reaffirmed that Article I applies to 'all scientific and technological developments in the life sciences and other fields of science relevant to the Convention'.[30]

---

[24] Sixth BTWC Review Conference, 'Prohibition of use of biological weapons, submitted by the Islamic Republic of Iran', document BWC/CONF.VI/WP.25, 23 Nov. 2006, paras 3–4. See also Zanders, J. P. and Eckstein, S., *The Prohibition of 'Use' under the BTWC: Backgrounder on Relevant Developments during the Negotiations, 1969–1972* (SIPRI: Stockholm, 3 Dec. 1996), URL <http://www.sipri.org/contents/cbwarfare/Publications/Publications/cbw-papersfactsheets.html>.

[25] The BTWC's preamble reaffirms the Geneva Protocol's principles and objectives. Iran's position implies that any divergence between how the 2 agreements are interpreted and implemented could constitute a loophole that states wishing to retain the option of using BW might exploit. However, this interpretation is contrary to the spirit of the BTWC and the general international understanding of its prohibitions, including that expressed in the final documents of both the fourth and sixth review conferences.

[26] Sixth BTWC Review Conference, 'Final document', document BWC/CONF.VI/6, 20 Nov.–8 Dec. 2006, p. 9.

[27] Tucker, J. B. (interview by P. Crail), Monterey Institute of International Studies Center for Nonproliferation Studies, 'The Sixth Review Conference of the Biological Weapons Convention: success or failure?', 4 Jan. 2007, URL <http://cns.miis.edu/pubs/week/070104.htm>.

[28] Regardless of its phrasing, a definition of BW that is narrower in scope than the general purpose criterion would risk narrowing the application of the BTWC's prohibition against such weapons.

[29] BTWC (note 1), Article I.

[30] Sixth BTWC Review Conference (note 26), p. 9. For background on scientific and technological challenges see Tucker, J. B. and Zilinskas, R. A., 'The promise and perils of synthetic biology', *New Atlantis*, spring 2006, pp. 25–45, URL <http://www.thenewatlantis.com/archive/12/tuckerzilinskas.htm>. See also Littlewood, J., *The Biological Weapons Convention: A Failed Revolution* (Ashgate: Aldershot, 2005).

The inter-sessional programme for 2007–10 will consist of four annual meetings of one-week duration to 'discuss, and promote common understanding and effective action' on: (*a*) ways and means to enhance national implementation, (*b*) regional and subregional cooperation on BTWC implementation, (*c*) national, regional and international measures to improve bio-safety and bio-security, (*d*) oversight, education, awareness raising and development of codes of conduct, (*e*) capacity building in the fields of disease surveillance, detection, diagnosis and containment of infectious diseases; and (*f*) assistance and coordination with relevant organizations at the request of any BTWC party in case of alleged BW use.[31] The issue of an institutionalized verification structure remains formally in abeyance despite concern that the absence of some such form of oversight could gradually erode the international legal norm against BW. The usefulness of the annual meetings will depend on the extent to which they promote effective implementation of the BTWC.[32]

III. Chemical weapon disarmament

As of December 2006, 181 states had ratified or acceded to the 1993 Chemical Weapons Convention; an additional 6 states had signed but not ratified the convention, and 8 states had neither signed nor ratified it.[33]

The Conference of the States Parties

The 11th Conference of the States Parties to the CWC met on 5–8 December 2006. The parties devoted much attention to the issue of the destruction of CW stockpiles and took a number of procedural decisions.[34] The verification of non-production of chemical weapons by the chemical industry—essential for maintaining the effectiveness of the convention—was also considered. The CSP approved the OPCW's 2007 budget of €75 025 751 ($99 700 000), a decrease of €588 490 ($765 000) over the 2006 budget. It is the second con-

---

[31] Sixth BTWC Review Conference (note 26), p. 21.

[32] On institutional issues see Zanders, J. P., 'Verification of the BTWC: seeking the impossible or impossible to seek?', ed. G. Lindstrom, *Enforcing Non-Proliferation: The European Union and the 2006 BTWC Review Conference*, Chaillot Paper no. 93 (European Union Institute for Security Studies: Paris, Nov. 2006), pp. 50–54.

[33] The Central African Republic, Comoros, Djibouti, Haiti, Liberia and Montenegro became parties to the CWC in 2006. The CWC entered into force for Montenegro on 3 June 2006, the date of the country's independence (until 2006 Montenegro was part of Serbia and Montenegro). The states that have signed, but not ratified the CWC are Bahamas, Republic of the Congo, Dominican Republic, Guinea-Bissau, Israel and Myanmar (Burma). The states that had not signed or ratified the CWC as of Dec. 2006 were Angola, Barbados, Egypt, Iraq, Lebanon, North Korea, Somalia and Syria. See also annex A in this volume.

[34] CW destruction in Russia is also a major focus of the Group of Eight (G8) industrialized countries' Global Partnership against the Spread of Weapons and Materials of Mass Destruction activities. On the Global Partnership see chapter 12 in this volume.

secutive 'zero nominal growth' budget. The CSP earmarked €37 545 676 ($49 900 000) to cover verification costs.[35]

The CSP granted the OPCW Director-General the authority, effective until 29 April 2012, to extend and renew employment contracts beyond the seven-year total length of service that was specified by a 2003 CSP decision.[36] The CSP also extended for one year the OPCW's Plan of Action for the implementation of the obligations of Article VII (national implementation measures).[37] As of 1 November 2006, 172 of the parties (95 per cent) had established or designated a national authority; 112 parties (62 per cent) had reported to the Technical Secretariat the adoption of legislative and administrative measures to implement the CWC; and 72 parties (40 per cent) had adopted and reported on national legislation covering all key areas required by the CWC.[38] The CSP also requested that all states parties and the Technical Secretariat intensify their efforts to promote the convention's universality with a view towards achieving universal adherence by 29 April 2007.[39] The Technical Secretariat continued to document its operating procedures and to facilitate the transfer of institutional memory and expertise to future staff.

Chemical industry verification

At the 11th CSP and an Executive Council meeting that met parallel to it much attention focused on the verification regime covering other chemical production facilities (OCPFs). The CWC verification regime covers some plant sites that produce by synthesis certain discrete organic chemicals some of which contain the elements phosphorus, sulphur or fluorine (DOC/PSFs). Facilities that produce DOC/PSFs according to the guidelines in the CWC Verification Annex are called OCPFs. They must be declared to the OPCW and are subject to inspection.[40] A credible methodology for OCPF site selection and the carrying out of a sufficient number of geographically balanced inspections of such sites are necessary in order to ensure the effectiveness of the CWC verification regime. Some OCPF facilities are multi-purpose chem-

[35] Organisation for the Prohibition of Chemical Weapons (OPCW), 'Decision, programme and budget of the OPCW for 2007', document C-11/DEC.11, 8 Dec. 2006. For OPCW documents see URL <http://www.opcw.org>.

[36] With the exception of local staff, translators and interpreters, no OPCW staff member may have a total length of service exceeding 7 years by 2012. OPCW, 'Decision, tenure policy of the OPCW', document C-SS-2/DEC.1, 30 Apr. 2003; and OPCW, 'Decision, future implementation of the tenure policy', document C-11/DEC.7, 7 Dec. 2006.

[37] OPCW, 'Decision, sustaining follow-up to the plan of action regarding the implementation of Article VII obligations', document C-11/DEC.4, 6 Dec. 2006.

[38] OPCW, 'Note by the Director-General, report to the Conference of the States Parties at its eleventh session on the status of implementation of Article VII of the Chemical Weapons Convention as at 1 November 2006', document C-11/DG.6, 23 Nov. 2006, p. 5.

[39] OPCW, 'Decision, universality of the Chemical Weapons Convention and the further implementation of the universality action plan', document C-11/DEC.8, 7 Dec. 2006. See Guthrie, R., Hart, J. and Kuhlau, F., 'Chemical and biological warfare developments and arms control', *SIPRI Yearbook 2006: Armaments, Disarmament and International Security* (Oxford University Press: Oxford, 2006), pp. 715–16.

[40] CWC (note 2), Verification Annex, Part IX.

ical production facilities that can be reconfigured on short notice in order to produce a wide range of toxic chemicals that could be diverted to purposes prohibited by the CWC.[41]

The listing of chemicals in the Annex on Chemicals is meant to balance the risk they pose to the object and purpose of the CWC against the fact that such chemicals can often be used for peaceful, including commercial, purposes. The annex comprises three schedules: schedule 1 chemicals pose a 'high risk' to the object and purpose of the convention and have the fewest applications for peaceful purposes; schedule 2 chemicals pose a 'significant risk'; and schedule 3 chemicals pose 'a risk', although they have the widest application for peaceful purposes.[42] The verification regime for OCPFs targets facilities that produce chemicals that are not listed on the schedules but that may nevertheless present a threat to the convention. Inspections focus on the facilities, rather than on the chemicals they produce, and their primary aim is to confirm the absence of activities involving schedule 1 chemicals.

The extent to which OCPF inspections are carried out on the territory of parties with developed or developing chemical industries is another implementation issue. Parties with developing chemical industries tend to emphasize maintaining the 'hierarchy of risk' embodied in the CWC Annex on Chemicals.[43] Parties with more developed chemical industries, however, often stress the need for a better spread of OCPF inspections in order to preserve the equitable geographic distribution principle inherent to the operation of UN bodies and to effectively address potential proliferation concerns. The CWC specifies 'equitable geographical distribution' as a criterion for the selection of DOC/PSF plant sites for inspection.[44] The low number of OCPF inspections, both in absolute terms and as a percentage of total declared facilities, is considered by some as putting at risk the credibility of the overall CWC verification regime. At present, the OPCW annually inspects fewer than 2 per cent of the more than 5000 OCPFs that are subject to inspection. The number of declared OCPFs is also continuing to rise.[45] The optimization of the OCPF

---

[41] In 2003 the OPCW Scientific Advisory Board concluded that it would be 'prudent' to increase the number of OCPF inspections while maintaining the effectiveness of the verification regime for chemicals listed in the CWC Annex on Chemicals. It also stated that 'suitable training must be provided' to ensure that OPCW inspectors are familiar with new chemical production routes and processes. OPCW, 'Note by the Director-General, report of the Scientific Advisory Board on developments in science and technology', document RC-1/DG.2, 23 Apr. 2003, para. 2.3, p. 2. Many OCPFs selected for inspection in the early years of the CWC's implementation were single-purpose facilities that produced bulk chemicals or chemicals such as urea which have little relevance to the CWC. The selection process was later improved to include more multi-purpose facilities. In response to the CWC parties' nominating sites for inspection—in accordance with the CWC Verification Annex, Part IX, para. 11(c)—concern has been expressed that plant site selection should not overly rely on nominations by the parties to be inspected.

[42] CWC (note 2), Annex on Chemicals, 'Guidelines for Schedules of Chemicals'.

[43] E.g. the parties periodically consider whether small laboratories that synthesize a few milligrams of a schedule 1 chemical annually should be considered as posing a greater risk to the object and purpose of the CWC than multi-purpose facilities that are capable of producing thousands of tonnes of toxic DOC/PSFs annually.

[44] CWC (note 2), Verification Annex, Part IX, para. 11(a).

[45] E.g. in 2005 the OPCW conducted 80 inspections of OCPF sites out of a total of 4702 OCPF sites that are subject to inspection. OPCW, 'Report of the OPCW on the implementation of the Convention on

verification regime offers insight into the challenges of implementing at the operational level the provisions of the CWC that are broadly phrased.

Destruction of chemical weapons

The verification of the destruction of chemical weapons is a core objective of the CWC: all CW stockpiles must be destroyed by 29 April 2007, although the deadline may be extended by up to five years (until 29 April 2012). As of 31 December 2006, of approximately 71 330 agent tonnes of declared chemical weapons, about 16 600 agent tonnes had been verifiably destroyed; and of approximately 8.67 million declared items, about 2.64 million munitions and containers had been destroyed.[46] As of the same date, 12 states had declared 65 chemical weapon production facilities, of which 39 had been destroyed and 18 converted to peaceful purposes not prohibited by the CWC.[47] The states that have declared their possession of chemical weapons are Albania, India, Libya, Russia, the USA and a state that has not been officially identified by the OPCW (generally understood to be South Korea). Indications increased that Russia and the USA will not be able to complete the destruction of their CW stockpiles by 29 April 2012.[48]

The CSP's willingness to extend the Russian and US deadlines to 2012 was facilitated by an understanding that, starting no later than 2008, the two countries will periodically host visits by representatives of the Executive Council to chemical weapon destruction facilities (CWDFs) or CWDF construction sites.[49] The Executive Council, which met parallel to the CSP, agreed the modalities for these visits.[50] The OPCW Director-General emphasized that the visits should supplement but not replace the OPCW inspection regime,[51] while the EU offered to provide financial support, on an individual basis, to promote 'adequate geographical' representation in the teams.[52]

---

the Prohibition of the Development, Production, Stockpiling and Use of Chemical Weapon and on their Destruction', document C-11/4, 6 Dec. 2006, pp. 4, 8.

[46] OPCW official, Communication with J. Hart, 12 Feb. 2007. For periodic updates see also OPCW, 'The chemical weapons ban: facts and figures', URL <http://www.opcw.org>.

[47] The states are Bosnia and Herzegovina, China, France, India, Iran, Japan, South Korea, Libya, Russia, Serbia, the UK and the USA. OPCW, 'The chemical weapons ban: facts and figures', URL <http://www.opcw.org>. The CWC defines a chemical weapon production facility as one that has produced chemical weapons at any time since 1 Jan. 1946. CWC (note 2), Article II, para. 8. For quantity and type of CW stockpiles and associated destruction programmes see CBW chapters in previous editions of the SIPRI Yearbook.

[48] Ember, L., 'Chemical weapons deadline at risk: Russia, even U.S., is not likely to destroy its arsenals completely by 2012 as mandated by treaty', *Chemical & Engineering News*, vol. 84, no. 16 (17 Apr. 2006), pp. 27–30.

[49] The circumstances under which other CW possessor states might receive such visits were unclear.

[50] OPCW, 'Decision, visits by representatives of the Executive Council', document C-11/DEC.20, 8 Dec. 2006.

[51] OPCW, 'Opening statement by the Director-General to the Conference of the States Parties at its eleventh session', document C-11/DG.9, 5 Dec. 2006, para. 10, p. 2.

[52] OPCW, 'Statement by H. E. Markus Lyra, Under-Secretary of State, Finland, on behalf of the European Union', 11th CSP, The Hague, 5–8 Dec. 2006, URL <http://www.opcw.org/docs/csp/csp11/en/FIN-en.pdf>.

Albania's stockpile, which consists mainly of sulphur mustard, will be destroyed through high-temperature pyrolysis. As of September 2006, the USA had spent $38.5 million to support CW destruction in Albania.[53] The 11th CSP granted Albania intermediate deadline extensions to destroy its category 1 chemical weapons.[54]

India declared a CW stockpile of approximately 1044 agent tonnes.[55] The 11th CSP granted India an extension to destroy its category 1 chemical weapons no later than 28 April 2009, on the condition that it periodically provides additional information to the OPCW on the progress of destruction.[56]

Libya's remaining CW stockpile consists primarily of CW precursors and sulphur mustard. The 11th CSP granted it an extension to destroy its category 1 chemical weapons by 31 December 2010, providing Libya supplies further information to the OPCW on the progress of destruction.[57] An extension of intermediate destruction deadlines was also granted for category 1 CWs on similar conditions.[58] The US Department of Defense (DOD) has estimated that assisting Libya to destroy its stockpile will cost $100 million.[59]

The *Russian* CW stockpile is stored at six locations.[60] In March 2006 a second unit at the Kambarka CWDF became operational, and the first unit of the CWDF at Maradikovsky became operational in September.[61] CWDFs at Leonidovka, Pochep and Shchuchye are scheduled to become operational in 2008, while the last CWDF, located at Kizner, is scheduled to become operational in

---

[53] Squassoni, S., *Globalizing Cooperative Threat Reduction: A Survey of Options*, US Library of Congress, Congressional Research Service (CRS) Report for Congress RL32359 (CRS: Washington, DC, 5 Oct. 2006), p. 1. See also chapter 12 in this volume.

[54] OPCW, 'Decision, extensions of the intermediate deadlines for the destruction by Albania of its category 1 chemical weapons', document C-11/DEC.19, 8 Dec. 2006. The definition of CW categories, which is partly based on what schedule a chemical may be listed under, is given in CWC (note 2), Verification Annex, Part IV(A), para. 16.

[55] Perry Robinson, J. P., 'Near-term development of governance regime for biological and chemical weapons', Science & Technology Policy Research Unit paper, item 456, Brighton, 4 Nov. 2006, ref. 77, URL <http://www.sussex.ac.uk/Units/spru/nonstateactors/uploads/GovernanceRegimePaper.pdf>.

[56] OPCW, 'Decision, request by India for an extension of the deadline for destroying all of its category 1 chemical weapons', document C-11/DEC.16, 8 Dec. 2006.

[57] See Hart, J. and Kile, S. N., 'Libya's renunciation of nuclear, biological and chemical weapons and ballistic missiles', *SIPRI Yearbook 2005: Armaments, Disarmament and International Security* (Oxford University Press: Oxford, 2005), pp. 643–45.

[58] OPCW, 'Decision, proposal by the Libyan Arab Jamahiriya for the establishment of specific dates for intermediate destruction deadlines, and its request for an extension of the final deadlines for the destruction of its category 1 chemical weapons', document C-11/DEC.15, 8 Dec. 2006.

[59] 'U.S. considers aiding Libyan CW disposal', *Global Security Newswire*, 31 Mar. 2006, URL <http://www.nti.org/d_newswire/issues/2006_3_31.html>.

[60] The locations are Kambarka, Udmurtia Republic; Kizner, Udmurtia Republic; Maradikovsky, Kirov oblast; Pochep, Bryansk oblast; Leonidovka, Penza oblast; and Shchuchye, Kurgan oblast. On Russian CW destruction see 'Unichtozhenie khimicheskogo oruzhiya v R.F.' [Destruction of chemical weapons in the Russian Federation], *Rossiiskaya Gazeta*, URL <http://www.rg.ru/ximiya.html>; and *Khimicheskoe Razoruzhenie: Otkrity Elektronny Zhurnal* [Chemical disarmament: open electronic journal], URL <http://www.chemicaldisarmament.ru/>. Destruction operations at Gorny, Saratov oblast, were completed in Dec. 2005.

[61] ITAR-TASS, Magasumavo, R., 'Ob'ekt po unichtozheniyu khimoruzhiya v Maradykovo pushchen v ekspluatatsiyu' [Chemical weapon destruction facility at Maradykovo enters operation], 8 Sep. 2006, URL <http://www.chemicaldisarmament.ru/print/695.html>.

2009.[62] The 11th CSP granted an extension for Russia to complete the destruction of 45 per cent of its category 1 chemical weapons by 31 December 2009, and 29 April 2012 was set as the deadline for Russia to complete the destruction of its CW stockpile.[63] As of 5 December 2006, Russia had destroyed 3123 tonnes of blister agent and 2925 tonnes of organophosphorus nerve agent, accounting for approximately 15 per cent of its original stockpile of 40 000 agent tonnes.[64]

One party to the CWC (widely understood to be *South Korea*) has declared possession of a CW stockpile but has declined to identify itself. The party in question has declared a stockpile of approximately 1056 agent tonnes.[65] The 11th CSP granted an extension to 'a state party' to destroy its category 1 chemical weapons by 31 December 2008, on the condition that it periodically provides additional information to the OPCW on the progress of destruction.[66]

The estimated cost of destroying *the United States*' stockpile, which is stored at seven locations, was expected to reach $35 billion.[67] Approximately 40 per cent of the US stockpile has been destroyed. In 2006 CW destruction was completed at Aberdeen, Maryland, the second storage and disposal site (of an original nine sites). On 10 April 2006, the Secretary of Defense, Donald Rumsfeld, notified the US Congress that current estimates indicate that the USA will be able to destroy approximately 66 per cent of its CW stockpile by 2012.[68] This implies that the USA will complete the destruction of its stockpiled chemical weapons by about 2017. The 11th CSP granted the USA an extension to destroy its category 1 chemical weapons no later than 29 April 2012, providing that it periodically supplies further information to the OPCW on the progress of destruction and that this progress be periodically reviewed

[62] For an update on the Shchuchye CWDF see US Government Accountability Office (GAO), *Cooperative Threat Reduction: DOD Needs More Reliable Data to Better Estimate the Cost and Schedule of the Shchuch'ye Facility*, Report no. GAO-06-692 (GAO: Washington, DC, May 2006).

[63] OPCW, 'Decision, proposal for a date for the completion of phase 3 of the destruction by the Russian Federation of its category 1 chemical weapons', document C-11/DEC.14, 8 Dec. 2006; and OPCW, 'Decision, proposal by the Russian Federation on setting a specific date for completion of the destruction of its stockpiles of category 1 chemical weapons', document C-11/DEC.18, 8 Dec. 2006.

[64] Statement of the Russian delegation to the OPCW, 'Statement by Mr. Victor Kholstov, Head of the Russian delegation to the eleventh session of the Conference of the States Parties to the Chemical Weapons Convention', The Hague, 5–8 Dec. 2006. Some parties maintain that the percentage should be lower because they do not consider that a single hydrolysis step is sufficient to meet the 'end point of destruction' criterion in the convention, which requires that destruction be 'essentially irreversible'. CWC (note 2), Verification Annex, Part IV(A), para. 12.

[65] Perry Robinson (note 55).

[66] OPCW, 'Decision, request by a state party for an extension of the final deadline for destroying all its category 1 chemical weapons', document C-11/DEC.12, 8 Dec. 2006.

[67] The locations are Anniston Chemical Agent Disposal Facility, Anniston, Alabama; Blue Grass Chemical Agent Disposal Pilot Plant, Blue Grass, Kentucky; Newport Chemical Agent Disposal Facility, Newport, Indiana; Pine Bluff Chemical Agent Disposal Facility, Pine Bluff, Arkansas; Pueblo Chemical Agent Disposal Plant, Pueblo, Colorado; Tooele Chemical Agent Disposal Facility, Tooele, Utah; and Umatilla Chemical Agent Disposal Facility, Umatilla, Oregon. US Department of State, 'US requests chemical weapons destruction deadline extension', Washington, DC, 7 July 2006, available at URL <http://usinfo.state.gov/>.

[68] 'U.S. can't destroy its chemical arms by 2012', *Chemical & Engineering News*, vol. 84, no. 16 (17 Apr. 2006), p. 26; and Ember, L., 'U.S. can't eliminate arsenal until 2017', *Chemical & Engineering News*, vol. 84, no. 17 (24 Apr. 2006), p. 9.

by the Executive Council and the results shared with other parties on request.[69] Much of the discussion about the US programme centred on the treatment and disposal of caustic VX (a nerve agent) hydrolysate from the Newport CW destruction facility and whether the US Army should transport it for off-site treatment.[70]

Old, abandoned and sea-dumped chemical weapons

As of 31 December 2006, three countries had declared that abandoned chemical weapons are present on their territories, and 13 countries had declared that they possess old chemical weapons.[71]

In 2006 *the United States* Congress drafted legislation to address issues connected with the disposal of chemical weapons by sea dumping. These issues include concern about chemical weapons dumped at three or more locations off the coast of Hawaii until the end of the 1960s,[72] as well as more general concerns arising from the 2001 publication of a US Army report on past CW dumping which indicated that the practice had been more frequent and widespread than previously thought.[73] In 2006 operations to dispose of at least

[69] OPCW, 'Decision, request by the United States of America for establishment of a revised date for the final deadline for destroying all of its category 1 chemical weapons', document C-11/DEC.17, 8 Dec. 2006. For background see US Department of State, 'United States of America, request for establishment of a revised date for the phase 4 deadline for the destruction of category 1 chemical weapons (CW) in the United States', Washington, DC, 2006, URL <http://www.state.gov/documents/organization/64997.pdf>.

[70] US Department of Health and Human Services, Centers for Disease Control and Prevention, 'Review of the revised plan for off-site treatment of Newport Chemical Agent Disposal Facility's caustic VX hydrolysate at DuPont Secure Environmental Treatment Facility in Deepwater, New Jersey', July 2006, URL <http://www.cdc.gov/nceh/demil/>.

[71] The countries that have declared abandoned chemical weapons to the OPCW are China, Italy and Panama. The countries that have declared old chemical weapons to the OPCW are Austria, Australia, Belgium, Canada, France, Germany, Italy, Japan, Marshall Islands, Russia, Slovenia, the UK and the USA. Abandoned chemical weapons are defined as CW that were abandoned by a state after 1 Jan. 1925 on the territory of another state without the permission of the latter. CWC (note 2), Article II, para. 6. Old chemical weapons are defined as CW that were produced before 1925 or CW produced between 1925 and 1946 that have deteriorated to such an extent that they are no longer usable for the purpose for which they were designed. CWC (note 2), Article II, para. 5.

[72] Bearden, D. M., *US Disposal of Chemical Weapons in the Ocean: Background and Issues for Congress*, US Library of Congress, Congressional Research Service (CRS) Report for Congress RL33432 (CRS: Washington, DC, 24 May 2006). CW munitions dumped off the US coasts included 1100 1000-pound (lb) (454-kg) cyanogen chloride-filled bombs; 20 1000-lb (454-kg) hydrogen cyanide-filled bombs; 125 500-lb (227-kg) cyanogen chloride-filled bombs; 15 000 115-lb (52-kg) sulphur mustard-filled bombs; 31 000 sulphur mustard-filled mortar shells; 1000 one-ton bulk storage containers filled with sulphur mustard; 190 one-ton bulk storage containers filled with lewisite; 16 000 100-lb (45-kg) sulphur mustard bombs; and 4220 tons of assorted ordnance filled with hydrogen cyanide. US Senate bill S.2295, 'Hawaiian waters chemical munitions safety act of 2006', 109th Congress (2005–2006), URL <http://www.govtrack.us/congress/billtext.xpd?bill=s109-2295>. As of Dec. 2006 the bill was apparently still in committee. The bill cites US Department of Defense, US Army Research, Development, and Engineering Command, Aberdeen Proving Ground, Md., Corporate Information Office, Historical Research and Development Team, 'Off-shore disposal of chemical agents and weapons conducted by the United States', 29 Mar. 2001.

[73] Kakesako, G., 'Isle lawmakers seeking survey of weapons sites', *Star Bulletin*, 17 Feb. 2006, URL <http://starbulletin.com/2006/02/17/news/story06.html>. CW produced after World War II that were dumped at sea are not considered to be old or abandoned chemical weapons. CWs dumped before 1 Jan. 1985 also need not be declared to the OPCW.

137 suspected CW munitions, including 4-inch (*c.* 10-cm) Stokes mortar rounds and at least one Livens Projector shell, continued at a military reservation on Oahu, Hawaii.[74] In addition to smoke rounds, some munitions contain chlorpicrin, a harassing agent (one designed to cause severe discomfort, but not death or permanent injury).[75]

In 2006 Japan sent four investigation teams and five excavation and recovery teams to *China*, where more than 1700 projectiles were recovered. Both countries are working to identify and destroy chemical weapons that were abandoned in China by Japan in the 1930s and 1940s.[76]

In *Germany* a third CWDF began operation in April 2006 at a facility on Lüneburg Heath near Munster. Small-calibre—2.3 kg trinitrotoluene (TNT) equivalent or less—conventional and CW munitions will be fed directly into the unit, an incinerator, without disassembly.[77]

IV. Allegations of chemical and biological weapon violations and past programmes

Most of the information dealing with allegations of CBW programmes is provided by the USA and contained in various reports and statements that tend to provide similar listings of states in any given year.[78] In 2006 the USA stated that it 'believes' that *Iran* 'probably has an offensive biological weapons program'; that it 'believes' that *North Korea* has a 'biological warfare capability and may have developed, produced, and weaponized for use biological weapons'; and that *Syria* has carried out research and development (R&D) for

[74] The Livens Projector, named for a British engineer, is a drum-and-tube CW- or smoke-delivery system developed during World War I. The Stokes Trench Mortar was a similar system used in World War I by the US Army's First Gas Regiment. Such systems were developed to be fired simultaneously in order to try to achieve sudden high concentrations of CW agent over enemy trench positions. See Foulkes, C. H., *"Gas!" The Story of the Special Brigade* (William Blackwood & Sons: Edinburgh, 1936).

[75] US Army Corps of Engineers, 'Chemical munitions encountered during Schofield Barracks Military Reservation range clearance', Presentation at the 9th International Chemical Weapons Demilitarisation Conference: CWD 2006, Lüneburg, 15–18 May 2006.

[76] Japanese delegation to the OPCW, 'Statement by H. E. Mr. Takeshi Nakane, Ambassador, Director-General, Disarmament, Non-Proliferation and Science Department, Ministry of Foreign Affairs at the eleventh session of the Conference of the States Parties [to] the OPCW', The Hague, 5 Dec. 2006, URL <http://www.opcw.org/docs/csp/csp11/en/JP-en.pdf>. On the type and quantity of CW in China see Nanaoka, S., Nomura, K. and Wada, T., 'Determination of mustard and lewisite related compounds in abandoned chemical weapons (yellow shells) from sources in China and Japan', *Journal of Chromatography A*, vol. 11101 (2006), pp. 268–77; and Science Council of Japan, *Risk Assessment of Old and Abandoned Chemical Weapons and Development of Safe Advanced Destruction Technologies* (Digital Print Co.: Ibaraki, Oct. 2006).

[77] Dynasafe, 'The DYNASAFE SK 2000 for chemical munitions in Munster: one step destruction of old chemical weapons', Presentation at the 9th International Chemical Weapons Demilitarisation Conference: CWD 2006 (note 75). Starting in World War I, the Munster military training ground was the principal German experimental and training area for CW. In 1919 approximately 1 million CW shells were scattered about the site when a train carrying munitions exploded. The site contains hundreds of thousands of World War I- and World War II-era conventional and CW munitions. The first CWDF (Munster I) began operation in the 1980s.

[78] On states not mentioned in this chapter see CBW chapters in previous editions of the SIPRI Yearbook.

an offensive BW programme.[79] Iran and Syria rejected the US allegations.[80] It is unclear what criteria the USA attaches to the term 'capability'.[81]

Evidence was given in the judicial proceedings against *Chile*'s former president, Augusto Pinochet, alleging that his government maintained a clandestine CBW programme that was run by the secret police. The programme allegedly produced sarin and the causative agents for anthrax and botulism. An unspecified lethal bacterial agent was also reportedly developed by the programme and used to assassinate former president Eduardo Frei Montalvo in January 1982.[82] If such a programme existed, it is not clear whether it was used to support a military BW capability or for assassination purposes.[83]

In September 2006 a US Department of State official testified to the US–China Economic Security Review Commission that the USA has 'reservations about *China*'s current research activities and dual-use capabilities, which raise the possibility that sophisticated CBW work could be underway' partly because of a possible capability to aerosolize CBW agents for offensive use and apparent Chinese military involvement in such research. The official stated that the USA believes that China maintains 'some elements of offensive BW capability in violation of its BWC obligations' and 'a CW production mobilization capacity'. She questioned China's commitment to effectively implementing export controls on dual-purpose items that could support offensive CBW programmes.[84] China responded that the 'accusations made by a

---

[79] Sixth BTWC Review Conference, 'USA: confronting noncompliance with the Biological Weapons Convention', document BWC/CONF.VI/WP.27* (reissued), 24 Nov. 2006, para. 7, p. 2. Iran and North Korea are parties to the BTWC; Syria has signed but not acceded to the convention.

[80] Sixth BTWC Review Conference, 'Statement by H. E. Mr. Ali Moaiyeri, Ambassador Extraordinary and Plenipotentiary and Permanent Representative of the Islamic Republic of Iran before the Sixth Review Conference of the States Parties to the Convention on the Prohibition of the Development, Production and Stockpiling of Bacteriological (Biological) and Toxin Weapons and on their Destruction (BWC)', Geneva, 20 Nov. 2006, URL <http://missions.itu.int/~missiran/sts2006/06112801BWC.pdf>; and Pearson, G., 'The Biological Weapons Convention Sixth Review Conference', *CBW Conventions Bulletin*, no. 74 (Dec. 2006), pp. 10, 16.

[81] US officials do not appear to have defined the term. Milton Leitenberg has stated that possible definitions include: (*a*) the procurement of dual-use equipment, (*b*) the possession of a well-developed pharmaceutical industry, and (*c*) various types of BW R&D work. See Leitenberg, M., *Assessing the Biological Weapons and Bioterrorism Threat* (Strategic Studies Institute, US Army War College: Carlisle, Pa., Dec. 2005), p. 15.

[82] In Mar. 2005 Frei's body was examined for traces of toxic chemicals after allegations by relatives that he was murdered with sarin. Three tissue samples, since discarded, reportedly indicated that he had been exposed to sulphur mustard. Spector, L. S., 'Allegations of Pinochet biological weapons (BW) program underscore challenges of BW control', *WMD Insights*, June 2006, URL <http://wmdinsights.org/I6/I6_LA1_AllegationsOfPinochet.htm>; Franklin, J., 'Pinochet accused over murder of ex-president', *The Guardian*, 18 May 2006; 'Pinochet charged in Chile for murder of secret police chemist Eugenio Barrios', *Santiago Times*, 12 May 2006, URL <http://www.tcgnews.com/santiagotimes/index.php?nav=story&story_id=11286&topic_id=1>; and MercoPress, 'Possible mustard gas poisoning of former Chilean president', 22 Jan. 2007, URL <http://www.mercopress.com/vernoticia.do?id=9693&formato=html>.

[83] Eugenio Berríos, the alleged founder of such a programme, was killed on a beach near Montevideo, Uruguay, in 1995. Franklin (note 82).

[84] DeSutter, P., Assistant Secretary for Verification, Compliance, and Implementation, 'The administration's perspective on China's record on nonproliferation', Testimony before the US–China Economic Security Review Commission, Washington, DC, 14 Sep. 2006, URL <http://www.state.gov/t/vci/rls/rm/72302.htm>.

handful of American officials' were 'groundless and irresponsible' and reiterated its commitment to its arms control and non-proliferation obligations.[85]

The trial in *Iraq* of members of Saddam Hussein's regime included charges of CW attacks against the Kurdish population of Iraq in the 1980s as part of the Anfal Campaign.[86] Saddam Hussein testified that the targets were not Iraqi citizens but Iranian agents and that 'any strike against Iran, be it with special ammunition, such as a chemical one, as it was alleged . . . I will take the responsibility with honor'.[87]

Former biological weapon activities

Further research was presented in 2006 on post-World War II BW work conducted by a number of states, including Canada, France, the Soviet Union, the UK and the USA.[88] A major study of the Soviet Anti-Plague System and its role in the Soviet BW programme was also published (together with Wendy Orent) by Igor Domaradskij, a scientist who worked in the system in Soviet times.[89] The system continues to conduct valuable disease surveillance and response and research work in Russia and the other former Soviet states. Knowledge of how past BW programmes were carried out and their rationale is useful in promoting better understanding of how threat perceptions can influence decisions to pursue offensive BW or bio-defence work. Such analyses can also assist in understanding the international disarmament and non-proliferation measures that must be taken in order to destroy infrastructure that formerly supported offensive BW work or how to ensure that such infrastructure is used for non-hostile purposes only.

V. Remaining verification issues in Iraq

The United Nations Monitoring, Verification and Inspection Commission, UNMOVIC, remained excluded from Iraq in 2006, but it continued to docu-

---

[85] Chinese Ministry of Foreign Affairs, 'Foreign Ministry spokesman Qin Gang's comment on accusation by American officials against China of non-proliferation', Beijing, 18 Sep. 2006, URL <http://www.fmprc.gov.cn/eng/xwfw/s2510/2535/t272376.htm>. The USA did not include China in its statement at the Sixth BTWC Review Conference listing the parties it believes to be violating the convention.

[86] See 'Timeline: Anfal trial', BBC News, 8 Jan. 2007, URL <http://news.bbc.co.uk/2/5272224.stm>.

[87] Daragahi, B., 'Memos outline chemical plans', *Los Angeles Times*, 19 Dec. 2006; and Santora, M., 'Hussein's trial sees videotapes of chemical attacks on Kurds', *New York Times*, 20 Dec. 2006.

[88] Wheelis, M., Rózsa, L. and Dando, M., *Deadly Cultures: Biological Weapons Since 1945* (Harvard University Press: Cambridge, Mass., 2006).

[89] In the late 1890s the Russian Government created a commission to develop and implement measures to fight plague, which was then endemic in much of the country. This was done partly by establishing a system of research institutes and field stations—the Anti-Plague System—elements of which were later used to support the Soviet BW programme. See the articles in *Critical Reviews in Microbiology*, vol. 32, no. 1 (Jan.–Mar. 2006). See also Domaradskij, I. V. and Orent, W., 'Achievements of the Soviet biological weapons programme and implications for the future', *Revue Scientifique et Technique de l'Office International des Epizooties*, vol. 25, no. 1 (2006), pp. 153–61; and Domaradskij, I. V. and Orent, W., *Biowarrior: Inside the Soviet/Russian Biological War Machine* (Prometheus Books: Amherst, N.Y., 2003), an English-language version of his self-published memoirs: *Perevyertysh* [Troublemaker] (Moscow, 1995).

ment and analyse the lessons learned from its inspection experiences—and those of its predecessor the United Nations Special Commission on Iraq (UNSCOM)—in the country beginning in 1991. The future of the organization remained uncertain. Although there were indications of an increased desire among UN Security Council members 'to wrap things up', they continued to disagree on UNMOVIC's future role, if any.[90] Discussions were also held on intelligence regarding Iraq's weapons of mass destruction (WMD) holdings and capabilities prior to the 2003 US-led invasion of the country. Although some questions relating to Iraq's CBW programmes remain unresolved, considerable progress has been made in verifying undeclared CW activities, including details about Iraq's production of VX and confirmation that large amounts of filled and unfilled munitions and chemical agents have been destroyed.[91] The BW programme was smaller than the other WMD programmes and BW production was not admitted by Iraq until 1995, when inspectors presented compelling evidence of such activities. UNMOVIC concluded that the BW programme may have been larger than declared by Iraq.[92]

In 2006 the OPCW conducted a second and third training course, both held in Jordan, to assist Iraqi officials to prepare for implementing the provisions of the CWC.[93] Iraq also sent an observer delegation to the 11th CSP. On 7 April the permanent representative of Iraq to the UN wrote to the acting executive chairman of UNMOVIC stating Iraq's intention to accede to the CWC, and on 30 May UNMOVIC provided Iraq with the relevant sections (edited to remove proliferation-sensitive content) of Iraq's December 2002 declaration.[94] On 15 September and 10 October Iraqi officials were provided with CD-ROMs containing 1200 pages of documents with information requested by Iraq.[95]

Pre-war intelligence and weapons of mass destruction

In 2006 the USA continued to debate the reliability of pre-war intelligence on Iraq. The debate focused on the organization of the intelligence community and the US Administration's alleged politicization of the intelligence process to make a public case for war.[96] US Senator Rick Santorum and Congressman

[90] Kerr, P., 'Three years later, Iraq investigations continue', *Arms Control Today*, vol. 36, no. 3 (Apr. 2006), pp. 38–39.

[91] UN Security Council, 'Summary of the compendium of Iraq's proscribed weapons programmes in the chemical, biological and missile areas', UN document S/2006/420, 21 June 2006, pp. 45–47. For this and other UNMOVIC documents cited in this chapter see the UNMOVIC website, URL <http://www.unmovic.org/>. See also the CBW chapters in previous editions of the SIPRI Yearbook.

[92] UN Security Council (note 91), pp. 59–68.

[93] OPCW, 'OPCW conducts second Chemical Weapons Convention training for Iraq officials', Press release no. 6, 15 Feb. 2006; and OPCW, 'OPCW conducts third OPCW training for Iraqi officials', Press release no. 99, 15 Dec. 2006.

[94] UN Security Council, 'UNMOVIC 25th quarterly report', UN document S/2006/342, 30 May 2006, pp. 2–3.

[95] UN Security Council, 'UNMOVIC 27th quarterly report', UN document S/2006/912, 22 Nov. 2006, p. 2.

[96] Pillar, P. R. , 'Intelligence, policy and the war in Iraq', *Foreign Affairs*, vol. 85, no. 2 (Mar./Apr. 2006), pp. 15–27. See also chapters 1 and 5 in this volume.

Peter Hoekstra made public declassified information to help stimulate further debate on whether any WMD had actually been found in Iraq.[97] The report stated that, since 2003, some 500 munitions filled with degraded sarin and sulphur mustard have been found in Iraq; that more such unrecovered weapons exist; and that they risk falling into the hands of terrorists or insurgent groups.[98] Further calls were made for greater declassification of intelligence information on these issues.[99] These developments also raised questions about the way in which WMD that were present in Iraq before the 1991 Gulf War were addressed in the 2005 report of the Iraq Survey Group (ISG), a US-led body that searched for WMD in Iraq.[100] Charles Duelfer, special advisor to the Director of the US Central Intelligence Agency (CIA), stated in his 2004 comprehensive report on Iraq's WMD that Iraq had completed the destruction of its CW stockpile that had been produced before 1991. However, small numbers of CW munitions were found in 2004 and more may be found in the future.[101] David Kay, who headed the ISG in 2003–2004, testified before the House Armed Services Committee that the chemical agents found were of such low quality that they did not constitute effective weapons and his report did not note them because the ISG did not concentrate on weapons that were produced before the 1991 Gulf War.[102]

Verification lessons learned

In 2006 UNMOVIC continued to compile information on Iraq's proscribed weapon programmes. Because some information gathered in the larger compendium was sensitive, a summary was prepared of the inspections carried out by UNMOVIC and UNSCOM and made public in 2006.[103]

Owing to the lack of procedures for conducting inspections, UNSCOM had to develop verification procedures to assess Iraq's compliance with its obligations under relevant UN Security Council resolutions. Key elements of and lessons learned about the verification process from the Iraq experience include

[97] US Office of the Director of National Intelligence, 'Unclassified, subject: Iraqi chemical munitions', 21 June 2006, URL <http://intelligence.house.gov/Media/PDFS/DNILetter.pdf>.

[98] US Office of the Director of National Intelligence (note 97). Such CW remnants will continue to be uncovered and did not constitute a military CW capability in 2003.

[99] E.g. Federation of American Scientists, Project on Government Secrecy, 'Iraq intelligence reports are over classified, senators say', *Secrecy News*, 12 Sep. 2006, URL <http://www.fas.org/blog/secrecy/2006/09/iraq_intelligence_reports_are.html>.

[100] See US Central Intelligence Agency, 'Comprehensive report of the Special Advisor to the DCI on Iraq's WMD', 30 Sep. 2004; and US Central Intelligence Agency, 'Addendums to the Comprehensive report of the Special Advisor to the DCI on Iraq's WMD', Mar. 2005, URL <https://www.cia.gov/cia/reports/iraq_wmd_2004/>.

[101] US Central Intelligence Agency, 'Key findings', vol. 3 (30 Sep. 2004), URL <https://www.cia.gov/cia/reports/iraq_wmd_2004/chap5.html#sect0>.

[102] Kay, D. A., 'Statement prepared for the House Armed Services Committee Hearing on reports of weapons of mass destruction findings in Iraq', 29 June 2006, URL <http://www.globalsecurity.org/wmd/library/congress/2006_h/>.

[103] UN Security Council, 'Summary of the compendium of Iraq's proscribed weapons programmes in the chemical, biological and missile areas', UN document S/2006/420, 21 June 2006, pp. 2–3.

the need to: draw on a variety of verification experiences in disarmament and arms control; maintain some degree of consistency in staffing in order to build institutional stability, objectivity and staff accountability; have sufficient resources to perform inspections and maintain relevant data and supporting documentation; and recognize the benefits of multidisciplinary inspections with a mix of complementary expertise.[104] When UNMOVIC replaced UNSCOM it acquired verification technology, equipment and the means of transport through UN procurement procedures, rather than directly from the member states. This facilitated the development and implementation of standardized verification procedures and a high degree of operational readiness when planning and preparing for inspections. It also reduced the risk of surveillance activities beyond the inspection mandate. UNMOVIC has now trained inspectors from about 50 countries and maintains a roster of trained inspectors to serve in Iraq on short-term contracts in case it should be asked to return to Iraq in future.[105]

Another lesson learned from the inspections in Iraq is the importance of understanding the verification conclusions that can be drawn from sampling and analysis results. These include: protecting against the perception that scientific results have proved or disproved an argument, guarding against both false-positive and false-negative test results, and implementing an agreed sampling and testing methodology at key points in a facility or location.[106] In one instance, UNSCOM found that the detection of conversion of a legitimate biological facility for BW purposes was 'especially difficult since such activities had taken place only for a short period of time, and the site required only minor adjustments for the production of a biological warfare agent'.[107] UNSCOM sometimes assumed that Iraq would not or could not carry out certain activities because to do so would risk the health and safety of facility workers.[108] Inspectors also might not always have understood what they were seeing. For example, inspectors missed the modification to some R-400A bombs that enabled them to be used to deliver BW agents. This was partly because Iraq had already declared the bombs as chemical munitions and partly because Iraq had denied producing BW munitions.[109] UNSCOM's experience demonstrated the importance of not relying excessively on sampling and

---

[104] UN Security Council (note 103), pp. 7–15.

[105] UN Security Council (note 103), pp. 17–18.

[106] UN Security Council (note 103), p. 66.

[107] UN Security Council (note 103), p. 67.

[108] E.g. UNSCOM was initially sceptical that Iraq had progressed beyond the R&D phase of a BW programme partly because, in the absence of conclusive evidence to the contrary, inspectors knew that, if liquid bacterial agent had been produced at al-Hakam, Iraqi workers would risk airborne contamination. However, it later became clear that Iraq had been prepared to accept such risks. UN Security Council (note 103), p. 67.

[109] UN Security Council (note 103), p. 67. The R-400 (a more general nomenclature for this type of munition) was designed for chemical fill and later as a binary CW. Most were empty at the time they were destroyed. In the mid-1990s it was revealed that Iraq had coated the interior of a small number of such munitions with a varnish in order to facilitate taking a BW fill.

analysis, of building an integrated information baseline and of being able to conduct interviews with Iraqis inside and outside the country.

UNMOVIC concluded that two major elements form the basis of an effective verification system: 'institutional knowledge encompassing the detailed experience and expertise gained from inspections and technical capabilities comprising verification technology and other necessary specialized assets'.[110] The need to preserve such know-how is a major factor in favour of prolonging UNMOVIC's mandate or transforming it into an organization to help support a general UN inspection capability.[111] Analysis of information gathered from systematic and comprehensive collections in areas relating to sites or activities can often reveal indications of possible undeclared proscribed activity or lead to investigations of less obvious sources, and UNMOVIC could carry out such analyses. Such analyses of indicators and how they have been used would be useful in helping to develop a more systematic approach to an overall inspection methodology.[112]

VI. Bio-terrorism prevention and remediation

Much of the current international focus on attempting to prevent the intentional misuse of biological materials emphasizes implementing measures to promote bio-safety and bio-security, terms that are used to cover a wide variety of activities and expectations.[113] Several types of institution and group have participated in activities in these fields, and each has a different perspective, mandate and set of institutional interests. Some cooperating institutions are partly concerned with acquiring new technology and equipment for themselves in the name of non-proliferation and safety efforts, while others are more interested in promoting increased transparency at biological defence establishments. Others are primarily interested in improving disease surveillance and response, pharmaceutical R&D, developing ethics and codes of conduct, or promoting good laboratory practice (GLP) and good manufacturing practice (GMP). For example, a survey of bio-security and bio-safety practices in Asia found that researchers were concerned mainly with accidental exposure to infectious agents, rather than intentional security breaches.[114] One of the difficulties of assessing the effectiveness of bio-security and bio-safety measures is the uncertainty associated with the BW threat and risk assessments.

---

[110] UN Security Council (note 103), p. 20.

[111] On the future of UNMOVIC see Guthrie, Hart and Kuhlau (note 39), pp. 725–27.

[112] UN Security Council (note 95), pp. 6–7.

[113] In some languages, one word covers both concepts: e.g. *biobezopasnost'* (Russian) and *biosäkerhet* (Swedish).

[114] Sandia National Laboratories, *A Survey of Asian Life Scientists: The State of Biosciences, Laboratory Biosecurity, and Biosafety in Asia*, Report no. SAND2006–0842 (Sandia National Laboratories: Albuquerque, N.M., Feb. 2006),

This is especially true in cases where little or no historical record exists to serve as a guide.[115]

Preventive bio-security activities

In 2006 the UN Secretary-General, Kofi Annan, called for a global forum to encourage the spread of legitimate biotechnology in order to eliminate infectious diseases, while at the same time recognizing the potential harm if biotechnology is put to destructive use by those seeking to develop diseases and pathogens for illegitimate purposes. Annan suggested that risks arising from negligence or deliberate misuse could be dealt with by several measures, such as voluntary codes of conduct, legally binding systems and regulatory bodies to oversee sensitive research.[116]

The World Health Organization (WHO) published a document on bio-risk management and laboratory bio-security guidance in September 2006. It focused on bio-risk management through bio-safety, laboratory bio-security and ethical responsibility and encouraged its member states to develop national frameworks for the security of biological materials. In the absence of national regulatory guidance, laboratory managers are urged to consider bio-risk management. The WHO has defined laboratory bio-safety as 'the containment principles, technologies and practices that are implemented to prevent the unintentional exposure of pathogens and toxins, or their accidental release'. Laboratory bio-security is defined as 'the protection, control and accountability for valuable biological materials ... within laboratories, in order to prevent their unauthorized access, loss, theft, misuse, diversion or intentional release'.[117]

On 8 September the UN General Assembly adopted the United Nations Global Counter-Terrorism Strategy, which provides an overarching systematic policy approach to combating terrorism. An attached plan of action 'encourage[s]' the Secretary-General to update the roster of experts and laboratories and technical guidelines and procedures in order to help ensure the 'timely and efficient' investigation of alleged CBW use; invites the UN system to develop a comprehensive database on biological incidents that is complementary to the planned Biocrimes Database being developed by the International Police Organization (Interpol); and encourages WHO to 'step up' its technical assistance to states to improve their public health systems in order to prevent and prepare for possible bio-terrorist attacks.[118]

---

[115] See Roffey, R. and Kuhlau, F., 'Enhancing bio-security: the need for a global strategy', *SIPRI Yearbook 2006* (note 39), pp. 732–48; and *Globalization, Biosecurity, and the Future of the Life Sciences* (National Academies Press: Washington, DC, 2006).

[116] UN News Centre, 'Accepting a prize, Annan proposes global forum to address biotechnology's benefits, risks', 17 Nov. 2006, URL <http://www.un.org/apps/news/story.asp?NewsID=20648&Cr=biotechnology&Cr1=>.

[117] World Health Organization (WHO), *Biorisk Management: Laboratory Biosecurity Guidance* (WHO: Geneva, Sep. 2006), pp. iii–iv, 6.

[118] United Nations, 'United Nations Global Counter-Terrorism Strategy', Plan of action: measures to prevent and combat terrorism, para. 11, and Measures to build states' capacity to prevent and combat

US activities

The US DOD issued an 'instruction' in 2006 on minimum security standards for safeguarding 'biological select agents and toxins' (BSATs). It establishes security standards for BSATs in the custody or possession of the DOD to ensure their security from attack, theft, wrongful use and inappropriate transfer to unauthorized receivers. The measures cover personnel, information, physical and transport security as well as the requirements for inventory and accountability.[119]

In 2004 the USA addressed the issue of dual-use research (research that can have peaceful or hostile application) partly by establishing an oversight body, the National Science Advisory Board for Biosecurity, to aid policymakers and researchers in assessing risks associated with US Government-funded research in the life sciences. A 2006 report questioned whether the available tools are sufficient and effectively implemented and if additional measures should be developed.[120]

The publication of a 2006 review of the US chemical industry infrastructure's vulnerability to possible terrorist attacks was delayed for several months by the US Department of Homeland Security out of concern that it contained classified information.[121] The report concluded that a single terrorist attack could result in catastrophic loss of life and injuries but would probably adversely affect only the operation of individual companies and local economies. However, multiple terrorist incidents would have national implications.[122] A bill authorizing more than $973 million of expenditure for homeland security was signed into law by President George W. Bush on 4 October 2006. It authorizes the Secretary of Homeland Security to issue risk-based security standards for high-risk chemical facilities.[123]

---

terrorism and to strengthen the role of the United Nations system in this regard, point 10, URL <http://www.un.org/terrorism/strategy/>. See also the Interpol bio-terrorism website, URL <http://www.interpol.int/Public/BioTerrorism/>; and the World Health Organization website on BW issues, URL <http://www.who.int/topics/biological_weapons/en/>.

[119] US Department of Defense, 'Instruction', no. 5210.89, 18 Apr. 2006, URL <http://www.fas.org/biosecurity/resource/reports.htm>. This instruction implements policy and assigns responsibilities under DOD directive 5210.88 on safeguarding biological select agents and toxins.

[120] Shea, D. A., *Oversight of Dual-use Biological Research: The National Science Advisory Board for Biosecurity*, US Library of Congress, Congressional Research Service (CRS) Report for Congress RL33342 (CRS: Washington, DC, 28 Mar. 2006), pp. 2, 7–12.

[121] National Research Council, Committee on Assessing Vulnerabilities Related to the Nation's Chemical Infrastructure, *Terrorism and the Chemical Infrastructure: Protecting People and Reducing Vulnerabilities* (National Academies Press: Washington, DC, 2006), URL <http://books.nap.edu/catalog/11597.html>; and Kosal, M., 'Terrorism targeting industrial chemical facilities: strategic motivations and the implications for US security', *Studies in Conflict and Terrorism*, vol. 30, no. 1 (Jan. 2007), pp. 41–73. See also Ember, L., 'Terrorism and the chemical industry', *Chemical & Engineering News*, vol. 84, no. 27 (3 July 2006), p. 25. The review investigated how best to invest in R&D and technology to make the chemical infrastructure more secure and able to withstand a terrorist attack or catastrophic accident. The committee was asked to focus on vulnerabilities of the chemical supply chain and the processes and key chemicals whose disruption might cause economic or human damage, and not the vulnerabilities of individual facilities, which would duplicate the work of other government efforts.

[122] National Research Council (note 121), pp. 2–4.

[123] Ember, L., 'Congress focuses on security before adjourning', *Chemical & Engineering News*, vol. 84, no. 41 (9 Oct. 2006), p. 10.

EU activities

A harmonized EU standard for biological 'select agents' does not exist. However, the European Commission Directorate-General for Justice, Freedom and Security is preparing a Green Paper on bio-preparedness (expected to be published in early 2007) that will call for preventive bio-security measures, and recommend the creation of a European strategy on bio-security.[124] This consultation paper will cover issues in the civil sector such as industry and research in the life sciences. A number of other relevant projects on bio-safety and bio-security have been launched, two of them in 2006, under the EU's Framework Programme 6 (FP6), the EU's main instrument for research funding in Europe. The Bio-safety–Europe project recently started an inventory of safety and security in P3 and P4 laboratories in Europe.[125] The project promotes the 'coordination, harmonisation and exchange of biosecurity practices within a pan European network'. It establishes a network of bio-safety experts and a website that includes an updatable inventory of information relevant to bio-safety and bio-security. A second FP6 project, BIOSAFE, is intended to strengthen the ability of public health and civil protection authorities to respond to the deliberate use of biological agents by terrorists, partly by establishing a European-wide network and a database information system. The project will evaluate the virulence factors of pathogens and toxins that could be used in acts of bio-terrorism.[126]

The 2001 anthrax letter attacks in the United States

It remains unclear whether the perpetrators of the 2001 attacks in the USA with anthrax spore-laden letters were domestic or foreign and, if domestic, the extent to which a non-state actor may have been involved.[127] It has been argued that a limited number of individuals with experience of working in US bio-defence programmes were responsible. This reasoning is partly based on the view that the *Bacillus anthracis* spores were 'highly refined'. In the view of some, the spores were also treated with additives to enhance the ability to aerosolize the particles (e.g. to prevent clumping). Both factors may suggest sophisticated engineering skills of a type that would normally only be found in a state-run R&D programme.[128]

---

[124] Bio-preparedness in this case is a general term that refers to both preventive and responsive measures such as bio-security, preparedness and response.

[125] EU Sixth Framework Programme, 'Project fact sheet: biosafety–Europe', URL <http://cordis.europa.eu/fp6/dc/index.cfm?fuseaction=UserSite.FP6HomePage>. P3 and P4 refer to the physical-containment levels of laboratories, with P4 being the most secure.

[126] EU Sixth Framework Programme (note 125), 'Project Fact sheet:BIOSAFE'. See also Kuhlau, F., *Countering Bio-Threats: EU Instruments for Managing Biological Materials, Technology and Knowledge*, SIPRI Policy Paper no. 19 (SIPRI: Stockholm, forthcoming 2007).

[127] For background see Zanders, J. P., Hart, J. and Kuhlau, F., 'Chemical and biological weapon developments and arms control', *SIPRI Yearbook 2002: Armaments, Disarmament and International Security* (Oxford University Press: Oxford, 2002), pp. 696–703.

[128] See Zanders, Hart and Kuhlau (note 127), p. 703.

The distinction between 'highly refined' and 'treated' spores is often confused. The former implies the removal of vegetative cells (cells that have not sporulated during the spore preparation process) and other debris. Thus, 'highly refined' implies a high concentration of spores only, while 'treated' implies that a substance has been added to the preparation in order to promote lower viscosity (resistance to flow) and to obtain a median number of spores having a certain diameter that is suitable for achieving deep lung penetration.[129] In 2006 a researcher at the Hazardous Materials Response Unit laboratory of the US Federal Bureau of Investigation (FBI) published a study on the sampling and analysis procedures used to investigate the attacks that also shed light on the above points. It includes a description of the challenges of integrating law enforcement and scientific and technical requirements when responding to bio-terrorism. According to the study, the understanding that the attacks involved sophisticated spore preparation is a 'widely circulated misconception' that is 'usually the basis for implying that the powders were inordinately dangerous compared to spores alone' and 'fosters erroneous misconceptions, which may misguide research and preparedness efforts and generally detract from the magnitude of hazards posed by simple spore preparations'.[130]

US developments in biological warfare prevention and defence

In December 2006 President Bush signed into law the Pandemic and All-Hazards Preparedness Act, which established the Biomedical Advanced Research and Development Authority (BARDA).[131] This authority is designed to identify vulnerabilities in existing medical and public health defences against chemical, biological, radiological and nuclear threats and to facilitate the development of countermeasures, including new medicines. BARDA will be part of the US Department of Health and Human Services, but its effect on existing drug R&D is unclear. Some of the information that BARDA possesses will be exempt from disclosure for at least five years.

This has been pointed to as an example of the lack of transparency in bio-defence activities, which creates concern that bio-defence and bio-terrorism preparedness programmes in some countries might serve as a general cover for an offensive BW capability.[132] In most countries there is also

[129] The size would be generally 1–5 microns in diameter (the optimal size for deep lung penetration through the alveolar sacs).

[130] Beecher, D. J., 'Forensic application of microbiological culture analysis to identify mail intentionally contaminated with *Bacillus anthracis* spores', *Applied and Environmental Microbiology*, vol. 72, no. 8 (Aug. 2006), pp. 5304–10.

[131] The White House, 'President Signs H.R. 5466, H.R. 6143, S. 843, and S. 3678 [the Pandemic and All-Hazards Preparedness Act]', News release, Washington, DC, 19 Dec. 2006, URL <http://www.whitehouse.gov/news/releases/2006/12/20061219-2.html>.

[132] Miller, J. D., 'New U.S. biodefense agency signed into law', *The Scientist*, 11 Jan. 2007, URL <http://www.the-scientist.com/news/home/40755/>; and Roffey, R., Hart, J. and Kuhlau, F., 'Crucial guidance: a code of conduct for biodefense scientists', *Arms Control Today*, vol. 36, no. 7 (Sep. 2006), pp. 17–20.

a lack of information about the size of such programmes. Funding of BW prevention and defence programmes in the USA, for which there is generally more information, has been estimated at $7905 million in 2006, and $8017 million has been requested for 2007. The cumulative funding for 2001–2007 is estimated to be $44 064 million.[133]

VII. Conclusions

The effectiveness of the annual meetings of the BTWC parties in 2007–10 will depend in part on whether they can agree measures and reach understandings that promote positive political or practical results. Such results are less likely if the meetings consist only of exchanges of views and information. The actions that states take will be affected by the extent to which the meetings are able to enhance national implementation of the BTWC's provisions and raise the level of political attention and importance attached to various preventive bio-security activities.

As CW stockpiles are further reduced, increased attention will focus on the overall purpose of the CWC and balancing convention activities, such as the extent to which efforts should concentrate on the verification of non-production of chemical weapons by the chemical industry and the implementation of scientific and technological assistance programmes.[134] The political willingness of the CW possessor states to accept visits may also be tested.

It is increasingly recognized that achieving universal adherence to the BTWC and the CWC and effectively implementing their provisions will substantially reduce the risk of CBW proliferation and terrorism. The fundamental CBW policy challenge remains how to define the threat posed by such weapons (both generally and in terms of specific cases) and what combination of national and international measures should be taken to best address the associated threats. A proper appreciation of the threats posed by CBW requires an interdisciplinary approach that encompasses historical, legal, political and technical factors. However, authoritative public information is lacking to enable assessment of the accusations that state and non-state actors wish to acquire, develop or use such weapons and possess the necessary expertise. The development of effective policies to implement threat assessments and risk-remediation strategies is not always well understood. The current increased focus on bio-safety and bio-security, national implementation of agreements, and outreach and awareness raising among the various scientific and technical communities (e.g. through codes of conduct) has highlighted a continued need to take practical and sustained measures in order to fulfil political commitments.

---

[133] Center for Arms Control and Non-Proliferation, 'Federal funding for biological weapons prevention and defense, fiscal years 2001 to 2007', Washington, DC, 21 June 2006, URL <http://www.arms controlcenter.org/archives/002259.php>, p. 1.

[134] See e.g. Thakur, R. and Haru, E. (eds), *The Chemical Weapons Convention: Implementation Challenges and Opportunities* (United Nations University Press: New York, N.Y., 2006).

14. Conventional arms control

ZDZISLAW LACHOWSKI and MARTIN SJÖGREN

I. Introduction

The year 2006 marked the seventh 'lean year' since the signing of the 1999 Agreement on Adaptation of the 1990 Treaty on Conventional Armed Forces in Europe (CFE Treaty), and no signs of further progress were evident at the Third CFE Treaty Review Conference in May. The 'hard' conventional arms control regime remains stalled by disagreements between Russia and the West over political texts adopted at the 1999 Istanbul Summit of the Organization for Security and Co-operation in Europe (OSCE).[1] As a result, entry into force of the adapted CFE Treaty remains hostage to the completion of Russia's promised military pullouts from Georgia and Moldova.[2] The March 2006 Russia–Georgia agreement, supplementing their 2005 agreement on the withdrawal of Russian military bases and other facilities from Georgia, indicated further progress in the withdrawal process, but deadlock persists over Russian personnel and equipment in Moldova.

In 2006 the OSCE continued to review and develop arms control-related endeavours, including confidence- and stability-building measures and other arrangements, to address the common risks and challenges facing Europe. Globally, progress on tackling 'inhumane weapons' continues, and Protocol V of the 1981 Certain Conventional Weapons (CCW) Convention on explosive remnants of war (ERW) entered into force.[3]

This chapter analyses the major issues and developments in conventional arms control in 2006. Section II discusses critical elements of the implementation of the CFE Treaty. Arms control-related efforts to promote confidence, render assistance and foster stability in the OSCE area and elsewhere are addressed in section III. The issue of mines and ERW is reviewed in sec-

---

[1] On conventional arms control in Europe before 1999 see the relevant chapters in previous editions of the SIPRI Yearbook. For the text of the CFE Treaty and Protocols see the OSCE website at URL <http://www.osce.org/fsc/documents.html>. For the text of the Agreement on Adaptation see *SIPRI Yearbook 2000: Armaments, Disarmament and International Security* (Oxford University Press: Oxford, 2000), pp. 627–42; and the OSCE website. See annex A in this volume for a brief summary of, and the parties to, the CFE Treaty, and the signatories of the Agreement on Adaptation.

[2] OSCE, Istanbul Summit Declaration, Istanbul, 17 Nov. 1999, para. 19; OSCE Final Act of the Conference of the States Parties to the Treaty on Conventional Armed Forces in Europe, Istanbul, 17 Nov. 1999. The text is reproduced in *SIPRI Yearbook 2000* (note 1), pp. 642–46. So far Russia has failed to implement the following Istanbul commitments: (*a*) to close the Gudauta base in Abkhazia, Georgia; (*b*) to withdraw all Russian troops from Moldova's Trans-Dniester region; and (*c*) to eliminate the stocks of ammunition and military equipment in the Trans-Dniester region.

[3] The 1981 Convention on Prohibitions or Restrictions on the Use of Certain Conventional Weapons which may be deemed to be Excessively Injurious or to have Indiscriminate Effects was signed on 10 Oct. 1980 at Geneva and entered into force on 2 Dec. 1983. For the signatories and parties to and basic information on this convention see annex A in this volume.

tion IV. Section V presents some conclusions regarding the status and future of conventional arms control.

II. European arms control

The CFE Treaty regime remains by far the most elaborate conventional arms control regime worldwide. Acclaimed as the cornerstone of European security, it has contributed significantly to removing the threat of large-scale military attack and has enhanced confidence, openness and mutual reassurance on the continent. The CFE Treaty process has also inspired regional arms control solutions in the Balkans and efforts elsewhere, such as in Central Asia.

The 1990 CFE Treaty set equal ceilings on the major categories of heavy conventional armaments and equipment of the two groups of states parties in the Atlantic-to-the-Urals (ATTU) zone of application. The Agreement on Adaptation discarded the original, bipolar concept of an equilibrium of forces between the North Atlantic Treaty Organization (NATO) and the now-defunct Warsaw Treaty Organization (Warsaw Pact), and introduced a new regime of arms control based on national and territorial ceilings codified as binding limits in the agreement's protocols. It increased the verifiability of its provisions and opened the adapted CFE Treaty regime to European states which were not parties to it. The Agreement on Adaptation has not yet entered into force because of the refusal of the members of NATO and other states to ratify it in the face of Russian non-compliance with its Istanbul commitments. Of the 30 signatories to the CFE Treaty, only Belarus, Kazakhstan and Russia have ratified the agreement. Ukraine has ratified the agreement but has not deposited its ratification document. The 1990 CFE Treaty and the associated agreed documents and decisions therefore remain binding on all parties. The Joint Consultative Group (JCG) is the body established by the states parties to monitor implementation, resolve issues arising from implementation and consider measures to enhance the viability and effectiveness of the treaty regime.

The Third CFE Treaty Review Conference, held in Vienna on 30 May–2 June 2006, failed to agree on a final document.

The Treaty on Conventional Armed Forces in Europe: implementation and adaptation issues

Operation and compliance

In spite of the stalemate over the completion of its adaptation, the CFE Treaty for the most part operates in a satisfactory manner. The Third Review Conference offered a balance sheet of the operation of the treaty in general and in the period since the previous review conference in 2001. It was noted that the overall holdings of conventional armaments and equipment within the area of application have been further reduced and a number of states parties have voluntarily reduced holdings to levels lower than those set in the treaty (table 14.1). At the Third Review Conference, Ukraine declared that it would voluntarily reduce its national levels for holdings of treaty-limited equipment (TLE) and of its national personnel limits. Since 1990, more than 5000 on-site inspections have been carried out and tens of thousands of documents of notification and annual information have been exchanged and submitted. A statement made on behalf of NATO at the conference summarized other aspects of implementation related to numerical limits as follows:[4] (*a*) the overall numerical ceilings for the TLE are generally observed; (*b*) all states parties comply with their overall maximum level for holdings (MLH); (*c*) national personnel limits laid down in the CFE-1A Agreement[5] are not exceeded; (*d*) by mid-2003 Russia had fulfilled the former Soviet Union's obligation pertaining to the TLE transferred east of the Urals, and in early 2005 it notified the OSCE of the destruction of the last equipment which had been declared to be non-combat capable and which had been held at the St Petersburg and Kushchevskaya maintenance facilities;[6] (*e*) no state party now exceeds the number of decommissioned TLE; and (*f*) all states parties comply with the numerical limitations applying to armoured vehicle-launched bridges in active units and with the political obligations regarding land-based naval aircraft. In addition, no state party maintains permanently land-based attack helicopters with its naval forces in the area of application.

With regard to notifications and inspections, the same statement noted that: (*a*) despite a lower number of inspection quotas (resulting from the reduction of TLE in states parties), the verification regime is being implemented with the same rigour and high intensity as before; (*b*) multinational inspection teams have provided an additional measure of transparency and cooperation; and (*c*) the exchange of information and notifications has provided a high degree of transparency. During declared site inspections, the counted holdings of equipment covered by the CFE Treaty were consistent with the data given in the exchanges of information almost without exception.

Attention was drawn at the review conference to a range of continuing political and technical implementation issues that remain of concern. These include: the stationing of forces on the territory of another state party without host-state agreement (i.e. Georgia and Moldova); the problem of uncontrolled and unaccounted-for TLE in the area of application (notably in territories with disputed sovereignty such as Nagorno-Karabakh in Azerbaijan, Abkhazia and South Ossetia in Georgia, and Trans-Dniester in Moldova); cases of unilateral reinterpretation of how to categorize and report items in the Protocol on

---

[4] Elaboration of elements for inclusion in a Final Document of 2006 CFE Review Conference as proposed to the Joint Consultative Group on behalf of Belgium [and the other NATO states], doc. JCG.DEL/4/06, 16 May 2006.

[5] The CFE-1A Agreement is the 1992 Concluding Act of the Negotiation on Personnel Strength of Conventional Armed Forces in Europe. It was signed on 10 July 1992 at Helsinki and entered into force simultaneously with the CFE Treaty. For a brief summary of this agreement see annex A in this volume.

[6] For more on the issue of 'non-combat-worthy' equipment see Lachowski, Z. 'Conventional arms control', *SIPRI Yearbook 1998: Armaments, Disarmament and International Security* (Oxford University Press: Oxford, 1998), p. 629.

Table 14.1. Treaty on Conventional Armed Forces limits and holdings as of 1 January 2006

	Tanks	ACVs	Artillery	Aircraft	Helicopters	Personnel
MLH/NPL	39 142	59 822	38 286	13 462	4 000	5 789 181
Holdings	24 774	44 140	28 236	7 135	1 971	2 892 667

ACVs = armoured combat vehicles; CFE = Treaty on Conventional Armed Forces in Europe; CFE-1A = Concluding Act of the Negotiation on Personnel Strength of Conventional Armed Forces in Europe; MLH = maximum level for holdings; NPL = national personnel limit.

Sources: Treaty on Conventional Armed Forces in Europe and the Concluding Act on the Negotiations on Personnel Strength of Conventional Armed Forces in Europe Joint Consultative Group, Group on Treaty Operation and Implementation, Consolidated matrix on the basis of data valid as of 1 Jan. 2006, JCG document JCG.TOI/21/06, 19 May 2006.

Existing Types of Conventional Armaments and Equipment (POET); reports of signatories exceeding current treaty limits for the flank region,[7] and exceeding overall and sub-zonal ceilings for equipment in active units; continued failure to account for TLE reportedly transferred from one CFE state party to another between 1994 and 1996 (i.e. Russian deliveries to Armenia); and the failure by some states to make notification of changes of 10 per cent or more in unit holdings, or to properly report the location of all objects of verification.[8]

Russia sought to reinterpret the CFE Treaty's definition of 'group of states'. In the light of successive enlargements of NATO, Russia has raised the issue of the numerical limits for NATO members, claiming that their present holdings of equipment in the five categories of TLE considerably exceeded the treaty's aggregate maximum levels for the countries in question. The same claim was made about Western ceilings for the flank zone.[9] All this reinforced Russia's argument that the immediate entry into force of the Agreement on Adaptation is the only sensible solution.

The issue of whether inspections should be paid for by the inspecting state remains outstanding.

---

[7] For background on and a discussion of the 'flank issue' see Lachowski, Z. 'Conventional arms control', *SIPRI Yearbook 1997: Armaments, Disarmament and International Security* (Oxford University Press: Oxford, 1997), pp. 476–79.

[8] It was suggested that the following implementation issues require further consideration and resolution in the JCG: mutual understanding of declared sites and common areas (designation of sensitive points/areas); photography rules; use of global positioning systems during inspections; documenting ambiguities; notification of certain types of armament and equipment; inability to conduct inspections in certain regions; interpretation of counting rules for export/re-export; differentiation between industrial testing and research and development; updating of POET; dealing with the problem of TLE unaccounted for and uncontrolled in the area of application; inspection costs; notification of final withdrawal of TLE and armoured vehicle launched bridges from designated permanent storage sites; and notification of changes to lists of inspectors and transport crew members. Elaboration of elements (note 4).

[9] Statements by the delegation of the Russian Federation under agenda items 3 and 5 of the Third CFE Treaty Review Conference, OSCE document CFE-TRC.3JOUR, annex 40, attachment, 2 June 2006.

Updating the POET lists

POET suffers from a lack of clarity as regards the types of TLE systems that are covered by the CFE Treaty. For many years this has adversely affected information exchange and hampered the work of inspectors. The JCG has not yet completed the mandate assigned to it by the 1996 and 2001 review conferences to update the lists of armaments and equipment in the protocol by, among other things, removing types, models and versions of equipment that do not meet treaty criteria. The POET sub-working group, formed in 2001, has so far agreed on four of the five categories in Section I of POET (TLE) and four of six categories in Section II (armaments and equipment not limited by the treaty, called 'lookalikes'). By the end of 2006, 'more than 99%' of all relevant armaments and equipment had reportedly been agreed.[10] In Section I, however, the problem of armoured combat vehicles (ACVs) remains unresolved; in Section II the outstanding issues are those of armoured personnel carrier lookalikes and armoured infantry fighting vehicle lookalikes. With regard to ACVs, the main sticking point concerns vehicles that have a gun with a calibre larger than 20 millimetres and a compartment too small to transport an infantry squad. These do not fall into any of the definitions under Article II of the CFE Treaty. With respect to the look-alikes, the argument is about specific types of equipment that have been in dispute for a long time.

The issue of an obligation to electronically exchange technical data and digitized photographs, as proposed in 2003, also remained unsettled in 2006.

The United States notified the JCG of the introduction into service of a new family of light armoured vehicles known as Stryker.

Treaty adaptation

In 2006 Russia continued to reject NATO's demand that ratification of the adapted CFE Treaty must be linked to the outstanding Istanbul commitments and also claimed that it has actually fulfilled all of the latter. Russian officials repeatedly argued that the lack of progress on the adapted CFE Treaty called into question the sense and purpose of the CFE regime, leaving it 'divorced from reality'. Since the beginning of the year, Russia on various occasions at various forums has warned that it could withdraw from the treaty 'in certain circumstances'.[11] Not surprisingly the Western position was the opposite: for example, Germany, a state party that has consistently sought a compromise

---

[10] Chairman's speaking points, POET working group meeting, OSCE document HCG.TOI/41/06, 12 Dec. 2006.

[11] See e.g. 'S. Ivanov: RF mozhet vyyti iz DOVSE' [S. Ivanov: Russia may leave the CFE], RosBiznesKonsalting, 24 Jan. 2006, URL <http://top.rbc.ru/index.shtml?/news/daythemes/2006/01/24/24000604_bod.shtml>. At the Third CFE Review Conference, Russia reserved the right to 'undertake a comprehensive analysis of the current situation' and inform the other states parties of the outcome of that analysis. Statement by the delegation of the Russian Federation at the Third CFE Treaty Review Conference, OSCE document CFE-TRC3.JOUR, annex 40, 2 June 2006.

solution to the deadlock, claimed that the treaty 'generally functions very well'.[12]

Before the review conference, Russia drafted its version of a conference final document suggesting that all states parties should provisionally apply the Agreement on Adaptation as from 1 October 2006, begin national ratification procedures, bring the adapted CFE Treaty into force in 2007 and discuss 'the possibility of accession of new participants'.[13] NATO rejected this, and the statement made by France on NATO's behalf at the OSCE ministerial meeting in Brussels at the end of the year reaffirmed the position that only fulfilment of the Istanbul commitments can 'create the conditions for the Allies and other States Parties to move forward on ratification of the Adapted CFE Treaty'.[14]

Georgia–Russia: the run-up to the 2008 deadline

On 30 May 2005 the ministers of foreign affairs of Georgia and Russia issued a joint statement regarding the closing of the Russian military bases and other military facilities and the withdrawal of Russian forces from Georgia.[15] The withdrawal is to take place in stages until 2008.

CFE-related developments in 2006 took place in the shadow of the growing political and economic tug of war between Georgia and Russia (which also backs Georgia's separatist entities, Abkhazia and South Ossetia).[16] On 31 March in Sochi two agreements were signed, one on the terms and rules of the temporary functioning and withdrawal of Russian military bases and other military facilities of the Group of Russian Forces in the Transcaucasus (GRFT), deployed on the territory of Georgia; and another on the transit of military cargo and personnel through its territory. The first agreement, however, failed to cover the Russian base in Gudauta, located in Abkhazia. Seeking to exempt the Russian 'peacekeepers' there from the obligation to withdraw, Russia proposed that an observation mission could be sent to Gudauta on condition that Georgia would then confirm that the military base had been closed there. Georgia declined the proposition. In July, through a parliamentary vote, Georgia called—in vain—for the replacement of Russian 'peacekeeping' troops by international police.

---

[12] Statement by the delegation of Germany at the Third CFE Treaty Review Conference, OSCE document CFE-TRC3.JOUR, annex 27, 31 May 2006. Other NATO delegations shared the view. E.g. the United Kingdom stated that the treaty remains 'both useful and relevant, chiefly in bringing greater certainty and predictability to an uncertain, unpredictable world'. Statement by the delegation of United Kingdom to the Joint Consultative Group, JCG document JCG.DEL/20/06, 19 Dec. 2006.

[13] Delegation of the Russian Federation to the Joint Consultative Group, Draft basic elements of the final document of the third conference to review the operation of the Treaty on Conventional Armed Forces in Europe, JCG document JCG.DEL/2/06, 9 May 2006.

[14] Statement by the delegation of France, OSCE Ministerial Council, Brussels 2006, OSCE document, MC(14). JOUR/2, 5 Dec. 2006.

[15] Joint Statement by the Ministers of Foreign Affairs of the Russian Federation and Georgia, 30 May 2005, available at the website of the Russian Ministry of Foreign Affairs, URL <http://www.ln.mid.ru /brp_4.nsf/clndr?OpenView&query=31.05.2005&Lang= ENGLISH>.

[16] For more on Georgia–Russia relations see chapter 1 in this volume.

In the early autumn tensions worsened between the two countries following the arrest of four Russian officers charged with espionage. The commander of the GRFT, Major General Andrei Popov, reportedly threatened to suspend the withdrawal of troops and armaments. However, Russian President Vladimir Putin quickly disavowed this statement.[17] All regional problems during the year notwithstanding, the pull-out of Russian armaments and troops continued, winning praise from the Western and other states. The withdrawal process was crowned at the end of 2006 with the removal, ahead of schedule, of the last personnel from the headquarters of the GRFT in Tbilisi.

Russian troops and ammunition in Moldova

In 2006 Moldova made no progress in its military relations with Russia. Under its 1994 constitution, Moldova is permanently neutral and refuses to host foreign forces on its territory. Withdrawal of Russian TLE was completed in 2003, but the failure to achieve a political settlement of the problem of the separatist Trans-Dniester region caused Russia to delay the withdrawal of its troops and the disposal of its approximately 20 000 tonnes of stockpiled ammunition and non-TLE in that area.

During 2006 Moldova intensified its challenge to the legitimacy of Russia's military presence. Russia's claims to legitimacy are based on a series of agreements reached in 1992–94, none of which Moldova accepts as legally valid. Russia continued to insist on making the withdrawal of its forces and ammunition contingent on a political settlement on the issue of the Trans-Dniester region, which Russia itself has made impossible to achieve by supporting the self-appointed authorities in the separatist entity.[18] CFE inspections to the Russian ammunition depots in the region continued to be obstructed. However, on 13 November 2006 a group of heads and deputy heads of OSCE delegations visited the Russian ammunition depot at Colbasna in Trans-Dniester. This was the first time OSCE representatives had been able to enter the depot since March 2004. The '5+2' format talks that attempted to find a solution to the Trans-Dniester problem in 2005 did not resume in 2006.[19] Ammunition removal activities also remained stalled during the year.

Moldova and other issues related to the Istanbul commitments were the main points on which efforts to agree on the political and 'regional'

---

[17] Dzhindzhikashvili, M., 'Russian arrests threaten pullout', *Washington Times*, 30 Sep. 2006; and 'Russian forces on high alert in Georgia', *International Herald Tribune*, 2 Oct. 2006.

[18] Russia has also claimed that 'the ammunition supplies are extremely hazardous and could be withdrawn only with cooperation of the local authorities and with guarantees of security on their part, and these, for familiar reasons, are not available at present'. Statement by Alexei Brodavkin, Permanent Representative of the Russian Federation at the meeting of the OSCE Permanent Council, OSCE document PC.DEL/531/06, 9 June 2006.

[19] These talks involved 5 directly engaged parties (Moldova, the OSCE, Russia, the Trans-Dniester entity and Ukraine) plus 2 observers (the European Union and the USA), and were launched in Oct. 2005 in an attempt to reach a political agreement.

declarations at the Brussels OSCE ministerial meeting in December 2006 foundered.[20]

The Baltic states and the Treaty on Conventional Armed Forces in Europe

Although Russia has declared itself (moderately) satisfied with the political assurances of military restraint that it has received from NATO since 1997, it still considers them insufficient in the context of the CFE Treaty regime. At the Third CFE Review Conference, despairing of the lack of progress on the adapted CFE Treaty and what it sees as the 'abstract' nature of Western commitments, Russia called on the West to re-address the situation created by the admission of the Baltic states to NATO in 2004, and to redress the 'balance' of commitments involving the latter.[21] Russia insisted on having more clarity on NATO's earlier promise not to permanently station 'substantial combat forces' on its Baltic members' territory (as on other new members' territories), and on the quantities of conventional armaments to be held there. It argued that fulfilment of the pledge made by the Baltic states to accede to the adapted CFE Treaty remained uncertain,[22] and that Russia's own commitments on restraint in the north-western part of its territory had therefore lost much of their political and military logic. Consequently, Russia demanded further concrete 'elements' in the treaty, including unilateral reductions in the national armament levels of the NATO countries. It stressed that it would judge how far NATO had taken into account its security interests and those of other states parties' in the light of the extent to which NATO established parameters to make concrete its restraint.[23]

Subregional arms control in the former Yugoslavia

By the end of 2006, around 9000 heavy weapons had been destroyed in the area of application of the Agreement on Sub-regional Arms Control, the so-called Florence Agreement (agreed under Article IV of Annex 1B of the General Framework Agreement for Peace in Bosnia and Herzegovina).[24] As of January 2006, new issues arose for the Florence Agreement after the dissolution of the defence ministries at the level of the two entities that comprise

---

[20] At the 2006 Brussels ministerial meeting, Moldova strongly called for the earliest transformation of the 'peacekeeping' force in the security zone into a multinational force under an international mandate, and reiterated that unless Moldova is free from any foreign military or quasi-military presence, it will not ratify the CFE Agreement on Adaptation. Statement by Andrei Stratan, Deputy Prime Minister and Minister of Foreign Affairs and European Integration of the Republic of Moldova at the 14th OSCE Ministerial Council Meeting, Brussels, 5 Dec. 2006, OSCE document MC.DEL/79/06.

[21] The 3 Baltic states—Estonia, Latvia and Lithuania—are not parties to the CFE Treaty.

[22] In effect, such Baltic action is blocked until the requirements set for ratification of the Agreement on Adaptation by NATO as a whole (i.e. fulfilment of the Istanbul commitments) are met.

[23] Statements by the delegation of the Russian Federation (note 8).

[24] The General Framework Agreement for Peace in Bosnia and Herzegovina (Dayton Agreement), was signed at Dayton, Ohio, 14 Dec. 1995. On Annex 1B, see URL <http://www.oscebih.org/essentials/gfap/eng/annex1b.asp>. The text of the Florence Agreement is available at URL <http://www.oscebih.org/security_cooperation/?d=4>.

Bosnia and Herzegovina (the Federation of Bosnia and Herzegovina and Republika Srpska), and the transfer of their competences to the newly created Bosnia and Herzegovina Ministry of Defence. All the parties to the Florence Agreement (Bosnia and Herzegovina, Croatia, and Serbia and Montenegro), agreed that, under its terms, as from 10 March 2006 Bosnia and Herzegovina should be represented only at state level. After Montenegro gained independence in June 2006 following the May 2006 referendum, it became party to the agreement on 16 January 2007 after all parties had notified their consent.[25]

III. Building confidence and stability

After disquieting signals from some OSCE states with respect to the evolution of the confidence- and security-building process in Europe, there was more optimism and activity in this area in 2006. The ongoing Security Dialogue in the OSCE's Forum for Security Cooperation (FSC) highlighted a range of issues, including those related to arms control and confidence-building. The OSCE's long-awaited fifth seminar on military doctrine was held at the beginning of the year. Two new Russia-sponsored confidence- and security-building measures (CSBMs) were proposed in the FSC. Confidence- and stability-building endeavours within the OSCE continued in the fields of small arms and conventional ammunition. Following a 2005 workshop, a special FSC meeting on the Code of Conduct (COC) on Politico-Military Aspects of Security took place in September.

The fifth OSCE military doctrine seminar

Military doctrine seminars are part of the OSCE's confidence-building 'toolbox'. In accordance with the recommendation included in the 1999 Vienna Document to hold 'periodic high-level military doctrine seminars similar to those already held',[26] the fifth OSCE seminar on military doctrine was held in Vienna on 14–15 February 2006 under the auspices of the FSC. High-level governmental and military representatives from all the OSCE member states, partner states and interested institutions, as well as independent experts, gathered for the seminar, which had the stated purpose of examining 'changes in military doctrine derived from evolving threats, changing forms of conflict and the emergence of new technologies'. The seminar also considered the consequences of such changes for armed forces and defence structures.[27] This

[25] Serbia and Montenegro will divide the agreement-limited armament ceilings. The agreement will be amended accordingly during 2007.

[26] OSCE, Vienna Document 1999 on the Negotiation of Confidence- and Security-Building Measures, chapter II, para. 15.7, URL <http://www.osce.org/documents/html/pdftohtml/4265_en.pdf.html>.

[27] Agenda, timetable and modalities for the OSCE high-level seminar on military doctrine, Decision no. 4/05, FSC document FSC.DEC/4/05, 16 Nov. 2005.

was the first such event since the seminal seminar of 2001. The first three were held in 1990, 1991 and 1998.[28]

Session one of the seminar dealt broadly with doctrinal change, focusing on such issues as changing threats, changing forms of conflict and the contribution made by politico-military instruments to tackling new challenges. It was broadly agreed that the security environment in the OSCE area was currently characterized by a mixture of 'old' and 'new' threats, with the latter including weapons of mass destruction (WMD) proliferation, terrorism, and trafficking in arms, people and narcotics.

Session two addressed technological changes and identified both benefits and challenges for militaries resulting from such changes. Among the benefits was the potential for modernization and transformation of military forces. However, the increased availability of advanced technologies (which might also be exploited by non-state actors) also creates increased vulnerability. Efforts to prevent such capacities falling into the wrong hands—whether state or non-state—were discussed, and special attention was paid to the implications of technological changes for defence capabilities, interoperability of national forces, and multinational operations.

Session three sought to draw lessons from the discussions in the preceding two sessions, focusing on the impact of the doctrinal and technological changes on military structures and activities, as well as on security and defence policy in a broad sense. There was general agreement that changes in military structures were necessary and that the armed forces should be reorganized with an emphasis on the quality, professionalism and flexibility of the troops, as well as their interoperability with the forces of other OSCE states. The challenge of reorganization will, however, be different for the various OSCE participating states, because some militaries are struggling to manage the rapid pace of change already taking place, while others are seeking to overcome the obstacles to speeding it up.[29]

Owing to the format of the military doctrine seminars, which are designed to encourage dialogue and discussion, no concrete decisions were taken. However, a number of issues that will have to be addressed were identified in the final session of the seminar. They included: (a) ways of dealing with the failure of the adapted CFE Treaty to enter into force; (b) extending the geographical coverage of the various OSCE CSBM mechanisms, such as the 1992 Treaty on Open Skies,[30] to include all the OSCE member states; (c) the further development of the Vienna Document; (d) exploring how to apply CSBMs and arms control to specific subregions of the OSCE area; (e) exchanges

---

[28] On the 2001 military doctrine seminar see Lachowski, Z., 'Conventional arms control', *SIPRI Yearbook 2002: Armaments, Disarmament and International Security* (Oxford University Press: Oxford, 2002), p. 720–21. On the 1990, 1991 and 1998 military doctrine seminars see the relevant chapters in the 1991, 1992 and 1999 editions of the SIPRI Yearbook.

[29] For more on the discussions in the various sessions at the seminar see the reports of the session rapporteurs in 'OSCE seminar on military doctrine: consolidated summary', OSCE document FSC.MDS/36/06, Vienna, 17 Mar. 2006.

[30] The Treaty of Open Skies was signed at on 24 Mar. 1992 at Helsinki and entered into force on 1 Jan. 2002. For the parties to and basic information on the treaty see annex A in this volume.

within the OSCE on norms and principles regarding defence relationships and military tasks within society, especially in dimensions where the private sector has come to play an extensive role; (*f*) discussing further the OSCE's role in international efforts to prevent WMD proliferation and conventional arms trafficking, in landmines control and in the task of safely destroying outdated and unwanted military equipment; (*g*) exploring the possibilities for cooperation within the OSCE on training for military adaptation to new tasks with emphasis on conflict-related missions; and (*h*) developing generic partnerships with other organizations and states, such as other European institutions, the United Nations, neighbouring states and partner states in other regions, and subregional groupings both within and across the OSCE's boundaries.[31]

In his closing remarks, the chairperson of the seminar expressed hope that the issues discussed would be followed up at the different forums of the OSCE.[32] Some of the topics were indeed addressed during 2006, both in the context of the FSC's Security Dialogue (e.g. rapidly deployable forces) and at the 2006 Annual Security Review Conference, especially in its working group on politico-military aspects.[33] It remains to be seen whether and how the thoughts and concepts presented at the seminar will influence the ongoing changes in participating states' military postures, policies and doctrines.

Confidence-building measures

Two particular developments in CSBMs engaged the OSCE participating states during the year. On 7 June 2006 Russia submitted two proposals for consideration on: (*a*) complementary measures for risk reduction during the deployment of foreign military forces in the OSCE area;[34] and (*b*) prior notification of a large-scale military transit in the same zone.[35] Both proposals were further clarified at the FSC meetings during the autumn.[36] The first document addressed the matter of foreign military presence in the territory of a number of OSCE states. Russia suggested that the existing mechanism regarding unusual military activity provided in Chapter III of the Vienna Document had been little used because it was too complex and easily politicized. Instead, Russia proposed that as well as using the existing (hopefully simplified) procedure applicable within national borders, a complementary procedure giving a more concrete meaning to the term 'militarily

[31] Statement by the moderator of session 4, OSCE seminar on military doctrine, FSC document FSC.MDS/36/06, 17 Mar. 2006, pp. 15–19.

[32] Closing remarks by the Chairperson of the OSCE seminar on military doctrine, OSCE seminar on military doctrine, Consolidated summary, FSC doucment FSC.MDS/36/06, 17 Mar. 2006.

[33] OSCE Annual Security Review Conference, Working group II: Challenges in the security environment—politico-military contributions, with emphasis on the proceedings and findings of the military doctrine seminar 2006 (Vienna, 27–28 June 2006), Chair's report, OSCE document, PC.DEL/779/06, 19 July 2006.

[34] FSC document FSC.DEL/233/06, 6 June 2006.

[35] FSC document FSC.DEL/233/06 (note 34), Proposing notification of a large-scale transfer (transit) of land formations is not new in the CSBM history. A similar proposal was made in 1998.

[36] FSC document FSC.DEL/475/06; and FSC document FSC.DEL/476/06. Russia presented drafts of both proposals on 27 Oct. 2006.

significant' deployments of foreign forces (i.e. movements at brigade level and above) could be applied to both unusual and scheduled activities in the OSCE area. Russia's second proposal called for any states involved in a large-scale (brigade level and above) trans-border redeployment of manpower and equipment to submit prior notification of the purpose, the destination point(s) and the scheduled time frame of the redeployment. Both documents were intensely discussed but were not adopted in 2006. However, they will be considered further in 2007.

Confidence-building agreements between Greece and Turkey

In recent years Greece and Turkey, still dogged by continuing disputes over Cyprus and the Aegean Sea, have made efforts to improve their level of mutual confidence. These efforts have resulted in a number of confidence-building measures CBMs.[37] At a meeting between the Greek and Turkish foreign ministers on 9 June 2006, agreement was reached on the following additional CBMs: the establishment of a direct telephone line between the respective military chiefs of staff; extension by a month of the moratorium on military exercises in the Aegean Sea; mutual visits and regular contacts between respective coastguard commanders; joint military and civilian exercises for natural disaster response;[38] a hotline between operational headquarters of the respective air forces; construction of a second bridge at a border crossing; and the creation of a committee to improve cooperation on flood prevention on the Meric River.[39]

However, tensions remain, and in 2006 mock dogfights continued to occur between the Greek and Turkish air forces over the Aegean Sea. In an incident in May a Greek aircraft and a Turkish aircraft collided, killing the Greek pilot.[40] While this incident highlighted the need for improved relations between the two states, it also made clear that the CBMs agreed so far have been largely symbolic and have done little to reduce tensions.

The OSCE Code of Conduct on Politico-Military Aspects of Security

A year after the special workshop on the occasion of its 10th anniversary, a special meeting on the Code of Conduct on Politico–Military Aspects of Security was held at Vienna on 27 September 2006. The discussions included

---

[37] For background on the conflict and the confidence-building process see Lachowski, Z. and Sjögren, M., 'Conventional arms control', *SIPRI Yearbook 2004: Armaments, Disarmament and International Security* (Oxford University Press: Oxford, 2004); Lachowski, Z., 'Conventional arms control', *SIPRI Yearbook 2001: Armaments, Disarmament and International Security* (Oxford University Press: Oxford, 2001); and Lachowski, Z. and Kronestedt, P., 'Confidence- and security-building in Europe', *SIPRI Yearbook 1999: Armaments, Disarmament and International Security* (Oxford University Press: Oxford, 1999).

[38] The first such exercise was held in Nov. 2006.

[39] 'Turkey, Greece take action to restore confidence', *Turkey News,* 7–14 June 2006, URL <http://www.tusiad.us/specific_page.cfm?CONTENT_ID=603>.

[40] Gatopoulos, D., 'Greek and Turkish fighter planes collide over Aegean Sea', *International Herald Tribune,* 23 May 2006.

contributions by experts from the various OSCE states and focused on three topics: review and assessment of implementation of the COC and its question-naire;[41] improving the implementation and effectiveness of the document, including practical suggestions, assistance and means, and complementary measures; and the COC's role in combating terrorism. The report of the meeting included a survey of suggestions and recommendations for measures that, in the view of the participants, could enhance the standing, operation and role of this valuable document. However, some of the views expressed were contradictory.[42] Some were in favour of reopening or renegotiating the document and bringing more clarity and precision into its wording and structure. Others warned against such a step and advocated additional protocols to better address the existing threats and challenges. Further measures and arrange-ments were proposed ranging from enhancing awareness of the COC in various environments (national, institutional, regional, and outside the OSCE area) to specific steps for improving the questionnaire, such as strengthening the COC's implementation review in the FSC. If nothing else, the intensive debate and almost 50 recommendations submitted at the meeting testify that this normative, cross-dimensional document retains its relevance.

Destruction of ammunition stockpiles and toxic fuel

Insecure or uncontrolled stockpiles of conventional ammunition and the liquid rocket fuel component ('mélange') pose multiple security, humanitarian, eco-nomic and environmental risks. Under the 2003 OSCE Document on Stock-piles of Conventional Ammunition (SCA Document), any OSCE state that has identified a security risk from its surplus stockpiles and needs help to address such a risk may request assistance from the international community through the OSCE.[43]

Up to the end of 2006, 10 requests for assistance with disposal had been submitted to the OSCE: for disposal of conventional ammunition from Bel-arus, Kazakhstan, Russia, Tajikistan and Ukraine,[44] and for the elimination of mélange from Armenia, Azerbaijan, Kazakhstan, Ukraine and Uzbekistan. Phase one of a small arms and light weapons (SALW) and conventional ammunition destruction project in Tajikistan was completed in 2006.

In 2006 the FSC completed two best practice guides: one on stockpiles management drafted by the USA,[45] which was adopted by the OSCE; and

---

[41] Participating states agree to share information on the implementation of their COC obligations through a questionnaire. An updated questionnaire was adopted in 2003.

[42] Summary of the special FSC meeting on the implementation of the Code of Conduct on Politico-Military Aspects of Security, Vienna, 27 Sep. 2006, FSC document FSC.GAL/98/06, 17 Oct. 2006.

[43] OSCE, OSCE document on stockpiles of conventional ammunition, 19 Nov. 2003, URL <http://www.osce.org/fsc/item_6_16338.html>.

[44] The explosions and fires in May 2004, July 2005 and Aug. 2006 at the ammunition depots in Novo-bohdanivka, Ukraine, show the urgency of international assistance in disposal of conventional ammu-nition. See appendix 14A on global efforts to control man-portable air defence systems (MANPADS).

[45] Decision no. 9/06, Best practice on stockpiles of conventional ammunition, FSC document FSC.DEC/9/06, 29 Nov. 2006.

another on the transport of ammunition drafted by Germany, which by the end of 2006 had not been agreed. The FSC also made progress on two other best practice guides: on marking, tracing and record-keeping; and on stockpile destruction, drafted by Germany and the Netherlands, respectively.

Small arms and light weapons

The 2000 OSCE Document on SALW,[46] along with other relevant documents,[47] remains an effective instrument for addressing the substance of SALW problems, fostering transparency and confidence among the participating states, and helping to combat terrorism and organized crime. In 2001–2005 the OSCE participating states destroyed more than 5.2 million items of small arms that were deemed surplus or were seized from illegal possession and trafficking.[48] In May 2006 the FSC held a special meeting on SALW to prepare for the UN Review Conference on the Programme of Action to Prevent, Combat and Eradicate the Illicit Trade in SALW in All Its Aspects (POA) in New York on 26 June–7 July.[49] The participating states exchanged views on the OSCE *acquis* in SALW and its implementation, and discussed the overall OSCE contribution to the review conference.

Two important related issues were addressed at the OSCE in 2006. To tackle the threat posed by unauthorized proliferation and use of MANPADS (man-portable air defence systems), the FSC adopted Annex C to the Handbook of Best Practices on SALW concerning the national procedures for stockpile management and security of MANPADS.[50] In November the FSC decided to hold a special meeting on combating illicit trafficking of SALW by air. Its aims are to develop a mechanism to exchange information on the national legislation and regulations of the participating states on import and export controls relating to the air transport sector; to develop a best practice guide in

---

[46] OSCE, OSCE Document on Small Arms and Light Weapons, Vienna, 24 Nov. 2000, URL <http://www.osce.org/fsc/13281.html>.

[47] These OSCE documents include the OSCE Document on Small Arms and Light Weapons (note 45); Principles for export controls of man-portable air defence systems (MANPADS); Standard elements on end-user certificates and verification procedures for SALW exports; and Principles on the control of brokering in SALW. For a discussion of MANPADS see appendix 14A; Lachowski and Sjögren (note 37); Anthony, I. and Bauer, S., 'Transfer control and destruction programmes' (note 37); and Lachowski, Z. and Dunay, P., 'Conventional arms control and military confidence building', *SIPRI Yearbook 2005: Armaments, Disarmament and International Security* (Oxford University Press: Oxford, 2005).

[48] FSC Chairperson's Progress Report to the Fourteenth Meeting of the Ministerial Council, Further implementation of the OSCE Document on Small Arms and Light Weapons, Dec. 2006, Brussels, FSC document, MC.GAL/4/06/Corr.2, 23 Nov. 2006.

[49] Many suggestions were made during the SALW special meeting on 17 May. See Special FSC Meeting on SALW, 17 May 2006, Survey of suggestions, FSC document FSC.GAL/49706/Corr.1, 1 June 2006. See also Report to the review conference on the implementation of the United Nations Programme of Action to Prevent, Combat and Eradicate the Illicit Trade in Small Arms and Light Weapons in All Its Aspects, FSC document FSC.GAL/59/06, 23 June 2006. On recent developments in the UN SALW process see appendix 10C in this volume.

[50] Decision no. 3/06, FSC document FSC.DEC/3/06, 29 Mar. 2006; and FSC document FSC.DEL/33/06, 3 Mar. 2006. For more on OSCE measures to control MANPADS see appendix 14A.

this respect; and to engage in a dialogue with private business in the air transport sector as well as with competent international organizations.[51]

The implementation of Section V of the SALW document on requests for assistance from the OSCE states in the field of stockpile management and reduction remains one of the most dynamic areas of implementation. Three requests were submitted to the FSC in 2006 to address problems related to SALW: two from Tajikistan and one from Belarus.

IV. Confidence-building efforts outside Europe

Latin America

Since the early 1990s there has been a security dialogue within the Organization of American States (OAS), and the promotion and adoption of CSBMs has been a central aspect of this process. The evolution of CSBMs in Latin America differs from that in Europe: measures are voluntary, consisting of a loose inventory of confidence-building measures, and are implemented more on a bilateral than regional or subregional basis. The most important agreements to date are: (a) the 1994 Buenos Aires Meeting of Governmental Experts, which produced an Illustrative List of CSBMs; (b) the 1995 Santiago CSBM conference, at which the Declaration of Santiago was adopted; (c) the 1998 San Salvador CSBM conference, which produced the Declaration of San Salvador; and (d) the 2003 Miami Meeting of Experts on CSBMs, which adopted the Consensus of Miami and a new Illustrative List of CSBMs.[52]

The second meeting of the Forum on CSBMs was held in November 2006.[53] The purpose of the Forum was to review and evaluate the implementation of agreed CSBMs in the region and to consider adopting further measures, especially from those in the Miami Illustrative List of CSBMs. The main issue at the meeting was the downward trend in reporting by member states of their implementation of CSBMs. In order to reverse this tendency, the use of one simplified reporting format (instead of the existing three) was proposed and received widespread agreement. A third meeting of the Forum on CSBMs will be held in 2007, and a high-level event is scheduled to take place in 2008.[54]

---

[51] Decision no. 7/06, Combating the illicit trafficking of small arms and light weapons by air, FSC document FSC.DEC/7/06, 15 Nov. 2006.

[52] For more on these declarations and agreements see the chapters on conventional arms control in the relevant editions of the SIPRI Yearbook. The texts of the declarations and agreements, as well as further information about the CSBM process, are available at the OAS website, URL <http://www.oas.org/csh/english/csbm.asp>.

[53] The Forum on CSBMs was convened in the wake of the 2003 Consensus of Miami. The first meeting of the forum was held in Apr. 2005. See Committee on Hemispheric Security of the Permanent Council of the Organization of American States, Forum on Confidence- and Security-Building Measures, First Meeting, Rapporteur's report, OEA/Ser.K/XXIX, CSH/FORO-I/doc.10/05, 27 Apr. 2005, URL <http://www.oas.org/csh/english/Foro.asp>.

[54] Committee on Hemispheric Security of the Permanent Council of the Organization of American States, Forum on Confidence- and Security-Building Measures, Second meeting, Rapporteur's report, OEA/Ser.K/XXIX, CSH/FORO-II/doc.11/06, 14 Dec. 2006. URL <http://www.oas.org/csh/english/Foro.asp>.

West Africa: the ECOWAS Convention

On 14 June 2006 in Abuja, Nigeria, the heads of state of the 15 member states of the Economic Community of West African States (ECOWAS) signed a legally binding convention on SALW.[55] It aims to 'prevent and combat the excessive and destabilizing accumulation of small arms and light weapons within ECOWAS' and builds on the 1998 ECOWAS Moratorium on Importation, Exportation and Manufacture of Light Weapons in West Africa. The convention sets out common standards on a range of issues relating to SALW, including imports, exports, brokering, and marking and tracing. In addition, the convention obliges states parties to establish national databases detailing transactions and holdings of SALW and to submit to the ECOWAS Executive Secretary an annual report detailing orders and purchases of SALW. The ECOWAS Convention and the mechanisms it has created offer a new opening to work for transparency and confidence-building processes in West Africa, a region where reliable information on the topic of defence and arms acquisitions has been lacking in recent years.[56]

V. Mines and unexploded ordnance

Anti-personnel mines

The 1997 Convention on the Prohibition of the Use, Stockpiling, Production and Transfer of Anti-Personnel Mines and on their Destruction (APM Convention), commits states parties to destroy their stockpiles and clear their territories of anti-personnel mines (APMs).[57] This process has been very successful since the entry into force of the convention in 1999, contributing to improvements in both human and conventional security. In 2006 a further four states ratified the convention and one acceded to it, bringing the total number of ratifications and accessions to 152.[58] The most significant ratification was that of Ukraine, which has the fourth largest stockpile in the world (6.7 million APMs). However, over 160 million APMs are still stockpiled by states that remain outside the APM Convention, including China (110 million), Russia (26.5 million), the USA (10.4 million), Pakistan (6 million) and India (4–5 million).

The states parties to the convention agreed to destroy their existing stockpiles within four years of ratification, and to clear their territory of deployed

---

[55] The text of the Convention on Small Arms and Light Weapons, their Ammunition and Other Related Materials is available at URL <http://www.iansa.org/regions/wafrica/documents/CONVENTION-CEDEAO-ENGLISH.PDF>. See also annex A in this volume.

[56] For a recent analysis of military finances in Africa see Omitoogun, W., and Hutchful, E. (eds), SIPRI, *Budgeting for the Military Sector in Africa: The Processes and Mechanisms of Control* (Oxford University Press: Oxford, 2006).

[57] For the parties to and basic information on the APM Convention see annex A in this volume.

[58] In 2006 ratifications were made by Brunei, the Cook Islands, Haiti and Ukraine. Montenegro acceded to the treaty in Oct. 2006.

APMs within 10 years. As of 2006, some 39.5 million stockpiled mines had been destroyed, leaving only 13 states parties with stockpiles. Of these, only Angola reported that it may not be able to complete the destruction before the deadline. More than 40 states parties still have to clear mines deployed on their territories, 29 of which have deadlines for this process in 2009–2010. In view of the magnitude of the task, as well as the lack of resources, about half of these states have suggested that they will not be able to meet their deadlines. A process for applying for time extensions was accordingly adopted at the seventh meeting of the states parties to the APM Convention, held in Geneva on 18–22 September. Extensions will be granted following a vote at the annual meetings of states parties or at review conferences, and should only be sought as a last resort.[59]

Most of the armed conflicts since the end of the cold war have been intra-state, and landmines have been used not only by states but also by non-state actors. The number of countries where non-state actors use APMs has, however, decreased, from 13 in 2005 to 10 in 2006. The Colombian Government points to the continued use of APMs by non-state actors on its territory to explain its difficulty with implementing its commitments under the APM Convention, and Georgia and Sri Lanka have used similar explanations for not acceding to the convention. Since 2001 the humanitarian organization Geneva Call has sought to engage non-state groups in a process that allows and encourages them to commit themselves to not using APMs. As of January 2007, 31 non-state groups in nine countries have made such commitments.[60]

The Third Review Conference of the Certain Conventional Weapons Convention

The 1981 Certain Conventional Weapons Convention, with its five protocols, prohibits or restricts the use of certain kinds of weapons deemed inhumane, including non-detectable fragment weapons (Protocol I); mines and booby-traps (amended Protocol II); incendiary weapons (Protocol III); laser weapons (Protocol IV); and explosive remnants of war (Protocol V).

On 7–17 November 2006 the Third Review Conference of the CCW Convention was held in Geneva, but it failed to achieve any major break-through on the issues that have dominated discussions in recent years, such as cluster munitions and mines other than anti-personnel mines (MOTAPM). The most significant CCW-related event in 2006 was, in fact, the entry into force of the 2003 Protocol V on ERW.[61] This protocol, which now has 23 states parties, calls for the clearing of ERW following armed conflicts. Although the primary responsibility for this is assigned to the state in control of the

[59] Boese, W., 'Landmine clearance deadlines looming', *Arms Control Today*, Nov. 2006. URL <http://www.armscontrol.org/act/2006_11/>.

[60] Geneva Call, *Armed Non-state Actors and Landmines, Volume II: A Global Report of NSA Mine Action* (Geneva Call: Geneva, Nov. 2006), URL <http://www.genevacall.org/news/testi-press-releases/gc-16nov2006-nsanews.htm>.

[61] See Lachowski and Sjögren (note 37).

territory, other states parties are obliged to assist in the process if able to do so. Since the adoption of Protocol V in 2003, regular discussions have taken place in the convention's Group of Governmental Experts on issues related to implementation of the agreement. These discussions have addressed assessments of specific types of munitions from an ERW perspective, technical preventive measures to reduce the humanitarian risk, and assistance and cooperation in relation to implementation of Protocol V.[62] These discussions will continue in 2007.

The entry into force of Protocol V notwithstanding, some states parties are seeking to further restrict the use of certain types of munitions, in particular cluster munitions, through the negotiation of an additional legally binding protocol to address humanitarian concerns.[63] At the review conference it was agreed that an intersessional meeting of governmental experts would be convened on 19–22 June 2007 'to consider further the application and implementation of existing international humanitarian law to specific munitions that may cause explosive remnants of war, with particular focus on cluster munitions'.[64]

Success in further negotiations on cluster munitions within the framework of the CCW Convention remains doubtful, however, since several states that still use them oppose any further restrictions. Among these states are the USA and Russia, the latter even questioning the seriousness of the humanitarian consequences of deploying cluster munitions, despite several reports detailing these consequences.[65] In the face of such objections the agreement to continue discussing the issue can be seen as at least a partial success.

Norway, anticipating the difficulty of reaching a global agreement on cluster munitions in the near future, has taken the lead with an initiative to hold a conference outside the CCW framework to draft a treaty banning the use of such weapons in the hope of persuading as many states as possible to sign up.[66] This approach would emulate the success of the 1997 APM Convention. Several states have already adopted national restrictions on the use of cluster munitions: Belgium has banned them; Germany has stopped procurement and aims to phase out its existing holdings by 2015; and Norway has called for a

---

[62] Group of Governmental Experts of the States Parties to the CCW Convention, Fifteenth Session, Geneva, 28 Aug.–6 Sep. 2006, Report on the work on explosive remnants of war, CCW/GGE/XV/6/Add.1, 13 Oct. 2006.

[63] These states are Austria, the Holy See, Ireland, Mexico, New Zealand, Norway and Sweden.

[64] Third Review Conference of the High Contracting Parties to the Convention on Prohibitions or Restrictions on the Use of Certain Conventional Weapons Which May Be Deemed to Be Excessively Injurious or to Have Indiscriminate Effects, Final declaration, Decision 1, Geneva, 17 Nov. 2006.

[65] For a comprehensive report on the humanitarian impact of cluster munitions see Handicap International, 'Fatal footprint: the global human impact of cluster munitions, preliminary report', Nov. 2006, URL <http://www.handicap-international.org.uk/page_597.php>. See also the website of the Cluster Munitions Coalition, a network of civil society organizations working to end the use of cluster munitions, URL <http://www.stopclustermunitions.org>.

[66] Norwegian Ministry of Foreign Affairs, 'Norway takes the initiative for a ban on cluster munitions', Press release no. 149/06, 17 Nov. 2006, URL <http://www.dep.no/ud/english/news/news/032171-070945/dok-bn.html>.

moratorium on their use. The debate on cluster munitions was further fuelled by Israel's extensive use of them in its 2006 war with Hezbollah in Lebanon.[67]

The Third CCW Convention Review Conference also failed to reach agreement on a proposal to adopt a protocol to restrict the use of mines other than anti-personnel mines (MOTAPM), notably anti-vehicle mines. First advocated by Denmark and the USA in 2001 but subject to much revision since, the proposal called for all MOTAPM used outside clearly marked perimeter areas to be easily detectable and equipped with self-destruct functions, and it would ban international transfers of mines that do not meet these requirements. However, several large states remain opposed to such a protocol. China pointed to the economic costs of fulfilling the requirements, while Russia questioned the humanitarian problems arising from such weapons. Other states, such as Pakistan, maintained that using undetectable and long-lasting MOTAPM remained important for their security.[68]

Owing to the failure to reach an agreement on the MOTAPM proposal at the review conference, the negotiations within the CCW framework on the proposal have been indefinitely suspended. The parties did, however, agree to spend up to two days discussing the issue at the 2007 meeting of the states parties.[69] Most of the co-sponsors of the proposal have meanwhile adopted its main provisions as national policy.[70]

Three concrete agreements were reached at the Third CCW Review Conference. First, the parties to the CCW Convention agreed to establish a compliance mechanism, which would include a pool of experts from which any party could seek help on issues regarding implementation of the convention and its protocols.[71] Second, a plan of action was agreed for promoting the universality of the convention and its protocols; an issue which will be prioritized in the coming five years. This plan of action calls for parties, among other things, to review their own participation in the regime with a view to adhering to any protocol they have so far remained outside. Furthermore, signatories will be encouraged to ratify the convention and states not yet parties will be encouraged to adhere to its provisions, especially in regions of conflict and other areas where participation is low, notably Africa, Asia and the Middle East.[72] Finally, agreement was reached on setting up a sponsorship programme. This will be used to support the participation of representatives from less developed countries in CCW-related activities, allowing signatory

---

[67] Nash, T., 'Foreseeable harm: The use and impact of cluster munitions in Lebanon, 2006. Landmine Action report 2006', 19 Oct. 2006, URL <http://www.landmineaction.org/resources/Foreseeable Harmfinal.pdf>.

[68] Boese, W., 'Cluster munition, anti-vehicle mine limits sought', *Arms Control Today*, Dec. 2006. URL <http://www.armscontrol.org/act/2006_12/Cluster.asp>.

[69] Third Review Conference (note 64), Decision 2.

[70] Third Review Conference (note 64), Declaration on anti-vehicle mines, CCW/CONF.III/WP.16, 16 Nov. 2006.

[71] Third Review Conference (note 64), Decision 3 and Annex B.

[72] Third Review Conference (note 64), Decision 4 and Annex C.

and non-member states a chance to become acquainted with them, as well as supporting the participation of experts in such activities.[73]

V. Conclusions

The current state of conventional arms control agreements and endeavours can only be called pitiful. In Europe, where arms control efforts are most advanced, the process is blocked and remains hostage to the Russia's non-compliance with its own commitments, the political tug of war between Russia and the NATO states, general arms control 'fatigue' and the deteriorating status of the OSCE.[74] It remains to be seen whether continued efforts by Russia, on the one hand, and Germany (which holds the EU Presidency in the first half of 2007), on the other, will resuscitate interest in a set of arms control and confidence-building measures more attuned to the new conditions in Europe.

The OSCE's 2006 military doctrine seminar was an important event because it allowed a relatively calm and non-adversarial discussion of the security thinking and military postures of OSCE participating states in the world security environment after the 2001 terrorist attacks on the USA. It should hopefully give impetus to further doctrinal changes that respond to rapid political and technological developments. Other confidence- and transparency-building and stability-enhancing steps tended to focus on the dangers created by stockpiles of small arms and ammunition. In Latin America interest in implementing and adopting confidence-building measures continues at a fairly steady pace.

The number of states adhering to the APM Convention is rising, although whether some states parties will meet the deadlines for the elimination of land-mine stockpiles is cause for concern, and time extensions may be needed. The successful entry into force of the protocol on explosive remnants of war and developments at the Third CCW Convention Review Conference in 2006 showed that, despite reluctance on the part of some powers, humanitarian efforts to contain the scourge of 'inhumane weapons' are drawing steadily growing interest worldwide.

---

[73] Third Review Conference (note 64), Decision 5 and Annex D.

[74] For a discussion of the OSCE's declining status see Dunay, P., 'The Organization for Security and Cooperation in Europe: constant adaptation but enduring problems', *SIPRI Yearbook 2005: Armaments, Disarmament and International Security* (Oxford University Press: Oxford, 2006).

Appendix 14A. Global efforts to control MANPADS

MATT SCHROEDER

I. Introduction

Preventing the acquisition and use of man-portable air defence systems (MANPADS) by terrorists and rebel groups has been a matter of concern since the early 1970s. However, despite the persistence of the threat MANPADS pose to aviation, it was the 2002 al-Qaeda attack on an Israeli civilian aircraft flying out of Mombassa, Kenya, that focused world attention on the issue.

This introductory section continues by providing some basic information on the development and main types of MANPADS and their capabilities. Section II of this appendix gives an overview of the main threats posed by the weapon. Section III reviews efforts to control the weapon prior to the Mombassa attack, and section IV examines contemporary counter-MANPADS efforts. Section V presents some concluding observations and recommendations for further action.

MANPADS fire short-range surface-to-air (SAM) missiles and are designed to be carried and operated by a single individual or a crew of several individuals. There are three basic types of missile used by MANPADS, which are often categorized by their guidance system: passive infrared seekers, laser-beam riders and command line-of-sight (CLOS) system (see table 14A). Most MANPADS missiles, including the Soviet/Russian SA series, the US Stinger and the Chinese Vanguard, are lightweight, 'fire-and-forget' missiles that home in on infrared light generated by heat from the target aircraft. Since the unveiling of the relatively primitive US FIM-43 Redeye and the Soviet SA-7 (Strela 2)[1] in the 1960s, weapons designers have steadily improved the range, altitude and guidance of infrared seekers. The latest version of the Stinger, for example, has a maximum range and altitude that are 2195 metres and 1585 metres longer, respectively, than the Redeye and an improved seeker that gives the missile an 'all aspect engagement capability'. It can hit a target from any direction (front, rear and side) and discriminate between aircraft and other heat sources, including protective flares.[2] The portability, ease of use and accuracy of infrared seekers have made them the most popular and the most widely proliferated type of MANPADS.

---

[1] The North Atlantic Treaty Organization and the USA use their own reporting names when referring to Russian or Soviet military equipment. E.g. 'SA-7' is the US designation for the Russian Strela missile. US designations are principally used in this appendix.

[2] Lyons, L., Long, D. and Chait, R., *Critical Technology Events in the Development of the Stinger and Javelin Missile Systems: Project Hindsight Revisited* (National Defense University: Washington, DC, July 2006), URL <http://www.ndu.edu/ctnsp/Defense_Tech_Papers.htm>, p. 10; Redstone Arsenal, 'Stinger avenger', URL <http://www.redstone.army.mil/history/systems/STINGER.html>; and Schaffer, M., *The Air Force Role in Reducing the Missile Threat to Civil Aviation* (RAND Corporation: Santa Monica, Calif., 2002).

Table 14A.1. MANPADS-producing countries and basic weapon specifications

Country	Designation	Guidance system	Range (m)[a]	Derivatives, copies and licensed production	
				Country	Designation
China	HN-5[b]	IR homing	4 400	Pakistan	Anza
				N. Korea	..
	QW-1/Vanguard	IR homing	5 000	Pakistan	Anza-2
				Iran	Misagh-1
	QW-2	IR homing	6 000		
	FN-6	IR homing	5 500		
France	Mistral	IR homing	6 000		
Japan	Type-91 Kin-sam	IR homing	5 000		
Poland	Grom-2	IR homing	5 200		
S. Korea	Chiron	IR homing	7 000		
Russia/ CIS	SA-7 (Strela-2)	IR homing	4 400	China	HN-5
				Egypt	Ayn-al-Saqr
				Romania	CA-94M
				Serbia	..
	SA-14 (Strela-3)	IR homing	5 500	Bulgaria	..
				N. Korea	..
	SA-18 (Igla)	IR homing	5 200		
	SA-16 (Igla-1)	IR homing	5 200	Bulgaria	..
				N. Korea	..
				Poland	Grom-1
				Singapore	..
				Viet Nam	..
Sweden	RBS-70	Laser-beam riding	7 000	Pakistan	RBS-70
	Bolide	Laser-beam riding	8 000		
UK	Blowpipe	Command line of sight	4 000		
	Javelin	Command line of sight	5 500		
	Starburst	Laser-beam riding	6 000		
	Starstreak	Laser-beam riding	7 000		
USA	FIM-43 Redeye	IR homing	4 500		
	FIM-92 Stinger	IR/UV homing	8 000	Europe	Fliegerfaust-2
				Switzerland	..
				N. Korea	Illegal copy

IR = Infra-red homing; UV = ultra violet; CIS = Commonwealth of Independent States;

[a] The range given is the maximum range. The effective range may be less.

[b] The Chinese HN-5 is a copy of the Soviet SA-7.

Sources: Small Arms Survey; and Foss, C. F. and O'Halloran, J. C. (eds), *Jane's Land-Based Air Defence 2006–2007* (Jane's Information Group: Coulsdon, 2006).

Laser-beam-riding missiles, the most common of which is the Swedish RBS-70, follow a laser beam projected onto the target by the operator. The system, which consists of a stand, a sight and a missile, is bulkier and more difficult to use than its infrared-seeking counterparts (which can generally be fired from the shoulder) but, in the hands of a skilled operator, is also more lethal. The new Swedish Bolide missile has a maximum range of 8000 m and a laser guidance system allowing the missile to be directed towards the most vulnerable part of an aircraft, increasing the probability of destroying the target to over 90 per cent in head-on engagements.[3] The RBS-70 is also impervious to aircraft-mounted anti-missile systems, making it a particularly worrisome threat in the hands of terrorists and insurgents. As of 2006, at least 20 countries have produced or imported laser-beam riding missiles, the vast majority of which are RBS-70 systems.[4] CLOS systems use radio-controlled missiles. The United Kingdom produced the only CLOS systems—the Javelin and the Blowpipe— neither of which is still in production.[5] In total, an estimated 1 million missiles for MANPADS have been produced, and it is estimated that 500 000–750 000 remain in the global inventory.[6]

II. Threats

Acquisition of MANPADS by non-state actors

Since the early 1970s terrorist and insurgent groups have acquired MANPADS from a variety of sources, including state sponsors, private arms dealers, poorly secured weapon depots, and other terrorists and insurgents. These missiles have been used to shoot down hundreds of military aircraft and dozens of civil aircraft.

While data on the acquisition of MANPADS by terrorists and insurgents are patchy, open-source literature suggests that, historically, transfers from governments to non-state actors have been a major, if not the largest, source of MANPADS for these groups. The Soviet Union provided its first-generation SA-7 missiles to North Viet Nam, who used them against US and South Vietnamese aircraft during the 1959–75 Viet-Nam War. In Afghanistan in the 1980s the USA shipped hundreds of US Stingers, British Blowpipes and even the Soviet Union's own SA series (which the Central Intelligence Agency, CIA, reportedly obtained from a corrupt Polish general)[7] to anti-Soviet rebels. By the time Soviet forces left Afghanistan in 1989, the Stinger missiles alone were credited with having downed nearly 270 Soviet planes and helicopters.[8]

Several former Soviet client states have also provided MANPADS to non-state actors. In the 1970s and 1980s, Libyan leader Muammar Qadhafi supplied his missiles to the Popular Front for the Liberation of Palestine (PFLP) and the Provisional Irish Republican Army (IRA). State-sanctioned shipments of MANPADS to non-state actors dropped off precipitously after the cold war, but did not end entirely. In 1998 Eritrea was accused of providing more than 40 SA-series missiles to the Somalian warlord Hussein Aideed, who was sheltering an Eritrean-backed Ethiopian

---

[3] See Saab Group, 'RBS 70', URL <http://www.saabgroup.com/en/capabilities>.

[4] Foss, C. F. and O'Halloran, J. C. (eds), *Jane's Land-Based Air Defence 2006–2007* (Jane's Information Group: Coulsdon, 2006).

[5] Foss and O'Halloran (note 4).

[6] Government Accountability Office (GAO), *Further Improvements Needed in US Efforts to Counter Threat from Man-Portable Air Defense Systems*, GAO-04-519 (GAO: Washington, DC, May 2004), URL <http://www.gao.gov/docdblite/details.php?rptno=GAO-04-519>, p. 10.

[7] Crile, G., *Charlie Wilson's War* (Grove Press: New York, N.Y., 2003), p. 159.

[8] Kuperman, A. J., 'The Stinger missile and US intervention in Afghanistan', *Political Science Quarterly*, vol. 114, no. 2 (summer 1999), pp. 219–63.

rebel group at the time.[9] More recently, United Nations investigators and Western intelligence officials have accused Iran of providing dozens of MANPADS to the Islamic Courts Union—an umbrella group of Islamic Somali militias—and of conspiring to supply advanced Russian-produced SAM systems to Hezbollah to transform the group 'into a coherent fighting force and a regional strategic arm'.[10]

The insidious combination of rogue arms brokers and weak national export controls is another cause of the proliferation of MANPADS to non-state actors. In May 2000, arms traffickers with ties to the Russian broker Viktor Bout reportedly delivered SA-series missiles to Liberia, which was under a UN arms embargo at the time. A few years later, UN investigators spotted what appeared to be nine of the missiles in film footage of Liberian rebels.[11] Similarly, arms traffickers working on behalf of an Angolan rebel group attempted to acquire advanced Igla SA missiles from Russia using false end-user certificates. In this case, however, the Russians suspected foul play and ended negotiations before any missiles were transferred.[12]

Poor stockpile security, battlefield losses, corruption and disorder following regime change also enable terrorists and insurgents to acquire MANPADS. According to Harvard University's Mark Kramer, guerrillas in Russia's restive province of Chechnya acquired Russian MANPADS from 'unguarded warehouses in southern Russia, from stockpiles captured during ambushes . . . from criminal gangs, and from Russian troops who sold them at a discount'.[13] The greatest threat to counter-MANPADS efforts, however, is the sudden collapse of well-armed regimes. In Iraq looters carried off many of the estimated 5000 MANPADS in Iraqi weapon depots after Saddam Hussein's government was overthrown by US troops in March 2003. One year later, US intelligence analysts revised their estimate of black-market MANPADS worldwide to reflect the sudden influx of Iraqi missiles, increasing it threefold to 6000 missiles.[14]

Use of MANPADS by terrorists and other non-state actors

Terrorists and other non-state actors began plotting MANPADS attacks almost immediately after the weapon was initially deployed in the late 1960s. In 1973 the first attack by non-state actors on a commercial airliner, which was reportedly organized by the PFLP and involved Libyan missiles, was narrowly averted when Italian authorities raided an apartment near Rome's Fiumicino airport. On the balcony,

---

[9] UN Security Council, Report of the Panel of Experts on Somalia pursuant to Security Council Resolution 1474, UN document S/2003/1035, 4 Nov. 2003. Most official UN documents are available at URL <http://documents.un.org/>.

[10] Hughes, R., 'Iran answers Hizbullah call for SAM systems', *Jane's Defense Weekly*, 9 Aug. 2006, URL <http://www.janes.com/defence/news/jdw/jdw060807_1_n.shtml>; and United Nations Security Council, Report of the Monitoring Group on Somalia pursuant to Security Council Resolution 1676, UN document S/2006/913, Nov. 2006. For more on Hezbollah and MANPADS see chapter 10 in this volume.

[11] See UN Security Council, Report of the Panel of Experts pursuant to Security Council Resolution 1343 (2001), UN document S/2001/1015, Oct. 2001, para. 19 on Liberia; and List of individuals subject to the measures imposed by paragraph 4 of Security Council Resolution 1521 (2003) concerning Liberia, updated 1 Aug. 2006, URL <http://www.un.org/sc/committees/1521/tblist.shtml>.

[12] UN Security Council, Report of the Panel of Experts on Violations of Security Council Sanctions Against UNITA, UN document S/2000/203, 28 Feb. 2000.

[13] Kramer, M., 'The perils of counterinsurgency: Russia's war in Chechnya', *International Security*, vol. 29, no. 3 (winter 2004), pp. 5–63.

[14] Jehl, D. and Sanger, D. E., 'US expands list of lost missiles', *New York Times*, 6 Nov. 2004.

police found two SA-7 missiles 'ready to shoot down an [Israeli] El Al plane after take-off'.[15] Kenyan authorities foiled a similar plot three years later.[16]

The first successful MANPADS attack on a commercial airliner occurred in September 1978 when members of the Patriotic Front, a Soviet-backed guerrilla movement fighting the Rhodesian Government, hit a Vickers Viscount turboprop aircraft owned by Air Rhodesia with an SA-7 missile. The plane crashed in rebel-controlled woodland about 65 kilometres from Kariba airport. Thirty-four of the 52 people on board died in the crash, and rebel gunmen killed 15 of the survivors a few hours later. Six months after the crash, Rhodesian rebels shot down another airliner, killing all 59 people on board and demonstrating to the world that the first attack was not a fluke.

Over the next 20 years, civilian aircraft flying over Afghanistan, Angola, Nicaragua, Sudan and other war zones came under fire from missile-wielding terrorists and rebel groups. Several dozen of these missiles found their targets, resulting in 25 downed aircraft and 600 fatalities.[17] Most notably, a MANPADS attack in April 1994 killed Rwandan President Juvénal Habyarimana and sparked the ethnic violence that led to the Rwandan genocide.[18]

III. Early efforts to control MANPADS

National and, to a lesser extent, international efforts to prevent terrorists from acquiring and using MANPADS date back to the advent of the new weapon. For example, by the 1970s the US Government had established strong export controls on MANPADS and stringent stockpile security requirements. Through diplomatic channels, it also attempted to coax the Soviet Union into exercising greater control over its missiles. The USA had also worked closely with the West German Government to address a potential MANPADS threat to Lufthansa airliners.[19] Until recently, however, such international cooperation was fitful, piecemeal, and often superseded by other foreign policy interests.

Early efforts to control MANPADS fell far short of what was needed for several reasons, primarily related to the cold war. The rift between the East and the West prevented the extensive global cooperation required to put pressure on irresponsible governments, dismantle international trafficking networks and establish global norms. The highly charged, zero-sum view of the conflict also resulted in myopic and contradictory foreign policies, a prime example of which was the USA's massive covert aid programme to the mujahedin in Afghanistan after 1979. Even as the USA was denying Jordanian and Saudi requests for Stingers for fear that the missiles would be diverted to terrorists, the CIA distributed hundreds of Stingers to rebel groups. The

---

[15] Schroeder, M., Stohl, R. and Smith, D., *The Small Arms Trade: A Beginner's Guide* (Oneworld Publications: Oxford, 2007) p. 64.

[16] Greenway, H. D. S., 'Israel admits 5 held over a year as terrorists', *Washington Post*, 15 Nov. 1977.

[17] US State Department, 'The MANPADS menace: combating the threat to global aviation from manportable air defense systems', Fact sheet, 20 Sep. 2005, URL <http://www.state.gov/t/pm/rls/fs/53558.htm>.

[18] The origin of the missiles used in the attack is not clear. It is reported that investigators acting on behalf of French judge Jean-Louis Bruguiere were able to trace the serial numbers of the two SA-16 missiles used to a batch sold to Uganda. See Swain, J., 'Riddle of the Rwandan assassins' trail', *Sunday Times*, 4 Apr. 2004.

[19] Schroeder, Stohl and Smith (note 15), pp. 65–66.

CIA exercised little direct control over these groups and, not surprisingly, the missiles spread widely, including to terrorists and state sponsors of terrorism.

It was not until the late 1990s that the first significant multilateral counter-MANPADS efforts got off the ground. Within the European Union (EU), the debate on small arms and light weapons (SALW) led in 1997 to a programme for preventing and combating illicit trafficking in conventional arms, followed by the December 1998 Joint Action on illicit arms trafficking in which MANPADS are treated as a specific element.[20] In the USA, the crash of TWA Flight 800 in July 1996 prompted US President Bill Clinton to establish the Commission on Aviation Security and Terrorism, which as part of its remit explored the threat to commercial aviation posed by MANPADS. The MANPADS threat was a side note in the commission's findings but was enough to prompt the US Department of State to begin negotiating a set of international standards for national controls on MANPADS exports.[21]

The forum favoured by both the USA and European countries for wider co-operation was the Wassenaar Arrangement (WA), the pre-eminent multilateral export control body for conventional armaments.[22] In December 2000 the WA produced the Elements for Export Controls of MANPADS—the first multilateral agreement on MANPADS.[23] This agreement laid out a set of controls and evaluation criteria that, if widely and effectively implemented by WA members (which include over half of the MANPADS-producing states), would help to prevent many of the most blatantly problematic MANPADS exports. The most important of these provisions was the de facto ban on transfers to non-state actors,[24] which have been a significant source of black market MANPADS. The ban is unprecedented and runs counter to the unyielding US opposition to restrictions on small arms transfers to non-state actors in other forums. Other important provisions include those that require exporters to ensure that recipients seek permission before re-exporting the missiles, promptly notify the exporter if the missiles are lost or stolen, and undertake specific physical security and stockpile management practices (PSSM), including physical inventories of all MANPADS and separate storage of missiles and launchers. The Elements also served as a foundation for the more rigorous, and widely adopted, set of controls pursued by the USA two years later.

Complementing the Elements were several regional and global initiatives aimed at stemming the illicit trade in SALW more generally, the most prominent of which was the UN Small Arms Process. Initiated in the mid-1990s, the process culminated in 2001 with the adoption of the Programme of Action to Prevent, Combat and Eradicate the Illicit Trade in Small Arms and Light Weapons in All its Aspects.[25] While not focused on MANPADS per se, the Programme of Action calls for a long list of

[20] European Union, Council Joint Action 1999/34/CFSP, 17 Dec. 1998, URL <http://europa.eu.int/eur-lex/en/archive/>.

[21] Schroeder, Stohl and Smith (note 15), pp. 105–106.

[22] On the Wassenaar Arrangement (WA) and a list of its participants see chapter 15 and the glossary in this volume.

[23] Wassenaar Arrangement, Elements for export controls of man-portable air defence systems (MANPADS), Vienna, Dec. 2003, URL <http://www.wassenaar.org/2003Plenary/MANPADS_2003.htm>. For a description of the negotiations that resulted in the Elements see Schroeder, Stohl and Smith (note 15), pp. 107–108.

[24] Section 2.1 of the Elements limits the export of MANPADS to 'foreign governments or to agents authorized by the government'.

[25] United Nations, Programme of Action to Prevent, Combat and Eradicate the Illicit Trade in Small Arms and Light Weapons in All its Aspects, UN document A/CONF.192/15, URL <http://www.http://disarmament.un.org/cab/poa.html>.

measures aimed at strengthening national, regional and international controls on SALW, many of which are applicable to shoulder-fired missiles. The UN Small Arms Process has also increased awareness of the threat posed by illicit arms trafficking and thrust the issue to the top of arms control, non-proliferation and counter-terrorism agendas worldwide.

Turning point: the Mombassa attack of November 2002

It was not until a pair of 24-year-old SA-7 missiles narrowly missed an Israeli airliner departing from Mombassa airport, Kenya, on 28 November 2002 that policymakers and the media became seriously concerned by the MANPADS threat. The attack marked a turning point in counter-MANPADS efforts.[26] In the USA there was a sea change in the emphasis and seriousness of existing inter-agency counter-MANPADS efforts. The attack prompted diplomatic efforts to expand the Elements and extend them to other international forums; the establishment of a multimillion-dollar programme for evaluating anti-missile systems for commercial airliners; and the expansion of foreign assistance programmes designed to secure foreign weapon stockpiles and destroy surplus weaponry. The attack had a similar (if more subdued) effect on the rest of the international community as well.

IV. Global counter-MANPADS efforts

Efforts to control the proliferation of MANPADS are truly global in scope. Over 100 countries are involved at some level, in ways that range from tacit support for one of the five multilateral agreements to the investment of significant diplomatic, budgetary and technical resources in a variety of initiatives. Israel, Russia, the USA and, more recently, Australia have been the most active states.[27] They have provided technical and financial assistance to other governments, spearheaded negotiations on regional and international agreements, and invested heavily in anti-missile systems for commercial aircraft. Together, these initiatives have significantly reduced the number of surplus and poorly secured MANPADS in national stockpiles and have taken hundreds of stray missiles out of circulation. The benefits from other initiatives are less certain, including the costly anti-missile programmes (see below). It appears that little progress has been made on other promising strategies, including the development and installation of launch control devices.

Below is a brief summary of each of these initiatives along with an assessment of their strengths and shortcomings. In isolation, none of these initiatives is sufficient to counter the MANPADS threat. However, if integrated into a coordinated multinational effort and supplemented with hitherto neglected tools such as launch control devices, these initiatives would provide a formidable layered defence against MANPADS attacks.

[26] Kuhn, D. A., 'Mombassa attack highlights increasing MANPADS threat', *Jane's Intelligence Review*, vol. 15, no. 2 (Feb. 2003), p. 29; UN Security Council (note 9); and Lacey, M., 'Investigation in Kenya: missiles fired at Israeli plane are recovered', *New York Times*, 7 Dec. 2002.

[27] In 2005 Australia launched an initiative to raise awareness of the threat, restrict MANPADS production capabilities, strengthen export controls, establish programmes to secure national arsenals and destroy surplus stocks, and improve airport perimeter security. See Downer, A., Australian Foreign Minister, 'Australia's International MANPADS Initiative', Speech at the Millennium Hotel, New York, 18 Jan. 2007, URL <http://www.foreignminister.gov.au/speeches/2007/070118_manpads.html>.

Export controls

Strong, harmonized, properly enforced national export controls are essential for preventing the diversion of weapons to irresponsible or unstable recipients. Unauthorized transfers arranged by globe-trotting arms brokers have resulted in the delivery of hundreds of weapons to rogue governments and rebel groups worldwide. In some cases, the complexity of the transaction and the extensive involvement of corrupt, high-ranking government officials make the diversion difficult to detect and foil.[28] In other cases, however, even minimal safeguards are enough to scuttle an attempted diversion. A good example is the shipment of 3000 Nicaraguan AK-47 assault rifles to Colombian paramilitaries in 2001. The broker who arranged the deal falsely claimed that his client was the Panamanian National Police—a claim that Nicaraguan officials failed to investigate. According to the Organization of American States (OAS) investigators, 'One telephone call [to Panama] could have prevented the entire arms diversion'.[29]

Since 2002 governments have taken several important steps towards strengthening national export controls on MANPADS, including regional and bilateral agreements aimed at promoting information exchanges on MANPADS transfers,[30] the expansion of the UN Register of Conventional Arms to include MANPADS, and, most significantly, the adoption of an expanded version of the Elements.[31] The expanded Elements, which have been adopted by members of the Asia–Pacific Economic Cooperation (APEC) forum, the OAS, the Organization for Security and Co-operation in Europe (OSCE) and the WA build on the original Elements by: (a) prohibiting the use of general supply agreements, thereby ensuring that each export request is properly vetted by trained government personnel; (b) banning the use of non-governmental brokers, who, as explained above, have diverted hundreds of weapons to embargoed states and non-state actors; (c) encouraging the development of technical performance or launch control features, which could limit the utility of lost, stolen or diverted missiles and reduce access to such missiles on the black market; (d) expanding the list of specific stockpile security procedures required of importers to include continuous (24-hour) surveillance and two-person entry requirements; (e) restricting access to hardware and related classified information to government personnel with proper security clearances and an established need to know; (f) sharing information on potential recipient governments that fail to satisfy these requirements and on non-state actors that are attempting to acquire MANPADS; and (g) imposing adequate (criminal) penalties for violations of national MANPADS export controls.

Particularly important is the provision calling for producer countries to 'implement technical performance and/or launch control features for newly designed MANPADS

---

[28] E.g. UN Security Council (note 9), pp. 46–9.

[29] Organization of American States, Report of the General Secretariat of the Organization of American States on the Diversion of Nicaraguan Arms to the United Defense Forces of Colombia, 29 Jan. 2003, URL <http://www.oas.org/OASpage/NI-COarmas/NI-COEnglish3687.htm>.

[30] E.g. the US–Russian arrangement on cooperation in enhancing control of MANPADS, which was signed at Bratislava on 24 Feb. 2005, URL <http://bratislava.usembassy.gov/pas/pr092en.html>; and the Commonwealth of Independent States resolution on measures to control the international transfer of Igla and Strela MANPADS, which was signed at Yalta on 19 Sep. 2003.

[31] The versions of the Elements adopted by the OAS, the OSCE and APEC differ slightly from the WA's version and from each other's. E.g. the OAS excluded the provision on launch control features but explicitly called for a ban on transfers to non-state entities. The Elements have also been endorsed by the UN General Assembly and the International Civil Aviation Organization.

as such technologies become available to them'. One such device touted for this role by Robert Sherman, the former director of the Advanced Projects Office at the US Arms Control and Disarmament Agency, is the controllable enabler—a device that requires the entry of a code to activate the missile. The missile could be enabled for any length of time, but after the code expires the missile will be useless until it is re-entered.[32] Installation of such devices would not only shorten the life of lost, stolen and diverted missiles but would also reduce black market trafficking. Terrorists are unlikely to plan attacks around weapons that may stop working before an attack, and arms traffickers are unlikely to invest tens of thousands of dollars in merchandise that may be useless a week later. Yet, despite their potential as tools for limiting proliferation, these features remain drawing-board concepts.

Several states have taken steps to implement the Elements. In 2004 South Korea 'put in place systematic control mechanisms for the international transactions of MANPADS prior to the adoption of the APEC guidelines', and New Zealand is 'looking to enhance existing end-user controls for MANPADS'.[33] Other governments have made changes to their export controls that go beyond what the Elements explicitly require. Russia recently started including provisions in its contracts for Igla missiles that give Russian inspectors the right to conduct physical inventories of exported missiles.[34] US end-use monitoring of Stingers is even more rigorous. While Russia simply reserves the right to inspect exported missiles, US regulations require annual inspections, and in 2003 the US Department of Defense (DOD) raised the percentage of exported Stinger missiles that its officials must annually inspect from 5 per cent to 100 per cent, meaning every exported missile must be inspected every year by a US team.[35]

In addition to their norm-building value, these agreements provide formal and informal opportunities for exchanging information, sharing best practices, and education and training. The OSCE has hosted a number of workshops, seminars and special meetings, during which the control of small arms—including MANPADS—was discussed.[36] The same goes for APEC, which has served as a venue for teaching members how to conduct MANPADS vulnerability assessments at airports and how to recognize MANPADS and their component parts.[37]

While these agreements are critically important, they also have significant limitations. APEC, the OAS, the OSCE and the WA lack the mandate, staffing and resources to systematically monitor and assess implementation, let alone to enforce compliance. However, there are informal mechanisms for self-policing among members of these organizations, such as information exchanges and opportunities to

---

[32] Sherman, R., 'The real terrorist missile threat, and what can be done about it', *FAS Public Interest Report*, vol. 56, no. 3 (autumn 2003), URL <http://www.fas.org/faspir/2003/v56n3/index.html>.

[33] See Asia–Pacific Economic Cooperation Counter-terrorism Task Force, 'Korea's response to leaders' and ministers' statements', Sep. 2005; and 'New Zealand efforts to respond to APEC leaders' and ministers' Statements', Sep. 2006—both available at URL <http://www.apec.org/apec/documents_reports/counter_terrorism_task_force.html>.

[34] Interview by the author with a Russian official, May 2005.

[35] US Defense Security Cooperation Agency, 'Revised guidance for stinger/man portable air defense systems (MANPADS)', 4 June 2003, URL <http://www.dsca.osd.mil/samm/policy_memo.htm>.

[36] E.g. Organization for Security and Co-operation in Europe, Technical Experts Workshop on Countering MANPADS Threat to Civil Aviation Security at Airports, 23 Jan. 2004, Vienna, URL <http://www.osce.org/item/3126.html>.

[37] Asia–Pacific Economic Cooperation Counter-terrorism Task Force, CTTF Chair's Summary Report, 14 Sep. 2005, URL <http:// www.apec.org/apec/documents_reports/senior_officials_meetings/2005.html>.

'name and shame' delinquent governments, but reports on implementation efforts are often vague or incomplete and the collegial nature of these institutions discourages direct confrontation.

Additionally, several key states—including producers such as Iran, North Korea and Pakistan—are not members of any of the multilateral institutions through which these agreements were negotiated and are therefore not obliged to follow them. At least one of these states (Iran) has allegedly acted against the most important provision of the Elements: the ban on transfers to non-state actors.[38]

Stockpile destruction

Since 2002, several countries and multilateral institutions have assisted with the process of destroying surplus, seized or obsolete MANPADS. The largest provider of such assistance is the USA, which has funded the destruction of approximately 29 000 missiles in 18 countries,[39] including 1300 as part of North Atlantic Treaty Organization (NATO) destruction programmes in Kazakhstan and Ukraine.[40]

The circumstances surrounding individual destruction projects vary significantly. In some cases, the missiles are part of massive, ageing, cold war-era government stockpiles intended for use against an enemy that no longer exists. Stockpiles in Nicaragua and Ukraine are good examples. Before the US-funded destruction programme began in 2003, Nicaragua had 2000 first- and second-generation Soviet missiles and no potential adversaries with more than a handful of functioning attack aircraft. Similarly, Ukraine, which served as the main Soviet military supply depot for the Western theatre, was saddled with over 2 million tonnes of surplus weapons— including thousands of MANPADS—after the cold war ended.[41] The Ukrainian missiles were destroyed as part of a 12-year, $27 million NATO programme to pare down the massive stockpiles, which have leaked into the black market and sparked accidental explosions that have killed several people and caused millions of dollars in damage to neighbouring towns.[42]

At the opposite end of the spectrum are the small caches of missiles in countries such as Bolivia and Liberia. Some of these missiles, like Bolivia's Chinese-made HN-5, are the remnants of legitimate but outdated and deteriorating national air defence systems. Others are the ill-gotten gains of rebel groups and embargoed governments, such as the regime of previous Liberian President Charles Taylor. In the case of Bolivia, US intelligence operatives worked closely with Bolivian officials to surreptitiously transport the 28 or so missiles to the USA,[43] where they were dis-

---

[38] On supplies of arms by states to rebel groups, see chapter 10 in this volume.

[39] This number includes 8000 missiles that, as of Mar. 2007, had not been destroyed but that the US State Department had received 'commitments' to destroy. Schroeder, M., 'Bush gets it right on small arms threat reduction', FAS Strategic Security Blog, 5 Feb. 2007, URL <http://www.fas.org/blog/ssp/2007/02/bush_gets_it_right_on_small_ar.php>.

[40] NATO Partnership for Peace Trust Fund, 'Status of trust fund projects', 9 Nov. 2006.

[41] Polyakov, L., *Aging Stocks of Ammunition and SALW in Ukraine: Risks and Challenges*, Paper 41 (Bonn International Center for Conversion: Bonn, 2005), URL <http://www.bicc.de/publications/papers/paper41/content.php>.

[42] US Department of State, 'Milestone reached in NATO Partnership for Peace arms destruction project in Ukraine', 21 Sep. 2006, URL <http://www.state.gov/r/pa/prs/ps/2006/72935.htm>; Polyakov (note 41).

[43] The number of missiles is a subject of debate. Estimates range from 19 to 38.

mantled and the pieces returned to Bolivia.[44] In Liberia, US officials sent to assist with the destruction of vast quantities of weapons left over from its civil war discovered 38 SA series missiles in Charles Taylor's presidential compound, which were described by one US official as 'the least secured MANPADS I had ever seen'.[45] The next day, they found four additional missiles in an unguarded shed on the private property of a high-ranking member of Taylor's government.

Destruction assistance programmes are straightforward, comparatively inexpensive and effective: a missile that is dismantled will never fall into terrorist hands. Particularly noteworthy is the US Department of State's SALW destruction programme. In just five years and with a total budget of less than $50 million, the programme has significantly reducing the pool of MANPADS and other small arms that are vulnerable to theft, loss and diversion by facilitating the destruction of nearly 1 million small arms, including 29 000 surplus and unsecured missiles.[46]

There are, however, inherent limitations to these programmes and it is not clear how many of the remaining stray and unsecured missiles are accessible to destruction teams. Many governments are hesitant to give up their MANPADS, which they view as a critical component of their air defence systems or (when sold) as a source of hard currency. Other governments are leery of the destruction process, which they fear will turn into a 'blatant intelligence-gathering exercise' by the donor state.[47] Poor relations between donor states and potential recipients also preclude the establishment (or completion) of destruction programmes. US law prohibits Iran, North Korea and Syria—all producers or importers of MANPADS—from receiving US foreign aid, including stockpile security and destruction assistance.[48] In other cases, unrelated political disputes delay or derail potential programmes. Decades-old hostility between the USA and the Sandinistas, for example, brought a promising US-funded programme to destroy Nicaragua's MANPADS to a grinding halt in late 2004 when the Sandinista-controlled National Assembly passed a law allowing it to block the destruction of the military's weapons.[49] The destruction programme has been frozen ever since.

Finally, destruction programmes are not mandated, and indeed are unable, to deal with the problem of missiles already in the hands of terrorists, insurgent groups or other non-state actors (except in the special case of disarmament, demobilization and reintegration, DDR, programmes after conflict). The threat from these missiles, which, according to some US intelligence analysts number around 6000, must be addressed in other ways.[50]

For these reasons, destruction programmes are a necessary but, in themselves, insufficient component of any successful counter-MANPADS strategy.

---

[44] The cooperation of the Bolivian officials was not sanctioned by the Bolivian Government, however. New Bolivian President Evo Morales pledged to evict US military advisers from Bolivia and punish the officials responsible.

[45] Schroeder, Stohl and Smith (note 15), p. 124.

[46] Schroeder (note 39).

[47] Interview by the author with US State Department official, Nov. 2006.

[48] Section 620A of the Foreign Assistance Act of 1961 prohibits the provision of foreign aid to countries that the Secretary of State has determined 'has repeatedly provided support for acts of international terrorism'. Cuba, Iran, North Korea, Sudan and Syria are on the State Department's list of 'state sponsors of terrorism'.

[49] Dellios, H., 'Sandinista election victories worry US', *Chicago Tribune*, 21 Nov. 2004.

[50] Jehl, D. and Sanger, D., 'The reach of war: weapons; US expands list of lost missiles', *New York Times*, 6 Nov. 2004.

Physical security and stockpile management practices

Effective stockpile security and management is the *sine qua non* of non-proliferation strategies and therefore a vital component of global counter-MANPADS efforts. Recently, the OSCE compiled the first multilateral best practice guide on stockpile management and security procedures for MANPADS.[51] This groundbreaking document provides, in great detail, best practice guidance on physical security, access control, handling and transport, and inventory management and accounting control prcedures for MANPADS. The document advises that MANPADS should be banded and sealed in their original containers and chained together in clusters weighing no less than 225 kilograms (so they cannot be easily carried away), and the containers kept in concrete ammunition storehouses equipped with intrusion detection devices, tamper-resistant locks and high-security doors. The storehouses should be surrounded by two sets—outer and inner—of fencing and be continuously monitored, ideally by armed guards via closed-circuit television. All vehicles entering and leaving the storage facility should be subject to inspection. Missiles and launchers should be stored separately and brought together only for training, lot testing or in the event of hostilities. Access to the missiles should be denied to everyone except authorized personnel operating in groups of two or more, and each entry to the storage area should be recorded. Physical inventories should be conducted at least once a month at the unit level and less frequently (but regularly) at the installation and depot levels.

Too often, however, procedures at the national level fall far short of these 'best practices'. In extreme cases, such as in Liberia under the Taylor regime, safeguards are non-existent. Other governments are more cognizant of the need to protect their MANPADS but also fail to establish adequate safeguards. In one such case the military stacked its MANPADS in the crawl space under a barracks, assuming that any attempt to steal the missiles would be heard by the soldiers in the rooms above.[52] Even militaries with comparatively rigorous physical security and accounting procedures occasionally fall foul of national and international standards. In 1987 the US General Accounting Office (GAO) documented such problems at ammunition storage sites in West Germany. At one site 'Stinger missiles were stored in lightweight corrugated metal sheds with the word "Stinger" stenciled on the side'.[53]

Since 2002 control advocates have pursued several complementary initiatives aimed at bolstering PSSM practices. At the international level, members of APEC, the OAS, the OSCE and the WA have agreed through the Elements to export eligibility criteria that establish minimum PSSM standards for MANPADS recipients. These standards require each individual exporter to 'take into account ... the adequacy and effectiveness of the physical security arrangements of the recipient government for the protection of military property, facilities, holdings, and inventories' and to 'satisfy itself' that the recipient is willing and able to securely store, handle, transport, use and dispose of its MANPADS by, among other things: (*a*) conducting monthly physical inventories of all MANPADS; (*b*) accounting by

---

[51] OSCE Forum for Security Co-operation, 'Annex C: man-portable air defense systems', *Best Practice Guide on National Procedures for Stockpile Management and Security* (OSCE: Vienna, Mar. 2006), URL <http://www.osce.org/fsc/item_11_13550. html>.

[52] 'Interview with David Diaz, Deputy Chief for conventional arms threat reduction at the US Defense Threat Reduction Agency', *FAS Public Interest Report*, vol. 59, no. 4 (2007).

[53] US Government Accounting Office, *Army Inventory Management: Inventory and Physical Security Problems Continue* (US Government Printing Office: Washington, DC, Oct. 1987), p. 37.

serial number for expended or damaged components; (c) storing missiles and firing mechanisms in separate locations and transporting them in separate containers; (d) providing 24-hour surveillance of MANPADS storage facilities; (e) allowing only groups of two or more authorized persons to enter storage sites; (f) bringing together missiles and launchers only for testing, training or use in battle; (g) limiting access to hardware and classified information to government and military personnel with proper security clearances; and (h) securely disposing of surplus stocks.[54] Through their membership in the above-mentioned institutions, nearly 95 countries, including all of the major MANPADS exporters, have agreed to these standards.

Complementing these initiatives are national and multilateral PSSM orientation and assistance programmes. Several countries—including Germany, the Netherlands, Norway, the UK and the USA—provide such assistance, either through bilateral initiatives or under the auspices of multilateral organizations such as NATO and the OSCE. Anecdotal evidence suggests that these programmes have resulted in many improvements to national PSSM practices. According to one US official, the USA's PSSM orientation and assistance programmes have helped to secure 'literally thousands' of MANPADS in every region of the world by helping foreign governments to 'complete 100 per cent inventories, institute regular surveys strengthened with external or senior-level audits, improve external security like fencing and lighting, improve staff training and rehearse security response, and standardize oversight procedures'.[55]

Other countries have unilaterally improved (or have committed themselves to improving) their PSSM practices since 2002. At the May 2006 meeting of APEC's Counter-terrorism Task Force, Russia pledged to '[optimize its] MANPADS storage facilities' through the installation of 'perimeter and site protection devices' and the introduction of 'strict rules regulating access to MANPADS'.[56]

However, the secrecy surrounding national PSSM practices and the absence of monitoring and enforcement mechanisms in international agreements precludes definitive conclusions about the extent and impact of these agreements and the improvements they have prompted. As explained above, the multilateral organizations through which the various iterations of the Elements and the OSCE's PSSM best practice guide were negotiated lack the mandate and the resources necessary to compile data on or assess implementation of the PSSM requirements. Some states provide detailed, publicly accessible summaries of their PSSM policies and procedures but they are the exception, and even in these cases it is often difficult, if not impossible, for outsiders to determine how widely and consistently the procedures are followed.

Interviews with knowledgeable government officials suggest that the PSSM practices of many governments fall short of international standards, and that the barriers to universal implementation of them are significant. A lack of political will and a reluctance to expose dysfunctional systems to outsiders hinder efforts to improve PSSM practices in some countries, while other countries are plagued by inadequate physical infrastructures and a lack of resources. Examples of the latter problem

---

[54] Wassenaar Arrangement (note 23).

[55] 'Q & A on shoulder-fired missile stockpile security', FAS Strategic Security Blog, 15 Mar. 2007, URL <http://www.fas.org/blog/ssp/2007/03/q_a_on_shoulderfired_missile_s.php>.

[56] Asia–Pacific Economic Cooperation Counter-terrorism Task Force, 'Counter-terrorism Action Plans: Russia', 26–27 May 2006, URL <http://www.apec.org/apec/documents_reports/counter_terrorism_task_force.html>.

include unreliable electrical grids, which preclude the establishment of automated export systems and reduce the utility of automatic lighting and alarm systems, and computer shortages, which complicate efforts by officials to monitor PSSM practices at depots in remote locations.[57] Foreign assistance programmes can address some of these shortcomings, but not all of them.

Furthermore, even the best systems are far from perfect, as evidenced by problems discovered by investigators at US shoulder-fired missile storage sites. In 1994 the US GAO found 'serious discrepancies in the quantities, locations, and serial numbers' of shoulder-fired missiles, including Stingers. They also found broken alarm systems, missing fencing, inadequate locks on magazines and lax inspections of vehicles leaving storage areas. Three years later the GAO reported that the DOD had made 'progress toward better oversight of handheld missiles', but also that 'weaknesses remained', including inventory discrepancies and violations of DOD physical security requirements.[58] For these reasons, strong physical security and stockpile management practices are a necessary but in themselves insufficient component of global counter-MANPADS efforts.

Buy-back programmes

Historically, MANPADS buy-back programmes have a mixed track record. They are least successful when the targeted missiles are numerous and widely dispersed, and when one or both sides in a regional conflict are threatened by enemy aircraft. The US-led buy-back programme in Afghanistan—Operation Missing in Action Stinger (MIAS)—is a good example. Operation MIAS was launched in 1990 to collect the hundreds of Stinger missiles left in circulation after the campaign to oust the Soviet forces from Afghanistan. Official accounts of the programme are still classified, but information gleaned from media accounts and interviews with former government officials suggests that, as of 1996, as many as 600 of the missiles distributed to the mujahedin had not been recovered.[59]

Many factors account for this failure, most of which had little to do with the programme itself. The decentralized nature of the Afghan resistance led to the widespread dispersal of missiles, and the need to maintain 'plausible deniability' limited direct US access to the battlefront and affected the ability of the CIA to track the missiles. Even when the CIA was able to locate stray missiles, the Afghan rebels' affinity for the Stinger—which became a status symbol in Afghanistan—and their ongoing struggle against the Afghan Air Force made it difficult to persuade the rebels to hand in the weapons.[60]

In contrast, the US operation to retrieve the missiles provided to Hussein Aideed, Somali National Alliance leader, by Eritrea in 1998 was very successful. In 2003 US operatives recovered 41 of the estimated 43 missiles given to the Somali warlord,[61]

---

[57] Interview by the author with US Government official, Nov. 2006.

[58] General Accounting Office (GAO), 'Vulnerability of sensitive defense material to theft', Sep. 1997, URL <http://www.gao.gov/docdblite/summary.php?rptno=NSIAD-97-175&accno=159446>.

[59] Coll, S., *Ghost Wars* (Penguin Books: New York, N.Y., 2005), p. 11.

[60] Schroeder, Stohl and Smith (note 15), pp. 91–96.

[61] The number of missiles originally provide to Aideed is a subject of debate. Aideed claims that he received only 41 missiles, but other sources claim that he received at least 43 and as many as 45. UN Security Council (note 9), pp. 29–30.

who reportedly decided to sell them for $500 000 in cash.[62] In this case, most of the missiles were still in the possession of the original recipient, who was willing to surrender them after signing a truce with the Ethiopian Government in 1999.

Examples of ongoing buy-back efforts include the US programme in Iraq and the Russian programme in Chechnya. Starting in 2003, US troops in Iraq set up collection points throughout Iraq at which they reportedly paid $250 for each launcher and $500 for each missile.[63] While the total number of MANPADS collected through this programme is classified, media accounts and DOD press releases document the collection of at least 300 missiles. Information on MANPADS collected through Russia's SALW buy-back programme in the Southern Federal District of Russia is also incomplete. According to a Russian government official, the authorities pay up to $1000 per MANPADS, depending on the condition of the weapon. He could not, however, reveal how many missiles had been collected through this programme.[64]

If history is any guide, many of the same problems that plagued Operation MIAS are hindering the ongoing buy-back programmes in Chechnya and Iraq. As in the Afghan example above, non-state groups in both countries face enemies with active air forces, providing a strong military incentive to hold on to their missiles. In Iraq the missiles are also plentiful and probably widely dispersed. Another potential problem is the low payouts offered in both countries. Insurgents who are aware of the price that similar missiles fetch on the international black market may be holding out (or may have already sold their missiles) for more money.

Yet even in cases where conditions are conducive to collecting MANPADS, buy-back programmes should not be the sole strategy for countering the threat from stray missiles. Even the highly successful operation to buy back Eritrea's missiles from Aideed may not have recovered all of them. According to UN investigators, the SA-7 missiles used in the Mombassa attack may have been missiles that Aideed sold on the black market in Mogadishu before receiving the USA's offer.[65]

Active defence measures: airports and airliners

Rigorous airport perimeter security can help deprive terrorists of access to the areas that are most conducive to MANPADS attacks. In 2005 each APEC member agreed to conduct one MANPADS vulnerability assessment of at least one of their own airports by the end of 2006.[66] To assist governments with their assessments, guidance material for conducting such assessments was drafted by the International Civil Aviation Organization and placed on a secure website. Several countries have already completed at least one assessment, and others, including Canada and the USA, have

---

[62] Carmony, P., 'Transforming globalization and security: Africa and America post-9/11', *Africa Today*, vol. 52, no. 1 (fall 2005), p. 100.

[63] US Army, 'Anti-aircraft weapons out of terrorists' hands', Press release, 24 Aug. 2003.

[64] Interview by the author with Russian official, May 2005.

[65] UN Security Council (note 9), p. 29–30.

[66] The purpose of the assessment is to 'identify the risk at each airport, and the recommended counter-measures that should be taken to deter a potential attack'. See Asia–Pacific Economic Cooperation (APEC), Joint Statement, 17th APEC Ministerial Meeting, Busan, South Korea (15–16 Nov. 2005), URL <http://www.apec.org/apec/ministerial_statements/annual_ministerial/2005_17th_apec_ministerial.htm>; and Asia–Pacific Economic Cooperation (APEC), APEC Initiative on Reducing the Threat of MANPADS to Aviation Security, URL <http://www.apec.org/content/apec/documents_reports/annual_ministerial_meetings/2005.html>.

assessed multiple airports. The USA has taken the additional step of assessing foreign airports.

Because many MANPADS have a range of 5 kilometres or more, even the best funded and most rigorous perimeter security cannot possibly detect and thwart every attempted MANPADS attack. A 2005 study of arrival and departure patterns at Los Angeles International Airport found that a terrorist armed with an SA-7 could engage aircraft anywhere within a 2250 km² area surrounding the airport. This area would expand to around 12 000 km² if the more advanced SA-18 missile were used.[67] Given the difficulty of patrolling so vast an area, airport perimeter security is not, in itself, a practical or cost-effective counter-MANPADS strategy.

The same is true for anti-missile systems, which, of the various counter-MANPADS strategies pursued since 2002, have attracted the most attention. There are several types of anti-missile system, of which the most widely deployed are plane-mounted infrared countermeasures that use lasers, lamps or flares to deflect heat-seeking missiles away from targeted aircraft. Other systems direct microwaves or high-energy lasers at the missile, shorting its circuitry or destroying it altogether.

Several countries are studying the possibility of deploying anti-missile systems at airports or on airliners. Israel's programme is probably the furthest along. In January 2006 the Israeli Civil Aviation Authority certified the Flight Guard system, which dispenses pyrophoric, or 'dark', flares designed to decoy infrared-seeking missiles, and El Al airlines has reportedly installed the system on several of its aircraft.[68] In 2003 the US Department of Homeland Security (DHS) established the largest such programme—a multi-year evaluation of aircraft-mounted, infrared countermeasure systems that is now in the operational testing phase. Three years later the DHS launched a parallel programme to assess emerging countermeasure technologies, including ground-based lasers and microwaves.[69]

Anti-missile systems are the last line of defence against a MANPADS attack and are therefore a potentially important part of the counter-MANPADS efforts at the global level. However, cost, logistical demands, export control issues and other challenges may prevent the widespread deployment of these systems, particularly in the developing world. In 2006 the DHS estimated that installation of aircraft-mounted laser systems would cost approximately $1 million by the thousandth installation, and $365 per flight to operate and maintain. The DHS also reported that, after two years of work on converting the systems from military to civilian use, 'The risk remains moderate to high that the commercial airline's economic business model, which emphasizes high reliability and low cost, would be adversely impacted by the current prototypes.'[70]

Even if the DHS programme yields anti-missile systems that are relatively affordable and reliable, other counter-MANPADS efforts would still be required. Aircraft-mounted systems are ineffective against laser-beam-riding and command-line-of-

---

[67] Chow, J. et al., *Protecting Commercial Aviation Against the Shoulder-fired Missile Threat* (RAND Corporation: Santa Monica, Calif., 2005), URL <http://www.rand.org/pubs/occasional_papers/OP106/>, p. 14.

[68] Ari, T., 'El Al flares alarm UK union', *Flight International*, 7 Mar. 2006.

[69] Other protection measures that have been proposed focus on safeguarding aircraft fuel tanks to minimize damage in the event of a missile strike. Such measures include: strengthening fuselages; 'honeycombing' fuel tanks; and replacing space in the fuel tank with an inert gas as fuel is used up. Altering aircraft take-off and landing paths can also limit the area around an airport from which a MANPADS attack can be launched.

[70] Kirby, M., 'DHS says more counter-MANPADS work needed', *Flight International*, 8 Aug. 2006.

sight missiles. Furthermore, such systems can be overcome by a large salvo of mis-siles, would take years to install on all commercial airliners and provide no protection to passengers flying on planes of countries that choose not to equip their airlines with the systems. Ground-based microwave and high-energy laser systems provide protection against all types of MANPADS, but they are not as technologically mature or time-tested, may not operate effectively in all weather conditions and only protect aircraft flying into or departing from airports equipped with the systems.[71]

V. Conclusions

Since 2002, the international community has made significant progress in the battle against the proliferation and misuse of MANPADS. More than 95 countries have adopted agreements that set minimum standards for controls on MANPADS exports and dozens more have endorsed them. At least 21 000 stray, surplus and poorly secured missiles have been destroyed, and programmes to improve stockpile security have reduced the threat that thousands more will be dispersed. Buy-back programmes and covert operations have captured hundreds of illicit missiles in Iraq, Afghanistan, Somalia, southern Russia, and probably other countries. Vulnerability assessments have been conducted at hundreds of airports worldwide, and military anti-missile systems are being converted for civilian use.

However, the MANPADS threat persists, as evidenced by recent attempted and successful attacks in El Salvador and Iraq, and the MANPADS scare at the 2003 APEC conference in Thailand. Furthermore, non-state actors are unlikely to stop trying to obtain MANPADS as long as they are a potent means of air defence and an effective tool of terror. Space constraints preclude a complete list of recommend-ations for countering this threat, but a few merit at least a brief mention.

First, producer states should heed the exhortation in the Elements for Export Controls of MANPADS to develop 'launch control features' for installation in MANPADS. As of January 2007, no producer had incorporated such features into its MANPADS, although Russia and the USA have reportedly done preliminary research on them. Feasibility studies should be undertaken immediately, and the most promis-ing technologies should be fast-tracked for production and installation.

Second, the OSCE's best practice guidelines for MANPADS stockpile manage-ment and security should be universalized, through either a global agreement or the adoption of binding agreements by other regional organizations. Ideally, any such agreement would include monitoring and enforcement mechanisms. As a minimum, regular information exchanges should be required and periodic implementation surveys conducted, and aggregate summaries of both should be made public when possible.

Third, export control, stockpile security and destruction assistance programmes should be expanded. Even US programmes—the largest and best funded in the world—operate on shoestring budgets. Their funding, and the funding of similar efforts by other governments, should be increased until they are commensurate with the size and seriousness of the threat they address.

[71] See Chow et al. (note 67), pp. 19–22.

15. Controls on security-related international transfers

IAN ANTHONY and SIBYLLE BAUER*

I. Introduction

International efforts to prevent the proliferation of nuclear, biological and chemical (NBC) weapons have become more multifaceted in recent years. Initiatives to increase the effectiveness of export controls have gone hand-in-hand with attempts to apply them alongside other instruments in order to address proliferation problems in a more coherent manner. These interlocking measures are designed both to address a small number of urgent proliferation 'hard cases' and to establish agreed rules for application on a global basis.

In his 2002 State of the Union Address, the President of the United States, George W. Bush, pledged to 'work closely with [allies] to deny terrorists and their state sponsors the materials, technology and expertise to make and deliver weapons of mass destruction' (WMD).[1] Since then US policy has focused on strengthening cooperation among like-minded states in informal groupings outside the framework of international organizations. However, while maintaining its approach of concentrating on countries designated to be 'of proliferation concern', the USA has increasingly promoted discussion in international organizations, notably the United Nations.

By adopting a steadily expanding catalogue of resolutions, the UN Security Council is playing an ever more prominent role in creating obligations in the area of non-proliferation for all UN member states. These include obligations of a general character, of which Security Council Resolution 1540 is a prominent example, as well as decisions that focus on particular countries.[2] In 2006 the Security Council adopted two resolutions that require UN member states to block transfers to the Democratic People's Republic of Korea (DPRK or North Korea) and Iran of items that are specified on control lists that form part of the respective resolution texts, both of which have direct implications for export controls.[3]

---

[1] The White House, 'President delivers State of the Union Address', News release, Washington, DC, 29 Jan. 2002, URL <http://www.whitehouse.gov/news/releases/2002/01/20020129-11.html>.

[2] UN Security Council Resolution 1540, 28 Apr. 2004, is reproduced in appendix 11B in this volume and is discussed in appendix 11A. For this and other UN Security Council resolutions cited in this chapter see URL <http://www.un.org/documents/scres.htm>.

[3] The resolution relating to North Korea is UN Security Council Resolution 1718, 14 Oct. 2006; and that to Iran is UN Security Council Resolution 1737, 23 Dec. 2006.

* The authors thank Lukasz Kulesa of the Polish Institute for International Affairs (PISM) for invaluable assistance in collecting information related to the Proliferation Security Initiative.

The greater role of the UN Security Council in countering NBC proliferation raises a question about the relationship between global efforts to control technology transfer and the efforts of the groups of states that work together in export control regimes and other forums for practical cooperation, such as the Proliferation Security Initiative (PSI).[4] In section II of this chapter recent developments in multilateral export control regimes and the PSI are examined. Changes in the export controls applied by the European Union (EU), including controls on transfers of both items specially designed and developed for military use and dual-use items, are discussed in section III. In section IV the recent decisions by the UN to use country-specific sanctions as part of the effort to prevent the proliferation of nuclear weapons are examined. The conclusions are presented in section V.

II. The control of international transfers of proliferation-sensitive items

Four of the informal multilateral export control arrangements tried to strengthen export control cooperation in 2006: the Australia Group (AG), the Missile Technology Control Regime (MTCR), the Nuclear Suppliers Group (NSG) and the Wassenaar Arrangement on Export Controls for Conventional Arms and Dual-Use Goods and Technologies (WA). The states participating in these arrangements and in the Zangger Committee are listed in table 15.1.[5] After a significant expansion in participation in these arrangements in 2005, no new countries joined them in 2006 (with one exception).[6] However, all the regimes conduct outreach efforts to non-participating states to emphasize the importance of modern and effective export controls. Outreach and increased transparency can help non-participating states to apply the guidelines, control lists, standards and procedures developed by regime partners to the extent that these are described in public documents.

Following the end of the cold war, export control regimes placed less emphasis on the targeting of controls on particular countries. Assuming that there was a widespread commitment to non-proliferation norms, public documents did not name countries of proliferation concern but focused instead on generic types of proliferation behaviour (e.g. non-participation in relevant agreements) as the trigger for given actions. This tendency began to change in the late 1990s: several of the regimes now routinely name countries of proliferation concern.[7] In another new development, the multilateral export control

---

[4] On efforts to control exports of civil materials with potential offensive applications see chapter 11 in this volume.

[5] The Zangger Committee participants seek to take account of the effect of 'changing security aspects' on the 1968 Treaty on the Non-proliferation of Nuclear Weapons (Non-Proliferation Treaty, NPT) and to 'adapt export control conditions and criteria' in that light, although it is not formally part of the NPT regime.

[6] Croatia joined the Zangger Committee on 30 June 2006.

[7] The WA is the exception. According to one of its founding documents, the Initial Elements, the WA 'will not be directed against any state or group of states'. Wassenaar Arrangement, 'Guidelines and pro-

cooperation arrangements have analysed how their work can help ensure that non-state actors are denied the items that they would need to gain access to or make use of NBC weapons and their means of delivery as well as conventional arms and related dual-use technology.

Developments in multilateral export control regimes

The Australia Group was established in 1985 in the light of the international concern about the use of chemical weapons (CW) in the 1980–88 Iraq–Iran War. At first, the participating states cooperated to maintain and develop their national export controls to prevent exports of chemicals that might be used for, or diverted to, CW programmes. The participating states now seek to prevent the intentional or inadvertent supply by their nationals of materials or equipment to CW or biological weapon (BW) programmes.[8]

In 2006 the USA imposed sanctions on two Indian companies that in the past had supplied customers in Iran with a chemical—tri-methyl phosphite— that, according to the USA, could contribute to a CW programme or be used to produce fuel for ballistic missiles.[9] The chemical is on an AG control list but was not controlled under Indian national export control law. While Indian officials underlined that the firms involved had not violated national laws or India's international obligations, in 2006 India signalled its intention to incorporate the AG guidelines and control lists in national export control legislation. The Indian Government also announced its plans to conduct outreach activities to national industry in order to familiarize companies with the export control regulations and to discuss how they can most easily comply with their obligations.[10]

At the 2006 plenary meeting the AG participating states agreed to modify control lists in the light of the development and spread of new technologies that are considered to pose a potential proliferation threat. The AG participating states will in future apply controls to chemical manufacturing equipment that is suitable for the production of CW made from the metal niobium or niobium alloys.[11] Two fungi (*Coccidioides immitis* and *Coccidioides posadasii*)

---

cedures, including the Initial Elements', Vienna, Dec. 2006, URL <http://www.wassenaar.org/guide lines/>.

[8] See the AG website at URL <http://www.australiagroup.net>.

[9] 'Imposition of nonproliferation measures against foreign entities', *Federal Register*, vol. 70, no. 250 (30 Dec. 2005), pp. 77441–42. In addition, the USA imposed sanctions on 5 Chinese and 1 Austrian company, alleging a range of different exports of proliferation-sensitive items to Iran. In the case that is relevant to the AG controls, the Indian company Sabero Organic Chemicals Gujarat exported tri-methyl phosphite to Iran according to a press release from the company, reproduced at 'US sanctions Indian firms for chem sales', 29 Dec. 2005, URL <http://www.armscontrolwonk.com/919/indian-firms-sanctioned-for-chemical-sale-to-iran>.

[10] Ramachandran, R., 'India will conform to Australia Group rules', *Asian Age*, 6 July 2006, World News Connection, National Technical Information Service (NTIS), US Department of Commerce.

[11] Australia Group, 'Control list of dual-use chemical manufacturing facilities and equipment and related technology', July 2006, URL <http://www.australiagroup.net/en/control_list/dual_chemicals.htm>.

Table 15.1. Membership of multilateral weapon and technology transfer control regimes, as of 1 January 2007

State	Zangger Committee[a] 1974	NSG[a] 1978	Australia Group[b] 1985	MTCR 1987	Wassenaar Arrangement 1996
Argentina	x	x	x	x	x
Australia	x	x	x	x	x
Austria	x	x	x	x	x
Belarus		x			
Belgium	x	x	x	x	x
Brazil		x		x	
Bulgaria	x	x	x	x	x
Canada	x	x	x	x	x
China	x	x			
Croatia	x[c]	x			x
Cyprus		x	x		
Czech Republic	x	x	x	x	x
Denmark	x	x	x	x	x
Estonia		x	x		x
Finland	x	x	x	x	x
France	x	x	x	x	x
Germany	x	x	x	x	x
Greece	x	x	x	x	x
Hungary	x	x	x	x	x
Iceland			x	x	
Ireland	x	x	x	x	x
Italy	x	x	x	x	x
Japan	x	x	x	x	x
Kazakhstan		x			
Korea, South	x	x	x	x	x
Latvia		x	x		x
Lithuania		x	x		x
Luxembourg	x	x	x	x	x
Malta		x	x		x
Netherlands	x	x	x	x	x
New Zealand		x	x	x	x
Norway	x	x	x	x	x
Poland	x	x	x	x	x
Portugal	x	x	x	x	x
Romania	x	x	x		x
Russia	x	x		x	x
Slovakia	x	x	x		x
Slovenia	x	x	x		x
South Africa	x	x		x	x
Spain	x	x	x	x	x
Sweden	x	x	x	x	x
Switzerland	x	x	x	x	x
Turkey	x	x	x	x	x
UK	x	x	x	x	x
Ukraine	x	x	x	x	x
USA	x	x	x	x	x
Total	**36**	**45**	**40**	**34**	**40**

NSG = Nuclear Suppliers Group; MTCR = Missile Technology Control Regime.

Note: The years in the column headings indicate when the export control regime was formally established, although the groups may have met on an informal basis before then.

a The European Commission is an observer in this regime.
b In addition to the 39 states listed, the European Commission participates in this regime.
c Joined in 2006.

were added to the core list of biological agents subject to export control.[12] In future, in order to help combat increasingly sophisticated procurement methods, the AG participants intend to focus on measures to control the activities of intermediaries that facilitate trade.[13]

The MTCR is an informal arrangement in which countries that share the goal of non-proliferation of unmanned delivery systems for NBC weapons cooperate to exchange information and coordinate their national export licensing processes.[14] Recognizing that significant investigative resources are needed to identify illegal exports of missile-related items, the MTCR established an ad hoc Enforcement Experts Meeting that convenes at the same time as the MTCR plenary meetings. In 2006 the MTCR participating states helped to draw attention to the significant number of ballistic missile tests that were carried out by India, Iran, North Korea and Pakistan during the year.[15]

On 5 July 2006 the North Korean Army test-launched seven ballistic missiles, in each case launching the missiles into the Sea of Japan. In July the UN Security Council adopted Resolution 1695, condemning the missile launches and requiring all UN member states 'to exercise vigilance and prevent missile and missile-related items, materials, goods and technology being transferred to North Korea's missile or WMD programmes'.[16] The resolution did not impose sanctions on North Korea, but it stressed the importance of the discussion in the Six-Party Talks (held by China, Japan, North Korea, South Korea, Russia and the USA) of the denuclearization of the Korean peninsula. The MTCR participating states drew attention to North Korea's missile programme in their October 2006 plenary statement, which expressed 'strong support' for the Security Council resolution and 'grave concern over the missile proliferation threat posed by the DPRK's missile activities'.[17] In the public documents that were agreed at the MTCR plenary meeting, oblique reference was also made to Iran's missile programme, although Iran is not named. Iran test-fired a Shahab ballistic missile in May 2006 and, in November 2006, Iranian armed forces carried out the 'Great Prophet-2' military exercise over the course of 10 days. As part of the exercise, 'several dozen' short- and medium-range ballistic missiles were launched, including an

[12] Australia Group, 'List of biological agents for export control', July 2006, URL <http://www.australiagroup.net/en/control_list/bio_agents.htm>.

[13] Australia Group, 'Media release: 2006 Australia Group plenary', Press release, Paris, 12–15 June 2006, URL <http://www.australiagroup.net/en/releases/press_2006.htm>.

[14] See the MTCR website at URL <http://www.mtcr.info/english/>.

[15] According to the Federation of American Scientists these 4 countries launched at least 15 ballistic missiles during 2006. It should be noted that China, France, Russia and the USA tested long-range ballistic missiles of far greater accuracy and range during 2006. Federation of American Scientists, 'Nuclear missile testing galore', 22 Dec. 2006, URL <http://www.fas.org/blog/ssp/2006/12/>. See also chapter 12 and appendix 12A in this volume.

[16] UN Security Council Resolution 1695, 15 July 2006.

[17] Missile Technology Control Regime, 'Plenary meeting of the Missile Technology Control Regime', Copenhagen, 2–6 Oct. 2006, URL <http://www.mtcr.info/english/press/copenhagen.html>.

extended-range variant of the Shahab missile that is believed to have a range of over 2000 kilometres.[18]

The aim of *the NSG* is to prevent the proliferation of nuclear weapons through export controls on nuclear and nuclear-related material, equipment, software and technology.[19] The export controls, which are implemented by the participating states through national legislation and procedures, are not intended to prevent or hinder international cooperation on peaceful uses of nuclear energy.

In 2006 the exchange of information on current proliferation challenges in the framework of the NSG focused mainly on Iran.[20] The NSG adopted decisions at its plenary meeting to revise the procedures for information sharing in the group and to continue discussing the relationship between nuclear export controls and the adoption by states of strengthened nuclear safeguards. The NSG agreed to consider proposals on the possibility of further strengthening the NSG Guidelines by placing special controls on items associated with particularly sensitive parts of the nuclear fuel cycle: uranium enrichment and the reprocessing of spent nuclear fuel. In the light of the commitment to expand bilateral activities in the field of civil nuclear energy contained in the July 2005 Indian–US Civil Nuclear Cooperation Initiative (CNCI), the NSG participants have begun to examine the inclusion of a provision in the NSG Guidelines (which might be either general or specific to India).[21]

The Wassenaar Arrangement was established by 33 states in December 1995 at a meeting in Wassenaar, the Netherlands. Its objective is to promote transparency and the exchange of information and views on transfers of an agreed range of items in order to promote responsibility in transfers of conventional arms and dual-use goods and technologies and to prevent 'destabilizing accumulations' of such items.

At the 2006 WA plenary session two new sets of guidelines to help implement effective export controls were agreed: (*a*) best practices for the control of intangible transfers of technology (ITT) or software; and (*b*) guidance on the use of global or general licences for less sensitive dual-use items where this would not undermine the purposes of the WA, national export control laws or other international commitments. In addition to introducing laws and regu-

---

[18] RIA Novosti, 'Iran successfully launches long-range ballistic missiles', Moscow, 2 Nov. 2006, URL <http://en.rian.ru/world/20061102/55318349.html>.

[19] On the NSG see Anthony, I., Ahlström, C. and Fedchenko, V., *Reforming Nuclear Export Controls: The Future of the Nuclear Suppliers Group*, SIPRI Research Report no. 22 (Oxford University Press: Oxford, 2007).

[20] Nuclear Suppliers Group, 'The NSG: strengthening the nuclear non-proliferation regime, Statement from the NSG plenary meeting', NSG–BSB/Statement/Final, Brasilia, 1–2 June, 2006, URL <http://www.nuclearsuppliersgroup.org/PRESS/2006-07-Brasilia.pdf>.

[21] US Department of State, 'Joint statement by President George W. Bush and Prime Minister Manmohan Singh', Washington, DC, 18 July 2005, URL <http://www.state.gov/p/sca/rls/pr/2005/49763.htm>. See also Ahlström, C., 'Legal aspects of the Indian–US Civil Nuclear Cooperation Initiative', *SIPRI Yearbook 2006: Armaments, Disarmament and International Security* (Oxford University Press: Oxford, 2006), pp. 669–85. Indian–US civil nuclear cooperation and its implications are discussed in chapter 12 in this volume. As of Jan. 2007 the NSG has not taken a position on either the need for or the form of its relationship with India.

lations to define and control ITT and raise awareness, the participating states acknowledged the importance of post-export monitoring and 'proportionate and dissuasive penalties to deter non-compliance'. To this end, the WA participating states' governments support record-keeping obligations for industry and academia; regular compliance checks; providing training to enforcement authorities on appropriate investigative techniques; and sanctioning those that have committed breaches of laws controlling ITT. [22]

According to the WA's best practice guidelines for licensing of controlled items, global and general licences or licence exceptions may be granted 'where a Participating State considers that authorisation of exports by such means would not undermine the purposes of the Wassenaar Arrangement and would not be inconsistent with its export control laws and regulations or its other international commitments'. WA participating states may impose reporting requirements on the use of such licences, and the exporter should be expected to keep documentation 'sufficient to enable the export licensing and/or enforcement authorities' to be satisfied 'that the terms and conditions of the licence or exception have been complied with'.[23]

The plenary meeting also set up task forces to prepare the regime's third assessment of its activities, to be conducted in 2007. (The second assessment took place in 2003.[24]) The WA control lists were amended to take into account technical and security developments. The munitions list includes 22 categories, covering close to 300 items. In 9 categories the WA dual-use list includes close to 1000 items to be controlled. Changes to the WA control lists are prepared at technical meetings held throughout the year and formally approved at the December plenary session. The 2006 plenary also agreed to initiate a dialogue between the WA experts group and its MTCR counterpart to examine overlap in list coverage, terminology and thresholds for control in order to clarify the scope of application of existing rules. Australia, the Plenary Chair of the WA in 2006, highlighted the need to strengthen controls on man-portable air defence systems (MANPADS) and promoted the Wassenaar Elements on Export Controls of MANPADS vis-à-vis non-participants.[25]

The Proliferation Security Initiative

In June 2006 the states that participate in the Proliferation Security Initiative marked its third anniversary with a high-level political meeting in Warsaw. On

---

[22] Wassenaar Arrangement, 'Best practices for implementing intangible transfer of technology controls', Vienna, 6 Dec. 2006, URL <http://www.wassenaar.org>.

[23] Wassenaar Arrangement, 'Best practice guidelines for the licensing of items on the basic list and sensitive list of dual-use goods and technologies', Vienna, Dec. 2006, URL <http://www.wassenaar.org>.

[24] See Anthony, I. and Bauer, S., 'Transfer controls and destruction programmes', *SIPRI Yearbook 2004: Armaments, Disarmament and International Security* (Oxford University Press: Oxford, 2004), pp. 744–47.

[25] Downer, A., Australian Foreign Minister, 'Australia's international MANPADS initiative', Speech at Millennium Hotel, New York, 18 Jan. 2007, URL <http://www.foreignminister.gov.au/speeches/2007/070118_manpads.html>. On international controls on MANPADS see appendix 14A in this volume.

behalf of the participating states, Canada stated that the PSI aims 'to impede and stop illegal shipments of weapons of mass destruction (WMD), their delivery systems and related materials'.[26] The contribution of the PSI to non-proliferation is not confined to interdiction of shipments. It also includes the development of informal cooperation networks of officials involved in counter-proliferation activities—such as customs officers and officials from ministries of defence and foreign affairs—and provides an opportunity to gain experience and test procedures in training exercises. The PSI meetings have also enabled the USA, in particular, to advocate and build support for various non-proliferation measures.

Participation in the Proliferation Security Initiative

The group that first met, in 2003, to form the PSI consisted of 11 'core states'.[27] According to the chairman's statement at the 2006 Warsaw meeting, 'more than 75' states have expressed support for the PSI Principles and committed themselves to actively support interdiction efforts whenever necessary.[28] However, only 65 states participated in the 2006 meeting and the core group had been disbanded in mid-2005. There is neither a public list of PSI partners nor a membership procedure.

The Statement of Interdiction Principles formulated under the PSI and pub-lished in October 2003 commits the participants to establish 'a more coordin-ated and effective basis through which to impede and stop shipments of WMD, delivery systems, and related materials flowing to and from states and non-state actors of proliferation concern, consistent with national legal author-ities and relevant international law and frameworks, including the UN Security Council'.[29] Within six months of the publication of the Statement of Interdic-tion Principles over 60 countries had expressed public support for it, signalling their intention to try to enforce existing national laws and international agree-ments (including mandatory decisions of the UN Security Council) more effectively. The private sector has been engaged in the PSI through annual meetings on particular subjects at which industry representatives contribute knowledge and expertise on relevant technical issues related to interdiction.[30]

---

[26] See the PSI website at URL <http://www.proliferationsecurity.info/introduction.html>. See also Ahlström, C., 'The Proliferation Security Initiative: international law aspects of the Statement of Inter-diction Principles', *SIPRI Yearbook 2005: Armaments, Disarmament and International Security* (Oxford University Press: Oxford, 2005), pp. 741–65; and the glossary in this volume.

[27] The states were Australia, France, Germany, Italy, Japan, the Netherlands, Poland, Portugal, Spain, the United Kingdom and the USA.

[28] Cracow Proliferation Security Initiative, High Level Political Meeting, 'Chairman's statement', Warsaw, 23 June 2006, URL <http://www.psi.msz.gov.pl/>.

[29] The statement is available on the PSI website (note 26).

[30] In Aug. 2004 a meeting in Copenhagen was dedicated to analysing ship container security; in Sep. 2005 a meeting in Los Angeles, Calif., was devoted to analysing air cargo security; and in Sep. 2006 a meeting in London focused on maritime security. See PSI Maritime Workshop, 'Preventing WMD pro-liferation', Press release 258/2006, London, 25–26 Sep. 2006, available at British Foreign and Common-wealth Office, URL <http://www.fco.gov.uk/>.

By June 2006, 20 states were regularly participating in PSI Operational Expert Group (OEG) meetings.[31] These states are understood to have the capabilities and expertise to develop the PSI, including the necessary national legal base and inter-agency coordination system, and they have also carried the main burden of organizing practical activities.[32]

Since the launch of the PSI in 2003 six countries have signed bilateral ship-boarding agreements with the USA—Belize, Croatia, Cyprus, Liberia, the Marshall Islands and Panama.[33] Except for Croatia, these states provide commercial shipping fleets with a flag of convenience according to the International Transport Workers Federation; and Liberia and Panama have the largest fleets of registered commercial vessels in the world.[34] The USA is engaged in discussions about signing such agreements with 20 other countries.

Almost all the European countries support the PSI, as does the EU. In 2004 Belarus declared that it shared the PSI objectives and was ready to cooperate within this framework. In Africa, Angola, Liberia, Libya and Tunisia have participated in PSI activities; and in Central and South America, Argentina, Belize and Panama support the PSI. PSI outreach activities have been carried out in key trans-shipment countries (i.e. countries that function as major hubs for the trading and shipment of cargo) and regions that are regarded as probable proliferation routes. Participation in PSI outreach activities has been undertaken by Azerbaijan and Georgia in the South Caucasus; Kazakhstan, Turkmenistan and Uzbekistan in Central Asia; Bahrain, Iraq, Israel, Jordan, Kuwait, Oman, the United Arab Emirates and Yemen in the Middle East; and Brunei, Cambodia, the Philippines and Thailand in South-East Asia.

There are noticeable gaps in participation. China, Egypt, India, Indonesia, South Korea and Malaysia (which control important shipping or transit routes of non-proliferation relevance) have not participated in the PSI. North Korean authorities have made it clear to China and South Korea that their support for PSI activities—which it has characterized as acts of piracy that can 'ignite military conflict and lead to the regional and worldwide instability'[35]—would jeopardize North Korean engagement in nuclear issues and negotiations on them.

[31] The 20 participants were the 11 'core states' as well as Argentina, Canada, Denmark, Greece, New Zealand, Norway, Russia, Singapore and Turkey. At OEG meetings representatives plan future activities and analyse past activities to consider the possible scope of action under international and domestic legal systems and to determine whether the necessary authority exists to conduct interdiction operations in different circumstances, including actual cases and hypothetical scenarios tested in exercises.

[32] All the 23 PSI exercises conducted prior to mid-2006 were organized or co-organized by a country in this group of 20 states.

[33] On these agreements see US Department of State, Bureau of International Security and Nonproliferation, 'Ship boarding agreements', URL <http://www.state.gov/t/isn/c12386.htm>.

[34] Together, the 6 countries that have signed ship-boarding agreements hold the registration of over one-quarter of world merchant shipping. Central Intelligence Agency (CIA), 'Rank order: merchant marine', *The World Factbook 2007* (CIA: Washington, DC, 2007), URL <https://www.cia.gov/cia/publications/factbook/>.

[35] North Korean Institute for Disarmament and Peace, 'Proliferation Security Initiative (PSI): nuclear energy and countering proliferation', Paper presented at the Third Meeting of the CSCAP Study Group on Countering the Proliferation of Weapons of Mass Destruction in the Asia Pacific, Singapore, 26–27 Mar. 2006.

The USA has frequently attempted to convince India to participate in the PSI as part of the wider strategy of engaging India in the global non-proliferation system. In 2005 India suggested to the USA that it would be willing to participate in the PSI on equal terms (i.e. if it was able to join the core group of PSI participants or if the group ceased to exist). After the core group's disbanding in 2005, India linked participation in the PSI to the process of negotiating amendments to the 1988 Convention for the Suppression of Unlawful Acts against the Safety of Maritime Navigation (SUA Convention), discussed below.[36] The SUA Convention was amended in October 2005. The US Congress discussed whether to make Indian participation in the PSI a condition of agreeing the US–India Peaceful Atomic Energy Cooperation Act—an agreement that was needed to enable civilian nuclear cooperation between the two countries.[37] This act was passed in December 2006, but references in it to the PSI were restricted to requiring a report from the US president on efforts and progress made towards achieving India's full participation in the PSI.

Indonesia and Malaysia have raised concern over the implications of the PSI for their jurisdiction over maritime routes and their sovereignty claims to the Strait of Malacca. Both countries are very suspicious of any foreign military presence in these waters and, when the question of Indonesian participation in the PSI was brought up by US Secretary of State Condoleezza Rice during her visit to Indonesia in March 2006, Indonesian Foreign Minister Hassan Wirajuda characterized the PSI as an initiative that would endanger Indonesian sovereignty.[38]

The scope of activities

President Bush proposed expanding PSI activities beyond intercepting goods in a 2004 speech at the National Defense University (NDU) in Washington, DC.[39] He suggested that the PSI participants and other interested states should explore more active use of law enforcement and criminal justice procedures to tackle illicit trafficking in proliferation-sensitive items. The 2004 Lisbon PSI meeting endorsed this objective and agreed to 'begin examining the key steps necessary for this expanded role', including a review of national tools available for this purpose.[40]

---

[36] The Convention for the Suppression of Unlawful Acts against the Safety of Maritime Navigation was opened for signature on 10 Mar. 1988 and entered into force on 1 Mar. 1992; for the text see URL <http://www.imo.org/>. It was amended in Oct. 2005 and the amended convention was opened for signature on 14 Feb. 2006. See also Ahlström (note 26), pp. 763–64.

[37] On the US–India Peaceful Atomic Energy Cooperation Act (Hyde Act) see chapter 12 in this volume.

[38] Indonesian Embassy, 'RI declines to join Proliferation Security Initiative', Canberra, 18 Mar. 2006, URL <http://www.kbri-canberra.org.au/brief/2006/mar/031806.htm>.

[39] The White House, 'President announces new measures to counter the threat of WMD: remarks by the President on weapons of mass destruction proliferation, Fort Lesley J. McNair, National Defense University', News release, Washington, DC, 11 Feb. 2004, URL <http://www.whitehouse.gov/news/releases/2004/02/20040211-4.html>.

[40] US Department of State, 'Proliferation Security Initiative: chairman's statement at the fifth meeting', Lisbon, 4–5 Mar. 2004, URL <http://www.state.gov/t/isn/rls/other/30960.htm>.

The PSI could promote discussion in the area of criminal justice and law enforcement by addressing the measures needed to implement the obligation introduced in UN Security Council Resolution 1540 for states to adopt and enforce appropriate, effective laws to criminalize the financing of non-state actors that would enable them to manufacture, acquire, possess, develop, transport, transfer or use NBC weapons and their means of delivery.[41] However, while Bush raised the freezing of assets associated with any aspect of NBC proliferation (state or non-state) in his NDU speech, there has so far not been much progress in this area of work under the PSI. Substantive discussions on this issue will need to include financial regulators, who are more used to cooperating in groups such as the Financial Action Task Force on Money Laundering, established in 1989 by the Group of Seven (G7) industrialized states,[42] or the Egmont Group of national finance intelligence units.[43]

In 2006 the USA suggested that the PSI could be expanded and tools created to interdict payments and financial flows between the parties to proliferation-sensitive transactions.[44] At the June 2006 PSI meeting in Warsaw, the participants examined some national efforts to disrupt the financial mechanisms that support proliferators. However, the meeting did not recommend a common approach but instead concluded that each participant should consider 'how their own national laws and authorities might be utilized or strengthened to identify, track or freeze the assets and transactions of WMD proliferators and their supporters'.[45]

Revision of the Convention for the Suppression of Unlawful Acts against the Safety of Maritime Navigation

The 1988 SUA Convention, together with a protocol on fixed platforms located on the continental shelf, is an anti-terrorist convention that was adopted within the framework of the UN.[46] Its parties are required to criminalize and prosecute a range of maritime terrorist offences.

After the 11 September 2001 terrorist attacks on the USA the international legal framework against terrorism was reviewed and, as part of that process, the Legal Committee of the International Maritime Organization (IMO) reassessed measures and procedures to prevent acts of terrorism at sea, includ-

---

[41] For the text of the resolution see appendix 11A in this volume.

[42] On the Financial Action Task Force on Money Laundering see URL <http://www.fatf-gafi.org/dataoecd/30/46/37627377.pdf>. See also Norgren, C., 'An international response to terrorism', eds A. J. K. Bailes and I. Frommelt, SIPRI, *Business and Security: Public–Private Sector Relationships in a New Security Environment* (Oxford University Press: Oxford, 2004), pp. 47–58.

[43] See the Egmont Group website at URL <http://www.egmontgroup.org/>.

[44] Executive Order no. 13382, issued in June 2005, gave US authorities the power to seize assets and property in the USA and block access to US financial system for designated foreign individuals and entities judged to be engaged in proliferation of NBC weapons and their means of delivery. The White House, 'Executive order: blocking property of weapons of mass destruction proliferators and their supporters', News release, Washington, DC, 29 June 2005, URL <http://www.whitehouse.gov/news/releases/2005/06/20050629.html>.

[45] Cracow Proliferation Security Initiative (note 28).

[46] SUA Convention (note 36).

ing the SUA Convention. In 2004 at PSI meetings the USA suggested amendments to the convention, and the meetings also served as a forum to promote and discuss those proposals. Amendments were adopted on 14 October 2005, and the amended convention was opened for signature on 14 February 2006.

Changes to the convention included widening the scope of offences to include not only the actual use of WMD against or on a ship but also the intentional transport of a range of proliferation-sensitive items on-board a ship. The amended convention establishes an international legal basis for action against a broad spectrum of proliferation-related maritime activities and includes provisions for boarding ships on the high seas that are modelled on bilateral ship-boarding agreements of the kind promoted by the PSI.

III. Supply-side measures in the European Union

In 2006 the EU continued its efforts to adopt the revision of its 1998 Code of Conduct on Arms Exports as a Common Position, which would strengthen its legal status.[47] The EU worked to strengthen the implementation and enforcement of dual-use export controls, following up recommendations from a 'peer review' of the regulation that is the legal basis for EU dual-use export control, including its national implementation. The EU also continued its outreach efforts to non-EU states on conventional and dual-use export controls. In the dual-use area, outreach efforts have increasingly been supported through technical assistance funded by the European Commission and implemented by EU member states.

The European Union Code of Conduct on Arms Exports

The EU Code of Conduct on Arms Exports was adopted in June 1998.[48] Beyond its application to the 27 members of the EU (as of January 2007), Bosnia and Herzegovina, Canada, Croatia, Iceland and the Former Yugoslav Republic of Macedonia (FYROM) have officially aligned themselves with its criteria and principles.[49] In addition, two countries in South-Eastern Europe (Montenegro and Serbia) have included an obligation to apply the EU Code criteria when assessing licence applications in their new export control laws adopted in 2006. Albania is about to adopt similar legislation.

---

[47] Council of the European Union, 'European Union Code of Conduct on Arms Exports', document 8675/2/98, Rev. 2, Brussels, 5 June 1998, URL <http://ue.eu.int/uedocs/cmsUpload/08675r2en8.pdf>. Unlike a Council Declaration, a Common Position is an instrument of the Common Foreign and Security Policy, which politically obliges member states to bring their legislation and policies in line with the agreed Common Position. While a Common Position would not transform the Code of Conduct into European law or make it subject to the jurisdiction of the European Court of Justice, it does have national legal implications for some member states.

[48] See Bauer, S. and Bromley, M., *The European Union Code of Conduct on Arms Exports: Improving the Annual Report*, SIPRI Policy Paper no. 8 (SIPRI: Stockholm, Nov. 2004), URL <http://www.sipri.org/>.

[49] 'Eighth annual report according to operative provision 8 of the European Union Code of Conduct on arms exports', *Official Journal of the European Union*, C 250 (16 Oct. 2005), pp. 1–346.

The EU Code of Conduct contains eight criteria for export licensing as well as operative provisions which outline reporting procedures and mechanisms for intergovernmental denial notification and consultation. The EU list of military equipment to which the Code is applied is revised every year to take into account the changes to the WA Munitions List.[50] The EU could include additional items but has not chosen to do this so far.

In 2004 the EU member states initiated a review of the 1998 Code of Conduct. The Council Working Party on Conventional Arms (COARM) prepared an updated and upgraded Code, which includes changes to its operative provisions, eight criteria and legal status.[51] A draft 'Council Common Position defining common rules governing the control of exports of military technology and equipment' was agreed at the technical level in the spring of 2005. The proposal by the Finnish EU Presidency to adopt the Common Position was vetoed by a number of member states, including France.[52] The delay was due to a political link between adopting the Common Position and lifting the arms embargo imposed on China in 1989. The adoption of the so-called toolbox of additional transparency and mutual control measures to be applied upon the lifting of an arms embargo, for inclusion in the User's Guide to the Council Common Position defining common rules governing the control of exports of military technology and equipment, has been held up for the same reason. This was in spite of the 2005 decision to apply it to Libya.[53]

The User's Guide to the EU Code, first published in November 2003, has been updated at least once a year since then. It further defines and interprets the terms and procedures outlined in the 1998 Code of Conduct. A number of important changes were made in 2006: best practice guidelines for the application of criteria 2 ('human rights'), 3 ('internal situation'), 4 ('regional stability') and 7 ('risk of diversion') were agreed. Work on best practice guides for the remaining criteria is ongoing.[54] The common elements for end-use certificates in the User's Guide were revised in alignment with the indicative list of end-use assurances agreed by the Wassenaar Arrangement.[55] A sur-

---

[50] 'Common Military List of the European Union (equipment covered by the European Union Code of Conduct on Arms Exports) adopted by the Council on 27 February 2006', *Official Journal of the European Union*, C66 (17 Mar. 2006), pp. 1–28.

[51] For a summary of changes see Anthony, I. and Bauer, S., 'Transfer controls', *SIPRI Yearbook 2005* (note 26), pp. 715–18.

[52] Rettman, A., 'France blocking plan for EU code on arms exports', *EUobserver*, 18 Jan. 2007, URL <http://euobserver.com/9/23296/?rk=1>; and Dombey, D., 'EU considers binding rules on arms sales', *Financial Times*, 18 Apr. 2005, p. 2.

[53] See Anthony and Bauer (note 51); and Anthony, I., 'Militarily relevant EU–China trade and technology transfers: issues and problems', Paper presented at the Conference on Chinese Military Modernization: East Asian Political, Economic, and Defense Industrial Responses, Maui, Hawaii, 19–20 May 2005, URL <http://www.sipri.org/contents/expcon/euchinapaper>.

[54] Council of the European Union, 'User's Guide to the European Union Code of Conduct on Arms Exports', document 16440/06, Brussels, 18 Dec. 2006, URL <http://www.consilium.europa.eu/export controls>. Best practice guidelines for criterion 8 on sustainable development were adopted in 2005.

[55] Wassenaar Arrangement, 'End-use assurances commonly used, consolidated indicative list', Vienna, updated at the 2005 WA plenary session, Dec. 2005, URL <http://www.wassenaar.org publicdocuments/>.

vey among member states on national requirements and policies for end-use certificates was initiated.

The development of the EU Code's implementation during 2006 is documented in the eighth annual report,[56] which was published considerably earlier than in previous years and was more comprehensive. The EU governments also held an experts meeting to discuss how to improve the data collection and reporting methods and initiated a survey on this subject.[57]

The member states use the EU's COREU system to circulate notifications of denials of exports and to consult with each other.[58] The EU Code of Conduct requires such consultations before authorizing a transaction that is essentially identical to an export previously denied by another EU member. According to the eighth annual report, such activities took place 'almost on a daily basis' in 2006.[59] Denial notifications and the results of bilateral consultations are included in a central database, which is managed by the EU Council Secretariat. In October 2006, 20 member states and acceding countries had legislation in place which fully implements Common Position 2003/468/CFSP on the control of arms brokering.[60] EU governments also exchanged information about national practices regarding post-shipment verification.

Among COARM's stated priorities for the near future are improvements in the clarity and transparency of annual reporting, in particular regarding the value of actual exports. The EU member states are also seeking to assist countries in the practical implementation of the Code's principles and criteria through, 'inter alia, the provision of practical and technical assistance to ensure the harmonisation of policies on arms export control'.[61]

The member states continued their outreach efforts to non-EU countries which are newly included in an annex to the annual report. The Austrian EU Presidency, in cooperation with SIPRI, organized a seminar on conventional and dual-use export controls for the Western Balkans countries in Vienna in May 2006. At the end of October 2006, the Finnish EU Presidency and the Government of Bosnia and Herzegovina, in cooperation with SIPRI, organized a regional seminar on the EU Code of Conduct in Sarajevo, during which working groups discussed the application of the Code criteria to hypothetical cases. In 2006 the EU also sent letters to authorities in Albania, Belarus, Bosnia and Herzegovina, Croatia, the FYROM, Moldova, Montenegro, Serbia, Switzerland, Turkey and Ukraine, in which it offered to strengthen the dialogue with these countries about the practical implementation of the EU Code of Conduct.

[56] 'Eighth annual report' (note 49).

[57] For further detail on the data in the eighth annual report and reporting methodologies see chapter 10 in this volume.

[58] COREU is the French abbreviation for European Correspondence, a telex network linking the foreign ministries of the EU member states.

[59] 'Eighth annual report' (note 49), p. 2.

[60] 'Council Common Position 2003/468/CFSP of 23 June 2003 on the control of arms brokering', Official Journal of the European Union, L156 (25 June 2003), pp. 79–80.

[61] 'Eighth annual report' (note 49), p. 4.

Strengthening European Union dual-use export controls

The participation of EU companies and individuals in the international nuclear trafficking ring coordinated by Abdul Qadeer Khan, a former senior scientific adviser to the Government of Pakistan on nuclear matters, underlined that more effective export controls are needed in Europe. Exports of dual-use items from the EU are controlled by a Council regulation (Regulation 1334/2000 as subsequently amended).[62] In 2004 the EU conducted a 'peer review' of the dual-use export control system and, in December 2004, EU leaders decided that the recommendations of the review, which were listed in nine categories, should be acted on without delay.

Subsequently, an electronic database was established on a pilot basis to record denial notices made by member states under EU law and in the international export control regimes. The database contains 'a growing number' of the valid denials issued by member states under Regulation 1334/2000 as well as those exchanged pursuant to rules created in the Australia Group and 'some' of those exchanged pursuant to rules created in the Nuclear Suppliers Group.[63]

Since the peer review of 2004, member states have got into the habit of informing one another about changes to national regulations and have established points of contact to make exchanges regular and systematic. A pool of technical experts has been designated to assist their colleagues to address specific questions on matters such as the classification and recognition of items subject to control as another practical step towards effective cooperation.

As regards Iran, prior to the adoption of sanctions by the UN Security Council in December 2006 (discussed below) the EU took steps to develop a specific approach to applying export controls. Regulation 1334/2000 applies to all exports of listed items but the EU has not prepared a list of countries to which particular measures would apply. However, the July 2006 Council Conclusions indicate that Iran has been the subject of special attention. The member states committed themselves to exercise 'the utmost vigilance in the application of existing export control mechanisms for sensitive material to prevent the transfer of goods, technology and materials that might be used, directly or indirectly, in fissile material programmes and missile programmes'.[64]

The Commission has prepared proposals to modify Regulation 1334/2000 that are intended to enhance security, simplify the task of industry in complying with the established rules and improve coordination of export controls at

---

[62] The regulation is normally amended on an annual basis to take into account changes in the control list that forms an integral part of the law. The most recent version at the time of writing is 'Council Regulation (EC) no. 394/2006 of 27 February 2006 amending and updating Regulation (EC) no. 1334/2000 setting up a Community regime for the control of exports of dual-use items and technology', *Official Journal of the European Union*, L73 (13 Mar. 2006), p. 1.

[63] Council of the European Union, 'Implementation of the recommendations of the Peer Review of Member States export control systems for dual-use goods', document 16507/06, Brussels, 12 Dec. 2006.

[64] Council of the European Union, 2743rd Council Meeting General Affairs and External Relations, Brussels, 17 July 2006, General Affairs, Press release 11574/06 (Presse 218), URL <http://www.consilium.eu.int>.

the international level.[65] These proposals, which address the issues highlighted in the peer review and take into account its recommendations, will be discussed by the Council of the European Union. UN Security Council Resolution 1540 requires appropriate and effective transit and trans-shipment controls over proliferation-sensitive items, including related services such as financing and transport. Neither transit and trans-shipment nor related services are controlled under existing EU law and thus action in this field will be necessary. The review of Regulation 1334/2000 also aims to clarify and update controls on intangible technology transfer. At present ITT falls under the scope of Regulation 1334/2000 when the means of transfer is electronic (including email, fax and via the Internet). However, the oral communication of intangible technology is controlled by each member state under national legislation in line with an undertaking made by EU member states in a Council Joint Action in June 2000.[66] Except for Cyprus, all EU member states participate in the Wassenaar Arrangement and have therefore committed themselves to implement the 'Best practices for implementing intangible transfer of technology controls' document agreed at the WA plenary meeting in December 2006 and discussed above.[67]

European Union export control outreach and assistance efforts

In recent years, outreach efforts to promote the adoption of modern and effective export controls have become more prominent on the agenda of the international export control regimes. A number of countries, Japan and the USA being the most prominent, have also offered technical assistance to help states that want to strengthen their export controls. While different EU organs have for some time cooperated with non-EU countries on dual-use export controls, there has been neither a systematic approach to coordinating such efforts nor support for them through a long-term technical assistance programme. Export control assistance at the EU level was given during the run-up to the 2004 enlargement, preparing countries to adopt the EU *acquis communautaire* for control of both dual-use and conventional exports, as expressed in the treaties, the secondary legislation and EU policies.

In December 2003 the threat-based approach adopted in the EU Strategy against Proliferation of Weapons of Mass Destruction widened the geograph-

---

[65] European Commission, 'New measures on export of Dual Use goods and technologies: summary of the proposals adopted by the Commission', Brussels, 19 Dec. 2006. URL <http://www.trade.ec.europa.eu/doclib/html/131958.htm>.

[66] 'Council Joint Action of 22 June 2000 concerning the control of technical assistance related to certain military end-uses', *Official Journal of the European Communities*, L159 (30 June 2000), pp. 1–2. According to the Joint Action, intangible technology transfer is to be controlled '*where it is provided outside the European Community* by a natural or legal person established in the European Community and is intended, or the provider is aware that it is intended, for use in connection with the development, production, handling, operation, maintenance, storage, detection, identification or dissemination of chemical, biological or nuclear weapons or other nuclear explosive devices or the development, production, maintenance or storage of missiles capable of delivering such weapons' (emphasis added). ITT that takes place within the EU (termed 'deemed export' in the USA) is not controlled under EU law.

[67] Wassenaar Arrangement (note 22).

ical scope of export control assistance within a more coherent EU non-proliferation policy.[68] The WMD Strategy contains a commitment to work with others on dual-use export controls, in the EU's immediate neighbour-hood, in strategic partner countries and in countries of proliferation concern. Export control assistance features prominently in the Action Plan that accompanies the WMD Strategy. During 2006 the EU took large strides towards implementing this commitment, most notably through the development of the Stability Instrument as one of the financial instruments in the Community budget cycle for 2007–13. The Stability Instrument will contain substantial funding to provide technical assistance to non-EU countries to set up or strengthen their dual-use export control systems.

Since 2003 EU assistance efforts have been carried out in a series of pilot projects authorized by the European Parliament. The first such project, which began in 2004 and was implemented by SIPRI, included activities to strengthen the national dual-use export controls of Bosnia and Herzegovina, Croatia, Montenegro and Serbia (initially, the State Union of Serbia and Montenegro) and to elaborate and test approaches to export control assistance that could offer guidance for the subsequent development of a larger pro-gramme.

Two pilot projects in the area of dual-use export control assistance are being implemented by the German Federal Office for Economics and Export Control (Bundesamt für Wirtschaft und Ausfuhrkontrolle, BAFA), with the support of officials from other EU countries. These projects focus on cooperation with China, Montenegro, Serbia, Ukraine and the United Arab Emirates. Albania, the FYROM and Morocco are included from 2007. The most recent pilot pro-ject aims to develop a training capability at BAFA to improve the delivery of EU assistance. In 2005 the European Commission also contracted BAFA to implement a project on export control of dual-use items in Russia financed under the Technical Aid to the Commonwealth of Independent States (TACIS) programme. The project has a contract budget of €3 million and is scheduled to last at least 30 months. Other EU member states will participate by contrib-uting experts in individual activities. The project's scope includes the legal and regulatory framework, institutional capacity-building and outreach to industry.

The Office of the High Representative's Personal Representative on Non-proliferation highlighted the importance of dual-use export controls for WMD non-proliferation during visits and workshops abroad, for example, in Ukraine in January 2006 and in Pakistan in December 2006.

---

[68] Council of the European Union, EU Strategy against Proliferation of Weapons of Mass Destruc-tion, Brussels, 12 Dec. 2003, URL <http://ue.eu.int/cms3_applications/Applications/newsRoom/Load Document.asp?directory=en/misc/&filename=78340.pdf>.

IV. The impact of UN sanctions against North Korea and Iran on export controls

In 2006 the UN Security Council adopted resolutions 1718 and 1737 as part of the effort to address nuclear and missile-related proliferation concerns in North Korea and Iran, respectively. In each case the resolution's targeted and limited measures were integrated into a package of measures including an attempt to conduct a dialogue on nuclear issues with the country concerned and to emphasize the rewards and the potential costs associated with alternative nuclear policies.[69] In spite of these efforts, at the end of 2006 Iran and North Korea continued to pursue nuclear programmes that create widespread international concern. While the countries engaged in this dialogue cannot accept the nuclear policies of Iran and North Korea, the use of sanctions has been examined because they offer 'something between words and war'.[70] The measures contained in the resolutions are intended to deny particular target groups the economic or material base with which to conduct activities of concern or to impose restrictions and costs directly on those deemed responsible for deciding the policies and programmes of concern.

UN Security Council Resolution 1718 was unanimously adopted on 14 October 2006 after North Korea carried out a nuclear weapon test.[71] It requires UN members to 'prevent the direct or indirect supply, sale or transfer to the DPRK, through their territories or by their nationals, or using their flag vessels or aircraft, and whether or not originating in their territories' of a range of different items. The resolution bans the supplying of major conventional weapons and of items set out in three lists that accompany the resolution, corresponding to the lists adopted by the AG, the MTCR and the NSG.[72] It also bans the provision of technical training, advice, services or assistance related to embargoed items. Supplying luxury goods to North Korea is also banned.

Resolution 1718 also states that North Korea 'shall cease the export' of the same items that may no longer be supplied to North Korea and instructs states to 'prohibit the procurement of such items from the DPRK by their nationals, or using their flagged vessels or aircraft, and whether or not originating in the territory of the DPRK'. In order to ensure compliance with these requirements,

---

[69] On the nuclear programmes of Iran and North Korea and the wider approaches to address concerns arising from them see chapter 12 in this volume.

[70] This formulation was used by Swedish State Secretary Hans Dahlgren in a presentation to the UN Security Council laying out the recommendations of a study that aimed to facilitate the more precise use of sanctions against threats to peace, while reducing collateral effects. United Nations, '"Stockholm Process" findings—year-long study on targeted sanctions—presented to Security Council', Press release, UN document SC/7672, 25 Feb. 2003, available at 'Minutes from the UNSC discussion', URL <http://www.smartsanctions.se/>. See also Speier, R. H., Chow, B. G. and Starr, S. R., *Nonproliferation Sanctions*, RAND Monograph Report no. MR-1285-OSD (RAND: Santa Monica, Calif., 2001), URL <http://www.rand.org/pubs/monograph_reports/MR1285/>.

[71] The nuclear weapon test is discussed in appendix 12B in this volume.

[72] The items covered are battle tanks, armoured combat vehicles, large calibre artillery systems, combat aircraft, attack helicopters, warships, and missiles or missile systems as defined for the purpose of the UN Register of Conventional Arms, URL <http://disarmament.un.org/cab/register.html>.

states are 'called upon to take, in accordance with their national authorities and legislation, and consistent with international law, cooperative action including through inspection of cargo to and from the DPRK, as necessary'.

The resolution also includes financial and travel sanctions. States are required to freeze funds, other financial assets and economic resources that are owned or controlled, directly or indirectly, by persons or entities that are listed in a document annexed to the resolution. The list contains the names of individuals and entities who are believed to be engaged in or providing support for North Korea's 'nuclear-related, other weapons of mass destruction-related and ballistic missile-related programmes', or 'acting on their behalf or at their direction'. Finally, states are instructed to prevent the 'entry into or transit through their territories' of people who are considered responsible for North Korea's 'nuclear-related, ballistic missile-related and other weapons of mass destruction-related programmes, together with their family members'.

In July 2006 the UN Security Council adopted Resolution 1696 which demanded that Iran 'suspend all enrichment-related and reprocessing activities, including research and development' and stipulated that this full suspension should be verified by the International Atomic Energy Agency (IAEA).[73] Resolution 1696 called on all states, 'in accordance with their national legal authorities and legislation and consistent with international law, to exercise vigilance and prevent the transfer of any items, materials, goods and technology that could contribute to Iran's enrichment-related and reprocessing activities and ballistic missile programmes'. The resolution did not prohibit nuclear or nuclear-related dual-use transfers to Iran but requested the Director General of the IAEA to report on whether Iran had established 'full and sustained suspension' of proliferation-sensitive activities. The Security Council made it clear that, if Iran did not comply with Resolution 1696, then 'appropriate measures' would subsequently be adopted 'to persuade Iran to comply with this resolution and the requirements of the IAEA'.[74]

In two subsequent reports the IAEA Director General stated that Iran had not established full and sustained suspension of all enrichment-related and reprocessing activities as set out in Resolution 1696.[75] In the light of these reports the UN Security Council passed Resolution 1737 on 23 December 2006, specifying and bringing into effect the 'appropriate measures' referred to in Resolution 1696.[76] Resolution 1737 bans states from supplying Iran with items that could contribute to enrichment-related, reprocessing or heavy water-related activities or to the development of nuclear weapon delivery systems. This embargo includes technical support that could assist banned activities. The resolution requires states to examine the activities of Iranian nationals

---

[73] UN Security Council Resolution 1696, 31 July 2006.

[74] UN Security Council Resolution 1696 (note 73).

[75] International Atomic Energy Agency (IAEA), 'Implementation of the NPT safeguards agreement in the Islamic Republic of Iran', document GOV/2006/53, Vienna, 31 Aug. 2006; and IAEA, 'Implementation of the NPT safeguards agreement in the Islamic Republic of Iran', document GOV/2006/64, Vienna, 14 Nov. 2006. Both are available on the IAEA's website at URL <http://www.iaea.org/Publications/Documents/>.

[76] UN Security Council Resolution 1737 (note 3).

who are resident in their countries and receiving technical education to minimize the risk that these people may acquire proliferation-sensitive knowledge.

The items that are banned for transfer to Iran are not the same as those that are banned for supply to North Korea. The lists applied in the case of Iran are derived from those of the MTCR and the NSG, but the resolution exempts items needed to complete the Iran–Russia project to build a light-water reactor at Bushehr. Under the terms of the resolution Iran is prohibited from exporting any items listed in two documents that conform to the MTCR and the NSG control lists, and states are also banned from importing these items from Iran.

The resolution includes targeted financial sanctions. States should freeze the financial assets of companies, organizations and individuals involved in Iran's nuclear and ballistic missile programmes and an annex to the resolution contains lists of the people and entities subject to these provisions. The resolution does not contain travel sanctions of the kind imposed on North Korea, but states are required to report the movement of designated individuals to the UN Security Council.

The export control implications of UN Security Council resolutions 1718 and 1737

Prior to the adoption of UN Security Council resolutions 1718 and 1737 North Korea and Iran were both subject to certain export restrictions because of their non-compliance with IAEA safeguards. However, the resolutions extend the restrictions to a wider range of items and increase the number of states obliged to implement them.

After April 1993, when the IAEA Board of Governors concluded that North Korea was in non-compliance with its safeguards agreement, the NSG participating states should have denied authorization for transfers of controlled items to North Korea in line with NSG guidelines. The NSG states should have applied the guidelines in a similarly restrictive manner with regard to Iran after September 2004, when the Board of Governors found that Iran was non-compliant with its safeguards agreement. Whereas the NSG guidelines are binding on the NSG participating states and some non-participating states that have made a voluntary decision to respect them, the Security Council resolutions of 2006 extend these restrictions to all states. Subsequent to Security Council resolutions 1781 and 1737, the EU adopted Common Positions concerning restrictive measures against both North Korea and Iran. The Common Positions describe how the UN decisions will be implemented by the EU through national laws in member states and under EU law, as appropriate.[77]

All parties to the 1968 Treaty on the Non-proliferation of Nuclear Weapons (Non-Proliferation Treaty, NPT)—that is, all states except India, Israel, North

[77] 'Council Common Position 2006/795/CFSP of 20 November 2006 concerning restrictive measures against the Democratic People's Republic of Korea', *Official Journal of the European Union*, L322 (22 Nov. 2006), pp. 32–35; and 'Council Common Position 2007/140/CFSP of 27 February 2007 concerning restrictive measures against Iran', *Official Journal of the European Union*, L61 (28 Feb. 2007), pp. 49–55

Korea and Pakistan—are bound by the undertaking in the NPT's Article III.2 not to provide source or special fissionable material, or equipment or material especially designed or prepared for the processing, use or production of special fissionable material, to any non-nuclear-weapon state for peaceful purposes, unless the source or special fissionable material 'shall be subject' to safeguards. The range of items that falls under the scope of this commitment is not specified in the NPT, but it is narrower than the contents of the lists linked to resolutions 1718 and 1737.

While the UN Security Council lacks the technical capacity to develop lists for sanctions purposes, one of the main tasks of the multilateral export control regimes has been to compile and update lists of items that should be subject to authorization prior to export. The lists that form critical elements of the sanctions imposed by the Security Council are closely modelled on the control lists developed in the regimes.[78] In order to prevent gaps emerging between the coverage of the national export control laws of important suppliers and the items to which UN Security Council resolutions apply, there should be regular updates of the UN lists in line with the changes agreed in multilateral export control regimes. In this way a valuable technical resource can be put at the disposal of the United Nations.

Unlike some previous sanctions resolutions that have a 'sunset clause', establishing a period of application, resolutions 1718 and 1737 are of unlimited duration. In each case, whether and when sanctions are lifted depend on a judgement by the Security Council about compliance with the terms of the resolution. Both resolutions anticipate that sanctions may be suspended or (partly or fully) lifted in case of compliance but also envisage the adoption of further measures in the event of non-compliance.

The implementation of Resolution 1737 is potentially complicated. Iran has important nuclear cooperation agreements with Russia, and the Russian representative to the UN has pointed out that the restrictions introduced by the Security Council only apply to the areas that are a cause for the IAEA's concern.[79] Cooperation with Iran in other areas should be subject to national authorization and control but should not be subject to additional restrictive measures imposed by the UN. Thus, Resolution 1737 exempts certain categories of items from the embargo and establishes the functional equivalent of an export licensing mechanism for others.

---

[78] The list contained in UN document S/2006/814 conforms with the NSG control lists; the list in UN document S/2006/815 conforms with the MTCR equipment and technology annex; and the list in UN document S/2006/853.Corr.1 conforms with the Australia Group lists. See UN, Letter dated 13 October 2006 from the Permanent Representative of France to the United Nations addressed to the President of the Security Council, UN documents S/2006/814 and S/2006/815, 13 Oct. 2006; and UN, Letter dated 1 November 2006 from the Chairman of the Security Council Committee established pursuant to resolution 1718 (2006) concerning the Democratic People's Republic of Korea addressed to the President of the Security Council, UN document S/2006/853/Corr.1, 14 Nov. 2006.

[79] United Nations, 'Security Council imposes sanctions on Iran for failure to halt uranium enrichment, unanimously adopting Resolution 1737 (2006)', UN Security Council document SC/8928, 23 Dec. 2006, URL <http://www.un.org/News/Press/docs/2006/sc8928.doc.htm>.

The Security Council's Resolution 1737 committee, comprising all Security Council members, is responsible for overseeing implementation of the UN sanctions. In certain cases controlled items may be transferred if the committee 'determines in advance and on a case-by-case basis that such supply, sale, transfer or provision of such items or assistance would clearly not contribute to the development of Iran's technologies in support of its proliferation sensitive nuclear activities and of development of nuclear weapon delivery systems'. In such a situation the state applying for permission is required to show that appropriate end-user guarantees are included in the contract. Iran is also required to provide a statement of end-use, pledging not to use the specified items in proliferation-sensitive nuclear activities or for the development of nuclear weapon delivery systems.

In order to give their informed consent as part of this licensing process the countries that serve on the Security Council will have to depend on support from their national export control systems, as the UN itself has little or no relevant expertise that can underpin specific decisions. The determination that a transfer does not pose an unacceptable proliferation risk would normally involve assessing the programme of the importing countries and the characteristics of the end-user (including ownership and management structures, its past and current operations and activities, and any record of involvement in activities of concern). The assessment would also involve a technical element to judge whether the specifications and the quantity of the items to be transferred are consistent with the stated end-use. Finally, the assessment would examine the national laws and procedures of the importing country to evaluate whether the assurances against unauthorized re-export are sufficient.

Resolutions 1718 and 1737 ban the export of listed items and open the way for cooperative enforcement action, including through the inspection of cargo that enters or leaves North Korea and Iran. As discussed above, the approach that China has adopted to the PSI has been strongly influenced by the direct link that North Korea has made between the PSI and participation in dialogue in the framework of the Six-Party Talks. North Korea's actions, not for the first time, have placed China in a difficult position. China felt compelled to support the resolution condemning the North Korean nuclear test, but in a statement immediately after the adoption of Resolution 1718 Wang Guangya, the Chinese ambassador to the United Nations, said that China did not approve of the practice of inspecting cargo to and from North Korea although this is specifically authorized in the resolution. The inspection of cargoes leaving North Korea could be a potential 'flashpoint'. The ambassador emphasized that China 'strongly urged the countries concerned to adopt a prudent and responsible attitude in that regard' and asked them to 'refrain from taking any provocative steps that could intensify the tension'.[80]

---

[80] United Nations, 'Security Council condemns nuclear test by Democratic People's Republic of Korea, unanimously adopting Resolution 1718', UN Security Council document SC/8853, 14 Oct. 2006, URL <http://www.un.org/News/Press/docs/2006/sc8853.doc.htm>.

Implementing the targeted financial sanctions that resolutions 1718 and 1737 impose on North Korea and Iran will depend on intrusive monitoring of their assets and on the availability of financial controls to block certain transactions. Targeting the transactions for which financing should be blocked will require the establishment of new links between the export control enforcement community and sanctions enforcement bodies.

V. Conclusions

The role of export controls in supporting the implementation of the main multilateral non-proliferation treaties is now supplemented by the important role that they will play in implementing decisions of the United Nations. The need for a progressively larger number of states to participate in export control cooperation is likely to create further momentum behind calls for a global legal framework for export controls that apply to nuclear, biological and chemical weapons.

The increasing integration of several different measures, of which export controls are only one, to achieve non-proliferation objectives will require cooperation between communities that have never previously worked closely together. This is perhaps particularly true for the communities that enforce export controls, criminal law and financial sanctions. The PSI is one mechanism by which focused dialogue can be organized internationally between different national enforcement agencies. It can also bring together different parts of the enforcement community on an as-needs basis to address specific cases of suspected trafficking. Export controls are being modernized to address changes in the way that international trade and economic cooperation are managed. In particular, there is a growing interest in bringing intangible transfers of technology under effective control.

Many countries may lack the practical capacity to implement Security Council decisions effectively. In particular, strengthening the national export control systems of countries that serve on UN sanctions committees would be a logical target for the various outreach and technical assistance processes that are being carried out around the world, including those of the European Union.

The need to focus on the effective enforcement of export controls has been discussed in the export control regimes, the EU and the UN, both for national capacity-building in the group of states that participate actively in export control cooperation and for technical assistance directed at other states. Such an approach requires the active and competent involvement of a range of national actors—customs, police, intelligence and prosecution services—and the appropriate legal framework, including civil and criminal penalties for export control violations. Adequate emphasis should also be given to building export control enforcement capacity when designing future assistance programmes.

Annexes

Annex A. Arms control and disarmament agreements

Annex B. Chronology 2006

Annex A. Arms control and disarmament agreements

NENNE BODELL

Notes

1. The agreements are listed in the order of the date on which they were adopted, signed or opened for signature (multilateral agreements) or signed (bilateral agreements). The date on which they entered into force and the depositary for multilateral treaties are also given. Information is as of mid-February 2007.

2. The main source of information is the lists of signatories and parties provided by the depositaries of the treaties.

3. For a few major treaties, the substantive parts of the most important reservations, declarations and/or interpretive statements made in connection with a state's signature, ratification, accession or succession are given in notes below the entry. For the 1925 Geneva Protocol, only 'explicit reservations' are listed here. For 'implicit reservations' and an explanation of the two categories see URL <http://www.sipri.org/contents/cbwarfare/cbw_research_doc/cbw_historical/cbw-hist-geneva-parties.html>.

4. States and organizations listed as parties have ratified, acceded or succeeded to the agreements. Former non-self-governing territories, upon attaining independence, sometimes make general statements of continuity to all agreements concluded by the former governing power. This annex lists as parties only those new states that have made an uncontested declaration on continuity or have notified the depositary about their succession.

5. Unless stated otherwise, the multilateral agreements listed in this annex are open to all states for signature, ratification, accession or succession.

6. A complete list of UN member states, with the year in which they became members, appears in the glossary at the front of this volume. Not all the signatories and parties listed in this annex are UN members.

7. Taiwan, while not recognized as a sovereign state by some countries, is listed as a party to those agreements which it has ratified.

8. In December 1991 the Russian Federation confirmed the continuity of international obligations assumed by the USSR. Treaties that were ratified by the USSR are in force for Russia.

9. In June 2006 Montenegro withdrew from its union with Serbia, established in Feb. 2003. Serbia continued the international obligations of the former State Union of Serbia and Montenegro.

Protocol for the Prohibition of the Use in War of Asphyxiating, Poisonous or Other Gases, and of Bacteriological Methods of Warfare (1925 Geneva Protocol)

Signed at Geneva on 17 June 1925; entered into force on 8 February 1928; depositary French Government

The protocol declares that the parties agree to be bound by the prohibition on the use of these weapons in war.

Parties (134): Afghanistan, Albania, Algeria[1], Angola[1], Antigua and Barbuda, Argentina, Australia, Austria, Bahrain[1], Bangladesh[1], Barbados, Belgium, Benin, Bhutan, Bolivia, Brazil, Bulgaria, Burkina Faso, Cambodia[1], Cameroon, Canada, Cape Verde, Central African Republic, Chile, China[1], Côte d'Ivoire, Cuba, Cyprus, Czech Republic, Denmark, Dominican Republic, Ecuador, Egypt, Equatorial Guinea, Estonia, Ethiopia, Fiji[1], Finland, France, Gambia, Germany, Ghana, Greece, Grenada, Guatemala, Guinea-Bissau, Holy See, Hungary, Iceland, India[1], Indonesia, Iran, Iraq[1], Ireland, Israel[2], Italy, Jamaica, Japan, Jordan[3], Kenya, Korea (North)[1], Korea (South)[5], Kuwait[1], Laos, Latvia, Lebanon, Lesotho, Liberia, Libya[1], Liechtenstein, Lithuania, Luxembourg, Madagascar, Malawi, Malaysia, Maldives, Malta, Mauritius, Mexico, Monaco, Mongolia, Morocco, Nepal, Netherlands, New Zealand, Nicaragua, Niger, Nigeria[1], Norway, Pakistan, Panama, Papua New Guinea[1], Paraguay, Peru, Philippines, Poland, Portugal, Qatar, Romania, Russia, Rwanda, Saint Kitts and Nevis, Saint Lucia, Saint Vincent and the Grenadines, Saudi Arabia, Senegal, Serbia[1], Sierra Leone, Slovakia, Solomon Islands[1], South Africa, Spain, Sri Lanka, Sudan, Swaziland, Sweden, Switzerland, Syria, Taiwan, Tanzania, Thailand[4], Togo, Tonga, Trinidad and Tobago, Tunisia, Turkey, Uganda, UK, Ukraine, Uruguay, USA[4], Venezuela, Viet Nam[1], Yemen

[1] The protocol is binding on this state only as regards states which have signed and ratified or acceded to it. The protocol will cease to be binding on this state in regard to any enemy state whose armed forces or whose allies fail to respect the prohibitions laid down in it.

[2] The protocol is binding on Israel only as regards states which have signed and ratified or acceded to it. The protocol shall cease to be binding on Israel in regard to any enemy state whose armed forces, or the armed forces of whose allies, or the regular or irregular forces, or groups or individuals operating from its territory, fail to respect the prohibitions which are the object of the protocol.

[3] Jordan undertakes to respect the obligations contained in the protocol with regard to states which have undertaken similar commitments. It is not bound by the protocol as regards states whose armed forces, regular or irregular, do not respect the provisions of the protocol.

[4] The protocol shall cease to be binding on this state with respect to use in war of asphyxiating, poisonous or other gases, and of all analogous liquids, materials or devices, in regard to any enemy state if such state or any of its allies fails to respect the prohibitions laid down in the protocol.

[5] South Korea withdrew its reservation concerning bacteriological and toxin weapons in 2002.

Signed but not ratified: El Salvador

Treaty for Collaboration in Economic, Social and Cultural Matters and for Collective Self-defence among Western European States (Brussels Treaty)

Signed at Brussels on 17 March 1948; entered into force on 25 August 1948; depositary Belgian Government

The treaty provides for close cooperation of the parties in the military, economic and political fields.

Parties (7): *Original parties:* Belgium, France, Luxembourg, Netherlands, UK

Germany and Italy acceded through the Protocols of 1954.

See also Modified Brussels Treaty and Protocols of 1954.

Convention on the Prevention and Punishment of the Crime of Genocide (Genocide Convention)

Adopted at Paris by the UN General Assembly on 9 December 1948; entered into force on 12 January 1951; depositary UN Secretary-General

Under the convention any commission of acts intended to destroy, in whole or in part, a national, ethnic, racial or religious group as such is declared to be a crime punishable under international law.

Parties (140): Afghanistan, Albania*, Algeria*, Andorra, Antigua and Barbuda, Argentina*, Armenia, Australia, Austria, Azerbaijan, Bahamas, Bahrain*, Bangladesh*, Barbados, Belarus*, Belgium, Belize, Bolivia, Bosnia and Herzegovina, Brazil, Bulgaria*, Burkina Faso, Burundi, Cambodia, Canada, Chile, China*, Colombia, Comoros, Congo (Democratic Republic of the), Costa Rica, Côte d'Ivoire, Croatia, Cuba, Cyprus, Czech Republic, Denmark, Ecuador, Egypt, El Salvador, Estonia, Ethiopia, Fiji, Finland, France, Gabon, Gambia, Georgia, Germany, Ghana, Greece, Guatemala, Guinea, Haiti, Honduras, Hungary*, Iceland, India*, Iran, Iraq, Ireland, Israel, Italy, Jamaica, Jordan, Kazakhstan, Korea (North), Korea (South), Kuwait, Kyrgyzstan, Laos, Latvia, Lebanon, Lesotho, Liberia, Libya, Liechtenstein, Lithuania, Luxembourg, Macedonia (Former Yugoslav Republic of), Malaysia*, Maldives, Mali, Mexico, Moldova, Monaco, Mongolia*, Montenegro*, Morocco*, Mozambique, Myanmar*, Namibia, Nepal, Netherlands, New Zealand, Nicaragua, Norway, Pakistan, Panama, Papua New Guinea, Paraguay, Peru, Philippines*, Poland*, Portugal*, Romania*, Russia*, Rwanda*, Saint Vincent and the Grenadines, Saudi Arabia, Senegal, Serbia*, Seychelles, Singapore*, Slovakia, Slovenia, South Africa, Spain*, Sri Lanka, Sudan, Sweden, Switzerland, Syria, Tanzania, Togo, Tonga, Trinidad and Tobago, Tunisia, Turkey, Uganda, UK, Ukraine*, United Arab Emirates, Uruguay, USA*, Uzbekistan, Venezuela*, Viet Nam*, Yemen*, Zimbabwe

* With reservation and/or declaration.

Signed but not ratified: Dominican Republic

Geneva Convention (IV) Relative to the Protection of Civilian Persons in Time of War

Signed at Geneva on 12 August 1949; entered into force on 21 October 1950; depositary Swiss Federal Council

The Geneva Convention (IV) establishes rules for the protection of civilians in areas covered by war and in occupied territories. This convention was formulated at the Diplomatic Conference held from 21 April to 12 August 1949. (Other conventions adopted at the same time were: Convention (I) for the Amelioration of the Condition of the Wounded and Sick in Armed Forces in the Field; Convention (II) for the Amelioration of the Condition of the Wounded, Sick and Shipwrecked Members of Armed Forces at Sea; and Convention (III) Relative to the Treatment of Prisoners of War.)

Parties (194): Afghanistan, Albania*, Algeria, Andorra, Angola*, Antigua and Barbuda, Argentina, Armenia, Australia*, Austria, Azerbaijan, Bahamas, Bahrain, Bangladesh*, Barbados*, Belarus, Belgium, Belize, Benin, Bhutan, Bolivia, Bosnia and Herzegovina, Botswana, Brazil, Brunei Darussalam, Bulgaria, Burkina Faso, Burundi, Cambodia, Cameroon, Canada, Cape Verde, Central African Republic, Chad, Chile, China*, Colombia, Comoros, Congo (Democratic Republic of the), Congo (Republic of), Cook Islands, Costa Rica, Côte d'Ivoire, Croatia, Cuba, Cyprus, Czech Republic*, Denmark, Djibouti, Dominica,

Dominican Republic, Ecuador, Egypt, El Salvador, Equatorial Guinea, Estonia, Eritrea, Ethiopia, Fiji, Finland, France, Gabon, Gambia, Georgia, Germany*, Ghana, Greece, Grenada, Guatemala, Guinea, Guinea-Bissau*, Guyana, Haiti, Holy See, Honduras, Hungary, Iceland, India, Indonesia, Iran*, Iraq, Ireland, Israel*, Italy, Jamaica, Japan, Jordan, Kazakhstan, Kenya, Kiribati, Korea (North)*, Korea (South)*, Kuwait*, Kyrgyzstan, Laos, Latvia, Lebanon, Lesotho, Liberia, Libya, Liechtenstein, Lithuania, Luxembourg, Macedonia (Former Yugoslav Republic of)*, Madagascar, Malawi, Malaysia, Maldives, Mali, Malta, Marshall Islands, Mauritania, Mauritius, Mexico, Micronesia, Moldova, Monaco, Mongolia, Montenegro, Morocco, Mozambique, Myanmar, Namibia, Nauru, Nepal, Netherlands, New Zealand*, Nicaragua, Niger, Nigeria, Norway, Oman, Pakistan*, Palau, Panama, Papua New Guinea, Paraguay, Peru, Philippines, Poland, Portugal*, Qatar, Romania, Russia*, Rwanda, Saint Kitts and Nevis, Saint Lucia, Saint Vincent and the Grenadines, Samoa, San Marino, Sao Tome and Principe, Saudi Arabia, Senegal, Serbia, Seychelles, Sierra Leone, Singapore, Slovakia, Slovenia, Solomon Islands, Somalia, South Africa, Spain, Sri Lanka, Sudan, Suriname*, Swaziland, Sweden, Switzerland, Syria, Tajikistan, Tanzania, Thailand, Timor-Leste, Togo, Tonga, Trinidad and Tobago, Tunisia, Turkey, Turkmenistan, Tuvalu, Uganda, UK*, Ukraine*, United Arab Emirates, Uruguay*, USA*, Uzbekistan, Vanuatu, Venezuela, Viet Nam*, Yemen*, Zambia, Zimbabwe

* With reservation and/or declaration.

In 1989 the Palestine Liberation Organization (PLO) informed the depositary that it had decided to adhere to the four Geneva conventions and the two protocols of 1977.

See also Protocols I and II of 1977.

Treaty of Economic, Social and Cultural Collaboration and Collective Self-defence among Western European States (Modified Brussels Treaty); Protocols to the 1948 Brussels Treaty (Paris Agreements)

Signed at Paris on 23 October 1954; entered into force on 6 May 1955; depositary Belgian Government

The 1948 Brussels Treaty was modified by four protocols which amended the original text to take account of political and military developments in Europe, allowing the Federal Republic of Germany (West Germany) and Italy to become parties in return for controls over German armaments and force levels (annulled, except for weapons of mass destruction, in 1984). The Western European Union (WEU) was created through the Modified Brussels Treaty. The treaty contains an obligation for collective defence of its members.

Members of the WEU: Belgium, France, Germany, Greece, Italy, Luxembourg, Netherlands, Portugal, Spain, UK

Antarctic Treaty

Signed at Washington, DC, on 1 December 1959; entered into force on 23 June 1961; depositary US Government

The treaty declares the Antarctic an area to be used exclusively for peaceful purposes. It prohibits any measure of a military nature in the Antarctic, such as the establishment of military bases and fortifications, and the carrying out of military manoeuvres or the testing of any type of weapon. The treaty bans any nuclear explosion as well as the disposal of radioactive waste material in Antarctica.

In accordance with Article IX, consultative meetings are convened at regular intervals to exchange information and hold consultations on matters pertaining to Antarctica, as well as to recommend to the governments measures in furtherance of the principles and objectives of the treaty.

The treaty is subject to ratification by the signatories and is open for accession by UN members or by other states invited to accede with the consent of all the parties entitled to participate in the consultative meetings provided for in Article IX. States demonstrating their interest in Antarctica by conducting substantial scientific research activity there, such as the establishment of a scientific station or the despatch of a scientific expedition, are entitled to become consultative members.

Parties (45): Argentina[†], Australia[†], Austria, Belgium[†], Brazil[†], Bulgaria[†], Canada, Chile[†], China[†], Colombia, Cuba, Czech Republic, Denmark, Ecuador[†], Estonia, Finland[†], France[†], Germany[†], Greece, Guatemala, Hungary, India[†], Italy[†], Japan[†], Korea (North), Korea (South)[†], Netherlands[†], New Zealand[†], Norway[†], Papua New Guinea, Peru[†], Poland[†], Romania, Russia[†], Slovakia, South Africa[†], Spain[†], Sweden[†], Switzerland, Turkey, UK[†], Ukraine[†], Uruguay[†], USA[†], Venezuela

[†] This state is a consultative member under Article IX of the treaty.

The Protocol on Environmental Protection (**1991 Madrid Protocol**) entered into force on 14 January 1998.

Treaty Banning Nuclear Weapon Tests in the Atmosphere, in Outer Space and Under Water (Partial Test-Ban Treaty, PTBT)

Signed at Moscow by three original parties on 5 August 1963 and opened for signature by other states at London, Moscow and Washington, DC, on 8 August 1963; entered into force on 10 October 1963; depositaries British, Russian and US governments

The treaty prohibits the carrying out of any nuclear weapon test explosion or any other nuclear explosion: (*a*) in the atmosphere, beyond its limits, including outer space, or under water, including territorial waters or high seas; and (*b*) in any other environment if such explosion causes radioactive debris to be present outside the territorial limits of the state under whose jurisdiction or control the explosion is conducted.

Parties (125): Afghanistan, Antigua and Barbuda, Argentina, Armenia, Australia, Austria, Bahamas, Bangladesh, Belarus, Belgium, Benin, Bhutan, Bolivia, Bosnia and Herzegovina, Botswana, Brazil, Bulgaria, Canada, Cape Verde, Central African Republic, Chad, Chile, Colombia, Congo (Democratic Republic of the), Costa Rica, Côte d'Ivoire, Croatia, Cyprus, Czech Republic, Denmark, Dominican Republic, Ecuador, Egypt, El Salvador, Equatorial Guinea, Fiji, Finland, Gabon, Gambia, Germany, Ghana, Greece, Guatemala, Guinea-Bissau, Honduras, Hungary, Iceland, India, Indonesia, Iran, Iraq, Ireland, Israel, Italy, Jamaica, Japan, Jordan, Kenya, Korea (South), Kuwait, Laos, Lebanon, Liberia, Libya, Luxembourg, Madagascar, Malawi, Malaysia, Malta, Mauritania, Mauritius, Mexico, Mongolia, Morocco, Myanmar, Nepal, Netherlands, New Zealand, Nicaragua, Niger, Nigeria, Norway, Pakistan, Panama, Papua New Guinea, Peru, Philippines, Poland, Romania, Russia, Rwanda, Samoa, San Marino, Senegal, Serbia, Seychelles, Sierra Leone, Singapore, Slovakia, Slovenia, South Africa, Spain, Sri Lanka, Sudan, Suriname, Swaziland, Sweden, Switzerland, Syria, Taiwan, Tanzania, Thailand, Togo, Tonga, Trinidad and Tobago, Tunisia, Turkey, Uganda, UK, Ukraine, Uruguay, USA, Venezuela, Yemen, Zambia

Signed but not ratified: Algeria, Burkina Faso, Burundi, Cameroon, Ethiopia, Haiti, Mali, Paraguay, Portugal, Somalia, Viet Nam

Treaty on Principles Governing the Activities of States in the Exploration and Use of Outer Space, Including the Moon and Other Celestial Bodies (Outer Space Treaty)

Opened for signature at London, Moscow and Washington, DC, on 27 January 1967; entered into force on 10 October 1967; depositaries British, Russian and US governments

The treaty prohibits the placing into orbit around the earth of any object carrying nuclear weapons or any other kind of weapons of mass destruction, the installation of such weapons on celestial bodies, or the stationing of them in outer space in any other manner. The establishment of military bases, installations and fortifications, the testing of any type of weapons and the conduct of military manoeuvres on celestial bodies are also forbidden.

Parties (107): Afghanistan, Algeria, Antigua and Barbuda, Argentina, Australia, Austria, Bahamas, Bangladesh, Barbados, Belarus, Belgium, Benin, Brazil, Brunei Darussalam, Bulgaria, Burkina Faso, Canada, Chile, China, Cuba, Cyprus, Czech Republic, Denmark, Dominica, Dominican Republic, Ecuador, Egypt, El Salvador, Equatorial Guinea, Fiji, Finland, France, Germany, Greece, Grenada, Guinea-Bissau, Hungary, Iceland, India, Indonesia, Iraq, Ireland, Israel, Italy, Jamaica, Japan, Kazakhstan, Kenya, Korea (South), Kuwait, Laos, Lebanon, Libya, Luxembourg, Madagascar, Mali, Mauritius, Mexico, Mongolia, Morocco, Myanmar, Nepal, Netherlands, New Zealand, Niger, Nigeria, Norway, Pakistan, Papua New Guinea, Peru, Poland, Portugal, Romania, Russia, Saint Kitts and Nevis, Saint Lucia, Saint Vincent and the Grenadines, San Marino, Saudi Arabia, Seychelles, Sierra Leone, Singapore, Slovakia, Solomon Islands, South Africa, Spain, Sri Lanka, Swaziland, Sweden, Switzerland, Syria, Taiwan, Thailand, Togo, Tonga, Tunisia, Turkey, Uganda, UK, Ukraine, United Arab Emirates, Uruguay, USA, Venezuela, Viet Nam, Yemen, Zambia

Signed but not ratified: Bolivia, Botswana, Burundi, Cameroon, Central African Republic, Colombia, Congo (Democratic Republic of the), Congo (Republic of), Ethiopia, Gambia, Ghana, Guyana, Haiti, Holy See, Honduras, Iran, Jordan, Lesotho, Macedonia (Former Yugoslav Republic of), Malaysia, Nicaragua, Panama, Philippines, Rwanda, Serbia, Somalia, Trinidad and Tobago

Treaty for the Prohibition of Nuclear Weapons in Latin America and the Caribbean (Treaty of Tlatelolco)

Original treaty opened for signature at Mexico City on 14 February 1967; entered into force. The treaty was amended in 1990, 1991 and 1992; depositary Mexican Government

The treaty prohibits the testing, use, manufacture, production or acquisition by any means, as well as the receipt, storage, installation, deployment and any form of possession of any nuclear weapons by Latin American and Caribbean countries.

The parties should conclude agreements with the IAEA for the application of safeguards to their nuclear activities. The IAEA has the exclusive power to carry out special inspections.

The treaty is open for signature by all the independent states of the region.

Under *Additional Protocol I* states with territories within the zone (France, the Netherlands, the UK and the USA) undertake to apply the statute of military denuclearization to these territories.

Under *Additional Protocol II* the recognized nuclear weapon states—China, France, Russia (at the time of signing, the USSR), the UK and the USA—undertake to respect the statute of military denuclearization of Latin America and the Caribbean and not to contribute to acts involving a violation of the treaty, nor to use or threaten to use nuclear weapons against the parties to the treaty.

Parties to the original treaty (33): Antigua and Barbuda, Argentina, Bahamas, Barbados, Belize, Bolivia, Brazil, Chile, Colombia, Costa Rica, Cuba, Dominica, Dominican Republic, Ecuador, El Salvador, Grenada, Guatemala, Guyana, Haiti, Honduras, Jamaica, Mexico, Nicaragua, Panama, Paraguay, Peru, Saint Kitts and Nevis, Saint Lucia, Saint Vincent and the Grenadines, Suriname, Trinidad and Tobago, Uruguay, Venezuela

Amendments ratified by: Argentina, Barbados, Belize, Brazil, Chile, Colombia, Costa Rica, Cuba, Dominican Republic, Ecuador, El Salvador, Grenada, Guatemala, Guyana, Jamaica, Mexico, Panama, Paraguay, Peru, Suriname, Uruguay, Venezuela

Note: Not all the countries listed had ratified all three amendments by 1 Feb. 2007.

Parties to Additional Protocol I: France[1], Netherlands, UK[2], USA[3]

Parties to Additional Protocol II: China[4], France[5], Russia[6], UK[2], USA[7]

[1] France declared that Protocol I shall not apply to transit across French territories situated within the zone of the treaty, and destined for other French territories. The protocol shall not limit the participation of the populations of the French territories in the activities mentioned in Article 1 of the treaty, and in efforts connected with the national defence of France. France does not consider the zone described in the treaty as established in accordance with international law; it cannot, therefore, agree that the treaty should apply to that zone.

[2] When signing and ratifying protocols I and II, the UK made the following declarations of understanding: The signing and ratification by the UK could not be regarded as affecting in any way the legal status of any territory for the international relations of which the UK is responsible, lying within the limits of the geographical zone established by the treaty. Should any party to the treaty carry out any act of aggression with the support of a nuclear weapon state, the UK would be free to reconsider the extent to which it could be regarded as bound by the provisions of Protocol II.

[3] The USA ratified Protocol I with the following understandings: The provisions of the treaty do not affect the exclusive power and legal competence under international law of a state adhering to this Protocol to grant or deny transit and transport privileges to its own or any other vessels or aircraft irrespective of cargo or armaments; the provisions do not affect rights under international law of a state adhering to this protocol regarding the exercise of the freedom of the seas, or regarding passage through or over waters subject to the sovereignty of a state. The declarations attached by the USA to its ratification of Protocol II apply also to Protocol I.

[4] China declared that it will never send its means of transportation and delivery carrying nuclear weapons to cross the territory, territorial sea or airspace of Latin American countries.

[5] France stated that it interprets the undertaking contained in Article 3 of Protocol II to mean that it presents no obstacle to the full exercise of the right of self-defence enshrined in Article 51 of the UN Charter; it takes note of the interpretation by the Preparatory Commission for the Denuclearization of Latin America according to which the treaty does not apply to transit, the granting or denying of which lies within the exclusive competence of each state party in accordance with international law. In 1974 France made a supplementary statement to the effect that it was prepared to consider its obligations under Protocol II as applying not only to the signatories of the treaty, but also to the territories for which the statute of denuclearization was in force in conformity with Protocol I.

[6] On signing and ratifying Protocol II, the USSR stated that it assumed that the effect of Article 1 of the treaty extends to any nuclear explosive device and that, accordingly, the carrying out by any party of nuclear explosions for peaceful purposes would be a violation of its obligations under Article 1 and would be incompatible with its non-nuclear weapon status. For states parties to the treaty, a solution to the problem of peaceful nuclear explosions can be found in accordance with the provisions of Article V of the NPT and within the framework of the international procedures of the IAEA. It declared that authorizing the transit of nuclear weapons in any form would be contrary to the objectives of the treaty.

Any actions undertaken by a state or states parties to the treaty which are not compatible with their non-nuclear weapon status, and also the commission by one or more states parties to the treaty of an act of aggression with the support of a state which is in possession of nuclear weapons or together with such a state, will be regarded by the USSR as incompatible with the obligations of those countries under the treaty. In such cases it would reserve the right to reconsider its obligations under Protocol II. It further reserves the right to reconsider its attitude to this protocol in the event of any actions on the part of other states possessing nuclear weapons which are incompatible with their obligations under the said protocol.

[7] The USA signed and ratified Protocol II with the following declarations and understandings: Each of the parties retains exclusive power and legal competence to grant or deny non-parties transit and transport privileges. As regards the undertaking not to use or threaten to use nuclear weapons against the parties, the USA would consider that an armed attack by a party, in which it was assisted by a nuclear weapon state, would be incompatible with the treaty.

Treaty on the Non-proliferation of Nuclear Weapons (Non-Proliferation Treaty, NPT)

Opened for signature at London, Moscow and Washington, DC, on 1 July 1968; entered into force on 5 March 1970; depositaries British, Russian and US governments

The treaty prohibits the transfer by a nuclear weapon state (defined in the treaty as those which have manufactured and exploded a nuclear weapon or other nuclear explosive device prior to 1 January 1967) to any recipient whatsoever of nuclear weapons or other nuclear explosive devices or of control over them, as well as the assistance, encouragement or inducement of any non-nuclear weapon state to manufacture or otherwise acquire such weapons or devices. It also prohibits the receipt by non-nuclear weapon states from any transferor whatsoever, as well as the manufacture or other acquisition by those states, of nuclear weapons or other nuclear explosive devices.

The parties undertake to facilitate the exchange of equipment, materials and scientific and technological information for the peaceful uses of nuclear energy and to ensure that potential benefits from peaceful applications of nuclear explosions will be made available to non-nuclear weapon parties to the treaty. They also undertake to pursue negotiations in good faith on effective measures relating to cessation of the nuclear arms race at an early date and to nuclear disarmament, and on a treaty on general and complete disarmament.

Non-nuclear weapon states undertake to conclude safeguard agreements with the International Atomic Energy Agency (IAEA) with a view to preventing diversion of nuclear energy from peaceful uses to nuclear weapons or other nuclear explosive devices. A Model Protocol Additional to the Safeguards Agreements, strengthening the measures, was approved in 1997; such Additional Safeguards Protocols are signed by states individually with the IAEA.

A Review and Extension Conference, convened in 1995 in accordance with the treaty, decided that the treaty should remain in force indefinitely.

Parties (189): Afghanistan[†], Albania[†], Algeria[†], Andorra, Angola, Antigua and Barbuda[†], Argentina[†], Armenia[†], Australia[†], Austria[†], Azerbaijan[†], Bahamas[†], Bahrain, Bangladesh[†], Barbados[†], Belarus[†], Belgium[†], Belize[†], Benin, Bhutan[†], Bolivia[†], Bosnia and Herzegovina[†], Botswana, Brazil[†], Brunei Darussalam[†], Bulgaria[†], Burkina Faso[†], Burundi, Cambodia[†], Cameroon[†], Canada[†], Cape Verde, Central African Republic, Chad, Chile[†], China[†], Colombia, Comoros, Congo (Democratic Republic of the)[†], Congo (Republic of), Costa Rica[†], Côte d'Ivoire[†], Croatia[†], Cuba[†], Cyprus[†], Czech Republic[†], Denmark[†], Djibouti, Dominica[†], Dominican Republic[†], Ecuador[†], Egypt[†], El Salvador[†], Equatorial Guinea, Eritrea,

Estonia[†], Ethiopia[†], Fiji[†], Finland[†], France[†], Gabon, Gambia[†], Georgia, Germany[†], Ghana[†], Greece[†], Grenada[†], Guatemala[†], Guinea, Guinea-Bissau, Guyana[†], Haiti, Holy See[†], Honduras[†], Hungary[†], Iceland[†], Indonesia[†], Iran[†], Iraq[†], Ireland[†], Italy[†], Jamaica[†], Japan[†], Jordan[†], Kazakhstan[†], Kenya, Kiribati[†], Korea (South)[†], Kuwait[†], Kyrgyzstan[†], Laos[†], Latvia[†], Lebanon[†], Lesotho[†], Liberia, Libya[†], Liechtenstein[†], Lithuania[†], Luxembourg[†], Macedonia[†] (Former Yugoslav Republic of), Madagascar[†], Malawi[†], Malaysia[†], Maldives[†], Mali[†], Malta[†], Marshall Islands, Mauritania, Mauritius[†], Mexico[†], Micronesia, Moldova, Monaco[†], Mongolia[†], Morocco[†], Mozambique, Myanmar[†], Namibia[†], Nauru[†], Nepal[†], Netherlands[†], New Zealand[†], Nicaragua[†], Niger, Nigeria[†], Norway[†], Oman, Palau, Panama, Papua New Guinea[†], Paraguay[†], Peru[†], Philippines[†], Poland[†], Portugal[†], Qatar, Romania[†], Russia[†], Rwanda, Saint Kitts and Nevis[†], Saint Lucia[†], Saint Vincent and the Grenadines[†], Samoa[†], San Marino[†], Sao Tome and Principe, Saudi Arabia, Senegal[†], Serbia[†], Seychelles[†], Sierra Leone, Singapore[†], Slovakia[†], Slovenia[†], Solomon Islands[†], Somalia, South Africa[†], Spain[†], Sri Lanka[†], Sudan[†], Suriname[†], Swaziland[†], Sweden[†], Switzerland[†], Syria[†], Taiwan, Tajikistan[†], Tanzania[†], Thailand[†], Togo, Timor-Leste, Tonga[†], Trinidad and Tobago[†], Tunisia[†], Turkey[†], Turkmenistan, Tuvalu[†], Uganda, UK[†], Ukraine[†], United Arab Emirates[†], Uruguay[†], USA[†], Uzbekistan[†], Vanuatu, Venezuela[†], Viet Nam[†], Yemen[†], Zambia[†], Zimbabwe[†]

[†] Party with safeguards agreements in force with the International Atomic Energy Agency (IAEA), as required by the treaty, or concluded by a nuclear weapon state on a voluntary basis.

77 Additional Safeguards Protocols in force: Afghanistan, Armenia, Australia, Austria, Azerbaijan, Bangladesh, Belgium, Bulgaria, Burkina Faso, Canada, Chile, China, Congo (Democratic Republic of the), Croatia, Cuba, Cyprus, Czech Republic, Denmark, Ecuador, El Salvador, Estonia, Fiji, Finland, France, Georgia, Germany, Ghana, Greece, Haiti, Holy See, Hungary, Iceland, Indonesia, Ireland, Italy, Jamaica, Japan, Jordan, Korea (South), Kuwait, Latvia, Libya, Lithuania, Luxembourg, Madagascar, Mali, Malta, Marshall Islands, Monaco, Mongolia, Netherlands, New Zealand, Nicaragua, Norway, Palau, Panama, Paraguay, Peru, Poland, Portugal, Romania, Seychelles, Slovakia, Slovenia, South Africa, Spain, Sweden, Switzerland, Tajikistan, Tanzania, Turkey, Turkmenistan, Uganda, UK, Ukraine, Uruguay, Uzbekistan

Note: On 6 February 2007 Iran informed the IAEA that it would no longer act in accordance with the provisions of the unratified Additional Safeguards Protocol. Taiwan, although it has not concluded a safeguards agreement, has agreed to apply the measures contained in the 1997 Model Additional Safeguards Protocol.

Treaty on the Prohibition of the Emplacement of Nuclear Weapons and other Weapons of Mass Destruction on the Seabed and the Ocean Floor and in the Subsoil thereof (Seabed Treaty)

Opened for signature at London, Moscow and Washington, DC, on 11 February 1971; entered into force on 18 May 1972; depositaries British, Russian and US governments

The treaty prohibits implanting or emplacing on the seabed and the ocean floor and in the subsoil thereof beyond the outer limit of a 12-mile seabed zone any nuclear weapons or any other types of weapons of mass destruction as well as structures, launching installations or any other facilities specifically designed for storing, testing or using such weapons.

Parties (94): Afghanistan, Algeria, Antigua and Barbuda, Argentina, Australia, Austria, Bahamas, Belarus, Belgium, Benin, Bosnia and Herzegovina, Botswana, Brazil[1], Bulgaria, Canada[2], Cape Verde, Central African Republic, China, Congo (Republic of), Côte d'Ivoire,

Croatia, Cuba, Cyprus, Czech Republic, Denmark, Dominican Republic, Ethiopia, Finland, Germany, Ghana, Greece, Guatemala, Guinea-Bissau, Hungary, Iceland, India[3], Iran, Iraq, Ireland, Italy[4], Jamaica, Japan, Jordan, Korea (South), Laos, Latvia, Lesotho, Libya, Liechtenstein, Luxembourg, Malaysia, Malta, Mauritius, Mexico[5], Mongolia, Morocco, Nepal, Netherlands, New Zealand, Nicaragua, Niger, Norway, Panama, Philippines, Poland, Portugal, Qatar, Romania, Russia, Rwanda, Saint Vincent and the Grenadines, Sao Tome and Principe, Saudi Arabia, Serbia[6], Seychelles, Singapore, Slovakia, Slovenia, Solomon Islands, South Africa, Spain, Swaziland, Sweden, Switzerland, Taiwan, Togo, Tunisia, Turkey[7], UK, Ukraine, USA, Viet Nam[8], Yemen, Zambia

[1] It is the understanding of Brazil that the word 'observation', as it appears in para. 1 of Article III of the treaty, refers only to observation that is incidental to the normal course of navigation in accordance with international law.

[2] Canada declared that Article I, para. 1, cannot be interpreted as indicating that any state has a right to implant or emplace any weapons not prohibited under Article I, para. 1, on the seabed and ocean floor, and in the subsoil thereof, beyond the limits of national jurisdiction, or as constituting any limitation on the principle that this area of the seabed and ocean floor and the subsoil thereof shall be reserved for exclusively peaceful purposes. Articles I, II and III cannot be interpreted as indicating that any state but the coastal state has any right to implant or emplace any weapon not prohibited under Article I, para. 1 on the continental shelf, or the subsoil thereof, appertaining to that coastal state, beyond the outer limit of the seabed zone referred to in Article I and defined in Article II. Article III cannot be interpreted as indicating any restrictions or limitation upon the rights of the coastal state, consistent with its exclusive sovereign rights with respect to the continental shelf, to verify, inspect or effect the removal of any weapon, structure, installation, facility or device implanted or emplaced on the continental shelf, or the subsoil thereof, appertaining to that coastal state, beyond the outer limit of the seabed zone referred to in Article I and defined in Article II.

[3] The accession by India is based on its position that it has full and exclusive rights over the continental shelf adjoining its territory and beyond its territorial waters and the subsoil thereof. There cannot, therefore, be any restriction on, or limitation of, the sovereign right of India as a coastal state to verify, inspect, remove or destroy any weapon, device, structure, installation or facility, which might be implanted or emplaced on or beneath its continental shelf by any other country, or to take such other steps as may be considered necessary to safeguard its security.

[4] Italy stated, *inter alia*, that in the case of agreements on further measures in the field of disarmament to prevent an arms race on the seabed and ocean floor and in their subsoil, the question of the delimitation of the area within which these measures would find application shall have to be examined and solved in each instance in accordance with the nature of the measures to be adopted.

[5] Mexico declared that the treaty cannot be interpreted to mean that a state has the right to emplace weapons of mass destruction, or arms or military equipment of any type, on the continental shelf of Mexico. It reserves the right to verify, inspect, remove or destroy any weapon, structure, installation, device or equipment placed on its continental shelf, including nuclear weapons or other weapons of mass destruction.

[6] In 1974, the Ambassador of Yugoslavia transmitted to the US Secretary of State a note stating that in the view of the Yugoslav Government, Article III, para. 1, of the treaty should be interpreted in such a way that a state exercising its right under this article shall be obliged to notify in advance the coastal state, in so far as its observations are to be carried out 'within the stretch of the sea extending above the continental shelf of the said state'. The USA objected to the Yugoslav reservation, which it considered incompatible with the object and purpose of the treaty.

[7] Turkey declared that the provisions of Article II cannot be used by a state party in support of claims other than those related to disarmament. Hence, Article II cannot be interpreted as establishing a link with the UN Convention on the Law of the Sea. Furthermore, no provision of the Seabed Treaty confers on parties the right to militarize zones which have been demilitarized by other international instruments. Nor can it be interpreted as conferring on either the coastal states or other states the right to emplace nuclear weapons or other weapons of mass destruction on the continental shelf of a demilitarized territory.

[8] Viet Nam stated that no provision of the treaty should be interpreted in a way that would contradict the rights of the coastal states with regard to their continental shelf, including the right to take measures to ensure their security.

Signed but not ratified: Bolivia, Burundi, Cambodia, Cameroon, Colombia, Costa Rica, Equatorial Guinea, Gambia, Guinea, Honduras, Lebanon, Liberia, Madagascar, Mali, Myanmar, Paraguay, Senegal, Sierra Leone, Sudan, Tanzania, Uruguay

Convention on the Prohibition of the Development, Production and Stockpiling of Bacteriological (Biological) and Toxin Weapons and on their Destruction (Biological and Toxin Weapons Convention, BTWC)

Opened for signature at London, Moscow and Washington, DC, on 10 April 1972; entered into force on 26 March 1975; depositaries British, Russian and US governments

The convention prohibits the development, production, stockpiling or acquisition by other means or retention of microbial or other biological agents or toxins whatever their origin or method of production of types and in quantities that have no justification of prophylactic, protective or other peaceful purposes, as well as weapons, equipment or means of delivery designed to use such agents or toxins for hostile purposes or in armed conflict. The destruction of the agents, toxins, weapons, equipment and means of delivery in the possession of the parties, or their diversion to peaceful purposes, should be effected not later than nine months after the entry into force of the convention for each country. According to a mandate from the 1996 BTWC Review Conference, verification and other measures to strengthen the convention are being discussed and considered in an ad hoc group.

Parties (155): Afghanistan, Albania, Algeria, Antigua and Barbuda, Argentina, Armenia, Australia, Austria, Azerbaijan, Bahamas, Bahrain, Bangladesh, Barbados, Belarus, Belgium, Belize, Benin, Bhutan, Bolivia, Bosnia and Herzegovina, Botswana, Brazil, Brunei Darussalam, Bulgaria, Burkina Faso, Cambodia, Canada, Cape Verde, Chile, China, Colombia, Congo (Democratic Republic of the), Congo (Republic of), Costa Rica, Croatia, Cuba, Cyprus, Czech Republic, Denmark, Dominica, Dominican Republic, Ecuador, El Salvador, Equatorial Guinea, Estonia, Ethiopia, Fiji, Finland, France, Gambia, Georgia, Germany, Ghana, Greece, Grenada, Guatemala, Guinea-Bissau, Holy See, Honduras, Hungary, Iceland, India, Indonesia, Iran, Iraq, Ireland, Italy, Jamaica, Japan, Jordan, Kenya, Korea (North), Korea (South), Kuwait, Kyrgyzstan, Laos, Latvia, Lebanon, Lesotho, Libya, Liechtenstein, Lithuania, Luxembourg, Macedonia (Former Yugoslav Republic of), Malaysia, Maldives, Mali, Malta, Mauritius, Mexico, Moldova, Monaco, Mongolia, Morocco, Netherlands, New Zealand, Nicaragua, Niger, Nigeria, Norway, Oman, Pakistan, Palau, Panama, Papua New Guinea, Paraguay, Peru, Philippines, Poland, Portugal, Qatar, Romania, Russia, Rwanda, Saint Kitts and Nevis, Saint Lucia, Saint Vincent and the Grenadines, San Marino, Sao Tome and Principe, Saudi Arabia, Senegal, Serbia, Seychelles, Sierra Leone, Singapore, Slovakia, Slovenia, Solomon Islands, South Africa, Spain, Sri Lanka, Sudan, Suriname, Swaziland, Sweden, Switzerland*, Taiwan, Thailand, Timor-Leste, Togo, Tonga, Tunisia, Turkey, Turkmenistan, Uganda, UK, Ukraine, Uruguay, USA, Uzbekistan, Vanuatu, Venezuela, Viet Nam, Yemen, Zimbabwe

* With reservation.

Signed but not ratified: Burundi, Central African Republic, Côte d'Ivoire, Egypt, Gabon, Guyana, Haiti, Liberia, Madagascar, Malawi, Myanmar, Nepal, Somalia, Syria, Tanzania, United Arab Emirates

Treaty on the Limitation of Anti-Ballistic Missile Systems (ABM Treaty)

Signed by the USA and the USSR at Moscow on 26 May 1972; entered into force on 3 October 1972; no longer in force as of 13 June 2002

The parties undertook not to build nationwide defences against ballistic missile attack and to limit the development and deployment of permitted strategic missile defences. The treaty prohibited the parties from giving air defence missiles, radars or launchers the technical ability to counter strategic ballistic missiles and from testing them in a strategic ABM mode.

The **1974 Protocol** to the ABM Treaty introduced further numerical restrictions on permitted ballistic missile defences.

In 1997 Russia and the USA signed a set of Agreed Statements, specifying the demarcation line between strategic missile defences, which are not permitted under the treaty, and non-strategic or theatre missile defences (TMD), which are permitted under the treaty. The set of 1997 agreements on anti-missile defence were ratified by Russia in April 2000, but because the USA did not ratify them they did not enter into force. On 13 December 2001 the USA announced its withdrawal from the ABM Treaty, which entered into effect on 13 June 2002.

Treaty on the Limitation of Underground Nuclear Weapon Tests (Threshold Test-Ban Treaty, TTBT)

Signed by the USA and the USSR at Moscow on 3 July 1974; entered into force on 11 December 1990

The parties—Russia and the USA—undertake not to carry out any underground nuclear weapon test having a yield exceeding 150 kilotons. The 1974 verification protocol was replaced in 1990 with a new protocol.

Treaty on Underground Nuclear Explosions for Peaceful Purposes (Peaceful Nuclear Explosions Treaty, PNET)

Signed by the USA and the USSR at Moscow and Washington, DC, on 28 May 1976; entered into force on 11 December 1990

The parties—Russia and the USA—undertake not to carry out any individual underground nuclear explosion for peaceful purposes having a yield exceeding 150 kilotons or any group explosion having an aggregate yield exceeding 150 kilotons; and not to carry out any group explosion having an aggregate yield exceeding 1500 kilotons unless the individual explosions in the group could be identified and measured by agreed verification procedures.

Convention on the Prohibition of Military or Any Other Hostile Use of Environmental Modification Techniques (Enmod Convention)

Opened for signature at Geneva on 18 May 1977; entered into force on 5 October 1978; depositary UN Secretary-General

The convention prohibits military or any other hostile use of environmental modification techniques having widespread, long-lasting or severe effects as the means of destruction, damage or injury to states party to the convention. The term 'environmental modification techniques' refers to any technique for changing—through the deliberate manipulation of natural processes—the dynamics, composition or structure of the earth, including its biota, lithosphere, hydrosphere and atmosphere, or of outer space. The understandings reached during the negotiations, but not written into the convention, define the terms 'widespread', 'long-lasting' and 'severe'.

Parties (72): Afghanistan, Algeria, Antigua and Barbuda, Argentina, Armenia, Australia, Austria, Bangladesh, Belarus, Belgium, Benin, Brazil, Bulgaria, Canada, Cape Verde, Chile, China*, Costa Rica, Cuba, Cyprus, Czech Republic, Denmark, Dominica, Egypt, Finland, Germany, Ghana, Greece, Guatemala, Hungary, India, Ireland, Italy, Japan, Kazakhstan, Korea (North), Korea (South)*, Kuwait, Lithuania, Laos, Malawi, Mauritius, Mongolia, Netherlands*, New Zealand, Niger, Norway, Pakistan, Panama, Papua New Guinea, Poland, Romania, Russia, Saint Lucia, Saint Vincent and the Grenadines, Sao Tome and Principe, Slovakia, Slovenia, Solomon Islands, Spain, Sri Lanka, Sweden, Switzerland, Tajikistan, Tunisia, UK, Ukraine, Uruguay, USA, Uzbekistan, Viet Nam, Yemen

* With declaration.

Signed but not ratified: Bolivia, Congo (Democratic Republic of the), Ethiopia, Holy See, Iceland, Iran, Iraq, Lebanon, Liberia, Luxembourg, Morocco, Nicaragua, Portugal, Sierra Leone, Syria, Turkey, Uganda

Protocol I Additional to the 1949 Geneva Conventions, and Relating to the Protection of Victims of International Armed Conflicts

Protocol II Additional to the 1949 Geneva Conventions, and Relating to the Protection of Victims of Non-International Armed Conflicts

Opened for signature at Bern on 12 December 1977; entered into force on 7 December 1978; depositary Swiss Federal Council

The protocols confirm that the right of the parties to international or non-international armed conflicts to choose methods or means of warfare is not unlimited and that it is prohibited to use weapons or means of warfare which cause superfluous injury or unnecessary suffering.

Parties to Protocol I (167) and Protocol II (163): Albania, Algeria*, Angola[1]*, Antigua and Barbuda, Argentina*, Armenia, Australia*, Austria*, Bahamas, Bahrain, Bangladesh, Barbados, Belarus, Belgium*, Belize, Benin, Bolivia, Bosnia and Herzegovina, Botswana, Brazil, Brunei Darussalam, Bulgaria, Burkina Faso, Burundi, Cambodia, Cameroon, Canada*, Cape Verde, Central African Republic, Chad, Chile, China*, Colombia, Comoros, Congo (Democratic Republic of the), Congo (Republic of), Cook Islands, Costa Rica, Côte d'Ivoire, Croatia, Cuba, Cyprus, Czech Republic, Denmark*, Djibouti, Dominica, Dominican Republic, Ecuador, Egypt*, El Salvador, Equatorial Guinea, Estonia, Ethiopia, Finland*, France*, Gabon, Gambia, Georgia, Germany*, Ghana, Greece, Grenada, Guatemala, Guinea, Guinea-Bissau, Guyana, Haiti, Holy See, Honduras, Hungary, Iceland*, Ireland, Italy*, Jamaica, Japan*, Jordan, Kazakhstan, Kenya, Korea (North)[1], Korea (South)*, Kuwait, Kyrgyzstan, Laos, Latvia, Lebanon, Lesotho, Liberia, Libya, Liechtenstein*, Lithuania, Luxembourg, Macedonia (Former Yugoslav Republic of), Madagascar, Malawi, Maldives, Mali, Malta*, Mauritania, Mauritius, Mexico[1], Micronesia, Moldova, Monaco, Mongolia, Montenegro, Mozambique, Namibia, Nauru, Netherlands*, New Zealand*, Nicaragua, Niger, Nigeria, Norway, Oman, Palau, Panama, Paraguay, Peru, Philippines[2], Poland, Portugal, Qatar*, Romania, Russia*, Rwanda, Saint Kitts and Nevis, Saint Lucia, Saint Vincent and the Grenadines, Samoa, San Marino, Sao Tome and Principe, Saudi Arabia*, Senegal, Serbia*,

Seychelles, Sierra Leone, Slovakia, Slovenia, Solomon Islands, South Africa, Spain*, Sudan, Suriname, Swaziland, Sweden*, Switzerland*, Syria*[1], Tajikistan, Tanzania, Timor-Leste, Togo, Tonga, Trinidad and Tobago*, Tunisia, Turkmenistan, Uganda, UK, Ukraine, United Arab Emirates*, Uruguay, Uzbekistan, Vanuatu, Venezuela, Viet Nam[1], Yemen, Zambia, Zimbabwe

* With reservation and/or declaration.

[1] Party only to Protocol I.
[2] Party only to Protocol II.

In 1989 the Palestine Liberation Organization (PLO) informed the depositary that it had decided to adhere to the four Geneva conventions and the two protocols.

Convention on the Physical Protection of Nuclear Material and Nuclear Facilities

Opened for signature at New York and Vienna on 3 March 1980; entered into force on 8 February 1987. The convention was amended in 2005; depositary IAEA Director General

The amended convention obligates the parties to protect nuclear facilities and material used for peaceful purposes while in storage as well as transport. The amendments will take effect 30 days after they have been ratified, accepted or approved by two-thirds of the parties to the original convention.

Parties to the original convention (122): Afghanistan, Albania, Algeria*, Andorra*, Antigua and Barbuda, Argentina*, Armenia, Australia, Austria*, Azerbaijan*, Bangladesh, Belarus, Belgium*, Bolivia, Bosnia and Herzegovina, Botswana, Brazil, Bulgaria, Burkina Faso, Cambodia, Cameroon, Canada, Chile, China*, Colombia, Congo (Democratic Republic of the), Costa Rica, Croatia, Cuba*, Cyprus*, Czech Republic, Denmark, Djibouti, Dominica, Ecuador, El Salvador*, Equatorial Guinea, Estonia, Euratom*, Finland*, France*, Georgia, Germany, Ghana, Greece*, Grenada, Guatemala*, Guinea, Honduras, Hungary, Iceland, India*, Indonesia*, Ireland*, Israel*, Italy*, Jamaica, Japan, Kazakhstan, Kenya, Korea (South)*, Kuwait*, Latvia, Lebanon, Liechtenstein, Libya, Lithuania, Luxembourg*, Macedonia (Former Yugoslav Republic of), Madagascar, Mali, Malta, Marshall Islands, Mexico, Moldova, Monaco, Mongolia, Morocco, Mozambique*, Namibia, Nauru, Netherlands*, New Zealand, Nicaragua, Niger, Norway*, Oman*, Panama, Pakistan*, Paraguay, Peru*, Philippines, Poland, Portugal*, Qatar*, Romania*, Russia*, Senegal, Serbia, Seychelles, Slovakia, Slovenia, Spain*, Sudan, Swaziland, Sweden*, Switzerland*, Tajikistan, Tanzania, Togo, Tonga, Trinidad and Tobago, Tunisia, Turkey*, Turkmenistan, Uganda, UK*, Ukraine, United Arab Emirates, Uruguay, USA, Uzbekistan

* With reservation and/or declaration.

Signed but not ratified: Dominican Republic, Haiti, South Africa*

7 ratifications, acceptances or approvals of the amended convention deposited: Austria, Bulgaria, Croatia, Libya, Romania, Seychelles, Turkmenistan

Convention on Prohibitions or Restrictions on the Use of Certain Conventional Weapons which may be Deemed to be Excessively Injurious or to have Indiscriminate Effects (CCW Convention, or 'Inhumane Weapons' Convention)

The convention, with protocols I, II and III, was opened for signature at New York on 10 April 1981; entered into force on 2 December 1983; depositary UN Secretary-General

The convention is an 'umbrella treaty', under which specific agreements can be concluded in the form of protocols. To become a party to the convention a state must ratify a minimum of two of the protocols.

The amendment to Article I of the original convention was opened for signature at Geneva on 21 November 2001. It expands the scope of application to non-international armed conflicts. The Amended Convention entered into force on 18 May 2004.

Protocol I prohibits the use of weapons intended to injure by fragments which are not detectable in the human body by X-rays.

Protocol II prohibits or restricts the use of mines, booby-traps and other devices.

Amended Protocol II, which entered into force on 3 December 1998, reinforces the constraints regarding landmines.

Protocol III restricts the use of incendiary weapons.

Protocol IV which entered into force on 30 July 1998, prohibits the employment of laser weapons specifically designed to cause permanent blindness to un-enhanced vision.

Protocol V, which entered into force on 12 November 2006, recognizes the need for measures of a generic nature to minimize the risks and effects of explosive remnants of war.

Parties to the original convention and protocols (102): Albania, Argentina*, Australia, Austria, Bangladesh, Belarus, Belgium, Benin[1], Bolivia, Bosnia and Herzegovina, Brazil, Bulgaria, Burkina Faso, Cambodia, Cameroon, Canada*, Cape Verde, Chile[1], China*, Colombia, Costa Rica, Croatia, Cuba, Cyprus*, Czech Republic, Denmark, Djibouti, Ecuador, El Salvador, Estonia[1], Finland, France*, Georgia, Germany, Greece, Guatemala, Holy See*, Honduras, Hungary, India, Ireland, Israel*[2], Italy*, Japan, Jordan[1], Korea (South)[3], Laos, Latvia, Lesotho, Liberia, Liechtenstein, Lithuania[1], Luxembourg, Macedonia (Former Yugoslav Republic of), Maldives[1], Mali, Malta, Mauritius, Mexico, Moldova, Monaco[3], Mongolia, Montenegro, Morocco[4], Nauru, Netherlands*, New Zealand, Nicaragua[1], Niger, Norway, Pakistan, Panama, Paraguay, Peru[1], Philippines, Poland, Portugal, Romania*, Russia, Senegal[5], Serbia, Seychelles, Sierra Leone[1], Slovakia, Slovenia, South Africa, Spain, Sri Lanka, Sweden, Switzerland, Tajikistan, Togo, Tunisia, Turkey*[3], Turkmenistan[2], Uganda, UK*, Ukraine, Uruguay, USA*[2], Uzbekistan, Venezuela

* With reservation and/or declaration.

[1] Party only to 1981 Protocols I and III.
[2] Party only to 1981 Protocols I and II.
[3] Party only to 1981 Protocol I.
[4] Party only to 1981 Protocol II.
[5] Party only to 1981 Protocol III.

Signed but not ratified the original convention and protocols: Afghanistan, Egypt, Iceland, Nigeria, Sudan, Viet Nam

Parties to the Amended Convention and original protocols (50): Albania, Argentina, Australia, Austria, Belgium, Bulgaria, Burkina Faso, Canada, China, Croatia, Czech Republic, Denmark, Estonia, Finland, France, Germany, Greece, Holy See*, Hungary, India, Ireland, Italy, Japan, Korea (South), Latvia, Liberia, Liechtenstein, Lithuania, Luxembourg, Malta, Mexico*, Moldova, Montenegro, Netherlands, Norway, Panama, Peru, Poland, Romania, Russia, Serbia, Sierra Leone, Slovakia, Spain, Sri Lanka, Sweden, Switzerland, Turkey, UK, Ukraine

* With reservation and/or declaration.

Parties to Amended Protocol II (87): Albania, Argentina, Australia, Austria, Bangladesh, Belarus, Belgium, Bolivia, Bosnia and Herzegovina, Brazil, Bulgaria, Burkina Faso, Cambodia, Cameroon, Canada, Cape Verde, Chile, China, Colombia, Costa Rica, Croatia, Cyprus, Czech Republic, Denmark, Ecuador, El Salvador, Estonia, Finland, France, Germany, Greece, Guatemala, Holy See, Honduras, Hungary, India, Ireland, Israel, Italy, Japan, Jordan, Korea (South), Latvia, Liberia, Liechtenstein, Lithuania, Luxembourg, Macedonia (Former Yugoslav Republic of), Maldives, Mali, Malta, Moldova, Monaco, Morocco, Nauru, Netherlands, New Zealand, Nicaragua, Norway, Pakistan, Panama, Paraguay, Peru, Philippines, Poland, Portugal, Romania, Russia, Senegal, Seychelles, Sierra Leone, Slovakia, Slovenia, South Africa, Spain, Sri Lanka, Sweden, Switzerland, Tajikistan, Tunisia, Turkey, Turkmenistan, UK, Ukraine, Uruguay, USA, Venezuela

Parties to Protocol IV (85): Albania, Argentina, Australia*, Austria*, Bangladesh, Belarus, Belgium*, Bolivia, Bosnia and Herzegovina, Brazil, Bulgaria, Burkina Faso, Cambodia, Cameroon, Canada*, Cape Verde, Chile, China, Colombia, Costa Rica, Croatia, Cyprus, Czech Republic, Denmark, Ecuador, El Salvador, Estonia, Finland, France, Georgia, Germany*, Greece*, Guatemala, Holy See, Honduras, Hungary, India, Ireland*, Israel*, Italy*, Japan, Latvia, Liberia, Liechtenstein*, Lithuania, Luxembourg, Maldives, Mali, Malta, Mauritius, Mexico, Moldova, Mongolia, Montenegro, Morocco, Nauru, Netherlands*, New Zealand, Nicaragua, Norway, Pakistan, Panama, Peru, Philippines, Poland*, Portugal, Romania, Russia, Serbia, Seychelles, Sierra Leone, Slovakia, Slovenia, South Africa*, Spain, Sri Lanka, Sweden*, Switzerland*, Tajikistan, Tunisia, Turkey, UK*, Ukraine, Uruguay, Uzbekistan

* With reservation and/or declaration.

Parties to Protocol V (29): Albania, Australia, Bulgaria, Croatia, Czech Republic, Denmark, El Salvador, Estonia, Finland, France, Germany, Holy See*, Hungary, India, Ireland, Liberia, Liechtenstein, Lithuania, Luxembourg, Malta, Netherlands, Nicaragua, Norway, Sierra Leone, Slovakia, Sweden, Switzerland, Tajikistan, Ukraine

* With reservation and/or declaration.

South Pacific Nuclear Free Zone Treaty (Treaty of Rarotonga)

Opened for signature at Rarotonga, Cook Islands, on 6 August 1985; entered into force on 11 December 1986; depositary Director of the Pacific Islands Forum Secretariat

The treaty prohibits the manufacture or acquisition by other means of any nuclear explosive device, as well as possession or control over such device by the parties anywhere inside or outside the zone area described in an annex. The parties also undertake not to supply nuclear material or equipment, unless subject to IAEA safeguards, and to prevent in their territories the stationing as well as the testing of any nuclear explosive device and undertake not to dump, and to prevent the dumping of, radioactive wastes and other radioactive matter at sea anywhere within the zone.

Each party remains free to allow visits, as well as transit, by foreign ships and aircraft.

The treaty is open for signature by the members of the Pacific Islands Forum.

Under *Protocol 1* France, the UK and the USA undertake to apply the treaty prohibitions relating to the manufacture, stationing and testing of nuclear explosive devices in the territories situated within the zone, for which they are internationally responsible.

Under *Protocol 2* China, France, Russia, the UK and the USA undertake not to use or threaten to use a nuclear explosive device against the parties to the treaty or against any territory within the zone for which a party to Protocol 1 is internationally responsible.

Under *Protocol 3* China, France, Russia, the UK and the USA undertake not to test any nuclear explosive device anywhere within the zone.

Parties (13): Australia, Cook Islands, Fiji, Kiribati, Nauru, New Zealand, Niue, Papua New Guinea, Samoa, Solomon Islands, Tonga, Tuvalu, Vanuatu

Parties to Protocol 1: France, UK; **signed but not ratified:** USA

Parties to Protocol 2: China, France[1], Russia, UK[2]; **signed but not ratified:** USA

Parties to Protocol 3: China, France, Russia, UK; **signed but not ratified:** USA

[1] France declared that the negative security guarantees set out in Protocol 2 are the same as the Conference on Disarmament (CD) declaration of 6 Apr. 1995 referred to in UN Security Council Resolution 984 of 11 Apr. 1995.

[2] On ratifying Protocol 2 in 1997, the UK declared that nothing in the treaty affects the rights under international law with regard to transit of the zone or visits to ports and airfields within the zone by ships and aircraft. The UK will not be bound by the undertakings in Protocol 2 in case of an invasion or any other attack on the UK, its territories, its armed forces or its allies, carried out or sustained by a party to the treaty in association or alliance with a nuclear weapon state or if a party violates its non-proliferation obligations under the treaty.

Treaty on the Elimination of Intermediate-Range and Shorter-Range Missiles (INF Treaty)

Signed by the USA and the USSR at Washington, DC, on 8 December 1987; entered into force on 1 June 1988

The treaty obligated the parties—Russia and the USA—to destroy all land-based missiles with a range of 500–5500 km (intermediate-range, 1000–5500 km; and shorter-range, 500–1000 km) and their launchers by 1 June 1991. A total of 2692 missiles were eliminated by May 1991. For 10 years after this date, on-site inspections were conducted to verify compliance; the inspections were ended on 31 May 2001.

Treaty on Conventional Armed Forces in Europe (CFE Treaty)

Original treaty signed at Paris on 19 November 1990; entered into force on 9 November 1992; depositary Netherlands Government

The treaty sets ceilings on five categories of treaty-limited equipment (TLE)—battle tanks, armoured combat vehicles, artillery of at least 100-mm calibre, combat aircraft and attack helicopters—in an area stretching from the Atlantic Ocean to the Ural Mountains (the Atlantic-to-the-Urals, ATTU, zone).

The treaty was negotiated and signed by the member states of the Warsaw Treaty Organization and NATO within the framework of the Conference on Security and

Co-operation in Europe (from 1995 the Organization for Security and Co-operation in Europe, OSCE).

The **1992 Tashkent Agreement**, adopted by the former Soviet republics (with the exception of the three Baltic states) with territories within the ATTU zone, and the **1992 Oslo Document** (Final Document of the Extraordinary Conference of the States Parties to the CFE Treaty) introduced modifications to the treaty required because of the emergence of new states after the break-up of the USSR.

Parties (30): Armenia, Azerbaijan, Belarus, Belgium, Bulgaria, Canada, Czech Republic, Denmark, France, Georgia, Germany, Greece, Hungary, Iceland, Italy, Kazakhstan, Luxembourg, Moldova, Netherlands, Norway, Poland, Portugal, Romania, Russia, Slovakia, Spain, Turkey, UK, Ukraine, USA

The first Review Conference of the CFE Treaty adopted the **1996 Flank Document**, which reorganized the flank areas geographically and numerically, allowing Russia and Ukraine to deploy more TLE.

The **1999 Agreement on Adaptation of the CFE Treaty** replaces the CFE Treaty bloc-to-bloc military balance with individual state limits on TLE holdings and provides for a new structure of limitations and new military flexibility mechanisms, flank sub-limits and enhanced transparency. It opens the CFE regime to all the other European states. It will enter into force when it has been ratified by all the signatories. The **1999 Final Act**, with annexes, contains politically binding arrangements with regard to the North Caucasus and Central and Eastern Europe, and withdrawals of armed forces from foreign territories.

3 ratifications of the Agreement on Adaptation deposited: Belarus, Kazakhstan, Russia*

* With reservation and/or declaration.

Concluding Act of the Negotiation on Personnel Strength of Conventional Armed Forces in Europe (CFE-1A Agreement)

Signed by the parties to the CFE Treaty at Helsinki on 10 July 1992; entered into force simultaneously with the CFE Treaty; depositary Netherlands Government

The agreement limits the personnel of the conventional land-based armed forces of the parties within the ATTU zone.

Treaty on the Reduction and Limitation of Strategic Offensive Arms (START I Treaty)

Signed by the USA and the USSR at Moscow on 31 July 1991; entered into force on 5 December 1994

The treaty obligated the parties—Russia and the USA—to make phased reductions in their offensive strategic nuclear forces over a seven-year period. It sets numerical limits on deployed strategic nuclear delivery vehicles (SNDVs)—ICBMs, SLBMs and heavy bombers—and the nuclear warheads they carry. In the Protocol to Facilitate the Implementation of the START Treaty (**1992 Lisbon Protocol**), which entered into force on 5 December 1994, Belarus, Kazakhstan and Ukraine also assumed the obligations of the former USSR under the treaty.

Treaty on Open Skies

Opened for signature at Helsinki on 24 March 1992; entered into force on 1 January 2002; depositaries Canadian and Hungarian governments

The treaty obligates the parties to submit their territories to short-notice unarmed surveillance flights. The area of application stretches from Vancouver, Canada, eastward to Vladivostok, Russia.

The treaty was negotiated between the member states of the Warsaw Treaty Organization and NATO. It was opened for signature by the NATO member states, former member states of the Warsaw Treaty Organization and the states of the former Soviet Union (except the three Baltic states). For six months after entry into force of the treaty, any other participating state of the Organization for Security and Co-operation in Europe could apply for accession to the treaty, and from 1 July 2002 any state can apply to accede to the treaty.

Parties (34): Belarus, Belgium, Bosnia and Herzegovina, Bulgaria, Canada, Croatia, Czech Republic, Denmark, Estonia, Finland, France, Georgia, Germany, Greece, Hungary, Iceland, Italy, Latvia, Lithuania, Luxembourg, Netherlands, Norway, Poland, Portugal, Romania, Russia, Slovakia, Slovenia, Spain, Sweden, Turkey, UK, Ukraine, USA

Signed but not ratified: Kyrgyzstan

Treaty on Further Reduction and Limitation of Strategic Offensive Arms (START II Treaty)

Signed by the USA and Russia at Moscow on 3 January 1993; not in force

The treaty obligated the parties to eliminate their MIRVed ICBMs and reduce the number of their deployed strategic nuclear warheads to no more than 3000–3500 each (of which no more than 1750 may be deployed on SLBMs) by 1 January 2003. On 26 September 1997 the two parties signed a *Protocol* to the treaty providing for the extension until the end of 2007 of the period of implementation of the treaty.

Note: The START II Treaty was ratified by the US Senate and the Russian Duma and Federation Council, but the two parties never exchanged the instruments of ratification. Hence the treaty never entered into force. On 14 June 2002, as a response to the taking effect on 13 June of the USA's withdrawal from the ABM Treaty, Russia declared that it will no longer be bound by the START II Treaty.

Convention on the Prohibition of the Development, Production, Stockpiling and Use of Chemical Weapons and on their Destruction (Chemical Weapons Convention, CWC)

Opened for signature at Paris on 13 January 1993; entered into force on 29 April 1997; depositary UN Secretary-General

The convention prohibits the use, development, production, acquisition, transfer and stockpiling of chemical weapons. Each party undertakes to destroy its chemical weapons and production facilities by 29 April 2012.

Parties (181): Afghanistan, Albania, Algeria, Andorra, Antigua and Barbuda, Argentina, Armenia, Australia, Austria, Azerbaijan, Bahrain, Bangladesh, Belarus, Belgium, Belize, Benin, Bhutan, Bolivia, Bosnia and Herzegovina, Botswana, Brazil, Brunei Darussalam, Bulgaria, Burkina Faso, Burundi, Cambodia, Cameroon, Canada, Cape Verde, Central African Republic, Chad, Chile, China, Colombia, Comoros, Congo (Democratic Republic of the), Cook Islands, Costa Rica, Côte d'Ivoire, Croatia, Cuba, Cyprus, Czech Republic, Denmark, Djibouti, Dominica, Ecuador, El Salvador, Equatorial Guinea, Eritrea, Estonia, Ethiopia, Fiji, Finland, France, Gabon, Gambia, Georgia, Germany, Ghana, Greece, Grenada, Guatemala, Guinea, Guyana, Haiti, Holy See, Honduras, Hungary, Iceland, India, Indonesia, Iran, Ireland, Italy, Jamaica, Japan, Jordan, Kazakhstan, Kenya, Kiribati, Korea (South), Kuwait, Kyrgyzstan, Laos, Latvia, Lesotho, Liberia, Libya, Liechtenstein, Lithuania, Luxembourg, Macedonia (Former Yugoslav Republic of), Madagascar, Malawi, Malaysia, Maldives, Mali, Malta, Marshall Islands, Mauritania, Mauritius, Mexico, Micronesia, Moldova, Monaco, Mongolia, Montenegro, Morocco, Mozambique, Namibia, Nauru, Nepal, Netherlands, New Zealand, Nicaragua, Niger, Nigeria, Niue, Norway, Oman, Pakistan, Palau, Panama, Papua New Guinea, Paraguay, Peru, Philippines, Poland, Portugal, Qatar, Romania, Russia, Rwanda, Saint Kitts and Nevis, Saint Lucia, Saint Vincent and the Grenadines, Samoa, San Marino, Sao Tome and Principe, Saudi Arabia, Senegal, Serbia, Seychelles, Sierra Leone, Singapore, Slovakia, Slovenia, Solomon Islands, South Africa, Spain, Sri Lanka, Sudan, Suriname, Swaziland, Sweden, Switzerland, Tajikistan, Tanzania, Thailand, Timor-Leste, Togo, Tonga, Trinidad and Tobago, Tunisia, Turkey, Turkmenistan, Tuvalu, Uganda, UK, Ukraine, United Arab Emirates, Uruguay, USA, Uzbekistan, Vanuatu, Venezuela, Viet Nam, Yemen, Zambia, Zimbabwe

Signed but not ratified: Bahamas, Congo (Republic of), Dominican Republic, Guinea-Bissau, Israel, Myanmar

Treaty on the Southeast Asia Nuclear Weapon-Free Zone (Treaty of Bangkok)

Signed at Bangkok on 15 December 1995; entered into force on 27 March 1997; depositary Thai Government

The treaty prohibits the development, manufacture, acquisition or testing of nuclear weapons inside or outside the zone area as well as the stationing and transport of nuclear weapons in or through the zone. Each state party may decide for itself whether to allow visits and transit by foreign ships and aircraft. The parties undertake not to dump at sea or discharge into the atmosphere anywhere within the zone any radioactive material or wastes or dispose of radioactive material on land. The parties should conclude an agreement with the IAEA for the application of full-scope safeguards to their peaceful nuclear activities.

The zone includes not only the territories but also the continental shelves and exclusive economic zones of the states parties.

The treaty is open for all states of South-East Asia.

Under a *Protocol* to the treaty China, France, Russia, the UK and the USA are to undertake not to use or threaten to use nuclear weapons against any state party to the treaty. They should further undertake not to use nuclear weapons within the Southeast Asia nuclear weapon-free zone. The protocol will enter into force for each state party on the date of its deposit of the instrument of ratification.

Parties (10): Brunei Darussalam, Cambodia, Indonesia, Laos, Malaysia, Myanmar, Philippines, Singapore, Thailand, Viet Nam

Protocol: no signatures, no parties

African Nuclear-Weapon-Free Zone Treaty (Treaty of Pelindaba)

Signed at Cairo on 11 April 1996; not in force as of 1 February 2007; depositary Secretary-General of the African Union

The treaty prohibits the research, development, manufacture and acquisition of nuclear explosive devices and the testing or stationing of any nuclear explosive device. Each party remains free to allow visits and transit by foreign ships and aircraft. The treaty also prohibits any attack against nuclear installations. The parties undertake not to dump or permit the dumping of radioactive waste and other radio-active matter anywhere within the zone. The parties should conclude each an agreement with the IAEA for the application of comprehensive safeguards to their peaceful nuclear activities.

The zone includes the territory of the continent of Africa, island states members of the African Union (AU) and all islands considered by the AU to be part of Africa.

The treaty is open for signature by all the states of Africa. It will enter into force upon the 28th ratification.

Under *Protocol I* China, France, Russia, the UK and the USA are to undertake not to use or threaten to use a nuclear explosive device against the parties to the treaty.

Under *Protocol II* China, France, Russia, the UK and the USA are to undertake not to test nuclear explosive devices anywhere within the zone.

Under *Protocol III* states with territories within the zone for which they are inter-nationally responsible are to undertake to observe certain provisions of the treaty with respect to these territories. This protocol is open for signature by France and Spain.

The protocols will enter into force simultaneously with the treaty for those protocol signatories that have deposited their instruments of ratification.

21 ratifications deposited: Algeria, Botswana, Burkina Faso, Côte d'Ivoire, Equatorial Guinea, Gambia, Guinea, Kenya, Lesotho, Libya, Madagascar, Mali, Mauritania, Mauritius, Nigeria, Senegal, South Africa, Swaziland, Tanzania, Togo, Zimbabwe

Signed but not ratified: Angola, Benin, Burundi, Cameroon, Cape Verde, Central African Republic, Chad, Comoros, Congo (Democratic Republic of the), Congo (Republic of), Djibouti, Egypt, Eritrea, Ethiopia, Gabon, Ghana, Guinea-Bissau, Liberia, Malawi, Morocco, Mozambique, Namibia, Niger, Rwanda, Sao Tome and Principe, Seychelles, Sierra Leone, Sudan, Tunisia, Uganda, Zambia

Protocol I: ratifications deposited: China, France[1], UK[2]; **signed but not ratified:** Russia[3], USA[4]

Protocol II: ratifications deposited: China, France, UK[2]; **signed but not ratified:** Russia[3], USA[4]

Protocol III: ratifications deposited: France

---

[1] France stated that the Protocols did not affect its right to self-defence, as stipulated in Article 51 of the UN Charter. It clarified that its commitment under Article 1 of Protocol I was equivalent to the nega-tive security assurances given by France to non-nuclear weapon states parties to the NPT, as confirmed in its declaration made on 6 Apr. 1995 at the Conference on Disarmament, and as referred to in UN Security Council Resolution 984 of 11 Apr. 1995.

[2] The UK stated that it did not accept the inclusion of the British Indian Ocean Territory within the African nuclear weapon-free zone without its consent, and did not accept, by its adherence to Protocols I and II, any legal obligations in respect of that territory. Moreover, it would not be bound by its under-taking under Article 1 of Protocol I in case of an invasion or any other attack on the UK, its dependent territories, its armed forces or other troops, its allies or a state towards which it had security commitment, carried out or sustained by a party to the treaty in association or alliance with a nuclear

weapon state, or if any party to the treaty was in material breach of its own non-proliferation obligations under the treaty.

[3] Russia stated that as long as a military base of a nuclear state was located on the islands of the Chagos archipelago these islands could not be regarded as fulfilling the requirements put forward by the treaty for nuclear-weapon-free territories. Moreover, since certain states declared that they would consider themselves free from the obligations under the protocols with regard to the mentioned territories, Russia could not consider itself to be bound by the obligations under Protocol I in respect to the same territories. Russia interpreted its obligations under Article 1 of Protocol I as follows: It would not use nuclear weapons against a state party to the treaty, except in the case of invasion or any other armed attack on Russia, its territory, its armed forces or other troops, its allies or a state towards which it had a security commitment, carried out or sustained by a non-nuclear weapon state party to the treaty, in association or alliance with a nuclear weapon state.

[4] The USA stated, with respect to Protocol I, that it would consider an invasion or any other attack on the USA, its territories, its armed forces or other troops, its allies or on a state toward which it had a security commitment, carried out or sustained by a party to the treaty in association or alliance with a nuclear-weapon state, to be incompatible with the treaty party's corresponding obligations. The USA also stated that neither the treaty nor Protocol II would apply to the activities of the UK, the USA or any other state not party to the treaty on the island of Diego Garcia or elsewhere in the British Indian Ocean Territory. No change was, therefore, required in US armed forces operations in Diego Garcia and elsewhere in these territories.

Agreement on Sub-Regional Arms Control (Florence Agreement)

Adopted at Florence and entered into force on 14 June 1996

The agreement was negotiated under the auspices of the OSCE in accordance with the mandate in the 1995 General Framework Agreement for Peace in Bosnia and Herzegovina (Dayton Agreement). It sets numerical ceilings on armaments of the former warring parties, now Bosnia and Herzegovina, Croatia, Montenegro and Serbia. Five categories of heavy conventional weapons are included: battle tanks, armoured combat vehicles, heavy artillery (75 mm and above), combat aircraft and attack helicopters. The reductions were completed by 31 October 1997. It is confirmed that 6580 weapon items were destroyed by that date.

Comprehensive Nuclear Test-Ban Treaty (CTBT)

Opened for signature at New York on 24 September 1996; not in force as of 1 February 2007; depositary UN Secretary-General

The treaty prohibits the carrying out of any nuclear weapon test explosion or any other nuclear explosion, and urges each party to prevent any such nuclear explosion at any place under its jurisdiction or control and refrain from causing, encouraging, or in any way participating in the carrying out of any nuclear weapon test explosion or any other nuclear explosion.

The treaty will enter into force 180 days after the date of the deposit of the instruments of ratification of the 44 states listed in an annex to the treaty. All the 44 states possess nuclear power reactors and/or nuclear research reactors.

The 44 states whose ratification is required for entry into force are: Algeria, Argentina, Australia, Austria, Bangladesh, Belgium, Brazil, Bulgaria, Canada, Chile, China*, Colombia*, Congo (Democratic Republic of the), Egypt*, Finland, France, Germany, Hungary, India*, Indonesia*, Iran*, Israel*, Italy, Japan, Korea (North)*, Korea (South), Mexico, Netherlands, Norway, Pakistan*, Peru, Poland, Romania, Russia, Slovakia, South Africa, Spain, Sweden, Switzerland, Turkey, UK, Ukraine, USA* and Viet Nam.

* States which as of 1 Feb. 2007 had not ratified the treaty.

138 ratifications deposited: Afghanistan, Albania, Algeria, Andorra, Antigua and Barbuda, Argentina, Armenia, Australia, Austria, Azerbaijan, Bahrain, Bangladesh, Belarus, Belgium, Belize, Benin, Bolivia, Bosnia and Herzegovina, Botswana, Brazil, Bulgaria, Burkina Faso, Cambodia, Cameroon, Canada, Cape Verde, Chile, Congo (Democratic Republic of the), Cook Islands, Costa Rica, Côte d'Ivoire, Croatia, Cyprus, Czech Republic, Denmark, Djibouti, Ecuador, El Salvador, Eritrea, Estonia, Ethiopia, Fiji, Finland, France, Gabon, Georgia, Germany, Greece, Grenada, Guyana, Haiti, Holy See, Honduras, Hungary, Iceland, Ireland, Italy, Jamaica, Japan, Jordan, Kazakhstan, Kenya, Kiribati, Korea (South), Kuwait, Kyrgyzstan, Laos, Latvia, Lesotho, Libya, Liechtenstein, Lithuania, Luxembourg, Macedonia (Former Yugoslav Republic of), Madagascar, Maldives, Mali, Malta, Mauritania, Mexico, Micronesia, Moldova, Monaco, Mongolia, Montenegro, Morocco, Namibia, Nauru, Netherlands, New Zealand, Nicaragua, Niger, Nigeria, Norway, Oman, Panama, Paraguay, Peru, Philippines, Poland, Portugal, Qatar, Romania, Russia, Rwanda, Saint Kitts and Nevis, Saint Lucia, Samoa, San Marino, Senegal, Serbia, Seychelles, Sierra Leone, Singapore, Slovakia, Slovenia, South Africa, Spain, Sudan, Suriname, Sweden, Switzerland, Tajikistan, Tanzania, Togo, Tunisia, Turkey, Turkmenistan, Uganda, UK, Ukraine, United Arab Emirates, Uruguay, Uzbekistan, Vanuatu, Venezuela, Viet Nam, Zambia

Signed but not ratified: Angola, Bahamas, Brunei Darussalam, Burundi, Central African Republic, Chad, China, Colombia, Comoros, Congo (Republic of), Dominican Republic, Egypt, Equatorial Guinea, Gambia, Ghana, Guatemala, Guinea, Guinea-Bissau, Indonesia, Iran, Israel, Lebanon, Liberia, Malawi, Malaysia, Marshall Islands, Mozambique, Myanmar, Nepal, Palau, Papua New Guinea, Sao Tome and Principe, Solomon Islands, Sri Lanka, Swaziland, Thailand, USA, Yemen, Zimbabwe

Inter-American Convention Against the Illicit Manufacturing of and Trafficking in Firearms, Ammunition, Explosives, and Other Related Materials

Adopted at Washington, DC, on 13 November 1997; opened for signature at Washington, DC, on 14 November 1997; entered into force on 1 July 1998; depositary General Secretariat of the Organization of American States

The purpose of the convention is to prevent, combat and eradicate the illicit manufacturing of and trafficking in firearms, ammunition, explosives and other related materials; and to promote and facilitate cooperation and the exchange of information and experience among the parties.

Parties (26): Antigua and Barbuda, Argentina*, Bahamas, Barbados, Belize, Bolivia, Brazil, Chile, Colombia, Costa Rica, Dominica, Ecuador, El Salvador, Grenada, Guatemala, Honduras, Mexico, Nicaragua, Panama, Paraguay, Peru, Saint Kitts and Nevis, Saint Lucia, Trinidad and Tobago, Uruguay, Venezuela

* With reservation.

Signed but not ratified: Canada, Dominican Republic, Guyana, Haiti, Jamaica, Saint Vincent and the Grenadines, Suriname, USA

Convention on the Prohibition of the Use, Stockpiling, Production and Transfer of Anti-Personnel Mines and on their Destruction (APM Convention)

Opened for signature at Ottawa on 3–4 December 1997 and at New York on 5 December 1997; entered into force on 1 March 1999; depositary UN Secretary-General

The convention prohibits anti-personnel mines, which are defined as mines designed to be exploded by the presence, proximity or contact of a person and which will incapacitate, injure or kill one or more persons.

Each party undertakes to destroy all its stockpiled anti-personnel mines as soon as possible but not later that four years after the entry into force of the convention for that state party. Each party also undertakes to destroy all anti-personnel mines in mined areas under its jurisdiction or control not later than 10 years after the entry into force of the convention for that state party.

Parties (152): Afghanistan, Albania, Algeria, Andorra, Angola, Antigua and Barbuda, Argentina, Australia, Austria, Bahamas, Bangladesh, Barbados, Belarus, Belgium, Belize, Benin, Bhutan, Bolivia, Bosnia and Herzegovina, Botswana, Brazil, Brunei Darussalam, Bulgaria, Burkina Faso, Burundi, Cambodia, Cameroon, Canada, Cape Verde, Central African Republic, Chad, Chile, Colombia, Comoros, Congo (Democratic Republic of the), Congo (Republic of), Cook Islands, Costa Rica, Côte d'Ivoire, Croatia, Cyprus, Czech Republic, Denmark, Djibouti, Dominica, Dominican Republic, Ecuador, El Salvador, Equatorial Guinea, Eritrea, Estonia, Ethiopia, Fiji, France, Gabon, Gambia, Germany, Ghana, Greece, Grenada, Guatemala, Guinea, Guinea-Bissau, Guyana, Haiti, Holy See, Honduras, Hungary, Iceland, Ireland, Italy, Jamaica, Japan, Jordan, Kenya, Kiribati, Latvia, Lesotho, Liberia, Liechtenstein, Lithuania, Luxembourg, Macedonia (Former Yugoslav Republic of), Madagascar, Malawi, Malaysia, Maldives, Mali, Malta, Mauritania, Mauritius, Mexico, Moldova, Monaco, Montenegro, Mozambique, Namibia, Nauru, Netherlands, New Zealand, Nicaragua, Niger, Nigeria, Niue, Norway, Panama, Papua New Guinea, Paraguay, Peru, Philippines, Portugal, Qatar, Romania, Rwanda, Saint Kitts and Nevis, Saint Lucia, Saint Vincent and the Grenadines, Samoa, San Marino, Sao Tome and Principe, Senegal, Serbia, Seychelles, Sierra Leone, Slovakia, Slovenia, Solomon Islands, South Africa, Spain, Sudan, Suriname, Swaziland, Sweden, Switzerland, Tajikistan, Tanzania, Thailand, Timor-Leste, Togo, Trinidad and Tobago, Tunisia, Turkey, Turkmenistan, Uganda, UK, Ukraine, Uruguay, Vanuatu, Venezuela, Yemen, Zambia, Zimbabwe

Signed but not ratified: Indonesia, Marshall Islands, Poland

Inter-American Convention on Transparency in Conventional Weapons Acquisitions

Adopted at Guatemala City on 7 June 1999; entered into force on 21 November 2002; depositary General Secretariat of the Organization of American States

The objective of the convention is to contribute more fully to regional openness and transparency in the acquisition of conventional weapons by exchanging information regarding such acquisitions, for the purpose of promoting confidence among states in the Americas.

Parties (12): Argentina, Brazil, Canada, Chile, Ecuador, El Salvador, Guatemala, Nicaragua, Paraguay, Peru, Uruguay, Venezuela

Signed but not ratified: Bolivia, Colombia, Costa Rica, Dominica, Haiti, Honduras, Mexico, USA

Vienna Document 1999 on Confidence- and Security-Building Measures

Adopted by the participating states of the Organization for Security and Co-operation in Europe at Istanbul on 16 November 1999; entered into force on 1 January 2000

The Vienna Document 1999 builds on the 1986 Stockholm Document on Confidence- and Security-Building Measures (CSBMs) and Disarmament in Europe and previous Vienna Documents (1990, 1992 and 1994). The Vienna Document 1990 provided for military budget exchange, risk reduction procedures, a communication network and an annual CSBM implementation assessment. The Vienna Documents 1992 and 1994 introduced new mechanisms and parameters for military activities, defence planning and military contacts.

The Vienna Document 1999 introduces regional measures aimed at increasing transparency and confidence in a bilateral, multilateral and regional context and some improvements, in particular regarding the constraining measures.

Treaty on Strategic Offensive Reductions (SORT)

Signed by Russia and the USA at Moscow on 24 May 2002; entered into force on 1 June 2003

The treaty obligates the parties to reduce the number of their operationally deployed strategic nuclear warheads so that the aggregate numbers do not exceed 1700–2200 for each party by 31 December 2012.

ECOWAS Convention on Small Arms, Light Weapons, their Ammunition and Other Related Materials

Adopted by the member states of ECOWAS at Abuja, on 14 June 2006; not in force as of 1 February 2007; depositary Executive Secretary of the Economic Community of West African States (ECOWAS)

The convention obligates the parties to prevent and combat the excessive and destabilizing accumulation of small arms and light weapons within the ECOWAS member states. The convention will enter into force on the date of deposit of the ninth instrument of ratification.

Treaty on a Nuclear-Weapon-Free Zone in Central Asia (Treaty of Semipalatinsk)

Signed at Semipalatinsk on 8 September 2006; not in force as of 1 February 2007; depositary Kyrgyz Government

The treaty and its protocol obligate the parties not to conduct research on, develop, manufacture, stockpile or otherwise acquire, possess or have control over any nuclear weapons or other nuclear explosive device by any means anywhere. The treaty will enter into force on the date of deposit of the fifth instrument of ratification.

Signed but not ratified: Kazakhstan, Kyrgyzstan, Tajikistan, Turkmenistan, Uzbekistan

Annex B. Chronology 2006

NENNE BODELL

For the convenience of the reader, keywords are indicated in the right-hand column, opposite each entry. Definitions of the abbreviations can be found on pages xviii–xx. The dates are according to local time.

1 Jan.	The EU Police Mission in the Palestinian Territories (EUPOL– COPPS) is launched in the West Bank and the Gaza Strip to support the Palestinian Authority in establishing sustainable and effective policing arrangements. It is a civilian mission within the framework of the European Security and Defence Policy (ESDP).	EU; Palestinians
10 Jan.	Following the 3 Jan. announcement of its intentions, Iran starts to remove the International Atomic Energy Agency (IAEA) seals from its uranium enrichment facility at Natanz and resumes its nuclear research and development programme, and ends a two-year voluntary suspension. The IAEA confirms the removal of the seals.	Iran; Nuclear programme; IAEA
10 Jan.– 6 Feb.	Cartoons depicting the Prophet Muhammad, first published in a Danish newspaper on 30 Sep. 2005, are reprinted in a Norwegian newspaper. The action sparks serious and sometimes violent protests around the Muslim world.	Islam
14 Jan.	Missiles fired from a US military aircraft on the village of Damadola, Pakistan, kill at least 18 people. US media claim that the attack was carried out by the Central Intelligence Agency, targeting the deputy leader of al-Qaeda, Ayman al-Zawahiri. The US military states that it is not aware of any US operations in the area. The attack sparks demonstrations against the USA in Karachi, Pakistan.	Pakistan; USA
14 Jan.	The Norwegian-led Sri Lanka Monitoring Mission (SLMM), set up by the Sri Lankan Government and the Liberation Tigers of Tamil Eelam (LTTE) rebel group under the 2002 ceasefire agreement, is attacked in a grenade blast at its headquarters in Batticaloa, Sri Lanka. The LTTE denies any involvement.	Sri Lanka
18 Jan.	During protests against a UN proposal to dissolve the Ivorian Parliament the UN Operation in Côte d'Ivoire (UNOCI) forces in Guiglo, are besieged and attacked by the Young Patriots group, supporting President Laurent Gbagbo. The UN forces respond with force, killing four people, and decide to leave Guiglo and withdraw to the demilitarized zone. President Gbagbo's ruling party, the Front populaire ivoirien (Ivorian Popular Front), leaves the UN-led peace talks and calls on the peacekeeping forces to leave the country.	UN; Côte d'Ivoire

25 Jan.	In the first Palestinian parliamentary elections since 1996, the Islamic militant group Hamas wins a majority of the seats in the 132-member Palestinian Legislative Council. Palestinian Prime Minister Ahmed Qurei announces his resignation on 26 Jan., following the Fatah party's defeat. — Palestinians
27 Jan.	Following the killing of eight peacekeepers of the UN Mission in the Democratic Republic of the Congo (MONUC) on 23 Jan., the UN Security Council unanimously adopts Resolution 1653, condemning the militias and other armed groups that are destabilizing the Great Lakes region by attacks on civilians and UN personnel, and stressing the need for disarmament and demobilization of these groups. — UN; DRC; Great Lakes region
31 Jan.	The UN Security Council unanimously adopts Resolution 1654, requesting the re-establishment of the expert group to monitor the arms embargo on the Democratic Republic of the Congo (DRC) that was imposed by Resolutions 1493 (2003) and 1596 (2005). — UN; DRC; Arms embargoes
3 Feb.	The third round of Asian Senior-level Talks on Non-Proliferation (ASTOP) is held in Tokyo, Japan. Building on the 2003 and 2005 ASTOP meetings, the aims of the meeting are to discuss North Korea's proliferation of weapons of mass destruction and Iran's nuclear programme; to follow up the measures taken to strengthen the existing non-proliferation regimes, export controls and the Proliferation Security Initiative; and to discuss cooperation to overcome problems in the implementation of treaties and norms relating to disarmament and non-proliferation. — Asia; Non-proliferation; North Korea; Iran
4 Feb.	The International Atomic Energy Agency (IAEA) Board of Governors adopts, by a vote of 27–3 (Cuba, Syria and Venezuela voting against), with 5 abstentions (Algeria, Belarus, Indonesia, Libya and South Africa), Resolution GOV/2006/14, requesting the IAEA Director General to send to the UN Security Council all IAEA reports and resolutions relating to the implementation of safeguards in Iran; and urging Iran to 'extend full and prompt cooperation' to the IAEA. — Iran; IAEA; UN; Safeguards
5 Feb.	Following the resolution passed by the International Atomic Energy Agency (IAEA) on 4 Feb. Iranian President Mahmoud Ahmadinejad orders an end to Iran's voluntary cooperation with the IAEA and IAEA inspections of its nuclear sites, and the continuation of its full-scale uranium enrichment programme. On 6 Feb. Iran orders the IAEA to remove its surveillance cameras and seals from Iranian sites and nuclear equipment by 17 Feb. — Iran; Nuclear programme; IAEA
14 Feb.	Two protocols amended to the 1988 Convention for the Suppression of Unlawful Acts against the Safety of Maritime Navigation (SUA Convention) are opened for signature. Under the protocols it will be illegal to use non-military ships to intentionally transport or launch attacks with weapons of mass destruction (WMD), and to use these types of weapons in attacks against or from a fixed platform at sea. — WMD

22 Feb.	Meeting in Geneva, Switzerland, under the leadership of the Norwegian Special Peace Envoy, Erik Solheim, representatives of the Sri Lankan Government and the Liberation Tigers of Tamil Eelam (LTTE) rebel group open peace negotiations for the first time since 2003.	Sri Lanka
22–24 Feb.	A bomb attack badly damages the al-Askari shrine in Samarra, Iraq, one of the holiest sites of Shia Islam, sparking protests in many cities throughout Iraq. In the aftermath Shia Muslims attack several Sunni mosques. At least 130 people are killed or injured as the violence escalates.	Iraq
28 Feb.	Meeting in Yamoussoukro, Côte d'Ivoire, the five main leaders in the Ivorian conflict—Prime Minister Charles Konan Bany, President Laurent Gbagbo, the leader of the News Forces rebel group, Guillaume Kigbafori Soro, and the main opposition leaders, Henri Konan Bédié and Alasanne Outtara—agree to support the peace plan contained in UN Security Council Resolution 1633 (2005), to acknowledge the necessity to update the timetable for the peace process and to immediately resume the five-party dialogue.	Côte d'Ivoire
2 Mar.	Meeting in New Delhi, India, US President George W. Bush and Indian Prime Minister Manmohan Singh sign the Indian–US Civil Nuclear Cooperation Initiative, announced in July 2005. Under the agreement India pledges to place its nuclear facilities under IAEA safeguards and adhere to the guidelines of the Nuclear Suppliers Group and the Missile Technology Control Regime, and will have access to US civil nuclear technology. The agreement will take effect after ratification by both India and the USA. The US Congress ratified it on 9 Dec.	India; USA; Nuclear energy
8 Mar.	The International Atomic Energy Agency (IAEA) Board of Governors decides to send the IAEA Director General's report on Iran's nuclear programme to the UN Security Council.	Iran; IAEA; UN; Safeguards
11 Mar.	Former Yugoslav President Slobodan Milosevic dies of a heart attack in his cell at the UN Detention Unit, Scheveningen, the Netherlands. The trial of Milosevic at the International Criminal Tribunal for the former Yugoslavia (ICTY) in The Hague was to be completed later in 2006.	Yugoslavia; ICTY
14 Mar.	The Israeli Army raids the Palestinian prison in Jericho, the West Bank, demolishes the building and moves the leader of the Popular Front for the Liberation of Palestine (PFLP), Ahmed Saadat, to an Israeli prison, claiming that he and other militants were about to be freed by the Palestinian authorities. Saadat is accused of killing the Israeli Tourism Minister in 2001. The raid sparks demonstrations and a general strike in the Gaza Strip and the West Bank.	Israel/ Palestinians
15 Mar.	The UN General Assembly adopts, by a vote of 170–4 (Israel, the Marshall Islands, Palau and the USA voting against), with 3 abstentions (Belarus, Iran and Venezuela), Resolution 60/251, establishing a Human Rights Council. The council was first proposed at the UN World Summit in Sep. 2005 and replaces the UN Commission for Human Rights.	UN; Human rights

15 Mar.	The US Government announces that it will withdraw its fighter aircraft and helicopters from the military base at Keflavík, Iceland, by the end of Sep. Iceland, a member of NATO, has no armed forces of its own.	USA; Iceland
16 Mar.	The USA, supported by Iraqi forces, launches Operation Swarmer, the largest airborne operation in Iraq since the US-led invasion in 2003, targeting suspected insurgents near Samarra.	USA/Iraq
22 Mar.	The Basque separatist group Euzkadi ta Azkatasuna (ETA, Basque Land and Liberty) releases a statement declaring a permanent ceasefire effective as of 24 Mar. and the start of 'a new democratic process in the Basque country'.	Spain
29 Mar.	The UN Security Council unanimously approves Presidential Statement S/PRST/2006/15, calling on Iran to re-establish the full and sustained suspension of all enrichment-related and reprocessing activities, including research and development, and requesting, within 30 days, a report from the Director General of the International Atomic Energy Agency (IAEA) on Iranian compliance with the steps required by the IAEA (see also *28 Apr.*).	Iran; IAEA; UN; Safeguards
29 Mar.	Former Liberian President Charles Taylor is detained in Nigeria (after nearly three years in exile in Calabar, Nigeria) and transferred to the Special Court for Sierra Leone, in Freetown, facing 17 charges of war crimes and crimes against humanity for his alleged role in Sierra Leone's civil war in 1991–2002.	Sierra Leone; Liberia; Special Court for Sierra Leone
31 Mar.	Georgia and Russia sign, in Sochi, Russia, two agreements: on the time limits for the closure of Russian military bases in Akhalkalaki and Batumi, Georgia, and on the passage of armaments across the territory of Georgia. The agreements are based on a joint statement that was issued in May 2005.	Georgia; Russia; Military bases
4 Apr.	The Iraqi Special Tribunal (IST), in Baghdad, announces that former Iraqi President Saddam Hussein and six other defendants will be charged with genocide for the 1986–89 Anfal Campaign, in which 180 000 civilians were killed and for the chemical gas attack on the Kurdish town of Halabja in 1988.	Iraq; IST
11 Apr.	The President of Iran, Mahmoud Ahmadinejad, officially announces that Iran has successfully produced enriched uranium to the level needed to make nuclear fuel (see *5 Feb.*).	Iran; Nuclear programme
17 Apr.	In a suicide bomb attack in Tel Aviv, Israel, 10 people are killed and around 50 are injured. The Islamic Jihad claims responsibility for the attack, but the Israeli Government holds the Hamas-led Palestinian Authority responsible. Palestinian President Mahmoud Abbas condemns the attack, while Hamas describes it as an act of self-defence.	Israel/ Palestinians
24 Apr.	At least 23 people are killed and 62 are wounded in three explosions in the resort town of Dahab, Egypt. Egyptian authorities claim that a militant group that is active in the Sinai, inspired by al-Qaeda, is responsible for the attacks.	Egypt

26 Apr.   Following a suicide bomb attack on 25 Apr. on the Sri Lankan   Sri Lanka
Army headquarters in Colombo, seriously wounding Army
Chief Sarath Fonseka, the armed forces carry out air strikes on
suspected Liberation Tigers of Tamil Eelam (LTTE) rebel
bases. The air strikes are the first army action since the signing
of the ceasefire agreement in 2002.

27 Apr.   The UN Security Council unanimously adopts Resolu-   UN; WMD
tion 1673, extending the mandate of the 1540 Committee for a
period of two years and deciding that the Committee shall
intensify its efforts to promote the full implementation by all
states of Security Council Resolution 1540 (2004).

28 Apr.   International Atomic Energy Agency (IAEA) Director General   Iran; IAEA;
Mohamed ElBaradei releases his report on Iranian non-   UN; Safeguards
compliance with the demands to suspend its enrichment and
reprocessing programme.

3 May   The EU freezes its talks on a Stability and Association Agree-   EU; Serbia and
ment with Serbia and Montenegro as the deadline for the arrest   Montenegro
of former Bosnian Serb General Ratko Mladic, set for 30 Apr.,
was not met. Mladic is indicted for genocide in the 1995
Srebrenica massacre.

5 May   Meeting in Abuja, Nigeria, under the auspices of the African   Sudan; AU
Union (AU), the Sudanese Government and the largest rebel
group, the Sudan Liberation Movement (SLM), sign the Darfur
Peace Agreement. Under the agreement the pro-government
Janjaweed militia is to be disbanded, the rebel fighters are to be
integrated into the armed forces, and a regional government is
to be created. Two rebel groups, a faction of the SLM and the
Justice and Equality Movement, refuse to sign the agreement.

11 May   Following a suicide attack on a navy convoy near Jaffna, the   Sri Lanka
Sri Lanka Monitoring Mission (SLMM) issues a statement
calling on the Liberation Tigers of Tamil Eelam (LTTE) to
cease all activities at sea. The SLMM blames the LTTE for
'gross violations' of the 2002 ceasefire agreement.

18 May   Up to 100 people are killed in several clashes between Taliban   Afghanistan/
fighters and forces from the US-led coalition and the Afghan   USA; Pakistan
Government in Helmand and Kandahar provinces. Afghan
President Hamid Karzai blames the Pakistan Inter Services
Intelligence for encouraging Taliban insurgents to mount
suicide attacks.

1 June   The Weapons of Mass Destruction Commission (WMDC),   WMD; Non-
initiated in 2003 and chaired by Hans Blix, of Sweden, presents   proliferation;
its report to the UN Secretary-General, Kofi Annan. The   CTBT
WMDC makes 60 recommendations and calls on all states to
work to achieve a ban on all WMD and to bring the Comprehensive Nuclear-Test-Ban Treaty (CTBT) into force.

3 June   Following a referendum on 21 May, Montenegro formally   Montenegro;
withdraws from its union with Serbia. In response to   Serbia
Montenegro's decision, Serbia formally declares its independence on 5 June.

14 June	The members of the Economic Community of West African States (ECOWAS) adopt, in Abuja, Nigeria, the ECOWAS Convention on Small Arms, Light Weapons, Their Ammunition and Other Related Materials, completing the transformation of the 1998 Moratorium on Light Weapons into a legally binding instrument. The convention will enter into force when 9 of the 15 ECOWAS members have ratified it.	ECOWAS; SALW
26 June– 7 July	The UN Conference to Review Progress Made in the Implementation of the 2001 Programme of Action to Prevent, Combat and Eradicate the Illicit Trade in Small Arms and Light Weapons in All Its Aspects is held in New York.	UN; SALW
27 June	The Parliamentary Assembly of the Council of Europe adopts Resolution 1507, Alleged Secret Detentions and Unlawful Inter-state Transfers of Detainees Involving Council of Europe Member States, urging the USA to dismantle its system of secret detentions and unlawful interstate transfers and condemning the USA's systematic exclusion of all forms of judicial protection.	Council of Europe; USA; Terrorism
28 June	The Israeli Army launches a major attack in the southern Gaza Strip, aimed at rescuing a captured Israeli soldier. The incursion comes less than a year after the Israeli pullout from Gaza. On 29 June, 64 ministers and other officials from the Hamas-led Palestinian Authority are detained by Israeli forces in the West Bank.	Israel/ Palestinians
5 July	North Korea test fires a series of ballistic missiles. On 15 July the UN Security Council unanimously adopts Resolution 1695, condemning the missile launches and demanding that North Korea suspend all its activities related to its ballistic missile programme and re-establish its pre-existing commitments to a moratorium on missile launches.	North Korea; Missiles
10 July	Chechen warlord Shamil Basayev is killed in an explosion in the Russian Republic of Ingushetia. Basayev was responsible for the 2004 hostage taking in Beslan, Russia, and for the 2005 attack in Nalchik, Russia.	Russia/ Chechnya
11 July	Seven near-simultaneous bomb attacks on the train network in Mumbai, India, kill over 180 people and injure several hundred.	India
12 July	Meeting in Paris, France, the foreign ministers of the five permanent members of the UN Security Council (China, France, Russia, the UK and the USA), together with Germany, decide to refer Iran back to the Security Council for possible sanctions for its non-compliance with the demands to suspend its enrichment and reprocessing activities.	Iran; Nuclear programme; UN

12 July– *14 Aug.*	Following the capture of two Israeli soldiers by Hezbollah rebels in Lebanon, Israel launches attacks into southern Lebanon, including Beirut, using aircraft, tanks and gunboats. This is the first Israeli land incursion into Lebanon since its unilateral withdrawal in 2000. The violence escalates as Hezbollah fires rockets on Haifa and Israel extends its air strikes to the northern Lebanese city of Tripoli. A large number of civilians are killed in the attacks.	Israel/Lebanon
15–17 July	The leaders of the Group of Eight (G8) industrialized nations, meeting in St Petersburg, Russia, adopt a special statement on non-proliferation, reaffirming that the proliferation of weapons of mass destruction (WMD) and international terrorism remain the pre-eminent threats to international peace and security. They also adopt a statement condemning the North Korean missile launches of 5 July.	G8; Non-proliferation; WMD; North Korea
24 July	Meeting in Vienna, Austria, under the leadership of UN Special Envoy for the Future Status Process for Kosovo Martti Ahtisaari, political leaders of Serbia and Kosovo begin the negotiations to determine the future status of Kosovo. (Lower-level talks took place in Feb. 2006 to determine issues such as the economy.)	UN; Kosovo
25 July	Four observers from the UN Interim Force in Lebanon (UNIFIL) are killed in an Israeli air strike on an observation post in southern Lebanon. UN Secretary-General Kofi Annan calls the attack an 'apparently deliberate targeting'.	Israel/Lebanon; UN
30 July– *22 Aug.*	The first democratic presidential elections since its independence, in 1960, are held in the Democratic Republic of the Congo (DRC). Following the announcement on 20 Aug. of the necessity of a run-off vote between President Joseph Kabila and Jean-Pierre Bemba, violent clashes between their supporters break out in Kinshasa. Forces from Operation EUFOR RD Congo support the patrolling of the streets by the UN Mission in the Democratic Republic of the Congo (MONUC). An agreement to stop the fighting is reached on 22 Aug. under the auspices of the UN. On 29 Oct., in the second round of the elections, President Joseph Kabila is re-elected.	DRC
31 July	The UN Security Council adopts, by a vote of 14–1 (Qatar voting against), Resolution 1696, demanding that Iran suspend all activities related to enrichment of uranium and reprocessing of plutonium, including research and development. The suspension is to be verified by the International Atomic Energy Agency (IAEA) by 31 Aug. and 'appropriate measures' will be taken if Iran does not comply with the resolution.	Iran; Nuclear programme; UN; IAEA
10 Aug.	The British police reveal a suspected 'terror plot' to bring down about 12 aircraft scheduled to fly from the UK to the USA. The suspects in the plot are reportedly UK-born Muslims of Pakistani origin, and 24 people are arrested in Birmingham and London. It is believed that the plot involved liquid explosives which were to be detonated using electrical devices such as mobile phones.	UK; Terrorism

11 Aug.	The UN Security Council unanimously adopts Resolution 1701, calling for a full cessation of hostilities in Lebanon between Israel and Hezbollah; calling for the deployment of Lebanese forces together with UN Interim Force in Lebanon (UNIFIL) in southern Lebanon and a parallel withdrawal of Israeli forces; and deciding to drastically increase the force size to 15 000 soldiers and the scope of the mandate of UNIFIL. The UN ceasefire plan is approved by both Hezbollah and Israel.	Israel/Lebanon; UN; Peacekeeping
14 Aug.	The ceasefire in Lebanon, drawn up by UN Security Council Resolution 1701, comes into force. On 16 Aug. the Lebanese Government approves a plan to deploy 15 000 Lebanese soldiers to the region of the Litani river, in southern Lebanon. France agrees to command the expanded UN Interim Force in Lebanon (UNIFIL).	Lebanon; UN; France
31 Aug.	The UN Security Council adopts, by a vote of 12–0, with 3 abstentions (China, Qatar and Russia), Resolution 1706, expanding the mandate of the UN Mission in Sudan (UNMIS) to include its deployment to Darfur. The Security Council invites the consent of the Sudanese Government to the deployment, but President Omar al-Bashir strongly reiterates his opposition and states that 'Sudan will not consent to any resolution that will violate its sovereignty'.	UN; Sudan; Peacekeeping
7 Sep.	Israel lifts its sea and air blockade of Lebanon, allowing the UN Interim Force in Lebanon (UNIFIL) to replace Israel at 'control positions'.	Israel/Lebanon
7 Sep.	The Government of Burundi and the Forces nationales de libération (FNL, National Liberation Forces) rebel group sign, in Dar es Salaam, Tanzania, a ceasefire agreement, ending 13 years of civil war between ethnic Tutsi and the Hutu majority. The agreement comes into effect on 11 Sep. (The FNL had rejected the power-sharing agreement signed by the other rebel groups of Burundi in Nov. 2003.)	Burundi
8 Sep.	The UN General Assembly unanimously adopts Resolution 60/288, UN Global Counter-Terrorism Strategy and an annexed Plan of Action, enhancing national, regional and international efforts to counter terrorism.	UN; Terrorism
8 Sep.	Meeting in Semipalatinsk, Kazakhstan, leaders from Kazakhstan, Kyrgyzstan, Tajikistan, Turkmenistan and Uzbekistan sign the Treaty of Semipalatinsk, establishing a Central Asia Nuclear Weapon-Free Zone.	Central Asia; NWFZ
5 Oct.	The NATO-led International Security Assistance Force (ISAF) expands its operations to include the east of Afghanistan. ISAF will now carry out its UN-mandated mission throughout the whole of Afghanistan, in order to extend the authority of the Afghan Government and to create the conditions for reconstruction and development.	NATO; ISAF; UN; Afghanistan

9 Oct.	North Korea carries out an underground nuclear weapon test in Gilju, Hamgyong province. An official statement is issued claiming that the test was successful and that there was no radioactive emission.	North Korea; Nuclear tests
14 Oct.	The UN Security Council unanimously adopts Resolution 1718, condemning the North Korean nuclear weapon test of 9 Oct.; demanding that North Korea not conduct further tests or launch ballistic missiles; imposing sanctions against the country and individuals supporting its military programme; and demanding that North Korea cease its pursuit of weapons of mass destruction (WMD).	UN; North Korea; Nuclear tests; WMD
16 Oct.	A suicide bomb attack at a military bus convoy kills nearly 100 people and wounds more than 150, in the deadliest rebel attack in Sri Lanka since the 2002 ceasefire agreement. On 18 Oct. the Liberation Tigers of Tamil Eelam (LTTE) carries out a suicide attack on a naval base in the tourist city of Galle in the south of Sri Lanka.	Sri Lanka
17 Oct.	US President George W. Bush signs the 2006 Military Commissions Act, setting standards for the interrogation and prosecution of foreign terror suspects held by the USA, setting out a system of special tribunals, forbidding the treatment of detainees that would constitute war crimes (torture, rape and biological experiments), but authorizing the president to decide which interrogation techniques to be used.	USA; Terrorism
22 Oct.	UN Secretary-General Special Representative for Sudan Jan Pronk is expelled from the country by the Sudanese Government after he claimed that the morale of the Sudanese Army was low and that it had recently lost two major battles to rebel groups. The UN protests to the Sudanese Government over the expulsion.	UN; Sudan
24 Oct.	In clashes in Kandahar, Afghanistan, between the NATO-led International Security Assistance Force (ISAF) and Taliban insurgents, 48 rebels and several civilians are killed.	NATO; ISAF; Afghanistan
26 Oct.	The UN First Committee votes, by a vote of 139–1 (the USA voting against), with 24 abstentions, in favour of beginning the work of drawing up an international arms trade treaty. The UN Secretary-General shall within a year produce a report on how to introduce common international standards for the import, export and transfer of conventional arms (see also *6 Dec.*).	UN; Arms trade
1 Nov.	Israel launches a major military offensive into Beit Hanoun, in the northern Gaza Strip, aiming at stopping Palestinian militants from firing rockets into Israel. By 7 Nov., when Israel withdraws its troops, more than 60 Palestinians are killed. On 8 Nov. the Israeli Army kills 18 civilians and wounds 40 people when it again fires rockets into the town.	Israel/ Palestinians
5 Nov.	The Iraqi Special Tribunal (IST), in Baghdad, finds former Iraqi President Saddam Hussein guilty of the charges of crimes against humanity and for ordering the killing of 148 Shia men in Dujail, Iraq, in 1982, and sentences him to death by hanging.	Iraq; IST

8 Nov.	Nepal's ruling Seven-Party Alliance, under Prime Minister Girija Prasad Koirala, and Maoist rebel leader Prachanda sign, in Kathmandu, an agreement under which the rebels will join a transitional government after having put their weapons under UN supervision. Under the agreement a constituent assembly will be elected in 2007, replacing the parliament restored by King Gyanendra. A comprehensive peace agreement is signed on 21 Nov., ending a 10-year rebel insurgency.	Nepal
9 Nov.	The first hearing of the confirmation of war crime charges is opened at the International Criminal Court (ICC), The Hague, the Netherlands, against the alleged founder and leader of the Union des Patriotes Congolais (Union of Congolese Patriots), Thomas Lubanga Dyilo. Lubanga Dyilo was the first person to be arrested on an ICC warrant issued on 17 Mar., on charges of war crimes committed in the Democratic Republic of the Congo (DRC) since July 2002.	ICC; DRC
12 Nov.	The Protocol on Explosive Remnants of War (ERW), Protocol V to the 1981 Convention on Prohibitions or Restrictions on the Use of Certain Conventional Weapons Which May be Deemed to be Excessively Injurious or to Have Indiscriminate Effects (CCW Convention), enters into force.	CCW
16 Nov.	Meeting in Addis Ababa, Ethiopia, the African Union (AU), the UN and the Sudanese Government agree to allow UN peacekeepers to enter into Darfur together with the AU Mission in Sudan (AMIS), already deployed there.	AU; UN; Peacekeeping; Sudan
20 Nov.– *8 Dec.*	The Sixth Review Conference of the States Parties to the 1972 Biological and Toxin Weapons Convention (BTWC) is held in Geneva. The conference adopts measures to promote effective implementation of the convention, to improve bio-safety and bio-security at biological facilities, and to improve national capabilities for disease surveillance, detection and diagnosis. The Seventh Review Conference will be held no later than the end of 2011.	BTWC
29 Nov.	Meeting in Riga, Latvia, NATO issues the Riga Summit Declaration, in which member states agree to ease their restrictions on deploying troops against the Taliban in Afghanistan; endorse the Comprehensive Political Guidance, providing a framework and political direction for NATO's continuing transformation; reaffirm the NATO Open Door accession policy; announce that the NATO Response Force is fully operational; and invites Bosnia and Herzegovina, Montenegro and Serbia to join the Partnership for Peace programme.	NATO
4 Dec.	British Prime Minister Tony Blair announces the British Government's plan to maintain its independent nuclear deterrent, based on a new and smaller fleet of submarines carrying Trident missiles. The plan must be approved by the British Parliament.	UK; Nuclear weapons

5 Dec.	In a coup d'état in Fiji, the armed forces, under Military Commander Frank Bainimarama dissolve the parliament, dismiss the prime minister, occupy government buildings and impose a state of emergency. In protest, the Commonwealth of Nations suspends Fiji from the organization on 8 Dec.	Fiji; Commonwealth of Nations
5–8 Dec.	Meeting in The Hague, the Netherlands, the Conference of the States Parties to the 1993 Chemical Weapons Convention (CWC) agrees that the final date for destruction of the chemical weapon stockpiles declared to the Organisation for the Prohibition of Chemical Weapons is extended from 2007 until 29 Apr. 2012.	CWC
6 Dec.	The Iraq Study Group, created in Mar. by the US Congress and co-chaired by James Baker and Lee Hamilton, issues its report, calling for new and enhanced diplomatic and political efforts in Iraq and the region (including Iran and Syria); and a change in the primary mission of US forces in Iraq that would enable the USA to begin moving its combat forces out of Iraq responsibly.	USA/Iraq
6 Dec.	The UN General Assembly adopts, by a vote of 153–1 (the USA voting against), with 24 abstentions, Resolution 61/89, *Towards an Arms Trade Treaty: Establishing Common International Standards for the Import, Export and Transfer of Conventional Arms* (see *26 Oct.*).	UN; Arms trade
6 Dec.	The UN Security Council unanimously adopts Resolution 1725, authorizing the Intergovernmental Authority on Development (IGAD) and the African Union (AU) to establish a protection and training mission in Somalia, with a mandate drawing on the relevant elements of the mandate and concept of operation specified in the Deployment Plan for the IGAD Peace Support Mission to Somalia (IGASOM).	UN; IGAD; AU; Somalia
11 Dec.	In an interview for German television, Israeli Prime Minister Ehud Olmert says that 'the Iranians are aspiring to have nuclear weapons just as America, France, Israel, Russia'. Israeli officials immediately deny that Israel has changed its policy of ambiguity on the possession of nuclear weapons.	Israel; Nuclear weapons
15–18 Dec.	Clashes erupt in the Gaza Strip between rival Palestinian factions, Hamas and Fatah, after accusations from Hamas that Fatah had tried to assassinate Prime Minister Ismail Haniya on 14 Dec. On 16 Dec. Palestinian President Mahmoud Abbas calls for new presidential and parliamentary elections to end the violence in the region. Hamas rejects the call as a 'coup attempt'. On 18 Dec. Hamas officials state that they have agreed a truce with Fatah.	Palestinians
18–22 Dec.	The sixth round of the Six-Party Talks (China, Japan, North Korea, South Korea, Russia and the USA) is held in Beijing, China. The USA puts forward a package of incentives for North Korea to end its nuclear programme, but North Korea insists that it wants the USA to lift its financial sanctions before considering any discussion of its nuclear programme. The meeting ends without results or a date for the resumption of the talks.	North Korea; Nuclear weapons

20–28 Dec.   Heavy fighting erupts in Baydhabo, Somalia, between troops   Somalia/
from the Transitional Federal Government of Somalia and the   Ethiopia
Union of Islamic Courts (UIC). On 24 Dec. Ethiopia admits
that its army is fighting in Somalia on the government side, and
on 28 Dec. Ethiopian-backed government forces capture the
Somalian capital, Mogadishu.

23 Dec.   The UN Security Council unanimously adopts Resolution   Iran; Nuclear
1737, imposing sanctions on Iran for its failure to comply with   programme;
Resolution 1696 and the requirements of the IAEA Board of   UN; IAEA
Governors to halt its enrichment and reprocessing activities.
The sanctions include a ban on the supply, sale or transfer of
nuclear-related technology and equipment and impose an asset
freeze on key individuals and companies (see *31 July*).

30 Dec.   Former Iraqi President Saddam Hussein is executed by hanging   Iraq
in Baghdad, convicted for crimes against humanity.

About the authors

Dr Christer Ahlström (Sweden) is Associate Professor of International Law at Uppsala University and a career diplomat in the Swedish foreign service. He was Deputy Director of SIPRI from 2002 to 2005. He previously served as a Deputy Director in the Swedish Ministry for Foreign Affairs on issues related to disarmament and non-proliferation of weapons of mass destruction. He has contributed to the SIPRI Yearbook since 2003.

Dr Ian Anthony (United Kingdom) is SIPRI Research Coordinator and Leader of the SIPRI Non-proliferation and Export Controls Project. His most recent publication for SIPRI is *Reducing Threats at the Source: A European Perspective on Cooperative Threat Reduction*, SIPRI Research Report no. 19 (2004). He is also editor of *Russia and the Arms Trade* (1998) and *The Future of Defence Industries in Central and Eastern Europe*, SIPRI Research Report no. 7 (1994), and a co-author of *Reforming Nuclear Export Controls: The Future of the Nuclear Suppliers Group*, SIPRI Research Report no. 22 (forthcoming 2007). He has contributed to the SIPRI Yearbook since 1988.

Alyson J. K. Bailes (United Kingdom) has been Director of SIPRI since July 2002. She was a member of the British Diplomatic Service for 33 years, ending as British Ambassador to Finland in 2000–2002. Her other diplomatic postings included the British Delegations to Beijing, Bonn, Budapest, Oslo and NATO. She spent several periods on detachment outside the Service, including two academic sabbaticals, a two-year period with the British Ministry of Defence, and assignments to the European Union and the Western European Union. Her main analytical interests are politico-military affairs, European integration and the role of business in security. She has published widely in international journals on these and on other, institutional and regional subjects. She is co-editor of *The Nordic Countries and the European Security and Defence Policy* (2006) and co-author of *The Shanghai Cooperation Organization*, SIPRI Policy Paper no. 17 (May 2007). She has contributed to the SIPRI Yearbook since 2003.

Vladimir Baranovsky (Russia) is Deputy Director of the Institute of World Economy and International Relations (IMEMO), Moscow. He was Leader of the SIPRI Project on Russia's Security Agenda from 1992 to 1997, and prior to that head of IMEMO's European Studies Department from 1988 to 1992. He is the author, editor or co-editor of several publications, including *Russia's Attitudes Towards the EU: Political Aspects* (Ulkopoliittinen Instituutti, 2002), *Mirovoi okean i strategicheskaya stabil'-nost'* [The world's ocean and strategic stability] (IMEMO, 2002) and the SIPRI book *Russia and Europe: The Emerging Security Agenda* (1997).

Dr Sibylle Bauer (Germany) is Head of the Export Control Programme of the SIPRI Non-proliferation and Export Controls Project. Previously, she was a Researcher with the Institute for European Studies in Brussels. She has published widely on European export control and armaments issues, including chapters in *The Restructuring of the European Defence Industry* (Office for Official Publications of the European Communities, 2001), *Annuaire français de relations internationales* [French yearbook of international relations] (Bruylant, 2001) and *The Path to European Defence* (Maklu, 2003). She is co-author of *The European Union Code of Conduct on Arms Exports: Improving the Annual Report*, SIPRI Policy Paper no. 8 (Nov. 2004). She has contributed to the SIPRI Yearbook since 2004.

Åsa Blomström (Sweden) joined SIPRI in 2005 as Project Secretary for the Military Expenditure, Arms Production and Arms Transfers projects. She is responsible for the electronic archive common to these three research areas, and maintains the SIPRI reporting system for military expenditure. She contributed to the SIPRI Yearbook in 2006.

Nenne Bodell (Sweden) is Head of the SIPRI Library and Documentation Department and of the SIPRI Arms Control and Disarmament Documentary Survey Project. She has contributed to the SIPRI Yearbook since 2003.

Dr Hans Born (Netherlands) is a Senior Fellow in Democratic Governance of the Security Sector at the Geneva Centre for the Democratic Control of Armed Forces (DCAF). He leads the DCAF working groups on parliamentary accountability of the security sector and on legal aspects of security sector governance. He is co-author or co-editor of *Civil–Military Relations in Europe* (Routledge, 2006), *Making Intelligence Accountable: Legal Standards and Best Practice for Oversight of Intelligence Agencies* (Norwegian Parliament, 2005), *Who's Watching the Spies? Establishing Intelligence Service Accountability* (Potomac, 2005) and *Parliamentary Oversight of the Security Sector: Principles, Mechanisms and Practices* (Inter-Parliamentary Union/DCAF, 2003). He is co-editor of and contributor to *Democratic Control of Intelligence Services: Containing Rogue Elephants* (Ashgate, 2007). He has contributed to the SIPRI Yearbook since 2005.

Mark Bromley (United Kingdom) is a Research Associate with the SIPRI Arms Transfers Project. Previously, he was a Policy Analyst for the British American Security Information Council (BASIC). While at BASIC he authored or co-authored a number of research reports and papers, including *Secrecy and Dependence: The UK Trident System in the 21st Century* (BASIC, 2001) and 'European missile defence: new emphasis, new roles' (BASIC, 2001). He is co-author of *The European Union Code of Conduct on Arms Exports: Improving the Annual Report*, SIPRI Policy Paper no. 8 (Nov. 2004) and has contributed to the SIPRI Yearbook since 2004.

Dr Michael Brzoska (Germany) is Director of the Institute for Peace Research and Security Policy at the University of Hamburg. He has also been a Researcher at the Centre for the Study of Wars, Armaments and Development at the University of Hamburg and Director of Research at the Bonn International Center for Conversion. From 1983 to 1986, he was a co-leader of the SIPRI Arms Trade and Arms Production Project. He has written articles in international academic journals including *International Peacekeeping*, *European Security*, the *Journal of Peace Research*, *Defence and Peace Economics*, *Global Dialogue* and the *International Journal of Regional Science*, and chapters in several edited volumes, including the SIPRI book

The Nordic Countries and the European Security and Defence Policy (2006). He is co-author of two SIPRI monographs—*Arms Transfers to the Third World, 1971–85* (1987) and *Arms Production in the Third World* (1986)—and co-editor of the SIPRI book *Restructuring of Arms Production in Western Europe* (1992).

Dr Pál Dunay (Hungary) is Director of the Hungarian Institute of International Affairs in Budapest. Until 2007 he was a Senior Researcher with the SIPRI Euro-Atlantic, Regional and Global Security Project. Before joining SIPRI he worked at the Geneva Centre for Security Policy between 1996 and 2004. He is co-author of *Ungarns Aussenpolitik 1990–1997: Zwischen Westintegration, Nachbarschafts- und Minderheitenpolitik* [Hungarian foreign policy 1990–1997: at the crossroads of Western integration, neighbourhood and minority policy] (Nomos Verlag, 1998) and *Open Skies: A Cooperative Approach to Military Transparency and Confidence-Building* (United Nations Institute for Disarmament Research, 2004). He has contributed to the SIPRI Yearbook since 2004.

Vitaly Fedchenko (Russia) is a Researcher with the SIPRI Non-proliferation and Export Controls Project, with responsibility for nuclear security issues and the political, technological and educational dimensions of nuclear arms control and non-proliferation. Previously, he was a visiting researcher at SIPRI, a Researcher and Project Coordinator at the Center for Policy Studies in Russia, and a Research Fellow at the Institute for Applied International Research in Moscow. He is the author or co-author of several publications on international non-proliferation and disarmament assistance, the international nuclear fuel cycle and Russian nuclear exports. He has contributed to the SIPRI Yearbook since 2005.

Harold A. Feiveson (United States) is a Senior Research Policy Scientist at Princeton University and a member of Princeton's Program on Science and Global Security of the Woodrow Wilson School of Public and International Affairs. He has taught regularly at the Woodrow Wilson School for the past 32 years on a range of topics, including arms control. From 1963 to 1967 he was a member of the Science Bureau of the US Arms Control and Disarmament Agency. His principal research interests are in the fields of nuclear weapons and nuclear-energy policy. He is editor and a principal author of *The Nuclear Turning Point: A Blueprint for Deep Cuts and De-alerting of Nuclear Weapons* (Brookings, 1999) and editor of the international journal *Science & Global Security*.

Ragnhild Ferm Hellgren (Sweden) was a Research Assistant and then Researcher at SIPRI between 1974 and 2001. She was Leader of the SIPRI Arms Control and Disarmament Documentary Survey Project from 1996 and wrote chapters for the SIPRI Yearbook on nuclear explosions and the comprehensive ban on nuclear testing, summaries of arms control agreements, and the annual chronologies of arms control and political events. She is also the author of several fact sheets in Swedish on SIPRI research topics.

Damien Fruchart (United Kingdom) is a Research Assistant with the SIPRI Arms Transfers Project. He has a BA in Chinese and Japanese Studies from the University of Leeds and a master's degree from Uppsala University. Previously, he held an internship with the European Commission's delegation in Beijing, China. He contributed to the SIPRI Yearbook in 2006.

Alexander Glaser (Germany) is a member of the research staff of Princeton University's Program on Science and Global Security. Previously, he was associated with the Interdisciplinary Research Group in Science, Technology, and Security (IANUS) of Darmstadt University of Technology, where he wrote his master's and doctoral theses on fissile material and nuclear non-proliferation issues. Between 2001 and 2003 he was an SSRC/MacArthur pre-doctoral fellow with the Technical Group of the Security Studies Program at the Massachusetts Institute of Technology. During 2000 and 2001 he was an adviser to the German Federal Ministry of Environment and Reactor Safety.

Lotta Harbom (Sweden) is a Research Assistant with the Uppsala Conflict Data Program at the Department of Peace and Conflict Research, Uppsala University. She has contributed to the SIPRI Yearbook since 2005.

John Hart (United States) is the Head of the Chemical and Biological Warfare Programme of the SIPRI Non-proliferation and Export Controls Project. He is a co-editor of *Chemical Weapon Destruction in Russia: Political, Legal and Technical Aspects*, SIPRI Chemical & Biological Warfare Studies no. 17 (1998); the author of 'The ALSOS Mission, 1943–1945: a secret U.S. scientific intelligence unit' in *International Journal of Intelligence and Counter Intelligence* (autumn 2005), and 'The Soviet biological weapons program' in *Deadly Cultures: Biological Weapons since 1945* (Harvard University Press, 2006); and co-author of the *Historical Dictionary of Nuclear, Biological and Chemical Warfare* (Scarecrow Press, 2007) and a chapter on verification in *Combating Weapons of Mass Destruction: The Future of International Non-Proliferation Policy* (University of Georgia Press, forthcoming 2007). He has contributed to the SIPRI Yearbook since 1997.

Dr Paul Holtom (United Kingdom) is a Researcher with the SIPRI Arms Transfers Project. Previously, he was a Research Fellow at the Centre for Border Studies at the University of Glamorgan. He has also been an International Expert for the Council of Europe's Transfrontier Co-operation Programme on the Kaliningrad Oblast and Lead Researcher on small arms and light weapons projects in north-eastern and south-eastern Europe for Saferworld. He is the author of several journal articles on the Baltic states, Kaliningrad and the Russian Federation, *Arms Transit Trade in the Baltic Sea Region* (Saferworld, 2003) and *Turning the Page: Small Arms and Light Weapons in Albania* (Saferworld, 2005).

Shannon N. Kile (USA) is a Senior Researcher with the Non-proliferation and Export Controls Project at SIPRI, where he has worked since 1991. His principal areas of research are nuclear arms control and non-proliferation with a special interest in Iran and North Korea. He has contributed to numerous SIPRI publications, including chapters on nuclear arms control and nuclear forces and weapon technology for the SIPRI Yearbook since 1995. His recent publications include, as editor, *Europe and Iran: Perspectives on Non-proliferation*, SIPRI Research Report no. 21 (2005).

Hans M. Kristensen (Denmark) is Director of the Nuclear Information Project at the Federation of American Scientists (FAS), Washington, DC. He is co-author of the 'Nuclear Notebook' column in the *Bulletin of the Atomic Scientists*. His recent publications include *Chinese Nuclear Forces and U.S. Nuclear War Planning* (FAS/ NRDC, November 2006), *Global Strike: A Chronology of the Pentagon's New Offensive Strike Plan* (FAS, 2006), 'Preparing for the failure of deterrence' in *SITREP* (November/December 2005) and 'New doctrine falls short of Bush pledge' in *Arms Control Today* (September 2005). He has contributed to the SIPRI Yearbook since 2001.

Frida Kuhlau (Sweden) was a member of the SIPRI Chemical and Biological Warfare Project from 2001 to 2007. She is the author of a report to the European Commission on bio-threat reduction and cooperation in biological proliferation prevention, *Countering Bio-Threats: EU Instruments for Managing Biological Materials, Technology and Knowledge*, SIPRI Policy Paper no. 19 (forthcoming 2007), and the chapter 'Disease outbreaks: managing threats to health and security' in *Health and Conflict Prevention* (Gidlunds Förlag, 2006). She is co-author of *Non-Compliance with the Chemical Weapons Convention: Lessons from and for Iraq?*, SIPRI Policy Paper no. 5 (2003), and the article 'Crucial guidance: a code of conduct for bio-defense scientists' in *Arms Control Today* (September 2006). She has contributed to the SIPRI Yearbook since 2002.

Dr Zdzislaw Lachowski (Poland) is a Senior Researcher with the SIPRI Euro-Atlantic, Regional and Global Security Project. He has published widely on the problems of European military security and arms control as well as on European politico-military integration. He is the co-editor of *International Security in a Time of Change: Threats–Concepts–Institutions* (Nomos, 2004) and author of *Confidence-and Security-Building Measures in the New Europe*, SIPRI Research Report no. 18 (2004), and *Foreign Military Bases in Eurasia*, SIPRI Policy Paper no. 18 (June 2007). In 2006 he led a project on confidence-building measures for North and South Korea. He has contributed to the SIPRI Yearbook since 1992.

Professor Ian Leigh (United Kingdom) is Professor of Law at the University of Durham, specializing in public law and human rights, and Co-Director of the Durham Human Rights Centre. He is the author of *Law, Politics and Local Democracy* (OUP, 2000); co-author of *In From the Cold: National Security and Parliamentary Democracy* (OUP, 1994), *Religious Freedom in the Liberal State* (OUP, 2005) and the policy report *Making Intelligence Accountable* (Norwegian Parliament, 2005); and co-editor of *Who's Watching the Spies? Establishing Intelligence Service Accountability* (Potomac, 2005). He is a consultant to the Organization for Security and Co-operation in Europe Office of Democratic Institutions and Human Rights on human rights in the armed forces and a member of the Venice Commission working party on democratic control of security and intelligence agencies in Council of Europe states.

Sara Lindberg (Sweden/United States) is a Research Assistant with the SIPRI Armed Conflict and Conflict Management Project. Since joining SIPRI in 2005 she has provided research support for conflict projects, compiled data for the Multilateral Peace Operations Database and authored a case study on Timor-Leste for a forthcoming SIPRI book on local ownership in the rule of law after conflict. She recently completed field research in Liberia as part of the Minor Field Studies programme sponsored by the Swedish International Development Cooperation Agency (SIDA).

Dr Neil J. Melvin (United Kingdom) is a Senior Research Fellow of the Centre for European Policy Studies (CEPS) in Brussels. He was Leader of the Armed Conflict and Conflict Management Project from 2006 to 2007. Prior to joining SIPRI he served as Senior Adviser to the High Commissioner on National Minorities of the Organization for Security and Co-operation in Europe. He is the author of a number of books and articles on security and conflict in Eurasia, including *Building Stability in the North Caucasus: Ways Forward for Russia and the European Union*, SIPRI Policy Paper no. 16 (May 2007), and co-author of 'Diaspora politics: ethnic linkages, foreign policy, and security in Eurasia' in *International Security* (winter 1999/2000). He contributed to the SIPRI Yearbook in 2006.

Zia Mian (Pakistan/United Kingdom) is a physicist with the Program on Science and Global Security, Woodrow Wilson School of Public and International Affairs, at Princeton University, where he directs the Project on Peace and Security in South Asia. For the past decade his work has focused on nuclear weapons, arms control and disarmament, and nuclear energy issues in Pakistan and India. He has previously worked at the Union of Concerned Scientists, the Sustainable Development Policy Institute and Quaid-e-Azam University, Islamabad. He contributed to the SIPRI Yearbook in 2003.

Catalina Perdomo (Colombia) is a Research Associate with the SIPRI Military Expenditure Project, responsible for monitoring military expenditure in Africa, Latin America and the Middle East. Previously, she worked at the Inter-American Development Bank (IADB) in Washington, DC, at the Washington, DC, office of the Fundación Ideas para la Paz of Colombia and at the Bogotá office of Management Sciences for Development. She is the author of several publications on security and development, including the chapter 'International assistance for security sector reform' in *Obsevatorio de Análisis de los Sistemas Internacionales 2007–2008* [Observatory for international systems analysis 2007–2008] (Universidad Externado de Colombia, 2007), and co-author of *Informe sobre la implementación de la estrategia de desarrollo subnacional* [Report on the implementation of subnational development strategy] (IADB, 2004). She has contributed to the SIPRI Yearbook since 2004.

Kamila Pronińska (Poland) is a PhD Fellow in Political Science at the Institute of International Relations of Warsaw University. She lectures on international security, armed conflicts and international negotiations. She is also coordinator for *Rocznik Strategiczny* [Strategic yearbook] (Scholar, annual). Her main areas of research are energy security, 'resource conflicts' and European Union–Russian energy relations. She is the author of several papers and articles published in various scientific journals in Poland. Her recent publications include the article 'Resource wars in contemporary international relations' in the *Polish Quarterly of International Affairs* (summer 2005) and the chapter on strategic aspects of energy security in international relations in *Stosunki międzynarodowe w XXI wieku* [International relations in the 21st century] (Scholar, 2006).

Matt Schroeder (United States) is Manager of the Arms Sales Monitoring Project at the Federation of American Scientists (FAS). Since joining the FAS in 2002 he has written extensively on the international arms trade, US arms export controls, the illicit trade in small arms and light weapons, and the terrorist threat from man-portable air defence systems (MANPADS). He is co-author of *The Small Arms Trade* (Oneworld, 2006). He contributed to the SIPRI Yearbook in 2005.

Martin Sjögren (Sweden) is a Research Assistant with the SIPRI Euro-Atlantic, Regional and Global Security Project. He recently co-authored a report on confidence-building measures for North and South Korea and has contributed to the SIPRI Yearbook since 2003.

Elisabeth Sköns (Sweden) is Leader of the SIPRI Military Expenditure and Arms Production projects. Her most recent publications outside SIPRI include papers on the costs of conflict and on the financing of peace missions for the International Task Force on Global Public Goods; and chapters on defence offsets in *Arms Trade and Economic Development: Theory and Policy in Offsets* (Routledge, 2004), on the restructuring of the West European defence industry in *Mot et avnasjonalisert forsvar?* [Towards a denationalized defence?] (Abstrakt, 2005), on the costs of armed conflict in *Peace and Security*, Expert Papers Series no. 5 (Secretariat of the International Task Force on Global Public Goods, 2006), on financing of security in *The Statesman's Yearbook 2007* (Palgrave Macmillan, 2006), and on the economics of arms production (with Paul Dunne) for the *Encyclopedia of Violence, Peace and Conflict*, 2nd edn (Academic Press, forthcoming 2007). She has contributed to the SIPRI Yearbook since 1983.

Kirsten Soder (Germany) is a Research Assistant with the SIPRI Armed Conflict and Conflict Management Project in 2006 and 2007. She supports the research work of the programme and compiles data for the SIPRI Multilateral Peace Operations Database.

Petter Stålenheim (Sweden) is a Researcher with the SIPRI Military Expenditure Project, responsible for monitoring data on military expenditure, with a special focus on Europe and Central Asia, and for the maintenance of the SIPRI Military Expenditure Database. In 2005–2006 he was acting Leader of the SIPRI Military Expenditure and Arms Production projects. He has previously worked as a consultant to the International Institute for Democracy and Electoral Assistance (IDEA) in Stockholm and lectured at the George C. Marshall Center in Germany. He is co-author of *Armament and Disarmament in the Caucasus and Central Asia*, SIPRI Policy Paper no. 3 (July 2003). He has contributed to the SIPRI Yearbook since 1998.

Eamon Surry (Australia) is a Research Associate with the SIPRI Arms Production Project. He is responsible for maintaining the project's arms industry databases and Internet site. Prior to joining SIPRI he worked as a Researcher for a broadcast media consultancy in London. He is the author of *Transparency in the Arms Industry*, SIPRI Policy Paper no. 12 (February 2006). He has contributed to the SIPRI Yearbook since 2004.

Frank von Hippel (United States) is a nuclear physicist and Professor of Public and International Affairs at Princeton University. He has worked for the past 30 years on fissile material policy issues, including those relating to commercialization of plutonium recycling, ending the production of plutonium and highly enriched uranium for weapons, and ending the use of highly enriched uranium as a reactor fuel. In 1993–94 he served as Assistant Director for National Security in the White House Office of Science and Technology Policy. He is currently Co-chair of the International Panel on Fissile Materials.

Connie Wall (United States) is Head of the SIPRI Editorial and Publications Department. She has edited or contributed to the SIPRI Yearbook since 1970.

Professor Peter Wallensteen (Sweden) has held the Dag Hammarskjöld Chair in Peace and Conflict Research at Uppsala University since 1985 and has been the Richard G. Starmann Sr Research Professor of Peace Studies at the University of Notre Dame since 2006. He directs the Uppsala Conflict Data Program and the Special Program on the Implementation of Targeted Sanctions. The second, updated edition of his book *Understanding Conflict Resolution: War, Peace and the Global System* (Sage) was published in 2007. He is co-editor of *International Sanctions: Between Words and Wars in the Global System* (Frank Cass, 2005). He has contributed to the SIPRI Yearbook since 1988.

Pieter D. Wezeman (Netherlands) is a Researcher with the SIPRI Arms Transfers Project. He rejoined SIPRI in 2006, having previously worked at the institute from 1994 to 2003. From 2003 to 2006 he was a Senior Analyst for the Dutch Ministry of Defence in the field of proliferation of conventional and nuclear weapons technology. He contributed to the SIPRI Yearbook between 1995 and 2003.

Siemon T. Wezeman (Netherlands) has worked in the SIPRI Arms Transfers Project since 1992 and has led the project since mid-2006. Among his publications are several relating to international transparency in arms transfers. He is author of *The Future of the United Nations Register of Conventional Arms*, SIPRI Policy Paper no. 4 (August 2003), and co-author of *Cluster Weapons: Necessity or Convenience?* (Pax Christi Netherlands, 2005). He has contributed to the SIPRI Yearbook since 1993.

Sharon Wiharta (Indonesia) is a Researcher with the SIPRI Armed Conflict and Conflict Management Project, working on peacekeeping and peacebuilding issues, particularly efforts to promote justice and to establish the rule of law in post-conflict situations. Recently, she co-led a study on local ownership and the rule of law during the peacebuilding process. Prior to joining SIPRI in 2001 she worked at the Center for International Affairs of the University of Washington, Seattle, where she conducted research on sustainable development issues. Her publications on peacekeeping and peacebuilding include *The Transition to a Just Order: Establishing Local Ownership after Conflict* (Folke Bernadotte Academy Publications, 2007), as co-author, and *Prospects for Peace Operations: Regional and National Dimensions* (Georgetown University Press, forthcoming 2007), as co-editor. She has contributed to the SIPRI Yearbook since 2002.

SIPRI Yearbook 2007: Armaments, Disarmament and International Security

Oxford University Press, Oxford, 2007, 752 pp.
(Stockholm International Peace Research Institute)
ISBN 978-0-19-923021-1

ABSTRACTS

BAILES, A. J. K., 'Introduction. A world of risk', in *SIPRI Yearbook 2007*, pp. 1–20.

The term 'risk' can be used in modern security analysis to cover many types of threat and hazard. Risk is often influenced by the subject's own behaviour, and comparing, assessing and prioritizing risks with different origins from different dimensions is open to many distortions. In trying to eliminate a given risk, an actor may misjudge the probability of backlash, of shifting the risk elsewhere, or of incurring legal or moral penalties. The post-cold war global environment makes risk taking (by the USA, among others) easier but has also underlined the need for self-restraint. Strategies based on the larger common interest may ultimately control risks most effectively.

DUNAY, P. and LACHOWSKI, Z., 'Euro-Atlantic security and institutions', in *SIPRI Yearbook 2007*, pp. 23–54.

Despite enduring differences, Euro-Atlantic security relations were largely pursued pragmatically in 2006. US security policy, including in Iraq, met increased domestic criticism. The European Union's agenda was dominated by the continued impasse over the 2003 Constitutional Treaty and enlargement issues. NATO increased its involvement in Afghanistan—in part to prove the alliance's continued relevance. The complexity of the Kosovo problem was highlighted when concrete proposals for the province's future were presented. Russia used its economic leverage to assert its interests more forcefully vis-à-vis the West and its own neighbours. Ukraine's politics, including its engagement with Western institutions, showed signs of a stalemate.

MELVIN, N. and LINDBERG, S., 'Major armed conflicts', in *SIPRI Yearbook 2007*, pp. 55–78.

The growing significance of transnational influences on armed conflict and the close links between localized violence and broader regional and global factors were highlighted in 2006. The involvement of proxy interests, transnational crime networks, terrorist groups, and other regional and international actors was evident in Afghanistan, Somalia and the Middle East, where continuing unrest was compounded by military confrontations involving Israel and Palestinian and Lebanese armed groups. These cases underlined the need to understand better the nature of such conflicts and to find ways to harness transnational phenomena to conflict resolution agendas.

HARBOM, L. and WALLENSTEEN, P., 'Patterns of major armed conflicts, 1997–2006', in *SIPRI Yearbook 2007*, pp. 79–90.

There were 17 major armed conflicts in 16 locations around the world in 2006. Both figures were the same as those in 2005, and the same conflicts were active in both years. No interstate conflicts were active in 2006, and Asia was for the second year the region with the highest number of conflicts. In the period 1997–2006 there were 34 different major armed conflicts. In all but three years of the period, the highest number of conflicts was in Africa. There was a decline in the total annual number of conflicts from 26 in 1998 to 17 in 2005.

BRZOSKA, M., 'Collective violence beyond the standard definition of armed conflict', in *SIPRI Yearbook 2007*, pp. 94–106.

The relevance of quantitative data on armed conflicts has been called into question by recent trends in warfare as well as by shifts in perceptions of the major threats to peace and security. From a human security perspective, for instance, all kinds of violence are important: not only those taking place in armed conflicts as they are traditionally defined but also various forms of non-state violence, including crime. Collectors of data on conflicts have responded by introducing new data sets. However, major gaps in the data remain. Although such data is difficult to collect, it could improve our understanding of current global trends in conflict.

WIHARTA, S., 'Peacekeeping: keeping pace with changes in conflict', in *SIPRI Yearbook 2007*, pp. 107–28.

The end of the cold war and the emergence of what have been called 'new wars' have resulted in significant developments in the conceptualization of peacekeeping, the articulation of mission mandates and the way in which those mandates are carried out, all of which were illustrated—and influenced—by events in 2006. Although the established principles of peacekeeping have withstood the test of time, they have undergone considerable reinterpretation. In 2006 the emerging principle that peacekeeping operations may use force in defence of their mandate, and not only in self-defence, arguably blurred the line between peacekeeping and war fighting in some peace operations, notably that in Afghanistan.

BAILES, A. J. K., BARANOVSKY, V. and DUNAY, P., 'Regional security cooperation in the former Soviet area', in *SIPRI Yearbook 2007*, pp. 165–92.

The former Soviet area has followed a general trend towards multilateral institution building, with two Russia-led groups—the Commonwealth of Independent States (CIS) and the Collective Security Treaty Organization (CSTO); one group formed by four states (GUAM); and the Shanghai Cooperation Organization (SCO), consisting of China, Russia and four Central Asian states. Unlike similar bodies created by the West, none of these except GUAM promotes governance norms (at least, any that threaten current regimes). The CSTO seems most coherent militarily. The SCO shows most vitality and scope for development. All are likely to shape their part of the Eurasian security architecture for some time.

BORN, H. and LEIGH, I., 'Democratic accountability of intelligence services', in *SIPRI Yearbook 2007*, pp. 193–214.

The 11 September 2001 terrorist attacks and the 2003 US-led invasion of Iraq focused international attention on Western intelligence services—particularly their professionalism, their relationship with national governments and alleged human rights abuses. A comparative study of several democratic countries reveals that during the past 30 years many countries have moved from control of their intelligence agencies by executive decree towards greater democratic accountability. Intelligence oversight systems now face a number of recurring challenges and problems. How far these systems are capable of addressing the challenges and problems in the post-September 2001 climate remains to be seen.

PRONIŃSKA, K., 'Energy and security: regional and global dimensions', in *SIPRI Yearbook 2007*, pp. 215–240.

Current concerns about energy security are motivated by a different and more complicated set of factors than in the 1970s. Concepts of energy security and ideas about the best national, regional and global policies to ensure it have both changed significantly. Some states understand the need for international cooperation; others take a nationalistic approach and are even ready to use force to protect their energy interests. Energy security is thus reshaping contemporary international relations. Energy security concerns have led to new strategic alliances and cooperation between states that are major energy market players—but they are also sources of international tension, rivalry and conflict.

SKÖNS, E., 'Analysing risks to human lives', in *SIPRI Yearbook 2007*, pp. 243–66.

Governments allocate large sums of money to their military sectors with the stated purpose of providing security for their citizens. Whether this purpose is achieved depends partly on how security is defined. An analysis from a public health perspective suggests that, if security is measured in terms of overall risk to human lives, a range of non-military interventions would be more cost-effective in providing security than military instruments alone. Furthermore, the overlaps between different types of risk factor open up the possibility of trade-offs between different types of security strategy.

STÅLENHEIM, P., PERDOMO, C. and SKÖNS, E., 'Military expenditure', in *SIPRI Yearbook 2007*, pp. 267–97.

World military expenditure in 2006 is estimated to have reached $1204 billion—3.5 per cent higher in real terms than in 2005 and 37 per cent higher than 10 years before, in 1997. The top 15 spenders accounted for 83 per cent of the world total, and the USA alone for 46 per cent, distantly followed by the UK and France. US outlays for national defence increased by 53 per cent between financial years 2001 and 2006, primarily as a result of massive supplemental appropriations to fund the military operations in Afghanistan and Iraq. A comparison of spending priorities between country income groups shows that the ratio of social to military expenditure increases with income per capita.

SKÖNS, E. and SURRY, E., 'Arms production', in *SIPRI Yearbook 2007*, pp. 345–73.

The combined arms sales of the world's 100 largest arms-producing companies (excluding Chinese companies)—the SIPRI Top 100—totalled $290 billion in 2005. In real terms this was 3 per cent more than the 2004 Top 100 and 18 per cent more than the 2002 Top 100. US companies dominate in world arms production and 40 US companies accounted for 63 per cent of the arms sales of the Top 100 in 2005. Six companies increased their arms sales by more than $1 billion in 2005, four of them US companies, one British and one Italian. IT companies and some Russian companies also increased their sales significantly.

WEZEMAN, S. T., BROMLEY, M., FRU-CHART, D., HOLTOM, P. and WEZEMAN, P. D., 'International arms transfers', in *SIPRI Yearbook 2007*, pp. 388–417.

Over the past four years there has been an almost 50-per cent increase in the volume of major arms transfers. The USA and Russia were the largest single suppliers in the period 2002–2006, accounting each for around 30 per cent of global deliveries. The EU members together accounted for 31 per cent of deliveries, making them combined the largest supplier during the period. Arms deliveries to Iran, mainly from Russia, attracted media attention in 2006, but deliveries from Europe and the USA to other Middle Eastern states are much larger and as worrisome. The problem of controlling state supplies of weapons to non-state actors was highlighted in 2006.

P. HOLTOM and S. T. WEZEMAN, 'Towards an arms trade treaty?', in *SIPRI Yearbook 2007*, pp. 431–39

In December 2006, 153 governments voted in favour of a UN General Assembly resolution towards creating an international arms trade treaty; the USA was the only country voting against At the July 2006 UN Small Arms Review Conference the USA also opposed expansion of the UN Programme of Action on Small Arms and Light Weapons (SALW). Both process have their origins in civil society campaigns that were later taken up by governments. Despite the diverse challenges that the arms trade treaty initiative faces, it remains the most significant global development in conventional arms transfer controls since the end of the cold war.

ANTHONY, I., 'Reducing security risks by controlling possession and use of civilian materials', in *SIPRI Yearbook 2007*, pp. 443–59.

There is a new tendency to enlist efforts by the private sector of industry in actions that supplement the traditional arms control framework in order to take into account the risks posed by non-state actors. Regulators and industry are taking action to address the risk that groups planning mass-impact terrorist acts will employ chemicals, bacteriological agents, radioactive materials and other hazardous items in their attacks. To help reduce these risks, industry is exploring the adoption of voluntary standards, including under the framework of the International Organization for Standardization (ISO), to demonstrate compliance with an increasingly complicated *acquis* of regulations.

AHLSTRÖM, C., 'United Nations Security Council Resolution 1540: non-proliferation by means of international legislation', in *SIPRI Yearbook 2007*, pp. 460–73.

United Nations Security Council Resolution 1540 was adopted by consensus on 28 April 2004. The aim of the resolution is to combat proliferation of weapons of mass destruction involving non-state actors. The adoption of Resolution 1540 raised important questions about the authority of the Security Council to adopt binding resolutions that contain 'legislative' elements under Chapter VII of the UN Charter. Resolution 1540 remains controversial: it is still far from universally accepted and full implementation of the resolution by all UN member states is probably still some way off.

KILE, S. N., 'Nuclear arms control and non-proliferation', in *SIPRI Yearbook 2007*, pp. 477–513.

In 2006 North Korea carried out a nuclear test explosion but did not dispel doubts about whether it could produce nuclear weapons. Questions remained about the scope and nature of Iran's nuclear programme and its compliance with its safeguards agreement with the International Atomic Energy Agency. The United Nations Security Council imposed sanctions on both countries targeting their activities of proliferation concern. Initial steps were taken towards implementing the controversial Indian–US Civil Nuclear Co-operation Initiative, which would exempt India from international nuclear supplier restrictions. Procedural disputes continued to delay the opening of negotiations on a global fissile material cut-off treaty at the Conference on Disarmament.

FEIVESON, H., GLASER, A., MIAN, Z., and VON HIPPEL, F., 'Fissile materials: global stocks, production and elimination', in *SIPRI Yearbook 2007*, pp. 558–76.

Today there are roughly 1700 tonnes of highly enriched uranium (HEU) and 500 tonnes of separated plutonium in the world, sufficient to make over 100 000 nuclear weapons. National declarations of stocks would facilitate further reductions in nuclear arsenals. It is necessary to confront the potential weapons use of the very large HEU stocks that Russia, the UK and the USA have reserved for naval reactors, and the 250 tonnes (and growing) global stock of separated civil plutonium, as well as the capacity of civilian nuclear fuel cycles to produce HEU and plutonium.

HART, J. and KUHLAU, F., 'Chemical and biological weapon developments and arms control', in *SIPRI Yearbook 2007*, pp. 577–601.

In 2006 the parties to the 1972 Biological and Toxin Weapons Convention agreed to meet annually in 2007–10 to consider measures such as improving bio-safety and bio-security at biological facilities and strengthening national capabilities for disease detection and diagnosis. The parties to the 1993 Chemical Weapons Convention agreed that states requesting extension of chemical weapon destruction deadlines should receive additional on-site visits. Increased focus on bio-safety and bio-security, national implementation of agreements, and outreach and awareness raising among the various scientific and technical communities has highlighted the need for practical and sustained measures in order to ensure that political commitments are met.

LACHOWSKI, Z. and SJÖGREN, M., 'Conventional arms control', in *SIPRI Yearbook 2007*, pp. 603–22.

Progress in European arms control was hampered in 2006 by, among others, Russia's failure to comply with its commitments, political competition between Russia and the North Atlantic Treaty Organization (NATO) and 'arms control fatigue'. The Vienna military doctrine seminar enabled clarification of the current military security thinking and postures of its participants. In Latin America there was continued interest in confidence-building measures. The entry into force of Protocol V on explosive remnants of war to the 1981 Certain Conventional Weapons (CCW) Convention, and developments at the Third CCW Convention Review Conference showed unabated worldwide interest in limiting 'inhumane' weapons.

SCHROEDER, M., 'Global efforts to control MANPADS', in *SIPRI Yearbook 2007*, pp. 623–39.

The unsuccessful attempt by terrorists to shoot down an Israeli airliner departing from Mombassa, Kenya in 2002 sparked a global campaign to address the threat posed by man-portable air defence systems (MANPADS). This campaign has already succeeded in establishing important norms, raising awareness of the threat of terrorist use of MANPADS, eliminating surplus missiles, improving airport perimeter and stockpile security, and strengthening export controls. However, none of the various control strategies pursued since 2002 are sufficient in themselves; a multi-faceted, multilateral approach is needed to significantly reduce the terrorist threat from MANPADS.

ANTHONY, I. and BAUER, S., 'Controls on security-related international transfers', in *SIPRI Yearbook 2007*, pp. 641–63.

In 2006 the number of countries that cooperate in informal groups to strengthen the national export controls of the participating states continued to grow when Croatia joined the Zangger Committee. These groups also continued to update the lists of items that are proliferation sensitive and that therefore require assessment and approval by national authorities prior to export. Enforcement communities have strengthened their cooperation under processes such as the Proliferation Security Initiative in an attempt to impede and stop illegal shipments of proliferation-sensitive items. The United Nations Security Council adopted resolutions restricting access by Iran and North Korea to international supplies of certain proliferation-sensitive items. These restrictions will require countries to apply effective national export controls.

Errata

SIPRI Yearbook 2006: Armaments, Disarmament and International Security

Page 173, CEMAC peace operations	*The budgeted cost in 2005 for the CEMAC mission FOMUC should read $10.2 million, not $6.2 million*
Page 212, footnote 54	*'UN Security Council Resolution 1371' should read 'UN Security Council Resolution 1373'*
Page 235, line 23	*'no-first-use' should read 'first-use'*
Page 397, lines 23–25 and footnote 51	*The sentence 'Indeed, world military spending in 2005 exceeded (in real terms) the peak of spending during the cold war' is incorrect; it should read 'Indeed, world military spending in 2004 was only 6 per cent lower in real terms than at the peak of the cold war'. Footnote 51 should read 'Sköns, E. et al., "Military expenditure", SIPRI Yearbook 2005 (note 4), p. 307.'*
Page 594, lines 7–8	*Russia has both signed and ratified the Comprehensive Nuclear Test-Ban Treaty (CTBT).*
Page 776, table 16.1	*The European Commission is an observer, not a participant, in the Zangger Committee*
Page 819, Chemical Weapons Convention	*Grenada has signed and ratified the 1993 Chemical Weapons Convention and so should only appear in the list of parties.*

Index